W9-BYQ-255

For Reference

Not to be taken from this room

DICTIONARY OF
American History

Third Edition

EDITORIAL BOARD

DICTIONARY OF
American History

Third Edition

Stanley I. Kutler, *Editor in Chief*

Volume 7
Quakers to Suburb

CHARLES SCRIBNER'S SONS®

GALE

New York • Detroit • San Diego • San Francisco • Cleveland • New Haven, Conn. • Waterville, Maine • London • Munich

Dictionary of American History, Third Edition

Stanley I. Kutler, *Editor*

For permission to use material from this
product, submit your request via Web at
http://www.gale-edit.com/permissions, or you
may download our Permissions Request form
and submit your request by fax or mail to:

Permissions Department
The Gale Group, Inc.
27500 Drake Rd.
Farmington Hills, MI 48331-3535
Permissions Hotline:
248-699-8006 or 800-877-4253, ext. 8006
Fax: 248-699-8074 or 800-762-4058

LIBRARY OF CONGRESS CATALOGING-IN-PUBLICATION DATA

Dictionary of American history / Stanley I. Kutler.—3rd ed.
    p.   cm.
Includes bibliographical references and index.
    ISBN 0-684-80533-2 (set : alk. paper)
    1. United States—History—Dictionaries.   I. Kutler, Stanley I.
E174 .D52   2003
973'.03—dc21

Printed in United States of America
10 9 8 7 6 5 4 3 2 1

CONTENTS

DICTIONARY OF
American History

Third Edition

QR

QUAKERS. The Society of Friends was the most enduring of several religious groups to emerge out of the social and religious turmoil of the English Puritan Revolution. The movement dates its origins from 1652, when George Fox announced he had received from God a vision of "a great people to be gathered" in northwest England. The movement spread to the American colonies soon thereafter.

The core of Friends' theology was the Inner Light, or the intervention of the Holy Spirit in the consciousness of ordinary men and women. Friends, or "Quakers" (so called because of the trembling said to follow divine illumination), agreed with the Puritans that the Anglican Church had not gone far enough toward purifying itself of the external forms of the Catholic Church. But Quakers went further than the Puritans in their effort to clear the path to a direct and personal religious experience. They rejected the need for clergy or outward sacraments and adopted a plain worship style. Community worship took place not in churches, but in "meetings," during which members sat in silence until one among them felt moved by the Inner Light to speak. Quaker ethics, or "testimonies," were rooted in the belief that pride and wastefulness obstructed the path of the purifying Light. Thus they opposed ostentatious dress and other signs of social hierarchy, such as formal greetings, titles, and "doffing the hat" before superiors; insisted on fair business dealings; and refused to take oaths. The Quaker "peace testimony" against raising money or men for wars (deriving from their belief that war, too, was a manifestation of pride) evolved over time to become one of the more distinctive Quaker beliefs. Quakers believed that theirs was the only true religion and that God was working through them to turn others to the Light of Christ within and thereby remake humanity and society.

Quakers in the colonies, as in England, faced severe persecution in response to their persistent challenges to existing religious and civil authority. Between 1659 and 1661, several Quaker missionaries were hanged in Massachusetts Bay Colony because the Puritan leaders considered them a threat to their Bible Commonwealth. Persecution abated there and elsewhere in the colonies in the 1660s, but Quakerism spread most successfully in Rhode Island, which granted religious freedom, and in those areas of Long Island, New Jersey, Maryland, Virginia, and North Carolina where the established church was weak. When George Fox visited America (1671–1673) he helped institutionalize the colonial meeting structure, establishing "Yearly Meetings" in New England (1671) and Maryland (1672). Quakers emigrated to America in the 1670s and early 1680s in large numbers, escaping harsh persecution in England and seeking new opportunities for religious and economic prosperity. They migrated in families and sometimes Quaker communities, the majority coming from the "middling ranks" of English, Irish, and Welsh society.

Pennsylvania, founded in 1681 by English Quaker convert William Penn, was the largest haven for emi-

William Penn. The seventeenth-century Quaker founder of Pennsylvania, a proprietary colony that welcomed Quakers but accepted freedom of religion. Archive Photos, Inc.

grating Quakers. Penn, who had been granted a royal charter (probably in payment of a debt), planned Pennsylvania as a "Holy Experiment"—a peaceful community formed in obedience to God, which, if successful, would prefigure Christ's reign on earth. Although Pennsylvanians expected conformity to Quaker moral codes, the colony allowed freedom of religion. Pennsylvania was to have no militia and to maintain peaceful relations with the local Delaware Indians. The early decades of the colony were characterized by internal conflict over how best to govern and collect revenue for the colony while maintaining religious commitments. Tensions peaked in the Keithian Controversy (1691–1692), in which George Keith challenged the ministerial authority of the Quaker leaders and was disowned. Quaker society in Pennsylvania and the Delaware River region achieved stability by the 1720s. Philadelphia, or the "City of Brotherly Love," became the center of temporal and religious power in the colonies.

Beginning in the 1720s Quaker strictures on plain dress and simple living increasingly gave way to visible signs of wealth and class difference. Quakers' fair business dealings and frugal habits had made them successful businessmen. By the 1740s Quaker "grandees," or wealthy Philadelphia merchants (many of whom owned slaves), dominated Philadelphia's legislative assembly. Beginning in the 1750s, in response to a perceived fall from "first principles," reformers within the Society brought about a quietist, sectarian turn in Quaker theology and practice. They worked to foster commitment to Quakerism within the community through strengthening the family and tightening enforcement of Quaker moral codes, or "disciplines"—particularly that forbidding marriage to non-Quakers. In this same period, Quakers withdrew from political leadership of Pennsylvania and sharpened their opposition to slavery and violence against Indians. During the French and Indian War (1754–1763), the Quaker-led Assembly battled with proprietor Thomas Penn (William Penn's son) and German and Scotch-Irish frontiersmen—long embittered by the Quakers' pacifist relations with the Indians—over appropriations to fight the Delawares, who had sided with the French. By 1756 the Quakers in the Assembly were forced to resign or compromise their peace testimony. Quakers never again controlled the Assembly.

While some Quakers had criticized slavery since the time of Fox, there was no consensus against it until the time of the American Revolution. Germantown Quakers had written the first protest against slavery in the colonies in 1688, and George Keith had spoken out against slavery; but not until the sectarian turn of the 1750s did Quakers as a group begin to condemn slavery. John Woolman's antislavery tract, "Some Considerations on the Keeping of Negroes" (1754), rallied Quaker meetings against slavery. In 1775 Philadelphia Quakers launched the first abolitionist society in America. By 1776 Quaker slaveholders who did not manumit their slaves were disowned. During the Revolution, Quakers incurred patriot hostility because of their pacifism. In these tumultuous years Quakers had become a religious sect, seeking to reform the world they inhabited without becoming contaminated by it.

In the nineteenth century, Quakers left southern states and migrated westward, relocating to the slave-free states of the Northwest Territory, and eventually farther west. In response to the pressures of the market revolution and the evangelical revivals of the Second Great Awakening, Quakers underwent a series of schisms in the nineteenth century that brought the majority into greater conformity with the broader evangelical culture.

By the 1840s Quakers were divided into "Hicksites," "Wilburites," and "Gurneyites." "Hicksite" followers broke off in 1827, when the "Orthodox" majority disowned Elias Hicks for rejecting the Atonement, Original Sin, and other standard Christian tenets for total obedience to the Inner Light. Orthodox Friends went on in the 1840s to divide over the evangelical innovations to Quakerism of English preacher Joseph John Gurney. Gurney emphasized the importance of Scripture and justification by simple act of faith, thus adopting the more immediate "conversion" experience of evangelical Christianity over the slow process of justification by Divine Light characterizing early Quaker belief. Gurney, closely associated with leaders of the British antislavery movement, also defended abolition and other philanthropic reform activities of the kind evangelicals were actively pursuing in the nineteenth century. Five hundred "Wilburites" followed John Wilbur in separating from the "Gurneyites" in 1843, calling for a return to a more quietist vision of Quakerism. A wave of revivalism influenced by the interdenominational Holiness movement coursed through Gurneyite Meetings in the 1870s, leading to further divisions, which presaged the Fundamentalist-Modernist divide. Holiness Friends, along with some "Conservative" Wilburites and Gurneyites rejected higher criticism of the Bible, the theory of evolution, and the immanence of God in human history. More moderately evangelical Friends embraced the social gospel and theological liberalism, finding a spokesperson in *American Friend* editor and Haverford professor Rufus M. Jones.

Quakers in the nineteenth century, particularly of the "Gurneyite" variety, sought to partake of the broader evangelical Protestant culture without losing Quaker distinctiveness. They strengthened Quaker commitment to secondary and higher education and extended the humanitarian implications of the doctrine of the Inner Light. While they devoted themselves most energetically to temperance reform, they also supported foreign and home philanthropic mission efforts, pioneered prison-reform activities, and fought to end slavery in the South. Many Quakers held leadership positions in the abolitionist movement, including John Greenleaf Whittier, Levi Coffin, and Angelina and Sarah Grimké. Quakers also dedicated themselves to freedmen's aid after the Civil War.

In response to the total wars of the twentieth century, Quakers sought to expand their peacemaking role in creative ways. In 1917 Gurneyites, Hicksites, and Philadel-

Sarah Grimké. A nineteenth-century daughter of slaveholders, Quaker convert, and, with her sister Angelina, important activist against slavery and for women's rights.
LIBRARY OF CONGRESS

phia Orthodox worked together to create the American Friends Service Committee (AFSC), modeled after British war-relief organizations, to provide conscientious objectors with alternative ways to serve their country in war—including civilian relief, reconstruction, and medical work overseas. The AFSC's youth work camps, starting in the 1930s, helped pave the way for the government's development of the Peace Corps in the 1960s. The AFSC has also assisted in arbitration efforts, defended the rights of conscientious objectors, and, back home, engaged in social welfare, prison reform, and civil rights activism.

A distinctive legacy of Quakers is their disproportionately large presence in the ranks of the early feminists. Although official Quakerism may not have abided the activities of many of these feminists, the Quaker belief that "in souls there is no sex," and the opportunities provided Quaker women to preach, hold meetings, and write epistles, gave rise to the high percentage of Quakers among the "mothers of feminism," including Angelina and Sarah Grimké, Lucretia Mott, Abby Kelley, Susan B. Anthony, and Alice Paul.

BIBLIOGRAPHY

Bacon, Margaret Hope. *Mothers of Feminism: The Story of Quaker Women in America.* San Francisco: Harper and Row, 1986.

Barbour, Hugh, and J. William Frost. *The Quakers.* New York: Greenwood Press, 1988.

Hamm, Thomas D. *The Transformation of American Quakerism: Orthodox Friends, 1800–1907.* Bloomington: Indiana University Press, 1988.

Marietta, Jack D. *The Reformation of American Quakerism, 1748–1783.* Philadelphia: University of Pennsylvania Press, 1984.

Soderlund, Jean R. *Quakers and Slavery: A Divided Spirit.* Princeton, N.J.: Princeton University Press, 1985.

Susan Haskell

See also **Awakening, Second; Evangelicalism and Revivalism; Puritans and Puritanism.**

QUALITY CIRCLES is a term used in human resources management that refers to the technique of motivating workers by allowing them input into decisions concerning the production process, thereby increasing productivity and profits. The underlying premise is that productivity will increase for two reasons: because the person best able to decide the most efficient way to do a job is the person who does it for a living and because employees who have greater control over the product will be more committed and effective workers.

Originating in Japan in 1962, quality circles were introduced in the United States in the early 1970s. By the mid-1990s thousands of manufacturing plants, banks, hospitals, and government agencies had implemented quality circles. A circle typically consists of three to twelve employees from a given department and a representative of management. The circle meets on a regular basis on company time to examine a limited range of issues related to the department, identify and analyze problems, and propose solutions. The focus of the circles is on improving both the quality of the product and the production process. Some critics view quality circles as antiunion corporate strategies, intended to make employees feel as though they have input while denying them real power in the workplace.

BIBLIOGRAPHY

Cole, Robert E. *Managing Quality Fads: How American Business Learned to Play the Quality Game.* New York: Oxford University Press, 1999.

Cotton, John L. *Employee Involvement: Methods for Improving Performance and Work Attitudes.* Newbury Park, Calif.: Sage Publications, 1993.

Giordano, Lorraine. *Beyond Taylorism: Computerization and the New Industrial Relations.* New York: St. Martin's Press, 1992.

Grenier, Guillermo J. *Inhuman Relations: Quality Circles and Anti-Unionism in American Industry.* Philadelphia: Temple University Press, 1988.

Jack Handler/D. B.

See also **Corporations; Industrial Management; Industrial Relations; Labor.**

QUANTRILL'S RAID.

William Clarke Quantrill, leading a band of 448 Missouri guerrillas, raided and plundered the undefended town of Lawrence, KANSAS, in the early dawn of 21 August 1863. The raiders killed more than 150 and burned all the business buildings and most of the dwellings. Pursued by federal troops, they escaped to Missouri.

Justified as revenge for an earlier raid on Osceola, Missouri, this was less a border raid than a general massacre, prompted by the old bitterness against Lawrence for its part in the Kansas conflict and the persistent contest between proslavery and abolitionist forces. Quantrill, who had lived in Lawrence under the name of Charlie Hart and had been driven out as an undesirable, was probably motivated by a personal grudge.

BIBLIOGRAPHY

Connelley, William E. *Quantrill and the Border Wars.* Cedar Rapids, Iowa.: Torch Press, 1910.

Goodrich, Thomas. *Bloody Dawn: The Story of the Lawrence Massacre.* Kent, Ohio: Kent State University Press, 1991.

Schultz, Duane P. *Quantrill's War: The Life and Times of William Clarke Quantrill, 1837–1865.* New York: St. Martin's Press, 1996.

Samuel A. Johnson / A. R.

See also **Border Wars; Civil War; Kansas Free-State Party; Kansas-Nebraska Act; Lawrence, Sack of; Popular Sovereignty; Slavery; Topeka Constitution.**

QUARTERING ACT.

The Quartering Act of 2 June 1774, one of the COERCION ACTS, was passed in Parliament after the BOSTON TEA PARTY in 1773. The Quartering Act provided that local authorities must provide quarters for British troops. If they failed to do so, the governor might compel the use of occupied buildings. Though two previous quartering acts had passed in the 1760s, this third act engendered greater opposition as tensions mounted between Parliament and Boston Whigs. The Boston patriots refused to repair the empty buildings that Gen. Thomas Gage had procured for quarters and thus forced the British troops to remain camped on the Boston Common until November 1774.

BIBLIOGRAPHY

Bailyn, Bernard. *The Ordeal of Thomas Hutchinson.* Cambridge, Mass.: Belknap Press, 1974.

Greene, Jack P. *Understanding the American Revolution: Issues and Actors.* Charlottesville: University Press of Virginia, 1995.

Middlekauff, Robert. *The Glorious Cause: The American Revolution, 1763–1789.* New York: Oxford University Press, 1982.

John C. Miller / H. S.

See also **Billeting; Revolution, American: Political History.**

QUASI-WAR.

See **France, Quasi-War with.**

QUEBEC, CAPTURE OF.

In 1759, the year after the fall of Louisburg, Nova Scotia, British General James Wolfe was given command of 9,280 men, mostly regulars, to capture Quebec. Wolfe's force sailed 4 June 1759, for the Saint Lawrence River landing on the circle d'Orléans below Quebec on 27 June. Wolfe's army partially encircled Quebec with soldiers on the east, batteries on the south bank, and the fleet upstream. His coordinated attacks by land and water in July and August were rebuffed.

On 3 September the British secretly moved 3,000 soldiers to ships upstream. On the night of 12 September, Wolfe slipped a strong force downstream in small boats and effected a surprise landing near the city. Wolfe's force overpowered a small guard, captured an adjacent battery, and made it possible for about 5,000 troops to land safely and climb to the heights of the Plains of Abraham by six o'clock in the morning.

In this position, Wolfe threatened Quebec's communications with Montreal and inner Canada. In the formal eighteenth-century manner, Wolfe arrayed his force by eight o'clock. At ten o'clock, the French under Marquis Louis-Joseph de Montcalm formed for a conventional assault, which was met by formal volleys from the British battalions. Shots were exchanged for a few moments only, then the French wavered. The British charged and the French fled. Wolfe was killed on the field and Montcalm was carried off mortally wounded. Wolfe's successor closed in, and the surrender of Quebec on 18 September made inevitable British hegemony in Canada and the close of the French and Indian War, with the capture of Montreal, the following year.

BIBLIOGRAPHY

Donaldson, Gordon. *Battle for a Continent, Quebec 1759.* Garden City, N.Y.: Doubleday, 1973.

LaPierre, Laurier L. *1759: The Battle for Canada.* Toronto: McClelland & Stewart Inc., 1990.

Parkman Jr., Francis. *Montcalm and Wolfe.* New York: Collier Books, 1962.

Elbridge Colby / A. R.

See also **Abraham, Plains of; Canada, Relations with; French and Indian War.**

QUIDS.

Adapted from *tertium quid* ("third something"), the term "quid" was used in the early nineteenth century

Star of Bethlehem. A museum-quality example of the ancient tradition of quilting; this pattern and variations of it, also known as the Lone Star and Rising Star, date back to about 1830. MUSEUM OF MODERN ART

to refer to a member of a third political party or faction composed of disaffected Jeffersonian (or Democratic) Republicans, who attracted Federalist support with varying success. Quids were most commonly so called in Pennsylvania and New York, although the term was occasionally used in other states. "Quid" was generally applied reproachfully by political opponents and was rarely used in self-designation. No national Quid party ever developed, and most Quids continued to regard themselves as Jeffersonian Republicans.

BIBLIOGRAPHY

Cunningham, Noble E., Jr. *The Jeffersonian Republicans in Power: Party Operation, 1801–1809.* Chapel Hill: University of North Carolina Press, 1963.

———. "Who Were the Quids?" *Mississippi Valley Historical Review* 50 (1963).

Noble E. Cunningham Jr. / A. G.

See also **Federalist Party; New York State; Pennsylvania; Political Parties; Republicans, Jeffersonian.**

QUILTING. A quilt is made by sewing two pieces of cloth together with a padding in between the two layers held in place by stitching that creates a design. The first quilts emerged in ancient Egypt, and the decorative art form traveled to Asia and later to Europe during the Crusades (c. 1100–1300). By 1300, quilting had spread to Italy, where women sewed bed quilts, and from there a long tradition of quilt making developed throughout Europe. Female European immigrants brought their quilting skills to the United States where the art form flourished during the colonial era. American women often created patchwork quilts made from scraps of fabric. Women also participated in quilting bees in which they worked together in groups to sew quilts. African American women began quilting as slaves with scraps from their masters and continued the art form after their emancipation. As Americans migrated west during the nineteenth century, women's quilting patterns reflected their new experiences and carried such names as wagon wheel, log cabin, and North Star. Picture quilts also emerged during this time with designs that looked like pictures sewn onto quilts. Women sewed "friendship" quilts to create an album for special events like weddings and births. The AIDS Memorial Quilt originated in 1987 as a friendship quilt to remember those who died from AIDS. Each panel of the quilt includes the name and date of death of a person who died from AIDS.

BIBLIOGRAPHY

Cooper, Patricia, and Norma Bradley Buferd. *The Quilters: Women and Domestic Art.* Garden City, N.Y.: Anchor Press, 1993.

Orlofsky, Patsy, and Myron Orlofsky. *Quilts in America.* New York: McGraw-Hill, 1974.

Jane E. Dabel

QUIZ SHOW SCANDALS. A quiz show craze swept the United States in the 1950s. Television programs, such as CBS's *The $64,000 Question*, turned contestants into instant celebrities. One contestant, Charles Van Doren, reigned for fifteen weeks as champion of NBC's *Twenty-One.* The handsome, bright college instructor created a national sensation, winning $129,000, and even landing the cover of *Time* magazine.

Quiz show ratings skyrocketed under the guise of honest competition, but two whistleblowers—Edward Hilgemeier and former *Twenty-One* champion Herb Stempel—revealed that the shows were rigged. Champions, such as Van Doren, were chosen for their dashing looks and personality, and were fed the answers beforehand. Contestants were even instructed when to pause for greatest dramatic effect.

Quiz show fraud tainted the television industry. Van Doren initially denied being coached, only later confessing under pressure from a congressional inquiry in 1959. Critics pointed to quiz shows as confirming the decline of American morals. As a result, television networks added more news and documentary programs during the 1960s. Robert Redford brought the quiz show scandal to life in the 1994 motion picture *Quiz Show*, starring Ralph Fiennes as Van Doren. Van Doren did not cooperate with Redford on the film version and has never spoken publicly about the scandals.

BIBLIOGRAPHY

Anderson, Kent. *Television Fraud: The History and Implications of the Quiz Show Scandals.* Westport, Conn.: Greenwood, 1978.

DeLong, Thomas A. *Quiz Craze: America's Infatuation with Game Shows.* Westport, Conn.: Praeger, 1991.

Bob Batchelor

See also **Scandals; Television: Programming and Influence.**

Charles Van Doren. The assistant professor of English at Columbia University (until the scandal broke in 1959) looks puzzled as he competes on the quiz show *Twenty-one*—but is he really? AP/WIDE WORLD PHOTOS

RABAUL CAMPAIGN (1943–1944). In August 1943, the Allies opted against a land assault on the key Japanese base of Rabaul, on New Britain, just east of New Guinea. Instead, beginning in October, the Allies launched a fierce air attack that effectively neutralized Rabaul as an offensive threat and provided cover for Allied operations to the west and south. Under almost daily attack, the Japanese began evacuating aircraft and shipping. By the end of the air campaign in March 1944, roughly 20,000 tons of bombs had been dropped. The nearly 100,000 Japanese troops still defending Rabaul were isolated and impotent, no longer factors in the war.

BIBLIOGRAPHY

Miller John, Jr. *Cartwheel: The Reduction of Rabaul, United States Army in World War II.* Washington, D.C.: Government Printing Office, 1959.

Murphy, James T. *Skip Bombing.* Westport, Conn.: Praeger Publishers, 1993.

Schaffer, Ronald. *Wings of Judgment: American Bombing in World War II.* New York: Oxford University Press, 1985.

Stanley L. Falk / A. R.

See also **Bismarck Sea, Battle of; Bougainville; Coral Sea, Battle of the; Guadalcanal Campaign; World War II; World War II, Air War against Japan; World War II, Navy in.**

RACE RELATIONS, in complex societies, such as that of the United States, involve patterns of behavior between members of large categories of human beings classified on the basis of similar observable physical traits, particularly skin color. Race is a social status that individuals occupy along with other statuses, such as ethnicity, occupation, religion, age, and sex. In the United States racial status has often been paramount, transcending all other symbols of status in human relations.

While it is virtually impossible to chronicle the history of American race relations in any single publication, this entry provides a brief glimpse at some of the events that played a major role in continually evolving relationships among America's various races.

Although there have been numerous instances of friendly and egalitarian relationships across racial lines in American history, the major pattern of race relations has been characterized by extreme dominant-subordinate relationships between whites and nonwhites. This relationship is seen in the control by whites of the major positions of policymaking in government, the existence of formal and informal rules restricting nonwhite membership in the most remunerative and prestigious occupations, the often forcible imposition of the culture of white Americans on nonwhites, the control by whites of the major positions and organizations in the economic sector, and the disproportionate membership of nonwhites in the lower-income categories. Race relations have also been characterized by extreme social distance between whites and nonwhites, as indicated by long-standing legal restrictions on racial intermarriage, racial restrictions in immigration laws, spatial segregation, the existence of racially homogeneous voluntary associations, extensive incidents of racially motivated conflict, and the presence of numerous forms of racial antipathy and stereotyping in literature, the press, and legal records. This pattern has varied by regions and in particular periods of time; it began diminishing in some measure after World War II.

Race Relations in Early America
Before the Europeans arrived in America, there were at least 1 million Indians divided into hundreds of tribes and bands and speaking at least 200 mutually unintelligible languages. However, the first discussion of race, or the categorization of individuals based on physical features, occurred when three historical occurrences converged in America. The first Europeans arrived on the continent and labeled the indigenous ethnic groups "Indians." Shortly thereafter, Europeans began referring to themselves as "whites." Ethnic groups that were, for the most part, indigenous to Africa were brought to America and labeled as "Negroes." Since this early effort at categorization, the subject of race relations has been a controversial topic ripe with dissenting opinions and actions.

The first Africans arrived in the English colonies in 1619. Debate over the status of these new arrivals has been substantial. Some scholars suggest that the first Africans were probably indentured servants, individuals bound to a person for a specific amount of time. This would infer that Africans who were called indentured servants had approximately the same status as white indentured servants, many of whom paid their way to America by binding themselves to service for a limited period. However, other equally learned scholars argue that historical records do not indicate the existence of indentured servant status for early Africans, and believe that this "legend" occurred because the word "slave" did not appear in Virginia records until 1656.

Prior to the arrival of Africans aboard a Dutch man-of-war, Europeans had attempted to enslave Native Americans. However, complex issues, including Native Americans' susceptibility to European diseases, the numerous avenues of escape available for Native Americans, and the lucrative nature of the African slave trade, led to a transition toward African slavery. Before this transition, numerous Native American nations—including the Pequot, Tuscarora, and Yamasee—and tens of thousands of individuals were displaced and relocated throughout the colonies. Colonists also drove Native Americans from their territories by signing treaties, which they quickly violated, and declaring war on the affected nations.

As relationships grew between Native Americans and African Americans and the evolution of Afro-Indian nations began to occur, colonists used the legislature to strengthen their hold on the enslavement of both integrating cultures. In 1662 the general assembly of Virginia had passed a law that ruled any child born of a slave mother would also be a slave, regardless of the father's legal status; by 1740 the South Carolina slave code declared that all Negroes and Indians in that particular province, as well as their descendents, would be and remain slaves for the rest of their lives.

Africans and Indians, however, began to protest their enslavement. Slave revolts began as early as 1657 when an African-Indian uprising occurred in Hartford, Connecticut. Other early revolts occurred in 1690 in Newbury, Massachusetts, and in Queens County, New York, in 1708. This spirit of uprising continued throughout the 1700s, culminating in slave revolts in 1712 and 1739.

Years later, a sense of historical irony came over the nation. During the time when the colonies were fighting for their freedom from British rule, Abigail Adams, the wife of founding father John Adams, told her husband that she could not understand how the colonists could fight for their own freedom while they were daily stealing the freedom of those who had as much right to freedom as anyone. Then, on 5 March 1770, former slave Crispus Attucks became the first person to die in the Boston Massacre, and became, to many, the martyr of the American Revolution. Despite this apparent show of bravery and the fact that 20 percent of the overall population in the thirteen colonies was of African descent, the Continental Congress in 1775 barred people of African descent from joining the Revolutionary Army.

On 4 July 1776, America issued its Declaration of Independence, which professed that all men were created equal, endowed with certain inalienable rights, and entitled to liberty. It was this act, which a number of African Americans considered hypocritical, that helped fuel the creation of an African American polity that would eventually lead the way for a civil rights movement.

Gabriel's Insurrection, Black Cultural Identity, and Race Relations

Africans and their descendants in the new United States outnumbered Europeans south of the Mason-Dixon line in 1800; in fact, close to 50 percent of all immigrants (including Europeans) who lived in the thirteen American colonies between 1700 and 1775 came from Africa. A forced migration of these proportions had an enormous impact on societies and cultures throughout the Americas and produced a diverse community of peoples of African descent.

An event known as Gabriel's Insurrection characterized race relations in the early nineteenth century. In the spring of 1800, the slave Gabriel Prosser, whose intention was to create a free black state in Virginia, organized a slave uprising. Prosser hoped that slaves from the surrounding territory would join him and his comrades and, eventually, that the uprising would reach such proportions that the whites would be forced to discuss Prosser's vision for a free black state. When Prosser's plans to attack the city of Richmond became known, Governor James Monroe ordered in the federal militia, which ultimately suppressed the insurrection. Prosser and fifteen of his followers were hanged in October of that year.

During this time, Africans and their descendants forged two distinct identities: one as black Virginians sharing a provincial culture, and a second as African Americans sharing a fate with enslaved peoples throughout the hemisphere. In his *Ploughshares into Swords* (1997), the historian James Sidbury contends that African ethnicity mattered in the New World. To highlight the absence of racial solidarity, Sidbury points to the refusal of slaves from one locality to aid those of another in resisting their common oppressor. Ironically, the lack of a broader collective identity was itself the primary "Africanism" in early Virginia.

In the half-century after 1750 four developments fostered a broader racial consciousness. First, as plantation slavery expanded into Piedmont counties, links between old and new quarters enlarged the boundaries of community. Second, evangelical Christianity created a network of the faithful, especially as black Baptists pushed to establish autonomous churches. At the same time, the American Revolution gave black Virginians a reason to see themselves as a cohesive people. In particular, Dunmore's Proclamation addressed the colony's slaves in collective terms. Finally, events in Saint Domingue, Haiti, provided a model of revolutionary racial justice that prompted black Virginians to situate themselves in a larger African diaspora.

By 1800 Prosser and his neighbors asserted a double consciousness that was at once provincial (black and Virginian) and global (black Virginian and African American). Sidbury carefully roots community and identity in concrete social relations, specific to time and place. People can simultaneously inhabit multiple, and potentially antagonistic, communities. Likewise, identities are "crosscutting," the term Sidbury uses to capture the tension among an individual's class, race, gender, status, nativity, and religious positions. Race was the foundation of many, but not all, of the communities to which enslaved Virginians belonged. When Haitian slaves arrived with their exiled masters in Richmond in 1793, local slaves skirmished with the strange, predominantly African refugees. In 1800 Prosser and his allies excluded women from their uprising. They also debated whether to spare Quakers, Methodists, Frenchmen, and white women. Not long after, two slaves alerted their master to the plot, another black man turned the fleeing Prosser over to the authorities, and several co-conspirators turned state's evidence. Where other historians have mythologized a homogeneous "slave community," Sidbury introduces complexity and conflict.

Native American Relations

After the American Revolution white Americans increased their migration into Indian territories to the West and into the Spanish Empire (and after 1821, Mexico). The policy of the federal government toward Indians before the Civil War was the removal of Indians to then unwanted territories west of the Mississippi River. By 1821 the tribes in the Great Lakes region had been forcibly relocated, and the Indians of the Southeast were forcibly removed between 1817 and 1835.

Settlers in Georgia coveted Spanish and Seminole land in Florida. The Georgians were also upset that when Britain controlled Florida the British often incited Seminoles against American settlers who were migrating south into Seminole territory. These old conflicts, combined with the safe-haven Seminoles provided Africans, caused the United States to support a group of recent settlers (mainly from Georgia) who lived in northeastern Florida and called themselves the Patriots. The Patriot War was unsuccessful in part because the United States became involved in the Creek War in Alabama. But soon attention turned again to Florida. One of the initial attacks of the First Seminole War (1817–1818) was the attack on the Negro Fort. The cry of "Negro Fort!" became a battle cry among Seminoles and Africans in Florida. By 1817 reports claimed that 600 blacks were training as soldiers and were highly regimented, an even larger number of

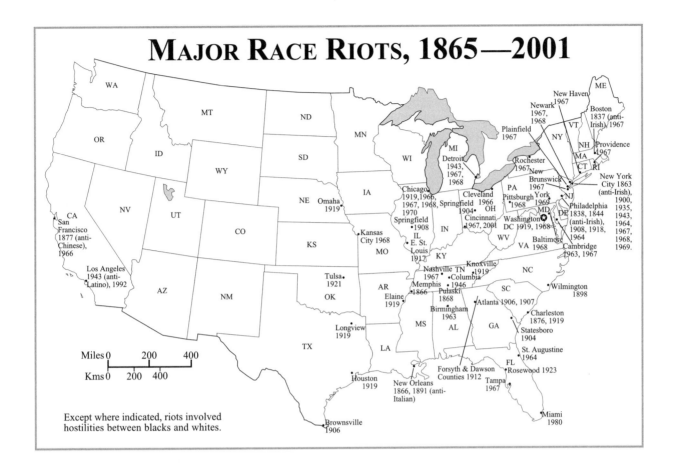

MAJOR RACE RIOTS, 1865—2001

Except where indicated, riots involved hostilities between blacks and whites.

Seminoles were preparing to fight invaders into their territory. Many Africans had decided that they would follow Bowlegs as king, and Nero was their commander. Forces under General Andrew Jackson fought the Seminoles for several years. Although the war officially ended in 1818, unofficial U.S. military expeditions into the territory continued until Spain formally ceded Florida to the United States in 1821. As soon as the United States acquired Florida, it began urging the Indians there to leave their lands and relocate along with other southeastern tribes to Indian Territory, in present-day Oklahoma. Some Seminole leaders signed a treaty in 1832, and part of the tribe moved. But other Seminoles refused to recognize the treaty and fled to the Florida Everglades.

The Second Seminole War (1835–1842), usually referred to as the Seminole War proper, was the fiercest war waged by the U.S. government against American Indians. The United States spent more than $20 million fighting the Seminoles. In 1842, a nominal end to the hostilities arrived, however no peace treaty was signed. By this time most Seminoles had been moved from Florida and relocated to Indian Territory. A Third Seminole War broke out in 1855, when conflicts—largely over land—arose between whites and some Seminoles who remained in Florida. Constant military patrols and rewards for the capture of Indians reduced the Seminole population in Florida to about 200 when the Third Seminole War ended in 1858.

In 1862 Indians were designated wards of the Bureau of Indian Affairs rather than enemies, and in 1871 Congress declared an end to the policy of signing treaties with Indian nations. Numerous conflicts took place during the nineteenth century as Indians resisted the invasion of their territories and their placement on reservations. Of the Indians in California, 70,000 were killed by war and disease between 1849 and 1859, and other groups were similarly devastated. The defeat of the Plains Indians was made possible, in part, by the reduction of the bison herds from an estimated 13 million in 1867 to 200 in 1883.

With the defeat of the Apache in 1886, the Indian wars came to an end; the Indian population had been reduced to about 200,000 and was forced into impoverishment on reservations under the paternalistic and often corrupt control of the Bureau of Indian Affairs. From 1887 to 1934 federal policy toward Indians was governed by the General Allotment Act (Dawes Severalty Act) of 1887, under which Indians were to be transformed into individualistic and responsible farmers on family owned plots. The policy reduced reservation acreage from 139 million acres in 1887 to 47 million acres by 1933.

African American Relations

Throughout the colonial period and until 1819, slaves escaped from the Lower South into East and West Florida. While the famous "Negro Fort," once the British Fort

Gadsden, was taken by American troops in 1816, it was not until 1819 that the United States made a bold play to take all of East Florida. In that year, Congress attempted to put a stop to slave runaways and Indian raids across the Florida border by sending General Jackson to make war on the encampments and communities of Africans and Native Americans. Jackson claimed all of Florida for the United States. Spain was not strong enough to reclaim Florida and the descendants of many fugitives moved on to Cuba or retreated into the swamps.

The bloodiest insurrection of all, in which some sixty whites were murdered, occurred in Southampton County, Virginia, in August 1831. Nat Turner, its leader, besides being a skilled carpenter, was a literate, mystical preacher. He had discovered particular relevance in the prophets of the Old Testament. Besides identifying with the slave experience of the Israelites, Turner and other slaves felt that the social righteousness preached by prophets related directly to the men's situation. Turner's growing hatred of slavery and his increasing concern for the plight of his brothers led him to believe he was one of God's chosen instruments. In early 1831 Turner collected a small band of followers, and in August they moved from farm to farm, slaughtering the white inhabitants, gaining many of the slaves who were freed in the process. When word of the massacre spread, they were met by armed resistance. Some of Turner's men were killed and wounded, and Turner and several of his followers were captured and executed.

The Turner massacre was universally depicted as the work of savages and brutes and, as a result, new laws controlling the slaves were passed throughout the South. Both the violence of the slaves and the verbal abuse of the abolitionists served only to strengthen the South in its defense of the institution of slavery. Slaves who revolted were depicted as beasts that could not be freed because they would endanger society. Submissive slaves were pictured as children in need of paternal protection from the evils of a complex, modern world. They were never seen as men whose rights and liberties had been proclaimed in the Declaration of Independence.

By 1804 all the northern states had either eliminated slavery or passed laws for its gradual abolition. But the humanitarian motives behind the antislavery laws were not sufficient to prevent the imposition of a system of severe discrimination and segregation on the 10 percent of the African American population that resided in the North. Before the Civil War, African Americans in the North were restricted from entering various states, given inadequate and segregated schooling, barred from most public facilities, excluded from jury service and denied the vote, and nursed in segregated hospitals and buried in segregated graveyards.

The Post–Civil War Period

After the Civil War, African Americans improved their economic status as a whole, engaged in civil rights efforts to enforce new antidiscrimination laws, and became politically active. However, between 1877, when the federal troops were withdrawn from the South, and 1910, a new system of segregation and discrimination was imposed on African Americans. With each depression in the late nineteenth century, African Americans lost their hard-won gains, were deserted by liberals, and saw a number of rights eliminated or curtailed by U.S. Supreme Court decisions in 1873, 1883, and 1896.

With the passage of numerous state and local ordinances dealing with segregation, the disfranchisement of the African American voter, and the economic relegation of African Americans to the lowest menial occupations, the apartheid system was complete, not to be seriously challenged by white liberals or African Americans until after World War II. In the North between 1865 and 1945, African Americans could vote and segregation was never formalized into the legal code; but de facto segregation and a disproportionate placement in the less desirable occupations were still a social reality for African Americans in the North.

With the end of the Mexican-American War in 1848, half of Mexico was annexed to the United States, and the estimated 150,000 Mexicans who lived in the territory rapidly became a numerical minority as Americans inundated the area. Most of this Mexican population was reduced to landless menial labor by 1900, through discriminatory property taxes and title laws. As the economic status of Mexicans was reduced, those of Spanish and of Indian-Spanish, or mestizo, descent were lumped together by Americans and viewed as a single, distinct, and inferior race—a view intensified by the entrance of over 700,000 legal immigrants from rural Mexico into the United States between 1900 and 1930. (In 1930 the U.S. Census Bureau, for the first and only time, divided Mexican Americans into 4.6 percent white and 95.4 percent colored.)

During the same period European and Asian immigrants arrived in the United States in increasing numbers to meet the demands of an expanding economy. Between 1820 and 1920 some 30 million Europeans entered America. Being white, most of them entered the American mainstream within two or three generations, the rate of assimilation being affected primarily by the degree to which their cultures approximated that of Americans of British descent.

Asian immigrants, however, had a different experience. The peak years of Chinese immigration were from 1861 to 1890 (249,213) and 1891 to 1920 (239,576) for the Japanese. All were met with resistance. The Chinese were barred from voting in California in 1848 and from testifying in court between 1854 and 1872. The California constitution banned Chinese persons from working in corporations and government, and forced them to pay discriminatory taxes and fees. This state-sanctioned discrimination made for an essentially lawless West that ig-

Race Relations. Blacks and whites sit together at the massive March on Washington rally in front of the Lincoln Memorial on 28 August 1963, the site of Martin Luther King Jr.'s famous "I Have a Dream" speech—envisioning a day when, finally, children will "not be judged by the color of their skin but by the content of their character." NATIONAL ARCHIVES AND RECORDS ADMINISTRATION

nored the numerous acts of violence committed against Asian immigrants.

By arriving in a more stable period, the Japanese avoided this "frontier" situation but were excluded from white unions and denied ownership of land by a number of western states (a practice declared constitutional by the U.S. Supreme Court in 1923). Further Chinese and Japanese immigration was almost terminated by congressional acts in 1902 and 1924.

The Twentieth Century

By the beginning of the twentieth century almost all nonwhites were in the lowest occupation and income categories in the United States and were attempting to accommodate themselves to this status within segregated areas—barrios, ghettoes, and reservations. The great majority of whites, including major educators and scientists, justified this condition on the grounds that nonwhites were biologically inferior to whites.

Although the period was largely characterized by the accommodation of nonwhites to subordination, a number of major incidents of racial conflict did occur: the mutiny and rioting of a number of African American soldiers in Houston, Texas, in 1917; African American–white conflict in twenty-five cities in the summer of 1919; and the de-

struction of white businesses in Harlem in New York City in 1935 and in Detroit in 1943. A major racist policy of the federal government was the forcible evacuation and internment of 110,000 Japanese living on the West Coast in 1942—a practice not utilized in Hawaii, and not utilized against Italians and German Americans.

Following World War II major changes occurred in the pattern of white dominance, segregation, and nonwhite accommodation that had been highly structured in the first half of the twentieth century. After the war a number of new nonwhite organizations were formed and, with the older organizations, sought changes in American race relations as varied as integration, sociocultural pluralism, and political independence. The government and the courts, largely reacting to the activities of these groups, ended the legality of segregation and discrimination in schools, public accommodations, the armed forces, housing, employment practices, eligibility for union membership, and marriage and voting laws. In addition, in March 1961 the federal government began a program of affirmative action in the hiring of minorities and committed itself to a policy of improving the economic basis of Indian reservations and, by 1969, promoting Indian self-determination within the reservation framework.

Although government efforts to enforce the new laws and court decisions were, at least at the outset, sporadic and inadequate, most overt forms of discrimination had been eliminated by the mid-1970s and racial minorities were becoming proportionally represented within the middle occupational and income levels. Changes in dominance and social distance were accompanied by white resistance at the local level, leading to considerable racial conflict in the postwar period. The Mississippi Summer Project to register African American voters in Lowndes County in 1965 resulted in the burning of 35 African American churches, 35 shootings, 30 bombings of buildings, 1,000 arrests, 80 beatings of African American and white workers, and 6 murders.

Between 1964 and 1968 there were 239 cases of hostile African American protest and outbursts in 215 cities. In 1972 Indian groups occupied Alcatraz, set up roadblocks in Washington, D.C., and occupied and damaged the offices of the Bureau of Indian Affairs in that city. The Alianza movement of Chicanos in New Mexico in 1967 attempted to reclaim Rio Arriba County as an independent republic by storming the courthouse in Tierra Amarilla. Mexican American students walked out of high schools in Los Angeles in 1968, and a number of Chicano organizations boycotted the Coors Brewery in Colorado between 1968 and 1972. During the 1970s Chinese youth organizations in San Francisco, California, staged a protest and engaged in violence, claiming the right to armed self-defense against the police and the release of all Asians in American prisons.

The major developments in the 1970s were the increased efforts on the part of federal agencies to enforce the civil rights laws of the 1960s; a greater implementation of affirmative action programs, involving efforts to direct employers to take positive actions to redress employment imbalances (through the use of quotas in some cases); and the resistance in numerous communities to busing as a device to achieve racial integration in the public schools. In the 1970s America saw an influx of 4 million immigrants, followed by 6 million more in the 1980s. Millions more arrived in the country illegally. Most of the immigrants originated in Asia and Latin America and, by 1999, California, which was the nation's most populous state, had a makeup that included more than 50 percent nonwhites.

Hate crimes continued to grow from the early 1980s to 2002. In 1982 Vincent Chin, a Chinese American, was beaten to death in Detroit, Michigan, by two out-of-work autoworkers. The men blamed the Japanese for their lack of work and mistakenly believed that Chin was Japanese. In July 1989 a young African American man was assaulted in the mostly white area of Glendale, California. Despite these and numerous other instances of hate crimes throughout these decades, race relations became embedded in America's social conscience with the Rodney King beating. On 3 March 1992, a young African American man named Rodney King was pulled over for reckless driving in Los Angeles. Several police officers beat King, and despite the videotape of a bystander, an all-white jury acquitted the officers. Riots erupted in Los Angeles, resulting in 53 deaths, 4,000 injuries, 500 fires, and more than $1 billion in property damage. When speaking to reporters, King uttered what are now some of the more famous words surrounding race relations: "People, I just want to say, you know, can we all get along? Can we just get along?"

BIBLIOGRAPHY

Kitano, Harry H. L. *The Japanese Americans.* New York: Chelsea House, 1987.

Marden, Charles F., Gladys Meyer, and Madeline H. Engel. *Minorities in American Society.* 6th ed. New York: Harper-Collins, 1992.

Moore, Joan W., with Harry Pachon. *Mexican Americans.* 2d ed. Englewood Cliffs, N.J.: Prentice-Hall, 1976.

Pinkney, Alphonso. *Black Americans.* 5th ed. Upper Saddle River, N.J.: Prentice-Hall, 2000.

Quarles, Benjamin. *The Negro in the Making of America.* 3d ed. New York: Simon and Schuster, 1996.

Sidbury, James. *Ploughshares into Swords: Race, Rebellion, and Identity in Gabriel's Virginia, 1730–1810.* New York: Cambridge University Press, 1997.

Simpson, George Eaton, and J. Milton Yinger. *Racial and Culture Minorities: An Analysis of Prejudice and Discrimination.* 5th ed. New York: Plenum Press, 1985.

Wax, Murray L. *Indian Americans: Unity and Diversity.* Englewood Cliffs, N.J.: Prentice-Hall, 1971.

James T. Scott

See also **Black Codes; Civil Rights Movement; Discrimination: Race; Jim Crow Laws; Racial Science; Riots; Segregation; Slavery.**

RACE RIOTS. *See* **Riots.**

RACIAL SCIENCE in America is nearly as old as the United States itself. Thomas Jefferson's *Notes on the State of Virginia* (1785) included a discourse on racial physiology (and supposed inequality) that was among the earliest intellectual treatments of the subject. Systematic scientific attention to the issue began in the early 1800s and has continued in various forms to the present day.

Two competing theories defined early nineteenth-century racial science debates: monogeny and polygeny. Monogeny, the idea that all humans derived from a single pair of ancestors and that racial differences arose from inherent adaptability, drew on biblical creation as well as enlightenment rationalist ideals of the unity and perfectibility of humankind. The foremost advocate of this theory exemplified its diverse influences: Samuel Stanhope Smith was both a minister and president of what is now Princeton University. Polygeny was the theory that human races were created separately and thus have innate and immutable differences. Influential support for this hypothesis came from anatomist Samuel George Morton's *Crania Americana* (1839) and *Crania Aegyptiaca* (1844), morphological analyses of hundreds of skulls that included the first racial cranial capacity studies. Josiah Nott and George Gliddon expanded upon these works in their landmark polygenist synthesis *Types of Mankind* (1854). This new and controversial "American School of Anthropology" received important scientific credibility when the world-renowned naturalist Louis Agassiz publicly espoused it from his position at Harvard. Proponents of this school used their quasi-scientific studies to justify slavery or the restriction of civil rights for non-whites, and decried miscegenation (racial intermarriage) as akin to interspecies mating.

Although Darwinian theory (1859) changed the parameters of debate, polygenist theory continued to thrive under the guise of human evolution. Racial hierarchies formerly explained by separate creations remained intact, justified instead as separate racial divergences from primitive ancestors. Investigators in the emerging field of physical anthropology adopted racial classification as their primary focus, utilizing large amounts of raw data collected from Civil War soldiers, Native Americans, immigrants, and other groups to reinforce older racial hierarchies and introduce new ones. Adding the new statistical and biological advances of the early twentieth century to their analytical arsenal, physical anthropologists, psychologists, and biologists sought to quantify and rank racial differences through head shape, I.Q. tests, blood type, and even the structure of internal organs. These studies not only reinforced prevailing stereotypes of non-whites, they also became purportedly impartial justifications for the exclusion of immigrants from "inferior" southern- and eastern-European groups.

Even as scientific racism reached its high tide, it faced serious challenges from a growing number of scientists. Johns Hopkins biologist Raymond Pearl, widely respected anatomist T. Wingate Todd, outspoken anthropologist M. F. Ashley Montagu, and famed Columbia anthropologist Franz Boas were among the leading figures in their fields who (along with their former students) sought to discredit racial determinism from a scientific standpoint. Between these critiques, the increasing unpopularity of German racial science under the Nazi regime, and the development of population biology and the neo-Darwinian evolutionary synthesis, defenses of racial inequality ceased to be part of mainstream scientific thought by the 1950s.

Despite its retreat, racial science has endured. Although the American Association of Physical Anthropologists officially rejected the concept of racial inferiority in 1956, its members still research human variation. In fact, great advances in biogenetic techniques from the 1980s on spurred a resurgence of ethnic and racial variation studies in physical anthropology and forensics, albeit without the overt inegalitarian overtones of the past. In contrast, workers from other fields continued to champion the idea of racial inequality. In the 1960s and 1970s,

University of California educational psychologist Arthur Jensen claimed to have proven racial differences in intellectual abilities. Similarly, political scientist Charles Murray and Harvard psychologist Richard J. Herrnstein asserted the existence of significant racial differences in I.Q. in their controversial book *The Bell Curve* (1994). Although the mainstream American scientific community (led by such notable figures as Harvard's Stephen Jay Gould) countered these works with detailed critiques, these well-publicized debates demonstrated that scientific racism, an idea tracing back to the birth of the United States, still lingered at the dawn of the twenty-first century.

BIBLIOGRAPHY

Barkan, Elazar. *The Retreat of Scientific Racism: Changing Concepts of Race in Britain and the United States between the World Wars.* Cambridge: Cambridge University Press, 1992.

Gould, Stephen Jay. *The Mismeasure of Man.* New York: Norton, 1981.

Haller, John S. *Outcasts from Evolution: Scientific Attitudes of Racial Inferiority, 1859–1900.* Urbana: University of Illinois Press, 1971.

Stanton, William. *The Leopard's Spots: Scientific Attitudes toward Race in America 1815–59.* Chicago: University of Chicago Press, 1960.

Kevin F. Kern

See also **Eugenics; Race Relations.**

RADAR, an acronym for "radio detection and ranging," is a method of locating distant targets by sending bursts of electromagnetic radiation and measuring their reflections. In the most common method, ultrashort radio waves are beamed toward the target by a scanning antenna. The resulting echoes are then displayed on a cathode-ray tube by means of a scanning signal synchronized with the antenna, so that the echo from each target appears as an illuminated dot, in the appropriate direction and at a proportional distance, on a map of the entire area being scanned. In other versions, continuous waves are used, and, in some, only moving targets are revealed (for example, in police sets used to detect speeding vehicles).

The science behind radar dates to the 1920s, when radio operators noticed perturbations caused by obstacles moving in a radio field. Such effects were familiar to both amateur and professional radio enthusiasts in many countries and were at first freely discussed in engineering journals. As the military significance of these observations dawned on researchers in government laboratories in the 1930s, such references grew rarer. Two American reports, in particular, helped shape the nascent science of radio detection: a 1933 report (by C. R. Englund and others in the *Proceedings of the Institute of Radio Engineers*) describing a systematic investigation of the interferences caused by overflying aircraft and a 1936 report (by C. W. Rice in the *General Electric Review*) on the uses of ultrahigh-

Radar Room. Men wearing headphones sit at a table in a carrier on the China Sea during World War II. © UPI/CORBIS-BETTMANN

frequency equipment, among which was listed "radio-echo location for navigation."

The first innovations came from the commercial sector. Radio altimeters were developed to gauge the altitude of planes; experimental equipment intended to prevent collisions was installed on the French Line's giant ship *Normandie*, producing considerable publicity but only moderate success. Scientists, as well, found applications for these early forms of radar technology. They used radio detection to locate storms, measure the height of the ionosphere, and survey rugged terrain. Essential technologies evolved from these experiments, such as ultrahigh-frequency (microwave) tubes, circuits, and antennas; cathode-ray (picture) display tubes; and wide-band receivers capable of amplifying and resolving extremely short pulses of one-millionth of one second (microsecond) or less.

As WORLD WAR II approached, military laboratories in several countries rushed to develop systems capable of locating unseen enemy ships and aircraft. Such a capability, military planners knew, would provide enormous tactical advantages on sea and in the air. Six countries led the race—the United States, Great Britain, France, Germany, Italy, and Japan—but there were doubtless others, including Canada, the Netherlands, and the Soviet Union. Great Britain made the swiftest progress before the outbreak of the war. A team assembled by the engineer Robert Watson-Watt devised a system of radar stations and backup information-processing centers. This complex was partly in place when war broke out in September 1939 and was rapidly extended to cover most of the eastern and south-ern coasts of England. By the time of the air Battle of Britain a year later, the system was fully operational. The British radar system is credited with swinging the balance in the defenders' favor by enabling them to optimize their dwindling air reserves.

American military developments had started even earlier, in the early 1930s, and were carried on at fairly low priority at the Naval Research Laboratory under R. M. Page and at the army's Signal Corps laboratories under W. D. Hershberger. By the time the United States entered the war, radar had been installed on several capital warships and in a number of critical shore installations. Indeed, a radar post in the hills above Pearl Harbor spotted the Japanese attack in December 1941, but the backup system was not in place and the warning did not reach the main forces in time. American forces in the Pacific quickly corrected this situation, and radar played a significant role six months later in the pivotal victory over a Japanese naval force at Midway Island.

British researchers had not been idle in the meantime. Great Britain made a great step forward with the invention of a high-power magnetron, a vacuum tube that, by enabling the use of even shorter centimetric wavelengths, improved resolution and reduced the size of the equipment. Even before the attack on Pearl Harbor, a British delegation led by Sir Henry Tizard had brought a number of devices, including the centimetric magnetron, to the United States in an effort to enroll U.S. industry in the war effort, since British industry was already strained to full capacity. The resulting agreement was not entirely one-sided, since it placed some American developments at the Allies' disposal: for instance, the transmit-receive (TR) tube, a switching device that made it possible for a single antenna to be used alternately for radar transmission and reception. From then on until the end of the war, British and U.S. radar developments were joined, and the resulting equipment was largely interchangeable between the forces of the two nations.

The principal U.S. radar research laboratories were the Radiation Laboratory at the Massachusetts Institute of Technology (MIT), directed by Lee Du Bridge, where major contributions to the development of centimetric radar (including sophisticated airborne equipment) were made; and the smaller Radio Research Laboratory at Harvard University, directed by F. E. Terman, which specialized in electronic countermeasures (i.e., methods of rendering enemy's radar ineffective and overcoming its countermeasures). The MIT group produced an elaborate and detailed twenty-eight-volume series of books during the late 1940s that established a solid foundation for worldwide radar developments for several decades.

Wartime industrial advances gave U.S. manufacturers a head start over foreign competitors, notably in the defeated nations, where war-related industries remained shut down for several years. Postwar developments were enhanced by commercial demand—there was soon scarcely an airport or harbor anywhere that was not equipped with radar—and by the exigencies of the space age, including astrophysics. Many of the basic inventions of World War II remained fundamental to new developments, but additional refinements were introduced by researchers in many countries. Among them, the contributions of Americans were perhaps the most numerous and ensured that American-made radar equipment could compete in world markets despite high production costs.

BIBLIOGRAPHY

Buderi, Robert. *The Invention that Changed the World.* New York: Simon and Schuster, 1996.

Burns, Russell, ed. *Radar Development to 1945.* London: Institution of Electrical Engineers, 1988.

Fisher, David E. *A Race on the Edge of Time.* New York: McGraw-Hill, 1988.

Page, Robert M. *The Origin of Radar.* Garden City, N.Y.: Anchor Books, 1962.

Charles Süsskind / A. R.

See also **Air Defense; Aircraft Industry; Signal Corps, U.S. Army; Weather Service, National.**

RADICAL REPUBLICANS.

The Radical Republicans were a wing of the Republican Party organized around an uncompromising opposition to slavery before and during the Civil War and a vigorous campaign to secure rights for freed slaves during Reconstruction.

In the late 1840s, before the Republican Party was created, a small group of antislavery radicals in Congress (including Salmon Chase and Charles Sumner in the Senate and Joshua Giddings, George Julian, and Thaddeus Stevens in the House) formed an unofficial alliance. They were ostracized at first, but as the decade wore on and the Fugitive Slave Law (1850), the Kansas-Nebraska Act (1854), and the Dred Scott decision (1857) seemed to prove to many northerners that the South was in fact conspiring against farmers and workers, their political fortunes improved. Radicals had already staked out the position to which moderates increasingly felt driven.

When the Republican Party was organized in 1854, it attracted antislavery advocates from the Free Soil and Democratic Parties and those left politically homeless by the collapse of the Whig Party. Many former Whigs wanted to turn the party into a new platform for their conservative economic policies, but the Radicals, who had belonged to all three antecedent parties, were determined to structure Republicanism around opposition to slavery. They largely succeeded.

When secession came in the winter of 1860–1861, the Radicals refused to pursue a compromise that might head off violent conflict. They agitated for vigorous prosecution of the war, emancipation, and the raising of black regiments. Though they considered President Abraham Lincoln too moderate for their tastes, he appointed Radicals Salmon Chase and Edwin Stanton to his cabinet.

Moreover, Lincoln often followed their recommendations, firing a succession of generals and issuing the Emancipation Proclamation, though he did so according to his own timetable and in his own more compromising style.

During Reconstruction the Radicals urged the full extension of rights, and especially the franchise, to blacks. But President Andrew Johnson imposed an extremely mild plan for Reconstruction that did not guarantee legal equality for freed slaves, and a majority of Republicans supported him at first. The southern states, however, exploited the leniency by using strict black codes to reduce former slaves to virtual servitude. Republican moderates again felt driven to the position already occupied by the Radicals, and Congress overrode presidential vetoes of the Freedmen's Bureau and the Civil Rights Act of 1866, and passed the Fourteenth Amendment (guaranteeing equality before the law), thus beginning the period of Congressional, or Radical, Reconstruction.

After President Ulysses Grant took office, the Radicals gradually lost influence. Their zealous yet unsuccessful campaign to remove Johnson from office had cast them as fanatics, and by the end of the decade, they were struggling against a fairly pervasive antiblack backlash and their own sense that they had done much of what they had set out to do. The Democrats won a majority in the House in 1874, and Reconstruction was ended in 1877.

Radicals finally pushed through the Fifteenth Amendment (1869), granting black men the franchise, but it would be another century before former slaves in the South were able to vote freely. Reconstruction stalled, and the racial climate got steadily worse, but for a brief moment around 1870, America looked something like what the Radical Republicans had imagined in 1854.

BIBLIOGRAPHY

Foner, Eric. *Free Soil, Free Labor, Free Men: The Ideology of the Republican Party before the Civil War.* New York: Oxford University Press, 1970.

———. *Reconstruction: America's Unfinished Revolution, 1863–1877.* New York: Harper and Row, 1988.

Trefousse, Hans L. *The Radical Republicans: Lincoln's Vanguard for Racial Justice.* New York: Knopf, 1968.

Jeremy Derfner

See also **Civil War; Reconstruction; Republican Party.**

RADICAL RIGHT.

The *radical right* is a term applied in the United States to sociopolitical movements and political factions and parties that develop in response to supposed threats against American values and interests. Such backlashes usually stem from rapid social or economic change that sparks a reaction among groups seeking to maintain or narrow lines of power and privilege. They justify their actions by discounting the legitimacy of their opponents, seeing them as agents of an un-American conspiracy not deserving of political respect or constitutional protection.

Threats to the religious values of the traditional evangelical groups gave rise in the late 1790s and again in the late 1820s to efforts to eliminate perceived irreligious elements and liberal forces. Fear of the Masons, for example, culminated in the formation of the Anti-Masonic party in 1830. For the next century, the most important source of rightist backlash in politics was anti-Catholicism, particularly among the Methodists and Baptists, who had become the dominant Protestant denominations.

Nativist movements sought to preserve existing institutions and traditional values against the threat of change—a threat that was attributed to the increased number of immigrant Catholics, and even to conspiracies directed by the Vatican. Groups espousing such NATIVISM included the Native Americans of the 1840s, the Know-Nothings of the 1850s, and the multimillion-member Ku Klux Klan of the 1920s. The decade of the 1930s—with its massive depression, unemployment, and political pressures linked to events in Europe—gave rise to many extremist movements. The most potent on the right was an anti-Semitic, pro-fascist movement led by a Catholic priest, Charles E. Coughlin.

After World War II the radical right turned its concerns from anti-Catholicism and anti-Semitism to communism and racial issues. The most prominent movement of the early 1950s followed the line of Sen. Joseph R. McCarthy's investigations into alleged communist infiltration of the government and the key opinion-forming and policy-controlling institutions. Right-wing resistance to the CIVIL RIGHTS MOVEMENT first centered in the postwar South in white citizens councils. Subsequently the largest and most important racially motivated rightist movement emerged in the presidential campaigns of Gov. George Wallace of Alabama. Wallace had strong showings in primary and general elections from 1964 to 1972, as he effected a coalition of disparate right-wing forces in support of the AMERICAN INDEPENDENT PARTY. In the 1990s radical right-wing sentiment focused on the presidential campaigns of the columnist and television commentator Patrick J. Buchanan.

Characteristically, radical-right movements, from the Anti-Masonic party to the American Independent party, have drawn their major support from poorer, less educated, more provincial, and more religiously traditional elements of American society. Lacking a power center, they have generally been taken over by the conservative elite, as when the Anti-Masons merged with the Whigs after the election of 1836. Thus, most of the mass-based radical-right groups have been short-lived, generally lasting about five years. Intense factional struggles, propensities to become more extreme and thus alienate moderate supporters, gradual solidification of opposition to their extremism, and occasional policy concessions in their direction by more established forces all reduce their capacity to maintain their strength.

BIBLIOGRAPHY

Bell, Daniel, ed. *The Radical Right*. Garden City, N.Y.: Doubleday, 1964.

Davis, David Brion, ed. *The Fear of Conspiracy: Images of Un-American Subversion from the Revolution to the Present*. Ithaca, N.Y.: Cornell University Press, 1971.

Lipset, Seymour M., and Earl Raab. *The Politics of Unreason: Right-Wing Extremism in America, 1790–1977*. Chicago: University of Chicago Press, 1978.

Nash, George. *The Conservative Intellectual Movement in America Since 1945*. Wilmington, Del.: Intercollegiate Studies Institute, 1996.

Reeves, Thomas C. *The Life and Times of Joe McCarthy: A Biography*. Lanham, Md.: Madison Books, 1997.

Seymour Martin Lipset / A. G.

See also **Anticommunism; Anti-Masonic Movements; Conservatism; Fascism, American; Immigration Restriction; McCarthyism; Radicals and Radicalism; Republican Party.**

RADICALS AND RADICALISM. The word "radical" is popularly used to designate individuals, parties, and movements that wish to alter drastically any existing practice, institution, or social system. In politics, radicals are often seen as individuals and/or parties reflecting "leftist" views. This meaning originated during the French Revolution (1787–1789), where those most opposed to the king sat in the National Assembly at the far left, and those most committed to the king at the far right. It is therefore common to designate points on the political spectrum, reading from left to right, as radical, liberal, conservative, and reactionary.

The Nineteenth Century

Immediately after the Civil War (1861–1865), the term "radical" gained widespread usage in the United States when it was applied to a powerful faction of the governing Republican Party who fought to reconstruct the defeated Confederacy. Their policies promoted social and political rights for the former slaves, and they opposed the return to power of former Confederates and members of the former slaveholder-planter class. The Radical Republicans impeached and nearly convicted President Andrew Johnson for his opposition to their Reconstruction policies. At their most militant, they advocated the redistribution of millions of acres of plantation land to the former slaves, a policy embodied in the slogan "forty acres and a mule," but instituted only limited land reform programs.

Radicalism in politics from the end of Reconstruction to the beginning of the Cold War was generally associated with proposals to fundamentally alter the capitalist economic and social system. In varying ways, radicals demanded far-reaching changes in property relations. Among the nonsocialist radical groups of the time were the Knights of Labor, Greenback Labor Party, and Populist Party, who advocated a wide variety of reforms, including more democracy in politics, various producer and consumer cooperatives, government ownership of railroads and telegraph lines, and antitrust legislation to protect farmers, skilled workers, and small businessmen threatened by the economic instability and political corruption that accompanied the rise of big business.

The Twentieth Century

The Marxist socialist tradition in America had its roots among refugees from the European revolutions of 1848. In 1901, a variety of socialist organizations and factions joined to create the Socialist Party of America. World War I (1914–1918) brought about widespread repression of the Socialist Party and other radical groups. The Russian Revolution intensified this "Red Scare," which continued into the postwar period against the new Communist Party, USA, founded initially out of radical factions of the Socialist Party in 1919.

Communists sought to advance the working-class movement and prepare the way for the eventual triumph of socialism. During the Great Depression, they achieved great success by leading struggles to organize unions,

Eugene V. Debs. The radical first president of the American Railway Union, cofounder of the Industrial Workers of the World and the Social Democratic Party, and Socialist presidential candidate five times between 1900 and 1920, winning more than 900,000 votes the last time—despite being in prison for opposing American involvement in World War I. LIBRARY OF CONGRESS

John Brown. The radical abolitionist, whose violent tactics horrified most Southerners and alienated even many antislavery advocates—until the Civil War, when Brown, who had been executed in 1859 for treason, was widely regarded as a martyr in the North. NATIONAL ARCHIVES AND RECORDS ADMINISTRATION

fight against racism and anti-Semitism, and fight for social reforms. After 1935, communist activists joined with liberals to build the industrial unions of the Congress of Industrial Organizations (CIO). Communists also joined with liberals and other radicals to fight segregation, racism, and isolationism at home.

The alliance of radicals and liberals in the 1930s produced a sharp backlash among conservative elements and business elites, leading to the creation of the House Un-American Activities Committee (HUAC) in 1938, which identified conservative policies with "Americanism" and New Deal policies with Soviet-directed communist conspiracies. With the development of the Cold War after World War II (1939–1945), the Soviet Union became a permanent enemy, and radicalism that could be associated with the Communist Party, USA, however far-fetched it might be, was portrayed as the "enemy within." What followed was the longest and most comprehensive campaign against radicals in American history. In 1947, President Harry S. Truman's administration established a federal "loyalty" program and an Attorney General's List of Subversive Organizations. In 1950, the McCarran Internal Security Act established a "Subversive Activities Control Board" to label and register alleged "Communist groups." Local "loyalty oaths," purges in the trade unions, blacklists in the arts, sciences, and professions, along with sporadic acts of vigilante violence against domestic radicals, characterized the period.

During the civil rights movement of the 1950s, the seeds of mass political protest and new alliances between liberals and radicals were sown. In 1955, the Reverend Martin Luther King Jr. led a successful mass strike against bus segregation in Montgomery, Alabama. In the after-

either through social revolution, or by, in the words of the writer Timothy Leary, "tun[ing] in, turn[ing] on, [and] drop[ping] out." The beat movement developed into the mass "hippie" counterculture, which championed "alternative" living arrangements and philosophies of life.

In 1963, Betty Friedan's groundbreaking book *The Feminine Mystique* challenged the exclusion of women from all areas of work and sought to change the role of women in the home. More radical feminist writers like Shulamith Firestone and organizations like Red Stockings joined with liberal feminists to fight for reproductive rights, affirmative action policies in employment, and the passage of an Equal Rights Amendment.

The social radicalism of the 1960s also produced consumer and environmental movements. Ralph Nader inspired and led a generation of activist researchers and attorneys to expose and challenge the abuses of corporate power. Although political power passed to conservatives in the 1980s, alliances of radicals and liberals challenged and pushed back the nuclear power industry, led campaigns for a nuclear freeze, and struggled to defend affirmative action for minorities and women and oppose President Ronald Reagan's "Star Wars" proposal.

What is radical in the political and cultural sense is born of the mainstream, of the gap between the rhetoric of democracy and opportunity and the reality of life. The function of American radicals and radical movements has been to challenge complacency, think the previously unthinkable, and open up space for society's mainstream to change and progress. As society changes, the meaning of radicalism itself changes. Proposals once considered radical—social security and unemployment insurance, equal rights for minorities and women—are now considered by many to be normal and necessary.

BIBLIOGRAPHY

Buhle, Mary Jo, Paul Buhle, and Dan Georgakas, eds. *Encyclopedia of the American Left*. New York: Garland Publishers, 1990.

Lasch, Christopher. *The New Radicalism in America, 1889–1963: The Intellectual As a Social Type*. New York: Alfred A. Knopf, 1965.

Lens, Sidney. *Radicalism in America*. New York: Crowell, 1969.

Lynd, Staughton. *Intellectual Origins of American Radicalism*. New York: Pantheon Books, 1968.

Norman Markowitz

See also **Antislavery; Civil Disobedience; Civil Rights Movement; Counterculture; Nader's Raiders.**

Black Panthers. Members of the radical group that advocated Black Power as well as community programs—*(left to right)* James Pelser, Jerry James, Greg Criner, and Robert Reynolds—walk in New Brunswick, N.J., in February 1969, during a period of increased violent confrontation between the Panthers and police around the country. AP/Wide World Photos

math of the strike, a Southern Christian Leadership Conference (SCLC) led by King organized against segregation throughout the South. Meanwhile a radical or militant northern group, the Congress of Racial Equality (CORE) grew in membership. In 1960, the Student Non-Violent Coordinating Committee (SNCC) was founded to mobilize student- and youth-led campaigns against segregation. SNCC and CORE led "Freedom Rides" against interstate bus segregation throughout the South in 1961, and King organized a mass strike against the whole system of segregation in Birmingham, Alabama. Although these campaigns produced a backlash of violence against civil rights activists, they resulted in the Civil Rights Act of 1964 and the Voting Rights Act of 1965, which ended the system of segregation and sharply reduced institutional and ideological expressions of racism.

During the 1960s, the civil rights movement and the beat cultural movement spawned what dissident sociologist C. Wright Mills called a New Left, as organizations like the SNCC and the Students for a Democratic Society (SDS) developed the concept of an activist participatory democracy and called for a radical restructuring of society,

RADIO. The Information Age began with the invention of the TELEGRAPH and TELEPHONE. These innovations led directly to the next important technological breakthrough—the arrival of commercial radio. Almost immediately, radio focused on listeners as consumers and the developing consumer culture, which would be replicated later with television, motion pictures, and most recently, the Internet. Radio transformed people's lives, changing the way living space was arranged, shaping family dynamics and leisure time, and reinforcing the ideals of the growing consumer culture.

Throughout its history, radio has not only been a driving force in American popular culture, but has basically provided the soundtrack for people's lives. Despite the all-encompassing influence of television, movies, and the Internet, radio remains at the core of the public's being. While some listeners tune in for music (spanning the spectrum from classic rock to rap) and others for talk (politics, sports, culture, and religion), radio continues to be a central component in shaping lives—musically, spiritually, politically, and culturally.

Early Days

Radio pioneers built on the success of telegraph and telephone inventors to conduct experiments with wire-based and wireless radio. Heinrich Hertz and Guglielmo Marconi carried out groundbreaking work. In 1901, Marconi gained international fame by sending a message across the Atlantic Ocean via wireless telephony. Early triumphs spurred greater advances. By the 1910s, Lee De Forest broadcast music and voice from his lab in New York. Early advocates championed the use of radio as an emergency device, citing how it was used when the *Titanic* sank in 1912 or during World War I (1914–1918).

In November 1920, Pittsburgh's station KDKA initiated America's first radio broadcast. Operated by the Westinghouse Corporation, KDKA was set up to encourage radio sales. Other large companies followed suit, including the Radio Corporation of America (RCA) and the phone company AT&T. Within two years, more than 500 stations were clogging the airwaves. The federal government stepped in to regulate radio stations with the Radio Act of 1927, which established the Federal Radio Commission to license stations. The need for regulating the entire telecommunications industry later led President Franklin D. Roosevelt to support the Communications Act of 1934, which established the FEDERAL COMMUNICATIONS COMMISSION (FCC).

Radio stations first sold advertising in 1922 at New York station WEAF. In 1926 and 1927, NBC (NBC-Red and NBC-Blue) and CBS were founded as national radio stations, although there were 700 other stations on the air at the time. Along with the Mutual Broadcasting System (MBS), these stations controlled the airwaves for most of radio's heyday. Since RCA owned both NBC stations, it was ordered by the FCC to divest one. In 1943, NBC-Blue became ABC.

Golden Age

The period leading up to the introduction of television is considered radio's Golden Age. Radio transformed people's lives from the late 1920s to late 1940s by providing news and entertainment to anyone who could afford a

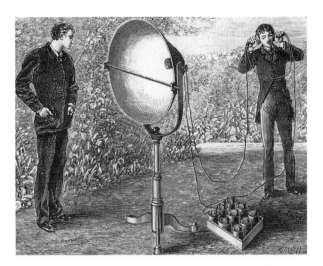

Early Days of Radio. Early radio research built upon knowledge gained from improvements in telegraph and telephone communication. Pioneers in the field, such as the two men shown with an amplifier and a listening device in this 1900 engraving, attempted to prove that radio waves could be used to transmit voice communication. In 1901 Guglielmo Marconi shocked the world when he successfully transmitted a radio broadcast across the Atlantic Ocean via wireless telephony; with that transmission, modern radio was born.
© UPI/CORBIS-BETTMANN

receiver. Specific audience-friendly programming was introduced to lure listeners, from half-hour sitcoms to daytime dramas and music programs. Radio had a grip on the nation's psyche, as seen on Halloween 1938 when Orson Welles narrated a dramatization of the book *War of the Worlds* by H. G. Wells. A panic ensued when listeners believed the news that invaders from Mars were attacking the world, despite many disclaimers that were run throughout the broadcast.

The national networks solidified their hold during the Golden Age. Local stations lost their monopolistic control over programming and as network affiliates, were contractually obliged to play the shows emanating from the larger stations. The networks delivered more sophisticated programs and made national stars of performers such as Will Rogers and Freeman Gosden and Charles Correll, better known as *Amos 'n' Andy*, the most popular show in America by 1929. The networks played an important cultural role, since they delivered the same programming nationwide. Radio helped promote national values and attitudes, making radio one of the few threads that tied the entire nation together. By the late 1940s, more than 90 percent of the homes in the nation had at least one radio and Americans spent more leisure time listening to the radio than doing anything else other than sleeping.

As radio developed, the kind of programs it offered changed as well. Action series, such as *The Shadow* and *The Green Hornet*, helped define how people thought about law enforcement. The medium endorsed a hero culture to listeners, from broadcasting the heroic efforts of baseball's Babe Ruth to the intergalactic exploits of Flash Gordon.

Radio had a tremendous impact on politics and journalism. President Franklin D. Roosevelt used the radio to mobilize support for his New Deal programs in "fireside chats" with the American people. As World War II (1939–1945) loomed, the president used the radio to stoke the public's patriotic fever. Once the war began, correspondents, such as Edward R. Murrow, Walter Cronkite, and Eric Sevareid, delivered reports from the European frontlines, forever changing reporting and in essence inventing broadcast journalism.

During World War II, most people experienced the war most forcefully through radio. In addition to the breaking news, presidential reports, and reports from the frontlines, celebrities used radio to pitch for war bonds and plead for scrap metal drives and other resources. Paper shortages during wartime limited the influence of

Short-Wave Radio. During World War II, the radio played an important part in the American war effort. On commercial radio, President Franklin Roosevelt gave his famous "Fireside Chats," and celebrities encouraged the public to buy war bonds and save their scrap metal for the war effort. In addition, radio technicians, like these men at the National Broadcasting Company (NBC), monitored short-wave radio broadcasts to listen to Japanese news reports in order to gain information about the enemy. © AP/WIDE WORLD PHOTOS

newspapers. Radio stations stepped into this void and provided a mix of news, reports, and patriotic messages that listeners craved.

Advertisers realized the power of radio and poured money into commercials. In 1928, radio garnered less than 1 percent of all advertising. By 1945, however, radio commanded 15 percent. In 1948, sponsors spent more than $400 million on radio advertising. The financial growth of radio was mimicked by the expansion of stations themselves. In 1930 there were 600 amplitude modulation (AM) stations. A decade later, the figure jumped to 765. But by 1948, it more than doubled to 1,612.

Radio in the Television Age

Frequency modulation (FM) radio developed in the late 1930s, when E. Howard Armstrong searched for a way to broadcast without the static common on AM dials. The AM dial also became overcrowded during radio's Golden Age. Inventors looked for an alternative to mainstream radio, which coincided with the anticommercialism of the 1960s.

The decade's youth culture helped spur the growth of FM stations. Listeners were antitelevision and anticonformity and could find a similar rebelliousness in the songs and programs on FM radio. Progressive rock stations took root in San Francisco, Los Angeles, New York, and Boston, eliminating advertising jingles and the antics of AM disc jockeys.

Gradually, the FM dial went through the same commercial transformation that occurred with AM. Initially, the networks started exerting their influence on FM, attempting to maintain a delicate balance between commercialism and FM's underground roots. By the end of the 1970s, however, the demand for profits and fall of the counterculture movement made FM radio look just like its AM predecessor, with the large networks squeezing out the remnants of the underground heritage. Revenues at FM stations, under $20 million in 1964, hit $284 million a decade later. There were more than 2,300 stations on air in 1972, but 3,700 by 1976. In 1977, FM revenues topped $543 million, but programming was done by committee and depended on computerization. An assembly line mentality took hold and the same rotations of hit songs were played over and over.

Modern Radio

Modern radio is far removed from its origins. At one time, pioneering entrepreneurs influenced radio and introduced diversity into programming. At the end of the twentieth century, corporate conglomerates governed the industry and a general uniformity had befallen radio. Despite the homogeneity of modern radio, however, its influence is still strong. By 2000, there were more than 12,000 AM and FM stations broadcast, with much of the programming distributed by satellite networks.

The cookie-cutter mentality at most radio stations from the 1980s onward led to the rise of talk radio, from

NATIONAL PUBLIC RADIO (NPR) to political and sports-oriented shows. Talk radio opened the airwaves to a variety of voices and made celebrities of hosts like Howard Stern, Rush Limbaugh, and Diane Rehm. Stern, in particular, gained notoriety as a "shock jock." His show is syndicated via satellite nationwide and features racy bits and an in-your-face attitude that launched a slew of imitators. The number of stations with all-talk or news and talk format topped 850 in 1994, and talk radio placed second among popular formats, with country music at the top.

The domination of the radio industry by large corporations was helped by the passage of the TELECOMMUNICATIONS ACT of 1996, which eliminated restrictions on radio ownership. Before, companies could only own two stations in any single market and 28 nationwide. All this changed after the Telecom Act passed. For example, as of 2002, Clear Channel Radio was the largest operator of radio stations in the United States with more than 1,350 stations and reaching 110 million listeners every week. Clear Channel also syndicated more than 100 programs to 7,800 stations, including Rush Limbaugh, sports talk leader Jim Rome, and Casey Kasem. Nearly half (625) of Clear Channel's radio stations were purchased in the 1999 Jacor acquisition.

The Telecom Act pushed radio acquisitions into overdrive. The feeding frenzy, driven by an influx of Wall Street money, enabled a handful of conglomerates to take control of the industry. Although radio is now more profitable, critics rebuke the conglomerates for forcing staid, automated music and formats on listeners, as well as for the elimination of countless radio jobs. Regardless of its shortcomings, however, radio continues to attract listeners and frames the way people think about music, sports, politics, and culture. In 2001, there were nearly 13,000 stations in the United States, which reached 77 percent of the people over 12 years old every day and 95 percent of consumers weekly.

BIBLIOGRAPHY

Barnouw, Erik. *A History of Broadcasting in the United States.* 3 Vols. New York: Oxford University Press, 1966–1970.

Douglas, Susan J. *Listening In: Radio and the American Imagination, from Amos 'n' Andy and Edward R. Murrow to Wolfman Jack and Howard Stern.* New York: Times Books, 1999.

Keith, Michael C. *Talking Radio: An Oral History of American Radio in the Television Age.* Armonk, N.Y.: M.E. Sharpe, 2000.

MacDonald, J. Fred. *Don't Touch That Dial! Radio Programming in American Life, 1920–1960.* Chicago: Nelson-Hall, 1979.

Bob Batchelor

RADIOCARBON DATING is the measurement of the age of dead matter by comparing the radiocarbon content with that in living matter. The method was discovered at the University of Chicago in the 1940s, but

Willard F. Libby. The 1960 recipient of the Nobel Prize in chemistry for his discovery of how to date once-living objects by measuring radioactive carbon. LIBRARY OF CONGRESS

further research had to wait until the end of World War II. Radiocarbon, or radioactive carbon (C-14), is produced by the cosmic rays in the atmosphere and is assimilated only by living beings. At death, the assimilation process stops. Living matter, wherever found on earth, always has the same ratio of radioactive carbon to ordinary carbon. This ratio is enough to be measured by sensitive instruments to about 1 percent accuracy.

The bold assumption that the concentration of radiocarbon in living matter remains constant over all of time appears to be nearly correct, although deviations of a few percentage points do occur. It has been possible to determine the accuracy of the basic assumption back some 8,000 years, and a correction curve has been produced that allows absolute dating by radiocarbon back 8,000 years. The deviation is about 8 percent, at maximum.

The discovery of the radiocarbon dating method has given a much firmer base to archaeology and anthropology. For example, human settlers, such as the big-game hunting Clovis peoples of the American High Plains and the Southwest, first came to the Americas in substantial numbers at least 12,000 years ago. On the other hand, the magnificent color paintings of the Lascaux Cave in France are 16,000 years old, made 4,000 years before the first substantial number of human beings came to the Americas. By the end of the twentieth century, firm radiocarbon dates for human occupation of North America had never exceeded 12,000 years—the famous Kennewick Man, discovered in Oregon in 1996, was determined to be 9,300 years old—whereas in Europe and Asia Minor these dates reached back to the limits of the radiocarbon method and well beyond, according to other dating methods.

BIBLIOGRAPHY

Libby, Willard F. *Radiocarbon Dating.* Chicago: University of Chicago Press, 1965.

Renfrew, Colin. *Before Civilization: The Radiocarbon Revolution and Prehistoric Europe.* Cambridge, U.K.: Cambridge University Press, 1979.

Willard F. Libby / A. R.

See also **Archaeology; Chemistry; Indian Mounds.**

RAFTS AND RAFTING. The raft, the simplest type of watercraft, was first constructed by lashing together several logs or reeds with vines or animal hide, and it served as water transportation as early as prehistoric times. In the United States, the simplest form of the raft, also called a flatboat, consisted of logs and planks fastened together to form a platform moved by river currents. The KEELBOAT, a more elaborate version of the raft that could be poled, rowed, and even sailed, had the ability to travel upstream as well. Both styles of raft were used in the Mississippi River Valley prior to the Civil War. Poor immigrants often used the flatboat to transport lumber, livestock, and fodder. The keelboat, used by Lewis and Clark in their expedition up the Missouri River in 1804–1805, was also used in the fur trade and to transport goods and people. The new steam-powered boat, invented in the early nineteenth century, almost entirely replaced the raft by the Civil War. Rafts, however, did not fall into complete obsolescence. At the beginning of the twenty-first century, rigid and inflatable rafts are used as emergency equipment on ships and airplanes as well as for recreation. Rafting, for some, no longer conjures up Mark Twain's Huckleberry Finn; instead, it carries with it the thrill and danger of navigating whitewater rapids.

BIBLIOGRAPHY
Baldwin, Leland Dewitt. *The Keelboat Age on Western Waters.* Pittsburgh, Pa.: University of Pittsburgh Press, 1941. Reprint, 1980.

Rafting. A group tackles the Chattahoochee River in Georgia, May 1972. NATIONAL ARCHIVES AND RECORDS ADMINISTRATION

Mueller, Edward. *Upper Mississippi River Rafting Steamboats.* Athens: Ohio University Press, 1995.

Lila Corwin Berman

See also **River Navigation.**

RAGTIME dominated American popular music style from the mid-1890s to about 1920. The word "ragtime" seems to have evolved from a compound term, "rag time" or "ragged time," describing the syncopated and percussive nature of the music. Ragtime's 1970s revival, boosted by the popularity of George Roy Hill's film *The Sting* (1973), whose soundtrack featured some of the most poignant and evocative of Scott Joplin's piano rags, put the piano at the center of popular perceptions of ragtime. Consequently, even some music historians have mistakenly privileged ragtime piano in assessing the genre. In fact, as Edward A. Berlin has argued, ragtime songs like "Mister Johnson Turn Me Loose" and "Under the Bamboo Tree" would probably have been cited by contemporaries as the most important ragtime compositions.

Ragtime's popularity crossed races, opening the way for the later appeal of BLUES and JAZZ and the prominence of African Americans as composers and performers of American popular music. Though black musicians and composers largely created ragtime, in its earlier years ragtime included songs with racially derogatory lyrics: "coon songs," in the terminology of the era used by both whites and blacks. Ironic and painful, this phenomenon also typifies the Jim Crow racial hierarchy of the new century.

Despite pockets of largely white resistance based on its identification with "Negro" music and its exciting rhythms, ragtime was adopted by both white and black Tin Pan Alley songwriters and classical composers, so that its distinctive sound has become a kind of shorthand for turn-of-the-century culture and society, first in the United States and then in Europe. Ragtime found a home in nightclubs, marching bands, bourgeois parlors, and concert halls. It helped elevate both the piano and the banjo as popular instruments. Among prominent ragtime composers, arrangers, and popularizers are Scott Joplin, James Scott, James Reese Europe, John Philip Sousa, Irving Berlin, Erik Satie, Claude Debussy, Igor Stravinsky, and Jelly Roll Morton.

BIBLIOGRAPHY
Badger, Reid. *A Life in Ragtime: A Biography of James Reese Europe.* New York: Oxford University Press, 1995.

Berlin, Edward A. *Ragtime: A Musical and Cultural History.* Berkeley: University of California Press, 1980.

Hasse, John Edward. *Ragtime: Its History, Composers, and Music.* New York: Schirmer, 1985.

Mina Carson

See also **Minstrel Shows; Music: Popular.**

"RAIL SPLITTER" was a nickname for Abraham Lincoln; it originated in the Illinois State Republican Convention at Decatur on 9 May 1860, when Richard J. Oglesby, later governor of Illinois, and John Hanks, who had lived with the Lincolns, marched into the convention hall with two fence rails placarded, "Abraham Lincoln, The Rail Candidate for President in 1860." Lincoln had worked as a soldier, a postmaster, a surveyor, a tavern keeper, and a rail splitter before pursuing law and politics, and the nickname capitalized on his humble beginnings. The sobriquet caught on at the national convention at Chicago, spread quickly over the North, and became a valuable campaign asset.

BIBLIOGRAPHY

Jaffa, Harry V. *A New Birth of Freedom: Abraham Lincoln and the Coming of the Civil War.* Lanham, Md.: Rowman and Littlefield, 2000.

Paul M. Angle / F. B.

See also **Conventions, Party Nominating; Elections, Presidential.**

RAILROAD ADMINISTRATION, U.S. established in December 1917 by proclamation of President Woodrow Wilson, to control and operate all rail transport for the duration of the war. The Railroad Administration was a direct response to the failure of the Railroads' War Board, which railroad executives had formed in April 1917 to achieve a coordinated "railway system" for the World War I emergency. Although this private effort to coordinate activities had resulted in some pooling of freight cars and coal supplies, it was difficult to unify other transportation resources without governmental intervention and was almost impossible to obtain adequate financial assistance.

Under the Railroad Administration, the government "leased" key facilities," which eventually totaled 532 properties with 366,000 miles of track, valued at $18 billion. This included terminal companies, an express company, and certain coastal and inland waterways and piers, although street cars, interurban lines, and industrial railroads were all excluded from the Railroad Administration's control. In general, the Railroad Administration retained the personnel and administrative machinery of each property under the direct charge of a federal manager, usually an officer of the corporation. Regional directors were in charge of coordinating operations, and the regional directors, in turn, answered to the director general (William Gibbs McAdoo, former secretary of the Treasury, and, later, railroad lawyer Walker D. Hines) and a central administration at Washington, D.C.

This episode of government enterprise was intended to be an emergency military measure to help win the war, and supporters carefully pointed out that they did not regard it as a socialist experiment. Certain efficiencies and economies did result, and centralization and standardization eliminated competitive wastes. The Railroad Administration organized unified terminals, notably at Chicago, and developed a "permit system" that prevented loading until shippers gave assurances for unloading. It standardized locomotives and freight cars, centralized the purchasing of equipment and supplies, and pooled repair shops and maintenance. A coal zoning plan helped to eliminate fuel wastes.

Passenger service, although discouraged because of the war, gained unifying devices such as consolidated ticket offices, the universal mileage book, and standard ticket forms and baggage rules. Finally, the Railroad Administration eliminated advertising while standardizing all statistical records. The government spent $1.12 billion in all, mostly for additions, betterments, and equipment. An act of 21 March 1918 guaranteed stockholders and bondholders compensation equal to the average annual net operating income during the preceding three years, 1914–1917. Wages generally rose, and the administration formally recognized the eight-hour day for 2 million railroad employees. In March 1920, sixteen months after the armistice, the government returned the railroads to private management under the supervision of the Interstate Commerce Commission and in accordance with the Transportation Act of 1920.

BIBLIOGRAPHY

Association of American Railroads. *United States Railroad Administration Publications: A Bibliography.* Washington, D.C.: 1952.

Hines, W. D. *War History of American Railroads.* New Haven, Conn.: Yale University Press, 1928.

U.S. Chamber of Commerce. *Organization of War Transportation Control.* Washington, D.C.: 1918.

Martin P. Claussen / C. W.

See also **Fuel Administration; Interstate Commerce Commission; Railroads; Transportation Act of 1920; World War I, Economic Mobilization for.**

RAILROAD BROTHERHOODS. Along with many other pioneering labor organizations in nineteenth-century America, organizations of railroad workers took the name "brotherhoods" in token of their partly fraternal purposes. The most powerful of the railroad brotherhoods were those formed in the operating trades—those directly involved in moving trains. These included the Brotherhood of Locomotive Engineers (founded in 1863), the Order of Railway Conductors (1868), the Brotherhood of Locomotive Firemen (1873), and the Brotherhood of Railroad Trainmen (founded in 1883 as the Brotherhood of Railroad Brakemen). Sometimes grouped along with "the Big Four" was the Switchmen's Union (1894), the men responsible for making up trains. Numerous other unions were founded to represent nonoperating railroad employees such as trackmen (1887), railway clerks

(1899), and sleeping car porters (1925). Though the operating brotherhoods represented fewer than one-fifth of all railroad employees, they dominated the early history of organized labor in the railroad industry.

Workers Organize as Partners to Industry

Like a great many wage-earners in the United States' rapidly industrializing economy, railroad workers found their market position increasingly eroded by mechanization, conditions of labor surplus, recurrent recessions and depressions, and the arbitrary power of employers. Like organizations in other skilled trades, the railroad brotherhoods formed to defend the interests of men in their crafts. But the brotherhoods held themselves aloof from other categories of workers: they seldom cooperated with unions outside their industry and none joined the American Federation of Labor (AFL) until 1957.

Serving what was then the nation's central industry, the brotherhoods relied on the indispensability of their skills and the respectability of their characters. This was especially true of the Brotherhood of Locomotive Engineers (BLE), whose members adopted "Sobriety, Truth, Justice, and Morality" as their motto. These organizations were entirely male and most of them barred blacks until the 1960s. A substantial majority of brotherhood members were native-born Protestants in a labor force that was rapidly filling with immigrants and non-Protestants.

From the brotherhoods' prideful self-image flowed a strategy of assuring loyal service in exchange for good treatment by their employers. The main aim of the newly formed BLE, Chief Grand Engineer Charles Wilson declared in 1864, was "to win the good graces of the employers through elevating the character of its members and thus raising their efficiency as workmen. The employer should be so pleased with their work that he would of his own free will provide better recognition of labor and higher pay." Similarly, the union publication of the Brotherhood of Railroad Trainmen declared in 1887, "Railway managers and superintendents recognize in the Brotherhood a school for the mental, moral and physical improvement of its members, and consequently a better and more desirable class of men. . . ." Leaders like the BLE's P. M. Arthur and the Brotherhood of Locomotive Firemen's (BLF) Frank Sargent sought partnership with the railroad companies. They regarded strikes and other adversarial actions as measures of last resort.

Most of the brotherhoods began as fraternal and mutual benefit societies, offering their members camaraderie, self-esteem, and insurance rather than the collective bargaining representation in which unions specialize. The BLF formed in 1873 "for strictly benevolent purposes" and vehemently opposed 1877's Great Strike by 100,000 rail workers; the union did not approve of its own lodges staging strikes until 1885. The Order of Railway Conductors, founded as a fraternal society in 1868, did not engage in collective bargaining until 1890.

Brotherhoods' Conservatism Is Challenged in Era of Strikes

The Great Strike of 1877 was a spontaneous, unorganized, sometimes violent walkout by railroad employees, and its collapse reinforced the conservative instincts of the brotherhoods. Cultivating harmonious relations with the railroads seemed to serve the brotherhoods well as long as the industry's expansion generated favorable terms of employment, as it did into the late 1880s. But as expansion slowed and railroad managers grew less accommodating, the brotherhoods began to feud among themselves and sometimes, though reluctantly, mounted strikes, which usually failed. In 1885 and 1886, the BLE and BLF rejected pleas to support strikes by railroad shopmen against companies run by the notorious railroad magnate Jay Gould. After bitter divisions among workers contributed to the failure of a major strike against the Chicago, Burlington, and Quincy line in 1888, many brotherhood members began chafing against the policies of their leaders. By 1892, the rising calls for federation among the brotherhoods to strengthen them in battles with the railroads had developed into a more radical proposal: the creation of a new industrial union, embracing railroad workers of all skills and trades, and which would replace the autonomous brotherhoods. Finally, in 1893, Eugene V. Debs, formerly the general secretary of the BLF, took the leadership of a militant new American Railway Union (ARU).

Men left the brotherhoods in droves to join the ARU, but the organization was soon shattered by its defeat in the epic Pullman boycott and strike of 1894. The brotherhoods expelled the deserters, stitched themselves together, and went back to selling themselves to the railroads as model workers. The federal Erdman Act of 1898 brought a new order to labor-management relations in the railroad industry. It provided for voluntary arbitration of disputes, banned antiunion practices, but also allowed for court injunctions to stop strikes. Hundreds of companies signed collective bargaining agreements with the brotherhoods, which grew from an aggregate membership of 100,000 in 1897 to 350,000 (in a total railroad workforce of 2 million) twenty years later.

Mounting costs of living, impatience with expensive arbitration proceedings, and demands for better conditions of work pushed the brotherhoods into a brief phase of militancy in the years around World War I. In 1916, the brotherhoods' threat of a national railroad strike impelled Congress to pass the ADAMSON ACT, giving them the eight-hour day. During the war, the Woodrow Wilson administration took over operation of the nation's rail system. Eager to retain the protections they enjoyed under federal control, the brotherhoods briefly supported the "Plumb plan" (named for the brotherhoods' chief legal counsel, Glen E. Plumb), which called for permanent nationalization of the industry. But enthusiasm for Plumb soon faded, and in the 1920s, both the industry and the brotherhoods began to shrink as alternative means of transportation took business away from the railroads.

The epitome of craft conservatism and business unionism, the railroad brotherhoods gained security and decent terms of employment for their members while steadfastly resisting efforts to organize less skilled men. Ultimately, the firemen, trainmen, switchmen, and conductors merged to form the United Transportation Union in 1969. Of the original brotherhoods, only the BLE remained an independent union in 2002.

BIBLIOGRAPHY

Licht, Walter. *Working for the Railroad: The Organization of Work in the Nineteenth Century.* Princeton, N.J.: Princeton University Press, 1983.

Montgomery, David. *The Fall of the House of Labor: The Workplace, the State, and American Labor Activism, 1865–1925.* New York: Cambridge University Press, 1987.

Richardson, Reed C. *The Locomotive Engineer, 1863–1963: A Century of Railway Labor Relations and Work Rules.* Ann Arbor: Bureau of Industrial Relations, Graduate School of Business Administration, University of Michigan, 1963.

Stromquist, Shelton. *A Generation of Boomers: The Pattern of Railroad Labor Conflict in Nineteenth-Century America.* Urbana: University of Illinois Press, 1987.

Eugene E. Leach

See also **American Federation of Labor-Congress of Industrial Organizations.**

RAILROAD CONVENTIONS

RAILROAD CONVENTIONS were phenomena of the early years of railroad promotion. They were held before the RAILROADS were built rather than after their completion, and they were composed not only of railway builders but also, and principally, of the public-spirited citizens of their vicinities.

The conventions were both a symptom and a cause of popular enthusiasm for better means of transportation. They probably did not greatly stimulate private investment in railroad securities, but they undoubtedly did yeoman service in the numerous campaigns for state or local aid. It was hoped in many cases that they would serve to reconcile conflicting interests and aspirations concerning routes and termini; nevertheless, they could only demonstrate or promote popular interest in particular projects.

Railroad conventions spread across the country in the antebellum period. Perhaps the most notable were the three great Pacific Railroad conventions in Saint Louis and Memphis in October 1849 and in Philadelphia in April 1850. They were held to demonstrate the strength of the popular demand for federal aid for a railroad to the Pacific coast, to formulate a practicable plan of financing it, and to assert claims for the eastern terminus; the Philadelphia convention supported the pretensions of the Saint Louis convention. But Congress gave their resolutions scant courtesy.

One of the most influential gatherings of the sort ever held was the Southwestern Railroad Convention in New Orleans in January 1852. It helped to launch Louisiana and New Orleans on ambitious programs of state and municipal aid and to make clear the broad outlines of a proper railroad system for the whole Southwest. The Pacific Railroad conventions in Sacramento, in September 1859 and February 1860, sought to unite the Pacific coast in support of a central route and to persuade the legislatures of California, Oregon, and Washington Territory to make provision for getting the western leg of the proposed railroad started. The Southwestern Convention in Memphis, in November 1845, was interested primarily in the improvement of western rivers; but it also endorsed the major railroad projects of the Southwest and broached the subject of a southern route for a Pacific railroad. Similarly the Chicago Rivers and Harbors Convention, in July 1847, gave secondary concern to railroad projects for connecting the East and the West.

BIBLIOGRAPHY

Ely, James W. *Railroads and American Law.* Lawrence: University Press of Kansas, 2002.

Fogel, Robert W. *Railroads and American Economic Growth.* Baltimore: Johns Hopkins University Press, 1964.

Hastings, Paul. *Railroads: An International History.* New York: Praeger, 1972.

Ward, James A. *Railroads and the Character of America: 1820–1887.* Knoxville: University of Tennessee Press, 1986.

R. R. Russel / A. G.

See also **Grand Central Terminal; Railways, Interurban; Transcontinental Railroad, Building of; Transportation and Travel.**

RAILROAD MEDIATION ACTS

RAILROAD MEDIATION ACTS. After a series of damaging railroad strikes, the federal government began in the 1890s to consider new ways to assure uninterrupted transportation service without denying the rights of workers to organize. In the Erdman Act of 1898 and the Newlands Act of 1913, Congress created mediation procedures and, in the Adamson Act of 1916, it established the eight-hour day on the railroads. The Transportation Act of 1920 founded the Railroad Labor Board. After the board failed to prevent the shopmen's strike of 1922, Congress passed the Railway Labor Act of 1926. As amended in 1934, it continues to be the basic legislation in the field.

The amended law created several procedures designed to resolve labor-management disputes. It established the National Railroad Adjustment Board to assert quasi-judicial authority over rates of pay, working conditions, and work rules in case of the failure of ordinary collective bargaining. It set up the National Mediation Board to assist labor and management in resolving differences. If all other procedures collapsed, the president was empowered to enforce a sixty-day cooling-off period in order to forestall a strike. The law also secured workers' right to organize unions of their own choosing.

In the 1960s, major strikes threatened railroad service. Congress enacted legislation to settle individual disputes, and it reviewed the idea of enforcing compulsory arbitration in labor disputes affecting transportation.

BIBLIOGRAPHY

Urofsky, Melvin I. "State Courts and Protective Legislation during the Progressive Era: A Reevaluation." *Journal of American History* 72 (June 1985).

Zieger, Robert H. *Republicans and Labor, 1919–1929.* Lexington: University of Kentucky Press, 1969.

K. Austin Kerr / A. R.

See also **Labor Legislation and Administration; Railroad Administration, U.S.; Railroads; Strikes.**

RAILROAD RATE LAW. Attempts to regulate railroad rates by law began at the state level. The so-called Granger laws of the 1870s were passed by the states in response to demands by farmers for lower rates on agricultural products from the Midwest to the eastern seaboard and by midwestern river towns (which had been hurt when river transport was displaced by the new East-West trunklines) that rates be based on mileage. The first demand was satisfied, not by laws but by the striking twenty-five-year decline in all railroad rates after 1873. The second demand was submerged in the economic boom after 1877, but it survived in the durable issue of discrimination in rates between long and short hauls. The SUPREME COURT, in *Munn v. Illinois* (1877), affirmed for the right of states to fix interstate rates so long as the federal government did not act. Anticipating the decision in *Wabash, Saint Louis and Pacific Railroad Company v. Illinois* (1886), which reversed *Munn*, Congress began studies that culminated in the Interstate Commerce Act of 1887. Support by business groups was broad, including some railroad men who sought the right to enter into legally enforceable agreements—that is, cartels—to pool revenues and/or freights.

The traditional view of the failure of the act of 1887 is that the INTERSTATE COMMERCE COMMISSION (ICC) was intended to fix specific maximum rates and energetically abolish discrimination between long and short hauls, powers of which it was deprived by two 1897 decisions of the Supreme Court. But neither Congress nor the affected interests had wanted the ICC to fix specific rates, nor did many want a literal application of the clause that prohibited discrimination between long and short hauls. (Although energetic attempts were made under subsequent legislation to abolish this ratemaking practice, they failed because the United States, a vast area in which trade is carried on free of regional barriers, was devoted to a tradition of low through rates arrived at under competitive conditions.) The fatal weakness of the act of 1887 was

that it prohibited pooling, even under ICC supervision, an anomaly that led contemporary experts to predict correctly that the only other antidote to rate chaos—consolidation of the railroads into a few systems—would be adopted.

While the ELKINS Act of 1903 enhanced the ICC's powers to deal with rebates as criminal acts, it was the overloading of the American railroad system after 1898 that effectively killed rate cutting. Reaction to a stable and moderately rising rate structure resulted in the HEPBURN ACT OF 1906, which gave the ICC power to fix specific maximum rates and broadened its jurisdiction. Before it was fully operative, the Hepburn Act was overshadowed by the Mann-Elkins Act of 1910, which enabled the ICC effectively to freeze rates at levels pervasive in the 1890s throughout the great inflation of the Progressive era, despite repeated concerted efforts by the railroads to raise rates. When the government took over the railroad system in December 1917, the ICC was as far from developing a criterion of "reasonableness" of rates as ever, and literal application of the SHERMAN ANTITRUST ACT of 1890 had rendered the carriers impotent to operate the system in a unified manner as a war measure. Without consulting either the ICC or the state commissions, the U.S. Railroad Administration raised rates by almost 60 percent, thereby returning them to about the level of the 1890s in real dollars. Meanwhile, in the *Shreveport* case (1914) the Supreme Court had completed the reversal of the *Munn* decision by giving the ICC power to set intrastate rates, arguing that they are economically linked to interstate rates.

Neither the power to pool revenues nor the encouragement of consolidation, both features of the TRANSPORTATION ACT OF 1920, was germane to postwar regulatory problems. But the power to fix specific minimum rates operated in a totally unforeseen manner. By 1933 the emergence of competition by trucks, which were not federally regulated until 1935, had become the crucial problem. Despite repeated declarations in the acts passed in 1940 and 1958 in favor of a balanced transportation system based on the "inherent advantages" of rail and highway modes, both the ICC and lawmakers shrank from giving railroads freedom to compete through lowering rates, and the Supreme Court failed consistently to enunciate a rule of ratemaking based on cost. As a result the railroads lost most of their profitable, high-class freight and came to be operated at a fraction of capacity; 60 percent of highway freight came to be carried by unregulated private carriers because, under the ICC's policy of high rates for railroads and regulated motor carriers, it was advantageous for the shippers; and the nation's transportation costs thus rose. Despite widespread belief among transportation economists that rate laws had failed, Congress attempted to solve the problem by a system of guaranteed loans, or quasi-subsidies.

BIBLIOGRAPHY

Hoogenboom, Ari Arthur. *A History of the ICC: From Panacea to Palliative.* New York: Norton, 1976.

Martin, Albro. *Railroads Triumphant: The Growth, Rejection, and Rebirth of a Vital American Force.* New York: Oxford University Press, 1992.

Albro Martin / a. g.

See also **Interstate Commerce Laws; Progressive Movement, Early Twentieth Century; Railroads; Railways, Interurban; Trade, Domestic; Transcontinental Railroad, Building of.**

RAILROAD RATE WARS. The rapid expansion after the Civil War added greatly to the number of communities, large and small, served by two or more railroads competing for the traffic between these communities and markets. The fact that many of the points served by competitive railroads were ports intensified competition by involving the water carriers serving the ports.

Competition led to rate cutting by the railroads and water carriers and caused widespread use of rebates. Railroad rebates were special low rates that a railroad carrier charged its favored customers. The intent of a carrier in granting a rebate was usually to discriminate in favor of a particular shipper by giving him a secret rate that was less than that charged his competitors. This practice developed in the mid-1850s and continued because of the spectacular railroad rate wars that took place during the second half of the nineteenth century and that often proved disastrous to carriers and public alike. These costly rate wars led carriers to avoid general rate cuts and to develop the practice of making secret agreements with certain shippers, whereby the shipper would get some form of rate reduction in exchange for his promise to ship his goods over the line offering the concession. Such concessions enabled the favored shippers to undersell their competitors and thus increase their business and the business of the railroad offering the rebates. The public objected bitterly to the practice of rebating because of its obvious unfairness and because the process of building up one shipper at the expense of others promoted the development of monopolies, with all of their attendant evils.

Competition among railroads serving the northern Atlantic ports—Boston, New York, Philadelphia, and Baltimore—resulted in rate wars among the railroads and between the railroads and the Erie Canal. In like manner competition among southern railroads intensified as several railroads reached inland points such as Atlanta. Severe competition occurred between railroads and water carriers at the principal ports on the Atlantic Ocean, Gulf of Mexico, Mississippi River, and Ohio River. Rate wars indeed threatened to demoralize the financial structures of rail and water carriers. In the West rate wars resulted from the multiplication of railroads and the struggle between the railroads and steamboat lines for freight at important traffic centers, such as Saint Louis, Kansas City, and Omaha.

The severity and destructiveness of rate wars was due to several factors: the overbuilding of railroads, the unregulated competition among railroads and between railroads and waterlines, the speculative management of some of these carriers, the inability of the railroads to temporarily suspend service until the excessive competition had abated, and the peculiar ability of railroads or other carriers in impaired financial condition to cause and exaggerate the effects of the rate-cutting contests. These latter carriers were usually bankrupt and had no interest charges to pay. They were not earning enough to pay these charges or dividends on capital stock. Freed of the burden of such charges, they were able to reduce rates in the hope of attracting traffic from their solvent rivals, which were meeting interest charges and sometimes paying dividends. They had little to lose and much to gain either through increasing their traffic and gross earnings or forcing their more vulnerable competitors to yield and divide traffic or earnings.

Railroad rate wars, accompanied by unjust and unreasonable discriminations among persons, communities, and kinds of traffic, led to the development of popular antagonism to railroads after 1870. One result of this popular protest was the enactment by a number of states, particularly the western Granger states, of severe and often restrictive and punitive railroad regulatory legislation and the organization of state regulatory commissions.

Another result of rate wars and their attendant abuses was the demand for federal railroad regulation. The Interstate Commerce Act (1887) prohibited rate discrimination and established a fine of five thousand dollars for each violation; two years later violation of the law was made a penitentiary offense. But it was necessary to prove that a rebate actually resulted in discrimination, and this was difficult to do. Furthermore, juries were reluctant to send men to prison for civil offenses even if proven guilty. Hence the act did not stop the practice of discrimination, and further legislation was necessary. Under the Elkins Act (1903) any departure from a printed rate was considered an offense, thus eliminating the necessity of proving that discrimination existed. At the same time the penalty of imprisonment was dropped, the maximum fine was raised to twenty thousand dollars; the law applied to shippers who received rebates as well as to carriers who granted them. The Hepburn Act (1906) restored the penalty of imprisonment and subjected the receiver of a rebate to a fine equal to three times the value of the rebates received during the preceding six years. Subsequent acts brought a further tightening of the law.

BIBLIOGRAPHY

Chernow, Ron. *Titan: The Life of John D. Rockefeller, Sr.* New York: Random House, 1998.

Hoogenboom, Ari Arthur. *A History of the ICC: From Panacea to Palliative.* New York: Norton, 1976.

Railroad Strike of 1877. An engraving of a rail yard in Pittsburgh during the short strike. On 21 July, the state militia killed or injured dozens of the strikers—who then set fires that destroyed nearly forty Pennsylvania Railroad buildings and more than 1,300 engines and passenger and freight cars. The U.S. Army broke the Pittsburgh strike five days later. GETTY IMAGES

Martin, Albro. *Enterprise Denied: Origins of the Decline of American Railroads, 1897–1917.* New York: Columbia University Press, 1971.

*G. Lloyd Wilson/*A. G.

See also **Corporations; Mergers and Acquisitions; Monopoly; Railroads; Railways, Interurban; Trade, Domestic; Transcontinental Railroad, Building of; Trusts.**

RAILROAD RETIREMENT ACTS.

President Franklin D. Roosevelt approved a railroad retirement act on 27 June 1934, with the comment that it was "crudely drawn" and would require revision. The act called for a federal board to oversee a system of retirement allowances for certain categories of employees, with two-thirds of the cost to be borne by employers and the balance by the employees. No adequate actuarial studies had been made; carriers claimed that their share would prove a crushing load on the finances of most railroads. In March 1935 the U.S. Supreme Court, in *Railroad Retirement Board v. Alton Railroad Company,* declared the act unconstitutional. Two bills were passed the following August, the first (Wagner-Crosser Railroad Retirement Act) providing a retirement plan and the second imposing special taxes for its support. These acts retained several features that the Supreme

Court had found objectionable in the earlier enactment. The railroads renewed their objections and won an injunction against the new acts on 30 June 1936. In May 1937, after protracted negotiation, new legislation gained the approval of both parties and a month later passed through Congress with little opposition.

BIBLIOGRAPHY

Graebner, William. *A History of Retirement: The Meaning and Function of an American Institution, 1885–1978.* New Haven, Conn.: Yale University Press, 1980.

Schreiber, David B. *The Legislative History of the Railroad Retirement and Railroad Unemployment Insurance Systems.* Washington, D.C.: U.S. Government Printing Office, 1978.

*W. A. Robinson/*A. R.

See also **Pension Plans;** *Railroad Retirement Board v. Alton Railroad Company;* **Railroads; Retirement.**

RAILROAD RETIREMENT BOARD V. ALTON RAILROAD COMPANY,

295 U.S. 330 (1935), a case in which the Supreme Court, divided five to four, invalidated the Railroad Pension Act of 1934. The majority opinion declared the act contrary to the due process clause of the Fifth Amendment because of a long series

of arbitrary impositions on the carriers and, furthermore, because "the pension plan thus imposed is in no proper sense a regulation of the activity of interstate transportation." The minority opinion, while agreeing that the retroactive feature of the law violated the Fifth Amendment, disagreed that Congress had exceeded the limits of its jurisdiction over interstate commerce when it created the pension system.

BIBLIOGRAPHY

Leuchtenburg, William E. *The Supreme Court Reborn: The Constitutional Revolution in the Age of Roosevelt.* New York: Oxford University Press, 1995.

W. A. Robinson / A. R.

See also **Due Process of Law; Pension Plans; Railroad Retirement Acts.**

RAILROAD STRIKE OF 1877.

After the panic of 1873, the railroads chose to pay dividends while imposing salary cuts on all nonmanagerial employees. The imposition of this cut, which was not the first, by the Baltimore and Ohio sparked a massive, national labor insurrection. Angry workers in Martinsburg, West Virginia, occupied the roundhouse. The rails carried the news to the urban rail centers, where the strike spread to other industries. This sparked major rioting in Pittsburgh, Pennsylvania, and in Chicago and brief insurrectionary seizures of power in St. Louis, Missouri, and Toledo, Ohio. Federal troops broke the strike movement.

BIBLIOGRAPHY

Bruce, Robert V. *1877: Year of Violence.* Chicago: Quadrangle Books, 1970.

Foner, Philip S. *The Great Labor Uprising of 1877.* New York: Monad, 1977.

Stowell, David O. *Streets, Railroads, and the Great Strike of 1877.* Chicago: University of Chicago Press, 1999.

Mark A. Lause

See also **Railroads; Strikes.**

RAILROAD STRIKE OF 1886.

Although the railroads had agreed not to discriminate against union members, Jay Gould maneuvered to break the hold of the Knights of Labor. When the Texas and Pacific Railroad fired a unionist, the Knights called a general strike on 1 March 1886, demanding recognition and a minimum daily wage of $1.50. Federal troops intervened, and the demoralized strike ended on 3 May. Backed by the government, employer ruthlessness broke an early form of industrial unionism. However, union reappearance in the

Railroad Strike of 1886. This engraving from a sketch by G. J. Nebinger, published in *Frank Leslie's Illustrated Newspaper* on 10 April 1886, shows U.S. marshals protecting a freight train in East St. Louis, Ill. There, as in Pittsburgh in 1877, strikers were fired on, railroad buildings and cars were burned, and the state militia soon arrived to break the strike. LIBRARY OF CONGRESS

1888 strike exacted a high price in public opinion and fostered the idea of arbitration.

BIBLIOGRAPHY

Foner, Philip S. *History of the Labor Movement in the United States.* Vol. 2. New York: International Publishers, 1972–1975.

Stromquist, Shelton. *A Generation of Boomers: The Pattern of Railroad Labor Conflict in Nineteenth-Century America.* Urbana: University of Illinois Press, 1987.

Mark A. Lause

See also **Knights of Labor; Railroads; Strikes.**

RAILROAD SURVEYS, GOVERNMENT.

Interest in a railroad to the Pacific coast became keen and widespread after the territorial expansion resulting from the Mexican cession of 1848. The question of the best route became the subject of a great deal of discussion, especially since each state along the Mississippi and most midwestern cities evinced an interest in the selection.

In 1853 Congress added the sum of $150,000 to an army appropriation bill to defray the expenses of SURVEYING feasible routes to the Pacific. Under the direction of Jefferson Davis, secretary of war, five routes were surveyed. The northernmost survey ran from Saint Paul to the mouth of the Columbia River. A party under Lt. E. G. Beckwith secured data for a route generally along the emigrant trail to California. Capt. John W. Gunnison surveyed a difficult route between the thirty-eighth and thirty-ninth parallels. Lt. Amiel W. Whipple conducted a survey following the thirty-fifth parallel from Fort Smith, in western Arkansas, to Los Angeles. Finally, parties under Capt. John Pope, Lt. John G. Parke, and others explored a far southern route along the thirty-second parallel.

The survey reports, later published in copiously illustrated volumes, contributed greatly to geographical and scientific knowledge concerning the Far West. But the surveys themselves did not bring agreement about a route. Davis championed the southernmost survey, but sectional rivalry was too great to permit the choice of a route until after the southern states had seceded from the Union. When the Pacific Railroad Bill was adopted in 1862, the central route from the western border of Iowa to the California-Nevada line was chosen for the construction of the transcontinental railroad.

BIBLIOGRAPHY

Goetzmann, William H. *Army Exploration in the American West.* Austin: Texas State Historical Association 1991.

Wallace, Edward S. *The Great Reconnaissance: Soldiers, Artists, and Scientists on the Frontier, 1848–1861.* Boston: Little, Brown, 1955.

Dan E. Clark/F. H.

See also **Gadsden Purchase; Land Grants: Land Grants for Railways; Railroads; Transcontinental Railroad, Building of; Western Exploration.**

RAILROADS.

Beginning in the nineteenth century in the United States, a vast system of railroads was developed that moved goods and people across great distances, facilitated the settlement of large portions of the country, created towns and cities, and unified a nation.

Early railways were a far cry from the great system of railroads that were built in the nineteenth century and that continue to be used today. The earliest railways in the United States were short, wooden railways built by quarries and mines along which horses pulled loads to nearby waterways. In 1827, quarry and mine operators in Quincy, Massachusetts, and Mauch Chunk, Pennsylvania, constructed the first full-size railways. The first locomotive for use on railways was imported from England in 1829. The English had been experimenting with steam-powered locomotives since the late eighteenth century and had developed a prototype by 1828. Horatio Allen, working for the Delaware & Hudson Canal Company, purchased four of these early steam locomotives and brought them to the United States. One, Stourbridge Lion, was tested on 8 August 1829, but proved to be too heavy for the tracks that had been constructed and was subsequently retired.

Undeterred, railroad companies continued to seek a viable steam-powered locomotive. By 1828, railroad track was being laid not only by the Delaware & Hudson, but also by the Baltimore & Ohio and the South Carolina Railroads. Locomotive engines were needed. Peter Cooper rose to the challenge and on 28 August 1830 drove his diminutive Tom Thumb locomotive at speeds approaching fifteen miles per hour while towing a car filled with thirty people. The thirteen-mile trip was made from Baltimore to Ellicot's Hill in Maryland.

With the viability of steam-powered locomotives proven, the race was on to build other, larger locomotives. The Baltimore & Ohio and the South Carolina railroads instituted contests for locomotive designs. E. L. Miller was commissioned by the South Carolina to construct what would be the first locomotive built in America for use on railroad. He named the locomotive The Best Friend of Charleston. Tested in October of 1830, the engine performed admirably. Unfortunately, The Best Friend exploded the following year, but not before the South Carolina Railroad inaugurated service on 25 December 1830. The Best Friend pulled train cars, the first locomotive to do so in the United States, along six miles of track out of Charleston. The age of the railroad in America had begun.

Other railroads quickly followed the South Carolina and the Baltimore & Ohio. Steam-powered railroads operating in the early 1830s included the Mohawk & Hudson, the earliest link in the future New York Central system, begun on 9 August 1831; the Camden and Amboy,

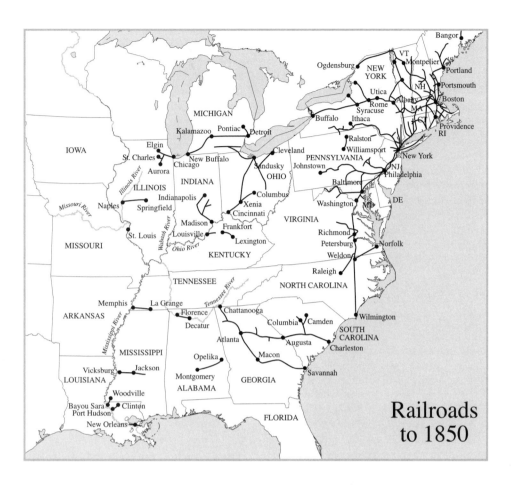

Railroads
to 1850

later part of the Pennsylvania system, in 1831; the Philadelphia, Germantown and Norristown in 1832; and the railroad connecting New Orleans with Lake Pontchartrain, afterward part of the Louisville and Nashville Railroad, on 17 September 1832. By 1835 railroads ran from Boston to Lowell, Massachusetts, the beginnings of the future Boston and Maine; to Worcester, Massachusetts, first link in the Boston and Albany Railroad; and to Providence, Rhode Island, the genesis of the New York, New Haven and Hartford Railroad. The Petersburg Railroad, later part of the Atantic Coast Line, ran from the Virginia City into North Carolina.

By 1840, railroad track in the United States had reached almost three thousand miles; by 1850, more than nine thousand miles; by 1860 over thirty thousand miles. During these decades, technology associated with the steam locomotive continued to improve, and innovations were made in the design of the tracks themselves. Early tracks were constructed of wood, which was not strong enough to support ever-heavier locomotives. Iron rails were developed that could carry the weight of large, steam-powered locomotives. These rails were originally laid on crossties made of blocks of stone, which were not only expensive, but also could not support the weight of locomotives. They were replaced by wooden crossties similar to those used today.

Several other innovations helped foster the growth of railroads between 1840 and 1860. These included T-shaped rails that distributed the weight of trains evenly and hook-headed spikes that grabbed the rail, thus attaching it securely to the crossties. Swiveling trucks under railroad cars created greater stability, allowing trains to travel over rough roadbed and high terrain. The development of truss and cantilever bridges provided a way to get railroads over waterways and other obstructions. By the 1860s, track could be laid virtually anywhere.

In the 1850s the ambitious efforts to reach the seaports of the Atlantic and to reach the West were successful. The Erie Railroad and the Albany & New York Central connected New York State and New York City with the Great Lakes. Philadelphia established an all-rail connection with Pittsburgh, and Baltimore reached the Ohio River at Wheeling, Virginia (now West Virginia), early in the 1850s. Other lines were built across the more open and level country of the Middle West. Two railroads, the Michigan Central and the Michigan Southern, reached Chicago from the east in 1852. Both were later incorporated into the New York Central system. Lines were also built west from Chicago. The Galena & Chicago Union (later the Chicago and North Western) reached the Mississippi River in February 1854. Only a year later a route between Chicago and East Saint Louis afforded another rail connection between the eastern seaboard and the Mississippi River, while in 1857 two more connections were added. A direct route from the Atlantic to Chicago was constructed from Baltimore via Cincinnati. In addition, a route between Charleston, South Carolina, and Savannah, Georgia, on the Atlantic coast and Memphis, Tennessee, on the Mississippi, was built.

Railroads were also being built from the far bank of the Mississippi River westward. On 9 December 1852, the Pacific Railroad of Missouri (later the Missouri Pacific) ran five miles westward from Saint Louis. In 1856, the locomotive The Iron Horse crossed the Mississippi on the first railroad bridge. The bridge belonged to the Rock Island line, later called the Chicago, Rock Island & Pacific. By 1860, the railroad had reached the Missouri River on the tracks of the Hannibal & Saint Joseph (later part of the Burlington lines).

Standardization

The thousands of miles of track laid and the locomotives and other railroad equipment built in the early years of the railroad in the United States were all done by private companies. These companies built their railroads to suit their needs and to specifications they determined. Tracks were built in a variety of gauges (the distance between the rails) ranging from two and one-half feet to six feet. By the 1870s, close to two dozen gauges of track were in use in the United States. Locomotives were built to fit the gauge of the track. In addition, the couplings used to attach one train car to another varied. The incompatibility of railroads was not a problem if the purpose of the railroads remained to move people and goods over short distances. However, when the potential of the railroad to travel greater distances, even to traverse the country, was realized, the need for industry standards became evident.

Track gauge was the first of such standards to be achieved. The standard gauge in the South was five feet. In the rest of the country, the predominant gauge was four feet eight and one-half inches—the standard English gauge that had been used because locomotives had been imported from England. In 1886, the South changed its gauge to conform to that of the rest of the country. Trains today run on this gauge of track except for a limited of number of narrow-gauge railroads.

Next came standardization of locomotives and railroad cars to fit the track; standardization of couplings followed. Early couplers were simple link and pin devices that were unsafe and unreliable. In 1885, forty-two improved couplers were tested in Buffalo, New York. In 1887, a coupler designed by Eli H. Janney was adopted as the standard; Janney's design remained in use until the 1970s.

Interchanging cars between railroads also required the standardization of brakes. Early train brakes were hand brakes operated by brakemen in each car. Efforts to standardize brakes were unsuccessful until 1869. In that year, George Westinghouse developed his first air brake.

In 1871, he designed an air brake that would immediately engage if cars became separated. Westinghouse's air brakes were designed only to work on passenger trains. Air brakes for freight trains were not developed until 1887, after testing on the Chicago, Burlington, & Quincy in Burlington, Iowa. These air brakes, with improvements, have remained an integral part of freight trains.

One final, crucial feature of rail transport needed to be standardized: time. Efforts were made in the 1870s to standardize rail schedules and timetables. In light of the increasing interconnection of railroad lines, the timing of trains became critical. Each railroad originally had its own "standard time." This time was usually that of the railroad headquarters or an important town on the line. In an era when people were still keeping local time, the idea of a standard time seemed implausible if not impossible, but local time was increasingly becoming railroad time. Each town had a "regulator" clock by which local people set their watches and clocks. This clock often hung in the railroad station. On 18 November 1883, the American Railway Association adopted a "standard time" with four time zones one hour apart. The standard time system remained under the auspices of the railroad until 1918, when the U.S. Congress adopted the system and put it under the control of the INTERSTATE COMMERCE COMMISSION (ICC).

The Growth of the Railroad, Railroad Towns, and the Population of the American Interior

Railroads began in the East, but quickly moved west, spider-webbing across the country. Wherever railroads went, people followed and towns grew. Previously uninhabited or sparsely inhabited areas of the country became towns almost overnight when the railroad came through. One striking example is the case of Terminus, Georgia. The small town of about thirty was chosen as the terminus for the Western & Atlantic Railroad. In 1845, it was renamed Atlanta and went on to become one of the most important cities in the South.

Railroads required land on which to lay tracks, build rail yards, and construct depots. Beginning in the 1850s, speculators bought land in the hopes that a railroad would come through an area and they could then resell the land at a much higher price. Also in the 1850s, the United States government realized the value of the railroads and the land associated with them. One of the first railroads built as a single unit was the Illinois Central. The line could be built as one unit partly because the government granted land to the rail company in a patchwork pattern of alternating one-mile-square sections, with the government retaining ownership of the intervening lands. The combination of public and private ownership created by the grant and others like it led to the use and settlement of vacant lands, the extension of railroads into underdeveloped areas, and increased production and wealth. In return for the land grants, the railroads transported gov-

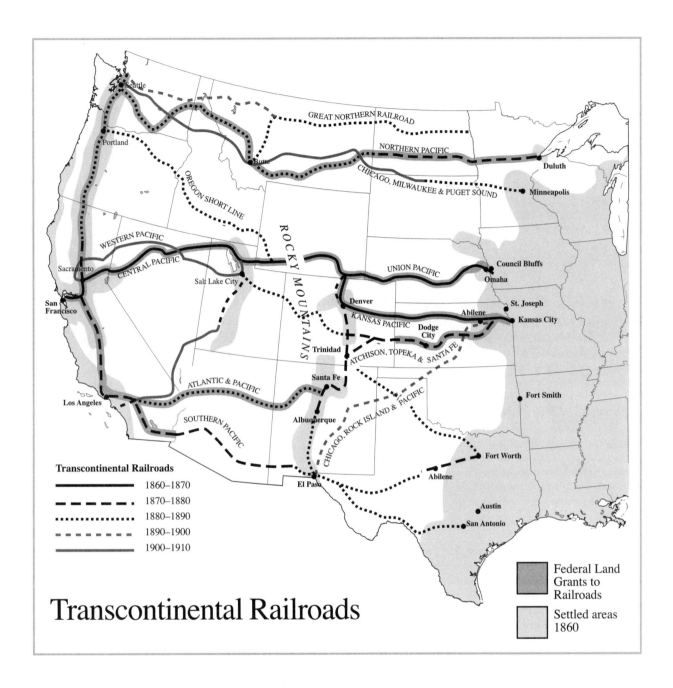

Transcontinental Railroads

Transcontinental Railroads

————————	1860–1870
– – – – – –	1870–1880
··············	1880–1890
- - - - - -	1890–1900
————————	1900–1910

Federal Land Grants to Railroads

Settled areas 1860

ernment freight, mail, and personnel, including military troops, until 1946.

The government further encouraged settlement in the wake of the railroads through the Homestead Act of 1862. Settlers were granted 160 acres of land in the West on the condition that they farm it for five years; they could also purchase the land for $1.25 an acre after farming it for only six months. Few farmers could afford to take advantage of the latter provision, but many land speculators could. Thousands of acres of homestead land were purchased by speculators at what were paltry sums, forcing new settlers, in turn, to purchase land at inflated prices from speculators.

Railroads were crucial in moving goods to markets. Cities in the East, like New York and Boston, and in the Midwest, like Chicago, that had begun life as ports, became the centers for railroad transport of agricultural and industrial products. Railroads freed trade of the constrictions of the natural sources of transport, such as rivers, because railroads could be constructed almost anywhere. Like canals before them, railroads became in essence man-made rivers. Railroads moved freight and people between urban centers in the East into the interior of the country and ultimately toward the West.

Towns in the center of the country became boomtowns, acting as railroad transshipment points for goods.

Golden Spike Ceremony. Men and engines of the Union Pacific and Central Pacific Railroads, approaching from opposite directions, meet face-to-face as the first transcontinental railroad is completed just north of the Great Salt Lake in Utah, 10 May 1869. GETTY IMAGES

Perhaps the best examples of this are the Kansas towns like Abilene and the infamous Dodge City. From the mid-1860s to the mid-1880s, Texas cowboys drove herds of longhorn cattle to these towns where they were loaded onto trains for shipment to stockyards and slaughterhouses in cities like Chicago. The cattle drives ended when the railroads moved even farther west and south to areas where the cattle were grazed and when farmers across whose lands the cattle were driven erected barbed-wire fences to keep out the trampling herds. Railroad towns that were no longer needed as access points for railroads often were abandoned as quickly as they arose or greatly reduced in population. Railroads brought boom and bust to towns and cities across the nation.

The Transcontinental Railroad
A large part of the effort to bring the railroad to the freight instead of the freight to the railroad culminated in the building of the first transcontinental railroad. On 1 July 1862, President Abraham Lincoln signed a bill authorizing the construction of a railroad between the Missouri River and California. The idea for a transcontinental railroad had been around since at least 1848. Engineers had mapped several routes by the 1850s and railroads had

been built along some portions of those routes. Rivalry between railroads had prevented the completion of a unified transcontinental route, however.

The outbreak of the Civil War removed the southern routes from consideration and increased the need for a transcontinental railroad for use by the military. Lincoln designated Council Bluffs, Iowa, as the starting place for the new railroad. Two railroads worked on the transcontinental railroad: The Union Pacific built westward from Omaha, Nebraska, and the Central Pacific built eastward from Sacramento, California. The two lines met on 10 May 1869 in Promontory, Utah, where the tracks were joined with a golden spike. The telegraph spread the news nationwide.

This first transcontinental route was built with government assistance in the form of land grants and loans. The line was intended for use by the military and was not expected to make money. Subsequent transcontinental railroads were built with the assistance of land grants but not governmental loans.

Several more transcontinental rail lines were completed between 1869 and 1910. In 1881, the Atchison, Topeka & Santa Fe building from the west met the

Southern Pacific at Deming, New Mexico. The Southern Pacific continued eastward until it met the Texas & Pacific at Sierra Blanca, Texas, in 1883. Through the acquisition of other railroads and further construction, including a line to New Orleans and to California from Albuquerque, New Mexico, the second transcontinental railroad was completed in 1883.

Three routes were built to the Pacific Northwest. The Northern Pacific Railroad completed the first in 1883. It ran through the northern tier states. The second opened a year later when the Oregon Short Line joined the Union Pacific with Oregon Railway and Navigation Company tracks. Both railroads later became part of the Union Pacific System. Great Northern completed the third route: the first transcontinental railroad to be built without land grants, the extension connected the West coast with the Chicago, Milwaukee & Saint Paul Railroad.

A Union Pacific route to southern California was completed by the San Pedro, Los Angeles & Salt Lake Railroad in 1905. In 1910, the Western Pacific joined with the Denver, Rio Grande & Western Railroad at Salt Lake City to complete yet another transcontinental route.

The fever for constructing transcontinental routes did not lead to other parts of the railroad system being neglected. In the 1860s, twenty-two thousand miles of new track were laid. Over the course of the decade of the 1870s, forty thousand miles of new rail lines were built. In the 1880s, more than seven thousand miles of new rail line were laid. By the end of the nineteenth century, railroads crisscrossed America, transporting freight to ports and markets at an unprecedented volume.

The Railroads and the U.S. Government
The relationship between the U.S. government and the railroads began in the 1850s with the land grants given to railroads. The government had a vested interest in seeing the expansion of the railroads because this expansion made use of previously unused or underused land, creating new, and taxable, wealth.

A more direct relationship between the government and the railroads was forged during the Civil War. Before 1860, the majority of the railroad track in the United States was in the North. Railroads ran west from the North to the interior of the country; when the war started in 1861, railroads lost their markets in the South, but gained an even bigger market, the military. Railroads in both the North and the South became vital to the Union and Confederate militaries, and large railroad termini, like Atlanta, became prime military targets.

Railroads were used to move large numbers of troops to the sites of major battles. The outcome of the First Battle of Bull Run was determined by troops shifted by rail from the Shenandoah Valley to the vicinity of Manassas, Virginia. In preparation for the launching of General Braxton Bragg's Kentucky campaign, the Confederate Army of Tennessee was moved by rail from Tupelo,

Mississippi, to Chattanooga, Tennessee. A more remarkable accomplishment was the movement of General James Longstreet's army corps by rail from Virginia through the Carolinas and Georgia, just in time to secure the Confederate victory of Chickamauga, Georgia. Most remarkable of all was the movement of General Joseph Hooker's two corps of twenty-two thousand men over a distance of twelve hundred miles from Virginia to the vicinity of Chattanooga, via Columbus, Indianapolis, Louisville, and Nashville.

More important even than these spectacular shifts of large army units from one strategic field to another was the part played by the railroads in the day-to-day movement of men, food, ammunition, matériel, and supplies from distant sources to the combat forces. Such movements reached their height during General William Tecumseh Sherman's campaign to capture Atlanta in the summer of 1864. His army of one hundred thousand men and thirty-five thousand animals was kept supplied and fit by a single-track railroad extending nearly five hundred miles from its base on the Ohio River at Louisville.

The military continued to use railroads in later wars. In April 1917, when railroad mileage in the United States was at its peak, the country entered World War I. A volunteer Railroads' War Board was established to coordinate the use of railroads to meet military requirements. When this board proved unsatisfactory, the railroads were taken over by the government on 1 January 1918; the takeover lasted twenty-six months.

During World War II, railroads initially remained under private directorship. Improvements made in the interwar years, perhaps in part because of needs realized during World War I, allowed the railroads to meet World War II military requirements despite less operational railroad track within the United States. Between the world wars, new, more powerful steam locomotives had been put into use; the diesel engine was introduced to passenger travel in 1934 and to freight service in 1941. Wooden cars had been replaced and passenger cars were air conditioned starting in 1929. Passenger train speeds increased and overnight service was instituted for freight service. Railroad signaling was centralized, increasing the capacity of rail lines. The organization and operation of car supply and distribution were improved to the extent that train car shortages became a thing of the past.

Railroad service was so improved that the government did not need to seize the railroads during World War II, but shortly after the war ended the situation changed. In 1946, President Harry S. Truman was forced to seize the railroads to handle a nationwide strike of engineers and trainmen that had paralyzed the railroads (and much of the nation) for two days. Strikes in 1948 and 1950 precipitated further government seizures. The intervention of the government in railroad-labor relations illustrates not only the importance of the railroads, but also the regulatory power the government wields in its relationship with the railroads.

U.S. Military Railroads Engine no. 137. One of the engines (built in 1864) that served a vital function in the Civil War, taking troops and supplies where they were needed—which made key railroad junctions and tracks the strategic targets of military attack and sabotage. NATIONAL ARCHIVES AND RECORDS ADMINISTRATION

Railroads and U.S. Government Regulation

Much of the history of the relationship between the U.S. government and railroads has involved regulation or its lack. Early in the growth of railroads, the government tended to ignore what were later seen to be the excesses of railroad developers. The desire to drive the railroad west in the 1860s overrode concerns about land speculators buying up homestead land and led to the distribution of millions of acres of government land to railroads at minimal prices. In the 1880s, railroads set about competing for business, using any means necessary, including special terms to companies who shipped a lot of freight. Planning was minimal—railroads ran everywhere and nowhere at all; railroads were spending a lot, but making little. Ultimately railroads' power to control land and access to markets resulted in farmers who could not afford to ship their goods to market.

In the 1890s, in part in response to the discontent of farmers and others with the disorganized state of the railroads, "ROBBER BARONS" (wealthy speculators and businessmen) bought companies in many industries, consolidating them into large, monopolistic corporations. The foremost of these businessmen in the railroad industry

was J. P. Morgan, who set up the House of Morgan in New York City. Morgan proceeded to merge railroads across the country, claiming to be attempting to stabilize the industry. In so doing, he created TRUSTS, virtual monopolies, with interlocking directorates. Investors flocked to trusts like Morgan's. The result for small businessmen was the same as under the previous, disorganized system: power over the railroads rested in the hands of a few individuals who gave preferential treatment to large industrial producers. The government watched these events more or less from the sidelines until, in 1902 President Theodore Roosevelt challenged Morgan's creation of Northern Securities, an entity set up to unite competing railroad moguls from the East and West coasts. Roosevelt used the power of the SHERMAN ANTITRUST ACT (1890), setting a precedent for dissolving railroad and other corporate monopolies.

Attempts to regulate the railroad industry had been made prior to the use of antitrust laws against railroads. Another means the government used to try to regulate railroads was control of interstate trade. Early attempts to regulate railroad rates and practices by states had been only partly successful, although in 1876 the so-called

Granger laws had been upheld by the Supreme Court for intrastate application. In 1886, however, the Court held, in *Wabash, Saint Louis and Pacific Railroad Company v. Illinois*, that Congress had exclusive jurisdiction over interstate commerce and that a state could not regulate even the intrastate portion of an interstate movement. Efforts had been made for a dozen years before to have Congress enact regulatory legislation. The decision in the Wabash case resulted in passage on 4 February 1887, of the Interstate Commerce Act, which created the Interstate Commerce Commission. Subsequent legislation broadened the commission's jurisdiction and responsibilities, increased its powers, and strengthened its organization.

Between 1890 and 1900 another 40,000 miles of track were added to the railroad net; after 1900, still another 60,000 miles of line were built, bringing the total of first main track to its peak of 254,000 miles in 1916. Mileage of all tracks, including additional main tracks, passing tracks, sidings, and yards, reached its maximum of 430,000 miles in 1930. By 1960, mileage of line declined to approximately 220,000, and miles of track of all kinds had declined 390,000. This reduction in mileage was the result of many factors, including the exhaustion of the mines, forests, and other natural resources that were the reason for being of many branch lines; intensified competition from water routes and highways; and the coordination and consolidations that made many lines unnecessary. In 1916 more than fourteen hundred companies operated 254,000 miles of line; in 1960, fewer than six hundred companies operated 220,000 miles of line—but the reduced mileage had more than double the effective carrying capacity of the earlier, more extensive network.

Congress voted to return the railroads to private operation and set up the terms of such operation in the TRANSPORTATION ACT OF 1920. Among the changes in government policy was recognition of a measure of responsibility for financial results, found in the direction to the ICC to fix rates at such a level as would enable the railroads, as a whole or in groups, to earn a fair return on the value of the properties devoted to public service. This provision was frequently described as a government guarantee of railroad profits, although there was no guarantee of earnings. Commercial conditions and competitive forces kept railway earnings well below the called-for level, and the government was not asked or required to make up the deficiency.

Another shift in government policy related to consolidation of railroads, which had initially been frowned on but was later encouraged by the Transportation Act of 1920. The change in policy stemmed from the fact that consolidation in one form or another had from early times been the way the major systems, some of which included properties originally built by a hundred or more companies, achieved growth. Accordingly the 1920 law directed the ICC to develop a plan of consolidation for the railroads; in 1933, the ICC requested that it be relieved of this requirement.

Leland Stanford. The cofounder and first president and director of the Central Pacific Railroad and later head of the Southern Pacific Railroad, as well as a governor and U.S. senator and the founder of what is now Stanford University. © CORBIS-BETTMANN

In passing the Transportation Act of 1958 Congress somewhat relaxed regulatory requirements on the railroads, providing, in effect, that competitive cost factors be given greater consideration in determining the lawfulness of rates, so long as the rates proposed were compensatory to the carrier and not discriminatory.

Railroads and Labor

The construction of a massive project like railroads requires a tremendous amount of labor. Once built, railroad upkeep and operation requires even more labor. Ancillary industries utilized large labor forces for the production of iron, and later steel, the felling of trees and processing of wood, and the production of other materials necessary for the manufacture of tracks, locomotives, and train cars. Service industries employed workers to fill jobs such as porters, waiters, and other functions on railroads. Finally, fuel had to be mined and processed to run the locomotives.

Relations between railroads and their workers have often been rancorous. Tension was present from the beginning because of the danger associated with many railroad jobs. One of the earliest and most dangerous was that of brakeman. Brakemen rode on top of freight cars, hopping down to stick wooden clubs into the spokes of the wheels of the train to bring it to a halt. The air brake ended this particularly hazardous employment, but other rail jobs were also dangerous. Not only were railroad jobs often dangerous, they usually did not pay well. In the 1870s, many rail workers were paid less than $2 per twelve-hour day.

The combination of dangerous work, long hours, and low pay led to railroads and labor often being at loggerheads. Railroad workers went on strike several times in the late nineteenth and early twentieth centuries. In 1877, one of the largest and most devastating strikes involved Baltimore & Ohio Railroad workers in Martinsburg, West Virginia, who went on strike to protest wage cuts. The strike spread to Baltimore, then to the Pittsburgh and the Pennsylvania railroads, and eventually to St. Louis. Although some national railroad labor unions disavowed the strike, local strikers held train stations and set them afire. State militias and the national guard were called out to break the strike in several locations. A thousand people were imprisoned during the strike, which eventually involved one hundred thousand workers. When the railroads rescinded the wage cuts, the strike, which had involved more than half the freight on the country's railroads, came to an end.

The Homestead and Pullman strikes of 1892 and 1894, respectively, further frayed relations between laborers and railroad management. Strikes and unrest in the railroad industry led the federal government to institute regulations that mitigated some of the labor problems. The first federal legislation addressing relations between railroads and their employees was passed in 1888. The law applied only to employees in train and engine service: the first railway employees to form successful unions—the Brotherhood of Locomotive Engineers in 1863, the Order of Railway Conductors in 1868, the Brotherhood of Locomotive Firemen and Enginemen in 1873, and the Brotherhood of Railroad Trainmen in 1883. These, with the addition of the Switchmen's Union of North America, organized in 1894, constitute the "operating" group of unions. "Nonoperating" crafts formed organizations at various dates—the telegraphers (1886), the six shop-craft unions (1888–1893), the maintenance-of-way employees (1891), the clerks and station employees (1898), the signalmen (1901).

The Erdman Act (1898) and the Newlands Act (1913), which provided various measures for mediation, conciliation, arbitration, and fact-finding in connection with railway labor disputes, dealt with train service cases only. The Transportation Act of 1920 that encouraged the consolidation of railroads also set up the U.S. Railroad Labor Board and granted it jurisdiction over all crafts of employees and power to determine wage rates and working conditions; however, the act did not grant the Labor Board the power to enforce its decisions. In 1922, the shopmen brought about the first nationwide strike on the railroads when they struck in response to a Labor Board decision reducing wages. The strike failed, but its aftereffects were such that in the Railway Labor Act of 1926, agreed to by the unions and the railroads, the Labor Board was abolished and the principles of earlier labor legislation, with their reliance on mediation and conciliation, were restored. The 1926 law was amended in important particulars in 1934, at the urging of the Railway Labor Executives Association, an organization of the "standard" railway unions formed in 1929.

In 1934, the Railroad Retirement Act was passed as the first of the Social Security measures of the New Deal. This legislation was declared unconstitutional, but in 1937 a retirement and unemployment insurance system was set up under legislation agreed upon by the Railway Labor Executives Association and the Association of American Railroads, an organization of the industry formed in 1934.

Strikes by the engineers and trainmen and other groups of unions in 1946, 1948, and 1950 led, in 1951, to amendment of the 1934 Railway Labor Act. The amendment removed the prohibition on requiring union membership as a condition of railroad employment, thus permitting the establishment of the union shop by negotiation. Such agreements were negotiated on most railroads.

Passenger Transport in the Early Twentieth Century
The romance of railroad travel extends perhaps as far back to the day when Tom Thumb pulled a train car with thirty people through the Maryland countryside. The first sleeper car, an innovation that provided some comfort on long rail journeys, was made for the Cumberland Valley Railroad that ran through Pennsylvania and Maryland. In 1856, the sleeper car that was to become an American classic was invented by George W. Pullman. The cars had an upper and lower berths and were improved by all-steel construction in 1859.

The heyday of passenger rail travel, however, did not begin until the 1920s. The year that kicked off that decade saw a record 1.2 billion passengers. The immense ridership was short lived; the automobile became more and more popular throughout the 1920s. In 1934, the Burlington, Chicago & Quincy line introduced the Zephyr—a streamlined, diesel-powered locomotive. The locomotive was unveiled at the Century of Progress Exhibition and was later featured in the 1934 movie, *The Silver Streak*. The country was transfixed, and by the end of the decade rail travel had again become fashionable. Many railroad lines ran streamlined trains and passenger travel increased by 38 percent between 1930 and 1939, though total ridership remained at less than half of the highs of 1920.

World War II again interrupted the popularity of rail travel. Railroads remained profitable during the war years because government used the railroads to move troops, supplies, and equipment and because of the scarcity of other means of transport during gas rationing. After World War II, railroads failed to recapture the American imagination and never recovered the phenomenal number of passengers of the early part of the century. Automobiles and airplanes took a firm hold as the preferred means of passenger transport in the United States. Railroads turned to more profitable freight business as their main source of income.

Throughout the postwar years the railroads made many capital improvements, spending, on average, more than $1 billion a year. The most significant change was the replacement of steam power by diesel-electric power. Continuous-welded rail in lengths of a quarter-mile, a half-mile, and even longer came into wider use. Railroads were increasingly maintained by more efficient off-track equipment. New freight cars that rode more smoothly were designed. An automatic terminal with electronic controls, known as the push-button yard, was developed. Container or trailer-on-flatcar service, commonly called piggybacking, was introduced. Containers today are used in the transport of much of the freight in the United States and abroad.

The Late Twentieth Century and Early Twenty-first Century

Fewer passengers and decreased freight and mail service in the second half of the twentieth century led to railroad bankruptcies as well as mergers and acquisitions designed to streamline the industry. By the 1970s, railroad passengers accounted for only 7.2 percent of travelers in the United States. By contrast, airline passengers represented 73 percent of travelers each year. Freight service has evolved differently. Between 1980 and 2000, while the number of miles of track decreased from 202,000 to approximately 173,000, the amount of freight transported annually increased from 918 billion ton-miles (one ton transported one mile) to 1.4 trillion ton-miles.

New types of freight service appeared in the 1960s. Although the number of freight cars in service dropped slightly, the average capacity per car increased by nearly 25 percent. In addition, container freight service continued to grow. Railroads also rebuilt a declining coal traffic by reducing rates through the introduction of "unit trains," which are whole trains of permanently coupled cars that carry bulk tonnage to a single destination on a regular schedule. Unit trains were so popular that they were soon in use for hauling a variety of commodities.

During the 1960s and early 1970s, total investment in the railroad industry grew only modestly. The rather bleak financial picture was in part relieved by technological advances. A major reduction in overheated locomotive engines ("hot boxes") was achieved during the 1960s. Improved lubrication plus infrared detection devices at trackside reduced the incidence of overheated engines by more than 90 percent.

Beginning in the late 1960s, railroad cars were tagged with automatic car identification, which allowed them to be tracked anywhere in the country. The use of computers to control train traffic burgeoned during the decade, with almost ten thousand miles of Centralized Traffic Control installed.

Passenger rail service dropped sharply in the 1960s. In 1961 passenger service was offered on more than 40 percent of the nation's railroads. By 1971 passenger trains were running on less than 20 percent of the national mileage. In an effort to save the failing passenger rail industry in the United States, the government sponsored a project for high-speed passenger service in the Northeast corridor from Boston to Washington, D.C., running through New York City and Philadelphia. The service was dubbed the Metroliner and is today part of the AMTRAK system.

Amtrak, National Railroad Passenger Corporation, is a federally sponsored entity that took control of most railroad passenger service in May 1971. In 2000, Amtrak had 22,000 miles of track and served forty-six states and over five hundred communities. Despite a ridership of over 22 million passengers in 2000, Amtrak faced a severe financial crisis. Amtrak and the government continue to work together to try to maintain passenger rail service across the United States.

The number of railroad employees declined steadily in tandem with declining ridership in the 1960s. At the beginning of the twenty-first century, the number of railroad employees hovers at slightly over one hundred thousand; the average annual income of a railroad employee is $60,000 per year.

Since the middle of the twentieth century, mergers have become a survival tactic for railroads. The aim was to achieve significant operational savings, which were projected and claimed for nearly every proposed merger. In 1960, 116 Class I, large freight, railroads operated in the United States; only nine were in operation by 1997. Class I railroads dropped from 106 to 76 between 1960 and 1965.

The federal government continued to play a role in railroad affairs in the second half of the twentieth century. In addition to sponsoring Amtrak, the federal government addressed regulatory issues. Federal controls had been somewhat lessened by the Transportation Act of 1958, but most railroad managers still believed their industry to be overregulated. In 1970, the Department of Transportation was established; in 1980, sweeping changes were made to federal government regulatory practices. The STAGGERS RAIL ACT (1980) forced partial deregulation of the industry. In addition, the decline in passenger service and a decreased need for freight service because of greater railroad efficiency, along with government support of the airlines and highway construction, led to the railroads becoming unable to compete effectively. Federal regulation also prevented railroads from reacting to changes in the marketplace.

Deregulation permitted railroads to make changes that increased their revenues. For example, unprofitable branch lines could be closed. Railroads were also forced into free competition with air and road carriers. Shippers could now demand better prices from railroad carriers. More recently, the small number of freight railroads has caused some concern among shippers, who have begun to question the competitiveness in the industry.

Recent technological advances are revolutionizing railroads in other areas. In the 1990s, the airbrake had its first significant change since the 1930s. The Electro-Pneumatic brake system now in use allows the command for the brakes on a train to be sent electronically by the engineer, thereby increasing braking control. Computers control many other phases of railroad operation; satellites monitor the position of trains to prevent collisions. Many trains, like those of the Metro-North commuter train in southern New York, are now equipped with a system that sends signals to a display in the train, eliminating the need for wayside signaling. Finally, high-speed passenger rail service has been developed. At present, it is in limited use by Amtrak in the Northeast corridor. The hope is that commuters and travelers will see high-speed rail as an alternative to air travel and automobiles, ushering in another great age of passenger train travel.

BIBLIOGRAPHY

Bianculli, Anthony J. *Trains and Technology: The American Railroad in the Nineteenth Century.* Vol. 1, *Trains and Technology.* Newark: University of Delaware Press, 2001.

Daniels, Rudolph. *Trains across the Continent: North American Railroad History.* Bloomington: Indiana University Press, 2000.

Del Vecchio, Mike. *Pictorial History of America's Railroads.* Osceola, Wis.: MBI Publishing, 2001.

Saunders, Richard, Jr. *Merging Lines: American Railroads, 1900–1970.* DeKalb: Northern Illinois University Press, 2001.

Schweiterman, Joseph P. *When the Railroad Leaves Town: American Communities in the Age of Rail Line Abandonment.* Kirksville, Mo.: Truman State University Press, 2001.

Stover, John F., and Mark C. Carnes. *The Routledge Historical Atlas of the American Railroads.* New York: Routledge, 1999.

Usselman, Steven W. *Regulating Railroad Innovation: Business, Technology, and Politics in America, 1840–1920.* New York: Cambridge University Press, 2002.

Williams, John Hoyt. *A Great and Shining Road: The Epic Story of the Transcontinental Railroad.* Lincoln: University of Nebraska Press, 1996

Christine K. Kimbrough

See also **Homestead Movement; Homestead Strike; Interstate Commerce Laws; Land Speculation; Monopoly;** *Northern Securities Company v. United States;* **Pullman Strike; Pullmans; Steam Power and Engines; Transcontinental Railroad, Building of; Transportation and Travel; Transportation, Department of; Trust-Busting.**

RAILROADS IN THE CIVIL WAR. Because of great distances separating armies, long supply lines, and a premium on quick troop movements, the Civil War became the first war to feature railroads prominently. Railroads connecting the North with the Ohio and Mississippi River valleys had insured the West's adherence to the Union. Southern railroads, however, mainly connected the Atlantic seaboard to the Mississippi River. The South's most important military lines connected the Gulf states to Richmond via Chattanooga, enabling shipment of supplies and munitions to Virginia and the transfer of troops on interior lines.

As early as 31 March 1861, the federal government began using strategic railroads. On 31 January 1862, Congress authorized President Abraham Lincoln to "take possession of [certain] railroad and telegraph lines." In contrast, states' rights enthusiasts restricted the Confederate government to "supervision and control" until February 1865.

The North held material advantages as well. Of 31,256 miles of rail in the United States in 1861, Confederate states controlled only 9,283 miles, which Union captures soon reduced to about 6,000 miles. Southern roads—poorly equipped; lacking trunk lines; local in character and purpose; and handicapped by disrepair, inferior track and roadbed, and worn-out equipment and bridges—suffered delays, accidents, and limited traffic. Northern lines, on the other hand, steadily transported men and supplies southward to the Virginia battlefront, as well as eastward from western terminals at Memphis, Saint Louis, and Vicksburg.

The Confederate government's failure to "fully utilize railroads for southern defense partly explains the Confederacy's final collapse. Superior Northern railroads, prompt federal control where necessary, and greater means made the railroads an effective military auxiliary for the Union.

BIBLIOGRAPHY

Abdill, George. *Civil War Railroads.* Seattle, Wash.: Superior Publishing, 1961.

Anderson, Carter S. *Train Running for the Confederacy.* Mineral, Va.: W. D. Swank, 1990.

Thomas Robson Hay
Christopher Wells

See also **Army, Confederate; Army, Union; Railroads.**

RAILWAY SHOPMEN'S STRIKE. The Railway Employees Department of the American Federation of Labor (AFL), representing 400,000 members, struck 1 July 1922 to protest the unfavorable decisions of the Federal Labor Board and the unpunished violations of the Transportation Act by the carriers. President Warren G. Harding issued a warning against interference with the mails and attempted unsuccessfully to mediate the strike. Attorney General Harry M. Daugherty supported the carriers by obtaining a sweeping injunction against the

Vital but Vulnerable. Union troops guard a train against possible Confederate attack.

strikers and their leadership. On 27 October a settlement was reached, largely in favor of the carriers, although both sides claimed victory.

BIBLIOGRAPHY

Davis, Colin J. *Power at Odds: The 1922 National Railroad Shopmen's Strike.* Urbana: University of Illinois Press, 1997.

Harvey Wish / A. R.

See also **Railroad Mediation Acts; Strikes; Transportation Act of 1920.**

RAILWAYS, INTERURBAN. Electric interurban trains grew out of city-based networks of electric streetcars, commonly known as trolleys. Transit companies nationwide began to electrify their lines following the successful installation of a so-called "Sprague" system in Richmond, Virginia, in 1888. Inventors had been experimenting with electricity as a source of motive power for at least fifty years prior, but their systems had proved unworkable or unreliable. Frank Sprague, a young graduate of the Naval Academy and former assistant to Thomas Edison, developed a system that made electrically powered streetcars feasible, and electricity quickly replaced animal, cable, and other motive systems. In 1890, 70 percent of streetcar power was supplied by animals, but by 1902, 97 percent of all streetcars were powered by electric motors. Because electrifying streetcar lines was expensive, a period of consolidation followed within the transit industry that often left a local transportation market with only one or two competitors, all of which were much better capitalized than their predecessors.

These larger companies were interested in and dependent upon expansion. Many generated the electricity that moved the streetcars themselves, and constantly sought new uses for excess capacity. The search for ways to use excess power along with other social forces such as urbanization, increasing literacy, industrial growth and consolidation, and the impending end of rural isolation combined to impel the extension of the electric networks into the countryside, and eventually into vast interurban networks that operated in competition with the ubiquitous steam railroad.

The first electric railroads that were consciously "interurban" originated in the Midwest, particularly Ohio and Indiana. While the actual definition of "interurban" was a matter of some confusion even then, the distinction that emerged over time is essentially based on the primary operating goal of the railroad: interurbans were electric trains that carried passengers (not freight) from one city

41

to another. The terrain of Ohio and Indiana was ideally suited for this kind of transportation, dotted, as it was, with small yet significant towns that needed quick and easy connections to the major metropolitan centers where most business took place.

Nationally, mileage increased quickly, yet sporadically. From 1900 to 1904, more than 5,000 miles of track were built, and a second boom from 1907 to 1908 added roughly 4,000 additional miles. These 9,000 miles of track represented over 55 percent of the eventual total of 16,000 miles. Ohio led all states with 2,798 miles of track, Indiana followed with 1,825 miles, and Illinois was also in the top five. Pennsylvania, New York, and California ranked three, five, and six in total mileage, demonstrating that interurbans grew outside the Midwest as well.

One such place was California, where Henry Huntington's Pacific Electric interurban network in Los Angeles had a profound impact on the nature of that city's famously decentralized spatial arrangement. Huntington used his interurban trains to spur residential and commercial development in his massive land holdings, creating a metropolitan network of smaller towns linked to central Los Angeles (whose streetcar system, the LARY, he also owned) and determining the directions in which this network would grow. While Huntington was not unique in this respect, the situation in which he operated was: Los Angeles was small, yet rapidly growing, and relatively free from legal restrictions that might have impeded the growth of the interurban network. As a result, interurbans in Los Angeles played a crucial role in determining the spatial arrangement of the city. The effect in other cities was important as well; in Milwaukee, Wisconsin, for example, the main interstate highway routing follows a right-of-way by which interurban trains once entered the city.

The replacement of an interurban right-of-way with an interstate highway is symbolic of the fate of the industry as a whole. The interurbans peaked at a time (reaching peak mileage in 1916) when fast intercity transportation was demanded by the regionalization and nationalization of business, but before the automobile brought an astonishing level of comfort, convenience, and flexibility to travel. Electric interurban trains always provided lower quality service than steam railroads, and competed on price and frequency of service. When both lower steam railroad fares and affordable automobiles threatened this niche, the industry was doomed. Some companies turned to freight hauling or express delivery service in an attempt to make up lost revenue, but the growth of both trucks and air delivery eroded any cost or frequency edge that they might have had. The industry declined almost as precipitously as it had climbed: more than 5,000 miles of track were abandoned, and by 1940 4,000 miles, at most, remained in service—only 25 percent of the peak total. By 1960, and throughout the 1970s, the South Shore Electric, between Chicago and South Bend, Indiana, was the only electric interurban railway in the country.

In many ways, interurbans were victims of their own success. Their promises of cheap, frequent service created expectations that made the automobile appealing to millions of Americans tired of the tyranny of railroad schedules. By 1950, the automobile had replaced local trolleys and interurbans for short-haul traffic, and commercial air service was a well-established competitor that was overtaking long-distance passenger rail service. The decline of electric interurban service is but one aspect of the marginalization of all forms of passenger rail service in the United States. Despite their almost total demise, interurbans have taken on a second life as a hobby. Enthusiasts across the nation restore, preserve, and recreate interurban cars, routes, and buildings, indicating the powerful hold that rail travel has on the American imagination, if not its travel dollars. Recent proposals for the revival of rail service are often simply calls to reinstitute old interurban service. Many of the runs, such as St. Louis to Chicago and Los Angeles to San Diego, were the sites of actual or proposed high-speed lines in 1910; and the Midwest is the site of an immense proposed high-speed rail network, much as it was once the site of the largest of the interurban networks.

BIBLIOGRAPHY

Friedricks, William B. *Henry E. Huntington and the Creation of Southern California.* Columbus: Ohio State University Press, 1992.

Harwood, Herbert, Jr., and Robert S. Korach. *The Lake Shore Electric Railway Story.* Bloomington: Indiana University Press, 2000.

Hilton, George W., and John F. Due. *The Electric Interurban Railways in America.* Stanford, Calif.: Stanford University Press, 1960.

Middleton, William D. *The Interurban Era.* Milwaukee, Wis.: Kalmbach, 1961.

Christopher Miller

See also **Automobile; Railways, Urban, and Rapid Transit; Suburbanization; Transportation and Travel; Urbanization.**

RAILWAYS, URBAN, AND RAPID TRANSIT

systems have since the 1830s been indispensable to large cities and advantageous to smaller ones, moving many people while using relatively little space. While sail-powered ferryboats served Manhattan in the colonial era, non-waterborne local mass transportation service in the United States began in 1827 with the introduction of a horse-drawn carriage in New York City. Abraham Brower's Accommodation held twelve passengers, charged one shilling, and initially ran 1.75 miles along Broadway between Battery and Bond Streets. In 1831, Brower designated his third coach an omnibus, a term first used in France around 1815 to designate horse carriages used for transit service. In North America the term was eventually truncated to "bus."

Similar horse-drawn carriage (or omnibus) service appeared in Philadelphia in 1831; Boston, 1835; and Baltimore, 1844. By 1836, New York City alone had over one hundred omnibuses. Generally, these carriages were similar in structure to stagecoaches. Drivers sat on an open raised bench, and passengers pulled a leather strap attached to the driver's leg to disembark.

Horse-powered Railways

In 1832, the New York and Harlem Railroad Company introduced the first horse-powered rail car, also designed by Abraham Brower, which ran between downtown Manhattan and Harlem. Cities subsequently adopted the street railway over the omnibus for the first large-scale urban mass transit systems, citing the quieter and more comfortable ride afforded by rail cars and the mechanical efficiency derived from less need for horsepower. Prominent streetcar manufacturing firms included J.G. Brill and Company of Philadelphia; Jackson and Sharp of Wilmington, Delaware; and the Saint Louis Car Company. Their designs shifted away from the stagecoach and omnibus prototype to structures more reminiscent of later electric streetcars. Horses maintained an average speed of four miles per hour and worked approximately five hours per day for five years; thus, a single streetcar running fifteen hours per day behind one or two animals required three or six horses for power.

The world's oldest continually operating street railway service began in New Orleans in 1835 and ran along St. Charles Street. Additional streetcar networks appeared in Brooklyn in 1853; Boston, 1856; Philadelphia, 1858; Baltimore, Pittsburgh, Chicago, and Cincinnati, 1859; and in other cities thereafter. In 1882, 415 street railway companies employed 35,000 workers who drove over 100,000 horses and mules, hauling 18,000 streetcars and carrying 1.2 billion annual passengers along 3,000 miles of track.

Weaknesses inherent in an industry relying on animal power were illustrated by the Civil War, when both Federal and Confederate governments requisitioned railway horses for military use, and by the Great Epizootic, an equine influenza epidemic in 1872 that killed thousands of horses in major cities. The development of alternate power sources spurred the decline of horse-drawn mass transit: although street railway mileage increased nationally between 1890 and 1902 from 8,000 to 22,500, the share of railway service relying on animal power fell from 75 percent to 1 percent. The final horse-drawn streetcar in revenue service operated in New York City on 26 July 1917.

Cable Railways

After the rise of horse-powered streetcars but before the widespread adoption of street railway electrification, some cities used moving cable to transmit mechanical energy from large steam engines to streetcars. In 1869, Andrew Hallidie invented a system in which a cable, running in a groove under the street and between railway tracks, gripped and released a streetcar to move it forward. Mechanical brakes stopped the car after the cable was released. While cable cars had previously been used in mines and for funiculars, San Francisco in 1873 began to implement them as components of a streetcar network along five lines totaling 11.2 miles. Eventually fifty-nine companies in twenty-seven cities operated cable-powered streetcars, including Denver, with forty-four miles of cable railway; St. Louis, fifty-five miles; and Chicago, eighty-six miles.

Cable-powered railways ran at an average speed of six to eight miles per hour, double that of horsecars. As workers, tempted by the faster rides, moved farther from their places of employment, property values along railway lines increased. The 1884 introduction of electrified streetcars, however, allowed railways to transmit energy through small copper wires instead of complex systems of large cables, wheels, pulleys, and underground vaults. The two technologies competed from 1888 to 1893, when total track mileage for cable railways peaked at 305. Soon after, most cities with cable systems switched to electric power, the last of which were Tacoma, 1938, and Seattle, 1940. Only 8.8 miles of cable railway remain along three lines in San Francisco.

Electric Street Railways

Werner Siemens in 1879 provided the world's first electric rail demonstration on a 350-yard track at the Berlin Industrial Exhibition. In the United States, revenue service on electric-powered streetcars appeared on the East Cleveland Street Railway in 1884, on the Baltimore and Hampden Railway in 1885, and on the Court Street Line in Montgomery, Alabama in 1886. Frank Sprague's Union Passenger Railway in Richmond, Virginia began service in 1888 over twelve miles of track, and is generally considered to be the first successful electric street railway. Other cities rapidly adopted Sprague's model; and by 1891 two hundred streetcar systems nationwide were electrified or were planning to electrify. The synonymous term "trolley" derives from early devices mounted atop overhead wires and pulled, or trolled, forward by the car's movement.

Between approximately 1880 and 1920, streetcars were an essential part of city life. Residents often depended on them for work, school, worship, shopping, and social activities. Ten-mile-per-hour electric railways effectively expanded residential city limits by allowing commuters to live farther from their workplace. Many street railways expanded into subsidiary ventures, including interurban railways, electric power companies, and amusement parks. Massachusetts street railway companies alone owned thirty-one such parks in 1902, generating profit from admissions as well as from additional streetcar ridership.

Major electric streetcar manufacturers included Brill, St. Louis, Pullman, Osgood-Bradley, and G.C. Kuhlman. Nineteenth-century cars were generally made of wood and were either "open," without sides for warm weather

Subway. Rush hour in New York City. National Archives and Records Administration

use, or "closed," with sides. Twentieth-century cars were primarily constructed from steel and included articulated models, in which two separate body sections connected into a single unit with a bend in the center, allowing for increased hauling capacity and productivity. Innovations included the 1916 Birney Safety Car, a smaller, lightweight model requiring one operator instead of two. Although the Stone and Webster Company built 6,000 Birney cars between 1916 and 1921, they quickly went out of favor because their low weight and small size led to choppy rides and insufficient capacity for passengers. In 1929, twenty-five industry leaders formed the Electric Railway Presidents' Conference Committee to research car design improvements. The resulting Presidents' Conference Committee, or PCC, streetcar featured improved electric propulsion, acceleration, and braking systems, and began to be distributed nationally in 1936.

Trackless Trolleys, Elevateds, and Subways

Several other forms of urban mass transit coexisted with the electric streetcars. Trackless trolleys were similarly powered by electricity, but ran on rubber tires and drew current from an overhead wire system rather than through steel rails. First used in Hollywood in 1910, they replaced electric streetcars on Staten Island in 1921 and spread to Philadelphia in 1923, Chicago in 1930, and elsewhere. National trackless trolley usage peaked in the early 1950s, with about 7,000 cars running along 3,700 route miles in thirty-two cities. By 1990, about 1,200 cars remained, operating on about 600 route miles.

Elevated railways of the late nineteenth century were variations on standard steam-powered rail, except for Manhattan's West Side and Yonkers Patent Railway, which began cable rail service in 1868 and switched to steam in 1871. Early elevated steam engines, called "dummies," wore shrouds resembling railroad coaches in order to avoid frightening horses below. Manhattan's so-called els, the West Side and the Manhattan Elevated Railway (1877),

carried 500,000 daily passengers by 1893 and facilitated residence farther from the workplace, but also darkened roads beneath and caused fires by dropping cinders. Additional elevated railways operated in Brooklyn (beginning 1870s); Kansas City (1886); Sioux City, Iowa (1891); and Chicago (1892).

The nation's early subways represented the first significant expenditures of public funds on urban mass transportation projects. Subways in Boston, New York, and Philadelphia all followed a public-private financing structure, in which a public body sold bonds to finance construction, then leased the system for operation to a private company. "Cut and cover" construction methods were standard: workers uprooted the street surface, excavated, constructed the facility, and rebuilt the pavement. This process severely limited access to adjacent businesses until the addition of temporary wooden plank surfaces in the 1910s.

Boston opened the first 1.7 miles of its Tremont Street subway in 1897, and three additional lines, each using different rolling stock, opened in 1901, 1904, and 1912. New York City's first 9.1 miles of track began service in 1904. Between 1913 and 1931, the Interborough Rapid Transit Company and the Brooklyn Rapid Transit Company constructed most of the city's modern subway network, and the city-owned Independent Subway System inaugurated service in 1932. All three systems were unified under municipal control in 1940. Philadelphia subway service, which included elevated rail outside the central city, comprised the Market Street Line (1907) and Broad Street Line (1928).

Decline of Urban Mass Transit

For several reasons, electric streetcars, which in 1920 dominated mass transit in virtually every city with a population over 10,000, declined in usage after 1926. Contributing problems within the industry included financial and political corruption, deliberate overbuilding and overcapitalization, and a flat five-cent fare that generated low revenue on long-haul trips. The industry faced competition from motorized buses, introduced in 1905 on Manhattan's Fifth Avenue, and from jitneys, large automobiles providing irregular transit service along popular streetcar lines beginning in 1913 in Phoenix. While street railway executives responded by initiating their own bus service and by advocating strong regulation of jitneys, they could not meet the challenges posed by the private automobile, which changed how people thought about urban travel and created desire for personalized service not held to fixed times and routes.

The demise of street railways was also fueled by government policies that invested heavily in road construction and improvement, levied especially high taxes on railways relative to public utilities and private businesses, and permitted low-density suburban development not conducive to profitable streetcar service. Decreased ridership resulted from the shrinking workweek (from five-and-a-half to five days after World War II) and from shifts in commuting patterns away from downtowns. Meanwhile, industry leaders were distracted from responding to these challenges as they struggled to appease their constituent groups quarreling over the primary duty of mass transit: riders and employees saw the railways as public service utilities, while investors and executives perceived them as profit-bearing private enterprises. Except for a spike in patronage during World War II, when fuel and tires for private automobiles were rationed and new car construction virtually ceased, urban mass transit declined steadily after 1926 before leveling off in 1973.

Federal Policy

The federal government entered the urban transit arena following passage of the Transportation Act of 1958, which facilitated the elimination of unprofitable railroad lines and resulted in the discontinuation of many commuter routes. Responding to calls for assistance from city officials, Congress passed the Housing Act of 1961, which authorized the dispersal of funds, under the jurisdiction of the Housing and Home Finance Agency (HHFA), for urban mass transit demonstration projects and capital improvement loans. The Urban Mass Transportation Act of 1964 and its 1966 amendments, which increased funding, signaled strong federal support for the development and improvement of urban transit and for the planning and construction of coordinated regional transportation networks. Still, between 1961 and 1966, federal expenditure

on urban transit under these acts totaled only $375 million against $24 billion allocated to highways, airways, and waterways.

In 1966 federal authority over mass transit shifted to the Department of Housing and Urban Development and in 1968 to the Urban Mass Transportation Administration within the Department of Transportation. Subsequent key legislation included the Highway Act of 1973, which gradually opened the previously sacrosanct Highway Trust Fund for transit use; the National Mass Transportation Assistance Act of 1974, which enabled use of federal funds for operating as well as capital expenses; and the Surface Transportation Assistance Act of 1982, which established the first guaranteed funding source for urban transit from a new one-cent gasoline tax. The Intermodal Surface Transportation and Efficiency Act of 1991 and the Transportation Equity Act for the Twenty-First Century (TEA-21) of 1998 increased federal funding for mass transit—TEA-21 authorized $41 billion for transit over six years, including funding for research on magnetic levitation for urban rapid transit use.

Transit Revival

Drawing on federal funds provided under the Urban Mass Transportation Act, cities including San Francisco, Miami, Baltimore, Washington, Atlanta, and Los Angeles built rapid transit systems in the second half of the twentieth century. Electric streetcar service, now called light rail, reappeared in San Diego in 1981 and thereafter in Buffalo, Sacramento, San Jose, Portland, St. Louis, Baltimore, Minneapolis, and elsewhere. Development of new rapid transit systems and expansion of old ones continued nationwide in the early twenty-first century as cities struggle to improve traffic conditions, rejuvenate central business districts, and improve access between virtually autonomous suburbs.

TABLE 1

U.S. Urban Mass Transit Patronage, by mode (1870–1980, in millions)

Year	Animal-powered street railway	Cable-powered street railway*	Electric-powered street railway*	Motor bus	Trackless trolley	Rapid transit
1870	140	—	—	—	—	—
1880	570	5	—	—	—	80
1890	1,295	65	410	—	—	250
1902	45	24	5,403	—	—	363
1912	—	18	11,091	—	—	1,041
1920	—	—	13,770	—	—	1,792
1926	—	—	12,895	2,009	—	2,350
1930	—	—	10,530	2,481	16	2,559
1940	—	—	5,951	4,255	542	2,382
1946	—	—	9,027	10,247	1,354	2,835
1950	—	—	3,904	9,447	1,686	2,264
1960	—	—	463	6,425	654	1,850
1970	—	—	235	5,034	182	1,881
1980	—	12	133	5,837	142	2,108

* Between 1920 and 1970, cable-powered street railway figures are included in the electric-powered street railway column.

SOURCE: Brian J. Cudahy, *Cash Tokens, and Transfers: A History of Urban Mass Transit in North America*, (New York: Fordham University Press, 1990), 249.

BIBLIOGRAPHY

Bianco, Martha J. "Technological Innovation and the Rise and Fall of Urban Mass Transit." *Journal of Urban History* 25, no. 3 (1999): 348–378.

Cheape, Charles W. *Moving the Masses: Urban Public Transit in New York, Boston, and Philadelphia, 1880–1912*. Cambridge, Mass.: Harvard University Press, 1980.

Cudahy, Brian J. *Cash, Tokens, and Transfers: A History of Urban Mass Transit in North America*. New York: Fordham University Press, 1990.

———. *Under the Sidewalks of New York: The Story of the World's Greatest Subway System*. Revised ed. New York: Stephen Greene Press/Pelham Books, 1988.

Mallach, Stanley. "The Origins of the Decline of Urban Mass Transportation in the United States, 1890–1930." *Urbanism Past and Present*, no. 8 (Summer, 1979): 1–17.

Middleton, William D. *The Time of the Trolley*. Milwaukee, Wisc.: Kalmbach, 1967.

Miller, John Anderson. *Fares, Please! A Popular History of Trolleys, Horse-Cars, Street-Cars, Buses, Elevateds, and Subways*. New York: Dover, 1960.

Smerk, George M. *The Federal Role in Urban Mass Transportation.* Bloomington: Indiana University Press, 1991.

Jeremy L. Korr

See also **Electricity and Electronics; Land Grants for Railways; Railways, Interurban; Suburbanization; Transportation and Travel; Urbanization.**

RAINBOW COALITION.

The Rainbow Coalition was a group developed within the Democratic Party during the 1984 presidential election. Led by the African American civil rights activist Jesse Jackson, it attracted blacks, Latinos, Asian Americans, American Indians, and poor whites. As the coalition's spokesperson (and candidate for president in the Democratic primaries), Jackson criticized the administration of President Ronald Reagan and called for cuts in defense spending, strengthening of AFFIRMATIVE ACTION, and federal assistance for urban workers and farmers. Although he received 3.3 million votes in 1984 and 6.8 million in a second presidential bid in 1988, the coalition's alliance fragmented, and its influence greatly diminished by 1992.

BIBLIOGRAPHY

Collins, Sheila. *The Rainbow Challenge: The Jackson Campaign and the Future of U.S. Politics.* New York: Monthly Review Press, 1986.

Germond, Jack W., and Jules Witcover. *Whose Broad Stripes and Bright Stars?: The Trivial Pursuit of the Presidency, 1988.* New York: Warner Books, 1989.

Jill Watts/A. G.

See also **Elections, Presidential: 1988; Federal Aid; Lobbies; Race Relations.**

Jesse Jackson. The longtime civil rights activist, candidate for the Democratic presidential nomination in the 1980s, and head of the Rainbow Coalition, shown here under arrest during a protest. AP/WIDE WORLD PHOTOS

RALEIGH, the capital of North Carolina, is located in the central PIEDMONT section of the state, midway between the coastal plain and the mountains. A committee appointed by the state legislature founded the city in 1792 as the state's first permanent capital. The city was named after Sir Walter Raleigh, the English explorer and author.

Raleigh quickly became a center of transportation and banking. On 20 May 1861, following Abraham Lincoln's call for volunteer troops from North Carolina, a convention met in Raleigh and voted for the state to secede from the Union. General William Tecumseh Sherman occupied the city on 13 April 1865. Raleigh suffered virtually no damage during the Civil War.

African Americans currently make up 28 percent of Raleigh's population. The city elected its first African American mayor in 1973. Raleigh is a center of government, education, and research. North Carolina State University, opened in 1887, has a current student population of 28,000. The 7,000-acre Research Triangle Park (RTP), established in 1959, is home to over one hundred technological, pharmaceutical, and other research firms. The city has experienced rapid growth since the establishment of RTP. The population grew from 93,931 in 1960 to 276,093 in 2000.

BIBLIOGRAPHY

Murray, Elizabeth Reid. *Wake: Capital County of North Carolina.* Vol. 1, *Prehistory through Centennial.* Raleigh: Capital County Publishing Co., 1983.

Perkins, David, ed. *The News & Observer's Raleigh: A Living History of North Carolina's Capital.* Winston-Salem, N.C.: John F. Blair, 1994.

Vickers, James. *Raleigh, City of Oaks: An Illustrated History.* Woodland Hills, Calif.: Windsor Publications, 1982.

Thomas Vincent

RALEIGH COLONIES.

Sir Walter Raleigh and his half brother, Sir Humphrey Gilbert, were authorized to colonize lands, and in 1578 they outfitted a fleet of privateering ships and sailed into the West Indies. Raleigh had a large interest in a 1583 Newfoundland voyage, on the return leg of which Gilbert was lost. In 1584, Raleigh planned an expedition, commanded by Philip Amadas and Arthur Barlowe. It arrived off the coast of what is now North Carolina on 13 July 1584; took possession of the area in the name of the queen; explored the inlets, islands, and mainland south of Chesapeake Bay; and returned to England with skins, a pearl necklace, and two young Indian men, Manteo and Wanchese. They were put on show in London and used to help raise support for Raleigh's next expedition. Queen Elizabeth I agreed to the land being named Virginia in her honor, knighted Raleigh on 6 January 1585 as a result of this expedition, and made him lord and governor of Virginia.

Queen Elizabeth would not allow Raleigh to risk hazardous voyages himself, so in 1585 he organized a colonial expedition to Roanoke Island, off the coast of North Carolina. It was led by Sir Richard Grenville, with Ralph Lane to be the governor. The landing in July was too late in the season and much of the seed brought along was spoiled by salt water. Grenville returned to England, taking further samples of Indian trade goods, leaving Lane in command of 107 men, including Manteo. Sir Francis Drake's 1586 expedition was primarily intended to capture Spanish treasure ships but it visited the Roanoke colony, possibly because the expedition was financed in part by Raleigh. Drake arrived off the coast on 10 June and had supplies sent to the colonists. Lane wanted to accept Drake's offer of further assistance, including food and boats, and move north to Chesapeake Bay. The planned relief ship from England was considerably overdue, and most of the colonists were desperate to leave. When Drake offered to take them home with his fleet, they all left the settlement. Grenville arrived in August 1586 to find nobody at the colony. He left fifteen men with plenty of provisions, but their fate is unknown. In 1587, Raleigh organized a second colony, one including women and children, with John White as governor. Raleigh instructed his captains to settle the colony one hundred miles farther north, at a site on Chesapeake Bay to be named after him. However, one of the captains, Simon Fernandez, overruled Raleigh and a colony was established once again at Roanoke Island. When White reluctantly left the colony to return home for supplies, there were eighty-five men, seventeen women, and eleven children. This colony disappeared sometime between White's departure in August 1587 and his return in August 1590. The members of White's relief expedition in 1590 saw smoke near the colony and thought it was a signal. They fired a cannon to indicate that they had arrived. Six of the relief crew, including Captain Edward Spicer, drowned during the landing at the colony; the survivors found nobody there. It had been agreed that the colonists would, if they had to leave, carve a message on the fort's palisade, to say where they had gone. White found a carving of the word "CROATOAN," the name of an island where Manteo had been born and still had friends. White, however, was unable to persuade Captain Abraham Cooke to check Croatoan. In the lost group was White's daughter, Ellinor, the mother of Virginia Dare, the first English child born in America. The Lumbee Indians (a mixed Indian-white people) of Robeson County, North Carolina, claim to be the direct descendants of the members of Raleigh's lost colony on what is now called Croatan Island.

Raleigh's last attempt at colonization was in 1603. Bartholomew Gilbert had instructions to establish a new colony in the Chesapeake Bay area. A group landed on 10 May, but Indians killed Gilbert. The rest of the crew were discouraged and went back to England in September. When they returned, Raleigh was in the Tower of London on conspiracy charges and his rights to the New World had reverted to the Crown.

BIBLIOGRAPHY

Durant, David N. *Raleigh's Lost Colony.* New York: Atheneum, 1981.

Quinn, David Beers. *Raleigh and the British Empire.* London: Hodder and Stoughton, 1947.

Quinn, David Beers, ed. *The Roanoke Voyages, 1584–1590.* 2 vols. Reprint. New York: Dover, 1991.

Winton, John. *Sir Walter Raleigh.* New York: Coward, McCann, 1975.

Michelle M. Mormul

See also **Explorations and Expeditions: British; North Carolina; South Carolina;** *and vol. 9:* **Charter to Sir Walter Raleigh.**

RAMS, CONFEDERATE. The *Virginia*, first and most famous ram (a warship with a heavy beak at the prow for piercing an enemy ship) of the Confederate fleet, was constructed on the salvaged hull of the U.S. frigate *Merrimack*, sunk at the evacuation of the Norfolk Navy Yard. The rams featured armor plated casemates with sloping sides to deflect enemy fire; their bows were fitted with massive iron beaks or rams, which enabled it to revive the smashing tactics of the ancient galleys. They were used with much success by the Confederates, who put in service or had under construction forty-four ironclad (armor four to eight inches) vessels of this general class.

BIBLIOGRAPHY

Melton, Maurice. *The Confederate Ironclads.* South Brunswick, N.J.: T. Yoseloff, 1968.

Still, William N. *Iron Afloat: The Story of the Confederate Armorclads.* Columbia: University of South Carolina Press, 1985.

William M. Robinson Jr. / A. R.

See also **Ironclad Warships;** *Monitor* **and** *Merrimack,* **Battle of; Navy, Confederate; Vicksburg in the Civil War; Warships.**

RANCHING. *See* **Cattle; Livestock Industry.**

RANDOLPH COMMISSION. In 1676, Edward Randolph was commissioned as the special agent of the king to carry to MASSACHUSETTS BAY COLONY the king's orders that agents be sent to England authorized to act for the colony concerning the boundary disputes with heirs of John Mason and of Ferdinando Gorges. As with the royal commission of 1664, he was also commanded to investigate conditions there, by which it was apparent that the real matter at issue was the king's decision to face the problem of the uncertainty and confusion about the relationship between Massachusetts and England. During Randolph's month in New England he was to make a complete investigation concerning the governments of the colonies; their methods of defense, finance, religion, and trade; the character of their laws; and their attitude in general toward each other and toward England.

Needless to say, Randolph did not meet with a cordial reception. The government of Massachusetts personally affronted Randolph and ignored the king's demands, although agents were reluctantly dispatched a few months after Randolph's departure. Many people had complained to him of religious and political discriminations, and neighboring colonies resented the arrogant attitude of Massachusets toward them. Most serious of all was that Randolph confirmed the flagrant breaches of the NAVIGATION ACTS and the denial of parliamentary legislative authority over the colony. On his return to England he made a comprehensive report, adverse as far as Massachusetts was concerned, recommending repealing its charter and making it into a royal province. In particular, the attitude that laws made in England did not apply in Massachusetts because it was not represented in Parliament caused grave concern at court and was chiefly responsible for the reopening of the fifty-year-old question as to the legal position of the Massachusetts Bay Company, which ended in the annulment of the charter in 1684.

BIBLIOGRAPHY

Hall, Michael G. *Edward Randolph and the American Colonies, 1676–1703.* Chapel Hill: Published for the Institute of Early American History and Culture by the University of North Carolina Press, 1960.

Randolph, Edward. *Edward Randolph; Including His Letters and Official Papers from the New England, Middle, and Southern Colonies in America, with Other Documents Relating Chiefly to the Vacating of the Royal Charter of the Colony of Massachusetts Bay, 1676–1703.* With historical illustrations and a memoir by Robert Noxon Toppan. New York: B. Franklin, 1967.

Viola F. Barnes
Michael Wala

See also **Massachusetts.**

RANGERS are specially trained infantry capable of acting in small groups to make rapid attacks against enemy forces and then withdraw without major engagement. Rangers have existed since before the American Revolution, when the British employed skilled marksmen learned in woodlore to gather intelligence and harass the French and Indians. Colonists on both sides of the conflict organized ranger groups to fight during the American Revolution. John Butler's Rangers and the Queen's American Rangers fought for the British, while Thomas Knowlton's Connecticut Rangers served in the Continental army.

Ranger units fought in the War of 1812, in the Black Hawk War, and in the Mexican War. In the Civil War, many units of both the North and South adopted the name. Rangers were not used again until World War II. During 1942–44, the American military organized six ranger battalions that saw action in Africa, Europe, and the Pacific. After the invasion of Korea, the armed forces organized sixteen ranger companies, seven of which served in the conflict. In 1951 the military decided that ranger-trained personnel would be better utilized if they were spread among standard infantry units. Since that time, selected officers and enlisted men have undergone intensive training at Fort Benning, Georgia, before being assigned to units throughout the army. In Vietnam, the army designated long-range infantry patrol units as ranger companies in 1969. The World War II ranger battalions, the First Special Service Force, and the Korean War ranger companies continued as part of the U.S. Army's Special Forces into the 1970s.

BIBLIOGRAPHY

Hogan, David W., Jr. *Raiders of Elite Infantry? The Changing Role of the U.S. Army Rangers from Dieppe to Grenada.* Westport, Conn.: Greenwood Press, 1992.

Johnson, James M. *Militiamen, Rangers, and Redcoats: The Military in Georgia, 1754–1776.* Macon, Ga.: Mercer University Press, 1992.

Robinson, Charles M., III. *The Men Who Wear the Star: The Story of the Texas Rangers.* New York: Random House, 2000.

John E. Jessup Jr. / E. M.

See also **Mosby's Rangers; Rogers' Rangers; Special Forces.**

RAPE is a crime of sexual coercion, most commonly committed by men and against women. While we have limited information about the incidence of rape in early America, there is strong evidence to suggest that many more rapes occur today, when rates are adjusted for population, than occurred in the colonial period. Estimates are that in the early twenty-first century at least one in eight women in America has been a victim of forcible rape, a crime that can cause acute and long-term trauma of both physical and psychological dimensions.

Between the eighteenth and mid-twentieth centuries, American rape law changed surprisingly little. Since the mid-1970s, however, the law has been modified considerably, largely due to the persuasive efforts of reformers who claimed that traditional rape law manifested biases and inadequacies.

Definition and Punishment

Throughout England and colonial America, rape was defined as the carnal knowledge of a woman obtained forcibly and against her will. From the seventeenth through the nineteenth centuries, rape was treated primarily as a crime committed by a male stranger against another man, an outsider's trespass against the property of the husband or father of the woman who was raped. Even in the twentieth century, after America had abandoned the formal notion of married women as property, its influence remained for many years in the form of the marital exemption from rape laws that irrefutably presumed a woman's consent even to forced intercourse with her husband. Because female slaves were the exclusive property of their owners, they too fell outside the reach of rape law.

In early English common law, rape was a misdemeanor punishable by fine or imprisonment. A statute enacted in England in 1285 made rape a capital felony. Likewise, in the American colonies, rape was exclusively a capital felony through the seventeenth and eighteenth centuries. A rape conviction obtained in the past century, however, was more frequently punished by imprisonment.

Seventeenth Century

The law of seventeenth- and eighteenth-century England treated woman's accusations of rape with considerable skepticism. This attitude is captured in the oft-quoted language of the seventeenth-century English jurist Sir Matthew Hale in his *History of the Pleas of the Crown:* "It must be remembered, that [rape] is an accusation easily to be made and hard to be proved, and harder to be defended by the party accused, tho never so innocent."

Although the skeptical approach to rape complaints characterized American law in the eighteenth and nineteenth centuries, it did not take hold instantly in the American colonies. Prior to 1700, when almost all sexual assault cases in colonial American courts involved attempted rape of white women by assailants they knew, conviction rates were quite high and magistrates articulated a philosophy of deterrence, often imposing severe corporal punishments on men convicted of attempted rape. In this Puritan regime, women who came to court alleging sexual violence that they had resisted were generally believed to be telling the truth. In the mid-1600s, Governor Theophilus Eaton of New Haven Colony explained that "a young girle [would not] bee so impudent as to charge such a carriage upon a young man when it was not so," especially when she would be subjected to intensive judicial questioning (Dayton, p. 239).

Although her account of sexual violation was generally deemed truthful, a woman who failed to report a sexual assault promptly might also receive corporal punishment, at a level less than her assailant, for concealing the offense for an unreasonable period. A woman pregnant out of wedlock who claimed to have been raped would not benefit from the presumption of truthfulness, as it was thought in that era that a woman could not conceive a child during a rape. These women, like those who were found to have encouraged or submitted to a man's sexual advances, were punished for fornication.

Eighteenth to Twentieth Centuries

After 1700, colonial judges began consulting English legal sources more frequently and importing into American legal procedures the suspicion toward rape complaints that prevailed in England. In the 1700s, unlike the previous century, the noncapital crime of attempted rape by acquaintances was rarely prosecuted, and both rape indictments and conviction rates were low, especially if the complainant was an unmarried woman who had charged an acquaintance. As Zephaniah Swift, author of an eighteenth century treatise on Connecticut's laws warned, "the vindictive spirit of lewd women" has frequently caused charges of rape to be made from "motives of malice and revenge" (Dayton, p. 265).

When defendants were non-whites, the reluctance to sentence them to death for the crime of rape was [somewhat]diminished. In the eighteenth century, most of the men indicted for rape and virtually all who were convicted and executed were blacks, Indians, foreigners, or transients. Rape evolved into a crime committed primarily by strangers against white women. After 1700, father-daughter incest, no longer a capital felony, was the only crime of sexual violence for which local white men might expect harsh corporal punishment.

Racialized enforcement of rape law continued through the nineteenth and twentieth centuries. Forbidden sexual access to white women and stereotyped as sexual predators, African American men alleged to have raped white women were often vigorously prosecuted, even in cases where there was reason to doubt the allegation's veracity. This is the scenario that underlies the infamous SCOTTSBORO CASE in which nine young African American men were falsely accused of gang rape in 1931 in a small town in Alabama, tried without some of the most minimal protections of fair process, convicted, and in eight of the cases, sentenced to death. Ultimately the Supreme Court reversed all the convictions, but not before the Scottsboro defendants had served many years of imprisonment. Statistics show that African Americans constituted approximately 90 percent of the men executed for rape in the United States in the twentieth century. The Supreme Court highlighted this racialized pattern of punishment when it declared the death penalty for rape unconstitutional in the case of *Coker v. Georgia* (1977).

By contrast, when complainants were African American women, rape laws were notoriously underenforced. The institutionalized rape of black females by white slave owners as part of the system of slavery is well documented. Since a slave woman was considered "unrapeable" by law, she could not control her sexual accessibility and had no lawful options to resist being raped. Hence in 1855, when a young slave named Celia repeatedly resisted forcible sexual advances by Robert Newsom, her sixty-five-year-old Missouri slave master, finally striking him with a large stick that caused his death, she was tried for capital murder, convicted, and executed by hanging.

Reform Efforts

Model Penal Code. While late-nineteenth-century women's groups succeeded in their lobbying to raise the age limit for statutory rape, the first twentieth-century effort to modernize rape law came with the revision of the Model Penal Code (MPC) in the 1950s. The MPC is an influential model statute drafted by a group of learned legal experts. In the MPC revision, the rape victim no longer had to resist "to the utmost," as many states had required, to prove her nonconsent. Following this lead, states began to abolish resistance requirements. The MPC also established three grades of sexual assaults. Felony rape in the first degree was violent stranger rape. Violent acquaintance rape was a second-degree felony, and other kinds of sexual coercion constituted the third-degree felony of "gross sexual imposition." Adapting this model, many states have graded rape offenses by degree of severity in their statutory schemes.

Feminist Critiques. Subsequent reforms of traditional rape law came largely as a response to the critiques that began to emerge from the woman's movement in the 1970s. Feminist reformers [first] raised awareness of the extent of rape and the degree of harm it inflicts, then analyzed how, despite harsh penalties for rape, the law had failed to hold accountable most perpetrators. These reformers suggested that misunderstandings about the crime of rape were operating within traditional rape law and impeding its effectiveness.

Feminist writings portrayed the evidentiary and procedural rules unique to rape law as reflections of patriarchal skepticism about rape victims' claims. This led to such virulent attacks on victims' character and behavior in rape cases that the rate at which victims reported rape was reduced, as were the rates at which police arrested, prosecutors charged, and judges and juries convicted and sentenced. Feminists observed that a direct consequence of this preoccupation with false accusations was dramatic underprotection of victims of sexual assault.

In her book, *Real Rape: How the Legal System Victimizes Women Who Say No* (1987), the law professor Susan Estrich asserts that only violent stranger rapes, which constitute a minority of rapes committed, are treated as serious crimes in the legal system. Estrich and others argue that disparate treatment of some rapes such as stranger rapes, and other rapes, such as acquaintance rapes, belies the fact that all of these actions violate the victim's bodily integrity and sexual autonomy.

Rape Law in the Early Twenty-First Century

Some rape law reforms have achieved broad acceptance. For example, state statutes tend to denominate rape by more descriptive terms such as "criminal sexual conduct" or "sexual assault," to define it in gender-neutral terms, and to encompass a broader array of conduct including oral and anal penetration. The age limit for statutory rape is typically the mid-teens, and the marital exemption from rape laws survives in a limited form only in a small number of states. Requirements that the victim's testimony be corroborated and that jurors be cautioned to give this testimony special scrutiny have largely disappeared. Rape shield laws that, with some exceptions, restrict admission of the victim's prior sexual conduct, have been widely adopted. Rarely is physical resistance formally required any longer to show nonconsent.

Other proposed reforms have received less widespread acceptance. For example, only a few states prohibit sexual coercion by certain types of fraud or by extortionate threats. A few states will not exonerate rape defendants who claim to have reasonably mistaken nonconsent for consent, while many others will. Whether and under what circumstances to permit mistakes about consent to provide a valid defense is an area of continuing controversy in rape law.

The impact of these reforms is unclear, as studies have detected only limited measurable effects from various reforms on victim behavior and case outcomes. This may reflect the fact that popular attitudes can be harder to change than written laws. Perhaps for similar reasons, the problem of rape in American penal institutions persists at high levels, with estimates that 350,000 sexual assaults are committed each year on male prisoners, typically by other prisoners. High levels of rape of female prisoners by male prison staff have also been reported.

Despite the fact that rape is largely an intraracial crime, studies suggest that cases involving black male suspects and white female victims still attract greatest attention from the courts and the press and are accorded the harshest punishment. This discriminatory treatment poses grave harm to African American men and contributes as well to cultural denial of the frequency and seriousness of other forms of rape. Studies also suggest that African American women remain least able of all rape complainants to obtain redress through legal process. Unfortunately, efforts to combat race bias in rape law enforcement are difficult to achieve through statutory reform. As with many of the other aspects of the problem of rape, they require deeper cultural change.

Two of the most famous rape trials of the late twentieth century, those of William Kennedy Smith in 1991 and heavyweight champion Mike Tyson in 1992, were based on allegations of date rape. In each trial, the victim testified that she was raped and the defendant testified that sex was consensual. In the Smith trial, the jury resolved credibility questions in favor of the defendant, finding Smith not guilty. In the Tyson trial, the jury resolved credibility questions in favor of the victim. As a result, Tyson was convicted and sentenced to a term of imprisonment. As American culture continues to struggle with issues of date rape and acquaintance rape, reform affecting cases such as these will likely continue.

BIBLIOGRAPHY

Dayton, Cornelia Hughes. *Women before the Bar: Gender, Law, and Society in Connecticut, 1639–1789.* Chapel Hill: University of North Carolina Press, 1995.

Estrich, Susan. *Real Rape: How the Legal System Victimizes Women Who Say No.* Cambridge, Mass.: Harvard University Press, 1987.

LaFree, Gary D. *Rape and Criminal Justice: The Social Construction of Sexual Assault.* Belmont, Calif.: Wadsworth, 1989.

MacKinnon, Catharine A. *Sex Equality: Rape Law.* New York: Foundation Press, 2001.

Schulhofer, Stephen J. *Unwanted Sex: The Culture of Intimidation and the Failure of Law*. Cambridge, Mass.: Harvard University Press, 1998.

Spohn, Cassia, and Julie Horney. *Rape Law Reform: A Grassroots Revolution and Its Impact*. New York: Plenum, 1992.

Phyllis Goldfarb

See also **Violence Against Women Act; Women's Rights Movement: The 20th Century.**

RAPE CRISIS CENTERS first appeared in 1972, when the first center opened in Washington, D.C. They originated in the commitment of second-wave feminists' (those whose views predominated during the 1960s and 1970s) "personal politics," which redefined as public issues the problems individual women experienced. Rape crisis centers, like women's health clinics and battered women's shelters, were designed to empower and serve women. Personnel at the centers counsel women who have been raped, provide information about medical and legal procedures, and act as advocates in hospitals, police stations, and courtrooms. At first, rape crisis centers were erratically funded and staffed by community volunteers. By the 1990s many centers were run by universities or local governments and employed professional counselors.

BIBLIOGRAPHY

Calhoun, Karen S. *Treatment of Rape Victims: Facilitating Psychosocial Adjustment*. New York: Pergamon Press, 1991.

Amy Fried / D. B.

See also **Sexual Harassment; Social Work; Violence Against Women Act; Women's Health; Women's Rights Movement: The 20th Century.**

RAPID TRANSIT. See **Railways, Urban, and Rapid Transit.**

READER'S DIGEST, founded in 1922 by husband and wife Dewitt Wallace and Lila Bell Acheson with the mission of providing selections of published articles and books to help readers cope with the flood of news and information. The *Digest* drastically "condensed" articles, often cutting by 75 percent before reprinting them.

The *Digest* conceived of reading material as information, not literature. One popular though widely criticized innovation was its publication of condensed fiction. Novels lost their subplots in the abridgement process. Publishers initially feared losing book buyers to *Digest* publication, but found that appearance in the *Reader's Digest* actually boosted sales.

Wallace refused advertising until 1955. Soliciting ads would entail revealing circulation figures, and revealing them could raise the prices the *Digest* paid for reprinting.

DeWitt and Lila Wallace. The founders of *Reader's Digest*.
GETTY IMAGES

Production costs were likewise kept low, and the magazine seemed a bargain, containing large quantities of articles shortened from the periodical press, printed in a handy size. Eventually, the *Digest* developed its own original articles, maintaining the illusion that these were reprints by first subsidizing their publication elsewhere. This strategy allowed it to promote its conservative views in other magazines. Its conservative crusades included an attack on Alfred Kinsey's 1948 *Sexual Behavior in the Human Male*, and it firmly supported U.S. government policy during the Vietnam War.

Although the *Digest*'s circulation dropped far below its high of 18 million, in 2000 it still had over 12.5 million subscribers, the third largest circulation of an American magazine. Editions in nineteen languages generated an enormous international circulation as well.

BIBLIOGRAPHY

Sharp, Joanne. *Condensing the Cold War: Reader's Digest and American Identity*. Minneapolis: University of Minnesota Press, 2001.

Tebbel, John, and Mary Ellen Zuckerman. *The Magazine in America 1741–1990*. New York: Oxford University Press, 1991.

Ellen Gruber Garvey

READJUSTER MOVEMENT. The readjuster movement in VIRGINIA had its inception in the contention of Rev. John E. Massey, Col. Frank G. Ruffin, and a few others that the antebellum state debt, which had been funded in 1871, ought to be readjusted so that it could be met without ruin to farmer taxpayers (already hard pressed by economic conditions) and without neglect of public schools and charities. Gen. William Mahone, seeking the Democratic gubernatorial nomination, endorsed the idea in 1877, swung the *Richmond Whig* to its support, and in 1879 organized the Readjuster party. Winning the legislature in 1879 with the help of disorganized Republican voters, and gaining the governorship in 1881 with William E. Cameron as its candidate, the new party scaled the debt by the Riddleberger Bill of 1882, enacted laws in the economic and social interest of the masses, and, carefully guided by Mahone, apportioned the offices among its leaders. Elected to the Senate in 1880 (where he was soon joined by H. H. Riddleberger), Mahone cooperated with the Republicans and received the federal patronage on the theory that he stood for anti-Bourbonism and a fair vote. Thus supported, blacks rallied unanimously to his standard, while many of the whites continued faithful. His political machine now seemed invincible. But the regular Democrats, led by John S. Barbour and John W. Daniel, accepted the debt settlement; welcomed back such sincere Readjusters as Massey and Ruffin, who would not brook Mahone's "bossism"; drew the color line; and won in 1883 and thereafter, although sometimes very narrowly. Perhaps the most lasting result of the movement, aside from the debt settlement, was the belief among the white masses that, while blacks could vote, white men must not be divided, however important the issues on which they differed and however "rotten" the Democratic machine.

BIBLIOGRAPHY

Moore, James T. *Two Paths to the New South: The Virginia Debt Controversy, 1870–1883.* Lexington: University Press of Kentucky, 1974.

C. C. Pearson / L. T.

See also **Confederate States of America; Debts, State; Reconstruction.**

REAGANOMICS denotes the economic policies of President Ronald Reagan in the 1980s. He sought to remedy the high inflation and recessions of the 1970s, which conservatives attributed to the heavy burden government imposed on private enterprise. Reagan called for sharp reductions in federal taxes, spending, and regulation as well as a monetary policy that strictly limited the growth of the money supply.

The administration implemented most of its program. The Federal Reserve pushed interest rates to historic highs in 1981, limiting monetary growth; Congress reduced tax rates in 1981 and again in 1986; and Reagan appointees relaxed many federal regulations. Reagan also secured immediate cuts in domestic spending, but he failed to arrest the growth of social security, Medicare, and Medicaid, which continued to grow automatically with the aging of the population and new medical technology.

Reaganomics was and remains controversial. The country suffered a severe recession in 1981–1982, but inflation fell from 13.5 percent to 3.2 percent. In 1983, the economy began a substantial boom that lasted through 1989, and unemployment gradually fell to 5.3 percent. Throughout, inflation remained under control, hovering between 3 and 4 percent a year. But Washington ran heavy deficits throughout the 1980s, with the federal debt tripling. The international balance of payments went from equilibrium to an annual deficit of over $100 billion, and the distribution of income became less equal.

BIBLIOGRAPHY

Stein, Herbert. *Presidential Economics: The Making of Economic Policy from Roosevelt to Clinton.* Washington, D.C.: American Enterprise Institute, 1994.

Wyatt Wells

See also **Supply-Side Economics.**

REAL ESTATE INDUSTRY. Real estate is land, all of the natural parts of land such as trees and water, and all permanently attached improvements such as fences and buildings. People use real estate for a wide variety of purposes, including retailing, offices, manufacturing, housing, ranching, farming, recreation, worship, and entertainment. The success or failure of these uses is dependent on many interrelated factors: economic conditions, demographics, transportation, management expertise, government regulations and tax policy, climate, and topography. The objective of those engaged in the real estate industry is to create value by developing land or land with attached structures to sell or to lease or by marketing real estate parcels and interests. The real estate industry employs developers, architects, designers, landscapers, engineers, surveyors, abstractors, attorneys, appraisers, market researchers, financial analysts, construction workers, sale and leasing personnel, managers, office support workers, and building and grounds maintenance workers. By the end of 2001, 1,544,000 were employed in the real estate industry.

The development and marketing of real estate, common in Europe since the Middle Ages, came with European colonists to the United States. For instance, in the seventeenth century Dr. Thomas Gerard, an owner of land in Maryland granted to him by the second Lord Baltimore, profited by leasing and selling land to other settlers. The new federal city of Washington, created in 1791, was subdivided and the lots offered for sale, although this enterprise proved disappointing to its sponsors. The first hotel constructed in the United States, an early example of commercial real estate development, was the seventy-three-room City Hotel at 115 Broadway in New York City, which opened in 1794. It served as a model for similar hotels in Boston, Philadelphia, and Baltimore. In the 1830s, William Butler Ogden came to investigate land his brother-in-law had purchased near the Chicago River and stayed on to become a real estate developer and Chicago's first mayor. The rapid growth of cities in the nineteenth century provided many opportunities for the real estate industry.

Real estate development is sensitive to fluctuations in the economy and in turn contributes to those cycles. The combination of a capitalist economy and a growing population makes the expansion of land uses inevitable, but developers can misjudge the market and produce too many office buildings, hotels, apartment buildings, or houses in any particular area. As a result rents and sale prices fall. The economic prosperity of the 1920s brought a huge expansion of real estate, especially in housing, but by the mid-1930s, 16 million people were unemployed and the demand for real estate of all types declined precipitously. World War II brought technological innovation and a backlog of demand for new construction. The mortgage stability introduced by federal legislation following the Great Depression and World War II greatly aided the huge expansion of suburban housing and shopping centers that followed the war. William Levitt started building Levittown on Long Island in 1947, with 17,447 standardized houses produced at the rate of 36 per day for a population of 82,000, and by 1955 this type of subdivision represented 75 percent of new housing starts. The 1950s also brought the nationwide development of Holiday Inns by Kemmons Wilson. In the continuation of a trend that had begun with the Empire State building in the 1930s, skyscraper office, apartment, and hotel building construction continued after World War II in urban centers, driving up site values. As population growth shifted to the West and the South after the war, investment in the real estate industry moved with it.

The restrictive monetary policies of the latter years of the 1960s, the energy crisis and inflation of the mid-1970s, inflation in the early 1980s, the savings and loan crisis of the late 1980s, and inflation and overproduction in the early 1990s, all negatively affected the real estate industry. However, a period of general economic prosperity began in 1992 and the real estate industry flourished in the remainder of the 1990s.

BIBLIOGRAPHY

Caplow, Theodore, Louis Hicks, and Ben J. Wattenberg. *The First Measured Century: An Illustrated Guide to Trends in America, 1900–2000.* Washington, D.C.: American Enterprise Press, 2001.

Gelernter, Mark. *A History of American Architecture: Buildings in Their Cultural and Technological Context.* Hanover, N.H.: University Press of New England, 1999.

Miles, M.E., et al. *Real Estate Development.* Washington, D.C.: Urban Land Institute, 1991.

Seldin, Maury, and Richard H. Swesnik. *Real Estate Investment Strategy.* 3d ed. New York: John Wiley and Sons, 1985.

White, John R., ed. *The Office Building: From Concept to Investment Reality.* Chicago: Appraisal Institute and the Counselors of Real Estate, 1993.

Judith Reynolds

See also **City Planning; Housing; Property.**

RECALL. A state and local constitutional provision allowing for the removal of public officials by the voters. Fifteen states, mostly western, include recall for state-level officers, and many more allow for the removal of local officials. Recall is most often grouped with the INITIATIVE and the REFERENDUM; taken together, the three measures formed a cornerstone of the Progressive-Era reforms aimed at promoting "direct democracy." The first state to adopt the recall was Oregon in 1908 (it had earlier adopted the initiative and referendum), although the 1903 Los Angeles city charter actually marked the first instance of its inclusion in a community's body of fundamental law. Recall usually applies to administrative (executive branch) officials, although it has occasionally been applied to judicial officers as well. Along with the other measures, the demand for recall arose in response to the feeling among Progressive reformers that officials, because they were beholden to the party machines and special interests, paid little heed to the public welfare once elected or appointed.

In contrast to impeachment proceedings, which allow for the removal of elected and appointed officials accused of high crimes and misdemeanors by a tribunal of their legislative peers, recall invests the power of removal directly with the voters. The procedure calls for the presentation of a petition signed by a stipulated number of registered voters (usually 25 percent of those participating in the last election) requesting the official's removal. No indictable criminal or civil charges need be brought against the official in order for the petition to be valid. After judicial review to ensure the petition's authenticity and procedural conformance, a recall election is scheduled and the voters decide either to remove or to retain the official. While simple in theory, the process is actually cumbersome since the petition requires voter mobilization, and its submittal inevitably prompts legal challenges by those opposed.

Since its inception nearly a century ago, recall has been used infrequently and most often without success. Of the three measures, it has proven the least popular. The majority of attempts have involved local officials. Notable cases in the last thirty years of the twentieth century include unsuccessful efforts to remove Philadelphia Mayor Frank Rizzo, Cleveland Mayor Dennis Kucinich, and San Francisco Mayor Dianne Feinstein. At the time of its adoption in the early twentieth century the issue of recall was hotly debated, with those opposed to the measure arguing that, along with the initiative and referendum, it undercut representative government and would lead to mob rule. Even supporters such as Theodore Roosevelt admitted the procedure opened up "undoubted possibilities for mischief," and, especially in the case of judges, should only be used as a last resort.

BIBLIOGRAPHY

Cronin, Thomas E. *Direct Democracy: The Politics of Initiative, Referendum, and Recall.* Cambridge, Mass.: Harvard University Press, 1989.

Zimmerman, Joseph F. *The Recall: Tribunal of the People.* Westport, Conn.: Praeger, 1997.

C. Wyatt Evans

See also **Progressive Movement.**

RECESSIONS. *See* **Business Cycles.**

RECIPROCAL TRADE AGREEMENTS. To help increase American exports at a time when worldwide depression had reduced international trade and many countries raised import tariffs, in June 1934 President Franklin D. Roosevelt's secretary of state Cordell Hull persuaded Congress to pass the Reciprocal Trade Agreements Act (RTAA). This amendment to the 1930 Smoot-Hawley Tariff Act granted the president the power to make foreign trade agreements with other nations on the basis of a mutual reduction of duties. This marked a departure from the historic approach of having Congress set import duties, usually at high protectionist levels.

Although Congress gave the State Department the primary responsibility for negotiating with other nations, it instructed the Tariff Commission and other government agencies to participate in developing a list of concessions that could be made to foreign countries or demanded from them in return. Each trade agreement was to incorporate the principle of "unconditional most-favored-nation treatment," and could permit a reduction of import duties of up to 50 percent of Smoot-Hawley levels.

In negotiating agreements under the RTAA, the United States usually proceeded by making direct concessions only to so-called chief suppliers—namely, countries that were, or probably would become, the main source, or a major source, of supply for the commodity under discussion. The concessions were granted in return for openings of foreign markets to American exports.

Secretary Hull's initial effort was to obtain reciprocal trade agreements with countries in Latin America, a region considered crucial to U.S. trade and security, where rival powers (especially Germany) were gaining ground at the expense of American exporters. However, Hull was able to negotiate agreements with only three of ten South American countries by September 1939, because the reciprocal trade program ran up against opposition from Latin Americans who opposed the most-favored-nation

requirement that they abandon all bilateral arrangements with other countries. Since pressure from Congress on behalf of special interests ensured that the Latin American countries were not granted unrestricted access to the U.S. market, these countries would have been seriously hampered in their efforts to sell their raw materials abroad had they eliminated the bilateral agreements with European countries that absorbed much of their exports.

Between 1934 and 1947 the United States made separate trade agreements with twenty-nine foreign countries. The Tariff Commission found that when it used dutiable imports in 1939 as its basis for comparison, U.S. tariffs were reduced from an average of 48 percent to an average of 25 percent during the thirteen-year period.

The General Agreement on Tariffs and Trade

During World War II the State Department and other government agencies worked on plans for the reconstruction of world trade and payments. They discovered important defects in the trade agreements program, and they concluded that they could make better headway through simultaneous multilateral negotiations. After the war, President Harry S. Truman used the RTAA to authorize the United States to join twenty-three separate countries conducting tariff negotiations bilaterally on a product-by-product basis, with each country negotiating its concessions on each import commodity with the principal supplier of that commodity. The various bilateral understandings were combined to form the General Agreement on Tariffs and Trade (GATT), signed in Geneva on 30 October 1947.

The RTAA was regularly renewed by Congress until it was replaced in 1962 by the Trade Expansion Act, which President John F. Kennedy sought to grant him wider authority to negotiate reciprocal trade agreements with the European Common Market. The Common Market had been established in 1957 to eliminate all trade barriers in six key countries of Western Europe: France, West Germany, Italy, Belgium, the Netherlands, and Luxembourg. Their economic strength, the increasing pressure on American balance of payments, and the threat of a Communist aid and trade offensive led Congress to pass the Trade Expansion Act. Whereas the United States had negotiated in the past on an item-by-item, rate-by-rate basis, in the future the president could decide to cut tariffs on an industry, or across-the-board, basis for all products, in exchange for similar reductions by the other countries. In order to deal with the tariff problems created by the European Common Market, the president was empowered to reduce tariffs on industrial products by more than 50 percent, or to eliminate them completely when the United States and the Common Market together accounted for 80 percent or more of the world export value.

From the original membership of 23 countries, GATT grew to include 128 countries responsible for about four-fifths of all world trade. During eight extended negotiating sessions or "rounds," GATT member countries further reduced tariffs, established antidumping regulations, and contributed to an upsurge in international trade levels.

World Trade Organization
In the final "Uruguay Round" (1986–1994), GATT created its own successor, the World Trade Organization (WTO), which established ground rules for replacing bilateral agreements with a multilateral trading system among more than 140 member countries. The WTO went beyond tariff reduction efforts to promote trade liberalization in areas such as global information technology and financial services. The WTO Secretariat is based in Geneva, but decisions are made by consensus among the member countries at biannual Ministerial Conferences. Because of the advantages of membership, even former Communist countries, including Russia and China, sought to join.

At the end of the twentieth century, the WTO came under fire from environmentalists, trade unions, and advocates of sustainable development in many countries because of the organization's ability to overrule national protective laws when these laws were deemed to be an impediment to free trade, and because critics argued that the WTO promoted an international economic system that favored rich countries and large private corporations at the expense of the poor. The ministerial conferences were often the scene of public demonstrations outside and clashes inside between the poorer countries of the third world and the wealthier industrialized nations. Together with the major international lending agencies—the World Bank and the International Monetary Fund—the WTO found itself obliged to defend the impartiality of policies designed to foster global economic growth.

BIBLIOGRAPHY
Butler, Michael A. *Cautious Visionary: Cordell Hull and Trade Reform, 1933–1937.* Kent, Ohio: Kent State University Press, 1998.
Hody, Cynthia A. *The Politics of Trade: American Political Development and Foreign Economic Policy.* Hanover, N.H.: University Press of New England, 1996.
Kunz, Diane B. *Butter and Guns: America's Cold War Economic Diplomacy.* New York: Free Press, 1997.
Steward, Dick. *Trade and Hemisphere: The Good Neighbor Policy and Reciprocal Trade.* Columbia: University of Missouri Press, 1975.

Max Paul Friedman
Sidney Ratner

See also **European Union; General Agreement on Tariffs and Trade; Tariff.**

RECLAMATION of arid lands by means of federally assisted irrigation began when Congress enacted the Desert Land Act of 1877. This law encouraged reclamation by offering 640 acres at $1.25 per acre to those citizens who would irrigate one-eighth of their newly purchased holdings within three years. Although 10 million acres passed from government ownership under the provisions of the act, widespread fraud limited its effectiveness. Somewhat more positive were the results of the Carey Act of 1894, which granted 1 million acres of the public domain to each of the western states on the condition that they irrigate them and sell them to settlers in maximum tracts of 160 acres. Under the provisions of that act, participants reclaimed 1,067,635 acres, 75 percent of them in Idaho and Wyoming.

By the middle of the 1890s, it was becoming apparent to westerners that the federal government needed to provide more positive assistance for constructing larger reservoirs and canals. In 1896 Congress appropriated $5,000 for a survey by the Corps of Engineers of reservoir sites in Colorado and Wyoming. Capt. Hiram M. Chittenden led the survey, and when he recommended the following year that the federal government construct the reservoirs, westerners under the leadership of George H. Maxwell organized the National Irrigation Association to champion the recommendation. On 26 January 1901, Rep. Francis G. Newlands of Nevada introduced a bill into Congress to provide for federal reclamation. With the support of President Theodore Roosevelt, it passed in a revised form and on 17 June 1902, became law.

The Reclamation Act of 1902 authorized the secretary of the interior to construct irrigation works in the sixteen western states and to pay for them from a revolving reclamation fund accumulated from the sales of public lands in those states. It stipulated that the reclaimable lands were to be disposed of under the Homestead Act of 1862 in tracts of 160 acres or fewer and that the settlers repay within ten years the costs of constructing the irrigation dams and canals. Ethan Allen Hitchcock, the secretary of the interior, did not delay implementation of the act. He created the Reclamation Service, with Frederick H. Newell of the Geological Survey in charge, and within one year had authorized the construction of three projects: the Newlands in Nevada, the Salt River in Arizona, and the Uncompahgre in Colorado.

As water became available to these and other projects, problems arose. Construction and land-acquisition costs were higher than anticipated, as were the expenses of settlement and the preparation of farms for irrigation. Consequently, settlers began to complain that they were unable to make their payments and petitioned the government for relief. Congress responded with the Reclamation Extension Act of 1914, which extended the repayment time from ten to twenty years.

When the postwar depression hit the settlers in 1920, they renewed their appeals, and Secretary of the Interior Hubert Work replied by appointing a fact-finding committee in 1923 under the chairmanship of Thomas E. Campbell of Arizona. It studied the situation and recommended reforms. In 1926 Congress extended the repayment period to forty years, and later it allowed even longer periods of time for some projects.

On 20 June 1923, Work renamed the Reclamation Service the Bureau of Reclamation and the next year appointed Elwood Mead its second commissioner. Under Mead's leadership, the bureau began to design multipurpose projects to provide, in addition to water for irrigation, flood control, hydroelectric power, municipal water, and recreational opportunities. The first of these projects was the Boulder Canyon project, with its 726-foot HOO-VER DAM and Lake Mead reservoir, designed to provide water for crops in Arizona and CALIFORNIA and 1,344,800 kilowatts of electric power. After its authorization in 1928 by Congress came authorizations of the Columbia Basin (1935), Central Valley (1935), Colorado–Big Thompson (1937), and Colorado River Storage (1956) projects, to name four of the larger ones.

By 1970 the bureau and its predecessor had built 276 storage reservoirs, which provided water for 8.5 million acres, producing nearly $2 billion worth of crops per year and water for an expanding urban population. In addition, they had constructed forty-nine hydroelectric power plants with sixteen thousand miles of high-voltage transmission lines to provide electric power for the industrialization of the western states, including the defense industries of California.

Another government agency involved in reclamation is the BUREAU OF INDIAN AFFAIRS, which in 1962 supervised projects irrigating 837,000 acres and producing crops valued at $67.3 million. Reclamation by this agency began with a congressional appropriation of $30,000 in 1891 for use on reservations in Arizona, Montana, and Nevada.

Despite the hydroelectric power and the water for agriculture and household use that these dams provide, reclamation of arid lands in the American west has proved a mixed blessing. As the population of the western United States continues to boom, debate over how best to allocate scarce water brings various interests into conflict. Although the myth of the west has always suggested that the area's natural resources are plentiful, land reclamation projects use water more quickly than natural processes can replace it. Much of the plains states' wheat industry depends on water for irrigation drawn from the subterranean Ogallala aquifer, a source that some experts believe will completely disappear within the next few decades.

Furthermore, the question remains of who deserves the water more. Should preference go to growing desert cities, such as LOS ANGELES, PHOENIX, and LAS VEGAS, or to western farmers and ranchers? How can the United States balance its needs for water with those of Mexico, into which many important western rivers eventually flow? Damming rivers for irrigation also interferes with salmon reproduction, limiting the availability of a natural resource especially important to American Indians. Of course, the complete cessation of reclamation would severely limit the economic livelihoods of western farmers, cut American agricultural production, and deprive many western regions of affordable electricity. Thus, an effective solution to these difficulties must consider both the needs of the American west as an ecosystem and of those Americans who use that ecosystem.

BIBLIOGRAPHY

Fleck, Richard F., ed. *A Colorado River Reader.* Salt Lake City: University of Utah Press, 2000.

Kromm, David E., and Stephen E. White, eds. *Groundwater Exploitation in the High Plains.* Lawrence: University Press of Kansas, 1992.

Lowitt, Richard, ed. *Politics in the Postwar American West.* Norman: University of Oklahoma Press, 1995.

Miller, Char, ed. *Fluid Arguments: Five Centuries of Western Water Conflict.* Tucson: University of Arizona Press, 2001.

Opie, John. *Ogallala: Water for a Dry Land.* Lincoln: University of Nebraska Press, 2000.

Tallmadge, John, and Henry Harrington, eds. *Reading Under the Sign of Nature: New Essays in Ecocriticism.* Salt Lake City: University of Utah Press, 2000.

Wolf, Donald E. *Big Dams and Other Dreams: The Six Companies Story.* Norman: University of Oklahoma Press, 1996.

Robert G. Dunbar / A. E.

See also **Climate; Hydroelectric Power; Interior, Department of the; Irrigation.**

RECOGNITION, POLICY OF. It has generally been accepted that the power of the president to recognize any country, mainly through his constitutional authority to appoint and receive ambassadors, is absolute. Congress has never seriously challenged this presidential prerogative.

The criteria for recognition were established by Secretary of State Thomas Jefferson in 1793, following the execution by the French of their king, Louis XVI, and the French Republic's declaration of war against Great Britain. The opening of the English phase of the French Revolution—Paris was already at war with her neighbors on the continent—launched the conflict upon the sea and brought it to the very shores of the United States. Aside from popular sentiment, which was pro-French in its commitment to republicanism and democracy, the United States had treaty obligations to France, in particular an obligation under certain circumstances to protect French possessions in America as well as an obligation to allow French naval vessels and privateers privileges denied to ships of Great Britain. To these forces, pulling the United States toward France, was added a British policy of ruthless interference with American trade at sea and consistent opposition to American interests on the frontier. To drift into war with England would be easy, but a war with England, when the United States was barely getting on its feet under the new Constitution, was certain to lead to disastrous consequences.

Secretary of the Treasury Alexander Hamilton thought the treaties invalid, since, among other reasons, the government with which they had been made was now destroyed. Even if the treaties were still in force, Hamilton added, the Treaty of Alliance (1778) was expressly a "defensive" one, and France, having declared war against England, was the aggressor. Jefferson opposed Hamilton's reasoning, arguing that the treaty had been made by the government of Louis XVI acting as the agent of the French people, and that a mere change of agents did not invalidate the agreement. On this point, Jefferson's position was the one now generally accepted in the conduct of international relations: a treaty is made with a nation and is not abrogated by a change in government. Still, while Jefferson would not repudiate the treaty, neither was he inclined to interpret it to involve the United States in the war on the side of France. For the most part, President George Washington followed Jefferson's counsel.

Jefferson's policy of de facto recognition was generally followed until President Woodrow Wilson changed direction from this practice, beginning in 1913. Shocked by the assassination of the leader of Mexico, Francisco I. Madero, a reformer and a man of good will, by General Victoriano Huerta, Wilson looked upon the new regime as "a government of butchers," unworthy of recognition. On 11 March 1913, Wilson announced in a press release that friendship and cooperation with the "sister republics" of Latin America would be possible only when supported by the orderly processes of just government based on the rule of law, not upon arbitrary or irregular force. Although called forth by rumors of revolutionary plots in Nicaragua, this statement was obviously also applicable to Mexico. In fact, it hinted at what was to become an established feature of Wilson's foreign policy regarding Latin America: a refusal to recognize governments that had attained power only by force and violence. Thus he deviated from the practice, followed quite consistently since Jefferson's day, of recognizing, regardless of origin, any government that was firmly seated and capable of performing its duties, internally and externally.

Several years later Wilson had an opportunity to further advance his moralistic approach to recognition. The United States had hailed with enthusiasm the overthrow of Nicholas II in March 1917 and the establishment of a liberal provisional government in Russia. However, the enthusiasm had turned to dislike and suspicion when the Bolshevists, led by V. I. Lenin and Leon Trotsky, seized power in November, made a separate peace with Imperial Germany, and adopted a program of world revolution. Communist Russia was excluded from the Paris Peace Conference in 1919 and was long refused recognition by the United States. The reasons for withholding recognition (after an initial period when the new regime was in doubt) were: the refusal of the Soviet Union to recognize the financial obligations of its predecessors; its refusal to recognize claims of American citizens for damages sustained as a result of the revolution; its denial of the validity of international agreements; and the subversive activities of the Communist International, the propaganda agency

of the Moscow government, operating through Communist parties in the United States and elsewhere.

By 1933, some of the arguments against recognition had lost part of their force. In Russia, Trotsky, the chief apostle of world revolution, had been expelled from the Communist Party and from the country while Stalin had adopted the slogan "Socialism in one country." To a considerable degree, the Soviet government had also settled many of the claims of American individuals and corporations, as the price of doing new business with them. Most importantly, the Great Depression of the early 1930s aroused a hope that official recognition of Russia would expand the Russian market for American producers. In any case, the administration of Franklin D. Roosevelt was not, like its predecessor, committed to a policy of nonrecognition. Consequently, at Roosevelt's invitation, the Soviet government sent Maxim Litvinov to Washington, D.C., and on 16 November 1933 the United States established regular diplomatic relations with Moscow. By an exchange of notes prior to recognition, the Soviet government agreed not to sponsor propaganda or any activity aimed at the overthrow of the United States, to allow religious freedom and protection in the courts of American nationals residing in the U.S.S.R., and to negotiate for a final settlement of debts and claims. The results were disappointing as Moscow-sponsored communist activity in the United States continued, a number of claims went unsettled, and trade figures fell well below expectations. The good news was that the United States had finally returned to the Jeffersonian criteria of de facto recognition that had served the nation so well.

BIBLIOGRAPHY

Coletta, Paul E. "Recognition." In *Encyclopedia of American Foreign Policy*. Edited by Alexander De Conde et al. 3 vols. 2d ed. New York: Scribners, 2002.

Goebel, Julius, Jr. *The Recognition Policy of the United States*. Buffalo, N.Y.: W.S. Hein, 2001. The original edition was published in 1915.

Jaffe, Louis, L. *Judicial Aspects of Foreign Relations, in Particular of the Recognition of Foreign Powers*. Cambridge, Mass.: Harvard University Press, 1933. A standard text in the field.

Moore, John Basset. *A Digest of International Law*. 8 vols. Washington, D.C.: Government Printing Office, 1906. Indispensable reference on international law.

Joseph M. Siracusa

See also **Foreign Policy; France, Relations with; Mexico, Relations with; Revolution, American: Diplomatic Aspects; Russia, Relations with.**

RECONSTRUCTION is the term applied to the restoration of the seceded states and the integration of the freedmen into American society during and especially after the Civil War.

The question of the restoration of the seceded states to the Union became an issue long before the surrender at Appomattox, Virginia, on 9 April 1865. According to the Crittenden-Johnson Resolutions of July 1861, the object of the war was to restore the Union with "all the dignity, equality, and rights of the several States unimpaired." But as the conflict progressed, it became evident that this objective was impossible to achieve. Congress refused to reaffirm its policy, President Abraham Lincoln appointed military governors for partially reconquered states, and moderate and radical Republicans debated the exact status of insurgent communities.

Presidential Reconstruction

The president viewed the process of wartime reconstruction as a weapon to detach Southerners from their allegiance to the Confederacy and thus shorten the war. Consequently, on 8 December 1863, he issued a proclamation of amnesty that promised full pardon to all disloyal citizens except a few leaders of the rebellion, former officers of the United States, and perpetrators of unlawful acts against prisoners of war. Whenever 10 percent of the voters of 1860 had taken the oath of allegiance, they were authorized to inaugurate new governments. All Lincoln required was their submission to the Union and their acceptance of the EMANCIPATION PROCLAMATION.

The president's plan encountered resistance in Congress. Perturbed by his failure to leave Reconstruction to the lawmakers and anxious to protect Republican interests in the South, Congress, on 2 July 1864, passed the WADE-DAVIS BILL, a more stringent measure than Lincoln's "ten-percent plan." Requiring an oath of allegiance from 50 percent, rather than 10 percent, of the electorate before new governments could be set up, the bill prescribed further conditions for prospective voters. Only those who were able to take an "iron-clad oath" of past loyalty were to be enfranchised, and slavery was to be abolished. When Lincoln pocket vetoed the measure, its authors bitterly attacked him in the Wade-Davis Manifesto. After the president's reelection, efforts to revive the Wade-Davis Bill in modified form failed. Congress refused to recognize the "free-state" governments established in accordance with Lincoln's plan in Louisiana and Arkansas, and so Lincoln's assassination of 14 April 1865 left the future of Reconstruction in doubt.

What Lincoln would have done if he had lived is difficult to establish. It is known that as soon as General Ulysses S. Grant had forced General Robert E. Lee to surrender, the president withdrew his invitation to members of the Confederate legislature to Virginia to reassemble: his wartime plans are evidently not necessarily a guide to his peacetime intentions. It is also clear that he was not averse to the enfranchisement of qualified blacks. He wrote to this effect to the governor of Louisiana and touched on the subject in his last public address on 11 April 1865. But, as he said in his second inaugural address, pleading for "malice toward none" and "charity for all," he was anxious for a speedy reconciliation between the sections.

With the end of the war, the problem of Reconstruction—both the restoration of the states and the integration of the freedmen—became more acute. If the seceded states were to be restored without any conditions, local whites would soon reestablish rule by the Democratic Party. They would seek to reverse the verdict of the sword and, by combining with their Northern associates, challenge Republican supremacy. Moreover, before long, because of the end of slavery and the lapse of the Three-Fifths Compromise, the South would obtain a larger influence in the councils of the nation than before the war.

The easiest way of solving this problem would have been to extend the suffrage to the freedmen. But in spite of an increasing radical commitment to votes for blacks, the majority of the party hesitated. Popular prejudice, not all of it in the South, was too strong, and many doubted the feasibility of enfranchising newly liberated slaves. Nevertheless, the integration of the blacks into American life now became one of the principal issues of Reconstruction.

Lincoln's successor, Andrew Johnson, was wholly out of sympathy with black suffrage, especially if conferred by the federal government. A Southerner and former slaveholder, Johnson held deep prejudices against blacks, who, he believed, should occupy an inferior place in society. In addition, as a firm adherent of states' rights, he was convinced that voting rights were the exclusive concern of the states, not the federal government. He was willing to have the states concede the vote to very few educated or propertied African Americans, but only to stop radical agitation. Based on his Jacksonian conviction of an indestructible Union of indestructible states, his Reconstruction policies in time of peace resembled those of his predecessor in time of war. But they were no longer appropriate.

Johnson's plan, published on 29 May 1865, called for the speedy restoration of Southern governments based on the (white) electorate of 1861. His proclamation of amnesty offered pardons to all insurgents swearing an oath of allegiance to the United States except for certain exempted classes, including high officers of the Confederacy and those owning property valued at more than $20,000, but even they were eligible for individual pardons. Appointing provisional governors—executives who were to call constitutional conventions—first for North Carolina and then for the other states, Johnson expected the restored states to ratify the Thirteenth Amendment abolishing slavery, nullify the secession ordinances, and repudiate the Confederate debt, although he did not even insist on these conditions.

In operation, the president's plan revealed that little had changed in the South. Not one of the states enfranchised even literate blacks. Some balked at nullifying the secession ordinances, others hesitated or failed to repudiate the Confederate debt, and Mississippi refused to ratify the Thirteenth Amendment. Former insurgent leaders, including Alexander H. Stephens, the vice president of the Confederacy, were elected to Congress. Several states passed Black Codes that in effect remanded the freedmen to a condition not far removed from slavery.

Congressional Reconstruction

The reaction of Northerners to these developments was not favorable. When Congress met in December, it refused to admit any of the representatives from the seceded states, even the most loyal ones, and created a Joint Committee of Fifteen on Reconstruction to which all matters pertaining to the restoration of the South were to be referred. It was clear that Congress would not acquiesce to Johnson's policy.

The president had to make a choice. As the Republican Party consisted of radicals, moderates, and conservatives, he could either cooperate with the moderate center of the party or, by opposing it, break with the overwhelming majority of Republicans and rely on the small minority of conservatives and the Democrats. Most Republicans were hoping to avoid a rift with Johnson, but the president left them little choice. When Lyman Trumbull, the moderate chairman of the Senate Judiciary Committee, framed a bill extending the powers and duration of the FREEDMEN's BUREAU, an agency established during

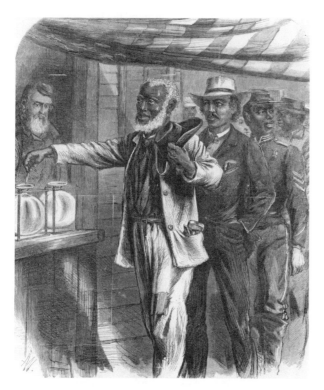

Reconstruction Voters. Freedmen—including an artisan, a professional, and a soldier—go to the polls in this engraving published in *Harper's Weekly* on 16 November 1867; by then, the Freedmen's Bureau had registered 700,000 blacks. Suffrage for blacks was soon dead throughout the South, however, not to return for nearly a century. LIBRARY OF CONGRESS

Lincoln's administration to succor freedmen and refugees, he vetoed it and delivered a speech comparing the leaders of the radicals to Jefferson Davis. The veto was upheld, but when, unwilling to compromise on the subjects of race and federal relations—he also vetoed Trumbull's civil rights bill, a measure to protect African Americans—his veto was overridden, and Congress thereafter tended to override most of his vetoes.

Congress then developed a Reconstruction plan of its own: the Fourteenth Amendment. Moderate in tone, it neither conferred suffrage upon the blacks nor exacted heavy penalties from Southern whites. Clearly defining citizenship, it made African Americans part of the body politic, sought to protect them from state interference, and provided for reduced representation for states disfranchising prospective voters. If Johnson had been willing to accept it, the struggle over Reconstruction might have ended. But the president was wholly opposed to the measure. Believing the amendment subversive of the Constitution and of white supremacy, he used his influence to procure its defeat in the Southern states, an effort that succeeded everywhere except in Tennessee, which was readmitted on 24 July 1866. At the same time, he sought to build up a new party consisting of conservative Republicans and moderate Democrats. The rival plans of Reconstruction thus became an issue in the midterm elections of 1866, during which four conventions met, while Johnson, on a trip to a monument to Stephen Douglas in Chicago, campaigned actively for his program and once more denigrated the radical leaders. His claims of having established peace in the South were weakened by serious riots in Memphis and New Orleans.

The elections resulted in a triumph for the Republican majority. Since the president was still unwilling to cooperate—he continued his opposition to the amendment—Congress, overriding his veto or opposition, proceeded to shackle him by restricting his powers of removal (see TENURE OF OFFICE ACT) and of military control (command of the army provisions of the Military Appropriations Act for 1867–1868). In addition, it passed a series of measures known as the Reconstruction Acts, which inaugurated the congressional, formerly called the "radical," phase of Reconstruction.

The first two Reconstruction Acts divided the South (except for Tennessee) into five military districts, enfranchised male African Americans, and required Southern states to draw up constitutions safeguarding black suffrage. The new legislatures were expected to ratify the Fourteenth Amendment, and certain Confederate officeholders were for a time barred from voting and holding office.

The president refused to concede defeat. After his vetoes of the Reconstruction Acts were not sustained, he sought to lessen their effect. His attorney general's lenient interpretation of the law led to the more stringent third Reconstruction Act (19 July 1867). Reaffirming that the Southern governments were only provisional and confer-

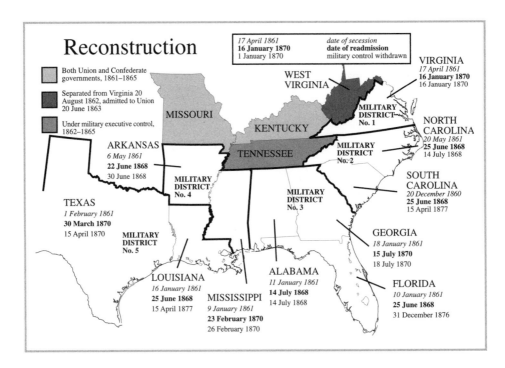

Reconstruction

17 April 1861	*date of secession*
16 January 1870	**date of readmission**
1 January 1870	military control withdrawn

Both Union and Confederate governments, 1861–1865

Separated from Virginia 20 August 1862, admitted to Union 20 June 1863

Under military executive control, 1862–1865

MISSOURI

WEST VIRGINIA

VIRGINIA
17 April 1861
16 January 1870
16 January 1870

MILITARY DISTRICT No. 1

KENTUCKY

ARKANSAS
6 May 1861
22 June 1868
30 June 1868

TENNESSEE

MILITARY DISTRICT No. 2

NORTH CAROLINA
20 May 1861
25 June 1868
14 July 1868

MILITARY DISTRICT No. 4

MILITARY DISTRICT No. 3

SOUTH CAROLINA
20 December 1860
25 June 1868
15 April 1877

TEXAS
1 February 1861
30 March 1870
15 April 1870

MILITARY DISTRICT No. 5

GEORGIA
18 January 1861
15 July 1870
18 July 1870

LOUISIANA
16 January 1861
25 June 1868
15 April 1877

MISSISSIPPI
9 January 1861
23 February 1870
26 February 1870

ALABAMA
11 January 1861
14 July 1868
14 July 1868

FLORIDA
10 January 1861
25 June 1868
31 December 1876

ring powers of removal of officers and alleged voters upon the commanding generals, the law only spurred Johnson to further resistance. On 12 August he suspended Edwin M. Stanton, his radical secretary of war. After appointing Grant secretary ad interim, he also removed some radical major generals in the South. Always believing that in the end the popular majority would sustain him, he was greatly encouraged by Democratic successes in the fall elections.

Johnson's intransigence resulted in a complete break with Congress and to efforts to remove him. Because the radicals lacked a majority, and because the charges against the president were too flimsy, the first attempt to impeach him, on 7 December 1867, failed. But when the Senate reinstated Stanton, and Johnson dismissed him again, this time in defiance of the Tenure of Office Act, as Congress was in session, the House acted. Passing a resolution of impeachment on 24 February 1868, it put the president on trial before the Senate. Because of the defection of seven moderate Republicans and the weakness of the case, on 16 and again on 26 May he was acquitted by one vote. His narrow escape once more encouraged Southern conservatives, so that it was difficult for Grant, elected president in November 1868, to carry congressional Reconstruction to a successful conclusion.

During 1867 and 1868 congressional Reconstruction had been gradually initiated. Despite conservative opposition—Congress had to pass a fourth Reconstruction Act requiring a majority of voters rather than of registrants before the constitution of Alabama was accepted—the electorate ratified the new charters in all but three states: Mississippi, Texas, and Virginia. Accordingly, in the summer of 1868 the compliant states were readmitted and the Fourteenth Amendment declared in force. Because Georgia later excluded African Americans from its legislature

and because Mississippi, Texas, and Virginia, for various local reasons, did not ratify their constitutions on time, those four states were subjected to additional requirements. These included ratification of the Fifteenth Amendment, prohibiting the denial of suffrage on account of race. After complying with the new demands, in 1870 these states too were restored to their place in the Union, and the amendment was added to the Constitution.

Historians have long argued about the nature of the governments Congress imposed upon the South. According to William A. Dunning and his school, they were characterized by vindictiveness, corruption, inefficiency, and ruthless exploitation of Southern whites. Northern CARPETBAGGERS, local SCALAWAGS, and their black tools supposedly trampled white civilization underfoot. Modern scholars have questioned these assumptions: pointing out that the governments imposed by Congress succeeded in establishing systems of public education, eleemosynary (charitable) institutions, and workable constitutions, they have discarded the concept of "black Reconstruction." Black legislators were in a majority only in South Carolina, and even there their white allies wielded considerable influence. Conceding the presence of corruption in the South, these historians have emphasized its nationwide scope. They have tended to show that the new governments deserved credit for making the first efforts to establish racial democracy in the South; that far from being vindictive, they speedily extended amnesty to former Confederates; and that many radical officeholders, black and white alike, did not compare unfavorably with their conservative colleagues. In addition, they no longer called congressional Reconstruction "radical," because the measures enacted by the moderate majority fell far short of radical demands. The Fourteenth Amendment did not

RADICAL MEMBERS
OF THE FIRST LEGISLATURE AFTER THE WAR

SOUTH

CAROLINA

Dusenberry	Mayes	Demars	Rivers	Miteford	Smith		Swails
McKinlay	Jillson	Brodie	Duncan	White	Pettengill		Percin
Dickson	Lomax	Hayes	BOOZER	Barton	Hyde		James
Wilder	Jackson	Cain	Smythe	Boston	Lee		Johnston
Hoyt	Thomas	Maxwell	Wright	Shrewsbury	Simonds		Wimbush
Randolph	Webb	Martin	MOSES	Mickey	Chesnut		Hayes
Harris	Bozeman	Cook	Sancho	Henderson	McDaniel		Farr
	Tomlinson	Miller	Sanders	Howell	Williams		Meade
	Wright *		Nuckles	Hayne	Gardner		Thompson
				Mobley			Rainey
				Hudson			
				Nash			
				Carmand			

* Afterwards associate Justice of the Supreme
Court of the State

Reconstruction Legislators. The African Americans who controlled the South Carolina House of Representatives for a few years after the Civil War; until the short-lived Reconstruction Acts, of course, there had been no black legislators in the South at all, and once Reconstruction ended in 1877, there would be none in South Carolina again until 1970. Library of Congress

enfranchise African Americans, the Fifteenth did not protect them from interpretations designed to deprive them of the vote, and the Reconstruction Acts did not impose stringent restrictions on former Confederate leaders.

The Waning of Reconstruction

But the experiment could not last. The rapid disappearance, by death or retirement, of the radical Republicans, the granting of amnesty to former Confederates, the con-

servatives' resort to terror, and a gradual loss of interest by the North would have made Reconstruction difficult in any case. These problems were complicated by the blacks' lack of economic power—Johnson had gone so far as to return to whites lands already occupied by freedmen. Factionalism within the dominant party increased with the rise of the Liberal Republicans in 1872, and the panic of 1873 eroded Republican majorities in the House. The Supreme Court, which had refused to interfere with Reconstruction in *Mississippi v. Johnson* (1867) and *Georgia v. Stanton* (1867), began to interpret the Fourteenth Amendment very narrowly, as in the *Slaughterhouse Cases* (1873). Such a tendency foreshadowed the Court's further weakening not only of the Fourteenth but also the Fifteenth Amendment in *United States v. Cruikshank* (1876) and *United States v. Reese* (1876) and its invalidation of the Civil Rights Act of 1875 in the *Civil Rights Cases* (1883).

The end of Reconstruction came at different times in several states. Despite the passage during 1870 and 1871 of three FORCE ACTS seeking to protect black voting rights and to outlaw the KU KLUX KLAN, the gradual collapse of the regimes imposed by Congress could not be arrested. In some cases terror instigated by the Klan and its violent successors overthrew Republican administrations; in others, conservatives regained control by more conventional means. By 1876 Republican administrators survived only in Florida, Louisiana, and South Carolina, all of which returned disputed election results in the fall. After a series of economic and political bargains enabled Rutherford B. Hayes, the Republican candidate, to be inaugurated president, he promptly withdrew remaining federal troops from the Southern statehouses, and Reconstruction in those states, already weakened by Northern unwillingness to interfere further, also came to an end. For a time, African Americans continued to vote, although in decreasing numbers, but by the turn of the century they had been almost completely eliminated from Southern politics.

Reconstruction thus seemed to end in failure, and the myth of radical misrule embittered relations between the sections. But in spite of their apparent lack of accomplishment, the radicals, spurring on the Republican majority, had succeeded in embedding the postwar amendments in the Constitution, amendments that were the foundation for the struggle for racial equality in the twentieth century.

BIBLIOGRAPHY

Belz, Herman. *Reconstructing the Union: Theory and Policy during the Civil War.* Ithaca, N.Y.: Cornell University Press, 1969.

Benedict, Michael Les. *A Compromise of Principle: Congressional Republicans and Reconstruction, 1863–1869.* New York: Norton, 1974.

Cox, LaWanda, and John H. Cox. *Politics, Principle, and Prejudice, 1865–1866: Dilemma of Reconstruction America.* New York: Free Press of Glencoe, 1963.

Donald, David Herbert, Jean Harvey Baker, and Michael F. Holt. *The Civil War and Reconstruction.* New York: Norton, 2001.

Foner, Eric. *Reconstruction, America's Unfinished Revolution, 1863–1877.* New York: Harper and Row, 1988.

McKitrick, Eric L. *Andrew Johnson and Reconstruction.* Chicago: University of Chicago Press, 1960.

Perman, Michael. *Reunion without Compromise: The South and Reconstruction, 1865–1868.* Cambridge, U.K.: Cambridge University Press, 1973.

———. *The Road to Redemption: Southern Politics, 1869–1879.* Chapel Hill: University of North Carolina Press, 1984.

Stampp, Kenneth M. *The Era of Reconstruction, 1865–1877.* New York: Knopf, 1965.

Simpson, Brooks D. *The Reconstruction Presidents.* Lawrence: University Press of Kansas, 1998.

Trefousse, Hans L. *Andrew Johnson: A Biography.* New York: Norton, 1989.

Hans L. Trefousse

See also **Civil War; *Georgia v. Stanton;* Impeachment Trial of Andrew Johnson; *Mississippi v. Johnson;* Race Relations; *Slaughterhouse Cases; United States v. Cruikshank; United States v. Reese;* and vol. 9: Black Code of Mississippi, November 1965; President Andrew Johnson's Civil Rights Bill Veto; Police Regulations of Saint Landry Parish, Louisiana.**

RECONSTRUCTION FINANCE CORPORATION.

After the 1929 stock market crash, the banking system verged on failure. Anxious depositors ran on banks to get their money out; banks had less money to give because they had invested in the collapsing stock market; more banks failed; depositors grew increasingly nervous; and banks continued selling off stocks, which depressed the market even further. In January 1932, on the recommendation of President Herbert Hoover, Congress created the Reconstruction Finance Corporation (RFC), which would use government money to make loans to banks, railroads, and insurance companies. In July, with the crisis deepening, the Emergency Relief and Reconstruction Act authorized the RFC to make loans directly to farmers, states, and public works projects.

Hoover was wary of any sort of government intervention in the marketplace. He was slow to propose the RFC because he hoped bankers could solve their own problem, and he never stopped viewing it as a temporary agency. Hoover's chairmen (Eugene Meyer and Atlee Pomerene) insisted on an overly conservative set of guidelines. The RFC's loans carried high interest rates (they did not want to compete with private lenders), and its collateral requirements were extremely rigid. Moreover, RFC-funded public works projects had to pay for themselves (hydroelectric plants or toll bridges, for example). According to Hoover and his advisers, the primary purpose of the RFC was to encourage banks to start making loans again so the private sector could initiate its own recovery. It lent almost $2 billion in its first year, which was enough to serve the immediate goal of delaying a banking catastrophe, but the money did not inspire the expected general economic upturn.

In February 1933 the banking system collapsed again. President Franklin Roosevelt, inaugurated in March, had none of Hoover's reservations about state capitalism. Roosevelt immediately declared a banking holiday and passed the Emergency Banking Relief Act, which empowered the RFC to oversee bank reorganizations and invest directly in struggling financial institutions through preferred stock purchases. President Roosevelt and RFC chairman Jesse Jones continually enlarged and modified the RFC's mission to meet specific needs, and the RFC played a vital role in the evolution of the New Deal. The federal Emergency Relief Administration was modeled on the RFC state grant program, and the Public Works Administration was spun off from its public works division. The RFC also helped to finance many New Deal agencies because its semi-independent status allowed President Roosevelt to work around Congress and to work quickly. The RFC made loans to the Home Owners' Loan Corporation ($200 million), the Farm Credit Administration ($40 million), and the Works Progress Administration ($1 billion). Even greatly expanded, however, the Depression-era RFC ultimately failed in its Hoover-conceived mission of reinvigorating private investment.

During World War II, Roosevelt converted the RFC from a recovery agency to a wartime agency. The RFC and its wartime subsidiaries, including the Rubber Reserve Company, the Defense Plant Corporation, and the War Damage Corporation, handed out $40 billion in loans during the war. The massive defense buildup finally generated the elusive economic recovery.

When Dwight Eisenhower was elected president (1952), memories of the Great Depression, the New Deal, and even World War II were becoming increasingly distant, and the idea of keeping government and business separate regained some of its Hoover-era popularity. Congress abolished the RFC in July 1953.

BIBLIOGRAPHY

Jones, Jesse H. *Fifty Billion Dollars: My Thirteen Years with the RFC (1932–1945)*. New York: Macmillan, 1951.

Olson, James Stuart. *Herbert Hoover and the Reconstruction Finance Corporation, 1931–1933*. Ames: Iowa State University Press, 1977.

———. *Saving Capitalism: The Reconstruction Finance Corporation and the New Deal, 1933–1940*. Princeton, N.J.: Princeton University Press, 1988.

Jeremy Derfner

See also **Banking: Banking Crisis of 1933; Great Depression; New Deal.**

RECREATION. America's indigenous peoples enjoyed a wide array of recreational activities. Indians in the upper Midwest played lacrosse, while those living in the Spanish borderlands played versions of a Mesoamerican ball game. Native Americans throughout California chewed milkweed gum for pleasure, while boys from some Wisconsin tribes made tops of acorns, nuts, and oval stones. Singing, dancing, drumming, gambling, and smoking all played important roles in the social lives of many native peoples.

When English settlers first arrived on the eastern shore of North America, their view of the continent's native inhabitants was powerfully shaped by differing attitudes towards work and leisure. While Indian women generally gathered plants and tilled fields, native men "for the most part live idlely, they doe nothing but hunt and fish," observed one New England minister. William Byrd II, the scion of a wealthy Virginia family, added that Indian men "are quite idle, or at most employ'd only in the Gentlemanly Diversions of Hunting and Fishing." As these quotes suggest, in England hunting and fishing were considered recreational and were generally reserved for members of the gentry. They were vital, however, to the subsistence of native peoples.

The Puritan Work Ethic

In New England, the colonists' view that Indians were "indolent" or "slothful" savages was reinforced by an attitude that came to be known as the "Puritan work ethic." For centuries, societies had viewed labor as a necessity, while seeing leisure as more conducive to happiness. After the Reformation, however, some radical Protestant sects came to see "honest toil" as a sign of God's "chosen" or "elect," and to equate most forms of recreation with idle sinfulness. New England Puritans feared that dancing and drinking would lead to promiscuity, and they banned gambling and smoking (except at dinner) as wasters of time. The Massachusetts Bay Colony forbid "unnecessary" walking on Sunday, and the governor of Plymouth required colonists to work on Christmas. When fur trader Thomas Morton celebrated a traditional English May Day in the mid-1600s, Puritans burned his compound, cut down his maypole, and exiled him from the colony. The Puritans did, however, embrace moderate exercise, and they encouraged their followers to sing Psalms and read the Bible. Puritan children played with toys and dolls, while youth engaged in ball games and cricket.

By the late seventeenth century, growing secularization and commercial success had eroded Puritan austerity. Nevertheless, the Puritan work ethic had a powerful lingering effect on American society. An emerging middle class embraced a secular version of the work ethic and used it to define themselves against both the working class, who often viewed labor as simply necessary for pleasure, and some elites, who saw labor as the degrading province of servants and slaves. In the mid-eighteenth century, Benjamin Franklin preached the work ethic in his widely read autobiography and *Poor Richard's Almanac*, and the religious Great Awakenings of the mid-eighteenth and early nineteenth centuries carried this attitude beyond New England.

In the late seventeenth and eighteenth centuries, colonists both north and south adapted traditional European recreational activities to their new home. Cockfighting spread through Virginia and the southern colonies, while New Englanders engaged in wrestling and cudgeling on the Boston Common. Fashionable New Yorkers paraded in powdered wigs and ruffles, while Southern gentry traveled to Williamsburg and Charleston for balls and plays.

Transforming hunting from an elite to a popular sport, frontiersmen engaged in wolf drives and "ring hunts," in which a crowd would encircle an area of up to forty square miles and gradually close in on all the game within the ring. (One such hunt reportedly netted sixty bears, twenty-five deer, one hundred turkeys, and assorted smaller animals.) County fairs, weddings, and religious camp meetings also provided opportunities for recreation and socializing.

The Impact of Industrialization

The Industrial Revolution that transformed the U.S. in the nineteenth century fundamentally altered the way many Americans spent their leisure time. As workers migrated from farms to cities and industrial towns, work—and thus recreation—became less dependent on the seasons. More importantly, the emergence of the factory system institutionalized the Puritan work ethic and imposed clock time on the masses. With employers dictating the length of their employees' days, the workday expanded to twelve hours or more in the early nineteenth century. Efforts to control workers were not entirely successful, however: At the Harper's Ferry Armory in western Virginia, for instance, many employees skipped work to go hunting or fishing.

The removal of work from the home and its centralization in factories also produced an increasingly sharp divide between work and recreation. For centuries, the line dividing the two had been porous. American Indians socialized while cooking or mending huts, and European colonists gathered for corn huskings, barn raisings, or candle-dipping parties. But just as factory owners tried to control their workers' hours, they also attempted to eliminate play from work. In 1846, for instance, a Pennsylvania textile factory banned "spiritous liquors, smoking or any kind of amusements" from its premises. Mill owners in Lowell, Massachusetts, required their female employees to live in dormitories and observe a strict 10 P.M. curfew. Children who worked long hours in factories or mines had little time or energy to play.

To a large degree, this separation of work and recreation was a gendered experience. Few middle-class women worked outside the home, and even female mill workers generally left the factory after they married and had children. Housewives—as well as women who took in boarders or did piecework in the home—tended to remain more task than time conscious. They visited with neighbors between household chores, and interspersed drudgery with decorative arts.

In middle-class Victorian families, leisure time increasingly focused on the home, and women planned recreation for the entire family. Instructed by new magazines like the *Godey's Lady's Book*, they organized board games, family picnics, sing-alongs, and lawn games like croquet. By transforming their homes into refuges, they attempted to provide moral training and emotional sustenance for their husbands and children. One result of this new emphasis on the home was the makeover of many American holidays. In the early nineteenth century, the Fourth of July was celebrated with riotous communal drinking, but by the 1850s it was a time for family picnics. The family Christmas, complete with trees, carols, and an exchange of gifts, also emerged during the Victorian Era. (In the late nineteenth century, middle-class reformers used settlement houses, "friendly visitors," and field matrons to spread such "wholesome" home-based recreation to immigrant workers and Native Americans.)

If middle-class families increasingly turned to the home for recreation in the nineteenth century, working-class men turned to the pub. Alcohol had been an important component of adult male leisure since colonial times, but with the advent of industrialization. the social life of many male workers came to revolve around the bar. Factory workers gathered at the pub after quitting time, and waited in taverns to be hired. Choral societies and sports clubs met in bars, as did fledgling trade unions. Laborers drank to escape urban loneliness, the boredom of factory jobs, and the anxieties of periodic unemployment. Beginning in the 1820s, both solo drinking and alcoholism rose, and by 1900, working-class districts boasted one beer hall for every fifty men.

Drinking was not the only recreational "vice" on the rise in the nineteenth century. The breakdown of community and parental controls in cities led to what some saw as an "epidemic" of extramarital sex. Working-class youth, no longer controlled by either parents or masters, dropped out of school and created a youth culture centered around gangs. Some of these engaged in juvenile crime.

Reforming Recreation

Such trends alarmed both middle-class reformers and many working-class families. Beginning in the 1830s, they responded with a series of campaigns designed to stamp out various forms of problematic recreation. A powerful temperance movement emerged, supported by ministers, businessmen, and even many workers. By the 1850s, it had restricted alcohol use in thirteen states and territories and established an alternative teetolling culture centered on music halls, coffee houses, and reading rooms. Although the movement faltered briefly, it was revived in 1874 with the founding of the Women's Christian Temperance Union and ultimately succeeded in passing a prohibition amendment to the Constitution. (Passed in 1919, the amendment was repealed in 1933.) Campaigns against prostitution also gained steam in the late nineteenth and early twentieth centuries.

Paralleling the temperance and antivice campaigns were a variety of efforts that sought to use recreation to foster self-improvement and inculcate moral values. Between the 1830s and the 1860s, the lyceum movement brought speakers to communities across the nation to lecture on history and philosophy, to give scientific demonstrations and dramatic performances, and to debate such topics as abolition, temperance, and women's rights.

Although the lyceum movement faded after the Civil War, the Chautauqua movement carried on the tradition of adult education through the 1920s. The Young Men's Christian Association, introduced to the United States in 1851, provided shelter, reading rooms, lectures, and eventually athletic programs for single men. Reformers pushed for both large downtown parks and smaller neighborhood green spaces in the belief that contact with nature encouraged moral uplift. The steel baron Andrew Carnegie endowed hundreds of public libraries across the country in the late nineteenth and early twentieth centuries, explaining, "How a man spends his time at work may be taken for granted but how he spends his hours of recreation is really the key to his progress in all the virtues."

Many such programs focused on children. In the 1870s, New York merchants organized a "Fresh Air Fund" which sent slum-dwelling children to live with Christian families in small towns and rural areas during the summer months. The Boy Scouts of America, incorporated in 1910, sought to inculcate loyalty and competitiveness in its largely middle-class clientele. (By contrast, the Girl Scouts, founded in 1912, taught feminine virtues and domestic skills.) The playground movement, launched in 1885, provided sandboxes, park programs, and playgrounds for children in poor urban areas.

The Commercialization of Leisure

The playground movement reflected the belief that government should provide a safe alternative both to the streets and to what many reformers saw as the degrading effects of commercial leisure. By the mid-nineteenth century, revolutions in transportation and technology, a growth in personal income, and the growing distinction between work time and leisure time catalyzed the emergence of new industries geared to providing recreation for the masses. Railroads made it possible for circuses and vaudeville acts to travel from city to city, spreading their costs over a wider market. They also allowed tourists to travel to new resorts like Atlantic City or extravaganzas like the 1893 Columbia Exposition in Chicago. The increasing concentration of people in towns and cities, together with the advent of the streetcar, provided a market for amusement parks, dance halls, wax museums, and theater districts. Neighborhood "nickelodeons" gave way to luxurious "movie palaces," and by the late 1920s an estimated 100 million people a week were watching motion pictures. In that decade, Americans spent more money on movies than on any other form of recreation.

Such developments transformed one of the nation's oldest leisure pastimes: sports. Americans had always played athletic games, and amateur sports were central to Victorian leisure. Many Victorians believed that, for males, athletic competition built character. Although women were generally seen as too frail to engage in vigorous physical activity, they took up more sedate sports such as hiking, bicycling, and lawn tennis. In the late nineteenth century, however, such participatory sports increasingly vied for attention with new "spectator" sports. Cities and streetcar travel helped fill the modern sports stadium, while mass newspapers created a cadre of fans. As early as 1858, some New Yorkers were willing to pay 50 cents to watch baseball teams battle, and in 1869 the Cincinatti Red Stockings became the first completely professional team. In the twentieth century, the new technologies of radio and television broadened the audience for spectator sports by allowing fans to follow teams—or individuals like boxer Jack Dempsey—without actually attending games or fights.

The divergent tracks taken by baseball and football also point to another feature of commercial, and indeed most, recreation: its stratification along class, race, and ethnic lines. Baseball, which probably originated in New York around 1845, quickly attracted a working-class following. When ballparks took off around the turn of the twentieth century, white-collar workers occupied most of the grandstand seats, while Irish- and German-American workers sat in the bleachers and African Americans of all incomes were relegated to segregated sections. Football, by contrast, was first played by students at Harvard, Yale, and Princeton. It remained a predominantly amateur, and comparatively elite, sport until after World War II.

Restructuring Leisure Time

The rise of commercial recreation both profited from and reinforced a "repackaging" of leisure time that ultimately produced the "weekend." In the nineteenth century, most industries had a six-day workweek, and a few (such as steel) operated on a seven-day schedule. Since few factory workers got much intrinsic satisfaction from work, they agitated for shorter hours. (By 1900, the average workday had fallen from twelve to nine hours.) Increasingly, they also argued for a holiday on Saturday, which they could spend with family or use for shopping, swimming, boating, bicycling, or trips to baseball games and amusement parks.

By 1900 some factories observed Saturday half-holidays in the summer months, mostly because the absence of air-conditioning made working conditions unbearable. In 1908, a New England spinning mill became the first factory to adopt a five-day work week, largely to accommodate its Jewish workers who observed a Saturday sabbath. The Saturday holiday was given a big boost in 1926, when Henry Ford adopted it in his automobile plants: Ford argued that an increase in leisure time would lead to more consumer spending, including more spending on cars and car travel. It took the Great Depression, however, to make the forty-hour work week and the two-day weekend an American standard; shorter hours were seen as the best cure for unemployment.

Increasingly, Americans spent at least part of each weekend in their cars. Ford's Model T, first introduced in 1908, put automobiles within reach of even the working class, while government investment in roads surged beginning in the 1920s. The car liberated Americans from timetables and streetcar routes and, like the railroad before it, revolutionized tourism. (The airplane had a similar impact after World War II, although the car remained more important to everyday recreation.) Americans took Sunday drives and weekend road trips on parkways designed to be aesthetically pleasing. Millions used cars to visit state and national parks in the West. Although the first such parks were established in the nineteenth century to preserve the country's most dramatic natural areas, governments in the twentieth century increasingly encouraged the public to use them for recreation. Motels, roadside campgrounds, drive-in restaurants, and drive-in movie theatres mushroomed between the 1930s and the 1950s, and in later decades, shopping malls replaced "main street" as centers for shopping and socializing. Older amusement parks like New York's Coney Island were tied to the streetcar. Newer amusement parks like Disneyland, which opened in 1955, were built at the conjunction of freeways.

The Privatization of Leisure

By providing "individualized mobility," the car contributed to the "privatization" of leisure in the twentieth century. Radios and television had a similar effect, homogenizing Americans' experience of recreation, while reducing the need for social contact. The first licensed radio station in the United States appeared in Pittsburgh in 1920; by 1930 one home in three had a radio. The radio initially opened the airwaves to a cacophony of local groups, but within a decade regulatory changes and financial pressures had produced the first national radio network. This ensured that Americans from coast to coast could tune in to the same sportscasts and soap operas. By the 1930s, family sing-alongs were beginning to disappear, and people increasingly planned their dinner hours around the latest episode of *Flash Gordon* or Drew Pearson's news program. When television spread after World War II, it employed the same genres as radio—the soap opera, the situation comedy, the western, the mystery, and the children's adventure program—and was developed largely by the same companies. By 1960, the television was on for at least five hours per day in 90 percent of American homes. In the mid-1950s, so many Americans stayed home to watch *I Love Lucy* on Monday nights that stores which had previously stayed open that evening closed their doors.

The final decades of the twentieth century saw both a continuation and reversal of earlier trends. Alcohol use remained widespread, while the use of recreational drugs, particularly by members of the middle class, climbed in the late 1960s and 1970s. (Recreational drug use dipped in the early 1990s, before rising again.) With the proliferation of state lotteries, riverboat casinos, and casinos on Indian reservations, legalized gambling became one of the nation's fastest growing industries. Videocassette recorders, video games, the explosion of cable channels, and the popularization of Internet "chat rooms" reinforced the

privatization of recreation, while reversing the trend toward a uniform experience.

Perhaps most surprisingly, the number of hours most Americans spent on recreation began to shrink in the 1970s for the first time in a century. As more women entered the paid workforce, the continuing need to do housework cut into time available for leisure activities. Clogged freeways and the growth of suburbs lengthened commuting times, while telephone answering machines, pagers, cell phones, and portable computers made it easier to take work home. With the growth of the leisure industry, Americans needed more money to spend on recreation; thus, the average workweek climbed as Americans increasingly shifted from "time intensive" to "goods intensive" recreation. One group bucked this overall trend: retired Americans were generally healthier and more affluent than their predecessors had been. Moving away from their families, many spent long hours on the golf course, in shopping malls and recreation centers, or as seasonal visitors to warm areas like Florida and Arizona.

BIBLIOGRAPHY

Axtell, James. *The European and the Indian: Essays in the Ethnohistory of Colonial North America.* New York: Oxford University Press, 1981.

Cross, Gary. *A Social History of Leisure since 1600.* State College, Penn.: Venture Publishing, 1990.

Nasaw, David. *Going Out: The Rise and Fall of Public Amusements.* New York: Basic Books, 1993.

Rybczynski, Witold. *Waiting for the Weekend.* New York: Viking, 1991.

Wendy Wall

See also **Consumerism; Sports.**

RECYCLING. The term "recycling" was virtually unused outside of industry before the late 1960s when voluntary programs were formed by counterculture communities. The emerging culture of hippies reapplied the age-old practice of collecting and reusing materials. For centuries, rag pickers collected worn out cloth and sold it to those who made paper. Not until the mid-nineteenth century did the demand for paper outstrip the quantity of rags. It was then that the method of making paper from wood was invented. Wood soon replaced textile fiber entirely in paper manufacturing, preparing the way for paper to become the most plentiful item in twentieth-century landfills.

The United States evolved from a nation of people who saved pieces of twine and reused nails (as Henry David Thoreau did, when building his cabin at Walden Pond) to a "throwaway society" of people who discarded containers, furniture, appliances, and even automobiles by the mid-twentieth century. The need to conserve and reuse materials, while stressed as a patriotic duty during World War II, was forgotten in the postwar boom.

Aluminum Recycling. This 1973 photograph by Flip Schulke shows a dump outside an aluminum recycling plant in Islamorada, on Upper Matecumbe Key in the Florida Keys; aluminum has been one of the few materials to provide a profit when recycled. NATIONAL ARCHIVES AND RECORDS ADMINISTRATION

"Fast food" emerged, sold in plastic and foam containers which, like so much else, was considered "disposable." Then, on the heels of the 1960s movements for civil rights and peace, came "the greening of America," a political movement to save the environment. The size of the environmental movement became apparent on 22 April 1970 when 20 million people turned out to celebrate the first Earth Day. Months later, Congress created the Environmental Protection Agency (EPA). Soon books like *Limits to Growth* by the Club of Rome (1972) began making the case that our American way of life was not sustainable.

The Truth about Consequences: Hard Choices
Recycling is the most obvious way individuals can assist in waste management, though source reduction can also be practiced. The "diaper wars" of the late 1980s exemplify the latter, reducing the amount of waste by using cloth diapers. But the makers of disposable diapers argued that washing cloth diapers used energy and water, offset-

ting any benefit. Making choices that "save the Earth" turned out to be complex.

Another hard choice for consumers was the "paper or plastic" question at the grocery store. This apparently ethical question became moot when it was discovered that neither would decompose in a landfill. Marketers promoted items as good for the environment because they were biodegradable, but consumers later found that the term had little meaning. One researcher dug up ten-year-old chicken bones in a landfill, demonstrating that in the absence of light and air, even organic waste does not decompose.

Recycling Goes Mainstream
In the late 1980s, news reports began referring to a "landfill crisis" and showed images of medical waste washing up on beaches. Support for recycling spread beyond the minority of environmentalists to the general population. By then most of the voluntary programs, unable to accommodate the quantity of recyclables and fluctuating prices, had disappeared. In their stead, large, efficient trash collection companies had begun to offer curbside recycling (often required by municipalities). This combination of widespread concern and the convenience of curbside collection led to increasing quantities of recycled trash.

Recycling is, of course, only one of many interrelated environmental issues, but it is the one to which everyone can contribute directly. Americans began to associate it with groundwater pollution, topsoil erosion, deforestation, and global warming. "Do you recycle?" became an ethical question, and curbside recycling grew rapidly in urban areas. By 1999, curbside recycling was available to over half the population of the United States. It was much more widespread in the urban Northeast (83 percent) than in the more rural South (39 percent), with the West and Midwest averaging 48 percent.

Thus the quantity of household waste which was recycled increased significantly in the United States. In 1980, the average weight of materials recycled per person per day was 0.35 pounds; it increased to 0.70 by 1990 and to 1.30 by 1999. At the same time, the amount of generated waste increased from 3.7 in 1980 to 4.5 in 1990; however, that figure stopped growing as rapidly and was only 4.6 pounds in 1999.

On Earth Day 1990, about 200 million people in 137 countries showed support. Recycling was declared "more popular than democracy" by the editor of *Resource Recycling* who claimed that more people recycled than voted in the November 1991 elections (September 1992 issue; qtd. in Ackerman, p. 8). Indeed, recycling had become so significant in the American conscience that a *Wall Street Journal* article connected the act of recycling with religious ritual: "For many, a little trash sorting has become a form of penance to acknowledge that the values of our high-consumption society don't always nurture the soul" (19 January 1995; quoted in Ackerman, pp. 9–10). The

Newspaper Recycling. This center in the Park Slope section of Brooklyn was handling three tons of newspapers per week when Gary Miller took this photograph in 1973; the revenue from this operation went to a program to fight drug addiction. NATIONAL ARCHIVES AND RECORDS ADMINISTRATION

title of the article, "Curbside Recycling Comforts the Soul, But Benefits Are Scant," suggests one of the basic points of contention: should recycling be profitable?

To Recycle or Not: The Argument

Challengers to recycling argue that we should allow the market to determine what is recycled. For the most part, curbside recycling does not pay for itself except for aluminum cans. The environmental advocates, however, list two kinds of benefits. First, in waste management, recycling reduces the amount of waste, thereby reducing both pollution from landfills and litter from improper disposal; second, on the production end, recycled materials reduce pollution and energy costs and extend the life of raw materials which cannot be replaced.

The "anti-recyclers" argue that the "landfill crisis" of the 1980s was largely exaggerated and that even with the added cost of containment, landfills are cheaper than recycling. However, many people balk at locating landfills near where they live: the NIMBY response ("Not In My Back Yard"). Further, recycling advocates point out, we must weigh the social value of recycling rather than measure it solely by economics, and if we do use economics, we must consider the hidden costs (such as cleaning up pollution and end-of-life disposal) and not just the immediate ones.

The continuing dialogue about recycling is well illustrated by the February 2002 response of the National Recycling Coalition (NRC)—one of many groups formed around this issue—to the white paper put out by the EPA. The NRC finds much to approve of in the EPA recommendations but returns to the fundamental issue of sustainability: can we go on producing and consuming and disposing of material goods at an ever-increasing rate?

BIBLIOGRAPHY

Ackerman, Frank. *Why Do We Recycle: Markets, Values, and Public Policy.* Washington, D.C.: Island Press, 1997.

Alexander, Judd H. *In Defense of Garbage.* Westport, Conn.: Praeger, 1993.

Strasser, Susan. *Waste and Want: A Social History of Trash.* New York: Metropolitan Books, 1999.

Strong, Debra L. *Recycling in America: A Reference Handbook.* 2d ed. Santa Barbara, Calif.: ABC-CLIO, 1997.

William E. King

See also **Waste Disposal.**

RED CROSS, AMERICAN. Clara Barton and associates founded the American Red Cross in Washington, D.C., on 21 May 1881. Barton first learned of the Swiss-inspired International Red Cross Movement while in Europe following the Civil War. Returning home, she campaigned for an American society and for ratification of the Geneva Convention protecting the war injured, which the United States ratified in 1882.

Barton led the Red Cross for twenty-three years, during which time it conducted its first domestic and overseas disaster relief efforts, aided the U.S. military during the Spanish-American War, and campaigned successfully for the inclusion of peacetime relief work as part of the International Red Cross Movement—the so-called American Amendment that some Europeans initially resisted.

The Red Cross received its first congressional charter in 1900 and a second in 1905, the year after Barton resigned from the organization. This charter—which remains in effect today—obligates the Red Cross to provide aid to the sick and wounded in war, give relief to and serve as a medium of communication between members of the American armed forces and their families, and provide national and international disaster relief and mitigation.

Prior to World War I, the Red Cross introduced its first aid, water safety, and public-health nursing programs. With the advent of war, the organization experienced phenomenal growth under the leadership of the banker Henry P. Davison and a War Council appointed by President Woodrow Wilson. The number of local chapters grew from 107 in 1914 to 3,864 in 1918, and membership jumped from 17,000 to more than 20 million adult and 11 million Junior Red Cross members. The public contributed $400 million in funds and material to support Red Cross programs, including those for U.S. and Allied forces and civilian refugees. The Red Cross staffed hospitals and ambulance companies and recruited 20,000 registered nurses to serve the military. Additional Red Cross nurses helped combat the worldwide influenza epidemic of 1918.

American Red Cross. Its service for Allied forces stationed in Great Britain during World War I included "Flying Squadron" units such as this one that could respond within three minutes of getting a call. NATIONAL ARCHIVES AND RECORDS ADMINISTRATION

After the war, the Red Cross focused on service to veterans and enhanced its programs in safety training, home care for the sick, accident prevention, and nutrition education. Major disasters also called for relief efforts, including the Mississippi River floods of 1927 and severe drought and economic depression during the 1930s.

In World War II, the Red Cross again provided services to the U.S. military, Allies, and civilian war victims. It enrolled more than 71,000 nurses for military service, prepared 27 million packages for U.S. and Allied prisoners of war, and shipped more than 300,000 tons of supplies overseas. At the military's request, the Red Cross also introduced a national blood program that collected 13.3 million pints of blood for use by the armed forces.

After World War II, the Red Cross initiated the first nationwide civilian blood program, which now supplies nearly 50 percent of the blood and blood products in this country. The Red Cross played an increasing role in biomedical research and expanded into the banking and distribution of human tissue. During the 1990s, it undertook

a massive modernization of its blood services operations to increase the safety of its blood products. It continued to provide services to members of the armed forces and their families, including during the Korean, Vietnam, and Persian Gulf wars. The Red Cross also entered new fields, such as civil defense, CPR/AED training, HIV/AIDS education, and the provision of emotional care and support to disaster victims and their survivors. It helped the federal government form the Federal Emergency Management Agency and serves as its principal supplier of mass care in federally declared disasters.

While closely associated with the federal government in the promotion of its objectives, the Red Cross is an independent, volunteer-led organization, financially supported by voluntary public contributions and cost-reimbursement charges. A fifty-member, all-volunteer board of governors leads the organization. The president of the United States, who is honorary chairman of the Red Cross, appoints eight governors, including the chairman of the board. The chairman nominates and the board

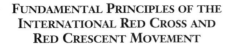

FUNDAMENTAL PRINCIPLES OF THE INTERNATIONAL RED CROSS AND RED CRESCENT MOVEMENT

Humanity. The International Red Cross and Red Crescent Movement, born of a desire to bring assistance without discrimination to the wounded on the battlefield, endeavors, in its international and national capacity, to prevent and alleviate human suffering wherever it may be found. Its purpose is to protect life and health and to ensure respect for the human being. It promotes mutual understanding, friendship, cooperation, and lasting peace amongst all peoples.

Impartiality. It makes no discrimination as to nationality, race, religious beliefs, class, or political opinions. It endeavors to relieve the suffering of individuals, being guided solely by their needs, and to give priority to the most urgent cases of distress.

Neutrality. In order to continue to enjoy the confidence of all, the Movement may not take sides in hostilities or engage at any time in controversies of a political, racial, religious, or ideological nature.

Independence. The Movement is independent. The National Societies, while auxiliaries in the humanitarian services of their governments and subject to the laws of their respective countries, must always maintain their autonomy so that they may be able at all times to act in accordance with the principles of the Movement.

Voluntary Service. It is a voluntary relief movement not prompted in any manner by desire for gain.

Unity. There can be only one Red Cross or one Red Crescent Society in any one country. It must be open to all. It must carry on its humanitarian work throughout its territory.

Universality. The International Red Cross and Red Crescent Movement, in which all Societies have equal status and share equal responsibilities and duties in helping each other, is worldwide.

BIBLIOGRAPHY

Dulles, Foster Rhea. *The American Red Cross: A History*. New York: Harper, 1950. Reprint, Westport, Conn.: Greenwood Press, 1971.

Gilbo, Patrick F. *The American Red Cross: The First Century*. New York: Harper and Row, 1981.

Hurd, Charles. *The Compact History of the American Red Cross*. New York: Hawthorn Books, 1959.

Pryor, Elizabeth Brown. *Clara Barton: Professional Angel*. Philadelphia: University of Pennsylvania Press, 1987.

Brien R. Williams

See also **Philanthropy.**

RED POWER, a movement that began with the 1969 occupation of Alcatraz Island in San Francisco Bay, awakened American Indian people to the possibilities of protest politics. Young Indian college students and Indian people from northern California joined in an organization that reflected their diversity. Named Indians of All Tribes, this group executed an occupation of the former prison island that lasted for nineteen months. Following the Alcatraz occupation, members of the American Indian Movement (AIM) in 1972 occupied the Bureau of Indian Affairs (BIA) headquarters in Washington, D.C., for seven days. In 1973, American Indians occupied Wounded Knee, South Dakota, for seventy-one days.

Protest at Alcatraz. Nine of the pan-Indian activists stand outside the former federal prison in late 1969, at the start of their nineteen-month occupation of the island. AP/WIDE WORLD PHOTOS

elects the president of the Red Cross, who is responsible for implementing the policies and programs of the board. The American Red Cross works closely with the International Committee of the Red Cross on matters of international conflict and social, political, and military unrest. As a member of the International Federation of Red Cross and Red Crescent Societies, which it helped found in 1919, the Red Cross joins more than 170 other national Red Cross organizations in bringing aid to victims of disasters throughout the world.

The Red Power movement set in motion a wave of American Indian militancy that ultimately resulted in abandonment of the U.S. government policy of termination and the adoption of a policy of Indian self-determination. During the WOUNDED KNEE occupation, President Richard Nixon returned Blue Lake and 48,000 acres of land to the Taos pueblo, 40 million acres of land to the Navajo Nation, 21,000 acres of Mount Adams in Washington State to the Yakima tribe, and some 60,000 acres to the Warm Springs tribes of Oregon. The Nixon administration also increased the budget of the BIA by 224 percent and doubled the funds for Indian health care. The Red Power movement ceased to exist as a coherent movement following the killing of two Federal Bureau of Investigation agents on the Pine Ridge, South Dakota, reservation in 1975. Three members of AIM were prosecuted for the crime. Two were acquitted, but the third, Leonard Peltier, was convicted. Peltier and his supporters insisted on his innocence and condemned the government's conduct at the trial.

BIBLIOGRAPHY

Johnson, Troy, Joane Nagel, and Duane Champagne, eds. *American Indian Activism: Alcatraz to the Longest Walk.* Urbana: University of Illinois Press, 1997.

Josephy, Alvin M., Joane Nagel, and Troy Johnson, eds. *Red Power: The American Indians' Fight for Freedom.* 2d ed. Lincoln: University of Nebraska Press, 1999.

Troy Johnson

See also **American Indian Movement; Indian Policy, U.S., 1900–2000; Indian Political Life.**

RED RIVER CAMPAIGN (1864). Early in 1864, Union General Henry W. Halleck ordered an invasion of the cotton-growing sections of Louisiana, Arkansas, and Texas. The thrust, to be under the command of General Nathaniel P. Banks, was to move up the Red River. Banks planned to begin the exedition in March to take advantage of the spring rise in the river.

Banks's command and a force from Mississippi under Union General Andrew Jackson Smith, together with a river fleet, were to converge on Alexandria, Louisiana, after which the combined force would move on to a junction with troops under General Frederick Steele coming southward from Arkansas. The two armies would then sweep up the Red River valley to Shreveport, the Confederate headquarters, and on into eastern Texas. Scattered Confederate troops—half the size of the Union army—under General Edmund Kirby-Smith, were available to oppose the invasion.

By the middle of March, the fleet and Banks's army had taken Fort DeRussy (14 March) and occupied Alexandria (16 March) to await the arrival of reinforcements marching overland from the Mississippi River. The retreating Confederate troops under General Richard Tay-lor—receiving reinforcements as they went—halted at Mansfield, south of Shreveport. Posted in good defensive positions, Taylor's force, with less than half his opponents' numbers, sustained Banks's attack on 8 April. The Union forces were defeated and driven back in confusion. The next day Taylor's troops advanced against Banks's army posted in a strong position at Pleasant Hill, southeast of Mansfield, and were repulsed. Banks failed to follow up his success. During the night, the Union army retreated to Grand Ecore near Natchitoches, and then to Alexandria. The withdrawal of the army placed the Union fleet in jeopardy. The river did not rise as anticipated, and it was uncertain if the ships could pass the rapids at Grand Ecore. Engineering skill and resourcefulness saw the ships safely through in time to escape capture or destruction.

When the threat of Banks's advance was removed, Kirby-Smith, at Shreveport, undertook both to pursue Banks and to crush Steele. On 30 April he attacked at Jenkins Ferry, Arkansas, on the Saline River. Steele retreated to Little Rock. Kirby-Smith then turned southward to join Taylor for a final blow against Banks, but Banks had already reembarked and started back to the Mississippi, where the troops were dispersed. The defeat of Banks's expedition brought important operations in the trans-Mississippi to a close. The Confederate forces held out until 26 May 1865, when Kirby-Smith surrendered, thus ending the war in that area.

BIBLIOGRAPHY

Brooksher, William R. *War Along the Bayous: The 1864 Red River Campaign in Louisiana.* Washington, D.C.: Brassey's, 1998.

Johnson, Ludwell H. *Red River Campaign: Politics and Cotton in the Civil War.* Kent, Ohio: Kent State University Press, 1993.

Thomas Robson Hay / A. R.

See also **Civil War; Mississippi Plan; Mississippi River.**

RED RIVER CART TRAFFIC. The Red River cart was a two-wheeled vehicle made entirely of wood, including the wheels, and carried a maximum load of one thousand pounds. An ox or Indian pony with a rude harness of rawhide drew each of them.

The traffic began by 1822 with the founding of Fort Snelling at what is now Saint Paul, MINNESOTA. Traders loaded the carts at Fort Garry in Winnipeg or at Pembina with buffalo robes, pemmican, dried meat, and furs, and exchanged these products at Fort Snelling for the trade goods needed at the fur trade posts tributary to Fort Garry. In 1843 the AMERICAN FUR COMPANY established a post at Pembina, and thereafter the traffic from this point grew rapidly in volume.

The most popular Red River cart trails were on the west side of the river. On the east side of the Red River, the trail ran southeast to Fort Snelling. Later, the trails crossed the Mississippi River at Sauk Rapids and reached

Saint Paul on the east side of the river. The Lake Traverse route ran southeast to the crossing of the Minnesota River at Bois de Sioux and then to Mendota, at its junction with the Mississippi. After 1850 ferries connected Fort Snelling with Mendota and Saint Paul.

The low cost of this form of transportation explains its popularity. The oxen and horses were pastured on the prairie grasses, and the drivers found abundant game along the entire route. One serious drawback arose from the fact that these trails traversed the area that was the battleground of two Indian tribes, the CHIPPEWA and the Dakota. Gradually, cart traffic gave way to flatboat and steamboat traffic, and the coming of the railroads in the 1860s completed the transformation.

BIBLIOGRAPHY

Ens, Gerhard John. *Homeland to Hinterland: The Changing Worlds of the Red River Metis in the Nineteenth Century.* Toronto: University of Toronto Press, 1996.

Lass, William E. *Minnesota: A History.* New York: W.W. Norton, 1998.

Wilkins, Robert P. *North Dakota: A Bicentennial History.* New York: Norton, 1977.

O. G. Libby / A. E.

See also **Fur Trade and Trapping; Hudson's Bay Company; North Dakota; Snelling, Fort.**

RED RIVER INDIAN WAR (1874–1875). In 1867 the Treaty of Medicine Lodge placed the Comanche, Kiowa, Arapaho, and Cheyenne tribes on reservations in western Oklahoma. The federal government systematically failed to meet the terms of the treaty by not providing supplies and by allowing white outlaws, cattle rustlers, and liquor merchants entry into tribal areas. The decline of the buffalo herds, particularly following the completion of the Union Pacific Railroad in 1819, and the neglect of the Indian Office and military officials produced widespread suffering among the tribes. The efforts of two Quaker federal agents, James M. Haworth and John D. Miles, to provide education and farming instruction were unsuccessful.

Encouraged by religious dances and leaders such as Quanah Parker, the tribes responded to white incursions by attacking military and civilian facilities. Fourteen battles took place from the Texas Panhandle to western Oklahoma and north Texas. Troops under the command of General Phil Sheridan and Colonel Ranald S. Mackenzie, with the advantage of superior weapons and favorable weather, subdued the Indian resistance by 1876. Following their surrender, some tribal leaders were sent to Fort Madison, Florida, under the supervision of Captain Richard Pratt. They were released in 1878. In the aftermath of the war, Indian and white ranchers came to dominate the southern Plains.

BIBLIOGRAPHY

Haley, James L. *The Buffalo War: The History of the Red River Indian Uprising of 1874.* Garden City, N.Y.: Doubleday, 1976. The best account of the conflict.

Hutton, Paul Andrew. *Phil Sheridan and His Army.* Lincoln: University of Nebraska Press, 1985.

Nye, W. S. *Carbine and Lance: The Story of Old Fort Sill.* 3d ed., revised. Norman: University of Oklahoma Press, 1969. A colorful account.

Utley, Robert M. *Frontier Regulars: The United States Army and the Indian, 1866–1891.* New York: Macmillian, 1974. A first-rate account of the overall conflict between the military and the Plains Indians.

Donald K. Pickens
Carl Coke Rister

See also **Buffalo (Bison); Indian Reservations.**

RED SHIRTS. Even though they wore shirts of various colors, this name was given to Democrat Wade Hampton's supporters, who in 1876 helped the former Confederate general become governor of South Carolina. Their core consisted of 290 clubs, composed of 14,350 men. They intimidated black voters and joined Hampton parades on foot or on horses or mules. Hundreds of uniformed blacks also joined Democratic parades in support of Hampton. Some thought Hampton, a paternalist, would bring peace and an end to corruption; others were bribed or intimidated into wearing red shirts. White and black Red Shirts also participated in Hampton's reelection in 1878.

BIBLIOGRAPHY

Drago, Edmund L. *Hurrah for Hampton: Black Red Shirts in South Carolina During Reconstruction.* Fayetteville: University of Arkansas Press, 1998.

Simkins, Francis Butler, and Robert Hilliard Woody. *South Carolina During Reconstruction.* Chapel Hill: University of North Carolina Press, 1932.

Zuczek, Richard. *State of Rebellion: Reconstruction in South Carolina.* Columbia: University of South Carolina Press, 1996.

Edmund L. Drago

REDLINING is discrimination against people trying to buy homes, finance businesses, or obtain bank services in minority neighborhoods. The term comes from banks allegedly drawing red lines on maps in the early 1970s to mark neighborhoods where they had offices to take deposits and provide bank services but where loans would not be made. Since the mid-1970s the megamergers that have transformed the banking industry have exacerbated the problem of redlining by reducing the number of bank offices in minority neighborhoods, often leaving only check-cashing stores and pawn shops to provide bank services.

At the same time, the megamergers have alleviated the problem of redlining by creating favorable conditions for increasing the flow of credit to minority neighborhoods. The 1977 Community Reinvestment Act gives community groups, like the more than 600 nonprofit organizations organized into the National Community Reinvestment Coalition, the authority to challenge the megamergers if the banks involved do not have good records of lending in minority neighborhoods. To avoid such challenges, banks have established partnerships with community groups to expand mortgage lending, new and rehabbed housing, and small business lending. The 1992 Federal Housing Enterprises Financial Safety and Soundness Act has also been helpful in this regard, by requiring government-sponsored credit agencies (Fannie Mae and Freddie Mac) to purchase more mortgages that banks issue in minority neighborhoods.

BIBLIOGRAPHY

Campen, Jim. "Neighborhoods, Banks, and Capital Flows: The Transformation of the U.S. Financial System and the Community Reinvestment Act." *Review of Radical Political Economics* 30, no. 4 (1998): 29–59.

National Community Reinvestment Coalition. *NCRC Reinvestment Compendium.* Bimonthly report on regulatory and legislative developments.

Yinger, John. *Closed Doors, Opportunities Lost: The Continuing Costs of Housing Discrimination.* New York: Russell Sage Foundation, 1995.

Edwin T. Dickens

See also **Discrimination: Race.**

REDWOOD. *See* Sequoia.

REED RULES, adopted by the House of Representatives on 14 February 1890, marked the successful conclusion of the protracted fight by Speaker of the House Thomas B. Reed for more efficient procedures in that body. The new rules permitted the suppression of dilatory tactics, substituted a "present" for a "voting" quorum, reduced the size of the Committee of the Whole, and provided sundry changes in the order of business. These measures brought an immediate increase in efficiency but greatly increased the power of the speaker; and the title of "czar" was promptly bestowed upon their author.

BIBLIOGRAPHY

Cheney, Richard B. *Kings of the Hill: Power and Personality in the House of Representatives.* New York: Simon and Schuster, 1996.

McCall, Samuel W. *The Life of Thomas Brackett Reed.* Boston: Houghton Mifflin, 1914.

Pyle, Christopher H. *The President, Congress, and the Constitution: Power and Legitimacy in American Politics.* New York: Free Press, 1984.

Robinson, William A. *Thomas B. Reed: Parliamentarian.* New York: Dodd, Mead, 1930.

William A. Robinson / A. G.

See also **Blocs; Colonial Assemblies; Delegation of Powers; Majority Rule; Rules of the House.**

REED V. REED, 404 U.S. 71 (1971), a case deriving from a provision of Idaho probate law preferring men as administrators of the estate of a deceased child, was the first in a series of 1970s cases associated with the future Supreme Court justice Ruth Bader Ginsburg that successfully challenged laws discriminating on the basis of sex. The case arose when Sally Reed sought to serve as administrator of her deceased teenage son's meager estate. Challenged by her divorced husband Cecil Reed, the boy's father, the case made its way through the Idaho courts to the Supreme Court. Writing the brief, Ginsburg argued that legislative classification by sex served no compelling state interest in this instance. Furthermore, it violated the right of Sally Reed to the even-handed application of governmental action guaranteed by the equal protection clause of the Fourteenth Amendment. In a unanimous decision, the Court agreed, although the justices differed as to whether the decision encouraged stricter scrutiny of legislation that discriminated on the basis of sex. Subsequent decisions, however, would confirm that *Reed* marked the beginning of a major effort, using equal protection analysis, to make the law gender neutral.

BIBLIOGRAPHY

Rhode, Deborah L. *Justice and Gender: Sex Discrimination and the Law.* Cambridge, Mass.: Harvard University Press, 1989.

Jane Sherron De Hart

See also **Civil Rights and Liberties; Discrimination: Sex; Equal Protection of the Law.**

REFERENDUM. A referendum is a provision permitting voters to accept or reject a public policy measure or policy question at a formal election. Its particulars vary from state to state: it may be binding or advisory, constitutional or legislative, and have local or statewide application; it may deal with amendments to state constitutions and city charters, statutes, and ordinances, or the financing of schools and public works projects through taxation or bonded indebtedness. In some states, the process can be set in motion only by the state legislatures; in others, it can be activated by voter-generated petition.

Although some scholars trace the referendum's modern beginnings back to Switzerland or to colonial New England, others locate its specific origins in the Massachusetts state constitution of 1780, which limited its application to the ratification of either new constitutions or amendments to existing ones. During the 1840s, Texas became the first state to permit the submission of proposed statutes, but the movement did not gain much momentum until the Populists and other agrarian radicals advocated it during the last decade of the century. With the onset of the Progressive Era in the late 1890s, the referendum, in common with the initiative, recall, primary elections, direct election of U.S. senators, and woman's suffrage, became a vital component of "direct democracy" or "power to the people" movement that swept the nation. Initiative and referendum together constituted the "direct legislation" segment of that movement, inspired by the growing belief that city councils and state legislatures—once considered the most representative of all branches of government—had become virtual tools of corrupt corporate and partisan interests. They could no longer be relied upon to enact legislation on behalf of general welfare, nor could they be prevented from passing laws that blatantly betrayed the public's trust in favor of special interests. One part of the putative solution—*initiative*—was designed to allow the general public to force popular measures upon legislature. The second component—*referendum*—was crafted to permit voters to undo pernicious work by legislature, as well as to demonstrate widespread support for progressive measures. Spearheaded by South Dakota in 1898, some twenty states adopted the referendum over the next two decades.

Despite its widespread adoption, the referendum has generally failed to justify the optimistic predictions of its Progressive Era proponents. Referenda have been used by legislators to postpone or prevent the enactment of legislation; they have functioned as "buck-passing" safety valves for lawmakers caught between two powerful pressure groups or between the competing demands of special interests and the general welfare. The precipitous decline in political participation in general has all but obviated the "democratic" nature of referenda, frequently reducing them to contests between two cohorts of special interest groups. The increasing reliance upon television, the Internet, and other forms of mass communication have greatly increased the cost of referendum campaigns, to the obvious advantage of those with "deep pockets." This has also tended to turn complex policy questions into simplistic slogans or sound bytes. The escalating revolt against "big government" has greatly exacerbated what has always been the conventional wisdom regarding referenda: if you do not understand the issue or suspect that it will raise your taxes vote NO! After thoroughly analyzing the operation of the referendum in California over the past century, political historian John M. Allswang has pessimistically concluded that "somewhere along the way direct legislation moved well beyond its original intent, to the point where it has overwhelmed the governing processes it was designed to monitor, to become in effect a 'fourth branch' of state government."

BIBLIOGRAPHY

Allswang, John M. *The Initiative and Referendum in California, 1898–1998.* Stanford, Calif.: Stanford University Press, 1999.

Munro, William B., ed. *The Initiative, Referendum, and Recall.* New York: Appleton, 1912.

John D. Buenker

See also **Initiative; Progressive Movement.**

REFORMATORIES are penal institutions meant to "reform" or "rehabilitate" the persons assigned to them. The difference between reformatories and prisons is best understood as aspirational. "Prison" connotes a purpose to detain inmates as punishment rather than to help them learn to function effectively in society. As a matter of experience, however, most modern prisons purport to offer inmates some opportunity for self-improvement through employment, education, and vocational training and thus appear to have reformative objectives, however secondary. Many prisons are formally named "correctional institutions," suggesting a reform mission.

By most accounts penal institutions of any designation rarely deliver on the promise of serious rehabilitative programs. Most are chiefly concerned with accommodating large numbers of inmates in minimally acceptable physical conditions at the least possible cost. Prisoners often work only inasmuch as they assist with housekeeping or labor in the kitchen or the laundry. At some institutions prisoners are employed in more meaningful and productive industrial jobs. Yet the primary objective still is not to teach prisoners skills they need to succeed in society but rather to relieve tensions and generate funds to pay the costs of their detention.

Historically three kinds of facilities were especially associated with the "reformatory" label: reform schools for juveniles, institutions for women, and institutions for young adult male convicts. New York established the first American facility for juvenile delinquents in 1825, roughly when the first adult penitentiaries appeared. Other states soon established similar institutions. At first boys and girls were housed in the same facilities. Later girls were diverted to separate institutions. Delinquency was loosely defined. Many of the boys had committed criminal offenses, but many of the girls had simply become pregnant out of wedlock. The working idea, borrowed from England and Europe, was that young delinquents were the victims of inadequate guidance and discipline. Their parents had failed them, and they had not been apprenticed to master craftspeople who might have taught them productive skills. Instead, they had been corrupted by drink, prostitution, or other vices. Juvenile detention facilities were meant to provide delinquents with the structured homes they had been denied. Assuming quasi-parental responsibility, those institutions also proposed to educate the children in their charge. Thus, reform "schools."

The proper curriculum for reform schools was controversial. Advocates debated, for example, whether children should be housed in dormitories or in small cottages that more closely resembled ideal family homes. Alternative organizational systems occasionally appeared. Some reform schools operated under a strict military-style discipline; others experimented with schemes under which children governed themselves. By common account, reform schools generally failed to realize their ambitions. Most ultimately concentrated on discipline and hard labor and in the process subordinated academic programs. By the late twentieth century penologists had come to distrust the very idea that troubled children could be helped by detention. Some states attempted finally to achieve results by creating special offices to orchestrate more effective programs. The California Youth Authority, founded in 1941, was the most famous example. Yet the demise of large reformatories was inexorable. By the twenty-first century juveniles were more commonly channeled to community-based programs or to small group homes.

Reformatories for female offenders developed from concerns about the squalid conditions under which women and their children suffered in jails and penitentiaries in the nineteenth century. All the children born to imprisoned women at Sing Sing died before their mothers were released. Quakers and Unitarians, most of them women themselves, insisted that women should be housed in separate facilities, where they could be supervised by female staff and offered some form of education or vocational training. Many states established separate women's institutions along these lines. Late in the twentieth century, however, most observers concluded that the women's reform facilities were unsuccessful. The crime rate among women increased dramatically in the last years of the twentieth century, yet few jurisdictions opened new penal institutions for female offenders.

Reformatories for young adult men were responsible for altering the meaning of "reform" in the penal context. Previously the idea had been to achieve religious transformation. The reformatories established in the late nineteenth century scarcely abandoned religious indoctrination. They made intensive efforts to instill the Protestant ethic. Yet they also contemplated that criminal offenders could be induced to change their ways if they were educated and trained to perform productive jobs. New York established the most famous reformatory for young men at Elmira in 1876. The warden, Zebulon Brockway, proposed to use that facility to implement policies and programs associated with the "rehabilitative ideal" that dominated American penology until the 1970s: the indeterminate sentence, under which prisoners were held as long as, but only as long as, it took to prepare them to function properly; the classification of incoming inmates to ensure that each received appropriate individualized treatment; educational and vocational programs to prepare prisoners for ultimate release; and parole supervision in the community thereafter.

By most accounts, however, reformatories for young men also were unsuccessful. Brockway promoted his program exceedingly well, and many states established institutions on the Elmira model. Yet too much crowding and too little money constantly undermined both Elmira itself and its sister facilities. Brockway proved a tyrant who personally made cavalier decisions about the programs appropriate for individual inmates without pausing to consider the results of interviews and the recommendations of his staff. Moreover, investigations of his methods revealed that he savagely whipped "recalcitrant" prisoners. Within a few years Elmira and other reformatories came to operate much like ordinary prisons, albeit stripped of the old "separate" and "silent" systems that had prevailed in the early penitentiaries in Pennsylvania and New York. Elmira became a general penal facility for confining male offenders, offering inmates no more than the usual limited employment and training opportunities.

BIBLIOGRAPHY

Allen, Francis A. *The Decline of the Rehabilitative Ideal: Penal Policy and Social Purpose.* New Haven, Conn.: Yale University Press, 1981.

McKelvey, Blake. *American Prisons: A History of Good Intentions.* Montclair, N.J.: Patterson Smith, 1977.

Morris, Norval, and David J. Rothman, eds. *The Oxford History of the Prison: The Practice of Punishment in Western Society.* New York: Oxford University Press, 1995.

Pisciotta, Alexander W. *Benevolent Repression: Social Control and the American Reformatory-Prison Movement.* New York: New York University Press, 1994.

Rothman, David J. *The Discovery of the Asylum: Social Order and Disorder in the New Republic.* Boston: Little, Brown, 1971.

Larry Yackle

See also **Prisons and Prison Reform; Punishment.**

REFORMED CHURCHES. The Reformed branch of the Protestant Reformation yielded two main streams in North America. Presbyterians, the English-speaking expression of Reformed Christianity, have always had a larger presence in American history thanks in part to language and culture. The second stream came to the United States by way of northern Europe, where the term "Reformed" signifies essentially the same thing as "Presbyterian" in Britain. Both Reformed and Presbyterians follow the reforms launched most notably by John Calvin in the sixteenth century. Theologically, they stress human depravity and dependence on divine mercy for salvation. Liturgically, they practice a simple form of worship that stresses the centrality of Scripture. Governmentally, these churches follow a presbyterian order that grants authority to elders through a series of graded ecclesiastical assemblies. For Reformed churches these are the consistory at the congregational level, the classis at the regional, and the synod for national purposes.

The first Dutch Reformed congregation was established in 1628 in New York City. The surrounding areas were centers of Dutch Calvinist strength throughout the colonial period. These churches remained generally uniform in their Dutch identity and piety, even after the English gained control of New York, until a new and more enthusiastic form of devotion began to divide ministers and laity alike. The revivals of the First Great Awakening fueled these tensions to the point that two identifiable parties emerged—the conferentie, who championed the order of inherited Dutch ways, and the coetus party, who favored zeal and autonomy from the Old World. By 1772, church leaders had effected a compromise that allowed the American churches greater autonomy from Dutch oversight while retaining the Dutch language for worship. Eventually, this led to the founding in 1792 of the Reformed Church in America (RCA) the oldest and largest of the Dutch Reformed bodies.

A new wave of Dutch immigration in the mid-nineteenth century, however, created strains on the established church, especially notable when American practices did not line up with those in the Netherlands. The recent immigrants became frustrated with the perceived laxness of the RCA and in 1857 founded the Christian Reformed Church (CRC), the second-largest Dutch Reformed denomination. In the 1920s, a debate in the CRC over worldliness and ecumenical relations precipitated the 1924 split that produced the Protestant Reformed Churches in America. In 1996, a number of congregations left the CRC over the issue of women's ordination to found the United Reformed Churches in North America. Subsequent twentieth-century migrations from the Netherlands have yielded several other Dutch Reformed denominations—the Free Reformed Churches, the Canadian and American Reformed Churches, the Netherlands Reformed Congregations, and the Heritage Netherlands Reformed Congregations.

German and Hungarian Reformed denominations have also been part of the ecclesiastical mosaic of the United States. The former traces its roots back to the formation of the Reformed Church in the United States (RCUS), a synod that first convened in 1793. The RCUS blossomed during the mid-nineteenth century under the theological leadership of John Williamson Nevin (1803–1886) and Philip Schaff (1819–1893), both of whom taught at the denomination's seminary in Mercersburg, Pennsylvania. From the beginning of the twentieth century, the RCUS participated actively in Protestant ecumenical conversations, and in 1934 joined the Evangelical Synod of North America to become the Evangelical and Reformed Church, the denomination in which brothers Reinhold (1892–1971) and H. Richard Niebuhr (1894–1962) ministered. In 1957, this body merged with the Congregational Christian Churches to form the United Church of Christ. The German Reformed tradition continues in another denomination with the name Reformed Church in the United States, a body that refused to join

the merger of 1934. First called the RCUS, Eureka Classis, the regional association of churches in the Dakotas and northern Iowa, these congregations eventually dropped the geographical descriptor to be simply the RCUS.

The history of the Hungarian Reformed churches is bound up with the German Reformed. The small number of Hungarian Reformed made the construction of a formal association of churches difficult. Consequently, from 1890 they received oversight from the RCUS. In 1904, the Hungarian Reformed churches withdrew from the RCUS and came under the supervision of the Reformed Church in Hungary. After World War I (1914–1918), maintaining relations with the church in the motherland became difficult. Some of the Hungarian Reformed churches reaffiliated with the RCUS and eventually became an ethnic synod within first the Evangelical and Reformed Church and then within the United Church of Christ. Other congregations in 1924 formed the Free Magyar Reformed Church in America. In 1958 this body adopted the name Hungarian Reformed Church in America.

BIBLIOGRAPHY

Balmer, Randall H. *A Perfect Babel of Confusion: Dutch Religion and English Culture in the Middle Colonies.* New York: Oxford University Press, 1989.

Bratt, James D. *Dutch Calvinism in Modern America: A History of a Conservative Subculture.* Grand Rapids, Mich.: W. B. Eerdmans Publishing Company, 1984.

Fabend, Firth Haring. *Zion on the Hudson: Dutch New York and New Jersey in the Age of Revivals.* New Brunswick, N.J.: Rutgers University Press, 2000.

Gunnemann, Louis H. *The Shaping of the United Church of Christ: An Essay in the History of American Christianity.* New York: United Church Press, 1977.

Parsons, William T. *The German Reformed Experience in Colonial America.* Philadelphia: United Church Press, 1976.

Piepkorn, Arthur Carl. *Profiles in Belief: The Religious Bodies of the United States and Canada.* New York: Harper and Row, 1977.

D. G. Hart

See also **Calvinism; United Church of Christ.**

REFRIGERATION. The preservation of winter ice, principally for cooling drinks in summer, was practiced from antiquity, when ice was stored in insulated caves. Ice cooling was so popular in America that, within a decade of the Revolution, the United States led the world in both the production and consumption of ice. As the use of ice was extended to the preservation of fish, meat, and dairy products, ice production became a major industry in the northern states, and ice was shipped not only to the southern states but to the West Indies and South America. By 1880 the demand in New York City exceeded the capacity of 160 large commercial icehouses on the Hudson River. This industry reached its peak in 1886, when 25 million pounds were "harvested" by cutting lake and river ice with

THE SELF-FEEDING ICE SAFE.

The PISTON FREEZING MACHINE and ICE COMPANY, 314 and 315c, Oxford-street, direct attention to

MR ASH'S NEW PATENT

SELF-FEEDING ICE SAFE

It produces perfectly dry, cold, ventilated air, no increase of temperature during the melting of the ice. The lowest temperature effected with, say 50lb. of ice, is fully maintained in every part of the Safe, even though the ice may have diminished to 10 or 12lb. In operation daily, and particulars obtained at the

OFFICES OF THE COMPANY,

314 and 315c, OXFORD-STREET (near Harewood Gates).

Freezing Machine, c. 1874.
Cr:Hulton Getty/Archive Photos

Piston Freezing Machine. An 1874 advertisement for an "ice safe." GETTY IMAGES/HULTON GETTY PICTURE LIBRARY

horse-drawn saws. The advent of mechanical refrigeration in the nineteenth century began a slow decline in the ice trade. The natural ice industry had expired by 1920.

A method of making ice artificially, lowering the temperature of water by accelerating its evaporation, had long been practiced in India, where water in porous clay dishes laid on straw evaporated at night so rapidly as to cause ice to form on the surface of the remaining water. This method endured until as late as 1871, when a U.S. patent utilized this principle for a refrigerator that depended on the evaporation of water from the porous lining of the food compartment. But previous scientific discoveries had suggested other, more efficient methods of cooling.

Several types of refrigeration machines were developed in the nineteenth century. All depended on the absorption of heat by expanding gases, which had been a subject of scientific research in the previous century. It had been observed that the release of humid compressed air was accompanied by a stream of pellets of ice and snow. This phenomenon, the cooling effect of expanding air, led to the development of the Gorrie ice machine in

the 1840s. John Gorrie, a physician in Apalachicola, Florida, sought ways to relieve the suffering of malaria victims in the southern summer climate. Gorrie's machine injected water into a cylinder in which air was compressed by a steam engine. This cooled the air. The air expanded in contact with coils containing brine, which was then used to freeze water. Gorrie's machine saw scarce use (although at least one was built—in England), but his 1851 patent, the first in the United States for an ice machine, served as a model for others, including the first large machines that in the 1880s began to compete with lakes and rivers as a source of ice.

More important were "absorption" machines, based on the observation, made by Sir John Leslie in 1810, that concentrated sulfuric acid, which absorbs water, could accelerate the evaporation of water in a dish to such a degree as to freeze the remaining water. This method of artificial ice production was patented in England in 1834. Scientists further increased the efficiency level by using ammonia as the evaporating fluid and water as the absorbing fluid. Ferdinand Carré developed the first important example in France in 1858. In this machine, Carré connected by tube a vessel containing a solution of ammonia in water to a second vessel. When the former heated and the latter cooled (by immersing it in cold water), the ammonia evaporated from the first vessel and condensed in the second. Heating was then terminated and the ammonia allowed to reevaporate, producing a refrigerating effect on the surface of the second (ammonia-containing) chamber. Such a "machine" was no automatic refrigerator, but it was inexpensive and simple and well suited for use in isolated areas. One of them, the Crosley "Icyball," was manufactured in large numbers in the United States in the 1930s. Supplied with a handle, the dumbbell-shaped apparatus had to occasionally be set on a kerosene burner, where the "hot ball" was warmed and then moved to the "ice box," where the "cold ball" exercised its cooling effect (the hot ball being allowed to hang outside).

The vapor compression system would soon replace all of these early designs. In a vapor compression machine, a volatile fluid is circulated while being alternately condensed (with the evolution of heat) and evaporated (with the absorption of heat). This is the principle of the modern refrigeration machine. Oliver Evans, an ingenious American mechanic, had proposed in 1805 to use ether in such a machine, and in 1834 Jacob Perkins, an American living in London, actually built one, using a volatile "ether" obtained by distilling rubber. Perkins built only one machine, but improved versions—based in large part on the patents of Alexander C. Twining of New Haven, Connecticut—were developed and actually manufactured in the 1850s.

The earliest demand for refrigeration machines came from breweries, from the Australian meat industry, and from southern states that wanted artificial ice. Only when the operation of such machinery was made reliably automatic could it serve the now familiar purpose of house-

Frigidaire. An early refrigerator used a wooden box with metal hinges. © UPI/CORBIS-BETTMANN

hold refrigeration, a step successfully taken by E. J. Copeland of Detroit in 1918. Another important step was the use of less hazardous fluids than the ethers common in commercial refrigerators. Ammonia replaced the ethers in a few machines from the 1860s and became the most common refrigerating fluid by 1900. But ammonia was only slightly less hazardous than ether. The problem was to be solved through a research program remarkable for its basis in theoretical science. In the 1920s, Thomas Midgley Jr., with the support of the General Motors Corporation, studied the relevant characteristics (volatility, toxicity, specific heat, etc.) of a large number of substances. The result was a description of an "ideal" refrigerating fluid, including a prediction of what its chemical composition would be. Midgley then proceeded to synthesize several hitherto unknown substances that his theory indicated would possess these ideal characteristics. In 1930 he announced his success with the compound dichlorodifluoromethane. Under the commercial name Freon 12, it became the most widely used refrigerant.

The most noteworthy subsequent development in the use of refrigeration has been the introduction of frozen foods. It began in 1924 with an apparatus in which prepared fish were carried through a freezing compartment on an endless belt, developed by Clarence Birdseye of Gloucester, Massachusetts. By 1929 Birdseye had modified the apparatus to freeze fresh fruit, and in 1934 frozen foods were introduced commercially. Since World War II, progress in refrigerator design has focused on efficiency. The energy crisis of the 1970s spurred the first state regulatory standard for refrigerator efficiency. A California law passed in 1976 over the objection of appliance manufacturers required that 18-cubic-foot refrigerators sold in the state conform to a minimum efficiency level of 1400 kilowatt-hours (kwh) per year. California's large market share made it relatively easy for the federal government to hold refrigerators to a standard of 900 kwh in 1990 and then 700 kwh in 1993. Advances in refrigerator design have improved the consumption of the average refrigerator by over 60 percent in the last three decades of the twentieth century.

BIBLIOGRAPHY

Anderson, Oscar E., Jr. *Refrigeration in America: A History of a New Technology and Its Impact.* Port Washington, N.Y.: Kennikat Press, 1972.

David, Elizabeth. *Harvest of the Cold Months: The Social History of Ice and Ices.* New York: Viking, 1995.

R. P. Multhauf/A. R.

See also **Air Pollution; Dairy Industry; Electrification, Household; Food Preservation; Meatpacking; Ozone Depletion.**

REFUGEE ACT OF 1980. The primary goal of the Refugee Act of 1980 was to bring U.S. law into compliance with the requirements of international law. Though domestic U.S. law has long contained provisions designed to protect certain persons fearing persecution, U.S. accession to the 1967 Refugee Protocol created certain specific legal obligations pursuant to the 1951 Convention relating to the Status of Refugees. Years of controversy about these obligations led to the passage of the Refugee Act.

The act contains a definition of the term "refugee" derived from the 1951 convention. The definition includes, in brief, any person unable or unwilling to return to his or her country because of persecution or a well-founded fear of persecution on account of race, religion, nationality, membership in a particular social group, or political opinion. The definition excludes those who have "ordered, incited, assisted or otherwise participated in [such] persecution." The act sought to prohibit the use of so-called "parole" power to admit groups of refugees, prescribing a complex formula and various procedures for refugee admissions that involves both the president and the Congress. In the late twentieth century over 100,000 refugees were authorized for admission pursuant to the act.

In addition the act permits individuals within the United States and at the U.S. border to apply for "asylum" or "restriction on removal," formerly known as "withholding of deportation." Asylum seekers, among other statutory and discretionary requirements, must qualify under the refugee definition. Applicants for restriction on removal, a form of relief derived from Article 33 of the Refugee Convention ("non-refoulement"), must prove a threat to life or freedom. Both refugees and those granted asylum may apply for lawful permanent residence status after they have been physically present in the United States for at least one year.

BIBLIOGRAPHY

Aleinikoff, Thomas Alexander, David A. Martin, and Hiroshi Motomura. *Immigration and Citizenship: Process and Policy.* 4th ed. St. Paul, Minn.: West Group, 1998.

Gordon, Charles, Stanley Mailman, and Stephen Yale-Loehr. *Immigration Law and Procedure.* New York: Matthew Bender, 1988; supplemented through 2002.

Musalo, Karen, Richard A. Boswell, and Jennifer Moore. *Refugee Law and Policy.* Durham, N.C.: Carolina Academic Press, 1997.

Daniel Kanstroom

See also **Green Card; Immigration; Refugees.**

REFUGEES. The idea of a refugee as a person who, for various possible reasons, can no longer live safely in a particular country and is therefore due special care has ancient religious roots. The humanitarian concept of special care owed to refugees has evolved substantially, however, to the point where it has anchored a fundamental shift in accepted notions of human rights under international law.

Ill-Fated Voyage. Two of the more than 900 hopeful German Jewish refugees aboard the *St. Louis*, an ocean liner that docked in Havana, Cuba, in 1939 while Cuban, U.S., and several South American governments refused highly publicized appeals to take them in; forced to return to Europe, most were killed during the German occupation of western Europe. UNITED STATES HOLOCAUST MEMORIAL MUSEUM PHOTO ARCHIVES

The problem of refugees is one of the most important public policy issues in the world today. It is estimated that more than 12 million refugees meet the currently accepted legal definition. However, tens of millions more are "internally displaced" refugees within their own countries. Millions more may be displaced for reasons that are not strictly within the current legal definition. Thus, to speak of refugees is to speak of an evolving set of extremely compelling moral and legal problems.

Refugees and World War II

The modern legal concept of a refugee may be most specifically traced back to 1921, when the League of Nations created a high commissioner for Russian refugees, which led to the development of a specific travel document. This sort of provision, however, proved woefully inadequate to deal with the massive persecutions and displacements of World War II. Part of the reason for this was a lack of public consciousness of and support for the plight of refugees. During the 1930s, the United States government resisted the strenuous efforts of various groups to permit Jewish refugees to flee Nazi persecution in Europe and seek safety in the United States. Although the reasons for this failure were complex, one legal aspect of the debate at the time involved the lack of a specific provision in U.S. immigration law to exempt refugees from generally applicable immigration quotas. During the war years, however, from 1941 to 1945, a series of ad hoc measures permitted more than 200,000 refugees to enter the United States.

After the war, it became clear that the problem of millions of "displaced persons" across Europe was a humanitarian crisis. At the Yalta conference, measures were agreed upon by the Allies that, by the end of 1948, resulted in the repatriation of millions to their native countries. Large numbers of people from Eastern Europe, however, opposed repatriation to their countries of origin because they feared persecution by new governments. Populations in displaced persons' camps grew at an unsustainable pace. At the same time, millions of ethnic Germans were forcibly transferred from various countries to Germany. It became clear that the newly developing West Germany could not and would not accommodate nearly a million displaced persons of various nationalities and ethnic groups. Thus, in 1947, the United Nations established the International Refugee Organization to facilitate the resettlement of the displaced persons in the United States, Canada, Australia, and Western Europe.

The U.S. government began to take the refugee problem more seriously as a matter of law and policy at this time. In 1948, the Displaced Persons Act was enacted, which authorized some 200,000 persons to enter the United States over a two-year period. The law, however, was limited to those who had registered as displaced persons on 22 December 1945, which excluded tens of thousands of people, primarily Jews, who had registered in 1946 and 1947. By 1950, a new law permitted 400,000 more refugees to enter, as it moved the cutoff date to 1 January 1949.

The Refugee Convention
Important developments also took place in international law in the early 1950s. In 1950, the United Nations formally established the Office of the United Nations High Commissioner for Refugees (UNHCR). The mandate of the UNHCR included "providing international protection" for refugees. In addition, permanent solutions were sought in a nonpolitical and humanitarian manner. In 1951, the United Nations adopted the 1951 Convention Relating to the Status of Refugees (the Refugee Convention). Article 1 of the Refugee Convention specifically defined the term "refugee" to include any person who, "as a result of events occurring before 1 January 1951 and owing to well-founded fear of being persecuted for reasons of race, religion, nationality, membership in a particular social group, or political opinion, is outside of the

country of his nationality and is unable, or owing to such fear, is unwilling to avail himself of the protection of that country." The definition also included those who had been considered refugees under certain prior laws and protected certain persons who had no nationality or had multiple nationalities.

The convention included provisions for civil rights for refugees in contracting states and protections against the expulsion of refugees lawfully in their territory "save on grounds of national security or public order." Article 33 specifically prohibited the expulsion or return ("refoulement") of a refugee "in any manner whatsoever to the frontiers of territories where his life or freedom would be threatened" on account of one of the grounds listed above. Article 34 provided that the contracting states "shall as far as possible facilitate the assimilation and naturalization of refugees." Protections under the convention, however, were denied to persons who had committed various types of crimes, especially war crimes, or who had been "guilty of acts contrary to the purposes and principles of the United Nations." Over time, strong sentiment developed to eliminate the 1951 dateline of the convention. Therefore, in 1967, a protocol entered into force that extended the provisions of the 1951 convention without the 1951 dateline.

U.S. Law
The United States did not become a party to the convention until 1968, when it acceded to the 1967 protocol as well. Thus, through the 1950s and 1960s, U.S. actions for refugees were largely ad hoc. Similarly, in the 1970s, though it had ratified the protocol, the United States had no specific statutory mechanism to implement its obligations under the Refugee Convention and Protocol. In 1965, amendments to the 1952 Immigration and Nationality Act had allocated 10,200 visas each year to refugees. However, the definition of refugee was limited to those who had fled "from any Communist or Communist-dominated country or area," from "any country within the general area of the Middle East," or those who were "uprooted by catastrophic natural calamity." As a result, throughout the 1970s, refugee admissions to the United States were highly ideologically biased in favor of those fleeing the Soviet Union and other communist regimes. Special laws continued to be passed for certain groups, such as Hungarians and Cubans. Indeed, to date, more than 500,000 Cubans have become lawful permanent residents as a result of the Cuban Adjustment Act of 1966.

The ostensible goal of the Refugee Act of 1980 was to bring U.S. law into compliance with the requirements of international law. For example, it removed the ideological requirement of flight from a communist country. The Refugee Act sought to prohibit the use of so-called "parole" power to admit groups of refugees as it prescribed a formula and procedures for refugee admissions that involve both the president and the Congress. The act contains a definition of the term "refugee" that is derived from that of the 1951 convention. It excludes those who have "ordered, incited, assisted or otherwise participated in [such] persecution." Since the passage of the act, some 70,000 to 100,000 refugees have been authorized for admission each year. Since its passage, more than a million refugees have obtained permanent resident status.

Such status can be obtained in two basic ways. In addition to overseas application, the law of the United States now permits individuals within the territory and at the border to apply for "asylum" or "restriction on removal" (formerly known as "withholding of deportation"). Both refugees and those granted asylum may apply for lawful permanent residence status after they have been physically present in the United States for at least one year. Asylum seekers must, among other statutory and discretionary requirements, qualify under the statutory refugee definition. Applicants for restriction on removal, a form of relief derived from Article 33 of the Refugee Convention ("non-refoulement"), must prove a threat to life or freedom.

In the decades since its passage, the Refugee Act has been subject to elaborate regulatory explication and extensive judicial interpretation. Among the most important issues in the 1980s were the relationship between the "well-founded fear" standard of proof in the refugee definition and the standard of former section 243(h) of the Immigration and Nationality Act that a person's life or freedom "would be threatened." In *INS v. Stevic* (1984) the Supreme Court held that a noncitizen seeking "withholding of deportation" under the latter standard had to prove a threat was "a clear probability," meaning "more likely than not." As applied to asylum-seekers this holding seemed to contradict accepted understandings about the burden of proof for a refugee claiming a "well-founded fear." The issue was resolved by the Supreme Court in *INS v. Cardoza-Fonseca* (1987). The Court made clear that a well-founded fear meant something less than "more likely than not." As the Court put it, "One can certainly have a well-founded fear of an event happening when there is less than a 50 percent chance of the occurrence taking place."

Since the passage of the Refugee Act the United States and other Western nations have confronted serious theoretical and practical problems in the development of refuge and asylum law. Throughout the 1980s, for example, according to many refugee rights advocates, considerable ideological bias remained in the supposedly objective refugee and asylum process of the United States. On the other hand, increasingly large numbers of asylum applicants caused political backlash, which was often accompanied by charges that the refugee/asylum system was being abused. One of the first major governmental responses to this allegation was an "interdiction" program, started during the Reagan administration, that authorized U.S. officials to board Haitian vessels on the high seas and forcibly return the vessel to Haiti. Although the United States agreed that it would not return any refugee

to Haiti, human rights organizations and others criticized the program as a violation of basic principles of human rights. The Supreme Court, however, ultimately upheld the interdiction program in *Sale v. Haitian Centers Council* (1993), holding that neither section 243(h) of the Immigration and Nationality Act nor Article 33 of the U.N. protocol apply to actions taken by the Coast Guard on the high seas. The program, however, was eventually discontinued by the Clinton administration.

In the mid-1990s, continuing criticism of asylum practices in the United States spawned further special measures such as increased authority to border personnel, known in the United States as "expedited removal," and time limits on filing claims. Such measures were designed to distinguish legitimate from fraudulent or frivolous claims and to discourage the latter. Another such measure, applied in Europe but not the United States as of 2002, is the development of lists of "safe" countries from which asylum claimants may be presumed ineligible. A variant on this theme is an agreement whereby states may agree on which country will adjudicate a claim made by a person who has traveled through signatory states en route to the place where asylum is finally claimed. The United States has authorized such agreements by statute but to date has concluded no such bilateral arrangement with another country.

Certain substantive issues have also generated great controversy. In 1996, for example, after years of debate and litigation over asylum claims arising out of China's so-called "one-couple, one-child" policy, the U.S. Congress amended the statutory definition of a refugee. The new definition includes "a person who has been forced to abort a pregnancy or to undergo involuntary sterilization, or who has been persecuted for failure or refusal to undergo such a procedure or for other resistance to a coercive population control program." The question whether neutrality can constitute a political opinion spawned years of complex litigation, though the Supreme Court's decision in *INS v. Elias-Zacarias* (1992) established some guidelines. In the 1990s powerful arguments were also made, with considerable success, to expand the protections of refugee and asylum law to women who face harsh or inhuman treatment due to their gender, women who suffer more specific physical and mental abuse by men in societies where legal protection may be unavailable, women who flee the practice of female genital mutilation, and people who fear persecution on account of their sexual orientation.

Among the more interesting recent legislative trends in the United States has been the ratification of the Convention Against Torture (CAT), which protects the removal or extradition of any person to a state "where there are substantial grounds for believing that he would be in danger of being subjected to torture." The United States passed implementing legislation in 1998 and CAT claims in the United States are now an important source of protection. Finally, special temporary protection laws, such as so-called "Temporary Protected Status" in the United States, have aided many persons fleeing natural disasters and others with compelling claims that do not fit within the refugee law parameters.

BIBLIOGRAPHY

Aleinkoff, T. Alexander, David A. Martin, and Hiroshi Motomura. *Immigration and Citizenship Process and Policy.* 4th ed. St. Paul, Minn.: West Group, 1998.

Goodwin-Gill, Guy S. *The Refugee in International Law.* 2d ed. Oxford: Clarendon Press, 1996.

Legomsky, Stephen H. *Immigration and Refugee Law and Policy.* 3d ed. New York: Foundation Press, 2002.

Musalo, Karen, Jennifer Moore, and Richard Boswell. *Refugee Law and Policy.* Durham, N.C.: Carolina Academic Press, 1997.

Daniel Kanstroom

See also **United Nations;** *and vol. 9:* **Excerpt from Maya in Exile: Guatemalans in Florida.**

REGULATORS were vigilantes. The term was used by the 5,000 to 6,000 Regulators in the Carolinas between 1767 and 1771, adopted from an earlier, short-lived London police auxiliary. Most American regulators sought to protect their communities from outlaws and tyrannical public officials. Some groups employed summary execution; more employed flogging and exile. Regulators were active in almost every state, peaking recurrently from the 1790s to the late 1850s. After 1865, a few Regulator groups flourished, mainly in Missouri, Kentucky, Indiana, and Florida. Some interfered with freedmen, but most concentrated on crime deterrence and punishment. Similar organizations included Slickers, law and order leagues, citizens' committees, vigilance committees, and committees of safety.

BIBLIOGRAPHY

Brown, Richard Maxwell. *The South Carolina Regulators.* Cambridge, Mass.: Harvard University Press, 1963.

———. "The American Vigilante Tradition." In *The History of Violence in America.* Edited by Hugh Davis Graham and Ted Robert Gurr. New York: Bantam Books, 1969.

Powell, William S., James K. Huhta, and Thomas J. Farnham. *The Regulators in North Carolina: A Documentary History, 1759–1776.* Raleigh, N.C.: State Department of Archives and History, 1971.

Steve Sheppard

See also **Vigilantes.**

REITMAN V. MULKEY, 387 U.S. 369 (1967). The 1963 California legislature, voting nearly along party lines, passed the Rumford Act prohibiting racial discrimination in the sale or rental of part of the state's housing. Soon after, the California Real Estate Association sponsored Proposition 14, a state constitutional amendment banning fair housing measures by California state or local governments. Strongly supported by the Republican Party, Proposition 14 was ratified by the state's voters in November 1964 by nearly two to one. The NAACP's challenge to Proposition 14 on behalf of Lincoln Mulkey failed in Orange County, but its appeal succeeded, by five votes to two, in the California Supreme Court and by five to four in the U.S. Supreme Court. Since 1967, housing discrimination has lessened, but not disappeared. Although the decision has never been explicitly overruled, it was silently sidestepped when the Ninth Circuit Court of Appeals, with the Supreme Court's acquiescence, rejected a challenge to California Proposition 209, which banned affirmative action to overcome past and present racial discrimination.

BIBLIOGRAPHY

Casstevens, Thomas W. *Politics, Housing, and Race Relations: California's Rumford Act and Proposition 14.* Berkeley: Institute for Governmental Studies, 1967.

Karst, Kenneth L., and Harold W. Horowitz. "Reitman v. Mulkey: A Telophase of Substantive Equal Protection." *Supreme Court Review* (1967): 39–80.

J. Morgan Kousser

RELIEF. *See* **Welfare System.**

RELIGION AND RELIGIOUS AFFILIATION. When European scholars and church leaders visited early-nineteenth-century America, they were quick to comment on the religious freedoms of the new nation. Reporting on his 1831–1832 visit in the now famous *Democracy in America*, Alexis de Tocqueville wrote that the "religious aspect of the country was the first thing that struck my attention." Tocqueville was not alone. Francis Grund from Austria, Andrew Reed from England, Philip Schaff of Germany, and many others commented on the "voluntary principle" of religion, the peculiar "religious economy," and the religious "exceptionalism" of the new nation. In their European homelands, church and state had strong formal ties. American churches, by contrast, received no financial support from the state and faced few regulations.

What most intrigued the visitors was that severing ties between church and state appeared to invigorate rather than decimate the religious life of the nation. Alexis de Tocqueville reported that it became his objective to discover how "the real authority of religion was increased by a state of things which diminished its apparent force." Writing for their European audiences, the visitors explained how the new religious freedoms of the voluntary principle contributed to a host of new preachers (many unpaid) and the building of more churches. With obvious enthusiasm they reported on the population's voluntary and generous contributions of time and money for their churches. Yet they expressed strong concerns over the proliferation of sects that were openly disagreeing over church teachings and aggressively competing for members. Finally, they marveled at the churches' ability to gain support from a broad cross-section of the population. They noted how the diversity of churches reflected the diversity of the population, with each of the major religious traditions of Europe being represented in the new nation. The consequences the European visitors associated with the new religious freedoms have persisted throughout American history.

The freedoms identified by the Europeans have continued to fuel religious changes. Indeed, the history of American religion is a story of constant change. For many observers, the most surprising change is that religious participation has dramatically increased over time. As shown in Figure 1 less than 20 percent of Americans were active in church affairs in 1776. Throughout the twentieth century, church membership included more than half of all Americans. Voluntary contributions and the value of church property have shown similar trends, with contributions to religious organizations still towering over other forms of voluntary charitable giving. But some of the most dramatic changes have occurred in the shape of the religious landscape. The dominant colonial mainline religions (Congregational, Presbyterian, and Anglican), holding the allegiance of more than half of colonial church adherents, plummeted in the nineteenth century and now claim the loyalties of approximately 5 percent of all adherents. Meanwhile, a handful of marginal religious minorities and ethnic religious enclaves of past eras have become powerful mainline denominations today. This proliferation and growth of sects, which so alarmed the European visitors, shows no signs of slowing. Religious diversity continues to mirror the diversity of the population as new religious movements frequently emerge and im-

migrants introduce and promote their religions. Gordon Melton's most recent *Encyclopedia of American Religions* reports on more than 1,500 religious movements in the United States.

This brief sketch of major changes in religious affiliation over the course of American history inevitably omits many important religions, eras, and events. For a more complete review, readers may consult the sources listed in the bibliography.

Colonial Religion

Americans are burdened with more nostalgic illusions about the colonial era than any other period in our history. Our conceptions of that era are dominated by a few powerful images, such as the Pilgrims walking through the woods to church and the first Thanksgiving. What these myths fail to illustrate is that the colonies were open frontiers, oriented toward commercial profits, and were typically filled with a high percentage of recent immigrants lacking social ties. As in other frontier areas throughout history this resulted in high levels of social deviance (crime, prostitution, and alcohol abuse) and low levels of church involvement. Even the celebrated Puritan settlements in New England, with their high initial levels of involvement, were showing increasing signs of religious apathy and dissent by the mid-1600s. Neither the second generation nor the new immigrants shared the fervor of the founders.

Levels of religious deviance as well as social deviance were high, including alternative religious practices outside the church and corrupt clergy within the church. Magic, the occult, and the practice of witchcraft were all part of the colonial experience. The witchcraft and witch hunts of New England are the most famous, but the practices were probably more common in other colonies. When Reverend Henry Muhlenberg arrived in 1742 to put the affairs of the Pennsylvania Lutherans in order, he was appalled by the religious deviance he found in and outside the church. He charged that Pennsylvania, the colony with the most Lutherans and one of the highest rates of religious adherence, had more necromancers than Christians. Muhlenberg's sharpest criticism, however, was aimed at the fraudulent clergy selling religious services, confessing faiths they did not hold, and taking part in activities prohibited by the church.

Lutherans were not alone in their struggle against fraudulent and immoral clergy. Anglican vestrymen complained that many of their clergy left England to avoid debts, wives, and onerous duties, viewing the colonies as a place of refuge and retirement. Both the Anglicans and the Lutherans faced a common problem: their reliance on European clergy resulted in a severe shortage, forcing them to accept any clergy who would make the trip across the Atlantic and allowing all forms of religious deviance to arise in the areas where clergy could not be provided.

Struggling to survive in this new frontier were the ill-equipped offshoots of Europe's state churches. In the

FIGURE 1

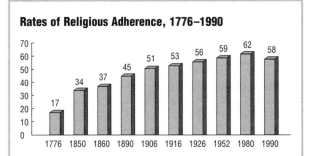

Rates of Religious Adherence, 1776–1990

SOURCE: For 1776 data, see Stark and Finke 1988; for 1850–1926, see Finke and Stark 1986 and 1992; for 1952, see Zelinsky 1961; and for 1980, see Stark 1987. Using the *Churches and Church Membership in the United States, 1990* and multiple other sources, the authors calculated the 1990 rate.

NOTE: Adherents include adult members and their children.

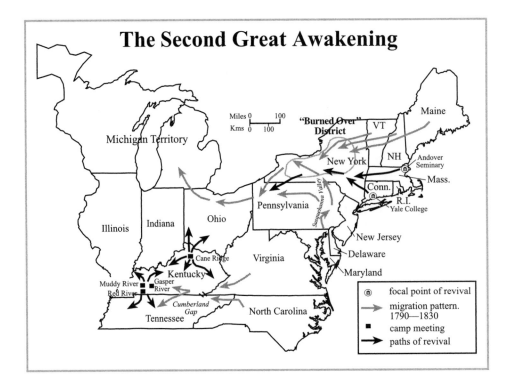

The Second Great Awakening

southern colonies, the Anglican Church (Church of England) attempted to serve as the official establishment. Despite receiving financial support from the state and sporadically regulating dissenters, the Anglican establishment proved ineffective in all of the southern colonies except Virginia. By 1776 (see Table 1) the dissenting religions had far more congregations than the Anglicans throughout the South.

In New England the Congregational establishment was substantially more effective in regulating dissenters, receiving state support, and appealing to the people. With the exception of Roger Williams's Rhode Island, where the Congregational Church was never the establishment, more than 60 percent of all New England churches were Congregational in 1776.

In the middle colonies, the picture is far more mixed. Pennsylvania, New Jersey, and Delaware had no religious establishments and were known as bastions of religious toleration. Although New York and Maryland supported Anglican establishments for most of the colonial era, New York began as a Dutch colony and Maryland was started as a haven for Catholics. Both retained a high level of religious diversity. The middle colonies were also ethnically diverse. Along with hosting religions of British origin, the middle colonies were home to the German and Dutch Reformed, the German and Swedish Lutherans, and the Moravians. When the first U.S. Census was conducted in 1790, only New York, New Jersey, and Pennsylvania had less than 65 percent of their population being of British descent

By the middle of the eighteenth century, three significant developments had occurred. First, religious toleration was increasingly practiced throughout the colonies. The growing diversity of the settlers and their religions,

TABLE 1

Percentages of All Adherents in 1776, by Geographical Region

	New England	Middle Colonies	Southern Colonies
Congregationalist	63.0%	0.3%	0.1%
Presbyterian	5.5	24.6	24.9
Baptist	15.3	7.6	28.0
Anglican (Episcopal)	8.4	12.9	27.8
Quaker	3.8	14.1	9.0
German Reformed	0.0	9.8	2.8
Lutheran	0.0	8.6	3.8
Dutch Reformed	0.0	8.9	0.0
Methodist	0.0	3.8	1.4
Roman Catholic	0.0	4.2	0.1
Moravian	0.0	1.8	0.6
Other	3.6	3.1	1.2

SOURCE: For 1776 data, see Stark and Finke 1988; for 1850–1926, see Finke and Stark 1986 and 1992; for 1952, see Zelinsky 1961; and for 1980, see Stark 1987. Using the *Churches and Church Membership in the United States, 1990* and multiple other sources, the authors calculated the 1990 rate.

NOTE: Adherents include adult members and their children.

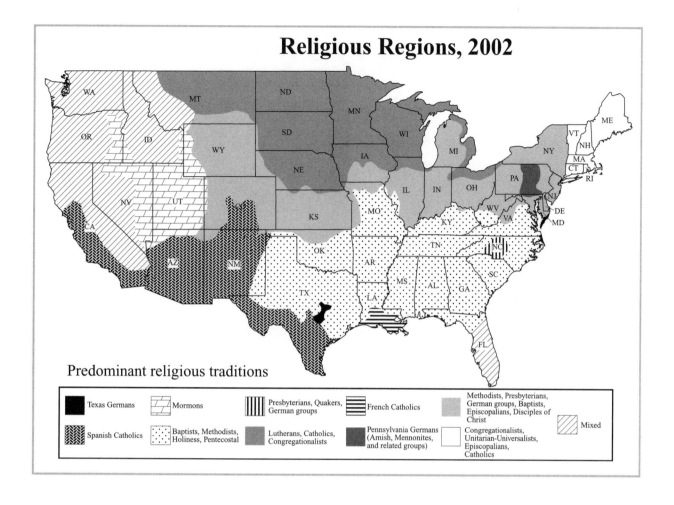

Religious Regions, 2002

Predominant religious traditions

■ Texas Germans	Mormons
Spanish Catholics	Baptists, Methodists, Holiness, Pentecostal
Presbyterians, Quakers, German groups	Lutherans, Catholics, Congregationalists
French Catholics	Pennsylvania Germans (Amish, Mennonites, and related groups)
Methodists, Presbyterians, German groups, Baptists, Episcopalians, Disciples of Christ	Congregationalists, Unitarian-Universalists, Episcopalians, Catholics
Mixed	

combined with the vast amount of space, a desire for profitable colonies, and the religious apathy of most residents, resulted in eroding support for the establishments. Second, the 1730s and 1740s introduced new methods for conducting religious revivals. George Whitefield, in particular, demonstrated how itinerant preaching, extensive promotions, and an emotional plea for conversion could appeal to the populace. Third, many of the distinctive Native American cultures and their religions were annihilated. The devastating effects of European diseases, combined with frequent warfare, resulted in the extinction of 100 to 200 Native American groups. Each of these developments would shape the religion of the new nation. Native American religions, like their cultures, would continue to face the threat of extinction; the new methods for conducting religious revivals, including itinerant preaching, would be openly embraced by new sects; and the eroding establishments would give way to a religious diversity that few could then imagine.

In 1776, there were an estimated 3,228 churches in the colonies and a total population of approximately 2.5 million. Even if we estimate 130 adherents per church, a number that exceeds the capacity of most colonial churches, less than one in five residents was active in a local church.

Unleashing the Upstart Sects

As geographic size, economic interests, and increasing religious diversity pushed the colonies toward an increased acceptance of religious toleration, an unlikely alliance between the rationalists (such as Thomas Jefferson) and the evangelical dissenting religions (such as Baptists) pulled the colonies toward religious freedom. Despite the disparity in the background and training of the rationalist and evangelical leaders, they agreed that religion was a concern for God and the individual, and that the state should not intervene. The rationalists often deplored the religious fervor of the new sects, and the evangelicals were clearly at odds with the beliefs of many rationalists, but the alliance proved effective as the rationalists provided legal justification for the emotional pleas of the evangelicals. In 1791 the First Amendment promised that "Congress shall make no law respecting an establishment of religion, or prohibiting the free exercise thereof." De facto establishments remained, and many states still refused to give religious liberties to Catholics, Jews, and those opposing a Protestant Christianity, but the regulation of religion was declining rapidly. There would be no national church, and the groundwork was laid for a continuing separation of church and state.

Camp Meeting. A few of the more than 5,000 worshipers, along with 50 members of the clergy, attending a religious camp meeting in Eastham, Mass., in 1851—part of the surge of nineteenth-century revivalism embraced by, and greatly benefiting, the Methodists and Baptists in particular.
© CORBIS

The first to take advantage of these new freedoms were the Methodists, Baptists, and other upstart sects. They quickly generated a legion of clergy throughout the new nation. Although few had seminary training, and many lacked even a grade-school education, they held an unbridled fervor for spreading their religious message. Both the Methodists and Baptists made it easy for gifted laymen to enter the ministry. Among the Baptists, the preacher was often a man of local origins whose call was ratified by his fellow congregants. The Baptist position was simple: God never called an unprepared man to preach. Receiving little or no pay, Baptist clergy typically earned their living behind a plow, like other members of the congregation. The Methodists' local church also relied on the voluntary services of class leaders and local preachers. Even the highly visible circuit riders, who supervised and coordinated the activities of the churches in their circuits, received little pay. One consequence of having untrained and often unpaid clergy was that their message was heartfelt and in the vernacular. Rather than offer an articulate and carefully drafted sermon based on years of seminary training, they used emotional pleas to arouse faith and call for spiritual conversion. This method of calling clergy also allowed the Methodists and Baptists to sustain a congregation anywhere a few people would gather. The clergy's low pay reduced the start-up costs of new churches, and because clergy could be called from the local congregation, there was seldom an absence of

clergy. The result was that the upstarts seemed to thrive everywhere.

But as the new sects thrived, the former colonial mainline denominations struggled. The two colonial establishments, the Anglicans (now Episcopalians) and Congregationalists, fared the worst. Accustomed to a parish system, where clergy and congregation received state support for serving a prescribed area, the old establishments were ill-prepared for the free-wheeling, no-holds barred approach of the upstarts. The Congregational clergy (and Harvard faculty) had objected to Whitefield's preaching in areas served by Congregational churches. Now they faced a more formidable challenge. Whereas Whitefield was content to preach revival, the upstarts were starting new churches and appealing to the membership of their churches. The Congregationalists, Episcopalians, and Presbyterians also failed to match the upstarts' supply of clergy. Relying on seminary-trained clergy, they faced a constant shortage. Moreover, because the clergy expected financial support from the congregation, they were less willing to go to the new frontiers where accommodations and support were lacking.

Finally, the old colonial mainline and the new upstarts differed in their acceptance of the new methods of revivalism. The upstarts openly embraced the new methods, but the new revivalism became a source of bitter dispute and schism for the colonial mainline. After helping to organize one of the earliest and most successful frontier revivals, Cane Ridge, Barton Stone, and other Presbyterian clergy were charged with insubordination for failing to affirm strict Calvinist doctrines. Stone and his followers soon began their own religious movement, which later joined the Cambellites to form the Christian Church. In sharp contrast, the Baptists and Methodists actively promoted revivals. The famous Methodist bishop Francis Asbury was effusive in his praise of camp meetings and advised his clergy to replace the circuit's summer quarterly meeting with a revivalist camp meeting. Writing in his *Journal and Letters*, he described camp meetings as "fishing with a large net" and the "battle ax and weapon of war" against wickedness. The Baptist and Christian Church movements agreed.

The differences in membership growth were dramatic. Figure 2 reports on religious adherents (membership including children) for each denomination as a percentage of all adherents in the nation. Of all Americans active in a religious denomination in 1776, more than half (55 percent) belonged to one of the three major colonial religions: Congregationalist, Episcopalian, or Presbyterian. By 1850 the percentage plummeted to 19 percent. All of the groups continued to gain members, but none could keep pace with the upstarts, and only the Presbyterians continued to grow at a pace roughly equal to the growth of the population.

The Methodists and Baptists, however, grew at a pace that far exceeded population growth throughout the new nation. The Methodists, in particular, skyrocketed from 2.5 percent to 34.2 percent. Part of this growth came from the upstarts' ability to adapt to the expanding frontiers, an area where the colonial mainline churches were slow to go. But they also showed sustained growth in areas where communities and congregations were well founded. Table 2 shows that even in New England, the heart of the Congregational stronghold, the upstarts were rapidly dominating the religious landscape. Regardless of the location, the Baptists and Methodists were appealing to a growing segment of the population.

The appeal of the Methodists and Baptists was also evident in the growing African American population. Prior to 1776, few enslaved Africans converted to Christianity. But following the Revolutionary era, the Methodists and Baptists began preaching, with results. *The Minutes of the Methodist Conferences in America, 1773–1813* reports that even as late as 1785 there were only 1,890 "colored" Methodists, or about 9 percent of all Methodists. By 1813 about 20 percent (42,859 members) of all Methodists were African American. The upstart churches offered an emotional worship style leading to a personal conversion experience and allowed African Americans to exercise a leadership that was denied in all other areas of their life. Overcoming numerous legal and social obstacles, African

FIGURE 2

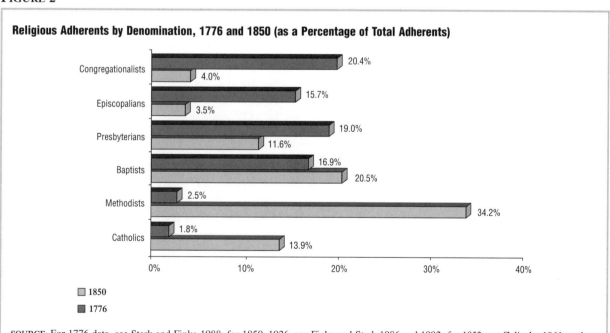

Religious Adherents by Denomination, 1776 and 1850 (as a Percentage of Total Adherents)

SOURCE: For 1776 data, see Stark and Finke 1988; for 1850–1926, see Finke and Stark 1986 and 1992; for 1952, see Zelinsky 1961; and for 1980, see Stark 1987. Using the *Churches and Church Membership in the United States, 1990* and multiple other sources, the authors calculated the 1990 rate.

NOTE: Adherents include adult members and their children.

TABLE 2

Percentages of All Adherents in Major Denominations, 1776 and 1850.

	1776	1850
NEW ENGLAND*		
Congregational Establishment	67%	28%
Baptist and Methodist	12%	41%
Roman Catholic	0%	11%
MAINE		
Congregational Establishment	61%	19%
Baptist and Methodist	8%	58%
Roman Catholics	0%	6%
NEW HAMPSHIRE		
Congregational Establishment	63%	30%
Baptist and Methodist	9%	46%
Roman Catholics	0%	3%
VERMONT		
Congregational Establishment	65%	29%
Baptist and Methodist	10%	4%
Roman Catholics	0%	6%
MASSACHUSETTS		
Congregational Establishment	72%	29%
Baptist and Methodist	15%	33%
Roman Catholics	0%	17%
CONNECTICUT		
Congregational Establishment	64%	37%
Baptist and Methodist	9%	39%
Roman Catholics	0%	11%

*New England totals exclude Rhode Island, which never supported an established church.

SOURCE: For 1776 data, see Stark and Finke 1988; for 1850–1926, see Finke and Stark 1986 and 1992; for 1952, see Zelinsky 1961; and for 1980, see Stark 1987. Using the *Churches and Church Membership in the United States, 1990* and multiple other sources, the authors calculated the 1990 rate.

NOTE: Adherents include adult members and their children.

Americans also began to form their own churches in the North.

Recall from Figure 1 that the percentage of the population active in a church jumped from 17 percent to 34 percent between 1776 and 1850. The rapid growth of the Protestant upstarts, especially the stunning growth of the Methodists, made this increase possible. But the Protestant upstarts were not the only groups growing. Figure 2 and Table 2 also reveal that the Catholics were showing sizable and rapid increases—a growth that would swell in the remainder of the century. A plethora of new religious movements was also emerging. Most would fall into decline or expire before the end of the century. But a few, such as the Mormons and Adventists, would experience a persistent growth throughout the nineteenth and twentieth centuries.

Building Religious Communities

The religious freedoms of the new nation not only allowed the new religions to compete for members without fear of persecution or penalty; they also forced the local churches to become more responsive to the people. Churches became an institutional free space where even oppressed minorities could build a church that was responsive to their needs. After the Civil War, the millions of new immigrants and freed slaves created churches that catered to unique language, political, social, and religious needs. Despite holding limited resources, they effectively built institutions that carried their unique religious identity and culture.

Annual immigration to the United States first exceeded 200,000 in 1847 and, with the exception of the Civil War era and a brief interval in the 1870s, immigration never dropped below 200,000 until 1931. The initial waves of immigrants were from Ireland, Germany, and later Scandinavia. By the end of the century, however, the boats were filled with central, eastern, and southern European immigrants. During an 80-year time span (1850–1930), more than 35 million immigrants arrived—immigrants who changed America.

The most dramatic shift in American religion was the rapid growth of Roman Catholics. As shown in Figure 3, Roman Catholicism was the largest denomination in the nation by the end of the nineteenth century. This might seem inevitable, with the heavy flow of immigrants from

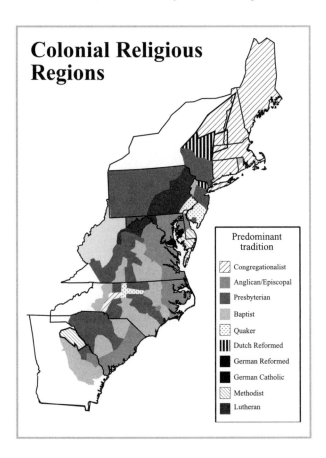

Colonial Religious Regions

Predominant tradition

- Congregationalist
- Anglican/Episcopal
- Presbyterian
- Baptist
- Quaker
- Dutch Reformed
- German Reformed
- German Catholic
- Methodist
- Lutheran

predominantly Catholic nations. In truth, however, most of the millions of immigrants from "Catholic" nations were at best potential American Catholic parishioners. To tap this potential, the Roman Catholic Church had to counteract the vigorous efforts of Protestant sects to recruit these immigrants and it had to activate them to entirely new levels of commitment and participation. The techniques they used were remarkably similar to their Protestant counterparts. At the center of this new evangelical surge was the Catholic revival campaign they called the parish mission. Using uniquely Catholic ritual, symbolism, and ceremony, the traveling evangelists would seek to stir the spirit and save the soul. Like the Protestants, Catholics aggressively recruited new members into the church.

Once they were recruited, the Catholic parish offered new parishioners a distinctive Catholic society. From social groups to schools to literature, American Catholicism created a subculture that was parallel yet separate from the hostile dominant culture. Like Protestant sectarian movements, they stressed a distinctive lifestyle and placed high demands on their membership. But the Catholic subculture was strengthened by yet another dimension: ethnicity. Deviating from strict territorial parishes, they also founded national churches organized around a common language and nationality. As late as 1916 nearly half (49 percent) of all Catholic parishes held worship services in a language other than English. Considering that English was the native tongue for Irish-American parishes, this is a strong testimony to the ethnic identity of the local parish.

The Protestant and Jewish immigrants would follow a similar pattern. The churches and synagogues quickly learned that they must appeal to the new immigrants or lose them to the aggressive sects. When Friedrich Wyneken wrote his *Notruf* (Distress Call) to German religious and social leaders in 1843, he warned of the "dangerous" and large number of sects in America. He explained that "there is hardly a Lutheran or Reformed congregation which does not suffer from these swarming pests." Like the Catholics, the Protestant and Jewish immigrants developed institutions (often emphasizing educational institutions) that paralleled those in the dominant culture and offered a unique appeal to the new immigrants.

For the Lutheran and Reformed traditions, denominations were soon formed around nationality and the recency of their immigration. Composed of recent Dutch immigrants, the Christian Reformed Church (CRC) split from the Reformed Church of America (RCA) to form a more distinctive Dutch Christian church. Not surprisingly, 90 percent of the CRC congregations held services in a foreign language, compared to only 35 percent in the RCA. The Lutherans were fractured into more than 20 different denominations based on nationality, recency of immigration, region of the country, and doctrine. The denominational nationalities included German, Norwegian, Swedish, Icelandic, Slovak, Danish, and Finnish.

Once again, the more recent immigrants retained a more distinctive ethnic subculture and more frequently held services in a foreign language.

Finally, Jewish immigrants faced similar divisions. The immigrants arriving before 1880 tended to be German, middle class, and were seeking to more fully assimilate. After 1880, a flood of poor, rural eastern European immigrants developed a distinctively Jewish enclave. Yiddish became the vernacular and, in New York alone, the number of Jews increased from 80,000 in 1880 to more than 1 million by 1910.

Protestant, Catholic, and Jewish enclaves all served a dual role. Despite separating the new immigrants from a foreign world and supporting a distinctive religious and ethnic subculture, the enclaves also served to assimilate immigrants into the larger culture. Many of the institutions in the immigrant enclaves paralleled those in the dominant culture, providing immigrants with the skills, information, and training needed for success in the new land. Educational, recreational, and social service institutions are the most obvious examples, but the mutual benefit societies, professional associations, and social networks all served to integrate immigrants into the new nation.

The most impressive institution building of this era, however, was the development and growth of African American churches. After the slave revolts in the 1830s, the slaves were seldom allowed to hold public religious services without white supervision—a restriction that limited the formal development of African American churches in the South before the Civil War. Following the Civil War, however, the African American churches became the key institution for uniting the former slaves, training new leaders, and building a new community. In 1890 the Bureau of the Census' *Report on Statistics of Churches* reported 19,448 churches in the Baptist and Methodist African American denominations alone, with well over 2 million adult members. When children are included in the membership count, the 1890 adherence rate for African Americans is 6 points higher (51 percent) than for the nation as a whole. Because many African Americans remained members in predominantly white denominations, the actual rate is even higher. In less than 25 years they built institutions that helped mobilize the African American community throughout the twentieth century.

As African Americans and new immigrants were making bold changes to the religious landscape, other, more subtle shifts were taking place. All of the major denominations were increasing their membership totals, but as a percentage of all Americans involved in religion their rates were falling (see Figure 3). The Episcopalians and Baptists showed a slight decline, the rates for Congregationalists, Presbyterians, and Methodists plummeted. A part of this change can be explained by the immigrants' attraction to churches supporting their language and ethnicity. Catholic, Lutheran, Reformed, and Jewish congregations, and their cultural enclaves, held a unique appeal.

FIGURE 3

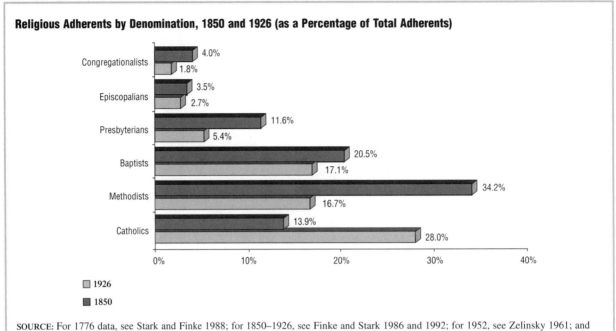

Religious Adherents by Denomination, 1850 and 1926 (as a Percentage of Total Adherents)

1926
1850

SOURCE: For 1776 data, see Stark and Finke 1988; for 1850–1926, see Finke and Stark 1986 and 1992; for 1952, see Zelinsky 1961; and for 1980, see Stark 1987. Using the *Churches and Church Membership in the United States, 1990* and multiple other sources, the authors calculated the 1990 rate.

NOTE: Adherents include adult members and their children.

But this doesn't explain the sudden changes for the Methodists. When they moved from a sect served by itinerant and untrained clergy promoting revivals to a mainstream denomination with settled and seminary-trained clergy, their growth rates began to resemble those of mainline churches. As they drifted from their moorings of holiness teachings and revivalism at the turn of the century, they also spawned a series of holiness sects protesting these changes. Most would fade away, but a few served as catalysts for growing denominations in the twentieth century.

Expanding Pluralism

With the Immigration Act of 1924 taking effect in 1929 and with the onset of the Great Depression, the pace of change in American religion seemed to slow. Immigration dropped sharply from more than 4.3 million in the 1920s to less than 700,000 in the 1930s, and the existing immigrants were gradually assimilating into the American culture. Even the mainline denominations seemed to receive a short reprieve from their long declines. As shown in Table 3, the changes between 1925 and 1950 were modest for all of the major denominations, with the Episcopalians even showing a substantial increase. This proved to be the calm before the storm.

In the latter portion of the twentieth century, major shifts in American Protestantism reemerged. First, the mainline Protestant religions continued their long decline. When measured as a percentage of the population,

the 1999 adherence rates of United Methodists, American Baptists, and the United Church of Christ (including the Congregationalists) were half or less of their 1950 rates. For the first time, their membership totals also showed significant declines. The other mainline denominations and Judaism also showed declines.

The Catholics and the older evangelical denominations, Southern Baptists and Lutheran Church–Missouri Synod, showed rapid growth until 1975 but have now started to plateau and even decline. The more recently emerging evangelical groups, however, have continued to show a rapid growth. Emerging in the early twentieth century, the two small pentecostal groups, Assemblies of God and Pentecostal Assemblies of the World, Inc., now outnumber the Congregationalists (United Church of Christ). The reliability of the data for African American denominations is weak, but the trend appears to be similar to the other Protestant denominations. The new African American pentecostal denomination, Church of God in Christ, is showing the most rapid growth.

Finally, the Church of Jesus Christ of the Latter-Day Saints (Mormons) and the Jehovah's Witnesses, which were minuscule religious outsiders in the nineteenth century, are showing consistent and rapid growth. Once largely confined to the state of Utah, the Mormons are now making a presence throughout the United States.

By the late 1960s, however, new religious outsiders were arriving in increasing numbers, once again altering

TABLE 3

Church Adherence Rates for Major Denominations (Adherents Per 1000 Population)

	1925	1950	1975	1999
Mainline Protestant Denominations				
The United Methodist Church	66	64	46	31
Evangelical Lutheran Church in America	15	26	25	19
Presbyterian Church (USA)	21	21	16	13
Episcopal Church	10	17 (1949)	13	9
Greek Orthodox Archdiocese of North and South America	2	7 (1947)	9	7 (1998)
American Baptist Churches in the USA	13	10	7	5
United Church of Christ	14	13 (1949)	8	5
The Orthodox Church in America	2	3	5	4
Evangelical Protestant Denominations				
Southern Baptist Convention	31	47	59	58
The Lutheran Church— Missouri Synod	5	11	13	10
Assemblies of God	.4	2	6	9
Pentecostal Assemblies of the World, Inc.	.06 (1937)	.3	2 (1989)	6 (1998)
African American Protestant Denominations				
Church of God in Christ	2 (1933)	N/A	14 (1973)	20
National Baptist Convention, USA, Inc.	29 (1936)	29	32 (1958)	30 (1989)
National Baptist Convention of America	26	17	16 (1956)	15 (1987)
African Methodist Episcopal Church	6	8	9 (1978)	9
African Methodist Episcopal Zion Church	4	4	5 (1973)	5
Other				
The Church of Jesus Christ of Latter-Day Saints	7	7	11	19
Jehovah's Witnesses	N/A	1 (1955)	3	7
The Catholic Church (Roman Catholic)	139	189	227	229
Judaism	32 (1937)	33	28	24 (1990)

SOURCE: All information is from the *Yearbook of American and Canadian Churches,* except for the most recent Jewish and National Baptist Convention, USA estimates and the 1973 estimate for the Church of God in Christ.

NOTES: 1) Reported rates are rates of church adherence per 1000 members of the population, rather than the percentage of church adherents reported elsewhere. Because the total number of adherents was unknown for most years, the percentage of total church adherents could not be calculated. 2) All estimates before 1999 adjust for mergers and splits among denominations by including all denominations that comprise the denomination in question in 1999.

the landscape of American religion. When the 1965 amendments to the Immigration and Nationality Act replaced country-of-origin quotas with a single quota for the Eastern and Western Hemisphere, immigration to the United States increased and the sources of immigration suddenly shifted. Immigration from India, for example, rose from 467 in 1965 to 2,293 the next year, and now runs around 30,000 a year. For Asia as a whole, immigration went from a modest 20,040 in 1965 to an average of nearly 150,000 per year in the 1970s and more than 250,000 in the 1980s. Immigration from Latin America, especially Mexico, was sizable before 1965, rose sharply throughout the 1970s, and remained the largest current of immigration in the 1980s and 1990s. In 1960 about 75 percent of all foreign-born residents were born in Europe. Forty years later (2000) 15 percent of the foreign-born were from Europe, 26 percent were from Asia, and 51 percent were from Latin America. This sudden shift in the nationality of immigrants has brought immediate changes to American religion.

One of the most potent effects of this new wave of immigrants is that world religions other than Christianity are being introduced to America. Buddhism and Hinduism are making a presence throughout the nation, with approximately 400 Hindu temples and more than 1,500 Buddhist temples rising. Estimates for Muslims are often erratic, but a series of major surveys projects their membership at approximately 2 million. These religions are also reaching beyond the confines of the immigrant enclaves. Although most were founded to serve the new immigrants, Buddhist temples have proven effective in appealing to middle-class whites, and the Islamic mosques are enrolling increasing numbers of African Americans. Although still small, these movements are having an impact on American religion.

Most immigrants, however, are reshaping the European foundations of American Christianity. The large flow of Latin Americans is redefining American Catholicism and is having a growing impact on American Protestantism, especially the pentecostal groups. More than 25 percent of all Americans identifying themselves as Catholic are now Hispanic. Even from nations where Christians are a minority, a disproportionate number of Christians emigrate and many convert to Christianity after they arrive. South Korea, for example, is 25 percent Christian, but an estimated 50 percent of Korean immigrants are Christian and half of the remainder join Christian churches after arriving in the United States. China holds only a small minority of Christians, yet the number of Chinese Protestant churches in the United States jumped from 66 in 1952 to 697 by 1994.

Often the immigrants bring distinctive versions of Catholicism and Protestantism. Many Chinese Christians find that the family-oriented and theologically conservative teachings of evangelical Protestantism are congruent with Confucian principles. Supporting more than 3,500 Spanish masses, Hispanics are giving new emphasis to the emotional or charismatic aspects of Catholicism. Immigrant churches that are members of the Protestant mainline (such as Presbyterian USA) often call for a return to more traditional teachings. In these and many other ways the new immigrant churches are remolding the foundation of American Christianity.

Yet for all of the changes that immigrant religions (Christian and non-Christian) bring to America, the immigrant faiths are adapting in ways that closely resemble past experience. Like the immigrant congregations before them, they seek to preserve the ethnic and religious identity of the new immigrants as they adapt to a new world. Congregations teach the younger generations to speak the native language as they teach the older generations to speak English. They hold worship services in the native tongue and promote traditional rituals as they assist members in getting citizenship, jobs, and training. They also know that membership is voluntary and the religious alternatives are many, leading them to actively recruit new members and to seek higher levels of commitment from their members. Finally, the congregations use community halls, recreational facilities, schools, and other organizations to promote tight social networks among their parishioners.

Conclusion

At the dawn of a new century, the religious pluralism of America continues to expand. As new faiths emerge from importation and inspiration, and other faiths fall into extinction, the profile of American religion is ever changing. Even the religions of prominence and power have shifted over time. The marginal minority faiths of one era have often become the prominent religions of the next.

The increasing religious pluralism is also forcing changes in the public arena. New rules for religious civility are slowly emerging. A Protestant America once strained to include Catholics and later Jews into the public faith. Now the Judeo-Christian faiths are struggling to incorporate Muslims, Hindus, and others into the public religion of America.

Yet many things have gone unchanged for more than two centuries. Endowed with religious freedoms, religious organizations and their clerics continue to appeal freely to the people. New faiths quickly emerge and seek out a following. Even the minority faiths can openly compete with other faiths. Free of state control, the local congregations remain a free space for institution-building and cater to the specific needs of their memberships. A result of this ongoing effort is a church adherence rate that has exceeded half of the population for the last century. As American religion undergoes an endless cycle of change, the consequences of religious freedoms remain the same.

BIBLIOGRAPHY

Ahlstrom, Sydney E. *A Religious History of the American People.* New Haven, Conn.: Yale University Press, 1972.

Albanese, Catherine L. *America, Religions and Religion.* 2d ed. Belmont, Calif.: Wadsworth, 1992.

Butler, Jon. *Religion in Colonial America.* New York: Oxford University Press, 2000.

Dolan, Jay P. *The American Catholic Experience: A History From Colonial Times to the Present.* Notre Dame, Ind.: University of Notre Dame Press, 1992.

Ebaugh, Helen Rose, and Janet Saltzman Chafetz, eds. *Religion and the New Immigrants: Continuities and Adaptations in Immigrant Congregations.* Walnut Creek, Calif.: AltaMira Press, 2000.

Finke, Roger, and Rodney Stark. *The Churching of America, 1776–1990: Winners and Losers in our Religious Economy.* New Brunswick, N.J.: Rutgers University Press, 1992.

Gaustad, Edwin Scott, and Philip L. Barlow. *New Historical Atlas of Religion in America.* New York: Oxford University Press, 2001.

Hatch, Nathan O. *The Democratization of American Christianity.* New Haven, Conn.: Yale University Press, 1989.

Lincoln, C. Eric, and Lawrence H. Mamiya. *The Black Church in the African American Experience.* Durham, N.C.: Duke University Press, 1990.

Mead, Sidney E. *The Lively Experiment: The Shaping of Christianity in America.* New York: Harper and Row, 1963.

Noll, Mark A.. *The Old Religion in a New World: The History of North American Christianity.* Grand Rapids, Mich.: Eerdmans, 2002.

Data Sources

Bureau of the Census. *Eleventh Census of the United States: 1890,* Vol. IX. Washington, D.C.: Government Printing Office, 1894.

Bureau of the Census. *Religious Bodies: 1906,* Vols. I and II. Washington, D.C.: Government Printing Office, 1910.

Bureau of the Census. *Religious Bodies: 1916,* Vols. I and II. Washington, D.C.: Government Printing Office, 1919.

Bureau of the Census. *Religious Bodies: 1926,* Vols. I and II. Washington, D.C.: Government Printing Office, 1930.

Churches and Church Membership in the United States, 1990. Glenmary Research Center, 1992. The 1952, 1971, 1980, and 1990 Churches and Church Membership surveys can be reviewed and downloaded from the American Religion Data Archive (http://www.TheARDA.com).

Finke, Roger, and Rodney Stark. "Turning Pews into People: Estimating 19th Century Church Membership." *Journal for the Scientific Study of Religion* 25 (1986): 180–192. Explains how census reports on churches were used to estimate 1850–1870 church membership.

Lindner, Eileen W., ed. *Yearbook of American & Canadian Churches 2001.* Nashville, Tenn.: Abingdon Press, 2001. Reported numbers are from various volumes of the *Yearbook,* from 1925 to 2001. Titles vary: 1924/25, *Year Book of the Churches.* 1926/27, *The Handbook of the Churches.* 1930/31, *The New Handbook of the Churches.* 1932–1972, *Yearbook of American Churches.*

Stark, Rodney. "Correcting Church Membership Rates: 1971 and 1980." *Review of Religious Research* 29 (1987): 69–77. The Churches and Church Membership surveys reviewed in this article can be reviewed and downloaded from the

American Religion Data Archive (http://www.TheARDA .com).

Stark, Rodney, and Roger Finke. "American Religion in 1776: A Statistical Portrait." *Sociological Analysis* 49 (1988): 39–51. Explains how 1776 church membership estimates were computed.

Zelinsky, Wilbur. "An Approach to the Religious Geography of the United States: Patterns in 1952." *Annals of the American Association of Geographers* 51 (1961): 139–193.

Roger Finke
Philip Schwadel

RELIGIOUS LIBERTY. The United States adopted a policy of religious liberty partly because influential people, including Thomas Jefferson and James Madison, advocated it, but partly because the sheer number of competing religious groups in eighteenth-century America made the possibility of religious uniformity remote. The nation's subsequent success in upholding the principle undermined the old European idea that an established church and a political state reinforced each other and that neither could thrive alone. In place of Europeans' attribution of divine right to their monarchs, Americans developed a civil religion, granting quasi-religious status to the Constitution, the flag, and the founders, but leaving plenty of room for citizens to practice their diverse particular religions.

Colonial Period

Colonial-era origins of American religious liberty are not hard to find. Separatist Puritans journeyed to the New World to escape religious persecution and in the expectation of finding a religious haven. Roger Williams, for whom the church was a purely spiritual phenomenon, detached religion from politics in early Rhode Island to prevent its political contamination. The Catholic founders of Maryland introduced a toleration law in 1649 for Christians of all types. William Penn's colony, Pennsylvania (1681), specified religious liberty not only for its original Quaker inhabitants but for all other settlers, and early became a shelter for Mennonites, Moravians, Baptists, and other dissenters from England and Germany.

These were no more than auguries, however, and it would be easy to overstate the degree of religious liberty in colonial America. The Church of England was established in Virginia and the Carolinas while the Congregationalist Church was established in most of New England. These establishments could be intolerant, as Massachusetts showed in executing four Quakers in 1659 and in hanging Salem's suspected witches in 1692–1693. Even after the Revolution, as the possibility of an Establishment disappeared, the widespread notion that America was a Protestant nation led to bursts of intense anti-Catholicism, in politics (the Know-Nothing Party) and in riots and the burning of Catholic churches and convents. Many churches, moreover, regarded religious liberty as a necessary evil rather than a positive good and looked forward to an era in which they would have spread their own particular brand of religious truth nationwide. Catholics themselves, despite recurrent persecution, sheltered under the American umbrella of religious liberty but aspired to a condition of Catholic unity, until Dignitatis Humanae, a document of the Second Vatican Council (1962–1965) finally recognized religious liberty as a positive good.

No denomination did more to promote religious liberty than the Baptists, whose growth in the eighteenth century spread opposition to the idea of an establishment. Flourishing among the less-well-educated population and in the colonial backcountry, some Baptists challenged the legitimacy of the coastal Anglican elite and substituted a democratic model of divinely chosen preachers for the establishment's staid, seminary-educated clergymen.

The growth of Baptist influence in the backcountry coincided with the spread of Enlightenment ideals among colonial elites. Thomas Jefferson, like many leaders in the Revolutionary generation, feared the imposition of a more rigorous establishment after 1770 and the threatened arrival of Anglican bishops. Eager to see the republic proclaimed on rational grounds, he traced the natural law to a Deist "Creator" in his draft of the Declaration of Independence but avoided doctrinal or denominational language. In 1786 he wrote the "Act for Establishing Religious Freedom." James Madison, his friend and principal drafter of the Constitution, understood that it was going to be difficult to win ratification from all the states and that the best approach to religious issues was to leave them alone completely. This approach succeeded and was codified in the First Amendment (1791), which precluded Congress from passing laws pertaining to the free exercise or the establishment of religion. Several states retained established churches but support for them weakened in an atmosphere supportive of religious liberty. The last of them, in Massachusetts, was abolished in 1833.

The constitutional separation of church and state and the promotion of religious liberty, however, did not imply a lack of interest in, or respect for, religion. An overwhelming majority of the revolutionary generation thought of themselves as Christians, and they saw no contradiction in describing America as a Christian nation or in holding Christian services in Congress.

Nineteenth Century

Early-nineteenth-century developments strengthened this belief in a Christian America but also strengthened the principle of religious liberty. The democratic revivalism of the Second Great Awakening placed a new emphasis on individual religious choice. In earlier Calvinist theology, the anxious soul had had to prepare in hope for the infusion of God's grace. In the teaching of Francis Asbury, Charles Finney, and other revivalists, by contrast, the individual was free to choose to turn towards God and to decide to embrace salvation rather than waiting on God. This change in theological emphasis gave additional support to the principle of religious liberty; the unsaved individual needed a setting in which his or her choice for God was in fact free.

As we have seen, the arrival of a large Catholic population tested the limits of American Protestants' commitment to religious freedom; anti-Catholic writers like Samuel Morse (inventor of the electric telegraph and Morse code) feared that Catholics' allegiance to the pope, whom they depicted as a foreign absolute monarch, made them incapable of true loyalty to the republic. Catholic leaders like Cardinal James Gibbons of Baltimore and Archbishop John Ireland of St. Paul reacted by emphasizing Catholics' absolute loyalty to the church in matters of religion and absolute loyalty to the republic as citizens. The arrival of a large Jewish population in the mid- and late-nineteenth century, from Germany, Russia, Poland, and the Austro-Hungarian Empire, tested the principle further still.

Twentieth Century

Despite widespread Protestant suspicion of Catholics and Jews, however, and frequent polemics, permanent divisions along religious lines never disfigured the republic; neither did any religious group suffer legislatively enforced persecution. Jewish success and upward social mobility in America, along with widespread revulsion against the Nazi Holocaust, contributed to the rapid decline of American anti-Semitism after 1945. By European standards it had never been intense. The idea of America as a "Judeo-Christian" nation replaced, for many observers, the older claim that America was a Christian nation. The American confrontation with the officially atheist Soviet Union during the Cold War stimulated the spread of "Judeo-Christian" rhetoric. When Congress added the words "under God" to the pledge of allegiance in the 1950s, it was in recognition that America was on the side of religion and that America's religious liberty stood in sharp contrast to Soviet anti-religious persecution. The God in question, however, was not attached to any particular church.

The Immigration and Naturalization Reform Act of 1965 led, in the later decades of the twentieth century, to a new wave of immigration and a further diversification of the American religious landscape. Large numbers of Hindus and Buddhists entered America for the first time, and the Islamic population grew rapidly, partly through immigration and partly through the adherence of African Americans to the Nation of Islam. Here again, the principle of religious liberty operated to ensure that these groups were free to worship as they wished, that their religious organizations were insulated from the state, and that they, like all other religious groups, enjoyed tax exemption. Court cases, such as *Sherbert v. Verner* (1963), adjudicated nettlesome issues to accommodate students' and employees' religious needs and observation of holy days. Recurrent frictions, especially when neighbors' religions were dissimilar, were offset by a widespread belief in religious civility.

There have been occasions throughout American history when the right to religious liberty appeared to threaten other rights, or when activities undertaken in the name of religion violated social or legal convention. In such cases, the limits of the liberty were tested. In the nineteenth century, for example, the Oneida Community's practice of "complex marriage" and the Mormons' practice of polygamy brought down persecution on their heads. Neighbors of the Oneida Community were horrified by complex marriage, regarding it as no better than sexual promiscuity. Their pressure, along with declining fervor in the community's second generation, prompted John Humphrey Noyes, the founder, to emigrate and the community to dissolve. Early Mormon communities in Missouri and Illinois faced recurrent attacks with the connivance of the local authorities, which culminated in the murder of their leader Joseph Smith.

In the 1970s Americans wrestled with the issue of "brainwashing" by cults. The counterculture of that decade gave rise to numerous religious organizations whose members lived in communes, often handing over their belongings to charismatic leaders. Were these cults—Jesus Freaks, Rajneeshis, Hare Krishnas, Moonies, and others—abusing the principle of religious liberty or were their unusual ways of life signs of its flexibility and continuing vitality? In the most notorious of these groups, the People's Temple, parents of young members claimed that their children had been brainwashed into parting with their property and were, in effect, prisoners rather than devotees. People's Temple leader Jim Jones, denying these allegations, led his community out of the United States to Guyana (just as Brigham Young had led his people out of the United States and into what was then Mexican territory 130 years before). When Congressman Leo Ryan of California went to Guyana to investigate parents' claims in 1978, Jones told his security guards to assassinate Ryan at the Jonestown airstrip, then ordered the entire community (about 900 people) to commit suicide by drinking poisoned Kool-Aid. All but a handful, who escaped into the jungle, followed his suicide order. The ensuing scandal led some states to consider anti-cult legislation but found themselves unable to define the difference between denomination, sect, cult, and church. The principle of religious liberty prevailed against legislative intrusion, even though the principle was clearly liable to abuse in extreme cases.

BIBLIOGRAPHY

Butler, Jon. *Awash in a Sea of Faith: Christianizing the American People.* Cambridge, Mass.: Harvard University Press, 1990.

Eastland, Terry, ed. *Religious Liberty in the Supreme Court: The Cases That Define the Debate over Church and State.* Grand Rapids, Mich.: Eerdman's, 1995.

Hanson, Charles P. *Necessary Virtue: The Pragmatic Origins of Religious Liberty in New England.* Charlottesville: University Press of Virginia, 1998.

Hatch, Nathan O. *The Democratization of American Christianity.* New Haven, Conn.: Yale University Press, 1989.

Hunter, James Davison, and Os Guinness, eds. *Articles of Faith, Articles of Peace: The Religious Liberty Clauses and the American Public Philosophy.* Washington D.C.: Brookings Institution, 1990.

Lee, Francis Graham, ed. *All Imaginable Liberty: The Religious Liberty Clauses of the First Amendment.* Lanham, Md.: University Press of America, 1995.

Patrick N. Allitt

See also **Discrimination: Religion;** *and vol. 9:* **An Act Concerning Religion.**

RELIGIOUS THOUGHT AND WRITINGS.

If Sydney E. Ahlstrom was correct when he wrote that "the country that declared its independence in 1776 was more clearly a product of Protestantism than any other country in the world" (*Theology in America,* p. 24), then it would hardly be surprising to find that Protestants have dominated those systematic and formal treatments of religion that have gained the widest circulation and been most influential in the United States. After 225 years of American history, Protestant hegemony in religious literature may be a source of embarrassment to scholars of religion. In a report of the National Endowment for the Humanities to Congress in 1985, *A Report to the Congress of the United States on the State of the Humanities,* for example, the American Academy of Religion—the professional scholarly organization devoted to the formal study of religion—concluded that writing about spiritual and divine matters had "taken a quantum leap" from "WASP theology" to the "unique religious vision of Blacks, of American Indians, of Chicanos, of American Orientals." But to ignore the former dominance of Protestantism in the religious thought and writings of the United States for the sake of contemporary religious diversity is to distort the nature of intellectual endeavor and overestimate the opportunity for religious reflection that has existed throughout the history of the United States. Furthermore, to ignore the institutional setting for such thought and writing is to obscure the purpose and character of the influential churchmen and scholars who put their ideas about divinity into print. For good or ill, throughout much of American history the occasion for most systematic treatments of religion has been the training of clergy. Without the context of church-sponsored ministerial training, attempts to make sense of the variety of religious literature would appear almost arbitrary.

Colonial Protestantism

As much as New England Puritanism receives credit for cultivating the life of the mind in America, the Puritans who in the early seventeenth century settled in Massachusetts Bay Colony inherited theological and educational patterns from England that colored the way religious thought was conducted in the New World. Training for ministry in the Church of England consisted primarily in a classical education with theology and spiritual counsel supplementing literary training. As such, English universities were not the sites of sustained reflection on religious topics. In fact, England did not develop posts in technical or academic religious learning until the nineteenth century. Instead, religious writing took place in the studies of pastor-theologians—that is, bishops or rectors of large parishes—and was decidedly occasional, conducted in response to particular controversies, whether over the prerogatives of the church or the dubious views of wayward priests. Consequently, Puritans had no model for establishing religious learning as part of higher education. Where it existed, it was either vocational or polemical, either training future ministers or protecting the views of those who already were.

This pattern prevailed throughout the British colonies in North America, Puritan New England included. Harvard and Yale Colleges perpetuated the English tradition of providing education for the governing class. Religious scholarship was only a minor part of this training. Graduates from Puritan colleges received religious instruction sufficient to maintain the commonwealth's godly ways. But the colleges themselves offered rare opportunities for sustained reflection or serious scholarship on religious matters. The same was true for William and Mary in Virginia. In this context, religious writing took place in response to particular issues of public or ecclesiastical significance and its practitioners were ministers with sufficient talent and resources. The only exception to this depiction was the sermon, a form of religious learning that in the hands of the Puritans was every bit as technical as scholastic theology. Puritan preaching, which functioned in many ways as the public discourse of New England villages, followed a set form that assumed a high degree of theological literacy. Because of Puritan notions about the importance and techniques of preaching, New England ministers were engaged weekly in the most sustained form of religious learning in colonial America, whether their sermons were printed or remained in manuscript.

For this reason, the religious literature of the British colonies in North America was far more likely to come from the pens of ministers than college professors. Noteworthy examples of the Puritan minister as pastor-theologian were John Cotton, Thomas Hooker, and Cotton Mather. Cotton (1585–1652) was pastor at Boston's First Church and was embroiled in a number of controversies owing both to his own endeavors as well as to the Puritan understanding of religion's importance to society. Even so, these conflicts afforded Cotton the opportunity to give masterful expression of Congregationalism as a system of church government and the ideal pattern of church life in Massachusetts Bay. Hooker (1586–1647), who arrived in Boston after Cotton, founded the colony of Hartford owing in part to rivalry with the older Puritan minister. A gifted preacher, Hooker's learning was manifest in a large body of published sermons and, as with

Cotton, in a book on Puritan church government. Mather (1663–1728) was the first native-born American religious thinker of significance. The grandson of John Cotton, Mather ministered at Boston's North Church and left behind a body of writing that exceeded his sermon preparations, with books on church history (*Magnalia Christi Americana*, 1702), moral theology (*Essays to Do Good*, 1721), and science (*The Christian Philosopher*, 1721).

These pastor-theologians, however, could not rival the accomplishments of Jonathan Edwards (1703–1758), whose achievements were all the more remarkable given his location in the town of Northampton, situated on the western frontier of colonial society. Like his predecessors, Edwards was first and foremost a pastor, having trained at Yale College before settling in western Massachusetts, where he ministered for most of his career. But he was no ordinary pastor. Edwards read widely in philosophy and attempted to turn Enlightenment thought to pious ends. The particular aim of much of the Northampton pastor's writing was a defense of the revivals that occurred locally in Northampton during the 1730s and then became a transatlantic phenomenon with George Whitefield's arrival in 1739. In one of his most important books, *A Treatise Concerning Religious Affections* (1746), Edwards used the philosophy of Nicolas de Malebranche and John Locke to argue that true religion began with a sense in the heart but that religious experience combined subjective and objective elements. In addition to advocating revivalism, Edwards attempted to express traditional Puritan divinity in the idiom of recent trends in philosophy. After a controversy with town officials in which Edwards lost his call in Northampton, he moved to nearby Stockbridge and while evangelizing among the Native American population wrote three important treatises on themes central to Calvinism: *Freedom of the Will* (1754); *The Great Christian Doctrine of Original Sin Defended* (1758); and *The Nature of True Virtue* (1765).

Aside from the significance of Edwards's thought in its own right, his work launched what Bruce Kuklick, in *Churchmen and Philosophers: From Jonathan Edwards to John Dewey* (1985), has called "the most sustained theological tradition that America has produced." Known as the New England Theology, or sometimes as the New Divinity, it arose informally with Edwards as its center and once again demonstrates that sustained and formal religious learning in the seventeenth and eighteenth centuries developed most often outside the colleges. The New Divinity's proponents were Congregationalist pastors laboring in the Connecticut River valley who often had apprenticed with Edwards or knew the great Northampton preacher directly. Its themes drew directly on Edwards's legacy: the restatement of Calvinism in philosophically informed expressions; the defense of revivalism's compatibility with Calvinist theology; and moral theology rooted in Edwardsian psychology.

Among the New Divinity's ablest proponents, Joseph Bellamy (1719–1790) and Samuel Hopkins (1721–1803),

both Yale graduates whom Edwards tutored in divinity, carried forward the Northampton pastor's experimental Calvinism to another generation of pastors by attempting to systematize their mentor's theology. Bellamy did this by writing books on Edwardsean themes, such as true piety and original sin, while Hopkins attempted a comprehensive system of doctrine. Because of the occasional nature of many of Edwards's writings and the sheer originality of his thought, trying to imitate or summarize his theology led to a number of ambiguities in the New Divinity movement. Even so, Bellamy and Hopkins instructed another set of disciples who extended Edwards's influence into the nineteenth century. These younger Edwardseans included Jonathan Edwards Jr. (1745–1801), the ninth child and namesake of Edwards, and Nathaniel Emmons (1745–1840), both of whom were too young to learn divinity from Edwards directly and so relied upon his closest colleagues. Like Bellamy and Hopkins, Edwards Jr. and Emmons perpetuated the themes of experimental Calvinism by trying to justify and restate Puritan divinity in the latest philosophical and ethical thought.

From Parsonage to Seminary

What may have accounted for the influence of the New Divinity, apart from Edwards's own genius, was the sustained reflection over time, accompanied by a series of texts, on a number of set themes of Protestant divinity. To be sure, ministers in New England who did not identify with the Edwardseans and others outside New England in other religious communions addressed the issues that animated the New Divinity theologians in similarly learned ways. But these other clerics lacked the institutional base and the network of apprenticeships and collegiality that the Edwardseans had possessed. This changed profoundly in the early nineteenth century with the rise of the theological seminary, which had the unintended consequence of professionalizing religious learning and moving it away from pastors and assigning it to full-time theologians.

The seminary emerged with lasting significance when Massachusetts Congregationalists founded Andover in 1808 and four years later, when Presbyterians began Princeton Seminary. Although the divinity school was under the governance of the college (later the university), like the seminary it gave Protestant divinity a degree of institutional muscle that it had previously lacked when it relied upon the unpredictable abilities of pastors. Yet at the same time, divinity schools and seminaries explicitly segregated formal religious learning in faculties outside the arts and sciences where the chief task was not academic but professional, namely, the training of ministers. Even so, the establishment of separate schools for ministerial preparation provided resources for the flourishing of theology among the largest Protestant denominations.

In New England three schools, Andover Seminary, Yale Divinity School, and Harvard Divinity School, were the main contenders for Protestant support. Andover was the most self-conscious of the three in attempting to preserve the heritage of Edwards. Here Edwards Amasa Park (1808–1900), his Christian name revealing the Northampton minister's ongoing influence, was the last of the line of Edwardsean theologians. Although Park had studied in Germany and begun to refashion New England Calvinism according to idealist philosophy, by the end of his tenure at Andover the faculty had grown restless with the metaphysical direction of the seminary's theology and fashioned a system of religious reflection geared toward experience, not scholastic categories. At Yale Divinity School, Nathaniel William Taylor (1786–1858) continued in paths established by Edwards, not always supplying the same answers but usually interacting with the same questions about the relationship between divine sovereignty and human responsibility and the nature of religious experience. Taylor's views became so dominant at Yale that when he died the divinity school experienced such a loss of students that administrators almost closed it. The pattern at Harvard was even graver than at Yale. At the beginning of the nineteenth century, Unitarians took control of the divinity school there, thus forcing orthodox Congregationalists to establish Andover. Andrews Norton (1786–1853), a biblical scholar who made use of new developments in German religious learning, was arguably the leading Unitarian scholar prior to the Civil War. But the divinity school's sway outside Unitarian circles was negligible and the rise of transcendentalism further weakened Harvard's reputation.

Outside New England, three theological seminaries—Princeton in New Jersey, Mercersburg in Pennsylvania, and Union in New York City—shaped the professionalization of religious inquiry. Charles Hodge (1797–1878) taught more students during his tenure at Princeton Seminary than any other nineteenth-century theologian. In contrast to New England theology, Princeton repudiated scholarly innovation and attempted to pass on the received views of Presbyterian orthodoxy to aspiring ministers while also carrying on extensive polemics with wayward academic peers. At Mercersburg Seminary, an institution of the German Reformed Church, John Williamson Nevin (1803–1886) and Philip Schaff (1819–1893) positively appropriated developments in German theology to emphasize the historical development of religious truth and negatively criticized the novelties of American Protestantism such as revivalism and denominational fragmentation. In New York City at the Union Seminary, a Presbyterian institution, Henry Boynton Smith (1815–1877) stood midway between the speculative efforts of New England theology and the conservatism of Princeton.

No matter what the differences in doctrine, the rise of the seminary replaced the pastor-scholar with the academic theologian. To be sure, theologians in Protestant seminaries and divinity schools were oriented primarily to the church by their function of training ministers. But

the urge to locate religious learning in formal academic structures was so great that even the revivalist Charles Grandison Finney (1792–1875), who fulminated against the scholastic theology of the Presbyterian Church, ended up teaching moral philosophy and theology to future pastors at Oberlin College. The pastor-scholar model only survived in such figures as William Ellery Channing (1780–1842), a Unitarian pastor in Boston, Ralph Waldo Emerson (1803–1882), a Unitarian pastor in Boston who left the church to become a popular lecturer and writer, and Horace Bushnell (1802–1876), a liberal Congregationalist pastor in Hartford.

Among Roman Catholics and Jews, however, religious learning and writings remained in the hands of able bishops, priests, and rabbis. The nonacademic character of Catholic and Jewish thought was partly the function of the poverty of the immigrants of those religions, which made formal learning a luxury, and partly the result of Protestant dominance in American higher education. In the case of Catholics the primacy of Rome in the training of clergy also restricted the development of professional theologians for the church in the United States. Although Catholic spokesmen often directed their thoughts more to the establishment of an American church than to formal Catholic teaching, such bishops as John Carroll (1735–1815) and John Hughes (1797–1864) provided a necessary foundation for advanced religious learning among American Catholics. A similar pattern prevailed among Jews, for whom the rabbi functioned as a jack-of-all-trades. Isaac Meyer Wise (1819–1900) was among the ablest and most vocal of American Jews during the nineteenth century and he founded in Cincinnati a preparatory school, Hebrew Union College, for training rabbis that became a model for Jewish learning. His understanding of Judaism in the New World did not receive unanimous assent and in 1886 a more conservative group, led by Sabato Morais (1823–1897), founded in New York City the Jewish Theological Seminary, a school that not only provided rabbinical education but also a place for sustained religious reflection.

From Seminary to University

Although the emergence of seminaries and divinity schools supplied institutional support for the task of formal religious learning, these schools could not overcome the Anglo-American legacy of religious scholars working in isolation from the university. The emergence of the research university after the Civil War only increased religious scholarship's seclusion. To be sure, new institutions such as the University of Chicago (1892) included a faculty of theology. But this was rare and turned out to be the equivalent of the divinity schools at Harvard and Yale, which although they may have granted doctorates, were primarily oriented to ministerial training. Formal religious learning, in effect, remained segregated from the arts and sciences.

Developments in the churches that the seminaries and divinity schools served did not make religious learning any more appealing in higher education. The modernist-fundamentalist controversy, which flared up visibly during the 1920s but had been evident from 1890 on, pitted traditionalists against progressives. The latter were eager to provide universities with a form of religious learning more in tune with the research and pragmatic aims of the university, but the former were unwilling to modify religious teaching. Over time the progressives won, in part because traditionalists either lost control or left the leading seminaries and divinity schools, founding instead Bible colleges that dispensed an egalitarian and arcane brand of religious thought. By 1935 progressive Protestants occupied the field of religious scholarship and over the course of the next three decades would consolidate their position by establishing the discipline of the academic study of religion.

The political and cultural climate of the United States during the middle decades of the twentieth century was one to which the Protestant initiative in religious studies could well adapt. Thanks to a renewed sense of liberal democracy's stake in the West's cultural heritage, the humanities and liberal arts reemerged as higher education's contribution to the battle with totalitarianism. At the same time, the study of religion received support because of Christianity's influence upon European society and the United States. Between 1940 and 1965 religious learning finally had moved from the periphery of the parsonage and seminary to a formal area of instruction and study in the modern research university. Yet because Protestants controlled the field, the curriculum in the newly founded departments of religion differed little from the sequence of courses at seminaries. As anomalous as the academic study of religion may appear in hindsight, this was an era when Reinhold Niebuhr (1892–1971) and H. Richard Niebuhr (1894–1962) were America's public theologians. Although the Niebuhr brothers taught in the seminary and divinity school setting, their ability to relate Christian concepts to politics and culture found a wide and receptive audience.

After 1965, around the same time that the United States entered a period described by many as post-Protestant, the academic study of religion moved outside Protestantism's orbit toward greater pluralism and scholarly sophistication. The result is that religious thought and learning in the United States became polarized between academic theories at one end and the practices of religious adherents at the other, with university departments of religion studying religion as an abstraction, clergy-scholars embedded in concrete religious traditions, and seminaries and divinity schools trying to harmonize generic and particular conceptions of belief. As such, the systematic study of religion in the United States continued to bear the consequences of religious learning's initial location in the colleges that English Puritans replicated in the New World.

BIBLIOGRAPHY

Ahlstrom, Sydney E., ed. *Theology in America: The Major Protestant Voices from Puritanism to Neo-Orthodoxy*. Indianapolis, Ind.: Bobbs-Merrill, 1967.

Brereton, Virginia Lieson. *Training God's Army: The American Bible School, 1880–1940*. Bloomington: Indiana University Press, 1990.

Cherry, Conrad. *Hurrying toward Zion: Universities, Divinity Schools, and American Protestantism*. Bloomington: Indiana University Press, 1995.

Fogarty, Gerald P. *American Catholic Biblical Scholarship: A History from the Early Republic to Vatican II*. San Francisco: Harper and Row, 1989.

Gilpin, W. Clark. *A Preface to Theology*. Chicago: University of Chicago Press, 1996.

Gleason, Philip. *Contending with Modernity: Catholic Higher Education in the Twentieth Century*. New York: Oxford University Press, 1995.

Hart, D. G. *The University Gets Religion: Religious Studies in American Higher Education*. Baltimore: Johns Hopkins University Press, 1999.

Kuklick, Bruce. *Churchmen and Philosophers: From Jonathan Edwards to John Dewey*. New Haven, Conn.: Yale University Press, 1985.

Miller, Glenn, and Robert Lynn. "Christian Theological Education." In *Encyclopedia of the American Religious Experience*. Edited by Charles H. Lippy and Peter W. Williams. Vol. 3. New York: Scribners, 1988.

Miller, Glenn. *Piety and Intellect: The Aims and Purposes of Ante-Bellum Theological Education*. Atlanta, Ga.: Scholars Press, 1990.

Noll, Mark A. *Between Faith and Criticism: Evangelicals, Scholarship, and the Bible in America*. San Francisco: Harper and Row, 1986.

Perko, F. Michael. "Religion and Collegiate Education." In *Encyclopedia of the American Religious Experience*. Edited by Charles H. Lippy and Peter W. Williams. Vol. 3. New York: Scribners, 1988.

Ritterbrand, Paul, and Harold S. Wechsler. *Jewish Learning in American Universities: The First Century*. Bloomington: Indiana University Press, 1994.

Sloan, Douglas. *Faith and Knowledge: Mainline Protestantism and American Higher Education*. Louisville, Ky.: Westminster John Knox Press, 1994.

Stout, Harry S. *The New England Soul: Preaching and Religious Culture in Colonial New England*. New York: Oxford University Press, 1986.

Toulouse, Mark G., and James O. Duke, eds. *Makers of Christian Theology in America*. Nashville, Tenn.: Abingdon Press, 1997.

———, eds. *Sources of Christian Theology in America*. Nashville, Tenn.: Abingdon Press, 1999.

D. G. Hart

See also **Catholicism; Education, Higher: Denominational Colleges; Edwardsean Theology; Evangelicism and Revivalism; Fundamentalism; Judaism; Modernists, Protestant; Protestantism; Puritans and Puritanism.**

RELOCATION, ITALIAN AMERICAN.

Voluntary relocation of enemy aliens (primarily Italians, Germans, and Japanese) who lived or worked in West Coast security zones began in mid-February 1942. In California, this amounted initially to between eight thousand and ten thousand persons, not including family members who accompanied the aliens. But the voluntary approach failed, and the army commenced enforcement of mandatory relocation in late February, as provided for by Executive Order 9066.

Lieutenant General John L. DeWitt, who led the Fourth Army and Western Defense Command, vehemently insisted that removal should embrace all enemy aliens, a position that mirrored local opinion. But DeWitt, the public, and the politicians were overruled. Within weeks, following an intense debate among War Department and Justice Department officials and owing principally to considerations of logistics, morale, and race, only Japanese aliens and U.S. citizens of Japanese ancestry would be subject to relocation in camps. Italian and German aliens (with or without their citizen-relatives) moved across streets, across towns, or to other communities outside the restricted zones.

By June 1942, most of the relocated Italians had returned home, and in October 1942 the Justice Department reclassified them as "friendly." The restrictions on German nationals ended in December 1942. In November 2000, President Bill Clinton signed legislation acknowledging that the U.S. government had violated the civil liberties of Italian Americans during World War II. A year later, the Justice Department issued a report on the matter, as the law required.

BIBLIOGRAPHY

DiStasi, Lawrence, ed. *Una Storia Sehgreta: The Secret History of Italian American Evacuation and Internment during World War II.* Berkeley, Calif.: Heyday Books, 2001.

Fox, Stephen C. "General John DeWitt and the Proposed Internment of German and Italian Aliens During World War II." *Pacific Historical Review* 57 (1988): 407–438.

———. *The Unknown Internment: An Oral History of the Relocation of Italian Americans During World War II.* Boston: Twayne, 1990. Revised as *UnCivil Liberties: Italian Americans under Siege during World War II.* Universal Publishers/uPUBLISH.com, 2000.

Stephen Fox

See also **Italian Americans; Japanese American Incarceration; Prisoners of War: Prison Camps, World War II.**

"REMEMBER THE ALAMO"

was a battle cry in which the bitterness of the Texans over the massacres by Mexican forces at the Alamo in San Antonio (6 March 1836) and at Goliad (27 March 1836) found expression. Use of the phrase has been attributed both to Gen. Sam Houston (who supposedly used the words in a stirring address to his men on 19 April 1836, two days before the Battle of San Jacinto) and to Col. Sidney Sherman, who fought in the battle.

BIBLIOGRAPHY

Flores, Richard R. *Remembering the Alamo: Memory, Modernity, and the Master Symbol.* Austin: University of Texas Press, 2002.

Roberts, Randy, and James S. Olson. *A Line in the Sand: The Alamo in Blood and Memory.* New York: Free Press, 2001.

*C. T. Neu/*ʟ. ᴛ.

See also **Alamo, Siege of the; Indian Missions; Mexico, Relations with; Texas;** *and vol. 9:* **The Story of Enrique Esparza.**

REMINGTON AND INDIAN AND WESTERN IMAGES.

Artists such as Frederic Remington (1861–1909) provided filmmakers with the lexicon for making Westerns. This lexicon has been used throughout the twentieth century and into the twenty-first. In his short career of only about twenty-five years, Remington produced a huge body of illustration, painting, sculpture, fiction, and nonfiction—most of which centered on imagining the nineteenth-century American West. For most of his life, Remington worked as a painter, producing close to three thousand paintings. Perhaps his most famous painting is *A Dash for the Timber* (1889). The painting depicts a group of cowboys scurrying away from avenging Indians. It creates a world of action and adventure that held and continues to hold great appeal for many Americans. Although Remington lived for short periods in the West, most of his depictions of the West were imagined rather than experienced directly.

Remington's work was celebrated in the late nineteenth century and is still celebrated for the way it captures what most white Americans believe about America's past. Since the 1890s, many Americans have adhered to the idea that the "real" West died and that with this event the nation had lost a romantic history marked not only by clashes between Indians and whites, but by lawlessness amongst whites, and by economic opportunity for whites. Remington, it was and still is believed, captured that conviction and celebrated a history that was both American and western. Remington immortalized the nostalgia white Americans invoked with memories of the frontier, the West, the cowboy, and the Indian. He captured a mythology that can be seen in all filmic depictions of the West as well as in cowboy-inspired fashion. Whites in the East needed to feel heroic about the conquest of the West, and Remington satisfied their desires through his art.

BIBLIOGRAPHY

Dippie, Brian W. *Remington and Russell: The Sid Richardson Collection.* Rev. ed. Austin: University of Texas Press, 1994.

Dippie, Brian W., et al. *The Frederic Remington Art Museum Collection.* New York: Abrams, 2001.

Western Art. Frederic Remington's popular 1908 painting *The Stampede* depicts cowboys trying to control panicking cattle during a thunderstorm. © CORBIS-BETTMANN

Nemerov, Alexander. *Frederic Remington and Turn-of-the-Century-America*. New Haven: Yale University Press, 1995.

White, Richard, and Patricia Nelson Limerick. *The Frontier in American Culture: An Exhibition at the Newberry Library*. Edited by James R. Grossman. Berkeley: University of California Press, 1994.

Liza Black

See also **Frontier; West, American; Westerns; Westward Migration.**

REMOVAL, EXECUTIVE POWER OF. Article 2, section 2 of the Constitution states that "by and with the Advice and Consent of the Senate," the president can appoint judges, ambassadors, and executive officials. The Constitution, however, says nothing about whether the president can subsequently fire these appointees. As a consequence, Congress and the courts have had to define the president's legal authority to remove officials.

During the First Congress, James Madison, then a member of the House, uncharacteristically argued that without the power to dismiss executive officials, the president would be rendered impotent. In the 1789 law establishing the Department of State, Madison inserted language that granted the president unqualified power to fire the secretary of state, who at the time was Madison's ally Thomas Jefferson. This provided the first statutory legitimation of the president's removal power. Though Senator Henry Clay tried unsuccessfully to curb President Andrew Jackson's removal power some 30 years later, not until after the Civil War did Congress revisit the "Decision of 1789."

In 1867 Congress enacted the Tenure of Office Act over President Andrew Johnson's veto. The act required the president to secure the Senate's approval to remove any official from government whose nomination had been confirmed by the Senate. When Johnson tested the act by unilaterally firing Secretary of War Edwin Stanton, Congress promptly initiated impeachment proceedings. The House voted 126 to 47 in favor of impeachment; the Senate, however, failed by just one vote. Two decades later, Congress repealed the Tenure of Office Act.

Throughout the nineteenth century, the federal courts sidestepped every opportunity to comment on the constitutionality of the president's removal power. In *Myers v. United States* (1926), however, the Supreme Court deemed unconstitutional an 1876 law that required presidents to secure the Senate's consent before firing "postmasters of the first, second, and third classes" (19 Stat. 78, 80). Chief Justice William Howard Taft, delivering the Court's opinion, noted that to fulfill his constitutional duty to "take care that the laws be faithfully executed," the president must retain an unrestricted power to remove subordinates.

Myers seemed to grant the president complete freedom to remove not only postmasters, but also officials throughout the executive branch—only judges appeared off limits. In 1933 President Franklin Roosevelt tested this freedom by firing William E. Humphrey from the Federal Trade Commission (FTC) because of policy differences. Under the terms of the Federal Trade Commission Act of 1914, members of the FTC were supposed to serve seven-year terms that could be revoked only for infractions involving "inefficiency, neglect of duty, or malfeasance in office." Though Humphrey died in 1934, the executor of his estate sued for lost wages and the case went to the Supreme Court. In *Humphrey's Executor v. United States* (1935), the Court unanimously voted in favor of Humphrey and limited the president's removal power to only those officials who immediately served him, such as White House aides. Congress, the Court ruled, could legally restrict the president's ability to remove anyone except "purely executive officers."

Two decades later, after President Dwight Eisenhower dismissed Myron Wiener from the War Claims Commission, the Supreme Court reaffirmed the legal limits to the president's removal powers. Though the legislation establishing the commission never stated when, or for what causes, members might be removed, the Court surmised that Congress did not intend commissioners to have to decide war claims while fearing "the Damocles' sword of removal by the President for no reason other than that he preferred to have . . . men of his own choosing." In *Wiener v. United States* (1958) the Court once again ruled against a president who tried to exercise his removal powers for expressly political purposes.

During the Watergate scandal, the president's removal power again took center stage. Congress had vested in the attorney general the power to appoint a special prosecutor to investigate and prosecute offenses relating to the Watergate Hotel break-in, the 1972 election, the president, and his subordinates. The regulations establishing the office stated that the special prosecutor would remain in office until the attorney general and himself deemed his investigative work complete, and that he would not be removed from office "except for extraordinary improprieties on his part." In the fall of 1973, however, shortly after the attorney general and deputy attorney general resigned, the solicitor general, assuming the title of acting attorney general and following President Richard Nixon's orders, fired the special prosecutor. Later, a district court ruled that the removal violated the regulations that initially established the office (*Nader v. Bork*, 1973).

Despite these various setbacks, presidents retain some say over when executive officials are removed from office. In *Bowsher v. Synar* (1986) the Court ruled that Congress cannot create an administrative agency that performs purely executive functions and retain full authority over the removal of its members. In subsequent cases, the Court has ruled that Congress cannot unduly restrict the president's power to remove officials from offices that immediately affect his ability to fulfill his constitutional responsibilities.

Through the beginning of the twenty-first century, however, no overarching principles dictate precisely when, and under what conditions, presidents can remove executive officials. Presidents enjoy broad discretion to fire cabinet secretaries and political appointees within the executive office. The president's freedom to dismiss directors of administrative agencies, however, is usually subject to terms set by Congress. The legislation creating some agencies, such as the President's Commission on Civil Rights and the Environmental Protection Agency, does not place any restrictions on the president's removal powers. For other agencies, however, the enacting legislation establishes certain guidelines. For example, the president can remove members of the Nuclear Regulatory Commission for "inefficiency, neglect of duty, or malfeasance in office," but can remove members of the Consumer Product Safety Commission "for neglect of duty or malfeasance in office but for no other cause."

When all is said and done, the president's power to remove executive officials may depend less upon formal principles than it does upon the practice of everyday politics. Congressional leaders, interest groups, and public opinion exert considerable influence over whether, and when, presidents opt to remove executive officials from office, and when they choose to withstand their continued service.

BIBLIOGRAPHY

Corwin, Edward S. *The President, Office and Powers, 1787–1957; History and Analysis of Practice and Opinion.* 4th ed. New York: New York University Press, 1957.

Fisher, Louis. *Constitutional Conflicts between Congress and the President.* 4th ed. Lawrence: University of Kansas Press, 1997.

Shane, Peter M., and Harold H. Bruff. *Separation of Powers Law: Cases and Materials.* Durham, N.C.: Carolina Academic Press, 1996.

William G. Howell

See also **Humphrey's Executor v. United States; Impeachment Trial of Andrew Johnson; Myers v. United States; Tenure of Office Act; Watergate.**

REMOVAL ACT OF 1830. On 28 May 1830 the Indian Removal Act became law, passed by Congress after

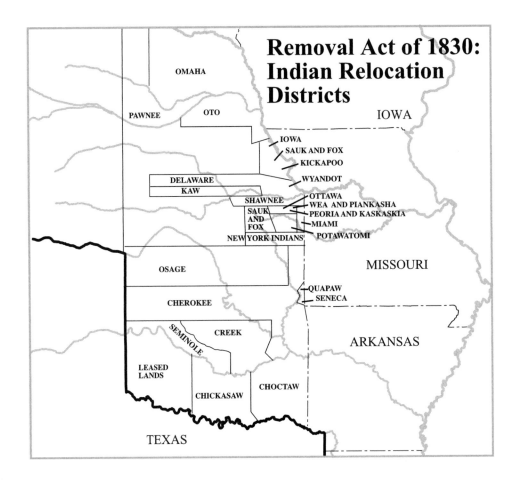

Removal Act of 1830: Indian Relocation Districts

heated debate and by a close vote. The purpose of this legislation was the removal of those Native Americans still residing east of the Mississippi to new homes west of that river. The measure had been proposed by President Andrew Jackson in his first message to Congress in 1829, but efforts to accomplish this ethnic cleansing go back at least to the presidency of Thomas Jefferson. In 1803 Jefferson proposed a constitutional amendment to permit turning the northern part of the Louisiana Purchase into a vast Indian reservation, relocating the white inhabitants to the east and the eastern tribes to the west of the Mississippi. The amendment failed, but Jefferson continued to encourage Indian emigration.

To effect the supposedly voluntary removal called for by the act, the U.S. government held treaty meetings, some grossly fraudulent, with the eastern tribes at which some in attendance were persuaded to agree to exchange their eastern lands for tracts in the Indian Territory in the present states of Oklahoma and Kansas. The actual emigration was to be supervised by federal agents supported by the U.S. Army. But resistance was immediate and intense, particularly among the tens of thousands of members of the Five Civilized Tribes of the Southeast, so-called because of their extensive adoption of white

economic and other institutions: the Cherokees in Georgia, the Choctaws and Chickasaws in Mississippi, the Creeks in Alabama, and the Seminoles in Florida. By the end of the decade federal authorities were prepared to use force. When most of the Cherokees refused to leave, thousands were rounded up at gunpoint, imprisoned in stockades, and escorted across the Mississippi in what became known as the Trail of Tears in remembrance of the thousands who died along the way. Creeks, Choctaws, and Chickasaws were tricked and coerced into removal, and numerous parties arrived in Indian Territory in bad weather and with few supplies. The Seminoles fought a war until 1842, when the United States called off its invasion after suffering hundreds of casualties.

In the South after removal a number of remnant tribal groups remained, Cherokees in North Carolina, Choctaws in Mississippi, and Seminoles in Florida. In the North, where far fewer Native Americans still lived in 1830, the pace of removal was slower. Miamis retained a reservation in Ohio until 1846; Ottawas, Potawatomis, and Chippewas remained in northern Michigan and Wisconsin; Menominees clung to Wisconsin; and Iroquois preserved several reservations in New York. The tribes in the Indian Territory gradually recovered under the supervision of the Bureau of Indian Affairs, which was bent on "civilizing" Indians.

The removal of the 1830s and 1840s was a disaster for Native Americans, but it also left scars on the body politic of the United States. Many religious groups and some politicians vehemently opposed removal, proposing instead to Christianize and "civilize" the Indians in their original homes. Others, like Jefferson and Jackson, saw nothing but doom for Indians who remained in contact with white settlers. Long after the demise of the Indian Territory, federal Indian policy remains a matter of debate.

BIBLIOGRAPHY

Foreman, Grant. *Indian Removal: The Emigration of the Five Civilized Tribes of Indians.* Norman: University of Oklahoma Press, 1932.

Wallace, Anthony F. C. *The Long, Bitter Trail: Andrew Jackson and the Indians.* New York: Hill and Wang, 1993.

Anthony F. C. Wallace

See also **Indian Policy, U.S.; Indian Removal; Indian Treaties; Trail of Tears.**

REMOVAL OF DEPOSITS.

The removal of deposits was the next step in President Andrew Jackson's campaign against the Second Bank of the United States after he vetoed its recharter in July 1832. Under its existing charter, due to expire in 1836, the bank acted as the exclusive fiscal agent of the federal government and the custodian of its funds. It was also the country's only truly national financial institution, with branches throughout the states. Deeply convinced of the bank's corrupting influence on politics, and fearful that it would use its favored position and tremendous financial leverage to again try to force a recharter, Jackson determined to defang the bank by removing public moneys from its control.

In the spring of 1833, following his election to a second term and the resolution of the South Carolina nullification crisis, Jackson consulted his cabinet on the advisability of removal. Most members, including the Treasury secretary Louis McLane, were opposed, but Attorney General Roger Taney strongly approved. The bank's charter gave sole authority to remove federal deposits to the secretary of the Treasury, reporting directly to Congress. In March the House of Representatives voted overwhelmingly that the deposits were safe where they were. Jackson paid no heed. To facilitate removal he elevated McLane to the State Department and appointed the bank opponent William John Duane secretary of the Treasury. When Duane unexpectedly balked at ordering the removal, Jackson dismissed him in turn and put in Taney. In September Taney duly ordered that federal receipts henceforth be deposited in selected state-chartered banks, while existing balances in the Bank of the United States were drawn down to meet current expenses.

Critics denounced the removal as financially reckless and politically high-handed, even tyrannical. The Bank of the United States president Nicholas Biddle retaliated by sharply curtailing loans, triggering a panic that sent businessmen crying to Congress for relief. There, reaction against the removal prompted Jackson's myriad political enemies to coalesce under the new name of Whigs. Whigs charged Jackson with undermining the country's financial system in pursuit of his vendetta against Biddle, with corruptly steering federal funds to politically favored state banks, and with brazenly usurping congressional and ministerial authority—all evidence, they said, of a despotic purpose that threatened the foundations of republican government. In March 1834 the Senate adopted unprecedented resolutions, sponsored by the Whig leader Henry Clay, censuring Jackson for having "assumed upon himself authority and power not conferred by the Constitution and laws, but in derogation of both."

Unifying Jackson's opponents while invigorating his supporters, the removal episode furthered the emergence of a national two-party system. Democrats, led by Jackson, made opposition to chartered banking, first at the federal and then at the state level, a central element in their creed. Despite Whig fulminations, the removal itself held up. The financial distress quickly subsided, while the Bank of the United States, discredited by Biddle's overreaction, was not rechartered and ceased to be a federal institution in 1836. Taney, rejected as Treasury secretary by an angry Senate in the wake of the removal, was later nominated and confirmed to succeed John Marshall as chief justice of the Supreme Court, while the Senate censure of Jackson was expunged just before he left office in 1837.

BIBLIOGRAPHY

Catterall, Ralph C. H. *The Second Bank of the United States.* 1902. Reprint, Chicago: University of Chicago Press, 1960. Classic account, sympathetic to the bank.

Hammond, Bray. *Banks and Politics in America from the Revolution to the Civil War.* Princeton, N.J.: Princeton University Press, 1957. Intensely anti-Jackson.

Remini, Robert V. *Andrew Jackson and the Bank War.* New York: Norton, 1967. Brief, even-handed treatment.

Daniel Feller

See also **Bank of the United States; Expunging Resolution.**

REORGANIZED CHURCH OF JESUS CHRIST OF LATTER-DAY SAINTS

(RLDS) was organized in April 1860 at Amboy, Illinois, under the leadership of Joseph Smith III. Its members had formerly belonged to the Church of Jesus Christ of Latter-day Saints (LDS), founded by the prophet Joseph Smith Jr. in 1830. After the murder of Joseph Smith Jr. in 1844, some church members refused to acknowledge the authority of Brigham Young as Smith's successor or join the migration to Utah Territory. Rejecting the claims of other dissenters, like

RLDS Headquarters. The world headquarters in Independence, Mo., of the Reorganized Church of Jesus Christ of Latter-day Saints—the Mormons who refused to follow Brigham Young. © CORBIS

In the early twentieth century, the RLDS moved to Independence, Missouri. There in 1909 the church created the United Order of Enoch, an attempt at cooperative living that stressed the community's responsibility for all its members. Before his death, Smith also established a strong executive leadership, sharply curtailing the right of administrators to report to the general conference. In 1914, when the leadership passed to Smith's son Frederick M. Smith, the church had seventy-one thousand members. Frederick Smith took an even more authoritarian course, which provoked some defections in 1925. During the Great Depression of the 1930s, the church was forced to cut back sharply on expenditures and personnel. Smith, however, stressed the social aspects of faith, encouraging the RLDS to support industry in providing work for church members and to encourage culture and the arts.

After World War II, the church demonstrated a new interest in world mission. It acquired financial stability and placed a new emphasis on worship and the training of future leaders. Under William W. Smith, the church expressed limited support for the civil rights movement during the 1960s. During the 1970s, it began to stress the fellowship of those who acknowledge Jesus Christ as its guiding principle and adopted a more decentralized approach to mission work in Haiti and South America. In 1984, the church accepted female ordination, and by 1991, three thousand women had entered the ministry. By 1999 the church had 137,038 members. President W. Grant McMurray succeeded President Wallace B. Smith in 1995, and delegates to the church's 2000 World Conference changed its name to the Community of Christ.

BIBLIOGRAPHY

Howard, Richard P. *The Church through the Years.* 2 vols. Independence, Mo.: Herald Publishing, 1992–1993.

Launius, Roger D. *Joseph Smith III: Pragmatic Prophet.* Urbana: University of Illinois Press, 1988.

Jeremy Bonner

See also **Latter-day Saints, Church of Jesus Christ of.**

James Strang, the group appealed to the prophet's son to take on the leadership of the new denomination. The RLDS acknowledged more congregational autonomy than its parent church but accepted the authority of the Bible, the Book of Mormon, and the doctrine and covenants.

In 1860, Joseph Smith III attended the RLDS General Conference and accepted the leadership. During his early years in office, Smith exerted great influence through his editorship of the *True Latter Day Saint Herald.* He worked unceasingly to divorce the memory of his father from the doctrine of polygamy and to make his denomination conform more readily to American social norms than the LDS church. During the 1880s, he cooperated with federal authorities in their prosecutions of the LDS church in Utah for polygamy. The reorganization adopted an orthodox notion of the Trinity, and in the twentieth century abandoned the notion of baptisms for the dead.

REPARATION COMMISSION. In accordance with Articles 231–235 of the Treaty of Versailles, the Reparation Commission was directed to estimate damage done by Germany to Allied civilians and their property during World War I and to formulate methods of collecting assessments. The Reparation Commission fixed German liability at 132 billion gold marks (equivalent to $10.3 trillion in 2002) to be paid in annual installments. The German people and national politicians were outraged by the size of the payments. Massive inflation and growing unemployment forced the German government to default on its reparations by the early 1920s.

Charles G. Dawes, an American banker, was asked by the Allied Reparation Commission to investigate the problems of payments. His report, published in April 1924, proposed that annual payments of reparations be paid on a fixed scale. The Dawes Plan was initially a great success because it stabilized the currency, brought inflation under control, and lowered unemployment in Germany.

The crash of the U.S. stock market in October 1929 created another financial crisis for the German economy and so another commission, under a banker named Owen Young, was set up to consider reparations. The Allies adopted the Young Plan which reduced Germany's liability to $3.1 trillion with installments paid annually until 1988. When the payments started in May 1930, the Reparation Commission ceased to exist.

BIBLIOGRAPHY

Dawes, Rufus Cutler. *The Dawes Plan in the Making.* Indianapolis, Ind.: Bobbs-Merrill, 1925.

Keynes, John Maynard. *The Economic Consequences of the Peace.* New York: Penguin, 1988.

Reparations Commission. Record Group 43, Series 56–57, Boxes 1–3, Records of International Conferences, Commissions and Expositions, National Archives.

Von Strandmann, Hartmut P., ed. *Walter Rathenau: Industrialist, Banker, Intellectual, and Politician: Notes and Diaries 1907–1922.* Translated by Hilary Von Strandmann. New York: Oxford University Press, 1987.

James F. Adomanis

See also **Dawes Plan; Young Plan.**

REPRESENTATION.

REPRESENTATION. Political representation in the United States reflects a central tension of American democracy. On the one hand, America is a democratic form of government. Democracy requires a close connection between the citizens and laws that govern them. On the other hand, from the time of its founding, the size of the nation has prohibited all but a very small minority to write and pass legislation. Thus, political representation provides the connective tissue between the democratic rule of American citizens and the aristocratic lawmaking of members of Congress, the executive, and the judiciary.

There are four key areas that are central to the history of representation in the United States: voting rights; electoral rules for the House; rules for the Senate; and nonlegislative political representation in the executive, judiciary, and interest groups.

The Right to Vote

The right to vote is a legal right that defines which groups or types of people shall be included or excluded from choosing representatives. Because the size of the electorate is so large that a single vote in any election for national office is unlikely to affect the outcome of an election, the right to vote is a powerfully symbolic expression of the nation's judgment about what qualifies as full democratic citizenship.

As early as 1763, the concept of political representation has been closely tied to the right to vote and the legitimacy of government through the colonial protests against the Stamp Act. In that case, the English Parliament justified taxing their colonial "subjects" because colonial interests were said to be "virtually" represented in Parliament. The rejection of this argument was summed up in the apocryphal "no taxation without representation"—the demand that taxes could only be legitimately levied by legislators who themselves were accountable to the voters whom they taxed.

At the founding, the right to vote for members of the U.S. House of Representatives was determined by state law. Anyone who could legally vote for a member of their own state's "most numerous branch of the State Legislature" was granted the right to vote for members of the House. In practice, this meant that voting requirements varied between states and that virtually all voters were white males, with some minimal financial means.

The decision to exclude groups of voters rested on principled and prejudicial grounds. In principle, the right to vote was denied to groups of citizens when that group was judged to lack wisdom, political independence, and a demonstrated stake in society. Prejudicially, this meant that nonwhite "citizens," slaves, women, and children, and in a few cases Jews, Catholics, and other non-Protestants, were, with some notable exceptions, denied the vote. Today children, felons (in some states), and noncitizens are denied the vote precisely because they are judged to lack the political maturity (or, in the case of felons, they have given up their rights) of full citizenship.

Voting laws since the founding of the United States were increasingly restrictive until roughly the period of Reconstruction. Women in New Jersey, for example, were allowed to vote until formally "disenfranchised" in 1807. In many states, laws were added post-founding that explicitly restrict the suffrage to white men. But it is less clear whether these restrictions in practice eliminated many voters from the rolls. In general, laws are not passed until legislators perceive a need—for example, the emergence of speed limits during the twentieth century is not evidence that anyone in nineteenth-century America was traveling 60 mph on a highway. Speed limits were instead a response to the new automobile. Similarly, it is quite likely that voting restrictions appeared in the early nineteenth century only when women, blacks, immigrants, and others began to take advantage of the unintended openness of local voting laws. Thus newly codified restrictions on suffrage through the early nineteenth century may have been more properly understood not as a formal "taking away" of rights but rather as a codification of the underlying but unstated intention. In any case, the restrictions were certainly a symbolic offense.

After this initial contraction, voting laws expanded during a century of progress, beginning with the Constitutional amendments passed at the start of Reconstruction. The Fourteenth Amendment (ratified 9 July 1868) was the first Constitutional enactment that linked citizenship rights to the right to vote for any "male citizens twenty-one years of age in such State." But the linkage was in the form of a penalty for noncompliance rather than a guarantee of a right to vote. States were still allowed to restrict their citizens from voting, but if they did so, they would receive fewer representatives in Congress directly proportionate to those whom they disenfranchised. The Fifteenth Amendment (ratified 3 February 1870) made such infringement illegal, providing an explicit guarantee, "The right of citizens of the United States to vote shall not be denied or abridged by the United States or by any State on account of race, color or previous condition of servitude."

While the Fifteenth Amendment ended legally sanctioned racial discrimination at the ballot box, state laws were enacted that made voting by former slaves and other nonwhites difficult, if not impossible. Literacy tests and poll taxes were legally allowed but unevenly applied to white and nonwhite citizens. Intimidation and informal coercion ensured that voting by blacks in particular would be treacherous even if they could pass the legal tests. Only through the various Civil Rights Acts of the 1960s, particularly the Voting Rights Act of 1965 (extended and expanded in 1982), did the law guarantee blacks the right to vote.

While blacks formally received the right to vote just after the Civil War, women had to wait until 1920, the United States being the last of the then-industrialized nations to so extend its suffrage. The move for national voting rights for women began in Seneca Falls, New York, in 1848 by Elizabeth Cady Stanton, Lucretia Mott, and Susan B. Anthony. Illustrating the earlier point that law is enacted in response to perceived need, debate around the Fourteenth Amendment resulted in the adoption of the first reference to gender in the U.S. Constitution. By the period of Reconstruction, women were seen as a sufficient "threat" that the word "male" qualified the linkage between citizens and voting rights in the language of that amendment.

In 1890, the women's movement unified to form the National American Woman Suffrage Association (NAWSA). While earlier campaigns had emphasized the equal standing of women and men, NAWSA engaged a new strategy: women had distinctive qualities that were themselves worthy of political representation. After an initial and failed strategy on making state-level changes in voting rights in 1915, they shifted their efforts toward a Constitutional amendment. Buoyed by both major political parties believing they stood to benefit most from the new electorate, the Nineteenth Amendment was adopted on 18 August 1920, guaranteeing voting rights to all citizens regardless of sex.

The last major expansion of the right to vote reduced the age of suffrage from twenty-one to eighteen. The age restriction again reflected the principle that only those of political maturity should be given the right to vote. The establishment of the age of twenty-one as the start of political maturity had been adopted in the American colonies from English practice and was the age restriction on every state voting law through the late 1960s. A political movement to decrease the voting age to eighteen emerged during almost every U.S. war because boys under twenty-one were ordered by their government to risk their lives. Although a Constitutional amendment had been proposed in 1942 by Senators Arthur Vandenberg and Jennings Randolph, it never made it out of committee. Indeed, while there were some proposals among state governments to lower the voting age during World War II, only Georgia succeeded in doing so. While there was some movement on the issue during the 1950s, the push to extend the suffrage to younger voters finally succeeded during the Vietnam War. An outgrowth of the social and political youth movements that arose during this time, Democrats and Republicans soon began campaigning to reduce the age of political maturity to eighteen. In 1970, as part of the expansion of the Voting Rights Act, Congress reduced the age of voting in all elections to eighteen.

Many, however, thought such a law was unconstitutional. The Supreme Court in *Oregon v. Mitchell* ruled in a 5 to 4 decision that the law was only constitutional when applied to federal elections. Following that decision there existed a two-tiered voting system in the United States: for federal elections, anyone over eighteen years could vote; with few exceptions, twenty-one was still the age of majority for state and local elections. Because of the cost of administering such a system, as well as the political sentiments that had been brewing, the Twenty-sixth Amendment, formally reducing the age of voting to eighteen, was adopted on 1 July 1971.

Representation in the House: Apportionment and Districting

Representation in the House of Representatives is determined by two features of the U.S. political landscape: apportionment and districting.

Apportionment. Apportionment refers to the number of representatives in the House of Representatives that each state receives based on its population. By linking representation to population, the House of Representatives was created as a body that represented individual persons. At the founding, each state was apportioned no more than one representative for every thirty thousand inhabitants, with a minimum guarantee of one representative each. How an "inhabitant" is counted has varied widely by state, and has sometimes included citizens and noncitizens.

Infamously, the U.S. Constitution did not include Native Americans in this count and only counted "three-fifths" of each slave. It is this clause (Article I, Section 2) that some people point to as evidence that the founders thought blacks were only three-fifths human. But this attribution of three-fifths human is apocryphal, and ignores the effects of the clause: were slaves to be counted as full persons for the sake of apportionment, southern states would have been apportioned that many more representatives and thus given that much more political power in Congress. Indeed, it was slave owners in the South who advocated counting each slave as a whole person. And it was abolitionists—people who thought slaves were both fully human and unjustly bound to a wicked institution—who wished not to count slaves at all. A compromise of three-fifths emerged between the two sides because the number of "inhabitants" also determined how much each state owed the federal government in taxes.

The ratio of population to representatives would determine how large or small the legislature would be. James Madison had earlier warned that the size of a legislature was independent of the underlying population. It must be large enough "to guard against the cabals of a few" but small enough "to guard against the confusion of a multitude" and the first Congress after the first apportionment saw a body of 106 members. But because the size of Congress was linked to population size, as the latter grew, so did the legislature, though in decreasing speed. By the turn of the twentieth century, the U.S. House of Representatives had more than quadrupled its size, and in the second decade passed a law to fix the number of seats at 435. That number has been maintained since, with the exception of the period just after Alaska and Hawaii were admitted to the union, when the number of House members briefly rose to 437.

Districting. While apportionment determines how many of the 435 representatives each state will receive, districting refers to drawing of electoral constituencies within each state. An "electoral constituency" is simply a group of people who vote for a particular seat. Electoral constituencies had originally been territorial because of the close affinity between where people lived and the set of political interests important to them. In the colonies, all political representation was based on the town, parish or county in which a citizen lived, a practice adopted from English political life going back at least as far as the Magna Charta. This practice well suited early American political life since populations tended not to be a mobile as they later would be, and the ratio between population and representatives could be relatively small.

Yet when the U.S. Congress was proposed, both opponents and supporters realized the nature of territorial representation would fundamentally change. A ratio of one representative to thirty thousand people—the minimum size of any Congressional district—was a roughly tenfold increase in the average size of the state electoral district. Even if citizens found their affinities close to home, the congressional district was far too big to represent them in the way it had in their state and colonial governments. Opponents of the Constitution saw the large size of the congressional district as undermining the "strong chords of sympathy" that representatives needed to have with their constituents, and undermining of the communal bonds that had justified territorial representation in the first place. Advocates of the Constitution admitted that the large district would make it much more difficult for constituents to attach to their national representative but viewed this to be a salutary check—representatives would have to earn their constituents' respect based on the quality of their service to the nation. Furthermore, as James Madison famously argued in "Federalist 10," large congressional districts would tend to check the emergence of electoral factions at the district level, allowing, he hoped, the emergence of people who would have strong incentives to act in the public good in order to get reelected.

Founding intent did not accurately predict the response within the states to the newly enacted federal laws. First among the unforeseen consequences of the institutional rules of the U.S. Constitution was the rise of political parties. Political parties essentially group together many different kinds of interests in order to represent them more efficiently in Congress. Their effect on political representation was direct: many states continued more forcefully the English and colonial practice of drawing district lines to maximize party advantage. In 1812, the Massachusetts legislature approved a districting map that was lampooned by a newspaper cartoonist who accentuated the features of its shape, making it appear as a salamander. Despite Governor Elbridge Gerry's reluctant support for the map, the cartoonist nevertheless labeled it after him, and thus arose the term "gerrymander."

A second response to the institutions of political representation was the creation of multi-member, statewide districts. During the first fifty years of the republic, party affiliation mapped closely to geographical location: Federalists and Whigs, for example, commanded much of the coastal and city votes, while Democrats were far more popular in the rural sections of each state. Single-member territorial districts ensured that these geographical differences were represented in Congress. Sensing an opportunity for greater influence, states began electing their delegations as a whole, through majority vote. Thus, states with a small majority of one party or another were able to elect and send a congressional delegation all of one party. Since 1842, electoral constituencies have been single-member districts by law, although violations of that and subsequent "single-member laws" were not unusual and seldom challenged. With some notable exceptions, representatives to the House have been elected in "single-member districts" by "first past the post" rules ever since.

Finally, during the industrial period of the late nineteenth and early twentieth centuries, rural Americans moved into cities, as did a continued influx of immigrants. This had unexpected consequences for political representation in the United States. Urban centers became more heavily populated relative to rural towns but district lines were not redrawn; the effect was to "over-represent" people in less populated rural areas relative to their urban counterparts. By the middle of the twentieth century, there were great disparities in district size: some rural congressional districts had only tens of thousands of people, other urban districts were ten times or more that size.

Advocates in Illinois and Tennessee, among other states, sued their respective states arguing that, coming from cities, they did not receive fair representation. After rejecting the argument in the 1940s and 1950s on the basis that districting was a "political question" and not for them to decide, the Supreme Court argued in *Baker v. Carr* (1962) that the equal protection clause of the Fourteenth Amendment required districts to be of roughly equal size. Writing in his last dissent on the bench, Justice Felix Frankfurter argued that the Fourteenth Amendment could not possibly apply to this case because it provided its own remedy for voting irregularities. Nevertheless, in 1964, in a collection of cases headed by *Reynolds v. Sims*, the Court established its standard of "one-person-one-vote," ultimately requiring states to come as close to equality of population between districts, and requiring them to redistrict every ten years.

The history of the redistricting cases up to that point was a remnant of the urban-rural split that emerged in the twentieth century and was largely unrelated to civil rights issues. Only after the decision in *Reynolds v. Sims* was the concept "one-person-one-vote" used as a forceful weapon in the fight for minority voting rights in the Voting Rights Acts of 1965 and 1982, and the upholding of much of their law by the Supreme Court. Increasingly, this has meant that districts can be drawn not only to equalize population, but also to produce desired electoral outcomes, particularly the securing of electoral success for minority candidates.

Representation in the Senate

The House of Representatives had been conceived of as a body to represent the people of the United States. In contrast, the U.S. Senate was animated by a very different conception of political representation. Emerging out of the "great compromise" during the Constitutional Convention of 1787, the Senate had originally been modeled on the House of Lords in England—as an aristocratic "upper house" meant to provide a more reflective space in which its members could check the cruder ambitions of the lower house. Much of these "aristocratic" origins of the institution still remain: members of the Senate serve longer terms than those in the House (six years to two years respectively); they must be an older minimum age (thirty compared to twenty-five in the House); and their functions were seen as requiring greater discretion and discernment (for example, ratification of treatises and advising and approving the executive's judicial nominees).

But even during the summer of 1787, the aristocratic nature of the Senate had shifted to something more practical. Owing to the "great compromise," the Senate was created in order to represent the states as political units, with each state receiving equal political representation (two senators per state) much as in the House, each person received equal political representation. Thus, from

the ratification of the Constitution until 1913, senators were elected by their state legislators rather than by the citizens of the state. In 1913, the Seventeenth Amendment was ratified after which individual voters were able to directly elect their U.S. senators.

Executive, Judicial, and Interest Group Representation

The executive and judicial branches must also be considered locations of political representation in the United States. In the executive branch, the nation as a whole is thought to be represented, and the symbols of that branch—the White House and the president—are regularly held to be symbols of the country. In the case of the judiciary as it has developed from its founding, the Constitution or supreme law of the land finds its representation.

Finally, the rights granted in the Bill of Rights, particularly the rights of free expression and congregation, have allowed citizens to form groups around various interests and to organize to persuade their elected representatives on issues that matter to them. The appropriateness of such "lobbying" activities—including giving money to political campaigns—has been debated throughout American history. In any case, there is little doubt that interest group lobbying remains a distinctive and important hallmark of political representation in the United States.

BIBLIOGRAPHY

Bybee, Keith J. *Mistaken Identity: The Supreme Court and the Politics of Minority Representation.* Princeton, N.J.: Princeton University Press, 1998.

Cooke, Jacob E., ed. *The Federalist.* Middletown, Conn.: Wesleyan University Press, 1982.

Foner, Eric. *Reconstruction: America's Unfinished Revolution: 1863–1877.* New York: Harper and Row, 1988.

Grofman, Bernard, and Chandler Davidson, eds. *Controversies in Minority Voting: The Voting Rights Act in Perspective.* Washington, D.C.: The Brookings Institution, 1992.

Keyssar, Alexander. *The Right to Vote: The Contested History of Democracy in the United States.* New York: Basic Books, 2000.

Nelson, William E. *The Fourteenth Amendment: From Political Principle to Judicial Doctrine.* Cambridge, Mass.: Harvard University Press, 1988.

Pole, Jack R. *Political Representation in England and the Origins of the American Republic.* Berkeley: University of California Press, 1971.

Rehfeld, Andrew. "Silence of the Land: On the Historical Irrelevance of Territory to Congressional Districting and Political Representation in the United States." *Studies in American Political Development* 15 (spring 2001): 53–87.

Storing, Herbert J., ed. *The Anti-Federalist: Writings by the Opponents of the Constitution.* Abridged by Murray Dry. Chicago: University of Chicago Press, 1985.

Andrew Rehfeld

See also **Elections; Federalist Papers; Representative Government; Stamp Act; Suffrage.**

REPRESENTATIVE GOVERNMENT has historically denoted a system in which people elect their lawmakers (representatives), who are then held accountable to them for their activity within government. Representative government, or the "republican form," as it is also known, has been widely accepted as the only practicable form of democracy.

In America, the acceptance of representative government as a legitimate democratic form has long-standing roots. The argument can be traced back to the English philosopher John Locke (1632–1704), whose *Second Treatise of Government* (1690) was widely read by the founders. Locke called for consent to government rather than direct consent to the laws. Thomas Jefferson reflected this in the Declaration of Independence (1776), writing that governments, rather than laws, derived their "just powers from the consent of the governed."

Most American colonial governments were representative in the sense of being ruled by elected lawmakers, though some, notably Pennsylvania's, were not. American federal and state governments have been representative since the founding in 1789 (or their admission into the union). Federal lawmakers are all regularly elected and must stand for reelection every two, four, or six years. All state governments are required and constitutionally guaranteed to be representative forms (U.S. Constitution, Article 3, section 4).

The fact that the size of the United States required representation did not sit well with a generation that had fought for the right to self-rule. Nor does it sit well with contemporary advocates of greater civic participation today. The central conceptual tension of representative government throughout American history may thus be posed as the question that animated the founding of its institutions: How close must the people be to the laws that govern them?

Problems of Size

The first answer to this question is practical necessity: there must be a considerable distance given the size of the nation. By the close of the seventeenth century, the colonies were simply too large to govern themselves directly. As Thomas Paine observed in *Common Sense* (1776), representative government was the only form of democracy practicable for 3 to 4 million people spread across such a large geographical space. It was simply impossible for such a large community to meet beneath one tree.

There were two other prudential reasons for preferring representative government. First, even if all the people could meet in one place, people had other things to do; representative government allowed division of labor. The English radical Algernon Sidney (1623–1683) presented a second reason in his *Discourses Concerning Government* (1698). Direct democracy would concentrate all the citizens of a nation in one place and leave it unprotected from foreign invaders. Representative government

thus allowed the people a role in government commensurate with national security.

Closing the Gap

After the War of Independence, some Americans argued against a large national government on the grounds that representative government would be unstable and too far removed from the people. This position would later become the basis for the opposition to the U.S. Constitution among a group of writers now known as the anti-federalists. The argument against a large national government derived from the French political philosopher Montesquieu's *The Spirit of the Laws* (1748). Montesquieu argued that democracy, even in the form of representative government, would be inherently unstable and thus unsuited for a nation much larger than the ancient city-states and the Italian republics where it had historically been successful.

The first government of the United States, embodied in the Articles of Confederation (1781–1789), reflected this teaching. First, the government under the articles was severely limited, requiring unanimity and taking state governments rather than the people as its objects. Representatives to the federal government were elected by state legislatures and not by the people directly. During this period, the people were governed by their states, and thus the distance between them and their laws was not as large as it would later be under the U.S. Constitution. Second, the practice of "instructions" was instituted in some states during this period. Instructions were binding commands from constituents to their representatives to vote in a manner the constituents prescribed. They were never widely adopted but did receive limited support, particularly in Maryland and New England.

Favoring Representative Government

The English politician and political theorist Edmund Burke articulated the alternative position in England. Burke argued that a representative had only the nation's best interest to guide him and should take the interests of his constituents only under advisement. While Burke's position was the extreme on this issue, by the time of the ratification of the U.S. Constitution (1789), the tide was turning toward representational independence.

As part of this turning, James Madison presented an argument refuting Montesquieu and establishing representative government as a preferable form. Madison's argument, presented in "Federalist No. 10," defended representative government precisely because of the buffer it created between the people and the laws that governed them. The grave threat to government was "factions," groups of citizens, whether a "majority or a minority of the whole," animated and organized against the "permanent and aggregate interests of the community." Direct democracies ensured that these factions would dominate, but representative government, however, especially over a large territory and population, would remove such a threat.

A larger nation meant extremely large constituencies for each representative, reducing the likelihood that constituents would be able to coordinate around a factional plan. Absent this coordination representatives would be more likely to pursue the common good, even if it went against some subgroup within their constituency. Madison thought that candidates themselves were more likely to succeed by appearing to be concerned with the public good than by trying to please a disparate group of partial interests. Men were not angels, Madison argued, but institutions might encourage them to act as if they were in order to be elected, and that would be an improvement.

The Continuing Tension
The subsequent emergence of political parties undercut much of Madison's argument, especially in the electoral dynamics of the congressional district. But by the time of the founding, the fact that people would be separated from their law was either grudgingly accepted as a necessary evil or warmly embraced as a beneficial consequence. Once representative government was established, the debate about representation, who should be granted the right to vote and how districts should be defined, became highly contentious.

But the central tension of representative government, striking a balance between the sovereignty of the people and the authority of their laws, has remained a prominent feature of the debate. Nowhere has this tension been more evident than in the case of the courts and the federal bureaucracy. These institutions are very far removed from the will of the people, yet both purportedly have the ability to craft legislation of a sort in the form of court orders and constitutional review (in the courts) and of regulations and statutes (in the federal bureaucracy). Representative government will always involve a distance between the people and the laws that govern them, even if the appropriate distance will remain a debated topic for some time.

BIBLIOGRAPHY
Manin, Bernard. *The Principles of Representative Government.* New York: Cambridge University Press, 1997.

Pitkin, Hanna Fenichel. *The Concept of Representation.* Berkeley: University of California Press, 1967.

Reid, John Phillip. *The Concept of Representation in the Age of the American Revolution.* Chicago: University of Chicago Press, 1989.

Storing, Herbert J. *What the Anti-Federalists Were for: The Political Thought of the Opponents of the Constitution.* Chicago: University of Chicago Press, 1981.

Andrew Rehfeld

See also **Antifederalists; Democracy; Federalist Party; Popular Sovereignty; Representation; Republic.**

REPTILES. *See* **Herpetology.**

REPUBLIC. The word *republic* derives from the Latin *res publica*; *res* means "thing" or "affair," and *publica* means "public," as opposed to "private." The word thus denotes government in which politics is a public affair and not the personal prerogative of a single ruler. There have been aristocratic republics and oligarchic republics, but, as applied to the United States government, this term usually connotes a democratic republic, one in which elected representatives carry out the functions of government. This conception of the terms derives both from classical philosophy and eighteenth-century liberal thought. In the context of the debate over the CONSTITUTION OF THE UNITED STATES in 1788, federalists refined the concept further so that the term *republic* referred to a particular kind of DEMOCRACY.

James Madison, Alexander Hamilton, and John Jay articulated this conception of a republic in their 1788 essays that were later compiled as *The Federalist Papers.* These essays, intended to support the ratification of the federal Constitution in New York, distinguished a republic from a pure democracy, describing the latter as "a society consisting of a small number of citizens, who assemble and administer the government in person." In the context of *The Federalist Papers*, a republic differed from a pure democracy only in that it was "a government in which the scheme of representation takes place." According to this interpretation, a republic was a representative democracy. As Madison pointed out, the representative principle militates against the irresponsible exercise of majority power, for it makes a large republic possible, and it is difficult in a large republic for any faction to become a majority. According to these authors, a large republic would foster the formation of many factions, and this sheer multiplicity of interests in turn would create shifting coalitions, which would hinder the formation of an oppressive or irresponsible majority. Furthermore, because of the checks and balances and separation of powers between different branches and levels of government, any upstart tyrannical faction would encounter many legal and institutional roadblocks.

Europeans had established partly or wholly representative governments before the American Revolution, but none was both wholly representative and wholly democratic. The republic of the United States achieved that novel combination. A danger remained, however, according to Alexis de Tocqueville, in its representative institutions: if representatives are little better than their constituents, he argued, the hoped-for improvement in the government of democracy might come to nothing.

BIBLIOGRAPHY
Bailyn, Bernard. *The Ideological Origins of the American Revolution.* Cambridge, Mass.: Belknap Press of Harvard University Press, 1992.

Banning, Lance. *The Sacred Fire of Liberty: James Madison and the Founding of the Federal Republic.* Ithaca, N.Y.: Cornell University Press, 1995.

Hamilton, Alexander, John Jay, and James Madison. *The Federalist Papers.* ed. Gary Wills. New York: Bantam Books, 1981.

Morton J. Frisch/s. b.

See also **Antifederalists; Citizenship; Constitution of the United States;** *Federalist Papers;* **Liberalism; Political Theory; Republicanism.**

REPUBLICAN PARTY.

The Republican Party began at a protest meeting in Ripon, Wisconsin, on 28 February 1854 as a group of ANTISLAVERY activists, known as Free Soilers, met to start a new grassroots movement. The first party convention took place in Jackson, Michigan, that same year on 6 July. The group adopted the name of the political party of Thomas Jefferson, which later evolved more directly into the Democratic Party. The Republican Party emerged directly out of the FREE SOIL PARTY in the North, a movement embraced at various times by such Democrats as Martin Van Buren, who ran unsuccessfully for the presidency on the Free Soil Party ticket in 1848, and David Wilmot, a member of the U.S. House of Representatives (1845–1851). Numerically more significant was the Republican Party's support from disillusioned northern Whigs. With the collapse of the WHIG PARTY in the 1850s, the Republicans emerged as one of the legatees of the Whig organization.

Ideological Roots

Ideologically the early Republican Party arose out of three traditions, the first of which was the reform tradition that followed on the heels of the Second Great Awakening. The Second Great Awakening was a religious revival movement that engulfed the early American republic in the first two decades of the nineteenth century. Many Second Great Awakening leaders came to abandon the orthodox Calvinist emphasis on predestination and human depravity in favor of a more optimistic view that the world could be made a better place by individuals seeking their own salvation. This doctrine connecting the individual to social progress was influential on a number of important reforms, many of them supported by the Whigs and others supported by third-party movements centered on a single issue. In temperance reform, public education, women's rights and antislavery efforts among others, this religious reform impulse was very important. Although most Republicans did not endorse equal rights for women, or immediate abolition of SLAVERY for that matter, they were more likely to see themselves as "their brother's keepers," a role entirely consistent with the Puritan tradition and anathematic to many others of a libertarian bent. This reform tradition helped inspire many of those who opposed slavery's extension into the territories. The LIBERTY PARTY and the Free Soil Party had previously served as the political vehicles for this movement. Nearly all the Republican leaders except Abraham Lincoln had strong connections to some of these antebellum reform movements.

The second important influence on the Republicans was the economic policies sponsored by Henry Clay and his allies in the Whig Party. Clay believed that the government should act to develop the American economy by promoting protective TARIFFS on "infant" industries such as textiles and iron. These protective tariffs would pay for internal improvements to the transportation infrastructure, such as roads, rivers, harbors, and most importantly in the 1850s, railroads. A rechartered Bank of the United States would provide a uniform currency with its banknotes and would channel investment throughout the Union.

The third influence on the Republican Party was NATIVISM. Since the 1790s the United States had gone through periods in which some Americans sought to define national identity tribally rather than by adherence to ideas or institutions. Founders such as John Jay thought only Protestants would make good Americans. With the tremendous influx of Irish and Germans, many of them Catholics, in the 1840s and 1850s, some Protestant Americans feared that American institutions would be "overrun" or destroyed entirely by illiterate paupers whose allegiance was to the Vatican.

Early Presidential Elections

The Republican Party nominated John C. Fremont as its first presidential candidate in 1856. Fremont was a hero of the Mexican-American War. Although the Democratic candidate, James Buchanan, enjoyed a landslide victory in that year, the Republicans made important gains in Congress and in the northern tier of states from New England to Wisconsin. While the Republicans in Congress and in the northern states tended to be radical free soilers, the party needed a candidate who appealed to northern moderates for the presidential election of 1860. In a field dominated by antislavery activists like William E. Seward and Salmon P. Chase, one candidate stood out: Abraham Lincoln of Illinois. Lincoln had shown himself to be a formidable debater and campaigner in the U.S. Senate contest against Stephen Douglas in 1858. He stood as a principled opponent of slavery's extension into the territories and he also stood with other economic interests that the Whigs had once favored and the Republican Party now represented: protective tariffs, a homestead law, federal land grants for higher education, federal sponsorship of internal improvements, and, most importantly, federal aid for a transcontinental railroad. Unlike some of the Know-Nothing converts to Republicanism, Lincoln opposed restrictions on immigration or any discrimination against Catholics.

The Republican Party was victorious in 1860 because it understood an electoral lesson the Democrats failed to remember: the presidential elections of the nineteenth and twentieth centuries were won in the Lower North, a region from New Jersey to Illinois. With those electoral votes, no candidate could be defeated. Without them, no candidate could win. Despite the fact that Lincoln won in a four-way race with only 39 percent of the popular vote, he would still have won in the Electoral College if all his opposition had united on a single candidate. For the rest of the century, the Republican Party represented the Lower North, and insofar as it represented its constituency well, it found itself usually in control of the presidency and the Senate, and for a significant portion of the time, in control of the House of Representatives.

Lincoln's reelection in 1864 was by no means assured until the string of Union victories in that year inspired confidence among wavering voters. Union voters strongly supported the Republicans, over the former commander of the Army of the Potomac, George McClellan. In the years after Lincoln's assassination, northern public opinion turned strongly against the conciliatory Reconstruction policy of Lincoln, and the inconsistent harsh and tepid policy of Andrew Johnson. With southern states reimposing chattel slavery in all but name and electing former Confederate generals to represent them in Congress, the tide of northern opinion turned against appeasement. In the elections of 1866 and 1868 the Radical faction of the Republicans gained control of the congressional party and used its power to enact sweeping changes in the post–Civil War United States. The Radicals, including Thaddeus Stevens and Charles Sumner, sponsored the Fourteenth and Fifteenth Amendments to the Constitution, which provided equal rights under the law and manhood suffrage for African Americans. Stevens went so far as to propose that freedmen who were heads of households be given forty acres and a mule from confiscated land of high Confederate military and civilian officers, by which they might establish their economic independence.

The Gilded Age

The next ten years after the CIVIL WAR saw Republicans' attempts to re-create a new society in the South, with black voters and officeholders supporting the Republican Party. After the election of 1876, however, with a compromise worked out to avoid disputed southern electoral votes to Republican Rutherford B. Hayes, the Republicans withdrew their support for the federal army's enforcement of RECONSTRUCTION. Within a short time the South began restricting black voting. Outside the mountain South, Republicans had almost no support among southern whites. The pattern of support for Republicans was set at this time until well into the twentieth century. Republicans enjoyed strong support among Yankee Protestants in every region of the United States, from New England and upstate New York, through the upper Midwest and into the Northwest. German Lutherans, Scots-Irish Presbyterians, and African Americans in the North tended to vote Republican as did mountain southerners. Among the newer immigrants, the Republican Party enjoyed some support among Italians, French Canadians,

and Russian Jews. Many skilled laborers, particularly in industries that enjoyed tariff protection voted for the Grand Old Party, as it came to be known in the GILDED AGE. Only two groups proved almost entirely immune to the attractions of the Republican Party: southern whites and Irish Catholics.

The Republican Party in the Gilded Age divided into two groups, set apart more by federal civil service patronage than by principle: the "Half Breeds" and the "STALWARTS." In the late-nineteenth century, in addition to protectionism, the Republican Party was best known for its advocacy of a high-profile foreign policy, particularly in the Caribbean and the Pacific. Republicans sponsored American annexation of HAWAII and a group of Republicans were the most vociferous advocates of war with Spain to liberate Cuba. Many of these same Republicans argued for retention of the conquered territories of Puerto Rico and the Philippines. Dissident voices against American overseas expansion and against "corruption" began to defect in the mid-1880s to the more reform-minded Democrats. These Republican defectors became known as "MUGWUMPS."

Populism and Progressivism

In the 1896 election, the Republicans successfully faced a challenge from the agrarian or "Populist" wing of the Democratic Party and the "People's Party." These Populists argued for an expansionary monetary policy based on the valuation of silver. In the midst of the depression of 1893, an easing of credit appealed to farmers in the South and West, but an inflationary money policy was adverse to the interests of wageworkers. With promises of prosperity and protectionism, the Republicans under William McKinley successfully appealed to workers, and new immigrants, particularly those non-evangelicals most alienated by William Jennings Bryan's religiously inspired rhetoric. The Republican Party held power for the better part of the next thirty-six years outside the South, interrupted only by Woodrow Wilson's two terms as president.

The Republican Party was divided over Progressivism. After McKinley's assassination, Theodore Roosevelt called for new initiatives in economic policy, designed to assert the power of the federal government in economic regulation. Roosevelt viewed the federal government as the arbiter when concentrated economic power threatened to overturn the limiting powers of the market.

At the end of Roosevelt's first elected term, he announced he would not seek reelection, and anointed William H. Taft as his successor. Although Taft embarked on a vigorous prosecution of trusts, Roosevelt soon grew disillusioned with him. Roosevelt's challenge to Taft in 1912, first within the Republican Party and then in forming the Progressive Party, split the Republican vote and allowed Democrat Woodrow Wilson to win the White House. After the outbreak of WORLD WAR I, Republicans proved eager to enter the war on the side of the Allies, but the party reverted to ISOLATIONISM after the end of the war.

Twentieth Century

From 1918 to 1932 the Republican Party was predominant in part because of the profound cultural alienation of Americans after World War I. Warren G. Harding promised a return to "normalcy" (not a word until Harding coined it). Republicans at this time linked themselves to the enduring values of the rural Old America: isolationism, nativism, Protestantism, Prohibition, and protection.

Under Calvin Coolidge, the Republicans rolled back corporate taxes and cut spending, reducing the size of government. Despite the Teapot Dome scandal affecting the Harding administration, Republicans continued to enjoy strong political support in 1924 and in 1928, in part because of the unprecedented prosperity of the United States in the 1920s. The Republican presidential and congressional elections gathered landslide support in all regions of the United States except the South.

The election of Herbert Hoover in 1928 was an important victory for the Republicans. While the Republicans had already won two elections in the 1920s, Hoover's victory was more substantive. Hoover had been director general of the American Relief Administration in the aftermath of World War I. In the midst of general prosperity, Hoover campaigned on the slogan, "A CHICKEN IN EVERY POT, a car in every garage." A Quaker, Hoover represented old-fashioned Protestant rectitude against everything his political opponent Al Smith stood for: urbanism, cosmopolitanism, and Catholicism. Hoover won an overwhelming victory. Smith captured only the heavily Catholic states of Massachusetts, Rhode Island, and Louisiana, and the Deep South states of Mississippi, Alabama, Georgia and South Carolina, that scorned Republicans more than they feared Catholics.

As the GREAT DEPRESSION deepened, Hoover's inability to mount an effective mustering of moral and rhetorical resources was his most significant failure. Hoover was a lukewarm Republican Progressive and, as such, he tried a few half-hearted attempts to stimulate the economy, most notably with the NATIONAL RECOVERY ADMINISTRATION. His worst failing was his insistence on old-fashioned budget balancing, calling for tax increases as the economy shrank, and reducing government spending as revenues declined. The Republican Congress responded with an equally shortsighted policy: a ruinous increase in protective tariffs under the Smoot-Hawley tariffs, a vindictive form of trade policy that generated trade reprisals from America's principal trading partners and made economic recovery—for Europe, Japan, and America—that much more difficult.

Franklin D. Roosevelt's landslide victories in 1932 and 1936 pushed the Republicans into near-eclipse. The Democrats cemented the loyalties of a new generation of Americans in the cities, particularly southern and eastern Europeans, Catholics, Jews, and, for the first time in American politics, the most reliably Republican of all ethnic blocs: African Americans. With Roosevelt's campaign for a third term in 1940, the Republicans nominated a likeable, internationalist former Democrat, Wendell Willkie, who reduced the Democratic majorities. In 1946 the Republicans were able to regain control of Congress for the first time in sixteen years. Thanks to the cooperation of President Harry Truman and Senator Arthur Vandenberg, bipartisan internationalism prevailed in foreign policy, and Republicans were instrumental in supporting the MARSHALL PLAN for European economic development, the NORTH ATLANTIC TREATY ORGANIZATION (NATO), the military alliance of Western Europe and North America organized against the Soviet Union, and the UNITED NATIONS. A group of Republicans in Congress under the leadership of Representative Richard Nixon of California held investigations into the charges that the Roosevelt and Truman administrations had coddled Communists in their midst. This accusation and particularly the charges against State Department undersecretary Alger Hiss created ill will between Truman and the Republicans.

The KOREAN WAR and Republican charges of "Korea, Communism, and Corruption," helped defeat the Democrats in both the presidential and congressional elections of 1952. Dwight D. Eisenhower, the popular Allied commander of the European theater in WORLD WAR II was elected president but his coattails did not allow for the control of Congress after the first two years. Republicans in the White House and in Congress proved unwilling, or unable to rein in Senator Joseph McCarthy's congressional investigations of Communists in government. McCarthy's hearings sometimes appeared both farcical and brutal at the same time. Only after the public became aware of his excesses did the repressive climate end.

In 1956, despite a heart attack, Eisenhower was elected to a second term. He provided international stability and attempted to engage in serous disarmament talks with Premier Nikita Khrushchev of the Soviet Union. In domestic policy, Eisenhower made great gains. Working in collaboration with a bipartisan coalition in Congress, the president promoted federal aid to education, sent troops to Little Rock, Arkansas, to enforce desegregation, and supported a national network of interstate highways. Nevertheless, Eisenhower's detached style of governing and the recession of the late 1950s contributed to a fall in his popularity.

In 1960 Democrat John F. Kennedy defeated Republican Richard Nixon. With Nixon's defeat, a group of new conservatives organized to overturn the Republican "Eastern Establishment." United under the banner of Senator Barry Goldwater, these conservatives secured Goldwater's nomination over the Establishment candidate Nelson Rockefeller. Although Goldwater was resoundingly defeated by Lyndon Johnson in 1964, the Republican Party was changed forever by the 1964 election: hereafter the party was more conservative, more issues-oriented, and more western and southern.

Richard Nixon was able to win election to the presidency in 1968 against a divided and discredited Demo-

113

cratic Party and with third-party candidate George Wallace taking the Deep South. In his first term Nixon united the conservatives and the moderates, and for the first time in the Republican Party's history, brought in large numbers of white southerners. This coalition, combined with conservative white ethnics in the North, brought Nixon a landslide victory in 1972. With the WATERGATE scandal and Nixon's resignation, the Republicans were badly defeated in congressional races in 1974 and Gerald Ford was defeated in the presidential race of 1976 by Jimmy Carter.

In 1980 Carter's difficulties with the Iranian government's refusal to return American hostages and the divisions within the Democrats weakened his claim on reelection in 1980. Ronald Reagan was elected president and succeeded in securing his legislative agenda, as no president had done for nearly twenty years. Working with a Republican Senate and a Democratic House of Representatives, Reagan sponsored a dramatic cut in taxes for those in the higher income brackets. His effort to scale back spending proved less effective, however. Nevertheless Reagan achieved impressive foreign policy triumphs. He negotiated substantial arms reduction with President Mikhail Gorbachev of the Soviet Union. He was triumphantly reelected in 1984, and he remained very popular personally, despite his administration's involvement in trading arms to Iran for hostages.

His successor, George H. W. Bush, was also successful in presiding over a coalition of Americans, Arab states, and Europeans that achieved a military victory against Iraq, when that country invaded Kuwait. Bush remained at record levels of public approval until shortly before the 1992 election. In a three-way race with Bill Clinton and Ross Perot, Bush was defeated.

In the first two years of the Clinton presidency the Republicans played a defensive strategy. With Clinton's failure to pass any form of his proposed health care legislation, the Republicans in Congress organized to defeat the Democratic majority in both houses. In what amounted to a public vote of no confidence in the Democratic Party, the Republicans took control of the Senate, and, for the first time in forty years, the House of Representatives as well. Under the effective electoral strategy of Speaker of the House Newt Gingrich, the Republicans maintained their majority in both houses for the rest of the decade. Their legislative strategy proved less effective. Republicans allowed the government to be shut down on two occasions in 1995, inconveniencing and alienating the public. Gingrich was unable to secure the passage of his CONTRACT WITH AMERICA, which promised term limits and greater legislative accountability. The Republican candidate for president, former Kansas senator Robert Dole, was resoundingly defeated in 1996.

President Clinton's admission of contradictions between his sworn testimony and his actual behavior in his sexual relationship with White House intern Monica Lewinsky allowed the Republican leadership to launch the impeachment of Clinton on the grounds that he committed perjury. In his Senate trial, however, Clinton was acquitted because a majority of the Senate, including some moderate Republicans, refused to vote for his removal.

The election of 2000, between Vice President Albert Gore and Texas governor George W. Bush, resulted in an indeterminate result. After much investigation, the disputed electoral votes of Florida were awarded to Bush in a U.S. Supreme Court decision split straight down ideological lines. The Republicans only enjoyed complete control of the Congress for a few months after the election. The defection of Senator James Jeffords of Vermont to Independent allowed the Democrats to organize the Senate, and the government was once again under divided control.

BIBLIOGRAPHY

Belz, Herman. *A New Birth of Freedom: The Republican Party and Freedmen's Rights, 1861 to 1866.* Westport, Conn.: Greenwood, 1976.

Gienapp, William E. *The Origins of the Republican Party, 1852–1856.* New York: Oxford University Press, 1986.

Marcus, Robert D. *Grand Old Party: Political Structure in the Gilded Age, 1880–1896.* New York, Oxford University Press, 1971.

Mayer, George H. *The Republican Party, 1854–1964.* New York: Oxford University Press, 1964.

McKinney, Gordon B. *Southern Mountain Republicans, 1865–1900: Politics and the Appalachian Community.* Chapel Hill: University of North Carolina Press, 1978.

Merrill, Horace Samuel, and Marion Galbraith Merrill. *The Republican Command, 1897–1913.* Lexington: University Press of Kentucky, 1971.

Mohr, James C., ed. *Radical Republicans in the North: State Politics during Reconstruction.* Baltimore: Johns Hopkins University Press, 1976.

Montgomery, David. *Beyond Equality: Labor and the Radical Republicans.* New York: Knopf, 1967.

Rae, Nicol C. *The Decline and Fall of the Liberal Republicans: From 1952 to the Present.* New York: Oxford University Press, 1989.

———. *Conservative Reformers: Republican Freshmen and the Lessons of the 104th Congress.* Armonk, N.Y.: M. E. Sharpe, 1998.

Richardson, Heather Cox. *The Death of Reconstruction: Race, Labor, and Politics in the Post–Civil War North, 1865–1901.* Cambridge, Mass.: Harvard University Press, 2001.

Rutland, Robert Allen. *The Republicans: From Lincoln to Bush.* Columbia: University of Missouri Press, 1996.

Andrew W. Robertson

See also **Democratic Party; Political Parties; Radical Republicans; Two-Party System.**

REPUBLICANISM is a term historians use to encompass the bundle of beliefs held by early Americans as they made the ideological transformation from loyal colonists to rebels and Patriots. Commonly applied to members of the elite, this protean word is easily adjusted to describe the ideological changes within the minds of common white men, Native Americans, African Americans, and women. Whether republicanism affects the structure of society from the top down or the bottom up is a matter of fierce debate. There is a consensus that republicanism infused the revolutionary generation and steered the debate over the writing of the Constitution—and the meaning of citizenship in the early republic.

The Basis of Republicanism

Classical republicanism insisted that civic virtue—the capacity to place the good of the commonwealth above one's own interest—became the key element of constitutional stability and liberty-seeking order. Only men who had a stake in society, preferably freeholder status of some magnitude, who were literate and familiar with major classical and Enlightenment thinkers, could lead society. Other people, including women, younger men, and the enslaved, had to depend on the elite's virtue to protect them against tyranny, conquest, and natural disasters. Americans understood that their newly arising state was part of history and thereby needed careful surveillance against the corruptions of time and excessive liberty. Ultimately, the American republican vision rested on four interlocking concepts. First, the ultimate goal of any political society should be the preservation of the public good or commonwealth; second, the citizens of a republic had to be capable of virtue, or the subordination of one's private interests in service of public needs; third, to be virtuous, citizens had to be independent of the political will of other men; fourth, citizens had to be active in the exercise of their citizenship.

Looking to the past for instructive examples, American thinkers searched the humanist legacies of Aristotle, Cicero, Tacitus, Plutarch, and others to bolster their beliefs that a simple, agricultural world nurtured civic humanism. Self-interest and patronage corrupted the simplicity of virtue and destroyed such past civilizations and would, if unchecked, ruin American society as well. While the American elite landed gentry and small farmers understood the advancing concept of capitalism and its concomitant qualities of self-interest, greed, and luxury, they believed that a hierarchical society led by the best men could curb excesses and preserve liberty for all.

A Struggle over Definition

As Joyce Appleby has noted, American scholars took to theories of republicanism as a chemist would to the discovery of a new element. For scholars, republicanism offered a solution for the divisive debate over the character of the revolutionary generation. One view, articulated during the Progressive Era by Charles and Mary Beard, was that interest groups were the "pistons in the engine of change," and that the Revolution was as much a conflict, as Carl Becker put it, over who shall rule at home as over who shall rule. Opposing this version of American

exceptionalism were scholars who noted the preponderance of English folkways. Moreover, Perry Miller and then Bernard Bailyn and Gordon Wood favored taking American writings seriously and accentuating their wrangling over their place in the British Empire. By the era of the American Revolution (1775–1783), this dissension had reached, as J. G. A. Pocock reported, a "Machiavellian moment," in which a new republican comprehension of history among the Patriots produced a powerful anxiety over English corruption. The biggest problems were the new moneymakers in London, their "corrupt and venal ministry," and a desire to enslave Americans.

Once Bailyn and other scholars started looking at the pamphlet wars in late colonial America, they found much to bolster their beliefs. In words and in symbols, early Americans articulated their themes and ideology. Bailyn showed how colonial Americans felt their virtue stemmed from the country faction of English politics and identified with its anxieties over court corruption, luxury, degeneration, and fear of enslavement. They felt a kinship with the country faction's critique of merchants and lawyers who set up international networks that ensnared the needy and unaware small producers, enslaved them, and weakened their civic humanism. As the revolutionary crisis of the 1760s and 1770s picked up steam, colonists argued about these anxieties in newspaper articles and pamphlets that were distributed widely along the Atlantic Coast. As subjects of the Crown, they had to be careful about identifying themselves and made plain their convictions through a series of pseudonyms. About half of the writers adopted monikers borrowed from republican Roman thought such as Publius, Brutus, and Cato. Two other significant groups took names from English Commonwealth heroes such as Harrington and Sidney or from such Greeks as Lycurgus, Solon, and Timeon. These ideas were expanded upon during the constitutional debates of the 1780s. Republican themes may also be found in the paper money, coins, state seals, and membership certificates of the era.

Further complicating these debates were the advents of modernization, population growth, and capitalism. Americans, like their European counterparts, were changing rapidly. Yeoman and gentry farmers, the prize proponents of republican ideology, were becoming capitalists and individualists by the 1750s. Because of this, republicanism might be construed as the last, nostalgic beliefs of a dying class of agrarian traditionalists. The American Revolution ensured that there would be wider distribution of land for common white males, who could offer greater support for their gentry leaders. Tradition-bound republicans adhered to a hierarchy of power. Noble birth, refinement, and money enhanced the dignity and purity of politics.

A Change in Power

Scholars of republicanism disagree sharply about when its power dissipated. Gordon Wood has contended that the defeat of the Anti-Federalists in the constitutional vote of 1787 was the last gasp of classical republicanism. Disagreeing with Wood are such scholars as Lance Banning and Joyce Appleby, who have uncovered the resurgence of classic ideals among the Jeffersonian republicans of the 1790s. While the Jeffersonians, Appleby contends, were capitalist and liberal, they used classical republicanism as a reaction to the more aristocratic forms of republicanism practiced by Alexander Hamilton and other Federalists.

Whenever republican power faded, its shadow fell across many people that Charles Beard might consider interest groups. One of the big tasks of social historians who have reacted to Bernard Bailyn's sweeping thesis has been to prove that ordinary Americans held ideologies as well and considered themselves fit to share power or displace the older elites. The Revolution did unleash greater expectations among the middling ranks of Americans. Because republicanism demanded more than mere mechanical exploration of the changes in power, scholars needed to identify the ideological power seeking of the middling and lower orders. Jesse Lemisch began this by showing how seamen in New York City felt grievances against the Crown as surely as did Virginia landowners. Richard Hofstedter argued that the Revolution actually produced a "status shift" in power, a concept used expertly by Edward Countryman in his *A People in Revolution: The American Revolution and Political Society in New York, 1760–1790* (1981), about the change in political power in postrevolutionary New York. Sean Wilentz subsequently showed how artisans added equality to the four precepts of republicanism listed earlier. The American Revolution instilled in common Americans the liberal idea that all citizens, at least all white male citizens, should be entitled to their natural civil and political rights under a representative, democratic system of laws. Artisan republicanism, as Wilentz described it, set off a generation of conflicts between elite politicians and ambitious mechanics over office holding, suffrage, and patronage. As capitalism transformed the craft traditions, these battles reared up between masters and journeymen as well.

Even groups who might be considered targets of enslavement or guided by the heavy hand of patronage, and thereby lacking in virtue, were capable of their own brand of republicanism. Consider the sturdy cartmen of New York City, who gained a monopoly on their semiskilled position by a bond of attachment via a freemanship with city officials. Throughout the colonial period, the carters, who gained the vote under the freemanship, exerted sizable political power alongside such brethren as butchers, bakers, and tavern keepers. After the Revolution, when the Federalist Party tried to channel the carters' votes, they rebelled because they believed that their stake in urban society came from their long-standing residence and their status as licensed workers.

Similar brands of republicanism could be found among African Americans. Republican-minded Americans often mentioned their fears of enslavement. The real slaves of early America responded with frustration over the lack of interest in their status displayed by republicans. African Americans found throughout the American Revolution and the constitutional period that conservative or radical republicans rarely gave much thought to the plight of enslaved Africans. Accordingly, they transferred their loyalties to the Crown. This does not mean that blacks were clients of the British. Rather, during the American Revolution, just as their white brothers did, African Americans sought participation in politics and demanded citizenship. When their hopes were rebuffed, several thousand of them sailed away with the departing British army in 1783, headed first to Nova Scotia, then to Sierra Leone to form a new nation in which they were the republican elite. Those left behind tried valiantly to persuade republicans in power to end the moral corruption of slavery and admit African Americans into the republican society. That they failed to convince speaks more about the sins of the founding fathers than of black inadequacies.

White American women were bound to a lesser status in the United States by their sex. During the American Revolution and its constitutional aftermath, little attention was paid to the political hopes of women. For many years, the colonial concept of the feme covert limited female political aspirations. As scholars have recently shown, however, women, in the same ways as African Americans, learned to exert their republicanism in churches, benevolent societies, schools, and above all, as the mothers of republicans. Their ideology stemmed perhaps from a protopsychology or from morals, but by the early nineteenth century, American women, white or black, were prepared to demand greater leadership.

Outside of European American society and well before the American Revolution, Native Americans created a unique brand of republicanism. In the Middle Ground, situated in the present-day upper Midwest, Indian republics coalesced from the migrations of survivors of war and plague. Outside of the French alliance and well beyond the shards of English power, Native American republicans in the 1740s and 1750s established an egalitarian political power that helped them defend against European incursions.

What these examples demonstrate is that republicanism is a protean concept with almost limitless possibilities. Early in the discussion about republicanism, scholars were delighted at its consensual potentials to explain Revolutionary and constitutional politics. The separateness of the examples described does not deny that consensual quality. Rather, each group, as American politics always does, requires the respect and understanding of its position.

BIBLIOGRAPHY

Appleby, Joyce. *Liberalism and Republicanism in the Historical Imagination.* Cambridge, Mass.: Harvard University Press, 1992.

Hodges, Graham Russell, ed. *The Black Loyalist Directory: African Americans in Exile after the Revolutionary War.* New York: Garland, 1996.

———. *New York City Cartmen, 1667–1850.* New York: New York University Press, 1986.

Pangle, Thomas L. *The Spirit of Modern Republicanism: The Moral Vision of the American Founders and the Philosophy of Locke.* Chicago: University of Chicago Press, 1988.

Pettit, Phillip. *Republicanism: A Theory of Freedom and Government.* Oxford: Clarendon Press, 1997.

Pocock, J. G. A. *The Machiavellian Moment: Florentine Political Thought and the Atlantic Republican Tradition.* Princeton, N.J.: Princeton University Press, 1975.

Sellers, M. N. S. *American Republicanism: Roman Ideology in the United States Constitution.* New York: New York University Press, 1994.

White, Richard. *The Middle Ground: Indians, Empires, and Republics in the Great Lakes Region, 1650–1815.* New York: Cambridge University Press, 1991.

Wilentz, Sean. *Chants Democratic: New York City and the Rise of the American Working Class, 1788–1850.* New York: Oxford University Press, 1984.

Graham Russell Hodges

See also **Agrarianism; Equality, Concept of; Liberty, Concept of; Locke's Political Philosophy.**

REPUBLICANS, JEFFERSONIAN.

The Jeffersonian Republicans emerged within three years of the inauguration of the Constitution, as Thomas Jefferson, James Madison, and lesser figures in the infant federal government united with, encouraged, and assumed the leadership of popular opposition to Alexander Hamilton's economic and financial programs. As their name implied, the coalition came together out of fear that the American experiment in popular self-governance—a revolutionary vision only twelve years old at the adoption of the Constitution—was profoundly threatened by the policies of the first secretary of the Treasury, the broad interpretation of the Constitution advanced in their behalf, and the antipopulistic sentiments expressed by some of Hamilton's supporters. After 1793, when revolutionary France and Britain entered into twenty years of war, the opposition deepened, broadened into foreign policy, and mobilized a large enough proportion of the population that the Jeffersonians are usually described as the first American political party. They defeated their Federalist opponents in the election of 1800 and vanquished them entirely in the years after the War of 1812. The modern Democratic Party, which celebrated its bicentennial in 1992, claims direct descent from these "Republican" progenitors. Today's Republicans did not originate until the 1850s, but might also fairly claim to be the heirs of Jeffersonian ideas.

Hamilton's proposals for the funding of the revolutionary war debt, federal assumption of the obligations of the states, creation of a national bank, and federal encouragement of native manufactures were intended to equip the new United States with economic and financial institutions similar to those on which Great Britain had been carried to the pinnacle of international prestige. Hamilton expected to secure the nation's freedom, promote prosperity and growth, and thus win the nation's firm allegiance to the fledgling Constitution. But Hamilton's proposals favored certain men and certain regions more immediately than others: states with large remaining debts, commercial and financial regions rather than the West and South, and the "moneyed" men whose fortunes swelled dramatically when bonds that they had purchased for a fraction of their value rose to par as a result of funding and could then be used to purchase bank stock. All of this, in Madison and Jefferson's opinions (and in that of numerous anonymous contributors to newspapers around the country), was profoundly incompatible with republican morality, with harmony among the nation's vastly different regions, and with the relatively modest differences between the rich and poor that seemed essential to a representative political regime. On top of that, the imitation of Great Britain, praise of institutions that were widely understood as driving Britain rapidly to ruin, a disregard for constitutional restraints (as these constraints were understood by others), and the obvious contempt of some of the most eager advocates of governmental measures for political involvement by the rabble all suggested that the pro-administration forces might prefer—and might, indeed, be secretly conspiring to promote—a gradual reintroduction of hereditary power.

By the end of 1791, the two Virginians and their allies in the Congress were reaching out for links with local politicians, and Jefferson had given part-time work in his State Department to Madison's college classmate, Philip Freneau, encouraging the revolutionary poet to move to Philadelphia to found a national newspaper that might counterbalance praise of the administration's course. In this *National Gazette*, during 1792, Madison and others, writing under pseudonyms, developed a coherent condemnation of the dangers they perceived and urged the people to support "the Republican interest" in the fall congressional elections.

Conflicting sympathies toward revolutionary France and Britain, both of which attempted to deny their enemy the benefits of neutral commerce, drew thousands of Americans into the party struggle during George Washington's second term, when war with Britain was averted only at the price of a demeaning treaty. During the administration of John Adams, who narrowly defeated Jefferson in the election of 1796, Jay's Treaty with Great Britain led to a limited, naval war with revolutionary France and to a Federalist attempt to repress the Jeffersonian opposition, culminating in the Alien and Sedition Acts of 1798 and Madison and Jefferson's Virginia and Kentucky Resolutions of that year. Wartime taxes and continuation of the program of repression even after Adams moved toward peace with France contributed importantly to the decisive Republican triumph in the elections of 1800.

The Jeffersonian ascendancy, stretching through the administrations of Jefferson and Madison and into that of James Monroe, during which the Federalists disintegrated as a party, was marked by quite consistent pursuit of the policies that had been outlined during the 1790s: quick retirement of the public debt, reduction of the diplomatic corps and military forces, retraction of the federal government within the limits that Republicans insisted had been set at the adoption of the Constitution, withdrawal of that government from guidance of the nation's economic life, expansion to the West (especially by way of the Louisiana Purchase of 1803), free trade, and commercial confrontation with nations that denied it. Economic warfare, mostly with Great Britain, climaxed in the Great Embargo of 1808, which failed as Madison succeeded Jefferson as president, and was eventually abandoned in favor of a declaration of war in 1812. Only after the conclusion of that conflict, as the Federalists collapsed and the country entered a period of single-party rule, did the Jeffersonians approve the creation of a second national bank, a moderate protective tariff, larger peacetime forces, and other policies they had initially opposed. By the middle 1820s both the National Republicans (later Whigs), who followed Henry Clay and John Quincy Adams, and their Jacksonian opponents claimed descent from Jeffersonian roots.

BIBLIOGRAPHY

Banning, Lance. *The Jeffersonian Persuasion: Evolution of a Party Ideology.* Ithaca, N.Y.: Cornell University Press, 1978.

Elkins, Stanley, and Eric McKitrick. *The Age of Federalism: The Early American Republic, 1788–1800.* New York: Columbia University Press, 1993.

McCoy, Drew R. *The Elusive Republic: Political Economy in Jeffersonian America.* Chapel Hill: University of North Carolina Press, 1980.

Lance G. Banning

See also **Alien and Sedition Laws; Federalist Party; France, Quasi-War with; Jeffersonian Democracy; War of 1812.**

REPUDIATION OF PUBLIC DEBT. When an individual goes bankrupt, he or she might pay one cent on the dollar, but when a nation goes bankrupt, it inflates its currency and pays in a one-cent dollar. That is approximately what the United States and many states did in the 1780s. To guard against a repetition, the Constitution of the United States permits only Congress to coin money.

The Constitution says nothing, however, about issuing legal-tender treasury notes. This silence discouraged the United States from printing paper money until the exigencies of the CIVIL WAR produced the first U.S. notes. This currency, dubbed GREENBACKS, were LEGAL TENDER for almost all payments but rapidly depreciated.

Thus, a series of challenges known as the LEGAL TENDER CASES questioned the constitutionality of the LEGAL TENDER ACT. Nonetheless, the SUPREME COURT eventually upheld the right of Congress to make treasury notes legal tender. One important exception to the new general rule was that the Legal Tender Act did not apply if an explicit "gold clause" in a contract required a borrower to repay the debt in gold and silver coin, so many agreements included such a stipulation.

On 19 April 1933, the government abandoned the gold-coin standard. On 5 June President Franklin D. Roosevelt signed a joint resolution of Congress declaring all specific gold contracts inoperative. This was necessary if the United States was to devalue, and devaluation was an important instrument of the administration's price-raising policy. On 31 January 1934, the government ordained a new gold dollar worth 1.69 times less than the old.

Four GOLD CLAUSE CASES came before the Supreme Court questioning the constitutionality of the resolution of 5 June 1933, and claiming for the creditors, on the basis of the gold clause, $1.69 for each dollar owed. The decisions were of vital importance because they affected about $100 billion of debt bearing the gold clause. On 18 February 1935, the Supreme Court held the resolution of 5 June unconstitutional because, although Congress could initially negotiate specific terms for paying back debt, it could not change them later. On the other hand, the Supreme Court refused to award damages because the plaintiff had not lost any buying power.

The buying-power theory was precedent breaking. "Value" under the Constitution had previously meant weight of gold, not purchasing power. This decision opened the way for suits against the government as soon as anyone could demonstrate loss in purchasing power because of INFLATION. So, on 27 August 1935, the president signed a joint resolution of Congress closing the Court of Claims to such suits but granting bondholders the temporary privilege of receiving cash payment for the par value of the bonds plus accrued interest. This move eliminated the financial confusion that would have resulted from the success of such suits, but according to many critics, it compromised national honor.

To the extent that a nation allows its currency to depreciate in value and pays its borrowings in that currency, it is also repudiating part of its public debt, even if it is not doing so as openly as the United States did in 1933–1934. Since March 1933 individuals have not had the right to demand gold coin for paper dollars, and on 15 August 1971, President Richard M. Nixon informed foreign central banks and treasuries that they had lost that right too. The American dollar has continued to depreciate over time.

BIBLIOGRAPHY

Eichengreen, Barry J. *Golden Fetters: The Gold Standard and the Great Depression, 1919–1939.* New York: Oxford University Press, 1992.

Gallarotti, Giulio M. *The Anatomy of an International Monetary Regime: The Classical Gold Standard, 1880–1914.* New York: Oxford University Press, 1995.

Markham, Jerry W. *A Financial History of the United States.* Armonk, N.Y.: M. E. Sharpe, 2002.

Timberlake, Richard H. *Monetary Policy in the United States: An Intellectual and Institutional History.* Chicago: University of Chicago Press, 1993.

Wilson, Thomas Frederick. *The Power "to Coin" Money: The Exercise of Monetary Powers by the Congress.* Armonk, N.Y.: M. E. Sharp, 1992.

Donald L. Kemmerer/A. E.

See also **Constitution of the United States; Debt, Public; Gold Standard.**

REPUDIATION OF STATE DEBTS

REPUDIATION OF STATE DEBTS was the subject of agitated discussion in the United States and abroad during the 1840s and the 1870s. In the 1830s various American states incurred heavy debts in the construction of canals and railroads and in the creation of banks. Frequently, in authorizing these loans, the faith of the state was pledged for the payment of the interest and the redemption of the principal. In many cases the laws specified that the bonds should not be sold below par. In negotiating these loans, authorized agents of the states violated the state statutes, and American bankers aided and abetted them. Foreign investors bought these securities with avidity because of the guaranty of the states, the high rate of interest they carried, the high standing of the national credit, and the confidence of foreign bankers in the Bank of the United States. When the American financial structure collapsed in the panic of 1837, European bankers tactlessly suggested that the U.S. government assume the state debts. Whatever merit the scheme might have possessed lost out to the hostility created by its supposedly foreign origin and the scramble for votes in the presidential election of 1840.

Between 1841 and 1842 eight states and one territory defaulted on their interest payments. There were many reasons for the growth of repudiation sentiment at this time. The sneers and jeers of the foreign press at American integrity fanned the flames of national prejudices while the universal indebtedness gave an impetus to the movement in favor of repudiation. Repudiation resulted from a series or combination of forces: speculative mania, ignorance of sound banking, a ruinous depression, blatantly demagogic leadership, and the stupidity of the bondholders in refusing to consider propositions that might have resulted in partial payments of their holdings. Although the meager resources of the American people at that time made it impossible for them to meet their obligations when they fell due, an inability to pay was no justification for refusal to pay.

The second attack of state repudiation came with the funding of the state debts incurred during the RECONSTRUCTION era. Governments that were not representative of the southern states issued these bonds. Foreign investors received warnings not to purchase them. The forced repudiation of the Confederate war debts by the Fourteenth Amendment strengthened the southerners' opposition to the payment of the "bayonet bonds," especially since "conquerors of the north" held a large proportion of these securities. The ravages of the Civil War, the misrule of the Reconstruction period, and the hard times following the panic of 1873 increased the heavy burdens of the southern people; but in no case were the debts scaled or repudiated until it was apparently impossible to discharge them.

The Eleventh Amendment to the U.S. Constitution prevented foreign creditors from seeking redress. In December 1933, Monaco, which possessed some repudiated Mississippi bonds, asked to bring suit in the U.S. Supreme Court against the state of Mississippi, but on 21 May 1934 the Court unanimously held that Monaco could not sue Mississippi.

BIBLIOGRAPHY

Foner, Eric. *A Short History of Reconstruction, 1863–1877.* New York: Harper and Row, 1990.

Hixson, William F. *Triumph of the Bankers: Money and Banking in the Eighteenth and Nineteenth Centuries.* Westport, Conn.: Praeger, 1993.

Markham, Jerry W. *A Financial History of the United States.* Armonk, N.Y.: M. E. Sharpe, 2002.

Reginald C. McGrane/A. E.

See also **Debts, State; Financial Panics; Foreign Investment in the United States.**

RESERVE OFFICERS' TRAINING CORPS

RESERVE OFFICERS' TRAINING CORPS (ROTC). The Morrill Act of 1862 required land grant colleges to provide military training for male students. As WORLD WAR I raged in Europe, the National Defense Act of 1916 provided for the establishment of the Reserve Officers' Training Corps (ROTC). Fully trained graduates received commissions in an OFFICERS' RESERVE CORPS that would become available for active duty in a major war.

Between World War I and WORLD WAR II, the army gave even stronger support than before to military training on college campuses. The navy began similar training in 1925. Some opposition to college military training arose, but it had no real effect on reserve officer production.

After 1945 the air force joined the army and navy in reviving campus military training. During the Cold War the substantial and seemingly permanent enlargement of the American military establishment changed the primary objective of college military training from reserve to active duty service. Then, from 1961 through the decade of conflict in Southeast Asia, the armed forces called almost all college military graduates to active duty, and only the cessation of American ground action promised a partial return to the reserve concept.

The unpopularity of the prolonged VIETNAM WAR led to widespread and sometimes violent opposition to military training on civilian campuses. Even before the truce of January 1973, enrollments had dropped by two-thirds, but more schools than ever, about 375, had military units. All three services had adopted the navy's method of providing scholarships and other inducements designed to assure a steady supply of college graduates for active duty despite reduced enrollments.

BIBLIOGRAPHY

Franke, Volker. *Preparing for Peace: Military Identity, Value Orientations, and Professional Military Education.* Westport, Conn.: Praeger, 1999.

Neiberg, Michael S. *Making Citizen-Soldiers: ROTC and the Ideology of American Military Service.* Cambridge, Mass.: Harvard University Press, 2000.

Stetson Conn / A. E.

See also **Army, United States; Kent State Protest; Morrill Act; Navy, United States.**

RESETTLEMENT ADMINISTRATION.

The Resettlement Administration (RA) was the New Deal's rural antipoverty agency (1935–1937). In 1935 President Franklin Roosevelt issued an executive order consolidating several farm programs into a single agency, the Resettlement Administration. Rexford Tugwell, the combative New Deal intellectual who became administrator of the RA, rejected a government policy that, as he saw it, maintained poor farmers on unproductive soil. At first he focused on long-term land reform: buying millions of acres of substandard land, converting it to more appropriate uses, and resettling displaced farm families in experimental communities and public housing (including controversial model farms and suburban greenbelt towns).

Congressional opponents of the New Deal, however, cast the RA's collectivist resettlement projects as dangerous experiments in socialism. Tugwell shifted the agency's attention to rural rehabilitation, a less controversial and shorter-term program assisting the rural poor with emergency grants, loans, and farm planning. By June 1936 the RA had more than two million clients, almost 10 percent of the total farm population.

In December 1936 Tugwell retired from government service, and the RA was transferred to the Department of Agriculture, where it could remain relatively safe from congressional attack. The RA became the Farm Security Administration in September 1937.

Back in 1935 Tugwell, knowing that the RA was likely to come under political attack, had formed an information division to distribute propaganda. Its artistic output, including the famous photographs of Walker Evans and Dorothea Lange, has survived longer than the land-reform policies it was meant to promote.

BIBLIOGRAPHY

Baldwin, Sidney. *Poverty and Politics: The Rise and Decline of the Farm Security Administration.* Chapel Hill: The University of North Carolina Press, 1968.

Jeremy Derfner

See also **Great Depression; New Deal.**

RESOLUTIONS, CONGRESSIONAL.

In each chamber of Congress, four forms of legislative measures may be introduced or submitted, and acted upon. These include bills, joint resolutions, concurrent resolutions, and simple resolutions. Both the House of Representatives and the Senate follow similar rules when making decisions on any of these actions. Both bills and joint resolutions are used when the focus is on making laws; a joint resolution can also be used to propose an amendment to the Constitution. Both concurrent and simple resolutions are used to delegate official internal Congressional business.

Although easily confused, resolutions are not laws but rather the statements of intent or declarations that affect the operations of Congress. Resolutions, which are not legislative in character, are used primarily to express principles, facts, opinions, and the purposes of both the House and the Senate—that is, until they pass both houses. When Congress seeks to pass a law, however, it uses either a bill or a joint resolution, which must be passed by both houses in identical form, and then presented to the president for approval or disapproval.

There are a variety of uses for each of the four types of measures. A bill, when presented to both the House and Senate, can be either an authorization or a reauthorization of federal policies or programs, or it may be a reconciliation bill, which alters spending authority. A bill follows a path originating from a member of either the House or the Senate, and then it must be approved by both chambers and the president. Similarly, a joint resolution, with the exception of those joint resolutions to amend the Constitution, follows the same path and could include measures such as transfer of appropriations; adjustment of debt limits; establishment of a date for the convening of Congress; declarations of war; abrogation of treaties; extensions of expirations or reporting dates for existing laws, including the dates for the president to submit budgets; and resolutions of either approval or disapproval. Joint resolutions can be used for important foreign policy measures, such as the delegation of broad powers to the president in the case of the Gulf of Tonkin Resolution in 1964, or the joint resolution authorizing the use of the U.S. military against those responsible for the attacks launched against the United States on 11 September 2001. Both bills and joint resolutions can eventually become laws or statutes if both chambers and the president approve. In the case of joint resolutions intended to amend the Constitution, the approval of the president is not required.

The two internal types of resolutions, concurrent and simple, also need only the approval of both houses, and do not become law. A concurrent resolution, introduced in either the House or the Senate, can call for the creation of a joint committee, provide for a joint session of Congress, call for a recess of either house of more than three days, or correct conference reports or enrolled bills. A resolution may also express an opinion of Congress, as in the example of the 1962 Berlin Resolution, which declared that all measures should be taken to prevent violations in Berlin by the Soviet Union. A simple resolution can establish a standing order, elect committee members, or create a special committee, such as an investigating committee.

BIBLIOGRAPHY

107th Congress of the United States. "Authorization for Use of Military Force." SJ 23 ES. Available from http://www.law .suffolk.edu/library/terrorism/SJRes23.html.

Beth, Richard S. "Bills and Resolutions: Examples of How Each Kind Is Used." Congressional Research Service, Library of Congress. 98-706 GOV (27 January 1999). Available from http://www.house.gov/rules/98_706.pdf.

———. "Bills, Resolutions, Nominations, and Treaties: Origins, Deadlines, Requirements, and Uses." Congressional Research Service, Library of Congress. 98-728 GOV (27 January 1999). Available from http://www.house.gov/rules/ 98_728.pdf.

Rundquist, Paul S. "'Sense of' Resolutions and Provisions." Congressional Research Service, Library of Congress. 98-825 GOV (2 March 1999). Available from http://www .house.gov/rules/98-825.pdf.

Sachs, Richard C. "Introducing a House Bill or Resolution." Congressional Research Service, Library of Congress. 98-458 GOV (3 August 1999). Available from http://www .house.gov/rules/98-458.pdf.

Jennifer Harrison

RESORTS AND SPAS. In the years following the end of the French and Indian War in 1763, mineral springs became as much a vogue in America as they were in England, because of their therapeutic promise—drinking, bathing, and inhaling were recommended for a variety of rheumatic, liver, kidney, alimentary, and other complaints—and because they had become a "fashionable indulgence" of the colonial gentry. Stafford Springs, Connecticut, with seventeenth-century roots, Berkeley Springs, Virginia, and many others locations with mineral springs conceded preeminence to Saratoga Springs, New York, in the nineteenth century.

Fort William Henry Hotel. A stagecoach full of vacationers prepares to leave the resort hotel at Lake George, N.Y., c. 1879. © BETTMANN/CORBIS

Springs, Seashores, and Esoteric Cures

As the country expanded westward, new spas attracted visitors. Early in the nineteenth century, numerous "temporary retreats" sprang up throughout the Mississippi Valley, among them Hot Springs, Arkansas (1804), and Blue Licks, Kentucky (1818). Later, the presence of springs coupled with salubrious climate brought health seekers to spas at such places as Colorado Springs, Colorado; Las Vegas, New Mexico; and the Napa Valley and Santa Barbara in California. All the states and the District of Columbia were included in a 1927 list of mineral water spas.

The twentieth century saw the development of resorts and spas (so-called) that dotted the country, many in unexpected places. They offered a whole gamut of attractions that reflected the hedonistic excesses, the obsessions with fitness, and especially the fascination for esoteric and mystic ways of escape and spiritual fulfillment of certain segments of American society. Most of the resorts were thematic, with their offerings running from strenuous ranch life to "palaces of pleasure" to virtual religious and meditative retreats. Everything was available, from Ayurvedic (Hindu) treatment to Zen meditation, from aerobics to "yoga with a kabalistic focus."

The seashore also offered some hope to the sick, but its attraction was more often recreational. Long Branch, New Jersey, claimed prerevolutionary roots, but by the mid-nineteenth century, the Atlantic Coast, and to a lesser extent the Gulf Coast, boasted many resorts. Long Branch and Cape May, New Jersey, catering to the gentry from New York City, Philadelphia, and the South, lost their fashionable position at the end of the century to Newport, Rhode Island, where only the wealthiest could build their "castles."

Steamships, railroads, stages, and eventually trolley cars brought excursionists even to the most exclusive resorts, and with the two-week vacation becoming more commonplace, the shore was no longer the domain of the elite. In the late 1800s, Atlantic City, New Jersey, began to flourish; by the 1950s it boasted 1,200 hotels and 12 million visitors a year.

Mountain Houses, Hotels, and Sanitariums

Still another type of resort—the mountain house—attracted easterners. The Catskill Mountain House in New York State opened in 1823. Late in the century, often under the stimulation of the railroads, the White Mountains, the Berkshires, the Adirondacks, and much of the Appalachian chain became studded with resort hotels, some very large and very fashionable.

In the settlement of the American West, the search for good health was turned into a business of immense proportions. Railroaders, real estate operators, and public officials (often with the help of the medical profession) puffed as virtually miraculous the climate of the Great Plains, the deserts, the Rocky Mountains, and southern California. Hotels and sanitariums, often indistinguishable, catered especially to the tubercular and the asthmatic and played a significant role in the growth of cities in Colorado, California, Arizona, and Texas in the last third of the nineteenth century. For the most part, only the well-to-do could afford the accommodations provided, but arrangements existed for a substantial "invalid traffic" of people of modest means and even of the indigent. By the 1890s, bitter experiences and new medical knowledge brought disillusionment. Resorts and hotels began to discourage the patronage of the sick.

Winter Resorts

The railroads, which had made it possible for easterners to winter in California, made Florida even more accessible. Florida had appealed to health seekers even before the Civil War, but its buildup as a major winter resort was the later work of entrepreneurs, who mixed railroading and the hotel business, and of speculators and promoters. The culmination came with the creation of Miami Beach out of a jungle in ten years, from 1913 to 1923. The automobile and then the airplane helped to turn Florida into a winter haven for many easterners and midwesterners.

One other type of winter resort was to flourish—that devoted to winter sports, especially skiing. Although skiing was not unknown earlier, it was not until the Olympic Winter Games of 1932 at Lake Placid, New York, that American interest in skiing began to skyrocket. Ski resorts first became popular in the Northeast. The introduction of uphill transportation in Vermont and New Hampshire in the 1930s, the weekend ski and snow trains from the seaboard cities, and the ease of automobile transportation all helped to popularize the sport and build up the resorts. At the end of the twentieth century, one ranking placed ten ski areas in Vermont and New Hampshire among the country's best fifty.

Colorado, with its ideal climate for skiing and its more than fifty peaks of over fourteen thousand feet, was not far behind in developing ski resort areas. The winter carnival at Steamboat Springs went back to 1913; Aspen built its first run in 1935. By the end of the century, according to the same ranking noted above, fifteen of the best fifty ski areas were in Colorado. Skiing, with its health as well as recreational aspects, continued to flourish. In Idaho, the Union Pacific Railroad turned the town of Ketchum into Sun Valley, a magnificent resort area, in 1936. In California, Yosemite National Park, Lake Tahoe, and Donner Summit were among the early ski areas. In the Northwest, ski lodges appeared in the vicinity of Mount Rainier in the State of Washington and Mount Hood in Oregon. From Butte, Montana, to San Diego, California, to Flagstaff, Arizona, ski resorts appeared.

The popularity of the Rocky and Sierra Nevada mountain regions resulted from the ease of air travel and the promotion of "package deals" by the airlines. One added feature was the development of the ski resort as a family vacation spot, as evidenced by the ready availability of children's rates, nurseries, and baby-sitters. Ingenuity in the East rose to meet the competition of the West: the snow-making machine was to turn every sizable hill within driving distance of any populous area into a ski resort.

BIBLIOGRAPHY

Amory, Cleveland. *The Last Resorts.* Westport, Conn.: Greenwood Press, 1973.

Corbett, Theodore. *The Making of American Resorts: Saratoga Springs, Ballston Spa, Lake George.* New Brunswick, N.J.: Rutgers University Press, 2001.

Holmes, Karen B. *101 Vacations to Change Your Life: A Guide to Wellness Centers, Spiritual Retreats, and Spas.* Secaucus, N.J.: Carol Publishing Group, 1999.

Jay, John C. *Skiing the Americas.* New York: Macmillan, 1947.

Jones, Billy M. *Health-Seekers in the Southwest, 1817–1900.* Norman: University of Oklahoma Press, 1967.

David L. Cowen

See also **Atlantic City; Medicine, Alternative; Miami; Saratoga Springs; Skiing.**

RESTRAINT OF TRADE refers to activity that obstructs, limits, or eliminates market competition. Restraints may affect particular occupations, industries, or commercial transactions. Though it carries a presumption of illegality, a restraint of trade may be legal or illegal, depending on its effect and intention. Restraints are prohibited by the first section of the Sherman Antitrust Act of 1890 (Title 15 of the United States Code), the main source of American antitrust law, which forbids "every contract, combination in the form of trust or otherwise, or conspiracy, in restraint of trade or commerce among the several States, or with foreign nations." The state attorneys general, under the direction of the federal Attorney General, have primary enforcement duties.

Restraint of trade takes a multitude of forms, ranging from private activity (e.g., contracts between two parties) to government regulation (e.g., licensing requirements or quotas). Common practices include noncompetition clauses, exclusive dealing arrangements, and price discrimination. Employers restrain trade by restricting the activity of their employees (e.g., through agreements controlling future dealings); employees restrain trade by disrupting the activity of their employers (e.g., through strikes and boycotts). As the above examples suggest, restraint of trade occurs regularly, even in a free market system. It is often difficult to distinguish between ordinary business transactions and trade-restricting agreements. It is not surprising, then, that both the definition of "restraint of trade" and what constitutes illegal action have been fluid, reflecting, among other things, economic conditions, legal and political attitudes, and industry preferences.

Restraint of trade was prohibited under English common law as early as the fifteenth century (the first known opinion, in the Dyer's Case, was issued in 1414). Courts, as a general rule, would not validate contracts restricting commercial capacity, even when all parties consented to the arrangement. These decisions promoted competition, but they were not only (or primarily) justified as free trade measures. Opinions refer to the importance of individual rights (particularly the right to labor) and the draining effect inactivity has on the community. Judges readily connected the public good to the full functioning of individuals; as stated in the case of the Tailors of Ipswich (1614), "the law abhors idleness, the mother of all evil . . . especially in young men, who ought . . . to learn useful sciences and trades which are profitable to the commonwealth."

English judges became more tolerant of voluntary restraints in the early eighteenth century. "Partial" restraints (i.e., agreements not restrictive in primary effect) were deemed enforceable, as were restraints that conformed to a flexible standard of reasonableness, that is, agreements that were self-contained, or limited in duration, or harmless to the public (the "rule of reason" was first stated in *Mitchel v. Reynolds*, 1711). Some historians stress the leniency of the common law during the eighteenth and nineteenth centuries, suggesting that new theories of laissez faire discouraged oversight of business. Others suggest that restraints were only tolerated in a narrow set of cases. It is clear, at least, that a conflict existed between flexible and rigid applications, reflecting the inherent tension between the right to freely contract and the right to freely trade.

The law of trade restraints, like the rest of common law, was incorporated by American states. Not surprisingly, American courts also developed competing interpretations. Irregularies between states and leniency in particular states (as well as the inability of states to control interstate trade) contributed to the passage of the SHERMAN ANTITRUST ACT, which was described in 1889 by its chief sponsor, Senator John Sherman, as setting forth "the rule of the common law" in federal statute (20 *Congressional Record* 1167). It may be noted, though, that the absolute prohibition in Section 1 of the Act against restraints went considerably beyond the common law; further, the Act's criminal penalties and enforcement mechanisms are foreign to the English tradition.

The Sherman Antitrust Act's strict terms are understandable in the late nineteenth-century context. Congressmen responded to ferocious opposition to trusts and "big business" by consumers, farmers, and small businesses. It was not long, however, before politicians, judges, and regulators demonstrated a willingness to moderate its meaning. President Theodore Roosevelt, for example, distinguished early in his administration between good and bad trusts, and showed little interest in discouraging the former. During the 1920s, Secretary of Commerce Herbert Hoover encouraged businessmen to conform to "codes of ethics" intended to eliminate unnecessary and ruinous competition.

It was ultimately federal courts, however, that shaped the law's meaning. The main task of the Supreme Court during the "formative period" of the Sherman Antitrust Act—1890 to 1911—was deciding which restraints "among the several States" are justifiable; support was brief, and weak, for absolute prohibition. Rules distinguishing acceptable from unacceptable restraints—the per se illegality rule, the rule of reason—were developed during this period, early evidence of the justices' willingness to make law, as well as interpret it, when considering commercial behavior. As antitrust law developed during the twentieth century, judges demonstrated an increasing tendency to assess specific market effects and the particulars of the public interest. While the Supreme Court categorically prohibited certain types of horizontal and vertical agreements, it generally adopted a tolerant, rule-of-reason analysis when considering trade restraints. It should be noted, however, that wide latitude in this area was not universally accepted: in the early twenty-first century attorneys general became increasingly aggressive in their antitrust enforcement activities.

BIBLIOGRAPHY

Gellhorn, Ernest, and Kovacic, William E. *Antitrust Law and Economics in a Nutshell*. 4th ed. St. Paul, Minn.: West, 1994.

Hovenkamp, Herbert. *Enterprise and American Law, 1836–1937*. Cambridge, Mass.: Harvard University Press, 1991.

Kinter, Earl W. *Federal Antitrust Law: A Treatise on the Antitrust Laws of the United States*. Volume 1: *Economic Theory, Common Law, and an Introduction to the Sherman Act*. Cincinnati, Ohio: Anderson, 1980.

Jones, Eliot. *The Trust Problem in the United States*. New York: Macmillan, 1921.

Shaffer, Butler D. *In Restraint of Trade: the Business Campaign against Competition, 1918–1938*. Lewisburg, PA: Bucknell University Press, 1997.

Kimberly A. Hendrickson

See also **Antitrust Laws; Fair-Trade Laws; Government Regulation of Business.**

RESUMPTION ACT.

Late in 1861, the federal government suspended specie payments, seeking to raise revenue for the war effort without exhausting its reserves of gold and silver. Early in 1862 the United States issued legal-tender notes, called greenbacks. By war's end a total of $431 million in greenbacks had been issued, and authorization had been given for another $50 million in small denominations, known as fractional currency or "shin plasters."

During Reconstruction a new coalition of agrarian and labor interests found common cause in the promotion of inflationary monetary policies. At the end of 1874, a total of $382 million of these notes still circulated. The Resumption Act of 14 January 1875 provided for the replacement of the Civil War fractional currency by silver coins. It also reduced the greenback total to $300 million. The secretary of the Treasury was directed to "redeem, in coin" legal-tender notes presented for redemption on and after 1 January 1879.

Riding a wave of electoral success in 1878, the inflationists, then organized as the Greenback Party, succeeded in modifying this law by securing the enactment of a measure stopping the destruction of greenbacks when the total outstanding stood at $346,681,000. Specie payments resumed during the presidency of Rutherford B. Hayes. Aided by the return of prosperity, Secretary of the Treasury John Sherman accumulated gold to carry out the intent of the Resumption Act. But when people found greenbacks to be on a par with gold, they lost their desire for redemption, thus making possible complete success for the legislation.

BIBLIOGRAPHY

Ritter, Gretchen. *Goldbugs and Greenbacks: The Antimonopoly Tradition and the Politics of Finance in America.* Cambridge: Cambridge University Press, 1997.

Weinstein, Allen. *Prelude to Populism: Origins of the Silver Issue, 1867–1878.* New Haven, Conn.: Yale University Press, 1970.

Erick McKinley Eriksson / A. R.

See also **Bland-Allison Act; Greenback Movement; Specie Payments, Suspension and Resumption of.**

RETAILING INDUSTRY.

The modern U.S. retail industry is dominated by huge retail giants owning thousands of stores in the United States and in other countries. According to the 1997 business census, retail sales in this country totaled nearly $2.5 trillion. This is fifty times the $48 billion of the 1929 business census. The size of individual stores has also grown enormously and there are actually fewer stores today than in 1929.

The roots of the industry in the United States go back to itinerant peddlers, small shopkeepers, and merchant importers that began in the early days of Boston, New York, and Philadelphia. Thousands of men walked the countryside selling the goods they could carry on their back. When profits permitted, they purchased horses and carts and expanded their assortments of goods. Henry W. Carter maintained five teams on the road and became known as the "Merchant Prince." Called "Yankee peddlers," many of the first merchants came from New England. Jewish immigrants became the most numerous peddlers in the nineteenth century. The development of the railroads, waterways, roads, and towns engendered stores that replaced the peddlers. Storekeepers even lobbied cities to pass laws outlawing peddlers.

Trading posts, established to trade furs with the Indians, became an important part of the frontier. The Hudson's Bay Company, founded in 1670 and headquartered in Canada, operated an extensive network in the western part of North America. The company still operates as The Bay department stores. Trading posts in the West lasted well into the twentieth century. The Hubbell Trading Post, on Arizona's Navajo Reservation, is owned by the National Park Service and operated by a nonprofit organization (see TRADING POSTS, FRONTIER).

In cities, stores often featured the products of craftsmen who sold their wares in spaces below their living quarters. They included tailors, apothecaries, stationers, importers, furniture makers, and tobacco merchants. Major cities also established markets where a large number of merchants would display their merchandise, starting with Boston in 1658. Smaller towns had general stores that attempted to carry everything customers wanted. The factories and artisans of England provided most of the consumer goods for America.

New Forms of Retailing

Three new forms of retailing that would dominate sales for the next century began in the second half of the nineteenth century: the modern department store, the chain store, and the mail-order business. Department stores evolved from dry goods and clothing stores as the owners expanded their operations by adding new classifications of merchandise. Dry goods merchants sold fabrics, sewing supplies (notions), blouses, and millinery (hats), mostly to women. Clothing stores specialized in ready-made clothing for men and boys that was manufactured in factories that made army uniforms during the Civil War. Marshall Field, who started his fancy dry goods business in Chicago in 1865, built a thriving wholesale business and the largest department store in the world in 1910. John Wanamaker of Philadelphia started in the wholesale men's clothing business before expanding his operation into a complete department store in 1877.

Growing cities provided large markets for the department stores. Mass circulation newspapers contributed an effective advertising medium. The invention of cast iron allowed for multi-floor buildings. Electricity powered the elevators, which moved customers to upper floors, and illuminated the far reaches of the large stores. The invention and local manufacture of plate glass provided show windows to entice customers into the store. Railroads brought people to the city and lowered transportation costs. Streetcars brought people to the stores and let them carry more merchandise home. In this industrial landscape, factories manufactured goods in larger quantities, allowing merchandise to be sold for lower prices to workers with more disposable income. The new American financial capital business provided needed funding for the larger operations.

These changes also enabled chain stores to develop. Described as a group of decentralized stores that handle similar lines of merchandise under one management, chain stores started slowly during the last forty years of the nineteenth century but built a base for phenomenal growth in the twentieth. The guiding principles of chain stores included mass purchasing and low operating costs. In 1859, tea sold at retail for $1 per pound. George Huntington Hartford and George Gilman decided to import tea directly and sell it for thirty cents. Their Great Atlantic & Pacific Tea Company developed into a grocery store (A&P) and became the first major chain-store organization. They had 200 stores by 1900. Frank W. Woolworth capitalized on the abundance of cheap merchandise to start his five-cent stores in 1879 (see DIME STORES).

Montgomery Ward and Richard W. Sears founded mail-order companies that greatly impacted the nation's marketplace (see MAIL-ORDER HOUSES). An employee of Marshall Field, Ward saw the opportunity to sell merchandise to farmers and started Montgomery Ward & Co. in 1872. A railway agent, Sears started his mail-order company by selling watches to other agents in 1886. While department stores attempted to build mail-order businesses with urban customers, Ward and Sears targeted the rural customer who did not have access to chain stores and department stores. Both made extravagant advertising claims, produced massive catalogs, and penetrated the rural market with great success (see SEARS ROEBUCK CATALOG).

During the first thirty years of the twentieth century merchant and consumer groups attempted unsuccessfully to limit the growth of department stores, chain stores, and mail-order houses by enacting laws and mounting public relations campaigns. Despite their efforts, the large companies prospered. The growth of the women's ready-to-wear business, increased consumer disposable income, and the desire to beautify the home attracted more and more customers to the department stores, who responded by erecting larger stores. Mass transit brought customers to downtowns that now featured several major department stores, variety stores, specialty stores, movie theaters, and restaurants.

The chain-store movement saw the advent of many new chains in the first decade of the twentieth century.

Among them were Lane Bryant (apparel), J. C. Penney (apparel), W. T. Grant (variety), Walgreen Company (drugs), and Louis K. Ligget (drugs). Opening stores in both small and large towns, the twenty leading chains totaled nearly 10,000 stores by 1920 and added another 25,000 in the next ten years. J. C. Penney, which started in 1902, had 676 apparel stores by 1930. That same year the F. W. Woolworth Company boasted 1,420 stores and A&P operated 14,034 stores. Four other food chains each had more than a thousand stores. The first business census in 1929 showed that chain stores controlled 22.2 percent of total sales.

Sears, Roebuck and Montgomery Ward continued to grow their catalog business and, recognizing changes brought about by the automobile and suburbanization, started their own retail stores. Ironically, mail-order sales reached their peak in 1926, although the two companies maintained their catalog operations for another sixty years.

Retail sales did decline from 1929 to 1934. However, none of the major department stores or chains closed during the Great Depression. Stores pressured suppliers for lower prices, and with the help of National Recovery Act regulations, many operations actually increased their profit margins during the 1930s.

The 1930s witnessed the movement to self-service food supermarkets. The first self-service stores started in 1911, but Clarence Saunders, who started Piggly Wiggly in 1916, is credited with innovations such as shopping baskets, open shelving, no clerks, and store layouts that led to the first self-service stores. A manager of a Kroger store, Michael Cullen, wrote a letter to the president in 1930 laying out the concept of a self-service supermarket. He never received an answer and instead opened the first supermarket, King Kullen, that year in Jamaica, New York. Sylvan Goldman, a grocery store operator in Oklahoma City, helped change the industry by inventing the shopping cart in 1937, enabling customers to carry more merchandise. The large chains such as A&P, Kroger, and Safeway had so many stores they did not want to embrace the supermarket concept. But they eventually relented and replaced smaller neighborhood stores with large units on major arteries.

Malls and Discount Stores

The 1950s ushered in two major changes in retailing: suburban shopping malls and discount stores. Favorable tax laws in the 1950s, together with the burgeoning suburbs and the start of the interstate highway program, encouraged the beginnings of suburban shopping malls. Mall developers gave low-rent terms to large, local department stores to anchor their malls and rented to smaller stores at high rents.

Proximity to affluent customers, ample parking, and night shopping hours quickly made malls the favored place for non-food shopping. Most cities did little to help their downtowns, which soon became retail wastelands with no department stores and many empty storefronts. Shopping centers grew larger and larger, with regional malls housing four to six anchor department stores and numerous specialty stores. The Mall of America in Bloomington, Minnesota, has more than 520 stores.

In 1953, Martin Chase converted the defunct New England Anne and Hope fabric mill into a huge self-service store with a wide assortment of off-price merchandise. Discount stores developed into the country's most successful retail outlets by the 1990s. Eugene Ferkauf expanded his New York City discount luggage store (E. J. Korvette) into a chain of full-line stores in the 1950s.

Many others started discount operations, but three stores that started in 1962 survived as the dominant chains. Sam Walton, a franchise operator of Ben Franklin dime stores, opened his first Wal-Mart in Rogers, Arkansas. Another dime store operator, S. S. Kresge, conceived K-Mart, and the Dayton Company of Minneapolis started Target. By 2000, Wal-Mart had become the largest retailer in the world (and the world's largest private employer) with annual sales of $200 million, the same amount as total retail sales in the United States in 1958.

Many downtown apparel specialty stores did not want to take the risk of opening in the new malls, leaving mall developers to look elsewhere for tenants. National chains such as Casual Corner, The Limited, Lane Bryant, and Lerner's began opening hundreds of stores to take advantage of mall traffic. Les Wexner opened his first Limited in Columbus, Ohio, in 1963. His company had 5,168 stores in 2001, including the Victoria's Secret lingerie chain. Donald and Doris Fisher opened a store in 1969 near San Francisco State University selling records and Levi's jeans. Their Gap Inc., operating under the names of Gap, Old Navy, and Banana Republic, had 4,024 stores in 2001.

Big-box stores started to dominate some of the retail sectors. Also known as "category killers," these retailers built very large stores to carry only a few lines of merchandise in great depth. In 1976, Bernard Marcus started Home Depot home improvement and lumber stores. By 2000, Home Depot had 1,127 stores, each averaging annual sales of more than $40 million. Big-box retailers such as Best Buy and Circuit City dominated the electronics business. Charles Tandy proved the exception—his Radio Shack chain had 7,200 small neighborhood electronic stores by 2002. The large retailers Staples and Office Depot dominated the office-supply business. Developers started grouping these stores in non-enclosed shopping centers known as power malls, often near the regional shopping centers.

Membership warehouse stores were another form of big-box store. Sol Price opened membership discount stores in San Diego in 1954. After selling his Fed-Mart chain in 1976, he developed the Price Club warehouse concept that carried bulk packaged food and non-food products. Consumer-goods manufacturers also began to compete with their retail customers and opened chains of retail outlets. After hiding these stores in remote factories, they soon began to group together in factory outlet malls on the outskirts of major cities. Some predicted that merchandise sales over the INTERNET would put stores out of business. However, E-commerce sales in 2000 accounted for only 2 percent of total sales.

The last twenty years have seen an acceleration of mergers between large operations. In 2001, Kroger had 3,660 supermarkets under sixteen different names and sales of $49 billion. Walgreens, the largest drugstore chain, operated 3,520 stores with $24.6 billion in sales. Federated Department Stores had 404 department stores (including Bloomingdale's and Macy's) and $18 million in sales. Industry analysts predict that the giant operations will continue to grow.

BIBLIOGRAPHY

Hendrickson, Robert. *The Grand Emporiums, The Illustrated History of America's Great Department Stores.* New York: Stein and Day, 1979.

Lebhar, Godfrey M. *Chain Stores in America, 1859–1962.* 3d ed. New York: Chain Store Publishing, 1963.

Jerry Brisco

RETALIATION IN INTERATIONAL LAW. Retaliation is a nonamicable action short of war taken by one state against another in response to conduct that the retaliating state considers injurious or unfriendly. It may be forcible or peaceful. The retaliation is generally in kind when in response to a legal act, such as discrimination in tariffs, restriction of immigration, closure of ports, or legislation against aliens; such action is called retortion. Reprisal, on the other hand, is a retaliatory action that seeks redress for an illegal act, such as refusal to arbitrate or to satisfy claims, confiscation or seizure of property, or injury to citizens of the retaliating state. Reprisal is generally not limited to retaliation in kind and need not be proportioned to the offense that prompted it. Reprisal may take one of several forms: withdrawal or severance of diplomatic relations, display of force, pacific blockade, embargo, nonintercourse, bombardment, or seizure and occupation of property.

The United States has usually taken reprisals in an effort to seek redress for injuries or wrongs after exhausting diplomatic channels for settlement. In 1807 President Thomas Jefferson, with congressional approval, placed an embargo on all American vessels as a reply to the illegal treatment of American merchant vessels on the high seas by France and England. That measure having failed after a year, the president tried nonintercourse as a means of forcing the two offending nations to mend their ways. In 1914 the U.S. Navy bombarded the port of Veracruz and U.S. Marines occupied the port for several months because the U.S. believed that Mexico had failed to make adequate amends for the arrest of three American sailors.

An example of retortion taken by the United States occurred in 1818 when, in response to restrictions placed on American vessels trading with British colonies in the Western Hemisphere, American ports were closed to British ships.

Retaliation takes place in wartime, too, by the belligerents who respond to the introduction by the enemy of measures deemed illegal; such actions include extending the contraband list, sowing mines, using submarines, bombing unfortified cities, invoking the doctrine of continuous voyage or ultimate destination, or blockading from long range. Finally, it may be said that fear of retaliation has played a role in determining the weapons used in warfare, as evidenced by the failure by both sides in WORLD WAR II to use biological and CHEMICAL WARFARE.

BIBLIOGRAPHY
Colbert, Evelyn Speyer. *Retaliation in International Law.* New York: King's Crown Press, 1948.

Armin Rappaport / F. B.

See also **Foreign Policy; General Agreement on Tariffs and Trade; International Law; Intervention; Trade, Foreign.**

RETIREMENT. Concerns for aging and the relevance of this issue for society seem to have had little impact on Americans before the beginning of the twentieth century. Although retirement contracts existed in colonial America, this was a gradual process that allowed the head of a household to transfer title to his property to an heir in exchange for money or services that might be required by the elderly couple or individual.

The Origins of Mandatory Retirement (1800–1900)

Mandatory retirement programs for public officials were introduced by some state legislatures between 1790 and 1820. In 1860, a few states required state judges to retire as they became elderly. Still, by the late 1800s, most businesses had no formal policies regarding retirement at a specific age, nor were there any laws requiring older persons to stop working once they reached a specified age. If a business chose to eliminate older workers, it normally did so through an informal process. However, in most cases, it seems as if people simply kept on working until they made the decision to stop, or until they were no longer capable of doing so. It is likely that older persons were also valued for their experience and knowledge, and this may have been especially true as the United States began to industrialize and was preparing to assume the role of world power. Additionally, the elderly could serve as a source of moral guidance for the young. On the farm, an older person still retained his or her knowledge about agriculture and might be useful by performing some needed chores.

It appears that before the twentieth century, the nature of American society made forced retirement unde-

sirable. Most businesses were far too small to assume the financial responsibility of offering pensions to their employees, who might only number a dozen or so. This small employee base also made it nearly impossible for employers and workers to share the cost of retirement. Second, it was not uncommon for close personal relations to develop between worker and employer, and this may have made discharging older workers unpleasant and, therefore, uncommon. Finally, as late as 1890, most Americans were still working on farms, which was not an occupation conducive to mandatory retirement. In general, skill and experience became effective substitutes for the loss of strength and endurance in later life. Society seems to have expected older Americans to remain productive and elderly individuals lived up to this expectation for as long as they could.

Further stunting the development of mandatory retirement through the turn of the twentieth century was the tendency of older workers to retire on their own. A few industries had grown large enough by then to employ enough people to make it possible to develop some sort of mandatory retirement system. The railroad industry inaugurated a pension system in the last part of the nineteenth century and the federal government offered pensions to Union Army veterans in 1890. Although these programs may have induced some workers to opt for retirement, a mandatory system of retirement was still decades away. Most who retired did so voluntarily, and often the decision was made because they no longer were able to work safely or efficiently. Notably, in 1840, about 70 percent of American males over age sixty-five were working; half a century later, with the American economy undergoing a dramatic transformation due to industrialization, the percentage of men over age sixty-five who were still working had hardly changed.

During the last two decades of the nineteenth century, meanwhile, the American business scene was being transformed. Corporations were becoming the dominant form of business organization; larger numbers of workers were moving to the nation's cities and taking jobs in factories and offices. The American marketplace had been unified by the railroads and with this came an increase in competition and a growing desire to eliminate business rivals. These alterations would make a mandatory system of retirement feasible, as workers were being organized into more efficiently managed groups. A system of mandatory retirement could solve problems such as reducing unemployment and turnover rates, while allowing management to sustain a younger and more efficient labor force. Labor, meanwhile, could utilize this system to transfer the burdens of work from one generation to another, especially in overcrowded labor markets.

This meant that while corporations were experimenting with ways to restrict competition through restraint of trade devices such as monopolies, trusts, and holding companies, they were also seeking to reduce the number of elderly workers employed. Restrictions on hiring the elderly were implemented and mandatory retirement programs were begun. An increase in competition and shorter workdays further aided the development of these policies.

Despite these measures, older workers were not retiring in sufficient numbers. The rate of unemployment for the elderly in the industrial 1890s was about the same as it had been in the agricultural 1840s. Retirement to an urban tenement flat or even the poorhouse in industrializing America was greatly different from retiring on the family farm half a century earlier. Older workers who had little in the way of savings, and who were unable to rely on community resources to assist them in easing the financial onus of retirement, clung to their jobs desperately.

The development of mandatory retirement in the United States was also affected by the economic transition from an economy based on productivity and agriculture to one focused on consumerism. The Panic of 1893 led businessmen and others to conclude that the nation was beginning to produce more goods than the domestic market could absorb. These beliefs led to an increased emphasis on advertising, marketing, and consumerism in an effort to develop untapped domestic markets. Later, the Great Depression strengthened this changeover from production to consumption, further pressuring the nation's elderly to retire and make way for a new generation of workers while spending their accumulated benefits. By the 1960s, retirement itself would become a consumer item, marketed to potential buyers just like any other product.

In the late nineteenth century, unemployment and poverty were thought of as being distinctly different. The term "unemployment" came into greater use as a result of the Panic of 1893, and this concept led employers to begin discriminating in their hiring and retention of employees. This was done by emphasizing the benefits of keeping outstanding workers and eliminating inefficient ones. Therefore, a shorter work life, aided by mandatory retirement, could help reduce unemployment. This idea began to gain acceptance in the 1890s and would become national policy with the development of railroad retirement and social security laws in the 1930s. However, some companies had begun to develop private pension plans well before then.

Early Pension Plans
The first railroad pension plan was established by the American Express Company in 1875. The Baltimore & Ohio (B&O) Railroad followed suit in 1880, while the Pennsylvania Railroad inaugurated a plan in 1900. The B&O plan provided for old-age income protection, allowing workers to retire voluntarily at age sixty-five, or, if they were disabled by illness, at age sixty. Because old age was commonly perceived and treated as a disabling illness, this plan gave retirees the same benefits workers who suffered long-term disabilities received. An innovative feature of the Pennsylvania Railroad retirement plan was

corporate control of the employee retirement plan. Earlier plans had left the administration of benefits to company relief associations. The Pennsylvania Railroad instead created a relief department that gave the company control of the plan, while permitting management total control over policy, administration and financial decisions. This set the precedent for the development of modern personnel supervision, which would directly affect the future of pension and retirement benefit packages. Pension plans such as these were put in place out of a desire to create a stable and efficient relationship between workers and management.

Despite these examples, only a handful of companies, especially those that were industrializing, had established some type of pension plan by 1900. One obstacle that may have discouraged more firms from implementing pension plans was the long-term commitment they required. Employers preferred profit-sharing plans, which shared benefits with the employees as a whole, over retirement plans that gave benefits only to the elderly and seemed like a far-off promise to younger workers. Long-term commitments of a crucial nature such as pension programs often led corporations to reject them outright.

As a result, many retired men in the nineteenth century were dependent upon their families for support. About half of all retired males in 1880 lived with their children or some other family member. Those who had no family, or whose families were unable to offer support, were often relegated to institutions run by charitable associations, often referred to as poorhouses. Songs, poems, and even films raised the issue of what the future might hold for unemployed elderly workers and they commonly concluded that his fate would be that of relegation to the poorhouse. Welfare reformers often referred to the likelihood of penniless elderly retired workers being forced to reside in poorhouses. The poorhouse became a symbol of the helplessness of the elderly in the industrial age in the minds of reformers, who feared that more and more people would be forced to enter these institutions until most old people resided in them. They argued that only old-age pensions could prevent this tragedy from occurring. Although reformers exaggerated the number of persons who were actually institutionalized in the late nineteenth and early twentieth centuries (about 2 percent), the fear of being placed in a poorhouse had a vivid and dramatic impact on public perceptions about the fate of the elderly and contributed to demands that the government should provide some sort of assistance.

Retirement and Scientific Business Management
As the Progressive Era took hold, a popular notion held that scientific management could result in the elimination of waste and inefficiency in business, government, and society. At the same time, rural poverty and other problems, such as poor health in the nation's cities, could be overcome. Business leaders especially approved of ideas that would improve efficiency, order, and organization.

One of the issues that came under consideration was the role of the elderly worker, not only in the workplace, but also in society in general. Arguments, which suggested that productivity began to decline after age forty, strengthened the view that workers should retire once they reached the age of sixty since they were likely to have become inefficient. Critics of this line of reasoning felt workers could remain productive past the age of sixty, yet still found a certain logic in the concept that one should retire in his or her later years.

Advocates of efficiency and progress argued for ideas that threatened the continued employment of workers who could be seen as sources of inefficiency. Younger persons undoubtedly thought of these ideas as a precursor to an age of opportunity, and those nearing an age where retirement might be an option could think of that state as a form of leisure earned from years of working. Resistance to the concept of retirement would continue to be strong until the 1930s. At this time, the shortage of employment opportunities combined with the greater availability of pensions and social security allowed the concept of retirement as a time of leisure to enter the mainstream. Promoters of efficiency in the workplace, however, helped contribute to the image of an aging population that would continue to threaten productivity in the United States. For the country to continue to progress, older workers would have to step aside to make way for younger ones.

One result of this was an increase in age discrimination in the country. Job applicants were more likely to have to take physical examinations, and some companies applied these rules more strictly to older men and women applying for work than to younger ones. Contributing to the rise in discrimination toward the elderly was a growing cult of youth in the 1920s. With the rapid spread of technology, particularly the automobile, the nation's young were increasingly expected to lead the way into the future, rather than the older population. The business community especially embraced these ideas, and employers began to look for vigorous and energetic employees. Some companies still recognized that older workers had a certain value, but the preference was for younger employees. Retirement now offered employers the chance to restructure the work force. Since it was impersonal and equal in application, retirement permitted businesses to offset the need for efficiency with labor-management relations that downplayed the more personal relationships of the past. After 1925, retirement was viewed as a useful tool for correcting the problems of unemployment in depressed industries as well as in the economy.

The Federal Government and Retirement (1900–1935)

The question of retirement also affected the federal government. The interest of Presidents Theodore Roosevelt and William Howard Taft led to the creation of a series of commissions to investigate the manner in which a federal retirement policy might be implemented. Due to op-position from the Woodrow Wilson administration, legislation enacting such a program was not passed by Congress until 1920. Under this law, civil service employees could retire at age seventy, as long as they had a minimum of fifteen years of service. Other employees, such as postal workers and clerks, could retire at sixty-five, and railway clerks at age sixty-two. Retirement benefits were determined by the number of years the retiree had worked. However, the law did not require mandatory retirement, and a person could work for as many as four years past his or her scheduled retirement date. The law was amended in 1926 to provide greater benefits, as the original pension was inadequate to meet the needs of those who had retired.

The Great Depression intensified the problem of unemployment and poverty among the elderly. By 1935, more than 50 percent of those workers over sixty-five were unemployed. Pension benefits offered little or no relief, as private plans were failing and state and local governments were cutting back or eliminating pension programs.

Plans to relieve this problem, such as the Townsend Plan and Lundeen Bill, were proposed, but not enacted. The Townsend Plan called for a monthly payment of $200 to older Americans, who would be expected to spend the money within thirty days. The Lundeen Bill proposed a payment for unemployed Americans who were eighteen or older, including elderly workers. But neither plan truly concentrated on retirement.

Social Security

From the beginning of the New Deal, members of Franklin D. Roosevelt's administration, led by Labor Secretary Frances Perkins, lobbied for a federal program that would provide social insurance for the elderly and unemployed. Roosevelt publicly expressed his support for such a program in 1935, and the Social Security Act was passed by Congress that same year. One of the most complex and far-reaching acts ever passed by Congress; the Social Security Act provided two types of aid to the elderly. Those who were impoverished at the time the act was passed received fifteen dollars in federal aid each month. Those Americans who were employed were placed in a national pension program funded by social security taxes. Eligible workers could begin receiving payments in 1942, and benefits ranged from ten dollars to forty-two dollars monthly. Many workers, including domestic servants, farm workers, and self-employed individuals were excluded, and there was no provision for health insurance. But, by encouraging older workers to retire, the Social Security Act helped open up jobs for younger workers.

The pace of retirement did not increase significantly at first, even with social security and the opportunity to receive federal benefits. As late as the 1950s, studies conducted by the Social Security Administration indicated that older workers based their decision to retire more for reasons of health than the availability of federal benefits.

The fact that the benefits were fixed was seen as a threat to financial security, especially as inflation could reduce the purchasing power of a retiree.

Retirement: An Increasing American Trend (1950–1980)

Even with the concerns about financial security, retirement was becoming more of a social occurrence in the 1950s. Private insurance companies began marketing programs designed to help people prepare for eventual retirement. Postwar prosperity contributed to the growing idea that retirement could be a time of pleasure and creativity that was society's reward to those who toiled for a lifetime. The growth of leisure industries, along with mass tourism and entertainment such as movies, television, golf, and many spectator sports, offered activities for the elderly at prices they could afford. Mandatory retirement became less of an issue; as early as 1956, women could retire at age sixty-two, while men received that opportunity in 1962. Reduced social security benefits accompanied early retirement in either case.

Concerns about poverty among older Americans led to passage of the Older Americans Act of 1965, during the administration of Lyndon Johnson. But the administration of Richard Nixon inaugurated the age of modern retirement. Although earlier amendments to social security had made more workers eligible, the benefits were no longer adequate. The benefit levels were increased five times between 1965 and 1975, and in 1972 benefits were tied to the Consumer Price Index. These adjustments allowed retired Americans to more closely maintain their standard of living, while legitimizing the concept of retirement as a social status that could be entered into voluntarily. Amendments to the Age Discrimination and Employment Act in 1978 raised the mandatory retirement age to seventy in most occupations, while the Employee Retirement Income Security Act (ERISA) offered some protection against loss of benefits in private pension plans.

Retirement in the Twenty-first Century

In general, retired Americans today have become a leisured class. Continued technological advances have created products designed to satisfy increasingly narrow portions of the retirement market and offer more leisure-time choices. Retirement communities, particularly in the Sunbelt, focus on the needs and interests of those residing in them. Recreation and leisure costs have fallen as new and better products have been introduced. Today's elderly, as a class, are also better able physically to partake of these options, and many leisure-time activities include various forms of exercise and sports. Travel opportunities have also increased. The tax-exempt status of retirement savings helps offer an incentive for retirement since it makes retirement income nearly the same as earning a salary, allowing the retired individual the maximum opportunity to take advantage of leisure-time activities that can replace the stimulus work satisfaction may have offered. Even so,

many senior citizens continue to work after retirement. They do so either to supplement inadequate benefit packages, to help support other family members or to sustain a level of status they held before retiring and that their benefits do not allow them to maintain otherwise.

Retirement has also allowed the elderly to enhance their political power. Political concerns of the elderly are promoted through senior citizens groups, of which AARP is the most prominent. Other groups, such as the Alliance for Retired Persons, founded in 2001, also lobby on behalf of the nation's elderly. Organizations such as these have been able to use their lobbying efforts successfully to protect social security, but have made little progress in regard to getting legislators to enact new programs for their benefit.

The future of retirement is difficult to predict. Growing concerns over the availability of social security payments to future generations has led to the feasibility that retirement may not be an option for the next generation. Improvements in medical technology and health care have resulted in increased lifespans, so that Americans can work efficiently and productively for more years. It may be that in this century many Americans will delay retirement as they are able to continue to play an important role in society and the workplace for a greater period of time.

BIBLIOGRAPHY

Carter, Susan B., and Richard Sutch. *Myth of the Industrial Scrap Heap: A Revisionist View of Turn-of-the-Century American Retirement.* Cambridge, Mass.: National Bureau of Economic Research, 1995.

Costa, Dora L. *The Evolution of Retirement: An American Economic History, 1880–1990.* Chicago: University of Chicago Press, 1998.

Graebner, William. *A History of Retirement: The Meaning and Function of an American Institution, 1885–1978.* New Haven, Conn.: Yale University Press, 1980.

Haber, Carole, and Brian Gratton. *Old Age and the Search for Security: An American Social History.* Bloomington: Indiana University Press, 1993.

Krajcinovic, Ivana. *From Company Doctors to Managed Care: The United Mine Workers' Noble Experiment.* Ithaca, N.Y.: ILR Press, 1997.

Price, Christine Ann. *Women and Retirement: The Unexplored Transition.* New York: Garland Publishers, 1998.

Ransom, Roger, and Richard Sutch. *The Trend in the Rate of Labor Force Participation of Older Men, 1870–1930: A Review of the Evidence.* Cambridge, Mass.: Harvard University Press, 1997.

Sass, Steven A. *The Promise of Private Pensions: The First Hundred Years.* Cambridge, Mass.: Harvard University Press, 1997.

Schaie, K. Warner, and W. Andrew Achenbaum. *Societal Impact on Aging: Historical Perspectives.* New York: Springer Publishing, 1993.

Schieber, Sylvester J., and John B. Shoven. *The Real Deal: The History and Future of Social Security.* New Haven, Conn.: Yale University Press, 1999.

Gregory Moore

See also **Old Age; Pension Plans; Retirement Plans; Social Security.**

RETIREMENT PLANS, a relatively new element in the emergence of modern retirement as a social process. Prior to the twentieth century, the concept of mandatory retirement, and therefore the need to plan for such an eventuality, did not exist. For the elderly, retirement in the agrarian society of the colonial and early national periods was essentially a slow transition that led to transferring the property of the head of a household to an heir in return for money or services that might be required by the aged couple. This also assured the continuation of family ownership of the land. In towns and cities before industrialization, the small size of businesses, and the limited numbers of employees they had, meant that the financial burden of creating a pension program of some sort was too great for them to assume. Even with industrialization, most Americans were still engaged in farming as late as 1890, limiting the number of persons who retired. Older Americans tended to stay with their jobs for as long as they could, substituting skills and experience for a loss of strength and stamina in their later years.

Even so, the onset of industrialization and the emergence of larger corporations led to growing concerns about productivity and efficiency on the part of business as well as employee apprehensions regarding their security. These issues helped fuel the move toward mandatory retirement programs. Yet, by 1900, only a few businesses had developed pension plans for their employees, or established programs for mandatory retirement.

In 1935, the Social Security Act established old-age pensions for workers, survivor's benefits for victims of industrial accidents, and aid for dependent mothers and children as well as the blind and disabled. The funds for this program came from taxes paid by employers and employees alike. However, social security did not immediately accelerate the process of retirement. Older workers continued a long-established pattern of delaying retirement until they were physically unable to continue working. This trend continued into the 1950s, although retirement as a social occurrence had begun to increase in this decade. The fixed benefits inherent in the social security program and in private pension plans offered little in the way of financial security for potential retirees, particularly as inflation reduced their spending power.

The ongoing problem of poverty among the elderly led to increases in the benefit levels of social security between 1965 and 1975. To allow adjustments for inflation, benefits were tied to the Consumer Price Index in 1972. At the same time, the private sector began reorganizing its pension plans. The enactment of the Employee Retirement Income Security Act (ERISA) permitted vesting plans, while it also provided workers with some protection against any loss of benefits. Retirement savings became tax-exempt and allowed tax deferments, which lowered the cost of saving for retirement by permitting pretax dollars to be put into a retirement plan and deferring taxation of the gains made from the plan's investments until withdrawal. Private insurance companies had begun offering programs in the 1950s to help individuals prepare for retirement; now they began to expand those programs to offer more options geared to take advantage of these new retirement savings opportunities.

Retirement plans offer workers various choices to plan for their eventual retirement. Often, employers and employees both contribute to these plans, although some may be funded entirely by either an employer or a firm's workers. In general, withdrawals made before age fifty-nine and a half are subject to a 10 percent penalty. Withdrawals normally have to begin no later than one year after a person turns seventy and a half. Income taxes usually become payable once withdrawal begins; taxes are paid on the amounts withdrawn and not on the entire sum in the plan.

Among the common qualified retirement plans in place at present are the following:

Defined benefit pensions generally provide a specific monthly payment from the time of retirement until death. The benefit is normally calculated on the basis of the retiree's final salary multiplied by the number of years of employment. The employer typically funds plans such as these.

Profit-sharing plans are also employer funded, with employee contributions an option. Upon retirement, a person will receive a lump-sum payment. The company's contributions, and therefore the employee's retirement benefit, are tied directly to the company's profits.

Lump-sum retirement benefits are also paid on savings plans. The employer, too, customarily funds these, although employees may contribute as well. Employees may be allowed to borrow a portion of their vested savings.

In employee stock ownership plans (ESOP), employers periodically contribute company stock toward an employee's retirement plan. When the employee retires, the plan may offer a single payment of stock shares. Employees may have additional options after a certain age and length of service (usually fifty-five and ten years) to diversify part of the portfolio.

Tax-sheltered annuities (403b) plans may be offered by tax-exempt and educational organizations for their employees. Retirees are offered a choice of a lump-sum or a series of monthly payments. Plans such as these are funded by tax-deductible employee contributions.

Employers fund money-purchase pensions, although employee contributions may be permitted. This type of plan provides either a lump-sum payment or a series of monthly payments, with the size of the payments dependent upon the size of the contributions to the plan.

Savings Incentive Match Plans (SIMPLE plans) are designed for small businesses. These may be set up either as Individual Retirement Accounts or in some sort of deferred plan such as a 401(k). Employees fund them on a pretax basis and employers are required to make matching contributions. The funds in the account grow on a tax-deferred basis.

For small businesses, there are Simplified Employee Pensions (SEPs). As with other plans, a retiree's withdrawals may be taken as a lump sum or periodically. The employer usually funds these programs, although employee contributions may be allowed.

Keogh plans are designed specifically for self-employed individuals. Funded entirely from the worker's contributions, which are tax-deductible for the most part, they, too, permit disbursement on a lump sum or periodic basis.

Among personal retirement savings programs, Individual Retirement Accounts (IRAs) are probably the most popular. These plans are funded entirely by personal contributions, which are tax-deferred. IRAs are most commonly held in an account with a bank, savings association, credit union brokerage firm, insurance company, or mutual fund company. As with the other plans, benefits may be withdrawn periodically or in a lump sum after retirement.

BIBLIOGRAPHY

Graebner, William. *A History of Retirement: The Meaning and Function of an American Institution, 1885–1978.* New Haven, Conn.: Yale University Press, 1980.

Haber, Carole, and Brian Gratton. *Old Age and the Search for Security: An American Social History.* Bloomington: Indiana University Press, 1993.

Sass, Steven A. *The Promise of Private Pensions: The First Hundred Years.* Cambridge, Mass.: Harvard University Press, 1997.

Schieber, Sylvester J., and John B. Shoven. *The Real Deal: The History and Future of Social Security.* New Haven, Conn.: Yale University Press, 1999.

Gregory Moore

See also **Pension Plans; Pensions, Military and Naval.**

REVENUE, PUBLIC. Public revenue has been derived from a changing array of tax sources in the United States. During the early national period, the FEDERAL GOVERNMENT placed taxes on distilled spirits, sugar, gold, watches, tobacco, property sold at auction, slaves, and corporate bonds. Nevertheless, the overall amount of federal revenue raised by taxation remained relatively modest. That changed in the 1860s. During the CIVIL WAR, the federal government levied the first income tax in the nation's history. At the war's close, the federal government

had netted more than $310 million in tax revenues. The Confederacy's defeat and the Union army's ensuing demobilization brought an end to the Civil War income tax. Consequently, between the late 1860s and the early 1910s, customs duties on imports and proceeds from the sale of public lands constituted the major part of the revenue of the federal government.

With the passage of the Sixteenth Amendment in 1913, the United States adopted the first permanent income tax in its history. Thereafter taxes on the income of individuals and corporations have remained the dominant source of government income since then. Excise taxes on the sale of selected commodities—notably alcohol, tobacco, and automobiles—provide an important but lesser source of revenue. After the 1930s a rapid expansion occurred in social security taxes and other employment-related "contributions" that are, in turn, dedicated to financing specific social insurance benefits. During World War II, tax revenues reached $7.3 billion. The Cold War defense budget and the expansion of domestic entitlement programs in the 1960s sent tax revenues soaring ever higher.

In the fiscal year 1972 the federal government received about $86 billion, or 43 percent of its total revenue of $198 billion, from the progressive personal income tax. Another $30 billion, or 15 percent, came from the corporate income tax. Social insurance taxes and contributions accounted for $54 billion, or 28 percent. Excise, estate, and gift taxes; customs duties; and miscellaneous receipts produced a total of $28 billion, or 14 percent.

A sluggish economy in the late 1970s led to taxpayer revolts throughout the United States. Indeed, Ronald Reagan won the 1980 presidential election in part on the fact that he promised voters that he would enact sweeping tax cuts. In 1981 Congress responded by passing $750 billion in tax cuts over six years, the largest tax reduction in the nation's history. However, a record national debt soon ensued, despite the fact that federal receipts reached more than $1.5 trillion by the end of the decade. Gradual tax hikes followed in an effort to reduce the national deficit. With the aid of a surging economy, annual federal revenue surpassed annual federal spending in the late 1990s, thus marking the first federal budget surplus in nearly forty years.

In contrast to the federal government, state governments have generally depended most heavily on sales taxes, although most have adopted personal and/or corporate income taxes as sources of supplementary revenue. Through grants-in-aid the federal government has financed major shares of state expenditures for highways and public assistance.

Cities, counties, and other local governments raise the bulk of their income from the traditional taxes on property values. The larger cities, particularly, have levied payroll taxes in an effort to obtain revenue from commuters who work in the central city but live in adjacent suburbs. State and federal governments have financed rising proportions of education and other local activities, in response to the slow growth in the yield of fixed-rate property taxation.

Overall, revenues raised by state and local governments rose from $18.8 billion in 1951 to $114.8 billion in 1971 to $1.5 trillion in 1999. These funds were supplemented by $2.3 billion of federal grants in 1951, $26.9 billion in 1971, and $270.6 billion in 1999.

The following table shows the growth of federal revenue, by ten-year periods (in millions):

1791	$ 4.4	1901	$587.7
1801	12.9	1911	701.8
1811	14.4	1921	5,624.9
1821	14.6	1931	3,189.6
1831	28.5	1941	7,995.6
1841	16.9	1951	53,368.6
1851	52.6	1961	94,371.0
1861	41.5	1971	188,392.0
1871	383.3	1981	606,799.1
1881	360.8	1991	1,086,851.4
1891	392.6	2001	2,019,000.0

Murray L. Weidenbaum / A. G.

See also **Banking Crisis of 1933; Debt and Investment, Foreign; Depression of 1920; Laissez-Faire; Office of Management and Budget; Share-the-Wealth Movements.**

REVENUE SHARING occurs when a government shares part of its tax income with other governments. State governments, for example, may share revenue with local governments, while national governments can share revenue with state governments. The amount of revenue shared is determined by law. Generally, the governments that receive the monies are free from any stipulations about or controls on how to use them. In some cases, however, the receiving government may be required to match the amount granted.

Forms of revenue sharing have been used in several countries, including Canada and Switzerland. In the United States, the idea of revenue sharing evolved in response to complaints that many of the vigorously monitored grant-in-aid programs created their own expensive and inefficient bureaucracies. Under the auspices of economist Walter Heller, the U.S. government created its own revenue-sharing programs. In October 1972, President Richard M. Nixon signed into law the State and Local Assistance Act, a modest revenue-sharing plan that allocated $30.2 billion to be spread over a five-year period. The funds were distributed so that one-third went to state governments and two-thirds to local governments. Matching funds were not required, and broad discretionary powers were given to the state and local governments in spending the funds.

However, not everyone embraced the idea of revenue sharing; critics of the program argued that revenue shar-

ing replaced rather than supplemented categorical grants and was inadequate to meet the needs of big cities. Nevertheless, the Gerald Ford and James Earl Carter administrations continued the experiment in revenue sharing. Between 1972 and 1986, money collected in federal taxes was given to state and local governments, with few restrictions placed on how those funds could be used. The notion guiding this practice was that local and state needs varied, and elected officials at either level would be more effective at identifying those needs than would officials of the federal government. Communities held public hearings on how the money ought to be spent. One of the few stipulations imposed upon localities and states was that there could be no racial discrimination on how the monies were dispersed. Public audits were also required. As a result, small towns and counties, as well as large cities, received direct federal aid.

During the fourteen years in which the program operated, administrative costs were extremely low and a total of $85 billion reached American communities. General revenue sharing continued into the 1980s, although the amounts allocated steadily diminished. Although still in use, revenue sharing was hampered by the general downturn in the economy that took place after September 2001, which left less money available to fund such programs.

BIBLIOGRAPHY
Dommel, Paul R. *The Politics of Revenue Sharing.* Bloomington: Indiana University Press, 1974.

Wallin, Bruce A. *From Revenue Sharing to Deficit Sharing: General Revenue Sharing and Cities.* Washington, D.C.: Georgetown University Press, 1998.

Meg Greene Malvasi

REVERE'S RIDE. Paul Revere, a Boston silversmith, engraver, and a messenger of the Massachusetts Committee of Safety, knew that British troops in Boston planned to seize the military stores collected in Concord, Massachusetts. On the night of 18 April 1775, Revere learned that the British attack had begun. After sending a signal to nearby friends, Revere headed for Lexington, sounding his alarm as he went. In Lexington, Revere teamed up with William Dawes and Samuel Prescott and started toward Concord. British officers intercepted the three, but Prescott escaped and continued on to Concord. Dawes fled back toward Lexington, and Revere was held for a few hours.

BIBLIOGRAPHY
Fischer, David Hackett. *Paul Revere's Ride.* New York: Oxford University Press, 1994.

Triber, Jayne E. *A True Republican: The Life of Paul Revere.* Amherst: University of Massachusetts Press, 1998.

Allen French / s. c.

Paul Revere. Robert Reid's painting depicts the well-known Boston silversmith's famous "midnight ride" to Lexington and Concord—made by William Dawes and Samuel Prescott as well—on 18–19 April 1775, to awaken fellow patriots and warn them that the British were coming. HULTON/GETTY IMAGES

See also **Lexington and Concord; Minutemen; Sons of Liberty (American Revolution);** *and vol. 9:* **Paul Revere's Account of His Ride.**

REVIVALISM. *See* **Evangelicalism and Revivalism.**

REVOLUTION, AMERICAN

This entry includes 5 subentries:
Political History
Military History
Diplomatic Aspects
Financial Aspects
Profiteering

POLITICAL HISTORY

The American Revolution transformed thirteen British colonies into fourteen states (including Vermont) and bound them into one republic. It changed the identity of millions of people, and transformed their dominant political idea from unequal subjection to equal citizenship. It began with a parochial dispute about being British. Its debates escalated to fundamental questions of human existence. By creating the United States, the Revolution gained world-historical significance.

The Revolution also created a continent-spanning empire. To the victors every denizen was a subject, though not necessarily a citizen, of the United States. To Indians, nothing of the sort was true. They remained their own peoples. The Revolution helped begin the worldwide as-

sault on slavery. It also let slavery spread across the Cotton Kingdom and gain enough strength that a southern republic nearly emerged out of the American republic's contradictions. Full of such contradictions, the Revolution was among the major modern transforming events.

British Power in the Colonies

At the end of the Seven Years' War in 1763, Great Britain stood triumphant among western European powers. But the war had been expensive, and the colonies had seemed insubordinate and uncooperative, even though colonials gloried in being Britons. Parliament's position, given formal statement in 1765 by Sir William Blackstone, was that it possessed power over all Britons. Vaunted British liberty merely meant that the Crown could not act without Parliament's consent.

After 1763 successive British administrations tried to tax the colonies directly to pay for imperial defense and administration and to assert Parliament's power. The Revenue or "Sugar" Act (1764) taxed all sugar and molasses brought to the mainland colonies. Despite sporadic protests and a great deal of smuggling, it took force. The STAMP ACT (1765) tried to tap colonial business by requiring official stamps on most transactions. Colonial resistance nullified it everywhere except Georgia, and it was repealed in 1766. The Declaratory Act (1766) announced that Parliament could legislate for the colonies "in all cases whatsoever." In 1767 the TOWNSHEND ACTS taxed imported glass, lead, paint, paper, and tea. Resistance led to the repeal of all except the tea duty in 1770. All of the British taxes were to be paid in scarce coin rather than colonial paper money, which was denied the status of legal tender. Violators would be tried in vice-admiralty courts, where a royal judge would decide all matters.

After 1767 an American Board of Customs Commissioners was based in Boston. Troops were stationed there in 1768 to protect customs officials. In 1773 Parliament combined the tea tax with rescuing the bankrupt East India Company by letting it market tea directly to America. Most towns simply turned the tea ships around before they entered the port limits and had to declare their cargoes. But Boston could not. When intense negotiations about sending it back finally failed on 16 December 1773, "Mohawks" dumped the tea into the Harbor.

The "destruction of the tea" (not called the Boston Tea Party until decades later) changed the British position. The issue no longer was taxes; it was punishing Boston and Massachusetts. Early in 1774 Parliament passed four "Coercive" or "Intolerable" Acts, which closed the port of Boston, altered the Massachusetts government, allowed troops to be billeted on civilians, and permitted trials of British officials to be heard in Nova Scotia or Britain, because they supposedly could not get a fair trial in the original colony. This was despite the acquittal by a Massachusetts court of the soldiers involved in the Boston Massacre. General Thomas Gage, commander in chief in America, became governor of Massachusetts, and British headquarters moved from New York to Boston. Meanwhile the Quebec Act recognized Catholicism and French customs there and gave jurisdiction over the Ohio and Great Lakes country to the government in Montreal.

The Rise of Resistance

Resistance received a strong lead from notable provincials. They had become used to making laws, raising taxes, setting public officials' salaries, and debating high policy. They regarded their assemblies as local equivalents of Parliament. Now Parliament itself threatened their power and pride. Provincial assemblies passed resolutions, established COMMITTEES OF CORRESPONDENCE, and called for days of fasting. The sort of white men who sat in them started to work out the position that we know as "taxation without representation is tyranny." The phrase was coined by the fiery Boston lawyer James Otis, but it was not widely used. The elite's lead was important, but resolutions and pamphlets would not alone have altered even one British policy, let alone start to change the fundamental terms of American life. From the Stamp Act in 1765 to the dumping of the tea, the resistance movement's "punch" came from the port cities, thanks to both ordinary people's grievances and well-organized popular leadership.

"Ordinary people" is a broad term. In the port towns it covered seafarers, laborers, apprentices, journeymen artisans, master craftsmen, tavern keepers, and even small merchants. In the right circumstances it could cover slaves, though describing a crowd as comprising "sailors, Negroes, and boys" was a standard way to disown it. Crowd action was a normal part of eighteenth-century urban life. Some crowds amounted to a whole community defending itself when the militia, the sheriff's posse, or the volunteer fire company could not. Even gentlemen might be involved, perhaps disguised in costume or a workingman's long trousers.

Crowd action also could have a class content. Seafarers, rather than all "town-born," frustrated an attempt in 1747 to impress them off the Boston streets into the Royal Navy. Crowds could be rough, but they also could be sophisticated. Boston workingmen paraded with effigies each autumn on "Pope's Day" (5 November), which celebrated the unmasking of the seventeenth-century Gunpowder Plot to bomb Parliament. They were keeping alive their sense that to be British meant more than doing whatever Parliament said. It was to be Protestant and free, and on that day the crowd of Protestant freemen ruled Boston's streets.

For the most part these uprisings were traditional, aimed at restoring how things ought to be, but during the Stamp Act crisis of 1765–1766 a transformation began. An intercolonial network of Sons of Liberty emerged, combining militancy with political direction. For the most part they were men in the middle, not real plebeians but not gentry either. In Boston Samuel Adams was Harvard educated but very much a popular politician. Adams could (and often did) argue with the governor, but he also could

talk to people like shoemaker Ebenezer Macintosh, who led one of the Pope's Day crowds. Macintosh brought out the crowds on 14 August 1765, in order to "convince" stamp distributor Andrew Oliver that he should resign before the Stamp Act even took force. Boston's depressed economy helps explain the crowd's intense anger.

Newport, New York City, and other places followed Boston's lead. Virginia's House of Burgesses passed powerful (if ambiguous) resolutions. These inspired more resolutions from other assemblies and from a congress of nine colonies that assembled in New York. Maryland pamphleteer Daniel Dulany demolished the British argument that the colonies were "virtually" represented in Parliament. Henceforth the British assertion would be simply that Parliament could do what it chose. Separate but coordinated nonimportation campaigns in the ports frustrated the Townshend Acts between 1768 and 1770, not completely but enough to bring repeal of all but the tax on tea.

Parallel to the tax problem, the issue of British soldiers became an irritant. Only New York had a long-standing garrison, and it was small until the Seven Years' War. When peace returned, the garrison remained so large that two separate barrack areas were needed to house the troops. Their off-duty competition for scarce jobs made them immensely unpopular, which also applied to the four-regiment garrison posted to Boston in 1768. Street brawls between soldiers seeking work and civilians broke out in New York in January 1770, and five Bostonians died when soldiers on guard duty at the customs house opened fire on a snowball-throwing crowd in Boston in March. Work was an issue there also, but Boston's bloodshed began when a customs informer fired into a hostile crowd, killing eleven-year-old Christopher Seider. Calm returned after the "Boston Massacre," but in 1772 Rhode Islanders captured and burned the revenue cutter *Gaspée* when it ran aground.

Resistance Becomes Revolution

The same year Boston named a committee to rouse awareness in backcountry towns. Initially the committee met with suspicion, but after the passage of the Coercive Acts country people reorganized their militias, closed the royal courts, and shut down the new government outside occupied Boston. This was the moment when ordinary country people first became directly involved. By shutting down the government rather than just resisting one law or policy, it also was the moment when resistance began turning into revolution. Committees of correspondence began to form outside Massachusetts, partly to exchange information and partly to rally support. The First Continental Congress met in Philadelphia at summer's end. It worked out the position that all colonials would support Massachusetts by direct aid and by boycotting British commerce, and it called for committees of association to guarantee compliance. During the autumn tense New

Englanders gathered supplies, conducted militia drills, and set up lines of quick communication.

They showed their temper by rallying quickly after a rumor of fighting at Boston spread through eastern New England in October. They showed their organization and their full readiness on 19 April 1775, when real fighting broke out at the towns of Lexington and Concord after a British expedition tried to seize supplies and capture leaders. Massachusetts men drove the troops back with heavy losses, gathered into an impromptu army, and besieged Boston, which the British army controlled. In June they inflicted massive injuries on another British force at Breed's (Bunker) Hill. Massachusetts had been in revolution since the closure of the courts the previous summer. Now it was at war.

When war broke out General and Governor Gage was under orders from London to act, even though he knew his troops were too few for the task. Each side knew the other's plans, and townsmen were ready for the alarm that Paul Revere spread as the troops prepared to move. Whoever fired first, the colonial militia gave the redcoats a terrible drubbing, besieged Boston, and gave British regulars another drubbing before they yielded Breed's (Bunker) Hill in June. Shortly after that, George Washington, who had appeared at the Second Continental Congress in uniform, arrived to take command. A stalemate followed until artillery captured from Fort Ticonderoga on Lake Champlain could be placed on Dorchester Heights. That made Boston untenable, and the British withdrew in March 1776.

Outside New England the news of fighting changed the mood from disquiet and support to angry solidarity. COMMITTEES OF SAFETY took form and began to drain power away from regular governments. The elite New Yorker Gouverneur Morris described one meeting to elect a committee as "the mob" beginning "to think and to reason." He likened the plebeians to "poor reptiles" and predicted that "'ere noon they will bite." When the news arrived from Lexington, a real mob broke open the city arsenal and seized the weapons stored there. Small farmers outside New England began to ponder their own interests. Slaves in Virginia quietly approached the royal governor and offered their services. They knew at least vaguely about Somerset's Case (1772), which seemed to outlaw slavery within Britain. As early as 1768 Ohio country Indians had been exploring the idea of unity. Now they and most others began considering which side to choose.

The Debate over Independence

Throughout the quarter-century from 1764, when the first protests against the Sugar Act appeared, until the end of the great debate about ratifying the federal Constitution in 1789, American writers argued. Until 1774 their debate was about the problem of being British while not dwelling in Britain. London set the terms of the argument even though writers like Daniel Dulany (Maryland) and

John Dickinson (Delaware and Pennsylvania) wrote with great power and usually won their points.

Thomas Jefferson's *A Summary View of the Rights of British America* (1774) broke free of that agenda. He, Thomas Paine, John Adams (*Thoughts on Government*, 1776) and others were declaring intellectual independence and beginning to address the problems that Americans would face as a separate people. The first result would be justifying independence in 1776. The second would be state-level arguments about how to be republican. The third would be the creation of the republic over a dozen intensely conflict-ridden but very creative years.

Paine's *COMMON SENSE* (1776) made the argument for independence and republicanism, calling for the simplest of political institutions to replace the old order. Not everybody was ready, and some people were moving to the king's side. Others dreaded Paine's call for extreme political simplicity, particularly Adams, whose *Thoughts on Government* made the call for institutional complexity and balance. That debate would continue until 1788. Adams also suggested that any new constitution would need some sort of popular ratification. New York artisans and farmers in western Massachusetts were making the same point. More immediately, doubters and moderates had to be convinced, particularly in New York and in Pennsylvania, whose old government continued to meet in the same building as Congress until May 1776.

Congress moved toward independence gradually between April and July, opening the ports to non-British trade, calling for remaining royal government to end, and finally naming the five-man committee that drafted its Declaration to the world. It also named committees to begin the business of foreign affairs, particularly with France, which already was giving clandestine aid, and to draft ARTICLES OF CONFEDERATION binding the separate states. Until that document was finally approved in 1781, there was no real basis for the United States to exist. Yet during those years Congress organized an army, supported a war, presided over the beginnings of a national economy, and won an alliance with France and financial aid from the Netherlands.

The DECLARATION OF INDEPENDENCE has three parts: an eloquent statement about human rights, a long bill of indictment against "the present king of Britain," and the formal statement of separation. Of these the most important at the time was the attack on King George. The Declaration did not attack monarchy in principle. That would have been foolish, given the need for French aid. What Jefferson wrote was not what Congress finally declared. To the Virginian's chagrin, his collective editor cut much of his impassioned rhetoric toward the document's end, including his attempt to blame slavery on King George, which Jefferson himself saw as the final and most powerful charge. Historically the charge was ridiculous; Virginians had wanted their slaves. But slavery was emerging as a moral and political problem that cut across all other lines of dispute, including that of loyal Briton and revolutionary American. When British writer Samuel Johnson asked in 1776 how it was "that we hear the loudest yelps for liberty from the drivers of Negroes," his revulsion was just as strong as Jefferson's.

The War Is Fought
Congress voted independence on July 2 and accepted the final draft on July 4. It was not fully signed until early August. By then an enormous fleet was discharging British and hired German troops on Staten Island, preparing to capture New York City. Expecting the invasion, George Washington had moved his half-trained and ill-equipped Continental Army to Brooklyn. His attempt to defend the city in the "Battle of Long Island" failed, but a superb retreat to Manhattan got most of his troops out of the way of capture. The Americans continued to retreat, first upstate and then across the Hudson River into New Jersey. Washington's strategy until 1781 would be to keep the army intact, rather than to win set pieces, unless a stroke was needed for purposes of military and civilian morale. He achieved two such strokes, one at Trenton in December 1776 and the other at Princeton in January 1777. New York City would remain in British hands until 1783.

The only great set-piece battles after Long Island were Saratoga in 1777, when American victory helped bring France into the conflict openly, and Yorktown in 1781. The French fleet made that possible by blocking the Chesapeake until a combined army under Washington could cut Lord Cornwallis and his troops off, breaking the British political will to continue.

By then the war had touched virtually everybody inside the whole zone that Britain had won in 1763. Even the Southwest, where Choctaws and Chickasaws were nominally pro-British but primarily interested in their own independence, saw an influx of loyalist refugees, as well as military aid from the Spanish authorities in New Orleans to the Americans farther east. Spain entered the war not as an outright ally of the United States, but rather to honor its own alliance with France. The "old northwest," New York State, eastern Pennsylvania, the Chesapeake, the southern backcountry, and the Carolina and Georgia lowlands all witnessed massive material destruction. Among all American wars, the struggle for independence was the second longest, after Vietnam. The rate of military casualties in relation to the population was the second highest after the Civil War.

The Revolution's Aftermath
At the war's end perhaps sixty thousand white refugees fled, going to Canada and Britain. Thousands of black people who had sought the king's freedom secured it by fleeing too, on the ships that left Savannah, Charleston, and New York late in 1783. The Mohawk Indians, who had been actively pro-British, went to Canada; most others believed they had lost nothing, whichever side they had chosen. The treaty signed in Paris that year provided almost everything the Americans could have wanted. It yielded not just the areas where American troops were in control but also the three major occupied ports. It also ceded the entire zone east of the Mississippi, south of the Great Lakes, and north of Florida, whatever Indians thought about it. Washington rightly called his fellow Americans "lords of a great empire" in 1784.

Within America changes were unfolding rapidly. Vermont abolished slavery in 1777 when it declared its own independence from New York. Pennsylvania began gradual abolition in 1780, to be completed in 1799. The Massachusetts Supreme Court decreed slavery's immediate abolition there in 1783. Women were starting to raise their voices about public affairs and about their own concerns. During the war all the states persecuted LOYALISTS, attainting them by name in statutes that confiscated their property and threatened them with death. The Penn family lost their feudal proprietorship over Pennsylvania. The material demands of the war generated a national economy, which simply had not existed prior to independence. The experiences of war as seen from the center of national politics and of diplomacy began turning the provincial gentlemen who had been mostly strangers when they first assembled in 1774 into a national elite with a common point of view and an increasingly common purpose.

Deciding on a New Political Order
The greatest immediate problem after independence was to work out the terms of a new political order. John Adams wanted to "glide insensibly" from the old order to the new, with minimal change in institutions or customs. That is what happened in Connecticut and Rhode Island, which already ran their own affairs entirely. But elsewhere the old institutions collapsed at independence, and new ones had to be built from the beginning. Thomas Paine thought that annual assemblies "with a president only" would do, and that is close to what came to be in Pennsylvania and Vermont. The idea horrified John Adams in Massachusetts, New York's John Jay, and Maryland leader Charles Carroll of Carrollton. Each state created complex institutions that their designers intended to balance society's elements against one another. Following British tradition and wanting to protect private property, they tried to define those elements in terms of "the few" and "the many," with property requirements for voting and holding public office.

The state constitutions of New York (1777) and Massachusetts (1780) foreshadowed the structure of executive branch, legislative branch, and judicial branch that the United States Constitution would establish. That document's authors intended to sort men who were qualified to rule from the rest. When they wrote it in 1787, they had come firmly to believe that ordinary people had shown themselves unfit to rule by their conduct in the separate states. But the Constitution says nothing about social distinctions among citizens, let alone about property requirements for voting and holding office. Its sorting out would be indirect, on the unproven premise that on a large stage only the truly qualified could emerge.

Perhaps the worst intellectual problem was figuring out how to be a republican people at all. It was not enough to depose the king, as the English had deposed James II in 1688. They had simply called new joint monarchs, James's daughter Mary and her husband, William, to the throne, but there would be no European prince for Americans. Nor was it enough to draw up a set of new institutions, call the document a constitution, and declare it in operation. Most states did try to do exactly that. The possible consequences became apparent when South Carolina's legislature repealed the state's two-year-old constitution in 1778. The governor vetoed the repeal and then resigned his office, leaving the state with neither a certain basis for its own institutions nor anybody in charge. Not until Massachusetts employed the devices of both a special convention to write a constitution and a special process to ratify it in 1780 did the notion of "the people" being its own sovereign begin to take on operational meaning. That device has underpinned American constitutional thinking ever since.

The movement for the federal Constitution sprang from the inadequacies of the Articles of Confederation, which rendered Congress nearly powerless, from foreign debts that could not be paid and treaty obligations that could not be met, from the Revolution's surge of "new men" into power at the state level, and from what those men did with the power they gained. That included continuing to persecute loyalists despite the peace treaty, cushioning the problems of debtors by staying suits and issuing cheap paper money, and looking to local needs ahead of national ones. The men we call "the Framers" already knew one another thanks to wartime experience, and they had developed a common perspective. To their minds the whole situation pointed toward disaster, particularly after Shays's Rebellion (1786) seemed to threaten the very government of Massachusetts.

Alexander Hamilton of New York began writing essays in favor of strong government as early as 1782. James Madison of Virginia retreated from the frustrations of serving in Congress to ponder political science. Serving as American minister in London, John Adams tried to defend "the constitutions of the United States." George Washington wrote worried letters to his friends. Informal meetings at Mount Vernon (1785) and Annapolis (1786) led to a call for a general convention to "propose amendments" to the Articles of Confederation, which would meet in Philadelphia in 1787.

That call had no legal basis, but Congress endorsed it, and only Rhode Island failed to send delegates. Even their absence could have been fatal, since amending the Articles required the legislatures of all thirteen founding states (excluding Vermont, which went unrecognized) to consent. The convention sidestepped that problem by providing that the Constitution would take effect when special conventions in nine states accepted it. The solu-

tion was strictly illegal, but by June 1788 nine states had ratified, though the majority of voters probably intended to reject it. Institutional stability finally returned when the United States Congress assembled and George Washington assumed the presidency early in 1789.

The Constitution solved the problems of political authority, political order, and political economy among the republic's citizens that the Revolution had raised. It created a huge common market within which a commercial economy could flourish. It gave the United States the strength to survive in a difficult, dangerous world and to create its own continent-spanning empire. The Northwest Ordinances adopted by the old Congress during the same period solved the problem of incorporating that American empire into the republic, both politically and economically. But the Constitution failed completely to address the issues of equality and freedom that people who were not white and not male had raised during the Revolution.

Those questions had had no place on the old agenda for discussion and action that had gone with being British in America. They would have very prominent places on the new agenda that sprang from the Revolution's proposition that to be American was to be equal and free. Part of what was revolutionary about American independence was that it happened at all, given Britain's strength and the amount of disruption required. Part was working out a way for republicanism to work over an enormous area. Part was opening up those questions of American equality, identity, and belonging, even though most would remain unanswered long after George Washington became president.

BIBLIOGRAPHY

Bailyn, Bernard. *The Ideological Origins of the American Revolution.* Cambridge, Mass.: Harvard University Press, 1967.

Calloway, Colin. *The American Revolution in Indian Country: Crisis and Diversity in Native American Communities.* Cambridge, U.K.: Cambridge University Press, 1995.

Countryman, Edward. *The American Revolution.* New York: Hill and Wang, 1985. Revised edition in preparation.

Frey, Sylvia. *Water from the Rock: Black Resistance in a Revolutionary Age.* Princeton, N.J.: Princeton University Press, 1991.

Greene, Jack P., and J. R. Pole, eds. *A Companion to the American Revolution.* Malden, Mass.: Blackwell, 2000.

Gross, Robert A. *The Minutemen and Their World.* Rev. ed. New York: Hill and Wang, 2001.

Holton, Woody. *Forced Founders: Indians, Debtors, Slaves, and the Making of the American Revolution in Virginia.* Chapel Hill: University of North Carolina Press, 1999.

Norton, Mary Beth. *Liberty's Daughters: The Revolutionary Experience of American Women, 1750–1800.* Rev. ed. Boston: Little, Brown, 1996.

Wood, Gordon S. *The Radicalism of the American Revolution.* New York: Vintage Books, 1993.

Young, Alfred F. *The Shoemaker and the Tea Party: Memory and the American Revolution.* Boston: Beacon Press, 1999.

Edward Countryman

See also **Constitution of the United States; Continental Congress; Intolerable Acts; Revolution, American: Military History; Sons of Liberty (American Revolution); Sugar Acts; "Taxation without Representation";** *and vol. 9:* **Address of the Continental Congress to Inhabitants of Canada; Declaration and Resolves of the First Continental Congress; Declaration of Independence;** *Common Sense;* **Letters of Abigail and John Adams; Massachusetts Circular Letter; Patrick Henry's Resolves; The Pennsylvania Farmer's Remedy; The Continental Association.**

MILITARY HISTORY

Without the War of Independence, there would have been no American Revolution and no American national state in the eighteenth century. Even if Britain had granted her disgruntled colonists separation from the empire in 1775 or 1776, the statement holds true. This generalization about the link between war and American state formation also applies to the creation of many nations since the Early Modern Era in Europe, which saw the emergence of the national state in something remotely approaching its modern form between the sixteenth and eighteenth centuries. America, in some measure, followed the pattern of weak kingdoms and other polities in Europe, since wars led to centralizing tendencies because of the heavy taxes, large armies, and bureaucratic agencies needed to energize and manage military undertakings. Some of those forms of centralization and bureaucratization remained permanently with the advent of peace in Spain, France, Sweden, and, in time, Britain.

It has seldom been noted that the earliest beginnings of war and state formation in America date back to almost a century before the War of Independence and other events that led to the Constitutional Convention in 1787. Britain's four imperial wars with France between 1689 and 1763 resulted in the growth of permanent powers for the thirteen British American legislative assemblies. Dependent on the colonies for men and money to defend the frontiers and to send expeditions against Canada, the colonial lawmakers became military policymakers by indicating the way monies were spent, the number of men to be raised, and the length and location of their service. In using wars as a way to increase their authority, the colonial legislatures seized greater control over military affairs than the House of Commons ever acquired in Britain. These were the bodies that led the resistance against Britain's new imperial program after 1763 and that produced American leaders in the War of Independence. Without the institutional gains from those previous wars in the New World, these assembles would hardly have been able to challenge Britain.

Beginning in 1774, after a decade of opposing British efforts to tax the colonies and to tighten the imperial system in other ways as well, the assemblies, meeting independently as de facto provincial congresses, took control of colonial governments, including the MILITIAS, and elected delegates to the First CONTINENTAL CONGRESS in Philadelphia. The following year, just after fighting erupted at LEXINGTON AND CONCORD in Massachusetts, the Second Continental Congress met and began to function as a quasi-central government. It took command of the New England colonial forces besieging the British in Boston, appointed George Washington commander in chief, and declared independence the following year. No organic growth of an American nation lay behind these actions, nor can American nationalism provide the explanation. Colonial rivalries and jealousies were deep and of long standing. Benjamin Franklin once remarked that the colonies had a greater dislike for one another than they had for Britain, and those sentiments hardly disappeared completely after independence. They were muted only to a limited degree by the war and the separation from Britain. Yet, concerns for self-preservation can propel people of different interests and traditions a vast distance—people who were reluctant revolutionaries, who found the break with the mother country a painful experience.

As for Britain, she had refused to work for a political solution to the problem of the constitutional relationship between London and her North American dependencies. That is why General Thomas Gage, stationed in Boston, received orders that resulted in his dispatching a troop column on 18 April 1775 to destroy the Massachusetts militia's military stores at Concord. The voices of conciliation and compromise in Parliament, led by Lord Chatham, never received a hearing, even though they prophetically warned of a difficult war of overwhelming costs and of French and Spanish intervention on the side of the rebellion.

The Resources of America

Unlike most revolutionaries in modern history, the Americans began the war in control of the infrastructure of the country. They did so through the provincial congresses, which provided written constitutions for the newly independent states, and through their command of the militias. Though often ineffective in pitched battles against British regulars, poorly trained militia performed a valuable constabulary role on the local scene in the Revolutionary War. As a result the loyalists, or tories, were always on the defensive, except when backed by the presence of a Royal Army. A South Carolina loyalist official, James Simpson, correctly observed that the great contribution of the militia was in sustaining civil governments; "their civil institutions" gave the rebels "the whole of their strength." Moreover, Americans fought on their own soil, very different from the relatively flat battlefields of western Europe, over which armies had swept back and forth for centuries. The militia and the Continental army knew the densely wooded country, with its mountains, valleys, swamps, and rivers, and made effective use of them. Americans, particularly the militia, sometimes used night

Battle of Lexington. This illustration by Amos Doolittle, a prominent artist of the time, shows the British firing at colonists on 19 April 1775—the start of the American Revolution. NATIONAL ARCHIVES AND RECORDS ADMINISTRATION

attacks and resorted to winter fighting. Another plus for the Americans was an abundance of manpower. Certainly most white men between ages eighteen and forty-five saw some military service, whether in the militia or the Continental army. The militia understandably preferred to serve under their own local officers, and the states usually limited their active service to anywhere from a few months to as much as a year. They were most valuable to Washington in the winter months when regular Continental enlistments usually ended and a virtually new army had yet to be raised for service in the following spring and summer.

One does not have to be slavishly devoted to a great man theory of history to maintain that Washington was the most valuable asset for the Americans—in any event, the greatest human asset. From the beginning, he showed his total commitment to civil control of the military. He himself was a former colonial legislator and a member of the Congress that appointed him in June 1775. He kept the lawmakers informed of his activities and unfailingly obeyed their instructions, although he was honest and open in making it known when he disagreed with his masters. Congress moved at a slower pace in the process of nation building than had been the case during the early

modern European wars. That fact frustrated Washington, but he knew the foremost problem was that the newly independent states were initially hesitant to create a strong central government. Congress, however, had wasted no time in 1776 in beginning the process, drafting the Articles of Confederation; however, disagreement about certain allocations of powers along with state jealousies kept the document from being formally ratified by all the thirteen states, as required, until 1781. Washington conceded that it was difficult to create an American constitutional union in the midst of war, at a time when Congress was deflected by its myriad military and diplomatic responsibilities. The loosely structured Confederation was a kind of federalism, more like the pre-1776 version of imperial federalism than the form of federalism to triumph after the war in 1787.

Washington himself was militarily conservative and so was Congress. A massive guerrilla war might well have spawned countless atrocities, the destruction of cities, and the weakening of American social and political institutions. As a FRENCH AND INDIAN WAR colonel, commanding the Virginia forces, he had sought to make his regiment as professional as possible, calling for strict discipline, rigorous training, and officers well read in European military literature. The same attitude shaped his thinking about the Continental army. The army suffered its share of defeats, but even on those occasions it often fought reasonably well. And it had open space in which to retreat and regroup. Washington escaped across New Jersey after the loss of New York City. General Nathanael Greene, pursued by Lord Cornwallis in the South, fled across the Dan River into Virginia. The army learned from its mistakes and steadily improved, displaying incredible staying power in a contest that lasted eight and one-half years. Much of the credit for its progress goes to Friedrich Wilhelm von Steuben, the so-called Prussian drillmaster, and to a cluster of French officers who constituted the corps of engineers.

If Washington's principal task was to hold his army together, he had two reasons for doing so. One was simply to outlast the British, to wear them down, to destroy their will to win a war that became an endlessly long contest of attrition. And it worked, just as North Vietnam's similar approach eventually spelled failure for the United States in Southeast Asia in the 1970s. For in both the earlier and later war, political pressures and public opinion generally led Britain and the United States, respectively, to withdraw from a quagmire, although both countries were still quite capable from a narrow military perspective of continuing the struggle. The second dimension of Washington's job was to foster a sense of unity in the army and, from his perspective, in the new nation as a whole. Washington urged the officers and men of the army to forsake religious, ethnic, and provincial jealousies. He contended with Protestants who did not like Catholics and Jews and conservative Protestant ministers who opposed the appointment of John Murray, the father of American Universalism, as an army chaplain. New England men did not want to serve under New York officers and frontier riflemen fought with Marblehead fishermen from Massachusetts. In his general orders, he constantly encouraged his soldiers to think of themselves first as Americans and not simply as Virginians or Pennsylvanians or Georgians. He enjoyed his greatest success in inculcating national identity and esprit in his officers, including Nathanael Greene, Henry Knox, Anthony Wayne, Henry Lee, and John Marshall. As a person, he emerged as the most visible symbol of unity for Americans. And as an institution, his army stood out as the most visible symbol of unity for his countrymen.

The Resources of Britain

Britain had certain formidable advantages over the colonies at the outbreak of the war. One was a growing sense of national identity that increased the unity of England, Scotland, and Wales. It was based on a mighty empire, economic growth, success in war, and anti-Catholicism. When had Britain ever lost a war? She was the dominant superpower in Europe after humiliating France and Spain in the Seven Years' War (the French and Indian War in North America). Her post-1688 imperial wars had been fueled by a dynamic economy stimulated by the Industrial

Revolution. At the same time, the government pioneered in new methods of taxation and deficit financing. The result was the development of a "fiscal-military state." The actual war machinery was headed by the king, George III, who was far from a figurehead. Ministers still had to be acceptable to him and so did military commanders. His job in wartime was to back his ministers and to dispense patronage to members of Parliament and other public figures who supported his government. He served as a cheerleader rather than as a planner of campaigns or as one involving himself in day-to-day decisions.

Humanpower constituted another plus for Britain. Her population came to eleven million, whereas there were fewer than three million colonials, of whom one-sixth were held in slavery. In 1775 the army numbered 48,000 men, of whom many were veterans of warfare and proud of their regiments and their traditions. The regimental officers were competent, some of them outstanding. The commanding generals who served in America, all veterans of the Seven Years' War, were sound by the standards of their day, but none displayed the talents of a Wolfe or a Wellington. The navy, long England's first line of defense and its pride, was the largest in the kingdom's history, although post-1763 budget restraints had led to its deterioration. It no longer in 1775 maintained the two-power standard: the numerical equal of Britain and Spain. But commanders were almost all reputable figures, superior to most senior officers of the Bourbon navies. If the Royal Navy used impressment to meet its critical manpower needs, the army turned to the German states, as did other countries needing foreign mercenaries. The ministry purchased the services of 33,000 from six principalities, the great majority of this human flesh coming from Brunswick and Hesse-Cassel. Valuable additions, they not surprisingly were of uneven quality. Having no real stake in the conflict, several thousand deserted and remained in America, lured by land and German American kinsmen in Pennsylvania and elsewhere. Additional human resources were found in America: loyalists and Native Americans. Perhaps two-thirds of the politically active Americans supported the Revolution. That left a sizable number who were neutralists or loyalists, and in fact colonials not uncommonly changed sides depending on who was winning and how they were treated. In the early years, Britain displayed a good deal of indifference to the king's friends, and in the later years, when French entry created a shortage of redcoats in North America, Britain turned too fully to the loyalists and exaggerated their strength, for by that time many Crown adherents had become angered by the army's indifference or mistreatment of them. Even so, perhaps some twenty thousand at one time or another took up arms against the revolutionaries. The Native Americans, as in the imperial wars, influenced the balance of power in the interior. Although both sides courted the tribesmen, the British were better versed in Indian affairs and benefited from the Native Americans' resentment against colonial encroachments on their lands. Consequently, the great majority of the participating Indians fought on the British side.

If the American disadvantages were obvious from the outset—their historic provincial jealousies, largely agricultural economy, and lack of a strong central government—British problems became apparent as the contest progressed. Lord North, the first minister, admitted he knew little of managing a war effort. The direction of military affairs then fell on the secretary of state for the colonies, Lord George Germain, able but prickly, hardly a dynamic war leader as William Pitt had been in the Seven Years' War. Problems of transportation, communication, and supply over the three-thousand-mile Atlantic increased in a war that lasted eight and one-half years. The generals and admirals, most of them members of Parliament, did not trust the ministry—the feeling was mutual—and were members of different factions in the House of Commons. The loyalists, as already indicated, contributed less than London officialdom had hoped. Even the Indians, although they wreaked havoc in the region later known as Kentucky, the Ohio country, and western New York, may have been more of a negative than a positive factor, for their depredations tended to unite and energize western settlers.

The War in New England

In general, the war moved from north to south in terms of where the brunt of the fighting took place between the regular armies of Britain and America. The first year of the conflict saw the colonists on the offensive. Even before Washington's arrival at the American camp at Cambridge in July 1775, the New Englanders, after forcing a British column back from Concord, laid siege to Boston and fought the bloody but inconclusive Battle of BUNKER HILL on 17 June. In that clash, General Thomas Gage, the British commander in chief, sanctioned an attack against the well-entrenched Americans that brought the redcoats a Pyrrhic victory. Before finally driving the colonials back, the British suffered their heaviest losses of any battle during the war, their casualties amounting to 42 percent of the 2,500 troops engaged. While Washington continued the siege, he sent a small American force from his camp through the Maine woods to attack Quebec. Its commander, Benedict Arnold, had gained recent renown, along with Ethan Allen, in seizing small British garrisons at Forts Ticonderoga and Crown Point on Lake Champlain in upper New York. Outside the Canadian city, he met a second American army under Richard Montgomery that had advanced up the Hudson–Lake Champlain waterway. On New Year's Eve, the two American columns were repulsed. Montgomery met death and Arnold took a bullet in the leg. The following year, the Americans were thrown out of Canada and thus ended Congress's serious effort to make the Canadians the fourteenth colony in rebellion.

During the siege of Boston, Washington forged an army out of what he described as a "mixed multitude of

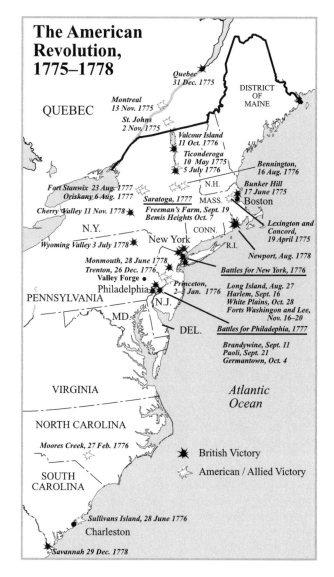

The American Revolution, 1775–1778

Quebec 31 Dec. 1775
DISTRICT OF MAINE
Montreal 13 Nov. 1775
QUEBEC
St. Johns 2 Nov. 1775
Valcour Island 11 Oct. 1776
Ticonderoga 10 May 1775 5 July 1776
Bennington, 16 Aug. 1776
N.H.
Fort Stanwix 23 Aug. 1777
Oriskany 6 Aug. 1777
Bunker Hill 17 June 1775
Saratoga, 1777
MASS. Boston
Cherry Valley 11 Nov. 1778
Freeman's Farm, Sept. 19 Bemis Heights Oct. 7
N.Y.
CONN.
Lexington and Concord, 19 April 1775
Wyoming Valley 3 July 1778
New York
R.I.
Newport, Aug. 1778
Monmouth, 28 June 1778
Trenton, 26 Dec. 1776
Valley Forge
Battles for New York, 1776
PENNSYLVANIA
Philadelphia
Princeton, 2–3 Jan. 1776
Long Island, Aug. 27
Harlem, Sept. 16
White Plains, Oct. 28
Forts Washington and Lee, Nov. 16–20
N.J.
MD.
DEL.
Battles for Philadelphia, 1777
Brandywine, Sept. 11
Paoli, Sept. 21
Germantown, Oct. 4
VIRGINIA
Atlantic Ocean
NORTH CAROLINA
Moores Creek, 27 Feb. 1776
★ British Victory
☆ American / Allied Victory
SOUTH CAROLINA
Sullivans Island, 28 June 1776
Charleston
Savannah 29 Dec. 1778

people," bringing order and discipline. He dismissed incompetent officers and elevated younger men with potential such as Henry Knox of Massachusetts and Nathanael Greene of Rhode Island, who became his most valuable subordinates and served throughout the war. He communicated regularly his needs and his objectives to the New England governments, and he deferred to their authority and their laws, winning their respect and esteem. He proved to New Englanders and to Congress that Americans need not fear an army composed of their own citizens. From his fortified positions surrounding Boston on the land side, he brought increasing pressure on British general William Howe, Gage's successor. After Washington planted artillery on Dorchester Heights, within range of the city, Howe evacuated his army by sea on 17 March. Retiring to Nova Scotia, he sought to regroup, await reinforcements, and attack New York City. Massachusetts appeared to be the center of the rebellion, and New York seemed to offer the prospect of greater success.

The War in the Middle States

Phase two of the struggle took place in the middle states, from 1776 to 1778. Except for the brief months of the Yorktown campaign in late 1781, Washington remained continuously in that theater. His balance sheet shows mixed results. In 1776 the London ministry elected to make a massive display of force, one that would quell the colonial uprising; it was the largest expeditionary undertaking in English history to that time. In the summer of that year General William Howe and his brother, Admiral Richard, Lord Howe appeared before New York City with seventy-three warships, several hundred transports, and 32,000 troops. The British plan was to take the New York capital, and cut off New England from the rest of the colonies. The Howes believed that if they could overwhelm the Puritan colonies, allegedly the most rebellious region, they would have a good chance of ending the uprising, especially if in the process they inflicted a decisive defeat on Washington, who had moved down from Boston to oppose them. But in some measure the Howes had mixed motives. They came as peace commissioners as well as conquerors. Both had been moderates on imperial questions and they seemingly hoped to bring the Americans to a cessation of hostilities by negotiation if possible. If so, they had little to offer in a meeting with a congressional delegation, only to accept an American agreement to stop the fighting before any London officials would consider concessions on policy.

For Britain, the campaign of 1776 began on a positive note and ended on a negative one. Washington suffered a series of setbacks in the New York City area between August and November and ran the risk of losing his army. Defeated on Long Island, he escaped to Manhattan and retreated up the island, fighting a series of battles at Kips Bay, Harlem Heights, and White Plains as the British unsuccessfully tried to get behind him and seal off his escape. But General Howe did capture Fort Washington, which Washington had unwisely left garrisoned on Manhattan. Washington then fled through New Jersey and reached safety by crossing the Delaware River to the Pennsylvania side. Even so, the year terminated with sparkling American counterstrokes. General Guy Carleton, after throwing the American invasion force of Montgomery and Arnold out of Canada, headed down Lake Champlain in hopes of linking up with Howe somewhere on the Hudson. But a setback at the hands of a tiny American fleet under Arnold on that lake, along with the lateness of the season, led Carleton to withdraw to Canada. And Washington, always an aggressive commander, was down but not out. At the end of December he struck back at the British, already settled into winter quarters, overwhelming their garrisons at Trenton and Princeton in New Jersey and then escaping in the first week of the new year into secure lodgings for the season in the hills around Morristown. The year 1777 displayed marked similarities to 1776, with two British armies in the field. The Canadian-based army, now under General John Burgoyne, pressed down the Lake Champlain–Hudson trough, but without a com-

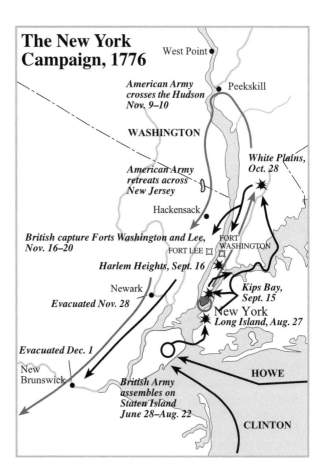

The New York Campaign, 1776

West Point

American Army crosses the Hudson Nov. 9–10

Peekskill

WASHINGTON

American Army retreats across New Jersey

White Plains, Oct. 28

Hackensack

British capture Forts Washington and Lee, Nov. 16–20

FORT WASHINGTON

FORT LEE

Harlem Heights, Sept. 16

Newark

Evacuated Nov. 28

Kips Bay, Sept. 15

New York

Long Island, Aug. 27

Evacuated Dec. 1

New Brunswick

British Army assembles on Staten Island June 28–Aug. 22

HOWE

CLINTON

mitment from General Howe to link up on the Hudson or elsewhere. Howe, leaving Sir Henry Clinton with a garrison in New York City, put to sea with most of his army for a strike at Philadelphia, leaving Burgoyne to his own devices. Lord Germain had sanctioned a campaign without a unifying concept, and Howe and Burgoyne did not trust each other. Overconfidence in the wilderness of upper New York led to Burgoyne's downfall. His army literally broke down in the heavily wooded terrain. Near Saratoga, New York, Burgoyne twice attacked General Horatio Gates's well-entrenched American northern army on Bemis Heights. Twice repulsed with heavy losses, Burgoyne surrendered at Saratoga on 17 October. His loss of over six thousand men demonstrated that European armies, with their bright uniforms and traditional linear formations, did not fare well in the interior of North America.

William Howe, smarter than Burgoyne in some respects, avoided the interior and recognized the importance of staying close to coastal urban areas to keep his supply lines open. Moreover, he won two battles in the fall of 1777. Landing his force at the head of Chesapeake Bay, he advanced on Philadelphia until Washington blocked his route at Brandywine Creek in southern Pennsylvania. After heavy fighting and turning Washington's right flank on 11 September, Howe pushed his opponent aside and occupied Philadelphia. Washington counterpunched on 4 October, staging a night assault on Howe's advance base at GERMANTOWN, Pennsylvania. Again the fighting was spirited, but Washington's battle plan was too complicated and he pulled back and soon went into winter quarters at VALLEY FORGE, some twenty miles from Philadelphia.

The campaigns of 1776 and 1777 revealed the weaknesses of Britain military planning—a lack of overall strategic thinking, an inadequate naval blockade, and a lack of coordination on land. The Howe brothers, increasingly pessimistic about military victory over America and resenting criticism in London circles, resigned and returned to the metropolis to defend their reputation and attribute their failures to Germain and others. Washington, in contrast, showed remarkable persistence and fortitude, keeping his army alive and using the winter and spring of 1777–1778 to survive the Valley Forge winter and to becoming more professional with each passing year through longer enlistments, larger bounties, and better training. It was at Valley Forge that Steuben, the drillmaster, made his mark on the army by standardizing drill and battlefield tactics.

The International War

Britain's failure to subdue New England and the middle states by the spring of 1778 combined with French entry on the side of America changed the scope and character of the conflict. Nursing old grievances against England, France moved from giving clandestine support to the revolutionaries—providing military stores funneled through a fictitious company and allowing the tiny Continental navy and rebel privateers use of her ports—to signing treaties of commerce and alliance with the United States in February 1778. Gallic dangers led Britain to spread her military and naval resources more thinly in America in order to protect the home kingdom and her valuable West Indian sugar islands. Sir Henry Clinton, General Howe's successor as commander in chief in America, evacuated Philadelphia in order to concentrate his forces at New York City and to send troops to the Caribbean. Breaking camp at Valley Forge, Washington pursued him across New Jersey, attacking his rear guard at MONMOUTH Courthouse on 28 June 1778. As the day wore on, a full-scale battle resulted. The Continental army, much enlarged and trained by Steuben, gave one of its best performances of the war. The outcome was indecisive, but the American regulars had more than held their own against veteran British troops, obtaining a moral victory that they sorely needed after their Brandywine and Germantown reversals. Washington's army followed behind Clinton and took up positions outside New York City at White Plains. The two armies were back in the same proximity of two years earlier, a sign that Howe's and Clinton's wanderings had little to show for. It was a matter of up and down and round and round, in the caustic words of the *London Evening Post*.

There were no more major battles in New England or the middle states after Monmouth, only skirmishes, raids, and Indian incursions on the fringes as Washington settled in to observing the British in New York City, although the British garrisoned Stony Point and other small posts on the Lower Hudson until they were dislodged or pressured to relinquish them. Unfortunately for Washington, although the French alliance resulted in a substantial increase in military supplies from France, his new allies failed to play an active role in the American part of the international war until quite late. In 1778 Admiral the Comte d'Estaing failed to intercept a British convoy bound from Philadelphia to New York City and a storm destroyed his chances of defeating Admiral Howe off the coast of Rhode Island. For over two years Washington remained in a holding pattern, not moving his base of operations until the YORKTOWN CAMPAIGN of 1781. The most traumatic event of those years was the treason of his ablest combat general, Benedict Arnold, whose plot to turn over the strategic bastion of West Point to Clinton in return for money and a British generalship fell through,

The American Revolution, 1779–1783

N.H.

NEW YORK

Indian Campaign, Aug–Sep 1779

Newburgh

MASS.

Boston

Stony Point, 31 May 1779

CONN.

New York

Newport 10 July 10 1780

R.I.

Paulus Hook, 19 Aug. 1779

PENNSYLVANIA   Philadelphia

Indian Campaign, 11 Aug. –14 Sept. 1779

N.J.

MD.

British troops leave America from New York 25 Nov. 1783

VIRGINIA

DEL.

Richmond burned, 5 Jan. 1781

Jamestown Ford, 6 July 1781

Battle of the Capes 5–9 Sept. 1781

Atlantic Ocean

Siege of Yorktown, 28 Sept.–19 Oct. 1781

Guilford Courthouse 15 March 1781

British troops withdraw to New York

Cowpens, 17 Jan. 1781

NORTH CAROLINA

Kings Mountain, 7 Oct. 1780

Siege of Fort Ninety-Six, 22 May–19 June 1781

Hobkirk's Hill, 25 April 1781

Camden, 16 Aug. 1780

Wilmington

Wilmington evacuated, January 1782

Augusta, 29 Jan. 1779

Eutaw Springs, 8 Sept. 1781

Kettle Creek 14 Feb. 1779

Briar Creek, 3 March 1779

Siege of Charleston, 11 Feb.–12 May 1780

Charleston

Charleston evacuated 14 Dec. 1782

Port Royal, 3 Feb. 1779

GEORGIA

Siege of Savannah 3 Sept.–2 Oct. 1779

Savannah evacuated 11 July 1782

FLORIDA (British)

★ British Victory

☆ American / Allied Victory

with Arnold himself escaping but his contact man, Major John Andre, being captured and executed as a spy.

The War in the South

In the winter of 1778–1779 the war began taking on a southern complexion. Unsuccessful in the north and fearful of French attacks in Europe and the West Indies, Britain tried its luck in the South. For several years southern loyalists had argued that the king's friends were most numerous in their region and that the South's agricultural resources were the most valuable part of the king's North American empire. With manpower resources stretched tissue thin, the idea of relying heavily on loyalists was beguiling. Yet there were reasons to question it, especially because of events there in 1776. A British naval assault on Charles Town, South Carolina, had been turned away and uprisings of loyalists in North Carolina and Cherokee in the backcountry had been crushed. The new southern policy was adopted only in piecemeal fashion, perhaps because Clinton was less enthusiastic about it than Germain. A small British expeditionary force overran Georgia at roughly the end of 1778, but in 1779 a lack of sufficient royal troops delayed a serious attempt to overwhelm South Carolina. Finally, Clinton himself brought several thousand additional men from New York and laid siege to Charles Town, which fell to Sir Henry on 12 May 1780, a devastating loss for the Americans since over five thousand continentals and militiamen were taken. A newly raised American southern army met a similar fate in upper South Carolina when it suffered a stinging defeat at Camden on 16 August and its remnant was scattered and demoralized. Clinton, by now back in New York City, had instructed Lord Cornwallis, commanding the southern operation, not to invade North Carolina and Virginia until he had secured the backcountry and had organized the loyalists into an effective constabulary for controlling the vast stretches behind the lines. But Cornwallis exaggerated the strength and effectiveness of the tories and underestimated the resistance movement led by partisan or guerrilla leaders such as Francis Marion, Thomas Sumter, and Andrew Pickens. On 7 October 1780, near the North Carolina border, Cornwallis's one-thousand-man loyalist left wing was destroyed by far-western frontiersmen at King's Mountain.

By December 1780 the southern conflict had become a duel between Cornwallis and Nathanael Greene, who regrouped and augmented the American southern forces. Dividing his small army, Greene sent General Daniel Morgan into the South Carolina backcountry, where he defeated Banastre Tarleton's Tory Legion on 17 January 1781. Greene then reunited his forces and escaped northward from Cornwallis into Virginia. Returning to North Carolina, he fought Cornwallis at Guilford Courthouse (later Greensboro) on 15 March, inflicting heavy casualties on the British, although neither side could claim a victory. Greene had played a cat-and-mouse game with his opponent. After wearing Cornwallis down, the British general limped to the North Carolina coast and then on

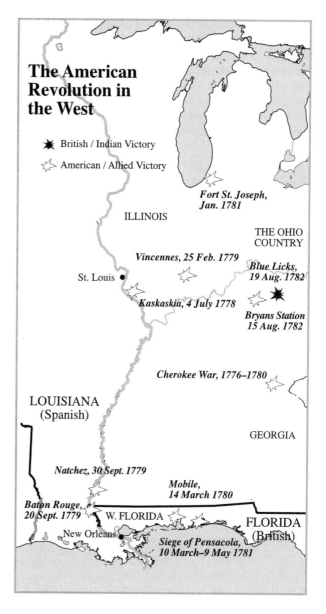

The American Revolution in the West

✷ British / Indian Victory

✩ American / Allied Victory

Fort St. Joseph, Jan. 1781

ILLINOIS

THE OHIO COUNTRY

Vincennes, 25 Feb. 1779

Blue Licks, 19 Aug. 1782

St. Louis

Kaskaskia, 4 July 1778

Bryans Station 15 Aug. 1782

Cherokee War, 1776–1780

LOUISIANA (Spanish)

GEORGIA

Natchez, 30 Sept. 1779

Mobile, 14 March 1780

Baton Rouge, 20 Sept. 1779

W. FLORIDA

FLORIDA (British)

New Orleans

Siege of Pensacola, 10 March–9 May 1781

to the Virginia Chesapeake. Greene continued his strategy of movement, isolating and picking off one by one British posts in South Carolina. His brilliant campaigning had left the enemy in control of only Charles Town and Savannah.

Washington too displayed boldness in 1781, racing south in an effort to trap Cornwallis on the Yorktown Peninsula in cooperation with French naval forces under Admiral the Comte de Grasse, and a French military force under General the Comte de Rochambeau. Cornwallis was doomed. His eight thousand men faced a Franco-American army of seventeen thousand, and Admiral de Grasse beat back British naval efforts to rescue the beleaguered Cornwallis. The month-long siege ended 17 October when Cornwallis surrendered. (Contrary to legend, British musicians did not play a tune called "The World Turned Upside Down" while redcoats stacked their arms.)

The outcome of the war was determined in the south, since Yorktown destroyed Britain's will to pursue the conflict in America, although fighting continued elsewhere between England and France and the latter's Bourbon ally Spain in 1782. British mistakes were their loyalist policy and Cornwallis's errors in abandoning South Carolina too quickly and moving to Virginia, where he became vulnerable to Franco-American land and sea cooperation. The year 1781 saw both Greene and Washington at their best and, for the first time, active French participation in America.

The War and American Society

The conflict impacted the lives of Americans in countless ways. In the short term, it did little for African Americans, although some hundreds of blacks fought in Washington's army, and thousands of bondsmen fled to the British, where some received their freedom but many were mistreated, a large percentage of them enslaved by royal authorities and tories. Women often assumed the responsibilities of men in shops and on farms as their sons and husbands took up arms. A comparative few even served in Washington's army and countless others moved with the army, fulfilling various needs such as washing and cooking. An organization of females founded by Esther Reed of Philadelphia raised money with the idea of providing soldiers some of the amenities of life. Some Americans acquired land for the first time by purchasing confiscated tory property, although most of that real estate went to the highest bidder to acquire money for war needs. Native Americans were losers without qualification. Without Britain as a buffer, the tide of American settlement rolled inexorably westward during and after the war, particularly into what became Tennessee, Kentucky, and Ohio. Inflation, paper money, and lack of specie hurt all sectors, including the officers and men of the Continental army. Late in the war there were small mutinies by the rank and file and grumbling by officers, especially at the field-grade level, seemed ominous. The desertion rate, about 20 percent of enlisted men, seems high but not by European standards. In March 1783 Washington doused the fires of officer discontent in a dramatic appearance before the officers at Newburgh, New York, promising to see that Congress addressed their legitimate grievances. In the final analysis, the army showed its loyalty to Washington and to civilian control, one of the great legacies of the Revolution. The officers and men returned peacefully to the civilian society from which they had come.

The most important consequences of the war itself, in addition to the precedent of civil control, were two in number. First, the treaty of peace in 1783 not only recognized America's independence but acknowledged its claims to the Mississippi River as the country's western boundary. Diplomats John Jay, John Adams, and Benjamin Franklin were tough at the bargaining table, but they profited by the rivalry between England and France, both of which sought American goodwill in the postwar world.

The last consequence saw the final phase of the process of state formation in America. The foremost political and military leaders, almost without exception, had become nationalists. They felt that the war showed that the Revolution could not reach its logical culmination without a central government with the authority to unite America and to protect it from domestic violence and foreign dangers. The result was the Constitution of 1787, which was both a political and a military document. The military provisions proved to be so comprehensive that amendments in that area have never been added to the original document.

BIBLIOGRAPHY

Carp, E. Wayne. *To Starve the Army at Pleasure: Continental Army Administration and American Political Culture, 1775–1783.* Chapel Hill: University of North Carolina Press, 1984.

Higginbotham, Don. *The War of American Independence: Military Attitudes, Policy, and Practice, 1763–1789.* New York: Macmillan, 1971.

———. *George Washington and the American Military Tradition.* Athens: University of Georgia Press, 1985.

Mackesy, Piers. *The War for America, 1775–1783.* Cambridge, Mass.: Harvard University Press, 1964.

Mayer, Holly A. *Belonging to the Army: Camp Followers and Community During the American Revolution.* Columbia: University of South Carolina Press, 1996.

Royster, Charles. *A Revolutionary People at War: The Continental Army and American Character, 1775–1783.* Chapel Hill: University of North Carolina Press, 1979.

Shy, John. *A People Numerous and Armed: Reflections on the Military Struggle for American Independence.* Rev. ed. Ann Arbor: University of Michigan Press, 1990.

Willcox, William B. *Portrait of a General: Sir Henry Clinton in the War of Independence.* New York: Knopf, 1964.

Don Higginbotham

See also **Brandywine Creek, Battle of; Camden, Battle of; Colonial Wars; French in the American Revolution; Guilford Courthouse, Battle of; Indians in the Revolution; Long Island, Battle of; New York City, Capture of; Newburgh Addresses; Paris, Treaty of (1783); Princeton, Battle of; Provincial Congresses; Saratoga Campaign; Savannah, Siege of (1779); Ticonderoga, Capture of; Trenton, Battle of; White Plains, Battle of;** *and* vol. 9: **Battle of Lexington, American and British Accounts; Correspondence Leading to British Surrender; Letters of Eliza Wilkinson; Life at Valley Forge, 1777–1778; A Soldier's Love Letter.**

DIPLOMATIC ASPECTS

During the decade before the American Revolution, European diplomacy was focused on the convulsions in eastern Europe that culminated in the first partition of Poland. Charles Gravier, comte de Vergennes, the French foreign minister in 1775, realized that the partition posed a danger to France. Unknown to the young King Louis XVI, Vergennes had been a charter member of a secret diplomatic organization devoted to restoring French influence in Poland and to blocking Russian expansion. Since he regarded Great Britain as Russia's chief backer, he believed that depriving Britain of her monopoly of American trade would weaken her and, hence, Russia.

In late 1775, a French agent, Julien-Alexandre Archard de Bonvouloir, met in Philadelphia with a committee of the Continental Congress. He assured them that France had no intention of retaking Canada and encouraged them to send ships to France; they in turn asked to purchase military supplies. Vergennes received the king's permission to sell supplies to Congress, and France subsequently loaned money to a trading company that planned to exchange military supplies for American tobacco. Simultaneously, France began to rebuild and resupply her navy, which would take until the end of 1777.

As Congress moved toward a declaration of independence, it became more ready to accept French assistance. It sent the congressional delegate Silas Deane to France to purchase supplies and then appointed Deane, Benjamin Franklin, and Arthur Lee as commissioners to negotiate a commercial treaty. At the beginning of 1777, the commissioners assembled in Paris. Initially, the French government was willing to loan them money but not to risk a premature war by signing a treaty. Naval rearmament permitted France to become directly involved in the war, but first Vergennes had to convince King Louis XVI. Luckily, news of the American victory at Saratoga arrived in early December. Vergennes argued that there was now a danger that the Americans would compromise with Britain and abandon independence. The commissioners played along by meeting with British agents. The king gave way and, in exchange for a treaty of amity and commerce, the commissioners would agree to a treaty of alliance, prohibiting the United States from abandoning independence or making a separate peace. Both treaties were signed on 6 February 1778.

By summer, France and Britain were at war. France hoped to win a quick victory by sending a fleet to attack British-held New York, but the attack failed. Knowing her navy would soon be badly outnumbered by the British, France sought the assistance of Spain, the only other great naval power. Spain distrusted the United States, but in mid-1779, the French promised to help retake Gibraltar from Britain and convinced her to join the war. A coalition was formed, and in 1781 a Dutch fleet in the North Sea and a Spanish-French fleet off the southern coast of England helped prevent Britain from sending the ships to rescue general Cornwallis at Yorktown.

The French government sent large sums to Congress to prevent its bankruptcy, which was handled by Benjamin Franklin, the sole American representative in Paris for most of the period from 1779 to mid-1782. American representatives John Jay in Spain and John Adams in the Netherlands procured smaller sums.

Cornwallis's capture led to the beginning of peace negotiations, which were largely the work of Franklin and the Earl of Shelburne, the British home secretary from March to July, 1782, and, thereafter, prime minister. Franklin refused to make a separate peace in exchange for British recognition of American independence, demanding in addition the Mississippi as a border and a share in the Newfoundland fishery. At the end of July, Shelburne accepted Franklin's conditions, hoping to use a separate peace to pressure France to make peace also. (If America made a separate peace, the British could send their large garrison at New York to attack the French West Indies.) Franklin, Jay, and Henry Laurens reached agreement with the British on 30 November 1782. Vergennes well realized that France now had to make peace or fight without American aid. Shelburne had offered him a carrot as well as a stick—future British help against Russia—but France could not make peace unless Spain also agreed. Luckily, Spain finally was convinced to accept the return of Florida and Minorca in lieu of Gibraltar. A general peace agreement was reached on 20 January 1783.

BIBLIOGRAPHY

Dull, Jonathan R. *A Diplomatic History of the American Revolution.* New Haven, Conn.: Yale University Press, 1985.

Hoffman, Ronald and Peter J. Albert, eds. *Diplomacy and Revolution: The Franco-American Alliance of 1778.* Charlottesville, Va.: University Press of Virginia, 1981.

———. *Peace and the Peacemakers: The Treaty of 1783.* Charlottesville, Va.: University Press of Virginia, 1986.

Hutson, James H. *John Adams and the Diplomacy of the American Revolution.* Lexington, Ky.: University Press of Kentucky, 1980.

Scott, H. M. *British Foreign Policy in the Age of the American Revolution.* New York: Oxford University Press, 1990.

Stinchcombe, William C. *The American Revolution and the French Alliance.* Syracuse, N.Y.: Syracuse University Press, 1969.

Jonathan R. Dull

FINANCIAL ASPECTS

Because of colonial hatred of any form of taxation, one of the most difficult tasks that faced the Continental Congress was raising money to finance the revolutionary war. Following hostilities at Bunker Hill in June 1775, an issue of $2 million in bills of credit was voted, based on the credit of the states. Depreciation set in shortly, and by March 1780, in spite of legal-tender laws and an attempt to fix prices, the value of continental currency in silver had fallen to forty to one. Debtors pursued their creditors and prices rose to unheard-of heights. "Not worth a continental" became a phrase of derision and stark reality.

A system of direct requisitions on the states for corn, beef, pork, and other supplies was resorted to in 1780 but proved equally discouraging, for it lacked an efficient plan of assessment and record. Other means used to obtain funds included domestic and foreign loans; quartermaster, commissary, and purchasing agent certificates; lotteries; and prize money received from the sale of captured enemy vessels. Foreign loans secured from France, Spain, and

Holland through the influence of Benjamin Franklin and John Adams proved invaluable. These, and an outright gift from France, did much to strengthen colonial morale and finance.

At war's close, Finance Superintendent Robert Morris was hampered by local jealousies, continued state refusal to levy taxes, and inadequate financial provisions of the Articles of Confederation. It remained for the new Constitution and the financial genius of Alexander Hamilton to place the United States on a firm national and international credit basis.

BIBLIOGRAPHY

Carp, E. Wayne. *To Starve the Army at Pleasure: Continental Army Administration and American Political Culture, 1775–1783.* Chapel Hill: University of North Carolina Press, 1984.

Ferguson, James E. *The Power of the Purse: A History of American Public Finance, 1776–1790.* Chapel Hill: University of North Carolina Press, 1961.

McDonald, Forrest. *We the People: The Economic Origins of the Constitution.* New Brunswick, N.J.: Transaction, 1992.

Elizabeth Warren / A. G.

See also **Debt, Public; Debts, Colonial and Continental; Debts, State; Repudiation of Public Debt; Repudiation of State Debts.**

PROFITEERING

The American Revolution left the colonies without hard currency and cut off from European trade. The Continental Congress repeatedly issued unbacked paper currency, creating rapid inflation. The increased risks and costs of importing goods, along with scarce supplies and overwhelming demand, added to inflationary pressures. Profiteers bought available commodities, held them until prices rose, and then sold for high profits. The Continental army suffered throughout the war from profiteers, but government efforts to halt them failed. Even the 1787 Constitutional Convention's resolution to protect public securities benefited profiteers, who bought up great amounts of the paper money that was almost worthless during the Revolution and gained fortunes by redeeming it at face value.

BIBLIOGRAPHY

Miller, John C. *Triumph of Freedom, 1775–1783.* Boston: Little, Brown, 1948.

Warner Stark / C. W.

See also **Constitution of the United States; Currency and Coinage; Profiteering.**

REVOLUTION, RIGHT OF.

Revolution is the overthrow of an established government, but to assert a right of revolution is to imply that such an upheaval is legitimate. It should therefore be distinguished from insurrection, coup d'état, and especially rebellion, for rebellion is opposition to all authority rather than resistance to unlawful power.

There are two major streams of thought that ultimately formed the right of revolution at the time of the American Revolution. The first came from the Protestant Reformation. John Calvin, while warning against popular insurrection, argued that magistrates had a positive duty to defend the people's freedoms against monarchs who disobeyed God's commands. John Knox expanded this doctrine, urging popular revolution in Scotland in 1560. The revolutionary faith of Scottish Presbyterianism strongly influenced English Puritans in their struggle against divine right monarchy, ultimately leading to the English Civil War and the execution of Charles I in 1649. The monarchy was restored in 1660, however, in reaction to the religious radicalism of the Commonwealth.

The second major stream of thought was developed in the 1680s against the increasing absolutism of the later Stuarts. Parliament established a constitutional monarchy in the Glorious Revolution of 1688, relying on John Locke's secular social contract theory. Individuals in a state of nature delegated power to government for the protection of their lives, liberties, and estates, but when lawmakers acted contrary to these ends, they used force without right and thus made themselves "rebels" in "a state of War with the People, who [were] thereupon absolved from any farther Obedience," as Locke argued in his *Second Treatise on Government* (1690). Power then reverted to the people, who had the sovereign right to dissolve the government and form it anew. Locke's was an ideology of successful revolution, but in the early eighteenth century a "country" opposition emerged against England's monarchy. John Trenchard and Thomas Gordon warned of government's inherent tendency to subvert popular liberty and corrupt the "mixed" constitution, but while this radical Whig ideology was marginal in England, it became the lens through which many Americans viewed British actions.

These streams were continually reinforced in addresses such as Jonathan Mayhew's *Discourse Concerning Unlimited Submission* (1750), given on the anniversary of Charles I's beheading. British efforts to tighten control of its empire after 1763 were interpreted by American revolutionaries as leading to arbitrary rule. Thomas Jefferson justified independence on Lockean grounds, arguing in the DECLARATION OF INDEPENDENCE that "when a long train of abuses and usurpations . . . evinces a design to reduce them under absolute Despotism," it is the right and duty of the people "to throw off such Government." In this respect, the goal of the American Revolution, wrote Bernard Bailyn in *The Ideological Origins of the American Revolution* (1967), was not "the overthrow or even the alteration of the existing social order but the preservation of political liberty threatened by the apparent corruption of the constitution."

These revolutionary ideas were exported to France, Haiti, and Latin America, in works such as Thomas Paine's

The Rights of Man (1791), although others like Edmund Burke, in his *Reflections on the Revolution in France* (1790), attempted to distance American doctrines from French radicalism. Jefferson himself recommended frequent recourse to revolution, although many Americans opposed it, especially when Southerners used the right of revolution to defend secession in the 1860s. Since the Civil War, the right of revolution has been interpreted by most Americans as having only limited application.

BIBLIOGRAPHY

Bailyn, Bernard. *The Ideological Origins of the American Revolution.* Cambridge, Mass.: Harvard University Press, 1967.

Wood, Gordon. *The Radicalism of the American Revolution.* New York: Knopf, 1992.

Fred W. Beuttler

See also **Locke's Political Philosophy; Political Theory.**

REVOLUTIONARY COMMITTEES.

REVOLUTIONARY COMMITTEES. From the beginnings of colonial protest in the aftermath of the Stamp Act, the American Revolution based its fundamental organization on committees. The most basic of these were the Committees of Correspondence, which originated in the need for colonies to keep each other informed of the progress in the boycott and protest of the Stamp Act. Later committees of correspondence formed an intelligence network among the leaders of the rebellion, keeping even the most remote communities abreast of what was happening in the capital or on the battlefields. The committees had a long historical pedigree, having been patterned on committees of security from the English civil war, the Revolution of 1688 in America, and the tax crises of the 1760s.

More crucial to the operation of the rebellion were the Committees of Safety, which generally were an extension of the assemblies elected by the colonies. Sometimes known as committees of recess, operating while assemblies were dismissed, the committees quickly began to act as an executive, handling some of the most crucial decisions of the colonies' resistance to Britain. The committees, the first organized by the Massachusetts legislature in November 1775, generally had the authority to draw money, to equip and raise militia, to grant militia commissions above the rank of captain, to set quotas of enlistment, to issue travel passes, and to solicit or demand supplies. In the southern colonies the committees also had the authority to deal with captured or escaped slaves. Sometimes the committees were responsible for identifying and trying Loyalists. In Vermont, which was not a colony, the committee of safety assumed the role of a de facto government that later became the nucleus of an independent state.

Other committees were formed ad hoc as needed to take care of problems, such as supply of the army and militias, overseeing the creation of a navy, and handling the dispatch of foreign documents and emissaries to Europe. Some informal groups, like Boston's Sons of Liberty, had the status if not the official standing of committees and served the political function of introducing the population of the colonies to revolution and its doctrines. The committees were frequently in contact with one another across colonial borders, and while not permanent bodies, they attracted some of the best leaders in the revolution, including Robert Morris, John Hancock, and Charles Carroll.

By 1781 the committees had solidified into executive departments staffed with professional bureaucrats under a department head. When the American colonies gained their independence, these committees were often adopted as cabinet offices, including the Department of State (the committee of foreign affairs), the Commerce Department (the secret committee), and the Board of War, which became the Department of War. These local organizations, which allowed management of the Revolution by more efficient groups than the legislatures as a whole, gradually transformed into the modern system of government departments under the authority of a single executive.

BIBLIOGRAPHY

Brown, Richard D. *Revolutionary Politics in Massachusetts.* Cambridge, Mass.: Harvard University Press, 1970.

Hunt, Agnes. *The Provincial Committees of Safety of the American Revolution.* New York: Haskell House, 1968. Originally published in 1904.

Margaret D. Sankey

See also **Cabinet.**

REYKJAVIK SUMMIT.

REYKJAVIK SUMMIT. The second summit meeting between President Ronald Reagan and Soviet Communist Party General Secretary Mikhail Gorbachev, held October 11–12, 1986, to discuss nuclear arms control. The meeting produced international controversy when news reports, later confirmed by U.S. officials, revealed that Reagan unexpectedly proposed the elimination of all nuclear weapons—to the dismay of NATO countries that depended on the American nuclear umbrella for security against overwhelming Soviet superiority in conventional forces.

The two sides made progress by agreeing to reduce intermediate-range nuclear missiles in Europe, but movement toward a major arms control agreement broke down in a dispute over the U.S. space-based antimissile program, the Strategic Defense Initiative (SDI). Gorbachev argued that SDI could render Soviet nuclear forces useless, eliminating the concept of mutual deterrence and leaving his country vulnerable to attack. Reagan offered to defer deployment of SDI for ten years, but was determined to continue research and development. The deadlock prevented a major arms control agreement. The two leaders did declare their agreement in principle to cut their offensive nuclear arsenals in half. At a third summit meeting in Washington in December 1987, the two leaders signed the Intermediate-Range Nuclear Forces (INF) Treaty, requiring the elimination of all U.S. and Soviet INF missiles.

BIBLIOGRAPHY

Beschloss, Michael R., and Strobe Talbott. *At the Highest Levels: The Inside Story of the Cold War.* Boston: Little, Brown, 1993.

Garthoff, Raymond L. *The Great Transition: American-Soviet Relations and the End of the Cold War.* Washington, D.C.: Brookings Institution, 1994.

Max Paul Friedman

See also **Cold War; Russia, Relations with; Summit Conferences, U.S. and Russian.**

REYNOLDS V. UNITED STATES, 98 U.S. 145 (1878),

was one of the Supreme Court's first decisions addressing the free exercise clause of the First Amendment of the U.S. Constitution, which prohibits Congress from making laws that infringe on the free exercise of religion. George Reynolds, a member of the Mormon religion, challenged a federal law that prohibited polygamy in the territories. He argued that his religion required him to have multiple wives and that to prohibit him from doing so was an infringement on his free exercise of religion. Chief Justice Morrison Waite, writing for the Supreme Court, held that to accept that argument would be to make religious beliefs superior to the laws of the United States and would allow any citizen to avoid compliance with the law. This case is credited with drawing a distinction between belief and action in holding that the free exercise clause protects the right of individuals to believe what they want but does not protect religious actions that conflict with the laws of the United States.

BIBLIOGRAPHY

Cannon, George Q. *A Review of the Decision of the Supreme Court of the United States, in the Case of Geo. Reynolds vs. the United States.* Salt Lake City, Utah: Deseret News Printing and Publishing Establishment, 1879.

Gordon, Sarah Barringer. *The Mormon Question: Polygamy and Constitutional Conflict in Nineteenth-Century America.* Chapel Hill: University of North Carolina Press, 2002.

Shira M. Diner

See also **First Amendment; Polygamy.**

RHODE ISLAND, located in the northeast part of the

United States, is the smallest state by size. The full name is the State of Rhode Island and Providence Plantations.

Geography

Although it is only 1,045 square miles, Rhode Island's geography is complex because of its large islands and a

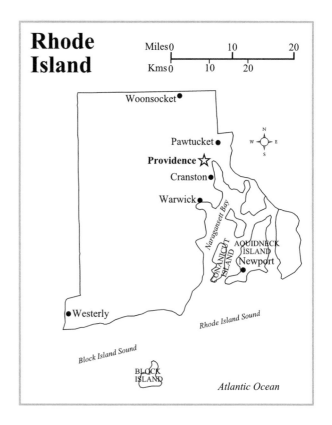

mainland carved by an ice-age glacier. While the state is not an island, it includes an island named Rhode Island that is also known as Aquidneck Island. It is the biggest island in Narragansett Bay, one of the world's greatest natural bays. The island stretches from north to south in the eastern bay; on its northeast coast is Portsmouth (also known as Pocasset) and on its southwest coast is Newport. To the west of Aquidneck Island are Prudence Island and Conanicut Island, roughly aligned northeast (Prudence) to southwest (Conanicut).

These islands and most of the mainland of Rhode Island are part of the Coastal Lowlands, a broad geological structure that extends along much of America's northeastern coast. The lowlands have many excellent areas for farming and during America's early history, Rhode Island's lowlands helped feed the nation. Northern Rhode Island is in the New England Uplands that extend south into Pennsylvania and north into Maine. When the state's most recent glacier pushed into Rhode Island, it carved into both the Coastal Lowlands and the New England Uplands; when it retreated roughly ten thousand years ago, it left behind not only Narragansett Bay but lakes and ponds, and valleys and hills. Newly formed rivers and streams ran through the valleys. The northeastern Blackstone River fed into Narragansett Bay near where the city of Providence was established. The rivers and streams, including the southwestern Pawtucket River, provided power for mills during the first several decades of Rhode

Island's industrialization; the lakes and ponds served to store water, especially when dammed.

Early Settlers

The first European settler in what is now Rhode Island was an Anglican minister, William Blackstone, who settled near what is now called Blackstone River, close to modern Lonsdale, in 1635. In June 1636, the father of Rhode Island, Roger Williams, brought some of his followers from Massachusetts to escape religious oppression. The people of Massachusetts were Congregationalists—Puritans who had fled England due to persecution by the Church of England. The freedom they sought was not freedom for all; it was freedom to practice their religion, consequently forcing non-Congregationalists to practice it too. They imprisoned, tortured, and even executed people who did not follow their church laws. Roger Williams wanted to establish a colony where people could worship freely. He believed that that one should not infringe on another's right to worship, and should have the ability to practice any religion of choice.

When he settled in Rhode Island, Williams named his settlement Providence. He took the time to learn the languages of the Native Americans, publishing the guide, *A Key into the Language of America* in 1643. Narragansetts populated most of the area, with a large tribe, the Wamponoags, to the south, and the Pequots in what is now Connecticut. There were also the small groups of Nipmucks, Niantics, Cowesetts, and Shawomets inhabiting the area. The tribes were part of the large cultural and language group, the Algonquins, who spread over much of eastern North American, from the future North Carolina into the future Canada. Williams and his followers negotiated treaties and bought land from the Native Americans; on 24 March 1638, they acquired a deed for their Providence "plantation" from the preeminent sachems (meaning chiefs) of the Narragansetts, Canonicus, and young Miantonomi. Williams always dealt with the Native Americans honestly, which the local tribes valued highly.

Williams's idea of a land of free religious practices attracted others. In 1638, Antinomians established Portsmouth on Aquidneck, which had been purchased that year. Nonconformist William Coddington established Newport on Aquidneck Island in 1639. The first American Baptist church was founded in Providence in 1839. In 1642, Samuel Gorton established Warwick. Small settlements of religious dissidents were established in the general area of Providence, becoming "plantations." They featured independent men and women, who insisted on practicing their faiths as they saw fit—much as Williams hoped they would. Prompted by continued Puritan harassment and claims to territory in Rhode Island, Williams went to England in 1643 to get a patent for the new townships and plantations. In 1644, the English Parliament granted Newport, Portsmouth, and Providence incorporation as "Providence Plantations in the Narragansett Bay in New England," often called "Warwick's Charter" after the Earl of Warwick. Plymouth and Massachusetts refused to recognize the validity of the charter.

From 19 to 21 May 1647, the First General Assembly met in Portsmouth, which established an anchor as a symbol of the colony's freedom and passed a modest number of laws. During the 1650s, Rhode Island attracted a wide variety of religious groups. Notable were the Jews who, in 1658, began establishing congregations (although the first synagogue in the state would not be built until 1763) and the Quakers, who were being executed and tortured in Massachusetts and Plymouth. In 1657, Plymouth demanded Rhode Island surrender its Quakers, and on 13 October 1657, Rhode Island refused, helping establish its reputation as a safe refuge from oppression.

By the 1670s, Williams's carefully wrought relationships with Native Americans began to fall apart. The Wampanoags, angered by the colonists who had cheated them out of much of their land, began to attack settlements. On 19 December 1675, a Narragansett traitor led Massachusetts soldiers into a Narragansett camp, and the soldiers slaughtered the almost 700 inhabitants, 400 of which were women and children burned to death in their wigwams. There followed King Philip's War named for a Wampanoag chief whose Native American name was Metacom. The alliance of Wampanoags and Narragansetts won a few battles and burned Providence (although taking special care not to harm Williams) and some villages. On 12 August 1676, a Wampanoag traitor murdered Metacom. War casualties diminished the populations of the tribes so much that they were never again threats to the settlers.

Independence

From 1686–1689, Rhode Island and other New England colonies were forced into the Dominion of New England by King James II. His governor for the Dominion, Edmund Andros, took control of Rhode Island on 22 December 1686, but on 18 April 1689 he was imprisoned in Boston, and the effort to gather the northern colonies into one unit failed. This may have marked the beginning of Rhode Island seeing its neighbors as allies against English oppression, rather than oppressors themselves.

On 1 March 1689, England and France went to war. The conflict was a world war, but in America, it was referred to as the French and Indian War. It had four separate outbreaks of hostilities that lasted from 1689–1763, when France finally lost its Canadian colonies. During this period, Newport became Rhode Island's major city, enriched by its shipping industry. It was the era of the notorious trade in rum, sugar, and slaves. Rhode Island's General Assembly had tried to outlaw slavery in 1674, but the law was ignored. Williams's vision of a prejudice-free society seemed lost during this era. For example, in February 1728, Jews, Muslims, pagans, and Roman Catholics were specifically given freedom of conscience but were denied the right to vote. In 1730, a census indicated

17,935 people lived in Rhode Island, but the count may have been low because some rural areas were not included. In 1764, the General Assembly authorized the establishment in Warren of "Rhode Island College," which was renamed Brown University in 1804.

Also in 1764, the English Parliament passed the Sugar Act, which required the American colonies to buy their sugar only from other British colonies. This hurt Rhode Island's economy since Britain's colonies did not produce nearly enough sugar to support the molasses and rum industries in Rhode Island. In response, the General Assembly passed a law in September 1765 declaring that only it could tax people in Rhode Island. Rhode Islanders burned the British ship, Liberty, in Newport's harbor on 19 July 1769. On 10 June 1772, the British ship Gaspee, which had been searching all ships was lured into running aground, seized, and burned. On 4 May 1776, aroused by the attacks of British soldiers on colonial militias and civilians, Rhode Island renounced its allegiance to England. The General Assembly approved the Declaration of Independence on 18 July 1776 and on 8 December 1776, the British army occupied Newport. Their looting and other depredations so ruined Newport that it lost its status as Rhode Island's most prosperous city, and thousands of citizens fled. The British looted and burned villages and towns, including, on 25 May 1778, Bristol and Warren. On 9 February 1778, the General Assembly declared that any slaves, black or Native American, who joined the first Rhode Island Regiment would be free; many slaves joined and the state government compensated their former owners. They became famous during the war as the "Black Regiment."

On 29 August 1778, the Continental Army and its new allies, the French, fought the British army in the Battle of Rhode Island. The battle was inconclusive, although the Black Regiment inflicted heavy casualties on the enemy's Hessians. On 25 October 1779, the British left Newport and moved to the southern colonies where the British army was suffering almost unendurable casualties in battles with the Army of the South, led by General Nathanael Greene, a Rhode Islander who had run an iron foundry in Warwick. Meanwhile, in 1778, Rhode Island ratified the Articles of Confederation.

When the Revolutionary War ended, Rhode Islanders wished to keep their independence from outside authority. Their history had included much suffering caused by those who had tried to rule them, and they were distrustful of any central national government. Thus, they resisted the imposition of a new American constitution and did not send delegates to the Constitutional Convention in Philadelphia in 1787. In 1784, Rhode Island enacted the Emancipation Act, which declared every child born to a slave to be free at age twenty-one. It was an imperfect abolition of slavery, with the last Rhode Island slave death in 1859. However, Rhode Islanders were angry that the Constitution of the United States of America allowed slavery. Long after other states had ratified the new federal constitution, Rhode Island, which had not acknowledged the validity of the Constitution Convention, refused to accept it. Several times it had been put to a vote in Rhode Island, and each time it had been voted down. Eventually, the federal government threatened to treat Rhode Island as an independent nation and to charge tariffs on its goods. In 1790, the General Assembly met twice to vote on the Constitution; the first time there were not enough votes, but on 29 May 1790, it ratified the Constitution by a vote of 34 to 32. By then, a federal election had already been held, and George Washington had been president since 1789.

Industry

In the 1790s, Rhode Island's economy began to move away from shipping to industrialization. Samuel Slater was a young engineer who had worked in an English cotton mill and had memorized every machine in it. It was illegal for engineers to leave England, but Slater managed to sneak out and come to America. In Moses Brown, a merchant from Providence, he found someone who was enthusiastic about building a cotton mill, and in 1790, they built Rhode Island's first. By 1804, manufacturing cloth was a major industry, and during the 1820s, the capital invested in the manufacturing of textiles surpassed that invested in shipping. By 1860, 80 percent of Rhode Island's capital was invested in manufacturing of jewelry and weapons and a host of other goods.

The growth of manufacturing in the state created significant social problems, exacerbated by an 1822 law that took the vote away from African Americans. Immigrants from all over Europe came to Rhode Island to work in factories, but even if they became naturalized American citizens they were denied the right to vote. By 1840, 60 percent of Rhode Island's adult males were disfranchised. This fostered the Dorr War of 1840–1842. A lawyer, Thomas Wilson Dorr argued that when a government fails to serve its people, the people have the right to overthrow it. He cited the Revolutionary War as an example. In 1841, his followers arranged for a plebiscite, without the permission of Rhode Island's government, to elect representatives to a People's Convention. They drafted the People's Constitution, which won a popular vote in December 1841. Thereafter, a government was elected with Dorr as governor. This created two governments in Rhode Island: the People's government and the Law and Order government led by Governor Samuel Ward King. On 17 May 1842, Dorr and a following of Irish immigrants tried to seize the state arsenal in Providence. They failed, partly because African Americans in the city came to the aid of the militia in defending the arsenal. Dorr's actions frightened many Rhode Islanders, and they supported Governor King. In 1842, the General Assembly offered voters a state constitution to replace a body of laws from 1663, which they passed. It liberalized voting rules and returned the vote to African American males. It also included a $134 "freehold suffrage qualification" for naturalized citizens as a way of punishing poor Irish immigrants for supporting Dorr.

During the 1850s, the Republican Party was formed. In Rhode Island, it attracted Whigs, disaffected Democrats, and some of the Know-Nothings—an anti-immigrant group. They were united in their abhorrence of slavery and in their belief that the Union must be preserved in order to maintain liberty throughout America. In 1860, voters rejected the antislavery Republican candidate for governor, Seth Padelford, electing instead the Conservative Party candidate, William Sprague, who was conciliatory toward slavery. On the other hand, he was a staunch Unionist. When the Civil War broke out, Rhode Island quickly began supplying the Union with goods it needed for the war effort. The state provided 25,236 servicemen, 1,685 of whom perished. During the war, the United States Naval Academy was moved from Annapolis, Maryland, to Newport, Rhode Island. In 1866, Rhode Island outlawed the segregation of races, but segregation would occur well into in the twenty-first century. For the rest of the nineteenth century, industry continued to grow, and immigration grew with it. In 1886, the legislature passed a state constitutional amendment giving the vote to adult women, but the amendment had to be approved by a plebiscite, and it lost 21,957 to 6,889. It was not until 1917 that Rhode Island passed a women's suffrage law. In an effort to end intimidation of workers by factory owners when voting, Rhode Island established the secret ballot in 1889. In the 1890s, French-Canadians moved to Rhode Island, and by 1895, there were over forty thousand of them residing in the state.

The Modern Era

In the first two decades of the twentieth century, tens of thousands each of Italians, Portuguese, and Poles emigrated to Rhode Island, adding colorful traditions to a society that was among the most culturally diverse in America. In 1900, Providence was made the state's permanent capital. By 1905, at 50.81 percent of the population, Roman Catholics were the largest religious group in Rhode Island. In 1909, the governor was given the right to veto legislation; this was an effort to even out the powers of the legislative and executive branches of the government.

Although Republicans had long controlled the state government, in 1935, Democrats staged the Bloodless Revolution. Led by Governor Theodore Francis Green, Lieutenant Governor Robert Emmet Quinn, and Pawtucket's Democrat party boss Thomas P. McCoy, the Bloodless Revolution replaced the members of the state's supreme court and restructured the government into departments rather than commissions. Further developments, such as calling a new state constitutional convention, fell to the wayside due to factional quarreling among Democrats. Disenchanted, voters elected Republicans, who in 1939 passed a civil service act protecting state employees from being arbitrarily fired.

In 1938, Rhode Island was hit by a hurricane with winds reaching 200 mph, killing 311 people and costing $100 million in damage. During World War II, Rhode Island's shipyards saw activity reminiscent of the Revolutionary War era. On Field's Point, the Walsh-Kaiser Shipyard employed about twenty-one thousand workers and built Liberty ships, cargo ships that hauled supplies to the United Kingdom. When the war ended and demand for new ships declined, many people were out of work. A sales tax was introduced in 1947 to help the government compensate for lost revenue. During the 1950s, many people moved out of cities and to the suburbs, causing steep declines in urban populations. For example, Providence's population from 1950 to 1960 dropped from 248,674 to 179,116.

The 1950s were marked by two devastating hurricanes. On 31 August 1954, Hurricane Carol killed nineteen people and caused $90 million in damage. On 19 August 1955, Hurricane Diane broke two dams and caused $170 million in damages. In 1966, a hurricane barrier was built on the Providence River.

Rhode Island held a state constitutional convention in 1964 to modernize its constitution, but its new constitution was rejected in a 1968 plebiscite. A state income tax took effect in February 1971 as a "temporary" measure; it was made permanent in July 1971. By the 1980s, corruption of public officials was causing a decline in the citizens' faith in Rhode Island's government. In 1985, mismanagement caused the Rhode Island Housing and Mortgage Finance Corporation to collapse; money intended to help low-income residents buy homes apparently went into the pockets of administrators. In 1986 and 1993 two state supreme court justices resigned because of their unethical conduct and the imminent prospect of impeachment. In 1991, a superior court judge was sent to prison for taking bribes. Also in 1991, the Rhode Island Share and Deposit Indemnity Corporation collapsed, taking credit unions it was supposed to protect down with it.

In 1984, the state held a constitutional convention. By May 1986, the new constitutional provisions approved by voters included a Constitutional Ethics Commission and a requirement that the General Assembly regulate campaign spending. A proposal of four-year terms for elected officials, including legislators, failed in 1986, but a 1992 amendment lengthening just the governor's and a few other executive branch officials' terms to four years passed in a popular vote. In 1994, voters approved an amendment that gave legislators $10,000 a year for their services and eliminated pensions for legislators. Further, the assembly was reorganized to have only seventy-five members in 2003, down from one hundred, and the senate was to have only thirty-eight senators, down from fifty.

BIBLIOGRAPHY

Bridenbaugh, Carl. *Fat Mutton and Liberty of Conscience: Society in Rhode Island, 1636–1690.* Providence, R.I.: Brown University Press, 1974.

153

Conley, Patrick T. *Democracy in Decline: Rhode Island's Constitutional Development, 1776–1841*. Providence: Rhode Island Historical Society, 1977.

Fradin, Dennis B. *The Rhode Island Colony*. Chicago: Children's Press, 1989.

James, Sydney V. *Colonial Rhode Island: A History*. New York: Scribners, 1975.

McLoughlin, William G. *Rhode Island: A Bicentennial History*. New York: Norton, 1978.

McNair, Sylvia. *Rhode Island*. New York: Children's Press, 2000.

Morgan, Edmund S. *Roger Williams, the Church and the State*. New York: Harcourt, Brace and World, 1967.

Nichols, Joan Kane. *A Matter of Conscience: The Trial of Anne Hutchinson*. Austin, Tex.: Raintree Steck-Vaughn, 1993.

Polishook, Irwin H. *Rhode Island and the Union, 1774–1795*. Evanston, Ill.: Northwestern University Press, 1969.

Rhode Island's official website. Available from http://www.state.ri.us.

Kirk H. Beetz

See also **Brown University; Providence Plantations, Rhode Island and.**

RHODES SCHOLARSHIPS were established by the will of Cecil J. Rhodes, English-born South African statesman and financier, who died in 1902. They provide appointments for study in the University of Oxford to students drawn from eighteen countries. Thirty-two students from the United States are selected annually. Rhodes Scholars are also chosen from Australia, Bermuda, the British Caribbean, Jamaica, Canada, Ceylon, Germany, Ghana, India, Malaysia, Malta, Nigeria, New Zealand, Pakistan, Rhodesia, South Africa, and Zambia.

Candidates for the Rhodes Scholarships in the United States are required to be unmarried citizens between the ages of eighteen and twenty-four, and they should have achieved at least junior standing in an accredited university or college. Competitions are held annually in each of the fifty states. Appointments to the scholarship are initially for a period of two years, with the possibility of renewal for a third. The stipend is calculated to cover all tuition expenses and to provide an allowance adequate to cover a student's living requirements.

Intellectual distinction is a necessary, but not the exclusive, condition for election to a Rhodes Scholarship. In keeping with the instructions of Rhodes's will, Rhodes Scholars are also expected to demonstrate qualities of character that promise potential service to others. Although less important than the other criteria for selection, Rhodes Scholars are further expected to possess physical vigor. The will further specifies that "no student shall be qualified or disqualified for election to a Scholarship on account of his race or religious opinions." As Rhodes Scholars are free to pursue any field of study available in the University of Oxford, so also have they chosen to enter a wide variety of professional careers.

Since 1904, when the first American delegation arrived at Oxford, and 2000, exactly 2,918 Americans had been awarded Rhodes Scholarships. Until 1975 the competition for the Rhodes Scholarships was restricted, by the terms of Rhodes's will, to male students. In 1976 changes in British law permitted the opening of the competition to women and Oxford admitted the first class of women Rhodes Scholars. By 2000 more than 298 women had won this scholarship.

BIBLIOGRAPHY
Rotberg, Robert I. *The Founder: Cecil Rhodes and the Pursuit of Power*. New York: Oxford University Press, 1988.

Thomas, Antony. *Rhodes: The Race for Africa*. New York: St. Martin's Press, 1997.

William J. Barber / H. S.

See also **Education, Higher: Colleges and Universities.**

RICE CULTURE AND TRADE. Rice culture defined the Lowcountry, a region including the coastal plains of Georgia, South Carolina, and North Carolina up to the Cape Fear River. Near present-day Charleston colonists experimented with rice along with other export products. Rice quickly emerged as a viable crop, with the first exports occurring during the 1690s. In the beginning, the West Indies and Europe provided the markets for Carolina rice. Once the profit-minded colonists recognized the value of rice as a staple they began forming plantations and importing slaves from West Africa to clear the land and cultivate the grain.

Rice cultivation

The earliest rice grown in Carolina was either *Oryza sativa*, originating in Asia, or *Oryza glaberrima*, native to Africa. It is clear that colonists in the Carolina colony preferred slaves from the rice-growing regions of West Africa. The enslaved Africans' knowledge of rice cultivation and technologies profoundly influenced the development of the plantations and resulted in a creolized African-European agriculture as well as a distinctive Lowcountry culture.

Planters and slaves employed three different agricultural systems during the history of Atlantic rice cultivation. In the earliest, lasting from the 1690s to the 1720s, they grew upland rice, which was rain fed. This method worked nicely in conjunction with cattle production, because cattle could graze the fields after harvest and provide manure for fertilizer. Then from the 1720s to the 1770s, Carolinians gradually shifted the locus of rice cultivation to freshwater swamps. Under this regime laborers collected rainfall in man-made reservoirs and released the water through sluices in a process that produced higher yields than did upland cultivation. The relocation along rivers meant that the shipping of rice to Charleston for export was carried out exclusively by coastal schooners. The swamp system coincided with the disappearance of Indian communities in the Lowcountry following the Yamasee War of 1715. This opened up prime plantation lands between the Ashepoo and Savannah Rivers, which were deeded to colonists through royal grants. As Carolinians spread rice cultivation to the Savannah River, Georgia colonists took notice of the growing prosperity of their neighbors and, in 1751, Georgia ended its prohibition of slavery. As a result, Georgians (along with migrating South Carolinians) began to pursue slave-based rice culture in their colony.

Gradually, beginning before the American Revolution, planters adopted a third cultivation system, tidal rice culture. Rice plantations required fresh water and several feet in pitch of tide (that is, the waterline difference between high and low tide). These restrictions meant that plantations could only be on rivers with substantial watersheds and, even then, could be neither too near the sea for the river to be saltwater nor far enough inland to lose the diurnal tidal pulse. By 1800 tidal rice culture dominated production because of much higher yields, greater water control, and the labor savings involved. By flooding rice fields at specific intervals during the growing season, rice planters negated the need for hoeing, freeing slaves for other work. However, the labor saved during the growing season went into the greater efforts required to create and maintain tidal rice plantations.

One rice planter famously captured the character of the Lowcountry plantation in describing it as "a huge hydraulic machine." Slaves created rice fields by clearing swamps made up of cypress and oak forest and building, over many years, plantations encompassing two hundred to a thousand acres of floodable land. Before rice could be planted, slaves had to build an elaborate system of canals, ditches, earthen banks, and flood gates to control the tides. Subsequent to construction, slaves had to maintain the entire system, which nature constantly eroded through freshets, storms, and river currents.

Plantation Slave Culture

Rice plantation slaves labored under a regimen unique to this region of the South: the task system, which grew out of a period of negotiation between slaves and planters over the customary patterns of work and reciprocity. Largely in place by the middle of the eighteenth century, the task system prescribed specific daily expectations for each type of labor. For example, a normal day's task was to hoe a quarter of an acre. Once a slave completed the day's task he or she could cultivate their own garden crops or perform plantation labor for which they were to be compensated in some way. This is not to say that the task system was a benign form of slavery, but it was distinctive, and it appears to have given rise to an underground market among slaves and to have been a contributing factor in the development and survival of the Gullah culture in the Lowcountry.

Demise of Lowcountry Rice Cultivation

Lowcountry rice culture ultimately perished in the early twentieth century. The Civil War certainly spurred the initial decline through war-related destruction, loss of plantation capital, emancipation, and the decay of plantations from neglect, but the rice economy was already stressed and would have faltered eventually in any case. European markets began to turn to competing sources of rice in Asia following the opening of the Suez Canal in 1869. The U.S. rice market grew starting around the time of the Civil War, but prices declined. In the 1880s, as Lowcountry rice culture began to recover from the war and adjust to a free labor system, new competitors appeared in Arkansas, Louisiana, and Texas. In these states rice production depended not on tides or rain but on pumped irrigation. Rice culture in the Gulf States differed from the Lowcountry in that it mechanized quickly and fully.

In the end, rice cultivation vanished due to a combination of economic factors, including the limited ability to mechanize and the losses inflicted by an intense period of hurricane activity that began in 1893. Planters and black laborers grew the final crops of Atlantic Coast rice in the 1920s along the Combahee River in South Carolina. Although it ultimately failed, rice culture shaped the economic, political, environmental, and cultural development of South Carolina and Georgia from an early date, and that history has ramifications in the region to the present day.

BIBLIOGRAPHY

Carney, Judith A. *Black Rice: The African Origins of Rice Cultivation in the Americas.* Cambridge, Mass: Harvard University Press, 2001.

Chaplin, Joyce E. *An Anxious Pursuit: Agricultural Innovation and Modernity in the Lower South, 1730–1815.* Chapel Hill, N.C.: Institute of Early American History and Culture, 1993.

Coclanis, Peter. *The Shadow of a Dream: Economic Life and Death in the South Carolina Low Country, 1670–1920.* New York: Oxford University Press, 1989.

Joyner, Charles. *Down By the Riverside: A South Carolina Slave Community.* Urbana: University of Illinois Press, 1984.

Schwalm, Leslie A. *A Hard Fight For We: Women's Transition from Slavery to Freedom in South Carolina.* Urbana: University of Illinois Press, 1997.

Stewart, Mart A. *"What Nature Suffers to Groe": Life, Labor, and Landscape on the Georgia Coast, 1680–1920.* Athens: University of Georgia Press, 1996.

James H. Tuten

See also **Agriculture.**

RICHMOND occupies the hilly terrain at the falls of the James River in Virginia. Native Americans inhabited that area, but the English created a series of temporary settlements there beginning in 1609 and erected a fort in the 1640s. Later, planter William Byrd I maintained a trad-

Richmond in Ruins. A scene of devastation in the largely burned-out Confederate capital in 1865, at the end of the Civil War. LIBRARY OF CONGRESS

ing post in the same vicinity. His son, William Byrd II, founded and named Richmond, incorporated in 1742. The meeting place for several notable Revolutionary War–era conventions, the town served as a storehouse for American armies, became the state capital in 1779, and suffered damage from two British raids in 1781.

After the Revolution, Richmond featured distinctive buildings, especially the state capitol, designed by Thomas Jefferson. The city was the scene of the Gabriel Prosser slave conspiracy of 1800, the Aaron Burr treason trial of 1807, and a deadly theater fire in 1811. During the antebellum period, Richmond became a manufacturing center known for its flour, iron, and tobacco products. Steamboat traffic, a westward canal, and railroads made the town a transportation and commercial hub. German and Irish immigrants augmented a workforce that included free blacks and African American slaves.

As the capital of the Confederate States of America during the Civil War, Richmond became the target of repeated Union military campaigns. Facing a population, swollen by military personnel, government officials, refugees, and Union prisoners, authorities struggled to provide such essential goods as food and vital services, including medical care for the many wounded soldiers. As retreating Confederates evacuated the city on 3 April 1865, fires that had been set to destroy warehouses spread and incinerated much of the downtown. Postwar commemorations gradually transformed Richmond into a shrine to the Confederacy. In addition to Hollywood and Oakwood cemeteries, the city featured countless statues, stately Monument Avenue, and numerous museums and historic sites.

Following Reconstruction, conservative politicians were dominant over dissenting groups, including blacks, and the city floundered economically. Despite their political suppression, African Americans developed successful secret societies, churches, and businesses. The early twentieth century brought renewed prosperity and growth fueled by diversified industries, resurgent commerce, and robust banking. Nationally acclaimed authors, significant educational institutions, and dynamic religious organizations made Richmond a cultural center. Reformers led local and statewide campaigns to improve education, health, and public welfare. Organized labor remained a political force until the 1920s, when politicians resumed a conservative course they upheld through the rest of the century. In the 1950s and 1960s, officials resisted and delayed desegregation of schools and other public facilities and whites relocated to nearby suburbs. In 1977 the black majority on the city council elected Richmond's first African American mayor. Despite post–World War II annexations, the population within the city limits shrank to 197,790 in 2000, down from 202,278 in 1990.

BIBLIOGRAPHY

Chesson, Michael B. *Richmond after the War, 1865–1890.* Richmond: Virginia State Library, 1981.

Kimball, Gregg D. *American City, Southern Place: A Cultural History of Antebellum Richmond.* Athens: University of Georgia Press, 2000.

Shepherd Samuel C., Jr. *Avenues of Faith: Shaping the Urban Religious Culture of Richmond, Virginia, 1900–1929.* Tuscaloosa: University of Alabama Press, 2001.

Tyler-McGraw, Marie. *At the Falls: Richmond, Virginia, and Its People.* Chapel Hill: University of North Carolina Press, 1994.

Samuel C. Shepherd Jr.

See also **Civil War; Slave Insurrections; South, the: New South; Virginia.**

RICHMOND CAMPAIGNS. The Battle of Richmond on 29 to 31 August 1862, fought in Kentucky, was one of the most one-sided victories of the Civil War. In August 1862, Confederate Brigadier General Edmund Kirby-Smith invaded Kentucky with 21,000 troops. Leaving Knoxville, Tennessee, on 14 August and bypassing the well-fortified Cumberland Gap, Kirby-Smith traveled 150 miles to Richmond, Kentucky, in two weeks. On 29 August, the Confederates were repulsed in a skirmish with Union cavalry at Rogersville, south of Richmond. Kirby-Smith pressed on and reached Richmond on 30 August. At Richmond, 6,000 Confederate troops faced a Union division of 6,500 under Major General William Nelson and Brigadier General Mahlon D. Manson. The Union soldiers were new recruits who had never experienced combat. The Confederates easily drove the Union force back on 30 August. The Union lost 206 killed, 844 wounded, and 4,303 captured. Additionally, the Confederates captured all of the Union wagon trains and supplies, nine pieces of artillery, and ten thousand small arms. The Confederates lost only 78 killed and 372 wounded. The victory at Richmond allowed Kirby-Smith to secure complete control over central Kentucky until early October. He periodically ordered cavalry raids into Louisville and Covington, Kentucky, just across the Ohio River from Cincinnati. Kirby-Smith's victory threw Cincinnati into a panic, with Richmond being only seventy-five miles south of this major Northern city. Businesses were shut down and citizens were impressed to construct fortifications. Major General Lew Wallace arrived to declare martial law in Cincinnati out of fear that Southern sympathizers in Ohio might rise. Kirby-Smith advanced to Richmond in conjunction with General Braxton Bragg's invasion of Kentucky. The Confederates intended to sway the border state to join the Confederacy. The invasion failed, however, after Major General Don Carlos Buell's Army of the Ohio fought Bragg to a bloody draw at Perryville, Kentucky, on 7 and 8 October.

BIBLIOGRAPHY

Hattaway, Herman, and Archer Jones. *How the North Won: A Military History of the Civil War.* Urbana: University of Illinois Press, 1983.

McPherson, James M. *Battle Cry of Freedom: The Civil War Era.* New York: Oxford University Press, 1988.

W. Scott Thomason

See also **Cincinnati; Civil War.**

RICHMOND JUNTO, headed by Thomas Ritchie, editor and publisher (1804–1845) of the *Richmond Enquirer,* was a group that controlled Virginia Democratic politics for more than a quarter century. Its membership included Ritchie's cousins Spencer Roane and John Brockenbrough. The junto allied with Thomas Jefferson, who, in his post-presidential years, described the *Enquirer* as the only newspaper in the country worth reading. Strongly states' rights in tone, the Richmond junto opposed the Missouri Compromise on the grounds that the federal government had no right to limit slavery's extension westward. It likewise opposed the tariff, the Bank of the United States, and internal improvements.

BIBLIOGRAPHY

Ambler, Charles H. *Thomas Ritchie: A Study in Virginia Politics.* Richmond, Va.: Bell Books, 1913.

Syndor, Charles S. *The Development of Southern Sectionalism, 1819–1848.* Baton Rouge, La.: 1948.

Alvin F. Harlow / A. G.

See also **Missouri Compromise; States' Rights.**

RICHMOND V. J. A. CROSON COMPANY, 488 U.S. 469 (1989), a Supreme Court case that considered whether the constitutionality of set-asides—affirmative action programs for minority businesses, permitted by a standard of strict scrutiny under the Fourteenth Amendment's equal protection clause—should continue. Since 1942, Congress had approved legislation requiring businesses with federal contracts to draw up action plans for hiring minority workers. Until *Croson,* however, the Court had not questioned this practice. In 1983 the Richmond, Virginia, city council instituted a set-aside to remedy past discrimination by requiring prime contractors (to whom the city awarded construction contracts) to subcontract at least 30 percent of each contract's dollar amount to minority business enterprises. Prime contractor J. A. Croson Company did not comply with the program, whereupon the city awarded the contract to another company. Croson challenged the city's 30 percent quota as a violation of the Fourteenth Amendment's equal protection clause. The city responded that the quota merely copied federal policy guidelines. In a six-to-three vote, the Court decided in favor of Croson. The opinion, combined with the decisions in *Wygant v. Jackson Board of Education* (1986) and *United States v. Paradise* (1987), signaled the Court's increased willingness to limit the states' use of quotas as a remedy for past discrimination. The Civil Rights Act of 1991 put an end to this trend and reaffirmed the national commitment to affirmative action.

BIBLIOGRAPHY

Kull, Andrew. *The Color-Blind Constitution.* Cambridge, Mass.: Harvard University Press, 1992.

Urofsky, Melvin I. *A Conflict of Rights: The Supreme Court and Affirmative Action.* New York: Charles Scribner's Sons, 1991.

Tony Freyer / A. R.

See also **Affirmative Action; Business, Minority; Civil Rights Act of 1991; Set-Asides.**

RICO. In 1970, Congress passed the Organized Crime Control Act, Title Nine of which is called the Racketeer Influenced and Corrupt Organizations Act, or RICO. RICO was the outgrowth of congressional studies of organized crime and the recommendations of a presidential commission. Although RICO was endorsed by President Richard Nixon and the American Bar Association, the American Civil Liberties Union raised concerns with its possible use against antiwar protesters.

The study of the Mafia was the occasion for RICO's enactment, but the statute is not limited to the classic mobster; it applies to all persons who engage in "patterns" of "predicate crimes" committed by, through, or against "enterprises" including legitimate and illegitimate organizations. Its "predicate crimes" include violence, such as murder, the provision of illegal goods or services, such as drugs, corruption in labor unions and government, such as extortion bribery, and commercial fraud, such as securities. Its criminal sanctions include fines, imprisonment, and forfeitures; its civil sanctions include injunctions, treble damages, and attorney fees for those injured in their property.

At first, the Department of Justice moved slowly to implement criminal RICO. By the end of the twentieth century, however, it was the prosecutor's tool of choice against sophisticated forms of crime. Of the 150 RICO prosecutions brought each year out of the 50,000-plus criminal prosecutions, 48 percent are brought in the area of white-collar crime (such as political corruption and Wall Street fraud), 39 percent are brought in the area of organized crime (not just the Mafia, but drug organizations, and so on.), and 13 percent are brought in the area of violent crimes (street gangs, white hate groups). Members of Congress, governors, mayors, and other governmental figures have been convicted under RICO. Wall Street securities firms have been convicted. Significant criminal groups (Mafia families, drug organizations, and white-hate groups) have been put out of business.

While RICO is not limited to the Mafia, it was one of RICO's targets. The Mafia's membership in the United States in 1963 was approximately 5,000 people, 2,500 of whom were in five families in New York City; 300 or more were in one family in Chicago. The other sixteen families were found in major cities throughout the nation. Not equal in power or status, the Mafia families were under the jurisdiction of a "commission," composed of the heads of four families in New York City and the bosses of the families in Chicago, Buffalo, Philadelphia, and Detroit.

The Mafia of the early twenty-first century is a tattered remnant of the 1963 organization. Membership is down to 1,150; 750 are in New York City, where the five families are mere shells; 40 to 50 are in Chicago. Segments of the economy that were once infiltrated by the Mafia (such as the garment industry in New York or its fish market) are now free of criminal domination. Garbage removal is now competitive. The families in cities besides New York and Chicago are basically destroyed, reduced to little more than street gangs. The reasons are various—death, old age, the rise of rival groups, changes in economic and social life—but most significant, law enforcement pressure brought about by criminal and civil prosecutions under RICO, the wiretapping of criminal conversations for evidence in court cases, and the witness protection program, which helps convince insiders to turn against higher figures in the family without fear of retribution. As of 2002, the "commission" had not met in ten years. In short, the Mafia no longer possessed any edge in an underworld teeming with Asians, Russians, South Americans, and others of varied ethnic background.

The Department of Justice also moved slowly to use RICO's civil provisions, it is using its injunctive provisions to deal with Mafia-dominated unions, placing them in trusteeships and forcing democratic elections. Federal courts are requiring reforms designed to weed out criminal influence in the Teamsters Union, the Hotel and Restaurants Worker's Union, the Laborer's Union, and the Longshoremen's Union.

RICO's private treble damage provisions were largely ignored until about 1985. When they were first used, a firestorm of controversy broke out. Objections were made to RICO's use beyond "organized crime" in "garden variety fraud." Fear was expressed that the statute would open a "floodgate" of new litigation and inundate already crowded court dockets. In *H. J. Inc. v. Northwestern Bell Telephone Co.* (1989), the U.S. Supreme Court clarified the scope of RICO's "pattern" requirement, holding that it is limited to systematic conduct, not isolated acts. Civil suits occur at about 750 per year out of about 275,000 civil filings. The flood did not happen.

Repeatedly challenged in court, RICO has been uniformly upheld. Defense attorneys sought to limit it to "organized crime." In its *H. J. Inc.* decision, the Supreme Court held: "The occasion for Congress' action was the perceived need to combat organized crime. But Congress for cogent reasons chose to enact a more general statute. . . . Congress drafted RICO broadly enough to encompass a wide range of criminal activity, taking many different forms and likely to attract a broad array of perpetrators." Defense lawyers, too, challenged its forfeiture provisions, alleging that they interfere with a defendant's right to counsel. In *Caplin & Drysdale v. United States*, (1989), the Court held: "A robbery suspect has no Sixth Amendment right to use funds he has stolen . . . to retain an attorney. . . . The privilege to practice law is not a license to steal." Vagueness challenges under due process are uniformly turned aside. In *Fort Wayne Books, Inc. v. Indiana* (1989), the Court observed that if RICO's predicate offenses were "not unconstitutionally vague, then RICO cannot be vague either." In short, since a violation of RICO depends on a violation of the predicate offense, fair notice is marked out by the predicate offense. Avoid such offenses and you avoid RICO. Abortion protesters are complaining that its use against them is unlawful. In *Now v. Scheidler* (1994), the Court held that the statute was broad enough to apply to unlawful protests. The American Civil Liberties Union was prescient.

BIBLIOGRAPHY

Blakey, G. Robert, and Brian Gettings. "Racketeer and Corrupt Organizations (RICO): Basic Concepts–Criminal and Civil Remedies." *Temple Law Quarterly* 53 (1980): 1009. Overview of the law at its inception.

Griffin, Joe, and Don DeNevi. *Mob Nemesis: How the F.B.I. Crippled Organized Crime.* Amherst, N.Y.: Prometheus Books, 2002. Personal story of F.B.I. efforts against Mafia families by a knowledgeable insider.

Jacobs, James B., et al. *Busting the Mob:* United States v. Cosa Nostra. New York: New York University Press, 1994. Best academic study of success of RICO in New York City.

Luccaro, Daniel et al. "Racketeer Influenced and Corrupt Organizations." 38 *American Criminal Law Review* (2001): 1212. Overview of the law as it has developed in the modern period.

President's Commission on Law Enforcement and Administration of Justice, Task Force: Organized Crime. Washington, D.C.: U.S. Government Printing Office, 1967. Comprehensive analysis of organized crime at the beginning of the modern period.

President's Commission on Organized Crime. Washington, D.C.: U.S. Government Printing Office, 1986. Comprehensive analysis of organized crime and RICO after the beginning of the modern period.

Raab, Selwyn. "A Battered and Ailing Mafia Is Losing Its Grip on America." *New York Times.* 22 Oct. 1990, p. A1. Popular presentation of the decline of the Mafia and RICO's use against the families of the Mafia in New York City.

G. Robert Blakey

See also **Organized Crime Control Act.**

RIDERS, LEGISLATIVE, are sections or clauses not germane to the subject matter of a bill that are added by amendment before passage for a specific strategic purpose—namely, that the sentiment favorable to the bill will be sufficient to sweep the whole enactment through the final vote and secure executive approval, even though the proposal would probably be defeated by vote or vetoed if submitted separately. For example, in 1913 Congress attached to an appropriation act a rider exempting labor unions from the SHERMAN ANTITRUST ACT. President William Howard Taft had to veto the whole bill to annul this provision.

BIBLIOGRAPHY

Luce, Robert. *Legislative Procedure: Parliamentary Practices and the Course of Business in the Framing of Statutes.* New York: DaCapo Press, 1972.

Harvey Walker/A. R.

See also **Congress, United States.**

RIFLE. The history of the rifle is a combination of technology, ideology, and the changing nature of war and military tactics. The first rifle barrels appeared during the sixteenth century. A spiraled groove allowed the bullet more accuracy and to travel farther than a bullet fired from a smooth barrel, as was characteristic of the musket. Until 1776 and the development of the Ferguson rifle, the first successful breech-loader, the rifle was loaded from the muzzle end, ramming the powder wadding and bullet down the barrel. Scottish soldier Patrick Ferguson's weapon changed the process of loading.

The eighteenth century gave rise to other significant changes. Through use of the rifle, control of battlefields was transferred from generals to smaller units, which could react on their own initiative. By the 1740s, the Germanic states enlisted game hunters who used rifles that later developed into the famous long rifle. These were accurate to 200 yards, far beyond the traditional musket,

Rifle. Near two dead Germans, a soldier reloads his M1 during World War II. NATIONAL ARCHIVES AND RECORDS ADMINISTRATION

which had to be fired from tight and coordinated military formations. In the rebel colonies of North America, German gunsmiths modified the long rifle, which they called the "Jaeger," into the accurate "Kentucky" or "Pennsylvania" rifle. Combined with the individualistic ethos in American culture, this weapon contributed to the legend of the minutemen—citizen sharpshooters who could answer the call for military assistance in a minute. Their contribution to the American Revolution is still being argued by historians. The musket was the basic weapon for the U.S. army until the War of 1812; the rifle was the weapon of special companies. Rifle ammunition was inadequate until Captain Claude-Étienne Minié invented the "Minié ball" in 1849. It was a bullet of modern conical form, with a hollow base and an iron cup in the base for use in muzzle-loading rifles. The first official military weapon was the U.S. Model 1803, manufactured at Harpers Ferry, Virginia (now West Virginia).

Warfare changed in the nineteenth century. Napoleon relied upon the musket as the prime weapon for his light infantry. He thought the volume of firepower supported by artillery would give him a psychological advantage. Learning from their experience in the American Revolution, the British used the rifle with great success. Technology supported the growth of democratic ideology, in which every man served in the military since every man was a part of the state. The rifle was foremost in the development of the democratic citizen-army, because every man could have one. Weapons took control of events and tactics. Firepower became massive and accurate.

Another significant factor in the history of the rifle was the American Civil War. Several types of breech-loading rifles, along with repeating rifles, were used in the conflict. The firepower increased as armies were enlarged to match the emerging doctrine of total war. The Model 1861 Springfield rifle, with a range of a thousand yards, was standard issue for the Union troops, and in the beginning the Confederacy was equally well equipped. Tactical considerations changed slowly, but the rifle proved itself an effective defensive weapon. Urged by a more aggressive doctrine of combat, the Confederacy suffered great losses and ultimately could not survive. Indeed the Rebel cause was lost to the superior impact of the Union rifle. The rifle, therefore, changed the role of artillery and ultimately reduced the cavalry charge to a romantic memory. Accurate rifle fire greatly damaged the traditional reliance on close military formations and allowed a less structured battlefield with initiative resting with smaller units.

Improvements to the rifle continued after the Civil War. The U.S. Rifle, Model 1873 was used in the Indian Wars (1869–1878), then the Krag-Jorgensen replaced it in 1892. Refinements in cartridges, loading systems, and general design created the need for an improved bolt-action. The invention of smokeless powder in the 1880s also gave more power to the bullet's projection. Eventually the U.S. Rifle, Model 1903 became the standard issue. With only slight modifications, the 1903 rifle was the standard until World War II. It was followed by the semi-automatic M1 Garland rifle. Its magazine held eight shots, and the weapon was used until 1957.

After the middle of the twentieth century, increased firepower from the individual rifle was the hallmark. The M14 rifle, with a 7.62-milimeter caliber bullet, replaced the M1. The M14 had a twenty-round magazine with the capacity for fully automatic fire. During the Vietnam War the AR-15 became the basic weapon with a 5.56-mm cartridge. After alleged issues of jamming were solved and other ammunition improvements were made, the weapon became the U.S. Rifle M16 Al in 1967. Despite air power, atomic weapons, and other military developments, an infantry equipped with some type of rifle remained essential to national defense and military posture into the twenty-first century.

BIBLIOGRAPHY

Kindig, Joe. *Thoughts on the Kentucky Rifle in Its Golden Age.* Wilmington, Del.: G. N. Hyatt, 1960.

O'Connell, Robert L. *Of Arms and Men: A History of War, Weapons, and Aggression.* New York: Oxford University Press, 1989. A masterful overview.

Smith, Graham, ed. *Military Small Arms.* London: Salamander Books, 1994. Impressive photographs.

Donald K. Pickens

RIFLE, RECOILLESS, a lightweight, air-cooled, manually operated, breech-loading, single-shot, direct-fire weapon used primarily for defense against tanks. The pressure to the front equals the force to the rear. The remaining gases are permitted to escape to the rear so that the RIFLE remains motionless when fired. First developed by the German army in World War II, the weapon saw further refinement as a form of antitank artillery for airborne units in the U.S. Army. After the Korean War, advances in armor indicated a need for heavier antitank weapons, and the 90-mm M67 and the 106-mm M40 A1 were introduced as a result.

BIBLIOGRAPHY

Baldwin, Ralph Belknap. *They Never Knew What Hit Them: The Story of the Best Kept Secret of World War II.* Naples, Fla.: Reynier Press, 1999.

Barker, Arthur James. *British and American Infantry Weapons of World War II.* London: Arms and Armour Press, 1973.

Warner Stark / H. S.

See also **Machine Guns; Munitions.**

"RIGHT TO DIE" CASES. "Right to die" does not refer to any general right of able-bodied and healthy people to commit suicide. Rather, the expression is conventionally used to refer to situations in which issues concerning physician-assisted suicide typically arise. The central question is whether, and under what circumstances, an individual whose illness is incapacitating will be allowed to die or be assisted in dying rather than be sustained on life support indefinitely.

Earlier generations presumably handled many of these difficult problems by having the doctor consult with the family or even possibly resolve the question without consultation. Currently, right to die cases often involve public discussion and the relatively transparent decision-making process characteristic of the present age. New technologies ranging from drugs to respirators increase the complexity of the problem. In 1997, the U.S. Supreme Court held in *Washington v. Glucksberg* that there was no constitutionally protected right to die assisted by a physician. Thus the issue is treated largely as a matter of state law. States often have statutes on substituted judgment, or living wills. One state, Oregon, has a Death with Dignity statute authorizing medical personnel to participate in the death of a patient, not by assisting, but by providing access to drugs.

One recurrent theme in the ongoing discussion is whether a judgment reached by a spouse or family is a judgment in which the surrogate (family or spouse typically) speaks for the patient, seeking to express the wishes of the patient, or speaks for the surrogate. The case of a comatose patient unable to speak for herself was at issue in both the case of Karen Quinlan, which in 1976 reached the New Jersey Supreme Court, and that of Missouri resident Nancy Cruzan, which reached the U.S. Supreme Court in 1990. A different question is whether the state will assist, or permit others to assist, those who directly communicate their wish to die. This issue was raised in the criminal prosecutions against Dr. Jack Kevorkian, who was convicted and sentenced to prison for assisting suicide. While some argue in terms of the state's interest in life, others are concerned that a right to die will translate into a duty to die, typically in the interest of the welfare of the next generation. The Assisted Suicide Funding Restriction Act of 1997 forbids the use of federal funds to support physician-assisted suicide.

Legislation in the Netherlands concerning the right to die has been widely discussed in the United States. The Dutch approach imposes a number of stringent requirements before any physician-assisted suicide is permitted and involves specific cases of people in intense pain or whose quality of life seems to them not to justify continued existence.

BIBLIOGRAPHY

Schneider, Carl E. *The Practice of Autonomy: Patients, Doctors, and Medical Decisions.* New York: Oxford University Press, 1998.

Carol Weisbrod

See also **Assisted Suicide; Euthanasia; *Washington v. Glucksberg* (1997).**

RIGHT WING. *See* **Radical Right.**

RIGHT-TO-WORK LAWS first appeared in a significant number of states after Congress enacted the 1935 National Labor Relations Act, also known as the Wagner Act, and they remain on the books in roughly twenty states today. The "right" these laws enshrine is the nineteenth-century liberal individualist conception of freedom of contract between employer and employee. They protect the individual worker's freedom to refuse to join or to help support a union, including one chosen by fellow employees as their bargaining representative. Thus, from the perspective animating the Wagner Act, they aim to undercut collective labor agreements.

More specifically, right-to-work laws are aimed against union security provisions in collective labor contracts. Such provisions may require that the employer hire only union members, ensuring a so-called "closed shop," or they may require that newly hired workers join the union within a certain period. Or union security provisions may not require union membership: they may only demand that employees contribute their share to the union's costs of bargaining on workers' behalf. Also, they may provide that the employer shall deduct union dues or fees from workers' paychecks. State right-to-work laws typically outlaw all such arrangements. Florida and Arkansas pioneered this field of legislation in 1944; other Southern and prairie states soon followed. According to most students of labor relations in post–World War II America, right-to-work laws have helped thwart union organizing in these antiunion regions, particularly in industries and among social groups with no union traditions.

Union security provisions adorned collective labor agreements long before the Wagner Act, but the law lent them no support. Indeed, many state and federal courts declared that strikes to secure or preserve the closed or union shop were illegal. The Wagner Act declared a new national policy in support of unionism and collective bargaining. The act cleared away old antiunion, judge-made law. It not only protected the rights to organize and to strike; it also required employers to recognize and to bargain in good faith with unions freely chosen by a majority of employees. The Wagner Act also provided that union security agreements were legal and enforceable. Then, in 1947, with passage of the Taft-Hartley Act over President Harry Truman's veto, Congress reversed its course and outlawed the closed shop, while permitting the union shop, which requires only that employees become union members within thirty days of initial employment. More controversially, Taft-Hartley also permitted the states to go much further than Congress had gone. Taft-Hartley allowed the states to outlaw the union shop or any other form of union security agreement, which would otherwise be legal under national law. Thus, Taft-Hartley opened the way for the rash of post–World War II right-to-work laws.

BIBLIOGRAPHY

Hardin, Patrick, et al. *The Developing Labor Law: The Board, the Courts, and the National Labor Relations Act.* Washington D.C.: Bureau of National Affairs, 2002.

Millis, Harry A., and Emily Clark Brown. *From the Wagner Act to Taft-Hartley.* Chicago: University of Chicago Press, 1950.

Zieger, Robert. *The CIO: 1935–1955.* Chapel Hill: University of North Carolina Press, 1995.

William E. Forbath

See also **Closed Shop; Labor.**

RIGHTS. *See* **Human Rights; Natural Rights.**

RIGHTS OF ENGLISHMEN were included in the colonial charters and were generally identified through English common law. The struggle against Gov. Edmund Andros's arbitrary rule in the Dominion of New England during the 1680s, as well as the publication of John Locke's *Two Treatises of Government* in 1690, popularized knowledge of these rights. After the Glorious Revolution (1688), colonists identified the English Bill of Rights and other new legislation as the foundation of English liberty–safeguards against tyranny at home and abroad, under laws that governed both king and Parliament. After 1763, colonists claimed the right of English subjects to be taxed internally only if they had representation in Parliament. Later, the patriot movement asserted English liberties to defend life, liberty, and property.

BIBLIOGRAPHY

Bailyn, Bernard. *The Ideological Origins of the American Revolution.* Cambridge, Mass.: Belknap Press of Harvard University Press, 1992.

Lovejoy, David Sherman. *The Glorious Revolution in America.* Middletown, Conn.: Wesleyan University Press, 1987.

William S. Carpenter / s. b.

See also **Locke's Political Philosophy; Natural Rights; Rights of the British Colonies Asserted and Proved; Stamp Act; Stamp Act Congress; "Taxation Without Representation."**

RIGHTS OF MAN, a defense of the French Revolution written by Thomas Paine in reply to Edmund Burke's *Reflections on the Revolution in France* (1790). The work appeared in two parts, the first in 1791 and the second in 1792. Its circulation was great, the number of copies sold in England alone being estimated at 1.5 million. Paine argued for natural rights, claiming that man "deposits his right in the common stock of society, and takes the arm of society, of which he is a part, in preference and in addition to his own. Society grants him nothing. Every man is a proprietor in society, and draws on the capital as a matter of right."

BIBLIOGRAPHY

Fennessy, R. R. *Burke, Paine, and the Rights of Man: A Difference of Political Opinion.* La Hague: M. Nijhoff, 1963.

Fruchtman, Jr., Jack. *Thomas Paine and the Religion of Nature.* Baltimore: Johns Hopkins University Press, 1993.

Philip, Mark. *Paine.* Oxford: Oxford University Press, 1989.

J. Harley Nichols / h. s.

See also **Bill of Rights; "Give me Liberty or Give me Death!"; Natural Rights; Revolution, American: Political History.**

RIGHTS OF THE BRITISH COLONIES ASSERTED AND PROVED, a tract by James Otis (1764), denied Parliament's authority to tax the colonies. At the same time, Otis favored parliamentary representation for the colonies. He based his claims on contemporary understandings of English liberties, which held that English constitutional law protected all subjects (at home and abroad) from tyranny, and that the king and Parliament had to act within these laws. Notable among English liberties were the protection from internal taxation without representation in Parliament and safeguards against illegal threats to life, liberty, and property. Otis declared void any acts of Parliament that violated natural equity or the British constitution.

BIBLIOGRAPHY

Bailyn, Bernard. *The Ideological Origins of the American Revolution.* Cambridge, Mass.: Belknap Press of Harvard University Press, 1992.

Martin, Thomas S. *Minds and Hearts: The American Revolution as a Philosophical Crisis.* Lanham, Md.: University Press of America, 1984.

Wood, Gordon. *The Creation of the American Republic.* Chapel Hill: University of North Carolina Press, 1998.

Richard B. Morris / s. b.

See also **Colonial Policy, British; Natural Rights; Pamphleteering; Revolution, American: Political History; Rights of Englishmen; "Taxation Without Representation."**

RINGS, POLITICAL. A political ring is a comparatively small group of persons, usually headed by a political boss, organized to control a city, county, or state, and primarily interested in deriving therefrom large personal monetary profit. Political rings became particularly notorious in American politics during the second half of the nineteenth century.

The TWEED RING of New York City was the most famous political ring of all time. As a young man on the New York Board of Aldermen in 1851, William Tweed joined a ring, known as the "Forty Thieves," whose purpose was to gain personal profit from the improper granting of franchises. As a member of the Board of Supervisors, Tweed belonged to several short-lived rings that stole rather moderately from the public. The famous political ring that bears his name, and that for boldness has probably never been surpassed, was organized in 1869 and composed of Tweed, Mayor A. Oakey "O. K." Hall, Comptroller Richard "Slippery Dick" Connolly, and Peter B. "Brains" Sweeny. In the early 1870s, the machinations of the Tweed Ring came to light and Tweed himself served time in prison.

Although less notorious than the Tweed Ring, the Philadelphia Gas Ring actually exerted greater political influence but indulged in less peculation. Whereas the Tweed Ring came to grief within three years of its founding, the Gas Ring wielded great political power from 1865 until 1887. Similar rings developed in Saint Louis, Minneapolis, and San Francisco, among other cities. During the twentieth century the term "political machine" replaced "political ring" in common usage.

BIBLIOGRAPHY

Callow, Alexander B., Jr. *The Tweed Ring.* New York: Oxford University Press, 1966.

Josephson, Matthew. *The Politicos, 1865–1896.* New York: Harcourt, Brace, 1963.

Mandelbaum, Seymour J. *Boss Tweed's New York.* Chicago: I. R. Dee, 1990.

Harold Zink / a. g.

See also **Civil Service; Corruption, Political; Gilded Age; Machine, Political.**

RIO DE JANEIRO CONFERENCE (15 August–2 September 1947), a meeting of nineteen American republics (Nicaragua and Ecuador did not take part) in Rio De Janeiro, Brazil, to discuss regional cooperation in a spirit of Pan-Americanism. Wishing to give permanent form to principles of hemispheric solidarity embodied in the Act of Chapultepec (March 1945), the participating countries signed the Inter-American Treaty of Reciprocal Assistance. The treaty had great significance because it was the first regional collective security agreement as authorized by Article 51 of the United Nations Charter. Each signatory nation agreed to assist in meeting an armed attack against an American country, or in the case of internal instability in an American country (for example, a revolution), the members would immediately meet to decide on what measures should be taken. The importance attached to the conference by the United States was indicated by President Harry S. Truman's journey to Brazil to address the final session.

BIBLIOGRAPHY

Green, David. *The Containment of Latin America: A History of the Myths and Realities of the Good Neighbor Policy.* Chicago: Quadrangle Books, 1971.

Stuart, Graham H., and James L. Tigner. *Latin America and the United States.* Englewood Cliffs, N.J.: Prentice-Hall, 1975.

Charles S. Campbell / A. G.

See also **Latin America, Relations with; Pan-American Union; Treaties with Foreign Nations; United Nations.**

RIO GRANDE, a North American river, thirteen hundred miles of which form the boundary separating the United States and Mexico. It is the fifth longest river in North America. It rises in the San Juan Mountains in southwestern Colorado and flows generally southward through New Mexico until it reaches El Paso, Texas. It then flows generally to the southeast until it empties into the Gulf of Mexico at Brownsville, Texas, and Matamoros, Mexico.

After the Louisiana Purchase, American expansionists claimed the Rio Grande as the southern and western border of the territory covered by that purchase, but Spain successfully insisted on the Sabine River as the border. After Mexican independence from Spain in 1821, numerous American colonies sprang up in Texas. Still, dispute over the Texas-Mexican border was one of the main causes of the Texas Revolution in 1835–1836.

The Texas Republic maintained that the Rio Grande constituted its southern and western boundaries. The United States inherited those claims with the annexation of Texas in 1845, but Mexico's unwillingness to accept the river as the boundary was an immediate cause of the Mexican-American War. The Treaty of Guadalupe Hidalgo, which ended the war, recognized the river as an international border.

Rio Grande. The steamer *Bessie* at Fort Ringgold (Rio Grande City, Texas), one of several forts along the border with Mexico, c. 1890. National Archives and Records Administration

The Rio Grande is not important as a trade route, but its waters have long been important for irrigation in the arid Southwest. In prehistoric times, the Pueblo of New Mexico built elaborate irrigation systems. In modern times, irrigation water from the Rio Grande supports the commercially important citrus and truck farm regions in the Rio Grande Valley in both Texas and Mexico. Cooperation between the two countries has resulted in various irrigation and flood-control projects, the most spectacular being the vast Amistad Dam.

BIBLIOGRAPHY

Francaviglia, Richard, and Douglas W. Richmond, eds. *Dueling Eagles: Reinterpreting the U.S.-Mexican War, 1846–1848.* Fort Worth: Texas Christian University Press, 2000.

Kelley, Pat. *River of Lost Dreams: Navigation on the Rio Grande.* Lincoln: University of Nebraska Press, 1986.

Rivera, José, A. *Acequia Culture: Water, Land, and Community in the Southwest.* Albuquerque: University of New Mexico Press, 1998.

Donald W. Hunt / A. E.

See also **Guadalupe Hidalgo, Treaty of; Rivers; Spain, Relations with.**

RIOTS. Though they usually involve spontaneous, wanton violence or disorder by an anonymous crowd, riots have also served as a noteworthy form of social protest in American history. While the American Revolution made popular revolt a "quasi-legitimate" aspect of American culture, the ideals of democracy privilege debate and representation over mob rule. Nevertheless, Americans have frequently brought disorder to the nation's streets to express opinions and demands. Crowds have sought to limit the rights of others as often as they have demanded equal rights. Riots are not by definition part of organized rebellions, but they sometimes occur when public demonstrations turn to physical violence.

Rioting in the Nation's Capital. Troops stand guard at a street in Washington, D.C., in April 1968; the assassination of Dr. Martin Luther King Jr. on 4 April sparked riots nationwide, but the worst was in Washington, where thousands of people were arrested, hundreds of buildings were destroyed, and some areas were left devastated for decades. LIBRARY OF CONGRESS

In the eighteenth century the American British colonies were frequently places of riot and protest against the British government. The Boston Massacre in 1770 is perhaps the most famous of the prerevolutionary civil disturbances. A riot erupted when a sailor named Crispus Attucks and a group of Boston artisans and sailors provoked British soldiers who they felt were taking the jobs of local workers. The uprising ended with British soldiers firing into a crowd of colonials, an incident that galvanized many against Britain's forceful rule over the colonies.

Once the United States became a sovereign country, it was forced to contend with riots directed against its own state and its citizens. The 1820s and 1830s were perhaps the most riot-filled decades of American history. Ethnic groups, mostly African and Irish Americans, became targets for others who sought to protect their jobs and social lives from incursions of immigrant and "non-white" Americans, as in the 1838 antiabolitionist riots in Philadelphia.

In July 1863 white and mostly poor workers throughout the country led demonstrations against the mandatory drafting of soldiers for the Civil War. Though the ability of the rich to buy soldier replacements was a major impetus for revolt, many demonstrators were protesting being forced to fight for the freedom of black slaves. Most dramatically, the demonstrations led to assaults on Republican Party representatives and African Americans in New York City. Five days of violence destroyed hundreds of homes and churches and led to the deaths of 105 people. The civil disturbance ended only when soldiers just returning from the battlefields of Gettysburg could muster the power to retake the city from the mob.

Intra-ethnic group conflict sometimes led to rioting as well, and in 1871, Irish Catholics and Protestants clashed over a religious conflict in New York City. That riot resulted in more than sixty deaths and over a hundred injuries when national guardsmen opened fire on the crowd. The battle among Irish Americans helped to stoke nativism in the city and throughout the nation.

Riots can also occur without a specific reason or disagreement. In 1919 Boston became enflamed when people used a policemen's strike as an opportunity for extensive criminal activity, such as robbery, stoning striking policemen, and other kinds of assaults. Highlighting the city's deep divisions, middle- and upper-class Bostonians formed vigilante posses to battle the rioters. The three-day period of chaos ended with eight deaths and dozens of injuries, many of which resulted from state guardsmen shooting into crowds of civilians. General public opinion was against the riots, and the court dealt harshly with the few rioters who were caught.

Though the end of World War I and the summer immediately following it saw racially motivated riots in East St. Louis and Chicago, Illinois, and Washington, D.C., and 1943 saw terrible bloodshed in Harlem and Detroit, the 1960s was the decade with the most widespread and pervasive race riots. Cities all over the country exploded with conflict between white and black citizens, from Harlem (1964) to Watts (1965), to Chicago and Cleveland (1966), to Newark and Detroit (1967), and finally to Washington, D.C. (1968). Unlike the earlier period of race riots, those in the 1960s involved mostly African Americans as white people fled the inner cities. Responding to the rhetoric of the Black Power Movement, desperation from the waning CIVIL RIGHTS MOVEMENT, economic deprivation, and, most importantly, the racism of whites in their cities, African Americans rose up to assert their rights as citizens and humans. The American Indian Movement had similar motivation in 1969 for its protests, most notably at Wounded Knee on the Pine Ridge reservation in South Dakota. In late June and early July of the same year, gay and lesbian protesters in New York City responded to homophobic raids by police with a riot at the Stonewall, a bar in Greenwich Village. Though many disowned the violence and chaos of the Stonewall Riots, the incident helped to insert gay rights into the national political agenda.

Major politically motivated riots also occurred, most notably those that protested the war in Vietnam. In the summer of 1968 civil rights and antiwar protesters joined in a march outside the Democratic National Convention in Chicago. One reason the civil rights and antiwar movements in the 1960s emphasized nonviolence was to make it more difficult for officials to declare a march or a demonstration a riot. In Chicago, however, city and party officials viewed the march as a potential riot, and Mayor Richard J. Daley sent busloads of police. Protesters and sympathizers described what happened as a police riot, claiming the protest was peaceful and nonviolent until police attacked demonstrators without provocation.

The most deadly prison riot in United States history occurred in 1971 at the state prison at Attica, New York. Like many prisons in the early 1970s, Attica became a riot scene as prisoners protested their treatment at the facility. The state militia used force to retake the prison, leaving in the end thirty-two inmates and eleven guards dead. All but four of the dead were killed by the militia.

Riots in the late twentieth century seemed especially senseless, partially because television coverage allowed many to view the chaos as it was happening. When Los Angeles went up in flames in April 1992, the riot was ostensibly caused by the acquittal of the white police officers accused of beating an African American, Rodney King, a year earlier. After five days of violence following the verdict, 54 people were dead, more than 2,000 others were injured, and property losses had reached approximately $900 million. Black-white racism seemed to lie at the heart of the controversy. However, Hispanic Americans were the largest group of rioters, and Korean-owned businesses were the most common target of vandals and looters. Many have asserted that these rioters were responding to economic, political, and social deprivation similar to that which led to the rioting in the 1960s. In the years following the riots, the Los Angeles Police Department underwent a massive review and changed many of its procedures regarding both arrests and riot control.

Looting became a common part of modern riots, as evidenced in Los Angeles and by the outbreak of mob violence at the World Trade Organization (WTO) protests in Seattle, Washington, in November and December 1999. Though peaceful demonstrators were on hand for the annual WTO meeting to protest numerous issues—from environmentalism to animal rights—a fringe group of youth activists espousing anarchism smashed storefront windows and spray-painted graffiti in the downtown area. A new element of protest was introduced in the Seattle riots when the Internet was used to call thousands to the city and spread the anarchistic gospel of the rioters. And as in the case of Los Angeles, millions throughout the world were able to watch the riots as they were happening, amplifying their affect on policy as well as the number of people offended by the violence. Random civil disorder has had a long but uneasy relationship with political, economic, and social protest in the nation's history, but it is certainly a relationship that continues to be a part of the functioning American republic.

BIBLIOGRAPHY

Gale, Dennis E. *Understanding Urban Unrest: From Reverend King to Rodney King.* Thousand Oaks, Calif.: Sage, 1996.

Gilje, Paul A. *Rioting in America.* Bloomington: Indiana University Press, 1996.

Smith, Kimberly K. *The Dominion of Voice: Riots, Reason, and Romance in Antebellum Politics.* Lawrence: University Press of Kansas, 1999.

Tager, Jack. *Boston Riots: Three Centuries of Social Violence.* Boston: Northeastern University Press, 2001.

Eric S. Yellin

See also **Civil Disobedience; Class Conflict; Race Relations.**

RIOTS, URBAN. Urban rioting in America antedates the Revolution and has been a part of the experience of American cities ever since. This is so because, from its inception, American politics always considered rioting—or, to use the older political terms, "crowd action" or "politics-out-of-doors"—to be a normal, if extreme, extension of the American political process. So race riots, ethnic upheavals, and economic conflagrations, or any

Urban Riots. This illustration, published in *Frank Leslie's Illustrated Newspaper,* shows mounted police driving "riotous communist workingmen" out of New York City's Tompkins Square Park on 13 January 1874; other sources say the police, without provocation, attacked a peaceful rally in order to suppress the emerging labor movement. LIBRARY OF CONGRESS

combination of these, have been part of the urban political landscape.

Even before the Revolution, New York City was afflicted by a major race riot, one in which at least a score of African American slaves and freedmen were killed or executed. The American nation was born of revolution, so it was that rioting marked the ultimate response to the Stamp Act of 1765 in New York, Boston, and elsewhere. Sporadic violence occurred in urbanizing America for the next half-century, and as cities matured in the Age of Jackson, cities exploded in violence. In 1834, called by the notable American diarist Philip Hone "the Great Riot Year," rioting from a variety of causes moved American politics to its most violent margins. There were anti-abolitionist riots in every major eastern and Midwestern American city, pitting immigrant Irish Catholics against native upper middle-class Protestants. Ethnic and racial riots (more than fifty in cities) persisted until 1835, when such "politics-out-of-doors" (a contemporary phrase) temporarily subsided. The anti-Draft Riot of 1863—the bloodiest in American history, with perhaps as many as two thousand dead—seemed to mark the end of the Age of Jackson.

After the Civil War, riots pitting labor against a developing and onerous factory system occurred with increasing frequency; for example, in 1877 and 1892, worker strikes in Pittsburgh turned violent. The cause of two riots during the Great Depression may also be traced to economic conditions. The violent repression of the Bonus Marchers in Washington D.C. (1931) and the United Auto Workers Sitdown Strike in Detroit (1936) also indicate a remarkable continuity with America's urban past.

Post-World War II American riots also demonstrated that continuity. Racial and class-related strife was evident in the tumultuous decade of the 1960s. The Weathermen's "Days of Rage" widespread racial violence in the Watts section of Los Angeles (1965), Newark, Detroit, New York City, and elsewhere (1967) all indicated the persistence of urban problems yet to be solved. In the more recent past, a bloody reprise occurred in Los Angeles in 1992, and a major race riot took place in Cincinnati in 2000.

BIBLIOGRAPHY

Gilje, Paul A. *Rioting in America.* Bloomington: Indiana University Press, 1996.

Carl E. Prince

RIOTS, URBAN, OF 1967. Beginning in April and continuing through the rest of the year, 159 race riots erupted across the United States. The first occurred in Cleveland, but by far the most devastating were those that took place in Newark, New Jersey, and Detroit, Michigan. The former took twenty-six lives and injured fifteen hundred; the latter resulted in forty deaths and two thousand injuries. Large swaths of ghetto in both places went up in flames. Television showed burning buildings and looted stores, with both National Guardsmen and paratroopers on the scenes.

These upheavals seemed to come out of nowhere, but that was not really the case. Urban violence, including race confrontation, was always present in America; "politics out of doors," as it was called in the nineteenth century, was evident in the coming of the American Revolution, the Age of Jackson, the Civil War, and the century following. In the long view, 1967's explosions were important but far from unique episodes of civil disorder in American history.

In a more immediate sense, the 1967 riots were part of the activist political culture of the 1960s. Agitations for civil rights seemed long overdue in America. It was a decade of upheaval and change involving not only black activism but also growing antiwar sentiment, street theater aimed at social change and class conflict, and the beginning of a women's rights movement. Within this mixture of activism, the civil rights movement, led by Reverend Martin Luther King, came into its own as a biracial effort to achieve full integration and political rights in American

society. The Civil Rights Act of 1964 and the Voting Rights Act of 1965 would seem to have met the demand, but that was not to be. Black activism remained alive and well and moved beyond the moderation of Dr. King to embrace the concept of Black Power evoked by militant radicals like Hughey Newton, Stokely Carmichael, and H. Rapp Brown. It was embodied in the Black Panthers as the foremost organizational vehicle for African Americans of the era. Radicalization of the civil rights struggle—seemingly encouraged by legislative progress under the aegis of President Lyndon Johnson's Great Society—led to the explosions of 1967 in black ghettos across America. It was euphemized most famously by Rapp Brown's oft-quoted epithet "Burn, baby, burn."

Yet even that destructive component of Black Power should not be taken out of context; the year 1967 ended with a final act of violence in late October, when antiwar protesters from around the country moved on Washington, D.C. Those who gathered at the Lincoln Memorial on 21 October were largely white, largely middle class, largely educated, and formerly mainstream in their politics. But, when U.S. Army units met them with fixed

Detroit. National Guardsmen, their bayonets ready, proceed through the West Side on 26 July 1967, during the city's second devastating race riot in a quarter century. © BETTMANN/CORBIS

bayonets, they took to the streets of the capital in an outbreak of destructive rioting and constructive confrontation, and 650 were arrested.

So, while 1967 was to go down in history as another major riot year like 1765, 1834, 1877, 1919, and 1931, it should be noted that not all of the riots were outpourings of racial confrontations that year. Violence was in the air in 1967, but so was free political expression as guaranteed by the U.S. Constitution.

BIBLIOGRAPHY

Paul Gilje. *Rioting in America*. Bloomington: Indiana University Press, 1996.

Carl E. Prince

See also **Black Panthers; Black Power; Civil Rights Movement; Insurrections, Domestic; National Association for the Advancement of Colored People; Riots, Urban.**

"RIPLEY'S BELIEVE IT OR NOT." Robert LeRoy Ripley (1893–1949) started out as a newspaper sports cartoonist for the *New York Globe*. Short of copy one day in December 1918, he created the first "Believe It or Not" column, which featured bizarre sports records. The feature quickly became a hit; signed by the head of King Features Syndicate at the behest of William Randolph Hearst, the column ran in 325 newspapers in 33 countries with an estimated readership of 80 million. Ripley earned half a million dollars a year by the mid-1930s and received thousands of letters per day, more than any other individual save Santa Claus. He also lectured, appeared in short films, and broadcast a weekly radio show starting in 1934. An international celebrity who made a fetish of the people and things of the Orient, Ripley can also be credited with providing the United States with its national anthem: in 1929, he alerted readers to the fact that "The Star-Spangled Banner" had never been officially adopted. Congress responded to more than five million letters of protest inspired by the column and rectified the situation in 1931. Ripley's personal collection of memorabilia is preserved in twenty-six museums worldwide.

BIBLIOGRAPHY

Considine, Robert B. *Ripley: The Modern Marco Polo*. Garden City, N.Y.: Doubleday, 1961.

Jackson, Donald Dale. "Believe It or Not, Rip Was Almost as Odd as His 'Items.'" *Smithsonian* 25, no. 10 (1995): 90–99.

Robbins, Peggy. "Believe It or Not! The Extraordinary World of Robert Ripley." *American History Illustrated* 17, no. 6 (1982): 34–41.

Jennifer Gold

RIPPER LEGISLATION, the name given to acts of state legislatures, motivated by partisan considerations, whereby local (usually city) officials of one party are turned out of office and replaced with political opponents. For example, Pennsylvania's Democratic legislature in 1937 sought to abolish the Philadelphia CIVIL SERVICE commission and municipal court, then in Republican control. These measures were later held unconstitutional by the state supreme court. Legislatures can forego frontal attacks on undesired employees by cutting an agency's budget drastically or imposing compulsory retirement ages, thereby forcing staff reductions and opening new slots for the majority party's minions.

BIBLIOGRAPHY

Shefter, Martin. *Political Parties and the State: The American Historical Experience*. Princeton, N.J.: Princeton University Press, 1994.

Charles H. Backstrom / A. R.

See also **City Manager Plan; Machine, Political; Municipal Government; Municipal Reform; Political Parties.**

RIVER AND HARBOR IMPROVEMENTS. Referring in 1783 to his country's extensive natural waterways, George Washington wrote, "Would to God we may have the wisdom to improve them." In colonial times, RIVERS and lakes were principal avenues of transit; schemes for their development abounded, but scarcities of money and engineering skills precluded large undertakings. With the formation of the federal government in 1789, the outlook brightened. The First Congress enacted legislation for "the establishment and support of the Lighthouses, Beacons, Buoys, and Public Piers." And in 1790, with congressional assent, states began levying tonnage duties to be used for deepening harbors and removing sunken vessels.

The administration of Thomas Jefferson pointed the way toward greater federal involvement with internal improvements. The founding of the U.S. Military Academy at WEST POINT, New York, in 1802 was auspicious. The first school of technology in the New World, the academy made possible a technically competent corps of engineers within the army that would be available for infrastructure development. In 1808, at the behest of Congress, Secretary of the Treasury Albert Gallatin produced a farsighted plan that envisaged a grand network of water routes binding together the seaboard states and linking the East Coast with the interior and the GREAT LAKES. The estimated cost was $20 million. Although the plan captured public interest, financial considerations, debate over the federal role in internal improvements, and the War of 1812 combined to forestall action.

The decade that followed the Treaty of Ghent (1814) witnessed significant changes. The War of 1812 had taught the value of interior lines of communication. Nationalism fostered by the war fired enthusiasm for public works. Navigation projects became important features both of Henry Clay's "American system" and of Secretary of War John C.

Calhoun's plans for an adequate defense. Presidential vetoes, based on constitutional scruples, curbed the will of Congress for a time and left the initiative largely to the states. Construction of the ERIE CANAL, the greatest undertaking of this period, began in 1817 under state auspices.

At length, in March 1824, the historic decision of the Supreme Court in GIBBONS V. OGDEN cleared the way for prompt enactment of two important laws. In that case, the Court applied an expansive definition of "commerce" to uphold the right of the holder of a federal coasting license to offer service on New York waters despite a state law granting a monopoly to Fulton-Livingston licensees. Congress responded to this broad understanding of its powers under the commerce clause of the Constitution by enacting the General Survey Act of 30 April 1824. That act authorized planning for roads and CANALS "of national importance in a commercial or military point of view" and empowered the president to employ army engineers in this work. Three weeks later, Congress enacted the appropriation act of 24 May, which provided $75,000 for navigation improvements on the Ohio and Mississippi Rivers. These acts marked the real beginning of the federal program for waterway development.

Over the next thirty-five years, state and federal governments enacted programs to facilitate commercial use of the nation's waterways. With federal subsidies and technical aid from army engineers, states and chartered companies soon began construction of such important canals as the Chesapeake and Delaware, the Chesapeake and Ohio, and the Louisville and Portland. Between 1824 and 1831, the War Department Board of Engineers for Internal Improvements outlined a comprehensive plan, segments of which were swiftly implemented. At the same time, the U.S. Army Corps of Engineers launched a nationwide endeavor to improve rivers that has continued to this day. Snagging on the MISSISSIPPI RIVER, opening up the log-choked Red River, deepening the Ohio, preserving SAINT LOUIS as a river port, and clearing harbors all along the Atlantic and Gulf coasts were among its early activities. In 1857, the corps introduced the seagoing hopper dredge at Charleston, South Carolina. The corps also entered the field of lighthouse construction, completing the famous Minots Ledge off the Massachusetts coast and many other lights. The Topographical Engineers, an independent branch from 1838 until the Civil War, also rendered impressive service. The Great Lakes survey, inaugurated in 1841, provided accurate information for shippers; and the Humphreys-Abbot study of the Mississippi, completed in 1861, was a major contribution to the science of hydraulics. Minuscule by latter-day standards (the total cost was less than $20 million), these antebellum programs nevertheless had a decided impact on commercial growth.

A great upsurge of activity followed the Civil War. During the last third of the nineteenth century, the Corps of Engineers expended nearly $333 million on rivers and harbors. To meet its enlarged responsibilities, the corps established a permanent, nationwide system of districts and divisions staffed by military and civilian engineers. Meanwhile, Congress created special organizations designed to meet special needs: the Mississippi River Commission (1879); the Missouri River Commission (1884–1902); the office of the supervisor, New York harbor (1888); and the California Debris Commission (1893). Among major projects of the period were improvement of the Mississippi River by wing dams, revetments, levees, and construction of the Eads Jetties that opened the river's South Pass to ocean traffic; canalization of the Ohio; provision of a ship channel to connect the waters of the Great Lakes between Buffalo, New York, Chicago, and Duluth, Minnesota; erection of the Tillamook (Oregon) and Stannard Rock (Michigan) lighthouses; and completion of the Muscle Shoals Canal in the Tennessee River and the "Soo" locks at Sault Sainte Marie, Michigan, both engineering marvels of the day. Virtually every major harbor on the oceans, the Great Lakes, the Mississippi, and the Ohio was improved for shipping.

A time of great accomplishment, these years were also the heyday of the pork barrel, when many schemes of marginal value won legislative sanction. The Civil War left many civil-works tasks for the Corps of Engineers, including fallen bridges, sunken vessels, twisted rails, broken levees, snags, and silt accumulation. But what began as an effort to restore river commerce turned into a deluge of projects that ensured the satisfaction of various interests in each region of the country. A year after the war ended, Congress appropriated $3.6 million for improvements and surveys at forty-nine sites. By 1882, the annual expenditure for rivers and harbors was more than $18 million and the corps was handling about five hundred assignments. That year, Congress authorized funding for eighteen projects that had received unfavorable reports from the corps. Mark Twain's fictional Columbus River, alias Goose Run, which if "widened, and deepened, and straightened, and made long enough . . . would be one of the finest rivers in the western country" had many a real life counterpart.

By the turn of the century, comprehensive planning and multiple-purpose projects started to become the focus of federal efforts. In 1902, Congress created the Board of Engineers for Rivers and Harbors, composed of officers of the corps, to review proposals for waterway development. Over the next seventy years the board turned down 57 percent of the proposals laid before it. Minor streams received progressively less attention; to win approval, projects generally had to promise far-reaching benefits. Symbolic of the new era was the Intracoastal Waterway, authorized in 1909, to connect all ports from Boston to the Rio Grande. The act of 3 March 1909, that also created the NATIONAL WATERWAYS COMMISSION, contained a little known, but highly significant, section directing the chief of engineers to aim in the future for multipurpose projects. Hence, the way was open to marry navigation improvement with hydropower development and flood protection. In 1917, flood control work on the Mississippi River, which had been carried on by the federal government since 1882 under the guise of navigation improvement, was formally recognized by Congress as a national responsibility. At the same time, Congress authorized the corps to undertake such work on the Sacramento River in California. The following year the Corps of Engineers began construction of their first multipurpose dam at Muscle Shoals, Alabama.

Noteworthy advances took place in the period between World War I and World War II. In 1927, Congress instructed the army to make a comprehensive survey of the multiple-use potentialities of the nation's rivers. During the next decade, the Corps of Engineers prepared some two hundred reports, known as "308 reports," outlining possible development of major river basins for navigation, flood control, irrigation, and power generation. These reports furnished basic guides for many valuable public works projects launched under the New Deal, among them such well-known dams as Bonneville (Oregon), Fort Peck (Montana), Norris (Tennessee), and Shasta (California). At the same time, federal programs for flood control expanded. In 1928, Congress adopted an extensive project for flood protection on the Mississippi, commonly called the Jadwin Plan. A year later, the Corps of Engineers established the U.S. Waterways Experiment Station at Vicksburg, Mississippi, to further the sciences of hydraulics and hydrology. In 1936, nationwide flood-control activities became a function of the corps. From this time forward, the federal government's waterway improvement goals steadily widened to encompass water supply, recreation, fish and wildlife CONSERVATION, pollution abatement, and flood plain management.

Programs implemented in the quarter century after World War II were larger in both size and scope than those of the first half of the twentieth century. From a curtailed wartime level of $100 million in 1945, annual expenditures for river and harbor improvements rose sharply to $1.8 billion in 1973. In these years, comprehensive planning attained full maturity. Authorization of the Pick-Sloan Plan for the Missouri River Basin, proposed jointly by the Corps of Engineers and the Bureau of Reclamation, launched the nation's first postwar attempt at comprehensive basin development. Constructed under the plan were extensive systems of levees and floodwalls; a nine-foot channel upstream on the Missouri to Sioux City, Iowa; and a series of dams and reservoirs, the largest being Garrison in North Dakota and Oahe, Big Bend, Fort Randall, and Gavins Point in South Dakota. Similar developments followed in the Columbia River and Arkansas River basins. Other projects of special importance in this period were construction of the SAINT LAWRENCE SEAWAY, recanalization of the Ohio, and modernization of the Black Warrior–Tombigbee Waterway in Alabama. Growing numbers of supertankers and giant cargo vessels spurred efforts to improve harbors and channels and called forth plans for superports.

But by the 1960s, a critical mass of the American public had come to demand that river development projects promote recreation, water quality, and environmental preservation as well as irrigation, navigation, and flood control. The strength of these new interests was reflected in several important laws Congress passed over the next decade including the Wilderness Act (1964), the Wild and Scenic Rivers Act (1968), and the National Environmental Policy Act (1969). During this period, the Corps of Engineers began using the Rivers and Harbors Act of 1899 to address water pollution, and those regulatory efforts helped lead to passage of the Federal Water Pollution Control Act of 1972. Environmental concerns also generated intense opposition to specific water projects and in a few cases, to their cancellation. In 1986, Congress passed the Water Resources Development Act, which modified approaches to financing and planning water programs as well as recognized that environmental considerations were an intrinsic factor in water resources planning. In the early 2000s, various organizations and some government agencies were promoting new approaches to river and harbor development including removal of dams, flood control through restoration of wetlands and floodplains, and community riverfront development for recreational and retail purposes.

A river and harbor improvement effort spanning nearly two centuries and embracing more than 4,000 projects has produced far-reaching benefits. Contributing materially to national defense as well as to national prosperity (as of 1998) were almost 300 deep-draft harbors; 25,000 miles of inland waterways, which carry more than 600 million tons of domestic freight each year; 383 reservoir and lake sites, with a total storage capacity of 329 million acre-feet; 75 hydropower dams, with installed capacity of 20.7 million kilowatts; 4,340 recreation sites at 456 corps projects handling 380 million visits per year; and more than 700 flood control projects, which have prevented approximately $6 worth of flood damage for every dollar spent since 1928 (adjusted for inflation).

BIBLIOGRAPHY

Bourne, Russell. *Americans on the Move: A History of Waterways, Railways, and Highways.* Golden, Colo.: Fulcrum Publishing, 1995.

Goodrich, Carter. *Government Promotion of American Canals and Railroads, 1800–1890.* New York: Columbia University Press, 1960.

Hull, William J., and Robert W. Hull. *The Origin and Development of the Waterways Policy of the United States.* Washington, D.C.: National Waterways Conference, 1967.

Reisner, Marc. *Cadillac Desert: The American West and Its Disappearing Water.* New York: Penguin Books, 1993.

Reuss, Martin. *Designing the Bayous: The Control of Water in the Atchafalaya Basin, 1800–1995.* Alexandria, Va.: Office of History, U.S. Army Corps of Engineers, 1998.

Scheiber, Harry N. *Ohio Canal Era: A Case Study of Government and the Economy, 1820–1861*. Athens: Ohio University Press, 1987.

Shallat, Todd. *Structures in the Stream: Water, Science, and the Rise of the U.S. Army Corps of Engineers*. Austin: University of Texas Press, 1994.

Smith, Frank Ellis. *The Politics of Conservation*. New York: Pantheon Books, 1966.

Stine, Jeffrey K. *Mixing the Waters: Environment, Politics, and the Building of the Tennessee–Tombigbee Waterway*. Akron, Ohio: University of Akron Press, 1993.

Lenore Fine
Jesse A. Remington / C. P.

See also **Engineers, Corps of; Gallatin's Report on Roads, Canals, Harbors, and Rivers; Hydroelectric Power; Inland Waterways Commission; Missouri River; Ohio River; Survey Act of 1824; Tennessee Valley Authority; Waterways, Inland.**

RIVER NAVIGATION. The continental United States is a network of water highways. Immense rivers thread the interior of the country for thousands of miles and empty into the vast seas at the nation's borders. At the time of initial contact with Europeans, Native Americans plied these RIVERS in bark canoes, bull-boats (tubs of buffalo hide stretched over a frame of willow), and pirogues (canoes made out of hollowed tree trunks).

The "keelboat age" began shortly after white colonists arrived on the continent. Taking its name from the long, narrow boat of shallow draft that rivermen propelled with poles, this was the period when humans had to rely on their own strength, wind, or water currents to drive their boats. Where the nature of the river permitted, the early settlers traveled on sailing craft, as on the Hudson, Delaware, and Potomac rivers; and it was often possible for ships to ascend far upstream. But on such waterways as the Connecticut and most of the western rivers,

Henry Miller Shreve. The steamboat captain who developed a vessel suitable for the relatively shallow Mississippi, Ohio, and Missouri Rivers in what was then the West. © CORBIS-BETTMANN

they used the bateau and KEELBOAT, because rowing or poling were more feasible than sailing. During this period, packet boats—vessels that traveled on a regular schedule between specific ports—were rare on the western rivers, and their services were not long continued, but in the East they existed on the Hudson and Delaware rivers.

Boatbuilding was among the earliest activities of the colonists, especially in New England, in New Amsterdam, and on Delaware Bay. In fact, by the start of the American Revolution, many English merchants owned vessels built in the colonies. But these sea-faring boats were much larger and faster than the boats that settlers built to traverse the continent. The crudest river craft were log rafts, one-way carriers that floated downstream ladened with produce, furs, and other items to sell. Once all was sold, the rafters broke up the raft, sold the logs for lumber, and returned home by foot or on another boat. Keelboats could make the return voyage, but typically took twice as long to travel upstream as down.

Flatboats, known also as arks and Kentucky boats, were the most numerous of the many types of river craft. Typically, they were larger than keelboats and could hold livestock in their hulls. Like rafts, flatboats were built at the headwaters of eastern and western rivers for downstream travel only. River crews used flatboats to transport produce, coal, cattle, and immigrants down American wa-

Clermont. A painting of the first commercially viable American steamboat, invented by Robert Fulton and launched in 1807 on the Hudson River. © BETTMANN/CORBIS

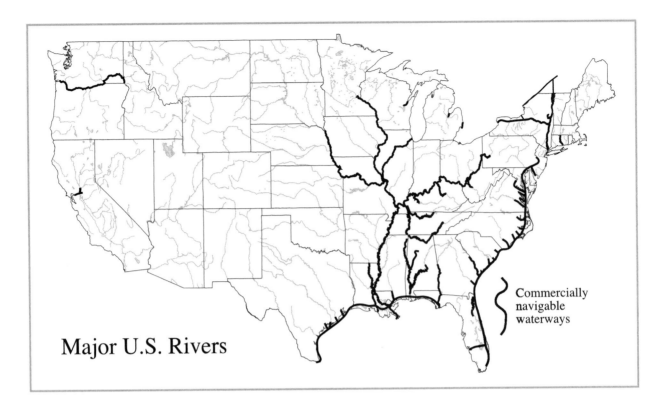

Major U.S. Rivers

Commercially
navigable
waterways

terways until after the Civil War. The number of flatboats that traveled the country's rivers is incalculable, and so too is the amount of freight they carried and the number of immigrants they transported. But flatboats were certainly a vital factor in the development and peopling of the West, particularly by way of the Ohio and Tennessee Rivers.

During the eighteenth and nineteenth centuries, western rivers were not only important avenues of commerce and settlement, but were also important lines of defense and the sites of crucial military battles. The French and the Spanish maintained fleets of galleys, boats propelled by both oars and sails, on the Mississippi for military purposes. The colonists built a number of GUNBOATS that plied western rivers during the Revolution and in the years following. One of the first STEAMBOATS, Fulton's *Orleans* or *New Orleans*, was of some assistance to Andrew Jackson's army in battles against the British in 1814 and 1815. The U.S. Army used gunboats and keelboats against the Indians on the western rivers as late as the War of 1812. Thereafter steamboats took their place. During the Civil War, few steamboats moved in civilian occupations on the lower MISSISSIPPI RIVER, because the waters ran red from the fires of burning boats and human blood as soldiers fought for control of the river and the forts and towns on its banks.

Long before the military battles of the Civil War, however, Americans engaged in competition of a different sort on the commercial inland waterways. When Robert Fulton launched the *Clermont* on the Hudson in 1807, he initiated a battle royal between river steamboats and

coastwise sailing packets, with the former destined to eventual victory. Although the first steamboat on western waters was Fulton's *Orleans*, it could not travel far upstream and other boats built on Fulton's patents had deep hulls, which were unsuited to the shallow western rivers. It was not until Henry Shreve's *Washington* was launched in 1816, with its boilers on the deck, that a craft was found suitable for western river navigation. In 1820, more than sixty steamboats were working the Mississippi, Missouri, and Ohio Rivers; two decades later, there were more than one thousand. By the 1840s, steamboats had also become much larger and evolved into floating entertainment palaces that boasted ornate cabins and private staterooms, bars, barbar shops, elegant food service, calliopes, bands, orchestras, and gambling tables. The largest boats could carry several thousand bales of cotton and several hundred passengers at the same time. But despite the advances in design, during the antebellum period, the title "packet" as applied to the western passenger steamboat was a misnomer, as they rarely operated on schedule. The eastern river steamboats were more reliable.

Nineteenth-century river travel was a dangerous enterprise. Swirling currents, bad weather, and underwater obstructions such as sunken tree trunks threatened to spin boats into river banks or rip holes in their hulls. Steamboats also brought onto the rivers high-pressure boilers that too frequently exploded. Early boilers were often defective. And boat captains and owners sometimes asked too much of the boilers by overloading the boat or trying to travel too fast. Between 1836 and 1848, there were approximately seventy-six steamboat explosions on western rivers. The use of high-pressure boilers resulted in so many explosions that in 1852 Congress set up a system of licensing and inspection. The average life of a western steamboat was about four years.

By 1850, the railroads had begun to sap the trade from the steamboats and from the canals both in the East and West. But, the tremendous volume of transport needed during the Civil War gave the steamboats a new lease on life. This continued for a couple of decades, since most railroads crossed rather than paralleled the rivers. During this second great age of the steamboat, lines of packets were formed and schedules became more honored by observance. "Low water boats" were even developed to cater to mail and passenger needs during the summer. And steamboats towed barges (the modern form of flatboat) laden with coal, oil, and other heavy goods. By the 1880s, however, the competition of the railroads parallel to the rivers was rapidly displacing steamboats in the West and had won a victory in the East.

It was partially in a desperate sectional effort to block the railroads that the federal government was pushed into western river improvements after 1879. A magnificent system of dams and other water controls have made the rivers of the Mississippi Basin important highways for heavy freight, carried chiefly in barges pushed in the early 2000s by tugboats fueled by diesel rather than steamboats. The Mississippi River system is connected with the SAINT LAWRENCE SEAWAY and the GREAT LAKES by the Illinois Waterway, completed in 1933, and the Ohio River system, and it extends to the Gulf of Mexico and the Gulf Intracoastal Waterway. This system—including the Ohio, Missouri, and Illinois rivers—saw a great increase in commercial traffic in the second half of the twentieth century.

On the Atlantic coast, the Hudson, Delaware, and Savannah rivers are linked to the Atlantic Intracoastal Waterway, which connects Boston and New York City with Key West, Florida. This system was especially important during World War II, since it enabled navigation to continue to and from Florida and Massachusetts unmenaced by German submarines. Commercial traffic on the Atlantic coastal rivers and canals also increased significantly in the second half of the twentieth century.

BIBLIOGRAPHY

Baldwin, Leland Dewitt. *The Keelboat Age on Western Waters.* Pittsburgh, Pa.: University of Pittsburgh Press, 1941.

Durant, John, and Alice Durant. *Pictorial History of American Ships on the High Seas and Inland Waters.* New York: A. S. Barnes and Company, 1953.

Gould, Emerson W. *Fifty Years on the Mississippi.* Columbus, Ohio: Long's College Book Co., 1951 (orig. pub. 1889).

Hunter, Louis C. *Steamboats on the Western Rivers: An Economic and Technological History.* New York: Dover Publications, 1993 (orig. pub. 1949).

Merrick, George B. *Old Times on the Upper Mississippi: The Recollections of a Steamboat Pilot from 1854 to 1863.* Minneapolis: University of Minnesota Press, 2002 (orig. pub. 1909).

Owens, Harry P. *Steamboats and the Cotton Economy: River Trade in the Yazoo-Mississippi Delta.* Jackson: University Press of Mississippi, 1990.

Robson, Nancy Taylor. *Woman in the Wheelhouse.* Centreville, Md.: Tidewater, 1985.

Skalley, Michael R. *Foss: Ninety Years of Towboating.* Seattle: Superior Publishing, 1981.

Leland D. Baldwin
Cynthia R. Poe

See also **Bargemen; Canoe; Flatboatmen; Galley Boats;** *New Orleans;* **Packets, Sailing; Rafts and Rafting; River and Harbor Improvements; Shipbuilding; Towboats and Barges; Waterways, Inland.**

RIVERS. America's rivers played a vital role in the early exploration, settlement, and development of the country. Long before white settlers arrived on American shores and began following river channels into the country's interior, Native peoples had been canoeing the waterways of the continent. Some of the detailed maps the indigenous cartographers created still exist today.

River Pathways to Exploration

The exploration of America via river travel boasts a history that includes nearly every major waterway. Among the first European explorers was Captain John Smith, who in 1608 traveled the POTOMAC RIVER, a body of water that traverses nearly 400 miles to form the fourth-largest watershed on the East Coast. Settlers established the colony of Maryland on the lower Potomac less than twenty-five years later, and colonization of the northern Virginia shore followed within a decade.

Commissioned by the Dutch East India Company, Captain Henry Hudson began his exploration of America's northeastern coast in 1609, eventually sailing into the mouth of a river near today's New York City. He hoped the river, now named the Hudson River, would offer a passage west to the Pacific. However, near the location of present-day Albany he found the river too shallow to continue and was forced to turn back.

The early seventeenth century also marked the first time the 1,200-mile-long Columbia River appeared on European maps—after Spanish maritime explorer Martin de Auguilar located it in the Pacific Northwest. That river would eventually become one of the many water highways used by the LEWIS AND CLARK EXPEDITION of 1804 to 1806. During that same expedition, Meriwether Lewis and William Clark depended heavily on the Missouri River, using it and its tributaries to transport them from St. Louis to the northern plains and on to Montana.

Without question, the Mississippi River has also played an important role in the European exploration of America. In 1673, Jacques Marquette and Louis Joliet traveled the Upper Mississippi River, descending the Wisconsin River and returning to Lake Michigan via present-day Illinois. Others soon followed, and the Mississippi quickly became a major artery of traffic.

Rivers As Sources for Early Industrial Transport and Power

The mid-1600s began to see rivers as major thoroughfares of transportation for moving both people and products, and there was scarcely a hamlet or a trading post that did not have water connection with the coast. Through the better part of three centuries, such rivers as the Saint Croix, Penobscot, Kennebec, Androscoggin, Saco, and Piscataqua bore millions of logs downstream from the vast forests of Maine until timber resources diminished.

The Merrimack River, until the coming of the railroads, carried a significant portion of New Hampshire's goods, principally timber and granite, to towns below, and especially to its nearest large market, Boston. Parts of New Hampshire and Vermont depended upon the Connecticut River. Northwestern Vermont and northern New York traded with Quebec and Montreal via the Richelieu and Saint Lawrence Rivers.

Rivers also became significant sources of power for sawmills and gristmills. Along the Piscataqua, which stretched from Maine to New Hampshire, a sawmill sprang up as early as 1631 that produced lumber, shingles, and barrel staves. A multitude of other sawmills that depended on river power followed.

Gristmills, or operations for grinding grain, also utilized rivers for generating power, as did rice and textile mills. In the early nineteenth century, the fast-running Willimantic River attracted many cotton manufacturers from Rhode Island and Massachusetts. They situated their water-powered cotton mills in Willimantic, Connecticut, and along the length of the Quinebaug and Shetucket Rivers. The city of Willimantic eventually became a major American center for silk thread and cloth production between the end of the Civil War and the outbreak of World War II.

Rivers As Sources of Transportation

During the eighteenth century, thousands of newcomers traveled up the western tributaries of the Susquehanna and Potomac Rivers, crossed the watershed, and followed the Youghiogheny, Monongahela, Conemaugh, and Allegheny Rivers downward to populate the Ohio Valley. The great Mississippi River system then became the settlers' highway, and their natural markets included the French communities of Saint Louis and New Orleans. Most were in favor of the War of 1812 because a conquest of Canada would add a new commercial outlet to the east through control of the Saint Lawrence River. George Washington and others warned that if better connections were not established with the Ohio Valley residents, their allegiance might follow their trade down the Mississippi to the Spaniards. The Mississippi River system played a significant role until the railroads began cutting across the natural trade routes.

Farther south, emigrants from Virginia and the Carolinas pushed up the James, Dan, Yadkin, and Catawba Rivers, through the mountains, to populate southwestern Virginia and northeastern Tennessee. The men of that region, in signifying their allegiance to the Revolution, spoke of themselves as "Men of the settlements beyond the Alleghenies, where the Watauga and the Holston flow to the Tennessee." Some of the earliest settlers of Nashville left a fort on the Holston River on 22 December 1779 and journeyed down the Holston and the Tennessee in flatboats. They worked up to the mouth of the Cumberland River, and traveled up the Cumberland to the site of Nashville, which they reached on 24 April 1780 after a journey of some 1,300 miles.

Down the lower Atlantic coast were many broad rivers, really estuaries, having tidewater far upstream from their mouths (Patuxent, Chester, Choptank, Nanticoke, Potomac, Rappahannock, York, James, Chowan, Roanoke, Pamlico, Cape Fear, Pee Dee, Santee, Cooper, Saint Johns, and others). These rivers were the chief highways for regular travel as well as for freight transport and saw much traffic in the early days. Great plantations clustered along them, with the mansions fronting the water.

Commercial River Transportation

With the coming of steam technology and before railroads replaced river transport, steamboats began to populate the rivers, particularly in the Midwest and South. Some steamboats traveled where channels were so narrow that they could not turn around except by backing into the mouth of a tributary stream; most could operate only in parts of the winter and spring, when the water was high. Rivers such as the Cumberland, where boats once ran 150 miles or more above Nashville, could pose difficulties for their navigators, and it was said that a town might hear a boat whistle across a bend in the early morning and not see the craft until late afternoon. Mark Twain, enamored with river travel and steamboats, once said a river is a "wonderful book [with] a new story to tell every day."

In California, when the gold rush began in 1849, the Sacramento and San Joaquin Rivers were almost the only feasible way to travel from San Francisco to the mining regions. There were no steamboats, and many gold-seekers paid high fees for passage upstream in a skiff or yawl, with the understanding that they were to help with the rowing. Others traveled in slow-moving sailing vessels. A steamer built in New York for the Atlantic coast trade went safely around Cape Horn and began operating on the Sacramento River; and until another one followed it four months later, its rates were so high that it earned $20,000 or more on a round trip. After 1855, the Columbia River likewise became the main route to and from the Pacific coast from the mining regions of Idaho and northeastern Washington.

Rivers' Role in Warfare

Rivers have played an important part in the nation's warfare. The French and Indian War took place almost entirely along rivers or intervening lakes. The French came down the Allegheny to seize the forks of the Ohio and build Fort Duquesne. Washington marched by the Potomac, Wills Creek, and the Youghiogheny on his ill-fated expedition of 1754.

The Ohio River was perhaps the most noted pathway of Indian warfare in American history. For decades, the upper Missouri River saw frequent Indian attacks upon white trappers, traders, and settlers. Much of the fighting of the Revolutionary War in New York State was done on, or immediately near, the Hudson and Mohawk Rivers.

In the Civil War the Potomac, the Rapidan, Rappahannock, North Anna, Chickahominy, and James Rivers served as important strategic barriers in the East, along which armies aligned themselves or fought. The division of Union Gen. George B. McClellan's army by the Chickahominy in the Seven Days' Battles came near being its ruin. The Potomac below Washington, D.C., provided a waterway by which the North could move armies quickly to block the mouth of the James. In the Midwest and South the Mississippi and its tributaries were among the chief objects of strategy. The seizure of the Mississippi in 1863 split the Confederacy in two and presaged its downfall. The Tennessee River furnished the route used by Gen. Ulysses S. Grant's army to reach Chattanooga in the autumn of 1863, and the Battle of Wauhatchie was fought to keep it open. The Red River (southern) witnessed an important but unsuccessful Union expedition in 1864 aimed at Texas.

Decline of River Transportation

In 1862, Congress passed the first of several railroad acts that would eventually connect the continent, lessening the need for rivers as a major mode of transportation within the commercial, public, and military sectors. At the beginning of the twenty-first century, the U.S. Army Corps of Engineers Navigation Data Center reported declining commercial traffic on many of the nation's waterways.

BIBLIOGRAPHY

Adams, Arthur G. *The Hudson through the Years.* Bronx, N.Y.: Fordham University Press, 1996.

Ambrose, Stephen E. *Undaunted Courage: Meriwether Lewis, Thomas Jefferson, and the Opening of the American West.* New York: Simon and Schuster, 1996.

Dietrich, William. *Northwest Passage: The Great Columbia River.* Seattle: University of Washington Press, 1996.

Hahn, Thomas F. *Cement Mills along the Potomac River.* Morgantown: West Virginia University Press, 1994.

Merrick, George Byron. *Old Times on the Upper Mississippi: Recollections of a Steamboat Pilot from 1854 to 1863.* Minneapolis: University of Minnesota Press, 2001.

Powell, John Wesley, and Anthony Brandt. *The Exploration of the Colorado River and Its Canyons.* Washington, D.C.: National Geographic Society, 2002.

Reps, John W. *Saint Louis Illustrated: Nineteenth-Century Engravings and Lithographs of a Mississippi River Metropolis.* Columbia: University of Missouri Press, 1989.

Worster, Donald. *A River Running West: The Life of John Wesley Powell.* New York: Oxford University Press, 2001.

Alvin F. Harlow
Kym O'Connell-Todd

ROADS.

Except for a brief spurt of road building around 1800, the continental United States was extended from the Atlantic coast to the Pacific without the benefit of good roads. The United States had few roads prior to the twentieth century, and most were of poor quality. In towns, most roads were unpaved until the late nineteenth century, and in rural areas most roads were little more than dirt paths into the twentieth century. Federal programs during the 1910s and again during the 1950s eventually provided the United States with adequate roads for motor vehicles.

Roads in Towns Before 1900

On maps, towns in colonial America and the newly independent nation appeared to have excellent roads. Colonial towns, such as Annapolis, Philadelphia, Savannah, and Williamsburg, were built according to founders' designs. Principal functions of the town, including court, church, market, and school, were placed at key locations, and main streets were laid out to connect the buildings.

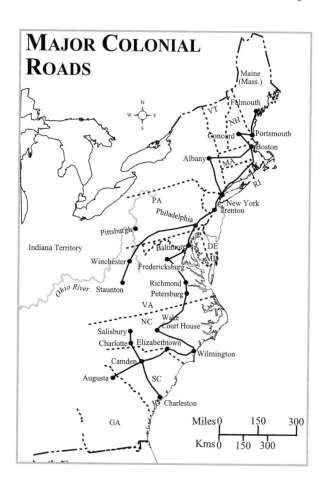

MAJOR COLONIAL ROADS

Squares and circles were placed at the points where the principal streets intersected. Other colonial towns, such as Boston and New York, had random mazes of streets said to be laid out by wandering cows.

Nineteenth-century cities were typically designed around a grid road pattern. Most dramatically, the Commissioners of Manhattan in 1811 laid out the entire island north of the colonial southern tip in a grid of wide avenues running north-south and narrow streets running east-west. As the city grew rapidly during the nineteenth century, the avenues were extended north and crossed by higher-numbered east-west streets. The rectangular blocks formed by the streets were more easily bought and sold by speculators and developers than the irregularly shaped parcels of most colonial settlements.

The main roads of colonial towns were laid with cobblestones obtained from ship ballast. Gravel and blocks made of wood or granite were also used for some road paving in nineteenth-century towns. Although travel on these uneven surfaces was jolting, stones and blocks were an improvement on the vast majority of roads made of dirt. In 1890 the percentage of unsurfaced roads exceeded 30 percent in Washington, D.C., 40 percent in Pittsburgh, and 80 percent in New Orleans and Kansas City. In smaller towns nearly all streets were dirt or gravel. Even Manhattan had many dirt roads in the late nineteenth century.

As cities grew rapidly during the nineteenth century, the poor condition of the roads became an important sanitary issue, not just an inconvenience. Excrement dropped by animals and waste thrown out windows by humans was ground into the dirt or the gaps between stones, spreading diseases such as cholera, typhoid, and dysentery through direct contact and contaminated water supplies.

Cities made major strides in paving roads during the last two decades of the nineteenth century. Brick was widely used beginning in the mid-1880s, especially in midwestern cities. Philadelphia had the highest number of bricks in 1898—2 million square yards—although Des Moines, Columbus, and Cleveland claimed more bricks per capita. Asphalt, already widely used in London and Paris, became a popular paving surface after the discovery of natural beds of pitch in Trinidad, and U.S. cities had 30 million square yards of asphalt paving in 1898. By 1900, after two decades of intensive improvements, Washington, D.C. boasted that it was the best-paved city in the world, and other U.S. cities, especially those along the East Coast, made similar claims.

Rural Roads Before 1900

The first rural routes were one-foot-wide paths traced by deer, buffalo, and other animals, or tamped down by Native Americans on foot. Pioneers of European heritage introduced horses and wheeled vehicles to the trails. Colonial governments, beginning with the Massachusetts General Court in 1639, laid out roads between towns, but few were actually constructed, and most long-distance travel in colonial times was by boat.

The most ambitious road project in the colonial era was the 1,300-mile King's Highway between Boston and Charleston, South Carolina, linking all thirteen colonies. The stretch between Boston and New York opened in 1673, and was widely known as the Boston Post Road because the route was used for postal delivery. Four years earlier, a post road had been opened from New York to Albany, and several others were constructed during the late seventeenth century to carry mail between the colonies. The entire King's Highway was completed in 1750.

Regular service to carry passengers and goods by horse-drawn covered wagon was inaugurated along the King's Highway and other POST ROADS in the years immediately before independence. The fastest service, called the "flying machine," took only a day and a half between Philadelphia and New York during the 1770s, but most intercity travel was difficult: the first regularly scheduled stagecoach route between New York and Boston in 1772 took one week, and it took George Washington twelve days to ride from Philadelphia to Boston to take command of the American army.

Fur traders and other European-descendent travelers to the West also followed paths created by animals and Native Americans. European Americans carved out new trails in the interior during the 1770s, including the Watauga Road from Virginia's Shenandoah Valley to east Tennessee in 1773, and the WILDERNESS ROAD into Kentucky in 1775. Hundreds of agents organized packhorse transportation along these trails, carrying tools, salt, and cloth west to settlers and returning east with farm products. Philadelphia became the center of packhorse transportation, utilizing such routes as the Forbes Trail across Pennsylvania.

Road building into the interior was extensive in the years immediately after independence, as the new country sought to tie together disparate colonies and a vast frontier. Lacking money to build and maintain roads, states turned to private companies beginning in 1790, when Pennsylvania offered a charter to the Philadelphia and Lancaster Turnpike Company. The company started building a road in 1792 and in 1794 opened the first sixty-two miles. The road was called a turnpike because a gatekeeper turned a pole armed with pikes to permit travelers to pass through after paying the toll.

When the Philadelphia and Lancaster Turnpike proved profitable, it was later extended further west, and hundreds of charters were awarded to turnpike companies by Pennsylvania and other states. Turnpike authorities were typically authorized to erect tollgates every five to ten miles and to charge ten to twenty-five cents. Tolls were used to pay for construction and maintenance.

The turnpike era culminated with the construction of the National Pike, authorized by Congress in 1806. The first 130-mile stretch between Cumberland, Mary-

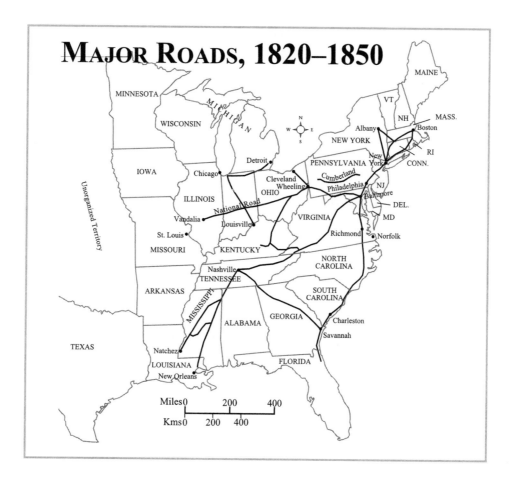

MAJOR ROADS, 1820–1850

land and Wheeling, West Virginia, known as the CUMBERLAND ROAD, followed a narrow dirt trail known as Nemacolin's Path, created around 1750 by the Delaware Indian chief Nemacolin and Colonel Thomas Cresap. Contracts were given out in 1811, but the War of 1812 delayed the start of construction until 1815, and it was completed in 1818. The National Pike was later extended across Ohio and Indiana and terminated in Vandalia, Illinois. A planned extension to Jefferson City, Missouri, was not built.

The Cumberland Road and other early turnpikes were constructed of crushed stone, but the rest of the National Pike and other later turnpikes were surfaced with macadam, named for Scottish engineer John McAdam, in which a layer of compacted small stones was cemented into a hard surface by stone dust and water. Wetlands and small streams were crossed by placing logs side by side, a style known as corduroy.

Taking advantage of the well-built turnpikes, large heavy vehicles that would have become stuck on dirt roads were placed in service beginning in the 1820s. Concord coaches, pulled by a team of four to six horses, were built in three sizes—six, nine, and twelve passenger coaches—while Conestoga wagons, pulled by six to eight horses, carried freight. A dozen stagecoach lines carried passengers along the National Pike from Washington, D.C. to

Wheeling in thirty hours, to Columbus, Ohio in forty-five hours, and to Indianapolis, Indiana in sixty hours.

Rural road construction came to a halt in the United States in the face of competition from canals and especially railroads. Many of the turnpike companies went bankrupt during the 1840s, and the roads deteriorated through neglect during the second half of the nineteenth century. Plank roads, made of wood, were constructed during the 1840s, but these quickly decayed and were not repaired.

Roads in the Automotive Age
The United States had the world's most extensive railroad network in 1900—and some of the world's worst roads. Through the twentieth century, road construction and motor-vehicle ownership reinforced each other. As motor-vehicle sales grew rapidly—exceeding 1,000 for the first time in 1899, 100,000 in 1909, and 1 million in 1916—Americans demanded and got good roads. At the same time, road construction stimulated increased usage of motor vehicles and, ultimately, dependence on them.

When the Office of Public Roads Inquiries undertook the first inventory of all U.S. roads in 1904, the country had 2,151,570 miles of rural public roads, but 1,997,908 miles, or 93 percent, were dirt. Of the 153,662 miles with any kind of surfacing, only 38,622 miles were stone or macadam, while the remainder included 108,232 miles of gravel and 6,810 of shell, sand, clay, brick, or other materials. Only a few hundred miles of roads in the entire country were suitable for motor vehicles.

A majority of Americans still lived in rural areas in the early twentieth century, but operating a motor vehicle there was nearly impossible because of poor-quality—or nonexistent—roads. Consequently, most vehicles were purchased by people living in cities, where streets were paved. Roads in rural areas served primarily as feeders into train stations. A few miles from stations, roads would terminate at streams or county lines or simply disappear into the mud. The cost of hauling grain ten miles from farm to station by road was higher than the cost of hauling it five hundred or one thousand miles by train to big-city markets. It could take an entire day to travel twenty miles in a rural area.

Good Roads Movement

Bicycling was booming as a leisure activity in 1900, and cyclists demanded good roads. The United States had 18 million horses in 1900, and many of their owners also demanded good roads. Bicycle and buggy owners were soon joined by millions of owners of Model Ts, produced on the Ford Motor Company's moving assembly line and sold at a price that was affordable for most American households.

Several organizations pushed for good roads. The League of American Wheelmen founded *Good Roads Magazine* in 1892 to promote the need for public roads. The National League of Good Roads lobbied for trained engineers to supervise road construction and educated farmers on the benefits of good roads. The National Good Roads Convention in St. Louis in 1903 heard President Theodore Roosevelt declare that a people who could tame a continent should be able to build good roads. In 1919 Colonel Dwight Eisenhower led an army convoy through the West to demonstrate the poor quality of roads and the resulting adverse impact on national security.

For motor vehicle owners, a top priority was construction of a highway linking the East and West Coasts. In the absence of public funding for highway construction, Indianapolis Motor Speedway owner Carl Fisher led a campaign to finance through private contributions the construction of a coast-to-coast highway named the Lincoln Highway, as a memorial to the slain president. For example, to promote the use of cement in highway construction, the Lehigh Cement Company donated 1.5 million barrels (the first cement highway was poured in Michigan in 1908). The Lincoln Highway was completed in 1923.

New Jersey was the first state to finance road construction through taxes, in 1891. Similar legislation was enacted by Massachusetts and Virginia a year later, and in twenty-seven states by 1913. Massachusetts and New York were the only two states collecting license fees from car owners in 1903.

At the federal level, the Office of Road Inquiry (later the Office of Public Road Inquiries, and then the Office of Public Roads) was established in 1893 in the U.S. Department of Agriculture. But the federal government did not fund rural road construction until the 1916 Federal Aid Road Act. The act appropriated $75 million over five years to pay half of the cost of building rural post roads, up to $10,000 per mile (later raised to $20,000 per mile). States had to agree to pay the remaining half, maintain them, and keep them free of tolls. The amount of surfaced roads in the United States increased from 257,291 miles in 1914 to 521,915 miles in 1926. When the system was completed during the 1930s, 90 percent of the population lived within ten miles of a Federal Aid road.

The Federal Highway Act of 1921 called for the designation of a national highway system of interconnected roads. No more than 7 percent of a state's public roads could be included in the system. The complete national system of 96,626 miles was approved in 1926 and identified by the U.S. highway numbers still in use. The Boston Post Road became part of U.S. 1, the Lincoln Highway part of U.S. 30, and the National Pike part of U.S. 40.

Limited-access parkways modeled on the German *autobahn* highways were built during the 1930s. The New York metropolitan area had a particularly large number of parkways, thanks to longtime parks commissioner Robert Moses, who wanted motorists to have access to the beaches of Long Island and the forests of Westchester County. Envisioning the New York parkways as for recreational driving only, Moses had the clearances under the bridges crossing the parkways designed too low for trucks. The Arroyo Seco Parkway (now the Pasadena Freeway), the first modern freeway in the Los Angeles area, opened in 1940, as did the Pennsylvania Turnpike, the first long-distance limited-access highway through rural areas. Toll roads were built throughout the Northeast between Maine and Illinois in the years immediately after World War II.

Federal interest in limited-access highways dates from the 1938 Federal Aid Highway Act, which proposed a 26,700-mile national system. The 1944 Federal Aid Highway Act expanded the proposed system to 40,000 miles, and the 1952 Federal Aid Highway Act provided the first token appropriation for their construction.

The landmark legislation was the Federal Aid Highway Act of 1956, which established a 44,000-mile toll-free National System of Interstate and Defense Highways and committed the federal government to pay 90 percent of the cost. Most of the miles of interstate highways were constructed to connect cities, but most of the dollars were spent to cross inside cities.

Impact of Interstate Highways

The trucking industry especially benefited from the interstate highways. Rail and truck shared in the growth of freight handling during the first half of the twentieth century about evenly, railroads going from 896 million tons in 1906 to 1.4 billion in 1950, and trucks from nil in 1906

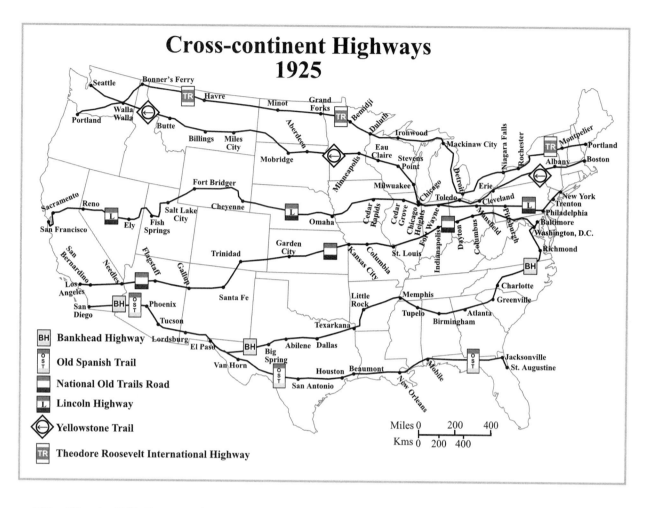

Cross-continent Highways 1925

- **BH** Bankhead Highway
- **OST** Old Spanish Trail
- National Old Trails Road
- **L** Lincoln Highway
- Yellowstone Trail
- **TR** Theodore Roosevelt International Highway

to 800 million in 1950. But over the next two decades, after most rural interstate highways were completed, truck haulage more than doubled to 1.9 billion tons, whereas railroads carried 1.5 billion tons, about the same as in 1950. Railroads were relegated to longer-distance hauling.

With construction of the interstate highways, the United States became a nation of suburbanites. The number of Americans living in suburbs increased from 30 million in 1950 to 120 million in 1990, whereas the number in cities of at least 50,000 inhabitants declined from 60 million to 40 million, and the number in rural areas declined from 60 million to 50 million. In 1950, 40 percent of Americans lived in rural areas, 40 percent in cities, and 20 percent in suburbs. A half-century later, after construction of the interstate highways, 20 percent of Americans lived in rural areas, 20 percent in cities, and 60 percent in suburbs.

People drove farther because they needed to do so to reach jobs, shops, and recreation. Taking advantage of the increased speeds afforded by cars, people chose to make longer trips rather than to reduce travel time. The average motorist drove 25 percent more per year in 2000 than in 1950. Average commuting distance increased 15 percent just between 1950 and 1960, offsetting a 15 percent in-

crease in average speed that decade. Private ownership of cars enabled Americans to move to suburban houses and travel to shops, jobs, and entertainment downtown. Soon the shops, jobs, and entertainment moved to the suburbs, where most of the people lived.

Interstate highways enabled more Americans to drive many more vehicles many more miles on a few more roads, and suburbanization required them to do so. In 1950, 150 million Americans drove 48 million vehicles 458 billion miles on 2 billion miles of paved roads. A half-century later, 250 million Americans drove 201 million vehicles 2.4 trillion miles on 4 billion miles of paved roads. Thus the number of Americans increased by two-thirds, the number of roads doubled, the number of vehicles quadrupled, and the number of miles driven increased six-fold.

Roads in the Twenty-First Century
Faced with the difficulty of increasing capacity through new road construction, engineers tried to ease congestion in the early twenty-first century by making more efficient use of existing highways through designating carpool lanes, building park-and-ride lots, and encouraging employers to stagger work hours. Technological improvements further helped traffic flow. A navigation system in the vehi-

cle, receiving continuously updated traffic data from satellites, alerted the driver to traffic jams and suggested alternate routes. Heavily used freeways were reconstructed with sensors in the pavement that could in the future control speed and distances between vehicles by regulating acceleration, braking, and steering.

Demand was also reduced by charging motorists for the use of existing roads and building new toll roads. Private or special-purpose public agencies gained authorization to construct new freeways during the 1990s, much as railroad companies did a century earlier and turnpike companies two centuries earlier. The California Private Transportation Company built a four-lane highway in Orange County parallel to the congested eight-lane Riverside Freeway (CA 91) between CA 55 on the west and the Riverside County line on the east. The company offered a money-back guarantee that the road would be congestion-free. The promise was kept by changing the toll by time of day, perhaps 25 cents at night and $4 during rush hour. A sign at the entrance to the road announced the cost at that moment to use the road. As the traffic volume increased, the cost was raised until sufficient motorists had chosen the old free road to maintain congestion-free driving on the toll road. Motorists could use the toll road only if they had purchased in advance windshield transponders that recorded the fares then in effect. Tolls were collected through monthly statements based on the records generated by the transponders rather than at tollbooths. Vehicles entering the road without transponders were noted by a sensor, and tickets of at least $100 were issued, either in person by highway patrol officers or through the mail.

Despite the wide variety of available technological strategies, congestion persisted, primarily because most Americans did not behave the way traffic engineers and economists thought they "should." In the 1950s, planners conducted elaborate studies to determine the optimal locations for new roads in response to travel demand patterns. The location of residences, shops, offices, and entertainment centers generated measurable amounts of traffic at specific times of the day. New roads were situated to accommodate existing and projected demand.

Ignored in the planning was the reciprocal relationship between roads and land uses. Roads were located in response to changing land uses, but in reality they also caused changing land uses. A highway built in the middle of nowhere soon sprouted commercial establishments and residential subdivisions near the interchanges. Engineers learned that if they built roads, motorists would come.

BIBLIOGRAPHY

Flink, James J. *The Automobile Age.* Cambridge, Mass.: MIT Press, 1988.

Garrison, William L., et al. *Studies of Highway Development and Geographic Change.* New York: Greenwood Press, 1969.

Goddard, Stephen B. *Getting There: The Epic Struggle Between Road and Rail in the American Century.* New York: Basic Books, 1994.

Hart, Virginia. *The Story of American Roads.* New York: Sloane, 1950.

Hokanson, Drake. *The Lincoln Highway: Main Street Across America.* Iowa City: University of Iowa Press, 1988.

Holbrook, Stewart Hall. *The Old Post Road: The Story of the Boston Post Road.* New York: McGraw-Hill, 1962.

Jordan, Philip D. *The National Road.* Indianapolis, Ind.: Bobbs-Merrill, 1948.

Kaszynski, William. *The American Highway: The History and Culture of Roads in the United States.* Jefferson, N.C.: McFarland, 2000.

Patton, Phil. *Open Road: A Celebration of the American Highway.* New York: Simon and Schuster, 1986.

Rae, John B. *The Road and the Car in American Life.* Cambridge, Mass.: M.I.T. Press, 1971.

Rubenstein, James M. *Making and Selling Cars: Innovation and Change in the U.S. Automotive Industry.* Baltimore: Johns Hopkins University Press, 2001.

James M. Rubenstein

See also **Conestoga Wagon; Federal-Aid Highway Program; Interstate Highway System; Stagecoach Travel; Suburbanization; Toll Bridges and Roads; Transportation and Travel.**

ROADS, MILITARY. From the colonial period to the beginning of the twentieth century, the construction of military ROADS resulted in many notable achievements: the Braddock Road, cut through the wilderness to Fort Duquesne in 1755; the backbreaking labors of Continental troops struggling to clear a path for guns captured at Fort Ticonderoga in the first year of the American Revolution; George Rogers Clark's road to Kaskaskia and Vincennes, built in 1778 and 1779; supply routes to the forts of the Old Northwest; the long stretches of corduroy road laid by the engineer battalion in the Civil War; the blazing of jungle trails in the Philippines during the insurrection of 1899–1902; and the road constructed in 1916 by engineers of the punitive expedition to Mexico, which made possible the first motorized movement by an army.

World War I and World War II called forth prodigious road-building efforts. In 1918, engineers of the American Expeditionary Forces repaired war-torn French highways and rebuilt and maintained roads across no-man's-land and beyond. World War I—the first conflict to require construction of substantial hard-surfaced roads—witnessed the debut of army engineer units trained especially for road building. In World War II, U.S. Army engineers completed more than ten thousand miles of road in the southwest Pacific area alone; and two projects of that war—the Ledo Road, linking India with China, and the Alcan, or Alaska, Highway, stretching across northwestern Canada and southeastern Alaska—rank

Ledo Road. U.S. Army trucks travel along the extraordinary, long, and vital supply route built under the command of General Joseph Stilwell (and later renamed after him) in 1942–44 from Ledo, India, to Burma, where it linked up with the Burma Road into China. NATIONAL ARCHIVES AND RECORDS ADMINISTRATION

BIBLIOGRAPHY

Beck, Alfred M., et al. *The Corps of Engineers: The War Against Germany.* Washington, D.C.: Center of Military History, 1985.

Hill, Forest G. *Roads, Rails, and Waterways: The Army Engineers and Early Transportation.* Norman: University of Oklahoma Press, 1957.

Jackson, William Turrentine. *Wagon Roads West: A Study of Federal Road Surveys and Construction in the Trans-Mississippi West.* Lincoln: University of Nebraska Press, 1979.

Morse Joseph E., and R. Duff Green, eds. *Thomas B. Searight's The Old Pike.* Orange, Va.: Green Tree Press, 1971.

Lenore Fine
Jesse A. Remington / c. w.

See also **Interstate Highway System; Overland Trail.**

among the greatest military roads ever. The U.S. armed forces' largest engineering project in a foreign country involved reconstruction of highways in the Republic of Vietnam. Their efforts there linked the major towns of that country with some three thousand miles of modern, high-speed, asphalt-surfaced roads capable of bearing heavy loads.

The term "military roads" also has broader connotations. Since ancient times, roads have served a dual purpose. The great Roman highway system facilitated both military movements and trade. Similarly, the first large road-building project undertaken in the United States, the National Road, or CUMBERLAND ROAD, served not only postal and commercial purposes but also functioned as a military route. As one congressional sponsor emphasized, its utility "in time of war for the transportation of the munitions of war, and the means of defense from one point of the country to another . . . must be palpable and plain to every reflecting mind." Later, the army built myriad wagon roads in the trans-Mississippi West that carried both military supply trains and caravans of prairie schooners. During the twentieth century, designers planned and built the vast interstate highway system with both military and commercial ends in view.

The army turned to good account in civil works the experience it gained on military projects. For example, the U.S. Army Corps of Engineers designed and contructed the systems of scenic roads in Yellowstone and Crater Lake national parks and the initial highway network in Alaska. And it was by no means coincidental that an army engineer, Francis V. Greene, perfected asphalt as a street-paving material and adapted it for use in the North American climate.

ROBBER BARONS. At the turn of the twentieth century, crusading journalists and other critics scornfully labeled the leading business titans of the age, the "Robber Barons." The term grew from the overwhelming power these industrial giants wielded over many aspects of society and the resentment those suffering under their yoke felt. Disgust with the power of corporate America and individuals like Andrew Carnegie, John D. Rockefeller, and J. P. Morgan led to the growth of the PROGRESSIVE MOVEMENT and to reform efforts, including antitrust legislation, and investigative journalism, or muckraking.

Robber Barons were vilified for using the capitalist system to exploit workers, form anti-competitive trusts, and place the accumulation of wealth above all else. The belief that the rich could use whatever means necessary to increase their riches seemed to counter the ideals upon which the United States was founded. Muckraking journalists such as Ida Tarbell, who wrote about the abuses of Rockefeller's Standard Oil, reinforced the idea that the Robber Barons were a destructive force, a group of soulless industrialists willing to circumvent laws to achieve supremacy.

Although the exact origin of the term is unknown, Edwin L. Godkin, an editor of *The Nation* used the term in 1869, while during the same time period Senator Carl Schurz of Missouri used it in a speech. The term became a permanent part of the nation's lexicon after Matthew Josephson's *The Robber Barons* (1934) gained wide readership, particularly among historians. Josephson wrote his book in reaction to the generally business-friendly works of the pre–GREAT DEPRESSION 1920s, which painted the Robber Barons as benevolent leaders. Josephson viewed the Robber Barons as unscrupulous pirates fighting to control the nation's economy.

The 1940s and 1950s witnessed a revival of the view of business leaders as industrial statesmen, which reflected the image of America's post–World War II economic, military, and cultural hegemony. A new school of historians wrote about these leaders as exemplary figures.

Works in this vein include *John D. Rockefeller: The Heroic Age of American Enterprise* (1940) by Allan Nevins and *Triumph of American Capitalism* (1942) by Louis M. Hacker. In the same vein, but not quite as fawning, are two national prizewinning works: *Morgan: American Financier* (1999) by Jean Strouse and *Titan: The Life of John D. Rockefeller, Sr.* (1998) by Ron Chernow.

In the early twenty-first century, the public once again looked back on the Robber Barons much more favorably than they were viewed in their own times. Morgan and Rockefeller, for example, acquired tremendous wealth, but also donated large sums to philanthropic and cultural causes, and both had an innate sense of the social responsibility that came with great prosperity. Both worked diligently throughout their later years to become civic patron saints, believing that donating money would soften the legacy of their business actions.

The Robber Barons also benefited from the generally favorable light many high-profile chief executives enjoyed during the early twenty-first century. Comparisons of Morgan and Rockefeller to Microsoft's Bill Gates or Berkshire Hathaway's Warren Buffett were not filled with scorn, but a sense of admiration and respect. In addition, the resurgence of the biography as America's favorite source of historical information helped soften the sharp edges of many Robber Barons. In recent years, most of the Robber Barons have been the subject of big general history biographies that have been predominantly favorable.

BIBLIOGRAPHY

Chernow, Ron. *Titan: The Life of John D. Rockefeller, Sr.* New York: Random House, 1998.

Josephson, Matthew. *The Robber Barons: The Great American Capitalists, 1861–1901.* New York: Harcourt, 1934. Reprint, New York: Harvest, 1962.

Porter, Glenn. *The Rise of Big Business, 1860–1920.* 2d ed. Arlington Heights, Ill.: Harlan Davidson, 1992.

Strouse, Jean. *Morgan: American Financier.* New York: Random House, 1999.

Bob Batchelor

See also **Antitrust Laws; Muckrakers.**

ROBBERIES. In the 1990s, the United States experienced a boom in bank robberies, and in 1991, banks reported the greatest number in American history. Los Angeles accounted for 20 percent of the robberies, with an average take of $3,000 and 85 percent of thieves caught. While robbers lacked the drama and flair of such bandits from earlier eras as Bonnie Parker and Clyde Barrow or Willie "The Actor" Sutton, the new generation brought about the reinstitution of past practices. A holdup that netted $434,000 drove a Wells Fargo bank to post a $10,000 reward, a practice unknown since the 1890s. Automatic teller machines (ATMs) brought theft increases. With more than seventy-seven thousand ATMs nationwide early in the 1990s, they became prime sites for small robberies. In some cases, hackers were able to crack computer codes and steal cash. In rare instances, thieves removed entire machines, opened them, and stole their contents.

While law enforcement officers were successful in tracking down most bank robbers, they were less successful with armored car robberies and solved only one-third of 340 armored car heists between 1988 and 1992. The nation's largest open-road armored car robbery, in which thieves netted $10.8 million, remains unsolved. The theft occurred 26 June 1990, outside a convenience store in Henrietta, New York. In January 1993, in nearby Rochester, New York, thieves held up a Brink's depot and escaped with $7.4 million. Authorities arrested four men, alleging that most of the money was funneled to the Irish Republican Army. In what may have been the largest cash theft in history, owners of Revere Armored Car, Inc., were charged in 1993 with stealing as much as $40 million from client businesses and banks over three years. Attempts to have charges dismissed because the government failed to preserve the company's records failed in 1994.

The Isabella Stewart Gardner Museum in Boston was the site of the biggest art heist in history on 18 March 1990. Thieves stole thirteen pieces worth an estimated $200 million, including five works by Degas, a Vermeer, a Manet, and three Rembrandts. The thieves made their way through the museum and sliced paintings out of frames. In June 2001, thieves took a small painting by Marc Chagall worth $1 million from the Jewish Museum in New York City. A ransom note that arrived four days later promised to return the work in exchange for peace in the Middle East. The painting later reappeared without explanation in a post office in Topeka, Kansas.

On 15 September 1993, a 1960s radical surrendered in one of the nation's most infamous robbery cases. Katherine Ann Power turned herself in to police twenty-three years after driving the getaway car in a small-time robbery that turned deadly. A student and Vietnam protester, Power was involved in a plot to rob a Boston bank on 23 September 1970. While she waited in the car, an accomplice killed Boston police officer Walter Schroeder, father of nine children. Power fled and lived as a fugitive in various cities before settling in Oregon in 1977 under the name Alice Metzinger. Unable to overcome her conscience, she surrendered to authorities and began serving an eight-to-twelve-year sentence in September 1993; she was released in 1999.

BIBLIOGRAPHY

Grabosky, Peter N., Russell G. Smith, and Gillian Dempsey. *Electronic Theft: Unlawful Acquisition in Cyberspace.* New York: Cambridge University Press, 2001.

King, Jeffery S. *The Life and Death of Pretty Boy Floyd.* Kent, Ohio: Kent State University Press, 1998.

Milner, E. R. *The Lives and Times of Bonnie and Clyde.* Carbondale: Southern Illinois University Press, 1996.

Palmer, Norman, ed. *The Recovery of Stolen Art: A Collection of Essays.* London: Kluwer Law International, 1998.

Kathleen B. Culver / A. E.

See also **Crime; Northfield Bank Robbery; Stagecoach Travel; Train Robberies; Wells, Fargo and Company.**

ROBERTS ET AL. V. UNITED STATES JAYCEES,

468 U.S. 609 (1984), a case in which the Supreme Court ruled that the states may forbid SEX DISCRIMINATION not only in public accommodations but also in private associations whose membership is restricted. The CIVIL RIGHTS ACT OF 1964 exempted private clubs from its coverage, but by the 1980s, California and Minnesota had extended their bans on sex discrimination to cover these groups. Minnesota's law led to a confrontation between the local and national organizations of the Junior Chamber of Commerce (the Jaycees), which encouraged members to participate in community activities, including running for office. Membership was open to any eligible person who paid dues, and the Jaycees had welcomed all races, religions, and nationalities since it was founded in 1920. However, only males between the ages of eighteen and thirty-five could be full members.

Women began demanding Jaycee membership in the 1970s, arguing that exclusion denied them equal professional and civic opportunities. Some local chapters began admitting women, and when the national organization threatened to revoke the charters of the Minneapolis and Saint Paul chapters, the case ended up in the Supreme Court. The justices ruled unanimously that, in light of the Jaycees's traditionally inclusive membership, they "have demonstrated no serious burden on their male members' freedom of association." *Roberts* did not ban all sex discrimination in private associations; it held only that the Constitution did not bar the states from prohibiting sex discrimination in a group like the Jaycees. Nevertheless, one month after the decision, the national organization voted to admit women.

BIBLIOGRAPHY

Baer, Judith A. *Women in American Law: The Struggle Toward Equality from the New Deal to the Present.* New York: Holmes and Meier, 2002.

Judith A. Baer / A. R.

See also **Chambers of Commerce; Clubs, Exclusionary; First Amendment; Fraternal and Service Organizations; *Rotary International v. Rotary Club of Duarte*; Women in Public Life, Business, and Professions; Women's Rights Movement: The 20th Century.**

ROBINSON-PATMAN ACT,

or Federal Anti-Price Discrimination Act, was passed by Congress in 1936 to supplement the Clayton Antitrust Act of 1914, the first federal statute to expressly prohibit certain forms of price discrimination. Twenty years after the Clayton Act, the growth of chain stores such as A&P and Sears, Roebuck led many to fear that retail chains presented a threat to smaller, independent retailers. Proponents of the legislation, including the bill's sponsors, Senator Joseph Robinson and Representative Wright Patman, argued that the size of the chains gave them an unfair advantage over their smaller independent competitors by enabling them to negotiate unfair price concessions and rebates from their suppliers. Opponents of the legislation argued that discounts to chain stores merely represented the increased efficiency of such operations.

The act contains certain exceptions, but, in general, it requires sellers to sell to everyone at the same price and requires buyers with knowledge of the circumstances to buy from a particular seller at the same price as everyone else. It also prohibits sellers and buyers from using devices such as brokerage fees or services to accomplish indirectly what the act prohibits them from doing directly. The Robinson-Patman Act has not always been vigorously enforced by antitrust authorities.

BIBLIOGRAPHY

Gellhorn, Ernest, and William E. Kovacik. *Antitrust Law and Economics in a Nutshell.* 4th ed. St. Paul, Minn.: West Publishing, 1994.

Peritz, Rudolph J. R. *Competition Policy in America, 1888–1992: History, Rhetoric, Law.* New York: Oxford University Press, 1996.

Katherine M. Jones

See also **Antitrust Laws; Chain Stores; Prices.**

ROBOTICS.

Several centuries ago, people envisioned and created mechanical automata. The development of digital computers, transistors, integrated circuits, and miniaturized components during the mid- to late twentieth century enabled electrical robots to be designed and programmed. Robotics is the use of programmable machines that gather information about their environment, interpret instructions, and perform repetitive, time-intensive, or physically demanding tasks as a substitute for human labor. Few Americans interact closely with robotics but many indirectly benefit from the use of industrial robotics.

American engineers at universities, industries, and government agencies have led advancements in robotic innovations. The Massachusetts Institute of Technology Artificial Intelligence Research Laboratory Director Rodney A. Brooks stated that by 2020 robots would have human qualities of consciousness. His robot, Genghis, was built with pyroelectric sensors on its six legs. Interacting with motors, the sensors detected infrared radiation such as body heat, causing Genghis to move toward or away from that stimulus and to appear to be acting in a predatory way. Interested in the role of vision, Brooks devised robots to move through cluttered areas. He programmed

Dante II. This tethered, eight-legged walking robot, developed by the Carnegie Mellon University Field Robotics Center (with help from the National Aeronautics and Space Administration) to explore hostile environments safely, successfully collects data inside volcanic Mount Spurr, Alaska, on 28 July 1994. CARNEGIE MELLON UNIVERSITY SCHOOL OF COMPUTER SCIENCE

his robots to look for clear routes instead of dealing with obstructions.

Because they are small, maneuverable, and invulnerable to smoke and toxins, robots are used during disaster recovery and to defuse explosives and detect radiation. After the 11 September 2001 terrorist attacks, robots entered the World Trade Center rubble in search of victims and to transmit video images to rescuers. Robotic sensors are sensitive to ultrasonic waves, magnetic fields, and gases undetectable to humans. Some robots are used for airport security screening of luggage. Military robotic applications include the prototype robotic plane, the X-45, which was introduced in 2002 for combat service. Micro Air Vehicle (MAV) flying insect robots were programmed to conduct military reconnaissance, filming enemy sites.

Other uses of robotics include robotic surgical tools inserted through small incisions. These robotics are steadier and more precise than humans. Engineers have devised ways for robots to have tactile abilities to palpate tissues undergoing surgery with pressure sensors.

The space shuttle is equipped with a robotic arm to retrieve and deploy satellites. The International Space Station (ISS) utilizes a 58-foot robotic arm for construction. The robotic Skyworker was developed to maintain the completed ISS. Engineers envisioned a future robotic space shuttle. The Sojourner robotic rover traversed Mars in 1997, and later missions prepared more sophisticated robots to send to that planet.

People have controlled telerobotics via the Internet. The iRobot-LE moves according to remote controls, enabling observers to monitor their homes with their work computers. Engineers have programmed robotic lawnmowers and vacuum cleaners. Robotic toys such as Sony's companionable AIBO dog have appealed to consumers. Inspired by RoboCup robotic soccer matches, enthusiasts have planned to develop humanoid robots to compete against human teams.

As computer processors have become faster and more powerful, robotics has advanced. Some researchers have investigated biorobotics, combining biological and engineering knowledge to explore animals' cognitive functions. Evolutionary robotics has studied autonomous robots being automatically refined based on performance fulfillment and evidence of desired skills and traits.

Researchers have programmed robots to master numerous tasks, make decisions, and perform more efficiently. Engineers, such as those working on the Honda Humanoid Project, have aspired to create universal robots, which have similar movement, versatility, and intelligence as humans. Hans Moravec, director of the Mobile Robot Laboratory at Carnegie Mellon University, hypothesized that robots will attain the equivalent of human intelligence by 2040.

BIBLIOGRAPHY

Brooks, Rodney A. *Flesh and Machines: How Robots Will Change Us.* New York: Pantheon Books, 2002.

Dorigo, Marco, and Marco Colombetti. *Robot Shaping : An Experiment in Behavior Engineering.* Cambridge, Mass.: MIT Press, 1998.

Goldberg, Ken, ed. *The Robot in the Garden: Telerobotics and Telepistemology in the Age of the Internet.* Cambridge, Mass.: MIT Press, 2000.

———, and Roland Siegwart, eds. *Beyond Webcams: An Introduction to Online Robots.* Cambridge, Mass.: MIT Press, 2002.

Menzel, Peter, and Faith D'Aluisio. *Robo Sapiens: Evolution of a New Species.* Cambridge, Mass.: MIT Press, 2000.

Moravec, Hans P. *Robot: Mere Machine to Transcendent Mind.* New York: Oxford University Press, 1999.

Nolfi, Stefano, and Dario Floreano. *Evolutionary Robotics: The Biology, Intelligence, and Technology of Self-Organizing Machines.* Cambridge, Mass.: MIT Press, 2000.

Rosheim, Mark E. *Robot Evolution: The Development of Anthrobotics.* New York: Wiley, 1994.

Schraft, Rolf-Dieter, and Gernot Schmierer. *Service Robots.* Natick, Mass.: A. K. Peters, 2000.

Webb, Barbara, and Thomas R. Consi, eds. *Biorobotics: Methods and Applications.* Menlo Park, Calif.: AAAI Press/MIT Press, 2001.

Elizabeth D. Schafer

See also **Artificial Intelligence; Automation.**

ROCK AND ROLL was originally a youth-based musical form. It is hybrid in origin, drawing from African American musical forms, such as the BLUES and gospel, as well as from white country and folk music. The path of rock and roll is inextricably linked to one of race in America, and as such, its history is complicated and contested. Although widely debated, Jackie Bernston's "Rocket 88," pressed in 1951, is often cited as the first rock and roll record, and it stands as an apt starting point for understanding the form. Breston was born in Clarksdale, Mississippi, center of the delta blues. Sam Phillips, who would introduce Elvis Presley to the world on his Memphis-based Sun Records label, produced "Rocket 88." At the Sun Records' studio, blues singers such as Howlin' Wolf and B. B. King created music that younger white artists like Presley incoporated into their country-based styles. The result was a cultural revolution feared by many white adults because of its black origins and its overt sexuality, while at the same time fervently embraced by American youth. Presley was undoubtedly at the center of this revolt. Covering many black musicians' songs, including Junior Parker's "Mystery Train" and Big Mama Thornton's "Hound Dog," Presley, a Mississippi native, recorded his first hits in the mid-1950s, and he dominated music charts for decades. His performances departed radically from the staid white ballad singers of the era. Presley swung his hips so wildly that when playing for television's *The Ed Sullivan Show* in 1956, it showed him only from the waist up. Presley's appearance caused a sensation and broke all of television's single-night ratings up to then.

Black artists also recorded rock music that appealed to teens, white and black, throughout the 1950s. Chuck Berry, perhaps the greatest of the rock and roll poets, created enduring standards such as "Johnny B. Goode" (1958), and Little Richard topped charts with hits such as "Good Golly Miss Molly." Richard also stunned audiences with his frantic, explosive performances, earning him wide popularity among youth while drawing the enmity of the white establishment. By the late 1950s, another distinctive sound that would last through the 1960s emerged at Detroit's Motown Records, a black-owned recording studio. The Motown sound was characterized by a lead singer delivering melodic story lines accompanied by the elegant, tight harmonies of a backup group. Popular Motown artists included the Temptations, Smokey Robinson and the Miracles, and Diana Ross and the Supremes. By the end of the 1950s, rock and roll, made by and for youth, had become big business, and the lyrics turned increasingly to safe topics, namely a host of teen-

Elvis Presley. Rock and roll's most famous white pioneer—and idolized worldwide as its king, even decades after his death in 1977—performs in 1956. © CORBIS-BETTMANN

age problems—school, summer vacation, cars, parents, and young love.

Rock and roll seemed to stagnate at the end of the 1950s. Presley had joined the Army, Berry was in prison, and Little Richard was in (temporary) retirement. Some mourned the supposed loss of rock and roll's original rebellious, gutsy quality. By the mid-1960s, however, the popularity of the music soared again with the emergence of a number of British rock groups. Known as the "British Invasion," this era began with the debut of the Beatles, who dominated American popular music charts after their 1964 smash hit, "I Want to Hold Your Hand." Influenced greatly by Sun Records' artists, the Beatles were followed by other British recording groups, including The Who and the Rolling Stones, whose music derived from American blues. These latter British bands initiated a return to rock's blues orientation, albeit in louder and more electric incarnations. Another important transformation in rock and roll occurred in 1965 at the Newport Folk Festival when Bob Dylan, noted folk and protest singer, appeared playing an electric guitar, backed by an electrified band. While many were outraged over his bastardization of acoustic folk, others were enthusiastic. A synthesis of rock and roll and the folk revival followed, becoming known as "folk rock." By the mid-1960s, rock and roll, which was no longer perceived as just for dancing, became known simply as rock.

In the 1960s, rock mirrored the social and political tensions of the Vietnam War era. The spirit-possessed performances of Otis Redding (crossover gospel singer) to the hyperkinetic screams of James Brown ("Say it Loud—I'm Black and I'm Proud," 1968) asserted black pride, gave expression to the CIVIL RIGHTS MOVEMENT, and stunned white audiences. Motown artists also employed the African American tradition of "masking" messages within their songs. Marvin Gaye and Kim Weston's hit, "It Takes Two" (1967), for example, was a love song as well as a masked call for desegregation. The lyrics of other rock songs turned toward rebellion, social protest, sex, and drugs. Groups, such as the Jimi Hendrix Experience, approximated in music the aural experience of psychedelic drugs, creating a genre known as "acid rock," featuring long, repetitive songs with surreal lyrics. During the later 1960s, rock festivals became a fixture of American popular culture and a site of important protest activity. The most famous of these was WOODSTOCK (1969), held in rural New York.

The 1970s and 1980s also witnessed turning points in rock music. The "punk rock" of the mid-1970s was a response to the perceived stagnation of the genre and a nihilistic political statement. Emergent among British bands such as the Sex Pistols and the Clash, punk quickly became popular in the United States and has had a lasting influence on rock music. Funk and disco also emerged in the 1970s. Both were based largely on the polyrhythmic grooves of Brown and his band, the JBs. Disco, which flourished in gay communities, was met with a strong backlash, fed by homophobia as well as by the racism that has always challenged rock and roll. Funk coalesced around artists like Stevie Wonder, the one-time child prodigy of Motown. But George Clinton's Parliament and Funkadelic groups likely left funk's most enduring influence. Not only did Clinton's music create enduring social commentary, his beats became among the most sampled in rap music, a dominant musical form of the 1980s and 1990s. Whether rap is actually rock is debated, but it clearly captures the earlier rebellious and socially conscious energy of Little Richard and Motown. The music video of the 1980s, played on cable network's Music Television (MTV), changed how rock was promoted and consumed. Artists such as Madonna successfully exploited this new medium, combining sexual provocation and steely business acumen to win huge commercial success.

Initially considered a passing fad and vilified as the devil's music, this now highly varied musical form is well entrenched and widely popular around the world among all ages. In 1995, the Rock and Roll Hall of Fame and Museum was opened in Cleveland, Ohio, where it receives thousands of visitors each year.

BIBLIOGRAPHY

Bangs, Lester. *Psychotic Reactions and Carburetor Dung.* New York: Knopf, 1987.

Baraka, Amiri. *Blues People: Negro Music in White America.* New York: Morrow, 1963.

Decurtis, Anthony, et al. *The Rolling Stone Illustrated History of Rock and Roll.* 3d ed. New York: Random House, 1992.

Marcus, Greil. *Mystery Train: Images of America in Rock 'n' Roll Music.* 4th. ed. New York: Plume, 1997.

Palmer, Robert. *Rock & Roll: An Unruly History.* New York: Harmony Books, 1995.

Werner, Craig Hansen. *A Change is Gonna Come: Music, Race and the Soul of America.* New York: Plume, 1999.

Lisa M. Tetrault

See also **Jazz; Music: African American; Music: Gospel; Music: Popular; Music Industry; Music Television.**

ROCKEFELLER COMMISSION REPORT. The National Commission on Children, created by Congress in 1987, began its deliberations two years later and presented its report in 1991. Chaired by Senator John D. "Jay" Rockefeller IV of West Virginia, the commission was broadly based and included representatives of all levels of government, business and civic leaders, and child welfare administrators. Its purpose was to "assess the status of children and families in the United States and propose new directions for policy and program development." The resulting assessment was bleak: one in five children lived in poverty, two out of five were at risk for failure in school, one out of four was being raised by a single parent, and millions were involved in sexual promiscuity, drug and alcohol abuse, and crime. The commission recommended early intervention, support through government programs and workplace benefits, and a general shoring up of families. Most controversial among the recommendations were a proposed $1,000-per-child tax credit and a proposal that employers provide unpaid parental leave for births, adoptions, and other family emergencies. The commission proposed new federal spending of $52 to $56 billion annually, which gave rise to substantial public criticism.

BIBLIOGRAPHY

Downs, Susan. *Child Welfare and Family Services: Policies and Practice.* Boston: Allyn and Bacon, 2000.

Harr, John Ensor. *The Rockefeller Conscience: An American Family in Public and Private.* New York: Scribners, 1991.

Stein, Theodore. *Child Welfare and the Law.* Washington, D.C.: CWLA Press, 1998.

Ellen Gray/A. G.

See also **Lost Generation; National Urban League; Society for the Prevention of Cruelty to Children; Youth Movements.**

ROCKEFELLER FOUNDATION was established on 14 May 1913 "to promote the well-being of mankind throughout the world." In 2000 the foundation was the nation's thirteenth largest, with assets of $3.8 billion and annual giving of around $150 million. Over its history it has paid out more than $2 billion and has assisted nearly 13,000 fellows.

The foundation is the product of a long history of giving by Standard Oil founder John D. Rockefeller (1839–1937), who in the course of his life donated $540 million to philanthropic purposes, of which $182 million capitalized the foundation. His first major project was supporting the University of Chicago, to which he eventually gave $35 million. In 1901 he founded the Rockefeller Institute for Medical Research (now Rockefeller University), and the following year established the General Education Board (GEB), which targeted rural schools in the South and among African Americans. The GEB eventually paid out $325 million before dissolving in 1965. In 1909, he launched a public-health program in the South called the Rockefeller Sanitary Commission for the Eradication of Hookworm Disease, and it was the success of this program that led him to establish the Rockefeller Foundation.

Once the foundation was organized, John D. Rockefeller delegated philanthropic responsibilities to its trustees, never attending a board meeting. His son, John D. Rockefeller Jr. (1874–1960), made philanthropic work his primary career, heading the foundation's board from its first meeting until 1940 and eventually donating over $530 million of his own resources to various causes.

For fifteen years the foundation devoted itself primarily to public health and medical science. Its field staff extended campaigns against hookworm into many countries and undertook similar measures against other communicable diseases, particularly malaria and yellow fever. The joint development of a yellow fever vaccine by the foundation's field staff and laboratory investigators in 1937 culminated two decades of worldwide health activities.

The foundation was a major supporter of Abraham Flexner's plan for a "full-time" system of medical education, which dramatically changed medicine by a strategic emphasis upon basic research. It applied this model worldwide, first in China with the founding of Peking Union Medical College in 1917. In the 1920s, the foundation funded numerous medical schools and schools of public health in Europe, Brazil, Southeast Asia, and the Pacific, with similar emphasis upon basic research. In 1932 the natural science division came under the direction of Warren Weaver, who focused funding on "vital processes," leading to the development of new disciplines, among them molecular biology.

Another early interest was in "social hygiene," that is, issues of maternal health, sex education, and birth control. In the 1930s it funded research in reproductive endocrinology, and after World War II it would be one of the first to support Albert Kinsey's research in sexual behavior. It also supported the Population Council, contraceptive development, and especially population control.

The social sciences began receiving foundation attention in the 1920s through a partnership with the Laura Spelman Rockefeller Memorial, established in honor of Rockefeller's wife. Under the direction of Beardsley Ruml, it funded the development of university research departments, especially in international relations, sociology, economics, and public administration, and also helped create the Social Science Research Council, the National Bureau of Economic Research, and the London School of Economics. The foundation's humanities division, in partnership with the GEB, established the American Council of Learned Societies.

In the late 1930s, the foundation assisted more than three hundred scholars and scientists in escaping from fascism in Europe, and helped many to gain positions in American universities. After World War II it increasingly shifted resources to the overwhelming problems of the developing world. It helped begin the first "area studies" program in 1946 and, in partnership with other large foundations, expanded such programs to numerous research universities.

Its work in agriculture began in Mexico in the 1940s, where the foundation supported research into increased production of basic food crops, a worldwide program that led to the Green Revolution of the 1950s and 1960s. Rockefeller Foundation field scientist Norman Borlaug was awarded the Nobel Peace Prize for this work, making him one of more than 170 Nobel Prize winners who had been assisted by the foundation.

The Rockefeller Foundation has frequently worked in partnership with other foundations and agencies, in such fields as environmental affairs, race issues, conflict resolution, and the arts. In 2000 it reorganized to concentrate more on poverty and involving the poor in the grant-making process, with four divisions focused on culture, working communities, food security, and health equity.

BIBLIOGRAPHY

Fosdick, Raymond B. *The Story of the Rockefeller Foundation.* New York: Harper, 1952. Reprint, New Brunswick, N.J.: Transaction, 1989.

Harr, John, and Peter Johnson. *The Rockefeller Century.* New York: Scribners, 1988.

———. *The Rockefeller Conscience: An American Family in Public and in Private.* New York: Scribners, 1991.

Fred W. Beuttler

See also **Philanthropy.**

ROCKEFELLER UNIVERSITY is a world-renowned center for research and graduate education in the biomedical sciences, chemistry, and physics, located in New York City. It was founded in 1901 as the Rockefeller Institute for Medical Research through the philanthropy of John D. Rockefeller. Over the course of a century, Rockefeller scientists received twenty-one Nobel Prizes for achievements such as revealing the microscopic structures inside cells, discovering the Rh factor in blood, developing novel methods for synthesizing proteins, and uncovering the workings of chemical transmitters in the brain.

The Rockefeller Institute was modeled on European research centers such as the Koch Institute, where in the late nineteenth century scientists had identified the bacterial causes of many infectious diseases. But the Rockefeller Institute's mission under its first director, Simon Flexner, was broader than bacteriology. Flexner created laboratories in chemistry, physiology, and other areas, each headed by an independent investigator, to study the underlying causes of disease. This administrative structure, of independent laboratories reporting directly to the institution's head, has remained in place throughout Rockefeller's history. In 1906, the institute's permanent laboratories opened at York Avenue and Sixty-Sixth Street in New York City.

In 1910, Rockefeller Hospital opened, the first hospital in the United States devoted completely to clinical research. Here physician-researchers combined the care of patients with laboratory investigation of disease. Polio, heart disease, and diabetes were among the first diseases studied. Dedication to studying the basic biology and chemistry of disease was rewarded in 1944 with one of the most dramatic scientific discoveries of the century: Oswald T. Avery and colleagues, in the course of searching for a cure for pneumococcal pneumonia, found that DNA carries genetic information. Rockefeller Hospital was a model for dozens of clinical research centers in university hospitals and elsewhere in the early decades of the twentieth century.

Always a center for postdoctoral training in the sciences, the Rockefeller Institute expanded and formalized its commitment to education under its third president, Detlev Bronk. In 1955, the first class of students was admitted into a new Ph.D. program. In 1965, the institute officially became Rockefeller University, and in the early 1970s, a M.D.–Ph.D. program was launched with Cornell University Medical College, now called Weill Medical College. The participation of the Sloan-Kettering Institute made the M.D.–Ph.D. program tri-institutional.

The transition from institute to university was also marked by expansion, both in size and in the areas of research supported. Physicists and mathematicians joined the faculty, as well as researchers studying animal behavior. As of 2002, there were seventy-five laboratories at the university, and approximately 160 Ph.D. and M.D.–Ph.D. students. The university draws from a diverse base of financial support, including its endowment, private gifts, and sponsored government and private contracts.

BIBLIOGRAPHY

Corner, George W. *A History of the Rockefeller Institute, 1901–1953: Origins and Growth.* New York: Rockefeller Institute Press, 1965.

Hanson, Elizabeth. *The Rockefeller University Achievements: A Century of Science for the Benefit of Humankind, 1901–2001.* New York: Rockefeller University Press, 2000.

Elizabeth Hanson

See also **Education, Higher: Colleges and Universities; Medical Education; Medical Research; Science Education.**

ROCKETS. In their most basic form, rockets are uncomplicated machines. They comprise a fuel supply, a combustion chamber in which the fuel is burnt, and a nozzle through which the products of combustion—mostly hot gasses—can escape. Early rockets were little more than tubes closed at one end and filled with gunpowder. They were used for fireworks and for maritime rescue (as signals and carriers of lifelines), but they lacked the power and accuracy to be useful beyond these highly specialized niches. Military interest in gunpowder rockets was sporadic and limited. The British use of them to bombard Fort McHenry, near Baltimore during the War of 1812, for example, did more for American culture (by inspiring Francis Scott Key to write "The Star Spangled Banner") than it did for British military objectives.

Modern rockets emerged between 1920 and 1960 from the confluence of several technological break-

Robert H. Goddard. The spiritual father of modern rocketry, at the historic launch of the first liquid-fuel rocket, on 16 March 1926 at Auburn, Mass.

throughs: more powerful fuels, lighter structural elements, steering mechanisms, onboard guidance systems, and multiple stages. These changes set the stage for the rocket's development, from the late 1950s on, into a range of powerful weapons and a versatile tool for scientific exploration.

The Birth of Modern Rocketry, 1920–1960

Robert H. Goddard was the spiritual father but not the true founder of American rocketry. He tested his first solid-fuel rocket on 7 November 1918 and the world's first liquid-fueled rocket (burning gasoline and liquid oxygen) on 16 March 1926. Trained as a physicist, Goddard produced rockets notable more for innovative design features than for sound engineering. He also feared that rivals might steal his ideas—an obsession that led him to publish few papers and keep potential collaborators at arm's length. His genius was prodigious, but his influence was slight.

The foundations of American rocketry were laid, in a practical sense, by four small groups of scientists and engineers scattered across the country. The first of these groups, the American Rocket Society, was formed as the American Interplanetary Society in 1930 by a group of technically minded New York City science fiction writers (they renamed their group in 1934). Its leading members went on to found Reaction Motors, one of America's first rocket-building companies. A second important group coalesced in the late 1930s around aerodynamics expert Theodore von Karman at the California Institute of Technology (Cal Tech). In time this group gave rise to another early rocket-building firm: Aerojet. A third group, led by naval officer Robert Truax, formed in the late 1930s at the Naval Research Laboratory in Annapolis, Maryland. The fourth group consisted of 115 scientists and engineers from Germany's wartime rocket program, led by the charismatic Wernher von Braun and hired by the U.S. Army to apply their expertise to its nascent rocket-building program. They brought with them boxes of technical documents and scores of V-2 rockets—then the world's most advanced—in various stages of assembly. Reassembling and test-firing the V-2s under the Germans' direction gave army rocket experts their first practical experience with large ballistic missiles.

All four groups worked closely with the military. Von Braun's and Truax's were directly supported by the army and navy, respectively. Von Karman worked closely with General Henry H. "Hap" Arnold, commander of the U. S. Army Air Forces. Reaction Motors supplied the engines for most of the Air Force's experimental rocket planes, including the Bell X-1 that broke the "sound barrier" in 1947. Through their military projects, the rocket designers also made connections with established defense contractors. The foundations of a robust aerospace industry had thus been laid even before the end of World War II.

Peacetime V-2 Launch. One of the many German rockets brought to the United States after World War II (along with 115 scientists and engineers) is test-fired from the USS *Midway* off the Atlantic coast, 6 September 1947. AP/WIDE WORLD PHOTOS

The rockets that emerged from these collaborations in the late 1940s and early 1950s established the basic design elements used by American rockets for the rest of the century. These included multiple stages (1947), lightweight aluminum rocket bodies that doubled as fuel tanks (1948), and swiveling engines for steering (1949). High-energy kerosene derivatives replaced gasoline and alcohol in liquid-fuel rockets. Research at Cal Tech produced a viscous solid fuel that produced more power and higher reliability than traditional powders. Thiokol Chemical Corporation improved it and by the 1950s had enabled solid-fuel rockets to match the power of liquid-fuel ones. Combined, these features created a new generation of rockets. The first representatives—such as the Vanguard and Jupiter of the late 1950s—carried the first small American satellites into space. Later examples—such as Atlas and Titan of the early 1960s—had the power to carry a nuclear warhead halfway around the world or put a manned spacecraft into orbit.

Refinements and Applications, 1960–2000

President John F. Kennedy's May 1961 call to land a man on the moon "before this decade is out" gave von Braun and his team—then working for the National Aeronautics and Space Administration (NASA)—a chance to develop the largest rockets in history. The result was the Saturn V, which made possible nine lunar missions (six of them landings) between December 1968 and December 1972. Taller than the Statue of Liberty and heavier than a navy destroyer, the Saturn V generated the equivalent of 180 million horsepower at the moment of liftoff. However, the Saturn series was a technological dead end. No branch of the military had a practical use for so large a rocket, and (without the spur of a presidential challenge) the civilian space program could not afford to use them for routine exploration. Experiments with nuclear-powered rockets, pursued in the mid-1960s, were discontinued for similar reasons.

Saturn was, therefore, atypical of American rocket development after 1960. Specialization, rather than a continual push for more power and heavier payloads, was the dominant trend. The navy, for example, developed the Polaris—a solid-fuel missile capable of being carried safely aboard submarines and launched underwater. The air force developed the Minuteman as a supplement to the Atlas and Titan. It was smaller, but (because it used solid fuel) easier to maintain and robust enough to be fired directly from underground "silos." All three armed services also developed compact solid-fuel missiles light enough to be carried by vehicles or even individual soldiers. Heat-seeking and radar-guided missiles had, by the Vietnam War (1964–1975), replaced guns as the principal weapon for air-to-air combat. They also emerged, in the course of that war, as the antiaircraft weapons most feared by combat pilots. Warships, after nearly four centuries serving principally as gun platforms, were redesigned as missile platforms in the 1960s and 1970s. "Wire-guided" missiles, first used in combat in October 1966, gave infantry units and army helicopter crews a combination of mobility, accuracy, and striking power once available only to tanks.

The space shuttle, NASA's follow-up to the Project Apollo moon landings, defined another line of rocket development. Conceived as a vehicle for cheap, reliable access to space, it was powered by three liquid-fuel engines aboard the winged orbiter and two large solid-fuel boosters jettisoned after launch. Both were designed to be reusable. The orbiter's engines would, according to the design specifications, be usable up to fifty times with only limited refurbishing between flights. The boosters, parachuted into the Atlantic Ocean after launch, would be cleaned, refurbished, and refilled with solid fuel for later reuse. By the early 2000s the shuttle, since becoming operational in 1981, had achieved neither the high flight rates nor the low costs its designers envisioned. Its reusability was, nonetheless, a significant achievement in a field where, for centuries, all rockets had been designed as disposable, single-use machines.

BIBLIOGRAPHY

Bromberg, Joan Lisa. *NASA and the Space Industry.* Baltimore: Johns Hopkins University Press, 1999. Surveys NASA's evolving partnership with aerospace companies.

Heppenheimer, T. A. *Countdown: A History of Space Flight.* New York: John Wiley, 1997. Places rocket development in its social, political, and military context.

Ley, Willy. *Rockets, Missiles, and Men into Space.* New York: Viking, 1968. Dated, but useful for its lucid explanations and insider's view of early rocketry.

MacDougall, Walter A. *The Heavens and the Earth.* New York: Basic Books, 1985. Definitive history of the interplay of Cold War politics, military missiles, and the U. S. space program.

Winter, Frank. *Rockets into Space.* Cambridge, Mass.: Harvard University Press, 1990. A compact, nontechnical history of rocket technology.

A. Bowdoin Van Riper

See also **Missiles, Military; National Aeronautics and Space Administration; Space Program; Space Shuttle.**

ROCKY MOUNTAINS, a vast system extending over three thousand miles from northern Mexico to Northwest Alaska, forms the western continental divide. The system varies from 70 to 400 miles wide and from 5,000 to 14,433 feet high. Mount Elbert in Colorado is its highest peak. The mountains uplifted about 63 million years ago during the Laramide Orogeny. During the last Ice Age, eleven thousand years ago, glaciers carved peaks and valleys.

Spanish explorers in Mexico were the first Europeans to see the Rockies, and Francisco Vásquez de Coronado was the first European to see the U.S. Rockies in 1540. Then came the French, hunting furs and new trade routes via the Great Lakes and Canadian streams. As early as 1743 members of the La Vérendrye family saw the "shining mountains" in the Wyoming region. The English followed, and pelt-hungry American trappers and traders came up the Missouri River and its tributaries, gathering beaver skins and later buffalo hides. These mountain men trail blazed the Central Rockies. In the years between 1825 and 1845 mountain men scoured the area for beaver, the difficult work made more so by weather, hunger, isolation, conflict with Native Americans, and grizzlies.

Although informal explorations of the Rockies occurred before the Louisiana Purchase (1803), what lay west of them was unknown. President Thomas Jefferson commissioned an expedition (1804–1805) led by Meriwether Lewis and William Clark to determine the commercial potential of northwestern natural resources and to investigate the possibility of a cross-continental water passage. Zebulon Pike led a similar expedition in the Southwest in 1806–1807. Reports from both expeditions were favorable. Following them came a long period of competition between American, Canadian, and British companies for control of the mountain fur trade. Another important explorer, Jedediah Smith, in 1823 rediscovered the forgotten South Pass across the continental divide, which allowed the settlement of Oregon and California, the Mormon trek of 1847, and the California gold rush of 1849. In 1850 the mountain man Jim Bridger discovered a shorter pass running south from the Great Basin, which became the route for overland mail, the Union Pacific Railroad, and Interstate 80.

Though the mountains and intervening plateaus were uninviting, gold discoveries during the 1850s and 1860s led to permanent settlement in the Rockies and eventually to the formation of mountain states. Agriculture followed mining in the West, helped by mountain snows that fed the rivers and the irrigation canals in the semiarid country to the east. Later the states undertook reservoir construction and water reclamation and diversion projects. The vital importance of mountain watershed protection led to national forest conservation, though lumbering became an important industry in the Rockies' more heavily wooded areas.

The federal government established four national parks in the Rocky Mountain region, Yellowstone National Park in Wyoming, Montana, and Idaho (1 March 1872), the world's greatest geyser area; Grand Teton National Park in Wyoming (26 February 1929); Glacier National Park in Montana (11 May 1910); and Rocky Mountain National Park in Colorado (26 January 1915).

BIBLIOGRAPHY

Alden, Peter, et al. *National Audubon Society Field Guide to the Rocky Mountain States.* New York: Knopf, 1999.

Chronic, Halka. *Pages of Stone.* Seattle: Mountaineers, 1984–1988.

McPhee, John. *Rising from the Plains.* New York: Farrar, Straus, Giroux, 1986.

Schmidt, Jeremy. *Adventuring in the Rockies: The Sierra Club Travel Guide to the Rocky Mountain Regions of the United States and Canada.* San Francisco: Sierra Club Books, 1986.

Deirdre Sheets

See also **Lewis and Clark Expedition; Mountain Men; Western Exploration.**

RODEOS were initially an aspect of open-range ranching in the late nineteenth century, contests of skill between cowhands. Although the rodeo eventually became a professional sport, it began as an amusement of working cowboys. Rodeos and roundups alike brought together people who led socially isolated lives and were festivals in which horsepeople proud of their occupation and expertise displayed fancy riding and expert roping. Cowboys played card games on blankets spread out in the firelight, exchanged songs, and occasionally engaged in "augering" matches, contests in storytelling.

"Rodeo" comes from the Spanish *rodear,* to round up. Spanish settlers began the first ranching in America on the open range, and open-range conditions existed throughout the long period of expansion in the western United States. Barbed wire, which effectively parceled the land, was not introduced until the late 1860s, but laws evolved to regulate gathering stock while Texas and California were still Mexican territories. Roundups were opportunities for ranchers to exchange livestock that had drifted into other herds. Cattle were selected for slaughter; colts, calves,

Flint Hills Rodeo. This 1974 photograph shows cowboys gathered around the chutes during this major annual event in Strong City, Kan., between Topeka and Wichita. NATIONAL ARCHIVES AND RECORDS ADMINISTRATION

and unbranded animals were branded; young horses were broken; mares were "shaped up"; and animals belonging on distant ranges were separated out. Cowboys saw the gatherings as a way to mitigate the monotony and loneliness of long cattle drives, and riders from far and near participated.

During the 1870s and 1880s, with the Great Plains still largely unfenced, annual cattle drives brought owners and their herds together on drives to slaughterhouses near urban railheads. Roundups regulated by cattle associations of the Plains states that dwarfed the original rodeos systematized times, limits, and procedures. Although lesser numbers were common, often as many as two hundred to three hundred riders representing scores of brands gathered, and the general roundup boss directed units to each day's work, combing the range for strays, branding, and preparing cattle for shipping.

By the 1880s, various western towns hosted formalized cowboy competitions. These events were distinguished from the contests held by cowboys themselves by the presence of paying spectators. Around the same time, wild west shows, elaborate exhibitions that sensationalized life on the western frontier, also became popular. The most famous was Buffalo Bill's Wild West Show. In 1897, Cheyenne, Wyoming, began its annual exhibition, which became famous all over the continent as Frontier Days. The Calgary Stampede (in Canada) and the Pendleton Roundup (Oregon), both of which started later, became equally famous.

Women competed in the same events as men in early rodeos. Women remained prominent until the 1930s, when female rodeo fatalities and gender values enforced by some rodeo promoters reduced the roles of women in rodeos. Eventually, women's events were dropped, and women's roles in modern rodeos became largely marginal.

By the beginning of the twenty-first century, rodeos drew millions of spectators annually. Professionals followed the big rodeos, but all over the range country communities held rodeos in which local talent participated each summer and fall.

BIBLIOGRAPHY

Fredriksson, Kristine. *American Rodeo: From Buffalo Bill to Big Business.* College Station: Texas A&M University Press, 1985.

Wooden, Wayne S., and Gavin Ehringer. *Rodeo in America: Wrangler, Roughstock, and Paydirt.* Lawrence: University Press of Kansas, 1996.

J. Frank Dobie
Deirdre Sheets

See also **Cattle Drives; Cowboys; Wild West Show.**

ROE V. WADE, 410 U.S. 113 (1973), the landmark case establishing a woman's constitutional right to an abortion, was initiated by attorneys Sarah Weddington and Linda Coffee with Norma McCorvey as one of the plaintiffs. A single pregnant woman known as "Jane Roe" to protect her privacy, McCorvey had been denied an abortion under a Texas law. The 7 to 3 decision, which also covered *Doe v. Bolton*, a Georgia case, upheld federal appeals court's decisions striking down provisions of both the Texas and Georgia laws. Effectively rendered unconstitutional were all statutes that either prohibited abortion (Texas) or encumbered legal abortions in such excessive regulation as to make then virtually unattainable (Georgia).

The decision was the culmination of ongoing efforts of several groups seeking decriminalization and reflected changing public opinion about abortion. Support for legal reform had grown stronger when the news broke that the drug thalidomide, extensively prescribed to alleviate morning sickness in the early stages of pregnancy, produced severe physical defects in children. In a much publicized incident, Sherry Finkbine, an Arizona woman who had taken thalidomide, requested an abortion with the support of her doctors. Because of the threat of prosecution by local authorities, the Finkbines, seeking a more favorable legal climate, fled to Sweden where abortion was legal. Her plight dramatized to both the medical profession and ordinary citizens the need for legal change, as did figures on illegal abortions, which ranged from 200,000 to 1,200,000 annually. Fatalities for the women undergoing the procedure, always estimates, were high. In 1955, the annual American loss of women's lives was put at from three thousand to eight thousand.

The justices, no longer able to avoid the issue, agonized over the decision—none more than Justice Harry Blackmun, who wrote the majority opinion resting the right to an abortion on the right to privacy. The right to privacy in sexual and reproductive matters, while not specified in the Bill of Rights, had recently evolved. Building on *Griswold v. Connecticut* (1965), a case involving the use of birth control by a married couple, abortion rights lawyers had persuaded the lower courts to extend the right of privacy implied in the Fourth Amendment's guarantee against unreasonable searches to other reproductive decisions, notably whether to carry a fetus to term. That right, however, was never intended by the Court to be absolute. After much internal debate concerning the cutoff point at which the state's interest in protecting potential life should take precedence over a woman's right to terminate a pregnancy, the majority reached a compromise that Blackmun tied to the trimester system. During the first three months of pregnancy, a woman was to be free to make the decision in consultation with her doctor. In the second trimester, the states could regulate abortion in order to protect maternal health, but could not prohibit the procedure. While rejecting the notion that the fetus from the moment of conception was a constitutionally protected "person" under the Fourteenth Amendment, the Court used the stage in fetal development when survival was possible outside the woman's body as the point at which state interest in protecting potential life took precedence. Since viability occurred at approximately the end of six months, *Roe* stipulated that states could prohibit abortions in the third trimester.

The decision, which imposed the Court's regulatory formula upon the states, evoked intense resentment and high praise. Irate legislators charged that their law-making function had been usurped. Abortion rights supporters, dismayed that only three states had legalized abortion by 1970, rejoiced. Catholic clergy attacked the decision as sanctioning the taking of a human life, while mainline Protestant clergy appreciated the option it offered the anguished women they counseled. Legal critics found the fragile textual backing for privacy to be weak constitutional grounding for abortion rights and the trimester formula to be problematic. Others argued that the Court had moved too far too fast. Its mistake, they argued, was abandoning an incremental approach to the abortion issue that would have produced smaller changes over time, allowing the public time to adjust. Pro-choice attorneys, while elated by the scope of the decision, also had legal concerns. Fearful that relying on privacy instead of equal protection made the decision constitutionally vulnerable, they further criticized *Roe* as too medicalized, privileging physicians' autonomy over women's. Concerned that state regulation in later trimesters would not take into account the needs of pregnant woman, feminists warned that the Court's compromise could lead to government coercion and involuntary motherhood.

What was indisputable was the immediate formation of a grassroots movement by opponents eager to erode the abortion rights conferred in *Roe*. Although the Court initially rejected state restrictions, in 1980 it upheld the "Hyde Amendment" by which Congress refused to fund even medically necessary abortions of indigent women (*Harris v. Mc Rae*, 488 U.S. 297), a practice that many states followed. And in *Webster v. Reproductive Health Services* (1989), the Court, by a 5 to 3 vote, upheld the right of Missouri legislators to deny the use of public employees and facilities to perform or assist abortions. In *Planned Parenthood of Southeastern Pennsylvania v. Casey* (1992), the Court finally reaffirmed *Roe* in a 5 to 3 vote. But though the formal right to an abortion had survived, other tactics of the antiabortion movement had reduced it as a practical option, especially for poor and rural women.

BIBLIOGRAPHY

Garrow, David J. *Liberty and Sexuality: The Right to Privacy and the Making of* Roe v. Wade. Updated and with a new preface and epilogue. Berkeley and Los Angeles: University of California Press, 1998.

Petchesky, Rosalind P. *Abortion and Woman's Choice: The State, Sexuality, and Reproductive Freedom.* Rev. ed. Boston: Northeastern University Press, 1990.

Siegel, Reva. "Reasoning from the Body: A Historical Perspective on Abortion Regulation and Questions of Equal Protection," 44 (Jan. 1992): 261–381.

Jane Sherron De Hart

See also **Abortion; Equal Rights Amendment.**

ROGERS' RANGERS were the most colorful corps in the British-American army during the FRENCH AND INDIAN WAR. Under the command of Maj. Robert Rogers, the Rangers served as the eyes of Gen. James Abercromby's and Gen. Jeffrey Amherst's armies, conducted raids, scouted enemy forces, and captured prisoners. The Rangers' effectiveness came from their adoption of guerilla warfare. They typically marched through forests in single file as skirmishers ranged around them and used the cover of shrubs and bushes. Each ranger was also highly mobile and self-sufficient. If outnumbered, they fled and reassembled at a designated rendezvous point. Rogers' Rangers' audacious reputation made them famous throughout Great Britain and the colonies.

BIBLIOGRAPHY

Roberts, Kenneth Lewis. *Northwest Passage.* Garden City, N.Y.: Doubleday, Doran and Co., 1937.

Rogers, Robert. *Reminiscences of the French War: With Robert Rogers' Journal and a Memoir of General Stark.* Freedom, N.H.: Freedom Historical Society, 1988.

Shy, John. *A People Numerous and Armed.* Ann Arbor: University of Michigan Press, 1990.

Edward P. Alexander / E. M.

See also **Lake Champlain; Rangers.**

ROLLERBLADING, or in-line skating, dates from 1979, when Scott and Brennan Olson, two brothers from Minnesota, discovered an antique in-line skate in a sporting goods store. Inspired by the design, the brothers forged

Rollerblading. A well-protected woman engages in in-line skating, a popular sport and recreational activity since the 1980s. © KARL WEATHERLY/CORBIS

a primitive rollerblade by attaching polyurethane wheels and a rubber toe-brake to a pair of ice-hockey boots. Four years later, Scott Olson founded Rollerblade, Inc., from which the sport of in-line skating takes its common name. Two decades later, competitive rollerblading attracted thousands of participants and viewers every year, while millions of Americans of all ages turned to rollerblading as a form of recreation and low-impact exercise.

BIBLIOGRAPHY

Powell, Mark, and John Svensson. *In-Line Skating.* 2d ed. Champaign, Ill: Human Kinetics, 1998.

John M. Kinder

ROMA. *See* **Gypsies.**

ROMANTICISM. Ever since A. O. Lovejoy explained the importance of "discriminating among" the strands, scholars have resisted treating "Romanticism" as a single unified historical movement. Without minimizing this variety, however, it is still possible to identify some emphases common to western Romanticisms, whether in the United States, England, or on the continent, especially in France and Germany. All celebrate the importance of the individual. Most represent human potential in terms of an organic link with the natural world. Many depict this capacity for human growth as the triumph of the intuitive over the methodical and rational. Some suppose that individual self-culture will lead to social progress, even political revolution.

The Beginnings of American Romanticism

In the United States, anticipations of Romanticism appear as early as the late eighteenth century—most notably in discussions of the sublime and the picturesque in landscape, and in the influence of the "moral sense" philosophy of such post-Lockeans as Francis Hutcheson, Dugald Stewart, and Thomas Reid. Although such proto-Romanticism can be found even in the works of Jonathan Edwards and Thomas Jefferson, it is most evident in the gothic and sentimental fictions that flourished in the late eighteenth and early nineteenth centuries. It is customary, however, to date the official beginning of American Romanticism from the rise of Bostonian "transcendentalism" in the 1830s. An outgrowth of liberal Christianity, transcendentalism began as occasional meetings among recent graduates of the Harvard Divinity School. The so-called Transcendental Club soon expanded into more inclusive discussions among men and (a few) women of general interests—primarily in philosophy, literature, and moral theology. From 1840 to 1844, the group published its own journal, *The Dial*. But its most important statement was one of its earliest: published in 1836, a few days before the club's first meeting, the little book *Nature* became the unofficial "credo" of transcendentalism, from its most influential spokesperson, Ralph Waldo Emerson.

Emerson's *Nature* was less concerned with the natural landscape than with the role that individual thought played in perceiving the world of substance. In his argument for the creative power of consciousness, Emerson drew not only on the Scottish moral sense philosophers, but also on European epistemology in general, with special emphasis on René Descartes, John Locke, and Immanuel Kant. He learned from Kant's *Critique of Pure Reason*, perhaps through intermediaries like Samuel Taylor Coleridge and Victor Cousin, to value the intuitions of Reason over the mechanical demonstrations of the Understanding. Most of the book outlined the value of idealism, with a complementary lack of interest in the material world. However radical Emerson's embrace of Kantian idealism, readers found more compelling the uplifting poetry of the prophetic final chapter "Prospects." When one's life conformed, Emerson claimed, to the "true idea" in one's mind, the influx of spirit would work a "corresponding revolution" in things. Not only did the disagreeable vanish; man, understood as a "god in ruins," once again established dominion over his kingdom.

Emerson was transcendentalism's most philosophical writer and its greatest advocate for unification with the Universal Spirit or the One. He was less interested in the practical consequences of that union. When invited to join a local reform group, he refused to lift "the siege of [my] hencoop" to "march baffled away to a pretended siege of Babylon." Most transcendentalists, however, saw spiritual purification as only the first step in political reform. Bronson Alcott and Elizabeth Palmer Peabody actively engaged in humanizing secondary education; while George Ripley put into practice the theories of French utopian Charles Fourier in his communal experiment at Brook Farm. Most influential in their politics were the two students most closely influenced by Emerson—Margaret Fuller and Henry David Thoreau. Emerson's coeditor at *The Dial*, Fuller was famous for her travel writing, reviews, and translations, and as part of the Italian unification movement. But her most celebrated work was "The Great Lawsuit: MAN versus MEN. WOMAN versus WOMEN," published first in *The Dial* in 1845 and expanded soon thereafter into the book-length *Woman in the Nineteenth Century*. The most influential feminist tract between those of Mary Wollstonecraft and Virginia Woolf, *Woman* explored gendered aspects of Emerson's sexless Universal. Just as Emerson foretold the advent of godlike American scholars and poets, so Fuller ended her work rhapsodically awaiting the second coming of woman as a daughter of God: "Would [woman] but assume her inheritance, Mary would not be the only Virgin Mother. . . . The soul is ever young, ever virgin."

Like Fuller, Thoreau introduced social realities into Emerson's abstract philosophy. In *A Week on the Concord and Merrimack Rivers* (1849), *Walden, or Life in the Woods* (1854), and numerous essays, he examined with microscopic attention the natural world that for Emerson remained merely ideal and phenomenal. More important, perhaps, was his early and unflinching opposition to slavery. Notorious in his age for his 1860 defense of John Brown, Thoreau has in later generations been more celebrated for his earlier piece, "Resistance to Civil Government" (1849), which under the posthumous title of "Civil Disobedience" helped shape Gandhi's and Martin Luther King Jr.'s policies of passive resistance. Taking to its logical conclusion the Emersonian proposition that society conspires against the "manhood" of its members, Thoreau announced that "that government is best which governs not at all."

Beyond Transcendentalism

Romanticism among American writers was not, however, restricted to the New England transcendentalists. Some Romantic novelists responded directly to transcendental theories—whether negatively as in Nathaniel Hawthorne's *The Blithedale Romance* (1852) or more ambivalently as in Herman Melville's *Moby-Dick* (1851). Romantic historians like George Bancroft, Francis Parkman, and William Prescott tempered fact with a gripping narrative style to celebrate a "democratic" vision of America. Most puzzling, especially in its regional allegiances with both the North and the South, was the work of Edgar Allan Poe.

Continuing older literary traditions, Poe's use of the gothic superimposed on a popular commercial genre a metaphysical density that was at times indistinguishable from Emerson's—by Poe's own account a Gothicism "not of Germany, but of the Mind."

The place of Romanticism outside of literature is harder to assess. Unitarianism shared many characteristics with the transcendentalist movement it spawned, particularly its distaste for the stern Calvinist image of God, and its support for liberal political reform. It was less comfortable, however, with Emersonian notions of the divinity in man, and openly opposed the transcendentalists' rejection of both the Holy Trinity and Christ's miracles. More generally, the religious intensity of the mid-century can be seen as broadly Romantic, and in fact transcendentalism has frequently been read as a more secular form of the revivalism that swept the Midwest and the "burned-over" district of upstate New York. Here the shifting allegiances of the Beecher family may be taken as representative. Firmly grounded in a Calvinist tradition of fire-and-brimstone preaching, Lyman Beecher openly rejected the "icy" rhetoric of Boston Unitarianism. Although his gradualist approach to both salvation and abolition seemed too cautious for the more fiery imagination of the frontier preacher Charles Grandison Finney, Beecher eventually became reconciled to Finney's evangelicalism to avoid the greater dangers of Bostonian secularism. By the next generation, Lyman's son Henry Ward Beecher was able to combine traditional Presbyterianism with a philosophical outlook not far from Emerson's own.

The point of convergence between religious and more secular Romanticisms was a shared sense of the perfectibility of man. Perfectibility had been a common theme of progressive Enlightenment philosophy. In mid-nineteenth-century America, however, the religious dimensions of programs for the betterment of individuals may have also reinforced conservative politics. The attempts of such benevolence societies as the American Bible Association and the American Tract Society to enlighten the lower classes also had the effect of bringing those previously ignored groups under more careful social surveillance. A similarly uncomfortable compromise between personal advancement and social control can be seen in the period's preoccupation with institutionalization, especially the prison reform movement.

The ambiguities by which Romantic reform of the individual also bound down the underprivileged are perhaps most evident in the women's movement. The most transcendental feminists like Fuller and Peabody eschewed any group activity to focus exclusively on self-cultivation. But more mainstream proponents like Catherine Beecher located female excellence in the special characteristics of women. This argument afforded the movement great power only at the expense of reinforcing domestic stereotypes. The limitations of this position informed much of mid-century women's fiction. The heroine's triumph over adversity in best-sellers like Susan Warner's *The Wide, Wide World* (1851) and Maria Cummins's *The Lamplighter* (1854) was accomplished by obedience to authority, spiritual and patriarchal. Even in Harriet Beecher Stowe's fierce *Uncle Tom's Cabin* (1851–1852), the conclusion—that slavery can be ended only through the reform of individuals into a state of "right feeling"—betrayed both its origins in Emerson's self-reliance and the insufficiency of transcendentalism as a political tool.

Eventually absorbed into the political ferment of antebellum culture, Romanticism as a movement was eclipsed by more pressing realities of secession and reconstruction. Yet the precepts of Romanticism continue to shape culture today. Modern Romanticism is most apparent in the poetic tradition, where the experiments of the late Romantic experimental poets Walt Whitman and Emily Dickinson stand as models for most subsequent poetry, not only of Ezra Pound and Wallace Stevens, but later of Elizabeth Bishop, Adrienne Rich, and John Ashbery. Even intellectual traditions like pragmatism and naturalism that define themselves in opposition to Romanticism still maintain clear links to the earlier tradition; there is as much of Emersonian individualism in William James, Theodore Dreiser, and Ernest Hemingway as in any of his Boston contemporaries. On the darker side, cynical readings of individualism and perfectibility are regularly used to justify contemporary laissez-faire economics and corporate greed. As a literary and philosophical movement, American Romanticism ended in 1865; as a cultural mentality, it is still very much with us.

BIBLIOGRAPHY

Davis, David Brion, ed. *Antebellum Reform*. New York: Harper and Row, 1967. Particularly fine essay by John L. Thomas on Romantic reform.

Hutchison, William R. *The Transcendentalist Ministers: Church Reform in the New England Renaissance*. New Haven, Conn.: Yale University Press, 1959.

Matthiessen, F. O. *American Renaissance: Art and Expression in the Age of Emerson and Whitman*. New York: Oxford University Press, 1941.

Packer, Barbara L. "The Transcendentalists." In *The Cambridge History of American Literature, Volume II; 1820–1865*. Edited by Sacvan Bercovitch. New York: Cambridge University Press, 1995.

Rose, Ann C. *Transcendentalism As a Social Movement, 1830–1850*. New Haven, Conn.: Yale University Press, 1981.

Tompkins, Jane. *Sensational Designs: The Cultural Work of American Fiction, 1790–1860*. New York: Oxford University Press, 1985. Fine feminist account of sentimental fiction.

David Van Leer

See also **Transcendentalism.**

ROMER V. EVANS (*Roy Romer, Governor of Colorado et al., v. Richard G. Evans et al.*, 517 U.S. 620, 1996). In 1992

Colorado citizens voted to adopt an amendment to the state constitution known as Amendment 2 that repealed all local ordinances banning discrimination on the basis of SEXUAL ORIENTATION. Amendment 2 also prohibited all state or local governmental actions designed to protect homosexual persons from discrimination. Soon after the amendment's adoption, municipalities that had adopted protective ordinances and various individual plaintiffs challenged it. A state trial court enjoined the enforcement of Amendment 2, and the Colorado Supreme Court affirmed. In *Romer v. Evans*, the U.S. Supreme Court affirmed by a 6–3 vote, holding that Amendment 2 violated the equal protection clause of the U.S. Constitution.

Justice Anthony Kennedy's opinion for the Court was surprising in that it struck down Amendment 2 while applying only "rational basis" scrutiny, the lowest level of constitutional review under the equal protection clause and a level of review that is ordinarily quite deferential. The Court held that Amendment 2 imposed special disabilities on homosexuals, that these disabilities were animated by "animosity" toward the class, and that animosity cannot itself be a "legitimate governmental interest." As the Court held, "a State cannot so deem a class of persons a stranger to its laws." The Court thus did not reach the question of whether to classify homosexuals as a "suspect class," making discrimination against them subject to heightened scrutiny.

Justice Antonin Scalia, joined by Chief Justice William Rehnquist and Justice Clarence Thomas, wrote a biting dissent. Scalia argued that the Court's decision was directly contradicted by *Bowers v. Hardwick*, 478 U.S.186 (1986), which held that the Constitution does not prohibit states from making homosexual conduct a crime.

BIBLIOGRAPHY

Rotunda, Ronald D., and John E. Nowak. *Treatise on Constitutional Law: Substance and Procedure.* 3d ed. Volume 3. St. Paul, Minn.: West, 1999.

Kent Greenfield

See also **Discrimination: Sexual Orientation.**

ROOSEVELT COROLLARY to the Monroe Doctrine, a unilateral declaration claiming a U.S. prerogative of exercising "international police power" in the Western Hemisphere, was first set forth by President Theodore Roosevelt on 20 May 1904 in a public letter to Secretary of War Elihu Root. Roosevelt was particularly alarmed in 1902 by the blockade and bombardment of Venezuela by Germany and Great Britain, writing Root, "Brutal wrongdoing, or an impotence which results in a general loosening of the ties of civilizing society, may finally require intervention by some civilized nation; and in the Western Hemisphere the United States cannot ignore this duty." In his annual messages of 6 December 1904 and 5 December 1905, he invoked the Monroe Doctrine in this regard. In March 1905, in order to forestall forced debt collection in Santo Domingo by Italy, France, and Belgium, he appointed a collector of customs in that indebted nation and established a de facto protectorate. Never before had the Monroe Doctrine, itself a unilateral pronouncement, been used to forbid temporary European intervention in order to collect debts or honor international obligations. During the presidencies of William Howard Taft and Woodrow Wilson, intervention in Honduras, the Dominican Republic, Haiti, and Nicaragua was defended on the basis of the Roosevelt Corollary.

BIBLIOGRAPHY

Collin, Richard H. *Theodore Roosevelt's Caribbean: The Panama Canal, the Monroe Doctrine, and the Latin American Context.* Baton Rouge: Louisiana State University Press, 1990.

Munro, Dana G. *Intervention and Dollar Diplomacy in the Caribbean, 1900–1921.* Princeton, N.J.: Princeton University Press, 1964.

Justus D. Doenecke

See also **Caribbean Policy; Dollar Diplomacy; Intervention; Latin America, Relations with; Monroe Doctrine.**

ROOT ARBITRATION TREATIES, a series of twenty-five bilateral pacts concluded in 1908 and 1909 during the tenure of Elihu Root as U.S. secretary of state. The pacts remained the chief bipartite nonaggression treaties to which the United States was a signatory until 1928, when Secretary of State Frank Kellogg negotiated with France the first pact of a new type. In general, the Root treaties obligated the parties to arbitrate differences of a legal nature and those relating to the interpretation of a treaty. They generally provided that controversies arbitrated under the treaty should be submitted to a tribunal of the Permanent Court of Arbitration.

BIBLIOGRAPHY

Gould, Lewis L. *The Presidency of Theodore Roosevelt.* Lawrence: University Press of Kansas, 1991.

Leopold, Richard W. *Elihu Root and the Conservative Tradition.* Boston: Little, Brown, 1954.

Philip C. Jessup / A. G.

See also **Kellogg-Briand Pact; Treaties with Foreign Nations; Treaties, Negotiation and Ratification of;** *and vol. 9:* **The Monroe Doctrine and the Roosevelt Corollary.**

ROOT MISSION. In April 1917, President Woodrow Wilson appointed a mission to go to Russia, chiefly for the purpose of ascertaining whether Russia's active participation in WORLD WAR I could be continued after the March revolution that had ousted Tsar Nicholas II. The mission, headed by former Secretary of State Elihu Root, arrived in Petrograd (now Saint Petersburg) in June. Greatly underestimating the strength of Nikolai Lenin and the Bolshevik party, the Root mission concentrated on developing contacts with moderates such as Aleksandr Kerenski. The mission thus reached the erroneous conclusion that an American-funded propaganda campaign could keep Russia in the war. The Bolshevik Revolution of November 1917 exposed the flawed strategy behind the Root mission and caught the Wilson administration almost completely unprepared. In March 1918, the Bolsheviks signed the Treaty of Brest-Litovsk, which established a separate peace between Russia and Germany, precisely what the Root mission had been intended to prevent in the first place.

BIBLIOGRAPHY

Kennan, George F. *Russia Leaves the War: Soviet-American Relations, 1917–1920.* Princeton, N.J.: Princeton University Press, 1989.

Leopold, Richard W. *Elihu Root and the Conservative Tradition.* Boston: Little, Brown, 1954.

Philip C. Jessup / A. G.

See also **Anticommunism; Russia, Relations with.**

ROOT-TAKAHIRA AGREEMENT,

an accord concluded on 30 November 1908 by U.S. Secretary of State Elihu Root and the Japanese ambassador Baron Kogoro Takahira. It declared the wish of the two governments to develop their commerce in the Pacific; their intention to defend the OPEN DOOR POLICY and the independence and integrity of China; their resolve to respect each other's territorial possessions in the Pacific; and their willingness to communicate with each other if these principles were threatened. (An earlier proposal for such an arrangement in October 1907 had been repudiated by the Japanese government, but the suggestion was renewed when Count Katsura became premier of Japan.) The proposal was welcomed by the United States as helpful in quieting the widely held belief that war between the two countries was imminent, a belief stimulated by the disputes over Japanese immigration, the anti-Japanese measures in California, and the American fleet's much-publicized voyage across the Pacific. The agreement was enthusiastically received in European capitals but did not please the Chinese, who feared that it would strengthen Japan's position in China. Through the agreement, the United States recognized Japanese primacy in Manchuria, while in return Japan conceded America's colonial domination of the Philippines.

BIBLIOGRAPHY

Esthus, Raymond A. *Theodore Roosevelt and Japan.* Seattle: University of Washington Press, 1966.

Leopold, Richard W. *Elihu Root and the Conservative Tradition.* Boston: Little, Brown, 1954.

Philip C. Jessup / A. G.

See also **Diplomatic Missions; Immigration Restriction; Japan, Relations with; Treaties with Foreign Nations.**

ROOTS: *The Saga of an American Family* (1976) was published after African American writer Alex Haley (1921–1992) spent twelve years researching his ancestry. Blending fact and fiction, *Roots* has been both widely heralded and fiercely criticized.

Most praise has concerned the way the book and, more importantly, the 1977 television miniseries, raised African Americans' consciousness of their heritage. Many African Americans who read the book or viewed the film experienced a new sense of pride in their ancestry and were inspired to compile their own genealogies. Consciousness was similarly raised among white Americans, particularly by the film's graphic scenes of the hardships and violence endured by slaves.

Criticism, however, has dominated recent decades' consideration of the work. Haley's biases are evident in his unfailingly noble and strong African characters; conversely, whites are virtually always portrayed as weak, foolish, and/or evil. Haley's historical scholarship is open to a number of attacks, as when he depicts Kunta Kinte enslaved on a cotton plantation in Virginia—a state that had virtually no cotton culture. Haley's writing style and the book's structure are both lackluster and, at times, amateurish.

Little scholarly or critical attention has been given to *Roots.* Its primary value has derived from its work as a cultural artifact rather than from any literary or historical merit.

BIBLIOGRAPHY

Shirley, David. *Alex Haley.* New York: Chelsea House Publishers, 1994.

Barbara Schwarz Wachal

ROSENBERG CASE.

Julius and Ethel Rosenberg, executed for World War II atomic espionage on behalf of the Soviet Union, were first exposed as spies after an investigation into security leaks from Los Alamos, New Mexico. As a result of this investigation, Klaus Fuchs, a German-born British scientist; Harry Gold, a courier; and David Greenglass, an army machinist, had all confessed to espionage. The latter implicated his brother-in-law, Julius Rosenberg. Although the evidence against Ethel was thinner, the FBI arrested her in the hope that Julius would also confess. Tried along with Morton Sobell, who was sentenced to thirty years' imprisonment, the Rosenbergs were convicted in April 1951 and sentenced to die. The most damning testimony came from Greenglass, who received a fifteen-year sentence, and his wife, Ruth.

A worldwide campaign to save the Rosenbergs emphasized the fate of their two young children and charged that the evidence was manufactured and the trial and sentence tainted by anti-Semitism. Nonetheless, they were executed at SING SING Prison on 19 June 1953. The re-

Ethel and Julius Rosenberg. ARCHIVE PHOTOS, INC.

lease of FBI files on the case in the late 1970s confirmed that Julius had headed a large ring of industrial spies and that Ethel was aware of his activities but had played only a minor role in the espionage, conclusions reinforced by decrypted Soviet cables released in 1995 and by revelations from Julius's KGB controller, Alexander Feklisov.

BIBLIOGRAPHY

Radosh, Ronald, and Joyce Milton. *The Rosenberg File: A Search for the Truth.* 2d. ed. New Haven, Conn.: Yale University Press, 1997. Contains revelations from National Security Agency and Soviet sources.

Harvey Klehr

See also **Anticommunism; Cold War; Subversion, Communist.**

ROTARY INTERNATIONAL V. ROTARY CLUB OF DUARTE,

107 Supreme Court 1940 (1987), upheld the second of two state laws prohibiting sex discrimination in private associations. This decision involved a California statute similar to the Minnesota law upheld in *ROBERTS ET AL. V. UNITED STATES JAYCEES* (1984). Like *Roberts*, the case represented a conflict between a local chapter and its parent organization. Two Supreme Court justices had to recuse themselves from the case—Harry A. Blackmun because he was a member of the Rotary and Sandra Day O'Connor because her husband was a member. Rotary, it was clear, was not a private club. It described itself as "inclusive, not exclusive" and, like the Jaycees, worked to remove racial, religious, and cultural barriers—among males. The difference between *Rotary* and *Roberts* was that the Rotary has always been a less political and more selective group than the Jaycees. Rotary

did not take positions on public issues, and local chapters determined their own admissions procedures (the international organization recommends selection committees).

In rejecting Rotary International's claim that the state law violated the constitutional right to privacy recognized in *Griswold v. Connecticut*, the Court emphasized "factors such as size, purpose, selectivity, and whether others are excluded from critical aspects of the relationship." A year later, the Court, in *New York State Club Association v. New York*, upheld an ordinance banning sex discrimination in even the most elite "city clubs." In the 1990s, the precedent of banning discrimination in large private associations on the grounds of gender was expanded to sexual orientation. Several state supreme court decisions in the 1990s ruled in favor of plaintiffs excluded from the Boy Scouts because they were gay.

BIBLIOGRAPHY

Abernathy, M. Glenn. *The Right of Assembly and Association.* Columbia: University of South Carolina Press, 1981.

Baer, Judith A. *Women in American Law: The Struggle Toward Equality from the New Deal to the Present.* New York: Holmes and Meier, 2002.

Judith A. Baer / A. R.

See also **Boy Scouts of America; Civil Rights Act of 1964; Clubs, Exclusionary; First Amendment; Fraternal and Service Organizations; Gender and Gender Roles; Women in Public Life, Business, and Professions.**

ROTATION IN OFFICE.

The premise of rotation in office is as old as the American republic and driven by two contrasting premises. The more exemplary reason offered by high-minded theorists and office seekers alike is that it underscores American democratic traditions by allowing as few as possible to be ensconced in remunerative and powerful lifetime government jobs. The second reason for the principle derives from the new administrations, at any level of government, who want open positions to reward their friends and punish their enemies. The first premise was invoked by no less a figure than George Washington, when, in 1796, he declined a third term as president on the grounds that a two-term limit by general informal agreement showed a healthy respect for American democratic institutions. Only a few years later, in 1801, Thomas Jefferson was the first president to sweep his Federalist enemies from office in wholesale numbers.

But it was President Andrew Jackson, a generation later, who laid the groundwork for what his opponents came to call the "spoils system." Beginning in 1829, Jackson invoked wholesale rotation in federal office as his guiding principle, saying plainly that "no one man has anymore intrinsic right to office than another." So, with that in mind, and in the name of (Jacksonian) Democracy, he cleansed the federal civil service of his predecessor John Quincy Adams's appointees, replacing them not with

"Teddy's Colts." Colonel Theodore Roosevelt *(center, wearing glasses)* and his Rough Riders pose at the summit after the Battle of San Juan Hill, 1898, which catapulted him to national prominence. NATIONAL ARCHIVES AND RECORDS ADMINISTRATION

the new democratic working class men who adored him, but with elite politicians who supported him, and who were indistinguishable, in class terms, from the men they succeeded. This occurred not only with cabinet and sub-cabinet level administrative positions in Washington, D.C., but with civil servants in the states and communities in America who staffed the customhouses, the Internal Revenue Service, the post offices, and the land offices.

Even with that principle put into wholesale practice, Jackson discovered what his successors in the nineteenth century would later learn as well. There were never enough jobs to go around, and many disappointed, politically connected office seekers turned on him. He said of them, "If I had a tit for every one of those PIGS to suck at, they would still be my friends." Only civil service reform, beginning at the turn of the twentieth century, would end the spoils system as the mechanism that drove the early premise of "rotation in office." The U.S. Civil Service laws mostly cleared that Augean stable of corruption, but it did nothing for the principle of rotation.

In the twentieth century, Franklin Roosevelt's decision in 1940 to run for a third (and then a fourth) term as president raised enough flags in the American electorate to launch a movement to legalize the two-term limit that George Washington had introduced by precedent. A constitutional amendment finally limited presidents to two terms, beginning with Lyndon Johnson.

In the 1990s, a term limits movement gained momentum in several states, imposing rotation in elective office at all levels of government. It limited elected office-holders in some places to terms that usually do not exceed eight years. Term limits, in the name of the principle of rotation, are still honored only here and there, but in a way they are a start toward a return to the more democratic process that George Washington wanted to establish at the inception of the American republic.

BIBLIOGRAPHY

Prince, Carl E. *The Federalists and the U.S. Civil Service.* New York: New York University Press, 1978.

Carl E. Prince

See also **Civil Service; Spoils System.**

ROTC. *See* **Reserve Officers' Training Corps.**

ROUGH RIDERS, officially the First U.S. Cavalry Volunteers, fought in the Spanish-American War and became the most widely publicized regiment in American military history. Its members came from the cattle ranges, mining camps, and law enforcement agencies of the Southwest. Such personnel offered brilliant copy for war correspondents and the unit's inexperienced but colorful commanding officers, particularly Theodore Roosevelt, enhanced its swashbuckling image. Although only half the regiment actually fought the Spanish, the fragment that reached Cuba lived up to its advance publicity. From Las Guásimas to San Juan Hill, the Rough Riders' attacks were often unconventional, but usually successful and helped romanticize the war in the United States.

BIBLIOGRAPHY

Hoganson, Kristin L. *Fighting for American Manhood: How Gender Politics Provoked the Spanish-American and Philippine-American Wars.* New Haven, Conn.: Yale University Press, 1998.

Samuels, Peggy, and Harold Samuels. *Teddy Roosevelt at San Juan: The Making of a President.* College Station: Texas A&M University Press, 1997.

Walker, Dale. *The Boys of '98: Theodore Roosevelt and the Rough Riders.* New York: Forge, 1998.

*Jim Dan Hill/*E. M.

See also **San Juan Hill and El Caney, Battles of; Spanish-American War; War Memorials;** *and vol. 9:* **A Soldier's Account of the Spanish-American War.**

ROYAL COLONIES were established in North America by England, France, the Netherlands, and Sweden over the course of the seventeenth and eighteenth centuries. The colonies were controlled by the king of the sovereign nation, who named a governor to each colony and, in English colonies, a council to assist him. The Crown was also responsible for appointing colonial judges, usually for life, though by 1760 they could be removed from office at will. The Crown controlled all unsold public lands, and the royal governor retained the power to disperse those lands. As a representative of the Crown in the colonies, the governor—who also could be removed at will by the king—and the council derived their authority from two key documents, the colonial commission and the set of royal instructions.

Some of the royal governors who worked at the will of the British Crown were well-trained bureaucrats. Others were just as likely to have gained their appointments solely through patronage. A majority of the royal governors had been born in England rather than the colonies; several chose to rule in absentia, despite instructions to the contrary. The average term for governors was five years. Although several royal governors developed positive and productive relationships with their colonial assemblies, most struggled to maintain control 3,000 miles from the Crown that had granted them the authority to rule.

In royal colonies, as in charter and proprietary governments, the assembly was popularly elected according to varying definitions of franchise. Though the governor and his council theoretically controlled appropriations and expenditures, in reality colonial assemblies undermined that power over time. By 1720, most colonial assemblies had wrested from the governor the power to initiate legislation, including laws governing taxation and the management of colonial revenue. With the exception of Georgia, established as a form of trusteeship supported directly by Parliamentary appropriation, most royal governors depended upon the assemblies for financial support. Colonial legislatures thus were in a position to challenge the authority of royal governors, most who lacked a network of patronage appointees sufficient to enable them to manipulate the local government.

By the eighteenth century, even as royal colonies became the standard form of colonial government, the governors themselves had begun to lodge complaints with the Crown that the assemblies were gaining too much power as governing bodies in and of themselves. Additionally they reported that the assemblies were much too inclined to reflect the will of the electorate rather than the king. Partially in an attempt to diffuse some of the financial control wielded by colonial assemblies, an act of Parliament in 1767 made colonial governors, councils, and judges independent of the assemblies; thereafter, they were paid directly from colonial revenue.

In theory, and according to royal instructions, laws passed by colonial assemblies had to be approved by both the governor and the Board of Trade in England. In practice, however, the vagaries of both distance and an inefficient hierarchy meant that years could pass before laws to which England objected could be repealed. Colonial assemblies learned rapidly how to articulate and defend their own interests.

With the exception of NEW FRANCE, established as a French royal colony in 1608, and several of the Caribbean islands, all of the original seventeenth-century Dutch and English colonies were corporate or proprietary. Between settlement and the American Revolution, however, the royal colony became the standard form of colonial government. By 1775, only Pennsylvania and Maryland (which had been a royal colony briefly from 1690 to 1715, until the proprietor converted to Anglicanism) retained their proprietary status, and only Connecticut and Rhode Island remained corporate colonies.

A majority of the original North American colonies were corporate. Virginia, established initially under a charter granted to the Virginia Company in 1607, was the first to cede its control to the Crown, in 1624. NEW NETHERLAND, settled by the Dutch under a corporate charter in 1613, became a proprietary colony under the Duke of York upon English conquest, and became a royal colony in 1685 with the accession to the thrown of James II. Plymouth (1620, annexed by Massachusetts in 1691), MASSACHUSETTS BAY (1630), Connecticut (1635), and

Rhode Island (1636) were all established according to religious charters; Massachusetts Bay became a royal colony under its second charter in 1691, in the aftermath of the Glorious Revolution.

Seventeenth-century proprietary colonies included Pennsylvania (on land granted to William Penn by Charles II in 1681), Maryland (Catholic, granted by Charles I to proprietor George Calvert, lord Baltimore and his heirs in 1632), New Jersey (given in two parcels by James, duke of York to Lord John Berkeley and Sir George Carteret), and Carolina (granted by Charles II to eight proprietors in 1663). Each would eventually become royal colonies. New Jersey became a single royal colony in 1702. Carolina was recognized as two distinct proprietary areas—North and South—according to a commission granted to Virginia agent Philip Ludwell, recruited by the proprietors in 1691. They became separate proprietary royal colonies in 1701. South Carolina became a royal colony in 1719, North Carolina in 1729.

BIBLIOGRAPHY

Greene, Jack P. *The Quest for Power: The Lower Houses of Assembly in the Southern Royal Colonies, 1689–1776.* Chapel Hill: University of North Carolina Press, 1963.

Labaree, Leonard Woods. *Royal Government in America: A Study of the British Colonial System before 1783.* 2d ed. New York: Frederick Ungar Publishing, 1964.

———, ed. *Royal Instructions to British Colonial Governors, 1670–1776.* New York: Octagon Books, 1967.

Leslie J. Lindenauer

See also **Colonial Assemblies; Colonial Councils; Colonial Policy, British; Proprietary Colonies.**

ROYAL DISALLOWANCE.

The King in Council held the power to approve or disallow colonial legislation. England disallowed colonial laws it judged contrary to English common or statute law, to a colonial charter, or to a governor's instructions, as well as laws deemed badly drafted. At heart, the Crown disallowed laws that diminished royal authority over local officials and governments, most especially representative assemblies.

Disallowance, exercised after a law's passage, differed from a royal veto, by which the Crown prevented a law from going into effect in the first place. The royal disapproval of a law functioned more like a repeal; though the law might be terminated, any acts instituted under the law would remain valid.

After its creation by Parliament in 1696, the Board of Trade undertook much of the work of considering colonial laws; most every approval or disapproval occurred as a result of its recommendations. Laws submitted to the PRIVY COUNCIL for review ultimately ended up in the hands of the Board of Trade. The Board, however, exercised direct control only over royal colonies, which included Virginia, Massachusetts, New Hampshire, New York, New Jersey, and the West Indies. Royal colonies submitted laws for approval promptly; charter and proprietary colonies, including Connecticut, Rhode Island, North and South Carolina, Maryland, and Pennsylvania, maintained special privileges with regard to the passage and approval of their laws. All colonial laws related to the effective enforcement of the Navigation Acts were subject to the Board and Council's approval.

Indeed, the Board of Trade exercised the greatest degree of control over laws regulating or promoting commerce. Many of the disallowed laws in the late seventeenth and eighteenth centuries were those that placed what was deemed an undue burden on British commerce, including laws establishing duties that discriminated against freight carried by nonprovincial ships, those that laid duties on European goods, those appointing seaports for lading and unlading of enumerated goods, and laws that regulated trade with Indians. Though representative assemblies and colonial merchants objected to what they saw as the Board's heavy hand, in some respects royal disallowance functioned as a check to the unrestrained power of the merchant class, and resulted in relative commercial harmony during much of the seventeenth and eighteenth centuries. Moreover, in some cases, the Crown disallowed colonial laws that encroached upon religious freedom, including those that resulted in the persecution of Quakers. The Crown also disallowed colonial slave laws it deemed too brutal or "contrary to nature."

Royal disallowance was relatively infrequent, and decreased over the course of the seventeenth century. The crown, however, repealed approximately one-sixth of the laws passed in Massachusetts in the 1690s, and over half of those passed in New Hampshire. In the corporate colonies of Connecticut and Rhode Island, not obliged to submit laws for royal approval, the Crown exerted control through its insistence on the right of appeal to the King in Council regardless of the legal status of the colony.

BIBLIOGRAPHY

Dickerson, Oliver Morton. *American Colonial Government, 1696–1765: A Study of the British Board of Trade in Its Relations to the American Colonies, Political, Industrial, Administrative.* New York: Russell and Russell, 1939.

Johnson, Richard R. *Adjustment to Empire: The New England Colonies, 1675–1715.* New Brunswick, N.J.: Rutgers University Press, 1981.

Leslie J. Lindenauer

See also **Board of Trade and Plantations; Instructions; Navigation Acts.**

RUBBER.

Although rubber-yielding plants are native to Africa and Asia as well as to the Americas, the first mention of rubber in the West was made by Pietro Martire d'Anghiera, the Italian representative to the court of Spain (*De Rebus Oceanicis et Novo Orbe*, 1516). In the early seventeenth century, Juan de Torquemada (*Monarquía In-*

diana, 1615) described how the Mexican Indians used a milk-like fluid drawn from a tree for religious rites and sport, and for making crude footwear, waterproof bottles, and garments. Although a little rubber was used in Europe in the eighteenth century to make erasers—it derived its name "rubber" for its property of rubbing out (erasing) pencil marks—along with elastic thread, surgical tubes, and experimental balloons, the rubber manufacturing industry was not established until the nineteenth century.

The first record of rubber in the United States is a patent for gum elastic varnish for footwear issued to Jacob F. Hummel in 1813. This was followed by a patent for a grinding and mixing machine granted to John J. Howe in 1820. Prompting these first steps was the profitable trade in crude rubber shoes imported into Boston and New York City from Brazil. By 1833, America's pioneering rubber factory was established at Roxbury, Massachusetts. Other rubber shoe and clothing factories soon appeared elsewhere in Massachusetts, as well as in New Jersey, Rhode Island, Connecticut, New York, and Pennsylvania. By 1840, the infant industry had experienced a speculative boom (about $2 million in stock was issued) and a disastrous collapse. The primary cause for the loss of confidence was that rubber products had not proven reliable—they softened in the heat and stiffened in the cold—but the downturn in general business conditions that began in the fall of 1837 only added to the industry's distress. So great were the industry's troubles that in 1843 the Roxbury Rubber Company sold the "monster" spreading machine (built by Edwin Marcus Chaffee in 1837) for $525; it had been purchased for $30,000.

Although experiments to cure rubber have been attributed to the eighteenth-century Swedish physician and pharmacist Petter-Jonas Bergius, it remained for Charles Goodyear to solve the basic technical problem confronting early rubber manufacturers. He did so in 1839, at Woburn, Massachusetts, when he developed the "vulcanization process," which gives rubber durability and consistent qualities across a broad range of temperatures by treating it with sulfur and white lead at a high temperature. His samples of "cured" rubber, with which he tried to raise funds in England, prompted the English inventor Thomas Hancock to make his own "discovery" of vulcanization. The "elastic metal" provided by these two inventors would soon prove indispensable to the Western world.

Nowhere was this more marked than in the development of the AUTOMOBILE INDUSTRY. Yet long before the automobile appeared at the end of the nineteenth century, America's consumption of raw rubber had grown twentyfold—from 1,120 short tons in 1850 to 23,000 tons in 1900 (two-fifths of the world total of 59,000 short tons). Wherever elastic, shock-absorbing, water-resistant, insulating, and air- and steam-tight properties were required, vulcanized rubber was used. Most of the raw rubber came from Brazil, with Africa the second-most important source. The problem was not to find rubber but to find the labor to collect it in the almost inaccessible forests and ship it to the factories of the Northern Hemisphere. Until the systematic development of plantation rubber in Southeast Asia in the twentieth century made collection and transportation a comparatively easy task, the growing demand for crude rubber could only be met at increased cost. In 1830, Para rubber was 20 cents a pound; in 1900 the annual average wholesale price had risen to about a dollar.

Between 1849 and 1900, the industry's output of manufactured goods—chiefly footwear, mechanicals (for use with machinery), proofed and elastic goods, surgical goods, bicycle tires, and toys—increased in value from $3 million to $53 million. In the same years, the industry's workforce grew from 2,500 to 22,000. Because of the economies of scale and the absence of product differentiation, the market for rubber products was fiercely competitive—hence the tendency for the early rubber manufacturers to band together. Before the CIVIL WAR, marketing arrangements were already in existence to control the sale of footwear and other products. By the eve of WORLD WAR I, production had come to be dominated by the "Big Four": Goodyear Tire and Rubber Company, United States Rubber Company, B. F. Goodrich Company, and Firestone Tire and Rubber Company. Partly to be close to the carriage-making industry—at the time the rubber industry's major consumer—the center of rubber manufacture had shifted from the towns of New England to Akron, Ohio. The industry's first branch factories were established in Western Europe in the 1850s.

The most dramatic phase of the industry's growth followed the introduction of the internal combustion engine, cheap petroleum, and the widespread use of the pneumatic tire in the early 1900s. Between 1900 and 1920, consumption of raw rubber increased tenfold—to 231,000 short tons. Even the world depression of the early 1930s only temporarily halted the industry's rapid expansion. By 1940, the United States was consuming 726,000 tons of a world total of 1,243,000 tons of crude rubber. Between 1900 (when the first four tons of Southeast Asia plantation rubber had reached the market) and 1910, the annual average wholesale price per pound of crude rubber doubled from $1 to $2. By 1915, more than twice as much rubber was coming from the plantations of Southeast Asia than from America and Africa combined, and prices had fallen to a quarter of their 1910 level; on 2 June 1932, the price was just three cents a pound.

Partly because of the great fluctuations in the price of crude rubber, and partly because the plantation industry of the Far East was largely in British hands, the industry began a search for rubber substitutes in the 1920s. In the next decade, manufacturers produced a few hundred tons a year of a special type of synthetic rubber. As Japan seized the rubber lands of Southeast Asia during WORLD WAR II, U.S. production of synthetic rubber increased a hundredfold—from 9,000 short tons in 1941 to

919,000 tons in 1945, at which point synthetic rubber met four-fifths of America's needs. By 1973, of a world output of 6.3 million metric tons, the United States produced about 40 percent, almost three times more than the next greatest producer, Japan. That year, the United States had consumed only 696,000 metric tons of a world output of approximately 3.5 million tons of natural rubber.

Chemists succeeded in not only synthesizing rubber by making a wide range of elastomers and plastomers available, they changed the character of the industry until it was no longer possible to distinguish between rubber and rubber substitutes. The price of the synthetic compared favorably with that of the natural product, and for some uses synthetic rubber was preferable.

The rise of other industrialized nations in the twentieth century reduced America's domination of the industry; even so, its output in 1970 (including plastics) was worth about $15 billion and the industry employed more than half a million workers. In 1987, the American rubber industry shipped $24.9 billion in goods, of which automobile tires accounted for $10.5 billion of that amount. According to the Environmental Protection Agency, more than 230,000 people were employed in the rubber industry in the United States in 1987. Although rubber was used in thousands of ways, automobile tires—with which the major technical developments in manufacture have been associated—continued to account for more than one-half of the industry's consumption of raw materials. The overwhelming size of the major rubber corporations (a fifth giant was added to the Big Four in 1915 when the General Tire and Rubber Corporation was formed at Akron) did not lessen the industry's competitive nature. After World War II, the tendency toward global expansion increased, and, in the late twentieth century, the major rubber manufacturers were worldwide in scope and operation.

BIBLIOGRAPHY

Allen, P. W. *Natural Rubber and the Synthetics.* New York: Wiley, 1972.

EPA Office of Compliance Sector. *Profile of the Rubber and Plastic Industry.* Washington, D.C.: U.S. Environmental Protection Agency, 1995.

Howard, Frank A. *Buna Rubber: The Birth of an Industry.* New York: Van Nostrand, 1947.

Phillips, Charles F. *Competition in the Synthetic Rubber Industry.* Chapel Hill: University of North Carolina Press, 1963.

Schidrowitz, Philip, and T. R. Dawson, eds. *History of the Rubber Industry.* Cambridge, U.K.: Heffer, 1952.

Woodruff, W. "Growth of the Rubber Industry of Great Britain and the United States." *Journal of Economic History* 15, no. 4 (1955): 376–391.

William Woodruff/c. w.

See also **Boot and Shoe Manufacturing; Chemical Industry; Indian Technology; Industrial Revolution; Petrochemical Industry.**

RUBY RIDGE. On 21 August 1992, a botched arrest attempt at Randy and Vicki Weaver's Ruby Ridge cabin in Idaho left a U.S. deputy marshal and Weaver's son dead. The next day FBI sniper Lon Horiuchi wounded Weaver and Kevin Harris, and killed Vicki Weaver. After an eleven-day standoff Weaver and Harris gave themselves up, and on 13 April 1993, their trial opened in Boise. On 8 July 1993 the jury acquitted Weaver and Harris of the murder and convicted Weaver on two lesser counts. Judge Edward Lodge sentenced Weaver to eighteen months and fined the federal government thousands of dollars for several procedural violations. Militia groups hailed the Weavers as martyrs.

BIBLIOGRAPHY

Walter, Jess. *Every Knee Shall Bow: The Truth and Tragedy of Ruby Ridge and the Randy Weaver Family.* New York: Harper, 1995.

Gordon Morris Bakken

See also **Waco Seige.**

RULE OF REASON, a judicial principle applicable when the purpose and intent of legislation are open to serious question. Application of the principle has been largely restricted to the interpretation of the SHERMAN ANTITRUST ACT of 1890. This measure, if taken literally, would be unenforceable, and possibly unconstitutional. To evade the issue of the law's constitutionality, the Supreme Court, in the 1911 cases *Standard Oil Company v. United States* and *United States v. American Tobacco Company*, enunciated the rule of reason and used it to conclude that the statutory prohibition of "all combinations in restraint of trade" set forth in the act actually meant "all unreasonable combinations in restraint of trade."

BIBLIOGRAPHY

Letwin, Willam. *Law and Economic Policy in America: The Evolution of the Sherman Antitrust Act.* Chicago: University of Chicago Press, 1981 [1965].

W. Brooke Graves/f. b.

See also **Restraint of Trade;** *Standard Oil Company of New Jersey v. United States.*

RULES OF THE HOUSE. The rules of the U.S. House of Representatives and the ever-increasing thousands of precedents that influence their interpretation constitute one of the most complete bodies of parliamentary law in the world, rivaled, perhaps, only by that of the British House of Commons. The size of the House (since 1912, fixed at 435 members) and its immense volume of proposed legislation require strict regulation of the actions of members while in session. The Constitution gives the House the right to make its own rules, which are adopted anew by each Congress, usually with few or no changes. The objectives of the rules are complex and hard to reconcile: to enable the majority to work its will while protecting the rights of the minority, and to legislate expeditiously while avoiding reckless haste.

BIBLIOGRAPHY

Currie, David P. *The Constitution in Congress: The Federalist Period, 1789–1801.* Chicago: University of Chicago Press, 1997.

Polsby, Nelson W. *Congress and the Presidency.* Englewood Cliffs, N.J.: Prentice Hall, 1986.

Pyle, Christopher H., and Richard M. Pious. *The President, Congress, and the Constitution: Power and Legitimacy in American Politics.* New York: Collier Macmillan, 1984.

D. B. Hardeman / A. G.

See also **Blocs; Colonial Assemblies; Delegation of Powers; Majority Rule; Reed Rules.**

RUM TRADE began in the NEW ENGLAND colonies in the seventeenth century and soon became vital to the existence of a people unable to produce staple crops beyond subsistence farms. Because the lumber and fishing industries of New England were unable to find sufficient markets in England, traders sought a market in the colonies of the West Indies. There, lumber and fish were exchanged for molasses, the main product of the islands. The molasses, in turn, was manufactured into rum, becoming one of the earliest of New England's industries.

The rum trade became part of a "triangular trade" between New England, the West Indies, and the African Gold Coast that maintained the prosperity of the northern colonies throughout the eighteenth century. In this TRIANGULAR TRADE, molasses was sent to New England, rum to Africa, and slaves to the West Indies.

The New England colonies soon came into conflict with Great Britain over the rum trade as traders found it more profitable to deal with the French, Dutch, and Spanish than with the English. The British Parliament attempted, through the MOLASSES ACT of 1733, to limit trade outside the empire by imposing high duties on non-British molasses imported into New England. This legislation was consistently evaded, and smuggling became an accepted practice.

In 1763 the conflict over molasses imports reached crisis proportions, largely because of the war between Great Britain and France. Parliament passed the Sugar Act, a stronger version of the Molasses Act, which attempted to enforce duties through the use of the British navy, the appointment of customs commissioners, and the issuance of writs of assistance. Opposition soared, and, by 1763, smuggling was regarded by New Englanders as a patriotic exercise.

BIBLIOGRAPHY

Loades, D. M. *England's Maritime Empire: Seapower, Commerce, and Policy 1490–1690.* New York: Longman, 2000.

McCusker, John. *Rum and the American Revolution: The Rum Trade and the Balance of Payments of the Thirteen Continental Colonies.* New York: Garland, 1989.

Temin, Peter, ed. *Engines of Enterprise: An Economic History of New England.* Cambridge, Mass.: Harvard University Press, 2000.

Roger Burlingame / H. S.

See also **Molasses Trade; Smuggling, Colonial; Sugar Acts; West Indies, British and French.**

RUNNING. Before bicycles and cars made transportation fast and easy, running was one of the only ways for a human being to move rapidly. According to the legend, Philippides ran twenty-six miles from Marathon to Athens in 490 B.C. to deliver the news that the Athenian army had defeated the Persians, making him the first famous runner in history. The first ancient Greek Olympics (776 B.C.) consisted of a foot race.

With the advent of mechanized locomotion, running in the United States today is almost exclusively a sport and a hobby. Official competitions in the United States include the sprint (the 100-, 200-, and 400-meter dash; the 400- and 1,600-meter relay; and the 100-, 110-, and 400-meter hurdles), middle-distance running (the 800-, 1,500-, and 3,000-meter run; the mile; and the 3,000-meter steeple chase), and long-distance running (the 5,000- and 10,000-meter run and the marathon). There are also running events in the triathlon, the pentathlon, the heptathlon, and the decathlon, as well as a variety of cross-country and road races. The most extreme of them,

Running for Fun and Fitness. With the 1967 publication of William J. Bowerman and W. E. Harris's *Jogging*, running became a popular hobby in the United States. By the 1970s an estimated 10 million Americans jogged regularly. Here Kenneth Cooper *(left)*, R. L. Bohannon *(second from left)*, and Hayes Jones *(right)* jog through New York City Plaza in 1969 accompanied by Bob Richard *(on bicycle)*, wearing National Jogging Association sweatshirts. © UPI/CORBIS-BETTMANN

appearing in 1978, is the Hawaiian Ironman contest, consisting of a 2.4-mile ocean swim, a 112-mile bike race, and a 26.2-mile run (1,427 contestants finished the race in 2000).

Track and field races never became as popular as baseball, basketball, golf and football, but U.S. athletes have performed extremely well in sprint competitions worldwide. Among famous U.S. Olympic heroes are Jesse Owens (four gold medals, 1936), Wilma Rudolph (three gold medals, 1960), and, more recently, Carl Lewis (nine gold medals, 1984–1996), Michael Johnson (five gold medals, 1992–2000), Florence Griffith Joyner (three gold medals, 1988), and Marion Jones (three gold medals, 2000).

Paradoxically, jogging has been a very popular sport in the United States while producing few world-class American long-distance runners (Billy Mills won the 10,000-meter Olympic race in 1964). The New Zealand coach Arthur Lydiard pioneered the idea that moderate continuous exercise could improve performance, allowing his country's athletes to dominate middle-distance running in the 1960s. William J. Bowerman, a track and field coach at the University of Oregon who had met Lydiard in 1962, and W. E. Harris, a heart specialist, popularized the concept in the United States when they published *Jogging* (1967). This book, as well as James Fixx's *The Complete Book of Running* (1977), launched a jogging and fitness craze. An estimated 10 million Americans jogged regularly by the 1970s. Bowerman, along with his student Phil Knight, also cofounded Blue Ribbon Sports (now Nike) in 1962 and invented the first modern running shoe, the Waffle Trainer, in 1972. Sales of running shoes in the United States amounted to $2.2 billion in 1998.

BIBLIOGRAPHY

Bowerman, William J., W. E. Harris, and James M. Shea. *Jogging*. New York: Grosset and Dunlap, 1967.

Fixx, James F. *The Complete Book of Running*. New York: Random House, 1977.

Henderson, Joe. *Better Runs: Twenty-five Years' Worth of Lessons for Running Faster and Farther*. Champaign, Ill: Human Kinetics, 1996.

Philippe R. Girard

See also **Marathons; Track and Field.**

RURAL FREE DELIVERY (RFD), a service designed to bring mail directly to people living in rural areas, was initiated on an experimental basis in 1896. Cities had enjoyed mail service for decades, but the cost of building a delivery network in remote areas, along with opposition from local merchants and postmasters, had delayed service to rural towns. Subscription magazines and mail-order stores had become staples for a growing middle class, and their emergence put new pressures on the federal government to expand its mail services. In addition, farmers' advocacy groups, well organized in the 1890s, amplified the call for reform.

Rep. Thomas E. Watson of Georgia, a friend of the FARMERS' ALLIANCE and vice presidential candidate for the Populists in 1896, was the author of the first free rural delivery legislation, enacted in 1893 and providing $10,000 for an experiment. (An earlier bill, based on the proposal of Postmaster Gen. John Wanamaker, would have provided $6 million, but the House Committee on Post Offices and Post Roads deemed it too expensive and killed it.) Opposition to RFD remained fierce. Service was delayed three years because of the intransigence of the new postmaster general, Wilson S. Bissell.

Congress had added $20,000 in 1894 and directed the postmaster general to make a report. The search for a postmaster general willing to start the experiment caused further delays. In the meantime, petitions poured in to Congress from local and state organizations of the National Grange and from other organizations of farmers. In 1896, Congress added another $10,000 appropriation, and Postmaster Gen. William L. Wilson, Bissell's successor, decided to test five rural routes in his home state of West Virginia. Between the autumn of 1896 and the spring of 1897, mail flowed along eighty-two pioneer routes, scattered through twenty-eight states and the territory of Arizona. Wilson laid the first routes in both sparse and populous areas, to better gauge the cost of the project. He estimated that extending the service nationally would cost between $40 million and $50 million.

After Wilson left office, Perry S. Heath, the first assistant postmaster general, and August W. Machen, superintendent of free delivery, adroit politicians who favored extension of the system, began active promotion of RFD. Securing an appropriation of $150,000 in 1898, they announced that any group of farmers wanting a mail route need only petition their congressman for it, sending a description of their communities and their roads. Congressmen were overwhelmed with petitions. In 1902, there were not more than eight thousand routes in the nation; three years later there were thirty-two thousand.

By 1915, the number of rural mail carriers was 43,718, as against 33,062 city mail carriers. Routes continued to be organized until the mid-1920s, and in 1925 the number of rural mail carriers reached 45,315. Afterward, consolidation of routes based on the use of automobiles brought sharp declines. In 1970, there were 31,346 rural routes extending 2,044,335 miles, or an average of about 65 miles per route.

Rural free delivery—by bringing daily delivery of newspapers with coverage of national and world events, changing fashions, and market quotations and by delivering mail-order catalogs—was of major importance in breaking down rural isolation. The rural free delivery system also contributed to the development of a parcel post system and played an important part in the good roads movement. True to some of the dire predictions of its early opponents, however, RFD cut into the profits of main street retailers; brought an exotic and sometimes threatening urban culture into rural living rooms; and added to the growing sense that residents of small towns lived at the margins of a consumer economy dominated by America's biggest cities.

BIBLIOGRAPHY

Barron, Hal S. *Mixed Harvest: The Second Great Transformation in the Rural North, 1870–1930.* Chapel Hill: University of North Carolina Press, 1997.

Fuller, Wayne E. *RFD: The Changing Face of Rural America.* Bloomington: Indiana University Press, 1964.

Gladys L. Baker / A. R.

See also **Advertising; Mail-Order Houses; Post Roads; Postal Service, United States; Rural Life.**

RURAL LIFE.

Rural life has been a central and defining aspect of the history of the United States, which has transformed from an agrarian-based society to a largely urban and industrial one. The term "rural life" broadly describes the lifestyle of residents of nonurban areas, defined by the U.S. Census Bureau as small towns and country areas with populations less than 2,500. Many changes have occurred in the day-to-day activities of rural residents from the colonial period, when virtually everyone in the United States either lived in rural areas or had a rural background. In the early twenty-first century, less than 25 percent of the American population lived in rural areas.

The Colonies and the Early United States

Colonists in North America spent their earliest years strictly as subsistence farmers, growing or making everything they might need—food, clothing, houses and furnishings, and farm implements. Water usually had to be hauled by hand from a nearby spring, well, or stream. As they became established, some rural residents had surplus production they were able to sell or use to barter in nearby towns.

By the time of the American Revolution there was more profit-oriented, commercial agriculture. Most rural residents lived in river areas to facilitate the movement of commodities and people, since roads and overland transportation were poor. To make a profit farmers had to be innovative, reducing labor needs and simplifying routine farming tasks. Where labor costs were high and market prices low, rural farmers used slave labor. The result was a caste system in which blacks were at the bottom of the social strata.

Distinctive regional customs quickly developed in rural life, partly due to differences in growing seasons and climatic conditions. For example, tobacco farmers in New England harvested their crops in late summer, while those in the South waited until fall. Southern colonists could do more chores and work outdoors than their Northern counterparts. Regardless of location, though, rural life was very isolated. The only regular break in the monotony was attending church services.

Life for rural women during this period was very difficult and physical. Women were called upon not only to keep the home and rear children, but also to help in the fields and to process the raw commodities of the farm. Theirs was a narrow focus, largely limited to domestic chores and making products such as cider and butter to provide additional income. Women had few rights by law and custom, and could not own property if married. Enslaved women led even more difficult lives and were often expected to carry out the same kind of work as male slaves.

As Americans spread across the Appalachian Mountains and along the Gulf Coast, settlers extended these characteristics of rural life into new areas. They increasingly came into contact, and sometimes conflict, with Indian groups. Many Indians were themselves rural farmers, and oftentimes showed the newly arrived farmers what seeds grew well in which areas and under which conditions. The settlers, however, very much wanted Indian lands for themselves. The result was decades of mixed federal policy involving purchase or seizure of Indian lands and relocation of whole tribes. This produced an unstable and sometimes fearful existence for both the settlers and the Indians in rural areas.

Influences of the Spanish

At its peak, Spain's reach included large portions of what would become Florida, Texas, New Mexico, and California. Spain's missions of exploration from Mexico and the Caribbean islands have been described by some historians as the search for "God, gold, and glory." Conquistadors sought wealth and honor for the Spanish crown. Accompanying them, or following close behind, were small groups of missionaries. These men, most often either members of the Franciscan or Jesuit religious orders of the Roman Catholic Church, established churches and missions where they could gather local Indians in an attempt to create an agrarian lifestyle and to convert them to the Catholic faith. The work of missionaries had only mixed success.

To encourage settlement in outlying areas of the Spanish Empire, the monarchy authorized large land grants. These tracts, often located along rivers, were in turn divided into areas for farms, homes, and communal uses, and became the centers of new colonial communities. Once established, rural life in and near these Spanish villages was not unlike the early subsistence existence of rural residents of the British colonies and the early United States.

In more developed communities, Spanish families slowly modified their surroundings to reflect their traditional culture, which was largely patriarchal and hierarchical. In households, men held authority over wives and children, but married Spanish women could own and maintain separate property and pass it on to their heirs. Most families followed Catholic custom and practice, faithfully attending mass and other church services.

Another critical element of Spanish rural life, particularly in the central and western colonies, was the building of dams and *acequias* (irrigation ditches) to divert river water for fields and the community. The presence and influence of these irrigation systems, and the accompanying system of water rights, remain a critical part of modern rural life in those communities.

The Spanish also brought with them a rigid caste system. This created strict separation of groups of people in a community based on their wealth and racial background. Spaniards (*españoles*) born in Spain (*peninsulares*) were at the apex of the social strata, followed by their children born in the Americas (*criollos*). *Mestizos*, those persons who were part Spanish and part Indian, were the largest group, particularly in rural colonial villages. Below them were Hispanicized Indians, freed or enslaved blacks, and other Indians. Only *españoles* enjoyed the privileges extended to colonists by the Spanish Crown. The further a community was from the formal rule of law in Spanish cities in Mexico or the Caribbean, though, the easier it was for settlers to transcend social barriers. Many rural villagers and farmers were unconcerned about social status or the legitimacy of relationships with each other, either as viewed by the Spanish Crown or by the church.

As early as the sixteenth century, the influence of the Spanish reached well beyond their explorations and settlements to affect other Indians of North America. A multitude of European plants, animals, and diseases spread well ahead of the physical presence of any European, creating major and long-lasting changes in Indian rural life. Both British and Spanish explorers "discovered" European watermelons and peaches under Indian cultivation. Cattle, horses, and sheep brought by European settlers spread throughout North America, especially in the arid Southwest, creating ecological changes to streams and grasslands. Several Indian tribes took advantage of these animals. The Comanche became accomplished horseback riders, while the Navaho began managing herds of *churro* sheep for their wool and their meat. These changes created lasting cultural influences among Indians, many of which are still reflected in their modern culture.

The Nineteenth Century

Rural life and agriculture in the nineteenth century remained very different from one region of the country to another and were still very much influenced by the seasons of the year. Families rejected subsistence agriculture, choosing to produce crops for economic gain in an effort to improve their standard of living. However, many rural families suffered from a combination of poverty and poor health. The supply of food was generally abundant, but included little variety or nutritious value. The introduction of various summer and winter vegetables, often tended in small gardens by women, offered some dietary im-

Farm Family. Four men stand behind four women, one of whom holds a baby, in front of a barn, c. 1890. INGRAM COLLECTION/GETTY IMAGES

provements. Numerous home remedies for illness developed throughout the rural United States.

The church was an important center for spiritual nourishment and social interaction. Families made regular trips to town to trade at the country store. Socializing often decreased from spring to fall because of the work that needed to be done at home and on the farm. It was important to many rural residents to live close to other family members, creating networks of kinship in communities. These provided support in hard times and help at peak times of labor. A family's "good name" was even good for credit in business transactions.

By the second half of the nineteenth century, rural residents had gained other venues for social interaction and education. Organized adult education programs like the lyceum and the Chautauqua movements offered programs and opportunities for rural residents to learn more about culture, the arts, and self-education. Similar activities were later organized through political-based organizations like the Grange and the Farmers' Alliance.

Through the nineteenth century, rural women's major roles were as housewife, mother, and helpmate. Women were responsible for making most domestic goods, such as clothing, and helping process farm products, such as butter and cheese. They were also called upon to work in the fields at crucial times such as the harvest. Slave women, found mostly in the cotton and tobacco-growing areas of the South, were expected to perform domestic tasks in addition to working in the fields.

Getting an education in a rural community was a great challenge. Most farm children attended school regularly only during the winter; fieldwork was more important during the growing season. Most children learned what they could from their parents, focusing on domestic and farm chores they would use when they were older. In most areas of the country, rural children often received no more than three or four years of formal education. An exception was in the New England states, where religious groups influenced the creation of public, tax-supported schools to teach basic writing, reading, and arithmetic to all children.

The U.S. Civil War ended slavery in the South and caused fundamental economic and social changes throughout the country. A system of sharecropping evolved to replace slavery in the South. Sharecropping often trapped families in an unending cycle of debt. The offer of free land in the West under the Homestead Act of 1862 encouraged many families to relocate from the Midwest and South in an effort to improve their economic standing. Rural life on the frontier, though, was often as difficult or worse than it had been in their former homes. Families worked hard to improve their new land so they could have extra income to purchase goods and services from nearby towns.

By the 1880s, the federal government had resettled much of the native Indian population on reservations in modern-day Oklahoma or remote corners of the West. The government forced Indians to "civilize" and adopt the American lifestyle. The Dawes Act of 1887 mandated that parts of reservations be divided into private property to aid efforts to turn Indians into modern, self-sufficient farmers. In most instances, reservation lands proved unsuitable for agriculture. The result was collective impoverishment that extended through Indian rural life, education, and employment. This continued to be a problem for Indians until the mid-1980s, when the development of reservation gambling and federal support for industrial and commercial development resulted in some improvements on reservations around the United States.

The late nineteenth and early twentieth centuries saw concern about rural life growing among urban-based educators, religious leaders, and public figures. The Country Life Movement sought ways to improve rural lifestyles, education, and agricultural practices. These efforts received a boost in 1907 when President Theodore Roosevelt created a commission to study the situation and recommend solutions. Rural people were wary of these outsiders, and change and reform came slowly.

New Conveniences in Rural Living

As the twentieth century began, a series of important developments and technologies relieved some of the isolation of rural life in the United States. In 1896 Congress instituted rural free delivery (RFD) mail service. This was

Rural Fixture. At the time this photograph was taken by Marion Post Wolcott in 1939, Mrs. Lloyd *(left)*, ninety-one years old (seen here with her daughter Nettie), had lived at this spot in Orange County, N.C., since her marriage sixty-nine years earlier. LIBRARY OF CONGRESS

a convenience long sought by farm organizations, and something that eager politicians were willing to provide to curry favor with voters. Some years later, in 1913, the parcel post system was introduced. RFD and parcel post opened the way for catalog services, such as those provided by Montgomery Ward and Sears, Roebuck, and Co. Now, families could order virtually anything from a catalog—farm equipment, clothing, household goods, and toys—and have it delivered to the farm without having to go to town. This resulted in lost business for merchants, who saw some families less frequently than before, but created an entire new industry—one that saw a resurgence in the late twentieth and early twenty-first centuries. RFD also literally brought the world to the doors of rural families, through correspondence, newspapers, and farm magazines.

Rural delivery and increasing numbers of automobiles and trucks, which were replacing farm wagons by the 1920s, brought rural support for the "good roads" movement. Farmers volunteered their time and equipment to help local road boards maintain and improve rural roads, and Congress began funding projects for federal roads and highways, starting with post roads for RFD routes.

The introduction of radio and movies in the early twentieth century brought the sounds of the world to rural families. Radio programs helped lessen the isolation of rural life, breaking the monotony of daily activities by providing a companion to help pass the time while chores and farm work were done. The radio also was a critical source of information: it provided timely market and weather reports. Farmers could better plan their work schedule for the next day and decide for themselves when to sell or hold their commodities. The number of farms with (mostly battery-powered) radios increased rapidly in the 1920s. Once acquired, the radio was one of the last things a rural family would part with, even during the hard times of the Great Depression. Movie houses came even to rural towns, and motion pictures provided rural residents entertainment and glimpses of what other parts of the world were like. The introduction of television in the 1950s had a similar effect in their homes. The popularity of movies, radio, and later television brought nineteenth-century-era educational and entertainment programs such as the Chautauqua to an end by the mid-twentieth century.

Another service long sought by farmers was electricity and its accompanying equipment and conveniences. Though electric service was becoming more common in cities in the early 1900s, electric lines were not being extended into rural areas. Companies felt that it cost too much to build lines to farms and small towns with little promise of financial return. This changed only with the creation of the Rural Electrification Administration (REA) in 1935. Subsidized by the federal government, local cooperatives were organized to build rural distribution systems. Though some farmers and power companies feared the REA as a socialistic enterprise, it brought electrical power to nearly every part of the United States by 1950. Some families used electric-powered pumps to establish indoor plumbing. Dietary habits and health improved as families began storing food in refrigerators. Some households acquired "labor-saving" devices, like vacuums and washing machines. Historians today debate whether these machines actually made home life easier or more complicated: because women were able to do chores more quickly, they did them more frequently.

Telephone service for rural areas followed a similar course as electrification. The Great Depression and a lack of interest from phone companies slowed the spread of telephone lines, leaving two out of three rural families without this new service. The Hill-Poage Act of 1949 authorized the REA to extend telephone service into rural areas. Initially introduced with party lines, where several households shared a single phone line, telephones quickly became a crucial part of rural life in the 1950s and 1960s.

The new technologies and services did not come to everyone, nor did the changes come uniformly. Rural residents of the South, because of their poverty and isolation, tended to be among the last to see any of these services or technologies. Families also could acquire these conveniences only if their finances permitted.

Despite these changes in rural life, many aspects remained the same for women and children. Many women still tended their butter and eggs for extra income and continued to be the housewife, mother, and extra farm hand. Child rearing, domestic chores, and food processing occupied most of their time. Some women received enough education to qualify for teaching positions. Many farm daughters took up teaching while still living at home so they could contribute to family earnings. Once married, though, women were often forced to give up teaching by school boards that believed husbands should provide for their wives, and wives should not be working so they could keep a home. The constant turnover of teachers, as well as financial difficulties due to increased tax delinquencies because of the poor economy, contributed to problems in rural education. As a result rural children, particularly African Americans in the racially segregated South, could get only the most basic education.

The problems with education and the shift away from sharecropper systems began to change the fabric of rural residency. Government crop subsidies introduced in the 1930s to support farmers offered the most benefit to landowners and large producers. Small farms increasingly were sold and consolidated into larger enterprises. Rural residents, particularly the poor and minorities, increasingly left the country behind and drifted into towns and cities looking for jobs and a different way of life. The increased industrial activity just before and during World War II further accelerated these migrations, resulting in a manpower shortage that further accelerated the mechanization of agricultural production. After the war, rural youth were more likely to leave for the appeal and grandeur of the cities than to stay and help with the farm or ranch and take it over when their parents died. This trend continued through the rest of the twentieth century.

No longer a large part of the population after the Korean War, rural families had little political influence and even less certainty about their lives. By 1990, farm families composed only 1.9 percent of the total population of the United States. Increasingly, farm families experienced an economic pinch because farming was more expensive and the returns smaller. Farm bankruptcies were numerous in the late 1970s and early 1980s. Rural women increasingly took on outside employment to provide needed extra income. Many families, though, stayed in the country because they believed the values of rural living were far better than what could be found in the city. However, in many areas of the country, school districts consolidated to combat high costs of building maintenance, teacher salaries, and administration, leaving some children to spend long hours of their day on a bus riding to school and back.

Rural Life Today

Rural life in the early twenty-first century is increasingly difficult to differentiate from urban life. Rural families make frequent trips to town to shop, attend church, and go to school. Many states have sponsored initiatives to extend Internet services into the country. With the proliferation of household goods and appliances, cable TV, and satellite dishes, there is little distinction between an urban home and a country home among families of similar economic standing. Rural residents wear the same clothes and eat the same foods as urbanites. Interestingly, some affluent families and retirees have begun acquiring country homes to escape the big city and to rediscover the slower pace and quieter way of life that they associate with America's rural past.

BIBLIOGRAPHY

Barron, Hal S. *Those Who Stayed Behind: Rural Society in Nineteenth-Century New England.* New York: Cambridge University Press, 1984.

Cotton, Barbara R., ed. *Symposium on the History of Rural Life in America.* Washington, D.C.: Agricultural History Society, 1986.

Cowan, Ruth Schwartz. *More Work for Mother: The Ironies of Household Technology from the Open Hearth to the Microwave.* New York: Basic Books, 1983.

Danbom, David B. *Born in the Country: A History of Rural America.* Baltimore: Johns Hopkins University Press, 1995.

Goreham, Gary A., ed. *Encyclopedia of Rural America: The Land and People.* Santa Barbara, Calif.: ABC-CLIO, 1997.

Hurt, R. Douglas. *American Agriculture: A Brief History.* Ames: Iowa State University Press, 1994.

Jensen, Joan M. *Promise to the Land: Essays on Rural Women.* Albuquerque: University of New Mexico Press, 1991.

Osterud, Nancy Grey. *Bonds of Community: The Lives of Farm Women in Nineteenth-Century New York.* Ithaca, N.Y.: Cornell University Press, 1991.

Shover, John L. *First Majority—Last Minority: The Transformation of Rural Life in America.* DeKalb: University of Northern Illinois Press, 1976.

Weber, David J. *The Spanish Frontier in North America.* New Haven, Conn.: Yale University Press, 1992.

Cameron L. Saffell

See also vol. 9: **The New American Poverty.**

RUSSIA, RELATIONS WITH. During the Revolutionary War, American leaders were eager to establish diplomatic ties with as many nations as possible, and Congress hoped that tsarist Russia might be willing to not only recognize the new nation diplomatically but also to help in its struggle for independence. Catherine the Great, although considered an enlightened monarch, despised both the British for their inability to crush the rebels in the colonies and the Americans because she was no friend of revolutions. When Catherine worked with Charles Gravier, comte de Vergennes, to set up a League of Armed Neutrality in 1780 to impede British commercial power, she did so because it aided Russian interests, not to support the American Revolution. In 1782 Congress sent Francis Dana to St. Petersburg in the hope of establishing diplomatic ties. Dana, speaking neither Russian nor French, the language of the diplomats, failed over the course of two years to persuade Russia to recognize the United States.

Formal Russian recognition of the United States did not come until 1809, when Russia entered into war against England on the side of France. Hoping for increased trade between the two nations, Washington was eager to establish friendly relations with Russia after the NONINTERCOURSE ACT of 1809 had prohibited U.S. trade with Great Britain and France. Exports to Russia increased noticeably during the next few years (from $12,000 before the EMBARGO ACT of 1807 to $6 million) but could not make up for the loss of transatlantic trade with traditional European commercial partners.

In September 1821, Russia issued a prohibition on all foreign trade within 100 miles of the Pacific coast of North America and claimed exclusive trading rights in the North Pacific as far south as the 51st parallel. The MONROE DOCTRINE, which was promulgated in 1823, declared the United States the dominating power in the Western Hemisphere and was a direct result both of Russia's attempts to restrain trade and also of its unwillingness to recognize the independence of the newly created republics in Latin America. The Russo-American Treaty of 1825, restricting Russian influence to north of 54° 40′, was negotiated between Russia and the United States; this was the first formal agreement between the two nations.

Relations remained friendly during most of the rest of the nineteenth century, despite differences over the Russian suppression of the Polish rebellion in 1830 and its support for Austria during the Hungarian uprising of 1848–1849. The arrival of Russian warships in Union ports in 1863 during the Civil War was hailed by many Northerners as a sign of support for their cause. However, the ships were not intended to reinforce the Union navy but to safeguard the Russian fleet and to be in place for possible use of American ports as bases for activities against Great Britain and France. When the American minister to St. Petersburg, Cassius Clay, approached his Russian counterparts after the war with an offer to buy Alaska, the Russian government responded eagerly because it believed that eventually America would take the area in any case. American commercial influence in that region had increased since the 1820s, and the Russian Trading Company, which ran Alaska, was highly dependent on American supplies. As early as 1856, Russia had considered selling Alaska; the Russian chargé d'àffaires in Washington, D.C., Baron Eduard von Stoekl, was authorized in December 1866 to sell the Russian colony for at least $5 million. Finding the Americans eager buyers, he pushed the price to $7.2 million; Alaska changed hands in an agreement signed on 30 March 1867.

The two nations became estranged around the turn of the twentieth century, when Russia's rejection of an OPEN DOOR POLICY in Asia became obvious and when news of anti-Jewish pogroms and discrimination against Jewish American businessmen in Russia reached the United States. Open friction erupted over China. Although all nations involved in putting down the BOXER REBELLION in 1900 had agreed to withdraw immediately after hostilities ceased, Russia continued to occupy Manchuria in an attempt to annex that region. With its own plans of expansion, Japan attacked Russian forces at Port Arthur on 8 February 1904. The United States sympathized with Japan because it hoped Japan would uphold the Open Door policy; President Theodore Roosevelt acting as mediator, helped negotiate the agreement that ended the war. The Portsmouth Treaty, signed on 5 September 1905, favored Japan, allowing it to become the dominant power in the Far East.

The fall of the tsarist regime in March 1917 was welcomed by many Americans, and the provisional government was immediately recognized. The weakness of the government of Aleksandr F. Kerenski, increased German pressure on the battlefield, and general war-weariness in Russia soon led to the Bolshevik seizure of power in November 1917. The Bolsheviks almost immediately announced their willingness to make a separate peace with Germany. That declaration and Soviet propaganda encouraging workers in all capitalist countries to stop fighting the capitalist's war and, instead, rise against their bourgeois oppressors, frightened and alienated many Americans. The United States did not recognize the new government. After Russia signed the Treaty of Brest Litovsk (March 1918) ending the war with Germany, the Allies intervened in order to maintain eastern front against the Central Powers. British and American forces were to secure Allied stores at Murmansk, Archangel, and Vladivostok, and they were assigned to support the so-called Czech legion, which was to leave Russia and be transported to the western front, where it could continue fighting against the Central Powers for an independent Czechoslovakia. Allied forces, some of which continued operating in northern Russia after the end of World War I (November 1918), did so, at least in part, in an effort to overthrow the Bolsheviks. Not until June 1919 did the United States extract all its troops from Russia; thus, by 1920, the United States was faced with a regime in Russia that was not only antagonistic to American society and its political system but also had been alienated by an obvious attempt to overthrow the Bolsheviks. This hostility was mirrored in the sharp anticommunism that culminated in the red scare and the PALMER RAIDS of the 1920s. Russia was not invited to participate in the Versailles peace talks ending World War I, and the United States continued to exclude the Soviet Union from other meetings long after the 1922 German-Soviet Treaty of Rapallo had led to the recognition of the communist regime in Russia by most nations. Attempts by the Soviets to establish diplomatic relations were brushed aside on legalistic grounds by the staunchly anticommunist administrations of Warren G. Harding, Calvin Coolidge, and Herbert Hoover. Nonetheless, semiprivate operations, such as the American Relief Administration, led by then-Secretary of Commerce Herbert Hoover, provided Russian famine relief from 1921 to 1923.

Official nonrecognition did not prevent increasing trade between the two nations. By 1925 the volume had expanded to $65 million, and in the 1930s, President Franklin D. Roosevelt saw an opportunity to stimulate exports to the Union of Soviet Socialist Republics (U.S.S.R.) through diplomatic recognition, thus creating jobs in the United States. He appointed William Bullitt as special assistant secretary of state for Soviet affairs. Agreement was reached on the settlements of debts and the propaganda disseminated by the supposedly independent international communist organization Comintern. At the end of 1933, Bullitt became the first U.S ambassador in communist Moscow. But constant friction with his Soviet hosts over domestic staff, who turned out to be Soviet agents; arrests of American citizens not reported to the embassy; and decreasing trade because of Soviet red tape soon dashed hopes of friendly relations. The signing of a nonaggression pact with Nazi Germany and the attack on Finland in 1939, the seizure of the Baltic states in 1940, and the Russo-Japanese Neutrality Pact of 1941 considerably strained relations between Washington and Moscow.

When Germany invaded the Soviet Union on 22 June 1941, public and official sympathy for the Soviet Union was high; the United States almost immediately announced support of the U.S.S.R., offering aid on a cash and carry basis. Lend-lease was offered on 7 November and, by the end of World War II, the United States had furnished $9.5 billion in aid. After Japan's attack on Pearl Harbor (7 December 1941) and the declaration of war on the United States by Germany and Italy on 11 December 1941, Roosevelt assured Joseph Stalin that a second front would be opened in France before the end of 1942 to help ease the pressure of German forces in the east. By mid-1942, it had become obvious that this promise could not be kept, and Soviet distrust of the United States and Britain, only slightly covered by the common goal of defeating Nazi Germany, resurfaced. Allied landings in Africa and in southern Italy did little to lessen the pressure on the Soviet Union until the invasion of Normandy on 6 June 1944.

In a series of wartime conferences—meetings of Roosevelt, Stalin, and British leader Winston Churchill in TEHERAN (November to December 1943) and in YALTA (February 1945)—the United States, the Soviet Union, and the United Kingdom agreed on war and on peace aims. The leaders affirmed their demand for unconditional surrender of the Axis powers. They also decided on the division of Germany into zones of occupation, the future of the eastern European states, and creation of a United Nations organization. The Soviet Union promised to enter the war against Japan as soon as Germany had been defeated. At the last of the "big three" conferences (17 July to 2 August 1945) in Potsdam, Harry S. Truman, who had become president on th death of Roosevelt in April, learned of the successful test of the atomic bomb. Great Britain and the United States had worked together in building the device but had agreed not to disclose the project to the Soviets. Without consulting Stalin, Truman ordered atomic bombs to be dropped on Nagasaki and Hiroshima to force Japan to surrender and also possibly as a show of power directed at the U.S.S.R.

Concurrently, the United Nations was being organized; it held its inaugural meeting on 25 April 1945 in San Francisco. It was agreed that the major powers—China, France, the Soviet Union, the United Kingdom and the United States—would be permanent members of a Security Council and have the right to veto a Council decision. The Soviet delegation, however, had initially insisted that these powers have the right to prevent Council discussion of an issue. Although the Soviet Union relented after Truman sent an envoy to Stalin, this conflict foreshadowed a number of confrontations in the coming years.

Wartime cooperation soon turned into bitter hostility when continued Soviet promulgation of world revolution and anticapitalist propaganda alienated the United States. The COLD WAR that developed was marked by the TRUMAN DOCTRINE of 1947, the MARSHALL PLAN of 1948–1952, the communist coup in Czechoslovakia in 1948, the Berlin Crisis of 1948–1949, the establishment of the North Atlantic Treaty Organization (NATO) in 1949, and the signing of the Warsaw Pact in 1955. In this period, the Soviet Union became viewed in the United States as an offshoot of Nazi Germany, an attitude that found expression in National Security Council document NSC-68 picturing the conflict as a struggle between good and evil and calling for a massive increase in military spending. Communism was envisioned as a monolithic bloc, its headquarters located in Moscow. Thus, the Chinese-supported invasion of South Korea by North Korean troops in 1950 was taken as a possible smokescreen for a Soviet attack on Western Europe. Political containment, as proclaimed in July 1947 by George F. Kennan Jr., turned into military containment, and nations were discouraged from trading with the Soviet Union.

After Stalin's death in 1953, a new Soviet leadership sent conciliatory signals to Washington. In 1959 Vice President Richard M. Nixon traveled to Moscow, and Nikita Khrushchev visited the United States. Only a year later, relations were again strained considerably when an American U-2 spy plane was shot down over Soviet territory on 1 May 1960. The failed American-backed invasion at the Bay of Pigs by CIA-trained Cuban refugees on 17 April 1961 and the erection of the Berlin Wall in August 1961 displayed on different continents the frictions between the two nations but also showed how careful both sides were to avoid slipping into direct military confrontation. Despite stark differences in character, President John F. Kennedy and Khrushchev had developed the beginnings of détente until the deployment of Soviet missiles on Cuba and the subsequent Cuban Missile Crisis in October 1962 brought the two nations to the brink of war. In 1963, the nations signed a nuclear test-ban treaty, and much of the antagonism of the preceding decade abated. Meanwhile, the Vietnam conflict was deepening. Partly because the Vietnam War was deemed to be guided by Soviet interests, Kennedy began shifting American resources to the region. President Lyndon B. Johnson, who

Cold War. The incommensurable ideologies and strategic aims of the United States and the Soviet Union swiftly drove the former World War II allies apart after the defeat of Germany and Japan. This photo shows Soviet premier Nikita Khrushchev *(left)* and U.S. President John F. Kennedy *(right)* in 1961—the year Kennedy staged the disastrous Bay of Pigs Invasion and Khrushchev built the Berlin Wall. The next year brought the Cuban Missile Crisis, in which the two nations brought the world to the brink of nuclear war—but managed to maintain the strained peace, which lasted until the fall of the Soviet Union three decades later. © AP/WIDE WORLD PHOTOS

had succeeded Kennedy after his assassination in late 1963, engaged the United States in the escalating conflict, paying little attention to other international issues.

After Khrushchev fell from power in October 1964, Leonid Brezhnev and Alexei Kosygin strove to achieve nuclear parity with the United States. In June 1967, Kosygin visited the United States, and a slow process of de-escalation and negotiations about arms reduction began. Rapprochement between the two nations was slightly set back when the reform movement in Czechoslovakia was suppressed by the Soviet Union in 1968, but both nations appeared to accept coexistence. Substantial American discontent with Soviet involvement in internal struggles in lesser-developed nations in Africa, Southeast Asia, Latin America, and the Caribbean; the establishment of diplomatic relations between the United States and the People's Republic of China; and, finally, the Soviet invasion in Afghanistan in December 1979, again led to a deterioration of relations.

When Ronald Reagan, an ardent anticommunist, became president in 1981, he denounced détente as a one-way street; in a speech on 8 March 1983, Reagan called the Soviet Union an "evil empire." This new Cold War only abated when Mikhail Gorbachev came to power in the Soviet Union in 1985. He seemed willing to re-establish friendly relations with the United States and to initiate democratization in the U.S.S.R. Reagan, seeing a chance to achieve a place in history as peacemaker, grasped the opportunity for personal diplomacy and, with a meeting in Reykjavik on 11 and 12 October 1986, began a process of mutual reassurance and accommodation that his successor, George H. W. Bush, continued after initial hesitation. Political changes in Eastern Europe, particularly in Bulgaria, Czechoslovakia, Romania, and the German Democratic Republic, and the disintegration of the power of the Communist Party in the U.S.S.R. led to unification of Germany and to a considerable lessening of the military threat the Soviet Union had posed to the United States. As the Soviet Union disintegrated in 1991 after a failed attempt by reactionaries to oust Gorbachev, the United States recognized the independence of the Baltic states. In December 1991, Boris Yeltsin, who had become the leading Soviet politician, conferred with leaders of Ukraine and Byelorussia to dissolve the Soviet Union and to form a Commonwealth of Independent States. On 31 December 1991, the U.S.S.R. ceased to exist.

The instability of the new regime, the fear that Yeltsin was much less predictable than Gorbachev, and anxiety about the safety of the nuclear arsenal, again led to strained relations between the United States and Russia. During the presidency of Bill Clinton (1993–2001), the integration of Russia with the West was thought likely; the administration of George W. Bush proved to be much cooler to that idea. However, the war against international terrorism after the attacks of 11 September 2001 on the United States led to increased cooperation, particularly in matters of intelligence. Despite unresolved issues, including the expansion of NATO, the missile defense system proposed by Bush, and the war in Chechnya, the United States and Russia signed an unprecedented arms reduction treaty in Moscow on 24 May 2002. The NATO-Russia Council was also established, and Russia was accepted as a junior partner in NATO at the Rome summit meeting on 28 May 2002.

BIBLIOGRAPHY

Boyle, Peter G. *American-Soviet Relations: From the Russian Revolution to the Fall of Communism.* New York: Routledge, 1993.

Jensen, Oliver, ed. *America and Russia: A Century and a Half of Dramatic Encounters.* New York: Simon and Schuster, 1962.

Laserson, Max M. *The American Impact on Russia: Diplomatic and Ideological, 1784–1917.* New York: Macmillan, 1950.

Loth, Wilfried. *Overcoming the Cold War: A History of Détente, 1950–1991.* New York: Palgrave, 2002.

Paterson, Thomas G. *Meeting the Communist Threat: America's Cold War History.* New York: Oxford University Press, 1988.

Tarsaïdzé, Alexandre. *Czars and Presidents.* New York: McDowell, Obolensky 1958.

Michael Wala

See also **North Atlantic Treaty Organization;** *and vol. 9:* **American Diplomacy.**

RUSSIAN AND SOVIET AMERICANS.

The entry of more than 243,000 émigrés from areas within the former Soviet Union between 1981 and 1993 represents the second large wave of Russian/Soviet IMMIGRATION to the United States. Between 1881 and 1920, 3.2 million people, the majority of them Jewish, came to the United States from areas of what became the Soviet Union. Between these two eras, immigration of both Soviet Jews and non-Jews was at very low levels. Public displays of anti-Semitism and lack of opportunities for social and economic advancement increased pressure on the Soviet government to allow the emigration of Soviet Jews during the late 1970s. The U.S. government responded by admitting more than fifty thousand refugees from the Soviet Union, the majority of whom were Jews, between 1972 and 1980. Since 1980, 96 percent of immigrants to the United States from areas within the Soviet Union have entered as refugees. Since the late 1980s, Soviet refugee streams have included increasing numbers of non-Jews as well as Jews. During the 1990s, refugee arrivals from areas within the former Soviet Union ranged between forty thousand and sixty thousand per year. For 1993, Congress authorized the admission of 49,775 Soviet refugees.

The communities of Russian and Soviet émigrés within the United States reflect each of these waves of large-scale migration. Between 1970 and 1990, the size of the U.S. population that had been born in the Soviet Union declined from 463,500 to 334,000, reflecting the aging of immigrants who entered at the turn of the century. Nearly two-fifths of the 1990 U.S. population of persons born in tsarist Russia or the Soviet Union had entered in the previous ten years.

Since 1992 the U.S. Immigration and Naturalization Service has reported immigration from specific areas in the former Soviet Union. Of the 58,600 immigrants admitted from the former U.S.S.R. in 1993, 31.3 percent were born in Ukraine, 20.6 percent in Russia, 10.7 percent in Armenia, and 8 percent in Belarus. More than half of recent Soviet immigrants are women and 30 percent are under the age of twenty, indicating the important role of the family in emigration.

As with other groups, Soviet émigrés are concentrated in specific geographic areas in the United States. In 1990, 48 percent of this population resided in the Northeast and 27 percent in western states; among Soviet immigrants arriving during the 1980s, 36 percent settled in California. The New York metropolitan region had the largest number of Soviet- and Russian-born people, and large communities of émigrés were formed in the Los

Russian Americans. These five women sitting in a wagon, their heads covered by lace shawls, wear a mix of Russian and American dress, 1947. © UPI/CORBIS-BETTMANN

Angeles–Long Beach area. Settlement of Soviet Jewish immigrants was aided in large part by private Jewish organizations in metropolitan areas throughout the United States. Results of survey research on resettled Jewish populations, moreover, indicate that Soviet Jewish émigrés to the United States expressed strong religious identities similar to Soviet émigrés to Israel.

Descendants of earlier waves of Russian immigration have been characterized by high levels of education and occupation. In the 1990 census, half of the Russian-ancestry male population reported either professional specialties or executive, administrative, or managerial occupations; among Russian-ancestry women, 40 percent were in these occupations. These levels are significantly higher than those for other ancestry groups. Recent immigrants also have been distinctive in levels of education and occupation. Among Soviet immigrants admitted to the United States in 1993, one-third of those reporting occupations listed professional, executive, administrative, or managerial occupations. Occupations among recent Soviet Jewish immigrants are estimated to be proportionally even higher. Estimates for immigrants aided by the Hebrew Aid Society in 1989 suggest that two-thirds of Soviet Jewish immigrants were in professional, scientific,

technical, and white-collar occupations prior to migrating. The population of people of Russian ancestry residing in the United States in 2000 was estimated at 2,980,776.

BIBLIOGRAPHY

Jones, Maldwyn A. *American Immigration.* Chicago: University of Chicago Press, 1992.

Lieberson, Stanley, and Mary C. Waters. *From Many Strands: Ethnic and Racial Groups in Contemporary America.* New York: Russell Sage Foundation, 1990.

Simon, Rita J., ed. *New Lives: The Adjustment of Soviet Jewish Immigrants in the United States and Israel.* Lexington, Mass.: Lexington Books, 1985.

Ellen Percy Kraly / A. G.

See also **Cold War; Immigration Restriction; Russia, Relations with.**

RUSSIAN CLAIMS. Tsar Paul I first defined Russia's claims to North America in his 1799 charter to the Russian-American Company, which established the territorial limits of the company's monopoly on Russian-American trade. These extended from the fifty-fifth parallel to the Bering Strait, but also empowered the company to explore south and north, and to trade with neighboring or attainable peoples, such as the Japanese. The company learned that the great market for furs was at Canton, China, and planned a great trade route to embrace the Asian islands and ALASKA.

The Russians looked south to secure supplies for their Alaskan establishments. After some exploration, in 1809, the company established Fort Ross on the northern California coast as a supply station for meat and grain. The company never traded with the Spaniards and in 1841 abandoned the settlement.

In 1821, upon renewing the Russian-American Company's charter, the Russian government claimed authority over the coast to fifty-one degrees north latitude, alarming Great Britain and the United States, both of which claimed territory there. The two countries succeeded in limiting Russia's exclusive claim to the southern line of 54°40′, and the British-Russian treaty of 1825 delimited Russian claims from the coast inland, thus establishing the basis for the boundary of Alaska as granted by Russia to the United States in 1867.

BIBLIOGRAPHY

Pomeroy, Earl. *The Pacific Slope: A History of California, Oregon, Washington, Idaho, Utah, and Nevada.* Lincoln: University of Nebraska Press, 1991.

Tikhmenev, Petr Aleksandrovich. *A History of the Russian-American Company.* Seattle: University of Washington Press, 1978.

Joseph Schafer / c. w.

See also **Explorations and Expeditions: Russian; Hudson's Bay Company; Russia, Relations with.**

RUST BELT refers to an economic region of the United States concentrated in the formerly dominant industrial states of Illinois, Indiana, Michigan, Ohio, and Pennsylvania. By the 1980s, the Rust Belt became what the DUST BOWL had been to an earlier generation—a symbolic name for a devastating economic change. The 1984 Democratic presidential candidate, Walter Mondale, is generally credited with coining the term. During the campaign, Mondale, the former vice president from Minnesota, attacked the economic policies of incumbent Republican president, Ronald Regan, stating that the president was "turning our great industrial Midwest and the industrial base of this country into a rust bowl." The media, however, repeated and reported the notion as "Rust Belt," and the phrase stuck as a good description of the declining industrial heartland, especially the steel- and automobile-producing regions in the Northeast and Midwest. The phrase became synonymous with industrial decline in the once-dominant U.S. heavy manufacturing and steel industries.

Rust Belt. Disgruntled workers in Pittsburgh, a steel-manufacturing center of the nation's declining industrial heartland in the Northeast and Midwest. CORBIS-BETTMANN

The Rust Belt has indefinite boundaries, although in 1979 Joel Garreau dubbed the same general region the "Foundry." Both terms aptly characterized the region's economic history and underpinnings. Readily available coal, labor, and inland waterways made the region ideal for steel manufacturing. Moreover, the automotive industry—a major buyer of steel—developed nearby. In the 1970s and 1980s, however, the U.S. steel industry rapidly fell from world dominance. The U.S. worldwide market share of manufactured steel went from 20 percent in 1970 to 12 percent by 1990, and American employment in the industry dropped from 400,000 to 140,000 over the same period. Starting in the late 1970s, steel factories began closing. Among the hardest hit of the communities was Youngstown, Ohio, where the closure of three steel mills starting in 1977 eliminated nearly 10,000 high-paying jobs. Also hurt were foundries in Buffalo, New York; and Johnstown and Pittsburgh, Pennsylvania, where the last outmoded steel plant closed in the late 1980s.

Although thirty-five states produce steel, the large steel plants in the Rust Belt faced particularly hard times because they relied upon large, unprofitable, and outdated open-hearth furnaces. Many were sulfur-burning, coal-fired plants, which had difficulty meeting stringent environmental regulations on smokestack emissions. Layoffs occurred even as worldwide demand for steel grew. Other countries, in particular Japan, met this demand with lower-cost and sometimes higher-quality steel. The American steel industry rebounded by developing low-cost, highly automated minimills, which used electric arc furnaces to turn scrap metal into wire rod and bar products, but the minimills employed fewer workers.

The region had been the nation's industrial heartland and contained many large, densely populated urban areas. These cities, which began showing signs of decline, initially had served as a destination for early European immigrants and tremendous numbers of African Americans who migrated north to join the industrial workforce following World War II. Industrial decline, however, permanently eliminated thousands of well-paid, benefit-laden, blue-collar jobs. Many families left the Rust Belt and relocated to the SUN BELT and the West, seeking jobs and better living conditions. The black populations in the Chicago and Pittsburgh metropolitan areas declined, reversing earlier patterns of northward migration from the Deep South. The population shift meant fewer congressional representatives from the region following the 1990 reapportionment.

BIBLIOGRAPHY

Cooke, Philip, ed. *The Rise of the Rustbelt.* London: UCL Press, 1995.

Florida, Richard, and Martin Kenney. *The Breakthrough Illusion: Corporate America's Failure to Move from Innovation to Mass Production.* New York: Basic Books, 1990.

Garreau, Joel. *The Nine Nations of North America.* Boston: Houghton Mifflin, 1981.

Brent Schondelmeyer / c. w.

See also **Automobile Industry; Immigration; Iron and Steel Industry; Japan, Relations with; Midwest; Migration, Internal.**

RUST V. SULLIVAN (111 Supreme Court 1759 [1991]). Congress enacted a law in 1970 that supported family-planning services by making available federal funds under Title X but forbade the use of those funds for abortions. Over a fifteen-year period, the Department of Health and Human Services (HHS) regulated use of the funds under the law and, in 1986, tightened regulations in an attempt to limit the ability of clinics to provide information about abortions. Two years later, with the strong support of President George H. W. Bush, HHS imposed a gag rule upon clinics and their physicians prohibiting references to abortion in family-planning programs.

The first issue in *Rust* was whether the 1970 law could be construed to allow the gag rule, although Congress had not granted federal authorities such power. The second was whether the regulations that imposed the rule violated freedom of expression guaranteed by the FIRST AMENDMENT and the DUE PROCESS OF LAW protected by the Fifth Amendment. On both issues, the SUPREME COURT decided in favor of the government. Conceding that the intent of Congress was ambiguous, the Court nonetheless held that it should defer to the judgment of those charged with applying the law. Also, regarding the second issue, the Court found that discussion of abortions could occur outside the federal program, and thus there was no violation of either the First or Fifth Amendments. *Rust* af-

fected 4,500 facilities serving nearly 4 million women and raised the question of whether the government could impose free-speech restrictions on other institutions receiving Title X funds. It marked a further limiting of a woman's right to an abortion since the Court's landmark decision of *ROE V. WADE* (1973).

The impact of the decision was lessened when President Bill Clinton's administration lifted the gag rule in 1993. The gag rule issue resurfaced during the political campaigns of 1994 and 1996. In 1999 Congressional Republicans linked repayment of the United Nations membership fee to a "global gag rule," banning the mention of abortion in international family planning literature.

BIBLIOGRAPHY

Garrow, David. *Liberty and Sexuality: The Right to Privacy and the Making of* Roe v. Wade. New York: Macmillan, 1994.

Tony Freyer / a. r.

See also **Abortion; Family; Health and Human Services, Department of;** *Planned Parenthood of Southeastern Pennsylvania v. Casey;* **Pro-Choice Movement; Pro-Life Movement;** *Webster v. Reproductive Health Services;* **Women's Health.**

RUSTLER WAR, a conflict centering in Johnson County, WYOMING. Local ranchers claimed it was impossible to secure convictions in the local courts for CATTLE rustling because jurors and county officials were either intimidated by or sympathized with the rustlers. Therefore, the cattlemen resolved to take matters into their own hands. In April 1892, they organized an expedition to kill some seventy supposed cattle thieves. The cattlemen soon met resistance and took refuge in the buildings of the T A Ranch, where a force of some two hundred men besieged them. President Benjamin Harrison sent in U.S. troops, and the desperate cattlemen gladly surrendered. They faced trial but were acquitted.

BIBLIOGRAPHY

Smith, Duane A. *Rocky Mountain West: Colorado, Wyoming, and Montana, 1859–1915.* Albuquerque: University of New Mexico Press, 1992.

Smith, Helena Huntington. *The War on Powder River.* New York: McGraw-Hill, 1966.

Edward Everett Dale / a. e.

See also **Cattle Rustlers; Homesteaders and the Cattle Industry.**

RUTGERS UNIVERSITY was chartered as Queens College in 1766 by the colonial governor of New Jersey, William Franklin. The college was located in New Brunswick on the banks of the Raritan River and was affiliated with the Dutch Reformed Church. In 1825, the college was renamed Rutgers College to honor a prominent church member and philanthropist from New York City named Henry Rutgers. During the nineteenth century the college gradually severed its religious ties and began receiving financial support from the state of New Jersey. In 1864 the New Jersey legislature named Rutgers the recipient of funding from the federal land grants of the MORRILL ACT, which allowed Rutgers to expand its scientific and agricultural educational offerings. In 1869, Rutgers played the first college football game with Princeton, winning by a score of 6 to 4. Through its ties to the Dutch Reformed Church, Rutgers became the site for more than 300 Japanese students who came to the United States in the late nineteenth century to study English and technical fields. The Rutgers faculty members William Elliot Griffis and David Murray traveled to Japan during the 1870s to advise the Meiji government on its modernization and educational projects.

During the early twentieth century New Jersey expanded its support for Rutgers to include a state-supported women's college. Thanks to a lobbying effort led by Mabel Smith Douglass, who was named the college's first dean, the New Jersey College for Women (renamed Douglass College in 1955) began operating in 1918. In 1921 the College of Agriculture (renamed Cook College in 1973) was formed. Soon after, engineering, arts and sciences, and education were all configured as colleges or schools, to organize what was now Rutgers University. Paul Robeson, a prominent African American entertainer and political activist, graduated from Rutgers in 1919 after distinguished academic and athletic achievement. Like most of American higher education, Rutgers experienced dramatic growth during the period following World War II with undergraduate enrollment reaching 8,656 during 1948 and expanding to nearly 48,000 graduates and undergraduates by 2000. The mid-twentieth century saw the expansion of Rutgers University to include campuses in Newark and Camden and the New Jersey legislature's official designation of Rutgers as the state

university. Selman Waksman, a professor in the College of Agriculture and a graduate of Rutgers College, was awarded the Nobel Prize in 1952 for his work in the discovery of antibiotics.

BIBLIOGRAPHY

McCormick, Richard. *Rutgers: A Bicentennial History.* New Brunswick, N.J.: Rutgers University Press, 1966.

Moffatt, Michael. *The Rutgers Picture Book: An Illustrated History of Student Life in the Changing College and University.* New Brunswick, N.J.: Rutgers University Press, 1985.

Robert Nelson Reddick

See also **Education, Higher: Colleges and Universities; New Jersey.**

RYSWICK, PEACE OF, signed 30 September 1697, ended KING WILLIAM'S WAR between the English and French and the Iroquois and French. By its provisions, all conquests made during the war were to be mutually restored to the status quo antebellum. However, ownership of the lands surrounding Hudson Bay was to be decided by an Anglo-French joint commission. Such a commission met in 1699 but failed to reach a decision. The Anglo-French rivalry for control of North America would continue for much of the eighteenth century, culminating in the FRENCH AND INDIAN WAR (1754–1763).

BIBLIOGRAPHY

Gipson, Lawrence. *The British Empire Before the American Revolution.* New York: Knopf, 1958

Hawke, David F. *The Colonial Experience.* Indianapolis, Ind.: Bobbs-Merrill, 1966.

Max Savelle / A. G.

See also **Colonial Wars; France, Relations with; Warfare, Indian.**

SABOTAGE.

SABOTAGE. A term borrowed from French syndicalists by American labor organizations at the turn of the century, sabotage means the hampering of productivity and efficiency of a factory, company, or organization by internal operatives. Often sabotage involves the destruction of property or machines by the workers who use them. In the United States, sabotage was seen first as a direct-action tactic for labor radicals against oppressive employers. The first organization to openly proclaim sabotage as a tactic, though by no means the only labor group to employ it, was the INDUSTRIAL WORKERS OF THE WORLD, known as the Wobblies. A Wobbly translated *Sabotage* by French syndicalist Émile Pouget and promulgated the various means of sabotage offered in the book and used by European radicals since the 1830s.

Though the Wobblies were the loudest advocates of sabotage tactics, such as playing dumb or tampering with machines, no state or federal authority ever established legal proof that they actually instigated sabotage. In fact, one historian has asserted that the American Federation of Laborers was linked more closely with industrial violence. Nevertheless, the Wobblies' association with syndicalism and socialism terrified industrialists, antisocialists, and other Americans who feared "red" infiltration of American society.

During World War I, American concern about sabotage turned to the military when operatives supported by the German government blew up the munitions supply terminal at Black Tom Pier on the New Jersey side of New York Harbor. Germany was hoping to coerce the United States into the war, a tactic that also involved the torpedoing of the *Lusitania*. The bombing at Black Tom in July 1916 and a second explosion at a shell manufacturing plant eight miles north in December broadened the definition of saboteur beyond socialists and anarchists.

In the 1950s, sabotage seemed to serve the purposes of workers as well as enemy nations when Americans believed that the Soviet Union was infiltrating United States labor and community organizations. In November 1950 the *Herald Tribune* reported that sardine cans discovered on a merchant marine ship were actually filled with how-to manuals for short-circuiting electrical lines, burning vital transformers, and other forms of industrial sabotage.

In the late twentieth and early twenty-first centuries, sabotage moved from the factory to cyberspace, as hackers frequently infiltrated computer systems to destroy data or embarrass companies. In one of the costliest acts of sabotage in American history, a computer programmer at a New Jersey engineering firm in 1998 allegedly planted a "computer bomb" that deleted software critical to the company's operations, leading to the loss of more than $10 million in sales and contracts. In the spring of 2001 hackers broke into California's electricity grid. There was little damage, but the system's vulnerability was apparent and embarrassing. Computer hackers, much like their syndicalist forerunners, developed their own antiauthoritarian culture based on infiltrating America's key computer systems. Though sabotage was originally a tactic promoted by intellectual subversives attacking specific economic and governmental systems in Europe, in America it became a tactic used by activists operating in numerous areas of society and for many different reasons.

BIBLIOGRAPHY

Dreyfus, Suelette. *Underground: Tales of Hacking, Madness, and Obsession in the Electronic Frontier.* Kew, Australia: Mandarin, 1997.

Dubofsky, Melvyn. *We Shall Be All: A History of the Industrial Workers of the World.* Abridged ed. Edited by Joseph A. McCartin. Urbana: University of Illinois Press, 2000.

Witcover, Jules. *Sabotage at Black Tom: Imperial Germany's War in America, 1914–1917.* New York: Algonquin, 1989.

Eric S. Yellin

SACCO-VANZETTI CASE.

SACCO-VANZETTI CASE. Nicola Sacco, a skilled shoeworker born in 1891, and Bartolomeo Vanzetti, a fish peddler born in 1888, were arrested on 5 May 1920, for a payroll holdup and murder in South Braintree, Massachusetts. A jury, sitting under Judge Webster Thayer, found the men guilty on 14 July 1921. Sacco and Vanzetti were executed on 23 August 1927 after several appeals and the recommendation of a special advisory commission serving the Massachusetts governor. The execution sparked worldwide protests against repression of Italian Americans, immigrants, labor militancy, and radical political beliefs.

Nicola Sacco and Bartolomeo Vanzetti. The Italian immigrants and self-declared anarchists, who were executed in 1927—unjustly, many people still believe. NATIONAL ARCHIVES AND RECORDS ADMINISTRATION

Numerous legal issues arose regarding the case's prosecution that sidelined the question of guilt or innocence, including prejudicial behavior of an unscrupulous district attorney, Frederick G. Katzmann, complemented by an often inept defense; and profane and violent prejudice by the judge against the defendants, expressed outside the courtroom and possibly implicit in his behavior on the bench. Other issues included alleged perjury by a state police captain; refusal to address circumstances pointing to a group of professional criminals; inexpert and potentially deceptive presentation of ballistics evidence; and failure of the evidence as a whole to remove "reasonable doubt." Throughout the trial, the men were disadvantaged by their avowed anarchism, their status as unassimilated alien workers, and the backdrop of the red scare following World War I. Scholarly legal opinion overwhelmingly holds that apart from the question of guilt or innocence, the case is an extremely serious instance of failure in the administration of justice.

Within the United States, Sacco and Vanzetti received from the start the help of compatriots, fellow anarchists, and scattered labor groups. By 1927 they had support in money, action, and words of concerned lawyers, numerous writers, prominent activists, organized labor, and the Communist Party leadership. Nevertheless, it is clear that the majority of persons in the United States who held an opinion, and they were in the millions, believed the verdict sound and approved of the death penalty.

The case has inspired writers and artists from the 1920s onward, including several novels, plays, television presentations, and over a hundred poems by such prominent writers as John Dos Passos, Countee Cullen, and Edna St. Vincent Millay. Upton Sinclair's novel *Boston* (1928) and Maxwell Anderson's prize-winning play *Winterset* (1935) reached particular fame, and Ben Shahn pro-

duced a notable series of gouaches on the two men. The letters Sacco and Vanzetti wrote during their seven years in prison are still regarded by many as the most profoundly human and genuinely literary commentary on the case.

BIBLIOGRAPHY

Avrich, Paul. *Sacco and Vanzetti: The Anarchist Background.* Princeton, N.J.: Princeton University Press, 1991.

Russell, Francis. *Sacco and Vanzetti: The Case Resolved.* New York: Harper and Row, 1986.

Sacco, Nicola, and Bartolomeo Vanzetti. *The Letters of Sacco and Vanzetti.* Edited by Marion Denman Frankfurter and Gardner Jackson. New York: Penguin Books, 1997.

Louis Joughin
Eric S. Yellin

See also **Anarchists; Italian Americans;** *and vol. 9:* **Vanzetti's Last Statement.**

SACHEM, a term drawn from Algonkin speakers of the Northeast. Although English colonists in NEW ENGLAND applied the term to most Indian leaders, the term truly applied to hereditary civil leaders as opposed to war leaders who acquired their status through prowess in combat. Much of a sachem's leadership depended on establishing consensus among the members of his village. Most sachems were men, but there are examples in New England history of women with the title. The term was adopted in the nineteenth century as a leadership title within the TAMMANY HALL political machine in New York City.

BIBLIOGRAPHY

Salisbury, Neal. *Manitou and Providence: Indians, Europeans, and the Making of New England, 1500–1643.* New York: Oxford University Press, 1982.

Robert F. Spencer/J. H.

See also **Indian Political Life.**

SACRAMENTO, the major urban center of California's Central Valley, is located at the confluence of the American and Sacramento Rivers. The region has been a crossroads of trade and commerce since its earliest habitation. John A. Sutter, a German-speaking Swiss adventurer, arrived in Sacramento in 1839 and built a fort as a frontier outpost for the Mexican government. The gold rush that began in 1848 led the following year to the platting of the city of Sacramento, which became the state capital in 1854. It was the western terminus of the Oregon Trail and of the first transcontinental railroad (completed 1869). By the late 1850s, agriculture had begun to supplant mining as the city's primary economic venture.

Located at the lower end of one of the world's highest-volume watersheds, Sacramento experienced its first flood in 1849. Completion of the Shasta Dam on the Sac-

Sacramento. A lithograph from a December 1849 drawing of the new California boomtown as seen from the foot of J Street, with the Sierra Nevada in the background. LIBRARY OF CONGRESS

ramento River in 1949, the Folsom Dam on the American in 1956, and the Oroville Dam on the Feather in 1968 led to extensive development on the floodplains. A major flood in 1989, which eclipsed all previous runoffs, and local flooding in January 1995 caused local, state, and federal agencies to reassess land use patterns.

The completion of Interstate Highways 5 and 80 in the 1960s reaffirmed Sacramento's role as a transportation hub. Several factors shielded the local economy from the problems that beset other regions of California after the Cold War. In the 1990s housing and land prices were one-third lower than in the San Francisco Bay area, approximately eighty miles to the southwest.

Local, state, and federal government employment provided a stable, albeit declining, share of the job market. With many institutions of higher learning, including community colleges, California State University, Sacramento, and the University of California, Davis, the region has a well-educated labor force. After the 1970s, data processing centers, high-tech manufacturing companies, biotechnology enterprises, and financial services companies were created in or relocated to Sacramento. The city's population increased from 275,741 in 1980 to 366,500 in 1990, when the Sacramento–Yolo County area had a population of nearly 1.5 million. From its inception Sacramento has had a multicultural population. Like the state of California, but at a much slower pace, Sacramento has experienced increased ethnic diversity since the 1970s.

BIBLIOGRAPHY

Kelley, Robert L. *Battling the Inland Sea: American Political Culture, Public Policy, and the Sacramento Valley, 1850–1986.* Berkeley: University of California Press, 1989.

McGowan, Joseph A., and Terry R. Willis. *Sacramento: Heart of the Golden State.* Woodland Hills, Calif.: Windsor Publications, 1983.

Gregg M. Campbell/ F. B.

See also **California; Gold Rush, California; Sutter's Fort.**

SADDLES have been of three principal types: (1) the English saddle—a flat tree with low pommel and cantle, introduced into America during the early colonial period; (2) the army saddle—first fully developed during the Civil War and, in its initial form (the McClellan), an English tree modified by heightening pommel and cantle, dishing the seat, and lengthening the stirrup leathers; and (3) the stock saddle—interchangeably termed "cowboy," "cow," "Mexican," "western," and "range" saddle.

Hernando Cortes brought the stock saddle to Mexico in 1519. The rider sat in it, rather than on it. On the pommel, Mexican vaqueros attached a vertical protuberance (the horn) to which the lariat could be fastened. White settlers in the American west adopted the Mexican saddle in the 1820s, and it soon became an important icon in America's western mythology.

During the colonial period, women sat facing sideways on a pillion (a pad fastened behind the saddle occupied by a rider), but the pillion was soon supplanted by the sidesaddle, an English tree altered by omitting the right-hand stirrup and adding hooked-shaped pommels. Once eastern women began riding astride, about 1900, the sidesaddle gradually disappeared.

BIBLIOGRAPHY

Ahlborn, Richard E., ed. *Man Made Mobile: Early Saddles of Western North America*. Washington, D.C.: Smithsonian Institution Press, 1980.

Philip Ashton Rollins / A. R.

See also **Horse; West, American.**

SAENZ V. ROE, 526 U.S. 489 (1999), 7 to 2 Supreme Court decision that found a constitutionally protected "right to travel" between the states. In 1992 California limited new residents' Aid to Families with Dependent Children (AFDC) benefits to the amount offered in their previous state of residence. A federal district court enjoined the U.S. Department of Health and Human Services' approval of the action, declaring it a violation of immigrants' right to be "treated equally with existing residents."

In 1996 Congress passed, and President Bill Clinton signed, the Personal Responsibility and Work Opportunity Reconciliation Act (PRWORA), replacing AFDC with Temporary Assistance to Needy Families (TANF). TANF authorized states to limit beneficiaries to the benefit of another state for a period of twelve months, and in light of its passage, California announced it would resume enforcement of the 1992 benefit change. The resulting class-action suit claimed that California's residency requirement, and PRWORA's apparent approval thereof, violated the constitutional "right to travel," constructed from Article IV of, and the Fourteenth Amendment to, the U.S. Constitution. The Court agreed with "Roe," and Justice John Paul Stevens's opinion declared that "Citizens of the United States, whether rich or poor, have the right to choose to be citizens 'of the State wherein they reside.' . . . The States, however, do not have any right to select their citizens."

BIBLIOGRAPHY

Ellis, Nan S., and Cheryl M. Miller. "A Welfare Waiting Periods: A Public Policy Analysis of Saenz v. Roe." *Stanford Law & Policy Review* 11, no. 2 (Spring 2000).

R. Volney Riser

See also **Welfare System.**

SAFETY FIRST MOVEMENT, a twentieth-century movement to reduce workplace hazards. Severe accidents were common—and much higher than in Europe—in the large industries of the nineteenth century. In 1877, Massachusetts pioneered in the establishment of factory safeguards and, in 1886, in the reporting of accidents. By the 1920s, nearly all states had workmen's compensation laws. In response, a number of large corporations launched safety programs, redesigned their equipment and workplace, sought to change workers' attitudes, and beefed up regulations for foremen and employees. Some, for instance the steel industry, made huge strides; after a stunningly high rate of industrial injury during 1907–1908, the industry cut accident rates to one-sixth within a decade or so.

A number of national, international, and governmental bodies began promoting safety in industry. The Iron and Steel Engineers' Association studied the safety problem in 1911 and in 1913 organized the National Safety Council, chartered by Congress in 1953, which carries on research in the development and standardization of safety methods and devices and collects and disseminates data pertaining to safety activities. The American Standards Association promulgates safety codes that are used by increasing numbers of administrative bodies. Though safety increased in some large industries, however, others—for instance, meatpacking—remained dangerous. Furthermore, the twenty-first century opened with a near epidemic of computer-related workplace injuries.

BIBLIOGRAPHY

Aldrich, Mark. *Safety First: Technology, Labor, and Business in the Building of American Work Safety, 1870–1939*. Baltimore: Johns Hopkins University Press, 1997.

Mogensen, Vernon L. *Office Politics: Computers, Labor, and the Fight for Safety and Health*. New Brunswick, N.J.: Rutgers University Press, 1996.

Joseph H. Foth / D. B.

See also **Industrial Management; Medicine, Occupational; Workers' Compensation.**

SAFETY FUND SYSTEM. The New York legislature passed the Safety Fund Act in 1829 to protect bank customers from losses incurred when the notoriously corrupt state banks failed. The Safety Fund System, as it came to be called, required that each bank incorporated in New York contribute to a common fund an amount equal to one-half of 1 percent of its capital stock, until such contributions aggregated 3 percent of its capital stock. Whenever a bank failed, this fund would be used to settle its debts. Should this safety fund be drained, the state comptroller was empowered to levy existing banks for additional contributions. The law was later refined to insure that holders of the defunct institution's bank notes would receive first consideration in the distribution of assets.

BIBLIOGRAPHY

Chaddock, Robert E. *The Safety-Fund Banking System in New York State, 1829–1866*. Washington, D.C.: Government Printing Office, 1910.

Wright, Robert E. "The First Phase of the Empire State's 'Triple Transition': Bank's Influence on the Market, Democracy, and Federalism in New York." *Social Science History* 21, 4 (1997): 521–558.

Frank Parker / A. R.

See also **Banking: Bank Failures; Banking: Overview.**

SAGADAHOC, COLONY AT.

SAGADAHOC, COLONY AT. The first attempt to establish an English colony in New England came in 1607, initiated when King James I chartered two ventures in 1606. The London Company established the Southern Colony, better known as the Jamestown Colony; despite severe difficulties, it thrived. The Plymouth Company established the Northern Colony, known as the Sagadahoc Colony, after the Indian name for the Kennebec River where it was situated in latter-day MAINE. It was also known as the Popham Colony, after Sir John Popham, the colony's chief patron and nephew of George Popham, its first leader; it lasted barely a year.

It is generally accepted that Sagadahoc Colony failed because of a lack of leadership. Some of the colonists were exiles from English prisons and disinclined to do the hard work necessary if the colony were to flourish. The colonists quarreled among themselves as well as with the natives, who refused either to come to their assistance or partner with them in trading endeavors. The colony was ill equipped to respond appropriately to the early arrival of a severe winter. Popham died in February 1608, barely six months after his arrival. Raleigh Gilbert took his place but fared little better, especially in his relations with the native Pemequids. In September, a supply ship from England brought news of the deaths of Sir John Popham and Gilbert's brother, at which point Gilbert abandoned the colony in order to claim his inheritance at home.

The *Virginia of Sagadahoc*, a ship built by the colonists during the settlement's first six months, successfully transported Gilbert and the remaining colonists home in the fall of 1608. The building of this ship marked the advent of Maine's subsequent shipbuilding industry. England would not attempt further colonization for more than a decade, until the Pilgrims arrived in 1620.

BIBLIOGRAPHY

Chandler, E. J. *Ancient Sagadahoc: A Narrative History*. Rev. ed. San Jose, Calif.: Authors Choice Press, 2000.

Judd, Richard W., Edwin A. Churchill, and Joel W. Eastman. *Maine: The Pine Tree State from Prehistory to the Present*. Orono: University of Maine Press, 1995.

Quinn, David B., "The Sagadahoc Colony of the Plymouth Company, 1607–1608." *New American World*, 1979.

Christine E. Hoffman

See also **Plymouth Colony; Plymouth, Virginia Company of; Virginia Company of London.**

SAILING AND YACHT RACING.

SAILING AND YACHT RACING. The Dutch brought their sailing traditions to New York during the seventeenth century. In 1939 the first American yacht club, the Detroit Boat Club, was founded. John C. Stevens founded the New York Yacht Club, the most famous club and one that has profoundly influenced yacht racing, in 1844.

Early sailboat racing pitted boats against each other on the basis of weight with a formula for handicapping at the finish line. In 1906 the Dixon Kemp Rule and the International Rule established a series of specifications under which racing boats fall into classes: six-meter, eight-meter, and twelve-meter. Each class has a design formula and specifications, with some variation allowed. The objective of standardization in construction, a movement led by Nathaniel G. Herreshoff among others, intended to reward the most skillful skipper.

In 1866 the American newspaper magnate James Gordon Bennett made history when he won the first transatlantic match race from Sandy Hook, Connecticut, to Cowes, Isle of Wight, England, on the schooner *Henrietta*. The race took thirteen days to complete. Alfred Johnson in 1876 completed the first single-handed transatlantic crossing in a six-meter boat. Francis Chichester attracted world attention when he won a single-handed race that was part of a series sponsored by the *London Observer* starting in 1960.

In an important benchmark for yacht racing, members of the New York Yacht Club challenged the British to a race around the Isle of Wight in 1851. The New York Club won the race on the schooner *America*. The trophy from this race was donated to the New York Yacht Club and became known as the America's Cup, the origin of the most prestigious sailboat racing event in the world. Every America's Cup race until 1983 was won by an American yacht, placing the United States at the head of world yacht racing. The American Dennis Connor is among the most successful skippers with four America's Cup victories. Other noteworthy personalities associated with yacht racing are Harold S. Vanderbilt, Bus Mosbacher, and Ted Turner. However, Connor has also been one of the most controversial yacht racers, challenging rules and creating controversy, especially during races in 1995.

In 1983 the Australians took the cup, and in the rest of the 1980s and the 1990s the race entered a period of controversy and turmoil. New technology, especially lighter materials and radical design techniques, including a controversy over the use of multihill yachts, created bitter conflicts and charges of design espionage and even sabotage of rivals' vessels. Moreover, the great costs associated with designing, building, and crewing yachts for such racing brought increasing corporate sponsorship and money to the sport. In 1987 the United States retook the cup only to lose it to New Zealand in 1995. New Zealand held on to the cup in the 2000 race.

In 1992 the new International America's Cup Class (IACC) was introduced. This class of boat is larger than the twelve-meter boats but with a much larger sail area, roughly 40 percent more accomplished, largely through higher masts. The objective of this new class was to create a more level playing field for syndicates involved in the America's Cup, including a boat that would sail faster at all points of sail, thus creating more exciting races. New design specifications and new dimensions for the yachts were established.

In addition to the America's Cup other ocean races and prestigious events, including the Whitbread Round the World Race, the Newport-Bermuda Race, the Fastnet Cup, the Golden Globe Race, the Sydney-Hobart, the Honolulu, and the Transpacific Race, have become prominent. As boats became lighter and competition more frequent and fierce, racers and racing organizations took greater risks with weather, resulting in increasing deaths and loss of yachts in storms. This led in the 1990s to a reexamination of racing practices and calls for reform of the rules.

Two basic types of sailboat races, "closed course" and "point-to-point," exist. The America's Cup and most small boat races, both on inland waters and on close-to-shore ocean racing, are closed-course races, usually consisting of a marked, triangular, timed course with elaborate right-of-way and other rules. Most transoceanic and global circumnavigation races, such as the Fastnet Cup, are point-to-point.

A different type of yacht racing has been part of the Olympic Games, where one-design, smaller sailboats competed beginning in 1900. At present nine classes of Olympic sailboats range in length from 12 feet, 1 inch (3.7 meters) to 26 feet, 9 inch (8.2 meter) vessels. Modern sailboats are lightweight and generally are manufactured of fiberglass to exact specifications. Sailboat racing classes are designated by the International Olympic Committee on recommendations of the International Yacht Racing Union, which was founded in 1907 to create a consistent set of international yacht racing standards and rules. They have included Star, Dragons, Finn, Laser, Soling, and Flying Dutchman class boats. Windsurfing, sailing on small sailboards, was added to the Olympics in 1984. The 2000 Olympics included three classes for men, Mistral or Sailboard, Finn, and 470; three classes for women, Mistral, Europe, and 470; and five mixed classes, Soling, Star, Laser, Tornado, and 49er.

BIBLIOGRAPHY

Bavier, Bob. *The America's Cup: An Insider's View—1930 to the Present.* New York: Dodd, Meade, 1986.

Johnson, Peter, ed. *Yachting World Handbook.* New York: St. Martin's Press, 1973.

Jourdane, John. *Icebergs, Port and Starboard: The Whitbread Round the World Yacht Race.* Long Beach, Calif.: Cape Horn Press, 1992.

Steffen W. Schmidt

See also **Olympic Games, American Participation In.**

SAINT ALBANS RAID. On 19 October 1864, Confederate Lt. Bennett H. Young led about thirty men not in uniform from Canada against the town of Saint Albans, in northwestern Vermont. The raid was in retaliation for the depredations of Union Gen. Philip H. Sheridan in Virginia. Three banks were looted of more than $200,000, but an attempt to burn the town failed. One citizen was killed. The raiders escaped into Canada pursued by an American posse. Young and twelve of his men were captured and held by the Canadian authorities, who released them 13 December but later rearrested five of them.

BIBLIOGRAPHY

Headley, John W. *Confederate Operations in Canada and New York.* Alexandria, Va.: Time-Life Books, 1984.

Wilson, Dennis K. *Justice Under Pressure: The Saint Albans Raid and Its Aftermath.* Lanham, Md.: University Press of America, 1992.

Charles H. Coleman / A. R.

See also **Canada, Confederate Activities in; Civil War; Confederate Agents; Northwest Conspiracy; Peace Movement of 1864; Shenandoah Campaign.**

SAINT AUGUSTINE, a city in northeastern Florida, is the oldest continually inhabited European settlement in North America. Pedro Menéndez de Avilés founded Saint Augustine in September 1565 to displace a French colony at Fort Caroline. The city's excellent strategic position above the Straits of Florida made it vital to the Spanish empire: the harbor provided protection for the plate fleets (the fleets that every year carried a fortune in American silver back to Spain), and as the English and French invaded the New World, Saint Augustine anchored Spanish interests in the area. The splendid fort, El Castillo de San Marcos, begun in 1672, withstood two English sieges. In 1763, Spain ceded Florida to the British, who made Saint Augustine the capital of East Florida.

Spain recovered Florida in 1783, only to sell it to the United States in 1819. When Florida became a state in 1845, Tallahassee was made the state capital. Occupied by Union troops early in the Civil War, Saint Augustine saw no action. In the 1880s, oil baron Henry Flagler, attracted by the mild climate and beautiful beaches, brought in the Florida East Coast Railway and built the extravagant Ponce de Leon Hotel, turning Saint Augustine into a fashionable winter resort for the wealthy. After 1937, restoration of the Castillo and the city's Old Town made Saint Augustine more appealing to modern sightseers. The population in the 2000 census was 11,592.

BIBLIOGRAPHY

Waterbury, Jean Parker, ed. *The Oldest City: Saint Augustine, Saga of Survival.* Saint Augustine, Fla.: Saint Augustine Historical Society, 1983.

Cecelia Holland

See also **Explorations and Expeditions: French, Spanish; Florida; Spanish Borderlands.**

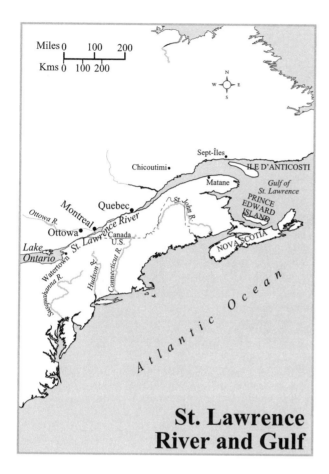

St. Lawrence River and Gulf

BIBLIOGRAPHY

Bosher, John Francis. *The Canada Merchants, 1713–1763.* Oxford: Clarendon Press; New York: Oxford University Press, 1987.

Eccles, William John. *The French in North America, 1500–1783.* East Lansing: Michigan State University Press, 1998.

Mackey, Frank. *Steamboat Connections: Montreal to Upper Canada, 1816–1843.* Montreal: McGill-Queen's University Press, 2000.

*Lawrence J. Burpee/*a. e.

See also **Canadian-American Waterways; Fur Companies; Fur Trade and Trapping; Portages and Water Routes.**

SAINT LAWRENCE RIVER, the largest river in North America, was explored between 1535 and 1541 by French explorer Jacques Cartier. During the seventeenth and eighteenth centuries, the Saint Lawrence, with its tributary, the Ottawa River, and with the GREAT LAKES, formed the main water thoroughfare from the sea to the interior of the continent. Explorers and missionaries, including Samuel de Champlain and Robert Cavelier, Sieur de LaSalle, set forth from Quebec or Montreal for the west or the southwest. Fur trading brigades left Montreal bound for Mackinac, Grand Portage, Lake Winnipeg, and the Saskatchewan and Columbia rivers. The combatants in the colonial wars, the American Revolution, and the War of 1812 each found the use or mastery of the Saint Lawrence waterways worth the fight.

During the nineteenth century, shipping developed on the Great Lakes as communities grew up about their shores and beyond. With the completion of a deep channel from the head of the lakes down to Lake Ontario, and from Montreal to the sea, a movement grew in the first half of the twentieth century for the removal of the only remaining barrier: the 182-mile extent between Lake Ontario and Montreal. The result was the SAINT LAWRENCE SEAWAY, begun in 1954 and opened in 1959.

SAINT LAWRENCE SEAWAY. Stretching 2,342 miles from Lake Superior to the Atlantic, the Saint Lawrence Seaway opens the industrial and agricultural heart of North America to deep-draft ocean vessels. Via the seaway and the great circle route, DETROIT is 400 miles closer to Amsterdam than New York is. The entire Great Lakes–Saint Lawrence Seaway system comprises 9,500 square miles of navigable waters, linked by three series of locks. A ship entering at Montreal rises to more than 600 feet above sea level at Lake Superior. The waterway accommodates vessels 730 feet long, with a seventy-six-foot beam and a draft of twenty-six feet.

The present seaway, opened to deep-draft navigation in 1959, evolved from the engineering efforts of several centuries. In 1534 the Lachine Rapids above Montreal turned back the ships of Jacques Cartier, but by 1783 a canal that afforded passage to flat-bottomed bateaux bypassed the rapids. By 1798 a small canal provided a route around the Sault Sainte Marie, on the Canadian side. In 1829 William Hamilton Merritt completed a chain of forty wooden locks across the Niagara peninsula. By 1861 ships were sailing regularly between the GREAT LAKES and Europe.

Increasing ship sizes and the rapidly growing economy of the Midwest created pressures for further improvements. Between 1913 and 1932, Canada built the Welland Canal to lift deep-draft ships from Lake Ontario to Lake Erie. Strong opposition from sectional interests blocked U.S. participation in proposals to develop the power-generating and navigation potential of the international rapids. The Wiley-Dondero Act of 1954 authorized the Saint Lawrence Seaway Development Corporation to construct that part of the seaway in the United States, and construction began under agreement with Canada.

Three initiatives in public policy distinguish the Saint Lawrence Seaway. First, it is international in character, with navigation facilities in both the United States and Canada. Second, entities of two governments, each with authority to negotiate with the other, operate it. Third, tolls assessed on shippers meet its operating expenses.

St. Louis Waterfront with the Gateway Arch. A 1979 picture of the city's downtown, highlighted by the landmark structure along the Mississippi River. © Franklin McMahon/corbis

Thompson, John Herd, and Stephen J. Randall. *Canada and the United States: Ambivalent Allies.* Athens: University of Georgia Press, 1994.

Willoughby, William R. *The Joint Organizations of Canada and the United States.* Toronto: University of Toronto Press, 1979.

D. W. Oberlin / A. E.

See also **Canadian-American Waterways; Fair Deal; Waterways, Inland.**

SAINT LOUIS. The city of Saint Louis, the heart of a large metropolitan area, lies on the western bank of the Mississippi River in east-central Missouri. Saint Louis's regional identification as a southern, western, and midwestern town has impacted its history since its origins as a French colonial fur trading post in 1764.

When New Orleans–based Pierre Laclède Liquest and René Auguste Chouteau founded Saint Louis on an elevated spot above the Mississippi and named it for the patron saint of King Louis XV of France, the area was home to the Missouri, Osage, Kansas, Otoe, Iowa, and Omaha peoples. Across the river in Illinois, a cluster of giant temple and burial mounds was all that was left of the long-dispersed Mississippians of Cahokia, once the largest settlement of indigenous peoples north of Mexico.

Although Saint Louis was part of the land France secretly ceded to Spain in 1762, colonial Saint Louis remained predominantly French, a legacy still visible in many Saint Louis street names. In 1770, the village population included 339 Creole families (American-born people of French or Spanish descent), along with 33 free blacks and 274 Native American and African slaves.

After Napoleon sold the Louisiana territory to the United States in 1803, Saint Louis's site as the gateway to the newly opened American West drew land speculators and other fortune seekers from the East. The city served as the territorial capital from 1804 until 1821. The introduction of STEAMBOATS on the Mississippi River in the early 1800s catapulted Saint Louis into the center of a national inland water system. By 1821, the city was a thriving commercial steamboat center of approximately four thousand people.

As in other midwestern cities, Saint Louis's population swelled from a wave of Irish and German immigrants in the 1840s. By the eve of the Civil War in 1861, Germans made up the city's largest ethnic group, evident by the publication of nine German language newspapers. Among these immigrants was Eberhard Anheuser, who, with son-in-law Adolphus Busch, founded the Anheuser-Busch Brewing Company in 1860 and built it into a major Saint Louis industry.

Missouri was a slave state, but the number of slaves in Saint Louis declined by the beginning of the Civil War.

Saint Louis Population, 1880–2000

1880	350,518
1890	451,770
1910	**687,029**
1930	821,960
1950	**856,796**
1970	**622,236**
2000	348,189

SOURCE: U.S. Department of Commerce, Bureau of the Census.

Although many transplanted New Englanders and German immigrants in Missouri actively opposed slavery, Confederate-leaning Saint Louisans had banned antislavery publisher Elijah Lovejoy, who was later murdered by a mob in nearby Alton, Illinois. The 1857 U.S. Supreme Court decision rejecting Saint Louis slaves Harriet and Dred Scott's suit for freedom (*Dred Scott v. Sandford*) further cast the city's image as a racially divided city.

Before railroads replaced steamboats and Chicago overshadowed Saint Louis, Saint Louis ranked as the fourth largest city in the United States. Its population climbed to more than 350,000 in 1880 and to 575,000 by 1900. That same year, Saint Louis had the largest percentage of African Americans outside Baltimore.

In segregated Saint Louis, a group of African American parents started Sumner High School in 1875, the first African American high school west of the Mississippi River. The 1904 Louisiana Purchase Exposition (World's Fair) may have boosted civic pride for white Saint Louisans, but the fair barred African American visitors. Ironically, Scott Joplin's "ragged time music" (ragtime), composed by one of the city's most famous African American migrants, was first introduced to mainstream Americans at the Saint Louis World's Fair.

By the mid-twentieth century, Saint Louis had evolved into a manufacturing hub—a leader in producing shoes, beer, steel, electronics, pet food and cereal, pesticides, and airplanes. After surviving Prohibition, Anheuser-Busch became the world's largest brewery; the Ralston Purina Company, which started as a horse feed company in 1894, manufactured its popular Chex cereals; and in 1939 James S. McDonnell established the McDonnell Aircraft Corporation, a major supplier of World War II jet fighters and later commercial jets.

By the early twentieth century, the once bustling riverfront was a neglected warehouse and industrial district. In 1939 the city cleared thirty-seven square blocks of the riverfront for the Jefferson National Expansion Memorial. Plans were delayed by World War II, but the 630-foot steel Gateway Arch (designed by architect Eero Saarinen) was finally completed in 1965. The following year, the new Busch Stadium opened with promises to revitalize downtown. But the urban renewal projects did little

to stem the outflow of businesses and residents to the outlying suburbs. In 1950, 60 percent of the population in the greater Saint Louis area lived in Saint Louis. After 1950, that proportion plummeted to just 15 percent.

After the late 1960s, urban homesteaders rehabilitated many of Saint Louis's older neighborhoods, which, along with the revitalized riverfront and Union Station, improved the city's face. Nevertheless, the population continued to shrink. From a peak of 856,796 in 1950, the population dropped to 348,189 in 2000. The impact of the loss of major corporate headquarters, including Southwestern Bell, McDonnell Douglas, TWA, and Ralston Purina, remained to be seen.

BIBLIOGRAPHY

Corbett, Katharine T. *In Her Place: A Guide to St. Louis Women's History*. St. Louis: Missouri Historical Society Press, 1999.

Fox, Tim, ed. *Where We Live: A Guide to St. Louis Communities*. St. Louis: Missouri Historical Society Press, 1995.

Hurley, Andrew. *Common Fields: An Environmental History of St. Louis*. St. Louis: Missouri Historical Society Press, 1997.

Lipsitz, George. *The Sidewalks of St. Louis: Places, People, and Politics in an American City*. Columbia: University of Missouri Press, 1991

Sandweiss, Eric. *St. Louis: The Evolution of an American Urban Landscape*. Philadelphia: Temple University Press, 2001

Elizabeth Armstrong Hall

See also **Dred Scott Case; Missouri.**

SAINT-LÔ, a town in France of about ten thousand people that marked the opening of the American invasion of German-held Normandy during WORLD WAR II. Gen. Omar N. Bradley's First U.S. Army initiated the battle in the Cotentin peninsula on 4 July 1944, and closed it, after taking forty thousand casualties, on 18 July, with the capture of Saint-Lô. One week later, Bradley launched Operation Cobra with the support of heavy bombers and broke the German defenses in Normandy. Allied forces spilled through the opening and by September had pushed the German forces to the SIEGFRIED LINE.

BIBLIOGRAPHY

Aron, Robert. *France Reborn: The History of the Liberation, June 1944–May 1945*. New York: Scribner, 1964.

Blumenson, Martin. *The Duel for France, 1944: The Men and Battles That Changed the Fate of Europe*. Cambridge, Mass.: Harvard University Press, 2000.

Martin Blumenson/A. R.

See also **Armored Vehicles; D Day; Normandy Invasion.**

SAINT-MIHIEL, CAMPAIGNS AT (12–16 September 1918). After the successful AISNE-MARNE OFFENSIVE on 10 August, the American First Army began gathering along the front between the Moselle River and Verdun Forest in France for a direct blow against the German salient at Saint-Mihiel. Under the command of Gen. John J. Pershing, nine American divisions, numbering 550,000 men, and four French divisions, numbering 70,000 men, faced about 60,000 German soldiers. On 12 September, the First Army advanced five miles into the salient. Just after daylight, 13 September, American divisions from the south and west converged at Vigneulles-les-Hattonchatel, trapping 16,000 Germans. Altogether 443 guns were captured. By 16 September, the salient was entirely obliterated. The Americans suffered 7,000 casualties.

BIBLIOGRAPHY

Hallas, James H. *Squandered Victory: The American First Army at St. Mihiel.* Westport, Conn.: Praeger, 1995.

Stallings, Lawrence. *The Story of the Doughboys: The AEF in World War I.* New York: Harper and Row, 1966.

Joseph Mills Hanson / A. R.

See also **American Expeditionary Forces; Champagne-Marne Operation; Meuse-Argonne Offensive; Somme Offensive; World War I.**

SAIPAN is the northernmost of the southern Mariana Islands and lies 1,270 miles south of Tokyo. In June 1944 it was the most heavily fortified Japanese outpost of the Marianas chain. Saipan figured imporantly in American war plans. Seizing it would bring Tokyo within flying range of the new U.S. Army Air Force B-29 very-long-range bomber. Also, to defend the island the Japanese were expected to dispatch a major fleet and thereby precipitate a sea battle with the U.S. fleet.

Saipan. U.S. Army reinforcements disembark from landing craft onto this strategically essential Pacific island, June–July 1944. NATIONAL ARCHIVES AND RECORDS ADMINISTRATION

Overall command of the operation to seize Saipan was given to Adm. Chester W. Nimitz, commander in chief of the U.S. Pacific Fleet and Pacific Ocean areas. After two days of intense preliminary bombardment, two marine divisions landed at dawn on 15 June 1944, on the eastern coast of the island, and by nightfall had established a defensible beachhead. While the U.S. Fifth Fleet defeated a Japanese carrier task force in the adjacent Philippine Sea on 18–19 June, marine and army units pushed rapidly to the western coast of Saipan and then deployed northward on a three-division front with the army in the center. By 9 July the attacking troops reached the northernmost point of the island, which was then declared secured.

Total American casualties came to an estimated 14,111 killed and wounded. Almost all of the Japanese garrison of 30,000 was destroyed. Premier Hideki Tojo and his entire war cabinet resigned immediately. The inner defense line of the Japanese empire had been cracked.

BIBLIOGRAPHY

Crowl, Philip A. *Campaign in the Marianas.* Washington, D.C.: Center of Military History, United States Army, 1993.

Isely, Jeter A. and Philip A. Crowl. *The U.S. Marines and Amphibious War: Its Theory and Its Practice in the Pacific.* Princeton, N.J.: Princeton University Press, 1951.

Morison, Samuel E. *History of United States Naval Operations in World War II.* Vol. VIII. Boston: Little, Brown, 1947–1962.

Spector, Ronald H. *Eagle Against the Sun: The American War with Japan.* New York: Free Press, 1985.

Philip A. Crowl / A. R.

See also **Philippine Sea, Battle of the; Tinian; World War II; World War II, Air War Against Japan; World War II, Navy in.**

SALEM. A port city in Essex County on the north shore of MASSACHUSETTS, Salem lies nineteen miles north of Boston. Salem is the site of one of the earliest European settlements in America, and it was a major trading port in the eighteenth century. It is perhaps best known as the site of the notorious SALEM WITCH TRIALS of 1692. Booming international trade soon overshadowed the Salem witch trials.

In 1626 a small group of settlers led by Roger Conant left Cape Ann (now Gloucester) and made their way south to a sheltered bay at the mouth of a river, a place Native Americans called Naumkeag or Comfort Haven. The group of settlers renamed the settlement "Salem" from the Hebrew word "shalom" or peace. Early settlers farmed and fished for cod.

By 1692 Salem had grown into a sprawling community, and divisions began to arise between Salem Village, the primarily agricultural outskirts, and Salem Town, the commercial and judicial heart of Essex County. Accusations of witchcraft were initially made against three

Salem Witch House. A 1902 photograph of the home not of a purported witch but of Jonathan Corwin, a judge in the notorious trials; built in 1642, it has been restored to the way it was when he questioned 185 accused witches there. LIBRARY OF CONGRESS

village women, but by the time the hysteria was brought under control a year later, 185 people had been accused of witchcraft. Nineteen women were executed on the gallows, and one man died while being interrogated. The Witch Trial Memorial was dedicated in 1992 by the Nobel laureate Elie Wiesel to commemorate the tercentenary of the Salem witch trials and to advocate for peace and tolerance.

Salem developed into a major shipbuilding, fishing, and trade port in the eighteenth century. The growth of the codfish trade with Europe and the West Indies brought wealth and prestige to the town. Salem, with its money and its ships, was poised to be a key player in the American Revolution. In 1774 the Provincial Congress was organized there. Salem merchant ships quickly equipped themselves for war and seized or sank over 450 British ships.

Salem reached its zenith between the Revolution and the War of 1812. It was the sixth largest city in the United States in 1790 and had the highest wealth per capita. Wealth from international trade, particularly with the Far East, led to the construction of magnificent mansions and stately homes. Many Salem captains and merchants commissioned Samuel McIntire (1757–1811), a great architect and woodworker, and Salem developed into the home to one of the most significant collections of Federal architecture in the world.

Salem became an industrial city in the mid-nineteenth century after shipping moved to deep-water ports. Immigrants came to Salem to work in cotton mills and leather and shoe factories.

By the twenty-first century tourism and retail were the base of Salem's economy. Its museums, magnificent architecture, numerous historical sites, and proximity to Boston made it a prime destination. It is also the home of Salem State College, and some industry remained in the area. Salem Harbor is used primarily by pleasure vessels and fishing boats, but they share the waterfront with the *Friendship*, a replica of a 1797 East India merchant tall ship. By 2000 Salem's population of thirty-eight thousand shared the city with over 1 million visitors every year.

BIBLIOGRAPHY

Flibbert, Joseph, et al. *Salem: Cornerstones of a Historic City.* Beverly, Mass.: Commonwealth Editions, 1999.

McAllister, Jim. *Salem: From Naumkeag to Witch City.* Beverly, Mass.: Commonwealth Editions, 1000.

"Salem, Massachusetts." Available at http://www.salemweb.com/guide.

Bethany Groff

See also **Merchant Marine.**

SALEM WITCH TRIALS. The witch panic began in Salem Village, in Essex County, Massachusetts, in the last weeks of 1691, when nine-year-old Betty Parris and eleven-year-old Abigail Williams—the daughter and niece, respectively, of the Reverend Samuel Parris of Salem Village—began to display odd behavior. Reverend Parris called upon local doctor William Griggs to determine the cause. Griggs informed Parris that he suspected the Devil's hand.

Under pressure from adults, the girls named three Village women as their tormentors: Sarah Good, Sarah Osborne, and Tituba, a West Indian slave who worked for the Parris household. On 29 February 1692, warrants went out for their arrest. Osborne and Good denied they were witches; Tituba confessed. All three were jailed in Boston.

Accusations, confessions, and trials escalated. At least forty-eight additional people testified to their own possession. Moreover, hundreds of non-possessed local residents testified against witches who had allegedly committed crimes, most especially *maleficium* (that is, causing misfortune, illness, accidents, or death). By early October, over 185 people from SALEM and the surrounding towns had been named as witches. Twenty-four women and six men had been tried and convicted. Nineteen of them, mostly women, had been executed by hanging, and one man had died under interrogation. Over 100 people remained in jail. Several of them died awaiting trial.

In the face of increasing skepticism about evidence, however, and because of the relatively high stature of some of the accused, growing numbers of clergymen and political leaders voiced their opposition to the trials, convictions, and executions. The Court of Oyer and Terminer was dismissed; most subsequent trials ended in acquittal and all prior convictions were overturned.

Most historians who have examined the Salem witchhunt maintain it was the result of underlying social tensions in late seventeenth-century Puritan Salem. Those tensions may have been rooted in gender conflict, dramatic economic change, or local politics. An accusation of WITCHCRAFT proved an effective way to control or punish a person labeled for a variety of reasons as an outsider.

BIBLIOGRAPHY

Boyer, Paul, and Stephen Nissenbaum. *Salem Possessed: The Social Origins of Witchcraft.* Cambridge, Mass.: Harvard University Press, 1974.

Demos, John Putnam. *Entertaining Satan: Witchcraft and the Culture of Early New England.* Oxford: Oxford University Press, 1982.

Godbeer, Richard. *The Devil's Dominion: Magic and Religion in Early New England.* Cambridge, U.K.: Cambridge University Press, 1992.

Hall, David D., ed. *Witch-hunting in Seventeenth-Century New England: A Documentary History, 1638–1692.* Boston: Northeastern University Press, 1991.

Karlsen, Carol. *The Devil in the Shape of a Woman: Witchcraft in Colonial New England.* New York: Vintage Books, 1989.

Leslie J. Lindenauer

See also vol. 9: **Evidence Used Against Witches.**

SALERNO. The Allied invasion of Salerno came the morning after the Italian government of Marshal Pietro Badoglio surrendered to the Allies. On 9 September 1943 the Germans assaulted an amphibious landing of the Fifth U.S. Army led by Lt. Gen. Mark W. Clark from the high ground ringing the shore. Another German attack on 13–14 September came close to reaching the beaches and splitting the British and American components at the Sele River. The arrival of reinforcements, air strikes, and naval gunfire support turned the tide for the Allies. On 20 September, German Field Marshal Albert Kesselring withdrew slowly to the north. On 1 October Allied troops entered Naples.

BIBLIOGRAPHY

Blumenson, Martin. *Salerno to Cassino.* Washington, D.C.: Office of the Chief of Military History, U.S. Army, 1969.

Morris, Eric. *Salerno: A Military Fiasco.* London: Stein and Day, 1983.

Martin Blumenson / A. R.

See also **Anzio; Gustav Line; Monte Cassino; World War II.**

SALES TAXES consist of two types: excise and general sales. The excise tax is placed on specified commodities and may be at specific rates or on an *ad valorem* basis.

The general sales tax may be a manufacturers' excise tax, a retail sales tax paid by consumers, a "gross income" tax applied to sales of goods and provision of services, or a "gross sales" tax applied to all sales of manufacturers and merchants.

During the nineteenth century several states adopted tax levies resembling sales taxes. The sales tax in its modern form was first adopted by West Virginia in a gross sales tax in 1921. During the 1930s, many states adopted the sales tax in its various forms as a replacement for the general property tax that had been their chief source of income.

The adoption of sales taxation slowed somewhat during the 1940s, but became more popular after World War II. At the end of 1971, forty-five states and the District of Columbia levied a sales tax in some form.

A corollary of the sales tax is the use tax. This is a charge levied on taxable items bought in a state other than the state of residence of the purchaser for the privilege of using the item in the state of residence. The rate structure is the same as that of the sales tax. Automotive vehicles are the most significant item in the yield of use taxes.

The rate structure used in the general sales tax is proportional; that is, the rate is constant as the base increases. For ease of administration and determination of the tax due, bracketing systems have been adopted by nearly all states. The rates in use in the mid-1970s varied from 2 percent to a high of 7 percent; 4 percent was the most common rate. A combination of state and local rates may exceed 7 percent. A selective sales tax applying to a single commodity may have much higher rates. At the time of initial adoption of many of the sales taxes in the 1930s, tokens were used for the collection of the tax on small sales where the tax was less than one cent. Ohio used stamps to show that the tax had been collected. Nearly all these systems have been abandoned in favor of collection of the tax in full-cent increments.

Several forms of sales taxes have been used abroad. Canada has used a manufacturers' excise in the belief that a levy at that level of the distribution process offers fewer administrative problems because of the small number of business units with which to deal. The value-added tax has been extensively used in Europe and has been adopted by the European Economic Community nations as a major revenue source with the goal of uniform rates within each member nation. During the 1950s and early 1960s, Michigan used a business receipts tax that was an adaptation of the value-added tax.

Specific sales taxes on selected commodities have long been used by the states. Selective sales taxes were used in the colonial period, with liquor the most frequently taxed commodity. Gasoline was selectively taxed by Oregon in 1919. The disadvantage of specific sales taxes is that they do not produce the revenues a general sales tax does. During World War II a national sales tax was proposed, but no action was taken by Congress. The proposal has been revived periodically, but changes in personal and corporate income taxes have been preferred over a national sales tax.

A great deal of attention is given to the regressive effect of the sales tax because an individual with a low income spends a greater portion of his or her income on consumption goods that are taxed than do those with higher incomes. When the necessities of food and clothing are excluded from the sales-tax base, the regressive effect is reduced.

The impact of sales taxes is on the seller, for in nearly all cases he makes the payment to the state. However, the incidence or final resting place of the tax burden is on the purchaser of the taxed commodity or service; the price increases or the price is constant, but the tax is stated separately on the sales slip and added to the sum collected from the purchaser. In fact, the laws of some states require forward shifting of the tax to the consumer.

In the late twentieth century, sales taxes became a preferred method of paying for publicly funded sports stadiums and arenas. A growing chorus of critics has argued that the use of sales taxes to finance professional sports facilities is tantamount to corporate welfare. They point out that the biggest financial beneficiaries of such facilities are the wealthy owners of professional sports franchises, who typically gain a controlling interest in the stadium's ownership. Nevertheless, sales taxes remain a popular way for state legislatures to avoid raising income tax rates, which usually alienate voters more than sales taxes do.

BIBLIOGRAPHY

Due, John F., and John L. Mikesell. *Sales Taxation: State and Local Structure and Administration.* Washington D.C.: Urban Institute Press, 1994.

Mikesell, John L. *Fiscal Administration: Analysis and Applications for the Public Sector.* Pacific Grove, Calif.: Brooks/Cole, 1991.

Chalmers A. Monteith / A. G.

See also **Duties, Ad Valorem and Specific; Gasoline Taxes; Negative Income Tax; Taxation.**

SALMON FISHERIES.

Commercial salmon fisheries provide consumers with a variety of products, including fresh, canned, frozen, smoked, and cured items. Sockeye (red) and pink salmon dominate the canned market, while chum salmon and silver (coho) salmon are mostly frozen. Chinook (king) salmon, the largest of the five Pacific species, is smoked and cured. During the short summer and fall seasons, all salmon species are shipped fresh to restaurant and retail trades. Cured salmon roe (eggs) is becoming increasingly popular, especially in sushi bars.

Salmon fisheries on both coasts of the United States have been important historically, but only the Alaska fishery continues to provide a significant commercial endeavor. The East Coast fishery for native Atlantic salmon was fished out or otherwise decimated by 1850. On the Pacific Coast, the five varieties of salmon have been fished and processed from Monterey Bay, California, to the Arctic Circle in Alaska since the 1860s. The first canning operation was established by the Hume brothers on the Sacramento River in California in 1864. Puget Sound saw its first salmon canning operation in 1877 and Alaska's first cannery opened in southeast Alaska in 1878.

Initially, salmon was captured with traditional Native American methods such as traps and fishwheels. European immigrants brought gillnet, purse seine, and trolling gear methods in the late nineteenth century. Canning production peaked in 1929 with more than 200 canneries operating on the Pacific Coast and Alaska producing more than 10 million cases (48 lbs. each). Alaska began dominating production at the turn of the twentieth century with the Alaska Packers Association the dominant company, producing more than 50 percent of the entire pack in 1903. By the 1930s, production in Alaska and the West Coast states began declining, with only two million cases produced in 1967. International agreements with Canada in 1930 and with other Pacific Rim nations in 1953 alleviated cross-boundary and high-seas conflicts.

The early 1970s saw a tremendous surge in the value of salmon fisheries as the emerging Japanese market for frozen salmon led a revitalization in the processing industry in Puget Sound and Alaska. However, Pacific coast fisheries declined to almost negligible commercial production through the end of the twentieth century, due to loss of spawning grounds, pollution, and overfishing. Alaska's fishery, however, saw high values and production in the 1980s and 1990s, with ex-vessel value peaking in 1988 at $780 million and landings peaking in 1995 with more than 1 billion pounds.

Today, the processing sector has consolidated to a few large companies, such as Trident Seafoods Corp., Peter Pan Seafoods, Icicle Seafoods, and Wards Cove Packing, all based in Seattle. However, more than 15,000 fishermen continue to operate directly in the salmon fisheries in the United States and 10,000 persons are employed in processing and marketing operations.

Finally, the early 2000s saw a downturn in value and profits as farmed salmon production from Norway, Chile, and Canada flooded the U.S. and world market with fresh salmon products. U.S. production in 2001 was 678 million pounds for an ex-vessel value of $268 million.

BIBLIOGRAPHY

Browning, R. J. *Fisheries of the North Pacific.* Anchorage: Alaska Northwest, 1973.

Johnson, H. M. *Annual Report of the U.S. Seafood Industry.* Jacksonville, Oreg.: HM Johnson and Associates, 2001.

Pacific Fishing Yearbook. Seattle, Wash.: FIS, 2001.

Pete Granger

See also **Mackerel Fisheries.**

SALOONS. *See* **Taverns and Saloons.**

SALT. As a commodity of near universal demand, common salt, or sodium chloride, has been produced and traded on a large scale in most countries throughout history. As a national industry in the United States, salt production can be studied in three distinct phases. First, salt served as a vital commodity drawn from oceans and surface waters by boiling. Second, producers discovered rock salt deep beneath the earth's surface and began large scale drilling operations. Finally, the salt industry moved into the realm of high technology as producers scientifically derived compounds from raw materials, reducing salt to—and marketing it as—its component chemicals.

Salt production in America dates from before colonial settlements, and it was vital to those settlements as a preservative and curing agent for perishable meats and other goods. The British colonies were well situated to produce sea salt; however, although there were saltworks at the Jamestown and Plymouth colonies, they were costly operations, and colonists therefore largely tended to import salt. During the American Revolution there was a frantic, and largely successful, attempt to produce salt on the American coast, either by the solar evaporation of seawater in lagoons laid out along the shore or, more commonly, by boiling it down in cast-iron pots. With the end of the war, these establishments became unable to compete economically with salt imported from England or the West Indies, and the United States again became a salt importer.

As settlement moved west and away from the coastline, inland sources of salt became more cost effective. Interior America possessed many brine springs, known as "licks" because wild animals, especially buffalo, congregated around them to lick the salt deposits. Buffalo trails to these licks became some of the first roads beyond the Appalachians. Many licks were known to the French, who largely controlled that region. Among the first salt-lick regions the British settlers appear to have paid attention to was the Onondaga country of central New York. French travelers reported that Indians were making a little salt there in the mid-eighteenth century, and, in 1788, the Anglo-Americans began to manufacture salt near present-day Syracuse, New York. A little later, buffalo licks gave rise to salt production from brine at two localities now known as Saltville, Virginia, and Charleston, West Virginia. Saltworks began as early as the late 1770s in the Kentucky settlements and quickly became a cornerstone of the frontier economy. Salt making employed scores of landless workers, and the salt produced became a vital currency in the cash-poor region. As late as the 1870s, salt was produced from buffalo licks in Kansas.

As in Europe, salt was regarded as important enough in the United States to justify government intervention, and most salt-producing lands were reserved to the states, which leased them to private producers. The state of New York provided brine to producers and applied a tax, which became a major source of funds for construction of the ERIE CANAL. Salt production from brine began on the Scioto River in Jackson County, Ohio, before 1800, and when the state was organized in 1803, the area was set aside as a state reservation. On the Wabash, near Shawneetown, Illinois, the federal government actually took on the operation of a saline works in the early nineteenth century. As salt proved plentiful, however, interest of governments waned. Salt exploration in Michigan began in 1838 under state auspices, but the actual production that began in 1860 was entirely private.

Salt became plentiful as a result of the discovery of rich in-ground sources at great depths. Salt production by well drilling appeared in the United States in the early nineteenth century in Kanawha country near present-day Charleston, West Virginia, through the effort of brothers David and Joseph Ruffner. From 1806–1808, their success in finding strong brine ninety-eight feet below the earth's surface made Kanawha a leading salt-producing region. Many other wells followed. By 1835, forty furnaces in the region boiled down brine, and, by 1845, one well reached 1,500 feet deep.

After reaching production of 2 million bushels (1 bushel equals 56 pounds) a year by 1850, Kanawha's output declined. Onondaga's output similarly declined after reaching 9 million bushels in 1862 and again dropped drastically after 1883. At that time, salt production began in Wyoming County, New York, from a deep well drilled originally in search of oil. Rock salt was found, however, and was produced at various places in New York from 1886.

Rock salt was not always deep, and it is now known that Indians mined salt at several shallow deposits in the Far West. During the emergency conditions of the Civil War, the Confederate government began to work a salt spring in Louisiana, and, in 1862, rock salt was found at a depth of only sixteen feet. Large-scale mining began, only to be terminated by the destruction of the works by Union troops in April 1863. Mining has been continuous at Avery Island since 1883.

Deep salt strata can either be mined or, often more economically, turned into brine by adding water. Michigan's salt production began in 1860 with a 636-foot well at East Saginaw. Near Hutchinson, Kansas, rock salt was found in 1887 by drilling to 800 feet. Drilling has also uncovered salt deposits in many other states—so many, in fact, that salt has lost its status as a precious commodity.

Since the 1850s, one of the most important sources of salt in the United States has been the tideland of San Francisco Bay. Here, solar salt production is successfully accomplished by a method practiced in France since the Middle Ages. Seawater is admitted to enclosed, rectangular basins and transferred to smaller and smaller enclosures as the sun reduces its volume. Ultimately, the water evaporates leaving the salt deposits.

Up to the mid-nineteenth century, nearly all salt was produced for human and animal consumption, although about half was used in meatpacking. In England, large quantities were used in making artificial soda, or sodium carbonate. This industry came to the United States in 1882 and, by 1900, consumed about half of the salt used in the country. By 1957, nearly 80 percent of salt consumed in the United States went to the chemical industry, and the artificial soda industry became the primary user in industries based on sodium and chloride, the elemental constituents of salt. Uses of sodium include the manufacture of caustic soda (sodium hydroxide), which is, in turn, used to make the artificial fiber rayon, to produce aluminum, and to manufacture plastics and detergents. The chlorine-consuming industries are even newer, although they depend on the mid-nineteenth-century discoveries of chlorinated hydrocarbons, organic compounds in which one or more carbon atoms have been replaced by chlorine. By the 1970s, more than half the salt used in the United States was broken down into chlorine and sodium. Chlorine is ultimately converted into the chlorinated hydrocarbons used in plastics, such as vinyl chloride; solvents for dry cleaning; automotive fluids such as antifreeze; and pesticides such as DDT.

Most of these uses date from about 1940. However, despite the growing chemical industry, the share of American salt used by the industry dropped to 63 percent by 1974 because of an even newer application for the product. Beginning in the 1950s, the salting of highways to remove snow and ice increased continuously until 1974 when 17 percent of all salt consumed was for this purpose. Since the automobile also accounts for the salt used in making automotive fluids and uses much of the plastics, it has clearly become the largest consumer of salt.

American salt production in 1974 was more than 46 million tons, by far the world's largest. Even so, to meet demand, 3 million tons were imported, an amount equal to the entire consumption of the country in 1900.

BIBLIOGRAPHY

Bathe, G. "The Onondaga Salt Works of New York State." *Transactions of the Newcomen Society* 25 (1945–1947): 17.

Chatard, Thomas Marean. *Salt-Making Processes in the United States.* Washington, D.C.: U.S. Government Printing Office, 1888.

Lonn, Ella. *Salt as a Factor in the Confederacy.* New York: Neale, 1933; Tuscaloosa: University of Alabama Press, 1965.

McMurtrie, D. C. "Negotiations for the Illinois Salt Springs, 1802–03." *Bulletin of the Chicago Historical Society.* (March 1937).

Quinn, William P. *The Saltworks of Historic Cape Cod: A Record of the Economic Boom in Nineteenth Century Barnstable County.* Orleans, Mass.: Parnassus Imprints, 1993.

Stealy, John E. *The Antebellum Kanawha Salt Business and Western Markets.* Lexington: University Press of Kentucky, 1993.

Robert P. Multhauf/ H. S.; A. E.

See also **Automobile Industry; Chemical Industry; Food Preservation; Industries, Colonial; Meatpacking.**

SALT I AND II. *See* **Strategic Arms Limitation Talks.**

SALT LAKE CITY was founded in July 1847 by Brigham Young and his followers, of the Church of Jesus Christ of Latter-day Saints (Mormon). The Latter-day Saints sought refuge from the religious persecution they had experienced in the eastern United States, and chose to settle in the interior basin of the Rocky Mountains, still formally part of Mexico.

The Salt Lake Valley had no settled population of American Indians, though Ute, Shoshoni, and Southern Paiute people had long inhabited the broader region. Although trappers and Mexican traders had traversed the Salt Lake Valley since 1824, and several immigrant parties had passed through on their way to California in 1846, the Mormons were the first to establish permanent settlements.

They began to plot out the city as soon as they arrived, and adapted a plan that had been proposed by Joseph Smith in 1833, called the "plat of the city of Zion." Surveyors set aside a large public square for a temple and other public use, and the grid pattern of streets was laid out. All locations were designated by their direction and distance from the southeast corner of the Temple Square. In 1850, the territorial legislature founded the University of Utah and the first classes met that fall, providing a foundation for cultural and scientific advance that would continue to thrive in the city. The Salt Lake Theater, built in 1861, was a major cultural institution in the West.

The completion of the transcontinental railroad in 1869 had enormous consequences for the city. Though

Salt Lake City. An early-twentieth-century view, photographed by Otto M. Jones, of the city founded by Mormons as a refuge from persecution. LIBRARY OF CONGRESS

the transcontinental route crossed fifty miles to the north, Brigham Young pushed for the completion of the Utah Central Railroad, a connecting line, by January 1870. The city's trade, business, and population all grew rapidly. The population almost doubled between 1870 and 1880, from 12,854 to 20,768, and again during the next decade to 44,834. Chinese and African American rail workers, Jews, and by the turn of the century, Italians, Greeks, Slavs, and others of the new immigration, created a variegated population.

The railroad stimulated both mining and smelting. Salt Lake City became the hub of a series of thriving mining districts in the nearby canyons that produced gold, silver, and copper. By 1910, the population had reached nearly 90,000. The 1920s and 1930s were a period of stagnation, but New Deal programs and war industries revived the economy. In the latter half of the twentieth century, recreation, especially skiing, and high-tech industries gave Salt Lake City a measure of economic stability. In February 2002, the Winter Olympic Games were held in Salt Lake City and brought unprecedented world attention.

BIBLIOGRAPHY

Alexander, Thomas G., and James B. Allen. *Mormons and Gentiles: A History of Salt Lake City.* Boulder, Colo.: Pruett, 1984.

Gottlieb, Robert, and Peter Wiley. *Empires in the Sun: The Rise of the New American West.* Woodland Hills, Calif.: Windsor, 1982.

McCormick, John S. *Salt Lake City, the Gathering Place: An Illustrated History.* New York: Putnam, 1980.

Dean L. May

See also **Latter-day Saints, Church of Jesus Christ of; Tabernacle, Mormon; Utah; Westward Migration;** *and vol. 9:* **An Expedition to the Valley of the Great Salt Lake of Utah.**

SALTON SEA. Originally named Lake Cahuila after the Indians living in the area, the Salton Sea was first called the Salton Sink in 1892. Located in Imperial County in southeastern California, the ancient lake bed would fill with water during rare rainstorms. The water would then evaporate, leaving pools and salt beds. In 1900, the California Development Company began diverting Colorado River water to the Imperial Valley through the Imperial Canal, a channel dug without adequate safeguards in case of flood. The company intended the water for the farmers buying its land. A series of floods from 1905 to 1907 caused the Colorado River to leave its course, break through the inadequate headgate, and head for the lowest point. Soon the sink became the Salton Sea. The Southern Pacific Railroad and the federal government spent millions of dollars to dam the diversion and return the river to its proper channel. By then the Salton Sea had expanded to some thirty-five miles in length and up to fifteen miles in width, with an average depth of some 230 feet below sea level.

During the twentieth century, as agricultural activity in the Imperial and Coachella Valleys expanded, so did use of Colorado River water. The All-American Canal, completed in 1941, provided water through a route that was entirely in the United States, unlike the earlier Imperial Canal that ran through Mexico. Agricultural development transformed the region from arid desert into fertile farmland, and one of the most productive areas in the world. However, runoff from irrigation ditches, carrying pesticides and other chemicals, led to the Salton Sea, increasing its salinity and polluting its water. Real estate promoters attempting to create a "Salton Riviera" in the 1960s failed, leaving abandoned lots and boarded-up buildings along the shore. In recent years there have been episodes of massive die-offs of fish and birds. The late Congressman Sonny Bono introduced legislation to restore the Salton Sea, but estimates to repair the ecological damage run as high as $500 million.

BIBLIOGRAPHY

De Buys, William E. *Salt Dreams: Land & Water in Low-Down California.* Albuquerque: University of New Mexico, 1999.

Fradkin, Philip L. *A River No More: The Colorado River and the West.* 2d ed. Berkeley: University of California Press, 1995.

Hundley, Norris. *The Great Thirst: Californians and Water: A History.* Berkeley: University of California Press, 2001.

Abraham Hoffman

SALVATION ARMY. The Salvation Army is an evangelistic organization created in 1865 by William Booth, a former adherent of METHODISM, to work among the poor of London. His book *In Darkest England and the Way Out* (1890) not only won popular support for his movement but also helped awaken public opinion to poverty in the world's richest city. The present military format of the group dates from the publication of *The Orders and Regulations for the Salvation Army* in 1878. The uniforms, designed by Booth's wife, Catherine Mumford Booth, were adopted in the early 1880s. A branch of the army was formed in the United States in 1880 and received leadership from Evangeline Cory Booth, the general's daughter, from 1904 to 1934. The group has been noted for the vigor of its preaching, its energetic use of music, and its crusades on behalf of the poor and oppressed. It has considered itself to have a special mission to alcoholics.

In 2001, as President George W. Bush proposed bringing "faith-based" charities into a federally coordinated program, the Salvation Army's stance on homosexuality caused concern. While the army condemns harassment based on sexual orientation, it nevertheless describes same-sex intimacy as sinful and has at times refused to hire homosexuals.

In the early twenty-first century the United States branch of the Salvation Army had 443,000 members and

William Booth. The founder and first general of the Salvation Army, the worldwide evangelistic charity organization. AP/WIDE WORLD PHOTOS

several million volunteers supporting its social service programs.

BIBLIOGRAPHY

Taiz, Lillian. *Hallelujah Lads & Lasses: Remaking the Salvation Army in America, 1880–1930.* Chapel Hill: University of North Carolina Press, 2001.

Winston, Diane H. *Red-Hot and Righteous: The Urban Religion of the Salvation Army.* Cambridge, Mass.: Harvard University Press, 1999.

Glenn T. Miller / s. c.

See also **Discrimination: Sexual Orientation; Evangelicalism and Revivalism; Methodism; Volunteerism.**

SAMOA, AMERICAN.

An unincorporated territory of the United States, located in the South Pacific and consisting of seven islands, American Samoa makes up the eastern portion of the Samoan archipelago; the western portion, known as Western Samoa or the Republic of Samoa, is an independent nation.

The first Polynesian colonists seem to have reached Samoa from Fiji around 1000 B.C. By the eighteenth century, Samoa supported a complex society with fortified villages, intensively cultivated fields, and extensive trade among the islands. In 1722, the Dutch explorer Jacob Roggeveen was the first European to visit the islands. Several other expeditions visited over the next century; European influence was minimal, however, until the 1830s, when the first English missionaries arrived. Thereafter, whalers, traders, and missionaries came in steadily increasing numbers.

By the 1870s, Great Britain and Germany were competing with the United States for commercial and diplomatic advantage in Samoa. In 1872 the Grant administration sent Col. Albert Steinberger as a "special commissioner" to "assist" the islanders and generally further American interests. Steinberger helped the Samoans draft a constitution but then installed himself as premier with near-dictatorial powers; he was deposed and deported by the British in 1876.

Samoa continued to be unstable, with various local factions bidding for support from the colonial powers. In 1889, Britain, Germany, and the United States attempted to settle their differences in the islands with the Berlin Treaty, which created a neutral and independent Samoa subject to the "advice" of the powers. This arrangement failed, and Samoa went through two rounds of civil war in the 1890s. In 1899 the three powers replaced the Berlin Treaty with the Tripartite Pact, which divided Samoa between Germany and the United States, with Britain withdrawing all claims in return for acknowledgement of its rights in other Pacific territories. The 1899 line of division, running along the 171st degree of longitude, remains the international boundary today between American Samoa and the independent Republic of Samoa.

The new colony was placed under the jurisdiction of the U.S. Navy, and executive authority was vested in a series of naval governors. American claims to the islands were strengthened by various Articles of Cession obtained from Samoan chiefs between 1900 and 1904, although Congress did not ratify these until 1929.

With the growth of Japanese militarism in the mid-1930s, Samoa began to acquire new strategic importance. By 1940 the Samoan islands had become a training area for the U.S. Marine Corps. After Pearl Harbor, the military facilities were rapidly and massively expanded, and Samoa became a rear staging area for U.S. offensives in the South Pacific. The military withdrew after the war's end, but this massive influx of American servicemen and goods had a lasting impact on Samoan society.

In 1951 control of the islands was shifted from the Navy to the Department of the Interior. The Samoans gained a measure of self-government when American Samoa approved its first constitution in 1966. This constitution is still in effect; it provides a tripartite system of government similar to the standard American model, albeit with some unique concessions to local custom. The islands' chief executive continued to be a governor appointed by Washington until 1977, when the position was made elective. Since then, the islands have had considerable autonomy, particularly in local affairs, although certain powers remain reserved to the Secretary of the Interior.

Samoans are American nationals, although not American citizens. They owe allegiance to the United States, and have American diplomatic and military protection, but are not entitled to a representative in Congress. Samoa is an "unincorporated" territory, meaning that not all provisions and protections of the United States Constitution apply there.

Samoans can travel freely to, and reside in, the United States. The 2000 Census gave the population of American Samoa as 57,291, of which 88.2 percent were ethnic Samoans. Ninety-six thousand Samoans were listed as living in the United States, with the largest groups in California and Hawaii. Samoa's economy has remained partly dependent upon American aid and is underdeveloped compared to the U.S. mainland or Hawaii.

BIBLIOGRAPHY
Gray, J. A. C. *Amerika Samoa: A History of American Samoa and Its United States Naval Administration.* Annapolis, Md.: United States Naval Institute, 1960.

Douglas M. Muir

See also **Insular Cases; Wilkes Expedition.**

SAMPLERS originated as a means of keeping together samples of stitches used in embroidering tablecloths, napkins, towels, pillowcases, and other household articles before books of patterns existed. The earliest known mention of a sampler dates from 1505, when Elizabeth of York paid eight pence for "an elne of lynnyn for a sampler for the queen." By the mid-sixteenth century samplers were popular in England. The will of Mary Thompson, dated 1546, read, "I gyve to Alys Pinchebeck my sampler with semes." The sampler appeared in the colonies with the arrival of Anne Gower in 1610. The first sampler known to have been made in America was the work of Laura Standish, daughter of Myles Standish.

American samplers, often created by children as young as five, were noted for their originality, inventiveness, and decorative quality. In the mid-eighteenth century, Adam and Eve were popular subjects for samplers. Later, family trees, shepherds, the sampler maker's house, and sometimes whole villages were depicted, with the designs becoming increasingly diverse. The American eagle was a popular motif in early nineteenth-century samplers. After 1830 the art of sampler making declined but did not completely disappear.

BIBLIOGRAPHY
Bolton, Ethel S., and Eva J. Coe. *American Samplers.* New York: Dover Publications, 1987.
Hersh, Tandy, and Charles Hersh. *Samplers of the Pennsylvania Germans.* Birdsboro: Pennsylvania German Society, 1991.

Ulrich, Laura Thatcher. "Pens and Needles: Documents and Artifacts in Women's History." *Uncoverings* 14 (1993): 221–228.

Katharine Metcalf Roof / A. R.

SAMPSON-SCHLEY CONTROVERSY. The Sampson-Schley controversy arose during the SPANISH-AMERICAN WAR, at the start of the the Battle of Santiago on 3 July 1898. At that time Adm. William T. Sampson, in his flagship *New York*, was seven miles to the east and unable to participate effectively in the battle. Sampson had signaled that the other ships should disregard the movement of the flagship, but he did not turn over command to Comdr. Winfield S. Schley. Nevertheless, Schley received popular credit for the victory. The resulting controversy raged bitterly. Upon final appeal, President Theodore Roosevelt declared Santiago "a captains' battle," in which "technically Sampson commanded" and movements followed standing orders.

BIBLIOGRAPHY
Musicant, Ivan. *Empire by Default: The Spanish-American War and the Dawn of the American Century.* New York: Holt, 1998.

Allan Westcott / A. E.

See also **Spain, Relations with; Spanish-American War, Navy in.**

SAN ANTONIO, Texas, was founded in 1718 as a mission outpost of the Spanish empire and has become the eighth largest city in the United States. The ready availability of water from the San Antonio River helped prompt the Spanish to establish an unusual concentration of five missions in the area, together with a presidio, or military post. Throughout the period of Spanish and Mexican rule, San Antonio served as the capital of Texas. In March 1836 the northernmost mission, popularly known as the Alamo, became the scene of the most celebrated battle of the Texas revolt. Today it remains the most visited tourist site in the state.

After independence in 1836, Texas relocated its capital northward, but San Antonio flourished during the post–Civil War boom in the cattle industry. The arrival of the railroad in 1877 somewhat compensated for the region's loss of preeminence as a national supplier of beef. Beginning in 1885, Mayor Bryan Callaghan II assembled a political coalition that promoted business development over competing interests. One harbinger of later growth was the federal government's establishment of Fort Sam Houston in 1879; it remains San Antonio's largest single employer. World War I brought a major expansion of military facilities in the city, notably with the founding of Kelly Field (later Kelly Air Force Base) in 1917. The growth of the military, especially aviation, was even more pronounced after 1941. Despite the closing of Kelly in

2001, more than 40,000 uniformed personnel remain based in San Antonio, and the military employs more than 31,000 civilians.

In addition, the city has become a major retirement center for veterans and their families, who are attracted by its mild winters, low cost of living, and urban services. The economy is dominated by the service sector, with tourism and government being especially prominent. Along with the Alamo, the nearby Riverwalk, a mixed-use urban park along the San Antonio River, is a leading tourist attraction.

The majority of San Antonio's population is Hispanic (58.7 percent according to the 2000 census) while African Americans comprise a fairly small proportion (6.8 percent) of the population. Ethnicity has been a major factor in the city's politics, intertwined with debates over economic development. The Hispanic population has been concentrated west of the downtown area, with African Americans on the near east side, although residential segregation has declined since 1970. This residential pattern resulted in part from flooding problems. Flood control had long been a major civic issue, but one addressed with considerable success in the last decades of the twentieth century. In the early 2000s management of the city's water supply in a period of economic development and rapid population growth (19.3 percent between1990 and 2000 to 1,144,646) emerged as a key issue.

BIBLIOGRAPHY

Davis, John L. *San Antonio: A Historical Portrait.* Austin, Tex.: Encino Press, 1978.

Johnson, David R., John A. Booth and Richard J. Harris, eds. *The Politics of San Antonio: Community, Progress, and Power.* Lincoln: University of Nebraska Press, 1983.

Poyo, Gerald E., and Gilberto M. Hinojosa, eds. *Tejano Origins in Eighteenth-Century San Antonio.* Austin: University of Texas Press, 1991.

James C. Schneider

See also **Alamo, Siege of the; "Remember the Alamo."**

SAN DIEGO. Located in Southern CALIFORNIA near the border with Mexico, San Diego boasts a pleasant, temperate climate and a magnificent natural harbor that has made the city a center of international commerce, a major U.S. naval base, and a popular destination for tourists. As of the 2000 Census, the city was home to some 1,223,400 people, making it the second largest city in California and the seventh largest in the United States.

The region was originally densely inhabited by Native American peoples, including the Cahuilla and the Kumeyaay. Europeans first came in 1542, when the Spanish explorer Juan Cabrillo landed there. He was followed in 1602 by Sebastián Vizcaíno, who gave San Diego its name. In 1769, when Spain finally decided to settle Alta California, San Diego became the site of the first Euro-

San Diego. A historical view of the city's harbor and part of its business district, c. 1911. LIBRARY OF CONGRESS

pean settlement. San Diego was incorporated as a city in 1850, following the American conquest. With the establishment of a connection to the Santa Fe Railroad in 1884, the city's population began to grow, but it remained in the shadow of Los Angeles, which had become the economic and demographic center of Southern California. Throughout the late nineteenth century, its economy remained rooted in agriculture, cattle ranching, and fishing.

In many ways the turning point for the city came in 1915, with the Panama-California Exposition. Designed to celebrate the opening of the Panama Canal, the Exposition also served to advertise the city's attractive climate, spurring TOURISM and settlement. A modest menagerie created as part of the celebration would become a permanent attraction, eventually blossoming into the world famous San Diego Zoo. In the late 1910s and early 1920s the city benefited from a growing military presence with the creation of naval and marine training centers and the designation of San Diego as the home port for the Eleventh Naval District.

During World War II the region's military facilities were hugely expanded to include a major new marine training center at Camp Pendleton, to the north of the city, and Miramar Naval Air Station. Equally important were wartime orders for aircraft that boosted the fortunes of several local companies, including Ryan Aeronautical and Consolidated Aircraft. In the postwar years, Cold War tensions sustained the region's military bases and fueled the federal government's orders for aircraft and sophisticated electronics. The establishment of the John Day Hopkins Laboratory and the U.S. Naval Electronics Laboratory helped provide the infrastructure to support the aerospace and high-technology industries. The University of California at San Diego, which opened in 1964 in the La Jolla section of the city, also quickly gained a reputation as a superior educational institution and a center for scientific research. In close proximity to the university were located the Salk Institute for Biological Studies, founded in 1960, and the Scripps Institute of

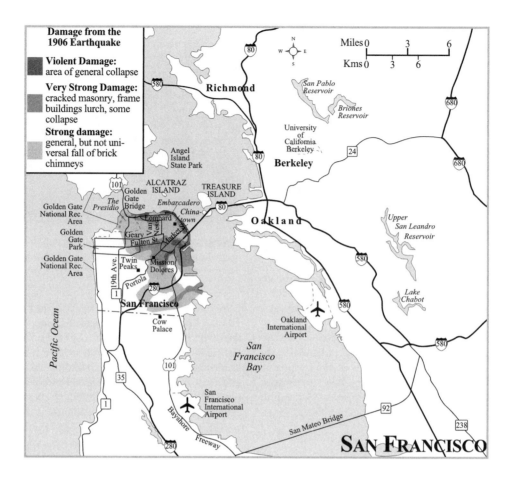

Damage from the
1906 Earthquake

Violent Damage:
area of general collapse

Very Strong Damage:
cracked masonry, frame
buildings lurch, some
collapse

Strong damage:
general, but not uni-
versal fall of brick
chimneys

SAN FRANCISCO

Oceanography, a famous aquatic research station established in 1903.

Although military spending provided the most important component of postwar growth, the city benefited as well from growing commercial ties with Asia and Latin America and a tuna fishing industry that by 1950 featured a fleet of some two-hundred ships and six canneries. By 1960 overseas competition had seriously eroded San Diego's significance as a fishing port, but a growing tourist trade helped to offset this. For decades the city's attractive climate and wide beaches had lured visitors, but during the 1960s concerted efforts were made to boost further the city's appeal, including the 1964 opening of Sea World, an amusement park with an aquatic theme; the revitalization of historic Old Town San Diego; and the unveiling of the San Diego Wild Animal Park in 1972. Since the late 1980s, cutbacks in defense spending have had an impact on the city's growth, but this has been moderated by the region's economic diversification, including a strong tourist industry and the city's strategic commercial location on the Pacific Rim.

BIBLIOGRAPHY

Lotchin, Roger W. *Fortress California, 1910–1961: From Warfare to Welfare.* New York: Oxford University Press, 1992.

McKeever, Michael. *A Short History of San Diego.* San Francisco: Lexikos, 1985.

Mills, James. *San Diego: Where California Began.* 5th ed. San Diego, Calif.: San Diego Historical Society, 1985.

Pourade, Richard F. *The History of San Diego.* 7 volumes. San Diego, Calif.: Union Tribune Publishing, 1960–1977.

Daniel J. Johnson

See also **Aircraft Industry; Laboratories; Marine Biology; Marine Corps, United States; Navy, United States; Oceanography; Zoological Parks.**

SAN FRANCISCO. Located on a forty-nine-square-mile peninsula in northern California, San Francisco grew from a small Spanish mission and military garrison (presidio) into one of the world's leading financial, technological, and cultural centers. The city's beauty, accentuated by its ocean and bay views, and Mediterranean climate have turned it into a beacon for tourists from all over the world. San Francisco's thriving economy, now based heavily on technology and finance, brings countless new arrivals into the city in search of their slice of the American pie.

Gaspar de Portolá discovered San Francisco Bay in 1769 on a journey north from San Diego. By 1776, Spanish settlers occupied San Francisco and set up a mission and military station. When Mexico gained independence from Spain in 1821, California became Mexican territory.

San Francisco. An early photograph of the city's famous cable cars (and one of its equally famous hills). Cable cars began operating on Clay Street in 1873; the first lines featured an open car and an enclosed one. © UPI/CORBIS-BETTMANN

In 1835, the small trading settlement of Yerba Buena was established, which became San Francisco in 1848. The United States took over in 1846 during the Mexican-American War and two years later, the gold rush turned the city into a burgeoning metropolis. San Francisco was incorporated as a city in 1850.

After the gold rush, San Francisco changed from a lawless frontier station into a financial, industrial, and commercial center. In 1906, an earthquake and fire leveled much of the city, killing more than 3,000 and leaving 250,000 homeless. Once rebuilt, though, San Francisco grew in financial prominence. The completion of the Panama Canal ensured that it would be closely tied to the money on the East Coast. Throughout the twentieth century, the city remained a hub for Pacific Rim finance, backed by Bank of America founder A. P. Giannini and the establishment of the Pacific Coast Stock Exchange. Bank of America financed the building of numerous businesses in the Bay area and major infrastructure developments, including the Golden Gate Bridge.

Culturally, San Francisco is well known for its progressiveness, diversity, and acceptance of a variety of political viewpoints, sexual preferences, and ethnicities. Since the mid-1800s, the city has had a large Asian and Pacific Island population, and now has a growing Hispanic community. Of San Francisco's 750,000 citizens, whites comprise only about 50 percent of the population, while African Americans make up about 10 to 15 percent. The

Bay area has also become a budding center for Middle Eastern and Indian immigrants.

San Francisco is known as a hotbed of liberalism—from its long history of labor unrest, exemplified by the general strike of 1934, to its place at the center of the 1960s counterculture, and today's large gay and lesbian communities, which make up about 20 percent of the population. The Democratic Party has dominated city politics since the early 1960s. San Francisco's challenges include finding a way to deal with rampant homelessness and striking the right balance between industrialism and tourism as the basis for the city's economy. The Bay area also has unusually high housing costs and the influx of people moving to the region has clogged its infrastructure.

Tourism remains a key facet of the San Francisco economy. Tourists flock to attractions such as Fisherman's Wharf, Chinatown, the cable cars, and a diverse mix of museums and sporting events. With its steep hills, water views, and historic landmarks, such as Alcatraz and the Golden Gate Bridge, the city has been the setting for numerous motion pictures, television shows, and novels.

Fueled by cowboy lore and the gold rush in the mid-nineteenth century, the city has long drawn the adventurous and courageous. Modern San Francisco still retains some of the old lure of the West. During the dot-com boom of the late 1990s, thousands of technologists poured into the city in search of untold wealth brought on by the

Information Age. Despite the implosion of the dot-com bubble, San Francisco and Silicon Valley remain centers for technological innovation.

BIBLIOGRAPHY

Issel, William and Robert W. Cherny. *San Francisco, 1865–1932: Politics, Power, and Urban Development.* Berkeley: University of California Press, 1986.

Kurzman, Dan. *Disaster!: The Great San Francisco Earthquake and Fire of 1906.* New York: William Morrow, 2001.

Richards, Rand. *Historic San Francisco: A Concise History and Guide.* San Francisco: Heritage House, 2001.

Bob Batchelor

See also **Counterculture; Gold Rush, California; Golden Gate Bridge;** *and vol. 9:* **Gentlemen's Agreement; Constitution of the Committee of Vigilantes of San Francisco.**

SAN FRANCISCO EARTHQUAKES. The city of San Francisco, California, rests on part of the San Andreas fault and endures hundreds of minor seismic tremors every year. One of the largest tremors occurred at 5:12 A.M. on 18 April 1906, when an earthquake measuring between 7.8 and 8.0 on the Richter scale ruptured the northernmost 430 kilometers of the San Andreas fault. San Francisco experienced unparalleled damage. Hit by falling masonry and buried beneath debris, at least 700 people died. Modern estimates suggest a final death toll in excess of 3,000. Losing its water supply from San Andreas Lake due to a broken pipeline, San Francisco was wracked by uncontrollable fires for four days. Looters pillaged stores and houses. The combination of violent shockwaves and multiple fires destroyed approximately 28,000 buildings and left 250,000 residents homeless. The 1906 earthquake resulted in a substantial rebuilding of the city and, due to its severity, became a lasting source of study into plate tectonics and seismic motion.

At 5:04 P.M. on 17 October 1989, San Francisco suffered another large earthquake. Geologists named it the Loma Prieta earthquake after its epicenter close to Mount Loma Prieta, sixty miles southeast of the city. The earthquake measured 7.1 on the Richter scale. Approximately thirty times less powerful than its 1906 precursor, the earthquake still tested the preparedness of northern Californians for a sizable seismic event. Famous for interrupting a live, televised World Series baseball game at Candlestick Park in San Francisco, the Loma Prieta earthquake caused substantial damage to communities in and around the city. Buildings in Santa Cruz and Watsonville, close to the epicenter, collapsed during a succession of wrenching shockwaves. In Oakland, across the bay from San Francisco, the Cypress Street section of Interstate 880, a two-tier freeway, collapsed. Seismic tremors damaged 18,000 houses and rendered 12,000 residents temporarily homeless. Officials later calculated the total cost of damage at $6 billion; sixty-three people died.

BIBLIOGRAPHY

Hansen, Gladys, and Emmet Condon. *Denial of Disaster: The Untold Story and Photographs of the San Francisco Earthquake and Fire of 1906.* San Francisco: Cameron, 1989.

McPhee, John. *Assembling California.* New York: Farrar, Straus, 1993.

Plafker, George, and John P. Galloway, eds. *Lessons Learned from the Loma Prieta, California, Earthquake of October 17, 1989.* United States Geological Survey Circular 1045. Washington, D.C.: Department of the Interior, 1989.

John Wills

See also **Disasters; Earthquakes.**

San Francisco Earthquake, 1906. A very small portion of the widespread destruction in the city caused by the earthquake on 18 April 1906 and the resulting fires. UNDERWOOD & UNDERWOOD/CORBIS-BETTMANN

SAN JACINTO, BATTLE OF (21 April 1836). On 11 March 1836, five days after the defeat of the Texas revolutionaries at the Alamo, General Sam Houston retreated with 374 men from Mexican general Antonio López de Santa Anna's advance. Houston recruited as he retreated, while Santa Anna divided his army in pursuit. On 20 April, Houston's force, now 800 strong, intercepted Santa Anna's force of about 1,200 men at Lynch's Ferry, which crossed the San Jacinto River. Destroying a bridge protecting his own as well as the Mexicans' avenue of retreat, Houston attacked. Santa Anna's surprise was complete. A thinly held barricade was quickly overrun, and organized resistance ended within twenty minutes.

San Juan Hill. This lithograph, published in *Harper's Weekly*, shows black soldiers of the 10th Regular Cavalry (whose white officers included Lieutenant John J. Pershing, of subsequent World War I renown) playing an important role in the most famous battle for Cuba during the Spanish-American War.

The rest was slaughter. Texas figures on enemy casualties—630 killed, 208 wounded, 730 prisoners—are inexact, the total reflecting more men than Santa Anna probably would have had on the field. Texan losses were 16 killed, 24 wounded, including Houston. Santa Anna, a prisoner, signed armistice terms under which the other divisions of his army immediately evacuated Texas.

BIBLIOGRAPHY

De Bruhl, Marshall. *Sword of San Jacinto: A Life of Sam Houston.* New York: Random House, 1993.

Pohl, James W. *The Battle of San Jacinto.* Austin: Texas State Historical Association, 1989.

Williams, John H. *Sam Houston: A Biography of the Father of Texas.* New York: Simon and Schuster, 1993.

Marquis James / A. R.

See also **Alamo, Siege of the; "Remember the Alamo."**

SAN JOSÉ, CALIFORNIA, is located seven miles below the southern tip of San Francisco Bay, on Coyote Creek and the Guadalupe River, fifty miles southeast of San Francisco. It is the seat of Santa Clara County. It was founded in 1777 as San José de Guadalupe under the Spanish Reglamento Provisional because the Spanish government wanted to lessen the dependency of the presidios (forts) on the missions for their food supply. It was the first civil town (pueblo) established by the Spanish in what was then known as Alta California. Until the gold rush of 1848 it was the most important town in the province. When California entered the union in 1850, the first state legislature met in San José, but only for a year. Major agricultural products included tree fruits, nuts, berries, vegetables, and livestock, and it was the world's largest dried-fruit packing and canning center.

Beginning with scientific development related to World War II, the entire county became a center for electronics research and space-related technology, ultimately acquiring the nickname Silicon Valley. San José is home to San José State University, the oldest public institution of higher learning in California, founded in 1857. The 2000 census listed the population of San José, the third-largest city in the state, as 894,943.

BIBLIOGRAPHY

Arbuckle, Clyde. *History of San Jose.* San Jose, Calif.: Smith and McKay, 1986.

McCarthy, Francis Florence. *A History of Mission San Jose, California, 1797–1835.* Fresno, Calif.: Academy Library Guild, 1958.

Mora Torres, Gregorio. *Los Mexicanos de San José, California: Life in a Mexican Pueblo, 1777–1846.* 1994.

Winther, Oscar Osburn. *Story of San Jose, 1777–1889, California's First Pueblo.* San Francisco: California Historical Society, 1935.

Carolle Carter

SAN JUAN HILL AND EL CANEY, BATTLES OF. After the Spanish withdrawal from Las Guásimas, Cuba, the key points defending Santiago de Cuba against U.S. general William Shafter's advance in June 1898 were

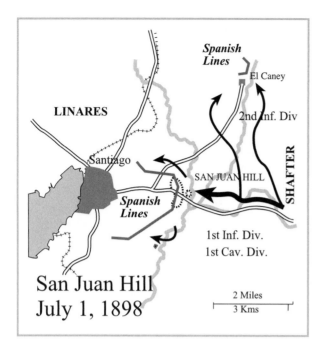

San Juan Hill
July 1, 1898

2 Miles
3 Kms

along a line from San Juan Hill northeast to El Caney. On 1 July the Americans attacked along the entire line. General Henry Lawton's division, on the right, carried El Caney. One division and Colonel Theodore Roosevelt's dismounted Rough Riders, advancing as much from desperation as by design, captured San Juan Hill. Admiral Pascual Cervera y Topete, alarmed by threat of American artillery on hills overlooking the harbor, sought safety on 3 July in a dash to the open sea. The Spanish fleet was overwhelmed by the U.S. Navy, under Admiral William T. Sampson. Santiago surrendered on 17 July.

BIBLIOGRAPHY

Dierks, Jack C. *A Leap to Arms: The Cuban Campaign of 1898.* Philadelphia: Lippincott, 1970.

Trask, David F. *The War with Spain in 1898.* New York: Macmillan, 1981.

Jim Dan Hill / A. R.

See also **Rough Riders; Spanish-American War.**

SAN JUAN ISLANDS. Approximately 172 islands make up the San Juan Islands, located eighty miles from Seattle in the northern reaches of Puget Sound. Together, they comprise San Juan County, one of the smallest but fastest-growing counties in Washington State. The islands cover 175 square miles and are home to roughly 13,000 residents. Friday Harbor, the county seat, is the islands' biggest and only incorporated town.

Native Americans, mostly of the Lummi nation, lived on the islands until Spanish explorers arrived and named the San Juans in the late 1700s. White settlers began to colonize in the 1850s. By 1859, the San Juan Boundary Dispute erupted over the boundary description between Canada and the United States, pitting the British against the Americans. After British warships arrived, Gen. Winfield Scott, commander in chief of American armies, stepped in and arranged for joint occupation on the islands. Germany's Kaiser Wilhelm I finally arbitrated the conflict in 1872, giving the San Juan archipelago to the United States and ending the last territorial conflict between the United States and Great Britain.

Historically, farmers, fishermen, and seafarers populated the islands. But by the 1970s, traditional occupations became less profitable than tourism. The San Juans in the early twenty-first century see a greater economic impact from visitors as well as from the mainlanders and retirees seeking an island alternative to city life.

BIBLIOGRAPHY

Bailey-Cummings, Jo, and Al Cummings. *San Juan: The Powder-Keg Island: The Settler's Own Stories.* Friday Harbor, Wash.: Beach Combers, 1987.

Miller, David Hunter, ed. *Northwest Water Boundary: Report of the Experts Summoned by the German Emperor as Arbitrator Under Articles 34-42 of the Treaty of Washington of May 8, 1871, Preliminary to His Award Dated October 21, 1872.* Seattle: University of Washington, 1942.

Richardson, David Blair. *Pig War Islands: The San Juans of Northwest Washington.* Eastsound, Wash.: Orcas Publishing Company, 1990.

———. *Magic Islands: A Treasure-Trove of San Juan Islands Lore.* Eastsound, Wash.: Orcas Publishing Company, 2000.

Kym O'Connell-Todd

See also **Puget Sound.**

SAN LORENZO, TREATY OF. *See* **Pinckney's Treaty.**

SAN QUENTIN. San Quentin State Prison in Marin County, known as the "Big House," is California's oldest penal institution. The original cell block, called "the Stones," was constructed in 1852 by a private lessee using prisoner labor. San Quentin initially housed both men and women. Women were moved outside the walls in the 1920s and to different facilities in the 1930s. Prisoners at San Quentin typically were employed in privately operated industries. For many years they made burlap bags in the prison jute mill.

Notorious offenders were confined at San Quentin, among them Sirhan Sirhan and Charles Manson. Eldridge Cleaver began his career as a leader of the BLACK PANTHER Party there. In 1970 George Jackson, one of the Soledad Brothers, was shot to death in an apparent escape attempt.

At the beginning of the twenty-first century San Quentin was a high-security prison for approximately six thousand male inmates, among them more than five hundred prisoners under sentence of death. Many prisoners were employed manufacturing furniture for state agencies. The coastal site of the prison on the Marin Peninsula is attractive to real estate developers, and it seems likely that San Quentin will ultimately be demolished to make its location available for private homes.

BIBLIOGRAPHY

Nichols, Nancy Ann. *San Quentin inside the Walls.* San Quentin, Calif.: San Quentin Museum Press, 1991.

Larry Yackle

See also **Prisons and Prison Reform.**

SAN SIMEON, the publisher William Randolph Hearst's estate, was designed by architect Julia Morgan. It is situated on the central coast of California, in the Santa Lucia Mountains, halfway between San Francisco and Los Angeles. Beginning in 1919 and for the next thirty years, Hearst spent hundreds of millions of dollars constructing a Mediterranean-style village, with swimming pools, tennis courts, and a full-sized zoo, enclosed within a working cattle ranch. The focal point of the estate was Casa Grande, or the "castle," and three guest villas, with 165 rooms in all. During the 1920s and 1930s Hearst's guests at San Simeon included movie stars, Hollywood producers, publishers, world leaders, and politicians.

San Simeon. A view of William Randolph Hearst's castle at his vast California estate—the thinly disguised model for "Xanadu" in the Orson Welles film *Citizen Kane.* AP/WIDE WORLD PHOTOS

BIBLIOGRAPHY

Kastner, Victoria. *Hearst Castle: The Biography of a Country House.* New York: H. N. Abrams, 2000.

Nasaw, David. *The Chief: The Life of William Randolph Hearst.* Boston: Houghton Mifflin, 2000.

David Nasaw

SAND CREEK MASSACRE, an attack on a village of sleeping Cheyenne Indians by a regiment of Colorado militiamen on 29 November 1864 that resulted in the death of more than 200 tribal members. About two-thirds of the dead were women and children. Many bodies were brutally mutilated and their scalps were strung across a Denver theater stage to the delight of an applauding audience.

By 1864, the previously united Cheyenne had divided into two bands that followed the northern and southern buffalo herds. In that year, with regular army troops redeployed for Civil War service and the borders between Indian and non-Indian settlements often in dispute, American settlers on the plains feared tribes like the Cheyenne who had access to weapons. In Colorado, Governor John Evans authorized the commander of the state's militia, a former Methodist minister named John M. Chivington, to patrol the eastern borders of the territory to guard against Indian attacks. Chivington's aggressive tactics worried the friendly Southern Cheyenne sufficiently that they sought out Major Edward Wynkoop at Fort Lyon on the Arkansas River. The Southern Cheyenne's leader, Black Kettle, turned four white captives over to Wynkoop and promised to live peacefully on a reservation. News of this breakthrough did not please Evans and Chivington, however, for they had just organized a new regiment of Colorado militiamen who had volunteered for 100 days of service and had been promised an Indian war.

Wynkoop brought Black Kettle to Denver to meet Chivington. On 28 September, Chivington met with the Cheyenne and invited them to establish a camp near Fort Lyon. By November nearly 230 lodges of peaceful Cheyenne and Arapaho had surrendered. Because of the need to hunt game, Black Kettle's group set up more than 100 of their lodges along Sand Creek. It was this camp that Chivington and his forces attacked on 29 November. When Chivington attacked, Black Kettle assumed it was a mistake. The chief raised an American flag and a white flag over his tipi in a sign of friendship. The Colorado volunteers rode on. Remarkably, Black Kettle was not killed at Sand Creek; he would die four years later in another unprovoked attack by American soldiers on the Washita River in Indian Territory.

While celebrated in Denver, a great many Americans met the Sand Creek Massacre with horror. Congress launched an investigation of the tragedy and within two years had established a Peace Commission to draw up equitable treaties with groups like the Cheyenne, Kiowa, and Sioux. Sand Creek remains a biting memory for both

Sand Creek Massacre. A depiction of the unprovoked 1864 attack by Colorado militia commander John M. Chivington, which killed more than 200 Cheyennes—most of them women and children. COLORADO HISTORICAL SOCIETY

the Cheyenne and non-Indians, but efforts to acquire the site of the massacre for a national park have only recently borne fruit.

BIBLIOGRAPHY

Moore, John H. *The Cheyenne.* Cambridge, Mass.: Blackwell, 1996.

Utley, Robert. *The Indian Frontier of the American West, 1846– 1890.* Albuquerque: University of New Mexico Press, 1984.

Frederick E. Hoxie

SANITARY COMMISSION, UNITED STATES.

The United States Sanitary Commission was created by executive order of President Abraham Lincoln on 13 June 1861. Its organization was the idea of a group of women and men who wanted to help the Union cause by developing a response to the inadequacy of the Army Medical Bureau in coping with the medical and sanitary needs of the army. On 29 April Dr. Elizabeth Blackwell, the first U.S. woman to earn an M.D., had organized a meeting of 3,000 women in New York City to form the Women's Central Association for Relief (WCAR), devoted to women's volunteer relief efforts. The WCAR would become the nucleus of the Sanitary Commission. But women, acting on their own, could not at that time hope to convince government to form a new national organization, so a group of men led to Washington by the Unitarian minister Henry Whitney Bellows convinced government officials to form the commission. Bellows was appointed president and Frederick Law Olmsted, the future designer of Central Park, was general secretary.

The commission worked through local affiliates. By 1863 there were 7,000 such branches throughout the north, all composed of and administered largely by women. Blackwell and the noted mental health reformer Dorothea Dix were early involved in recruiting volunteer nurses, but lost their influence as men took control of the commission. The commission's 500 paid agents were men, while tens of thousands of women labored as unpaid volunteers. These volunteers held bazaars and organized Sanitary Fairs to raise money to purchase medical supplies, clothing, and food to send to army camps and hospitals and to support the 3,000 women who served as army nurses. The work of the Sanitary Commission eventually helped to make nursing a respectable profession for women, advanced medical care within the army, and taught many women the organizational skills they would apply to founding thousands of women's voluntary groups after the war.

BIBLIOGRAPHY

Giesberg, Judith Ann. *Civil War Sisterhood: The U.S. Sanitary Commission and Women's Politics in Transition.* Boston: Northeastern University Press, 2000.

McPherson, James. *Battle Cry of Freedom: The Civil War Era.* New York: Oxford University Press, 1988.

Maureen A. Flanagan

See also **Women in Military Service; Women's Rights Movement: The Nineteenth Century.**

SANITATION, ENVIRONMENTAL.

To the first settlers the fresh clean air and sparkling waters of the New World contrasted sharply with the ingrained dirt and filth of ancient European cities, and the vast reaches of the new continent made it difficult for them to contemplate the possibility of dirt and crowding. Nevertheless, humanity's unhappy faculty for befouling its environment soon made governmental action necessary. Shortly after the establishment of the Dutch colony of New Amsterdam, a law in 1644 forbade its residents from urinating and depositing filth within the fort. In 1657 other ordinances prohibited throwing dead animals, rubbish, and filth into the streets and canals of the town. The following year another ordinance decreed that certain privies that were causing an outrageous stench should be torn down. Boston and other early colonial towns soon enacted similar sanitary measures. As early as 1634 Boston prohibited depositing garbage or dead fish in the vicinity of the common landing place and passed other measures seeking to eliminate the "loathsome smells" arising from privies, slaughterhouses, and the so-called nuisance trades.

The connection between filth and disease had been made early in history and informed American colonists argued for sanitary measures on both aesthetic and health grounds. In the eighteenth century, YELLOW FEVER, which struck most heavily in the crowded and dirty dock areas, gave emphasis to the prevailing miasmatic thesis, the theory that a mysterious and invisible gas or miasma emanating from putrefying organic substances caused disease. Cadwallader Colden, a physician best known for his political activities and historical writings, warned in 1743 that New York City, because of its deleterious atmosphere and unsanitary condition, was in grave danger of yellow fever, and he urged a massive drainage and sanitary program to restore the city to a healthful state.

The pleas of Colden and other intelligent observers went unheeded, and, as the colonial settlements grew, their sanitary problems intensified at an even faster rate. The records are full of complaints about the deplorable condition of the streets and the offensive stenches arising from slaughterhouses, tanners, fat and bone boilers, and other trades. Despite a series of ordinances prohibiting the practice, drainage ditches, canals, docks, gutters, and vacant lots remained repositories for garbage, offal, carrion, rubbish, and human waste. Municipal authorities began assuming some responsibility for street cleaning and sewage removal, but their efforts rarely achieved more than temporary success.

The first tentative steps in the direction of sewer systems arose from the offensive condition of the drainage ditches and canals. In despair, local residents began demanding that these ditches be covered. In one response to a petition in 1703, New York City constructed a "Common Sewer," approximately 1,200 feet long, along Broad Street. In the succeeding years, New York and other colonial towns gradually built more of these sewers. These structures were originally meant to be conduits for draining surface water, but so much sewage flowed into the gutters that they were in actuality sewers. Since they poured their contents into the docks or onto the shores

and banks of adjacent bodies of water, they created almost as much of a nuisance as the one they sought to remedy.

Water supplies were an equally grave problem. The more fortunate towns in the colonial period drew their water from fast-flowing streams or large rivers, but the majority of colonists relied on public and private wells. With the contents of privies and cesspools constantly seeping into the ground and overflowing into the gutters, these wells seldom ran dry. Not surprisingly, the consequence was endemic enteric diseases that affected all segments of the population but took their heaviest toll among infants and young children. By the 1790s Boston, Philadelphia, New York, and other cities were developing elementary water systems. Wooden pipes and primitive steam engines supplied water to the homes of the well-to-do citizens, and occasional hydrants appeared in the poorer neighborhoods. Unfortunately, the water sources were often polluted, and even when they were safe, the frequent loss of pressure combined with leaking pipe connections led to contamination.

The nineteenth century saw sanitary conditions, particularly in towns and cities, grow steadily worse. The twin movements of industrialization and urbanization crowded the working poor into squalid warrens and created an ideal environment for Asiatic CHOLERA and other enteric disorders. During the first half of the century, temporary health boards emerged. Although they functioned only when epidemics threatened, they occasionally initiated massive sanitary programs. These programs involved removing garbage and dead animals from the streets and lots, emptying privies and cesspools, and draining the many stagnant pools. In addition, quicklime and other substances were spread in the gutters, graveyards, and all possible sources of noxious miasmas.

Despite the efforts of these health boards, the sheer size of the garbage and human waste problems made the fight for a cleaner environment a losing battle. Municipal governments were ineffective, the prevailing technology was inadequate, the upper classes were reluctant to pay for large-scale sanitary programs, and the degradation of the poor was such that they made few protests. Not until the affluent perceived as a threat to themselves the diseases that were so rampant among the poor did they make serious efforts to improve the situation. Two dramatic epidemic diseases, Asiatic cholera and yellow fever, provided the chief impetus to sanitary reform.

Agitation for sanitary reform resulted in the formation of the Louisiana State Board of Health and a series of national sanitary conventions in the 1850s, but the Civil War cut short these promising developments. With NEW YORK CITY leading the way in the postwar years, municipal health departments and state boards of health rapidly began to appear. Although the bacteriological revolution was under way during these years, health boards still considered their major task to be that of improving the physical environment.

During the later years of the nineteenth century, water systems were improved and extended. Sewer systems began replacing the haphazard construction of individual conduits, and street paving improved drainage and facilitated the collection of garbage and rubbish. Furthermore, technological improvements eliminated many of the former nuisances that had outraged sensibilities and threatened health.

By the advent of the twentieth century, the discovery of pathogenic organisms had provided health authorities with a better rationale for their efforts. They no longer concentrated their attacks on dirt per se but rather on pathogenic organisms and disease-producing conditions. The old fears of miasmas and sewer gas disappeared in the face of equally grave apprehensions about germs. While dirt was no longer the bête noire of health authorities, environmental sanitation benefited from the rising standard of living that brought higher standards of personal and public HYGIENE.

During the twentieth century technology solved the problem of safe water supplies through the introduction of rapid sand filtration and chlorination, making effective sewer systems possible in the major cities. Major cities eliminated horses and dairy cows from built-up areas and supplanted noisy, dirty steam engines with electric trolley cars. Garbage collection and street cleaning improved, and there were profound changes in the food-processing industry. On the other hand, technology also resulted in food adulteration through dangerous chemical additives and led to new forms of air and WATER POLLUTION. The internal combustion engine and the electric motor combined to eliminate the stench and flies that characterized nineteenth-century towns. Nonetheless, they, along with other technological developments, helped raise noise to dangerous levels and posed both immediate and more subtle threats to humanity's environment.

Among the subtle threats to health are carcinogens spewed forth by petrochemical and other industries; pollution of air and water by trace elements of lead, mercury, arsenicals, and asbestos; and the residues from tons of insecticides and herbicides that annually drench the landscape. A growing public awareness of the need for a concerted attack on environmental dangers led Congress to establish the ENVIRONMENTAL PROTECTION AGENCY (EPA) on 2 December 1970. The major purpose of the agency is to coordinate the work of the many government and private institutions and agencies involved in studying, monitoring, and enforcing antipollution activities. The EPA's attempts to control pollution inevitably have brought it into sharp conflict with strong vested interests, and it has enjoyed only qualified success.

Nonetheless, the EPA played a role in combatting a new hazard to world health that emerged in the 1970s: the widespread use of Freon compounds (otherwise known as chlorofluorocarbons) in aerosol cans, refrigeration, industrial solvents, and the production of plastic foam. These chemicals destroy the protective blanket of ozone surrounding the earth and have created a hole over the South Pole. The ozone layer limits the effect of ultraviolet rays, and some scientists suspect that the recent rise in skin cancer in Australia and southern Argentina and Chile stems from this thinning of the ozone layer. The scientific community has long been aware of the deleterious effect of chlorofluorocarbons on ozone, but it wasn't until the late 1970s that governments began to act on scientific findings. In 1987 the United States, along with 162 other countries, signed the Montreal Protocol. This agreement, amended various times in the 1990s, committed participating nations to phasing out the production and use of many chlorofluorocarbons. By 2001 the Montreal Protocol appeared to be working because the size of the hole in the ozone layer had stabilized, and leading researchers predicted that the hole would disappear within about fifty years.

During the 1970s the EPA also took part in the successful push to remove lead from paint and gasoline. In 1978 the federal government forbade the use of lead paint in housing, but the toxic metal remains a potential hazard in many dwellings built before the ban went into effect. Between 1973 and 1996 the EPA also gradually restricted the level of lead allowable in gasoline and finally banned it as a fuel additive in 1996. Because of these limits the average level of lead in American children's blood has fallen from 15 micrograms of lead per 100 cubic centimeters of blood in 1976 to only 2.7 per 1,000 in 2000. Unfortunately, lead remains a public health threat, albeit on a smaller scale, because of old-fashioned lead water pipes that may contaminate household supplies. Thus, the need for environmental sanitation measures persists despite the control of more obvious sources of pollution.

BIBLIOGRAPHY

Benedick, Richard Elliot. *Ozone Diplomacy: New Directions in Safeguarding the Planet.* Cambridge, Mass.: Harvard University Press, 1998.

Landy, Marc K. *The Environmental Protection Agency: Asking the Wrong Questions from Nixon to Clinton.* New York: Oxford University Press, 1994.

Melosi, Martin V. *The Sanitary City: Urban Infrastructure in America from Colonial Times to the Present.* Baltimore: Johns Hopkins University Press, 2000.

Powell, J. H. *Bring out Your Dead: The Great Plague of Yellow Fever in Philadelphia in 1793.* Philadelphia: University of Pennsylvania Press, 1993.

Rosen, George. *A History of Public Health.* Baltimore: Johns Hopkins University Press, 1993.

Warren, Christian. *Brush with Death: A Social History of Lead Poisoning.* Baltimore: Johns Hopkins University Press, 2000.

John Duffy/A. E.

See also **Air Pollution; Epidemics and Public Health; Hazardous Waste; Hygiene; Ozone Depletion; Waste Disposal; Water Supply and Conservation.**

SANTA CLARA PUEBLO V. MARTINEZ, 436 U.S. 49 (1978), a landmark case regarding the federal government's jurisdiction over Indian tribes, arose from tribal disputes over membership. A woman member of the Santa Clara Pueblo tribe married a Navajo and had seven children. The Santa Clara Pueblo denied membership to the woman's children based on a tribal ordinance excluding the children of female, but not male, members who married outside the tribe. Excluded children could neither vote, hold secular office, remain on the reservation in event of the mother's death, nor inherit their mother's house or interest in communal lands. The mother asked the federal district court to enjoin enforcement of this gendered ordinance. The district court decided in favor of the mother, contending that the INDIAN CIVIL RIGHTS ACT granted it implied jurisdiction to do so. Congress passed the act in 1968 to apply certain provisions of the BILL OF RIGHTS IN THE U.S. CONSTITUTION to tribal governments in criminal cases. Santa Clara Pueblo appealed the federal court's decision, arguing that the 1968 law did not authorize civil actions in federal court for relief against a tribe or its officials. The SUPREME COURT agreed, guaranteeing strong tribal autonomy except when Congress provided for federal judicial review.

BIBLIOGRAPHY

MacKinnon, Catherine A. *Feminism Unmodified: Discourses on Life and Law.* Cambridge, Mass.: Harvard University Press, 1987.

Molander, Susan Sanders. "Case Notes: Indian Civil Rights Act and Sex Discrimination." *Arizona State Law Journal* 1 (1977).

Tony Freyer/J. H.

See also **Bureau of Indian Affairs; Native Americans; Women in Public Life, Business, and Professions.**

SANTA FE, capital city of NEW MEXICO, population 62,203 (U.S. Census, 2000). Ancestors of Pueblo Indians inhabited the northern central region of New Mexico, where Santa Fe is located, as early as the eleventh century. Juan de Onate led Spanish colonists to settle the region in 1598, and in 1609 Pedro de Peralta founded Santa Fe. The city has a rich political, military, and cultural heritage as the seat of government, the site of armed struggle and political conflict, and the source of artistic production.

Pueblo Indians built the Palace of Governors, which is considered the oldest public building in the United States. The harsh treatment of the Native Americans led to the Great Pueblo Revolt of 1680, resulting in the siege of Santa Fe, and the expulsion of the colonial settlers from the region. Diego de Vargas recaptured the capital in 1692.

The region experienced an economic boom in the 1820s, with the opening of the Santa Fe Trail. The Army of the West entered the capital in 1846, and it was declared a U.S. territory. The territorial period is marked by economic growth with the advent of the Atchison, Topeka, and Santa Fe Railroad in 1880. New Mexico statehood was granted in 1912, with Santa Fe as the capital city.

Writers Harvey and Erna Ferguson were among the first locals to extol New Mexico's "exotic" natural and cultural environment. Other early writers and artists who resettled in the area included Alice Corbin, Mabel Dodge Luhan, John Sloan, Witter Brynner, and Mary Austin, who founded the Santa Fe writer's colony. The Georgia O'Keefe Museum in Santa Fe holds a collection of her paintings inspired by the region's landscape. Santa Fe's unique combination of indigenous, colonial, and territorial cultures attracts one to two million visitors each year.

BIBLIOGRAPHY

Kessell, John. *Spain in the Southwest: A Narrative History of Colonial New Mexico, Arizona, Texas, and California.* Norman: University of Oklahoma Press, 2002.

Weber, David J. *The Spanish Frontier in North America.* New Haven, Conn.: Yale University Press, 1992.

Wilson, Chris. *The Myth of Santa Fe: Creating a Modern Regional Tradition.* Albuquerque: University of New Mexico Press, 1997.

Barbara O. Reyes

See also vol. 9: **Glimpse of New Mexico.**

SANTA FE TRAIL. The Santa Fe Trail was an important commerce route between 1821 and 1880 that extended from Missouri to Santa Fe, New Mexico. The trail extended south from SANTA FE for an additional thousand miles through El Paso to the Mexican towns of Chihua-

The Santa Fe Trail

The Santa Fe Trail in the Fra Cristobal Mountains. This lithograph shows soldiers riding single file up a hill while escorting a wagon in southern New Mexico along the trail's extension, between Santa Fe and El Paso, Texas. © CORBIS

hua and Durango, following the natural roads wagon masters found along the entire distance.

Prior to the opening of the trail, the city of Santa Fe was supplied with goods brought by mule at great expense from the Mexican seaport of Veracruz. Pierre and Paul Mallet of Canada crossed the Plains to Santa Fe in 1739, followed by more Frenchmen passing from the Missouri River or from Arkansas Post to the Rio Grande. The American army lieutenant Zebulon M. Pike arrived in 1807.

American attempts at Santa Fe trade met with summary action by Spanish authorities, who arrested twelve men from Saint Louis in 1812 and imprisoned them for nine years, and arrested Auguste Pierre Chouteau's Saint Louis fur brigade in 1815 for trapping on the Upper Arkansas. After Mexico overthrew Spanish rule, news spread that traders were welcome in Santa Fe. First to arrive was William Becknell of Missouri, who reached Santa Fe on 16 November 1821, and sold his Indian trade goods at from ten to twenty times higher than Saint Louis prices. Becknell started from the steamboat landing of Franklin, Missouri, followed the prairie divide between the tributaries of the Kansas and Arkansas rivers to the Great Bend of the Arkansas, and then followed the Arkansas almost to the mountains before turning south to NEW MEXICO. His route became known as the Santa Fe Trail. The MIS-

SOURI RIVER terminus later became Westport, now KANSAS CITY. At the western end the trail turned south to Santa Fe from the Arkansas by different routes touching the Colorado–New Mexico border and another near Kansas.

Merchants traveled in caravans, moving wagons in parallel columns so that they might be quickly formed into a circular corral, with livestock inside, in the event of an Indian attack. Josiah Gregg reported that up to 1843 Indians killed but eleven men on the trail. Losses were greatest from 1864 to 1869, the bloodiest year being 1868, when seventeen stagecoach passengers were captured and burned at Cimarron Crossing.

Santa Fe trade brought to the United States muchneeded silver, gave America the Missouri mule, and paved the way for American claims to New Mexico in the MEXICAN-AMERICAN WAR. Estimates of the heavy volume of westward-bound traffic on the trail vary. Gregg reported in *Commerce of the Prairies* that 350 persons transported $450,000 worth of goods at Saint Louis prices in 1843. Lt. Col. William Gilpin's register shows 3,000 wagons, 12,000 persons, and 50,000 animals between 1849–1859, a large part of the number bound for California. The register at Council Grove, Kansas, in 1860 showed 3,514 persons, 61 carriages and stagecoaches, 5,819 mules, and 22,738 oxen. Federal mail service by stagecoach was instituted in 1849. Completion of the last section of the

Santería. A voodoo doll and beaded necklaces sit in a pot next to this adherent, a Mrs. Lemus, as she cradles her child in Hialeah, Fla., in 1987; it was a Santería church in Hialeah that won a U.S. Supreme Court decision overturning municipal laws and allowing animal sacrifice for religious reasons. ARCHIVE PHOTOS, INC.

Atchison, Topeka, and Santa Fe Railroad in 1880 ended the importance of the wagon road.

BIBLIOGRAPHY

Boyle, Susan Calafate. *Los Capitalistas: Hispano Merchants and the Santa Fe Trade.* Albaquerque: University of New Mexico Press, 1997.

Chalafant, William Y. *Dangerous Passage: The Santa Fe Trail and the Mexican War.* Norman: University of Oklahoma Press, 1994.

Dary, David. *The Santa Fe Trail: Its History, Legends, and Lore.* New York: Knopf, 2000.

Gregg, Josiah. *Commerce of the Prairies.* Philadelphia: Lippincott, 1962.

Simmons, Marc. *The Old Trail to Santa Fe: Collected Essays.* Albequerque: University of New Mexico Press, 1996.

Bliss Isely / H. S.

See also **Southwest.**

SANTA MARIA. The *Santa Maria,* the flagship of Christopher Columbus, headed the fleet of three vessels that reached the New World on 12 October 1492. Two months later, on Christmas Eve, it ran aground off the coast of Hispaniola, in the present-day Dominican Republic. From the ship's wreckage Columbus had a fort erected at La Navidad before he left for Spain. He found the fort destroyed and its garrison murdered when he returned in November 1493. Although the colony established there faltered and Columbus soon lost the favor of his patron, Queen Isabella of Castile, the voyage of the *Santa Maria* inaugurated European IMPERIALISM in the New World.

BIBLIOGRAPHY

Pastor, Xavier. *The Ships of Christopher Columbus: Santa Maria, Niña, Pinta.* Annapolis, Md.: Naval Institute Press; London: Conway Maritime Press, 1992.

Wilford, John N. *The Mysterious History of Columbus: An Exploration of the Man, the Myth, the Legacy.* New York: Knopf, 1991.

Francis Borgia Steck / A. R.

See also **Expeditions and Explorations: Spanish.**

SANTERÍA is a religious tradition brought to the United States by immigrants from Cuba in the latter half of the twentieth century. It originated among the Yoruba peoples of present-day Nigeria. The Yoruba were enslaved in large numbers in the first decades of the nineteenth century and brought to Cuba to labor in the island's expanding sugar industry. Perhaps as many as 500,000 Yoruba men and women came to Cuba, where they were called "Lucumi." The Lucumi established a strong ethnic presence in Cuba and created important cultural institutions that survived their enslavement and flourish today.

The word "santería" means "way of the saints" in Spanish and reflects the tendency of the Lucumi to correspond their deities from Africa, called "orishas," with the saints of the Roman Catholic traditions into which they were indoctrinated. This tragic history of forced acculturation has led some contemporary practitioners to reject the name "santería" as a colonial misnomer for an independent African tradition that might preferably be called "Lucumi religion," after its ethnic heritage, or "Orisha religion," after its deities.

The orishas are personal, cosmic forces that inhabit and energize the world of nature: mineral, vegetable, animal, and human. In theory, there are innumerable orishas—1,600 is a traditional number used to show the vastness of the pantheon—but in practice there are some sixteen that are widely known and venerated. Each orisha has a distinct personality, and is approached through its own songs and dances with appropriate ritual foods, plants, and altar displays. The orisha Ogun, for example, is a hard, masculine deity, who as the cosmic blacksmith transforms the world through metals and tools. The orisha Oshun, by contrast, is a cool, feminine deity of the river, who works through the pliant, but no less powerful medium of water. Each orisha offers blessings and benefits to its devotees ranging from spiritual experience to practical assistance in finding jobs or maintaining health. The lore of the orishas contains a very large pharmacopoeia and this tradition has been of inestimable aid in providing medical and mental health care to the urban poor. In the late twentieth century, hospitals in Miami and New York established cooperative programs with orisha devotees to try to meet the needs of people often poorly served by established health institutions.

Since its introduction to the United States in the latter half of the twentieth century, the veneration of the orishas has spread well beyond the original Afro-Cuban population. In the early years of the twenty-first century, Puerto Ricans, Dominicans, and other Latin Americans, as well as significant numbers of African Americans and white Americans have embraced it. It is difficult to estimate the number of practitioners, as there are few public organizations or groups of congregations beyond the individual "houses," which typically claim twenty or thirty active participants. In the United States, the number of initiated priests and priestesses may number 50,000, while active participants are likely ten times that. As for those who might consult a priest or priestess for help, they number in the millions. Kindred orisha traditions are practiced throughout Latin America, particularly in Cuba, Brazil, Argentina, and Venezuela, making "santería" a world religion of growing influence.

BIBLIOGRAPHY

Brandon, George. *Santería from Africa to the New World: The Dead Sell Memories.* Bloomington: Indiana University Press, 1993.

Murphy, Joseph M. *Santería: An African Religion in America.* Boston: Beacon Press, 1988.

Joseph M. Murphy

See also **African American Religions and Sects.**

SARATOGA CAMPAIGN. Stung by their inability to end the American rebellion in 1776, the British government ordered an invasion of the colonies from Canada, meant to surgically separate New England from the other colonies. Unfortunately, General Sir William Howe, insistent on invading Pennsylvania from his base in New York, left the army sent from Canada, under General John Burgoyne, unsupported as it marched south. Marching out of Quebec in July 1777, Burgoyne's 9,000 men faced the enormous problems inherent in a 350-mile march: river crossings, hostile Indians, and poor support from French Canadians, as well as transporting an overloaded baggage train and heavy artillery. Although he displaced the Americans from Fort Ticonderoga, Burgoyne delayed en route to the Hudson River in order to gather supplies, allowing the rebels time to place obstacles along the route and plan an attack, which came when a detachment under Lieutenant Colonel Friederich Baum was defeated by rebels while on a foraging mission in Bennington, Vermont.

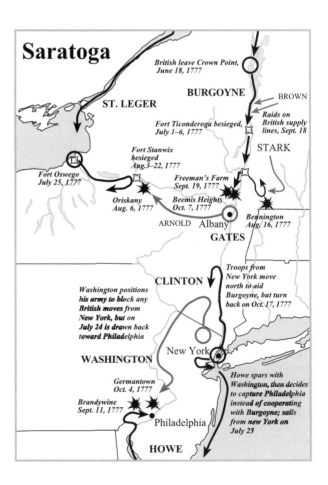

Benedict Arnold, Hero. Wounded on 7 October 1777 during his crucial assault on a Hessian-held redoubt, General Arnold rests atop a horse amid the frenzy of battle; before he became the first traitor in American history, Arnold was one of its first heroes, at Saratoga and in other campaigns.
© Bettmann/corbis

Advancing towards Albany, New York, Burgoyne learned that an American army under Horatio Gates had entrenched itself at Bemis Heights, also called Freeman's Farm, and had approximately the same number of men (5,500) as himself. The first battle of Saratoga, fought on 19 September 1777, began when Burgoyne ordered his army to attack the American fortifications. While Gates kept his troops behind their entrenchments, his more flamboyant second in command, Benedict Arnold, sent his left wing to fight in the woods in front of the entrenchments. The battle ended in a curious situation—although the British held the field, they had lost 600 men, while the Americans, unable to advance against the artillery commanded by Hessian General Friederich Riedesel, retreated to their fortifications on Bemis Heights and gathered more men and supplies.

Eighteen days later, while Gates waited for the British to weaken through lack of supplies and attrition from sniping, Burgoyne waited with increasing desperation for help from General Sir Henry Clinton in New York. Reaching the end of his patience on 7 October, Burgoyne sent out a reconnaissance force of 1,500 men to push the left wing of the American fortifications on Bemis Heights. Attacked by the Americans under the command of Arnold, who had been relieved of command after arguing with Gates, Burgoyne's men were routed. Burgoyne began a costly retreat back to Canada, but was surrounded by Gates's army on 12 October and compelled to negotiate a surrender.

These battles, later collectively known as Saratoga, were a major turning point in the Revolutionary War. The capture of a British army raised morale at a time when George Washington's army had been defeated by Howe in Pennsylvania. When news reached Europe, the American victory encouraged open French and Spanish aid to the rebels. The campaign also sparked the differences between Arnold and the American command, which were later to lead to his defection to the British. On the British side, the defeat led to the replacement of Howe with Clinton, and after the loss of so many men and resources, the British turned increasingly to the Royal Navy to press their advantage on the American coastline, particularly in the southern colonies.

BIBLIOGRAPHY

Elting, John R. *The Battles of Saratoga.* Monmouth Beach, N.J.: Philip Freneau Press, 1977.

Ketchum, Richard M. *Saratoga: Turning Point of America's Revolutionary War.* New York: Holt, 1997.

Mintz, Max M. *The Generals of Saratoga: John Burgoyne and Horatio Gates.* New Haven, Conn.: Yale University Press, 1990.

Margaret D. Sankey

See also **Revolution, American: Military History.**

SARATOGA SPRINGS is a city in east central New York State with more than one hundred natural MINERAL

SPRINGS. Discovered by whites in the late eighteenth century, the town offered few accommodations before 1802, when Gideon Putnam began construction of the Grand Union Hotel. Other hotels followed, and the springs rapidly increased in popularity. Incorporated as a village in 1826, Saratoga was known as a "resort of wealth, intelligence and fashion—a political observatory." Madam Eliza Bowen Jumel, Martin Van Buren, Stephen Douglas, De Witt Clinton, Daniel Webster, and Joseph Bonaparte were frequent visitors. Lavish display became the order of the day, replacing the medicinal properties of the springs in significance. During the 1860s profiteers discovered Saratoga Springs and started drilling six new springs, opened several new hotels, and ran the first horse races at the Travers track. After 1863 the annual races of the Saratoga Association for the Improvement of the Breed of Horses began to draw large crowds.

Throughout the last quarter of the nineteenth century, Saratoga Springs was the most fashionable spa in the United States. Commercial bottling of the waters nearly depleted the springs, but New York State acquired the property in 1909 and placed the springs in the charge of a CONSERVATION commission in 1916. Saratoga Springs continues as a popular tourist resort, mainly for its summer horse races and its historical sites.

BIBLIOGRAPHY

Amory, Cleveland. *The Last Resorts*. New York: Harper, 1952.

Spiegel, Ted. *Saratoga, The Place and Its People: Essays by Peter Andrews, Jennifer Dunning, and Whitney Tower*. New York: Abrams, 1988.

A. C. Flick / c. w.

See also **Horse Racing and Showing; Resorts and Spas; Tourism.**

SAT (formerly Scholastic Aptitude Test), a multiple-choice exam, consisting of math and verbal components. Invented by Carl C. Brigham, the SAT was first administered experimentally to high school students in 1926. In 1934, Harvard University began using the exam as a means of selecting scholarship students. Following World War II, the SAT expanded, becoming part of the admissions process at universities and colleges throughout the country. Despite criticisms that it is biased against women, students of color, and students from low-income backgrounds, the SAT continued to thrive in the twenty-first century and was administered to more than two million students each year. In June 2002, significant changes to the exam were approved, including making the math section more difficult, the addition of an essay section, and an increase in the total possible score from 1600 to 2400.

BIBLIOGRAPHY

Lemann, Nicholas. *The Big Test: The Secret History of American Meritocracy*. New York: Farrar, Straus, 1999.

Justin T. Lorts

See also **Educational Testing Service; Intelligence Tests.**

SATURDAY EVENING POST. The modern *Saturday Evening Post* dates from 1897, when publisher Cyrus H. K. Curtis bought the failing periodical for $1,000. Curtis immediately cobbled together a suspect genealogy, alleging Ben Franklin as the *Post*'s founder and pushing the masthead date back from 1821 to 1728. In 1898, Curtis appointed George Horace Lorimer as editor, a position he held through 1936. Under his leadership, the *Post* became America's most successful and most influential magazine, achieving a weekly circulation of 1,000,000 as early as 1908. In the 1920s, riding on a sea of advertising that exceeded $50 million annually, issues frequently offered over 200 pages carrying more than 20 stories, articles, and serial installments—all for a nickel.

The nickel was part of Curtis's plan: to finance a magazine through advertising rather than subscriptions. Lor-

An American Icon. Founded in 1821 and completely revamped in 1897, the *Saturday Evening Post* offered up more than 20 stories, articles, and serial installments each week, all for just one nickel. In this photo taken in 1910, a young boy in snowy Rochester, New York, sells the *Post* out of the bag slung over his shoulder. © CORBIS

imer's own financial plan was equally novel; the *Post* responded to submissions within two weeks and paid on acceptance rather than publication. That policy, along with Lorimer's recruitment of writers, paid off in a roster of talent. Nonfiction writers, especially strong in politics and business, included Albert Beveridge, Sam Blythe, Irvin S. Cobb, Emerson Hough, Will Irwin, Isaac F. Marcosson, and Will Payne. Short stories and serialized fiction were supplied by some of the most popular writers of the time, among them Thomas Beer, Earl Derr Biggers, G. K. Chesterton, Agatha Christie, William Faulkner, F. Scott Fitzgerald, Harold Frederic, Joseph Hergesheimer, Robert Herrick, Sinclair Lewis, J. P. Marquand, Mary Roberts Rinehart, Kenneth L. Roberts, and Arthur Train. Another attraction was the *Post*'s cover, painted over the years by the country's most successful and popular illustrators, most notably J. C. Leyendecker and Norman Rockwell.

The *Post*'s audience was broad, with the magazine reaching middle-class and middle-brow Americans from coast to coast. The magazine gave its audience entertainment and information, along with strong doses of politics. Up to World War I (1914–1918), those politics were essentially Progressive. After the war, the magazine turned sharply right, mixing a conservative social message with fiercely reactionary political views. The 1929 stock market crash and the Great Depression confirmed Lorimer's views of the nation's missteps, and President Franklin D. Roosevelt's election only blackened his outlook. By 1936 the *Post* virtually ran an opposition campaign to Roosevelt's reelection.

After Lorimer's retirement early in 1937 and under a series of editors, the *Post* gradually lost its dominant position among the media. Although fiction and illustration, especially cover art, remained attractive throughout the 1950s, by the 1960s the magazine found itself in deep financial trouble and, early in 1969, America's most popular weekly magazine ended publication.

BIBLIOGRAPHY

Cohn, Jan. *Creating America: George Horace Lorimer and "The Saturday Evening Post."* Pittsburgh, Pa.: University of Pittsburgh Press, 1989.

———. *Covers of "The Saturday Evening Post": Seventy Years of Outstanding Illustration from America's Favorite Magazine.* New York: Viking, 1995.

Tebbel, John. *George Horace Lorimer and "The Saturday Evening Post."* Garden City, N.Y.: Doubleday, 1948.

Jan Cohn

See also **Magazines.**

SATURDAY NIGHT LIVE (*SNL*) is a ninety-minute comedy and music television series that has been broadcast live from New York City on NBC since 11 October 1975. It employs an ensemble of versatile comic actors in

"Live from New York, it's Saturday Night!" With those seven words, a talented cast of young comics would launch into an hour and a half of often risqué, always timely, and sometimes controversial sketch comedy. In this photo, original cast members Jane Curtin (*left*), Dan Aykroyd (*center*), and Laraine Newman perform their popular "Coneheads" skit. © Archive Photos, Inc.

topical sketches and parodies punctuated by musical performances by guest artists. Because it airs late at night (11:30 P.M. EST), it has been free to present content and language that may not have been acceptable in prime time. The original group of actors consisted of Chevy Chase, John Belushi, Dan Aykroyd, Gilda Radner, Garrett Morris, Jane Curtin, and Laraine Newman. All of that cast were gone after 1980, and since then over seventy people have spent some time in the *SNL* troupe. Many of those went on to significant careers in film and television, including Bill Murray, Eddie Murphy, Julia Louis-Dreyfus, Chris Rock, and Adam Sandler. Several recurring sketches introduced on *SNL* were developed into motion pictures, most notably *Wayne's World* (1992). The eclectic list of weekly guest hosts has included comics, actors, and political leaders.

Saturday Night Live achieved a large and loyal following, especially among young viewers. It became a national forum for political satire, with presidential politics a particular specialty. Chevy Chase's impersonations of a stumbling Gerald Ford in the earliest seasons provided some of the most memorable moments from the show. Lorne Michaels was the show's producer, guiding force, and occasional on-screen presence. He left temporarily in 1980, but returned in 1985.

BIBLIOGRAPHY

Hill, Doug, and Jeff Weingrad. *Saturday Night: A Backstage History of Saturday Night Live.* New York: William Morrow, 1986.

Robert Thompson

See also **Television: Programming and Influence.**

SAUK. The Sauks, or Sacs, originally spoke a Central Algonquian dialect and referred to themselves as *asa·ki·waki*, meaning "People of the Outlet." They left their central Michigan location for northern Wisconsin after Iroquois attacks in the mid-seventeenth century. The tribe first contacted the French in 1667 at Chequamegon Bay, Lake Superior. Population estimates fluctuated between several thousand after contact and several hundred during the 1800s. Closely related to the Foxes culturally and allied with them politically between 1733 and 1850, the Sauks nonetheless always maintained a distinctive tribal identity.

The Native enemies of the Sauks included the Iroquois, Illinois, Osages, and Siouxes. The Sauk maintained good relations with the French (until the Fox wars of 1712–1736) and the English but divided over supporting the United States. The most famous Sauk leaders included Keokuk, a tribal chief who curried favor with the United States, and Black Hawk, a rival war chief who led his faction during the disastrous BLACK HAWK WAR (1832).

The Sauks maintained numerous clans and distributed themselves into "moieties" (two complementary divisions of the tribal group). Traditional economic gender definitions found women engaged in agriculture and gathering, while men concentrated on hunting. After residing in Illinois, Iowa, Missouri, and Kansas, the majority of the Sauks settled in Oklahoma and lost most of their traditional culture. Today approximately 2,700 Sauks (*Thâkîwâki*) live in central Oklahoma as the Sac and Fox tribe.

BIBLIOGRAPHY

Callender, Charles. "Sauk." In *Handbook of North American Indians.* Edited by William C. Sturtevant et al. Vol. 15: *Northeast,* edited by Bruce G. Trigger. Washington, D.C.: Smithsonian Institution, 1978. This most useful and authoritative account was prepared by an anthropologist.

Hagan, William T. *The Sac and Fox Indians.* Norman: University of Oklahoma Press, 1958. Reprint, 1980.

Jackson, Donald, ed. *Black Hawk: An Autobiography.* Urbana: University of Illinois Press, 1955. Black Hawk's autobiography was first published in 1833 under the title *Life of Ma-ka-tai-me-she-kia-kiak.*

Raymond E. Hauser

See also **Fox War;** *and vol. 9:* **Life of Ma-ka-tai-me-she-kai-kiak, or Black Hawk.**

SAUK PRAIRIE. A broad, fertile region of central WISCONSIN, Sauk Prairie is found along the north banks of the lower Wisconsin River. The combination of its geology, climate, and Native American field burning created fourteen thousand acres of prairie and oak savanna at the time of European arrival to the region beginning in the 1670s.

The name originates with the Sac tribe, who moved into the region in the eighteenth century, pushed by war, disease, and other conflicts farther east. They shared Sauk Prairie with the Ho Chunk tribe (formerly known as the Winnebagos). The New England writer and explorer Jonathan Carver noted a large Sac village when he traveled down the Wisconsin River in 1766. Several hundred occupants maintained an agricultural and trading center there. Sauk Prairie, situated where the fertile midwestern prairie merges into the woodlands of the northern regions and along a critical trading route connecting the Great Lakes and the Mississippi Valley, provided a strategic and economic advantage for the Sac villagers. Although the Sacs were later pushed beyond the Mississippi River, a renegade band led by Black Hawk boldly returned to their former homeland in the Black Hawk War of 1832.

Agricultural settlers began to move into Sauk Prairie in the 1840s. Ho Chunks ceded the land to the United States by treaty in 1837 and were removed westward, though many returned in the twentieth century. By the 1900s immigrant communities of predominantly German origin created a prosperous economy of mixed farming.

World War II reshaped Sauk Prairie with the creation of the Badger Army Ammunition Plant in 1941. The federal government removed eighty farm families to construct the ten-thousand-acre facility, which produced munitions until the end of the Cold War. At the beginning of the twenty-first century several community groups, including the Ho Chunk tribe, sought to restore the remaining 7,500 acres to an environment of mixed grasslands and agriculture. At that time the population of the region was approximately six thousand people living mainly in the two cities of Sauk City and Prairie du Sac.

BIBLIOGRAPHY

Lange, Kenneth I. *A County Called Sauk: A Human History of Sauk County, Wisconsin.* Baraboo, Wis.: Sauk County Historical Society, 1976.

Wyman, Mark. *The Wisconsin Frontier.* Bloomington: Indiana University Press, 1998.

Kevin R. Marsh

SAVANNAH. In May and June 1819, the SS *Savannah* became the first steam-powered ship to cross the Atlantic Ocean. The *Savannah* was the idea of steamboat captain Moses Rogers, who convinced Savannah, Georgia, entrepreneurs to back the venture. The Speedwell Iron Works at Morristown, New Jersey, built the engine.

The *Savannah* was a 100-foot-long packet ship fitted with steam boilers, a seventeen-foot smokestack, and paddle wheels that could be collapsed and taken on deck in case of a storm. The *Savannah* also had three masts and full sail rigging in case of a boiler malfunction.

Rogers took the ship to sea on 22 May 1819. It reached England in twenty-nine days without incident.

While the *Savannah* had spent much of its time under sail, it had proved such a design could safely cross an ocean. However, not until 1838 did anyone attempt another steam crossing.

The *Savannah* spawned several namesakes: a U.S. Navy cruiser that served in World War II; an oiler used from 1970 to 1995; and, in 1959, the first nuclear-powered merchant ship.

BIBLIOGRAPHY
Braynard, Frank O. *Famous American Ships.* New York: Hastings House, 1978.

Historic Speedwell. Homepage at http://www.Speedwell.org.

Philip, Cynthia Owen. *Robert Fulton: A Biography.* New York: Watts, 1955.

R. Steven Jones

SAVANNAH is a city in GEORGIA located on Yamacraw Bluff, eighteen miles inland from the Atlantic Ocean, above the Savannah River for which it is named. Since the mid-1700s, Savannah has been an important port of call for ships from all over the world.

In January 1733, an expedition of English settlers led by James Edward Oglethorpe sailed to the mouth of the Savannah River, hiking along the river until they found a good site for a new town, and in February 1733, the first immigrants settled in Savannah. The safe port Savannah offered enabled it to quickly increase its importance. In 1776, pressured by American patriots, the English governor James Wright fled Savannah, only to return in 1778, when British troops seized the city. In August 1779, French and American troops tried to retake Savannah, and were badly beaten. But in May 1782, the Savannah royalists negotiated a peaceful surrender to General Anthony Wayne.

Between the American Revolution and the Civil War, Savannah became one of America's jewels, dazzling visitors with its architecture, arts, and international commerce. Late in the Civil War, the city's leaders surrendered to Union General William Tecumseh Sherman, who spared Savannah the terrible destruction his troops had wreaked in their notorious march to the sea.

After the Civil War, Savannah's port suffered because many shippers had found alternative ports of call during the conflict. In a dark and difficult period, the city established a system of segregating the black and white races. In 1944, fifty African American students refused to surrender their seats to white passengers, sparking a protest movement in the city. With the civil rights movement of the 1950s came an openness that sparked a revival in the arts. In 1966, Savannah created a 2.2-square-mile historic district; in 1977, it turned its waterfront into a vibrant retail area. By the beginning of the twenty-first century, nearly seven million people a year were visiting Savannah, again regarded as one of America's shining jewels.

BIBLIOGRAPHY
Harden, William. *A History of Savannah and South Georgia.* Atlanta: Cherokee, 1969.

Martin, Harold H. *Georgia: A Bicentennial History.* New York: Norton, 1977.

Savannah. Homepage at http://www.savannahgeorgia.com.

Vedder, O. F. *History of Savannah, Ga.: From Its Settlement to the Close of the Eighteenth Century.* Syracuse, N.Y.: D. Mason, 1890.

Wills, Charles A. *A Historical Album of Georgia.* Brookfield, Conn.: Mildbrook, 1996.

Kirk H. Beetz

SAVANNAH, SIEGE OF (1779). Comte Jean Baptiste Hector d'Estaing with about 4,500 soldiers, joined by Benjamin Lincoln with about 2,100 Americans, sought to wrest Savannah from the British, who had about 2,500 defenders. After a siege of three weeks, on 9 October 1779 a general assault resulted in a disastrous failure. More than 1,000 of the attacking forces were killed, including Count Casimir Pulaski and Sergeant William Jasper, of Fort Moultrie fame. Lack of coordination and understanding between the French and Americans was considered to be the reason for the defeat.

BIBLIOGRAPHY
Lawrence, Alexander A. *Storm over Savannah.* Athens: University of Georgia Press, 1951.

Nadelhaft, Jerome J. *The Disorders of War: The Revolution in South Carolina.* Orono: University of Maine at Orono Press, 1981.

E. Merton Coulter/A. R.

See also **Moultrie, Fort, Battle of; Southern Campaigns.**

SAVANNAH, SIEGE OF (1864). On 10 December, Union general William Tecumseh Sherman approached Savannah. A skillful Confederate defense at Honey Hill kept the railroad open to Charleston, South Carolina. But Fort McAllister, eighteen miles southwest of Savannah and commanding the southern water approach, was captured, and connection was established with the Union supply fleet. Greatly outnumbered, but his line of escape still open, General William J. Hardee, the Confederate commander, after a brief defense on the night of 20 December, withdrew into South Carolina. Sherman telegraphed President Abraham Lincoln: "I beg to present you, as a Christmas gift, the City of Savannah."

BIBLIOGRAPHY
Glatthaar, Joseph T. *The March to the Sea and Beyond.* New York: New York University Press, 1985.

Jones, Charles C. *The Siege of Savannah in December 1864.* Albany, N.Y.: J. Munsell, 1874.

Royster, Charles. *The Destructive War.* New York: Knopf, 1991.

Thomas Robson Hay / A. R.

See also **Sherman's March to the Sea.**

SAVINGS AND LOAN ASSOCIATIONS (S&Ls) under various names were among the self-help organizations that so impressed Alexis de Tocqueville on his visits to the United States in the 1800s. Pioneered in the Northeast in the 1830s, which was also the era of "free banking," when bank charters were available for the asking, savings and loan associations spread through the country after the Civil War. Their dual purpose was to provide a safe place for a community's savings and a source of financing for the construction of houses. In most instances, their charters restricted S&Ls to loans secured by residential property. A symmetry emerged here as the American financial system developed, for until 1927 nationally chartered commercial banks and most state-chartered commercial banks were prohibited from making loans secured by real property.

S&Ls in most states were cooperatives or "mutuals." The significant exceptions were California, Texas, and Ohio. In theory and law, if not in reality, their depositors "owned" them, except that until 1966 the word "deposit" was wrong, as was the word "interest" as the reward for the deposit. By law, what the S&L "depositor" received was "shares" in an enterprise that paid "dividends" from interest earned on the mortgages in which the savings were invested. The boards of these institutions normally consisted of a builder, a real estate broker, a real estate lawyer, a real estate appraiser, a real estate insurer, and a real estate accountant who audited the books. Conflicts of interest were accommodated at all times. Self-dealing could be even worse in states that permitted for-profit operation of S&Ls by individual and corporate owners, especially in California, where the law permitted the payment of dividends beyond what the S&L actually earned.

Most charters for mutual S&Ls limited the institution's loans to residential real estate located within fifty miles of the office. California for-profit S&Ls could and did invest in other things, including corporate equity. Prior to the New Deal, these real estate loans were not "self-amortizing" mortgages. Typically, they ran for five years with a "balloon" payment at the end to be refinanced by the householder.

Until the 1970s these institutions did not offer third-party payment services, and they reserved the right to make "shareholders" wait as long as a year to get their money back. But participants expected that they could take their money out when they wanted it, and sometimes they could not. Mortgages on residential property could not be sold to get cash in times of trouble. The danger of a run was ever present, portrayed most memorably in the 1946 film *It's a Wonderful Life.* The earnings potential of a well-run S&L was limited by the need to keep substantial reserves in cash or U.S. government paper.

More than a third of the 16,000 such institutions in the United States at the end of the 1920s were sucked into the whirlpool of the Great Depression, stimulating the most long-lived of President Herbert Hoover's efforts to combat it. The Hoover administration created eleven geographically scattered Federal Home Loan Banks to be owned by the S&Ls of the district, as the Federal Reserve Banks are owned by the banks in their districts, but supervised by the Federal Home Loan Bank Board, as the Federal Reserve district banks are supervised by the board of governors of the Federal Reserve. Funded by the sale of notes in the money markets, these Home Loan Banks would make cash advances to the S&Ls in their jurisdiction, collateralized with mortgages.

The act also authorized the board to issue federal charters for mutual S&Ls and to establish the Federal Savings and Loan Insurance Corporation (FSLIC) to insure the par value of "shares" in S&Ls to the same $2,500 maximum the Federal Deposit Insurance Corporation (FDIC) would insure bank deposits. In 1974 the law was amended to permit corporate federal S&Ls. The Home Owners' Loan Corporation was formed to buy mortgages from S&Ls to liquefy the system, and the secretary of the treasury was encouraged to use public funds to purchase preferred stock in S&Ls that otherwise would be unable to write mortgages for their neighborhoods.

In 1934 the Federal Housing Administration (FHA) was created to insure mortgages on modest one-family homes, and after World War II the federal government subsidized Veterans Administration mortgages to reduce down payments on a home to 5 percent or less of the selling price. Government-insured mortgages were more likely to be sold to an insurance company or a bank, but S&Ls financed from a quarter to a third of the housing boom that changed the face of the country in the two decades after World War II and through the 1970s held more than two-fifths by face value of all home mortgages in the United States.

Precipitous Decline, Cushioned Fall

The legislation that created the FHA authorized a privately owned national mortgage administration to issue bonds for the purchase of mortgages. Nobody formed one, and in 1938 the government itself launched the Federal National Mortgage Administration (FNMA). Thirty years later, after the comptroller general required the Bureau of the Budget to count the purchase of these mortgages as a government expense, making the government deficit look worse, President Lyndon Johnson spun off Fannie Mae as a government-sponsored enterprise owned by shareholders with a small but symbolically important line of credit from the Treasury. FNMA, especially after it was privatized, was competition for the S&Ls. In response, the bank board in 1972 formed the Federal Home

Loan Mortgage Corporation, known in the market as "Freddie Mac," which could buy mortgages from S&Ls and package them for sale to the markets.

These institutions eventually made S&Ls essentially obsolete. By the year 2000, they financed between them two-thirds of all home mortgages. Funding mortgages in the market through the agency of mortgage brokers was a lot cheaper than mobilizing deposits for the purpose, and fixed-rate mortgages were bad assets for the investment of deposits in a world of computer-driven, low-cost money markets. When interest rates fell, borrowers refinanced their mortgages, depriving the S&Ls of their higher-yielding assets. When interest rates rose, depositors demanded higher rates or dividends for their money, which could mean that an S&L had to pay more for funds than it was earning on its old mortgages.

The extent of the peril was first revealed in California in 1966, when one of the largest state-chartered S&Ls had to be rescued from insolvency. The FSLIC agreed to consider S&L shares as a kind of deposit and to provide immediate redemption of the shares in a failed institution. In return for the rescue and the FSLIC agreement, the S&Ls accepted the same sort of government controls over the interest they could pay that the Federal Reserve imposed on banks. The rates S&Ls could pay depositors were set usually a quarter of a point higher than the rates banks were permitted to pay as part of the government's policy to encourage housing.

In 1980, Congress passed the Depository Institutions Deregulation and Monetary Control Act, which looked toward the complete elimination of controls on the interest rates banks and S&Ls could pay and authorized checking accounts at S&Ls, homogenizing what had been a divided banking industry. As the Federal Reserve drove rates ever higher in the fight against inflation in the early 1980s, the S&L industry with few exceptions became insolvent.

Nobody could think of an exit strategy other than a desperate effort for the S&Ls to "grow out of their problem" by acquiring high-yielding assets like junk bonds and real estate developments. Capital rules and accounting conventions were shattered by new regulations from the Home Loan Bank Board and by Congress in the 1982 Garn–St. Germain Act, which permitted S&Ls to avoid the recognition of losses in their portfolios and to expand their asset bases even when they were insolvent. Newcomers as well as established institutions were necessarily the beneficiaries of these changes, and the S&L industry drew a remarkable collection of crooks and Wall Street sharpies. Seen from their point of view, deposit insurance was a guarantee that, however worthless the asset they created with their loans, the government would buy it for its valuation on the books to make sure depositors were paid.

In 1987, Congress authorized the sale of $10.8 billion of special notes to cover the losses of the Federal Savings and Loan Insurance Corporation. The money was ludicrously too little. Finally, in 1989, the George H. W. Bush administration and Congress created the Financial Institutions Reform, Recovery, and Enforcement Act, which eliminated the bank board and awarded control of S&Ls to the Office of Thrift Supervision in the Treasury, made FSLIC a subsidiary of FDIC, and authorized about $125 billion of borrowings to keep FSLIC afloat as it spent good money for bad assets. The district Home Loan Banks were kept in existence partly to reinforce flows of money to housing and partly because they had committed $300 million a year to the Treasury to mitigate the drain of the S&L rescue, but they were made service institutions for all banks that invested in home mortgages, not just for S&Ls.

By 1999, the S&L industry no longer existed. Because nonfinancial companies could own holding companies built on S&Ls but not holding companies that included banks, the charter retained its value for entrepreneurs, but most thrifts decided to call themselves "banks" and were banks. In the fall of 1999, Congress, contemplating a world where commerce and finance would blend together in the great definitional mix of the law, passed the Gram-Leach-Bliley Act, which empowered all financial service holding companies to include securities underwriting and insurance subsidiaries. As the twenty-first century dawned, the S&L industry became the Cheshire Cat of finance, vanishing into the forest, smiling at its own disappearance.

BIBLIOGRAPHY

Brumbaugh, R. Dan, Jr. *Thrifts Under Siege: Restoring Order to American Banking.* Cambridge, Mass.: Ballinger, 1988.

Carron, Andrew S. *The Plight of the Thrift Institutions.* Washington, D.C.: Brookings Institution, 1982.

Change in the Savings and Loan Industry: Proceedings of the Second Annual Conference, December 9–10, 1976, San Francisco, California. San Francisco: Federal Home Loan Bank of San Francisco, 1977.

Eichler, Ned. *The Thrift Debacle.* Berkeley: University of California Press, 1989.

Expanded Competitive Markets and the Thrift Industry: Proceedings of the Thirteenth Annual Conference, December 10–11, 1987, San Francisco, California. San Francisco: Federal Home Loan Bank of San Francisco, 1988.

Kane, Edward J. *The Gathering Crisis in Federal Deposit Insurance.* Cambridge, Mass.: MIT Press, 1985.

Marvell, Thomas B. *The Federal Home Loan Bank Board.* New York: Praeger, 1969.

Mayer, Martin. *The Greatest-Ever Bank Robbery.* New York: Scribner, 1990.

President's Commission on Housing. *The Report of the President's Commission on Housing.* Washington, D.C.: President's Commission on Housing, 1982.

Strunk, Norman, and Fred Case. *Where Deregulation Went Wrong: A Look at the Causes Behind Savings and Loan Failures in the 1980s.* Chicago: U.S. League of Savings Institutions, 1988.

Martin Mayer

See also **Banking: Bank Failures, Savings Banks, State Banks; Federal Reserve System; Financial Services Industry; Home Owners' Loan Corporation; Mortgage Relief Legislation.**

SAVINGS BONDS. During WORLD WAR I the United States lent money to its allies in Europe to allow them to continue fighting. In order to raise the funds for these loans, the FEDERAL GOVERNMENT in turn borrowed money from its citizens by issuing U.S. Treasury bonds, also called Liberty Bonds or LIBERTY LOANS. In the end the United States government lost money on Liberty Bonds because, although it paid back citizens at the promised rate of interest, its allies in the war either could not make payments, as was the case with tsarist Russia, or made them at a much lower rate interest than originally

War Bonds. This 1943 poster shows one of the Tuskegee Airmen, the first African Americans trained to be pilots, navigators, bombardiers, and other air-support personnel during World War II. NATIONAL ARCHIVES AND RECORDS ADMINISTRATION

promised, as did the United Kingdom, France, Italy, and Belgium. Nevertheless, the Allies could not have won the war without American money. Indeed, financial support from the United States most likely contributed more to the war effort than did American military victories.

After the discontinuation of liberty loans, the federal government made no similar offering until 1935. Between March 1935 and April 1941, it issued $3.95 billion worth of "baby bonds," as they were called, in denominations ranging from twenty-five dollars to a thousand dollars. On 30 April 1941 the federal government took the baby bonds off the market and the following day issued the first of the defense savings bonds, in the same denominations and bearing the same 2.9 percent interest. Secretary of the Treasury Henry Morgenthau, Jr., sold the first bond to President Franklin D. Roosevelt. In December, when the United States entered WORLD WAR II, defense savings bonds took on a new name: war savings bonds. After the war they were once again known as defense bonds. After the Korean War the federal government simply termed them savings bonds.

Interest rates on savings bonds rose periodically to reflect rising rates in the general market, but they were always lower than prevailing interest rates. Thus, savings bonds have tended to appeal to cautious investors who value security over high return rates. Between 1952 and 1956 the general public could also buy bonds in denominations as high as ten thousand dollars. Beginning in 1954, trustees of employee savings plans were able to buy hundred-thousand-dollar bonds.

In April 1941 savings stamps, introduced during World War I, reemerged in a different form. They were available in denominations ranging from 10 cents to five dollars. They bore no interest, but purchasers could exchange them for bonds in units of $18.75, the price of a bond redeemable at maturity for $25. The purpose of the stamp program, which ended on 30 June 1970, was to foster patriotism and thrift in schoolchildren.

In December 1941 the federal government established the payroll savings plan, whereby employees voluntarily arrange for regular deductions from their salaries for the purchase of savings bonds. The plan became the major source for sales of bonds in denominations ranging from twenty-five dollars to one thousand dollars both during and after World War II. By the end of 1975, Americans had bought almost $68 billion worth of bonds. Savings bonds lost popularity during the 1990s, when a strong stock market appeared to offer a better return on investors' money, but they began to regain some of their allure in the early twenty-first century once the stock market slowed and the United States entered a military conflict with Afghanistan.

BIBLIOGRAPHY

Eichengreen, Barry and Peter H. Lindert, eds. *The International Debt Crisis in Historical Perspective.* Cambridge, MA: MIT Press, 1989.

Papayoanou, Paul A. *Power Ties: Economic Interdependence, Balancing, and War.* Ann Arbor: University of Michigan Press, 1999.

Rundell, Walter, Jr. *Military Money: A Fiscal History of the U.S. Army Overseas in World War II.* College Station: Texas A&M University Press, 1980.

Samuel, Lawrence R. *Pledging Allegiance: American Identity and the Bond Drive of World War II.* Washington, D.C.: Smithsonian Institution Press, 1997.

Sessions, Gene A. *Prophesying upon the Bones: J. Reuben Clark and the Foreign Debt Crisis, 1933–39.* Urbana: University of Illinois Press, 1992.

Norma Frankel / A. E.

See also **Banking: Overview; Treasury, Department of the; World War I War Debts.**

SAWMILLS. In 1634 a sawmill was in operation on the Piscataqua River between Maine and New Hampshire. By 1706 there were seventy operating in the colonies. A primitive type had a single sash saw pulled downward by a waterwheel and upward by an elastic pole, but more usually waterpower moved the saw both up and down. A few colonial mills had gangs, or parallel saws, set in one frame so as to cut several boards simultaneously. Muley saws, with a lighter guiding mechanism, were also used. Sawmills multiplied, but their technology did not greatly improve in colonial times. They handled principally soft timber of moderate dimensions, and operators were satisfied if a sawmill cut one thousand board feet a day.

Shortly before 1810 Oliver Evans's wood-burning, high-pressure steam engines began to appear in sawmills. These engines made it possible to manufacture lumber where waterpower was not available, as in the forested flatlands of the southern United States. Indeed, the portable engine owes its development in the United States partly to its usefulness for sawing timber. Circular saws, introduced about the middle of the nineteenth century, increased mill capacity because of their higher speed, but they were wasteful because they turned too much of the log into sawdust. Band saws, though invented earlier, did not become widespread in the United States until after the Civil War. They are now highly popular because they are faster, create less sawdust and more usable wood with their narrower kerf, or cut, and can handle logs of the largest size.

The giant sawmills developed for the most part in the great forest regions west of the Appalachia: in the white-pine belt of the Great Lakes Basin, in the yellow-pine area of the southern United States, and in the fir and redwood forests of the Pacific Northwest. By the end of the twentieth century, the South had nearly caught up with the West as a producer of lumber, largely because of falling production in the West. New technologies, such as optical scanners to ensure a clean cutting edge, had increased the production capacity of American sawmills, which produced an average of 7.6 million board feet per factory.

BIBLIOGRAPHY

Andrews, Ralph. *This Was Sawmilling.* New York: Bonanza Books, 1957.

Cox, Thomas R. *Mills and Markets: A History of the Pacific Coast Lumber Industry to 1900.* Seattle: University of Washington Press, 1974.

Smith, Kenneth L. *Sawmill: The Story of Cutting the Last Great Virgin Forest East of the Rockies.* Fayetteville: University of Arkansas Press, 1986.

Victor S. Clark / A. E.

See also **Lumber Industry.**

SAYBROOK PLATFORM, a revision of the ecclesiastical polity of the colony of Connecticut, drawn up by a synod meeting at the call of the legislature in Saybrook, 9 September 1708. Those in conservative circles, fearing that the Cambridge Platform (1648) did not furnish adequate authority for keeping all churches in line, reorganized the church into county associations ruled by a council of ministers and lay delegates empowered to discipline erring congregations and to supervise the choice of new pastors; county associations then sent delegates to a colony-wide regulatory assembly. Governmental support of the platform in Connecticut effectively transformed the eighteenth-century polity into a centrally administered unit, making the church practically a form of Presbyterianism.

BIBLIOGRAPHY

Walker, Williston, ed. *The Creeds and Platforms of Congregationalism.* Philadelphia: Pilgrim Press, 1960.

Perry Miller / A. R.

See also **Cambridge Platform; Congregationalism; New England Way.**

SCAB, a term of opprobrium for one who takes the job of a union worker during a strike. The word was used in 1806 at a trial in Philadelphia, where a journeyman shoemaker testified that when he came to America from England in 1794, the local shoemakers' union notified him that he must either join them or be considered a "scab" and be forbidden to work with union men (see PHILADELPHIA CORDWAINERS' CASE). The word "scab" did not come into public notice until about 1885–1886, when unions were coalescing into great national organizations. Its meaning had to be explained to a congressional committee in the latter year.

Scalping Victim. An illustration of the well-embroidered myth of Jane McCrea, whose scalping in mid-1777—under disputed circumstances—by Indian allies of Britain's General John Burgoyne quickly became an American propaganda weapon shortly before the pivotal Battle of Saratoga. (Ironically, McCrea was in love not with the revolutionary cause but with one of Burgoyne's officers.) ARCHIVE PHOTOS, INC.

BIBLIOGRAPHY

Kimeldorf, Howard. *Battling for American Labor.* Berkeley: University of California Press, 1999.

Alvin F. Harlow / C. W.

See also **Labor; Strikes.**

SCALAWAG, originally used to describe runty or diseased cattle, was the term of opprobrium applied to white southerners who joined with former slaves and carpetbaggers in support of Republican policies during the Reconstruction period that followed the CIVIL WAR. In the states of the upper South, white Republicans were generally hill-country farmers with Unionist sympathies. Those in the Deep South came from elements of the planter-business aristocracy with Whig antecedents. Neither group was committed to black rights or suffrage, but their role in Reconstruction was important. Constituting approximately 20 percent of the white electorate, they often provided the crucial margin of victory for the Republicans. In the constitutional conventions of 1867–1868 and in the subsequent state governments, they exerted leadership disproportionate to their popular strength.

BIBLIOGRAPHY

Foner, Eric. *Reconstruction: America's Unfinished Revolution 1863–1877.* New York: Harper and Row, 1988.

William G. Shade / C. P.

See also **Ku Klux Klan; Reconstruction; Sectionalism.**

SCALPING. Scalping is the removal of the skin and hair from atop the victim's skull, usually accomplished with a knife. While long believed to be a traditional Native American practice, modern apologists have argued that Europeans introduced the custom of taking scalps from slain or captive enemies in America. Nevertheless, references to Indians' scalping made by the earliest of European explorers, the elaborate methods and rituals often surrounding Indian scalping, and archaeological evidence in the form of telltale cut marks on pre-Columbian skulls indicate that scalping was a native practice prior to 1492. Various scalping traditions can be traced from Alaska to Mexico, and sporadically even into South America.

Following their entry into the New World, Europeans both adopted and encouraged scalping. During King Philip's War (1675–1676) in New England, the colonies of Connecticut and Massachusetts offered bounties for the scalps of their Wampanoag enemies. Colonial authorities would pay ten shillings to Indians and thirty shillings to non-Indians for every enemy scalp. The French in Canada appear to have been the first to encourage the scalping of whites. In 1688 they offered ten beaver pelts for every scalp—Indian or Puritan—brought to them. While Indians had practiced scalping for centuries, these bounties probably did encourage the spread of scalping to tribes who had not previously done so, or who had scalped only infrequently in the past.

Scalping and scalp bounties continued through the colonial wars of the eighteenth century, with a noticeable increase in colonists' willingness to scalp Indian enemies. During the American Revolution, British Colonel Henry Hamilton at Detroit drew the derisive nickname "hair buyer" because he encouraged his Indian allies to attack the rebels and to exchange enemy scalps for bounties. But he was not alone in the practice. South Carolina's legislature offered seventy-five pounds for male scalps, and Pennsylvania's offered one thousand dollars for every Indian scalp. Kentuckians invading Shawnee villages in southern Ohio dug up graves to take scalps for trophies. Scalp bounties and scalp-taking also took place during the War of 1812 and in the American invasion of the West. Reports of scalping cease with the close of the Plains Wars at the end of the nineteenth century.

For the Indians of the North American Plains and their neighbors to the east, those of the Great Lakes, the Eastern Woodlands, and the Gulf Coast, war was a major social tradition. Combatants in all these areas took scalps in the course of warfare, although how a scalp was taken and handled varied according to local customs. Plains Indians generally took scalps from the center of the victim's head, pulling hair and a silver dollar-sized piece of skin away after a circular incision. There are numerous instances of survival after such treatment, a reflection of the point that Plains Indian warfare was less directed at killing the enemy and more toward touching him, that is, counting "coup." Engaging an enemy hand-to-hand and then touching him while he was down but still alive confirmed a warrior's courage. Only the Teton Dakota regarded killing and scalping as the coup of highest worth. The Chiricahua Apache saw the taking of an enemy's scalp as disgusting, and declined the practice.

BIBLIOGRAPHY

Axtell, James, and William C. Sturtevant. "The Unkindest Cut, or Who Invented Scalping?" *William and Mary Quarterly* 37 (1980): 451–472.

Grinnell, George Bird. "Coup and Scalp Among the Plains Indians." *American Anthropologist* 12 (1910): 296–310.

Stockel, H. Henrietta. "Scalping." *Military History of the West* 27 (1997): 83–86.

Robert M. Owens

See also **Wars with Indian Nations: Colonial Era to 1783, Early Nineteenth Century (1783–1840), Later Nineteenth Century (1840–1900).**

SCANDALS. U.S. history is filled with stories of political, financial, and sexual misconduct. The general public has always been fascinated with the lives of those in power, including politicians, entertainers, and business leaders, particularly when these people fall from grace. Before WATERGATE (1972–1974), the mainstream media did not rush to expose the shortcomings of influential people. Beginning in the 1970s and intensifying with the advent of the Information Age, however, the national media, under the guise of exposing dishonesty or hypocrisy, focused on sensational stories, ultimately making misconduct and public scandal a part of everyday life.

The Vietnam War and Watergate changed journalism forever. The combination of an unpopular war and criminal behavior in the president's office expanded the scope of what broadcasters chose to expose about their leaders. The Internet also fueled the sensationalist aspects of society, since people now have almost instantaneous access to news and opinion. The public no longer expects movie stars, politicians, athletes, chief executive officers, or even the president of the United States to remain free of scandal. The idea that everyone has skeletons in their closet waiting to be exposed is pretty much universal.

Political scandal remains a constant reminder of human frailty. After Watergate forced President Richard M. Nixon to resign from office in 1974, investigations into political misconduct expanded. The Iran-Contra scandal of the mid-1980s not only destroyed the careers of several high-ranking officials in the Ronald Reagan administration, it caused a national crisis of confidence in the democratic system.

A number of scandals during the presidency of Bill Clinton (1993–2001), from the Whitewater real estate scheme to the president's affair with White House intern Monica Lewinsky, revealed the way public opinion about misconduct had changed. Initially, scandal focused primarily on criminal or financial wrongdoing. During the Clinton years, however, presidential scandal turned more intimate as the press reported on the president's numerous sexual liaisons, including open discussions of oral sex and semen-stained dresses. Many pop culture experts agreed that salacious television programs, such as *The Jerry Springer Show*, which featured crude behavior, incest, fistfights, and the glorification of the lowest common denominator, fueled the public craving for this kind of detail.

As a result of ever-intensifying media coverage and instantaneous access to information, the United States now thrives on a culture of scandal. Many individuals ride to great heights of fame based on disgrace, and infamy now seems part of an overall plan to increase the "buzz" around a given entertainer, politician, or public figure as part of a campaign to make the person even more well known.

The fruits of the scandal culture are an increase in public distrust and cynicism and fewer figures that people can look to for strong leadership in times of crisis. In an increasingly competitive media landscape and the twenty-four-hour information age, however, a culture of scandal seems to be here to stay.

BIBLIOGRAPHY

Garment, Suzanne. *Scandal: The Culture of Mistrust in American Politics.* New York: Anchor Books, 1992.

Kohn, George C. *The New Encyclopedia of American Scandal.* New York: Facts On File, 2001.

Ross, Shelley. *Fall From Grace: Sex, Scandal, and Corruption in American Politics from 1702 to the Present.* New York: Ballantine Books, 1988.

Bob Batchelor

See also **Clinton Scandals;** *Clinton v. Jones;* **Iran-Contra Affair; Teapot Dome Oil Scandal.**

SCANDINAVIAN AMERICANS. In 1970, the total number of first- and second-generation Scandinavian Americans included 806,138 Swedes, 614,649 Norwegians, 325,561 Danes, and 203,826 Finns. Scandinavian immigration to America ran at above 10,000 each year between 1866 and 1930, with a high of 105,326 in 1882. Before 1860, this immigration was driven largely by a desire for religious freedom, but from 1865 to 1910 the motivation was primarily economic. Population growth, land enclosure, Russian suppression of Finnish identity, and political repression in Denmark all contributed to the migration. Scandinavian immigrants were generally welcome in nineteenth-century America and most settled in the Midwest or Pacific Northwest.

Swedes came to America with the lifting of restrictions on emigration in the 1850s and headed for the Midwest, with Illinois as a favored destination. Many Swedes who joined the Union army settled in the Midwest during the 1870s. By 1900, 850,000 Swedes had migrated to America; they cleared ten million acres of farmland, more than any other ethnic group. Perhaps because of their growing urban population, Swedish Americans quickly learned English and entered higher education in large numbers, although they sought to preserve Swedish culture through fraternities such as the Vasa Order of America.

Following poor harvests and a famine in Norway during the 1830s, many Norwegians settled in Illinois and Wisconsin. By 1930, more than one million Norwegian immigrants had reached the United States, the largest proportion of any Scandinavian nation's population. In the late nineteenth century, many moved into the Pacific Northwest. The migration marked a significant change in occupation for most Norwegians, as wheat farming replaced fishing, although the ancestral skill of shipbuilding was practiced in settlements in New York. Norwegians were generally hostile to Americanization and the use of English, and worked to preserve the use of their own language with a network of schools and colleges and an ethnic press.

Danish migration was much less marked before the 1870s than that of either the Swedes or the Norwegians. The most distinctive early migrants were the roughly three thousand converts to Mormonism who migrated to Utah between 1850 and 1880, where they assimilated into that society and helped to establish religious cooperatives. The same impulse was manifested by those non-Mormon Danes who helped establish cooperative creameries in the Midwest in the 1880s. In contrast to other Scandinavians, assimilation came comparatively fast for the roughly 360,000 Danes who migrated to the United States.

Finnish migration to America came mostly between 1870 and 1914, and constituted only about 300,000 persons. Economic motivations drove the Finns, for American wages were much better than those in Finland and the ease of obtaining land was extremely appealing. Most Finnish communities worked to keep their culture alive through church life and religious and socialist newspapers. While Finns were much more heterogeneous in their interests than other Scandinavian groups, they proved much less easily assimilable and were regarded with suspicion by Anglo-Americans.

By the twentieth century, Scandinavians had largely embraced Americanization and upward mobility. New

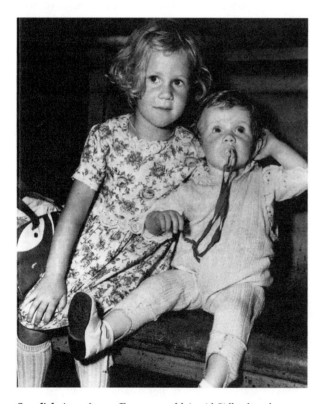

Swedish Americans. Four-year-old Astrid Sjdbeck and one-year-old Ingrid, in New York in 1949, are two of the thousands of Swedish immigrants to America each year.
© CORBIS

Norwegian Americans. In New York, officers of the Saga Lodge of the Sons of Norway draw up a protest against the German invasion of their country in 1940. © CORBIS

Scandinavian urban communities appeared in Chicago, New York City, Seattle, and Duluth. Many Scandinavian Americans worked in building, woodworking, and engineering, but over time they entered industry, as evidenced by William Knudsen, who rose to the presidency of General Motors. Most Scandinavians have leaned Republican in politics and many have been politically active. Political luminaries include Charles A. Lindbergh Sr., Andrew Volstead, Earl Warren, and Hubert Humphrey.

BIBLIOGRAPHY

Franck, Irene M. *The Scandinavian-American Heritage*. New York: Facts on File, 1988.

Hale, Frederick, ed. *Danes in North America*. Seattle: University of Washington Press, 1984.

Hoglund, A. William. *Finnish Immigrants in America, 1880–1920*. New York: Arno Press, 1979.

Lovoll, Odd S. *The Promise of America: A History of the Norwegian-American People*. Minneapolis: University of Minnesota Press, 1984.

Runblom, Harald, and Hans Norman, eds. *From Sweden to America: A History of the Migration*. Minneapolis: University of Minnesota Press, 1976.

Jeremy Bonner

See also **Immigration; Norwegian Churches.**

SCARLET LETTER, THE. Written by Nathaniel Hawthorne and published in 1850, the year in which the Clay Compromise postponed the American Civil War, *The Scarlet Letter* is a romance set in the years from 1642 to 1649, when Puritans were fighting the English civil war over the ultimate meaning of England, and Puritans in the Boston of Hawthorne's story were attempting to label Hester Prynne. A woman taken in adultery, she must wear the letter A on her chest for all to see, yet she surrounds it with beautiful stitching, so that it advertises not only her shame, but also her skill as a seamstress. She refuses to name her lover, the Reverend Mr. Arthur Dimmesdale; keeps her word not to reveal the identity of her husband, now calling himself Roger Chillingworth; and raises her daughter, Pearl, on her own, living at the edge of town, near the wild forest and the open sea.

As its title suggests, the book is about labeling, about the Puritan and later the American desire to eliminate ambiguity, to get the meanings right. The tale shows that even so simple a label as the first letter of the alphabet is full of burgeoning meanings dependent upon changing contexts. After Hester's competence and usefulness to the community become evident, some think the letter stands for "able." When an A appears in the sky at Governor John Winthrop's death, they think it stands for "angel." Since historical Puritans convicted of adultery were made to wear the letters AD on their sleeves, critics have noted that these are Dimmesdale's initials and concluded that the A also represents Arthur. Anne Hutchinson of the Antinomian Controversy is explicitly mentioned in the text, so the letter also represents Anne and Antinomian. Readers may well conclude that the A can mean almost anything, even America, where we still struggle to reinscribe the labels that others put on us.

Destroyed by his lie and guilt, Dimmesdale dies in Hester's arms, and some see a scarlet A on his chest. Destroyed by his single-minded quest for vengeance, Chillingworth bequeaths his vast estates to Pearl, who leaves America to live abroad, depriving America of all she represents. The book ends with an allusion to Andrew Marvell's poem "The Unfortunate Lover," in which the lover lives on in story. So does Hester Prynne, perhaps the first fully realized female character in American fiction, whose meanings continue to attract new readers.

BIBLIOGRAPHY

Colacurcio, Michael J., ed. *New Essays on "The Scarlet Letter."* New York: Cambridge University Press, 1985.

Crain, Patricia. *The Story of A: The Alphabetization of America from "The New England Primer" to "The Scarlet Letter."* Stanford, Calif.: Stanford University Press, 2000.

Reynolds, Larry J., ed. *A Historical Guide to Nathaniel Hawthorne*. Oxford: Oxford University Press, 2001.

Robert Daly

See also **Literature.**

SCHECHTER POULTRY CORPORATION V. UNITED STATES, 295 U.S. 495 (1935), unanimously held the National Industrial Recovery Act (NIRA) unconstitutional. With the NIRA, one of the two pillars of the early New Deal, Congress authorized codes of fair competition, cartel-like agreements among industrywide trade groups that set prices, regulated wages, controlled production, and apportioned markets under presidential authority.

Chief Justice Charles Evans Hughes, writing for the Court, rejected arguments based on *Home Building and Loan Association v. Blaisdell* (1934) that the Great Depression authorized emergency measures: "Extraordinary conditions do not create or enlarge constitutional power." Hughes held that the regulations involved in this case, the poultry code, involved local matters, not interstate commerce, relying on the direct and indirect impact distinction that supposedly apportioned the authority in the commerce clause and the Tenth Amendment. Finally, he wrote that Congress had excessively delegated its authority to the president and through him to private groups. "This is delegation running riot," wrote Justice Benjamin N. Cardozo, concurring.

Although the NIRA was collapsing under its own flaws, President Franklin D. Roosevelt denounced the result as throwing industrial America back into "the horse and buggy age." Within two years, the Court abandoned the direct and indirect criterion for measuring the regulatory authority of Congress. Similarly, the delegation issue seemed aberrational until it was revived in arguments in *Browner v. American Trucking Association* (2001).

BIBLIOGRAPHY

Cushman, Barry. *Rethinking the New Deal Court: The Structure of a Constitutional Revolution.* New York: Oxford University Press, 1998.

William M. Wiecek

See also **Great Depression; Interstate Commerce Laws; New Deal.**

SCHENCK V. UNITED STATES, 249 U.S. 47 (1919). A landmark in the development of free speech law, this case is the product of the prosecution of socialists Charles Schenck and Elizabeth Barr during World War I for conspiracy and violation of provisions of the ESPIONAGE ACT OF 1917, which made it a crime to mail certain kinds of material. The Socialist Party had sent men that passed their draft physicals an impassioned leaflet, which, after declaring that conscription was despotic and violated the Thirteenth Amendment, urged them to assert their rights. Convicted by a federal district court in Philadelphia, Schenck and Barr argued on appeal that the circular was protected by the FIRST AMENDMENT. Speaking through Justice Oliver Wendell Holmes, Jr., a unanimous Supreme Court rejected their contention. According to Holmes, "The question in every case is whether the words used are used in such circumstances and are of such a nature as to create a clear and present danger that they will bring about the substantive evils that Congress has a right to prevent." This "clear and present danger test," as refined

by Holmes and Justice Louis Brandeis in subsequent cases, became by the late 1930s the rule used to determine what violated the First Amendment. By then it was regarded as protective of free speech, but in *Schenck* the test was satisfied simply because America was at war.

BIBLIOGRAPHY

Polenberg, Richard. *Fighting Faiths: The Abrams Case, the Supreme Court, and Free Speech.* New York: Viking, 1987.

Rabban, David M. *Free Speech in its Forgotten Years.* New York: Cambridge University Press, 1997.

Michal R. Belknap

See also **Antiwar Movements; Socialist Party of America.**

SCHOLASTIC APTITUDE TEST. *See* SAT.

SCHOOL CHOICE MOVEMENT. *See* **Education, Parental Choice in.**

SCHOOL, DISTRICT. A district school is a small country school organized to serve the needs of a particular neighborhood rather than a whole township. It was the original form of public school in colonial NEW ENGLAND and New York. As the population increased, roads and transportation improved, and wild animals became less of a danger, the population scattered over the area of the towns. Most New England towns contained several villages as well as a widely distributed farm population. A town tax in whole or in part supported the school. Those who voted for and paid the tax required that the school be accessible to their children. Initially, the moving school, in which the teacher went to the pupils, emerged. The divided school developed next, in which the school went for a portion of the year to a village. When these short school terms became permanent, the school district came into existence.

Problems in the early district schools were numerous. Short terms, poorly equipped and poorly paid teachers, sometimes unruly schoolchildren, bad hygienic conditions, a multiplicity of textbooks, too many or too few pupils, an impossibly long program of recitations for the teacher, and lack of discipline were the leading drawbacks of the district system. Nontheless, the district school was probably the only basis on which democracy could build up a public school system.

While some critics have called the district school system of the early nineteenth century the low point in American EDUCATION, it at least made possible the development of a school system controlled and supported by the public that patronized it. It was against the evils of the system that Horace Mann and Henry Barnard labored in their educational reforms. Westward settlers, however, still carried the district school system from New England into nearly all the new states west of the Alleghenies. Thomas Jefferson advocated it, along with the town political organization, as the basis of a free society. In most western states, after the middle of the nineteenth century, the superimposition of either the township system or the county system or both modified the district system. In the mid-1800s, the union or county school appeared in New York, Massachusetts, and Connecticut. By the close of the nineteenth century, good roads made possible the consolidated school, which gradually replaced the one-room, ungraded district school throughout most of the country.

BIBLIOGRAPHY

Kaestle, Carl F., and Maris A. Vinovskis. *Education and Social Change in Nineteenth-Century Massachusetts.* Cambridge: Cambridge University Press, 1980.

McClellan, B. Edward, and William J. Reese, eds. *The Social History of American Education.* Urbana: University of Illinois Press, 1988.

Nasaw, David. *Schooled to Order: A Social History of Public Schooling in the United States.* New York: Oxford University Press, 1979.

Spring, Joel H. *The American School, 1642–2000.* 5th ed. Boston: McGraw-Hill, 2001.

Paul Monroe / A. E.

See also **Little Red Schoolhouse; New England; New York State; Textbooks, Early.**

SCHOOL LANDS.

When Congress created new states out of the public domain, it retained the authority to manage and dispose of the public land within their boundaries. One way in which the government exercised its authority was through land grants to the states for the purpose of funding elementary schools. Beginning with the Ordinance of 1785, Congress granted one out of thirty-six sections in each township to new states. In 1848, Congress increased the grant to two sections in each township, and, in 1896, it increased the grant to four sections. Eventually, Congress handed over more than one hundred million acres to the states under this system.

Public pressure induced state legislatures to dispose of this land, often by leasing parcels at below-market rates. Some states, like Ohio, held the lands and proceeds from them as trustees for the townships, while others, like Indiana, turned them over to the townships. Local management generally led to favoritism, careless administration, and reckless use of the funds, whereas state management often played into the hands of large speculator groups. Despite these problems the lands did fund elementary schools in communities where the tax base could not support EDUCATION or where residents opposed school taxes.

Management of school lands in the newer states of the Far West was more successful than it was in the old Northwest, partly because of heightened federal regula-

tions and partly because the states have been more prudent in their administration of land grants. Many western states have accumulated large funds from their school lands, the income from which makes up a substantial part of the state contribution to the public schools.

BIBLIOGRAPHY

Gates, Paul. *The Jeffersonian Dream: Studies in the History of American Land Policy and Development.* Edited by Allan G. and Margaret Beattie Bogue. Albuquerque: University of New Mexico Press, 1996.

Kaestle, Carl F. *Pillars of the Republic: Common Schools and American Society, 1780–1860.* New York: Hill and Wang, 1983.

Parkerson, Donald H., and Jo Ann Parkerson. *The Emergence of the Common School in the U.S. Countryside.* Lewiston, N.Y.: E. Mellen Press, 1998.

Paul W. Gates / s. b.

See also **Land Grants: Land Grants for Education; Land Policy; Northwest Territory; Ordinances of 1784, 1785, and 1787.**

SCHOOL PRAYER.

Although the First Amendment prohibited the establishment of religion, state-mandated religious practices such as prayer and Bible reading became established in public schools across the United States. Not until the 1960s did the issue of government support of religion become the impetus for challenges brought before the Supreme Court as violations of the First Amendment, although such opposition dates back to the late nineteenth century. An early opponent was Rabbi Isaac Wise, who opposed religious teaching and Bible reading in public schools on the grounds that it violated the separation of church and state.

The issue was first brought before the Supreme Court in *Engel v. Vitale*, 370 U.S. 421 (1962), in which the Court decided that government may not sponsor prayer in public schools because it is a violation of the First Amendment clause stating that "Congress shall make no law respecting an establishment of religion, or prohibiting the free exercise thereof." Further, in *School District of Abington Township v. Schempp*, 374 U.S. 203 (1963), the Court ruled that the government may not sponsor Bible reading and recitation of the Lord's Prayer in public school. Throughout the 1960s the debate continued. Then, in *Lemon v. Kurtzman*, 403 U.S. 602 (1971), the Court established the so-called "Lemon test," which set forth three conditions that had to be met for a challenged governmental action to be constitutional. First, the government, whether federal or state, may not sponsor or aid in the establishment of a state religion; second, the action must be secular in purpose and in its impact; and lastly, the action could not excessively entangle government with religion. This, in effect, made it difficult to introduce prayer into schools.

In the early 1980s a concerted effort was made to reintroduce voluntary prayer into public schools. Under the leadership of Jerry Falwell, Howard Phillips, Ed McAteer, and Paul Weyrich, and with the support of the Reagan administration, conservative religious groups such as the Moral Majority sought to overturn the legal limits set forth in *Engel* and *Abington Township*. Attempts were made to reintroduce prayer in school through legislation and by amending the Constitution. Legislation was proposed that would have limited the jurisdiction of the Supreme Court, and a constitutional prayer amendment was introduced. Each measure was defeated, and in *Wallace v. Jaffree*, 472 U.S. 38 (1985), the Court ruled that a state law authorizing a moment of silence in public schools was unconstitutional. In the late 1980s and early 1990s the religious right made sporadic efforts to reintroduce school prayer legislation but were unsuccessful.

BIBLIOGRAPHY

Alley, Robert S. *School Prayer: The Court, the Congress, and the First Amendment*. Buffalo, N.Y.: Prometheus, 1994.

Haynes, Charles C. "Religion in the Public Schools." *School Administrator* 56, no. 1 (January 1999): 6–10.

McCarthy, Tom H. "Prayer and Bible Reading in the Public Schools: Perspectives, Assumptions, and Implications." *Educational Foundations* 14, no. 1 (winter 2000): 65–87.

Keith A. Leitich

See also **Church and State, Separation of; Education; Moral Majority**.

SCHOOL VOUCHERS, state-funded tuition payments for students at private or public elementary and secondary schools emerged in the late 1900s as the most sweeping of the so-called parental choice reforms, and encompass divergent groups of supporters. The history of school vouchers dates back to 1792 when the revolutionary Thomas Paine proposed a voucher-like plan for England, but popular and legislative support in the United States did not begin until the early 1950s, when states in the Deep South and Virginia established tuition grants to counter anticipated school desegregation. In a 1955 article, economist Milton Friedman proposed vouchers as free-market education, to separate government financing of schools from their administration. Segregationists justified tuition grants on such grounds, but in a series of decisions between 1964 and 1969, the federal courts rejected them as evasions of the 1954 BROWN V. BOARD OF EDUCATION OF TOPEKA decision. Vouchers gained favor outside the South in the 1960s, with advocates of alternative schools, liberals seeking educational equity, and defenders of urban parochial schools among the supporters. The U.S. Office of Economic Opportunity sponsored a 1970 study that recommended compensatory vouchers, culminating in a five-year, public school-only demonstration program in Alum Rock, California. In *Committee for Public Education v. Nyquist* (1973), the Supreme Court set aside a New York tuition reimbursement program for parochial school students. In the 1980s, with support from the executive branch, vouchers had resurgence, via alliances of free-market conservatives, local activists, and private school supporters responding to inadequate academic achievement in urban public schools. Although voters rejected school vouchers in several statewide referenda in the 1990s, legislatures established pilot programs in three states. Wisconsin established a program for students at private secular schools in Milwaukee in 1990, followed in 1995 by an Ohio program that encompassed religious schools in Cleveland, and a 1999 statewide program in Florida for students in low-achieving school districts that also included sectarian schools. In *Zelman v. Simmons-Harris* (2002), the Supreme Court ruled the Cleveland program constitutional, paving the way for expansion to religious schools elsewhere.

BIBLIOGRAPHY

Friedman, Milton. "The Role of Government in Education." In *Economics and the Public Interest*, edited by Robert A. Solo. Rutgers, N.J.: Rutgers University Press, 1955.

O'Brien, Molly Townes. "Private School Tuition Vouchers and the Realities of Racial Politics." *Tennessee Law Review* 64, no. 2 (1997): 359–407.

Witte, John F. *The Market Approach to Education*. Princeton, N.J.: Princeton University Press, 2000.

Jim Carl

SCHOOLS, COMMUNITY. Community schools are committed to broad education and are characterized by home, school, and community collaboration to achieve learning. Beginning in the mid-1960s, thousands of small alternative schools sprang up across the United States and Canada. They varied widely in programs and policies, but common factors were a disenchantment with conventional schooling, a desire to reform education, and the belief that schools should be controlled by the population served, including students, parents, teachers, and community members. The National Coalition of Alternative Community Schools was formed in 1976. Community schools include rural schools that serve as community centers, featuring educational and social programs; others are independent neighborhood schools meeting academic, social, and cultural needs of children of African Americans, Hispanic Americans, Latino Americans, Native Americans, and Asian Americans. The New York State Community School Program organized public inner-city schools as sites for the delivery of social services to needy children and their families. Community schools described as "integrative" have sought to bring disabled students into the regular school program. Corporate community schools created partnerships among business executives, educators, and community leaders to establish and operate business-sponsored elementary schools in inner cities. Their goal is to reform urban public education by setting standards and demonstrating instructional methods and school management that can be used across the country.

BIBLIOGRAPHY

Leue, Mary, ed. *Challenging the Giant: The Best of* SKOLE, *the Journal of Alternative Education.* 4 vols. Ashfield, MA: Down-to-Earth Books, 1992.

Owen, Heleen. "Community Schools and Service Integration in New York." *Equity and Choice* 6 (1990).

Mary Deane Sorcinelli / A. R.

See also **Disabled, Education of the; Education, African American; Education, Experimental.**

SCHOOLS, DESEGREGATION OF. *See* Desegregation.

SCHOOLS, FOR-PROFIT.

The idea of schools for profit is rooted in the growing discontent with public schools that began in the 1960s, but an experiment in performance contracting, the hiring by public schools of private companies to provide instruction with remuneration dependent on student achievement, was deemed ineffective in a 1972 government report. Responding to widespread calls in the late 1980s for broad educational reforms, the media entrepreneur Christopher Whittle and the businessman John Golle offered for-profit school plans to redesign U.S. schools. In May 1991 Whittle announced the Edison Project, a plan for a multibillion-dollar chain of 150 to 200 private schools, which, he declared, would provide better instruction at lower per-pupil cost than public schools. A year later, Whittle hired Benno C. Schmidt, Jr., president of Yale University, to head the project. After failing to raise sufficient capital, the project was scaled back, focusing instead on obtaining management contracts with existing schools or winning public funds to establish new schools. In March 1994 Massachusetts became the first state to award charters for the project to operate schools. Meanwhile, Golle started Education Alternatives, Inc. (EAI), in 1986. His first schools, which opened in 1987, did not make money, so he turned to managing public schools. Following mixed results in Miami, Florida, and Duluth, Minnesota, EAI obtained a $133 million contract to operate nine inner-city schools in Baltimore, Maryland. At the end of its second year of operation, EAI showed significant positive changes in parent involvement, facilities maintenance, and student performance on standardized tests. Supporters of for-profit schools envision positive changes resulting from incentive management.

Edison Schools, Inc., flush with new capital, opened four schools in August 1995. By 2000 the company taught 38,000 enrolled students and ran seventy-nine schools in sixteen states and the District of Columbia. Edison's contracts, which paid it approximately $5,500 per student, were paid by diverting money previously earmarked for the school districts or for charter schools. Although the company boasted of improved test scores, it was losing tens of millions of dollars. Some analysts estimated it would reach profitability if it grew to three hundred schools. Detractors continued to express dismay at the admixture of pedagogy and the profit motive and believe that the proliferation of private schools would further undermine the public schools and widen the existing chasm in educational quality between children from affluent and less-well-off families. Teachers' unions almost universally oppose for-profit schools.

BIBLIOGRAPHY

Ascher, Carol. *Hard Lessons: Public Schools and Privatization.* New York: Twentieth Century Fund Press, 1996.

Hakim, Simon, et al., eds. *Privatizing Education and Educational Choice: Concepts, Plans, and Experiences.* Westport, Conn.: Praeger, 1994.

Henig, Jeffrey R. *Rethinking School Choice: Limits of the Market Metaphor.* Princeton, N.J.: Princeton University Press, 1994.

Myrna W. Merron / A. R.

See also **American Federation of Teachers; Education; Education and Intelligence Testing.**

SCHOOLS, MAGNET. *See* Magnet Schools.

SCHOOLS, PRIVATE.

Private, nonpublic, or independent schools do not receive governmental funding and are usually administered by denominational or secular boards; others are operated for profit. Before the advent of public education, all schools were private. During the eighteenth century private academies for boys such as Phillips Andover (1778), Phillips Exeter (1778), and Deerfield (1799) pioneered the teaching of modern and practical subjects, from astronomy to trigonometry. Religious schools were opened by the Quakers, Episcopalians, and Lutherans in the various colonies. A group of Jews opened a school in New York City in 1731, and Roman Catholic schools were under way later in the eighteenth century.

The Free (later Public) School Society opened and operated private schools (1806–1853) that were taken over by the New York City Board of Education. An independent Catholic parochial school system took shape in the late nineteenth century, especially after the Third Plenary Council at Baltimore (1884). Some of the most innovative schools could be found outside the emerging public school system, such as John Dewey's laboratory (1896) schools, noted for their progressive ideas and practices; the first kindergarten (1856); and female academies and seminaries.

The Magna Carta of the private school was the decision by the U.S. SUPREME COURT in *Pierce v. Society of Sisters* (1925), which upheld the constitutionality of private and parochial schools. The parochial schools experienced great financial difficulty after 1945, partially as a result of judicial bans on public support, and many Roman Catholic institutions were forced to close. Enrollment in private elementary and secondary schools in the United States rose to nearly 6.4 million students in 1965, fell to 5 million during the 1970s, and since then has fluctuated between 5 and 5.7 million (approximately 10 to 13 percent of the total school population). Much of the decline was in inner-city Catholic schools, many of which closed as Catholics migrated to the suburbs. A growing number of non-Catholic religious schools, 11,476 by 1990 (46 percent of private schools), offset the Catholic school decline. Still, they enrolled only 31 percent of private school students. Nonsectarian schools served the rest. Preparatory schools, military academies, and Waldorf and Montessori schools addressed particular educational concerns. The increased number of non-Catholic religious schools came largely from the growth of evangelical Christian academies. These academies responded to the perception of moral decline, which some critics attributed to an advancing secular humanist ideology in the public schools. For similar reasons, a rapidly increasing number of families—estimated in the 1990s at about 300,000—engaged in home schooling.

Private preschools also experienced a boom in the late twentieth century. These centers responded to the increased demand for child care created when growing numbers of women entered the labor force out of economic necessity or personal preference.

Critics of the public schools proposed such reforms as tuition tax credits and school vouchers to enable private schools to compete for government funds, thereby pressuring public schools to operate more efficiently. President George H. W. Bush included "school choice" in the America 2000 Excellence in Education Act that he introduced in 1991. The religious nature of many private schools led to protests that school choice, besides undermining public education, would violate separation of church and state. President Bill Clinton consequently excluded school choice measures from his educational proposals. Nonetheless, several states—including California, Minnesota, New York, and Wisconsin—adopted or tested school choice programs.

BIBLIOGRAPHY

Carper, James C., and Thomas C. Hunt, eds. *Religious Schooling in America.* Birmingham, Ala.: Religious Education Press, 1984.

Cookson, Peter W. *School Choice: The Struggle for the Soul of American Education.* New Haven, Conn.: Yale University Press, 1994.

Hanus, Jerome J., and Peter W. Cookson, Jr. *Choosing Schools: Vouchers and American Education.* Washington, D.C.: American University Press, 1996.

Kraushaar, Otto F. *American Nonpublic Schools: Patterns of Diversity.* Baltimore: Johns Hopkins University Press, 1972.

McLachlan, James S. *American Boarding Schools: A Historical Study.* New York: Scribner, 1970.

William W. Brickman
Alfred Lindsay Skerpan / A. R.

See also **Church and State, Separation of; Education.**

SCHOOLS, SINGLE-SEX.

Once the educational norm, single-sex schooling largely disappeared in the United States by the end of the twentieth century. Boys only attended Boston Latin, the first school founded in the United States (1635). The nation's first public schools, founded shortly thereafter, also admitted only boys. Girls of means could attend informal "Dames schools," but their curricula focused mainly on manners and morals rather than literacy. In some locations, especially New England, teachers offered summer school for girls or taught their female pupils before or after regular school hours. By and large, however, formal schooling was reserved for males of families who could afford to spare their labor.

In the aftermath of the American Revolution, heightened emphasis on democracy led to increased concern with schooling. Males needed to be educated to participate actively in the new Republic, and females required learning to rear intelligent, knowledgeable sons. As the common school movement developed in the 1800s, many education thinkers recognized the necessity if not the virtue of educating members of both sexes. Need caused by a lack of funds as well as political or personal expediency prompted many communities to adopt "mixed classes" rather than build separate schools for boys and girls. Slowly, often haphazardly, and against the wishes of white, middle-class and upper-class parents, who did not want their daughters educated alongside poor, ethnically diverse boys, coeducation took hold in the mid- and late 1800s. By the nineteenth century's close, only 12 of 628 American public school districts reported having single-sex schools. Private and parochial schools were the last remaining sites of single-sex education.

The twentieth century, with its democratization of education in the 1920s and 1950s and cries for equality in the women's movement, witnessed the further decline of single-sex schooling. In 1963, 166 of 682 schools belonging to the National Association of Independent Schools admitted only girls, but that number had shrunk to 109 out of 870 in 1992. Half of the nation's Catholic schools were single-sex in 1988, but only ten years later that number had dropped to 40 percent.

Movements in the late twentieth and early twenty-first century to revive single-sex public schooling met mixed responses on both the social and the judicial fronts. Proponents of educating African American males and underprivileged females separately faced successful challenges in court for violating the Fourteenth Amendment's equal protection clause or Title IX of the Educational Amendments of 1972. Despite growing opposition, supporters of single-sex schooling continued to argue that educating girls and boys separately allows members of each sex to reach their maximum academic, social, and personal potential.

BIBLIOGRAPHY

American Association of University Women Educational Foundation. *Separated by Sex: A Critical Look at Single-Sex Education for Girls.* Washington, D.C.: American Association of University Women Educational Foundation, 1998.

Riordan, Cornelius. *Girls and Boys in School: Together or Separate?* New York: Teachers College Press, Columbia University, 1990.

Shmurak, Carole B. *Voices of Hope: Adolescent Girls at Single Sex and Coeducational Schools.* Adolescent Cultures, School, and Society series, vol. 4. New York: Peter Lang, 1998.

Streitmatter, Janice L. *For Girls Only: Making a Case for Single-Sex Schooling.* Albany: State University of New York Press, 1999.

Tyack, David, and Elisabeth Hansot. *Learning Together: A History of Coeducation in American Public Schools.* New York: Russell Sage Foundation, 1992.

Diana B. Turk

See also **Education; Education, Higher: Women's Colleges.**

SCHOONER.

A schooner is a sailing vessel that, in its pure form, originated at Gloucester, Massachusetts, in 1713–1714. It is a fore-and-aft-rigged craft, originally small (fifty to one hundred tons), with two masts, designed for coastwise trade. It developed in the 1880s and 1890s into vessels of two to three thousand tons, having four, five, and even six masts. Only one seven-master was attempted (1901–1902), the *Thomas W. Lawson,* which was 368 feet long and 5,200 tons.

The use of schooners began to decline gradually in the mid-1800s with the advent of steam-powered vessels, but the schooner has always stood as the favorite and distinctive rig of American waters.

BIBLIOGRAPHY

Hahn, Harold M. *The Colonial Schooner, 1763–1775.* Annapolis, Md.: Naval Institute Press, 1981.

MacGregor, David R. *Schooners in Four Centuries.* Annapolis, Md.; Naval Institute Press, 1982.

William Lincoln Brown / A. R.

See also **Colonial Ships; Shipbuilding; Transportation and Travel.**

SCIENCE AND RELIGION, RELATIONS OF,

have been a feature of American thought since colonial times. British settlers began colonizing North America in the 1600s just as the mechanical philosophy was transforming Western science. Earlier European natural philosophers accepted an organic view of matter in which spirits pervaded nature. In contrast, the mechanical philosophy stripped matter of intelligence and purpose. Except for God, human souls, and spiritual beings, the universe consisted of inanimate matter moving in accordance with natural law. For some, this pushed God back to the beginning—a perfect, divine clockmaker who created matter and set it moving in accord with his rational laws. Others, while seeing matter as utterly passive, maintained that God not only created the physical universe but also actively maintained it and could miraculously intervene in its workings. Both views carried profound theological implications. Colonists carried this debate with them to the New World.

To the extent that they participated in these debates, most colonists followed the prevailing British view, associated with the preeminent British scientists Isaac Newton (1642–1727) and Robert Boyle (1627–1691), that saw God actively intervening in nature. The Massachusetts divine Cotton Mather (1663–1728), noted in Europe for his scientific observations of New World phenomena, exemplified this viewpoint. Such scientists typically stressed the need for observation and experiment to discover how God actually designed and maintained nature. Seeing the creation in this way encouraged them to study it for proof of God's existence and evidence of his goodness. Second only to God's revealed word in the Bible, natural theology gave insight into the divine.

In contrast, deists like Benjamin Franklin (1709–1790), whose analysis of electricity made him the best-known colonial scientist, followed the continental view most commonly associated with such French thinkers as René Descartes (1596–1650), Voltaire (1694–1778), and Pierre Laplace (1748–1827), who saw God as rationally creating the universe but no longer involved with its operation. For these scientists, reason tended to play a larger role than experiment in finding truth, and revelation typically played no part at all. Biblical miracles, including Christ's resurrection, became an object of scientific scorn for many deists, including Franklin and his younger revolutionary-era patriot colleagues Thomas Jefferson (1743–1826) and Thomas Paine (1737–1809). Among scientists, the Philadelphia physician Benjamin Rush (1746–1813) and the English émigré chemist Joseph Priestley (1733–1804) pushed the rational critique of revelation into the early national period.

Antebellum America

Cordial relations between science and religion generally prevailed through the first half of the nineteenth century. Excesses of the French Revolution undermined the appeal of continental thought in the United States, leaving the field open to British ideas. Rational deism, with its scientific assaults on revealed religion, gave way to a more emotional, and sometimes near pantheistic, romanticism among such American intellectuals as the Unitarian philosopher Ralph Waldo Emerson (1803–1882). Science did not feature prominently in their critique of traditional religion. Indeed, they were more likely to criticize science and technology than to appeal to them.

During the early nineteenth century, science found an institutional home in the growing number of small colleges dotting the American landscape. These colleges, even state-supported ones, typically functioned as an intellectual arm of evangelical Protestantism. Science was stressed as a means to instruct students in natural theology. The Yale College president Timothy Dwight (1752–1817), for example, used science to counter skepticism. The Bible was God's word, Dwight argued, and science studied God's creation: there could be no real conflict between them. Any apparent conflict must come from misinterpretations of scripture or science. Thus inspired, academic scientists took the lead in harmonizing new scientific theories with the Bible. America's two leading geologists, Yale's James Dwight Dana (1813–1895) and the Amherst College president Edward Hitchcock (1793–1864), reconciled new scientific evidence of a long earth history with the Biblical account of creation by suggesting that the days of creation in Genesis symbolized geologic epochs or that a gap existed in the scriptural account. Other scientists made similar efforts to reconcile evidence of ancient and diverse human races with the Genesis account of Adam and Eve. Antebellum American Protestants, impressed by the Biblical orthodoxy of these scientists, generally accepted that good science supported sound religion.

The Advent of Darwinism

The theories of the British naturalist Charles Darwin (1809–1882) began splitting science from religion in the late nineteenth century. Darwin announced his theory of organic evolution by natural selection in 1858. The concept that biological species evolved from preexisting species by natural processes, rather than each being separately created, necessarily pushed God's role back in time. It also challenged conventional readings of Genesis. Nevertheless, most American scientists, including such traditional Christians as Dana and the Harvard botanist Asa Gray (1810–1888), quickly accepted it. The popular Congregational minister Henry Ward Beecher (1813–1887) soon hailed evolution as "God's way of doing things," a view widely shared by liberal Protestants. Roman Catholics and conservative Protestants were more guarded, but many of their leading theologians, including Princeton's Benjamin B. Warfield (1851–1921), ultimately conceded that Genesis could be reconciled with evolution so long as the human soul remained a supernatural creation.

The enthusiasm of late-nineteenth-century Americans for the theory of evolution was tempered by their doubts about the process of natural selection. Darwin postulated evolution operating through chance inborn variations selected by a survival-of-the-fittest process. For believers schooled in natural theology, in which nature

exhibited God's character, a random, cruel process of creation all but damned the Creator—and the Princeton theologian Charles Hodge (1797–1878) said as much in his influential 1874 book, *What Is Darwinism?* Many American scientists devised evolutionary mechanisms more compatible with their concept of creation. Gray, for example, proposed a theory of theistic evolution in which a transcendent God guided evolution. The geologist Joseph LeConte (1823–1901) favored a form of theistic evolution driven by spiritual forces within nature. The paleontologist Edward D. Cope (1840–1897) revived notions of acquired variations and vital forces derived from the French naturalist Lamarck (1744–1829). Until the development of genetics early in the twentieth century, legitimate scientific problems with the Darwinian concept of natural selection left ample room for alternatives. During the late nineteenth century, these alternatives dominated American science, rendering it less threatening to religion. Gray, LeConte, and Cope authored popular books harmonizing their views of evolution with religious belief.

At least for LeConte and Cope, however, coming to terms with the theory of evolution proved corrosive of religious orthodoxy. Cope abandoned his Quaker roots for theistic Unitarianism. LeConte renounced all "anthropomorphic notions of Deity." Although other evolutionists retained traditional religious beliefs, they increasingly segregated them from their scientific pursuits. Evolution in biology, uniformitarianism in geology (which holds that present geological processes are sufficient to explain all past geological changes), and positivism in physics (which sees ultimate reality as unknowable) pointed scientists toward seeking immediate natural (rather than remote supernatural) causes for physical phenomena. "It is the aim of science to narrow the domain of the supernatural, by bringing all phenomena within the scope of natural laws and secondary causes," argued the Wesleyan University geologist William North Rice (1845–1928), a theist. The practical success of this approach in producing useful technology and new theories inevitably pushed God out of science and natural theology out of science education. The expansion and professionalization of science departments within American universities contributed to these trends. By the turn of the twentieth century, most American scientists had abandoned efforts to harmonize science with revelation and stopped talking professionally about their religious beliefs.

Twentieth-Century America

The divide between science and religion widened in the twentieth century, with both flourishing in their separate spheres. Housed in ever expanding research universities and fueled by unprecedented public funding, American science assumed intellectual leadership in virtually every field. The technological payoff transformed industry, agriculture, and warfare. During the same period, surveys found that a greater percentage of Americans regularly attended religious services and professed belief in God than the people of any other scientifically advanced nation. Yet surveys also suggested that these percentages dropped off for American scientists, particularly at the higher echelons of the profession. The Darwinian biologist Ernst Mayr (1904–), an atheist, attributed this to methodological naturalism. Science focused on finding naturalistic answers to physical phenomena and left supernatural issues to religion.

Mainline Protestantism disengaged from its historic dialogue with science and abandoned natural theology. The foremost Protestant theologians of the twentieth century, such as Karl Barth (1886–1968), Paul Tillich (1886–1965), and Reinhold Niebuhr (1892–1971), wrote virtually nothing about science in an era of triumphant scientism. Liberal and neoorthodox Protestants joined most Catholics in largely reserving their comment for ethical issues raised by technological applications of science, from biotechnology to nuclear weapons, and to general observations that modern science theories, like the big bang and quantum indeterminacy, leave room for God.

Conservative Christians generally accepted modern science too, though many maintained doubts about the theory of evolution, particularly Darwinian conceptions of natural selection gained general acceptance among biologists during the second quarter of the twentieth century. Periodically during the century, lay Christians stirred mass movements against Darwinism. The Presbyterian politician William Jennings Bryan (1860–1925) did so most effectively in the 1920s, resulting in widespread limits on the teaching of evolution in public schools and the 1925 trial of the high school teacher John Scopes (1900–1970) for violating one such law in Tennessee. Beginning in the 1960s, the Baptist engineering professor Henry M. Morris (1918–) helped revive a literal reading of the Genesis account of creation among fundamentalists, leading to widespread demands for the inclusion of so-called "creation science" in public school biology classes. In the 1990s, the Presbyterian law professor Phillip Johnson (1940–) rekindled widespread interest among conservative Protestants and Catholics for pre-Darwinian concepts of intelligent design in nature. America's rapidly expanding Pentecostal and Holiness denominations sympathized with these movements, though their members rarely took a lead in them. Antievolutionism also characterized Islam, with its sizable following among African Americans, and such Protestant offshoots as Mormonism, the Jehovah's Witnesses, and Seventh-Day Adventism. These popular faiths insure that America's long encounter between science and religion will continue.

BIBLIOGRAPHY

Bozeman, Theodore Dwight. *Protestants in an Age of Science: The Baconian Ideal and Ante-Bellum American Religious Thought.* Chapel Hill: University of North Carolina Press, 1977.

Conkin, Paul K. *When All the Gods Trembled: Darwinism, Scopes, and American Intellectuals.* Lanham, Md.: Rowman and Littlefield, 1998.

Greene, John C. *American Science in the Age of Jefferson.* Ames: Iowa State University Press, 1984.

Hovenkamp, Herbert. *Science and Religion in America, 1800–1860.* Philadelphia: University of Pennsylvania Press, 1978.

Larson, Edward J. *Summer for the Gods: The Scopes Trial and America's Continuing Debate over Science and Religion.* New York: Basic Books, 1997.

Numbers, Ronald L. *Darwinism Comes to America.* Cambridge, Mass.: Harvard University Press, 1998.

Roberts, Jon H., and James Turner. *The Sacred and Secular University.* Princeton, N.J.: Princeton University Press, 2000.

Szasz, Ferenc M. *The Divided Mind of Protestant America, 1880–1930.* University: University of Alabama Press, 1982.

Edward J. Larson

See also **Bioethics; Creationism; Evolutionism; Scopes Trial.**

SCIENCE EDUCATION.

Although advanced science education did not begin to thrive in the United States until the last third of the nineteenth century, scientific learning has long been a part of American intellectual and cultural life. In colonial America, mathematics and natural philosophy formed a standard part of a college education. As a Harvard student in the 1750s, John Adams studied both subjects, as did Thomas Jefferson and James Madison at William and Mary and the College of New Jersey (later Princeton), respectively. Natural history entered the university curriculum toward the end of the eighteenth century, and in 1802, the establishment of the United States Military Academy at West Point provided a center for engineering education to meet the new nation's military engineering needs.

Social settings outside the colleges and universities also provided important forums for learning and discussing the truths of the natural world. In Europe, the rise of print culture and an active literary public sphere, and the creation of new institutions such as London's Royal Society, with its gentlemanly forms of discourse, or the Parisian salon where men and women pursued science as a form of entertainment, all played a central role in disseminating the natural philosophy of the Enlightenment during the seventeenth and eighteenth centuries. Similar developments characterized scientific learning in America during the colonial and early national periods, through learned societies such as Philadelphia's American Philosophical Society, public lecture-demonstrations by men of science, and newly established museums with natural history collections.

Nevertheless, by the middle of the nineteenth century the boosters of American science remained acutely aware that scientific learning in the United States was still distinctly second-rate. Books were scarce, and standard sources in European libraries were absent from American shelves. In universities, the prohibitively high cost of scientific apparatus meant that laboratory instruction was almost nonexistent. Natural history flourished thanks to the wealth of living organisms and fossils that required identification and classification, but American science had little to celebrate in fields such as chemistry, physics, and mathematics. Opportunities for advanced science education were few, and Europe remained the preferred option for those who wanted high-quality training.

With the nationwide trend toward professionalization in the 1840s, opportunities for higher education in science and engineering gradually increased. West Point's engineering program had declined by the 1830s, but in 1835, the Rensselaer Institute (renamed Rensselaer Polytechnic Institute in 1851) helped fill the gap by awarding the nation's first civil engineering degrees. Engineering education expanded further in the 1850s and 1860s with the founding of new engineering schools such as Brooklyn Polytechnic Institute and MASSACHUSETTS INSTITUTE OF TECHNOLOGY. By the 1870s, there were eighty-five engineering schools in the United States. Scientific schools proliferated as well. Yale founded its School of Applied Chemistry in 1847, which evolved into the Sheffield Scientific School in 1861 (the same year that Yale awarded the nation's first Ph.D.s, one in physics and two outside the sciences), and other universities followed suit. The United States could boast seventy such schools by 1873. The passage of the MORRILL ACT in 1862 provided an additional boost to science and engineering by providing states with land grants to endow colleges and universities "for the benefit of agriculture and the mechanic arts." More than seventy institutions were either established or assisted under the Morrill Act, including Cornell University, University of Minnesota, and University of Wisconsin.

This expansion of science and engineering education represented a change in scale, but less a change in kind. The opening of JOHNS HOPKINS UNIVERSITY in 1876, however, signaled the creation of a new kind of institution: the American research university, dedicated primarily to graduate education and the generation of new knowledge, particularly in the sciences. By the turn of the century, research had become a central criterion for all universities that aspired to academic excellence. In the early twentieth century, other institutions, particularly philanthropic foundations, began to combine forces with the universities to promote advanced scientific education and research. The ROCKEFELLER FOUNDATION, launched in 1913, played a major role in building American leadership in science. During the 1920s, for example, a generation of brilliant young American physicists studied in Europe, most with support from the Rockefeller-funded National Research Council fellowship program, and their return to American academic positions turned the United States into a major center of physics where aspiring physicists could find high-quality training. A few years later, the rise of fascism forced many of Europe's best physicists

to seek refuge in the United States, and American physics reached even greater heights.

Ultimately, however, World War II and the Cold War played the most important role in transforming American science education into its currently recognizable form. Leading research universities in science and engineering fields built their reputations upon the foundations of wartime and postwar funding for research. Wartime defense spending, for example, helped transform MIT into a truly distinguished research center. MIT led universities with $117 million in defense contracts during the war, and with the rise of the Cold War and the permanent mobilization of science by the federal government, the institute continued to be a center of military-sponsored research. Stanford University also benefited immensely from the new relationship between science and the federal government. Although STANFORD UNIVERSITY held few wartime defense contracts, after the war its administrators aggressively pursued Cold War defense dollars in order to turn their university into a first-rate research institution. Within a few years Stanford rivaled MIT for preeminence in electrical engineering and other fields that commanded generous defense contracts.

Cold War funding and the massive expansion of university-based research transformed science education in a variety of ways. The physical sciences received well over 90 percent of their research funds from military sources in the 1950s and 1960s. As military needs shifted disciplinary priorities, science and engineering students gained a new sense of the kinds of research problems that earned professional acclaim. For example, the entire discipline of electrical engineering redefined itself around military problems. At MIT, a significant number of students wrote dissertations on classified projects, and even the textbooks reflected military topics. Its aeronautical engineering program turned away from questions of safety to an almost exclusive concern with high-performance aircraft. Such Cold War trends reproduced themselves, to varying degrees, at the major research universities across the country.

As a result of federal support for university research, postwar America could boast the best advanced scientific education in the world. There did not always seem to be enough students to take advantage of that education, however, and throughout the Cold War, policymakers continually worried about shortages in scientific manpower. They responded with educational initiatives designed to ensure a steady supply of scientists. In 1948 the Atomic Energy Commission established the largest program for advanced science education in the nation's history by providing generous fellowship support to hundreds of students each year for graduate and postdoctoral work in physics, mathematics, biology, and medicine. Federal educational support increased further after the Soviet launch of *Sputnik* prompted a nervous Congress to pass the National Defense Education Act of 1958. The act appropriated more than $370 million to promote education in science, engineering, and other areas, such as foreign language study, deemed necessary to provide expertise for waging the Cold War.

After the 1960s, government efforts increasingly focused on creating educational opportunities for women and minorities in order to augment the scientific talent pool. Government policies helped growing numbers of women and racial minorities to pursue scientific careers, but African Americans, Latinos, and Native Americans still report the persistence of systemic barriers and subtle forms of discrimination. By 1999, members of underrepresented minority groups—African Americans, Latinos, and Native Americans—still earned less than 10 percent of science and engineering doctorates. In physics these minorities accounted for only 3.6 percent of doctorates, or just twenty-six physics degrees across the entire nation. Women have become increasingly visible in the life sciences, where in 1999 they earned over 40 percent of doctoral degrees, but only 23 percent of Ph.D.s in the physical sciences (and less than 13 percent in physics) went to women. In the meantime, a heavy influx of science and engineering students from abroad played a key role in providing the United States with scientific talent. By the 1990s, foreigners constituted nearly 40 percent of science and engineering doctoral students in the United States, and two-thirds accepted American employment after earning their degrees. Among Chinese and Indians, nearly 80 percent chose to remain in the United States. Immigration also contributed to the relatively large percentage of Asian Americans who have earned science and engineering doctorates, since the highly educated Asian immigrants who came to the United States in large numbers beginning in the 1960s viewed science and engineering as means of upward mobility, and they encouraged their children to follow similar career paths. In 1999, Asian Americans earned over 11 percent of science and engineering doctorates, even though their percentage of the total U.S. population stood in the low single digits.

The evolution of science education has thus moved in tandem with larger social and political currents—transformed not only by institutional change but by domestic social change, which has led radically different groups of people to pursue science and engineering degrees in twenty-first-century America.

BIBLIOGRAPHY

Bruce, Robert V. *The Launching of Modern American Science, 1846–1876.* New York: Knopf, 1987.

Cohen, I. Bernard. *Science and the Founding Fathers: Science in the Political Thought of Jefferson, Franklin, Adams, and Madison.* New York and London: Norton, 1995.

Greene, John C. *American Science in the Age of Jefferson.* Ames: Iowa State University Press, 1984.

Kevles, Daniel J. *The Physicists: The History of a Scientific Community in Modern America.* New York: Knopf, 1978. Reprint with new preface, Cambridge, Mass., and London: Harvard University Press, 1995.

Kohler, Robert E. *Partners in Science: Foundations and Natural Scientists, 1900–1945.* Chicago and London: University of Chicago Press, 1991.

Leslie, Stuart W. *The Cold War and American Science: The Military-Industrial-Academic Complex at MIT and Stanford.* New York: Columbia University Press, 1993.

Lowen, Rebecca S. *Creating the Cold War University: The Transformation of Stanford.* Berkeley and Los Angeles: University of California Press, 1997.

Jessica Wang

See also **Education, Higher: Colleges and Universities.**

SCIENCE JOURNALISM AND TELEVISION.

Scientific knowledge and the accomplishments of scientists have long attracted the attention of the media in the United States. Newspapers have described the latest discoveries and chronicled the progress of research; books and magazines have explained scientific concepts and examined the lives of scientists. In interviews broadcast on radio and television, scientists have discussed their current research and commented on science-related ethical and political issues. And on television, science has often been presented as entertainment laced with educational content.

Print

In early American magazines, attention to science reflected ideals of progress and national pride. During the 1790s, articles by botanists, geologists, and explorers sought to satisfy curiosity about the vast North American continent. In the 1800s, a growing cadre of experimentalists and inventors described their discoveries to other interested amateurs; popular articles trumpeted innovative agricultural techniques or explained the medicinal value of certain herbs. By the end of the nineteenth century, literary monthlies like *Harper's*, *Atlantic*, and *Scribner's*, and general-content weeklies like the *Saturday Evening Post* and *Collier's* carried increasingly more forecasts of how advances in research would benefit public health, agriculture, and industry, many written by scientists themselves.

Specialized periodicals like *Scientific American* (founded in 1845) and *National Geographic Magazine* (1888) sought to translate science for interested laypeople. *Scientific American*'s focus reflected nineteenth-century interest in invention and technology, while *National Geographic* tapped Americans' growing fascination with people and places elsewhere in the world. From its first issue in 1872, *Popular Science Monthly* also promoted the cause of popularizing science, drawing authority from close connections to the scientific community. Its first two editors, Edward L. Youmans and James McKeen Cattell, emphasized the importance of expertise through publication of essays by the greatest scientists of the day.

By the early twentieth century, readers were seeking more practical information—how to operate (and repair) technological innovations, from typewriters and automobiles to radios and electric irons. Periodicals like *Popular Mechanics*, founded by Henry Haven Windsor in 1902, met this demand with articles that explained the "mechanics" behind new inventions and consumer devices. After 1915, as part of the same marketing trend, *Popular Science Monthly* began to focus more on technology and on the scientific concepts believed to interest amateurs or hobbyists, rather than only those deemed important by scientists.

Newspaper coverage of science rose and, by the 1920s, more professional journalists were specializing in science and medicine. Some of the increased press attention derived from science's expansion and from genuine public interest, but the scientific community's promotional efforts also played a role. Even though many scientists approached the popularization process with skepticism, others, such as physicist Robert A. Millikan and astronomer George Ellery Hale, believed that positive publicity would help in attracting federal government support and in erasing the negative public images associated with development of chemical weapons for World War I (1914–1918). The American Chemical Society, for example, joined with various chemical corporations and private foundations in a public relations campaign to popularize chemistry. The Society established its permanent News Service in 1919, the first of many such operations created by scientific associations.

The founding in 1921 of Science Service, a nonprofit news syndicate underwritten by newspaper publisher E. W. Scripps, was a direct outgrowth of the scientists' public relations campaigns. Directed by chemist E. E. Slosson and science writer Watson C. Davis, Science Service initially sought to assist journalists and news operations by issuing press releases and providing photos and other illustrations, but the organization's ultimate goal was to influence coverage overall. Eventually, Science Service engaged in radio production, providing programs to stations at no cost and thereby disseminating science's message to millions of listeners.

A few newspapers, like the *New York Times*, began to assign reporters to cover science exclusively. One influential journalist, Waldemar Kaempffert, started his career in 1897 at *Scientific American*, leaving in 1915 to become editor of *Popular Science Monthly* and then turning to newspaper journalism in the 1920s. Kaempffert served as Science Editor of the *New York Times* from 1927–1928 and 1931–1956. Another *Times* reporter, William L. Laurence, who worked at the paper from 1930–1964, helped to found the National Association of Science Writers in 1934, a further sign of science journalism's growing professionalism.

Many of these reporters also published frequently in popular magazines or wrote books for the growing numbers of Americans fascinated by what scientists were doing. The success of books like Paul de Kruif's *Microbe Hunters* (1926), which recounted the achievements of pioneers in bacteriology, had sparked a market for popular science texts. *The March of Science* (1936), by *New York Times* reporter H. Gordon Garbedian, explored the work of prominent researchers like anthropologist Franz Boas, physicist Michael Pupin, and chemist Harold C. Urey, and trumpeted the benefits of scientific progress.

Radio Broadcasting

Events such as the Scopes trial in 1925 heightened public interest in science, stimulating numerous newspaper columns, magazine articles, and books debating the viability of the concept of evolution and whether it should be taught in schools. That trial also featured one of the first remote news broadcasts; the open microphones of WGN, a station owned by the *Chicago Tribune*, allowed Americans all over the country to listen to the testimony, arguments, and judge's decision.

From its earliest days, radio offered an important platform for scientific discourse, to the extent that in 1925 opponents of evolution attempted to ban discussions of it from radio altogether. The approach to broadcasting science initially differed little from how scientists had been performing in public lecture halls for years; but as various scientific organizations began to engage in educational outreach through radio, they realized that, to compete for audience attention, science would have to be presented in more engaging and interesting formats. They began to work directly with commercial networks to develop such programming. Science Service's *Adventures in Science*, broadcast on CBS from 1938 until 1957, attempted to infuse drama into descriptions of the latest discoveries. The Smithsonian Institution's radio program *The World Is Yours* (1936–1942) included segments on its own scientific research, part of an experimental Works Progress Administration project with the U.S. Office of Education. The American Association for the Advancement of Science worked with NBC on three separate programs— *Science Everywhere* (1937–1938), *Science on the March* (1938), and *Science in the News* (1936–1940)—which the association perceived as a way for scientists to speak directly to the public and thereby to encourage confidence in research and scientific reasoning.

Universities and corporations sponsored radio talks by scientists, sometimes during the intermissions of symphony concerts. These talks were then printed and distributed to interested listeners. General Electric's program *Excursions in Science*, which ran nationally from 1936 to 1949, took this conventional lecture and interview approach as it emphasized the science behind the company's engineering work.

Radio played a significant role in public education in other science-related areas. From the beginning of commercial broadcasting, farm market reports included scientific advice on such things as pest control and soil enhancement. For thirty-two years, beginning in 1928, NBC's *National Farm and Home Hour* integrated agricultural news and educational presentations with entertainment, alternating segments produced by the U.S. Department of Agriculture with the network's commercially sponsored ones.

By the early 1930s, government agencies, dairy councils, pharmaceutical companies, and insurance firms were all producing public health broadcasts. The most significant contribution toward improvement of medical news and information on radio was made by the American Medical Association, which underwrote production of various weekly series from the 1930s through the 1950s. The Association's programs like *Your Health* (1935–1940) combined dramatizations with expert discussions and were distributed to stations at no cost.

The use of dramatization represented an important change in popular science's tone and techniques, one not always welcomed by the scientific community, even though its own organizations adopted similar approaches. Radio producers attempted to emphasize science's inherent dramatic aspects in order to satisfy audiences accustomed to fast-paced comedies, mysteries, and quiz shows. One successful and highly acclaimed series, *The Human Adventure*, produced by the University of Chicago from 1939 to 1946, re-created moments of discovery and used dramatizations to explain complex theories; other science programs employed orchestras and Hollywood actors to attract their audiences. With radio broadcasts, the popularization of science shifted from efforts driven solely by educational goals and the interests of the scientific community to communications designed to attract and sustain large audiences.

Explaining the Atom

World War II (1939–1945) interrupted the flow of some scientific information to the public. It also stimulated the publication of technical material related to wartime training programs for engineers, factory workers, and military personnel. Guidelines developed by the U.S. Office of Censorship strove not to inhibit all discussion of science and technology. Government officials also recognized the importance of informed publicity. *New York Times* reporter William L. Laurence was invited to be the only journalist present at the Trinity test at Alamogordo, asked to write the official press releases about the test, and allowed to travel with the mission to bomb Nagasaki, Japan (winning a Pulitzer prize for his eyewitness accounts of these events).

After the war, American publishers moved quickly to produce articles and books to "explain" the atom, while conforming to new government restrictions on the discussion of atomic energy. Among the first publications were Pocket Books' *The Atomic Age Opens!* (August 1945) and *Life* magazine's 20 August 1945 issue on the atomic bomb. Although the U.S. Atomic Energy Commission and other agencies established public information staffs to assist writers, publishers, and broadcasters in interpreting government restrictions, it is emblematic of postwar changes in science communication that the same of-

fices also engaged in promotional activities intended to increase media attention to government research.

Science had undeniable relevance to human life, welfare, and survival. Information about science was also an instrument of political and national power. Scientists, government officials, and the media did not always agree on when or if scientific information should be shared with the public. Science journalists, once inclined to be protective and promoting of science, began engaging in sharper, more investigative reporting about research organizations and research policies and paying closer attention to science's social and political context. *Scientific American*'s circulation increased dramatically after 1947 when its new owners and editors broadened the scope to include technical discussion of political issues like arms control and environmental policy, alongside explanations of theoretical work in physics, chemistry, and mathematics.

Magazine articles and radio documentaries played important roles in enhancing public discussion of the political and moral issues raised by the development of nuclear weapons because they could include more technical details than newspaper accounts. During the 1940s, the Federation of American Scientists and other action groups encouraged scientists to give media interviews and they developed public service broadcasts for their disarmament campaigns. By 1949, hundreds of separate documentaries about atomic energy had been broadcast on American radio stations, sometimes combining dramatizations by famous actors like Bob Hope with interviews of real scientists and politicians.

Television

Television offered an unparalleled platform for visualizing science for the public. Technical explanations could be supplemented with illustrations and animation; programs could include film of natural phenomena, show the insides of laboratories, and even project images directly from microscopes and telescopes. Early series like NBC's *The Nature of Things* (1948–1954), starring astronomer Roy K. Marshall, featured illustrated talks and interviews with guest scientists. Even more popular were programs in which scientists demonstrated simple experiments, as in the primetime show *The Johns Hopkins Science Review* (1948–1954), created by university administrator Lynn Poole, and the children's series *Watch Mr. Wizard* (1951–1965), starring Donald H. Herbert. Each week, "Mr. Wizard" would explain one or two simple scientific principles to children who acted as his helpers.

With a few notable exceptions, the majority of science on American television has appeared not in regular commercial series, but within news reports or in special programming subsidized by corporations and charitable foundations. In the 1960s, network news operations began to employ their own science and medical correspondents, often with professional degrees, to produce special reports or comment on emerging controversies, and television science coverage increased slightly. More entertaining science came via special programming. From 1956 to 1962, for example, the Bell Telephone System underwrote production and primetime broadcast of nine specials that combined animation, films of natural phenomena, and scientists' explanations of technical concepts. Beginning with *Our Mr. Sun* (1956) and *Hemo the Magnificent* (1957), the popular programs featured a professor of English literature, Frank H. Baxter, as the host; film and video versions have been distributed and shown in American classrooms ever since.

Other references to science occurred in the nature series that became popular following the success of *Zooparade* (1949–1957) and *Wild Kingdom* (1953–1976), starring zoo director Marlin Perkins. Beginning in 1965, television specials produced by the National Geographic Society set high standards for photographic quality, and exploited television's ability to transport viewers to exotic places, visiting natural habitats and archaeological digs around the world. Television's nature programs did not merely display beautiful natural scenes or discuss the lives of animals; they also espoused conservation and environmental values, with varying attention to the underlying science.

Television has offered three important venues for informing the public about medicine and public health: news and public affairs coverage of advances in medical research; educational programming about public health topics; and attention to ethical issues within medical drama shows. Fictional drama shows have freely incorporated factual material, including film footage of real surgery, within their plots, and they routinely address contemporary medical issues, from fetal alcohol syndrome to AIDS research and the treatment of Alzheimer's disease.

Despite national campaigns to improve science education, the amount of science programming on American television has been modest at best, much of it sustained by external underwriting rather than commercial sponsorship. Television transformed coverage of space launches into show business, culminating in the *Apollo* Moon landing of 1969, but network broadcasts included only minor amounts of science information. Public television became a dominant source of popularized science in the 1970s, beginning with the premiere of the *NOVA* series in 1974. American broadcast of the British miniseries *Ascent of Man* (1975), followed in 1980 by astronomer Carl Sagan's *Cosmos*, established a model of lavish science documentaries, distinguished by their charismatic scientist-hosts, expensive computer-generated graphics and animation, and reliance on government, corporate, and charitable support.

Television science programming in the 1980s and 1990s demonstrated the dominance of entertainment approaches. The children's educational series *3-2-1 Contact* (1980–1992), created for public broadcasting by Children's Television Workshop, used celebrities and popular music to teach science. The advent of cable channels provided new opportunities for reaching both children and adults. Don Herbert rejuvenated his old children's series for the Nickelodeon cable channel; *Mr. Wizard's World* ran from 1983–1991, wholly underwritten by government and corporate grants. Both The Learning Channel, created in 1981, and the Discovery Channel, started in 1985, feature a full schedule of science series and specials. Two other acclaimed noncommercial series are *Nature*, which premiered in 1982, and *Scientific American Frontiers*, which premiered in 1990. Like the magazine for which it is named, *Scientific American Frontiers* presents technical material for educated adult audiences. Science broadcasts also now routinely offer information in print and on the World Wide Web, for both teachers and regular viewers, to supplement their program content.

Late-Twentieth-Century Science Journalism

Although print and broadcast news enthusiastically tracked the advances of science, a number of controversies in the 1970s and 1980s, such as the debate over regulation of recombinant DNA research and the accident at the Three Mile Island nuclear facility, in Pennsylvania, chilled previously warm relations between scientists and the reporters who covered their activities. Scientific organizations became more protective of their public image and more skillful in their media relations. Other situations, such as the onset of the AIDS epidemic, focused attention on the importance of accurate reporting and on the adverse consequences of sensationalism. Starting in the 1970s, many U.S. newspapers initiated regular science pages or sections; online news operations now regularly include sections on science or health.

Through the years, prominent scientists have ventured into the mass media, gaining public visibility as they write articles for popular magazines, give interviews for radio and television, or host television shows. These scientists have become celebrities not because of their scientific accomplishments (although that expertise underlines their authority in a public forum), but because they are articulate, photogenic, and knowledgeable about the media; they have also helped to shape the public's image of what scientists are like. Through the 1990s, however, few of these visible scientists were female or were members of ethnic or racial minorities.

Books and popular magazines have continued to be important sources for public information about science, thanks to writers like biologist Stephen Jay Gould and physicist Stephen Hawking and to publications like *Discover* and *Scientific American*. Americans interested in learning more about science can sample continuously from a wide range of print, broadcast, and Internet sources, many of them now cross-linked to assist in the search for information. Most of these are produced by commercial groups or private foundations rather than scientists and their organizations, representing an important change in who presents science to the public.

BIBLIOGRAPHY

Burnham, John C. *How Superstition Won and Science Lost: Popularizing Science and Health in the United States.* New Brunswick, N.J.: Rutgers University Press, 1987.

Foust, James C. "E. W. Scripps and the Science Service." *Journalism History* 21, no. 2 (Summer 1995): 58–64.

Goodell, Rae S. *The Visible Scientists.* Boston: Little, Brown, 1977.

Kreighbaum, Hillier. *Science and the Mass Media.* New York: New York University Press, 1967.

LaFollette, Marcel C. *Making Science Our Own: Public Images of Science, 1910–1955.* Chicago: University of Chicago Press, 1990.

Mitman, Gregg. *Reel Nature: America's Romance with Wildlife on Film.* Cambridge, Mass.: Harvard University Press, 1999.

National Association of Science Writers. *Science; Who Gets What Science News—The News, Where They Get It, What They Think About It—And the Public.* New York: New York University Press, 1958.

Poole, Lynn. *Science via Television.* Baltimore: Johns Hopkins Press, 1950.

Tobey, Ronald C. *The American Ideology of National Science, 1919–1930.* Pittsburgh, Pa.: University of Pittsburgh Press, 1971.

Washburn, Patrick S. "The Office of Censorship's Attempt to Control Press Coverage of the Atomic Bomb During World War II." *Journalism Monographs*, no. 120 (April 1990).

Marcel C. LaFollette

SCIENCE MUSEUMS. The first public science museum was the Ashmolean Museum, founded at Oxford University in 1683 and created to educate and entertain the British public. In the United States the FRANKLIN INSTITUTE in Philadelphia (1824) and the American Institute of New York (1828) were among the first organizations to hold exhibitions of scientific developments. For many years, only natural history science MUSEUMS existed, such as the SMITHSONIAN INSTITUTION (1846), the AMERICAN MUSEUM OF NATURAL HISTORY (1869), and Chicago's Field Museum of Natural History (1893), which served as depositories for rich collections of specimens ranging from plants and animals to geological materials and human artifacts. By 1969 two different types of science museums existed—the traditional natural science museum, with its collections for viewing, and the science museum that incorporated science and technology with participatory activities. Most science and technology institutions are not engaged in research but rather in the hands-on interpretation of science. The traditional natural science museum is deeply involved in research and the care of collections, and are storehouses for the world's natural treasures.

Many science museums had their beginnings in world fairs. The first major international exhibition of a world fair of science was the 1851 Crystal Palace Exhibition, sponsored by the Royal Society of Arts in London. A similar exhibition was held in New York City in 1853. The well-known Museum of Science and Industry in Chicago occupies the sole surviving building from the 1893 World's Columbian Exhibition. Moreover, the idea for the Field Museum of Natural History also developed along with the plans for the World's Columbian Exhibition. The participatory science movement in the United States began in the 1970s, and by the 1990s there were twenty-three major science and technology centers and some 260 smaller institutions. The first major science and technology museum that did not house any collections was the Exploratorium in San Francisco, which opened its doors in the early 1970s. Most science centers that have opened since that time have copied the Exploratorium's style of hands-on exhibits.

These museums are constantly seeking ways to involve visitors. Many have gone through major additions, such as the Saint Louis Science Center (1959), which, in addition to pre-Columbian North American Indian artifacts, has modern interactive exhibits. Discovery Place (1981) in Charlotte, North Carolina, has a living rain forest and in 1991 added an Omnimax theater and a large planetarium. Traditional planetariums, such as the Adler Planetarium (1930) in Chicago, have also added interactive science exhibits. The California Museum of Science and Industry (1880) in Los Angeles houses exhibits on aerospace and computer-aided design and manufacturing. The Oregon Museum of Science and Industry (1944) in Portland has exhibits on earthquakes, computers, and electricity.

BIBLIOGRAPHY

Conn, Steven. *Museums and American Intellectual Life, 1876–1926.* Chicago: University of Chicago Press, 1998.

Danilov, Victor J. *America's Science Museums.* New York: Greenwood Press, 1990.

Hein, Hilde S. *The Exploratorium: The Museum as Laboratory.* Washington, D.C.: Smithsonian Institution Press, 1990.

Macdonald, Sharon, ed. *The Politics of Display: Museums, Science, Culture.* London; New York: Routledge, 1998.

Orosz, Joel J. *Curators and Culture: The Museum Movement in America, 1740–1870.* Tuscaloosa: University of Alabama Press, 1990.

Freda H. Nicholson / A. E.

See also **American Association for the Advancement of Science; Museum of Science and Industry.**

SCIENTIFIC FRAUD. The term "scientific fraud" is used to describe intentional misrepresentation of the methods, procedures, or results of scientific research. Behavior characterized as scientific fraud includes fabrication, falsification, or plagiarism in proposing, performing, or reviewing scientific research, or in reporting research results. Scientific fraud is unethical and often illegal. When discovered and proven, fraud can end the scientific careers of researchers who engage in it. Nonetheless, the substantial financial and reputational rewards that can accrue to scientists who produce novel and important research or who obtain certain desired results have induced some scientists to engage in scientific fraud.

Policing of Scientific Fraud

Before 1980, only a handful of accusations of scientific fraud were ever proven. In 1981, however, following press reports of a "crime wave" of scientific fraud, the U.S. House of Representatives conducted the first-ever congressional hearings on the subject. These hearings revealed a wide gap in perception of the magnitude of the problem. Prominent scientists testified that fraud in science was rare; that individual allegations were best investigated on an ad hoc, case-by-case basis; and that government intrusion into the evaluation of scientific fraud would place bureaucrats in charge of declaring scientific truth. Prominent journalists and other critics, in contrast, testified that many cases of scientific fraud had likely gone undetected; that the scientific system of self-policing responded inadequately to fraud; and that the government's substantial financial investment in basic scientific research necessitated undertaking measures to ensure the integrity of the scientific enterprise.

Congress, siding with the critics, enacted the Health Research Extension Act of 1985. The Act required federally supported research institutions to develop internal procedures for handling allegations of scientific fraud, and also mandated the establishment of a new government agency to receive and respond to such allegations. That agency, the Office of Scientific Integrity, was established in 1989, and was renamed the Office of Research Integrity (ORI) in 1992. In 1993, the ORI became part of the U.S. Department of Health and Human Services (HHS). In 1999, the ORI ceased conducting its own fact-finding operations, instead ceding that role to the inspector general of HHS. ORI continues, however, to oversee all scientific fraud investigations. From 1994 to 2000, ORI processed 1,205 allegations of scientific misconduct, and sustained findings of scientific misconduct and/or took administrative action in ninety-five cases.

Fabrication of Data or Physical Evidence

There are several varieties of scientific fraud. Perhaps the most egregious incidents involve "fabrication" or "forgery," for example, situations in which researchers deliberately invent or falsify data, or report results of experiments that were never conducted.

A modern incident of "fabrication" arose in 1981, when Dr. John R. Darsee of Harvard Medical School reported the results of experiments in which dogs with induced myocardial infarction were said to have been injected with experimental heart disease medications. In 1982, however, two investigating committees determined that the reported experiments had never taken place. In a similar case, from 1973 to 1977, Dr. John Long of the Massachusetts General Hospital published several papers in which he claimed to have "subcultured" certain permanent lines of malignant tumor cells taken from patients with Hodgkins disease. In 1980–1981, Dr. Long confessed that these claims were fabricated, and that no such cell subcultures had ever been created.

Occasionally, scientists have gone beyond fabrication of data, and have actually fabricated physical evidence to bolster their fraudulent claims. One infamous example of such possible fakery was perpetrated between 1912 and 1915. Amateur archaeologist Charles Dawson discovered two skulls said to belong to primitive hominoid ancestors of man in the Piltdown quarry in Sussex, England. For decades, the "Piltdown man" was widely accepted by the international scientific community as the "missing link" between human and ape, with the noble brow of *Homo sapiens* and a primitive jaw. In the 1930s, however, the discoveries in Asia and Africa of other, incompatible hominid fossils cast doubt on the authenticity of the "Piltdown man" skulls. Finally, in 1953, an international congress of paleontologists, relying in part on modern dating technology, pronounced "Piltdown man" a hoax. To this day, however, the identity of the perpetrator(s), whether Dawson or others, remains disputed.

A more recent case involving fabrication of physical evidence involved medical research into skin grafting, a process that can enhance the safety of organ transplantation. During the period from 1967 to 1974, Dr. William A. Summerlin of New York's prestigious Sloan Kettering Institute reported that he had successfully transplanted skin from black mice to genetically distinct white ones. In 1974, however, under pressure from his colleagues, Dr. Summerlin confessed that he had used a black felt-tip pen to darken an area of graft that he had actually transplanted from one white mouse to another. Subsequently, a committee of Sloan Kettering researchers determined that Summerlin had also misrepresented the results of his earlier work on corneal transplantation from human cadavers to rabbits.

Misrepresentation of Experimental Results

More prevalent and more vexing than outright fabrication is the "fudging" or "massaging" of data, in which collected data or mathematical computations are manipulated modestly, so as to make the data appear to conform more closely with the researcher's conclusions. A related offense occurs when researchers "cook" or "finagle" data by reporting only part of their findings, while omitting to report data or experimental results that do not support their conclusions. In one famous example, data may have been "cooked" by Robert A. Millikan, the University of Chicago physicist who was awarded the Nobel Prize in 1923 for computing the charge of subatomic particles called electrons. Millikan's computations were based on data that he obtained by charting the movements of oil droplets across electrically charged brass plates. In the 1913 paper that led to his Nobel Prize, Millikan stated that his data "represented all the drops experimented upon." In

1978 and 1981, however, researchers reviewing Millikan's original unpublished notebooks discovered that Millikan had, in fact, failed to report data from 49 of the 140 oil drop observations that he performed, and that the apparent clarity and elegance of his computations were enhanced by the omissions.

By today's standards, omission of data that inexplicably conflicts with other data or with a scientist's proposed interpretation is considered scientific fraud. In Millikan's time, however, scientific measurement technologies were relatively crude, and scientists commonly exercised judgment concerning which of their observations were valid, and which were tainted by laboratory error. In this regard, Millikan's judgment appears in retrospect to have been sound; his exclusion of the forty-nine "bad" data points did indeed enhance the accuracy of his computations of an electron's charge. Millikan's case thus illustrates the inherent difficulty of drawing a line between scientific fraud on the one hand, and the exercise of creative judgment and the force of conviction that remain integral to scientific achievement on the other hand.

The "Baltimore Case"

The difficulty in drawing a line between scientific fraud and honest error was illustrated by a prominent controversy involving another Nobel Laureate, the virologist David Baltimore. In 1975, at age thirty-seven, Baltimore was awarded the Nobel Prize in Medicine for his discovery of retroviruses and their means of reproduction. A decade later, while affiliated with the Massachusetts Institute of Technology, Baltimore coauthored a paper that concluded that a mouse's immune system could be altered by injection of a special mouse gene—a finding that raised the possibility of genetic modification of the human immune system. The data analyzed in this paper were derived from laboratory experiments performed on mice by Dr. Thereza Imanishi-Kari, Baltimore's assistant.

In 1985, Dr. Margot O'Toole, a postdoctoral fellow working in Baltimore's laboratory, was assigned to perform additional experiments on mouse genes for a proposed follow-up paper. When O'Toole could not reproduce Imanishi-Kari's original results, however, O'Toole became convinced that Imanishi-Kari's results were "fudged." O'Toole's suspicions seemed to be confirmed when inspection of laboratory notebooks revealed certain discrepancies with the published results. After Baltimore and Imanishi-Kari stood by Imanishi-Kari's original results, O'Toole complained to an acquaintance, who in turn alerted authorities at the National Institutes of Health (NIH) that Imanishi-Kari might have committed scientific fraud.

O'Toole's allegations sparked further congressional hearings in 1989 and 1990, during which Baltimore vigorously defended Imanishi-Kari's integrity, and argued that the government investigation represented a threat to scientific inquiry. Although no one ever accused Baltimore himself of fudging any experimental data, many sci-

entists initially credited the allegations against Imanishi-Kari, who was declared guilty of scientific fraud by both the House Subcommittee on Oversight and Investigations and the Office of Scientific Integrity of the NIH (now the ORI). Tarred with complicity in an alleged cover-up, Baltimore was forced in 1991 to resign from his recently acquired position as president of Rockefeller University in New York City.

In 1996, however, an NIH appeals board wrote a 183-page opinion analyzing the Baltimore case in great detail. The board fully exonerated Imanishi-Kari of engaging in any misconduct, but noted that the research paper at issue had contained errors that Baltimore and Imanishi-Kari had subsequently acknowledged. With some exceptions, scientists generally were persuaded by the board's disposition, and came to view the government investigations of 1989–1991 as "scientific McCarthyism," spearheaded by reckless politicians who sought to obtain publicity as crusaders by humiliating leading members of the academic establishment. In 1997, Imanishi-Kari received a tenured faculty position at Tufts University, while Baltimore was appointed president of the California Institute of Technology.

BIBLIOGRAPHY

Broad, William, and Nicholas Wade. *Betrayers of the Truth*. New York: Simon and Schuster, 1982.

Kevles, Daniel J. *The Baltimore Case*. New York: Norton, 1998.

Kohn, Alexander. *False Prophets: Fraud and Error in Science and Medicine*. New York: Basil Blackwell, 1986.

Steinberg, Nisan A. "Regulation of Scientific Misconduct in Federally Funded Research." *Southern California Interdisciplinary Law Journal* 10, no. 1 (2000): 39–105.

United States Department of Health and Human Services, Office of Research Integrity. Home page at http://ori.dhhs.gov.

United States Office of Science and Technology Policy. "Federal Policy on Research Misconduct." *Federal Register 65*, no. 235 (Dec. 6, 2000): 76260–76264.

Kenneth Katkin

SCIENTIFIC INFORMATION RETRIEVAL

is generally meant to cover the entire problem of recovering from recorded scientific and engineering knowledge those particular pieces of information that may be required for particular purposes at particular times. In this context it usually includes a wide range of techniques and devices used to collect, index, store, retrieve, and disseminate specialized information resulting from scientific research and development. Scientific information may be text- or multimedia-based (for example, sound, video, or imagery combined with text). Scientific information retrieval systems are generally automated by computers and computer networks.

Vannevar Bush is a pioneer in the development of automated retrieval systems. In his seminal article, "As

We May Think," published in the July 1945 issue of the *Atlantic Monthly*, he proposed the ground-breaking concept of an easily accessible, individually configurable automated storehouse of knowledge, which would operate like the human brain. Bush's article inspired subsequent generations of information systems researchers, including Ted Nelson and Doug Engelbart. During the late 1950s Nelson researched methods by which computers could manipulate text. This research was dubbed "Xanadu," and in a 1965 paper on Xanadu he coined the term "hypertext," a method that allows computer users to retrieve information contained in separate text documents. Today, almost all documents found on the World Wide Web are hypertext. Engelbart's contribution to the field of information retrieval was the oN-Line System (NLS), which he developed in the 1960s at Stanford University. NLS was the first computer system to use a mouse. Engelbart invented the mouse so that users could point and click on hypertext links displayed on the system's computer screen. From the 1960s until the 1990s, computers could only store and retrieve information at individual research sites. Scientists had limited ability to access needed information stored on another computer at a different facility or from one at a separate location within the same facility. Overcoming the limits on scientists' ability to access all relevant information stored on computerized systems led Tim Berners-Lee to invent the World Wide Web. In the early 1980s Berners-Lee was hired as a computer consultant by the Swiss scientific research center European Organization for Nuclear Research (CERN). To help researchers access the center's vast store of information, he first invented the Enquire system, which used hypertext and was able to access documents stored in all of CERN's various information systems.

Berners-Lee wanted to expand the scope of Enquire's capabilities so it could retrieve information stored at other research facilities. He was aware of the Internet and how it was enabling universities throughout the world to exchange information in a limited way through text file transfers and electronic mail. By adapting the Enquire system for use on the Internet, Berners-Lee invented the World Wide Web, which has revolutionized more than just the field of scientific information retrieval.

The World Wide Web uses hypertext, hyperlinks, and the hypertext transfer protocol (HTTP) for retrieving information, and universal record locators (URLs) for uniquely identifying pieces of information. Its retrieval capabilities are enhanced by search engines that use key words and indexes for storing, identifying, and retrieving information.

The World Wide Web is very effective at delivering large amounts of information to its users. However, it is not so effective at retrieving specific information that users request. As of the early 2000s, Berners-Lee and other researchers at the World Wide Web Consortium, headquartered at the Massachusetts Institute of Technology, were trying to solve this problem by developing the Se-

mantic Web, which is an enhanced version of the World Wide Web. In the Semantic Web, a user submits a request for information to a search program called an intelligent agent. Semantic Web documents give the information contained in them a well-defined meaning from which the intelligent agent has the ability to determine the relevancy of the information to the user's request. Thus, the Semantic Web would be more efficient at retrieving the specific type of information a user may need.

BIBLIOGRAPHY

Berners-Lee, Tim, and Mark Fischetti. *Weaving the Web: The Original Design and Ultimate Destiny of the World Wide Web by Its Inventor.* San Francisco: Harper San Francisco, 1999.

Maybury, Mark T., ed. *Intelligent Multimedia Information Retrieval.* Cambridge, Mass.: MIT Press, 1997.

Sparck-Jones, Karen, and Peter Willets, eds. *Readings in Information Retrieval.* San Francisco: Morgan-Kaufman, 1997.

John Wyzalek

See also **Internet**.

SCIENTIFIC MANAGEMENT is a term coined in 1910 to describe the system of industrial management created and promoted by Frederick W. Taylor (1856–1915) and his followers. Though Taylor had used the term informally to describe his contributions to factory or "shop" management, Morris L. Cooke, a friend and professional associate, and Louis Brandeis, a prominent attorney, deliberately chose the adjective "scientific" to promote their contention that Taylor's methods were an alternative to railroad price increases in a rate case they were preparing for the Interstate Commerce Commission. The term also came to mean any system of organization that clearly spelled out the functions of individuals and groups. With even less fidelity to the original meaning, it has been used to describe any situation where jobs are subdivided and individuals perform repetitive tasks.

Origins

The nineteenth-century factory system was characterized by ad hoc organization, decentralized management, informal relations between employers and employees, and casually defined jobs and job assignments. By the end of the nineteenth century, however, increased competition, novel technologies, pressures from government and labor, and a growing consciousness of the potential of the factory had inspired a wide-ranging effort to improve organization and management. The focus of this activity was the introduction of carefully defined procedures and tasks. Historians have labeled these innovations "systematic management."

The central figure in this movement was the American engineer, inventor, and management theorist Frederick W. Taylor. Born in 1856 to an aristocratic Philadelphia family, Taylor started his career in the machine shop of the Midvale Steel Company in 1878, rose rapidly, and began to introduce novel methods. In the next decade he devised numerous organizational and technical innovations, including a method of timing workers with a stopwatch to calculate optimum times. After a brief career as the manager of a paper company, Taylor became a self-employed consultant, devoted to improving plant management.

During these years Taylor, an 1883 engineering graduate of the Stevens Institute of Technology, also became a major figure in the engineering profession, whose adherents sought an identity based on rigorous formal education, mutually accepted standards of behavior, and social responsibility. In factories, mines, and railroad yards, engineers rejected the experiential knowledge of the practitioner for scientific experimentation and analysis. They became the principal proponents of systematic management.

In the 1890s, Taylor became the most ambitious and vigorous proponent of systematic management. As a consultant he introduced accounting systems that permitted managers to use operating records with greater effectiveness, production systems that allowed managers to know more precisely what was happening on the shop floor, time studies to determine what workers were able to do, piece-rate systems to encourage employees to follow instructions, and many related measures. Between 1898 and 1901, as a consultant to the Bethlehem Iron Company (later Bethlehem Steel), Taylor introduced all of his systems and engaged in a vigorous plan of engineering research. This experience was the capstone of his creative career. Two developments were of special importance. His discovery of "high-speed steel," which improved the performance of metal cutting tools, assured his fame as an inventor, and his efforts to introduce systematic methods led to an integrated view of managerial innovation. By 1901, Taylor had fashioned scientific management from systematic management.

As the events of Taylor's career indicate, systematic management and scientific management were intimately related. They had common roots, attracted the same kinds of people, and had the same objectives. Their differences also stand out. Systematic management was diffuse and utilitarian, a number of isolated measures that did not add up to a larger whole. Scientific management added significant detail and a comprehensive view. In 1901, when he left Bethlehem, Taylor resolved to devote his time and ample fortune to promoting both. His first extensive report on his work, "Shop Management," published in 1903 in the journal of the American Society of Mechanical Engineers, portrayed an integrated complex of systematic management methods, supplemented by refinements and additions, such as time study.

The Diffusion of Scientific Management

After 1901, Taylor devoted his time to publicizing his work and attracting clients, whom he would refer to as trusted lieutenants, such as Henry L. Gantt, Carl G.

Barth, Morris L. Cooke, and Frank B. Gilbreth. Taylor and his followers emphasized the importance of introducing the entire system. Most manufacturers, however, only wanted solutions to specific problems. They were particularly drawn to time study and the incentive wage, seemingly the most novel features of Taylor's system, which they had hoped would raise output and wean employees from organized labor. Taylor and his followers had little sympathy for unions and were slow to realize the implications of this course. By 1910, the metal trade unions and the American Federation of Labor (AFL) had become outspoken enemies of scientific management and Taylor and his followers were embroiled in a controversy that would continue for another five years. These developments had a substantial influence on Taylor's efforts to publicize his work. To respond to opportunities like the 1911 rate case hearings, as well as the union attacks, Taylor (with Cooke's assistance) prepared a new account of his system that he called *The Principles of Scientific Management* (1911). He embraced the term "scientific management," made time study its centerpiece, and used it as a metaphor for the system as a whole. Taylor argued that he had discovered universal "principles" of management: the substitution of scientific for "rule-of-thumb" methods, the "scientific selection and training of the workmen," and an equal division of work between managers and workers. To implement the principles successfully, managers and workers had to undergo a "complete revolution in mental attitude."

The Principles of Scientific Management was an immediate success. Its simplicity, colorful anecdotes, and insistence that the details of factory management were applicable to other activities captured the imaginations of readers. Translated into many languages, it became the best-selling business book of the first half of the twentieth century.

Two additional developments greatly extended Taylor's influence in the following years. First, other writers restated his principles in more inclusive terms and explored their implications. The most notable example was Henri Fayol, a prominent French mine manager who discussed the functions of top executives in several technical papers and in *General and Industrial Administration* (1916). Though Fayol operated independently of Taylor, he demonstrated that Taylor's ideas applied to the entire organization, not just the factory. Second, a growing corps of consultants installed scientific management in industry. Gantt, Barth, Cooke, Gilbreth, and others closely associated with Taylor initially dominated this activity, but outsiders such as Harrington Emerson and Charles Bedaux, who took a more flexible and opportunistic approach to the application of Taylor's methods, became increasingly popular.

Scientific Management in Industry

Between 1901 and 1915, the year Taylor died, his close associates introduced scientific management in at least

181 American factories. Some of the plants were large and modern, like those of the Pullman Railcar and Remington Typewriter companies; others were small and technologically primitive. Most of the 181 companies fell into one of two broad categories: first were those whose activities required the movement of large quantities of materials between numerous work stations (such as textile mills, railroad repair shops, and automobile plants); the second group consisted of innovative firms, mostly small, that were already committed to managerial innovation. Executives at these latter firms were attracted to Taylor's promise of social harmony and improved working conditions.

The history of scientific management in these 181 plants provides little support for the contention, common to many later accounts, that Taylor's central concern was the individual employee. Consultants devoted most of their time and energies to machine operations, tools and materials, production schedules, routing plans, and record systems. In one-third of the factories, these activities generated such controversy that time and motion studies were never undertaken. In others, such as the Franklin automobile company and several textile mills, the installation consisted almost exclusively of improvements in production planning and scheduling. As a result, one-half or more of all employees were passive participants. They may have experienced fewer delays, used different tools, or worked for less powerful supervisors, but their own activities were unaffected. Taylor promised that those workers directly affected would receive higher wages and have less reason for conflict with their supervisors. Most assessments of these claims have concluded that Taylor promised more than he could deliver.

The experiences of the 181 firms suggest that union leaders and other critics also exaggerated the dangers of scientific management. One example was the argument that skilled workers would lose their autonomy and opportunities for creativity. In the relatively few cases where skilled workers were timed and placed on an incentive wage, they devoted more time to their specialties, while less-skilled employees took over other activities. Critics were on firmer ground when they argued that scientific management would lead to speedups, rate cuts, and the elimination of employees whose skills or motivation were below average. In theory, only the most inferior workers had to worry. But many employers were less scrupulous or less patient. They gave lip service to Taylor's idea of an interrelated whole, but looked to the employees for immediate results. The association of time study with rate cuts sparked a famous strike at Watertown Arsenal in 1911, and was the apparent cause of strikes at the Joseph and Feiss Company and at three American Locomotive Company plants. Outside the Taylor circle the problem was even more widespread.

In summary, the available data from these early examples suggest that (1) first-line supervisors lost much of their authority to higher-level managers and their staffs; (2) the proportion of the work day devoted to production increased as delays were eliminated; (3) fewer decisions depended on personal judgments, biases, and subjective evaluations; (4) individual jobs were more carefully defined and some workers exercised less discretion; (5) in most cases earnings rose, but there were enough exceptions to blur the effect; (6) the level of skill required in production did not change, though the most highly skilled employees, like foremen, lost some of their de facto managerial functions; (7) some unskilled jobs disappeared as improved scheduling and accounting reduced the need for laborers.

Though the initial impact of scientific management would have seemed surprisingly modest to a contemporary reader of *The Principles*, in retrospect it is clear that Taylor and his associates provided a forecast and a blueprint for changes that would occur in most large industrial organizations over the next quarter century.

After 1915, scientific management—usually features of scientific management rather than the Taylor system—spread rapidly in the United States. There were undoubtedly wide variations in practice and, in the work of Charles Bedaux and others like him, efforts to exploit time study and the incentive wage to achieve immediate cost reductions at the workers' expense. But the surviving evidence suggests substantial continuity between the early experiences, reviewed above, and those of the 1910s and 1920s. One ironic measure of this continuity was the alliance between organized labor and scientific management that emerged after Taylor's death. By the mid-1910s, union leaders, with considerable prodding from Taylor's more liberal followers like Morris Cooke—realized that they had more to gain than lose from scientific management. Experience had shown that supervisors, not workers, were the real targets of scientific management and that the structured relationships characteristic of scientifically managed plants were compatible with collective bargaining.

Conclusion

By the 1920s, self-conscious management, systematic planning, specialization of function, and highly structured, formal relationships between managers and workers had become the hallmarks of modern industry. These features of the twentieth-century factory system were the legacy of systematic management and especially of Taylor and his disciples, the most important contributors to the campaign for order and rationality in industry. In the process of reorganizing the factory they made scientific management a malleable symbol of the potential of modern organization for changing virtually every facet of contemporary life.

BIBLIOGRAPHY

Aitken, Hugh G. J. *Taylorism at Watertown Arsenal: Scientific Management in Action, 1908–1915.* Cambridge, Mass.: Harvard University Press, 1960. Case study of famous incident at the height of Taylor's career.

Kanigel, Robert. *The One Best Way: Frederick W. Taylor and the Enigma of Efficiency*. New York: Viking, 1997. A readable, comprehensive biography.

Nadworthy, Milton J. *Scientific Management and the Unions, 1900–1932*. Cambridge, Mass.: Harvard University Press, 1955. Traces the great controversy of Taylor's later years.

Nelson, Daniel. *Frederick W. Taylor and the Rise of Scientific Management*. Madison: University of Wisconsin Press, 1980. Taylor's career as a manager and a theorist.

———. *A Mental Revolution: Scientific Management since Taylor*. Columbus: Ohio State University Press, 1992. The evolution of scientific management after 1915.

Schachter, Hindy Lauer. *Frederick Taylor and the Public Administration Community: A Reevaluation*. Albany: State University of New York Press, 1989. Scientific management and government administration.

Taylor, Frederick W. *Scientific Management*. New York: Harper, 1947. A collection of Taylor's major publications.

Daniel Nelson

See also **Capitalism; Industrial Management; Industrial Revolution; Mass Production; Productivity, Concept of;** *and vol. 9:* **The Principles of Scientific Management.**

SCIENTIFIC SOCIETIES. *See* Learned Societies.

SCIENTOLOGY.

The religious movement known as Scientology originated in the United States with the 1950 publication of *Dianetics: The Modern Science of Mental Health*. The book's author, L. Ron Hubbard (1911–1986), was a popular science fiction writer who envisioned Dianetics as an alternative to traditional therapy. Like other human potential systems, Dianetics promised its followers both enhanced survival mechanisms and new modes of self-expression. Drawing heavily on modern psychology, Hubbard claimed that detailed memory records of past traumatic experiences, called Engrams, are the cause of irrational and aberrant behavior. Subjects could uncover and eliminate their Engrams to become Clear through a process of Auditing, overseen by a practitioner of Dianetics using a device called an E-meter.

The more explicitly religious dimensions of Scientology evolved from Dianetic theory, as Hubbard and his followers began to make wider claims about the nature and meaning of human life. Hubbard posited that in addition to a body and a mind, each person is also an immortal spiritual entity called a Thetan, which spans lifetimes and has the power to create the basic elements of existence: matter, energy, space, and time. With the help of Scientology, church members move along a path to spiritual enlightenment known as the Bridge to Total Freedom. The aim of this spiritual pilgrimage is to attain higher states of consciousness, marked by successive levels of Operating Thetan status.

Since its founding in Los Angeles in 1954, the Church of Scientology has grown steadily, enjoying a high profile

Scientology Celebrities. Adherents John Travolta, his wife, Kelly Preston (right), and Jenna Elfman are among the actors attending a Scientology gala in Hollywood, 5 August 2000. AP/WIDE WORLD PHOTOS/E. J. FLYNN

due to its appeal among well-known entertainers. Membership estimates range from fifty thousand to several million. The church operates in more than one hundred countries and maintains an elaborate and well-funded network of institutions dedicated to promoting religious practice, the training of practitioners, and moral and political reform. Scientology has tirelessly sought legal status as a religion and has consistently assumed an aggressive posture toward its critics.

BIBLIOGRAPHY

The Church of Scientology International. *Scientology: Theology and Practice of a Contemporary Religion*. Los Angeles, Calif.: Bridge Publications, 1998.

Jenkins, Philip. *Mystics and Messiahs: Cults and New Religions in American History*. New York: Oxford University Press, 2000.

Miller, Russell. *Bare-Faced Messiah: A Biography of L. Ron Hubbard*. London: Michael Joseph, 1987.

SCOPES TRIAL.

Since the American public witnessed the dramatic testimony of William Jennings Bryan in the blistering heat of Dayton, Tennessee, in the summer of 1925, the Scopes Trial has come to represent the controversy over the teaching of evolutionary theories and Darwinism in the American public schools. John Scopes, a local biology teacher, agreed to serve as a defendant in an American Civil Liberties Union test case of Tennessee's antievolutionary law. He was arrested for teaching evolution and held for a jury trial in July of 1925. The issue at stake—whether the state could proscribe the teaching of any science that appeared to contradict the

Bible—predated the trial and has remained a source of bitter controversy.

Since the publication of the *Origin of Species* in 1859 and the *Descent of Man* in 1871, Charles Darwin's concepts of an ancient Earth and a gradual development of new species have been seen as particularly threatening by some groups of Christians, particularly in the United States. Seen to deny the story of Genesis and bolster a materialist interpretation of the appearance of life on Earth, evolution has become, for some important Protestant religious sects, symbolic of growing social disorder, immorality, and the decline of traditional culture in modern America.

The Scopes Trial occurred as a result of the Tennessee legislature's passage of the Butler Act in March 1925. The law, designed to prevent the teaching of Darwinian evolution in the public schools, was not the first of its kind; Oklahoma had passed a similar statute in 1923, while several other states had considered doing so. This series of antievolutionary measures could be attributed in part to the activism of the former Populist leader, three-time presidential candidate, and former secretary of state William Jennings Bryan. After World War I Bryan had become a leader of the newly organized fundamentalist tendency in American Protestantism and a leading opponent of evolutionary theory, which he saw as an immoral science that had legitimated German ruthlessness during the war. Throughout the early 1920s he used his fame and rhetorical gifts to further the antievolutionary cause.

The forces that met and clashed in Dayton, Tennessee, were remarkably like those that have continued to debate the issue throughout the twentieth century. Both prosecution and defense decided to use the occasion to score larger points for their cause. Local prosecutors invited Bryan to join their case, while defense attorneys brought in the famed trial lawyer Clarence Darrow. A large group of reporters, as well as spectators from the local countryside, descended on the small town, and the proceedings were broadcast over WGN radio in Chicago.

The trial's most dramatic moment came when Bryan agreed to testify about the Biblical account of creation. In his testimony he revealed, to the consternation of many fundamentalists, his belief in the "day/age" theory, which interpreted the days referred to in the Biblical account of creation as metaphors for much larger ages. Bryan, the town of Dayton, and much of rural America were mocked in the urban press, led by the journalist H. L. Mencken, who attended the trial. But none of this mattered to the outcome of the proceedings, which established that Scopes had indeed broken the law. While the Tennessee Supreme Court overturned the conviction on appeal, it set aside the lower court's verdict on a technicality rather than on the merits of the case or the constitutionality of the law. The ACLU thus failed to establish the legal precedent against antievolutionary laws that it had sought.

The events of Dayton and the decline of efforts to outlaw evolution did not mean that evolution could be taught widely in American schools. In fact, after 1925 and well into the 1960s, most public school textbooks removed any mention of Darwin or evolution. Biblical literalists did not budge in their opposition to evolutionary science. But they did change their tactics. Rather than simply attacking evolution, they borrowed the language of science to present the Biblical story of creation in a new, more respectable guise. While this new "creation science" made no headway among established biologists and geologists, it proved convincing to many other Americans. With considerable public support, fundamentalists and creation scientists sought "equal time" to present their views in science classes. Focused first at a statewide and later at a local level, their agitation won temporary victories in the South, the Midwest, and California over the course of several decades. In 1987, however, a 7 to 2 ruling by the United States Supreme Court in *Edwards v. Aguillard* rejected the equal time proposal and judged mandatory creation science to be an unconstitutional intrusion of religion into public schools.

The Supreme Court's powerful and far-reaching opinion notwithstanding, creation science has continued to win approval from many Americans, while the teaching of evolution and its mechanisms has lagged in the public schools. For example, in 1999 the Kansas Board of Education, by a narrow majority, approved a new science curriculum that eliminated the required teaching of evolutionary theory. Although the ruling was rescinded in early 2001, it does not appear that threats to American science education will disappear anytime soon.

BIBLIOGRAPHY

Conkin, Paul K. *When All the Gods Trembled: Darwinism, Scopes and American Intellectuals.* Lanham, Md.: Rowman and Littlefield, 1998.

Eve, Raymond A., and Francis B. Harrold. *The Creationist Movement in Modern America.* Boston: Twayne Publishers, 1990.

Larson, Edward J. *Trial and Error: The American Controversy over Creation and Evolution.* New York: Oxford University Press, 1985.

Numbers, Ronald L. *The Creationists.* Berkeley: University of California Press, 1993.

Webb, George E. *The Evolution Controversy in America.* Lexington: University Press of Kentucky, 1994.

James B. Gilbert

See also **Creationism; Evolutionism; Fundamentalism; Science and Religion, Relations of.**

SCOTCH-IRISH, a term referring to a migrant group of Protestant settlers from Scotland to northern Ireland in the seventeenth century and their subsequent migration to the American colonies in the eighteenth century, is an Americanism, a term seldom heard in Ireland and the United Kingdom and seldom used by British historians. Although it was first used during the colonial period—alongside "Irish," "Ulster Irish," "Northern Irish," and "Irish Presbyterians"—to describe the Irish in America, it fell out of general use by the time of the early republic, only to be renewed after the mass migration of Irish Catholics to the United States (1846–1856) as a means of distinguishing Irish Americans in terms of religion, culture, and class.

From 1606 to the end of the seventeenth century, a large number of migrants, mostly from the lowlands of Scotland, settled in the province of Ulster, northern Ireland, where many of them became tenant farmers. Though the lands originated as a private venture for Scottish investors, James I placed them under royal authority, claiming the lands of the defeated Irish rebels for the crown in 1607 and backing the colonial scheme in a royal missive to the Scottish Privy Council in 1609. His aim was to pacify the Scottish borders, relieving the kingdom of "reivers" ("rustlers") and the dispossessed of the borderlands. What is more, he anticipated that the largely Presbyterian emigrants would provide a buffer zone against the Irish Catholics, to be God's bulldogs, as it were. His plan worked and the plantation flourished for much of the century. By 1620, as many as 50,000 lowland Scots had settled in the Ulster province, followed by another 50,000 by the beginning of the English civil wars (1640). Economic, religious, and political conditions in northern Ireland by the end of the century, however, brought the enterprise to a standstill, instigating yet another migration—this time to the New World.

The migration of the Scotch-Irish to the American colonies, sometimes called the "great migration" by American historians, took place approximately between the years 1717 and 1776 and was largely the result of high rents, low wages, and parliamentary regulation. Although small pockets of Scotch-Irish were already arriving in America during the seventeenth century, it was not until 1717, with the transplantation of 5,000 Ulstermen to Pennsylvania, that the "great migration" got underway, culminating in about 200,000 Scotch-Irishmen in America by the beginning of the Revolution. Most of them entered the colonies by way of Philadelphia and settled in the rolling hills of western Pennsylvania. Others moved to the backcountry of Maryland, Virginia, the Carolinas, and Georgia, where they built a buffer zone against the French and Indians as far north as western Pennsylvania and parts of New York. Smaller pockets also settled in New England and along the eastern seaboard, but their numbers were dwarfed by the migration en masse to the backcountry, where the Scotch-Irish became the dominant group and the vanguard of the frontier movement in the nineteenth century.

Culturally, the Scotch-Irish were known as independent frontiersmen who carried a rifle in one hand and the Bible in the other. As the councilman of Pittsburgh, Robert Garland, summarized their coming to America, "They were pioneers, frontiersmen, these Scotch-Irish: their general equipment consisted of a rifle, the Bible, and the Psalms of David." Most were Presbyterians, but some converted to other noncomformist religions, like Methodism and Baptism, and sided with the new side revival movements of the eighteenth and nineteenth centuries. As Presbyterians, the Scotch-Irish, though not with the same intensity as that of their puritan neighbors, promoted literacy and higher education—literacy, that is, in the sense of allowing one to read the scriptures, and higher education in the sense of supplying an educated ministry. Besides the dissenting academies, which were usually built in the back parts of America, the Scotch-Irish were involved in the founding of the colleges of New Jersey (now Princeton), Dickinson, Allegheny, and Hampden-Sydney, and the universities of Delaware, Pittsburgh, Pennsylvania, Virginia, and North Carolina. Their support of literacy and education, however, had its limits. As God's frontiersmen, they applauded virility and physical strength more profusely. "Honor in this society," as one historian described it, "meant a pride of manhood in masculine courage, physical strength, and warrior virtue" (Fischer, p. 690). Considering the long history of warfare in the borderlands of Scotland and Ireland, physical strength and manly courage were not simply a matter of honor, but a means of survival, which the Scotch-Irish transplanted to the borderlands of America during the colonial period and to the conquest of the West in the nineteenth century.

The significance of the Scotch-Irish in North America might be summarized by their numbers at the end of the "great migration." Comprising no less than 10 to 15 percent of the population in the United States by 1776, they became ardent supporters of the American Revolution and were the backbone of Washington's army. Perhaps their fierce independence and family histories of parliamentary regulation between the years 1665 and 1680—as well as the Woolens Act of 1699 and the religious test of 1704—heightened their anti-British sentiment. Whatever the case, the Scotch-Irish were ardent supporters of the revolutionary cause from the very beginning. As the historian George Bancroft summarized their support in the early years of the war, "the first voice publicly raised in America to dissolve all connection with Great Britain came, not from the Puritans of New England, nor from the Dutch of New York, nor from the cavaliers from Virginia, but from the Scotch-Irish Presbyterians."

Notable Americans of Scotch-Irish descent include the composer Stephen C. Foster, the financier and statesman Andrew W. Mellon, the frontiersman Davy Crockett, the inventors Robert Fulton, Samuel Morse, and Cyrus McCormack, and the writers Mark Twain, Edgar Allan Poe, and F. Scott Fitzgerald. Of the U.S. presidents, those who can claim some sort of Scotch-Irish lineage are James Monroe, Andrew Jackson, James Polk, James Buchanan, Andrew Johnson, Ulysses S. Grant, Chester Arthur, Grover Cleveland, Benjamin Harrison, William McKinley, Theodore Roosevelt, Woodrow Wilson, Harry Truman, Dwight Eisenhower, Richard Nixon, Jimmy Carter, George H. W. Bush, Bill Clinton, and George W. Bush. That is to say, about 47 percent of U.S. presidents were of Scotch-Irish descent, and of 216 years of the presidency, 113 of those years were occupied by a president of Scotch-Irish descent.

BIBLIOGRAPHY

Bailyn, Bernard. *The Peopling of British North America: An Introduction.* New York: Knopf, 1986.

———. *Voyagers to the West: A Passage in the Peopling of America on the Eve of the Revolution.* New York: Knopf, 1986.

Chepesiuk, Ronald. *The Scotch-Irish: From the North of Ireland to the Making of America.* Jefferson, N.C.: McFarland, 2000.

Fischer, David H. *Albion's Seed: Four British Folkways in America.* New York: Oxford University Press, 1989.

Garland, Robert. "The Scotch Irish in Western Pennsylvania," *Western Pennsylvania Historical Magazine* 6 (1923): 65–105.

Glasgow, Maude. *The Scotch-Irish in Northern Ireland and in the American Colonies.* New York: Putnam, 1936.

Green, E. R. R., ed. *Essays in Scotch-Irish History.* London: Routledge and Kegan Paul, 1969.

Jackson, Carlton. *A Social History of the Scotch-Irish.* Lanham, Md.: Madison Books, 1993.

Leyburn, James G. *The Scotch-Irish: A Social History.* Chapel Hill: University of North Carolina Press, 1962.

Montgomery, Eric. *The Scotch-Irish in America's History.* Belfast: Ulster-Scot Historical Society, 1965.

Michael A. Sletcher

SCOTTSBORO CASE.

On 25 March 1931 nine black teenagers, after having fought with some white youths on a freight train traveling through northern Alabama, were apprehended. Also on the train were two young white women who accused the black youths of rape. Within two weeks the accused were put on trial in Scottsboro, Alabama, and eight of the nine were convicted and sentenced to death for rape. The ninth was sentenced to life imprisonment. From 1931 to 1937, during a series of appeals and new trials, the case grew to an international cause célèbre as the International Labor Defense (ILD) and the Communist Party of the U.S.A. spearheaded efforts to free "the Scottsboro boys." In 1932 the U.S. Supreme Court concluded that the defendants had been denied adequate counsel *(Powell v. Alabama),* and the following year Alabama judge James Edwin Horton ordered a new trial because of insufficient evidence. In 1935 the Supreme Court again ruled in favor of the defendants by overturning the convictions on the grounds that Alabama had systematically excluded blacks from jury service *(Norris v. Alabama).*

But white public opinion in Alabama had solidified against the Scottsboro youths and their backers, and each successful appeal was followed by retrial and reconviction. Finally, in 1937, defense attorney Samuel Leibowitz and the nonpartisan Scottsboro Defense Committee arranged a compromise whereby four of the defendants were released and five were given sentences ranging from twenty

Scottsboro Defendant. Ozzie Powell, one of the nine "Scottsboro boys"—and the one whose name is on the 1932 U.S. Supreme Court decision *Powell v. Alabama,* setting aside the initial convictions because they were denied adequate counsel—sits in a courthouse in Decatur, Ala., in 1936. After testifying at a codefendant's retrial, Powell was shot in the head during a scuffle with a sheriff's deputy, leaving him with permanent brain damage. He was paroled in 1946. LIBRARY OF CONGRESS

years to life. Four of the five defendants serving prison sentences were released on parole from 1943 to 1950. The fifth escaped prison in 1948 and fled to Michigan. In 1966 Judge Horton revealed theretofore confidential information that conclusively proved the innocence of the nine defendants.

BIBLIOGRAPHY

Carter, Dan T. *Scottsboro: A Tragedy of the American South.* Rev. ed. Baton Rouge: Louisiana State University Press, 1979.

Goodman, James E. *Stories of Scottsboro.* New York: Pantheon Books, 1994.

Dan T. Carter/c. p.

See also **Alabama; Race Relations.**

SCOUTING ON THE PLAINS.

Early fur trappers and hunters in the West, such as Kit Carson and William F. ("Buffalo Bill") Cody, acquired a remarkable knowledge of the geography and Indian tribes of the country, fitting them to be scouts and guides in later military campaigns on the Plains. For all the skill of these frontiersmen, however, friendly Indian scouts proved essential to the army—from General George Armstrong Custer's march in the Washita campaign of 1868 to the Sitting Bull Sioux war of 1876–1877, and later in the Ghost Dance uprising of 1890–1891. In the Southwest, Indian scouts bore the brunt of many campaigns in the Geronimo wars of 1881–1883 and 1885–1886.

BIBLIOGRAPHY

Wooster, Robert A. *The Military and United States Indian Policy, 1865–1903.* New Haven, Conn.: Yale University Press, 1988.

Paul I. Wellman
Christopher Wells

See also **Frontier Defense; Ghost Dance.**

SCRABBLE® is a board game of interlocking word building. Invented by Alfred Mosher Butts, the game was originally called *Criss Cross Words*; however, Butts was unsuccessful in marketing the game. In 1948 James Brunot bought the right to produce the game and trademarked it with some minor adjustments under its new name, *Scrabble*. In 1952 demand for the game outgrew Brunot's production capacities seemingly overnight, and he licensed game manufacturer Selchow and Righter to produce *Scrabble*. Today *Scrabble* is second only to *Monopoly* as the best-selling American board game of all time. The National Scrabble Association, founded in 1978, organizes tournaments nationwide and had more than 19,000 members in 2000.

BIBLIOGRAPHY

Edley, Joe, and John D. Williams Jr. *Everything Scrabble.* New York: Pocket Books, 1994.

Fatsis, Stefan. *Word Freak: Heartbreak, Triumph, Genius, and Obsession in the World of Competitive Scrabble Players.* Boston: Houghton Mifflin, 2001.

Eli Moses Diner

See also **Toys and Games.**

SCULPTURE. *See* **Art: Sculpture.**

SCURVY, a deficiency disease caused by lack of vitamin C (ascorbic acid), was once the scourge of sailors on long voyages. It afflicted the crew of Sebastián Vizcaíno when he explored the coast of California (1602–1603), and it decimated the companions of California's first physician, Don Pedro Prat (1769). Scurvy continued to flourish even though the simple remedy for its control—plenty of fresh fruits and vegetables in one's diet—was well-known by the mid-seventeenth century. Scurvy ravaged the passengers who came to California by boat during the gold rush (1848–1853), and ship captains admitted to health officers that shipowners would not permit them to stop on the way to take fresh vegetables on board. The first person in the United States to describe night blindness (1842) as one of the symptoms of scurvy was Edward Coale, who noted that deck work had to be discontinued because so many men of the frigate *Columbia* could not see after sundown. Modern methods of food preservation and distribution coupled with improved eating habits have made a diet rich in vitamin C accessible to most people, and scurvy has ceased to be a major American public health problem.

BIBLIOGRAPHY

Hess, Alfred Fabian. *Scurvy, Past and Present.* Philadelphia: Lippincott, 1920. Reprint, New York: Academic Press, 1982.

Watt, J., E. J. Freeman, and W. F. Bynum. *Starving Sailors: The Influence of Nutrition upon Naval and Maritime History.* London: National Maritime Museum, 1981.

Victor Robinson / c. w.

See also **Exploration of America, Early; Food Preservation; Gold Rush, California.**

SEA OTTER TRADE. Europeans and Americans first ventured to the North Pacific coast of America in the late eighteenth century in pursuit of sea otter skins. As the Pacific counterpart to the Atlantic beaver trade, the sea otter trade led trappers into the North Pacific, where they established bases from the Aleutian Islands to Baja California. In China, sea otter furs were exchanged at good profit for prized Oriental goods.

Russia and Spain were the pioneer nations to engage in the sea otter trade. After Vitus Bering's expeditions in the early eighteenth century, *promyshlenniki* (fur traders) pushed eastward, and in 1784 they established the first permanent Russian settlement in America, on Kodiak Island. In the same year, Spain organized a sea otter trade between California and China. At the opening of the nineteenth century, American and Russian traders entered the California sea otter fields, where in the face of strong opposition they poached throughout the Spanish period. After 1821 the liberal commercial policy of independent Mexico stimulated the California sea otter trade, and many Americans became Mexican citizens to participate in the business. Between 1804 and 1807 it is estimated that almost 60,000 furs were taken by American vessels, while the period 1808–1812 yielded nearly 50,000.

The sea otter trade ended once hunting nearly exterminated the animals. In general, the fur areas were exhausted in the order they were opened. Kamchatka and the Aleutians were depleted by 1790, Kodiak by 1805, Sitka to Nootka Sound by 1820, and California by 1840. A treaty signed in 1910 by the United States, Great Britain, Russia, and Japan banned the hunting of sea otters. In the 1930s several sea otter colonies were discovered in the Aleutians and along the California coast, and by the mid-1970s the sea otter population numbered about 50,000.

BIBLIOGRAPHY

Buell, Robert Kingery. *Sea Otters and the China Trade.* New York: D. McKay, 1968.

Gibson, James R. *Otter Skins, Boston Ships, and China Goods: The Maritime Fur Trade of the Northwest Coast, 1785–1841.* Seattle: University of Washington Press, 1992.

Ogden, Adele. *The California Sea Otter Trade, 1784–1848.* Berkeley: University of California Press, 1941.

Adele Ogden / H. S.

See also **Alaska; Aleutian Islands; Fur Trade and Trapping.**

SEAL OF THE CONFEDERATE STATES OF AMERICA.

The seal of the Confederate States of America was the official embossed emblem of the Confederacy. On 30 April 1863, the Confederate congress commissioned the seal. It depicted Thomas Crawford's equestrian statue of George Washington in RICHMOND, Virginia, with the date 22 February 1862, Jefferson Davis's inauguration day, and the motto *Deo Vindice* ("God will vindicate"). Joseph Shepherd Wyon of London cut the seal in solid silver. It reached Richmond in September 1864, but the Confederate government never affixed it to any document. The seal disappeared during the evacuation of Richmond at the end of the CIVIL WAR, but it was recovered and is now displayed in Richmond's Museum of the Confederacy.

BIBLIOGRAPHY

Ballard, Michael B. *A Long Shadow: Jefferson Davis and the Final Days of the Confederacy.* Jackson: University Press of Mississippi, 1986.

Grimsley, Mark, and Brooks D. Simpson, eds. *The Collapse of the Confederacy.* Lincoln: University of Nebraska Press, 2001.

John C. Fitzpatrick / A. E.

See also **Confederate States of America.**

SEAL OF THE UNITED STATES.

The seal of the United States, or the Great Seal, is the official embossed emblem that validates a U.S. government document. On 4 July 1776, the CONTINENTAL CONGRESS appointed a committee to design the seal, but it took Congress six years more to obtain a satisfactory design. The obverse of the seal that was finally adopted is still in use; it depicts the American eagle, as Charles Thomson suggested, while the reverse displays a pyramid and the Eternal Eye of God (symbols of the FREEMASONS), as proposed by William Barton. The secretary of state keeps the seal and affixes it to such documents as foreign treaties and presidential proclamations.

Seal of the United States. The first publication of Charles Thomson's design was this engraving by James Trenchard in *The Columbian Magazine* of Philadelphia, September 1786. LIBRARY OF CONGRESS

BIBLIOGRAPHY

Jillson, Calvin C. *Congressional Dynamics: Structure, Coordination, and Choice in the First American Congress, 1774–1789.* Stanford, Calif.: Stanford University Press, 1994.

Schlenther, Boyd Stanley. *Charles Thomson: A Patriot's Pursuit.* Newark: University of Delaware Press; London: Associated University Presses, 1990.

John C. Fitzpatrick / A. E.

See also **E Pluribus Unum; Eagle, American; State, Department of.**

SEALING

was accepted for centuries as an accepted means of extracting wealth from the sea. Sealing in subarctic waters of the North Atlantic began in connection with whaling early in the seventeenth century and developed into a separate occupation late in the eighteenth century. The hunting of the small hair seals, which include the harp and hooded seals, became an important commercial activity in the late eighteenth and early nineteenth centuries. Nonetheless, their numbers, as a result of reckless exploitation, have steadily declined. The seals of Antarctic waters, mainly the southern elephant and South American fur seal, were nearly exterminated during the nineteenth century by hunters but began to recover when regulations were introduced in 1881. In 1972 twelve nations signed a treaty giving complete protection to some varieties of seals and restricting the killing of others.

American sealing interests have traditionally centered on the PRIBILOF ISLANDS of Saint Paul and Saint George in the Bering Sea. After EARTH DAY in 1970, however, U.S. citizens began to see sealing as cruel and unnecessary. Environmental groups that opposed sealing effectively used the media to gain support in the United States, where few people earned their livings from the pursuit. Sealing, nevertheless, had long been an important livelihood on the northeast and northwest coasts of North America, where Aleuts harvested adolescent male fur seals for the fashion industry. In 1984 the government discontinued the harvest when protests against sealing and the fur industry intensified.

The harvesting of harp seal pups on the other side of the American subcontinent also created a storm of protest. Young harp seals have beautiful, almost pure white coats that serve as excellent camouflage on ice floes against natural predators. Each spring, fishermen from Newfoundland seeking to supplement their meager incomes headed out to the ice floes to gather seal pelts, which involved clubbing the animal on the head and removing the skin. The killing spawned criticism from environmentalists, who noted that furs were luxury items and that continued harvesting of the young threatened the species. Television crews filmed the appalling scenes of slaughter. Although harvesting of young seals was a minor problem in the long list of environmental crises facing the global community, the undeniable appeal of baby mammals made it a headline issue that fueled the growth of the ENVIRONMENTAL MOVEMENT and the ANIMAL RIGHTS MOVEMENT.

BIBLIOGRAPHY

Busch, Briton Cooper. *The War against the Seals: A History of the North American Seal Fishery.* Kingston, Ontario, Canada: McGill-Queen's University Press, 1985.

Lavinge, D. M., and Kit M. Kovacs. *Harps and Hoods: Ice-breeding Seals of the Northwest Atlantic.* Waterloo, Ontario, Canada: University of Waterloo Press, 1988.

Pelly, David F. *Sacred Hunt: A Portrait of the Relationship between Seals and Inuit.* Vancouver: Greystone Books, 2001.

Joseph Schafer / A. E.

See also **Alaska; Aleut; Aleutian Islands; Tribes: Alaskan.**

SEALS. *See* **Special Forces.**

SEAMEN'S ACT (1915), also known as the Furuseth Act and as the La Follette Seaman's Act, designed to counteract fears for the safety of American sailors during the early years of World War I. In order to improve living and working conditions for the crews of vessels registered in the United States, it abolished imprisonment for desertion; reduced penalties for disobedience; regulated hours of work at sea and in port; fixed a minimum quality of rations; regulated the payment of wages; required a certain number of lifeboats; increased the fraction of able seamen on board; and required 75 percent of each ship department to understand the language spoken by the officers.

BIBLIOGRAPHY

Bunker, John. *Heroes in Dungarees: The Story of the American Merchant Marine in World War II.* Annapolis, Md.: Naval Institute Press, 1995.

Hobart S. Perry / A. R.

See also ***Lusitania,* Sinking of the; Merchant Marine; World War I.**

SEARCH AND SEIZURE, UNREASONABLE.
The Fourth Amendment to the CONSTITUTION OF THE UNITED STATES prohibits "unreasonable searches and seizures." To circumvent this prohibition, the government must obtain a warrant to search and possibly seize one's person or property. The Fourth Amendment demands that such a warrant must be based on the sworn or affirmed testimony of a law enforcement official, must be specific as to the place to be searched and the person or thing to be seized, and will not be issued "but upon probable cause."

These strong protections against intrusion by the federal government into personal space have their origins in the hated writs of assistance that had been issued by Great Britain beginning more than a hundred years before America declared its independence. These writs were broad, general search warrants that the British Crown used to discourage colonial smugglers who were trying to evade various tax and trade restrictions. According to leading patriots such as James Otis and Samuel Adams, these writs of assistance were one of the prime reasons that anti-British feelings proliferated in the colonies. After American independence, most American state constitutions incorporated some form of protection against unreasonable searches and seizures, and the First Congress in which the Bill of Rights was debated and the conventions that ratified those amendments easily agreed to include in the Constitution of the United States protections against unreasonable searches and seizures.

The meaning of the Fourth Amendment was rarely at issue in the first century after it was adopted. Beginning in the early twentieth century, however, the Supreme Court began to grapple with the questions of what constitutes an "unreasonable" search and seizure, and what is encompassed in the notion of "probable cause." It has also made various exceptions to the general rule requiring a warrant. The Court has held that there are other kinds of searches that, despite the absence of a warrant, are still reasonable under the terms of the Fourth Amendment.

One of these exceptions is a search during a valid arrest. If a police officer arrests someone without a warrant, incident to that arrest, the law enforcement officer may search that suspect for a variety of reasons, including the protection of the personal safety of the officer and to prevent the arrested suspect from getting rid of important evidence. These so-called "stop and frisk" cases, beginning with *Terry v. Ohio* (1968), ruled that police officers, even if they do not have adequate grounds to arrest the person in question, may conduct a limited search of a person's outer layers of clothing by "patting them down."

More generally, police may act quickly to see that justice is done. For example, law enforcement officials may conduct a search to prevent the possible loss of evidence, even if they have not yet arrested someone. In the 1973 case of *Cupp v. Murphy*, the Supreme Court allowed the warrantless testing of a dark substance under the fingernails of the estranged husband of a woman who had just been murdered. The Court reasoned that there was sufficient probable cause to outweigh the absence of a warrant. When law enforcement officials are in hot pursuit of a suspect, they also need not take the time to appear before a judge and obtain a warrant. The same generally holds true when police enter a home using a valid search warrant to look for a weapon used in a crime and during the search find illegal drugs in plain view. The drugs can be reasonably used as evidence because they were not hidden and therefore did not require an additional warrant.

A more difficult set of issues and cases relates to those who are not suspects in criminal activity but who find themselves subjected to unwanted searches. A recent example is random testing for illegal drugs. Since those tested for illegal drugs are often not criminal suspects, are such searches and seizures of one's bodily fluids by state or federal agencies a violation of the Fourth Amendment? The Supreme Court has ruled that in certain circumstances drug testing is permissible, such as in the case of railroad employees involved in accidents or breaches of safety regulations. In the 2002 case of *Board of Education of Independent School District No. 92 of Pottawatomie County v. Earls*, the Court also allowed testing in the case of students participating in extracurricular activities in public schools.

The most controversial aspect of searches and seizures occurs when clearly damning evidence is excluded from use against a suspect because it was illegally obtained. In the 1914 case of *Weeks v. United States*, the "exclusionary rule" was created, which barred the use by federal officials and federal courts of evidence gathered in violation of the Fourth Amendment. In the 1961 case of

Mapp v. Ohio, the Supreme Court, led by Chief Justice Earl W. Warren, issued the strong version of the exclusionary rule, which excludes the use of evidence obtained unconstitutionally by state and local governments. On occasion, the exclusionary rule has led to the release of guilty criminals. In the face of significant public opposition to the release of criminals on the basis of such "technicalities," the exclusionary rule has been weakened by the two subsequent, more conservative Courts, led by chief justices Warren E. Burger and William H. Rehnquist.

BIBLIOGRAPHY

Amar, Akhil Ree. *The Constitution and Criminal Procedure: First Principles.* New Haven, Conn.: Yale University Press, 1997.

Bacigal, Ronald. *Criminal Law and Procedure: An Introduction.* Clifton Park, N.Y.: OnWord Press, 2001.

Israel, Jerold H., Yale Kamisar, and Wayne LaFave. *Criminal Procedure and the Constitution: Leading Supreme Court Cases and Introductory Text.* St. Paul, Minn.: West Wadsworth, 2001.

Akiba J. Covitz
Esa Lianne Sferra
Meredith L. Stewart

See also **Bill of Rights in U.S. Constitution.**

SEARS ROEBUCK CATALOG.

In 1886, Richard W. Sears, a railroad agent in North Redwood, Minnesota, purchased an unclaimed shipment of watches, which he sold for a profit to other agents. He ordered more watches and, within a year, he expanded into jewelry, moving his fledgling business to Chicago. His company eventually grew into the largest retail business in the world.

Mail-order companies answered midwestern farmers' prayers for a chance to buy products at lower prices than those charged by small-town stores. Montgomery Ward had started a dry goods business in 1872 that began to publish a catalog and by 1888 had annual sales of $1.8 million. Sears hired Alvah C. Roebuck as a watchmaker in 1887, and the two became partners, officially becoming Sears, Roebuck and Company in 1893. Expanding into numerous fields of merchandise, they produced a general catalog in 1896 and attained sales in 1900 of over $11 million, surpassing Montgomery Ward.

Sears provided the advertising genius for the firm, designing a cover that proclaimed Sears "The Cheapest Supply House on Earth." The huge catalogs, over 500 pages, made extravagant claims for the performance and value of their products, particularly patent medicines. Sears would sometimes advertise products the company had not yet purchased.

Julius Rosenwald, a men's suit manufacturer, joined the firm in 1895, combining his manufacturing and organizational talents with Sears's promotional brilliance. Rosenwald reorganized the shipping department, attracting the attention of Henry Ford, who copied the Sears

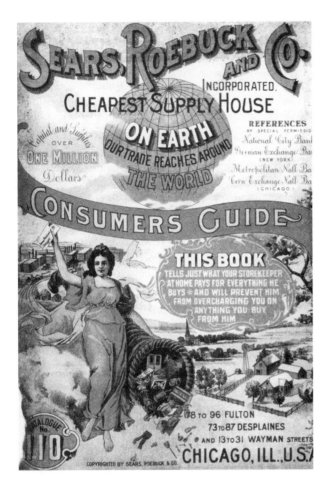

Sears Roebuck Catalog. Cover of an edition from c. 1910–20. ARCHIVE PHOTOS, INC.

BIBLIOGRAPHY

Hendrickson, Robert. *The Grand Emporiums: The Illustrated History of America's Great Department Stores.* New York: Stein and Day, 1980.

Hoge, Cecil C., Sr. *The First Hundred Years Are the Toughest: What We Can Learn from the Competition between Sears and Wards.* Berkeley, Calif.: Ten Speed Press, 1988.

Jerry Brisco

See also **Retailing Industry.**

SEARS TOWER was built in downtown Chicago as the headquarters of Sears, Roebuck & Co. It opened in 1974 as the world's tallest building, 1,474 feet, with 110 stories and 4.5 million square feet of office space. The building was designed by architects Skidmore, Owings & Merrill, and constructed in only thirty months. Engineer Fazlur Khan structured the building as nine square tubes of varying heights, bundled together to resist high winds. Most Sears operations were moved to a suburban location

Sears Tower. The world's tallest building when it opened in 1974 in Chicago, and still the tallest in the United States. AP/ WIDE WORLD PHOTOS

assembly line for his automobile plant. Rosenwald took over in 1910, continuing to grow the business while taking a more cautious advertising stance. He even phased out patent medicines in 1913.

The catalog displayed an incredible array of items, from groceries to cars and even prefabricated "house kits." As an example of the company's methods, when Sears sold houses, the company owned a lumber mill, a lumberyard, and a millwright plant. The house kit even included a kitchen sink. At its peak, the Sears catalog had 11 million customers, produced 75 million catalogs a year, and had annual sales over $250 million. It reached a record of 180,000 orders in one day.

As more and more people moved to the city, catalog sales started to decline in 1927. General Robert E. Wood, the new leader, quickly moved Sears into the retail store business, while trying to maintain the catalog business. In 1931 catalog sales took second place to retail store sales at Sears, and although the catalog continued for many years, it eventually became unprofitable. In 1993, after several years of losses, Sears closed the catalog operation, ending a unique chapter of American history.

in 1995. In 1998, Sears Tower was officially surpassed as the world's tallest building by the Petronas Towers in Kuala Lumpur, Malaysia.

BIBLIOGRAPHY

Pridmore, Jay. *Sears Tower: A Building Book from the Chicago Architecture Foundation.* San Francisco: Pomegranate, 2002.

Saliga, Pauline A., ed. *The Sky's the Limit: A Century of Chicago Skyscrapers.* New York: Rizzoli, 1990.

Dennis McClendon

SEATTLE, WASHINGTON (pop. 563,374; metropolitan area 3,275,847), the largest city and most prominent commercial center in the Pacific Northwest, lies on a narrow strip of land between PUGET SOUND and Lake Washington, framed by the Olympic and Cascade Mountains. Euro-Americans settled in the area in 1851 and encountered the Duwamish leader, Chief Sealth, for whom the city is named. Early business leaders exploited natural resources, including lumber and coal, and developed a successful shipping industry on Puget Sound and along the west coast. Seattle weathered an Indian war (1856), losing the transcontinental railroad to Tacoma (1873), anti-Chinese riots (1886), and a fire that destroyed the commercial district (1889). The arrival of the Great Northern Railroad terminus and the discovery of gold in the Klondike in the 1890s occasioned exceptional growth through the first decade of the twentieth century, as Seattle became the supply center for the Alaskan gold rush.

The struggle between the forces of social and civic order and those advocating a wide-open town tolerating some forms of vice dominated Seattle politics. However, by the 1920s, a strong middle class had gained ascendancy over the city's rough and tumble elements. A generation of public works, including street grading, land reclamation, sophisticated water and sewer system creation, parks

Seattle. This photograph by Asahel Curtis, c. 1910, shows the leveling of hills to facilitate the development of the city as a commercial center and seaport. LIBRARY OF CONGRESS

system development, sluicing Denny Hill, and culminating in the Lake Washington Ship Canal dedication in 1917, changed the physical face of the city. Early labor organizing and agitation, especially by the International Workers of the World, climaxed in the 1919 General Strike that shut down all but emergency services for five days.

Seattle pioneered municipal ownership of utilities and was a national leader in the development of public power. During and after World War II, the Boeing Company became a powerful economic force through its commercial and military airplane manufacturing. Seattle's economy, tied closely to Boeing's fortunes in the 1970s, diversified in the 1980s and 1990s into technology, biotechnology, banking, insurance, medical services, and tourism.

Seattle is home to the University of Washington, Seattle Pacific University, Seattle University, and a strong community college system. The city supports an array of professional sports franchises and cultural institutions including ballet, opera, symphony, and numerous theater companies. The natural beauty of the region sustains active outdoor recreation. Seattle's casual, middle-class lifestyle was rocked at the turn of the twenty-first century by the World Trade Organization and Mardi Gras riots, and the cancellation of millennium celebration in fear of a terrorist attack on the Space Needle, Seattle's most visible monument. The 2000 census revealed increased ethnic and racial diversity as minorities and foreign-born populations grew to comprise 30 percent of the city's residents.

BIBLIOGRAPHY

Berner, Richard C. *Seattle in the 20th Century.* 3 vols. Seattle: Charles Press, 1991–1999.

Buerge, David. *Seattle in the 1880s.* Seattle: Historical Society of Seattle and King County, 1986.

Morgan, Murray. *Skid Road: An Informal Portrait of Seattle.* Seattle: University of Washington Press, 1982.

Sale, Roger. *Seattle Past and Present.* Seattle: University of Washington Press, 1976.

Scott Cline

SECESSION in American history is best defined as the removal of a political entity from the federal Union. It is closely related to, but not synonymous with, NULLIFICATION; it can only be understood in contrast with Unionism.

The precedent for secession had, in the eyes of its advocates, been established with the American Revolution (1775–1783). Thus the possibility of secession from the federal Union was broached almost as soon as that union was formed. In 1790, faced with the economic threat of Alexander Hamilton's proposal for an assumption of debts, the Virginia legislature warned that it might be necessary at some future point to sunder ties. In 1798 and 1799 the Virginia and Kentucky resolutions (drafted anonymously by Thomas Jefferson and James Madison) proclaimed the rights of states to nullify federal legislation. This right was based on a "compact theory of union" that held that the union was simply an agreement between the sovereign communities of states. It indicated to many federalists that republicans were prepared to sever the union.

Yet it was the federalists themselves who first came to contemplate the possibility of secession. The greatest threat of secession prior to the Civil War (1861–1865) was made by New England federalists. Dismayed by the prospect of Jefferson's reelection, they secretly considered the possibility of withdrawing from the Union, only to be restrained by Alexander Hamilton in 1804. The federalists' fears had new focus with the War of 1812 (1812–1815). From the beginning, federalists considered it to be "Mr. Madison's War," created by the ineptitude of Republican administrations. With the British occupation of Nantucket, their annexation of Maine east of the Penobscot, and increasingly frequent raids on the New England coast, it seemed to federalists that there was no longer any protection that the federal government could offer states. This led to the Hartford Convention of December 1814, where measures were taken toward the formation of a "Dominion of New England." Secession was not immediately threatened but was intimated. News of peace arrived in Washington on the same day as a list of the Convention's ultimatums, ending New England's flirtation with secession.

Previous dalliances with the idea of secession were overwhelmed by the enormity of subsequent events. The South's long fight to preserve the slave system that its leaders saw as its cohering center, both economically and culturally, did not tend inevitably toward secession. That it did eventually has obscured the tortuous process by which secession came eventually to be seen by Southerners as their only possible relief from Northern domination.

Foremost in the fight to preserve slavery was John C. Calhoun. Yet while Calhoun was the theorist who revivified Madison's idea of nullification for use against tariff acts in 1828 and 1832, he was also staunchly against secession. As a member of Monroe's cabinet, he had pushed for national improvements such as canals and roads. Even when Calhoun no longer advocated federal power for such ends, he ran for president three times. He was not interested in seceding from the Union over which he hoped to one day preside.

Yet Calhoun found himself surrounded by critics of nullification. An aging Madison denounced Calhoun's philosophy and renounced the Virginia and Kentucky resolutions that he had drafted. He now claimed that they were only to be understood within the context of federal union. Thus, "nullification" could be nothing more than the appeal of a state to public opinion within the Union. The nullification that Calhoun proposed would only, Madison feared, lead to the dissolution of the Union. A small number of states could not seek to override the desires of the majority. Calhoun's theories could only give

The Hercules of the Union, Slaying the Great Dragon of Secession. This 1861 Currier and Ives lithograph shows Winfield Scott, general-in-chief of the U.S. Army at the start of the Civil War (he retired in November 1861), wielding the club of "Liberty and Union" against the Hydra of Confederate leaders such as President Jefferson Davis *(third from top).*
LIBRARY OF CONGRESS

comfort to those in the South seized by "madness," which drove them to look for "greater safety in disunion."

Those who did seek such comfort found no succor from Calhoun. Men such as Robert Barnwell Rhett and Jefferson Davis, who believed with varying degrees of firmness in the right of a state to secede from the Union, found Calhoun's doctrines of nullification to be both mystifying and useless. Nonetheless, he remained an unopposable force in Southern politics until his death in 1850. Unable to muster support across the South for nullification, Calhoun also prevented his more radical juniors from uttering threats of secession. What Southern union there was came only in response to the threats of Northern abolitionists.

With Calhoun's death, South Carolinian politicians once again planned to secede. In May of 1851, a conference of politicians met in Charleston to advocate secession as the only cure for abolitionist corruption from the North. Yet the conference failed; no other Southern state chose to follow South Carolina's lead. It was only the election of Abraham Lincoln that provided the initiative to override the proslavery Unionists in the South.

Secession has thus never had any cohering power inherent to itself at any point in American history. It required great external threats against a regional community to spur them toward secession from the federal Union. Since the carnage of the Civil War, no state or region has seriously contemplated secession.

BIBLIOGRAPHY

Banner, James M. Jr. *To the Hartford Convention: The Federalists and the Origins of Party Politics in Massachusetts, 1789–1815.* New York: Knopf, 1970.

Freehling, William W. *The Road to Disunion.* New York: Oxford University Press, 1990.

McDonald, Forrest. *States Rights and the Union: Imperium in Imperio, 1776–1876.* Lawrence: University Press of Kansas, 2000.

Albert Louis Zambone

See also **Antislavery; Federalist Party; South, the: The Antebellum South;** *and vol. 9:* **South Carolina Declaration of Causes of Secession.**

SECRET SERVICE. On 5 July 1865, the Secret Service was established as a division of the Department of the Treasury to combat the widespread counterfeiting of United States currency. At the time, a loosely organized monetary system contributed greatly to the instability of the nation's currency. State governments issued their own bank notes through private banks. During the early 1860s, more than 1,600 of these banks designed and printed their own bills. Efforts to adopt a national currency were also hampered by counterfeiters. The result was that during the Civil War, as much as one-third of American currency was counterfeit.

With the appointment of William P. Wood as its first chief, the Treasury Department's Secret Service used organized investigative efforts that produced a considerable impact in suppressing counterfeiting. The Secret Service also was asked to investigate other crimes that, in time, would be tasked to other government agencies. These included mail fraud, armed robberies, Ku Klux Klan activities, drug smuggling, naturalization scams, peonage cases, fraud involving land and oil reserves, and counterespionage during the Spanish-American War and World Wars I and II.

After President William McKinley was assassinated in 1901, presidential protection of Theodore Roosevelt became part of the Secret Service mission. In 1906, Congress passed legislation that officially delegated the Secret Service to provide Presidential protection. This was extended to the President-elect in 1913, and for members of the President's immediate family beginning in 1917. In that same year, Congress enacted legislation making it a

Secret Service. Agents, constantly on the alert, accompany the presidential motorcade.

crime to threaten the President by mail or by any other manner.

The Secret Service is now authorized to protect the president, vice president, president-elect, vice president-elect; the immediate families of these individuals; former presidents and their spouses (presidents taking office after 1996 receive protection for ten years following the end of their term); children of former presidents until age sixteen; visiting heads of foreign state or governments and their spouses; major presidential and vice presidential candidates; and other individuals as directed by the president.

The United States Secret Service Uniformed Division assists in the organization's protective mission. Its mission includes providing protection at the White House and surrounding buildings; numerous embassies and missions in the Washington, D.C., area; and the vice president's residence. This is accomplished through a series of fixed posts, vehicular and foot patrols, and specialized support units.

On 16 July 1951, Public Law 82-79 was passed making the Secret Service a permanent organization of the federal government. Until that time, the Secret Service existed without the benefit of a basic enabling act being passed by Congress. Prior to the passage of PL 82-79, the Secret Service's operational duties and responsibilities derived from annual appropriation acts.

The organization has expanded its role to investigate the dramatic rise in financial crimes. Other criminal activities that have fallen under the purview of the Secret Service include telecommunication fraud, computer crime, and fraudulent identification usage.

The effects of globalization combined with advances in communications, technology, and transportation have allowed such crimes to expand to new areas, both geographic and technological. Open economies, growing interdependence, and the instantaneous nature of financial transactions can all be exploited by criminals. The explosive growth of these crimes has resulted in the evolution of the Secret Service into an agency that is recognized worldwide for its expertise in the investigation of all types of financial and electronic crime.

Terry Samway

See also **Assassinations, Presidential; Counterfeiting.**

SECRET SOCIETIES

SECRET SOCIETIES are voluntary associations possessing arcane knowledge known only to their exclusive initiates. Alexis de Tocqueville got it wrong when he proclaimed that American society brooked no cabals or conspiracies. Benjamin Franklin's *Autobiography* (unfinished) first presented the concept of a network of secret cells used to influence public opinion.

Secret societies claim glamorous genealogies to enhance their sense of deep purpose. The Improved Order of Red Men (1834, Baltimore) traces itself to the Boston Tea Party. Rosicrucians, the Ancient Mystical Order Rosae Crucis, or AMORC (1915, New York City) claim a pedigree going back to Benjamin Franklin. The Cheyenne tribes of the Great Plains take their societies back to the mystical teachings of an orphaned boy named Sweet Medicine about 1000 B.C. Freemasons claim they go back to Solomon's temple.

Indigenous American tribes maintained secret societies. The men formed societies for warriors, religious societies, and hunting clubs. Women formed agrarian societies, often centered on the buffalo and corn, and crafts guilds. Both sexes joined mystery cults utilizing dreams and hallucinations. Initiates freely traveled from band to band and even between tribes for society meetings.

The importance of British freemasonry to American secret societies cannot be overemphasized. In 1730 Daniel Coxe became the first provincial grand master for New York, New Jersey, and Pennsylvania. Masonry grew to a national membership of two million men by 2000.

The golden age of fraternal and secret societies lasted until the 1960s. Several hundred societies existed during this period. The Independent Order of Odd Fellows, founded in Baltimore by Thomas Wildey in 1819, and the Knights of Pythias, founded in Washington, D.C., by Justus H. Rathbone in 1864, rivaled the Masons. Other "friendly" societies allowed only one nationality. They included the German Sons of Hermann (1852, New York City, by Dr. Philip Merkel), the Irish Ancient Order of Hibernians (1836, New York City), and the Hebrew B'nai B'rith (1843, New York City, by Henry Jones). In 1900 over 40 percent of all white males in America belonged to one or more of the freemasonry-based societies.

Those generally denied membership in these societies found others to join or created their own. Women joined the "Order of the Eastern Star" (1853, by Dr. Robert Morris) and the Order of Rebekah for female Odd Fellows (1851, Washington, D.C., by Schuyler Colfax). Prince Hall and fourteen other blacks in Boston received a freemason lodge charter from the Grand Lodge of England in 1784. E. A. Lightfoot, T. W. Stringer, and others founded the Knights of Phythias of North and South America, Europe, Asia, and Africa for blacks (1869, Philadelphia). The Reverend Michael J. McGivney and others incorporated the Roman Catholic Knights of Columbus (1882, New Haven, Connecticut). American-born Chinese began forming Tong (assembly hall) societies for mutual protection in San Francisco in 1874.

Popular twentieth-century fraternal orders stressed tangible benefits for members and civic benevolence rather than secrecy. Such societies as the Fraternal Order of Eagles (1898, Seattle, by John Cort), the Benevolent and Protective Order of the Elks (1868, New York, by Charles Vivian), and the Loyal Order of the Moose (1888) became immensely popular because they stressed family social events and public benevolence. In 2000 more than nine million people belonged to one or more American secret or fraternal societies worldwide.

BIBLIOGRAPHY

Mails, Thomas E. *Dog Soldiers, Bear Men, and Buffalo Women: A Study of the Societies and Cults of the Plains Indians.* Englewood Cliffs, N.J.: Prentice-Hall, 1973.

Stevens, Albert C. *The Cyclopedia of Fraternities.* 2d ed. Detroit, Mich.: Gale Research, 1966.

Whalen, William J. *Handbook of Secret Organizations.* Milwaukee, Wisc.: Bruce Publishing, 1966.

Bill Olbrich

See also **Fraternal and Service Organizations.**

SECTIONALISM

SECTIONALISM is identification with a geographic section of the United States and the cultural, social, economic, and political interests of that section. During the Revolutionary era, Americans already perceived that the thirteen colonies could be classed into three sectional categories: southern, middle, and New England. At the Constitutional Convention of 1787, Virginia's Edmund Randolph suggested a three-person executive for the United States with executive officers drawn from different sections of the nation. Gouverneur Morris expressed eastern fears of an emerging western section when he proposed a scheme for apportioning congressional seats that favored the eastern states over the new western commonwealths, thus ensuring eastern control of the nation's future. Neither Randolph nor Morris won approval for their proposals, and the convention's compromise over the enumeration of slaves for apportionment of congressional seats settled an incipient sectional clash between North and South. In the resulting Constitution of 1787, there was no formal recognition of sections. The Constitution conceived of the new nation as a federation of states, not sections.

Growth of Sectional Identities

During the early nineteenth century, sectional tensions mounted. New Englanders expressed increasing anxiety over the growing prominence of the western states and the policies of the Jefferson and Madison administrations regarding the Napoleonic conflict in Europe. Slow population growth owing to westward migration and an insecure economy dependent on international trade left New England vulnerable. In a pattern evident in future decades, perceptions of declining fortunes exacerbated sectionalism. Throughout American history, sectionalism seemed most significant in those sections that felt threatened, exploited, or oppressed. Sectionalism in the United States was primarily a defensive rather than an offensive stance. It was a raw nerve in the American identity; when irritated, it was felt sharply.

During the second quarter of the nineteenth century, the South grew increasingly insecure and defensive about its cultural and economic interests and, most notably, its "peculiar institution" of slavery. The rapid population growth and industrialization of the North seemed to doom the South to an inferior and vulnerable status in the nation. Moreover, northern gains increased the political leverage of abolitionists who were dedicated to eliminating the slave system of the South. Meanwhile, in the states west of the Appalachians, a sense of sectional identity was emerging as residents recognized their special economic needs. Westerners battled in Congress for aid in the construction of internal improvements and sought eastern money to advance their section's economic development. In the U.S. Senate, three great spokesmen personified the sectional clash and became sectional heroes. Daniel Webster was the proponent of the East, Henry Clay the idol of the West, and John C. Calhoun the statesman of the South. Each section rallied around its hero, yet until the 1850s periodic sectional crises produced compromises that patched the rifts in the union and held the nation together for a few more years.

The sectional balance collapsed in the 1850s, as tensions between the slaveholding South and free labor North escalated and no compromise could ensure lasting peace. Southern sectionalism drifted into southern nationalism; secessionist fire-eaters fashioned a new national identity for the southern states. The Kansas-Nebraska Act (1854), the Dred Scott Case (1857), and the Lecompton controversy (1857–1858) were each landmarks along the road to disunion; each pitted northerners against southerners over the issue of westward expansion of slavery, creating differences that some deemed irreconcilable.

Civil War and Reconstruction

The result was the Civil War, the nation's ultimate sectional drama. After four years of fighting, the North triumphed, forever squelching southern designs for a separate nation. The union was preserved, but southern sectionalism remained powerful. White southerners abandoned the struggle for independence, yet they did not repudiate their "lost cause." Instead, they canonized the Southern heroes of the Civil War and clung to memories of victory at Bull Run and in the Peninsula campaign while harboring resentment toward Northern generals such as William Tecumseh Sherman and their seemingly gratuitous acts of destruction. The South was defeated, but not mollified, and the resentment and romance arising from the Civil War fueled southern sectionalism in future decades.

Adding to the sectional resentment was the humiliation of Reconstruction. Northern military occupation of the South and rule by northern carpetbaggers and their black allies did little to bridge the sectional chasm between the North and white southerners. In the mind of white southerners, Reconstruction was proof that the North could not be trusted and the rebels of 1861 were correct: northerners seemed dedicated to oppressing and humiliating the South.

Following the withdrawal of federal troops from the South in 1877, sectional feelings did not diminish. For the following seventy-five years, the Republican party of Lincoln could make no substantial headway in the South, but remained a sectional party appealing only to the North and the West. The only political party with some following throughout the nation, the Democrats, remained in the minority for most of the period from 1861 to 1933. Thus the government of the nation was largely in the hands of leaders who could not win white southern support. The South remained an impoverished, conquered region in a nation dominated by the party of Abraham Lincoln and the Grand Army of the Republic.

Western Discontent and Populism

In the late nineteenth century, many westerners also grew increasingly resentful of their subordinate position within the nation. The silver mining states of the Rocky Mountain West joined with the Great Plains states in a sectional revolt against the perceived imperialism of eastern capitalists. Known as the Populist movement, this revolt of the late 1880s and 1890s expressed the resentment of miners and farmers who produced the raw materials vital to the nation's prosperity, but seemed to receive little in return. The supposed tyrants of New York's Wall Street were exploiting the economic colonies of the Great Plains and Rocky Mountain West, and the "colonists" were rising in yet another American revolution. These discontented westerners found their hero in the Nebraskan William Jennings Bryan. Securing both the Democratic and the Populist nominations for President in 1896, Bryan was able to combine unreconstructed white southerners and bitter westerners in an alliance that frightened eastern business leaders. In 1896 and in his later presidential bids of 1900 and 1908, however, Bryan was unable to win the support of a majority of the nation's voters. In the minds of discontented southerners and westerners, the East remained the nation's selfish master, a master that Bryan could not unseat.

As westerners rebelled, the nation's greatest historian of the West, Frederick Jackson Turner, was fashioning his views on sectionalism. In a series of essays written during the first three decades of the twentieth century and collected in *The Significance of Sections in American History* in 1932, Turner argued, "Our politics and society have been shaped by sectional complexity and interplay not unlike what goes on between European nations" (p. 50). Sectionalism was the preeminent factor explaining American history, and Turner conceived of the national government as "a League of Sections, comparable to a League of Nations" (p. 51). Moreover, he did not perceive a decline in sectionalism. "Statesmen in the future, as in the past, will achieve their leadership by voicing the interests and ideas of the sections which have shaped their leaders," he contended, "and they will exert their influence nationally by making combinations between sections" (p. 314). According to Turner, "Congressional legislation will be shaped by compromises and combinations, which will in effect be treaties between rival sections" (p. 314). In other words, the future, like the past would produce Clays, Calhouns, and Websters, sectional spokespersons who would achieve ascendancy through their ability to accommodate sectional interests and yet preserve the national union.

During the early twentieth century, however, the forces of sectionalism seemed less troublesome. The Populist revolt collapsed, and Americans rallied behind Theodore Roosevelt, a New Yorker who had once ranched in the Dakotas and projected the image of both eastern patrician and western cowboy. The North abdicated any responsibility for southern blacks, leaving white southerners in charge and avoiding a sectional clash over race. During the 1920s, a midwestern farm bloc in Congress expressed its section's resentment over the supposed mistreatment of farmers, but the farm bloc senators did not pose as formidable a threat as the fire-eaters or Populists of the past.

Cultural Regionalism

A cultural regionalism, however, was simmering during the 1920s, and in the 1930s it came to a boil. Following the stock market crash of 1929, southerners and midwesterners rose in revolt against the Northeast and its cultural dominion. Wall Street had long been a symbol of northeastern domination, and now this hated symbol was in disrepute as it seemingly dragged the nation into its worst economic crisis. Leading the revolt in the South were the Nashville agrarians, twelve Southern intellectuals who in 1930 issued their manifesto, *I'll Take My Stand*. Dedicated to maintaining the rural traditions and identity of the South, the twelve agreed that Southerners had to be on guard against the homogenizing influences of industrialization. In their statement of principles, the twelve affirmed "a Southern way of life against what may be called the American or prevailing way," and they summed up the distinction between the South and America as a whole in the phrase "Agrarian *versus* Industrial." One of the twelve, the poet John Crowe Ransom, described industrialism as "a foreign invasion of Southern soil, which is capable of doing more devastation than was wrought when Sherman marched to sea." Despite the rhetoric harkening back to earlier sectional strife, the twelve conceded: "Nobody now proposes for the South . . . an independent political destiny." But they questioned, "How far shall the South surrender its moral, social, and economic autonomy to the victorious principle of Union?"

Meanwhile, the social scientist Howard Odum was establishing the University of North Carolina as a center of regional studies, collecting data and publishing works on the South and its peculiar traditions and culture. This culminated in two large volumes by Odum: *Southern Regions of the United States*, published in 1936, and *American Regionalism: A Cultural-Historical Approach to National Integration*, coauthored with Harry Estill Moore, which appeared in 1938. The preferred term for the new focus on southern roots and culture was regionalism. But in his regionalist classic *The Attack on Leviathan*, Donald Davidson, one of the Nashville twelve, admitted that this was "really sectionalism under another name." "Sectionalism" was laden with too many negative connotations of violent conflict and hatred; "regionalism" seemed a more benign term that asserted southern cultural autonomy without raising political specters from the past. The Texas historian Walter Prescott Webb, however, was not squeamish about the term and unabashedly wrote of the persistent sectionalism in the United States and of the economic enslavement of the South and West by the North. With a strong sense of southern distinctiveness and a foreboding of change in the southern way of life, the regionalists south of the Mason-Dixon line were, in fact, raising once again the standard of sectionalism and asserting that the South was indeed different, a world apart from the industrialized North.

Regionalism, however, was not confined to the South. In the trans-Mississippi Midwest, some were celebrating their region's supposedly distinctive way of life. During the 1920s, *The Midland*, a literary journal based in Iowa, led a revolt against the dominance of the New York publishing world, urging young writers to remain in the Midwest, record the life of their region, and eschew the debilitating commercial influence of eastern publishers. In the 1930s, a triumvirate of midwestern artists, Grant Wood, Thomas Hart Benton, and John Steuart Curry, won fame for canvases that depicted the life and landscape of their native region. An outspoken statement of regionalism, Wood's manifesto "The Revolt Against the City," lauded those who escaped from the grip of the Europeanized East. At the Stone City Art Colony in Iowa, Wood and Curry created their works of art dressed in farmers' overalls. Their art was self-consciously midwestern, the creation of men in overalls working along the Wapsipin-icon River rather than on the banks of the Hudson.

Ironically, the federal government proved a formidable ally of the regionalists. Though Franklin Roosevelt's New Deal radically broadened the powers of the federal government, it also espoused the regional faith, paying artists across the country to paint post office murals with regional themes and writers to compile state guides that emphasized the art, the literature, and the folklore of each state. Grant Wood himself favored the creation of federally funded schools in the various sections of the country to teach artists to express their regional heritage and culture. The centralizing federal government was, then, deemed an instrument for making Americans aware that they were not only Americans, but, for example, southerners or midwesterners as well, with a regional baggage from the past that should not be jettisoned.

Economic Sectionalism

During the 1940s, 1950s, and 1960s, regionalism fell from favor. As the nation united to combat first fascism and then Communism and as millions abandoned the farm for the factory and office, the appeal of agrarian roots and regional folklore diminished. Whereas cultural regionalism attracted less attention, political and economic sectionalism heated up. The post–World War II clash over racial segregation pitted the North against a defensive South, and the southern crusade to lure northern industries embittered equally defensive northerners. New England sent Freedom Riders south of the Mason-Dixon line to dismantle the southern structure of racial separation; at the same time southern governors headed north on industry-hunting trips, dedicated to bagging Yankee factories for their perennially poor states. Southern politicians attacked northern interference in the South's race relations, and northern spokespersons deplored southern forays that damaged the economies of New York, Pennsylvania, Ohio, and Massachusetts. Meanwhile, a booming West was attracting people and business and challenging the traditional preeminence of the East. When baseball's New York Giants and Brooklyn Dodgers moved to the Pacific Coast in the late 1950s, it was a vivid reminder to the Northeast that it was losing ground.

By the 1970s, commentators were writing of the Sun Belt and Rust Belt, the former comprising the rising South and West and the latter composed of the declining Northeast and Midwest. In a reversal of fortunes, those sections that had traditionally complained of economic colonialism now enjoyed the advantage, whereas the Northeast and Midwest were losing assets. The Conference of Midwestern Governors issued statements deploring the concentration of federal defense spending in the South and West just as the governors' antebellum predecessors had complained of the national government's failure to invest in trans-Appalachian internal improvements. Bankrupt cities in the Northeast and Midwest likewise bewailed the lack of federal aid, and by the 1970s the once imperial financial capital of New York City seemed more in need of help than Mississippi or Montana.

Conclusion

Though sectional divisions had not disappeared, they commanded less attention from historians. Like his beloved Midwest, Frederick Jackson Turner had fallen from favor, and academic historians of the late twentieth century were more likely to focus on the divisions wrought by race, class, or gender rather than on sectional clashes or differences. In fact, as racial segregation disappeared from the South and both the South and West became wealthier and more urbanized, some observers noted a decline in sectionalism. Supposedly the mass media, and especially television, was creating an increasingly homogenized America. Residents of Georgia, Colorado, and New York all ate the same standardized cheeseburgers and fries at look-alike McDonald's and shopped at malls containing the same national chain stores selling the same wares.

Despite such superficial signs of homogeneity, the nation remained divided sectionally, and life in the Berkshires was not identical to that in the Ozarks, nor was Birmingham a clone of Boston. In the presidential elections of the 1990s and 2000, the nation divided sectionally with the South, the Great Plains, and the Rocky Mountain states lining up behind the Republican candidate and the Northeast and Pacific Coast opting for the Democrat. In fact, the sectional alliances in the election of 2000 were remarkably similar to those of 1900, with William Jennings Bryan country backing George W. Bush and William McKinley territory in the Al Gore column. The regions had reversed their partisan allegiances, but in 2000 as in 1900 the map of the United States was not a political checkerboard with Republican and Democratic states distributed in regular intervals across the nation. Instead, there were broad sections of Republican strength and of Democratic strength. There may have been some gender gap in politics, but there was a greater gap between New York and Nebraska, between Massachusetts and Mississippi.

At the close of the twentieth century, there was a "New South," with racially integrated institutions and more tailored suits and fewer overalls, but southern Baptism remained a powerful force, differentiating southerners from Yankees. Easterners still viewed the vast interior of the nation as flyover country, an expanse of corn inhabited largely by farmers. And many westerners still flocked to rodeos, resented federal control of their wide-open spaces, and regarded easterners as effete dudes. Sectional biases persisted, and most Americans still regarded themselves not only as belonging to the larger nation, but also as residents of a section—southerners, westerners, midwesterners, or easterners.

BIBLIOGRAPHY

Ayers, Edward L., Patricia Nelson Limerick, Stephen Nissenbaum, and Peter S. Onuf. *All Over the Map: Rethinking*

American Regions. Baltimore: Johns Hopkins University Press, 1996.

Cobb, James C. *The Selling of the South: The Southern Crusade for Industrial Development, 1936–1990.* 2d ed. Urbana: University of Illinois Press, 1993.

Davidson, Donald. *The Attack on Leviathan: Regionalism and Nationalism in the United States.* Chapel Hill: University of North Carolina Press, 1938.

Dorman, Robert L. *Revolt of the Provinces: The Regionalist Movement in America, 1920–1945.* Chapel Hill: University of North Carolina Press, 1993.

Fehrenbacher, Don Edward. *Sectional Crisis and Southern Constitutionalism.* Baton Rouge: Louisiana State University Press, 1995.

Hesseltine, William B. "Sectionalism and Regionalism in American History." *Journal of Southern History* 26 (1960): 25–34.

Sewell, Richard H. *The House Divided: Sectionalism and Civil War, 1848–1865.* Baltimore: Johns Hopkins University Press, 1988.

Sydnor, Charles S. *The Development of Southern Sectionalism, 1819–1848.* Baton Rouge: Louisiana State University Press, 1948.

Turner, Frederick Jackson. *The Significance of Sections in American History.* New York: Holt, 1932.

Twelve Southerners. *I'll Take My Stand: The South and the Agrarian Tradition.* New York: Harper, 1930.

Webb, Walter Prescott. *Divided We Stand: The Crisis of a Frontierless Democracy.* Rev. ed. Austin, Tex.: Acorn, 1944.

Jon C. Teaford

See also **Antislavery; Civil War; Compromise of 1850; Demography and Demographic Trends; Migrations, Internal; New England; Nullification; Reconstruction; Rust Belt; South, the; Sun Belt; West, American.**

SECULARIZATION. On 15 February 2000, the Kentucky Senate passed a bill on a 37 to 1 vote that instructed the state's board of education to prevent the "suppression and censorship" of "Christianity's influence on colonial America." As the bill's sponsor, the Republican state senator Albert Robinson, explained, secular squeamishness about religion, along with distorted demands for inclusiveness, had created a "terrible injustice" to "Christians and the Christian history of this nation." This legislative episode suggests what a battleground narratives about the religious history of the United States have become, and much of that conflict centers on the sorts of assumptions held dear by Robinson and most of his allies: namely, that the nation was in its beginnings a predominantly Christian land, but that over time the paired forces of secularization and pluralism slowly eroded the foundations of a Christian America. Questions about the wider secularization of American culture as well as questions about the historical drift from a Bible commonwealth to a pluralistic, post-Christian present became political footballs. As historical problems, they were hardly less contentious.

Part of what makes these questions so vexing for historians is a statistical puzzle presented by changing rates of religious adherence from the colonial period forward. According to most calculations, church membership at the time of the American Revolution hovered around a mere 15 percent of the population, suggesting a nation at best thinly Christianized at its birth. In the nineteenth century, adherence rates climbed steadily, growing to about 35 percent of the population at the time of the Civil War. That upward march continued throughout most of the twentieth century, with membership rates leveling off at around 60 percent by the 1970s and 1980s. Little evidence can be found in these statistical measures for either a solidly Christian founding or a gradual secularization of the culture. With these calculations in hand, many sociologists and historians are ready to bury both the conservative vision of a once Christian America and the liberal delight in the forward march of secularization. As story lines, both appear vestigial—the one a residue of nineteenth-century Protestant presumptions of empire and dominion, and the other a hangover from freethinking Enlightenment toasts to secular progress.

The continuing growth and vitality of religion in the United States shifted much of the attention away from accounts of secularization and placed the historical emphasis instead on the growing "Christianization" or (more generally) "sacralization" of the culture. Whereas, in the other industrial nations of the north Atlantic world, rates of church attendance and adherence have moved downward, often dramatically, the American case stands in direct opposition. Why, historians ask, has religion, particularly Christianity, proven so resilient and booming in the United States? What explains the upward climb of religious adherence, the movement from sparsely planted and weakly established churches in the colonial period to the vital, oversubscribed religious groups of the present? Why did secular worldviews that accented religion's eclipse, which had become commonplace among European intellectuals from Karl Marx and Auguste Comte to Max Weber, Emile Durkheim, and Sigmund Freud, make so little headway in American social and political life?

The most common answer hinges on an economic analogy to a free market. With the elimination of any established church through the First Amendment and through the gradual legal and cultural elaboration of that principle, religious groups were thrown into an open marketplace of sectarian competition and denominational rivalry. The loss of a monopoly, feared by many as a potential disaster for Christianity, proved instead a great boon, unleashing a voluntaristic ferment in religion unlike anything known in Europe. The free market combined with a heady dose of democratization to reverse the colonial fortunes of the churches and to chase away the specter of radical Enlightenment secularism. The Deist Thomas Paine's revolutionary proposal at the end of *The Age of Reason* (1794–1796) that every preacher become a philosopher and "every house of devotion a school of science" proved uncompetitive in the new religious marketplace that evangelical Protestants took by storm.

This free-market paradigm, as persuasive as it has proven to be, carries limits. First, there are various ways to challenge the statistics of ever-rising rates of religious adherence. At a basic level, some sociologists have argued that telephone polls estimating current levels of religious adherence and attendance are grossly inflated. When self-reporting, people claim levels of religious involvement that are not borne out by on-the-ground studies in church parking lots and sanctuaries. Also, being "churched" or "unchurched" could mean vastly different things from one period to another. The baseline of biblical literacy or doctrinal knowledge, for example, might well be much higher for both the affiliated and the unaffiliated at 1750 than at 1950. Gauging the gravity of devotional practices from one period to another—from prayers to sacraments to sermons to Bible reading—is much harder than calculating adherence rates.

When qualitative rather than quantitative concerns are made primary, the rates of religious adherence appear as something of a distraction from deeper, more thoroughgoing questions about the day-to-day realities of American religious life. From this angle of vision, the stories about secularization and de-Christianization remain highly relevant, particularly the ways in which secularizing, rationalistic, consumerist, and therapeutic values have transformed American Christianity from within. The Protestant theologian Reinhold Niebuhr put this matter in plain terms in a diary entry in 1921 about a "good toastmaster" who "pathetically described his pastor's successful ministry by explaining that under his leadership the congregation had 'doubled its membership, installed a new organ, built a parsonage, decorated the church and wiped out its debt.'" The minister's success was measured wholly in business terms, and it left Niebuhr wondering if he was only being "foolish" to worry over "these inevitable secularizations of religious values." To give another example, one could in 1900 still prepare for the high holy day of Easter by penitential fasting or even by carrying a large cross in a Holy Week procession. One was more likely, though, to prepare for it by shopping for just the right fashions to parade in after church. Religion, not least Christianity, flourished in the American marketplace, but it often came to carry a substantially different set of cultural values and secular associations within that milieu. Secularization might move forward under the cloak of religion itself.

On another point, would-be defenders of the secularization thesis appear to be on shakier ground, and that is on the question of "privatization." By this line of reasoning, the formal separation of church and state has effectively cut religion off from the public domain. It has been rendered a private, domestic matter of little consequence to social policy, state agencies, and learned public discourse. In this voluntaristic setting, people's religious commitments become their own personal concern with limited public consequence, and that privatization of faith is taken to be a potent measure of secularization. "My own mind is my own church," Thomas Paine had insisted, or "I am of a sect by myself, as far as I know," Thomas Jefferson had concluded. Religion was thus safely tucked away within the confines of the individual conscience. The assumptions about gender that often inform such privatizing discourses render them problematic: that is, the more religion is associated with the private, the more it is also associated with women and domesticity, and hence somehow the less significant it becomes. This kind of secularization argument—religion has become a private, domestic affair, and it has been diminished thereby—is, as the historian Ann Braude suggests, almost inevitably also a negative commentary on the feminization of religion in American culture. There is little evidence to sustain the claim that domestic religion, supported especially by women (as was the case throughout the nineteenth century), is religion in decline. The home, as a religious location all its own and as a springboard to moral reform, has proven one of the most enduringly vital religious sites in the culture.

The old stories about secularization continually advancing at religion's expense have proven unsatisfying in making sense of American history. Whether the story moves from Puritan to Yankee or from superstition to science or from Protestant producers to insatiable consumers or from Social Gospel reform to state welfare or from Bible college to research university, stories of secularization founder on religion's tenacity and malleability. At the same time, newer stories about Christianization and sacralization, about ever new heights of religious growth and free-market buoyancy, fall short as well. What counts as the religious and what counts as the secular keep crisscrossing and blurring, so that marking out their respective domains is at best an elusive enterprise: Is a Nativity scene surrounded by reindeer and candy-striped poles really a secular cultural symbol as the Supreme Court decided in *Lynch v. Donnelly* in 1984? Clean distinctions are hard to come by, and what abides instead is the shifting, negotiable relationship between things secular and things religious in American history and culture. Whether couched as a woeful tale of decline from the glories of a once-Christian America or as a hopeful story of liberal progress against theocracy, bigotry, and ignorance, the secularization thesis serves to tidy up American history. American religion and American secularism are too messy, intertwined, and recombinant for such orderliness.

BIBLIOGRAPHY

Braude, Ann. "Women's History Is American Religious History." In *Retelling U.S. Religious History*. Edited by Thomas A. Tweed. Berkeley: University of California Press, 1997.

Bruce, Steve, ed. *Religion and Modernization: Sociologists and Historians Debate the Secularization Thesis*. Oxford: Oxford University Press, 1992.

Finke, Roger, and Rodney Stark. *The Churching of America, 1776–1990: Winners and Losers in Our Religious Economy.* New Brunswick, N.J.: Rutgers University Press, 1992.

Hatch, Nathan O. *The Democratization of American Christianity.* New Haven, Conn.: Yale University Press, 1989.

Hollinger, David A. *Science, Jews, and Secular Culture: Studies in Mid-Twentieth-Century American Intellectual History.* Princeton, N.J.: Princeton University Press, 1996.

———. "The 'Secularization' Question and the United States in the Twentieth Century." *Church History: Studies in Christianity and Culture* 70, no. 1 (2001): 132–143.

McLeod, Hugh. *Secularisation in Western Europe, 1848–1914.* New York: St. Martin's Press, 2000.

Leigh E. Schmidt

See also **Christianity; Religion and Religious Affiliation; Science and Religion, Relations of.**

SEDITION ACTS. Two national sedition acts had been passed in the United States by the end of the twentieth century. The first, passed by the Federalist-dominated Congress of 1798, aimed to halt Republican attacks on the government and to ferret out pro-French sympathizers in case of war with France. Two complementary alien acts allowed the government to deport French and pro-French foreigners who were generally supporters of the Democratic-Republican Party. The second sedition act, passed during WORLD WAR I, targeted subversives, such as pacifists or "Bolsheviks," who interfered with the war effort.

The Sedition Act of 1798 reestablished the English common law on seditious libel, with some important changes. The new law accepted the idea of jury determination of sedition and also allowed truth to be considered in defense. But the Sedition Act did not clearly differentiate between malicious libel and political opinionation. The conviction of several newspaper editors and a Republican congressman confirmed fears that the law was being used to settle political scores. The act expired in 1801, before its constitutionality could be tested, and during President Thomas Jefferson's tenure in office, all persons convicted under the act were pardoned. In 1964 the SUPREME COURT flatly declared it inconsistent with the First Amendment in *New York Times v. Sullivan.*

The Sedition Act of 1918 made it a felony to interfere in the war effort; to insult the government, the Constitution, or the armed forces; or "by word or act [to] oppose the cause of the United States." This act departed from the 1798 measure in its emphasis on criticism of the government and its symbols. Justices Oliver Wendell Holmes and Louis D. Brandeis opposed the Sedition Act of 1918 in their dissenting opinions in *Abrams v. United States* (1919). The Sedition Act hastened the spread of wartime xenophobic hysteria, climaxing in the red scare and the PALMER RAIDS. The scare had run its course by the early 1920s, and the Sedition Act was repealed in 1921. Similar acts passed by the states resulted in litigation reaching the Supreme Court. The most notable decision in this area was *Gitlow v. New York* (1925), in which the Court began extending the strictures of the First Amendment to the states.

Although the Alien Registration Act of 1940, better known as the Smith Act, is not called a sedition act, it had that as a major purpose. Rather than forbidding criticism of government officers, the Smith Act prohibited advocacy of forceful overthrow of the government and made it a crime to belong to an organization subsequently found to advocate forceful removal of the government. Rarely used during WORLD WAR II, in the late 1940s the Smith Act became the main legal weapon in the government's battle against communists. In the late 1950s and 1960s, the Supreme Court blunted the Smith Act by raising the evidentiary standard for prosecutions brought under it. And in *Brandenburg v. Ohio* (1969) the Court dismantled the theoretical underpinning of seditious libel when it ruled that even the most extremist political speech, apart from political action, was protected under the First Amendment.

BIBLIOGRAPHY

De Conde, Alexander. *The Quasi-War: The Politics and Diplomacy of the Undeclared War with France, 1797–1801.* New York: Scribners, 1966.

Levy, Leonard W. *Legacy of Suppression.* Cambridge, Mass.: Belknap Press of Harvard University Press, 1960.

———. *Emergence of a Free Press.* New York: Oxford University Press, 1985.

Miller, John C. *Crisis in Freedom: The Alien and Sedition Acts.* Boston: Little, Brown, 1951.

Steele, Richard W. *Free Speech in the Good War.* New York: St. Martin's Press, 1999.

*Joseph A. Dowling/*A. R.

See also **Alien and Sedition Laws; Enemy Aliens in the World Wars; Federalist Party; First Amendment; France, Quasi-War with; Loyalty Oaths; Newspapers; Pacifism; Smith Act.**

SEGREGATION. The practice of segregating people by race and gender has taken two forms. De jure segregation is separation enforced by law, while de facto segregation occurs when widespread individual preferences, sometimes backed up with private pressure, lead to separation. De jure racial segregation was a practice designed to perpetuate racial subordination; de facto segregation of African Americans had similar effects, but sometimes could be defended as a result simply of private choice, itself an important American value. Separation of men and women occurred primarily in the workplace and in education. It contributed to the subordinate status of women, but less directly than racial segregation contributed to racial hierarchy.

Racial segregation as such was not a significant social practice before slavery was abolished because slavery itself was a system of subordination. Some northern states prohibited the immigration of free African Americans, reflecting the near-universal desire among whites to live apart from African Americans who would be socially and politically equal. In some northern cities, African Americans tended to live in neighborhoods that were racially identifiable, but de jure segregation was rare because it was unnecessary; there were few public programs of any sort that might be segregated, and de facto segregation produced the same results that de jure segregation would have. The city of Boston maintained a segregated school system from the beginning of the nineteenth century, and in 1845 the state supreme court found that doing so did not violate the state constitution's guarantee of equal liberty, but the state outlawed segregation in public schools in 1855. De facto segregation in railroads and steamboats was common. The practice of taking land from Indians and forcing them to live on reservations was a type of segregation enforced by law, although the U.S. Supreme Court's treatment of Indian tribes as semi-sovereign nations lent a certain theoretical sense to separating Indians and whites into different territories.

The Emergence of Southern Racial Segregation

Slavery's abolition meant that racial subordination could persist only with new kinds of support. Informal practices of racial segregation soon sprang up throughout the South, particularly in railroads and other places generally open to the public. In response, Congress enacted the Civil Rights Act of 1875, which made discrimination in places of public accommodation illegal. The Supreme Court held the act unconstitutional in the Civil Rights Cases (1883), concluding that the Fourteenth Amendment, which prohibited states from denying equal protection of the law, did not authorize Congress to adopt laws dealing with private discrimination.

After Reconstruction, whites sought to reinforce patterns of racial hierarchy. Many southern states adopted laws expressly requiring racial segregation in transportation, schools, and elsewhere. The Supreme Court upheld such laws in *Plessy v. Ferguson* (1896), arguing that the Fourteenth Amendment prohibited discrimination only in connection with civil and political rights but not in connection with social rights such as were involved in education and transportation. The Court's doctrine indicated that states could require racial segregation only if the facilities provided the races were actually equal, but no state took the requirement of equality seriously, and the segregated schools and railroad cars available to African Americans were, typically, substantially worse than those available to whites. The Supreme Court's approval of segregation spurred southern legislatures to extend the Jim Crow system much more substantially to include separate seating in courtrooms; separate water fountains from which to drink; separate Bibles for swearing oaths

in court; and separate swimming pools, parks, and golf courses.

De Jure Racial Segregation Declines, De Facto Racial Segregation Rises

African Americans continually mounted legal challenges to segregation, focusing at first on the inequality of facilities. Eventually, in *Brown v. Board of Education of Topeka* (1954), the Supreme Court became convinced that separate facilities could never be equal. As the social importance of de jure segregation declined with the repeal or invalidation of statutes specifically discriminating on the basis of race, the importance of de facto segregation increased. Migration of African Americans from the rural South to urban areas in the South and North led to significant increases in residential segregation, and—in a society where children went to their neighborhood schools—to de facto segregation in education.

Sometimes residential segregation was reinforced by law. In *Buchanan v. Warley* (1917), the Supreme Court held unconstitutional ordinances that effectively required residential segregation. In response, real estate agents and private developers began to include provisions, called restrictive covenants, in contracts for the purchase of housing that barred resale to purchasers of a race different from that of the homeowner. The Supreme Court eventually, in *Shelley v. Kraemer* (1948), held restrictive covenants unconstitutional, but not before patterns of residential segregation had become entrenched. National housing policy from the 1930s through the 1950s also reinforced residential segregation, as federal housing authorities required developers to include restrictive covenants and supported decisions by local housing authorities to segregate the buildings they owned. When combined with differences in the wealth of African Americans and whites, these policies helped create urban ghettos in which African Americans and, in some parts of the country, Hispanic Americans were concentrated.

Some antidiscrimination laws enacted in the 1960s provided the legal basis for challenging de facto segregation, but in general such attacks failed. Legislatures and courts regarded de facto segregation as resulting from private choices by people with different amounts of money to spend on housing, and therefore as less morally questionable than de jure segregation. The Supreme Court held that only de jure segregation violated the Constitution. By the early 1970s, Justice William O. Douglas, a liberal, and Justice Lewis F. Powell, a moderate conservative, urged their colleagues to abandon the distinction between de jure and de facto discrimination. The Court never did, however, in part because liberals were concerned that the courts could not successfully take on the challenge of eliminating de facto segregation, while conservatives were concerned that the courts would try to do so.

White Waiting Room. The police chief of McComb, Miss., looks at a sign aimed at passengers within the state, posted at the town's Greyhound Bus Depot, in 1961. AP/WIDE WORLD PHOTOS

Gender Segregation

Separation of men and women was also common. Often influenced by labor unions and early feminists, state legislatures adopted what were known as protective labor laws, barring women from particular occupations regarded as inappropriate for women, or restricting the hours women could work while leaving untouched employers' ability to contract with men for longer hours. In *Muller v. Oregon* (1908), the Supreme Court upheld a state law limiting the hours women could work, noting the extensive information about workplace safety submitted by public advocate Louis Brandeis. In *Goesaert v. Cleary* (1948), the Court upheld a law barring women from working as bartenders, except when their husbands owned the bars. Sincerely defended as being in the best interests of women who would become ill if they worked long hours, or morally degraded if they worked in certain occupations, the protective labor laws rested on assumptions about women's proper role that were part of a system of gender hierarchy.

The creation of separate educational institutions for girls and women had even more complex effects on the gender system. Women typically took different courses than men did, specializing in subjects that were thought particularly suitable for women who would be running households and caring for others, including children. Separate educational institutions, however, also provided women students a space within which they could develop free from competition with men, and their instructors gave women students models of intellectually engaged mature women whom the students could emulate.

The Civil Rights Act of 1964, banning workplace discrimination based on sex, led courts to invalidate protective labor laws and employer work rules that had the effect of creating different departments for men and women. The feminist movement of the mid-twentieth century discredited the assumptions on which protective legislation rested and began to undermine the assumptions that had justified separate educational institutions for girls and women. From the 1960s on, colleges that had been segregated by gender voluntarily abandoned the practice, leaving only a handful of private colleges that admitted only men or only women. In *United States v. Virginia* (1996), the Supreme Court held unconstitutional the exclusion of women from the Virginia Military Institute, one of the remaining state-run schools that did so—although the Court's opinion suggested that separate education for women might have more justification than did schools for men only.

Voluntary Segregation

In the 1990s, a minor flurry of interest arose in the creation of public schools for young African American men, which would have revived a form of de jure racial segregation. No such schools were created, largely because the nation's commitment against de jure racial segregation was so strong. Voluntary programs of racial separation, in the form of separate dormitories for African Americans at private colleges, had somewhat more support, and defenders of separate educational institutions for women and separate sports programs for men and women could be found even more easily. The different ways that de jure and de facto segregation contribute to creating racial and gender hierarchy seem to account for the stronger opposition to de jure than to de facto segregation, with de jure segregation expressing more clearly a social preference for hierarchy.

BIBLIOGRAPHY

Kerber, Linda. *No Constitutional Right to Be Ladies: Women and the Obligations of Citizenship.* New York: Hill and Wang, 1998.

Kousser, J. Morgan. "'The Supremacy of Equal Rights': The Struggle Against Racial Discrimination in Antebellum Massachusetts and the Foundations of the Fourteenth Amendment." *Northwestern University Law Review* 82 (Summer 1988): 941–1010.

Welke, Barbara Y. "When All the Women Were White, and All the Blacks Were Men: Gender, Class, Race and the Road to *Plessy*, 1855–1914." *Law and History Review* 13 (1995): 261–316.

Woodward, C. Vann. *The Strange Career of Jim Crow.* 3d rev. ed. New York: Oxford University Press, 1974.

Mark V. Tushnet

See also **Brown v. Board of Education of Topeka; Civil Rights and Liberties; Civil Rights Act of 1875; Civil Rights Act of 1964; Civil Rights Movement; Desegregation; Education, Higher: Women's Colleges;** *Muller v. Oregon; Plessy v. Ferguson;* **Schools, Resegregation of;** *and vol. 9:* **The Arrest of Rosa Parks; Pachucos in the Making.**

SELDEN PATENT, the first and most bitterly contested of all the automobile patents. The original application for a patent on a vehicle propelled by an internal combustion engine was filed in 1879 by George B. Selden of Rochester, New York, and issued in 1895. Rights to the patent shifted from the Pope Manufacturing Company to the Electric Vehicle Company, which in 1900 vigorously enforced its patent rights by filing suit against the Winton Motor Carriage Company. The case was abandoned when Winton and nine other companies formed the Association of Licensed Automobile Manufacturers and agreed to pay royalties.

Henry Ford refused to participate in the agreement, and in 1903 an infringement suit was filed against him. After eight years of litigation, Ford finally prevailed. The court of appeals, overturning a lower court judgment, ruled that although the Seldon patent was valid for two-cycle motors as per the design specifications of the original patent, it was not being infringed by Ford, whose vehicles used four-cycle engines.

BIBLIOGRAPHY

Doolittle, James Rood. *The Romance of the Automobile Industry.* Baltimore: Johns Hopkins University Press, 1984.

Richard W. Tupper / A. R.

See also **Automobile; Automobile Industry; Ford Motor Company; Patents and U.S. Patent Office.**

SELECTMEN were elected in town meetings to administer local government in many New England communities from the 1630s to the present. Specific responsibilities differed from one place to another and changed over time, but in general in the seventeenth and eighteenth centuries, selectmen were responsible for local licensing, the town watch, and poor relief. In less hospitable communities, this would also include "warning out" "sick, weary and hungry souls who tramped the roads into the town." Numbers of selectmen in a given town ranged from three to nine. They differ from modern town council members, in that New England's selectmen have always exercised executive as well as legislative responsibilities.

Selectmen are still alive and well in some New England communities. For example, during the 1990s, in the nation's wealthiest community, Greenwich, Connecticut, the town's selectmen (and women) have been on the job preventing outsiders from using town beaches. Employing complicated legal stratagems to evade the littoral rights of all Americans, they succeeded until 2001 in keeping undesired classes from their sea front.

BIBLIOGRAPHY

Nash, Gary B. *The Urban Crucible: The Northern Seaports and the Origins of the American Revolution.* Cambridge, Mass.: Harvard University Press, 1986.

Trattner, Walter I. *From Poor Law to Welfare State: A History of Social Welfare in America.* New York: Free Press, 1999.

Carl E. Prince

SELF-HELP MOVEMENT, the development of a philosophy and groups based on this philosophy whereby individuals who share like problems or situations work together to understand and/or improve their situations. The member-owned and -operated groups offer participants experiential knowledge, information, education, and emotional support. Leadership comes from the group's membership. These leaders are not paid, and membership is free or nominal. Groups may also provide material aid and/or social advocacy.

Historical Overview

The self-help movement began with the establishment of ALCOHOLICS ANONYMOUS in 1935. In terms of treating alcoholics, the group's accomplishments far exceeded those of the medical profession. Although the success of Alcoholics Anonymous was impressive, other groups did not develop in abundance until after World War II.

The civil rights movement in the 1960s introduced more people to the power of group initiatives. By the 1970s, people moved toward small-group efforts where individuals could work together in more intimate, immediate environments and on problems more specific to small groups. At the time, the government was also being challenged for its continually increasing public expenditures and its inefficiency. The response to this was a desire for less spending and more self-advocacy. Self-help groups filled the bill.

In 1976, self-help groups appeared to come into their own. Books such as *Support Systems and Mutual Help: Multidisciplinary Explorations*, edited by Gerald Caplan and Marie Killilea, and *The Strength in Us: Self-Help Groups in the Modern World*, edited by Alfred H. Katz and Eugene I. Bender, were published, and people became more aware of the value of the mutual support available to participants in self-help groups. This movement was not taking place only in the United States; the number of self-help groups was also expanding in western Europe and Japan.

By the 1980s, self-help clearinghouses had begun to pop up. They not only offered information as to how to locate appropriate groups but also provided information on how to begin a new group. Also during the 1980s, international networks of self-help support groups were created. An outgrowth of these groups was an international conference held in 1992 in Ottawa, Canada. From this meeting came a book of compiled papers including ones from eastern Europe, Japan, Israel, and Hong Kong.

In the 1990s, online self-help became an alternative avenue for support. Individual Web sites for both specific self-help groups and online clearinghouses were created for those seeking help and/or direction.

Attendance at self-help meetings remained strong into the twenty-first century. In the United States alone, over 25 million people had attended over 400 different types of self-help groups by the early 2000s. By that time, there were over 500,000 active self-help groups in the United States.

Positives and Negatives of Self-Help Groups

There are many reasons that self-help groups are so valuable to their participants. Most obviously the groups offer information and education about specific problems or situations and how to deal with them. Possibly the most valuable information offered is experiential. Here, members share how they have coped or are coping with their problems or situations. What the members often offer is a different perspective from what one might receive with professional help. Certainly, in many cases, more empathy is in evidence. A valuable addition to this is that, as information is shared, the sharers benefit as well, as they deepen their own personal understanding and commitment. In addition, as the members interact, new social bonds may form, allowing individuals to establish a new network of friends who have like problems or situations.

Another valuable component offered by many self-help groups is social advocacy. Through the group's efforts, members establish an avenue to spread understanding of their specific concern.

Online self-help groups offer their own sets of positives and negatives. On the positive side, they offer individuals who are housebound, such as agoraphobics (people who fear open or public places) and people with physical disabilities, an opportunity to participate in a group. Similarly, people with time constraints due to work schedules and/or child-care problems, as well as those who lack transportation, may have a difficult time attending a meeting in person, and online groups can offer these people the support they need—often on a twenty-four-hour-a-day basis—without their having to leave home. In addition, people with certain rare diseases or unusual problems who have difficulty pulling together enough people in a given area to attend a group meeting can cover a huge area online, making it easier to find enough people to establish a group. Another plus is that online self-help groups offer a certain degree of anonymity for those who are uncomfortable discussing their problems in a more public forum.

A negative is that online groups offer a somewhat less personal environment. In addition, another obvious drawback is that those without computers or who are not computer literate are not able to participate.

Areas of Support

Self-help groups offer help, support, and insight in a variety of areas. Mental health, one of the largest areas, includes groups that support those suffering with problems such as manic depression, anxiety disorders, phobias, and compulsive disorders. There are also groups offering support to family members of people with these kinds of problems. Illnesses such as diabetes, muscular sclerosis, cancer, AIDS, and chronic pain disorders are another large arena where many self-help groups are available. Problems of addiction such as alcohol, gambling, and narcotics are also dealt with well through the means of self-help groups.

Another large segment consists of weight management groups. These groups support people with problems such as obesity, compulsive overeating, bulimia, and anorexia. In addition, there are groups that deal with temporary emotional problems such as bereavement due to the loss of a loved one, divorce, or the stress that can result from a catastrophic event such as that which occurred on 11 September 2001. Another large category consists of groups in which the members have a common challenge in their lives with which they must deal. Examples of such groups include Parents without Partners, Mothers of Twins, and various women's, caregiver, and senior citizen support groups.

Numerous studies have been conducted to determine the value of various types of self-help groups. Consistently, studies have shown that these groups have been extremely helpful for the majority of those who commit to attend meetings and participate. Oftentimes, group members find far greater success with these groups than they do with professional care. Even in studies that have indicated equal success between the results of self-help group support and the care of a professional, it has been shown that there is still an advantage to taking the self-help route in that the cost is far less than that of professional care.

BIBLIOGRAPHY

"About Online Self-Help." Making Daughters Safe Again. Available at http://mdsasupport.homestead.com/why online-ns4.html.

Caplan, Gerald, and Marie Killilea, eds. *Support Systems and Mutual Help: Multidisciplinary Explorations.* New York: Grune and Stratton, 1976.

Katz, Alfred H., and Eugene I. Bender, eds. *The Strength in Us: Self-Help Groups in the Modern World.* New York: New Viewpoints, 1976.

Kyrouz, Elaina M., and Keith Humphreys. "Research on Self-Help/Mutual Aid Groups." Available at http://www.mentalhelp.net.

Oka, Tomofumi, and Thomasina Borkman. "The History, Concepts, and Theories of Self-Help Groups: From an International Perspective." Available at http://pweb.sophia.ac.jp/~t-oka/papers/2000/jjot.html.

Dawn Duquès

SELF-SERVICE STORES. *See* **Retailing Industry.**

SEMICONDUCTORS are solid materials with a level of electrical conductivity between that of insulators and conductors. Beginning with semiconducting elements found in nature, such as silicon or germanium, scientists learned to enhance and manipulate conductivity by changing the configuration of electrons in the material through the combination of materials and the precise introduction of impurities. Because of their ability to control electrical currents, semiconductors have been used in the manufacture of a wide range of electronic devices—including computers—that changed American life during the second half of the twentieth century.

Although the scientific study of semiconductors began in the nineteenth century, concentrated investigation of their use did not begin until the 1930s. The development of quantum physics during the first third of the twentieth century gave scientists the theoretical tools necessary to understand the behavior of atoms in solids, including semiconductors. But it was a commercial need that really stimulated semiconductor research in the United States. The rapid growth of the national telephone network had by 1930 made the replacement of mechanical switches—too large and too slow for the expanding system—highly desirable. Vacuum tubes, used in radios and other devices, were too expensive and fragile for use in the telephone network, so researchers turned their focus to solid crystals. Radar research during World War II, through efforts to make reliable and sensitive transmitters and receivers, advanced understanding of the relative merits of different crystal substances. Germanium and silicon showed the most promise. Scientists at Bell Laboratories, the research arm of the AT&T Corporation, built upon wartime investigations done there and elsewhere to design the first transistor using the semiconductor germanium. A prototype was produced in 1947, and innovation followed rapidly. William Shockley, Walter Brattain, and John Bardeen, all Bell Labs researchers, were awarded the 1956 Nobel Prize in physics for their research on semiconductors and the design of the transistor.

Transistors replaced vacuum tubes in electronic devices slowly at first. Hearing aids were the first technology to use the new, small transistors, but it was inexpensive portable radios that created the first large commercial market for the device. Initially manufactured by the Texas Instruments Company, the first large semiconductor company, "transistor" radios soon became a specialty of manufacturers in the Far East. Not limiting themselves to these consumer products and military signal devices, American researchers and manufacturers sought ways to use germanium-based transistors in computing machines. The more versatile silicon, however, ultimately replaced germanium to satisfy the needs of evolving computer technology.

The semiconductor silicon gave its name to a region—an area between San Jose and San Francisco, California, that became known as Silicon Valley—and fomented revolutions in technology, business, and culture. Silicon Valley grew outward from Palo Alto, home to Stanford University and host to a number of electronic pioneers beginning in the 1920s with the vacuum tube researcher Lee De Forest. Once scientists had determined that silicon had the necessary properties for applications in computing, practical concerns took center stage. Although silicon is one of the most common elements on earth—sand is made of silicon and oxygen—isolating and purifying it is notoriously difficult. But interest in silicon-based devices was very strong, and by the late 1950s a diversified semiconductor industry was developing, centered in California but serving government and commercial clients throughout the country.

The electronics industry initially turned to semiconducting materials to replace large, slow, electromechanical switches and fragile, unreliable vacuum tubes. But the new technology proved to be far more than an incremental improvement. Semiconductors showed promise for miniaturization and acceleration that previously seemed fanciful. An insatiable desire for faster, smaller devices became the driving force for the semiconductor industry.

An impressive stream of innovations in theory, design, and manufacturing led the semiconductor industry to make ever-smaller, ever-faster devices for the next half century. Improvements in semiconductor devices led to faster, cheaper electronics of all kinds, and to the spread of the semiconductor and its dependent industries throughout the world.

Although the semiconductor industry was born and developed in the United States, manufacturing of silicon-based devices—including the "memory chips" that are most essential to computer and other electronic technologies—began to move overseas in the 1970s. Japan was a particularly strong participant in the manufacture of high-quality chips. While American companies were eager to buy from Japanese manufacturers, American semiconductor manufacturers turned to the government for support and market intervention. Struggles in the industry continued throughout the 1970s and 1980s but the great expansion of the market for computers and continuing innovation kept semiconductor-based businesses flourishing both in the United States and abroad.

Silicon, the premier semiconductor, belongs among a small number of other substances that have changed the course of history. Unlike earlier, comparably influential materials—salt and gold, for example—mastering the use of silicon required an enormous amount of research. In fact, silicon is the most studied substance in history. Semiconductor science, and the industry it spawned, drew upon uniquely American elements in their development. Industrial research labs such as those at AT&T, IBM, and the entrepreneurial companies of Silicon Valley were vital to the development of the semiconductor industry, as was the government support of research during and after World War II. The military also influenced development as an important customer to the industry. The future will likely bring a replacement for silicon in the ongoing search for smaller, faster electronic devices, but silicon has earned a most valuable place in the history of technology and twentieth-century culture.

Bassett, Ross. *To the Digital Age: Research Labs, Startup Companies, and the Rise of MOS Technology.* Baltimore: Johns Hopkins University Press, 2002.

Misa, Thomas J. "Military Needs, Commercial Realities, and the Development of the Transistor." In *Military Enterprise and Technological Change: Perspectives on the American Experience.* Edited by Merritt Roe Smith. Cambridge, Mass.: MIT Press, 1987.

Queisser, Hans. *The Conquest of the Microchip.* Cambridge, Mass.: Harvard University Press, 1990.

Loren Butler Feffer

SEMINOLE. The Seminole tribe lives primarily in Oklahoma and Florida. They separated from the Creeks, migrating into northern Florida beginning in the early

Osceola. An 1838 lithograph made by George Catlin from his own portrait of the leader of those Seminoles who fought in the Second Seminole War, which continued for years after Osceola himself was captured and put in prison, where he died in 1838. LIBRARY OF CONGRESS

1700s and establishing full autonomy by 1800. The Seminoles spoke Muskogee and Hichiti, languages belonging to the Muskogean family. Their name derives from the Spanish word *cimarrón*, meaning "wild" or "runaway." The name "Seminole" originally designated only one group near Gainesville, but Europeans applied it to all Florida Indians by the late 1700s.

The earliest Seminole settlers came from the Lower Creek towns on the middle Chattahoochee River and included previously incorporated groups. From the 1770s, the Seminoles adopted escaped slaves, who lived in separate towns. Upper Creek refugees also joined the Seminoles following the Red Stick War (also called the Creek War) of 1813–1814.

The Seminoles organized their towns into chiefdoms—one around Tallahassee and Lake Miccosukee and one south of Gainesville—ruled by paramount chiefs. Around 1800, Creek towns in the forks of the Apalachicola River also formed a separate chiefdom, later assimilated into the Seminoles. These chiefdoms were known as the Talahassi or Mikkosuki, the Alachua or Seminole, and the Apalachicola.

Seminole, Florida Red Stick, and Lower Creek settlements on the Flint River engaged in mutual raiding with American border settlements from 1790 to 1818. General Andrew Jackson took advantage of this situation to invade Florida, destroying a few Indian and black towns and conquering the Spanish posts at St. Marks and Pensacola.

Spain ceded Florida to the United States through the Adams-Ónis Treaty (1819), bringing the Seminoles under American rule. The Treaty of Moultrie Creek (1823) relocated most Seminoles to a reservation in central Florida. A separate agreement allowed five chiefs to remain on the Apalachicola and lower Chattahoochee Rivers. Most western Seminoles moved in 1825 and a unified Seminole government formed at that time.

Under the Treaty of Payne's Landing (1832), the Seminoles agreed to consider emigration to Indian Territory, which is now Oklahoma. The Seminoles overwhelmingly rejected emigration, and mounting tensions culminated in the Second Seminole War (1835–1842). A few Seminoles voluntarily emigrated to Indian Territory in 1838, but most were sent west as prisoners of war. By the end of the war, 3,612 Seminoles lived in Indian Territory, while about 350 to 500 Seminoles remained in Florida.

The removed Seminoles reestablished their communities and their government, living as they had before. They relocated their settlements several times and experienced considerable hardships, as well as conflicts with the Creeks. Some Seminoles rejoined the Creeks, while others under Kowakochi (Wildcat) and John Horse (Gopher John) emigrated to northern Mexico in 1849.

The removed Seminoles signed a treaty with the Confederacy in August 1861, after the Union abandoned Indian Territory. Dissident leaders fled to Kansas and allied with the Union that autumn. Both Seminole factions fought in the Civil War (1861–1865) and the Seminole Nation was laid to waste. By the punitive Seminole Treaty of 1866, they relinquished their existing lands for a tract one-tenth the size purchased from the Creeks.

The Seminoles reestablished their lives on the new reservation and a written constitution was adopted in 1871. By 1880, the number of towns declined from 24 to 14 (including two black towns). Christian missionaries had opened schools and missions in 1848, but met little success during the nineteenth century.

In 1898, the Seminoles signed an agreement with the United States, dividing their lands among the 3,000 tribal members and formally dissolving the tribal government,

Seminole Braves. An early-twentieth-century photograph of a group posing in native garb. LIBRARY OF CONGRESS

although the latter operated administratively until 1915. The Seminoles became citizens of the United States in 1901 and six years later, became citizens of Oklahoma. Federal protections for allottees proved inadequate and the Seminoles lost 80 percent of their lands by 1920, retaining less than 10 percent at the end of the twentieth century. The tribal government was reestablished in 1935 and reorganized in 1970.

After allotment, earlier settlements broke up and many Seminoles left the area in the early twentieth century. Most Oklahoma Seminoles also converted to Christianity, primarily Baptist sects, and many ceased speaking their native language. About one quarter of Oklahoma Seminoles still follow the native religion and at least 20 percent speak Muskogee. As of 2002, Oklahoma Seminoles numbered almost 15,000, including over two thousand Freedmen or black Seminoles. Educational and income levels remain low and economic development projects have met little success, though the tribe's Class II gaming operations have generated considerable revenues since the late 1990s. The tribe also has a multimillion-dollar trust fund, from the land claims settlement for the loss of Florida.

After removal, the Florida Seminoles scattered to small settlements south of their former territory, generally avoiding Americans. Foraging became more important in their economy, owing to a lack of suitable farmlands. Since most chiefs were removed during the Second Seminole War, leadership shifted to the priests (*hilishaya*) and war leaders (*tastanaki*) and ritual unity and informal leadership by religious leaders replaced political unity and formal government.

Because American officials had little success removing the remaining Florida Seminoles, Executive Order 1379 (1911) created reservations at Brighton, Big Cypress, and Dania. Other Seminoles lived off-reservation along the Tamiami Trail (U.S. Highway 41) and south in the Everglades. The Seminole Tribe of Florida organized in 1957 and the Miccosukee Tribe of Florida incorporated separately in 1965. About 2,600 Seminoles and Miccosukees lived in Florida at the end of the twentieth century. Economic development on the Florida reservations generally has met little success, except for high-stakes bingo at the Hollywood (Dania) reservation, which has made the Florida Seminoles a successful gaming tribe.

BIBLIOGRAPHY

Fairbanks, Charles H. *Ethnohistorical Report on the Florida Indians.* New York: Garland Publishing, 1974.

Kersey, Harry A., Jr. *Pelts, Plumes, and Hides: White Traders among the Seminole Indians, 1870–1930.* Gainesville: University of Florida Press, 1975.

Mahon, John K. *History of the Second Seminole War, 1835–1842.* Gainesville: University of Florida Press, 1967.

McReynolds, Edwin C. *The Seminoles.* Norman: University of Oklahoma Press, 1957.

Richard A. Sattler

SEMINOLE TRIBE V. FLORIDA

SEMINOLE TRIBE V. FLORIDA 517 U.S. 44. In an attempt to overcome decades of chronic poverty and underemployment, American Indian communities began in the 1970s to exert forms of economic independence. Since Indian reservations are not subject to state and municipal jurisdictions, including state taxes and gaming prohibitions, many reservation communities established bingo and casino gaming facilities, often in the face of intense resistance by state and local governments. In 1988, Congress passed the Indian Gaming Regulatory Act (IGRA), which established the legal, or statutory, foundations for Indian gaming, including provisions for negotiated "compacts" between state and Indian governments. While many Indian casinos quickly attracted unprecedented capital, others languished. Increasingly, state and local governments resisted attempts by Indian nations to exert their economic sovereignty. In Florida, the state government refused the Seminoles' attempts to negotiate the required compacts as outlined by the IGRA. In 1991, the Seminoles sued the state of Florida for not complying with the IGRA. Reversing lower court rulings that denied the state's motion to dismiss, the Supreme Court ruled in *Seminole Tribe v. Florida* that the IGRA did not apply to "a State that does not consent to be sued." States, the court maintained, remained immune to prosecution under the IGRA. The ruling dealt a severe blow to Indian legal and economic sovereignty and reinforced some of the limited powers of state governments over Indian affairs.

BIBLIOGRAPHY

Mason, W. Dale. *Indian Gaming: Tribal Sovereignty and American Politics.* Norman: University of Oklahoma Press, 2000.

Ned Blackhawk

See also **Indian Reservations.**

SEMINOLE WARS.

SEMINOLE WARS. In the first decades of the nineteenth century, Seminole Indians in the Spanish colony of Florida faced numerous pressures. With the Spanish and then the French expelled from Louisiana, interior southeastern Indians no longer had European allies for protection or as markets for their goods. Everywhere, Americans were turning Indian lands into farms—particularly along the fertile rivers of the South, where cotton plantations mushroomed. Many Seminole communities increasingly incorporated runaway African American slaves into their societies, in which the escapees became productive community members. Meanwhile, as southern plantation owners became more militant, raids and counterraids across the U.S.–Florida border characterized Seminole–white relations.

In 1816, detachments of the U.S. Army began pursuing runaways into Florida, and in March 1818, General Andrew Jackson assumed control of nearly three thousand men in an invasion of Seminole Florida that began the First Seminole War. Focusing on several Seminole communities in northern Florida, Jackson marched southward, burning Seminole fields, villages, and houses. As Seminoles abandoned their settled communities and retreated into the interior, Jackson turned west, capturing St. Marks in April 1818 and Pensacola the following month. In 1819, Spain relinquished control of Florida to the United States, and when Florida became a territory of the United States in 1822, thousands of settlers rushed south to claim plantation lands. Jackson became the first governor of the Florida Territory.

Throughout the 1820s and into the 1830s, Florida officials attempted to pressure Seminole groups to leave their lands and move westward. The Seminoles, however, were required to leave behind their black community members, who were to become the slaves of whites. Refusing to leave their homelands and to break up their families—many runaway slaves had intermarried with Seminoles—Seminole leaders defied all attempts to force their removal. In 1835, as U.S. officials attempted a final drive to displace the Seminoles, a young warrior, Osceola, was arrested after failing to sign a removal treaty. After his arrest, Osceola killed a proremoval leader and called on his community members to join him in driving out white officials. This began the Second Seminole War.

From 1835 to 1842, Osceola and other Seminole leaders orchestrated guerrilla campaigns against U.S. Army stations throughout north-central Florida. Often overwhelming vastly superior forces, Seminoles became renowned for their military prowess and strategy. In the last week of 1835, Osceola led his forces to three stunning victories over the Americans, culminating in his triumph at Withlacoochee on 31 December, when the Seminoles dispersed a force of about 750 whites under General Duncan Clinch. Andrew Jackson, now president of the United States, appointed nine commanders before finally capturing Osceola, who died in captivity in 1838.

The Second Seminole War continued until 1842, when the U.S. government at last accepted the futility of its campaign. Although three thousand Seminoles were removed west to Indian Territory, with about a thousand left behind, the government lost just under fifteen hundred soldiers and spent nearly $40 million, including fighting the Third Seminole War in 1855. Although enduring recurrent infringements on their lands, the remaining Seminole groups created lasting communities in the Florida Everglades.

BIBLIOGRAPHY

Walton, George. *Fearless and Free: The Seminole Indian War, 1835–1842.* Indianapolis, Ind.: Bobbs-Merrill, 1977.

Weisman, Brent Richards. *Like Beads on a String: A Cultural History of the Seminole Indians in North Peninsular Florida.* Tuscaloosa: University of Alabama Press, 1989.

Ned Blackhawk

See also **Florida; Indian Policy, U.S.: 1775–1830, 1830–1900; Indian Removal; Indians and Slavery; Wars with Indian**

Nations: Early Nineteenth Century (1783–1840), Later Nineteenth Century (1840–1900).

SENATE. *See* **Congress, United States.**

SENECA FALLS CONVENTION was the first public gathering in the United States called explicitly for the purpose of debating the issue of women's rights. Meeting in Seneca Falls, New York, on 19–20 July 1848, a group of almost three hundred women and men passed a series of resolutions that protested against the moral, political, social, and legal status of women.

The American Revolution indirectly raised the question of women's rights by bringing the issues of equality and natural rights to the fore. In response, some Americans began to discuss the meaning of women's rights. However, their discussions occurred largely in private, and no organized, collective feminist movement emerged. Women remained largely invisible under the law, unable to vote, hold public office, or enjoy the same social or professional opportunities as men. In most states women were not even legally entitled to possess the wages they had earned.

Attitudes began to change in the early nineteenth century as women joined various social reform groups, such as temperance societies, anti-prostitution leagues, and antislavery organizations. The abolitionist movement, in particular, became a magnet for women committed to eradicating social evils. However, because women could not vote or hold office, they could advocate their position only through indirect means, such as petitioning, moral suasion, or by using their influence over male politicians. Over time women began to feel the limits of these constraints. They began to see analogies between the plight of slaves held in bondage and their own condition. Some of the more radical members of the antislavery organizations concluded that they must agitate for the rights of women along with the abolition of slavery.

The antislavery advocates Lucretia Mott and Elizabeth Cady Stanton were the prime movers behind the Seneca Falls Convention. During a casual visit by Mott at Stanton's home in Seneca Falls, the two shared their common frustration with the slow pace of progress for women. Deciding to act, they placed an advertisement in a local newspaper calling for a meeting on the subject of women's rights to be convened the very next week. In preparation, they met with other local women, including Mott's sister, Martha Wright, as well as Jane Hunt and Mary Ann McClintock, to draft the declarations, resolutions, and speeches that would be presented to the gathering.

On 19 July 1848 the convention convened in the Wesleyan Methodist Church to discuss women's rights. James Mott, Lucretia Mott's husband and a respected Quaker leader, chaired the session. The convention voted

Elizabeth Cady Stanton and Susan B. Anthony. The two most prominent figures in the nineteenth-century women's rights movement, which emerged in 1848 when Stanton *(seated)* and Lucretia Mott organized the Seneca Falls Convention. In 1851 Anthony joined the long struggle for woman's suffrage—but none of the three women lived to see it. LIBRARY OF CONGRESS

on a variety of measures, including the DECLARATION OF SENTIMENTS. Modeled on the Declaration of Independence, this document asserted women's equality with men and protested against the "long train of abuses" that "reduce [women] under absolute despotism." The convention unanimously passed a series of resolutions that challenged women's current status. They opposed women's exclusion from the rights of citizenship; rejected their second-class legal position; objected to the moral double standard; and inveighed against their inability to obtain the same educational and professional opportunities as men.

Stanton, however, proposed one resolution that aroused a great deal of controversy. She insisted that women be permitted to exercise "their sacred right to the elective franchise." Many participants, including Lucretia Mott, feared that this demand would be too radical and might alienate potential supporters. Ultimately the proposal did pass by a narrow margin. Sixty-eight women and thirty-two men signed the convention's final statement.

Seneca Falls represented the beginning of the country's first feminist movement. Subsequently throughout the 1840s and 1850s, conventions met all over the country to discuss the issue of women's rights. Yet not until 1920, with passage of the Nineteenth Amendment, did women gain the right to vote.

BIBLIOGRAPHY

Anderson, Bonnie S. *Joyous Greetings: The First International Women's Movement, 1830–1860.* Oxford, U.K., and New York: Oxford University Press, 2000.

DuBois, Ellen Carol. *Feminism and Suffrage: The Emergence of an Independent Women's Movement in America, 1848–1869.* Ithaca, N.Y.: Cornell University Press, 1978; reprint, 1999.

Isenberg, Nancy. *Sex and Citizenship in Antebellum America.* Chapel Hill: University of North Carolina Press, 1998.

Stanton, Elizabeth Cady, Susan B. Anthony, Ida Husted Harper, and Matilda Joslyn Gage, eds. *History of Woman Suffrage.* 6 vols. New York: Fowler and Wells, 1881. Reprint, Salem, N.H.: Ayer, 1985.

Rosemarie Zagarri

See also **Women's Rights Movement: The Nineteenth Century;** *and vol. 9:* **Seneca Falls Declaration of Rights and Sentiments.**

SENIORITY RIGHTS. Seniority establishes a clear and nondiscretionary system by which participating employers must implement layoffs, schedule vacation time, assign shifts, and promote employees. Normally, an employee accrues seniority commensurate with her tenure of employment with her current employer. Seniority may be conditioned on the employee's job performance, and is not transferable from one employer to another. Federal law provides that seniority continues to accrue while an employee takes up to five years of unpaid military leave.

Employment security was one of the early goals of labor unions. In the late nineteenth and early twentieth centuries, unions sought to prevent employers from replacing older, higher paid workers with younger, lower-paid ones. Seniority provisions are thus a hallmark of union collective bargaining agreements. However, many employers of nonunion workers also have adopted seniority systems, particularly for implementing layoffs. In 1934, the automobile industry introduced seniority in layoffs a few years before its workers became unionized.

In the late twentieth and early twenty-first centuries workers experienced relatively greater job turnover (both voluntary and involuntary) that made seniority rules less significant. Moreover, seniority systems sometimes conflicted with other societal goals, such as racial equality or disability rights. In 1979, the Supreme Court in *United Steelworkers of America v. Weber* permitted private sector employers to implement race-based affirmative action programs, which supersede seniority systems by promoting some minority employees ahead of more senior white employees. In 2002, however, the Supreme Court in *U.S.*

Airways Inc. v. Barnett held that employers need not supersede their seniority systems to accommodate disabled employees. Thus, a laborer who becomes disabled while working need not be given priority to obtain a sedentary "desk job" over a more senior non-disabled employee.

BIBLIOGRAPHY

Brody, David. "Workplace Contractualism." In *Industrial Democracy in America*, edited by Nelson Lichtenstein and Howell John Harris. New York: Cambridge University Press, 1993.

Linda Dynan

SEPARATION OF POWERS.   Separation of powers is a doctrine that is often believed to rest at the foundation of the U.S. Constitution. It holds that liberty is best preserved if the three functions of government—legislation, law enforcement, and adjudication—are in different hands. The modern idea of separation of powers is to be found in one of the most important eighteenth-century works on political science, the Baron de Montesquieu's *The Spirit of the Laws* (1748), which states that "There can be no liberty where the legislative and executive powers are united in the same person, or body of magistrates . . . [or] if the power of judging be not separated from the legislative and executive powers." In *Federalist No. 47* (1788) James Madison, commenting on Montesquieu's views and seeking to reconcile them with the Constitution's provisions, states that "The accumulation of all powers, legislative, executive, and judiciary, in the same hands, whether of one, a few, or many, and whether hereditary, selfappointed [sic], or elective, may justly be pronounced the very definition of tyranny."

In truth, however, the Constitution does not strictly adhere to the separation of powers, as the three branches of the government—Congress, the president, and the courts—have some overlap in their constitutionally assigned functions. Thus, although Congress is charged with legislation, a bill does not become law until the president affixes his signature, and the president may veto the legislation, which can be overridden only by a two-thirds vote of the House and Senate. Similarly, the courts came to be recognized to have the power of judicial review, pursuant to which they may declare laws or executive acts to exceed the authorization of the Constitution, and thus to be null and void. Congress is given the power to impeach and try executive and judicial branch officials for misconduct; if found guilty, they are removed from office. Presidential appointments to the judiciary or to the cabinet require the approval of a majority vote in the Senate; treaties negotiated by the president require a two-thirds Senate majority. These and other provisions are the famed "CHECKS AND BALANCES" within the Constitution, which are believed to prevent the exercise of arbitrary power by each of the branches.

Separation of Powers: Eighteenth- and Nineteenth-Century Issues

Nevertheless, whether or not the branches occasionally are involved in each other's assigned tasks, Montesquieu's idea that separation of powers should still be preserved whenever possible has been an important one throughout American history. In *Hayden's Case* (1792), for example, one of the earliest matters to be brought before the federal courts, the judges refused to perform the task a federal statute assigned them of reviewing applicants for Revolutionary War pensions. The reason was that their review was subject to overturning by the secretary of war, an executive branch official. The judges stated that to participate would be to compromise the independence of the judiciary. Similarly, in the early years of the Washington administration, the U.S. Supreme Court declined to announce advisory opinions because it felt its task should be limited to adjudication of actual cases.

Until about 1798 the federal courts decided cases based on the assumed existence of a federal common law of crimes, meaning that acts considered criminal in England would be considered so in the United States although no statute had been passed to prohibit them. Critics of this procedure argued that the American scheme of government required that the legislature first define a crime and affix a punishment before the courts could act. This matter became an important political issue in the period leading up to the presidential election of 1800, and the Supreme Court rejected the practice in *U.S. v. Hudson and Goodwin* (1812).

Separation of powers resurfaced from time to time in the nineteenth century as a cause of concern. It arose, for example, in the impeachment of President Andrew Johnson. Congress had passed, over the president's veto, the TENURE OF OFFICE ACT (1867), which prevented him from replacing cabinet officials before the Senate had confirmed their successors. Congress's aim was to ensure that Johnson was not able to replace officials whom Congress believed to be more committed to congressional policies than was the president himself. President Johnson fired his secretary of war in defiance of the statute, and was impeached by the House and brought for trial before the Senate. His defense was that the independence of the executive required that he have the power to fire as well as nominate executive branch officials, and his narrow acquittal on the impeachment charges at his Senate trial was generally seen as a vindication of the separation of powers principle.

Separation of Powers in the Twentieth Century

In the twentieth century, similar sporadic attention was paid to separation of powers. For example, when President Franklin D. Roosevelt sought legislative authorization for increasing the number of justices on the Supreme Court, he was accused of attempting to "pack the Court" in order to cobble together a majority of justices to end the Court's consistent pattern of rejecting key New Deal measures. The court-packing measure was never passed. One reason was the blistering criticism of the president for seeking to compromise the independence of the judiciary. Another was that the Supreme Court, probably taking the hint, reversed course on several key issues of constitutional interpretation. The principle of separation of powers was preserved in that the president's bill failed, although it was clear that the president had managed to change the course of Supreme Court adjudication. The Court itself sought to rein in executive authority on separation of powers grounds when in *Youngstown Sheet and Tube Co. v. Sawyer* (1952) it invalidated President Harry Truman's attempt to seize and operate the nation's steel mills without statutory authority.

In reaction to the growing military power wielded by the president in the late twentieth century and the tendency of the executive to involve the country's armed forces in foreign adventures, Congress passed the WAR POWERS ACT of 1973 as a means of subordinating the president to the constitutionally granted power of the Congress to declare war. Congress's concern with the exercise of executive power was also reflected in the passage, following the Watergate scandal, of the Independent Counsel Act of 1978, which created the Office of Independent Counsel to investigate executive misconduct and report on possible impeachable offenses to the Congress. Shortly after its passage, the law was challenged before the Supreme Court as a violation of separation of powers, on the grounds that the prosecutorial authority it created was, by definition, independent of the executive branch (to which branch the Constitution assigns the prosecutorial task) and that it involved members of the judiciary in the selection of the independent counsels. The act was upheld by a 7 to 1 vote of the Supreme Court in *Morrison v. Olson* (1988). Justice Antonin Scalia's lone dissent in that case (on separation of powers grounds) was belatedly recognized as prescient, following the operation of a brace of independent counsels appointed during the Clinton administration and the expenditure of many millions of dollars in investigations perceived as yielding few valuable results. When the Independent Counsel Act came up for renewal in 1999, and when even one of the most prominent independent counsels, Kenneth Starr, appeared before Congress to testify against it on separation of powers grounds, it was allowed to expire.

A final matter involving the separation of powers, and an important political issue in the late twentieth and early twenty-first century, was whether state and federal judges had, for most of preceding seven decades, been making rather than simply interpreting the law. Republican presidential candidates tended to run on platforms that were critical of the expansionist interpretations of the Warren and Burger courts and that obliged the nominees to rein in "judicial activism." When George W. Bush became president in 2001, his commitment to appoint judges in the mold of the Supreme Court's most conservative members, Justices Scalia and Clarence Thomas—justices publicly committed to altering much of the jurisprudence of the late twentieth century—raised separation of powers difficulties. The question of "judicial ideology" became the subject of congressional hearings, and none of the new president's nominees for the federal judiciary were confirmed for his first nine months in office. Republicans tended to argue—invoking separation of powers rhetoric in support of the president's position—that the Senate was now seeking wrongly to dictate what the judiciary should do in particular substantive areas of the law. Key Senate Democrats responded that they were simply seeking to fulfill their constitutional obligations to review judicial nominees in light of their fitness for office. Two centuries after the writing of the Constitution, then, the tension between the principle of separation of powers and its imperfect implementation in that document, a tension with which Madison sought to grapple in *Federalist No. 47*, had yet to be resolved.

BIBLIOGRAPHY

Fisher, Louis. *Constitutional Conflicts between Congress and the President.* Princeton, N.J.: Princeton University Press, 1985.

Kutler, Stanley I. *The Wars of Watergate: The Last Crisis of Richard Nixon.* New York: Knopf, 1990.

Marcus, Maeva. *Truman and the Steel Seizure Case: The Limits of Presidential Power.* New York: Columbia University Press, 1977.

Presser, Stephen B. *The Original Misunderstanding: The English, the Americans, and the Dialectic of Federalist Jurisprudence.* Durham, N.C.: Carolina Academic Press, 1991.

Vile, M. J. C. *Constitutionalism and the Separation of Powers.* Oxford: Clarendon Press, 1967.

Whittington, Keith E. *Constitutional Construction: Divided Powers and Constitutional Meaning.* Cambridge, Mass.: Harvard University Press, 1999.

Wolfe, Christopher. *The Rise of Modern Judicial Review: From Constitutional Interpretation to Judge-Made Law.* Rev. ed. Lanham, Md.: Rowman and Littlefield, 1994.

Wood, Gordon S. *The Creation of the American Republic, 1776–1787.* Chapel Hill: University of North Carolina Press, 1969.

Stephen B. Presser

See also **Constitution of the United States; Impeachment Trial of Andrew Johnson.**

SEPARATISTS, PURITAN. The Separatists, or Independents, were radical Puritans who, in the late sixteenth century, advocated a thorough reform within the Church of England. Dissatisfied with the slow pace of official reform, they set up churches outside the established order. Robert Browne gathered the first Separatist church at Norfolk, England, in 1581; later Separatists were dubbed "Brownists," but the groups did not constitute an organized movement. In the main Separatists proposed a congregational or independent form of church polity, wherein each church was to be autonomous, founded upon a formal covenant, electing its own officers, and restricting the membership to "visible saints." In England during the 1640s, the minority wing of the Puritan party maintained CONGREGATIONALISM against the majority in the Westminster Assembly and the Parliament, and were known as Independents, but the multitude of sects that arose out of the disorders of the time also took unto themselves the title of Independents, so that the term came to be a vague designation for opponents of PRESBYTERIANISM. Orthodox New England Puritans, although practicing a congregational discipline, always denied that they were either Separatists or Independents.

BIBLIOGRAPHY

Cooper, James F. *Tenacious of their Liberties: The Congregationalists in Colonial Massachusetts.* New York: Oxford University Press, 1999.

Miller, Perry. *Orthodoxy in Massachusetts, 1630–1650.* Boston: Beacon Press. 1959.

Perry Miller / A. R.

See also **Brownists; Church of England in the Colonies; Puritans and Puritanism.**

SEQUOIA, a genus of coniferous trees, comprising the species *Sequoia sempervirens* (the redwood) and *Sequoiadendron giganteum* (the giant sequoia), thought to be named for Sequoyah, the Cherokee Indian blacksmith and silversmith who invented the Cherokee alphabet about 1809. Both species average 275 feet in height, with trunks from 15 to 35 feet in diameter. Sequoias are the largest of all American forest trees, with the tallest redwoods attaining heights of more than 350 feet and the giant sequoia generally containing the largest total volume of wood. The redwood is found in the Pacific Coast region, from California to Oregon; the giant sequoia grows wild only on the western slope of the Sierra Nevada in California, generally between five thousand and seven thousand feet in elevation, where it finds a mix of mild temperatures and adequate rainfall. Sequoia wood is soft, light, and of a reddish color that darkens on exposure. Once believed to be the world's oldest living things—some are more than three thousand years old—sequoias have very thick bark that makes them highly resistant to insects, fire, and fungi. They have a very shallow root system, however, and rely on a straight trunk and well-balanced limbs to stay upright; most fall to their death.

Sequoias probably first became known to the white man in 1833, when Captain Joseph Walker's expedition sighted them. A. T. Dowd is credited with discovering the Calaveras grove in 1852. In less than a decade, loggers began extensive cutting of the sequoia, and cutting continued into the twentieth century, although on a lesser scale. The Sequoia National Park in the Sierra Nevada was established on 25 September 1890 to protect the groves of giant sequoia. The General Sherman tree in the park is 272 feet high and one of the oldest living things in the world; another famous tree had a hole bored through its trunk, allowing automobiles to drive through.

BIBLIOGRAPHY

Dilsaver, Lary M. *Challenge of the Big Trees.* Three Rivers, Calif.: Sequoia Natural History Association, 1990.

Orsi, Richard J., Alfred Runte, and Marlene Smith-Baranzini, eds. *Yosemite and Sequoia: A Century of California National Parks.* Berkeley: University of California Press, 1993.

John Francis Jr. / C. W.

See also **Lumber Industry; National Park System.**

SEQUOYAH, PROPOSED STATE OF. In April 1905, President Theodore Roosevelt made a railroad campaign throughout Indian Territory, encouraging the Five Civilized Tribes to unite with Oklahoma Territory into one state. Most Indian leaders, however, opposed uniting; they feared losing their land yet again and felt the United States was reneging on its treaty. Instead, they proposed a separate state of Sequoyah. The leaders of the Cherokees, Creeks, Choctaws, Seminoles, and Osages ignored Roosevelt's wish and held their own constitutional convention. The chief of the Chickasaws was in favor of joint statehood and refused to participate, though later he sent his private secretary to attend. On 22 August 1905, the convention was held at the Hinton Theater in downtown Muskogee, with 182 Native and non-Native elected delegates. This constitutional convention was the first such cooperative effort between whites and Natives. They published the Sequoyah Constitution on 14 October 1905, and held an election on 7 November. Of the 65,352 votes cast, 56,279 were for the ratification of the constitution. A copy of the constitution and the election results were sent to Congress, but they refused to consider the document. In 1907, the Indian and Oklahoma Territories became one state, Oklahoma, the Choctaw word for "home of the red man."

BIBLIOGRAPHY

Faulk, Odie B. *Oklahoma: Land of the Fair God.* Northridge, Calif.: Windsor Publications, 1986.

Gibson, Arrell Morgan. *The History of Oklahoma.* Norman: University of Oklahoma Press, 1984.

———. *Oklahoma: A History of Five Centuries.* Norman: University of Oklahoma Press, 1981.

Mary Anne Hansen

See also **Indian Policy, U.S.: 1900–2000; Indian Territory.**

SERBIA. See **Yugoslavia, Relations with.**

SERIAL KILLINGS. According to the National Institute of Justice, serial killings, or serial murders, are series of two or more murders committed as separate events, usually by one offender acting alone over a period of time ranging from hours to years. Often the motive is psychological, with the offender's behavior reflecting sadistic sexual overtones, and the victims—children, the insane, the elderly—being relatively powerless. Law enforcement officials estimate that in the 1990s there were between thirty and fifty serial killers active at any given time in the United States.

Records of serial killings in the fifteenth and sixteenth centuries and the murders by Jack the Ripper in 1888 attest that the practice is not new, nor are serial killings strictly a U.S. phenomenon. The former Soviet Union bred a number of serial killers, although their existence did not become manifest until the collapse of Communism in 1990. Andrei Chikatilo, a schoolteacher and factory procurer from the small coal-mining town of Shakti, committed fifty-two known killings, the victims mostly children under age twelve.

The largest number of serial killers, however, have been North American, with the United States producing an estimated 85 percent of the world's serial killers. Although victims of serial murders are few in comparison with other murders—an estimated 3,500 to 5,000 annually in the 1990s—the twentieth century saw a marked increase in serial killings. Although experts disagree on why this was the case, many suggest that the media's tendency to portray graphic violence may influence psychologically unstable individuals, while others suggest that American freedoms, including easy access to weapons, may make it easier for serial murderers to operate.

Serial murders are committed by members of all races and both genders, acting in pairs or even in gangs, but the greatest number are committed by single white males between twenty-five and thirty-five years of age. A small percentage of serial murderers act because of greed or the possibility of gain. Curiously, the number of female killers in the United States with such purposes is almost triple that for female serial killers who act for other reasons. Serial killings, once recognized, receive great attention from the media.

Among the most notorious serial killers of the second half of the twentieth century were Ted Bundy, who raped and murdered women in several states in the 1970s and 1980s (executed in 1989); Albert DeSalvo, known as the Boston Strangler; New York's David Berkowitz, known as Son of Sam; Wayne Williams of Atlanta; Richard Ramirez of southern California; and Jeffrey L. Dahmer, who by his own admission tortured, killed, and dismembered men and boys in Milwaukee and was convicted in 1992 of killing fifteen. Sentenced to fifteen consecutive life terms, Dahmer was bludgeoned to death in prison in 1994.

BIBLIOGRAPHY

Lester, David. *Serial Killers.* Philadelphia: Charles Press, 1995.

Newton, Michael. *Hunting Humans.* 2 vols. New York: Avon, 1990.

Norris, Joel. *Serial Killers.* New York: Doubleday, 1988.

Robert M. Guth
Christopher Wells

See also **Kidnapping; Rape; Violence.**

SESAME STREET is a daily series for children that has been airing on Public Broadcasting Service (PBS) stations since 10 November 1969. The series was created by Joan Ganz Cooney for the Children's Television Workshop, a company formed in 1967 with support from the Corporation for Public Broadcasting, the U.S. Office of Education, and a variety of foundations. *Sesame Street* often employs the style of TV commercials in segments designed to teach numbers, letters, and other preschool concepts. The hour-long show is a mixture of live-action scenes set in a fictional urban neighborhood, short documentary and animated sequences, and segments featuring Muppets, puppet characters created by Jim Henson.

Sesame Street quickly developed a large audience of both children and their parents. Muppet characters like Ernie, Bert, Oscar the Grouch, the Cookie Monster, and Big Bird have penetrated children's culture almost to the degree that Disney characters have. The Children's Television Workshop continues to earn income from licensing agreements with manufacturers of toys, garments, food products, and other items bearing these characters' images.

Arguments are occasionally made that the frenetic and highly entertaining style of the show has contributed to a decrease in the attention spans of children. Nevertheless, most people agree that the show set a high standard for instructional TV for children.

BIBLIOGRAPHY

Polsky, Richard M. *Getting to* Sesame Street: *Origins of the Children's Television Workshop.* New York: Praeger, 1974.

Robert Thompson

See also **Television: Programming and Influence;** *and picture (overleaf).*

SET-ASIDES are a form of AFFIRMATIVE ACTION used by governments in contracting government business; they include programs that typically designate a percentage of government contracts or funds (either for services or construction of public works) for minority-owned businesses. In 1977 Congress passed a law that directed 10 percent of federal public works funds to minority-controlled businesses, which the Public Works Employment Act defined as ones in which 50 percent of the business was held by AFRICAN AMERICANS, HISPANIC AMERICANS, ASIAN AMER-

Big Bird Revolutionizes Children's Television. Combining live action with colorful puppets (called Muppets) created by Jim Henson, *Sesame Street* combined learning with singing and colorful skits starring humans and Muppets. Created by the Children's Television Workshop with support from the Corporation for Public Broadcasting, the show was an instant hit with children and adults and was still going strong in 2002. © CORBIS

ICANS, NATIVE AMERICANS, Eskimos, or Aleuts. In 2000, FEDERAL AGENCIES purchased more than $13 billion in goods and services from minority-owned businesses as part of the program.

Like affirmative action programs generally, set-aside programs are controversial and have raised constitutional challenges. Opponents claim that such programs constitute reverse discrimination and are not cost-efficient because contracts go to businesses that may not have been the lowest or the most qualified bidder. Proponents believe that such programs help overcome the traditional economic disadvantages minorities have faced and promote economic development in minority communities. In 1995, the SUPREME COURT, ruling in *Adarand Constructors, Inc. v. Pena*, held that the FEDERAL GOVERNMENT must be subject to the same "strict scrutiny" as state and local governments when attempting to remedy discrimination. However, what initially appeared to be a victory for the white owner of Adarand Construction was modified by the Clinton administration, which overhauled certain programs while leaving the minority-contracting program in place. Since then, the Adarand case has gone back to the Colorado court, through federal appeals courts, and back to the Supreme Court, which, in the fall of 2001, refused to rule on the merits of the case. At the beginning of the twenty-first century, numerous other challenges to the set-aside program were brewing in state courts.

BIBLIOGRAPHY

Lassiter, Christo. "The New Race Cases and the Politics of Public Policy." *Journal of Law and Politics* 12 (1996): 411–458.

Orfield, Gary, ed. *Diversity Challenged: Evidence on the Impact of Affirmative Action.* Cambridge, Mass.: Civil Rights Project, Harvard University, 2001.

Katy J. Harriger / D. B.

See also **Business, Minority; Constitution of the United States; Discrimination: Race; Federal Aid; Indian Economic Life; Small Business Administration.**

SETTLEMENT HOUSE MOVEMENT. Between the late 1880s and the end of World War I, the settlement house movement was an influential Progressive-era response to the massive urban social problems of the day, The United States was in a period of rapid growth, economic distress, labor unrest, unemployment, low wages, unfair labor practices, and squalid living conditions. Large numbers of immigrants arrived daily to work in this newly established industrialized society. Ethnic enclaves sheltered immigrants who were experiencing isolation, new customs, and a strange language.

Established in large cities, settlement houses were privately supported institutions that focused on helping the poor and disadvantaged by addressing the environmental factors involved in poverty. The basic settlement-house ideal was to have wealthy people move into poor neighborhoods so that both groups could learn from one another. Canon Samuel Barnett, pastor of the poorest parish in London's notorious East End, established the first settlement house in 1884. In the midst of this neighborhood (settlement), Toynbee Hall housed educated and wealthy people who served as examples, teachers, and providers of basic human services to the poor residents of the settlement. Toynbee Hall was based on the social gospel movement and attracted young theologians and other middle-class people to emulate Jesus in living among the poor.

Inspired by Barnett's efforts, Dr. Stanton Coit and Charles B. Stover founded the first American settlement house, the Neighborhood Guild of New York City (1886). Other settlements quickly followed: Hull-House, Chicago, 1889 (Jane Addams and Ellen Gates Starr); College Settlement, a club for girls in New York City, 1889 (Vida Dutton Scudder and Jean G. Fine); East Side House, New York, 1891; Northwestern University Settlement, 1891 (Harriet Vittum); South End House, Boston, 1892 (Robert Archey Woods); and Henry Street Settlement, New York, 1893 (Lillian D. Wald). New settlements were established almost every year: University of Chicago Settlement, 1894 (Mary McDowell); Chicago Commons, 1894 (Graham Taylor); Hudson Guild, New York, 1897 (John Lovejoy Elliot); Hiram House, Cleveland, 1896 (George A. Bellamy); and Greenwich House, New York, 1902 (Mary Kingsbury Simkhovitch).

Although settlement houses have often been characterized as largely secular in nature, many of them grew from religious roots. Some settlement house workers who came from a faith perspective included moral teachings, at a minimum, in their work with community residents. Probably the best-known example is Chicago Commons, founded in 1894 by the Reverend Graham Taylor, who was the first professor of Christian sociology at the Chicago Theological Seminary. He founded Chicago Commons partially as a social laboratory for his students. As Allen F. Davis has pointed out, of the more than 400 settlements established by 1910, 167 (more than 40 percent) were identified as religious, 31 Methodist, 29 Episcopal, 24 Jewish, 22 Roman Catholic, 20 Presbyterian, 10 Congregational, and 31 unspecified. In 1930, there were approximately 460 settlement houses, and most of these were church supported.

Settlement houses were run in part by client groups. They emphasized social reform rather than relief or assistance. (Residence, research, and reform were the three

Rs of the movement.) Early sources of funding were wealthy individuals or clubs such as the Junior League. Settlement house workers were educated poor persons, both children and adults, who often engaged in social action on behalf of the community. In attaining their goals, the settlement house reformers had an enviable record. They had a realistic understanding of the social forces and the political structures of the city and nation. They battled in legislative halls as well as in urban slums, and they became successful initiators and organizers of reform.

Settlement workers tried to improve housing conditions, organized protests, offered job-training and labor searches, supported organized labor, worked against child labor, and fought against corrupt politicians. They provided classes in art and music and offered lectures on topics of interest. They established playgrounds, day care, kindergartens, and classes in English literacy. Settlement workers were also heavily involved in research to identify the factors causing need and in activities intended to eliminate the factors that caused the need.

Settlement houses assumed as their operational base the adequate functioning of the families they served, many of whom were migrants and immigrants whose problems were associated with making the transition from rural to urban living and from a known to an unknown culture. Whatever their problems, clients of settlement houses were viewed as able, normal, working-class families with whom the wealthier classes were joined in mutual dependence. When such families could not cope, settlement leaders assumed that society itself was at fault, and this assumption led quite naturally to a drive for societal reform.

The most famous settlement house in America was Hull-House of Chicago. Although it was not the first American settlement, Hull-House came to exemplify the particular brand of research, service, and reform that was to characterize much of the American settlement house movement. Jane Addams and her friend, Ellen Gates Starr, moved into a poor immigrant neighborhood in Chicago. They had vague notions of being "good neighbors" to the poor around them and studying the conditions in which they lived. As they observed the structural elements of poverty, however, the two began to create a specific agenda of services and reform. Exploitation of immigrants from southern and eastern Europe, poor employment conditions and inadequate wages, lack of educational opportunities, substandard housing, and inefficient city government were the factors that contributed greatly to the poverty of the area and called for specific responses. Hull-House soon offered a day nursery for children, a club for working girls, lectures and cultural programs, and meeting space for neighborhood political groups.

Along with a remarkable group of reformers who came to live at the settlement, Addams supported labor union activity, lobbied city officials for sanitary and housing reforms, and established the Immigrants' Protective League to fight discrimination in employment and other

317

exploitation of newcomers. In addition, Hull-House members carried on an active program of research. Residents surveyed conditions in tenements and workplaces. They publicized their results widely, attempting to create an atmosphere conducive to governmental and legislative reform.

Under Addams's leadership a powerful network of women social reformers emerged from the Hull-House setting that was influential throughout the United States. Three-fourths of settlement workers in America were women; most were well educated and dedicated to working on problems of urban poverty. These included Julia Lathrop and Grace Abbott, prominent figures in the U.S. Children's Bureau; Florence Kelley, labor and consumer advocate; Alice Hamilton, physician and social activist; and Edith Abbott and Sophonisba Breckinridge, social researchers and key leaders in the development of social work education. In addition to these women, Mary O'Sullivan, a labor leader and reformer, organized the Chicago Women's Bindery Workers' Union in 1889. In 1892, she became the American Federation of Labor's first woman organizer. Additionally, Lucy Flower helped found the Illinois Training School for Nurses, the Chicago Bureau of Charities, the Cook County Juvenile Court, the Protective Agency for Women and Children, and the Lake Geneva Fresh Air Association for poor urban children.

World War I had an adverse effect on the settlement house movement. The settlement houses declined in importance and there seemed to be less need of them. Gradually organizations such as the Young Men's Christian Association, summer camps, neighborhood youth centers, and other local and national agencies were established to carry on similar work. The settlement house movement gradually broadened into a national federation of neighborhood centers. By the early twentieth century, settlement houses were beginning to cooperate with, and merge into, "social work." The settlement house movement led the way to community organization and group work practice within the newly proclaimed profession of social work.

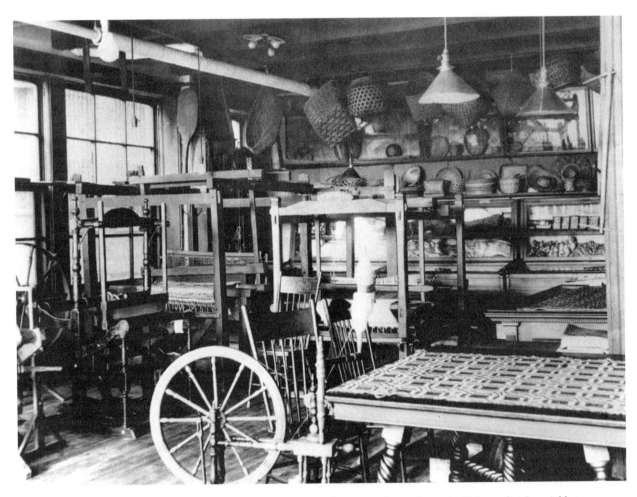

Hull-House. The workroom, used for spinning and sewing, in the famous settlement house in Chicago that Jane Addams cofounded and ran. UPI/CORBIS-BETTMANN

BIBLIOGRAPHY

Axinn, June, and Herman Levin. *Social Welfare: A History of the American Response to Need.* 4th ed. White Plains, N.Y.: Longman, 1997.

Davis, Allen F. *Spearheads for Reform: The Social Settlements and the Progressive Movement, 1890–1914.* New York: Oxford University Press, 1967.

Day, Phyllis J. *A New History of Social Welfare.* 4th ed. Boston: Allyn and Bacon, 2002.

Handel, Gerald. *Social Welfare in Western Society.* New York: Random House, 1982.

Popple, Philip R., and Leslie Leighninger. *Social Work, Social Welfare, and American Society.* 4th ed. Boston: Allyn and Bacon, 1999.

Trattner, Walter I. *From Poor Law to Welfare State: A History of Social Welfare in America.* 6th ed. New York: The Free Press, 1999.

Gaynor Yancey

SEVEN DAYS' BATTLES. The Seven Days' Battles (25 June–1 July 1862) were the succession of CIVIL WAR battles in which the Confederate Gen. Robert E. Lee forced the Union Gen. George B. McClellan to abandon his threatening position east of Richmond, Virginia, and retreat to the James River. McClellan's forces were repulsed by the Confederates at Mechanicsville on 26 June and Gaines's Mill on 27 June. Pursued across the Chickahominy River, his troops repelled Confederate attacks at Savage's Station on 29 June. Discovering that McLellan was retiring on the James, Lee and Gen. Thomas J. "Stonewall" Jackson hurried columns to Frayser's Farm. Here on 30 June and at Malvern Hill on 1 July, the Confederate assaults were beaten back decisively. Confederate losses over the seven days of fighting were 3,286 killed, 15,909 wounded, and 940 captured or missing; Union losses were 1,734 killed, 8,062 wounded, and 6,053 captured or missing.

BIBLIOGRAPHY

Dowdey, Clifford. *The Seven Days: The Emergence of Lee.* Boston: Little, Brown, 1964.

Martin, David G. *The Peninsula Campaign: March–July 1862.* Conshohocken, Pa.: Combined Books, 1992.

Sears, Stephen W. *To the Gates of Richmond: The Peninsula Campaign.* New York: Ticknor and Fields, 1992.

Joseph Mills Hanson / A. R.

See also **Army of Northern Virginia; Peninsular Campaign; Richmond.**

SEVEN SISTERS COLLEGES. The Seven Sisters Colleges are prestigious northeastern liberal arts institutions founded in the nineteenth century to educate women. While the schools often drew on each other's alumnae for faculty and consulted each other on matters of policy, the colleges did not officially become Seven Sisters until the 1926 organization of a Seven College Conference to create a united appeal for donations. The Seven Sisters are Smith, Wellesley, Mount Holyoke, Barnard, Bryn Mawr, Radcliffe, and Vassar Colleges.

The oldest of the colleges, Mount Holyoke, was established by Mary Lyon and opened in South Hadley, Massachusetts, in 1837. As the mother of the other schools, it set the pattern for them by instituting rigorous admission standards and emphasizing the sciences. Vassar, the brainchild of Matthew Vassar, opened in Poughkeepsie, New York, in 1865. It became the first institution to include an art museum among its facilities. Financial worries prompted Vassar to open its doors to men in 1969; it thereby became the first women's college in the country to turn coeducational. Wellesley, located in Wellesley, Massachusetts, was founded by Henry Fowle Durant in 1870 and opened in 1875. It has long been noted for its strong science program. Smith, a Northhampton, Massachusetts, school begun by a bequest of Sophia Smith in 1871, elected to admit men as graduate students in the 1970s but refused to accept them as undergraduates for fear of detracting from the founding goal of providing the best possible education for women. Smith is noted for two firsts in educational leadership: the first woman college president, Jill Ker Conway, in 1975, and the first black woman to head any top-ranked college or university, Ruth Simmons, in 1995.

Radcliffe, founded in Cambridge, Massachusetts, by students seeking instruction from Harvard University, began in 1879 as the Harvard Annex. In 1894 it became a separate women's college with Harvard professors as its faculty. In 1999, it officially merged with Harvard and, with a commitment to study women, gender, and society, became the Radcliffe Institute for Advanced Study. Bryn Mawr, founded by Joseph W. Taylor in 1885 to provide education to Quaker women, eventually became the leader of the Seven Sisters because of its innovative curriculum. This Bryn Mawr, Pennsylvania, college became the first institution in the United States to offer a Ph.D. in social work and the first to offer fellowships for graduate study to women. Also, from 1921 to 1938 it ran a Summer School for Women Workers in Industry to teach science and literature to factory workers. Barnard, located in Manhattan, was begun in 1889 as an independent college affiliated with Columbia University. Founded by Frederick Barnard, who had argued unsuccessfully for the admission of women to Columbia, the school was included in the educational system of Columbia in 1900 with provisions unique among women's colleges: it was governed by its own trustees, faculty, and dean, and was responsible for its own endowment and facilities, while sharing instruction, the library, and the degree of the university.

Graduates of Seven Sisters schools have more opportunities than women at coeducational institutions to hold leadership positions and they develop measurably higher levels of self-esteem. In addition, a higher proportion of them earn diplomas in traditionally male fields, like math and science. Seven Sisters alumnae include the founder of *Ms.* magazine, Gloria Steinem (Smith); the first woman secretary of state, Madeleine Albright, and the former first lady, Hilary Rodham Clinton (Wellesley); the playwright Suzan-Lori Parks and the first woman governor of Connecticut, Ella Grasso (Mount Holyoke); the first woman UN ambassador, Jeane J. Kirkpatrick, and the novelist Anne Bernays (Barnard); the actor Katherine Hepburn, the neurosurgeon Dorothy Klenke, and the poet Marianne Moore (Bryn Mawr); the blind activist Helen Keller and the newspaper columnist Katha Pollitt (Radcliffe); and the author Edna St. Vincent Millay (Vassar).

BIBLIOGRAPHY

Horowitz, Helen Lefkowitz. *Alma Mater: Design and Experience in the Women's Colleges from their Nineteenth-Century Beginnings to the 1930s.* New York: Knopf, 1984.

Howells, Dorothy Elia. *A Century to Celebrate: Radcliffe College, 1879–1979.* Cambridge, Mass.: Radcliffe College, 1978.

Plum, Dorothy A., and George B. Dowell. *The Great Experiment: A Chronicle of Vassar.* Poughkeepsie, N.Y.: Vassar College, 1961.

White, Marian Churchill. *A History of Barnard College.* New York: Columbia University Press, 1954.

Caryn E. Neumann

See also **American Association of University Women; Coeducation Movement; Education, Higher: Women's Colleges.**

SEVEN YEARS' WAR. *See* **French and Indian War.**

SEWING MACHINE. After almost one hundred years of trials, failures, and partial successes in Europe, the sewing machine in its practical form evolved as a mid-nineteenth-century American invention. Elias Howe, Jr., usually credited as the inventor, was not the first person to patent an American sewing machine. John J. Greenough, Benjamin W. Bean, and several others patented ideas for sewing machines in the early 1840s, before Howe was granted the first patent for the two-thread, lockstitch sewing machine in 1846. Howe's machine was far from adaptable for commercial production, and he met with little success in America at the time. The machine stitched only straight seams for the length of the baster plate, which then had to be reset. Taking his machine to England, Howe was unable to adapt it to British manufacturing needs, and he finally sold the patent rights in that country to William Thomas, a corset manufacturer.

When Howe returned home, he found that several other inventors had entered the field. John Bachelder had patented a continuous-feed, vertical-needle machine in 1849; Isaac M. Singer had used earlier ideas with his heart-shaped cam to move the needle and received a pat-

Singer Sewing Machine. The majority of American homes once had one of these revolutionary and widely advertised machines, made by over 200 companies and often purchased on an installment plan. HENRY FORD MUSEUM & GREENFIELD VILLAGE

ent in 1851; and A. B. Wilson patented the stationary rotary bobbin in 1852 and the four-motion feed in 1854. The principal technical problems had been solved, but no single manufacturer could make a practical machine without being sued for infringement of patent by another. In 1856, Orlando B. Potter, lawyer and president of the Grover and Baker Sewing Machine Company, suggested the idea of pooling the patents. This was accomplished, but each company maintained itself separately, and there was competition in the manufacturing and improving of the various machines. The four members of the "sewing-machine combination" were Elias Howe, Jr.; Wheeler and Wilson Manufacturing Company; I. M. Singer and Company; and Grover and Baker Sewing Machine Company. All four members had to agree on which companies would be licensed to build sewing machines, and a fee of fifteen per machine was charged. Howe received five dollars of this amount, a portion was held in reserve for possible litigation costs, and the money left was divided equally among the four parties. In 1860, the fee was dropped to seven and Howe's share to one dollar. In 1867 Howe's renewed patent expired, and only the three companies were left. The combination remained active until 1877, when all the major patents expired. Although the combination had been accused of retarding the development of the sewing machine, hundreds of thousands of good machines were produced in the 1850s and 1860s.

The sewing machines were used by manufacturers for shirts, dresses, aprons, cloaks, collars, and many other items. Details such as pleating and tucking could be produced by machine very quickly and were popularly added to many costumes. While the sewing machine revolutionized the ready-made garment industry, it produced mixed results for workers. It initially reduced the number of laborers required, and it attracted unskilled men into sectors of the garment industry formerly reserved for women. Already poorly paid, women who subcontracted piece work at home now bore the additional expense of purchasing or renting equipment, and unscrupulous subcontractors often deducted payments on machines from meager wages, causing women to default. Contractors would then repossess the machine and "sell" it to the next job applicant. Those who could not afford a machine sought work in large shops where their work habits and productivity could be tightly controlled. By 1900 tents, awnings, sails, books, umbrellas, mattresses, hose, trunks, shoes, and flags were all stitched by machine.

The sewing machine was the first widely advertised consumer product. Because of the high initial cost of the machine, the Singer company introduced the hire-purchase plan, and installment buying placed a sewing machine in almost every home. Competition for this ready market encouraged more and more manufacturers to enter the field. At the height of this competition in the 1870s, there were well over two hundred American sewing-

Garment Worker. The garment industry has long relied on a vast army of employees like this sewing machine operator—many of them working under oppressive conditions for low wages. THE TERRY WILD STUDIO

machine companies. But foreign competition began to invade the field in the twentieth century. The high cost of skilled labor in America made it difficult to compete. Nevertheless, ingenious sewing machines are still in production, including those that "sew" without thread, but most of the machines produced in the United States are highly specialized manufacturing machines.

BIBLIOGRAPHY

Bissell, Don. *The First Conglomerate: 145 Years of the Singer Sewing Machine Company.* Brunswick, Maine: Audenreed Press, 1999.

Brandon, Ruth. *Singer and the Sewing Machine: A Capitalist Romance.* London: Barrie and Jenkins, 1977.

Brewer, Priscilla J. *The Queen of Inventions.* Pawtucket, R.I.: Slater Mill Historic Site, 1986.

Cooper, Grace R. *The Sewing Machine: Its Invention and Development.* Washington, D.C.: Smithsonian, 1976.

Godfrey, Frank P. *An International History of the Sewing Machine.* London: R. Hale, 1982.

Grace R. Cooper / L. T.

See also **Clothing Industry; Industrial Revolution; International Ladies Garment Workers Union.**

SEX DISCRIMINATION. *See* **Discrimination: Sex.**

SEX EDUCATION. The movement for sex education, also at times known as sexuality education, began in the United States in the late nineteenth and early twentieth centuries. Dr. Prince Morrow developed the impetus for some of the first formal sex education curricula with an emphasis on the prevention of venereal disease, a focus that had its roots in the scientific social-hygiene and purity movements of the Progressive Era. In 1905, he established the American Society of Sanitary and Moral Prophylaxis, focusing on private agencies outside of schools, working with youth on sexually transmitted disease prevention. For the most part, Morrow's approach to sex education sought to discourage sexual activity and to emphasize the dangers of sex while also providing instruction about human anatomy and physiology. During this same time, Margaret Sanger began her pioneering work dispensing birth control information to young women in New York City.

In 1914, the National Educational Association began to endorse sex education, usually referred to as sex hygiene, in the schools. The NEA resolution stated that public school sex hygiene classes should be conducted by "persons qualified by scientific training and teaching experience in order to assure a safe moral point of view." By the second and third decades of the twentieth century, sex education in the public schools had become more institutionalized and had begun to shift from the earlier disease prevention model to a focus on helping young people relate sex to love, marriage, and family life. There was a strong proscriptive bent to most of these programs— "worthwhile" sexual experiences were only those that led to mature love and marriage. Sex educators in this era generally viewed bodily pleasure unto itself as morally dangerous.

In the 1940s, sex education continued to be taught primarily as part of social-hygiene classes and often existed in classes called "homemaking," "character building," or "moral or spiritual values." These classes were frequently sex segregated, although sex education specialists debated this issue. The post–World War II era witnessed a major social movement in support of a more explicit, normative, and nonjudgmental approach to sexuality education. The development of the Sex Information and Education Council of the United States in the early 1960s, followed by the American Association of Sex Educators and a number of other organizations, transformed the teaching of sex education in the schools. The pioneering work in the fields of human sexuality by Alfred Kinsey and William H. Masters and Virginia E. Johnson also had an enormous influence in promoting sex education. These organizations and individuals sought to develop programs that encouraged healthy sexuality to enhance individual growth and fulfillment. In addition, the women's movement challenged and transformed many previous assumptions about the teaching of female sexuality.

Nevertheless, sex education programs continued to be subject to considerable controversy. Some religious organizations voiced strenuous objections to teaching young people about issues such as contraception, abortion, or masturbation, or to framing homosexuality as an acceptable lifestyle in sex education classes. Throughout the 1980s and 1990s, local school boards waged protracted and divisive battles over the content of sex education curricula. In addition, political conservatives in the United States sought, at times successfully, to restrict the content of sex education programs and to limit explicit discussions of birth control in favor of an emphasis on abstinence. These controversies over the content of sex education curricula took on a more fevered pitch with the advent of the AIDS virus.

BIBLIOGRAPHY

Hottois, James, and Neal A. Milner. *The Sex Education Controversy.* Lexington, Mass.: Lexington Books, 1975.

Scales, Peter. "Historical Review of Sex Education Efforts and Barriers." In *Facilitating Community Support for Sex Education, Centers for Disease Control Final Report.* Bethesda, Md.: 1981.

Strong, Bryan. "Ideas of the Early Sex Education Movement in America, 1890–1920." *History of Education Quarterly* 12 (1972): 129–161.

John S. Berman

See also **Birth Control; Birth Control Movement; Kinsey Report.**

SEXUAL HARASSMENT is generally understood to be the attempt to influence, dominate, or injure an individual or a class of individuals through sexually inflected or sexually charged behaviors or environmental conditions. Currently, sexual harassment charges have achieved legal standing in the context of work, housing, and educational settings. Alleged harassers often proclaim their innocence by asserting that their intentions are amiable, innocuous, collegial, flattering, or humorous and have been misconstrued by accusers (victims) and observers. Over the last thirty years, the definition of sexual harassment and its standing in law and in educational and workplace regulation have become flash points for individuals and organizations contending over the impact of feminist ideologies on their own philosophies, rights, and behaviors.

Although "sexual harassment" is a recently formulated concept, using sex to establish and maintain power and status has a long history. Harassment of domestic and industrial female employees by male supervisors has plentiful, though sometimes veiled, documentation through workingwomen's narratives and court records. White men's power to rape, impregnate, and otherwise sexually control black women was a pillar of American slavery. The sexual exploitation, domination, and interpretation of African Americans by whites continued beyond slavery. A notable variant of these patterns was the frequent lynchings in the post–Civil War South; mobs often justified their extralegal actions by alleging that a black man had raped or sexually offended a white woman.

Sexual harassment emerged as a classification of certain patterns of behavior, and of pervasive environmental conditions, in the late 1960s and 1970s, with the women's rights movement and the extension of federal civil rights legislation to include sex as a protected class. Legal statistics and anecdotal evidence confirm what most theory addresses, from varying perspectives: harassers are usually men, while victims or targets are usually women. This pattern reflects prevalent social power relations. But as a way of establishing or affirming dominance over another person through intimidation and embarrassment, sexual harassment has been practiced by anybody on anybody.

Title VII of the Civil Rights Act of 1964 laid the basis for legal claims of sexual harassment by prohibiting employment discrimination on the basis of sex. After earlier lawsuits failed to establish sexual harassment as a variety of sex discrimination, several court decisions in the mid-1970s established a legal interpretation of quid pro quo ("this for that," or trading "favors") sexual harassment. In *Williams v. Saxbe* (1976), a Washington, D.C., court used Title VII to recognize quid pro quo sexual harassment as sex discrimination, on the grounds that sexual advances by a male supervisor to a female employee would constitute artificial barriers to employment placed before one gender and not the other. In *Alexander v. Yale University* (1977), a Connecticut court recognized quid pro quo sexual harassment as sex discrimination in education. *Brown v. City of Gutherie* (1980) and *Bundy v. Jackson* (1981) recognized another form of sexual harassment, the "hostile work environment." The Eleventh Circuit Court's decision in *Henson v. City of Dundee* (1982) elaborated this trend by delineating the conditions a plaintiff must establish to prove a hostile work environment, and the Supreme Court in *Meritor Savings Bank v. Mechelle Vinson* (1986) adopted these standards and affirmed that to gain a favorable decision the plaintiff need not prove that she lost economic benefits associated with the harassment.

The *Meritor* decision was a landmark in several ways. First, plaintiff Mechelle Vinson's case was argued by Patricia J. Barry, joined by Catharine A. MacKinnon, the author of *Sexual Harassment of Working Women* (1979), in which MacKinnon argued that the "hostile work environment" was often in effect a prelude to "quid pro quo" harassment. In this scenario, women who tired of "hostile work environment" sexual advances resisted or protested, which led to "quid pro quo" threats to their jobs or work conditions. Secondly, the Rehnquist Court unanimously upheld the favorable appeals court decision. Rehnquist's opinion cited previous interpretations of Title VII and the EEOC (Equal Employment Opportunity Commission) in regard to eliminating workplace differentials between men and women. The Court also found that whether the victim acquiesced in sexual intercourse was irrelevant to the district court's finding against her claim of "hostile environment," since that claim turned on whether the sexual advances were in fact "unwelcome."

The early 1990s brought a number of public, contentious, and soon infamous accusations of sexual harassment, largely among federal employees. In 1991, the courts developed new definitions of the content and possible victims of sexual harassment. In *Robinson v. Jacksonville Shipyards*, the Sixth Circuit Court ruled that pictures displayed in the workplace need not be "pornography" to create a hostile or offensive work environment; a pose calling attention to private parts of the body was sufficient. *Ellison v. Brady* (1991) adopted the "reasonable woman" standard in recognition that women's and men's perspectives might differ on what constituted pervasive harassment. And in *Jenson v. Eveleth Taconite*, the Eighth Circuit Court decided positively in a class action sexual harassment suit brought by women miners, although meager damages were awarded, and the National Organization for Women filed an amicus brief during the appeal, arguing that the judge showed bias against women and pushing for higher punitive damages. The parties eventually reached a settlement.

In June 1991, Thurgood Marshall, until that time the first and only black Supreme Court justice, announced his retirement, which initiated a string of events that would profoundly affect dialogue and litigation regarding sexual harassment. President George Bush nominated Clarence Thomas, former head of the EEOC (created in 1964 to administer Title VII of the Civil Rights Act) and a federal judge for two years, to replace Marshall. Thomas's nomination was controversial because of his inexperience on

the bench, his reluctance to explain apparent discrepancies in his statements on divisive social issues, and liberals' anger at Bush's disingenuous replacement of a black liberal by a black conservative. An evenly split Senate Judiciary Committee forwarded Thomas's nomination to the Senate floor on 27 September. In early October, as Senate proceedings began, Anita Hill, an African American law professor at the University of Oklahoma, filed a confidential affidavit accusing Thomas of sexual harassment ten years earlier, when he was her supervisor at the Department of Education and then at the EEOC. After the initial revelation, Judiciary Committee hearings were reopened in what Thomas would call, in his closing statement, a "high-tech lynching" of him, and what contemporary and subsequent commentators have analyzed as an extended and humiliating challenge to the possibility that Anita Hill might be telling the truth.

Thomas's confirmation undoubtedly played a role in the 62 percent increase in EEOC sexual harassment complaints between 1991 and 1992, and the significant increase in women running for political office in 1992. Winners included six senators, twenty-nine representatives, and more than a thousand local officials and representatives. Four male U.S. senators (Adams, Packwood, Inouye, and Durenberger) were accused of sexual harassment. In 1993, the U.S. Navy issued a final report of its investigation of the so-called Tailhook scandal, the egregious harassment and abuse of eighty-one women and seven men officers by more than a hundred of their fellow naval aviation officers at the Tailhook Association convention two years earlier. Seven officers were disciplined, Secretary of the Navy Garrett resigned over the episode, and the assistant chief of naval operations retired at reduced rank.

Educational settings from elementary school through graduate programs became another battleground over definitions of sexual harassment. In their book *The Lecherous Professor* (1984), Billie Wright Dziech and Linda Weiner ventured a portrait of the power imbalances and gender ideologies that created the context for sexual harassment of female students by male professors. In 1993 the American Association of University Women sponsored a survey of more than a thousand high school students that found that 85 percent of girls, and 76 percent of boys, reported being sexually harassed in school. In 1992 the Supreme Court held that students could hold their schools liable for monetary damages for sexual harassment under Title IX of the Education Amendments of 1972 (*Franklin v. Gwinnett County Public Schools*). In *Doe v. Petaluma* (1994) a California federal court asserted that the school could be held liable for peer-to-peer sexual harassment if the school had notice of the harassment and failed to act. In the same year, however, the New Hampshire District Court ordered the University of New Hampshire to reinstate a tenured professor fired for sexual harassment under the university's guidelines (*J. Donald Silva v. the University of New Hampshire*). Public responses to the case, which originated with students offended by a professor's use of sexually explicit imagery to teach rhetoric, typify the impassioned rhetoric sparked by the topic of sexual harassment. Anthony Lewis, the liberal columnist for the *New York Times*, adjured Americans to "grow up" and stop resorting to the law to protect their tender sensibilities. Other less prominent commentators hailed the decision as a victory for beleaguered free speech against the massed forces of political correctness.

As American society became more egalitarian, and at the same time certain influential interests continued to resist gender-based power analyses, dispassionate studies of the effects of harassment on men and boy victims, as well as women and girl victims, began to emerge; a salient example is Billie Wright Dziech's chapter on "Male Students: The Invisible Casualties" in *Sexual Harassment in Higher Education* (1998). The Court kept pace with this trend in *Oncale v. Sundowner Offshore Services* (1998), which upheld a plaintiff's right to seek damages for same-sex sexual harassment, holding that the prohibition of discrimination "because of sex" can apply to men as well as women.

BIBLIOGRAPHY

Crouch, Margaret A. *Thinking about Sexual Harassment: A Guide for the Perplexed.* New York: Oxford University Press, 2001.

Dziech, Billie Wright, and Michael W. Hawkins. *Sexual Harassment in Higher Education: Reflections and New Perspectives.* New York: Garland, 1998.

Hartel, Lynda Jones, and Helena M. VonVille. *Sexual Harassment: A Selected, Annotated Bibliography.* Westport, Conn.: Greenwood Press, 1995.

Wyatt, Nancy. "Information on Sexual Harassment." Available from http://www.de.psu.edu/harassment/.

Mina Julia Carson

See also **Discrimination: Sex; *Meritor Savings Bank v. Mechelle Vinson*; Tailhook Incident; Women's Rights Movement: The Twentieth Century.**

SEXUAL ORIENTATION. During the late twentieth century, "sexual orientation," rather than "sexual preference," became the preferred term among lesbian/gay civil rights activists in the United States for the classification they hoped to add to existing civil rights law. The terms of the debate grew out of the mix of moral, psychiatric, and legal discourses that had framed debates about sexual practice, sexual identity, and their significance since the 1860s. Those terms emerged from a much larger nexus of deeply embedded assumptions that began to undergo major changes during the second half of the nineteenth century as improving middle-class professionals conducted research and developed conceptual frameworks for organizing the varieties of human sexual functioning.

The prospect of building one's identity to some significant degree around the gender of one's sexual object choice is in all likelihood a mostly modern and urban phenomenon. Evidence clearly indicates that many cultures institutionalize same-sex sexual activity in some form. Much scholarly debate erupted during the 1980s and 1990s over whether other cultures ever developed meanings and practices around the belief that the gender of one's sexual object choice marks one as a particular type of person—a "homosexual" or a "heterosexual"—with identifiable personality characteristics and, in some accounts, some form of psychopathology if one's choices differ from the majority's.

Before the Twentieth Century

Historical evidence indicates that in the United States and western Europe, notions of "sexual orientation" in psychiatry, law, and politics emerged in the last third of the nineteenth century and have continued to develop since. Yet other evidence indicates remarkable continuity in the composition of gay male subcultures in the major cities of the United States and western Europe as far back as the seventeenth century. While many members of those subcultures were married, the subcultures' existence depended on the increased separation of economic production from family life that came about during the early modern period. That gay men were far more readily visible than lesbians reflects the extent to which cultural formations around same-sex desire were creations of individuals with significant access to disposable income and/or public space. Periodic police repression of those subcultures' denizens and institutions did not produce any systematic political organizing around a shared identity until the late nineteenth and early twentieth centuries in Germany and England.

Researchers first coined the terms we now associate with sexual orientation—"homosexual" and "heterosexual"—in 1869, with much of the important early work taking place in Europe. Richard von Krafft-Ebing and Havelock Ellis wrote systematically about variations in sexual practice; their work paralleled, but remained distinct from, related developments in other areas of psychology. Germans Karl Heinrich Ulrichs and Magnus Hirschfeld and Englishmen John Addington Symonds and Edward Carpenter pioneered advocacy of equal treatment for sexual minorities, borrowing from and modifying the ideas of Krafft-Ebing and Ellis. Krafft-Ebing and Ellis, Ulrichs, Hirschfeld, Symonds, and Carpenter also inspired the Chicago activist Henry Gerber, who in 1924 founded the Society for Human Rights, the first known homophile organization in the United States. In 1925 police raided his apartment, arrested him, and confiscated his membership list, all without a warrant.

Similarly, lesbian couples existed throughout early modern European and American history. The large cohort of never-married women who led the social reform movements of the late nineteenth and early twentieth centuries in the United States produced numerous "Boston marriages" of female couples who shared households. Any sexual activity these women engaged in typically caused little if any suspicion at the time, but has since produced considerable historical debate. More famous were such unapologetically lesbian expatriates as Gertrude Stein, Alice B. Toklas, and Natalie Barney.

Categories of Sexual Identity
The much-publicized 1929 trial to determine if British novelist Radclyffe Hall's *The Well of Loneliness* violated New York obscenity statutes with its depiction of a lesbian life encapsulated the debates of the previous sixty years and presaged future disputes about the characteristics associated with homosexual identity. The disinclination to attribute a sexual component to the intense romantic friendships between men and between women of the late nineteen century had increasingly given way to a strong suspicion about same-sex relationships as sexologists and psychiatrists began to impute sexual activity to such relationships with or without evidence. Contemporary observers found in *The Well of Loneliness* an overly positive portrayal of lesbian identity (in contrast to late-twentieth-century critics, who found in the novel the worst sort of negative stereotype), which they understood exclusively in terms of psychopathology. As indicated by the cases of Gerber and Hall, however, the emergence of a medical explanation for homosexuality in terms of mental illness did not automatically settle the question of how the law in the United States should treat such persons. Most sexologists and psychiatrists called for an end to legal persecution of what they called homosexuals in favor of treatment designed to "cure" what they considered a developmental failure. But major legislative and policy changes would have to await the increasingly militant social movement of lesbian, gay, bisexual, and transgender persons that emerged after World War II.

Indeed, the efforts of certain medical experts notwithstanding, the new notion that acts of sodomy indicated a homosexual person served more often to buttress than undermine the sorts of moral condemnation that led to legal restrictions. The framework for efforts to cure lesbians and gay men, and to continue legal sanctions against them, rested heavily on psychoanalytic theory, which posited heterosexual identity and practice as the only "mature" outcome of sexual development. Sigmund Freud, the originator of psychoanalysis, famously wrote to an American woman in response to a letter asking about her gay son. Freud stated that he considered homosexual identity a failure of development, but he also stated that he saw no reason for either treatment or prosecution of homosexuals. American psychiatrists and psychoanalysts mostly disagreed until the 1970s.

From their own perspective, sexologists, psychiatrists, and others who conducted research into the proliferating categories of sexual identity from roughly 1869 to 1970 rigorously separated their scientific work from political considerations. They saw their proliferating taxonomies of sexual perversions as empirical reflections of the cases they observed. To modern historians, though, the conceptual frameworks that researchers brought to questions of sexual practice and identity clearly reveal anxieties and assumptions about proper gender roles and social order, especially in terms of race and class, as well as proper sexual activity. The first late-nineteenth-century studies of women who passed as men and/or engaged in sexual relationships with other women described those women as "inverts" and emphasized their gender nonconformity as much as their sexual practice. In the context of official assumptions about male sexual aggressiveness and female sexual passivity, any sexual initiative by a woman could be read only as her adoption of an inappropriately masculine identity. Such research into sexuality during the late nineteenth and early twentieth centuries paralleled other attempts to naturalize the existing order by finding the roots not only of sexual identity, but also of racial, gender, and class identity and even of the propensity for criminal activity, in the physiological dictates of a biological body.

The conjunction between sexual and racial identity, on one hand, and national identity on the other became clear with restrictions on immigration, beginning with the Chinese Exclusion Act of 1882. In 1917, Congress adopted a set of exclusions based on the medical expertise of public health officials. The "constitutional psychopathic inferiority" category included "constitutional psychopaths and inferiors, the moral imbeciles, the pathological liars and swindlers, the defective delinquents, many of the vagrants and cranks, and persons with abnormal sexual instincts," according to a Public Health Service report. Exclusions aimed at lesbian and gay aliens, variously defined, would remain in American immigration law until 1990.

Debates among legal and medical elites had relatively little impact outside the self-improving middle class before World War II. Major cities continued to harbor significant subcultures of men and women for whom same-sex relationships were central to their lives, but the evidence from New York City indicates that it was still possible, especially for working-class men, to enjoy the occasional sexual encounter with a "fairy" or "faggot," a man who accepted a feminized gender identity as part of his decision to reveal his sexual attraction to other men. The man who played the insertive role, whether in oral or anal intercourse, could retain his identity as "normal," not "heterosexual," because that category was as class-specific and as recent as "homosexual."

Anti-Gay and Lesbian Policies and Practices
Henry Gerber's pioneering resistance to persecution based on sexual identity remained unemulated in the United States until after World War II, a conflict that would prove as significant for notions of sexual orientation—and for political organizing around them—as it did for all other areas of American life. During the 1930s, the Nazis systematically destroyed the work of sex researcher and

reformer Magnus Hirschfeld, a Jewish physician who led a vigorous civil rights movement in Germany until Hitler assumed power in January 1933. The following May, Nazi youth raided Hirschfeld's Institute of Sexual Research and publicly burned its contents. The Nazis strengthened existing laws against same-sex sexual activity and sent violators to concentration camps.

In the United States, anti-gay policies were less heavy-handed. Before World War II, various state and local laws prohibited not only sodomy, but also such practices as appearing publicly in the dress of the "opposite" gender. Sodomy laws provided justification for arresting lesbians as well as gay men in those jurisdictions where the courts applied the laws to cunnilingus or other lesbian sexual activity. The vagueness of those laws, often relying on terms such as "crimes against nature," left wide latitude for decisions about enforcement. Even in the absence of arrest and trial, however, lesbians and gay men suffered by the existence of such legislation, which served as de facto permission for various forms of harassment, from garden-variety taunting on the street through denial of child custody to lesbian mothers, whom the court presumed to violate sodomy laws.

Despite the legal obstacles, lesbians and gay men managed to create relatively visible identities and enclaves at least in major American cities before World War II. A flourishing, highly visible gay male subculture emerged in New York City during the 1890s and continued through the beginnings of the Great Depression of the 1930s. Economic hardship brought cultural conservatism and a consequent crackdown on the bars, drag balls, and other spaces where gay men had congregated—often entertaining large crowds of "straight" or "normal" people in the process—during the preceding decades. Undoubtedly, New York City was unique in this respect as in many others, but evidence indicates the existence of lesbian and gay networks and subcultures in other cities during this period as well.

World War II and the Emergence of Political Activity

During World War II military leaders for the first time relied heavily on psychiatric classifications as the basis for excluding various "undesirables" from the military and for discharging those who managed to get in anyway. However, wide variation in the attitudes of military psychiatrists and officers combined with a dire need for personnel to produce huge discrepancies in the treatment of men and women whose same-sex activity became known. Official policy called for their dishonorable discharge, but many either conducted themselves such that they never got caught or had the good fortune to serve under a commander who looked the other way.

The war contributed to future political organizing around issues of sexual practice and identity in at least two ways. It created a pool of increasingly politicized veterans who saw their dishonorable discharges for homosexuality as an injustice. It also left large numbers of discharged military personnel and wartime industrial workers in major cities where they could build their identities around their sexual desires. During the 1950s, two major divisions emerged that through the rest of the twentieth century would undermine the social and political solidarity among homosexuals that the diagnostic term implied. These divisions were reflected in the creation of the first two major postwar homophile organizations, the Mattachine Society and the Daughters of Bilitis.

The existence of two separate organizations was the result of distinct sets of priorities for lesbians and gay men, which constituted the first division. The mostly male Mattachine Society focused on the police entrapment and prosecution of men who cruised for sex in public places. The women who formed the Daughters of Bilitis were more concerned about problems such as child custody and the needs for social interaction of their members, who were less likely to have the sorts of public outlets that gay men had created. The two organizations adopted very similar approaches to reform, emphasizing education and efforts at conformity. But tensions between lesbians and gay men in political organizations persisted.

The second division lay in the distinction between radical and reformist agendas. The five men who formed the Mattachine Society in Los Angeles in 1950 were all current or former members of the Communist Party who used organizing techniques and tools of political analysis that they had learned from their Party work. They began to develop an account of homosexual identity as a distinct cultural and political phenomenon around which they could build a movement of resistance to oppression, including open challenges to police entrapment and other forms of discrimination. During the second Red Scare, the period of McCarthyism from roughly 1950 to 1954, the federal government fired more workers for suspicion of homosexuality than for suspicion of communism. But most members of the Mattachine Society proved unwilling to fight both battles at once. In 1953, conservative members took over as the communist founders and their allies left the organization. The conservatives chose to minimize the differences between homosexuals and the heterosexual majority by using activities such as blood drives to establish themselves as solid citizens. Just as gender difference would continue to define lesbian and gay civil rights organizing, so the movement would continue to split between those who saw sexual minorities as one among many that labored under an oppressive system in dire need of fundamental change and those who hoped to assimilate as lesbians and gay men with the surrounding society.

A surprising element entered the debate with the publication of the Kinsey Reports on the sexual behavior of human males in 1948 and of human females in 1953. Alfred Kinsey, an entomologist by training, changed dramatically the study of sex by focusing on individuals' reports of their activities without relying on a predetermined moral or developmental framework. He concluded that 95 percent of the population violated the law with their sexual activity, that one-third of adult males had had some sort of homosexual experience, and that roughly 10 percent of the United States population was lesbian or gay. Kinsey's figures, especially the estimate of the lesbian/gay population, would continue to play a central role in debates over lesbian/gay civil rights, with activists trumpeting the 10 percent figure as part of their demand for political recognition and opponents disputing it with their own estimates, while vilifying Kinsey himself at every opportunity.

Growing Militance and Growing Success

Discrimination in federal employment and security clearances became a major focal point for homophile organizing during the late 1950s and early 1960s. The Washington, D.C., chapter of the Mattachine Society organized pickets at various major public buildings, including the White House, in 1965. Though small, these demonstrations involved public acknowledgment of lesbian and gay identity, which was a huge step at the time, even for activists. That same year, in a general liberalizing of immigration law that removed the racist national origins quota system, Congress reinforced the prohibition on lesbian and gay aliens. Ten years later, however, after losing a federal court decision, the Civil Service Commission announced that it would no longer claim homosexual identity as a basis for discrimination in federal employment. Therefore, President William Jefferson Clinton technically added nothing new in 1998 when he put "sexual orientation" on a list of categories by which federal employers must not discriminate. But the symbolic gesture did precipitate an amendment in the House of Representatives to repeal it, which failed by a vote of 252 to 176. The issue at that point had solidified into a dispute between those who supported extending protections against discrimination based on race and gender to include sexual orientation and those who opposed such extension.

A major prop used to justify discrimination based on sexual orientation was the claim that all homosexuals suffered some psychopathology. During the 1950s, psychologist Evelyn Hooker had established that mental health professionals using standard diagnostic techniques could not reliably distinguish homosexual from heterosexual men. Critics of the psychopathology claim noted that its proponents consistently based all of their findings on populations that were incarcerated or had sought counseling without bothering to determine if those populations were representative of homosexuals as a whole. With the growing militance of the lesbian and gay civil rights movement after the still-celebrated Stonewall Riots of June 1969, the official characterization of homosexuality as mental illness by the American Psychiatric Association (APA) became a target for protest. Activists at first disrupted APA meetings, shouting down psychiatrists who claimed to have cured lesbians and gay men by making heterosexuals of them. Sympathetic psychiatrists arranged

for panels at subsequent meetings on which lesbian and gay activists could present evidence and argument for their mental health. In 1973, the APA officially decided to eliminate homosexuality as a diagnosis, but a significant minority dissented. Adherents of the thesis that homosexuality is a psychopathology increasingly allied themselves with political conservatives, emerging again during the late 1990s to support the Christian right's "ex-gay" movement of individuals who claimed to have converted to heterosexuality as part of their conversion to Christianity.

During the early 1970s, lesbian and gay activists enjoyed several successes, getting sodomy laws repealed and rights laws enacted in numerous jurisdictions. In 1977, however, voters in Dade County, Florida, repealed a lesbian and gay rights ordinance by almost 70 percent, setting off a series of similar repeals in Wichita, Kansas, St. Paul, Minnesota, and other locations. Christian conservatives led the charge in repeal efforts, claiming that homosexuality was a moral failing, not a minority identity, and therefore deserved no civil rights protections. Although the National Gay Task Force had existed since 1973, the Dade County ordinance fight was a major event in forging a national sense of political solidarity among lesbians and gay men. Similarly, the election of gay activist Harvey Milk to the San Francisco Board of Supervisors in 1978 cemented that city's status as the center of lesbian and gay culture and politics in the United States.

During the 1980s, the epidemic of Acquired Immune Deficiency Syndrome (AIDS) dramatically increased the sense of political solidarity among lesbians and gay men around the nation. Persons with AIDS, facing indifference to their situation from the administration of President Ronald Reagan, began lobbying Congress successfully for increased spending on research and treatment. In 1986, the U.S. Supreme Court further galvanized the political movement of gays and lesbians by upholding Georgia's sodomy statute against a privacy rights challenge. By 2000, however, nine state supreme courts, including Georgia's, had struck down sodomy laws under state constitutions, while twenty-six state legislatures had repealed their sodomy laws.

The 1990s proved a banner decade. The Hate Crimes Statistics Act included crimes motivated by bias against the victim's sexual orientation; it was the first federal law to use the category. Also, Congress passed both the Ryan White CARES Act to provide major funds for AIDS services and treatment and an immigration reform law that removed the prohibition on lesbian and gay aliens. The 1992 presidential election brought about a resurgence of debate over various lesbian and gay rights issues, but especially the ban on openly lesbian and gay military personnel. Colin Powell, the African American chairman of the Joint Chiefs of Staff, claimed that race was a "benign" characteristic for military service, but that sexual orientation was not. That year, Colorado voters amended their constitution to repeal all existing local lesbian and gay rights ordinances and to forbid their enactment in the future. In *Romer v. Evans* (1996), the U.S. Supreme Court struck down that amendment on equal protection grounds but without specifying sexual orientation as a "suspect classification," which would have placed sexual orientation on a par with race as a category that automatically triggers the highest level of judicial scrutiny.

By the end of the twentieth century, much lesbian and gay rights organizing focused on same-sex marriage and the Employment Nondiscrimination Act, a bill to prohibit employment discrimination based on sexual orientation. Twenty-six years of organizing and lobbying had produced major changes in public understanding around issues of sexual orientation, but as yet, few of the public policy changes that the lesbian and gay rights movement sought.

BIBLIOGRAPHY

Abelove, Henry, Michele Aina Barale, and David M. Halperin, eds. *The Lesbian and Gay Studies Reader.* New York: Routledge, 1993.

Bérubé, Allan. *Coming Out Under Fire: The History of Gay Men and Women during World War II.* New York: Free Press, 1990.

Chauncey, George. *Gay New York: Gender, Urban Culture, and the Makings of the Gay Male World, 1890–1940.* New York: Basic Books, 1994.

Clendinen, Dudley, and Adam Nagourney. *Out for Good: The Struggle to Build a Gay Rights Movement in America.* New York: Simon and Schuster, 1999.

D'Emilio, John. *Sexual Politics, Sexual Communities: The Making of a Homosexual Minority in the United States, 1945–1970.* Chicago: University of Chicago Press, 1983.

———, and Estelle Freedman. *Intimate Matters: A History of Sexuality in America.* New York: Harper and Row, 1988.

———, William B. Turner, and Urvashi Vaid, eds. *Creating Change: Sexuality, Public Policy, and Civil Rights.* New York: St. Martin's Press, 2000.

Duberman, Martin. *Stonewall.* New York: Dutton, 1993.

Eskridge, William N., Jr. *Gaylaw: Challenging the Apartheid of the Closet.* Cambridge, Mass.: Harvard University Press, 1999.

Faderman, Lillian. "The Morbidification of Love between Women by 19th-Century Sexologists." *Journal of Homosexuality* 4 (1978): 73–90.

Foucault, Michel. *The History of Sexuality: An Introduction.* Volume 1: *An Introduction.* New York: Random House, 1978.

Halperin, David M. *One Hundred Years of Homosexuality and Other Essays on Greek Love.* New York: Routledge, 1990.

Katz, Jonathan Ned. *Gay American History: Lesbians and Gay Men in the U.S.A.: A Documentary History.* Rev. ed. New York: Meridian, 1992.

———. *The Invention of Heterosexuality.* New York: Dutton, 1995.

Murdoch, Joyce, and Deb Price. *Courting Justice: Gay Men and Lesbians v. the Supreme Court.* New York: Basic Books, 2001.

Roscoe, Will. *Changing Ones: Third and Fourth Genders in Native North America.* New York: St. Martin's Press, 1998.

Shilts, Randy. *And the Band Played On: People, Politics, and the AIDS Epidemic.* New York: St. Martin's Press, 1987.

Turner, William B. *A Genealogy of Queer Theory.* Philadelphia: Temple University Press, 2000.

William B. Turner

See also **Civil Rights and Civil Liberties; Discrimination: Sexual Orientation; Gay and Lesbian Movement; Hate Crimes.**

SEXUALITY, along with race and gender, is an aspect of identity that historians paid relatively little attention to before 1975. Since then, however, it has become a very important topic for historical investigation, albeit one around which considerable theoretical debate swirls. Perhaps more than any other area of historical scholarship, the history of sexuality necessarily involves not only historians but anthropologists, literary critics, classicists, and philosophers. It is impossible to describe sexuality as a topic for historical inquiry in the United States without attending more than usual to historiographical debates, and to larger theoretical questions that encompass multiple disciplines. Regardless of whether one agrees that sexuality itself has a history, the history of sexuality as a topic for inquiry and debate in the late twentieth century is undoubtedly a major event in the intellectual and cultural history of the period. Recent research has demonstrated considerable variation in sexual practices and identities among different racial, ethnic, regional, and class groups even as it has demonstrated the centrality of sexuality to definitions of American national identity.

Indigenous Americans and Europeans

European conquerors and colonists saw sexual practice as distinguishing them from indigenous Americans starting with Columbus's first landing. About 1516, Vasco Nunez de Balboa, an early Spanish explorer of Central America, discovered men dressed as women and fed forty of them to his dogs. In North America and the United States, sexuality has consistently served since the beginning of European colonization as a basis for differentiating among racial and ethnic groups. This is so in the empirical sense that observers noted significant differences among the sexual practices and identity categories available to indigenous Americans, Africans and their descendents, and Europeans and their descendents in America. It is also the case in the sense that Europeans and their descendents have consistently relied on attributions of sexual immorality as justifications for discrimination against racial and ethnic minorities. Thus, sexuality has been a key to American national identity, and a major site for establishing and negotiating differences of power along lines of gender, race, and class, since 1607. The accounts of European observers throughout the Americas from the sixteenth century forward make clear that they could not separate their observations of indigenous sexuality from their European worldview, in which Christian prescriptions for proper gender roles and prohibitions on sodomy played a prominent role.

Consequently, understanding of indigenous and African sexual practices and identities in early America will always remain more partial and provisional than most historical understanding because the vast majority of the sources are highly moralizing or voyeuristic accounts by Europeans that tell us more about the European observers than about those they observed. However, most, if not all, of the indigenous peoples of North America had some institutionalized identity and role for males who wished to adopt a female role, and for females who wished to adopt a male role. Contemporary anthropologists and historians use "berdache" to describe this phenomenon. The specifics of the identity and role that these third-gendered natives assumed varied among tribes. In some instances parallel identities existed both for males who lived as females and females who lived as males, while others only institutionalized males living as females. In some cases berdaches had clearly defined social roles, such as undertaking and other funereal services in the Chumash and neighboring cultures around what is now Santa Barbara, California.

Sexual practice served not only to differentiate Europeans from native and African Americans, but as a vehicle for establishing and perpetuating European control over conquered peoples. Troops accompanying Columbus and later Spanish conquerors routinely used rape as one tactic for subjugating native populations. Venereal diseases, along with more well known infections, may have contributed to European dominance of the Americas. The Catholic Church as well as the Spanish and French governments tried to prohibit sexual contact between settlers and natives, but to little avail. French missionaries in Quebec complained that marriages between fur traders and Native women typically produced nativized Frenchmen rather than Frenchified Native women.

British North America

Slave owners routinely assumed sexual exploitation as a lagniappe of ownership. Beginning with the expectations of British planters in the Caribbean, however, North American planters started out relying primarily on male slaves and were slow to recognize the profit potential in slave women's reproduction. Slave sex ratios began to even out in North America during the middle of the eighteenth century primarily because of the fertility of those slave women whom traders brought over. The presence of wives and children helped solidify owners' control over male slaves by creating the threat of retribution against loved ones for the slave's misconduct, even as owners' sexual exploitation of slave women served as further demonstration of male slaves' powerlessness.

Europeans' voyeuristic attitudes toward images of naked, virile Native Americans and Africans as contrasted to supposedly more civilized Europeans, combined with the other deeply entrenched power differentials of slavery,

made attributions of sexual prowess and immorality key parts of the racist stereotypes that white Americans consistently used to justify and perpetuate discrimination against black Americans. After slavery, the charge that a black man had raped a white woman was the most reliable way to initiate a lynching. In some senses, black women could enjoy greater sexual freedom than white women, as reflected in the songs and other self-representations of black singers from Bessie Smith to Aretha Franklin. On the other hand, the overwhelming desire for respectability as an avenue to equal opportunity and treatment led many African American leaders to deny black sexuality altogether, creating difficulties for African American lesbian, gay, bisexual, and transgender persons and for efforts to reduce the spread of HIV starting in the late twentieth century.

Puritans strove to confine sexual activity within marriage, but encouraged it there. Changes in sexual practices and expectations contributed to the new sense of American identity in religious and political matters that emerged with the great awakening of the early eighteenth century. Times of political and social upheaval tend generally to reduce the effectiveness of restraints on sexual activity; the American Revolution was no exception. Judged by reports of children born too soon after marriage, premarital sex increased significantly in British North America during the late eighteenth century even as a longer-term shift from a general perception of women as morally weaker than men to a perception that women were sources of moral uplift and instruction for men generally, and especially for sons, took hold during the early national period. Regional variations became more pronounced as the growing distinction between public and private in the commercial north allowed women a measure of power in their homes that predominantly rural women of the south continued to lack.

Birth rates among European Americans remained unusually high in North America and the United States until 1800, at which point they began to drop steadily. In 1900, the birth rate was half its 1800 level, and it continued to fall, dropping below the replacement rate during the Great Depression and rebounding only during the Baby Boom from 1946 to 1964. Although historian Nancy Cott described a nineteenth-century ideal of "passionlessness" for middle-class white women, this notion can easily be overblown. One should emphasize its specificity in terms of race and class. The earliest explorations in the history of sexuality relied primarily on the elite discourse of magazines and marriage manuals. Subsequent research has revealed much greater variation in practice, with significant populations that either disregarded or remained largely unaware of white, middle-class ideals in matters of sexuality.

Birth rates consistently remained higher in the South than in the North and for black than white women. The birth rate decline long preceded significant declines in infant mortality. At the frontier, the birth rate was very low because almost all inhabitants were men. Recently settled areas just behind the frontier tended to have very high birth rates while urban commercial areas had low rates. Thus, race, class, and geography helped to determine the spread of sexual practices that reflected women's demands for increased autonomy, as in the burned-over district of New York and New England, and/or the calculation for middle-class urbanites that children were becoming a long-term cost rather than an asset because of their educational needs. This attitude contrasted with that of farmers, for whom children could provide labor at the earliest possible age.

The late nineteenth century produced both the largest cohort of never-married women in U.S. history and the idea of "voluntary motherhood," according to which women should control sexual activity in marriage as a means of controlling fertility. Although reforming middle-class women's efforts to "rescue" prostitutes dated to the antebellum period, some evidence indicates that voluntary motherhood carried with it a tacit acceptance that men who respected their wives' periodic demands for celibacy in the name of birth control would turn to prostitutes. While it is impossible to establish any clear links, the correlation between never-married women and the reform movements of the Progressive Era suggests that women's sexual relationships with men have political consequences at numerous levels. Whether they had sexual relationships with each other or not, many of the prominent women reformers of the late nineteenth and early twentieth centuries drew strength and inspiration from networks of close women friends. Changes in women's expectations and in men's roles in the new industrial, managerial economy contributed to the development of companionate marriage, more egalitarian and based on the expectation of love and fidelity, as the ideal for middle-class white couples beginning in the late nineteenth century. For many working-class white, immigrant, and African American couples, however, marriage remained as much an economic as an emotional and psychological arrangement.

The Administration of Sexuality

Sexual practice and identity attracted growing attention from the researchers and clinicians of the emerging biological, psychological, and social sciences and related professions during the Gilded Age and Progressive Era. Concerns about women's increased autonomy, combined with fears for the implications of absorbing an enormous number of immigrants, contributed to the pathologizing of intense romantic friendships between women as part of a larger move to connect deviant sexual activity with psychiatric diagnoses. Modern terminology for describing persons in terms of their sexual practices and presumed identities, such as "homosexual" and "heterosexual," emerged after 1870 as part of this new sexological discourse. Concerns and discussions about the relationship between sexual practice and national identity spread rapidly among professional and political elites. In 1905, President Theodore Roosevelt expressed concerns about "race

suicide," because he noted that native-born middle- and upper-class white women typically had far fewer children than immigrant women. He did not notice that the children of immigrants usually adopted the fertility patterns of their new land. In 1917, Congress created for the first time a category to exclude aliens with "abnormal sexual instincts," which would remain in immigration law in varying forms until 1990.

Mirroring Roosevelt, pioneering birth control advocate Margaret Sanger initially linked contraception to radical politics with her newspaper, *The Woman Rebel*, which she published briefly in 1914. Sanger learned of contraception after working with "Big Bill" Haywood of the Industrial Workers of the World and anarchist Emma Goldman in the early years of the twentieth century. She traveled to France, where she discovered that women routinely practiced contraception. She initially characterized contraception as a form of class warfare in which workers would deprive capitalists of wage slaves. Sanger's agitation accompanied a significant shift in sexual mores in the United States, at least in the major cities, beginning around 1910. Sexual experimentation outside of marriage increased, and popularized discussions of Sigmund Freud's psychoanalytic theories provided a new vocabulary of sexual repression as an omnipresent motivation in human action. Sanger's own career paralleled a general increase in the spread of knowledge about sexuality as both gradually lost their radical associations and the field became more professionalized from World War I on.

World War I precipitated further French surprises for Americans, as military leaders resisted the French solution to venereal disease—inspecting and licensing prostitutes. The large-scale population movements, such as African Americans moving from south to north, and workers generally moving to cities, contributed to the social disruption that created new opportunities for sexual experimentation among many Americans, especially young adults. In this respect as in many others, World War I anticipated trends that would occur on an even larger scale during World War II. The 1920s typically have a reputation as a decade of sexual permissiveness, with women smoking in public and wearing shorter skirts, but the same decade saw the recrudescence of a Ku Klux Klan that policed illicit sexual relationships, especially across racial and ethnic lines, as part of its culturally conservative program to sustain its ideal of American identity. With the onset of the Great Depression, employers including the federal government fired married women in order to create jobs for men. Virtually all couples began to count more closely the cost of each child, driving the birth rate to its lowest point in U.S. history.

World War II

World War II demanded long work hours from parents, leaving them less time to supervise their children. It also inspired some female adolescents to demonstrate their patriotism by bestowing sexual favors on soldiers. The war put large numbers of young adults, mostly men, but many women as well, into sex-segregated military environments and perhaps in large cities, away from parental supervision, for the first time. These changes contributed substantially to increased sexual activity among opposite-sex couples, but also among same-sex couples. At the same time, World War II saw the first use by the U.S. military of psychological tests and diagnoses in order to determine soldiers' aptitude as well as to exclude undesirables, especially lesbians and gay men. The effort largely failed, but it did result in significant punishments for many soldiers who got caught in same-sex activity, which in turn contributed to the growth of postwar lesbian and gay civil rights movements by creating a self-conscious group of veterans who saw their dishonorable discharges as an injustice.

Post World War II

The post–World War II period has seen an explosion of interest in and discussion about sexuality in the United States. The publication of the Kinsey reports on the sexual behavior of males (1948) and of females (1953), with claims that many women engaged in premarital intercourse and many men had at least some same-sex activity, touched off a frenzy of debate and revealed the capacity of the American public to find fascination in information about its own sexual practices. During the red scare of the 1950s, political leaders equated the foreign threat of communism with the domestic threat of homosexuality as part of a general effort to restore "normality" to American life via domesticity. The federal government fired more workers for suspicion of homosexuality than for suspicion of communist activity. One fired federal worker, Franklin Kameny, would spend the next thirty-five years fighting discrimination in federal employment and security clearances. The early 1950s also saw the formation of the first two "homophile" organizations, the Mattachine Society and the Daughters of Bilitis, which approached lesbian and gay civil rights as a reformist campaign for respectability through cooperation with psychiatrists and other influential professionals.

Most observers identify the 1960s as a key decade for changes in Americans' sexual attitudes. The anovulent pill became available as a means of contraception, protest on college campuses included resistance to curfews and restrictions on visitation, and theorists such as Herbert Marcuse linked sexual repression to other political problems. Feminists and lesbian and gay rights activists drew inspiration from the civil rights movement to make their demands and their tactics more militant. On the other hand, federal policymakers, lacking historical information about Africans' adaptation of their family forms under slavery and refusing to acknowledge the ongoing effects of racism, claimed that overly powerful black women were responsible for the widespread breakdown of black families.

Late Twentieth Century

From the 1970s onward, sexual practices and identities became major topics of cultural and political debate in the United States. The conservative movement that had coalesced around opposition to communism and support for Barry Goldwater took up lesbian and gay civil rights, the Equal Rights Amendment, and abortion as causes that, in their view, undermined long-standing moral principles that buttressed the American way of life. They pointed to the rising divorce rate, widespread use of sexual imagery in advertising and television programs, and the increasing visibility of lesbians and gay men as indicators of a nation in moral decline. Conservative President Ronald Reagan routinely made statements supporting "traditional" ideals of gender and sexuality, cut off the access to the White House that lesbian/gay civil rights activists had enjoyed during the Carter administration, and steadfastly ignored the new epidemic of Acquired Immune Deficiency Syndrome (AIDS) that emerged during his first year in office, 1981, because the vast majority of victims in the United States were gay men who transmitted the AIDS virus via anal intercourse.

During the closing years of the twentieth century, technological advance spread debates over sexuality into new areas. In vitro fertilization and surrogate motherhood raised legal issues that American institutions proved ill prepared for. The U.S. government granted an asylum request to a woman who feared she would suffer genital mutilation if she returned to her home country. Transgender activists, including transsexuals but also others who defied gender norms, struggled for recognition even from the lesbian and gay civil rights movement, much less conventional political and legal institutions. Intersexed persons, born with ambiguous genitalia, began to speak publicly against the medical practice of surgically assigning a sex to such babies at birth.

Sexuality as a Topic for History and Theory

Amidst such political confusion, major scholarly work on the history of sexuality began to emerge. Carroll Smith Rosenberg, Jonathan Ned Katz, Lillian Faderman, Jeffrey Weeks, and John D'Emilio all published important articles and books that explored sexual practice and identity as historical topics between 1975 and 1983. Much the way the African American and women's movements sparked increased interest in African American and women's history, so the increased visibility of the lesbian and gay civil rights movement after 1969 led a growing number of scholars to wonder about the history of sexual minorities. Historical study of sexuality depended on the belief that sexual minorities merited study and that sexuality was as much a historical as a medical or psychological topic. Both the politics of the scholars who conducted the research, and the evidence they found, contributed to the conclusion that definitions of sexuality varied not only on their own terms and with respect to gender, but in relation to race and class as well. The *Radical History Review* published a special issue on the history of sexuality in 1979.

Because of his status as an established scholar in France and his willingness to make provocative claims, Michel Foucault came to overshadow most American scholars during the 1980s and to define the field with volume one of *The History of Sexuality*, which appeared in English in 1978. Foucault's work has proven more valuable for the conceptual framework it provides than for the empirical claims it makes. It has also provoked considerable intellectual and political debate, with important scholars such as John Boswell dissenting vigorously from the claim for the recent provenance of "homosexuality" and "heterosexuality" as identity categories. Regardless, sexuality as a matter of individual, cultural, and national identity will continue to motivate considerable historical research for the foreseeable future.

BIBLIOGRAPHY

Abelove, Henry, Michele Aina Barale, and David M. Halperin, eds. *The Lesbian and Gay Studies Reader.* New York: Routledge, 1993.

Bailey, Beth. *Sex in the Heartland.* Cambridge, Mass.: Harvard University Press, 1999.

Berube, Allan. *Coming Out Under Fire: The History of Gay Men and Women during World War II.* New York: Free Press, 1990.

Chauncey, George. *Gay New York: Gender, Urban Culture, and the Making of the Gay Male World, 1890–1940.* New York: Basic Books, 1994.

D'Emilio, John, and Estelle B. Freedman. *Intimate Matters: A History of Sexuality in America.* New York: Harper and Row, 1988.

D'Emilio, John, William B. Turner, and Urvashi Vaid, eds. *Creating Change: Sexuality, Public Policy, and Civil Rights.* New York: St. Martin's Press, 2000.

Duberman, Martin Bauml, Martha Vicinus, and George Chauncey, Jr. *Hidden from History: Reclaiming the Gay and Lesbian Past.* New York: New American Library, 1989.

Foucault, Michel. *The History of Sexuality: An Introduction.* Volume 1. New York: Random House, 1978.

Gordon, Linda. *Woman's Body, Woman's Right: A Social History of Birth Control in America.* New York: Penguin Books, 1977.

Howard, John, ed. *Carryin' on in the Lesbian and Gay South.* New York: New York University Press, 1997.

Katz, Jonathan Ned. *Gay American History: Lesbians and Gay Men in the U.S.A., a Documentary History.* New York: Meridian, 1976; rev. ed., 1992.

———. *The Invention of Heterosexuality.* New York: Dutton, 1995.

Peiss, Kathy, and Christina Simmons, eds., with Robert A. Padgug. *Passion and Power: Sexuality in History.* Philadelphia: Temple University Press, 1989.

Roscoe, Will. *Changing Ones: Third and Fourth Genders in Native North America.* New York: St. Martin's Griffin, 1998.

Smith, Merril D., ed. *Sex and Sexuality in Early America.* New York: New York University Press, 1998.

Turner, William B. *A Genealogy of Queer Theory.* Philadelphia: Temple University Press, 2000.

William B. Turner

See also **Birth Control Movement; Gay and Lesbian Movement; Gender and Gender Roles; Military Service and Minorities: Homosexuals; Pornography; Prostitution.**

SEXUALLY TRANSMITTED DISEASES.

Sexually transmitted diseases (STDs) are infections communicated between persons through sexual intercourse or other intimate sexual contact. In the early 1970s, as the number of recognized STDs grew, the World Health Organization adopted the term to supersede the five diseases that collectively had been called venereal diseases (VD), chancroid, gonorrhea, granuloma inguinal, lymphogranuloma venereum, and syphilis. More than sixty other infections of bacteria, protozoa, fungi, and viruses that can be transmitted sexually have been added to the designation.

Of the venereal diseases, gonorrhea and syphilis were the most prevalent in the United States before World War II. Because of the social stigma attached to the diseases and the difficulty in diagnosing them, statistics of their incidence are often unreliable when available at all. One 1901 study concluded that as many as eighty of every one hundred men in New York City suffered an infection of gonorrhea at some time. The same study reported 5 to 18 percent of all men had syphilitic infections. Progressive Era reformers and social critics pointed to the high incidence of venereal diseases and the moral and public health threats they posed to families and communities as evidence of a cultural crisis. Combating venereal diseases was an important component of the social hygiene movement during this period. The high rates of venereal diseases among military personnel also led the U.S. War Department to institute far-reaching anti-VD campaigns during World Wars I and II. Soldiers were told that VD, like the enemy on the battlefield, threatened not only their health but America's military strength.

The reform impulse that began during the Progressive Era and World War I subsided until the 1930s, when the U.S. Public Health Service renewed efforts against syphilis and gonorrhea, resulting in the 1938 passage of the National Venereal Disease Control Act. Disease control efforts in the 1930s included requiring mandatory premarital tests for VD in many states. Widespread disease testing and the introduction of penicillin in 1943 contributed to declining VD rates after World War II. But by the late 1950s the rates began a steady increase that persisted with liberal sexual attitudes in the 1960s and 1970s.

During the 1980s the global pandemic of ACQUIRED IMMUNE DEFICIENCY SYNDROME (AIDS) overshadowed other STDs. Between 1981 and 2000, 774,467 cases of AIDS were reported in the United States; 448,060 people

Syphilis. A curable disease, but one of the most prevalent sexually transmitted diseases (or "venereal diseases," as they were called at the time) in the United States until the 1940s, when rates started to decline. This 1941 poster urges those suffering from syphilis to seek treatment. LIBRARY OF CONGRESS

nosis, chlamydia, gonorrhea, hepatitis B, herpes, human papillomavirus (hpv), syphilis, and trichomoniasis.

Incidence and prevalence vary dramatically from disease to disease. The incidence of some diseases, such as syphilis, reached a historic low in the late 1990s, while those of other diseases, such as chlamydia, genital herpes, and gonorrhea, continued to increase during the same period. STDs also pose an economic cost. The costs of the major STDs and their complications totaled almost $17 billion in 1994. With the emergence of antibiotic-resistant strains of once-treatable STDs, the problem has persisted as a major public health concern.

BIBLIOGRAPHY

Brandt, Allan M. *No Magic Bullet: A Social History of Venereal Disease in the United States since 1880.* New York: Oxford University Press, 1985.

National Center for HIV, STD, and TB Prevention, Division of Sexually Transmitted Diseases. *Tracking the Hidden Epidemics, 2000: Trends in STDs in the United States.* Atlanta: Centers for Disease Control and Prevention, 2001.

Poirier, Suzanne. *Chicago's War on Syphilis, 1937–40: The Times, The Trib, and the Clap Doctor.* Urbana: University of Illinois Press, 1995.

Shilts, Randy. *And the Band Played On: Politics, People, and the AIDS Epidemic.* New York: St. Martin's Press, 1987.

Smith, Raymond A., ed. *Encyclopedia of AIDS: A Social, Political, Cultural, and Scientific Record of the HIV Epidemic.* New York: Penguin, 2001.

D. George Joseph

See also **Sex Education.**

died of AIDS. Nearly 1 million other Americans were also infected by the human immunodeficiency virus (HIV), the virus that causes AIDS. The development of powerful antiretroviral therapies during the 1990s prolonged the lives of many Americans infected by HIV or suffering from AIDS.

In 2000, 65 million people in the United States were living with an incurable STD, and annually approximately 15 million new cases of STDs were diagnosed, of which nearly half were incurable. Of particular concern to public health officials was that nearly one-fourth of new STD infections occurred in teenagers. Also of concern was that STDs affected women and African Americans in disproportionately greater numbers and with more complications. The rates of gonorrhea and syphilis, for instance, were thirty times higher for African Americans than for whites. The most common STDs were bacterial vagi-

SHAKERS. The United Society of Believers in Christ's Second Appearing was a small sect founded by working-class men and women in Manchester, England, in the late 1740s. These "Believers," as they called themselves, were derided as "Shakers" because their bodies shook and trembled in religious devotion. Convinced that the Day of Judgment was nigh, they expressed contempt for earthly authority and respectable churches. Ann Lee, the illiterate woman who would become the sect's revered American leader, was jailed twice for disturbing Anglican services.

In 1774 a small cohort immigrated to New York and eventually clustered in the Hudson Valley, north of Albany, but they had not escaped repression. Shakers were arrested as troublemakers whose pacifism undermined the revolutionary cause. They were whipped, beaten, and accused of witchcraft. As they began to draw American converts, "Mother Ann" Lee's prophecies and teachings set the rules and defined the goals of life within the United Society. After her death in 1784, some believers regarded her as the second incarnation of God.

The two American converts who followed Mother Ann as Lead Elder—Joseph Meacham (1787–1796) and

Shakers. Rows of male and female "Believers," usually strictly separated, dance in lines at their upstate New York village. © CORBIS

Lucy Wright (1796–1821)—developed an institutional structure for less antagonistic relations with society. A village erected in the 1780s on a mountainside overlooking New Lebanon, New York, became the movement's headquarters. Emissaries supervised the "gathering" of new communities in hill country regions of Connecticut, Massachusetts, New Hampshire, and Maine. In the early nineteenth century the movement expanded into Ohio, Indiana, and Kentucky. By the mid-1820s about 4,000 believers lived in sixteen communal villages, usually with residential "Great Houses" surrounded by meetinghouses, barns, mills, workshops, and smaller residences for children and probationary members. A hierarchy of elders and eldresses who had completely abandoned the sinful world were in charge.

The practical arrangement of life in these communities was more important than any wrangling over theology. The goals were separation from unbelievers, a simple and harmonious life, and equality of men and women. In practice, believers gave up private property and worked for the common benefit in a rotation of tasks. Sexual relations were prohibited and men and women lived in strictly enforced separation.

In the early decades believers faced hardship together. But they proved to be skilled at marketing a wide variety of products, such as seeds and herbs, diapers and cloaks, and tools and furniture. Life among the believers reached levels of comfort and security that drew admiration from utopian socialist communities. The most prominent mid-nineteenth century Shaker leader, Elder Frederick Evans, had been a radical New York labor leader before he was converted by a series of nightly visitations by angels. He spoke for "progressive" Shakers who wished to see their movement more active in reform of society. An opposing faction feared that material success would lure "lukewarm" converts and undermine the pursuit of holy simplicity.

In fact, there were too few converts and too many defectors. After peaking at about 6,000 in the 1840s, membership declined steadily to about 855 in 1900, 40 in

Shaker Meetinghouse. The building, designed by Moses Johnson and built in 1794, is in Sabbathday Lake, Maine. © CORBIS

1950, and 8 in 2000. Some Shaker villages became tourist sites. Shaker songs, furniture, and recipes became American favorites. Popular nostalgia converted the once-persecuted Shakers into a charming sect.

BIBLIOGRAPHY
Brewer, Priscilla J. *Shaker Communities, Shaker Lives.* Hanover, N.H.: University Press of New England, 1986.
Stein, Stephen J. *The Shaker Experience in America: A History of the United Society of Believers.* New Haven, Conn.: Yale University Press, 1992.

Lewis Perry

SHANTY TOWNS as an American social phenomenon first appeared during the lag in reemployment after WORLD WAR I, rising on dump heaps or wastelands within or at the edges of large industrial cities. Such communities also existed during the GREAT DEPRESSION, when they received the indulgence if not the approval of officials. The shanties were constructed and occupied by single men who had fitted into an economy of abundance as transient workers. Forced to stay in one place, they built crude homes of any free material available, such as boxes, waste lumber, and tin cans. Some occupied abandoned boilers, boxcars, and caves. They continued to take odd jobs when they could be found, living on the scant wages with the extra aid of social agencies.

BIBLIOGRAPHY
Fearis, Donald F. *The California Farm Worker, 1930–1942.* Ph.D thesis. University of California-Davis, 1971.

Charles J. Finger / A. R.

See also **Bonus Army; Depression of 1920; Poverty.**

SHARE-THE-WEALTH MOVEMENTS. At the lowest point of the GREAT DEPRESSION in 1932–1933, the popular mind embraced two contradictory notions: a prophecy of impending doom and a promise of potential utopia. These ideas, together with high UNEMPLOYMENT, an insecure middle class, and the deepening plight of the aged, formed the common basis of appeal for the great mass organizations that sprang into existence in the South and West between 1933 and 1936. Among those promoting the redistribution of wealth were Francis E. Townsend's plan; Louisiana Sen. Huey P. Long's Share-Our-Wealth Clubs; the NATIONAL UNION FOR SOCIAL JUSTICE party, started by Father Charles E. Coughlin, Townsend, and Rev. Gerald L. K. Smith; and Upton Sinclair's EPIC (End Poverty in California).

Differing widely in their proposals, all but the EPIC depended on inflationist doctrine, and all utilized national radio hookups, skilled pressure politics, huge mass meetings, and frenzied emotionalism. Moving in and out of alliance with the New Deal and with one another, they ran the gamut of reform tactics: charismatic leaders driving for power, attempts to capture an old party, forming a third party, backing candidates of either party who supported "the plan," and attempts to perfect schemes within single states. All these movements shared anxious disillusionment, distress, an experimental frame of mind, and the complete unreality of party divisions in the United States.

BIBLIOGRAPHY
Brinkley, Alan. *Voices of Protest: Huey Long, Father Coughlin, and the Great Depression.* New York: Knopf, 1982.
Burns, James MacGregor. *The Crosswinds of Freedom.* New York: Knopf, 1989.

C. Vann Woodward / C. W.

See also **Technocracy Movement; Third Parties.**

SHARECROPPERS were agricultural wage laborers who raised crops on farm plots owned by large landowners in the post–Civil War era. Both landless whites and blacks worked as sharecroppers, although the majority of sharecroppers were African Americans. The system of sharecropping primarily existed in the southern states and was the end result of struggles between former planters and recently freed slaves over the terms of a new labor system. On one level, sharecropping was a compromise between planters who wanted a docile labor force and freedmen who wanted to purchase and work their own farmlands. In this arrangement, the planter supplied the sharecropper with the land, housing, tools, and seeds, and assumed chief supervision of the farming operations. The planter also retained legal rights to the crop. Sharecroppers brought only their labor to the bargaining table. After harvest, the sharecropper would be paid a share of the produce in lieu of cash wages. Typically he would receive one-third to one-half of the crops.

The sharecropping system was financially oppressive and most sharecroppers were unable to break out of a cycle of poverty and debt. Sharecroppers were responsible for providing their own board and clothing. Landlords would sometimes extend credit for food and living necessities at exorbitant interest rates, either through a local storekeeper or at a plantation commissary. Often the amount a sharecropper owed the landlord at "settling time" exceeded the value of his share of the crop. Unable to support himself or his family until the next harvest, the sharecropper would have to ask for more credit. Bad weather, poor crops, or declining prices on the cotton market could also make it difficult to get ahead. Occasionally, planters would pass punitive laws restricting the farm laborers' mobility, thereby increasing the chance that sharecroppers might find themselves tied to the land in a perpetual cycle of debt.

By the time of the Great Depression the sharecropping system was beginning to break down. The Agricultural Adjustment Act under the New Deal encouraged planters to reduce their acreage production in exchange for government payments. Landlords rarely shared these payments with their sharecroppers. Instead, many sharecroppers were evicted from the land and migrated to urban areas. In the 1940s the increasing mechanization of farm production, including the introduction of tractors and cotton pickers, made sharecropping all but obsolete. Rather than relying on sharecroppers, landlords employed wageworkers to meet their limited labor needs.

BIBLIOGRAPHY

Conrad, David Eugene. *The Forgotten Farmers: The Story of Sharecroppers in the New Deal.* Urbana: University of Illinois Press, 1965.

Woodman, Harold D. *New South, New Law: The Legal Foundations of Credit and Labor Relations in the Postbellum Agricultural South.* Baton Rouge: Louisiana State University Press, 1995.

Natalie J. Ring

See also **Feudalism; New Deal.**

SHAWNEE. Ancient residents of the Ohio Valley, the Shawnees ("Shawanos" or "Southerners") are an Alqonquian-speaking people who were living in villages scattered across southern Ohio, Indiana, and Illinois when they first encountered the French in the 1670s. During the next two decades, as the Iroquois expanded west, part of the Shawnees sought refuge among the Creeks in Georgia and Alabama, while others fled to northern Illinois, where they established new villages near Fort St. Louis, a French post at Starved Rock, on the Illinois River. By 1715, the Shawnees had reassembled in southern Pennsylvania, erecting villages along the Susquehanna and Monongahela rivers. As the Iroquois threat diminished, they gradually reoccupied their old homelands along the Muskingum, Scioto, and Mad Rivers in southern and central Ohio, often crossing the Ohio River to hunt deer and bison in the Bluegrass region of Kentucky.

During the colonial period the Shawnees divided their loyalties between the British and French, often attempting to "play off" both sides to their own advantage. Although ostensibly friendly to the French, they readily

Sharecroppers. A destitute family of nine, in torn clothes and worn-out shoes. © CORBIS-BETTMANN

accepted presents from colonial legislatures in Pennsylvania and Virginia and welcomed British traders into their villages. At the beginning of the Seven Years' War, the Shawnees participated in Braddock's Defeat and initially raided the Virginia frontier, but after the British captured Fort Duquesne, they temporarily withdrew from the fighting. In 1763 they joined with other tribes to support Pontiac's Rebellion and besieged Fort Pitt, but were defeated by the British at the Battle of Bushy Run (August 1763) and again made a reluctant peace with the Redcoats. Yet in the early 1770s, as the Virginians, or "Long Knives," crossed the mountains onto Shawnee hunting lands in Kentucky, Shawnees resisted, precipitating what the colonists called Lord Dunmore's War. The Shawnees eventually were defeated at the Battle of Point Pleasant (October 1774) and reduced their attacks upon American settlements in the Bluegrass region, but their bitterness toward the Long Knives continued.

The American Revolution provided the Shawnees with arms and allies to renew their war against Virginia. Led by their war chief Black Fish, the Shawnees assisted the British and spearheaded Indian attacks upon the settlements in Kentucky. In return, their villages were attacked by the Americans, and in 1779, about 1,000 Shawnees (one-third of the tribe) abandoned their Ohio villages and migrated to Spanish Missouri. The Shawnees who remained in Ohio continued to raid Kentucky throughout the war, and following the Treaty of Paris, they opposed any American settlement north of the Ohio. During the early 1790s, they combined with other tribes to defeat American armies led by Josiah Harmer (October 1790) and Arthur St. Clair (November 1791). In August 1794, they were defeated by Anthony Wayne at the Battle of Fallen Timbers, and with no prospect of further British support, they signed the Treaty of Greenville, relinquishing most of Ohio to the United States.

In the first decade of the nineteenth century, the Shawnee Prophet and his brother Tecumseh attempted to unite the tribes of the Midwest and Southeast into a pan-Indian coalition designed to prevent the further sale of Indian lands to the government. Their efforts were thwarted by the jealousy of traditional tribal chiefs, and by William Henry Harrison who attacked and destroyed their village, Prophetstown, at the Battle of Tippecanoe, in November 1811. During the War of 1812, part of the Shawnees supported Tecumseh who allied with the British, but the majority of the group followed Black Hoof, who sided with the Americans. When Tecumseh was killed by American militia at the Battle of the Thames (October 1813), Shawnee resistance to the Americans crumbled.

In the decades following the War of 1812, most Shawnees were removed from Ohio to Kansas and Missouri. Some sought temporary refuge with Cherokees in Texas, but after Texas became independent of Mexico, they returned to the United States. In the aftermath of the Civil War, most were assigned reservations in Okla-

The Prophet. A portrait of Tenskwatawa ("Open Door"), also called the Prophet, whose visions inspired many Indians to join his brother Tecumseh in an effort to drive Americans out of tribal lands. He was in command at the Shawnee defeat along the Tippecanoe River, and he lived for two decades after Tecumseh was killed and the resistance ended. ARCHIVE PHOTOS

homa where they formed three separate bands. Today the Absentee Shawnees maintain a tribal office at Shawnee, Oklahoma; the Loyal Shawnees, closely allied with the Western Cherokees, have a tribal building at White Oak Oklahoma; while the Eastern Shawnee Tribe is headquartered at Seneca, Missouri, near the Oklahoma border. Other small communities of Shawnees, while not officially recognized by the federal government, still reside in Kansas, Missouri, and Ohio.

BIBLIOGRAPHY

Edmunds, R. David. *The Shawnee Prophet.* Lincoln: University of Nebraska Press, 1983.

———. *Tecumseh and the Quest for Indian Leadership.* Boston: Little, Brown and Co., 1984.

Kohn, Rita, and W. Lynwood Montell, eds. *Always a People: Oral Histories of Contemporary Woodland Indians.* Bloomington: Indiana University Press, 1997.

McConnell, Michael M. *A Country Between: The Upper Ohio Valley and Its People, 1724–1774.* Lincoln: University of Nebraska Press, 1992.

Sugden, John. *Blue Jacket: Warrior of the Shawnees*. Lincoln: University of Nebraska Press, 2000.

———. *Tecumseh: A Life*. New York: Holt, 1998.

See also **Battle of Tippecanoe; Dunmore's War; French and Indian War; Pontiac's War; Tecumseh, Crusade of.**

SHAYS'S REBELLION, an agrarian rebellion centered in Massachusetts and committed to debt relief for small farmers and rural artisans, August 1786–June 1787. Though former Continental Army Captain Daniel Shays was its nominal leader, the rebellion was relatively loose and decentralized.

After the American Revolution, the new United States suffered from a severe cash-flow problem. Merchants no longer enjoyed access to British markets and were stuck with large inventories. Unable to repay English creditors, they demanded money from numerous customers carrying small debts. At the same time, the state and Confederation governments were raising taxes to fund their own war debts.

Thus farmers and rural artisans, who were accustomed to a barter economy, owed creditors and tax collectors cash they did not have. As the economy worsened, they increasingly found themselves hauled into debtors'

Daniel Shays. An engraving of the nominal leader of the 1786–1787 rebellion conducted by hard-hit farmers and rural artisans protesting debt collection in Massachusetts after the American Revolution. THE GRANGER COLLECTION

courts or prisons. (Shays himself was sued twice.) Beginning in 1784, members of an inchoate agrarian movement peacefully proposed through town petitions and county conventions that states issue paper money or pass tender laws, which would allow debt payment in goods and services as well as hard currency. But with the exception of Rhode Island, New England's legislatures were dominated by commercial interests and refused to enact reform.

In the late summer and fall of 1786, armed Shaysites, adopting the symbols and rhetoric of the Revolution, started raiding and closing down various courts, aiming to suspend debt collection until states addressed their grievances. An estimated 9,000 people throughout New England participated in these early stages of rebellion.

Legislators reacted aggressively, arresting a number of Shaysites, calling out militias, suspending habeas corpus, and passing harsh laws, including the Riot Act (limiting public assembly) and the Treason Act (penalizing anti-government violence by death). Unable to requisition money to raise a proposed federal militia, local merchants funded an army of local troops.

In January, the Shaysites abandoned their policy of raiding courthouses in favor of wider rebellion. Talking now about overthrowing state government and not simply reforming debtors' courts and the tax system, about 2,500 farmers and artisans attacked the Massachusetts state arsenal at Springfield. The Shaysites were easily defeated in battle, but over the next four months small bands raided market towns such as Stockbridge and Great Barrington, kidnapping and terrorizing lawyers, merchants, military leaders, and politicians.

By June, however, the hostilities had come to an end. A number of frustrated rebels, including Shays, moved farther West where they could continue subsistence farming. In addition, the new legislature and a new governor passed a one-year tender act, and the economy started to show signs of improvement.

The rebellion, which was winding down as the Constitutional Convention met in Philadelphia in May, helped the federalists gain control of the proceedings. Convinced that unchecked democracy and a weak national government would enable a tyranny of the majority, the delegates wrote a constitution that rolled back some of the most radical revolutionary reforms by providing for a strong, indirectly elected president, an indirectly elected senate, and appointed judges.

Szatmary, David. *Shays' Rebellion: The Making of an Agrarian Insurrection*. Amherst: University of Massachusetts Press, 1980.

Taylor, Robert Joseph. *Western Massachusetts in the Revolution*. Providence, R.I.: Brown University Press, 1954.

See also **Constitution of the United States; Insurrections, Domestic;** *and vol. 9:* **Shays's Rebellion.**

SHEEP. Sixteenth-century European colonists introduced sheep into the Americas. They accompanied the Spanish to Mexico, while the English brought sheep to Virginia and Massachusetts. They came along with the Dutch to New York and with the Swedes to New Jersey. These animals were unimproved, however, because farmers had yet to begin selective breeding of their sheep.

In colonial times, famers raised sheep as a part of self-sufficient agriculture to supply wool for homespun clothing and not for commercial purposes. Because of wolves, improper care, and British competition, the number of sheep remained relatively few and the quality and quantity of the wool poor. The industry improved somewhat during the American Revolution but slumped after peace and the resumption of British trade.

The first decades of the nineteenth century witnessed a marked change. Two events of importance occurred: the introduction of merino sheep and the exclusion of British competitors from the American market by the various nonintercourse acts and the War of 1812. In 1801–1802, the first merinos arrived from France and Spain. In 1807, with the passage of the EMBARGO ACT, native mills increased, wool prices skyrocketed, and the demand for fine-wool sheep became insatiable. A merino craze followed. Merino wool sold for $2 a pound, and the early importers sold sheep for $1,000 a head. In the midst of this craze, the Napoleonic armies broke the Spanish restrictions on the exportation of merinos, and between 1808 and 1811, importers brought approximately 24,000 merinos into the United States. Sheep raising had entered its commercial phase.

After 1815 British woolen importations again depressed the industry. Soon, however, the growth of the factory system and the tariff of 1828 revived it. Woolen manufactures doubled in a decade, the price of wool went up, and eastern flocks increased tremendously. In the 1830s, 60 percent of American sheep were in New England and the middle Atlantic states. After 1840, because of westward migration, improved transportation facilities, easy access to cheap western land, and an increase in the prices of foodstuffs, the center of sheep raising shifted westward. By 1850 it was in the OHIO VALLEY.

The Civil War produced a second merino craze. After the war, the type of sheep raised in the United States underwent improvement through importations of European breeds and selective breeding. Sheep raising continued to expand west to the Rocky Mountains and Pacific coast states. Farmers in this region at first concentrated on wool production, while those of the eastern United States, under the stimulus of growing urban markets, shifted to mutton production. Eastern sheep farmers turned to new English mutton breeds, including the Leicester and Shropshire. After 1890 sheep growers of the western United States began to place more emphasis on dual-purpose sheep, and mutton production and lamb feeding developed in this area as well.

The importance of western states in the raising of sheep continued into the twentieth century, and by 1935, 60 percent of all the sheep in the United States were in that region. The total number of sheep raised throughout the country reached a peak of 51.8 million that same year. By 1973 the number of sheep had declined to 17.7 million. Of these, only 48 percent were coming from the western states, which represented a shift away from the region. By 2000 the number had fallen even more steeply to only 7 million, but the western United States had regained its dominance of the industry, with Texas leading the nation in both number of sheep-raising operations and animals. Currently, 80 percent of sheep in the United States are raised for consumption, but because few Americans regularly eat lamb or mutton, Mexico imports the vast majority of the meat. Nonetheless, the burgeoning Hispanic and Middle Eastern population in the United States, which does frequently consume lamb and mutton, is increasing the domestic demand for the product.

BIBLIOGRAPHY

Carlson, Paul Howard. *Texas Woollybacks: The Range Sheep and Goat Industry.* College Station: Texas A&M University Press, 1982.

Crockett, Norman L. *The Woolen Industry of the Midwest.* Lexington: University Press of Kentucky, 1970.

Gemming, Elizabeth. *Wool Gathering: Sheep Raising in Old New England.* New York: Coward, McCann, and Geoghegan, 1979.

Miller, Char, ed. *Fluid Arguments: Five Centuries of Western Water Conflict.* Tucson: University of Arizona Press, 2001.

Wagner, Frederic H. *Predator Control and the Sheep Industry: The Role of Science in Policy Formation.* Claremont, Calif.: Regina Books, 1988.

Robert G. Dunbar / A. E.

See also **Agriculture; Food and Cuisines; Livestock Industry; Meatpacking; Tariff; Textiles; Wool Growing and Manufacture.**

SHEEP WARS. The Sheep Wars were range battles fought in the American West between CATTLE and SHEEP ranchers. Although some of the confrontations undoubtedly grew out of mere disputes over land and water rights, the main cause was the propensity of sheep to overgraze the range, sometimes making the lands unusable to cattle herds for months. Moreover, sheep polluted watering places used by cattle.

Spanish colonists introduced the sheep industry to the American West in the early seventeenth century, although conflict between the needs of sheep and cattle did not peak until long after the intrusion of Anglo-Americans. By 1875 clashes between cattlemen and sheepmen occurred regularly along the New Mexico–Texas boundary. New Mexican sheepmen drove their flocks onto the range of Charles Goodnight; Goodnight's cowhands, in retaliation, drove more than four hundred sheep into the Canadian River, where they drowned. In 1876 Goodnight and the sheepmen agreed to divide the Staked Plain range, giving the sheepmen the Canadian River valley, and giving Goodnight undisturbed access to the Palo Duro Canyon area of northwestern Texas.

Other range controversies ended in bloodshed. In Colorado, Nevada, Idaho, Wyoming, and Montana wars killed many cowboys and shepherds, along with thousands of sheep. During the 1880s and 1890s, sheepmen controlled the Arizona range, and they threatened to drive the cowmen from other choice ranges. This prompted the Graham-Tewksbury feud that killed twenty-six cattlemen and six sheepmen. Cattlemen in Wyoming attacked shepherds and drove more than ten thousand sheep into the mountains, where they perished. In another clash, near North Rock Springs, the cowmen drove twelve thousand sheep over a cliff. The sheep wars subsided only when landowners occupied and began to fence off the disputed areas.

BIBLIOGRAPHY

Haley, J. Evetts. *Charles Goodnight, Cowman and Plainsman.* Norman: University of Oklahoma Press, 1949.

Johnson, Dorothy M. *Some Went West.* Lincoln: University of Nebraska Press, 1997.

C. C. Rister / c. w.

See also **Cattle Associations.**

SHEFFIELD SCIENTIFIC SCHOOL originated in two professorships established by Yale College in 1846: agricultural chemistry (John Pitkin Norton) and practical chemistry (Benjamin Silliman Jr.). As the School of Applied Chemistry, it opened in 1847 under Yale's new Department of Philosophy and the Arts. Silliman left in 1853; Norton, carrying the school alone, died in 1852, at the age of thirty.

Norton's successor, John Addison Porter, professor of chemistry at Yale, interested his father-in-law in the School. Joseph E. Sheffield, the wealthy railroad builder and philanthropist, shared the founders' belief in the importance of science to America's agricultural and industrial development. As the school's principal benefactor, his gifts ultimately amounted to $1.1 million. William A. Norton established the School of Engineering in 1852; in 1854 the Yale Scientific School consisted of the School of Engineering and the School of Applied Chemistry. It became the Sheffield Scientific School in 1861.

The importance of Sheffield lay in its innovations in both graduate and scientific education. Like most colleges of that era, Yale gave its undergraduates a classical education, with the goal of building character and inculcating mental discipline through the teaching of Greek, Latin, philosophy, and theology. Engineering and science had an "applied" nature, a practical connotation at odds with classical concepts.

In 1852 Yale offered the bachelor of philosophy degree to students of the Scientific School, following a three-year course of study; in 1861 the doctor of philosophy degree was granted, the first Ph.D. in America. Sheffield thus pioneered graduate education in America. Daniel Coit Gilman, later the first president of Johns Hopkins University, joined the Sheffield faculty in 1861, remaining until 1872. He later stated that Hopkins owed much to lessons learned during his Sheffield years.

In 1860 the undergraduate Select Course was established, offering science, mathematics, history, English, geography, economics, political science, and, later, social science, instead of classical studies, in which Yale College persisted. The School introduced modern languages and philology studies into the curriculum, another innovation. Over the years Sheffield added courses of study for different engineering fields.

In 1863 the Scientific School became the Connecticut beneficiary of the Morrill Act (a land grant act). This money helped finance faculty expansion. The School inaugurated a series of lectures for the public on scientific subjects and issues in 1866. Adding more agricultural courses to its curriculum, Sheffield also commenced a traveling lecture series for farmers across Connecticut in 1867 under State Board of Agriculture auspices. By 1886 the State Grange, with interests in applied agriculture only, mounted continuing attacks against the School's land grant college status. The General Assembly voted another institution as beneficiary of land grant funds in 1893, thus ending a thirty-year relationship with a court awarding damages to the School in 1895 for abrogating the contract.

Yale's "Great Reorganization" (1918–1920) profoundly changed the School, ending budgetary autonomy and transferring most of its programs to the University, including the Master of Science program and the School of Engineering. Sheffield became a postgraduate institution after 1945.

BIBLIOGRAPHY

Chittenden, Russell H. *History of the Sheffield Scientific School of Yale University, 1846–1922.* New Haven, Conn.: Yale University Press, 1928.

Furniss, Edgar S. *The Graduate School of Yale: A Brief History.* New Haven, Conn.: Purington Rollins, 1965.

Veysey, Laurence R. *The Emergence of the American University.* Chicago: University of Chicago Press, 1965.

Warren, Charles H. "The Sheffield Scientific School from 1847 to 1947." *In The Centennial of the Sheffield Scientific School.* Edited by George Alfred Baitsell. New Haven, Conn.: Yale University Press, 1950.

Shelby Shapiro
Elizabeth H. Thomson

SHELBY'S MEXICAN EXPEDITION. After the downfall of the Confederacy in April 1865, Gen. Joseph

O. Shelby called on his men to follow him into Mexico rather than surrender. With one thousand men, including four generals and the governors of Texas, Kentucky, and Louisiana, Shelby crossed the Rio Grande from Eagle Pass, Texas, to Piedras Negras, in northeastern Mexico. Their plan was to enlist in the army of Emperor Maximilian. En route to Monterrey, Shelby's expedition was assaulted by rebel guerrillas supporting Benito Juárez.

At Monterrey, the expedition broke up, with parts going to Canada, British Honduras, the Mexican state of Sonora, and parts even joining the French army in Mexico. Shelby, with the remnant of his men, marched to Mexico City. Maximilian refused the offer of Shelby's sword, fearing the displeasure of the United States. The Confederates attempted to establish a colony on land given them by the Empress Carlota. The overthrow of Maximilian and his execution on 19 June 1867 made the colony untenable, and most of the Confederate exiles returned to the United States or went elsewhere.

BIBLIOGRAPHY

Edwards, John N. *Shelby's Expedition to Mexico.* Kansas City, Mo., 1872.

O'Flaherty, Daniel. *General Jo Shelby, Undefeated Rebel.* Chapel Hill: University of North Carolina Press, 1954.

Shalhope, Robert E. "Race, Class, Slavery, and the Antebellum Southern Mind." *The Journal of Southern History* 37 (1971): 557–574.

Paul I. Wellman / A. R.

See also **Civil War; Mexico, Confederate Migration to; Mexico, French in; Mexico, Relations with.**

SHENANDOAH CAMPAIGN

(1864). Coincident with General Ulysses S. Grant's advance, Union forces in western Virginia moved eastward to clear the SHENANDOAH VALLEY and cut General Robert E. Lee's supply communications. After engagements at Cloyd's Mountain (9 May), New Market (15 May), and Piedmont (5 June), the Union columns under General David Hunter were united for an advance on Lynchburg. To meet this threat, Lee detached General Jubal A. Early's corps with instructions to threaten Washington, D.C. Early drove Hunter into the mountains, crossed the Potomac, and defeated Union General Lew Wallace at Monocacy, Maryland, on 4–5 July. Too weak for a direct assault on Washington's defenses, Early interrupted railroad traffic, destroyed vast supplies, burned Chambersburg, Pennsylvania (30 July), and then safely withdrew.

Alarmed by Early's successes, Grant consolidated all Union troops in the valley under General Philip H. Sheridan. A month of maneuvers followed. On 19 September Sheridan, with a three-to-one superiority, defeated Early at Opequon and at Fisher's Hill. Instead of destroying his opponent, Sheridan spent several weeks burning crops, provisions, factories, and farm property. On 19 October,

Early attacked during Sheridan's absence (Battle of Cedar Creek) but was repulsed and retreated up the valley. By mid-December 1864, both Early and Sheridan had been recalled to Virginia.

Early had saved Lynchburg, collected immense supplies, diverted a large force from Grant's army, and preserved Lee's western line of supply. Sheridan, despite his great superiority, never seriously interfered with Lee's defense of Richmond.

BIBLIOGRAPHY

Cooling, Benjamin F. *Jubal Early's Raid on Washington, 1864.* Baltimore: Nautical and Aviation Pub. Co. of America, 1989.

Gallagher, Gary W., ed. *Struggle for the Shenandoah: Essays on the 1864 Valley Campaign.* Kent, Ohio: Kent State University Press, 1991.

Heatwole, John L. *The Burning: Sheridan in the Shenandoah Valley.* Charlottesville, Va.: Rockbridge, 1998.

Thomas Robson Hay / A. R.

See also **Civil War; Petersburg, Siege of; Saint Albans Raid; Sheridan's Ride; Wilderness, Battles of the.**

SHENANDOAH VALLEY

is located in Northern Virginia between the Blue Ridge and ALLEGHENY MOUNTAINS and is divided by the Massanutten Mountains. The valley is defined by the Shenandoah River, which flows 150 miles northeastward from Lexington, Virginia, to the Potomac River at Harpers Ferry, West Virginia. The valleys, formed on limestone, produced fertile soils that attracted European settlement by 1717. The northern part was settled by Tidewater Anglicans, the central part by Protestant Germans, and the southern part by Presbyterian Scots-Irish. By the American Revolution, agriculture was flourishing in the region. During the Civil War, the valley was known as the "Granary of the Confederacy" yet both sides contested the region and much was laid waste by General Philip Sheridan in 1864. At the beginning of the twenty-first century, the valley is a beautiful rural landscape with prosperous farms and attractive towns.

BIBLIOGRAPHY

Davis, Julia. *The Shenandoah.* New York: Farrar & Rinehart, 1945. From the excellent *Rivers of America* series.

Hart, Freeman Hansford. *The Valley of Virginia in the American Revolution, 1763–1789.* Chapel Hill: University of North Carolina Press, 1942.

Kercheval, Samuel. *A History of the Valley of Virginia.* Woodstock, Va.: W. N. Grabill, 1902. The original edition was published in 1833.

Mitchell, Robert D. *Commercialism and Frontier: Perspectives on the Early Shenandoah Valley.* Charlottesville: University of Virginia Press, 1977.

Stanley W. Trimble

See also **Virginia.**

SHEPPARD-TOWNER MATERNITY AND INFANCY PROTECTION ACT

of 1921 provided a system of federal funding to enhance the health and welfare of women and children. Grace Abbott, Julia Lathrop, and other feminist activists worked to get the statute adopted, and it was consistent with the social goals of the women's movement of the nineteenth century. Various medical groups, including the American Medical Association, opposed passage. Funding under the act ended in 1929, and the effort to achieve further federal support of such programs was not successful until the New Deal.

In addition to its role in the history of women and welfare, the Sheppard-Towner Act has a significant place in the history of federalism and the expanded role of the federal government. The act for the first time said it was appropriate for the federal government to respond directly to the needs of women and children. This was and has remained a contested issue.

There are continuities between the Sheppard-Towner Act and subsequent efforts to promote women's welfare, such as the attempt to establish federal support for displaced homemakers and women's health equity. The Displaced Homemakers Act was not funded, however, and the Women's Health Equity Act was not adopted in the form originally proposed, though some elements were incorporated in other statutes.

BIBLIOGRAPHY

Kessler-Harris, Alice. *In Pursuit of Equity: Women, Men, and the Quest for Economic Citizenship in Twentieth-Century America.* New York: Oxford University Press, 2001.

Rude, Anna Elizabeth. *The Sheppard-Towner Act in Relation to Public Health.* Washington, D.C.: Government Printing Office, 1921.

Carol Weisbrod

See also **Women's Health.**

SHERIDAN'S RIDE.

During the Shenandoah campaign of 1864, Confederate Gen. Jubal A. Early attacked Union Gen. Philip H. Sheridan's army at dawn on 19 October along Cedar Creek, near Strasburg, Virginia, throwing two Union corps into panic. Sheridan, returning from Washington, D.C., had stopped at Winchester on the night of the eighteenth. Awakened the next morning by the distant sound of artillery, he left for the front and soon encountered his routed commands. He reached the battlefield about 10:30 A.M., and his presence quickly restored confidence. By midafternoon the Confederates were in retreat. A poem written several months later by Thomas Buchanan Read, with its refrain, "And Sheridan twenty miles away," fixed his ride in the public mind as one of the heroic events of the war.

BIBLIOGRAPHY

Gallagher, Gary W., ed. *Struggle for the Shenandoah.* Kent, Ohio: Kent State Universty Press, 1991.

Heatwole, John L. *The Burning: Sheridan in the Shenandoah Valley.* Charlottesville, Va.: Rockbridge Publications, 1998.

Lewis, Thomas A. *The Guns of Cedar Creek.* New York: Harper and Row, 1988.

Alvin F. Harlow / A. R.

See also **Army, Confederate; Army, Union; Civil War; Petersburg, Siege of; Shenandoah Campaign; Wilderness, Battles of the.**

SHERMAN ANTITRUST ACT

was passed by Congress and signed into law by President Benjamin Harrison on 2 July 1890. Introduced and vigorously promoted by Senator John Sherman (R–Ohio), the law was designed to discourage "trusts," broadly understood as large industrial combinations that curtail competition. Its first section declares "every contract, combination in the form of trust or otherwise, or conspiracy in restraint of trade" to be illegal. The second section makes monopolistic behavior a felony subject to imprisonment ("not exceeding three years") and/or fines (not exceeding $10 million for corporations and $350,000 for private individuals). Civil actions may be brought by both the government and private parties. The act vests federal district courts with primary jurisdiction, and assigns the U.S. attorney general and "the several United States attorneys" chief enforcement authority.

Trusts were seemingly ubiquitous in the 1880s: thousands of businesses combined to control product pricing, distribution, and production. These associations were formed, among other reasons, to counter uncertainty created by rapid market change, such as uncoordinated advancements in transportation, manufacturing, and production. While many of these trusts were small in scale and managerially thin, the most notorious were controlled by industry giants such as Standard Oil, American Tobacco, and United States Steel. These large-scale, long-term trusts were seen as coercive and rapacious, dominating markets and eliminating competition.

The trust "problem" varied in the late nineteenth century, depending on who was describing it. For some, trusts perverted market forces and posed a threat to the nation's consumers—only big business gained from restricting free commerce and manipulating prices. (Some proponents of this view admitted, however, that the rise of the trusts corresponded with a general lowering of prices.) Popular journalists such as Henry Demarest Lloyd and Ida Tarbell stoked this distrust, arguing that trusts held back needed goods in order to make a profit under the ruse of overproduction. Others stressed the threat trusts posed to individual liberty by constricting citizens' ability to freely enter into trades and contracts. Many considered the threat to small businesses an assault on American values. Trusts were also seen as the cause of profound political problems. The money of men like Jay Gould and John D. Rockefeller was thought to corrupt politicians and democratic institutions, a view growing out of an American tradition equating concentrated power with tyranny and despotism. Fighting the trusts offered a way to combat new and pernicious versions of prerogative and corruption.

Prior to 1890, trusts were regulated exclusively at the state level, part of the general police power held by municipalities and states. States tackled the trust problem in various ways. Some attempted to eliminate collusion through the use of regulation; fifteen antitrust laws were passed between 1888 and 1891. More frequently they tried to limit business behavior without enacting legislation. State judges were receptive to arguments, raised by state attorneys general, that trusts violated long-standing legal principles; the common law provided a useful tool in battling "unreasonable" restraints of trade. However, several states, like New Jersey, Delaware, and New York, passed incorporation statutes allowing trusts and holding companies within their jurisdictions with the goal of attracting businesses.

Pressure to enact a federal antitrust law came from many quarters. Farmers and wage laborers, for example, saw industrialists as the major threat to their political and economic power; national control of trusts, under the banner of social justice, promised to increase their bargaining position. Small companies lobbied heavily for a federal antitrust law because they welcomed the chance to limit the power of their large competitors—competitors who disproportionately benefited from revolutions in distribution and production. Many were simply dissatisfied with state regulation, arguing that only the federal government could effectively control unfair business practices. Interestingly, evidence suggests that the trusts themselves were in favor of central regulation. They may have hoped a national law would discourage state antitrust activity, or, more cynically, serve as a useful distraction while they pursued more important goals. The *New York Times* of October 1890 called the Sherman Act a "humbug and a sham" that was "passed to deceive the people and to clear the way" for other laws, like a high protective tariff, that clearly benefited businesses.

When it was introduced, the Sherman Act raised serious objections in Congress. Like the Interstate Commerce Act of 1887, it was one of the first national laws designed to control private business behavior, and its legitimacy was uncertain. Concerns were allayed by three arguments. First, the law was needed: states were unable to fight trusts that operated outside their borders. Second, it was constitutional: antitrust activity was a legitimate exercise of Congress's authority to regulate interstate commerce. Finally, defenders argued that it did not threaten state sovereignty. The act, instead of preempting state antitrust activity, merely supplemented it.

Although the act passed by overwhelming margins in both the House (242–0) and Senate (52–1), many battles were fought between its introduction and final passage. The Senate Finance and Judiciary committees heavily re-

The general government is not placed by the Constitution in such a condition of helplessness that it must fold its arms and remain inactive while capital combines, under the name of a corporation, to destroy competition. . . . The doctrine of the autonomy of the states cannot properly be invoked to justify a denial of power in the national government to meet such an emergency, involving, as it does, that freedom of commercial intercourse among the states which the Constitution sought to attain.

SOURCE: From *United States v. E. C. Knight Company* (1895), Justice Harlan dissenting.

vised the original bill, and both chambers added and withdrew numerous amendments. Senator Sherman, for example, supported an amendment exempting farm groups and labor unions from the law's reach, and Senator Nelson W. Aldrich (R–Rhode Island) proposed that the law not be applied to combinations that "lessen the cost of production" or reduce the price of the life's "necessaries." Some historians argue that the debate leading up to the Sherman Act reflected an ideological split between proponents of the traditional economic order and a new one. Congressmen divided sharply over the value of free competition in a rapidly industrializing society and, more generally, over the value of laissez-faire approaches to social and economic problems. Not surprisingly, the final language of the Sherman Act was broad, allowing a good deal of enforcement discretion.

The Sherman Act's effects on trusts were minimal for the first fifteen years after enactment. Indeed, large-scale monopolies grew rapidly during this period. There was no concerted drive to prosecute trusts, nor was there an agency charged to oversee industry behavior until a special division in the Justice Department was created in 1903 under President Theodore Roosevelt. (The Bureau of Corporations was formed the same year within the Department of Commerce and Labor to gather industry information.) "Trust busting," however, was not neglected during this period. States continued to pass antitrust laws after 1890, many far more aggressive than the federal version. More importantly, federal courts assumed a leadership role in interpreting the act's broad provisions, a role that they have never abandoned.

Supreme Court justices openly debated the act's meaning from 1890 to 1911, an era now known as the law's formative period. Two prominent justices, John Marshall Harlan and Chief Justice Melville W. Fuller, differed over the scope of federal power granted under the act, specifically, how much authority Congress has to regulate in-state business behavior. Fuller's insistence on

> That which belongs to commerce is within the jurisdiction of the United States, but that which does not belong to commerce is within the jurisdiction of the police power of the state. . . . It is vital that the independence of the commercial power and of the police power, and the delimitation between them, however sometimes perplexing, should always be recognized and observed, for, while the one furnishes the strongest bond of union, the other is essential to the preservation of the autonomy of the states as required by our dual form of government; and acknowledged evils, however grave and urgent they may appear to be, had better be borne, than the risk be run, in the effort to suppress them, of more serious consequences by resort to expedients of even doubtful constitutionality.
>
> SOURCE: From *United States v. E. C. Knight Company* (1895), Chief Justice Fuller, majority opinion.

clear lines of distinction between state power and federal power (or police powers and the commerce power) reflected his strong attachment to dual federalism and informed decisions such as UNITED STATES V. E. C. KNIGHT COMPANY (1895). For Fuller, manufacture itself is not a commercial activity and thus cannot be regulated under Congress's commerce power. According to this view, the federal government has no authority over things that have merely an "indirect" effect on commerce. Harlan's alternative position—that monopolistic behavior is pervasive, blurring distinctions between in-state and interstate activities—held sway in cases like NORTHERN SECURITIES COMPANY V. UNITED STATES (1904) and *Swift and Company v. United States* (1905). This understanding significantly broadened Congress's commerce power and was accepted conclusively by the Court in the 1920s under the stewardship of Chief Justice William Howard Taft in STAFFORD V. WALLACE (1922) and *Board of Trade of City of Chicago v. Olsen* (1923).

In addition to disagreements over the reach of federal power, the justices differed over the intent of the act itself, namely what types of trade restraints were forbidden. The Court concluded that the section 1 prohibition against "every" contract and combination in restraint of trade was a rule that must admit of exceptions. Justices advocated prohibitions by type (the per se rule) and a more flexible, case-by-case analysis. A compromise was reached in STANDARD OIL COMPANY OF NEW JERSEY V. UNITED STATES (1911) known as the "rule of reason": the Sherman Act only prohibits trade restraints that the judges deem unreasonable. Some anticompetitive activity is acceptable, according to the rule. The harm of collusion may be outweighed by its pro-competitive ramifications.

The rule of reason may have solved an internal debate among the justices, but it did little to eliminate the ambiguity of federal antitrust enforcement. Indeed, internal Court debate before 1912 convinced many observers that the act invited too much judicial discretion. Proposals to toughen the law were prevalent during the Progressive Era and were a central feature of the presidential contest of 1912. The Clayton Antitrust Act of 1914 clarified the ambiguities of the law by specifically enumerating prohibited practices (such as the interlinking of companies and price fixing). The Federal Trade Commission Act, passed the same year, created a body to act, as President Woodrow Wilson explained, as a "clearinghouse for the facts . . . and as an instrumentality for doing justice to business" (see FEDERAL TRADE COMMISSION). Antitrust law from that point on was to be developed by administrators as well as by federal judges.

The reach of the Sherman Act has varied with time, paralleling judicial and political developments. Sections have been added and repealed, but it continues to be the main source of American antitrust law. Civil and criminal provisions have been extended to activity occurring outside of the United States, and indications suggest its international reach may become as important as its domestic application.

BIBLIOGRAPHY

Bork, Robert. *The Antitrust Paradox: A Policy at War with Itself.* New York: Basic Books, 1978.

Hovenkamp, Herbert. *Enterprise and American Law, 1836–1937.* Cambridge, Mass.: Harvard University Press, 1991.

McCraw, Thomas K. *Prophets of Regulation.* Cambridge, Mass.: Harvard University Press, 1984.

Peritz, Rudolph J. R. *Competition Policy in America, 1888–1992: History, Rhetoric, Law.* New York: Oxford University Press, 1996.

Thorelli, Hans B. *The Federal Antitrust Policy: Origination of an American Tradition.* Baltimore: Johns Hopkins Press, 1954.

Troesken, Werner. "Did the Trusts Want a Federal Antitrust Law? An Event Study of State Antitrust Enforcement and Passage of the Sherman Act." In *Public Choice Interpretations of American Economic History.* Edited by Jac C. Heckelman et al. Boston: Kluwer Academic Press, 2000.

Wiebe, Robert H. *The Search for Order, 1877–1920.* New York: Hill and Wang, 1967. Reprint, Westport, Conn: Greenwood Press, 1980.

Kimberly Hendrickson

See also **Business, Big; Corporations; Monopoly; Trusts.**

SHERMAN SILVER PURCHASE ACT.

In the late nineteenth century, years of falling prices and economic contraction gave rise to a strongly prosilver wing of the Democratic Party. These "silver Democrats" advocated the notion that the free coinage of silver would combat deflation and promote economic expansion, particularly for hard-pressed farmers in the South and West, a core constituency of the Democratic Party. Although some western Republicans also advocated the free coinage of silver, most Republicans staunchly supported the gold standard as the basis of the national currency. In 1890 prosilver Democrats began negotiations with protariff Republicans to reach a compromise. The Democrats pledged to support the McKinley tariff bill in return for Republican support of a bill for the free coinage of silver. The White House, however, constituted a major obstacle to the compromise. Although the silver advocates had a majority in the Senate powerful enough to force the House into line, they feared that President Benjamin Harrison, a GOLD STANDARD Republican, would veto a free coinage bill, even if it were attached as a rider to a tariff bill that he otherwise favored. As a practical solution to this dilemma the "silver" senators determined to adopt not a free coinage measure but the nearest possible approach to it. A compromise bill, the Sherman Silver Purchase Act, named for Senator John Sherman of Ohio, became law on 14 July 1890. The act provided for the issuance of legal tender notes sufficient in amount to pay for 4.5 million ounces of silver bullion each month at the prevailing market price. Then, enough silver dollars were to be coined from the bullion purchased to redeem all the outstanding U.S. Treasury notes issued in this manner. The notes were made full legal tender and were redeemable on demand either in gold or silver coin at the discretion of the secretary of the Treasury.

The passage of the Sherman Act failed to achieve its objectives. Although it increased the circulation of redeemable paper currency in the form of treasury notes by $156 million, it simultaneously accentuated the drain on the government's gold reserves by requiring that the treasury notes be redeemed in gold as long as the treasury had gold in its possession. A financial crisis in Argentina led to the failure of the British banking house of Baring Brothers and Company, which in turn eventually forced an exportation of gold from the United States to Great Britain. This exodus, coupled with an extraordinarily tight money market, created a situation bordering on panic in the latter part of 1890.

The marked growth of U.S. indebtedness to foreign nations and the reduction in custom receipts brought about by the McKinley Tariff compounded the crisis. The cumulative effect of the foregoing factors culminated in the panic of 1893, which was characterized by a fear of the abandonment of the gold standard because of the depletion of the government's gold reserve. The panic was checked in the autumn of 1893 by the repeal of the Sherman Act.

BIBLIOGRAPHY

Brands, H. W. *The Reckless Decade: America in the 1890s.* New York: St. Martin's Press, 1995.

Glad, Paul W. *McKinley, Bryan, and the People.* Philadelphia: Lippincott, 1964.

Hollingsworth, J. Rogers. *The Whirligig of Politics: The Democracy of Cleveland and Bryan.* Chicago: University of Chicago Press, 1963.

Palmer, Bruce. *"Man over Money": The Southern Populist Critique of American Capitalism.* Chapel Hill: University of North Carolina Press, 1980.

Anthony Gaughan
Frank Parker

See also **Silver Democrats; Silver Legislation.**

SHERMAN'S MARCH TO THE SEA. From 15 November to 21 December 1864 the Union general William T. Sherman and his 62,000 soldiers waged a purposeful war of destruction in Georgia from Atlanta to Savannah. Sherman destroyed property to convince Southerners that their cause was hopeless and that they should surrender. He believed that this psychological warfare would end the Civil War more quickly and with less loss of life than traditional battlefield conflicts.

Sherman began the march following his successful capture of Atlanta on 2 September 1864. When the Confederate general John Bell Hood tried to cut Sherman's railroad supply line, forcing Sherman to chase him, Sherman decided to try a new approach. He proposed to leave sixty thousand soldiers under General George H. Thomas to handle Hood. Cutting himself off from the railroad, Sherman intended to live off the land while waging a psychological war of destruction. The commanding general, Ulysses S. Grant, reluctantly went along with the plan.

Implementing the strategy he had used in the Meridian, Mississippi, campaign (3 February to 4 March 1864), Sherman divided his army into two wings, the right or southern wing under O. O. Howard and the left or

Sherman's March Nov. 15–Dec. 21, 1864

William T. Sherman. George N. Barnard's photograph shows the Union general at Federal Fort no. 7, Atlanta, Ga., in the fall of 1864. LIBRARY OF CONGRESS

sertions in Robert E. Lee's army increased. Sherman's psychological warfare of destruction had a major effect on the outcome of the war. It also made Sherman a brute to many Southerners and a hero to Union supporters. By the twenty-first century the purpose for the march was forgotten, but Sherman's methods remained the subject of spirited debate.

BIBLIOGRAPHY

Bailey, Anne J. *The Chessboard of War: Sherman and Hood in the Autumn Campaigns of 1864.* Lincoln: University of Nebraska Press, 2000.

Glatthaar, Joseph T. *The March to the Sea and Beyond: Sherman's Troops in the Savannah and Carolinas Campaigns.* New York: New York University Press, 1985.

Kennett, Lee. *Marching through Georgia: The Story of Soldiers and Civilians during Sherman's Campaign.* New York: Harper-Collins, 1995.

Marszalek, John F. *Sherman: A Soldier's Passion for Order.* New York: Free Press, 1993.

John F. Marszalek

See also **Atlanta Campaign; Nashville, Battle of; Savannah, Siege of (1864).**

northern wing under Henry W. Slocum. Judson Kilpatrick commanded the cavalry, which acted as a screen for the marching army. The two wings moved along separate paths from twenty to fifty miles apart, in four parallel corps columns, the left wing moving toward Augusta and the right wing toward Macon. They merged at Milledgeville, the state capital, and at Savannah. With no major Confederate army in the state, Joe Wheeler's Confederate cavalry and the weak Georgia militia provided ineffective opposition.

Sherman did not burn Atlanta to the ground when he began his march, and he did not destroy everything in his path through Georgia. His army systematically destroyed only property connected with the Confederate war effort, Union prisoners of war, or slavery. However, Sherman's Union soldiers, Wheeler's Confederate cavalry, deserters from both sides, fugitive slaves, and pillaging Southern civilians wantonly destroyed property. The anarchy aided Sherman's psychological cause and resulted in heavy though not total damage. Military and civilian casualties were extremely low. When Sherman completed his march, he offered the captured city of Savannah to Abraham Lincoln as a Christmas present. Meanwhile Thomas crushed Hood at the battle of Nashville on 15 December 1864.

Sherman's march to the sea brought the Civil War home to Southern civilians. Few became casualties, but many lost property and felt demoralized. In Virginia, de-

SHILOH, BATTLE OF. Gen. Ulysses S. Grant's capture of Fort Henry on 6 February 1862 and Fort Donelson on 15–16 February in northwestern Tennessee opened the Cumberland and Tennessee Rivers to Union water traffic and pierced the center of the Confederate defensive line, so that Columbus, Kentucky, had to be evacuated. Union Gen. Don Carlos Buell occupied Nashville with the Army of the Ohio, and Gen. Henry W. Halleck on 1 March ordered Gen. Charles F. Smith, with thirty thousand troops of the Army of the Tennessee, to concentrate at Shiloh (or Pittsburg Landing), twenty-five miles north of the Confederates under the command of Gen. Albert S. Johnston at Corinth, Mississippi. Buell's twenty-five thousand troops were to join by marching overland from Nashville.

On 3 April Johnston moved out of Corinth, fifty thousand strong, to strike Grant's force before the junction with Buell could be effected. Early on 6 April Johnston made a surprise attack against the unfortified Union position. Vigorous Confederate attacks drove in Grant's outlying units, shattered the hastily formed lines, and pushed the Union troops against the river.

Buell arrived that night. In the morning Grant launched his reorganized army into the Confederate lines. Grant's strike, with the fresh troops of Buell and Gen. Lew Wallace and aided by portions of Gen. William Tecumseh Sherman's and Gen. John A. McClernand's commands, killed Johnston and swept the Confederates from the field toward Corinth.

BIBLIOGRAPHY

Bannister, Donald. *Long Day at Shiloh*. New York: Knopf, 1981.

Daniel, Larry J. *Shiloh: The Battle that Changed the Civil War.* New York: Simon and Schuster, 1997.

Sword, Wiley. *Shiloh: Bloody April.* New York: Morrow, 1974.

Elbridge Colby / A. R.

See also **Civil War; Cumberland, Army of the; Donelson, Fort, Capture of; Henry, Fort; Tennessee, Army of.**

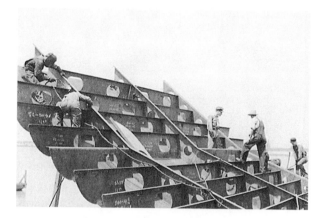

Building a Barge. A 1942 photograph by Jack Delano showing workers at the Ingalls Shipbuilding Company in Decatur, Ala., creating the stern of an oceangoing barge. LIBRARY OF CONGRESS

SHIPBUILDING. Shipbuilding in the United States began out of necessity, flourished as maritime trade expanded, declined when industrialization attracted its investors, then revived in World War II. Shipyards grew from barren eighteenth-century establishments with a few workers using hand tools even for "large" ships (200 tons) to huge twentieth-century organizations where thousands of employees use ever-changing technology to build aircraft carriers of 70,000 tons. Today the United States no longer leads the world in ship production, but it is still a major force in marine technology and engineering.

American shipbuilding began when Spanish sailors constructed replacements for ships wrecked on the North Carolina coast in the 1520s. Other Europeans launched small vessels for exploration and trade. In the 1640s the trading ventures of Massachusetts built vessels that established New England as a shipbuilding region. By the 1720s, however, New England shipyards faced competition from Pennsylvania and later from other colonies with growing merchant communities, such as Virginia, where slave labor boosted production.

The typical eighteenth-century urban shipyard was a small waterfront lot with few if any permanent structures. Rural yards, where land was cheap and theft less of a problem, often had covered sawpits, storage sheds, and wharfs. The labor force consisted of about half a dozen men, sawyers and shipbuilders as well as apprentices, servants, or slaves. Work was sporadic, and accidents, sometimes fatal, were common. Yet from such facilities came 40 percent of Great Britain's oceangoing tonnage on the eve of the Revolution. After Independence, shipbuilding stagnated until European wars in the 1790s enabled American shipyards to launch neutral vessels for their countrymen and merchant ships or privateers for French and British buyers.

During the Golden Age of American shipbuilding, from the mid-1790s through the mid-1850s, shipping reached its highest proportional levels, the navy expanded, and the clipper ship became a symbol of national pride. New technology entered the shipyard: the steam engine supplied supplementary power for some sailing vessels and the sole power for others; iron first reinforced and then replaced some wooden hulls. Many shipowners, attracted to the promised economy of size, ordered larger ships that required more labor, raw materials, and technology. Meanwhile, a transportation revolution compelled coastal vessels to connect with and compete with canal barges, inland river trade, and railroads. At this time, many New England merchants turned to manufacturing for higher and steadier returns.

By the late 1850s, the glory days had begun to fade. Maine and Massachusetts shipyards launched more tonnage than anyone else, but they did not construct steamships, while builders outside New England recognized that the future belonged to steam, not sail. The Civil War promoted naval construction, with both sides making remarkable innovations, but the war devastated commercial shipbuilding. Confederate raids on Union ships convinced some Yankee merchants to sell their ships to foreign owners. By 1865, American tonnage in foreign trade was half that of the late 1850s; at the end of the decade it was down to a third.

In 1880, Pennsylvania shipyards launched almost half of what the top ten states constructed. Iron, not steam, now represented the future; most shipyards could not afford the transition from wood to iron. Massachusetts builders held on by mass-producing small boats for offshore fishing schooners. Capital investments per yard many times greater than those of other states allowed Pennsylvania and Delaware yards to succeed. With yards in six of the ten states producing at a rate of less than two vessels per year, many establishments did not survive the introduction of iron.

Two successful shipyards of the period, William Cramp and Sons in Philadelphia and Newport News Shipbuilding and Drydock Company of Virginia, embraced the new technology and benefited from the naval modernization program of the 1890s. Naval contracts proved vital to these builders' success, and the strength of the navy depended upon such shipyards.

When the United States entered World War I, it undertook an unprecedented shipbuilding program. After the war, builders watched maritime trade decline through

Launching the *Abraham Clark*. The "Liberty" ship, built by the California Shipbuilding Corporation in Wilmington, Calif., slides into the water in 1942. LIBRARY OF CONGRESS

the 1920s as the coastal trade gave way to trains and trucks and quotas restricted the once profitable immigrant trade. The Newport News Shipbuilding and Drydock Company survived by performing non-maritime work such as building traffic lights. Relief did not come until the 1930s, when the U.S. government began ordering aircraft carriers to serve the dual purpose of strengthening the navy and providing jobs for the unemployed.

At the outbreak of World War II, Great Britain asked the United States to mass-produce an outdated English freighter design that had many deficiencies but possessed the all-important virtue of simplicity. Thanks to new welding techniques and modular construction, the "Liberty" ship became the most copied vessel in history. More than 2,700 were built—many completed in less than two months, some in a few weeks. This remarkable feat, accomplished by a hastily trained workforce using parts produced across the nation, was directed by Henry Kaiser, who had never before built a vessel. American shipyards also produced 800 Victory ships (a faster, more economical freighter), more than 300 tankers, and hundreds of other warships. American shipbuilding, a key factor in the Allied victory, increased 1,000 percent by war's end, making the United States the world's undisputed maritime power.

Following World War II, America abandoned maritime interests and focused on highways, factories, and planes. During the 1950s, Japanese, European, and Latin American shipbuilders outperformed American shipyards, while American Atlantic passenger liners succumbed to passenger jets. A nuclear-powered freighter, *Savannah*, proved both a commercial and public relations failure. While Americans pioneered development of the very economical container ship, it was quickly adopted by foreign competitors. Despite technical advances, shipbuilding continued to decline in the face of waning public and private support.

Today, Japan, Korea, and China build over 90 percent of the world's commercial tonnage; the U.S. share is only 0.2 percent. Since 1992, U.S. shipyards have averaged fewer than nine new commercial ships per year of 1,000 tons or more. Submarines and aircraft carriers are still under construction, although in reduced numbers; guided-missile destroyers and support vessels are on the rise. Modern maritime technology requires significant resources and expertise. Unlike the colonial years, when every seaport, however small, had a few shipyards, today the nation has just half a dozen major shipyards in total. The United States still enjoys an abundance of materials, skilled labor, and engineering ingenuity. It requires only large-scale public and private support to reignite interest in this once flourishing industry.

BIBLIOGRAPHY

Chapelle, Howard I. *The National Watercraft Collection.* Washington, D.C.: United States National Museum, 1960. 2d ed., Washington, D.C.: Smithsonian Institution Press, 1976.

Goldenberg, Joseph A. *Shipbuilding in Colonial America.* Charlottesville, Va.: University Press of Virginia, 1976.

Hutchins, John G. B. *The American Maritime Industries and Public Policy, 1789–1914.* Cambridge, Mass.: Harvard University Press, 1941.

Pedraja, René de la. *The Rise and Decline of U.S. Merchant Shipping in the Twentieth Century.* New York: Macmillan, 1992.

Joseph Goldenberg

See also **Armored Ships; Clipper Ships; Packets, Sailing; *Savannah*; Steamboats.**

SHIPPING. *See* **Merchant Marine.**

SHIPPING, OCEAN. From early colonial times to about 1870, there was little change in American cargo ships. The conventional major carrier in those early years was the three-masted, square-rigged ship, or bark. The earlier ones, like the *Mayflower*, had abnormally high poops and forecastles, which gradually gave way during the eighteenth century to relatively flush decks. But basically they were much the same, about one hundred feet long and thirty feet wide, measuring about three hundred tons, with hulls of oak and masts of pine or fir; they carried crews of about thirty men. Off the transatlantic main line, smaller vessels were used: two-masted, square-rigged brigs for runs to the Mediterranean or the West Indies and still smaller fore- and aft-rigged schooners or sloops for coastal and other short runs. Ownership of such ships was divided into sixty-four shares; sometimes a single person owned all shares, sometimes the shares were divided among dozens of people. In 1818 the American Black Ball Line innovated shipping by sailing on fixed schedules between New York City and Liverpool, England, with passengers, mail, and fine freight, but still using conventional ships. This new line pattern, highly profitable, expanded, but chiefly from New York.

The coming of steam gradually led to a new pattern. Robert Fulton's *Clermont* first plied the Hudson River in 1807, and in 1838 regular transatlantic service by steam-driven ships began. The early engines used so much fuel that governments were forced to subsidize steamers; consequently, ordinary cargoes continued to go by square-riggers.

A quiet revolution occurred about 1870 with the compound engine, which, by using the steam twice (and later three or four times), cut costs, so that a freighter could profitably carry such heavy cargoes as grain, coal, and sugar. These new freighters gradually drove the square-riggers from their older runs. Measuring only a few thousand tons, with iron (and later steel) hulls, some served on regular line runs, but most of them were operated as tramp steamers, picking up cargoes wherever they could find them. The American shipbuilders, who had done well with the wooden square-riggers, now could not compete with the cheaper British building costs of the new freighters.

The smaller freighters were particularly hard hit by German submarines in World War I, but their design became the basis for the type of ship that restored America to top the MERCHANT MARINE position after the war. The thousands of Liberty and Victory ships built in U.S. shipyards during World War II were essentially the same type, although by that time they were fueled by oil rather than coal.

By the 1920s, the oil tanker was a prominent part of ocean shipping, and older freighters became known as dry cargo ships. The rapid development of the automobile stimulated a worldwide demand for oil, and during World War II the U.S. produced numerous 16,000-ton T-2 tankers. Because of high American crew wages, many oil companies registered their tankers in the merchant marines of Panama and Liberia.

In the 1960s labor costs became the crucial factor in most merchant marines, and shippers began to seek cheaper methods of loading and unloading ships. The previous cargo ships had open holds into which longshoremen loaded the individual bags, boxes, and bales that made up a cargo, a time-consuming process. The shippers cut the loading time by assembling the cargo beforehand and sending it aboard in a single container, a process called containerization. Another innovation was the so-called "sea train," where loaded freight cars could be run aboard on tracks and run off at the other end. Later came other "roll on–roll off" devices for the same purpose. Even with these changes, the ship had to be put into port to load or unload, and a ship's stay in port could cost several thousand dollars a day. To save more time shippers inaugurated the LASH (lighter-aboard-ship) system, whereby scores of self-operating little lighters could be hoisted over the side to run into port while the mother ship kept on without loss of time.

Another innovation during the 1960s was the vastly increased tonnage of tankers and bulk carriers. The T-2 tanker of World War II measured 16,000 tons. Tonnage increased gradually after that; about 1970 the designation "very large crude carrier" (VLCC) was applied to ships of 150,000 tons or more. By the autumn of 1972, six ships measuring more than 250,000 tons were under construction, and one of nearly 500,000 tons was planned. Two factors brought on this expansion. The first was the closing of the Suez Canal in the Arab-Israeli war of 1967. Some tankers from the Persian Gulf had already been getting rather large for the canal, and, because of the war, there was no choice except to go around the Cape of Good Hope. The longer Good Hope route meant higher tanker earnings, stimulating new construction of larger tankers. The second factor was American concern about its overseas supplies of raw materials. U.S. oil reserves were dropping, and the old self-sufficiency in iron ore was dwindling, with substitute ore supplies necessary from Venezuela and northeastern Canada. Large numbers of bulk carriers began operating. Tankers also began carrying oil one way and ore or bulk grain the other. Few ports could provide the necessary draft for the larger tankers. Offshore loading into pipe facilities seemed one answer. Coastal communities, moreover, were concerned with the danger of oil spills. With the help of a subsidy act passed in 1970, the United States began to build some new types of oceangoing ships. Special ships were developed for natural gas, and bulk carriers were developed to bring iron and other ore from overseas. President Richard Nixon cut the subsidy program in 1973, which temporarily forced a decline in shipping's expansion.

Nonetheless, shipping remains an important source of revenue and employment in the nation's ports. The leading U.S. ports on the East Coast are New York–New Jersey, with 38 percent of the North Atlantic trade, mostly containerized cargo; Norfolk, Virginia; Philadelphia; and Baltimore. In the Gulf of Mexico, the principal port is Houston. New Orleans leads on the Mississippi. On the West Coast the leading ports are Seattle-Tacoma, San Francisco (including Oakland), Long Beach, and Los Angeles.

BIBLIOGRAPHY

Albion, R. G. *Seaports South of Sahara: The Achievements of an American Steamship Service.* New York: Appleton-Century-Crofts, 1959.

Gibson, Andrew, and Arthur Donovan. *The Abandoned Ocean: A History of United States' Maritime Policy.* Columbia: University of South Carolina Press, 2000.

Kendall, Lane C. *The Business of Shipping.* Centreville, Md.: Cornell Maritime Press, 1992.

Lawrence, Samuel A. *United States Merchant Shipping, Policies and Politics.* Washington, D.C.: Brookings Institution, 1966.

Robert G. Albion / f. b.

See also **Cape Horn; Embargo Act; Emergency Fleet Corporation; Maritime Commission, Federal; River and**

Harbor Improvements; River Navigation; Trade, Foreign.

SHIPPING BOARD, U.S.

SHIPPING BOARD, U.S. The Shipping Board, created by the Shipping Act of 1916, was the first body specifically charged with the supervision of the MERCHANT MARINE. It controlled the EMERGENCY FLEET CORPORATION, later the Merchant Fleet Corporation, established in 1917, and carried out World War I and postwar merchant marine policy, particularly an ambitious building policy to set up new yards. The largest of these was Hog Island, near Philadelphia. The board was superseded in 1933 by the U.S. Shipping Board Bureau of the Department of Commerce, which in 1936 gave way to the U.S. Maritime Commission.

BIBLIOGRAPHY

Lawrence, Samuel H. *United States Merchant Shipping, Policies and Politics.* Washington, D.C.: Brookings Institution, 1966.

Frank A. Southard Jr./ F. B.

See also **Maritime Commission, Federal.**

SHIPS OF THE LINE,

SHIPS OF THE LINE, or line-of-battle ships, were the eighteenth- and early nineteenth-century counterparts of modern first-class battleships. The first U.S. ship of this type, the *America*, was launched at Portsmouth, New Hampshire on 5 November 1782, and was given to the French. In 1813 Congress authorized four more, none of which saw action. In 1816 Congress authorized nine more ships of the line, including the *Vermont*, *North Carolina*, and *Ohio*, all burned at the Norfolk Navy Yard on 20 April 1861. None of these ships was ever engaged in battle. The introduction of steam, explosive shells, and armor plate rendered them obsolete before they could be used in warfare.

BIBLIOGRAPHY

Lavery, Brian. *The Ship of the Line.* Annapolis, Md.: Naval Institute Press, 1984.

Louis H. Bolander/ A. R.

See also **Armored Ships; Ironclad Warships; Navy, United States; Warships.**

SHOSHONE

SHOSHONE Indians span widely dispersed geographical and cultural areas. Eastern Shoshones live on the Wind River Reservation in Wyoming, Shoshone-Bannock tribes are at Fort Hall in Idaho, and Western Shoshones reside on reservations in Nevada. While the Shoshones' linguistic roots may have originated in the Great Basin of Utah and Nevada, archaeological evidence suggests a Shoshonean presence eight thousand years ago in the Bitterroot, Yellowstone, Absoroka, Wind River, and Bighorn Mountains.

Shoshones began migrating onto the Plains beginning around A.D. 1500, although the mountain Shoshones (Sheepeaters) did not venture to the Plains. They acquired horses in the late 1600s and then split into Comanche and Eastern Shoshone divisions in the early 1700s. As Plains horse-and-buffalo cultures, they celebrated the Sun Dance and leadership that valued military prowess. Shoshones of eastern and northern Idaho occasionally hunted buffalo and other large game, but staples were fish and camas roots. Western Shoshones did not use horses, but hunted small game and harvested wild vegetables and piñon nuts.

Shoshones in Idaho and Wyoming rapidly integrated into the European-American fur trade during the years from 1825 to 1845. The Fort Bridger Treaty of 1868 created the Wind River and Fort Hall Reservations. There are approximately 5,700 enrolled Eastern Shoshones at Wind River (with about 4,300 in residence) and about 4,500 Shoshone-Bannock people at Fort Hall. Most Shoshones are employed in ranching and farming.

BIBLIOGRAPHY

Crum, Steven J. *The Road on Which We Came: A History of the Western Shoshones.* Salt Lake City: University of Utah Press, 1994.

Madsen, Brigham D. *The Shoshoni Frontier and the Bear River Massacre.* Salt Lake City: University of Utah Press, 1985.

Stamm, Henry E., IV. *People of the Wind River: The Eastern Shoshones, 1825–1900.* Norman: University of Oklahoma Press, 1999.

Henry E. Stamm IV

See also **Fur Trade and Trapping; Indian Economic Life; Indians and the Horse.**

SHOWBOATS,

SHOWBOATS, also called floating theaters, floating operas, or boat-shows, were theaters on boats that brought entertainment primarily to small towns along the inland waterways of the midwestern and southern United States, chiefly along the Mississippi and Ohio Rivers. The showboat era lasted from 1831 to the 1940s, with a pause during the Civil War. Their heyday was the early twentieth century.

The original showboats were family owned and ventured to small, isolated river frontier locations. Family showboats were modest crafts of simple construction with seating for between one hundred and three hundred people. They did not carry passengers or transport goods, only culture and entertainment. Eventually, enormous floating theaters, with up to fourteen hundred seats, competed with the smaller family ventures.

The Chapman family from England launched the first showboat in 1831 in Pittsburgh. The Chapman boat floated with the current down the Ohio and Mississippi Rivers, tying up for one-night performances at river landings where there might be a viable audience. The nine-

Fort Washakie, Wyo. This 1892 photograph shows Eastern Shoshone, some dancing, and American soldiers at the fort renamed in 1878 in honor of the Shoshone chief *(pointing at left)*, whose warriors fought their Sioux enemies as Indian auxiliaries of U.S. troops under General George Crook, Colonel (later General) Nelson Miles, and others. NATIONAL ARCHIVES AND RECORDS ADMINISTRATION

person Chapman family served as the entire cast and crew. Admission to the show, although preferred in coins, was also accepted in the form of foodstuffs from the small river bottom farms.

Resembling a garage on a barge, the Chapman boat was one hundred feet wide and sixteen feet long. Performances included August von Kotzebue's *The Stranger*, William Shakespeare's *Hamlet* and *The Taming of the Shrew*, and the fairy tale "Cinderella." Popular songs were also frequent features. The Chapmans were successful in their venture and by 1836 were able to upgrade their operation to a small steamboat.

Other floating theaters soon followed the Chapman boat onto the waterways, as did circus boats featuring animal acts in addition to plays. The largest of these was the Floating Circus Palace of Gilbert R. Spaulding and Charles J. Rogers, built in 1851, which featured an impressive equestrian exhibition.

However, by the mid-nineteenth century the popularity of showboats had begun to diminish and with the Civil War they disappeared from the crowded waterways, which were disputed territories during the War. Showboats were revived beginning in 1878 with the building

of the *New Sensation* and the use of steamer tows and the beckoning sound of calliopes increased their territory and audience.

Early in the showboat era, comedies, back-to-nature plays, circuses, freak shows, and vaudeville acts were popular. After the Civil War minstrel shows and maudlin, nostalgic songs prevailed. During the Gilded Age and Progressive Era the melodrama proved to be the most successful style of showboat entertainment.

In the early twentieth century better roads, automobiles, and motion pictures provided river towns with other forms of entertainment. To compete with land entertainment, and one another, the boats and shows became larger, more lavish, and heavily advertised. The big boats featured musical comedy and full-length dramas as well as extravagant costumes. The most famous boats of this era were the *Grand Floating Palace*, the *Sunny South*, and the *Goldenrod*. Known as the Big Three, they belonged to W. R. Markle of Ohio. In the 1930s showboats changed their programs to burlesque in order to attract a new and more sophisticated, less family oriented audience, but ultimately high operating costs, a disappearing river frontier, and changing audience tastes brought the

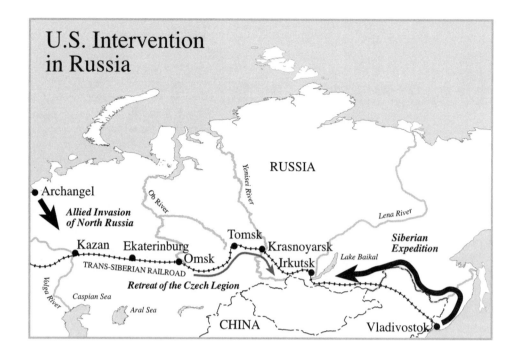

U.S. Intervention in Russia

showboat era to an end by the early 1940s. The *Goldenrod*, the last known showboat to be on the water, was tied permanently at St. Louis in 1943. Jerome Kern's 1927 musical, *Show Boat* (made into film versions in 1929, 1936, and 1951), dramatized the type of entertainment that showboats provided and depicted the lives of the showboat families and entertainers.

BIBLIOGRAPHY

Bryant, Betty. *Here Comes the Showboat!* Lexington: The University Press of Kentucky, 1994

Graham, Philip. *Showboats: The History of an American Institution.* Austin: University of Texas Press, 1951.

Deirdre Sheets

SHREVEPORT RATE CASE, officially known as *Houston, East and West Texas Railway Company v. United States* and *Texas and Pacific Railway Co. v. United States* 234 US 342 (1914), substantially increased federal control over interstate commerce. The case arose from a dispute between merchants in Shreveport, Louisiana, and several Texas railroad companies. At issue were freight rates set by the Texas Railroad Commission that were significantly higher for out-of-state merchants using Texas rail lines than for in-state companies. Encouraged by Progressive federal legislation such as the Hepburn Act (1906) and Mann-Elkins Act (1910), which had revitalized the Interstate Commerce Commission (ICC), the Shreveport Chamber of Commerce and the Railroad Commission of Louisiana brought federal suits against two Texas railroad firms. Whereas the prosecutors argued that the lower Texas rates undercut interstate trade, railroad attorneys

countered that the ICC lacked authority to control intrastate rates of interstate carriers. After losing in Federal Commerce Court, the railroad companies appealed to the U.S. Supreme Court, which ruled by a vote of 7 to 2 that Congress through the ICC, not individual states, wielded final authority over interstate trade. Although criticized by some states' rights advocates, the ruling proved popular with both business interests and the general public.

BIBLIOGRAPHY

Thompson, Alan S. "The Shreveport Rate Case." In *Grassroots Constitutionalism: Shreveport, the South, and the Supreme Law of the Land.* Edited by Norman W. Provizer and William D. Peterson. Lanham, N.Y.: University Press of America, 1988.

Thomas H. Cox

See also **Hepburn Act of 1906; Interstate Commerce Commission; Railroad Rate Law.**

SIBERIAN EXPEDITION. On 18 August 1918, near the end of World War I and five months after the Bolsheviks had signed the Treaty of Brest Litovsk with the Germans on 3 March 1918, an American expeditionary force landed in Siberia. Part of a joint Japanese–American agreement negotiated by President Woodrow Wilson, it was organized to help "rescue" a body of Czecho-Slovak soldiers, who had been fighting alongside the Bolsheviks against the Germans and were now seeking to reach the Western Front to fight for their freedom from Austria-Hungary. Although the Allies and the Supreme War Council (the chief agency for the direction of the war) had sought for six months to win Wilson's approval for an Allied intervention, designed to reestablish the Eastern Front, Wilson's public announcement of 3 August (known as the *aide memoire*) made clear that the United States would not support such an action.

Furious, the British and French proceeded with their own plans. The Czechs, under the command of the French, had secured from the Bolsheviks right of passage through Siberia. They were stopped in their tortuous journey, however, when the Germans forced the Bolsheviks to seek Czech disarmament, and when fighting broke out between Czech forces and Austro-Hungarian prisoners of war. Successful in occupying a major part of the Trans-Siberian Railway, the Czechs were persuaded by the Allies and counterrevolutionary White forces to remain at least temporarily in Siberia, to aid in the reestablishment of the Eastern Front.

Major General William S. Graves sailed from San Francisco with a contingent of U.S. troops on 2 September 1918 to join the U.S. regular 27th and 31st Infantry Regiments from Manila in the Philippines. He had been instructed to remain neutral and beware of Japanese imperialistic designs. Immediately upon his arrival, the divergence of views concerning the purpose of intervention became clearly apparent. Great Britain and France were attempting to extend the scope of military and political action in Siberia and co-opt the Czechs into reestablishing the Eastern Front, while Japan, under the terms of a secret Sino-Japanese military agreement of May 1918 (leaked by the Chinese to the State Department), was proceeding with its plans to occupy Manchuria and the Russian Far East. The United States, for its part, was attempting to limit and restrain its own independent operations. By the time the armistice was signed on 11 November 1918, Japan had sent some three divisions, or 72,400 men, all of them under the direct control of the General Staff in Tokyo. Fearing that Japan would succeed in gaining control of the railways, the United States initiated plans to have them administered by the U.S. military and operated by the Russian Railway Service Corps, a body of 300 American engineers (dispatched at the request of the Provisional Government in September 1917 to operate the Trans-Siberian Railway). The primary purpose of American military forces now became the restoration and protection of the railways, with Czech cooperation and support. Between 18 November 1918 and 27 December 1919, from the rise to the fall of Admiral Aleksandr V. Kolchak (would-be dictator of Siberia), General Graves scrupulously refrained from endorsing either the Whites or the Reds.

After the armistice, the defeat of the Bolsheviks became paramount in Allied decision making. Wilson soon found it impossible to keep American troops in Siberia without actively aiding Kolchak. Eventually, the Bolsheviks themselves conceded America's justification in following such a policy when in 1933, after being shown certain documents concerning American policy, they agreed to drop all claims against the United States for its

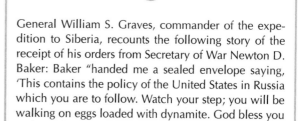

General William S. Graves, commander of the expedition to Siberia, recounts the following story of the receipt of his orders from Secretary of War Newton D. Baker: Baker "handed me a sealed envelope saying, 'This contains the policy of the United States in Russia which you are to follow. Watch your step; you will be walking on eggs loaded with dynamite. God bless you and goodbye.'"

SOURCE: William S. Graves. *America's Siberian Adventure,* p. 4.

part in the Siberian intervention. When U.S. troops left Siberia with the last contingent of Czech troops in April 1920, Japan remained in occupation of eastern Siberia and partial occupation of the Trans-Siberian Railway until 1922.

BIBLIOGRAPHY

Graves, William S. *America's Siberian Adventure, 1918–1920.* New York: Jonathan Cape and Harrison Smith, 1931. Reprint, New York: Arno Press, 1971. General Graves's personal account showing the divergence of American policy from that of its Allies.

Kennan, George F. *The Decision to Intervene.* Monograph published as part of *Soviet–American Relations, 1917–1920.* Princeton, N.J.: Princeton University Press, 1956–1958. A classic account of America's decision to intervene in both north Russia and Siberia.

Unterberger, Betty M. *America's Siberian Expedition, 1918–1920: A Study of National Policy.* Durham, N.C.: Duke University Press, 1956. Reprint, New York: Greenwood Press, 1969. Remains the classic account of the Siberian intervention.

———. *The United States, Revolutionary Russia, and the Rise of Czechoslovakia.* Chapel Hill: University of North Carolina Press, 1989. Paperback edition with *A 2000 Year Perspective.* College Station: Texas A&M University Press, 2000. Provides the complex setting for and the role of all participants in the Siberian intervention.

Betty Miller Unterberger

See also **Russia, Relations with; World War I.**

SICILIAN CAMPAIGN. In accordance with a decision made at the CASABLANCA CONFERENCE in January 1943, combined British and American ground, naval, and air forces under Lt. Gen. Dwight D. Eisenhower invaded Sicily on 10 July 1943 and conquered the island in thirty-eight days. Field Marshal Bernard L. Montgomery's British Eighth Army landed on the eastern coast; Lt. Gen. George S. Patton's Seventh U.S. Army came ashore on the southern coast. They were opposed by Gen. Alfredo

Sicilian Campaign. African American soldiers arrive at Gela, on the southern coast, on 26 July 1943, about two weeks after the start of the Allied invasion of Sicily. AP/WIDE WORLD PHOTOS

Guzzoni's Sixth Army of 200,000 Italians plus 30,000 Germans. A counterattack at Gela was quickly contained, and the beachheads were secured.

Montgomery advanced through Syracuse and Augusta to Catania in order to seize Messina. Patton was to protect his flank, but he obtained permission from Gen. Harold Alexander, the Allied ground commander, to extend westward toward Palermo. On 22 July he took the city. Montgomery was halted by strong defenses before Catania.

On 25 July in Rome, Benito Mussolini was deposed and imprisoned. Marshal Pietro Badoglio, the new Italian leader, soon sought terms of surrender. The Germans assumed control of Guzzoni's defense force, and by August the Axis effort in Sicily became a delaying action to cover an orderly withdrawal to the mainland. Axis troop withdrawal from Sicily started 11 August. Meticulously planned, the operation successfully transported about 125,000 men to the mainland.

With Patton already in Palermo, Alexander gave him permission, on 25 July, to advance on Messina. Thus began a contest between Montgomery and Patton to reach Messina. Launching three amphibious end runs to help his forces forward, Patton entered Messina first on 17 August. However, it was soon revealed that he had slapped two soldiers hospitalized for combat exhaustion. The unfavorable publicity marred his Sicily triumph and almost ended his military career.

BIBLIOGRAPHY

D'Este, Carlo. *Bitter Victory: The Battle for Sicily, July–August 1943.* London: Collins, 1988.

Garland, Albert N., Howard M. Smyth, and Martin Blumenson. *Sicily and the Surrender of Italy.* Washington, D.C.: Office of the Chief of Military History, Department of the Army, 1965.

Mitcham, Samuel W., and Friedrich von Stauffenberg. *Battle of Sicily.* New York: Orion Books, 1991.

Martin Blumenson / A. R.

See also **Anzio; North African Campaign; World War II.**

SIEGFRIED LINE. The Siegfried Line was the name given by Allied troops to fortifications erected before WORLD WAR II along Germany's western frontier. The name derived either from a German defensive position of WORLD WAR I, the *Siegfriedstellung*, or from the Siegfried legend celebrated in Richard Wagner's operas; it was popularized by a British music hall tune, "We're Going to Hang Out the Washing on the Siegfried Line." Known to the Germans as the Westwall, it was begun in 1938 as a short belt of fortifications opposite France's Maginot Line but later was extended to the Swiss and Dutch frontiers. It was a band three miles deep of more than three thousand concrete pillboxes, troop shelters, and command posts. Where no natural antitank obstacles existed, a belt of pyramidal concrete projections called "dragon's teeth" barred access across the terrain. Touted by German propagandists as impregnable, the line contributed to German success in bluffing France and Great Britain at Munich in 1938.

The line was neglected following German victory over France in 1940; but as Allied armies approached in September 1944, Adolf Hitler decreed that it be held. American attacks concentrated near AACHEN penetrated the line, only to be contained by German reserves. An attempt to outflank the line with an airborne attack in the Netherlands failed. Not until early spring of 1945, after German strength had been dissipated in a futile counteroffensive (the Battle of the Bulge), was the line pierced along its full length.

BIBLIOGRAPHY

MacDonald, Charles B. *The Mighty Endeavor: American Armed Forces in the European Theater in World War II.* New York: Oxford University Press, 1969.

———. *The Siegfried Line Campaign.* Washington, D.C.: The Center for Military History, United States Army, 1984.

Prefer, Nathan. *Patton's Ghost Corps: Cracking the Siegfried Line.* Novato, Calif.: Presidio, 1998.

Charles B. Macdonald / A. R.

See also **Bulge, Battle of the; Normandy Invasion.**

SIERRA CLUB. John Muir, the apostle of the American preservationist movement, cofounded the Sierra Club in 1892 and became its first president. The club's 182 charter members believed that by bringing people to the mountains and educating those who would not come, they could convince Americans to safeguard California's

activities to support new environmental laws to protect human health and welfare. To this end the club supplemented lobbying with litigation, which, for example, led to a ban on the widely used carcinogenic DDT in 1972. Club membership climbed to 114,000 by 1970 and to 200,000 by 1980.

Although concern over the Ronald Reagan administration's antienvironmentalism drove membership to 325,000 by 1982, the Sierra Club struggled during the 1980s just to defend what had been accomplished. During the 1990s, the club resumed the offensive, fighting to protect the Arctic National Wildlife Refuge, to strengthen the Clean Air Act, and to create the California Desert Protection Act. At the same time, the club again expanded its agenda by speaking out against global warming, the depletion of the ozone layer, and global trade without environmental controls and by linking environmentalism with human rights abuses worldwide. By 2000, club membership had reached 600,000. What had begun as a small group of outdoor enthusiasts dedicated to protecting Yosemite Valley became by the end of the twentieth century one of the largest and most influential environmental organizations in the world.

BIBLIOGRAPHY

Cohen, Michael P. *The History of the Sierra Club, 1892–1970.* San Francisco: Sierra Club Books, 1988.

Fox, Stephen R. *The American Conservation Movement: John Muir and His Legacy.* Madison: University of Wisconsin Press, 1985.

Shannon C. Petersen

See also **Conservation; National Park System; Yosemite National Park.**

John Muir. The influential naturalist, writer, and cofounder and first president of the Sierra Club. LIBRARY OF CONGRESS

wildlands. Foremost, the new club strove to protect the recently established Yosemite National Park, which faced its greatest threat from a proposal to dam the nearby Hetch Hetchy Valley. The ensuing controversy exposed a rift between preservationists, who believed in defending wilderness from most uses except recreation, and progressive conservationists, who advocated the "wise use" of the nation's resources.

During the first half of the twentieth century, the Sierra Club stood at the vanguard of the preservationist movement. The club lobbied hard for the creation and protection of such national parks as Mount Rainier, Glacier, and the Grand Canyon, and club member Steven Mather became the first director of the National Park Service. Yet the Sierra Club remained relatively small and localized.

Led by the so-called "Young Turks," including David Brower and Ansel Adams, during the 1950s, the Sierra Club became more aggressive and national. The club's focus, however, remained on preservation as it fought to stop a dam at Dinosaur National Monument and pushed for passage of the Wilderness Act. From 1955 to 1965, club membership grew from 10,000 to 33,000.

During the 1960s and the 1970s, the Sierra Club retained its leadership role only by broadening its lobbying

SIGN LANGUAGE, AMERICAN. American Sign Language (ASL) is a visual-gestural language used primarily by deaf residents of the United States and parts of Canada. It became a fully developed communication system only in the early nineteenth century, following contact between the American reformer Thomas Hopkins Gallaudet and deaf Frenchman Laurent Clerc. In 1815, Gallaudet, an evangelical Protestant minister from Hartford, Connecticut, traveled to England and then to France to learn how to instruct deaf children. Gallaudet became acquainted with Clerc at the National Institute for the Deaf in Paris, where Clerc taught, and in 1816 invited him to return to the United States. The next year, Gallaudet, Clerc, and a group of philanthropists opened a school for deaf children in Hartford, today's American School for the Deaf. The American School became the incubator for ASL.

Clerc's influence on the new language was enormous. He taught sign language to the American School's first principal, Gallaudet, to the first generation of the school's teachers, and to several generations of deaf students. For decades, his finest pupils became the lead teachers at other deaf schools in the United States, employing the signing that Clerc taught them. Modern examination of the lexical similarity of ASL and Clerc's native French Sign Language suggests that the languages share more than 50 percent of their vocabularies, reinforcing the historical evidence of Clerc's role. Indeed, in the late nineteenth century, critic Alexander Graham Bell charged that ASL was foreign, an import from France, and therefore fundamentally subversive of American culture and institutions.

Yet ASL's origins lie in both Europe and the United States. Clerc stated that he modified the sign language he brought from his homeland to fit American customs. School records indicate that many of the students who first attended the American School came from families with other deaf members; it is well known that in such situations deaf people typically create a shared system of gestures. These probably influenced ASL's early development, although the mechanism and the results—on ASL's lexicon, morphology, or syntax, for example—are not understood.

Natural change through time has influenced ASL. Many signs initially were close visual representations of the physical world of actions and things. Early nineteenth century ASL practitioners claimed that its power lay in the language's obvious mimetic characteristics. Studies of late-twentieth-century ASL, however, indicated that its signs by then were not in the least transparent to naive observers. Modern linguistic studies suggest that, in general, signs become smaller, more symmetrical, and more centrally located as sign languages mature and as iconicity is sacrificed for ease of production and comprehension.

ASL also reflects the influence of English. Initialized signs, made with a handshape that represents a particular letter in an English word, are common in ASL. The handshape for the letter G thus is used in the formation of the sign for the color "green," and the handshape for the letter B is necessary to produce the signs for "blue," "brown," and "beer." Furthermore, modern ASL incorporates a number of signs derived from the modification of finger-spelled English words. The usual ASL sign meaning affirmation or agreement, for instance, is a contraction of three finger-spelled letters, Y-E-S, into a single movement from the Y handshape to the S handshape. Similarly, word order in ASL may be undergoing modification, losing its dominant subject-object-verb pattern for the common English subject-verb-object.

The relationship between ASL and English has been contentious and negotiated throughout the language's history, and the boundary between ASL and English in a signed form is neither agreed upon nor unchanging. Clerc brought from France not only the language of deaf Parisians but also "methodical signs." The Abbé Charles Michel de l'Epée, founder of the National Institute in Paris in the 1770s, invented the latter to modify French Sign Language to conform to the rules of written French. For example, Epée appended elaborate grammatical markers to lexical terms borrowed from French Sign Language, and every word of spoken or written French had a direct equivalent in Epée's usage. Clerc learned methodical signs while a student at the Paris Institute. After arrival in the United States, he altered these to conform to English grammar. Clerc led the American School to use both English-like methodical signs and the "natural" or "colloquial" sign language of deaf people for instruction.

American educators debated the relative merits of methodical signs and ASL from the 1830s until after the Civil War. ASL proponents claimed that English-like signing taught students to create the forms of English without understanding. They noted that outside of the classroom deaf people used only natural sign language, as ASL was then called, for it conveyed meaning quickly, clearly, and easily. They believed that it should be allowed to remain separate and distinct from English. Others claimed that methodical signing's close relationship to English provided deaf children with greater access to written language. This argument eventually lost its urgency, however, as changing cultural attitudes condemned all signed communication.

Beginning in the 1870s, Alexander Graham Bell led a loose coalition of progressive educational reformers, nationalists, and eugenicists who attacked ASL and advocated the use of speech and speech reading in its place. They claimed that signing was primitive, associated with backward peoples; that its ease of use prevented deaf people from learning to speak; that it nurtured among deaf people a culture apart from the mainstream and thus threatened American cultural homogeneity; and that it encouraged deaf people to marry among themselves, possibly threatening the nation with the birth of more deaf children. Most hearing educators, hearing parents of deaf children, and school governing boards accepted these claims for decades. By the 1890s, schools were firing deaf teachers and banishing ASL from classrooms. Serious study of ASL, which had marked its early years, ceased.

Deaf Americans nevertheless kept ASL vibrant as the twentieth century began, passing it from pupil to pupil in school dormitories and playgrounds and from adult to adult in deaf clubs. Deaf leaders produced ASL dictionaries, and they filmed ASL masters to preserve classic forms for future generations. Various local deaf communities argued for ASL's reacceptance into schools. The educational failure of speech and speech reading, moreover, became increasingly obvious in the late twentieth century.

ASL's rehabilitation began about 1960 with the studies of William C. Stokoe and his colleagues at Gallaudet University. Stokoe showed that ASL, which was commonly used by his deaf students, was not a corrupt form of English but a language in its own right. Subsequent studies confirmed and developed Stokoe's insight and identified the qualities that distinguish true signed languages, like ASL, from other forms of visual communication, such as gesture or semaphore.

The Sign Language. Frederic Remington's illustration shows a white man using gestures to communicate with an Indian. NORTH WIND PICTURE ARCHIVES

The American civil rights movement provided the broader context within which ASL achieved scholarly and cultural acceptance in the late twentieth century. Public policy was no longer openly hostile to ethnic and linguistic diversity, affording deaf people some success in their demand to use their preferred language in social and legal contexts. By the 1970s, some schools had begun experimenting with the introduction of signed forms of English in the classroom. The next step was the introduction of ASL itself as the language of instruction. The old argument about the educational advantages of ASL versus English-like signing reemerged.

Some of the same cultural shifts that assisted ASL in gaining recognition in the late twentieth century, however, suggested that its future as a means of everyday discourse was not assured in the twenty-first century. Educational structures that concentrated deaf people in separate residential schools were no longer in favor. Technical devices to improve hearing, called cochlear implants, had made progress, and medical discoveries raised the possibility of eliminating genetic causes of deafness. Together, these changes had the potential to weaken or destroy the American deaf community.

BIBLIOGRAPHY

Baynton, Douglas C. *Forbidden Signs: American Culture and the Campaign against Sign Language.* Chicago: University of Chicago Press, 1996. The most important source for the history of ASL.

Lane, Harlan. *When the Mind Hears: A History of the Deaf.* New York: Random House, 1984.

Padden, Carol, and Tom Humphries. *Deaf in America: Voices from a Culture.* Cambridge, Mass.: Harvard University Press, 1988. See for the linguistics of ASL and for ASL's place in American deaf culture.

Stedt, Joseph D., and Donald F. Moores. "Manual Codes on English and American Sign Language: Historical Perspectives and Current Realities." In *Manual Communication: Implications for Educators.* Edited by Harry Bornstein. Washington, D.C.: Gallaudet University Press, 1990.

Van Cleve, John Vickrey, and Barry A. Crouch. *A Place of Their Own: Creating the Deaf Community in America.* Washington, D.C.: Gallaudet University Press, 1989.

John Vickrey Van Cleve

See also **Gallaudet University.**

SIGN LANGUAGE, INDIAN, also known as Plains Sign Talk, an intertribal language of gestural signs used by American Indians of the Great Plains region. Although origins remain obscure, Spanish explorers documented its use on the southern Plains during the sixteenth century. Extensive trade networks and political alliances brought tribes who spoke many different languages into regular contact with each other. Vocal communication was difficult and people probably maximized the panhuman tendency to resort to gestures in such contexts. Over time, such gestures were conventionalized into a language with a unique visual vocabulary and spatial grammar.

The sign language became so widespread that, despite dialect differences, a Blackfoot from the Canadian border could communicate with a Comanche from Texas, although neither understood the other's spoken language. The impetus for widespread standardization came from intertribal functions, but people within the same tribe integrated speech and signs, especially during storytelling and public oratory, and in communication with deaf and elderly persons. Plains Sign Talk flourished particularly during the eighteenth and nineteenth centuries, along with many other aspects of Plains cultures, as horse nomadism and the permanent population of the Plains increased.

Although simple spoken trade "jargons" (pidgins) developed in other regions of the continent, for example, Mobilian jargon in the Southeast and Chinook jargon on the Northwest Coast, the Plains area was unique in developing a signed *lingua franca*. Three factors shed some light on how and why it developed. First, no one nation in the Plains area was economically or politically dominant, so no one spoken language became widespread. Second, in contrast to philosophical and religious biases against the body in European thought, Plains peoples traditionally did not consider gestures to be more "primitive" than speech as a means of communicating. Third, sign languages have properties that make them easier to learn than spoken languages. Extensive use is made of signs that look like the objects and actions to which they refer (iconic signs), in addition to signs that are grammaticalized pointing gestures (indexical signs). This makes signs quicker to learn than the abstract sound combinations of spoken language. Contrary to popular misconceptions about the universality of gestural signs, however, Plains Sign Language is unique among the many sign languages of the world. It is not mutually intelligible with American Sign Language, the language used by members of the American Deaf community.

Colonial suppression of indigenous languages and forced accommodation to English led to a gradual decline in the use of Plains Sign Language during the twentieth century. Fluent sign talkers are rare, but the language remains active in numerous contexts, including storytelling, public oratory, ritual events, games, dances, and other social events, and wherever deafness is present. When speaking their native language, Plains people often continue to accompany their speech with signs. On the Northern Plains, educators working to revitalize the endangered spoken languages of the region, for example, Blackfoot, Assiniboine, Crow, and Cheyenne, incorporate Plains Sign Language in their language-maintenance programs.

BIBLIOGRAPHY

Clark, William P. *The Indian Sign Language.* Philadelphia: Hamersly, 1885.

Farnell, Brenda. *Do You See What I Mean? Plains Indian Sign Talk and the Embodiment of Action.* Austin: University of Texas Press, 1995.

———. *WIYUTA: Assiniboine Storytelling with Signs.* Austin: University of Texas Press, 1995. An award-winning interactive multimedia CD-ROM.

Taylor, Alan. "Non-Speech Communication Systems." In *Handbook of North American Indians.* Edited by William C. Sturtevant et al. Volume 17: *Languages,* edited by Ives Goddard. Washington, D.C.: Smithsonian Institution, 1996.

Umiker-Sebeok, Jean, and Thomas Sebeok, eds. *Aboriginal Sign Languages of the Americas and Australia,* Vol. 1: *North America.* New York: Plenum Press, 1978.

Brenda Farnell

See also **Indian Languages; Tribes: Great Plains.**

SIGNAL CORPS, U.S. ARMY. Congress created the U.S. Army Signal Corps on 21 June 1860. For more than a century, the term "Signal Corps" referred to both a separate unit within the War Department and the units having primary responsibility for army signal communications.

The Signal Corps first used a wigwag system of visual signaling developed by Albert James Myer, the first signal officer. In 1862 the corps began using the Beardslee magnetoelectric tactical telegraph machine. Following the Civil War the corps became responsible for army photography, established a pigeon service, and adapted to its uses the conventional electric telegraph; in subsequent decades it also incorporated the heliograph, telephone, radio, radar, and the communications satellite. From 1870 to 1891, the Signal Corps provided the United States with its first national weather service, which in 1891 became the Weather Bureau.

Beginning in 1962 a series of changes led to the elimination of the Signal Corps as a bureau. That year the Signal Corps lost responsibility for training, research and development, and procurement, and on 1 March 1964, the chief signal officer became the chief of communications-electronics (CC-E). The newly established U.S. Army Strategic Communications Command (USASTRATCOM) took over the corps command functions while the CC-E remained responsible for supervising staff. In 1973 USASTRATCOM became the U.S. Army Communications Command (USACC). On 16 September 1967 the CC-E became the assistant chief of staff for communications-electronics (ACSC-E), a position filled by a major general of the Signal Corps until elimination of the position in a major staff reorganization and transfer of functions in 1974.

BIBLIOGRAPHY

History of the U.S. Signal Corps. New York: Putnam, 1961.

Raines, Rebecca Robbins. *Getting the Message Through: A Branch History of the U.S. Army Signal Corps.* Washington D.C.: Center of Military History, U.S. Army, 1996.

Paul J. Scheips / F. B.

See also **Army, United States; Intelligence, Military and Strategic; Radar.**

SILENT SPRING. The biologist Rachel Carson (1907–1964) published *Silent Spring* in 1962, first as a series in *The New Yorker*, then as a book. She had become concerned during the 1950s at the rapid increase in artificial pesticide and herbicide spraying by farmers and government agencies. Carson, an elegant writer, already famous for the best-selling *The Sea Around Us* (1951), singled out DDT (dichloro-diphenyl-trichloro-ethane) as a particularly toxic chemical and criticized its widespread and indiscriminate use. Not only did such chemicals kill benign insects and birds and work their way into the food chain, she argued, they also encouraged the evolution of resistant strains of the pest insects and the displacement of indigenous flora by opportunistic weeds. Worse, they reached high levels of concentration in lakes, killed fish populations, and were slow to biodegrade. Even on purely economic grounds they made no sense because spraying, once begun, had to be done annually, at great cost. She recognized that pest control was sometimes necessary but made the case for introducing natural predators, including imported insects, and for neutering male insects in laboratories to reduce populations.

The book's commercial success took Carson and her publisher by surprise. Its success is not hard to explain, however. *Silent Spring* contained not only the relevant chemical equations but also a forcefully argued moral case, invoking the grand tradition of America's natural beauty under threat and pointing to the danger that even mothers, breast-feeding their infants, might inadvertently pass the poisons along. Here was a problem affecting every citizen's life and safety. The book took its title from the opening chapter, a dystopian vision of a rural community rendered silent in springtime, its habitual birdsong silenced by the mass poisoning of all the birds. The Audubon Society and the National Wildlife Federation both honored the book with prizes, and 600,000 copies were sold in the first year of publication.

American chemical manufacturers were afraid that Carson's work would damage their reputation as purveyors of progress and that they would be exposed to tighter government regulation. The former secretary of agriculture Ezra Taft Benson dismissed her as a "hysterical female." President John F. Kennedy's secretary of the interior, Stewart Udall, by contrast, praised the book and organized an investigation of the industry, which led ultimately to the Pesticide Control Act of 1972. Carson did not live to see this consequence of her work, dying of cancer in 1964. Environmental historians today recognize *Silent Spring* as the first literary salvo of the new environmental movement.

BIBLIOGRAPHY

Gartner, Carol. *Rachel Carson*. New York: Ungar, 1983.

Lear, Linda. *Rachel Carson: Witness for Nature*. New York: Henry Holt, 1997.

McKay, Mary A. *Rachel Carson*. New York: Twayne, 1993.

Patrick N. Allitt

See also **Conservation; Environmental Movement.**

SILHOUETTES—black profile portraits cut out of paper or painted on cards—were used as wall decorations during the first half-century of the republic. Well-known silhouettists included William M. S. Doyle and Henry Williams, both of whom worked in Boston, and William Bache, who was an itinerant. Another itinerant was the boy silhouettist Master Hubard, who cut profiles in 20 seconds. Auguste Edouart, a French visitor to America, cut full-length silhouettes. William Henry Brown, who was born in Charleston, South Carolina, likewise cut full-length silhouettes, and he published a *Portrait Gallery of Distinguished American Citizens* in 1855.

BIBLIOGRAPHY

Carrick, Alice Van Leer. *Shades of Our Ancestors*. Boston: Little, Brown, and Company, 1928.

Verplanck, Anne Ayer. "Facing Philadelphia: The Social Functions of Silhouettes, Miniatures, and Daguerrotypes." Ph.D. diss., College of William and Mary, 1996

Theodore Bolton / A. R.

See also **Folk Art.**

Mr. Shaw's Blackman. Moses Williams, the creator of this rare early-nineteenth-century silhouette of an African American, was a pupil and employee—and former slave—of the renowned Philadelphia portrait painter and museum owner Charles Willson Peale; Williams eventually earned enough to buy his own house. LIBRARY COMPANY OF PHILADELPHIA

SILICON VALLEY, located around Santa Clara and San Jose, California, is the home of many key U.S. corporations that specialize in advanced electronic and information technologies. First called "Silicon Valley" in 1971 by a local newsletter writer, Donald C. Hoefler, the "Valley" became the center of newly developing technologies that many believed would revolutionize computers, telecommunications, manufacturing procedures, warfare, and even U.S. society itself. The name came to symbolize a type of high-risk business characterized by rapid success or failure, extensive job mobility, and informal behavior, traits thought by some to be the wave of the future. The location of such high-tech research, development, and manufacturing in a formerly agricultural area—once known as the "prune capital of America"—grew mainly from its proximity to STANFORD UNIVERSITY in nearby Palo Alto. Stanford, a research-oriented institution with active departments in engineering and electronics, decided in 1951 to establish a "research park," a place where companies could build facilities and conduct research in cooperation with the university, the first such enterprise in the country.

If there was a single founder of Silicon Valley it was William Shockley, an English-born physicist who worked on early concepts of the transistor at Bell Laboratories before World War II and who went on to become the director of Bell's Transistor Physics Research Group. A restless person whose inquisitive mind and entrepreneurial aspirations did not find satisfaction in the larger corporation, he became a visiting professor at the CALIFORNIA INSTITUTE OF TECHNOLOGY in 1954. The following year he founded Shockley Semiconductor Laboratories just south of Palo Alto in the north end of Silicon Valley. Shockley's business acumen did not equal his skills in science and engineering, however, and in 1957 eight of his engineers defected to create Fairchild Semiconductor, supported by Fairchild Camera and Instrument.

Their departure established a pattern of job mobility that came to characterize careers in Silicon Valley in particular and in the electronics companies in general, with employees shunning ties of corporate loyalty in favor of personal fulfillment and financial reward. Reinforcing this pattern, Robert Noyce, Gordon Moore, and Andrew Grove left Fairchild Semiconductor in 1968 to establish Intel. Another Fairchild employee, W. J. Sanders III, founded Advanced Micro Devices soon thereafter. In the early 1970s one survey found forty-one companies in Silicon Valley headed by former Fairchild employees. This pattern continued into the 1980s with such companies as National Semiconductor, Atari, Apple Computer, LSI Logic, and Cypress Semiconductor having all or part of their origins in Silicon Valley.

To many observers the California location was central to the success and, later, the problems of Silicon Valley. The popular image of California, with its promise of individual and professional renewal, played a part, as did the cultural climate of the 1960s, which criticized large organizations for suppressing personal expression. The moderate climate of Silicon Valley, combined with a pool of educated talent from California universities and a largely nonunion workforce, attracted investors and corporations alike. Publicity about Silicon Valley in the 1970s generated discussion about new opportunities for U.S. industry, especially in electronics. In this respect the Valley represented a significant demographic change in American society: a shift in political and economic power from the older industrialized Northeast and Midwest to the Pacific Coast. The rise of Silicon Valley occurred at a time when major changes in financial markets and the availability of capital were affecting many established electronics companies.

During the 1950s and early 1960s, much of the valley relied on military contracts, but this dependence declined as commercial and then personal markets for computers emerged. Investors hoping for a very high rate of return increasingly were willing to risk supporting the new electronics companies even though as many as 25 percent of them failed within a few years. Demand for capital increased as the size of electronic components, such as memory chips, decreased. Hand in hand with smaller components developed the need for more sophisticated and costly technologies in manufacturing. By the late 1980s companies estimated that they needed as much as $1 billion to establish a manufacturing facility for the latest generation of SEMICONDUCTORS. Observers of investment practices and corporate strategies began to worry that this reliance on venture capital had created a pattern in U.S. business that stressed short-term profits rather than longer-term concerns about product development and competition from foreign corporations. Silicon Valley's success and the boost it gave to California's image and economy led such states as Oregon, Michigan, Texas, Colorado, New York, and Minnesota to invite or promote advanced electronic firms. In the 1990s, however, companies in Silicon Valley remained the major indicator of the health of the industry.

Products such as memory and logic chips, microprocessors, and custom-made circuits are expensive to manufacture, subject to price-cutting in the market, and have a short product life (sometimes two years or less) before the next generation appears. Their sale depends on the health of important segments of U.S. industry, including computers, telecommunications systems, automobiles, and military contractors. Silicon Valley and its counterparts elsewhere in the United States thus are subject to cycles of boom and bust. The latter occurred in 1984–1986, when many of the valley's companies found themselves with surplus products after a drop in the U.S. personal computer market. Companies had to lay off workers and some went out of business.

Foreign competition, especially from Japan, caused perhaps the greatest problems for Silicon Valley. Business and political leaders debated whether or not trade policy needed to defend the interests of U.S. electronics firms more aggressively and whether U.S. companies should receive government funding to make them more competitive in the international market. Silicon Valley had begun to worry about Japanese competition by the late 1970s. In 1981, U.S. companies controlled 51.4 percent of the world's semiconductor market; Japan's share was 35.5 percent. Within seven years the figures had virtually reversed themselves, with Japan at 51 percent and the United States 36.5 percent. U.S. companies charged their Japanese counterparts with dumping semiconductors onto the U.S. market at low prices to undercut U.S. manufacturers while Japan kept much of its home market closed. The Semiconductor Industry Association, which represented many companies in Silicon Valley, urged bilateral agreements to open Japan's market. The first of these was signed in 1986, and a second followed in 1992. By the early 1990s it appeared that U.S. industry had started to recover some of the ground lost to Japan. A boom cycle began in the mid-1990s with the emergence of the INTERNET and ELECTRONIC COMMERCE, sending technology stocks skyward and leading to the rapid rise of new businesses in the software and electronics industries.

Several factors reduced the lure of Silicon Valley as the center of the electronics and computer industry, among them new technologies, the ascent of successful electronic-component manufacturing elsewhere in the United States, and foreign competition. People learned that the manufacturing of electronic components was not as environmentally clean or safe as some thought, and the growth of the Valley led to traffic congestion and air pollution. Silicon Valley remained a center of research, development, and manufacturing in the electronics industry, however, and the rise of the Internet-based "dot.coms" of the mid- and late 1990s reenergized the area's symbolic role as a frontier of industrial and social organization and sent property values soaring. When technology stocks began to implode in early 2001, however, massive layoffs swept through Silicon Valley, again casting a shadow over the the area's immediate future and underlining the region's dependence on a sector of the economy that seems to be particularly susceptible to boom-and-bust cycles.

BIBLIOGRAPHY

Findlay, John M. *Magic Lands: Western Cityscapes and American Culture after 1940.* Berkeley: University of California Press, 1992.

Forester, Tom. *High-Tech Society: The Story of the Information Technology Revolution.* Cambridge, Mass.: MIT Press, 1987.

Saxby, Stephen. *The Age of Information: The Past Development and Future Significance of Computing and Communications.* New York: New York University Press, 1990.

Teitelman, Robert. *Profits of Science: The American Marriage of Business and Technology.* New York: Basic Books, 1994.

Kenneth B. Moss / c. w.

See also **Computers and Computer Industry; Demography and Demographic Trends; Electricity and Electronics; Japan, Relations with.**

SILICONE BREAST IMPLANTS. *See* **Breast Implants.**

SILK CULTURE AND MANUFACTURE.

Long known as the Queen of Textiles, silk is valued for its luster, soft hand, and drapability. It is used for both clothing and home décor in a wide range of fabrics including taffeta, chiffon, satin, brocade, and damask, as well as for trimmings such as ribbon and braid.

Silk filaments are harvested from a special caterpillar known as the silkworm, which lives in and feeds on the leaves of the white mulberry tree. Its cocoon is made of a single strand of delicate silk filament, which can be unwound and converted into thread to produce some of the most luxurious fabrics in the world. When first introduced, the fabrics were reserved for royalty.

While world production of silk goes back to China more than 4,500 years ago, the silk industry (or sericulture) in what is now the United States began in 1603. Having determined that the American climate was better suited to silk culture than that of Britain, and anxious to compete successfully with the French and Italian silk industry, King James I of England sent silkworm eggs and mulberry tree seeds to the new colonists in Virginia. Although cotton and tobacco proved to be more profitable crops, there was some limited silk production in Virginia and Georgia from 1603 to 1760.

In 1762, the struggling industry got a boost when Nathan Aspinwald decided to expand his white mulberry orchard from Long Island, New York, to include his native town of Mansfield, Connecticut. A silk farm and silk-spinning industry sprang up there, and by 1830—once other entrepreneurs became aware of the potential for high profits—the industry spread all along the Atlantic coast.

Small mills in New England produced primarily silk thread, ribbon, and trim such as braid around 1810. In 1827, Edmund Golding brought new technology to Mansfield, Connecticut, from his home in Macclesfield, England (center of a once-thriving silk industry). Using new machinery for doubling and twisting silk that replaced hand spinning, he and his partners opened the first successful silk mill in America.

Favorable trade agreements with China and a blight on mulberry trees from 1840 to 1844 forced American factories to switch to importing raw silk, and the silk fiber industry crashed. The advent of sewing machines in the mid-1800s, however, created a greater demand for silk sewing thread.

Christopher Cross of Connecticut introduced silk production to Paterson, New Jersey, in 1840. Prior to that (since 1807), Paterson's cotton textile mills had been producing silk ribbons. Although his Old Gun Mill silk enterprise eventually failed, there followed a large immigration of skilled workers and manufacturers who brought new silk machinery from Great Britain to Paterson between 1860 and 1880. In 1860, Paterson was home to six silk companies, employing 600 workers in the various tasks of twisting, weaving, and dyeing silk.

By the turn of the century, Paterson was becoming known as "Silk City," the capital of the silk industry in America, as more than one-third of the city's total workforce of 73,000 was employed in the silk business. The lure of work and the desire to escape from poverty brought immigrants, including skilled workers, not only from England, but also from France, Italy, Poland, Germany, and Russia.

The handloom for silk weaving was completely replaced by automation around 1905, and Paterson mills were thus able to steal business away from the European silk industry, which was less mechanized. There were 121 businesses in Paterson, which employed thousands of workers, all making silk products and machinery for textile production. By 1940, more than 175 silk companies were operating in Paterson, with 20,000 workers manufacturing products such as yard goods, ribbons, drapery and upholstery, veiling, linings, braid, and yarn.

Earlier on, however, Paterson had some notable competition. By 1890, there had been fierce rivalry from mills in northeastern Pennsylvania—prices dropped, profits dipped, and labor conflicts were intense. By the end of World War I, Pennsylvania had surpassed Paterson in spindlage and Philadelphia was making knitted silk hosiery, an industry that would sustain it for the next generation.

In 1913, a major labor strike in Paterson by silk workers captured national attention, and expanded to include 50,000 workers in New Jersey, Pennsylvania, New York, and Connecticut. Although it was the result of years of struggle, it was ignited by mill owners' demands that workers operate four looms instead of two, leading to longer hours, lower pay, layoffs, and an incensed labor force. This difficult period of labor problems culminated in many silk mills either closing their doors or moving south in the period from 1930 to 1940.

Also, consolidation of the silk industry in Paterson had been taking place since the early part of the twentieth century. Larger manufacturers, such as the Standard Silk Dyeing Company and Allied Textile Printers, had acquired many smaller businesses. The main focus of these operations was the wet processing of undyed woven cloth, called gray goods. Meanwhile, widespread substitutions of synthetic fabrics like rayon, nylon, and acetate for silk contributed to the end of silk production in Paterson and the United States. Allied Textile Printers closed in 1983.

Consumption of raw silk in the United States fell from an annual high of eighty-one million pounds in 1930 to forty-eight million in 1940, seven million in 1960, and only two million in 1970. Competition from China and Japan began to phase out the American silk industry around the end of the 1980s. By the early 2000s, the silk industry in the United States had virtually disappeared.

BIBLIOGRAPHY

Hellwig Silk Dyeing Company homepage. Available from http://homepages.rootsweb.com/~wdstock/hellwig.htm.

Paterson Friends of the Great Falls. Available from http://patersongreatfalls.com.

"Paterson Strike." National Archives Learning Curve. Available from http://www.spartacus.schoolnet.co.uk.

Scranton, Phillip B., ed. *Silk City: Studies on the Paterson Silk Industry 1860–1940.* Newark: New Jersey Historical Society, 1985.

Silk Association of India homepage. Available from http://www.silkassociation.com.

"Silk Industry in Mansfield, Conn." Mansfield Historical Society. Available from http://www.mansfield-history.org/silk industry.

Rosalie Jackson Regni

SILVER. *See* **Metalwork.**

SILVER DEMOCRATS was a term used at various times after 1878 to refer to those members of the DEMOCRATIC PARTY who advocated replacing the GOLD STANDARD with a policy of bimetallism. The Silver Democrats believed that the free coinage of silver at a ratio of sixteen to one would inflate prices and thus relieve the burden on the nation's depressed farmers. More general use of the term "Silver Democrats" followed the 1893 inauguration of President Grover Cleveland, a Gold Democrat, and his support for repeal of the SHERMAN SILVER PURCHASE ACT of 1890. Cleveland's position polarized the party into two factions: a proadministration gold faction based in the industrial Northeast and an antiadministration silver faction based in the agrarian South and Great Plains. The rift between pro-Cleveland GOLD DEMOCRATS and anti-Cleveland Silver Democrats reached a climax at the 1896 Democratic convention in Chicago, where the two sides met to nominate a presidential candidate. Silverites dominated the convention and secured the nomination of William Jennings Bryan as the party's presidential candidate. Bryan's free-silver stand also won the endorsement of the Populist party convention, but it alienated Gold Democrats so severely that many bolted the party. Some Gold Democrats supported the third-party candidacy of Gold Democrat John Palmer, but most turned to the Republican candidate William McKinley. The November election results broke down along regional lines, as McKinley captured the presidency on the strength of his support in the Midwest and Northeast. Bryan's defeat, coupled with growing inflation, led to silver's demise as a major issue in the early twentieth century.

BIBLIOGRAPHY

Durden, Robert. *The Climax of Populism: The Election of 1896.* Lexington: University of Kentucky Press, 1965.

Goodwyn, Lawrence. *Democratic Promise: The Populist Moment in America*. New York: Oxford University Press, 1976.

Ritter, Gretchen. *Goldbugs and Greenbacks: The Antimonopoly Tradition and the Politics of Finance in America*. New York: Cambridge University Press, 1997.

Elmer Ellis / A. G.

See also **Conventions, Party Nominating; Gold Bugs; Populism.**

SILVER LEGISLATION refers to U.S. statutes regulating silver coinage and/or affecting the interests of silver miners as a class. Both types of legislation have loomed large in American history.

It was the intention of the founders of the nation to establish a genuine bimetallism: that is, a monetary system in which both gold and silver were legal tender. It has been generally accepted by historians that this policy was based on the theory—offered by Alexander Hamilton, the first secretary of the treasury, in his *Mint Report*—that under bimetallism there is a more plentiful supply of money. Another reason for bimetallism was the fact that the principle of subsidiary silver coinage (that is, the use of silver alloys for coins of smaller denomination than the currency unit) was unknown to science or to history, and bimetallism was a necessity if small units of silver were to be coined.

The bimetallic system was a failure. Revision of the legal ratio between the values of gold and silver in 1834 and 1837 created an adequate gold coinage but drove out the limited silver coinage in circulation, since the free-market value of silver was higher than its monetary value. From 1834 on, American silver coins as standard money ceased to play a part in the life of the nation. The establishment by Congress of subsidiary silver coinage in 1853 confirmed this situation legally. But the 1853 statute accidentally left the silver dollar as a standard coin, although the market value of silver continued to make its coinage impossible. In a revision of the statutes in 1873, the unknown piece was dropped.

In 1873 the world market ratio of silver to gold fell below sixteen to one for the first time in history. This decline coincided with the opening of rich silver mines in the West, with the post–Civil War deflation, and with a deep depression that sorely afflicted the country. The consequence was a political movement, promoted by the silver interests and embraced by agrarian and pro-inflation elements, for the restoration of bimetallism. Eventually there developed in the Senate, and more tentatively in the House, a nonpartisan "silver bloc," led by members from the sparsely populated western states in which mine owners gained great political influence.

In the 1870s, 1890s, and 1930s, the efforts of this pressure group, reinforced by the popular clamor for INFLATION, almost achieved bimetallism and succeeded in extracting from Congress legislation giving a cash subsidy of some sort to the producers of silver. For example, the BLAND-ALLISON ACT of 1878 (passed over President Rutherford B. Hayes's veto) required the U.S. Treasury to buy $2 million to $4 million worth of silver a month. The SHERMAN SILVER PURCHASE ACT of 1890 (signed by President Benjamin Harrison but repealed at the insistence of President Grover Cleveland in 1893) mandated treasury purchases of 4.5 million ounces of silver a month, an amount roughly equivalent to the total estimated U.S. production in 1890.

The Silver Purchase Act of 1934 followed an unprecedented decline in the price of silver during the GREAT DEPRESSION that began in 1929. A flood of proposals for subsidies to silver miners was urged on Congress. The futile 1933 WORLD ECONOMIC CONFERENCE at London enacted, under pressure from U.S. participants, an agreement for stabilizing silver prices, under cover of which, by presidential proclamation, the United States paid from 64.64 cents to 77 cents per ounce for domestic silver, which had a market value of 45 cents. Unable to achieve bimetallism at sixteen to one (the market ratio was seventy to one), the silver interests finally forced the passage of the Silver Purchase Act. It provided for the nationalization of domestic stocks of silver and for the purchase of silver by the treasury until the price should reach $1.2929 per ounce or the value of the amount held should equal one-third of the value of the government's gold holdings. The immediate effect of the legislation was a speculative rise in the market price of silver to 81 cents an ounce, which destroyed the currency systems of China and Mexico.

In 1939 the president's powers to debase the gold standard and buy silver were renewed, and Congress was allowed to set the price for domestic silver. It was pegged initially at 71 cents an ounce, 36 cents above the market price. In WORLD WAR II, a shortage of silver developed, and the price rose rapidly. Under the leadership of Senator Patrick McCarran of Nevada, measures were blocked that would have provided government silver for defense production, for industrial use in nonwar industries, and for use by U.S. allies. Finally, in 1943, the Green Act provided that U.S. industries might buy silver from the treasury at the price originally paid for it, and large amounts of silver, all of which were returned, were lent to U.S. allies.

In the 1960s, when strong industrial demand for silver created another worldwide shortage, the metal was nearly eliminated from the U.S. monetary system. The Silver Purchase Act was repealed in 1963. Two years later, under the Coinage Act of 1965, silver was eliminated from two subsidiary coins (the quarter and dime), and its content in the half-dollar was reduced from 90 percent to 40 percent. By another act of Congress, U.S. Treasury certificates could no longer be redeemed in silver after 28 June 1968, and in 1970 the Bank Holding Company Act withdrew silver from the dollar and replaced it with copper and nickel. These later changes passed without the controversy that had accompanied previous silver legislation, suggesting a national acceptance of government fiat coins that, in the late nineteenth century, seemed impossible.

BIBLIOGRAPHY

Carothers, Neil. *Fractional Money: A History of the Small Coins and Fractional Paper Currency of the United States.* New York: Wiley, 1930.

Friedman, Milton, and Anna Jacobson Schwartz. *A Monetary History of the United States, 1867–1960.* Princeton, N.J.: Princeton University Press, 1963.

Schwartz, Anna Jacobson. *Money in Historical Perspective.* Chicago: University of Chicago Press, 1987.

Weinstein, Allen. *Prelude to Populism: Origins of the Silver Issue, 1867–1878.* New Haven, Conn.: Yale University Press, 1970.

Wilson, Thomas F. *The Power "To Coin" Money: The Exercise of Monetary Powers by the Congress.* Armonk, N.Y.: M. E. Sharp, 1992.

Neil Carothers/f. b.

See also **Crime of 1873; Currency and Coinage; Financial Panics; Gold Democrats; Greenback Movement; Populism.**

SILVER PROSPECTING AND MINING.

Silver mining in North America began when the Spanish worked small mines during their occupation of New Mexico, California, and Texas. New Hampshire produced small amounts of silver after 1828, as well as Virginia and Tennessee after 1832. Large-scale silver mining had its beginning in Nevada after 1859, when Peter O'Riley and Patrick McLaughlin prospected the area eastward from the California gold fields and staked what would become known as the Comstock lode. Though looking for gold, their discovery developed into a bonanza mine that yielded ores so rich that within two decades more than $300 million worth of silver and gold had been extracted.

The Comstock pattern, in which prospectors discovered silver while searching for gold, was repeated in various parts of the American West. At Georgetown, Colorado, an original gold placer camp developed as the center of a silver-producing district after the opening of the Belmont lode in 1864. Also in Colorado, the gold camp of Oro City was almost a ghost town when prospectors discovered carbonate of lead ores with rich silver content in 1877, rapidly transforming the town into the greatest of Colorado silver cities, Leadville. Gold prospectors also accidentally discovered the Bunker Hill and Sullivan mines in the Coeur d'Alene district of Idaho.

Silver occurs in lodes or veins that run to great depths underground. Prospectors identify the lode by the outcroppings of such ores. The silver can be recovered by crushing the ore in a stamp mill. This process passes the ore over copper plates coated with mercury and then separates the amalgam by driving off the mercury with heat. Other, more complex, forms of silver are chemically combined with gold, lead, copper, or other metals. The identification of these ores is much more difficult and requires more intricate metallurgical processes for separation. Mills and smelters necessary for treating complex silver ores were not available in the United States until 1866–1868. Thomas H. Selby in San Francisco, W. S. Keyes in Eureka, Nevada, A. W. Nason in Oreana, Nevada, and Nathaniel P. Hill in Blackhawk, Colorado, were all pioneers of the smelting industry in the United States. As a result of their advances in smelting technology, recovered metals such as lead and copper became increasingly significant by-products of the silver smelters.

The prosperity of the silver mining industry in the United States during the nineteenth century was intimately related to the currency policy of the federal government, particularly after the demonetization of silver in 1873. Many of the largest producing silver mines in the country opened after 1873. During the quarter of a century that followed, the nation debated the questions of silver purchases and coinage. The huge quantities of silver produced by these mines depressed the price, and, with the repeal of the Sherman Silver Purchase Act in 1893, the domestic silver market fell to levels so low that many mines suspended operations.

The industry recovered sufficiently to make the years 1911–1918 the peak years in volume of production. An annual average of 69,735,000 fine ounces of silver were produced during those years. After those boom years the continuing low prices for silver and high production costs limited activity in mining. After 1920 the Coeur d'Alene district of Idaho was the leading silver-producing region in the country. In 1970 Idaho produced 42 percent of the 45,006,000 fine ounces of silver mined in the United States, while most of the other silver came from mines in Arizona, Utah, and Montana.

BIBLIOGRAPHY

Bakewell, Peter, ed. *Mines of Silver and Gold in the Americas.* Brookfield, Vt.: Variorum, 1997.

Paul, Rodman W. *Mining Frontiers of the Far West, 1848–1880.* New York: Holt, Rinehart, and Winston, 1963.

Rickard, T. A. *A History of American Mining.* New York: McGraw-Hill, 1932.

Smith, Duane A. *Mining America: The Industry and the Environment, 1800–1980.* Lawrence: University Press of Kansas, 1987.

Carl Ubbelohde/h. s.

See also **Leadville Mining District; Mining Towns;** *and vol. 9:* **Roughing It.**

SILVER REPUBLICAN PARTY.

The Silver Republican party was an organization formed by the delegates who bolted from the Republican party convention of 1896 after its adoption of the gold standard as the basis of the U.S. monetary system. The Silver Republicans later issued an endorsement of the Democratic presidential candidate William Jennings Bryan. In 1900 the party met in its first and only national convention. The party's leaders hoped to secure a common ticket with the Democrats, but they failed when the Democrats refused to accept a Silver Republican as the vice-presidential candidate. In March 1901 the party's members in Congress joined in an address urging all supporters to unite with the DEMOCRATIC PARTY.

BIBLIOGRAPHY

Durden, Robert Franklin. *The Climax of Populism: The Election of 1896.* Lexington: University of Kentucky Press, 1965.

Ritter, Gretchen. *Goldbugs and Greenbacks: The Antimonopoly Tradition and the Politics of Finance in America.* New York: Cambridge University Press, 1997.

Elmer Ellis / A. G.

See also **Conventions, Party Nominating; Gold Bugs; Gold Democrats; Populism.**

SIMPSON MURDER TRIALS. On 12 June 1994, Nicole Brown Simpson and Ronald Goldman died of multiple stab wounds in Brentwood, California. Nicole's ex-husband, O. J. Simpson, a football celebrity, was questioned by the police. On 17 June, prior to his arrest, Simpson departed on a low-speed chase on the Los Angeles and Orange County freeways. He entered a plea of not guilty on 22 July, and Judge Lance A. Ito was assigned to hear the case. The trial opened on 24 January 1995 with the prosecutors Marcia Clark and Christopher Darden delivering opening statements. Three days later Simpson's book *I Want to Tell You* appeared, offering his story in print while the trial was on television. A media feeding frenzy was only starting.

O. J. Simpson. The former football star and accused murderer sits in the courtroom between Robert Shapiro (*right*) and Johnnie Cochran, two of his attorneys. © CORBIS

In the trial, the prosecution emphasized Simpson's long-term spousal violence, and the defense attacked the prosecution's physical evidence by forcing disclosure of procedural errors by the police. The Simpson defense team prevailed. On 2 October, after four hours of deliberation, the overwhelmingly African American jury acquitted Simpson. Long-standing differences and hostility between the police and the black community always hovered near the surface of the trial.

On 4 May 1995 the Goldman family filed a wrongful death civil suit against Simpson. That trial opened on 23 October 1996, and on 4 February 1997 the jury awarded the plaintiffs $8.5 million. Four years later, the plaintiffs still sought to collect the judgment, while Simpson claimed to be looking for the "real killer."

BIBLIOGRAPHY

Dershowitz, Alan M. *Reasonable Doubts.* New York: Simon and Schuster, 1996.

Schuetz, Janice, and Lin S. Lilley. *The O. J. Simpson Trials: Rhetoric, Media, and the Law.* Carbondale: Southern Illinois University Press, 1999.

Gordon Morris Bakken

SING SING is the familiar name of New York State's notorious prison, located at Ossining on the Hudson River north of New York City. The description of imprisonment as being "sent up the river" originated there. Sing Sing was constructed in the 1820s by inmate labor under the direction of the first warden, Elan Lynds. Initially the institution operated under the "silent" system. By night prisoners were confined to single-occupancy cells of less than thirty square feet. By day they worked together quarrying stone. They were required to remain silent at all times. When they moved about, they marched in lockstep with their eyes downcast. They were brutally whipped for any transgression.

The "silent" system was abolished at the end of the nineteenth century. In the 1930s Sing Sing provided the model for gangster movies, which created vivid imagery of the harsh prison culture. New York's electric chair was located at Sing Sing, and Ethel and Julius ROSENBERG were executed there in 1953.

Sing Sing remains a maximum-security prison for violent offenders. Most of the original structure has been replaced, but the first cell block is preserved and is listed in the National Registry of Historic Sites.

BIBLIOGRAPHY

Conover, Ted. *Newjack: Guarding Sing Sing.* New York: Random House, 2000.

Lewis, W. David. *From Newgate to Dannemora: The Rise of the Penitentiary in New York, 1796–1848*. Ithaca, N.Y.: Cornell University Press, 1965.

Larry Yackle

See also **Prisons and Prison Reform.**

SINGING SCHOOLS could be found in every region of the United States in the nineteenth century, but were especially common in the rural districts of the South and West. They were usually conducted by an itinerant teacher of music, who collected a small fee from each student enrolled. A session commonly continued from two to four weeks, with a meeting held each evening. Nominally formed to teach singing, the singing school also served as a social and often a matrimonial agency.

BIBLIOGRAPHY

Seeger, Charles. "Music and Class Structure in the United States." *American Quarterly* 9 (Autumn, 1957): 281–294.

Edward Everett Dale / A. R.

See also **Education; Music: Early American.**

SINGLE TAX. The single tax is the name of a levy proposed by Henry George in his book *Progress and Poverty*, published in 1879. In place of all other taxes, George advocated a single tax that would appropriate for government use all rent on land. His proposal was intended as much more than a mere fiscal device; it was set forth as a vehicle for social reform.

On the ground that land was a gift of nature, not a product of human effort, George condemned private ownership of land, which he considered the cause of economic and social ills. Land values, he held, were attributable to social or community factors. The state, therefore, and not the individual, should be the beneficiary of these values and any increases therein. The single tax, George wrote, would do no less than abolish poverty, elevate morals, and "carry civilization to yet nobler heights." George was undoubtedly influenced by his years in CALIFORNIA, where he had observed the speculation in land and the rapid rise in land values following the gold rush of 1849. He was not content merely to expound his views in writing. He made his single-tax plan the core of his unsuccessful campaigns for mayor of New York City in 1886 and 1897.

The single-tax program had but limited acceptance in the United States despite vigorous attempts to promote it through political campaigns, legislative action, and general publicity. The single-tax cause was aided by large financial contributions from the philanthropist Joseph Fels. In California in the early twentieth century, the single-tax plan came before the voters on seven occasions; each time it was rejected. Agitation for the single tax, or for a partial application of it, was also carried on in Oregon, Washington, Colorado, Missouri, New York, Pennsylvania, and Texas.

BIBLIOGRAPHY

Barker, Charles A. *Henry George*. New York: Oxford University Press, 1955.

George, Henry. *Progress and Poverty*. New York: Robert Schalkenbach Foundation, 1979.

Marvel M. Stockwell / A. R.

See also **Land Speculation; Radicals and Radicalism; Taxation.**

SINGLETON PEACE PLAN. In the winter and spring of 1865, James Washington Singleton, a native of Virginia, was the bearer of confidential messages between President Abraham Lincoln and Confederate authorities. These messages dealt at first with the achievement of peace and later with respect to the return of the South to the Union. Singleton's mission was ended by Lincoln's death. The Confederate government's unwillingness to accept any terms other than complete Southern independence, and the Lincoln administration's demand of national reunion and slave emancipation, doomed all efforts at a peaceful resolution of the CIVIL WAR. The collapse of the Confederacy in April 1865 made such efforts unnecessary in any event.

BIBLIOGRAPHY

Donald, David Herbert. *Lincoln*. New York: Simon and Schuster, 1995.

Paludan, Phillip Shaw. *The Presidency of Abraham Lincoln*. Lawrence: University of Kansas Press, 1994.

Matthew Page Andrews / A. G.

See also **Confederate States of America; Hampton Roads Conference; Peace Movement of 1864.**

SINKING FUND, NATIONAL, a fund established under the Funding Act of 1790 to pay off the public debt. Administered by high government officers, it drew its funds from surplus revenue from customs duties and $2 million of borrowed money. Alexander Hamilton checked the panic of 1792 by purchasing securities at market rate, below par, for the sinking fund.

On recommendation of Albert Gallatin, Thomas Jefferson's secretary of the Treasury, Congress reorganized the sinking fund in 1802. The years 1801 to 1812 brought America prosperity as chief neutral carrier during the Napoleonic Wars. Gallatin reduced the public debt by $40 million, although the War of 1812 ran up the debt to $119.5 million by 1815. Increased imports and mounting land sales after the war allowed Congress to make large appropriations to the sinking fund, and by 1837 the Treasury had a surplus of more than $42 million, of which it distributed $28 million to the states.

The prosperity of 1848 to 1857 ended with the panic of 1857, and the debt rose sharply during the Civil War. In the prosperous 1920s, appropriations to the sinking fund grew from $261 to $388 million, but the Great Depression ushered in an era of deficit spending, prolonged by World War II and the Korean and Vietnam wars. Congress regularly raised the debt ceiling and systematized refunding, and though Ronald Reagan made the public debt an issue during his successful bid for the presidency in 1980, the debt tripled during his administration. Surpluses in the late 1990s allowed President William Clinton to pay down the debt for the first time since 1972, but the debt stood at over $5 trillion in 1999.

BIBLIOGRAPHY

Kimmel, H. Lewis. *Federal Budget and Fiscal Policy.* Washington, D.C.: Brookings Institution, 1959.

Studenski, Paul, and Herman E. Krooss. *Financial History of the United States: Fiscal, Monetary, Banking, and Tariff, Including Financial Administration and State and Local Finance.* New York: McGraw-Hill, 1963.

Broadus Mitchell / c. w.

See also **Debt, Public; Financial Panics; Hamilton's Economic Policies.**

SINO-JAPANESE WAR. The eruption of war between China and Japan in 1894 did not directly involve the United States, but the resulting regional instability spurred the Cleveland administration to intervene diplomatically. Although it would not formulate the OPEN DOOR POLICY until 1899, Washington feared European powers would exploit for their own economic benefit the instability caused by the Sino-Japanese rivalry. Thus, the United States had rejected British overtures for foreign intervention to prevent the war. Once hostilities began, however, Washington advised Japan to moderate its ambitions in Asia or face international condemnation. In 1895 the Cleveland administration's efforts succeeded in bringing Japan and China to the peace table.

BIBLIOGRAPHY

Beisner Robert L. *From the Old Diplomacy to the New, 1865–1900.* New York: Crowell, 1975.

McCormick, Thomas J. *China Market: America's Quest for Informal Empire, 1893–1901.* Chicago: Quadrangle Books, 1967.

Foster Rhea Dulles / a. g.

See also **China, Relations with; Diplomatic Missions; Japan, Relations with; Trade, Foreign.**

SIOUX. Referred to collectively by outsiders as Sioux, a French rendition of the Ottawa name *na·towe·ssiwak,* meaning "enemy," the Sioux call themselves Lakota or Dakota, depending on dialect, signifying "allies." While linguists trace their origins to the southeastern United

Red Cloud. A powerful chief of the Oglala Sioux; his long siege of Fort Phil Kearny (in present-day Wyoming) and killing of Captain William Fetterman's entire eighty-man detachment led to the Fort Laramie Treaty of 1868, in which the U.S. government agreed to close the Bozeman Trail and establish the Great Sioux Reservation (what is now the western half of South Dakota). © BETTMANN-CORBIS

States, some Lakotas and Dakotas today say they emerged from the Black Hills, where they have lived for millennia. At the time of early European contact these groups were found in southern Minnesota, extending east to western Wisconsin and south to northern Iowa and westward across the prairies of North and South Dakota. By the late nineteenth century some Sioux had made their way west as far as eastern Montana. The total Sioux population reached its nadir in 1890 at 25,920. In the 2000 U.S. Census, 153,360 people self-identified as Sioux or Sioux and other tribal affiliations.

The Sioux conceptualize themselves as the Seven Council Fires. The easternmost division, the Santees, consist of four tribes: Mdewakanton (Spirit Lake Village), Wahpeton (Leaf Village), Wahpekute (Leaf Shooters), and Sisseton (sometimes translated as Fish Scale Village). The central division, the Yanktons, are made up of two tribes, Yankton (End Village) and Yanktonai (Little End Village). The westernmost division, the Tetons, consists of seven tribes: Sicangu (also Brule, Burnt Thighs), Hunk-

Wounded Knee. The tragic bloodbath on 29 December 1890—which left more than 150 Indian men, women, and children dead at the scene—ended a brief period marked by mass starvation, the religious fervor of the Ghost Dance Movement, the murder of the militant chief Sitting Bull, and the desperate flight of a band of Sioux from their reservation. LIBRARY OF CONGRESS

papa (End of the Camp Circle), Miniconjou (Planters by the Water), Oglala (They Scatter Their Own), Oohenonpa (Two Kettles), Itazipco (also Sans Arcs, Without Bows), and Sihasapa (Blackfeet). The Assiniboine and Sioux were formerly one people but at the time of European contact the Assiniboines allied themselves with the Crees and moved north and west, settling by the early nineteenth century in Saskatchewan and northeastern Montana. The westernmost Assiniboines moved to the Rocky Mountains in Alberta and became a separate tribe, the Stoneys.

The Sioux maintained their own historical records through oral traditions. The Yanktons and Tetons also preserved winter counts, pictographic records that associated each year (winter) with an event significant to the group. The Dakotas are first mentioned in European writings in 1640, and the first recorded contact with them was by French explorers in about 1660. The Dakotas and Lakotas encountered Lewis and Clark in 1804.

All the Sioux were primarily nomadic hunters and gatherers whose lives focused on the buffalo, a pattern that intensified with the introduction of European horses and guns in the eighteenth century. Each of the Dakota and Lakota tribes was organized into bands that were composed of families related by blood, marriage, and adoption. Each band established its own territory for hunting and gathering. These bands were largely independent but allied into larger groups for communal hunts and warfare. All the Sioux shared a common culture, but some of the Santees and Yanktons borrowed elements of Woodlands and Missouri River cultures, most significantly the Chippewa *midewiwin*, or medicine dance, and earth lodges from the riverine tribes. These Santee and Yankton bands constructed permanent villages, gathered wild rice, fished, and engaged in limited agriculture. Religious rituals practiced by all the Sioux include the sun dance, vision quest, and sweat lodge. While they practiced a rigidly defined sexual division of labor, respect was accorded to both gender groups for successful fulfillment of their respective roles. Contemporary Lakotas and Dakotas continue to stress the separate but complementary roles of men and women in their society.

Warfare was both a political and ritual act, and military service continues to be considered prestigious among these peoples. After sporadic contacts with the French and British, the Lakotas and Dakotas dealt primarily with the United States, first through the fur trade and then in the struggle to maintain their lands and traditions. As the United States expanded westward, a series of treaties resulted in significant land loss for the Sioux. The treaties of Mendota and Traverse des Sioux in 1851 placed the Santees in difficult circumstances, precipitating the Minnesota Conflict of 1862. The majority of the Santees fled into Canada or were exiled to a reservation in Nebraska. As Americans pressed farther west, the Yanktons and Lakotas entered into the Fort Laramie Treaty of 1851. Further American expansion through Lakota territory led to a series of conflicts sometimes called Red Cloud's War, which ended with the Fort Laramie Treaty of 1868. The insistence by the United States that the Lakotas leave their hunting territories to settle on their reservation precipitated the Battle of the Little Bighorn on 25 June 1876. Lakota lands diminished when the Black Hills were alienated through the Agreement of 1876, and much more land was forfeited through the Agreement of 1889, which broke up the Great Sioux Reservation into small units. Cultural disruption, mistreatment, and famine in 1889 all encouraged the spread of the Ghost Dance Movement among these peoples and culminated in the tragic WOUNDED KNEE MASSACRE in 1890.

Although some history books mark the "end" of the Lakota and Dakota tribes with Wounded Knee, this is clearly not the case. The persistence of the Lakotas as well as the dire conditions of reservation life came into public prominence through the Wounded Knee Occupation of 1973. The Lakotas continue to pursue various land claims, most significantly the claim for the Black Hills. In 1980 the Supreme Court recognized the rank illegality of the alienation of the Black Hills and awarded the Lakotas $106 million. The Lakotas, however, have refused to accept the money, seeking instead the return of the land. Lakotas and Dakotas today live on reservations in North and South Dakota, Nebraska, Minnesota, Montana, and the Canadian provinces of Manitoba and Saskatchewan as well as in urban areas throughout the United States and Canada. They continue to shape their own lives and struggle to maintain their distinct legal, linguistic, and cultural identity as they negotiate their relationships with the rest of the world.

BIBLIOGRAPHY

Sturtevant, William C., gen. ed. *Handbook of North American Indians.* Vol. 13 (2 parts): *Plains,* edited by Raymond J. DeMallie. Washington, D.C.: Smithsonian Institution, 2001. The following articles are relevant to the Sioux: Part 1: Raymond J. DeMallie and David Reed Miller, "Assiniboine"; Ian A. L. Getty and Erik D. Gooding, "Stoney." Part 2: Raymond J. DeMallie, "Sioux until 1850," "Teton," "Yankton and Yanktonai"; Patricia Albers, "Santee"; Dennis N. Christafferson, "Sioux, 1930–2000." This volume is the most authoritative and comprehensive written work on the Sioux.

Bucko, Raymond A. "Lakota Dakota Bibliography." http://puffin .creighton.edu/lakota/biblio.html. Contains an extensive bibliography of Lakota and Dakota materials.

Raymond A. Bucko

See also **Lakota Language; Laramie, Fort, Treaty of (1851); Laramie, Fort, Treaty of (1868); Wounded Knee (1973); *and vol. 9:* Account of the Battle at Little Bighorn; Fort Laramie Treaty of 1851; A Letter from Wovoka; Speech of Little Crow on the Eve of the Great Sioux Uprising.**

SIOUX UPRISING IN MINNESOTA.

The easternmost group of the Sioux peoples, known as the Dakota, controlled the northern Mississippi River valley throughout the first half of the nineteenth century, living in semi-sedentary communities along the river's tributaries in Minnesota and Iowa. In the Treaty of Traverse des Sioux of 1851, the Dakota ceded millions of acres to the U.S. government in exchange for federally protected reservation lands in Minnesota. The treaty also set forth extensive terms of payment by which the U.S. government would annually compensate Dakota groups for their ceded lands.

As tens of thousands of American settlers began moving into Minnesota, the Dakota increasingly found their game depleted and came to rely upon guaranteed government provisions for subsistence. When corrupt government officials began withholding provisions in 1862, Dakota children starved while government storehouses remained filled. Dakota resentment grew. Under the leadership of Little Crow, Dakota communities prepared for conflict, particularly following a series of insults by res-

Refugees of the Sioux Uprising. Fearful white settlers in Minnesota flee their homes after a rapid series of violent attacks by mistreated Dakota warriors. LIBRARY OF CONGRESS

ervation agents, including Andrew Myrick's infamous remark: "So far as I am concerned, if they are hungry, let them eat grass" (Meyer, p. 114).

After several Dakota warriors attacked a white ranch near Acton, Minnesota, on 17 August 1862 while in search of food, Dakota–white conflicts erupted throughout southwestern Minnesota. Reservation officials were killed and their hoarded provisions distributed to hungry Dakota families. At Lower Agency at Redwood along the Minnesota River, Dakota warriors killed Myrick and filled his mouth with grass in retribution. Quickly, white settlements along the Minnesota River retreated east as fear of the "uprising" shook the entire state.

Little Crow and Dakota leaders never imagined retaking all of Minnesota; they had lived alongside whites for years. They primarily wanted to feed their families, drive out corrupt officials and white farmers, and have the government fulfill its treaty obligations. White settlers and territorial leaders, however, thought otherwise and called in the army under Colonel Henry Sibley. Before Sibley arrived, the Dakota had won some small battles but failed to take the heavily defended town of New Ulm in a series of attacks from 19 to 26 August. After Sibley and his fourteen hundred well-equipped soldiers arrived, Little Crow and his warriors lost a succession of battles in September and then retreated.

After Sibley drove further into Dakota lands, hundreds of Dakota families surrendered and their warriors were imprisoned. With more than 800 settlers dead, white leaders called for revenge, and 303 Dakota warriors were sentenced to death at Mankato. After years of starvation, the loss of resources, and the loss of hundreds of warriors in conflict, the call for so many more Dakota lives was tantamount to ethnic cleansing. Despite the carefully negotiated treaties of the federal government, many recently arrived immigrants could no longer countenance living near autonomous Dakota groups. Heeding Indian policy reformers and advocates, President Abraham Lincoln commuted the sentences of all but thirty-eight of the Dakota. On 26 December 1862, the thirty-eight were hung at Mankato in the largest mass execution in U.S. history. Little Crow retreated onto the Plains but was murdered in 1863 by white bounty hunters after rewards of up to two hundred dollars were offered for Dakota scalps. Little Crow's scalp was exhibited in the Minnesota State Historical Society beginning in 1868. Many Dakota moved out of the state to join Lakota kinsmen on the Plains.

BIBLIOGRAPHY

Meyer, Roy W. *History of the Santee Sioux: United States Indian Policy on Trial.* Rev. ed. Lincoln: University of Nebraska Press, 1993.

Ned Blackhawk

See also **Indian Agents; Indian Land Cessions; Indian Policy, U.S.: 1830–1900; Indian Removal; Indian Reservations; Indian Treaties; Wars with Indian Nations: Later Nineteenth Century (1840–1900);** *and vol. 9:* **Speech of Little Crow.**

SIOUX WARS. Throughout the nineteenth century the linguistically and culturally related Dakota, Lakota, and Nakota, or Sioux, Indians spread throughout the northern Plains. Consolidating control of prime buffalo-grazing grasslands, the Lakota-speaking Teton Sioux controlled the region for more than a century. When the U.S. government claimed possession of Lakota territory in the mid-1800s, conflicts ensued. Initially, the Lakota and allied Cheyenne, Arapaho, and Shoshone groups entered into peace treaties with the government. At Fort Laramie in the Wyoming Territory, the government in 1851 negotiated the first Fort Laramie Treaty, which established mechanisms for annual payments to Indian groups for the safe passage of white settlers through Indian lands. Although white settlers heading to the Oregon Territory and later the Washington Territory passed through Lakota lands, in the early 1850s neither the U.S. government nor its citizens wanted to colonize those lands. Fearing that agreeing to any government treaties would result in permanent land losses, the Lakota refused to sign.

By the mid-1850s, Lakota groups increasingly came into conflict with growing numbers of white emigrants who disrupted buffalo migrations and damaged fragile river ecologies. In 1854, Lakota warriors fought and killed Lieutenant John L. Grattan and eighteen of his men at Fort Laramie. In revenge, General William S. Harney attacked a Brulé Lakota encampment near Ash Hollow,

Nebraska, the following year, killing more than one hundred Lakota, including women and children.

At the beginning of the Civil War, regular U.S. Army troops were removed from western forts and replaced by territorial and state militia, many of whom held deep suspicions and hatred of Indians. In Minnesota, for example, after the defeat of the Dakota in September 1862 during the Sioux Uprising, Minnesota military leaders rounded up surrendered Dakota warriors and sentenced nearly 303 to death—a sizable percentage of the remaining Dakota male population. Eventually, only 38 were executed, but deep animosities endured as many remaining Dakota families migrated onto the Plains to join their Lakota kinsmen.

During the Civil War, Lakota dominance of the northern Plains continued. As more and more white emigrants poured into Montana following the discovery of gold, Lakota groups attacked them as well as forts along the Bozeman Trail, routinely defeating army units. Under the political and military leadership of Red Cloud, Lakota groups in 1865 beat federal troops at Platte Bridge, cutting off an important portion of the Bozeman.

With several thousand warriors under their command, Lakota leaders throughout the 1860s remained confident of their ability to control their homelands. In 1866, when army troops attempted to erect forts along the Bozeman, the Lakota again resisted, initiating a series of conflicts known as Red Cloud's War. The Lakota effectively halted efforts to fortify the Bozeman, destroying army outposts, including Captain William Fetterman's unit of nearly one hundred soldiers at Fort Phil Kearny in the Wyoming Territory in December 1866. Brilliantly orchestrated by the Lakota warrior Crazy Horse, Fetterman's unit was lured out of the fort and then destroyed along a narrow passage. After several army reprisals, Red Cloud and other Lakota leaders negotiated peace with the federal government, and in 1868, in the second Fort Laramie Treaty, the U.S. government agreed to abandon its forts along the Bozeman Trail and to establish protected Indian reservations within which no whites would be allowed to settle. The Lakota had fought the government to a standstill and extracted the provisions they demanded. Red Cloud vowed to honor the treaty and moved to the new Great Sioux Reservation that included all the lands west of the Missouri River in the Dakota Territory, including the sacred Black Hills.

In the 1870s, Crazy Horse and other Lakota leaders, including Sitting Bull, grew increasingly suspicious of the government's intentions, especially after federal troops in 1874 under Colonel George Armstrong Custer accompanied white prospectors into the Black Hills, in direct violation of the second Fort Laramie Treaty. After gold was discovered, whites rushed into the Lakota territories and a series of new conflicts erupted. In early 1876, government troops inconclusively fought Lakota and allied Cheyenne groups, and on 25 June 1876, a combined Lakota-Cheyenne force entirely destroyed Custer's twelve

Sit-Down Strike. The tactic was widely used by rubber, steel, and autoworkers, especially in 1936 and 1937. © CORBIS

companies of the Seventh Cavalry along the Little Big-horn River in Montana. As news spread of Custer's defeat, the government resolved to pursue and punish remaining Lakota groups, and in January 1877, Crazy Horse and his Oglala Lakota surrendered to General Nelson Miles in Canada, where they had sought refuge.

The last military conflict of the Sioux Wars came more than a decade later. In 1890, after years of reservation confinement, members of Big Foot's Hunkpapa band attempted to flee the reservation after learning of Sitting Bull's assassination. Pursued to the creek of Wounded Knee, Big Foot and his band were massacred in December 1890. The Wounded Knee massacre marked the end of Lakota efforts to live entirely independent of the federal government. The Lakota wars, however, continue politically and culturally as Lakota communities demand redress for the unconstitutional violations of the Fort Laramie Treaty of 1868.

BIBLIOGRAPHY

Brown, Dee. *Bury My Heart at Wounded Knee: An Indian History of the American West.* New York: Holt, Rinehart, 1971.

Hedren, Paul L., ed. *The Great Sioux War, 1867–77.* Helena: Montana Historical Society Press, 1991.

Utley, Robert M. *Indian Frontier of the American West, 1846–1890.* Albuquerque: University of New Mexico Press, 1984.

Ned Blackhawk

See also **Indian Land Cessions; Indian Policy, U.S.: 1830–1900; Indian Removal; Indian Reservations; Indian Treaties; Laramie, Fort, Treaty of (1868); Little Big-horn, Battle of; Wars with Indian Nations: Later Nineteenth Century (1840–1900); Wounded Knee Massacre.**

SIT-DOWN STRIKES of 1936 and 1937 stood at the heart of the social movement that enabled the Committee for Industrial Organization (CIO) to unionize hundreds of thousands of workers in that era's industries. CIO rubber workers briefly deployed the sit-down as part of a recognition strike in February and March 1936, but this union stratagem did not rivet the nation's attention until late in the fall of that year. CIO organizers met fierce resistance from the nation's leading corporations, many supporters of the anti–New Deal Liberty League, which expected the Supreme Court to declare the Wagner Act unconstitutional. This growing polarization made Franklin Roosevelt's landslide reelection as president seem a referendum on the industrial New Deal, especially in working-class communities. "You voted New Deal at the polls and defeated the auto barons," organizers told Michigan workers late in 1936. "Now get a New Deal in the shop."

In November and December 1936, sit-down strikes took place at Midland Steel and Kelsey-Hayes in Detroit,

Michigan, and at Bendex in South Bend, Indiana. During the week after Christmas, sit-down strikes occurred at General Motors (GM), the most important at the Fisher Body and Chevrolet Motor plants in Flint, Michigan, the center of GM production. The strikes were not "spontaneous," neither were they planned by top union leaders. Socialists, communists, and other shop radicals led the way, then leaders of the United Automobile Workers (UAW) and the CIO took command. The factory occupations stopped production even though only a minority of the workforce participated. Supported by thousands of unionists on the outside, the Flint sit-downers organized food deliveries, policed the factories to avoid damage, and conducted classes and plays to sustain morale during the six-week stay-in. They won favorable press because of the legitimacy of their cause. The strikes were designed to force management to obey the labor law and to recognize the stake workers held in a secure and humane job. Frank Murphy, the New Deal governor of Michigan, kept the National Guard at bay. Backed by Roosevelt, Murphy sought to avoid a bloody confrontation and refused to enforce an antistrike injunction secured by GM. Although the sit-downers and their allies fought several celebrated battles with the Flint police, the unionists outnumbered their foes, and they were never dislodged from the factories.

GM reached a settlement with the UAW on 11 February 1937. The corporation recognized the union as the sole voice of its employees and agreed to negotiate with UAW leaders on a multiplant basis. Thousands of heretofore hesitant auto workers poured into the UAW. Across industrial America the settlement transformed the expectations of workers and managers alike. There were 47 sit-down strikes in March, 170 in April, and 52 in May. In Detroit, workers occupied every Chrysler factory, twenty-five auto parts plants, four downtown hotels, nine lumberyards, ten meat-packing plants, twelve laundries, and two department stores. To avoid such an upheaval, U.S. Steel and scores of other big firms agreed to recognize CIO unions during the next few months.

Although the sit-down strikes violated corporate property rights, many workers justified them as an ethical counter to management's failure to recognize the Wagner Act and to bargain with the unions. Given the industrial crisis of early 1937, such sentiments may well have contributed to the Supreme Court's 12 April 1937 decision in *National Labor Relations Board v. Jones and Laughlin Steel Corporation* to hold the Wagner Act constitutional. But in the more conservative climate that prevailed two years later, the Court declared sit-downs illegal in *National Labor Relations Board v. Fansteel Metallurgical Corporation* (1939).

BIBLIOGRAPHY

Fine, Sidney. *Sit-Down: The General Motors Strike of 1936–1937.* Ann Arbor: University of Michigan Press, 1969.

Pope, James Gray. "The Thirteenth Amendment versus the Commerce Clause: Labor and the Shaping of American Constitutional Law, 1921–1957." *Columbia Law Review* 102 (January 2002): 3–122.

Zieger, Robert H. *The CIO: 1935–1955.* Chapel Hill: University of North Carolina Press, 1995.

Nelson Lichtenstein

See also **American Federation of Labor–Congress of Industrial Organizations; Labor;** *National Labor Relations Board v. Jones and Laughlin Steel Corporation;* **Strikes; United Automobile Workers of America.**

60 MINUTES.   The first of the modern "newsmagazines," *60 Minutes* debuted on 24 September 1968 over the CBS television network. By 1975, it settled into the Sunday evening time slot, where it remained. *60 Minutes* presented two or three separately produced short documentaries each week, all under the editorial supervision of executive producer Don Hewitt, who had been with the show from its outset. The correspondents who have appeared on the show are Mike Wallace (1968–), Harry Reasoner (1968–1970, 1978–1991), Morley Safer (1970–), Dan Rather (1975–1981), Ed Bradley (1981–), Diane Sawyer (1984–1989), Meredith Vieira (1989–1991), Steve Kroft (1989–), and Leslie Stahl (1991–). Beginning in

Tick, Tick, Tick, Tick . . . It was that sound—a ticking watch—that signaled the arrival each Sunday night of one of the longest-running television shows of all time, the newsmagazine show *60 Minutes.* Beginning in 1978, Andy Rooney, shown here in his first season, would offer a wry, often humorous look at life's little absurdities to close out the show. © AP/WIDE WORLD PHOTOS

1978, Andy Rooney began offering short observational segments.

Providing a prime-time venue for serious investigative reporting, for a while *60 Minutes* was known for the confrontational manner in which correspondents like Mike Wallace approached their interview subjects-victims. What is most surprising about the show, however, is its extraordinary commercial success. It spent nineteen straight seasons in the Nielsen top ten (from 1977 to 1996), five as the most watched program on network television. Other networks, hoping for similar successes, introduced a variety of newsmagazines based on the *60 Minutes* model. In 1999, CBS introduced *60 Minutes II.*

BIBLIOGRAPHY

Madsen, Axel. 60 Minutes: *The Power and Politics of America's Most Popular TV News Show.* New York: Dodd, Mead, 1984.

Robert Thompson

See also **Television: Programming and Influence.**

SKATEBOARDING. Skateboarding first achieved widespread popularity in the United States during the

Skid Row. This 1937 photograph by Dorothea Lange shows transients loitering along Howard Street in San Francisco during the Great Depression. LIBRARY OF CONGRESS

1960s. Manufactured to resemble miniature surfboards, early skateboards were plastic with slippery, clay wheels. The introduction of wooden decks, precision bearings, and urethane wheels over the next decade gave skateboarders greater control and speed, allowing them to perform increasingly complex maneuvers both on vertical ramps and in the street. Although skateboarding's popularity waned in the late 1970s, the early 1980s saw the emergence of an entire skateboarding subculture with its own magazines, music, aesthetics, and jargon. Today, skateboarding is a multi-million-dollar industry attracting top athletes and media attention around the globe.

BIBLIOGRAPHY

Brooke, Michael. *The Concrete Wave: The History of Skateboarding.* Toronto: Warwick, 1999.

John M. Kinder

See also **Sports.**

Skateboarding. Dressed for impact, a youngster takes his board through the motions. © CORBIS

SKID ROW refers to the area of a city with a concentration of cheap hotels, pawnshops, secondhand stores, and missions that cater to the transient. Skid rows first emerged in America after the Civil War, when an influx of unskilled European immigrants and a series of financial depressions created a large pool of migratory workers. The term itself originated in Seattle, where Henry Yesler's logging company used oxen to haul timber across pole "skids" to its waterfront mill. The saloons, brothels, and cheap lodging houses used by itinerant foresters, miners, and railroaders clustered along this original "Skid Road."

In the twentieth century, skid rows gradually lost their role as clearinghouses for unskilled laborers and came to be populated by alcoholics, drug addicts, and the mentally disabled.

BIBLIOGRAPHY

Allsop, Kenneth. *Hard Travellin': The Hobo and His History*. New York: New American Library, 1967.

Bahr, Howard M. *Skid Row: An Introduction to Disaffiliation*. New York: Oxford University Press, 1973.

Wendy Wall

SKIING. Petroglyphs and archaeological evidence suggest that skiing emerged at least 5,000 years ago in Finland, Norway, Sweden, and the northern reaches of Russia and China. The first skis were probably ten feet long and had only loose willow or leather toe straps, which made it nearly impossible for the skier to turn or jump while in motion. Early skiers—hunters, midwives, priests, and others who had to travel across deep winter snow—dragged a single long pole to slow themselves down.

The Norwegians developed modern skiing in the late eighteenth and early nineteenth centuries. By adding heel straps to skis, they were able to gain more control on descents and make quicker, tighter turns. These first rough bindings allowed skiers to use shorter skis and two poles instead of one. Around 1820, Norwegians began racing each other and staged the first ski-jumping competitions.

When Norwegians emigrated to the United States in the mid-1800s, they brought skiing with them. Many flocked to lumber and mining camps, where their ability to move quickly through the mountains in mid-winter proved to be an invaluable asset. In 1856, a Norwegian farmer named John "Snowshoe" Thompson responded to a plea from the U.S. postal service for someone to carry mail across California's Sierra Nevada range in mid-winter, a route that lay under as much as twenty feet of snow. Thompson made the ninety-mile trip across 10,000-foot passes in three days. He continued to deliver mail this way until the transcontinental railroad was completed in 1869.

Thompson's legendary treks inspired many miners to take up ski racing as a diversion during long snowbound winters. They experimented with "dope"—early ski wax concocted from cedar oil, tar, beeswax, sperm, and other ingredients—to coax more speed out of their skis. In 1867, the town of La Porte, California, formed the nation's first ski club. Norwegian immigrants also introduced ski jumping to the United States in the 1880s, and in 1888, Ishpeming, Michigan, hosted the first formal ski-jumping tournament held in America. In 1904, jumpers and cross-country skiers founded the National Ski Association, which now encompasses all aspects of the sport.

Skiing. In Ron Hoffman's 1974 photograph, chairlifts ascend 11,800 feet on Aspen Highlands Mountain in Colorado. NATIONAL ARCHIVES AND RECORDS ADMINISTRATION

The "Nordic" events of ski jumping and cross-country skiing dominated U.S. slopes until the 1920s. In that decade, "Alpine" or downhill skiing began to make inroads, fanned in part by skiing enthusiasm among Ivy League college students. Wealthy Americans often sent their sons to Europe between high school and college, and some returned with an interest in the downhill. Dartmouth College, where the first outings club was founded in 1909, hired a series of Bavarian ski coaches who encouraged this trend. In 1927, Dartmouth racers staged the first modern American downhill race on a carriage road on Mt. Moosilauke, New Hampshire.

Downhill skiing and technological change fed each other. The invention of the steel edge in 1928 made it easier to ski on hard snow, leading to better control and faster speeds. The development of the ski lift helped popularize "downhill-only" skiing, which broadened the sport's appeal. (The rope tow, introduced to the United States in Woodstock, Vermont, in 1934, was simple, quick, and cheap.) Since Alpine skiers no longer had to walk uphill, they could use stiffer boots and bindings that attached firmly to the heel. These, in turn, allowed for unprecedented control and made possible the parallel turn.

By the late 1920s, skiing's commercial possibilities were becoming apparent. The first ski shop opened in Boston in 1926, and an inn in Franconia, New Hampshire, organized the first ski school three years later. Railroads began to sponsor ski trains and used their vast publicity networks to promote the sport. In the 1930s, skiing spread swiftly across New England and upstate New York, and in 1932 Lake Placid, New York, hosted the Third Winter Olympics. In 1936, a new resort in Sun Valley, Idaho, introduced chair lifts, swimming pools, private cottages, and other glamorous touches. The brainchild of W. Averell Harriman, president of the Union Pacific Railroad, Sun Valley foreshadowed the development of ski resorts across the country.

World War II further accelerated the popularization of Alpine skiing in the United States. The Tenth Mountain Division drafted many of the nation's best skiers and trained others for ski mountaineering in Europe. After the war, veterans of the unit joined the National Ski Patrol and established the nation's first major Alpine ski areas. Meanwhile, the division's surplus equipment was sold to the general public, giving newcomers an affordable way to take up the sport.

The surge in skiers on postwar slopes led inevitably to changes in technique. As large numbers of skiers began turning in the same spots, fields of "moguls" or snow bumps appeared, requiring tighter turns. The new skiers also demanded more amenities, and resort developers responded by installing high-capacity, high-speed lifts and mechanically grooming slopes. Some tried to lure intermediate skiers by cutting wide, gentle swaths through the trees from the top of the mountain to the bottom.

In the 1970s, such practices increasingly brought resort developers into head-on conflict with environmentalists. The environmental movement and the decade's fitness boom also led to the rediscovery of cross-country skiing. New equipment, which combined attributes of Alpine and Nordic gear, opened the new field of "telemark" or cross-country downhill skiing. Some skiers began hiring helicopters to drop them on otherwise inaccessible mountaintops.

In the postwar years, Americans began to challenge Europeans in international competitions. In 1948, Gretchen Fraser became the first American to win an Olympic gold medal in skiing, and in 1984, the United States collected an unprecedented three gold medals. When Squaw Valley, California, hosted the Winter Olympics in 1960, ski racing was televised live for the first time in the United States and it soon emerged as a popular spectator sport. Its popularity was propelled by gutsy and likeable stars such as Picabo Street, the freckle-faced racer who recovered from a crash and concussion in 1998 to win a gold medal in the downhill Super G.

Although Alpine and Nordic skiing remained popular in the 1980s and 1990s, they increasingly competed for space on the slopes with new variations like snowboarding, mogul skiing, tree skiing, aerial freestyle, slopestyle (riding over jumps, rails, and picnic tables), and halfpipe (in which skiers or snowboarders perform aerial acrobatics in a carved-out tube of snow and ice). U.S. skiers generally did well in these "extreme" events as they began to be added to the Olympics in the 1990s. In 1998, Jonny Moseley took gold in the freestyle mogul event, while Eric Bergoust flipped and twisted his way to a gold medal in the aerial freestyle. In 2002, the U.S. team captured silver in the men's and women's moguls and in the men's aerial freestyle.

BIBLIOGRAPHY

Berry, I. William. *The Great North American Ski Book*. New York: Scribner's, 1982.

Gullion, Laurie. *The Cross-Country Primer*. New York: Lyons and Burford, 1990.

Kamm, Herbert, ed. *The Junior Illustrated Encyclopedia of Sports*. Indianapolis, Ind.: Bobbs-Merrill, 1970.

Wendy Wall

SKYSCRAPERS entered American parlance around 1890, describing ten- to fifteen-story commercial buildings mostly in Chicago and New York. Dependent on the passenger elevator, telephone, and incandescent bulb for internal circulation, communication, and illumination, the structural potential of its steel frame ensured that the economic benefit of multiplying lot size twenty, fifty, or one hundred times would render municipal height restrictions obsolete. Well before New York's 1913 Woolworth Building opened at 792 feet (54 stories), the world's tallest edifice excepting the Eiffel Tower in Paris, it was a social convention to wonder if the only limit to upward growth were the heavens themselves.

Artistic hesitation characterized skyscraper design from the beginning, less so in Chicago than in New York. Although skyscrapers' determining features were steel and height, architects were inclined to hide steel inside highly decorated, thick masonry walls. In addition, they negated height by wrapping every few stories with a protruding cornice interrupting vertical flow or by periodically shifting styles, so, as a building ascended, it resembled a stack of small structures. Those willing to embrace height tended to base form on historical analogies, usually French gothic cathedrals or Italian medieval towers.

In Chicago, Louis Sullivan referred to the classical column, but in his pioneering search for a self-referential skyscraper aesthetic, he transformed base, shaft, and capital into commercial ground floor, office tier, and attic for ancillary services, each function indicated externally. By recessing windows and walls a few inches behind columns and mullions, he privileged vertical elements of the frame to create, he wrote in 1896, "a proud and soaring thing" that was "every inch of it tall." Although highly regarded by critics, Sullivan's "system of vertical construction" was not widely adopted by architects, not even his Chicago School (c. 1885–1915) colleagues, whose so-called "utilitarian" building facades, less ornamented and more fenestrated than Sullivan's, closely followed in composition the grid pattern of the frame, which in reality is nondirectional.

Chicago School buildings were America's principal contribution to the formative stages of what was soon labeled "modern architecture." The implication, which might be encapsulated in the phrase "form follows structure," was disregarded in the United States during the 1920s, but it was taken up in Europe, particularly in Ger-

Chrysler Building. The art deco skyscraper (*left*), designed by William Van Alen and briefly the tallest building in the world upon completion in 1930, is a distinctive highlight of the New York City skyline. LIBRARY OF CONGRESS

many, where in 1921 and 1922 Ludwig Mies van der Rohe proposed free-form skyscrapers entirely encased with glass panels clipped to the edges of floor slabs. Of the 265 entries from 23 countries to the 1922 *Chicago Tribune* headquarters competition, 37 were German, notable among them Walter Gropius and Adolf Meyer's grid of reinforced concrete completely filled with windows. These and other European designs conclusively demonstrated what Chicagoans had almost perceived. Since load-bearing walls were structurally unnecessary, a skyscraper's facade could be reduced to little more than frame and glazing. The lesson was ignored when the Tribune Company selected Raymond Hood and John Mead Howells's decidedly unglassy, neogothic cousin to the Woolworth Building.

Until large-scale private sector construction halted during the Great Depression, American skyscrapers were either historical pastiches or tips of the hat to European art deco. Most famous were New York's Chrysler, EMPIRE STATE, and Rockefeller Center buildings (of 1930 and 1931), featuring diagonal or zigzag "jazz age" ornament

and equal amounts of glass and masonry in alternating vertical or horizontal strips forming crisp, rectilinear facades that nonetheless hide the frame. Two exceptions were noteworthy: Hood's 1929–1931 McGraw-Hill Building, designed with André Fouilhoux, in New York; and William Lescaze's 1929–1932 Philadelphia Savings Fund Society Building, designed with George Howe. Both were in what was labeled "the international style," which made structurally determined form something of a fetish.

It was fitting that the European émigrés Fouilhoux (from Paris) and Lescaze (from Zurich) figured prominently in the reconfiguration of American skyscrapers, because a third European, Mies van der Rohe, who arrived in Chicago in 1938, almost single-handedly completed the process, beginning with his 1946–1949 Promontory Apartments. More than any other edifice, his 1954–1958 Seagram Building in New York made the flat-roofed, glass-walled, steel- or concrete-framed, minimally ornamented box a corporate signature as well as an indication that derivations of European modernism had captured the mainstream of American architecture.

A comparison of the two McGraw-Hill Buildings in New York suggests how much had changed since 1929. The first, by Hood with Fouilhoux, is bluish-green glazed terra-cotta and steps back five times before reaching its penthouse, which is sided with huge firm-name graphics. Its thirty-five richly textured, horizontally articulated stories complement the vertical thrust of the elevator shafts and stairwell. Although resolutely international in style, it resembles no other building. The four identical facades of the second McGraw-Hill Building, built in 1973 by Harrison, Abramovitz, and Harris, soar without interruption or variation through forty-five stories of closely spaced reddish granite columns. Devoid of graphics, it is a clone of the flanking Celanese and Exxon Buildings by the same architects. In less than half a century, collective anonymity replaced architectural individuality in every American city.

The low profile adopted by American corporations after World War II gave way in the 1980s to a more assertive public posture expressed architecturally in postmodernism (POMO): the return of polychrome, ornament, and historical reference enlivened by mixtures of nonorthogonal with rectilinear geometries. Rejecting the Mies-inspired modernist box and companion frame-based aesthetic, POMO recaptured a spirit of experimentation akin to that of the European 1920s but enhanced by an array of new materials and technologies, including computer-assisted design. The sky was again the limit in terms not of height but of artistic possibility.

Globalization of capital internationalized the profession. For example, four architects were invited in 2000 to submit proposals for a new *New York Times* headquarters: Norman Foster of London; Renzo Piano with offices in Paris and Genoa; Cesar Pelli, the Argentina-born dean of the Yale School of Art and Architecture; and Frank Gehry, a Toronto native residing in California. Gehry produced a twisting, undulating, concave and convex agglomeration of sinewy, computer-generated, non-Euclidean shapes that appears to be one tower or three, depending on the viewer's vantage point. Like the other submissions, it makes no reference except for signage to site or function, suggesting that any one of the four could be erected anywhere to serve any purpose. Sharing only the absence of similarity, they are as far removed from the modernist box as that was from the Woolworth Building.

During the course of a century, an American commercial building type, stylistically conditioned by historical precedent or by the steel frame, became an omnifunctional symbol of globalization conditioned only by architectural imagination. Technical limits to skyscraper height may be approaching, but form has no limits at all.

BIBLIOGRAPHY

Goldberger, Paul. *The Skyscraper.* New York: Knopf, 1981.

Scuri, Piera. *Late-Twentieth-Century Skyscrapers.* New York: Van Nostrand Reinhold, 1990.

Twombly, Robert. *Power and Style: A Critique of Twentieth-Century Architecture in the United States.* New York: Hill and Wang, 1995.

Van Leeuwen, Thomas A. P. *The Skyward Trend of Thought: The Metaphysics of the American Skyscraper.* Cambridge, Mass.: MIT Press, 1988.

Robert Twombly

See also **Architecture; World Trade Center.**

SLANG, the carbonation that often puts fizz into everyday language, usually does not last. "Twenty-three skiddoo" of the 1920s, "Daddy-O" of the 1950s, and "far out" of the 1960s are gone, but other slang terms such as "cool" continue to live. Some even lose the label "slang" in the new dictionaries, as did "peter out" (from miners' argot) and "jazz" (originally a slang expression for "sexual intercourse" in juke joints in the South). The shelf life of slang may depend on the environment that produces it. Connie Eble found that four words had endured in college slang at the University of North Carolina from 1972 to 1989: "bad" (good); "bummer" (an unpleasant experience); "slide" (an easy course); and "wheels" (car).

Slang should be distinguished from dialect, speech peculiar to a region. "I got screwed by that used car salesman," is slang. "I reckon so," is Southern dialect. The essence of slang, according to the iconoclast H. L. Mencken, in his classic *The American Language* (1918), is its "outsiderness." Slang works to prove that the speaker is "hip" or "with it" or "in the know." Can you dig it? Along with being "outside" comes the quality of being "disreputable." After all, an "outsider" has to be outside of something and that something is (in 1960s slang) the Establishment.

Outsiders whose slang has found acceptance by the Establishment include circus folk (guys, geeks), hoboes (handout), criminals (cop, the third degree), actors (make-up, star), aviators (to bail out, tail spin), and deep-sea sailors (aboveboard, shipshape, to keel over). Eric Partridge, whose *Slang Today and Yesterday* (1970) remains a valuable (if stylistically dated) study, refers to this process of acceptance as "ennobling."

Such language is usually referred to as argot while used within the group itself. Picked up by others, these terms become slang. As noted in *Webster's Third New International Dictionary of the English Language, Unabridged,* "There is no completely satisfactory objective test for slang, especially in application to a word out of context. No word is invariably slang, and many standard words can be given slang connotations or used so inappropriately as to become slang." The word "screw," for example, which in a hardware store has a specific standard English denotation, was often used as vulgar term for sexual intercourse, but during the late twentieth century it came into widespread use meaning "to take advantage of; cheat" according to *The American Heritage College Dictionary* (1997)—which, however, still labels it as slang.

While some slang is borrowed from a group, it is often created by shortening a word, as "mike" for "microphone." This kind of slang becomes more surprising when the stressed instead of the unstressed syllable is dropped: "ig" for ignore, "za" for pizza. This form seems startlingly modern until we recall wig (now standard English), a shortening of "periwig."

Sources of slang at the turn of the twenty-first century have included advertising, cyberspace, and media. "Where's the beef?" evolved from a hamburger slogan to a political slogan. Online conversations have elicited their own shorthand: TTYTT (to tell you the truth), IRL (in real life) and BTW (by the way). This extreme form of shortening is seen in college acronyms: TAN for an aggressive male (tough as nails); MLA for passionate kissing (major lip action). Movies often make a slang expression popular (as with "bodacious ta-tas" for large female breasts, from *An Officer and a Gentleman*), but like bell-bottom trousers, these fads quickly passed.

Many scholars see slang, because it is powerfully metaphoric, as "the poetry of everyday language" or "the plain man's poetry." Others, especially those of Victorian vintage, were much more negative. George H. McKnight (1923) finds it "akin to profanity." There is a certain in-your-face quality about slang, since it often, as Mencken notes, "embodies a kind of social criticism." As the late twentieth century American public grew more comfortable with satire and sexual innuendo, slang became more acceptable, though *The Random House Dictionary of the English Language* (1987) comments, "Because slang expressions are characterized by a sort of general irreverence, raciness, or figurative zest, their use is often avoided in the presence of social or hierarchical superiors."

NTC's Dictionary of American Slang and Colloquial Expressions (2000) is an accessible and up-to-date resource for tracking down the meaning of contemporary slang terms, but many can be found in standard dictionaries. Currentness is the key. For example, the 1986 edition of *Webster's Third International Dictionary* provides only the standard English meaning for "geek": a circus performer who performs bizarre acts such as biting off the heads of chickens. *The American Heritage Dictionary of the English Language* (2000) includes the new slang association with technology (as in computer geek).

In addition to general dictionaries of slang, there are specialized ones for cowboy slang, sexual slang, British and American slang, even Vietnam War slang. *The Dictionary of Sexual Slang* claims that "no other language can rival the variety, color, or sheer number of sexual terms to be found in English."

BIBLIOGRAPHY

Clark, Gregory R. *Words of the Vietnam War: The Slang, Jargon, Abbreviations, Acronyms, Nomenclature, Nicknames, Pseudonyms, Slogans, Specs, Euphemisms, Double-Talk, Chants, and Names and Places of the Era of United States Involvement in Vietnam.* Jefferson, N.C.: McFarland, 1990.

Eble, Connie. *College Slang 101.* Georgetown, Conn.: Spectacle Lane Press, 1989.

Hayakawa, S. I. *Language in Thought and Action.* 4th ed. New York: Harcourt Brace Jovanovich, 1978.

Lewin, Albert, and Esther Lewin, eds. *The Thesaurus of Slang: Revised and Expanded Edition.* New York: Facts on File, 1994.

Mencken, H. L. *The American Language: An Inquiry into the Development of English in the United States.* One-volume abridged edition. Edited by Raven I. McDavid. New York: Knopf, 1963. Includes a chapter on "American Slang."

Partridge, Eric. *Slang Today and Yesterday, with a Short Historical Sketch and Vocabularies of English, American, and Australian Slang.* New York: Barnes and Noble, 1970. Dated, but thorough.

Richter, Alan. *The Dictionary of Sexual Slang: Words, Phrases, and Idioms from AC/DC to Zig-zag.* New York: Wiley, 1992.

Spears, Richard A., ed. *NTC's Dictionary of American Slang and Colloquial Expressions.* 3d ed. Chicago: NTC Publishing Group, 2000. Accessible and up-to-date.

William E. King

SLAUGHTERHOUSE CASES, 16 WALL. (83 U.S.) 36 (1873).

The *Slaughterhouse Cases* (1873) provided the U.S. Supreme Court its first opportunity to interpret the Fourteenth Amendment, which had been adopted in 1868. The 5 to 4 majority held that New Orleans butchers did not have the right to pursue their occupation without utilizing a state-licensed central slaughterhouse, rejecting arguments based upon the common law of monopolies, the Thirteenth Amendment, and the Fourteenth Amendment. Justice Samuel F. Miller, writing for the majority, stated that the "one pervading purpose" of the Reconstruction amendments was to protect "the slave race" and expressed

doubts that any circumstances could arise in which the amendments applied to any other race. In three separate opinions, four dissenters supported butchers' claims and three of the dissenters suggested that the Fourteenth Amendment enforced the Bill of Rights against the states.

The split among the justices was over the extent to which the Fourteenth Amendment changed state-federal relations. Previously, Justice Miller had supported a conservative alternative version of the Fourteenth Amendment, implying opposition to the amendment actually adopted, while dissenters Chief Justice Salmon P. Chase and Justice Stephen J. Field had favored the amendment's adoption. Because this case attempted to define the boundary between state and federal power, its meaning and the motivation of the justices is the subject of continuing scholarly debate.

Although largely discredited, the case has never been overruled. In *Saenz v. Roe* (1999), the Supreme Court used the amendment's "privileges or immunities" clause to uphold a right to travel claim, opening the possibility of future reconsideration of the *Slaughterhouse Cases*.

BIBLIOGRAPHY

Aynes, Richard L. "Constricting the Law of Freedom: Justice Miller, the Fourteenth Amendment, and the Slaughter-House Cases." *Chicago-Kent Law Review* 70 (1994): 627–688.

Brandwein, Pamela. *Reconstructing Reconstruction: The Supreme Court and the Production of Historical Truth.* Durham, N.C.: Duke University Press, 1999. See especially pp. 61–95.

Fairman, Charles. *Reconstruction and Reunion, 1864–88.* Part I. New York: Macmillan Company, 1971. See especially pp. 1324–1363.

Richard L. Aynes

See also **Reconstruction; *Saenz v. Roe.***

SLAVE INSURRECTIONS.

For enslaved people in America, protest against the injustice of chattel SLAVERY took many forms. Most subtle were the individual acts of resistance against a cruel master or overseer, including theft, sabotage, feigned sickness, work slowdowns, and escape. The privacy of the slave quarters nurtured a culture of endurance, even defiance, in slave song, folktale, and religion. The most dramatic acts of resistance, however, were the organized conspiracies and rebellions against the system of slavery. They involved careful planning, collective action, and bravery. Indeed, few struggles for individual freedom and human dignity in America have ever entailed more personal risk.

Until well into the twentieth century, historians tended to play down unrest among slaves and to picture insurrections as aberrant. The mythology of the "happy slave" reflected a continuing paternalism in racial attitudes and helped to justify the Jim Crow practices that followed emancipation. Since World War II historians critical of racial injustice approached the issue with a new sympathy to the plight of enslaved people.

More than 250 cases have been identified that can be classified as insurrections. Such numbers are bound to be imprecise. Among the factors thwarting the quest for statistical certainty are the policy of silence, the bias of the records, the difficulty of distinguishing between personal crimes and organized revolts, and the quick spread of rumors. However, it is clear that insurrection was more frequent than earlier historians had acknowledged. According to a unique record of slave convictions in the state of Virginia for the period 1780–1864, of 1,418 convictions, 91 were for insurrection and 346 for murder. When this is added to the several recorded examples of plots and revolts in the state in the seventeenth and early eighteenth centuries, the record for that state alone is impressive.

The first slave revolt in territory now part of the United States took place in 1526 in a Spanish settlement near the mouth of the Pee Dee River in what is now South Carolina. Several slaves rebelled and fled to live with Indians of the area. The following year the colonists left the area without having recaptured the slaves. Insurrection in the British colonies began with the development of slavery and continued into the American Revolution. The most serious occurred in New York and in South Carolina. In 1712 a slave conspiracy in New York City led to the death of nine whites and the wounding of five or six others. Six of the rebels killed themselves to avoid capture. Of those taken into custody, twenty-one were executed in a variety of ways. Some were hanged, others burned, one broken on the wheel, and one hanged in chains as an example to other would-be insurrectionists. In 1739 Cato's Revolt (also known as the Stono Rebellion)

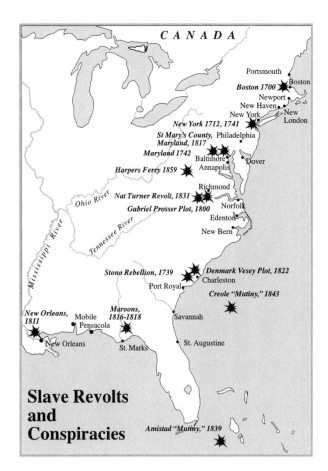

Slave Revolts and Conspiracies

Slave Revolt. This 1844 drawing depicts fighting on a slave ship; the best known of these rare incidents was the 1839 seizure of the *Amistad* by the African captives, which eventually resulted in their legal freedom and return to Africa.
© CORBIS

took place at Stono, South Carolina, near Charleston. Blacks seized guns and ammunition and fought the militia before being defeated. Approximately twenty-five whites and fifty blacks were killed. In 1741 a conspiracy among slaves and white servants in New York City led to the execution of thirty-one blacks and four whites. These events set a gruesome precedent—the retributions were usually far bloodier than the actual uprisings.

The successful slave revolt in Haiti during the French Revolution led to a series of plots in the South. Others followed up to the Civil War. Of these GABRIEL'S INSURRECTION, the plot of Denmark Vesey, and NAT TURNER'S REBELLION were the most significant.

In 1800 Gabriel Prosser, a blacksmith, and Jack Bowler planned a revolt to involve thousands of slaves in the Richmond area. Authorities became aware that something was afoot, and James Monroe, then governor of Virginia, ordered that precautions be taken. Nevertheless, the leaders planned to proceed on Saturday, 30 August. It rained heavily, and when more than a thousand armed slaves gathered, they found that a bridge over which they had to pass had been washed away. On the same day, an informer gave specifics of the plot to authorities. Many rebels were arrested, including Prosser and Bowler. Thirty-six slaves, including the leaders, were executed.

379

Negro Conspiracy. This illustration shows a black man being burned to death, one of thirty-five executed after a plot by slaves and white servants was uncovered in New York in 1741. GETTY IMAGES

In 1822 Denmark Vesey, a black carpenter who had purchased his freedom in 1800, planned an uprising in the area of Charleston. An active churchgoer in Charleston, Vesey was convinced that slavery violated the principles of the Bible. With able assistance from such leaders as Peter Poyas and Mingo Harth, many slaves over a large area were involved. The plan was to attack Charleston on the second Sunday in July, Sunday being a day on which it was customary for many blacks to be in the city and July being a time when many whites were vacationing outside the city. Weapons were made and information secured as to the location where arms and ammunition were stored. However, betrayal led Vesey to move the date ahead one month; before action could be taken, further information led to the arrest of the leaders. Vesey and thirty-four others were found guilty and hanged.

In August 1831 Nat Turner led the most famous revolt ever in Southampton County, Virginia. Turner and five others, with no clear plan of action, embarked on a killing spree. Turner's marauding army swelled to ap-

proximately seventy-five. They killed over seventy whites, many women and children, and caused panic over a wide area. Soldiers defeated the rebels, and Turner, his accomplices, and scores of innocent blacks were executed. The Virginia legislature tightened the slave codes in response. Thereafter, black preachers could not conduct religious services without the presence of a white.

These insurrections involved mainly slaves, with occasional participation by free blacks and rare involvement of whites. Usually the leaders, notably Prosser, Vesey, and Turner, were better educated than their peers. Many rebels were inspired by religious beliefs and borrowed biblical language and imagery to help unify their followers behind the cause. They were also stimulated by factors and events external to the local situation—such as the revolution in Haiti—and each uprising brought a new crop of repressive laws. From Turner's uprising in 1831 through the CIVIL WAR, slave owners curtailed slave rebellions by tightening the surveillance over black religion, travel, and expression.

BIBLIOGRAPHY

Aptheker, Herbert. *American Negro Slave Revolts.* New York: International Publishers, 1983.

Genovese, Eugene D. *From Rebellion to Revolution: Afro-American Slave Revolts in the Making of the Modern World.* Baton Rouge: Louisiana State University Press 1992.

Katz, William L. *Breaking the Chains: African-American Slave Resistance.* New York: Macmillan, 1990.

Oates, Stephen B. *The Fires of Jubilee: Nat Turner's Fierce Rebellion.* New York: Harper and Row, 1975.

Wood, Peter H. *Black Majority: Negroes in Colonial South Carolina from 1670 through the Stono Rebellion.* New York: Knopf, 1974.

Henry N. Drewry/A. R.

See also **African American Religions and Sects; Education, African American; Insurrections, Domestic; South, the: The Antebellum South; Vesey Rebellion; Virginia;** *and* vol. 9: **John Brown's Last Speech; The Nat Turner Insurrection.**

SLAVE RESCUE CASES. In eighteenth- and nineteenth-century North America, slave rescue cases were a source of sensational reportage and popular heroism. Concealment in attics, ships, and even boxes; cross-dressing, wearing disguises, passing for white or free black—all were familiar to the escape stories of fugitive slaves, including those of the most famous, such as Frederick Douglass, Henry "Box" Brown, William Wells Brown, and William and Ellen Crafts.

The first fugitive slave law was passed in 1787 as part of the Northwest Ordinance. Although this legislation nominally prohibited slavery, it permitted all masters to "lawfully reclaim" runaway slaves and avowed that the Constitution would work to suppress the threat of slave

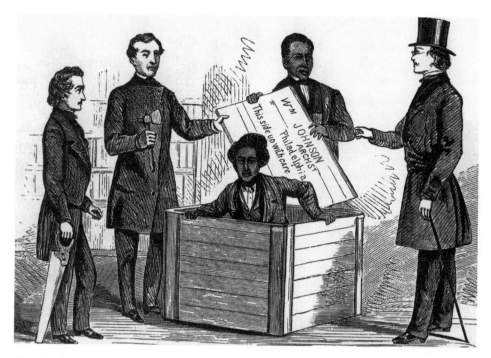

Slave Escape. Henry "Box" Brown emerges from the two-by-three-foot crate in which the slave, with another man's help, secretly shipped himself by rail, boat, and wagon from Richmond, Va., to the antislavery advocate James McKim *(right)* in Philadelphia in 1849; his 1851 narrative describes his twenty-seven-hour, 350-mile journey to freedom. © Bettmann/Corbis

insurrection. The Fugitive Slave Act passed in 1850 was much more effective than its predecessor, though, as it systematized the return of runaways on a national scale and gave slaveholders the right to appear in court and bear witness to the escape of their "property." Court officials then produced a description of the runaway, which could be used as legal proof of his or her slave status even in free states. Significantly, courts were expected only to verify an individual's identity and not to determine their slave status. The financial rewards for the return of fugitive slaves—authorities received $10 if the fugitive was returned to the slave owner and $5 if not—betray the injustices of the system. Not surprisingly, this legislation produced an abolitionist outcry and inspired a wealth of antislavery literature including Harriet Beecher Stowe's novel, *Uncle Tom's Cabin* (1852), as well as the first novel by an African American, *Clotel; or, The President's Daughter* (1853) by William Wells Brown. Stowe's work became famous for its hairbreadth escapes, as the flight of "the slave mother," Eliza, and her son across the frozen Ohio River, in particular, became a major attraction in theatrical adaptations. By comparison, Brown's novel adopted a much bleaker tone as he documented that the only escape from slavery for his title heroine was death by her own hand. As well as the literary outpourings prompted by this legislation, abolitionist protest meetings were held in states such as Massachusetts, New York, and Pennsylvania, while support for black- and white-run Vigilance Committees, as well as for the UNDERGROUND RAILROAD—

a large network of "stations" run by abolitionists including Harriet Tubman and William Still—intensified. The case of Solomon Northup, a free black kidnapped and sold into slavery for twelve years, proved abolitionist fears that the Fugitive Slave Act encouraged the unlawful kidnapping of free blacks. Finally, the famous cases of slave rescue—the fugitive slaves Frederick "Shadrach" Wilkins (1851), Anthony Burns (1854), and Dred Scott (1857) among them—not only converted large numbers to abolition as a means to register their resentment toward the domination of Southern slave power, but also contributed to the same escalating sectional differences that foreshadowed the American Civil War.

BIBLIOGRAPHY

Brown, Henry "Box." *Narrative of the Life of Henry Box Brown, Written by Himself.* New York: Oxford University Press, 2002. The original edition was published in 1851.

Craft, William. *Running a Thousand Miles for Freedom: The Escape of William and Ellen Craft from Slavery.* Baton Rouge: Louisiana State University Press, 1999. The original edition was published in 1860.

Franklin, John Hope, and Loren Schweninger. *Runaway Slaves: Rebels on the Plantation, 1790–1860.* New York: Oxford University Press, 1999.

Grover, Kathryn. *The Fugitive's Gibraltar: Escaping Slaves and Abolitionism in New Bedford, Massachusetts.* Amherst: University of Massachusetts Press, 2001.

Celeste-Marie Bernier

381

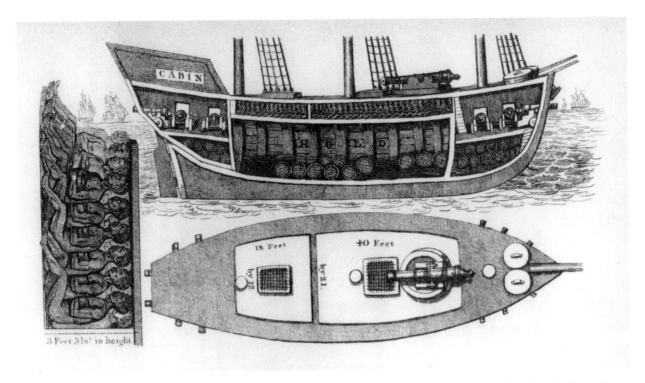

Sections of a Slave Ship. Cutaway drawings of a slave ship, showing captured Africans crammed into a deck described as only "3 Feet 3 Ins. in height." BRITISH LIBRARY

SLAVE SHIPS.

The earliest ships used to transport human beings from Africa to enslavement in North America were converted merchantmen; later, special vessels were built, equipped with air scuttles, ports, and open gratings. The first American ship to carry enslaved Africans was the seventy-nine-foot long *Desire*, sailing out of Salem, Massachusetts, in 1638. The *Hannibal*, an English slaver of 1693, was 450 tons and mounted thirty-six guns, which it was frequently forced to use; seven hundred human beings could be forced into its hold. Many slavers rigged shelves in the middle called a "slave deck," leaving only twenty inches of headroom, so that individuals were unable even to sit upright during the entire voyage.

When the SLAVE TRADE was made illegal in 1808, traders turned to fast ships, largely topsail schooners or brigs, to outrun the British frigates guarding the African coast. With such vessels every consideration was sacrificed for speed, and the accommodations for the enslaved people were even worse than on earlier vessels. The last American slaver was probably the *Huntress* of New York, which landed a cargo of enslaved men and women in Cuba in 1864.

BIBLIOGRAPHY

Cottman, Michael H. *The Wreck of the Henrietta Marie: An African-American's Spiritual Journey to Uncover a Sunken Slave Ship's Past.* New York: Harmony Books, 1999.

Dow, George Francis. *Slave Ships and Slaving.* New York: Dover Publications, 1970.

Daniel Mannix / A. R.

SLAVE TRADE.

The widespread enslavement of diverse peoples for economic and political gain has played a fundamental role throughout human history in the development of nations. Ancient Greek and Roman societies operated by using slave labor, as did many European countries in the modern period. As early as the Middle Ages, Mediterranean cities were supplied with "Moorish" black slaves from Muslim countries in North Africa. By comparison, the "slave trade" is a term which has grown to be associated specifically with the "transatlantic" or "triangular" trade that spanned four centuries (roughly between 1518 and 1865), involved three continents (Europe, Africa, and the Americas), and was responsible for human suffering on an unprecedented scale.

Slavery Comes to the New World

African slaves were first brought to the New World shortly after its discovery by Christopher Columbus—legend has it that one slave was included in his original crew—and they could be found on Hispaniola, site of present-day Haiti, as early as 1501. Upon his arrival in the Bahamas, Columbus himself captured seven of the natives for their "education" on his return to Spain. However, the slave trade proper only began in 1518, when the first black cargo direct from Africa landed in the West Indies. The importation of black slaves to work in the Americas was the inspiration of the Spanish bishop, Bartolomé de Las Casas, whose support of black slavery was motivated by "humanitarian" concerns. He argued that the enslavement of Africans and even of some whites—proving that in the early period slavery did not operate according to exclusive racial demarcations—would save the indigenous Amerindian populations, which were not only dying out but engaging in large-scale resistance as they opposed their excessively harsh conditions. As a result, Charles V, then king of Spain, agreed to the *asiento* or slave trading license (1513), which later represented the most coveted prize in European wars as it gave to those who possessed it a monopoly in slave trafficking.

The widespread expansion of the oceanic slave trade can be attributed to the enormous labor demanded by sugarcane, one of the first and most successful agricultural

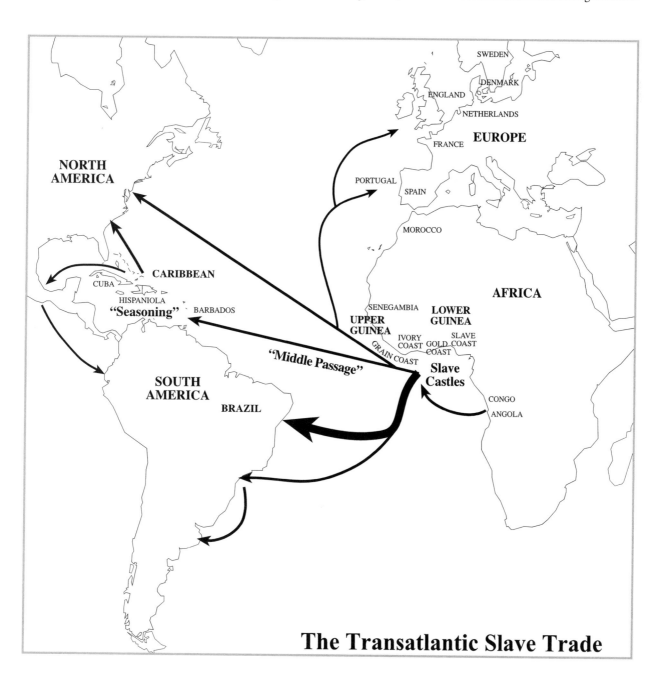

The Transatlantic Slave Trade

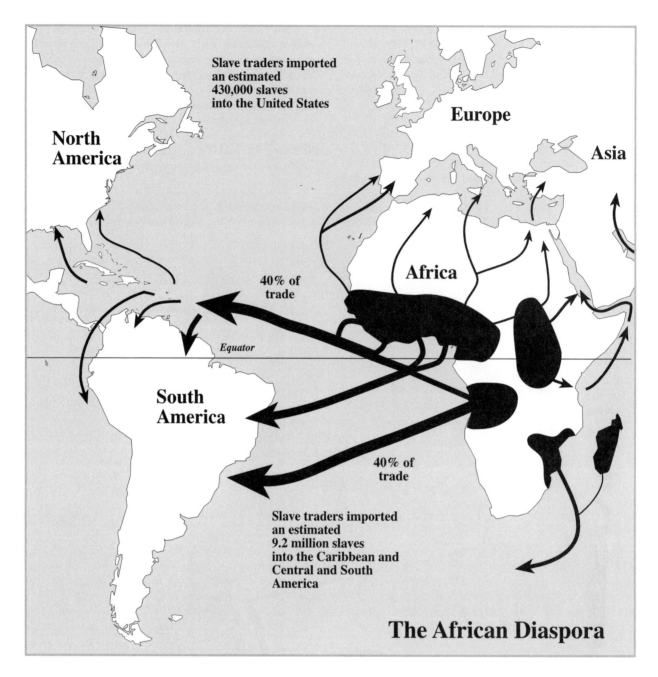

Slave traders imported an estimated 430,000 slaves into the United States

North America

Europe

Asia

Africa

40% of trade

Equator

South America

40% of trade

Slave traders imported an estimated 9.2 million slaves into the Caribbean and Central and South America

The African Diaspora

crops to be cultivated by slaves. The earliest lucrative Spanish sugar plantations were in the Caribbean and West Indies on the islands of Haiti, Cuba, and Jamaica, while Portugal controlled large areas of Brazil. However, Spanish and Portuguese domination of the trade was soon challenged by other Europeans, including the British. One of their earliest adventurers, Sir John Hawkins, undertook his first voyage between 1562 and 1563, and as a direct consequence of his gains was knighted by Elizabeth I. By the late sixteenth and early seventeenth centuries, the Dutch had also secured prominence by founding the Dutch West India Company, taking control of northern Brazil, and conquering the slave-holding fort of Elmina on the West African coast. Among Britain's major slave-

trading successes was Barbados (and later Jamaica, seized from Spain), upon which sugar was cultivated by Africans imported by the Royal African Company, founded in 1672 to protect a British monopoly in the trade. Throughout the seventeenth and eighteenth centuries, Britain's transatlantic slaveholding empire was unrivaled. By using vessels that embarked from the ports of Liverpool, Bristol, and London, Britain traded slaves from diverse areas of the African continent: from Senegambia south to the Gambia River as well as within Sierra Leone (later a settlement of British missionaries), the Gold Coast, the Bight of Benin, and West-Central Africa. The main African tribes associated with the slave trade were the Ibo, Mandingo, Ashanti, Yoruba, and Ewe—and each responded very differently, with various consequences, to white processes of enslavement.

Height and Decline of the Slave Trade

According to Philip Curtin, a recent statistician of the "transatlantic" slave trade, the eighteenth century both represented the height of the trade and also marked the beginnings of its decline. As far as the practice of negotiations between African and European sellers and buyers was concerned, the trade was made possible by "middlemen." These were usually mixed-race in origin or lower-class whites, who traveled deep into the interior and bartered with local African peoples. The sale of weapons in exchange for slaves represented the preferred commodity of Africans, as these were needed to maintain the trade and to protect their communities from raids and incursions by illegal traders and kidnappers (many of them European). The slave trade stimulated divisions within Africa as European rivalry encouraged various nations to enslave, kidnap, or wage war on each other while—as part of its more prolonged legacy—it devastated indigenous populations and economic structures. From a European point of view, it greatly stimulated national wealth and laid the foundations for modern capitalism as, in particular, the financial infrastructures required by the slave trade inaugurated new systems of banking and insurance.

Throughout the period, the slave trade remained closely linked to advances in the sugar plantation system as, for example, major production areas were transferred from offshore African islands to northeastern Brazil by the mid-sixteenth century. As the arrival of the first Africans in Jamestown, Virginia, in 1619 attests, slave populations working tobacco crops in the British colonies of Virginia and Maryland, as well as rice plantations in the Carolinas of mainland North America, in the seventeenth and eighteenth centuries, could only be sustained by the transatlantic slave trade.

The major reasons for the need of a trade in slaves on such a scale can be traced to the much smaller populations of the Americas in comparison with those of the Old World. For white immigrants (including paupers, criminals, and some kidnapped children) who arrived in the seventeenth and eighteenth century as indentured servants, the conditions were so harsh that they were unable, and in many cases refused, to fulfill the existing labor market; they frequently opposed the renewal of their contracts or simply died out.

While the first Africans who were imported to the Americas were described somewhat euphemistically as "apprentices for life," as labor demands increased and racist rhetoric became more deeply entrenched in everyday life,

Tippu Tip and the East African Slave Trade. This 1975 book by Leda Farrant (published by Hamish Hamilton) includes this illustration of the notorious Arab-African Tippu Tip's slave traders taking captives to Zanzibar for sale to the Portuguese after the end of the Atlantic slave trade; some were smuggled illegally into the United States. Hamish Hamilton, 1975

they acquired an unambiguous "chattel" status. It was not long before slavery in the Americas operated according to, and was legitimated by, white racist discourses of "natural black inferiority." Proponents of slavery ideology, including such prominent nineteenth-century figures as John C. Calhoun and even Thomas Jefferson, argued that slavery (or the "peculiar institution," as it became known in North America) served a "civilizing" and "christianizing" process (the Portuguese were well known for the baptism of their slaves) by educating the "heathen" and "barbarous" African while instilling both discipline and a religious sensibility. Thus, Europeans and Euro-Americans did not try to impose slavery on the poor, on victims of war, or on those imprisoned for crimes in their own continent. Instead, they undertook extremely expensive and hazardous journeys in merchant ships to buy peoples from the African coast.

In addition to their being subject to racist definitions of cultural differences, Africans were selected for other reasons, including the widespread belief that they were better able to withstand the climate and disease; however, it is unlikely that many Africans outlived Europeans in plantation areas of the Americas. One historian has commented perceptively that the "African slave trade appears rooted as much in cultural perceptions and social norms as in economic and demographic imperatives."

The slave trade's contribution to European and American understanding of Africans as "property" with "no rights that they were bound to respect" left behind a legacy that has continued well into the twentieth century, arguably undergirding the racial politics of the civil rights movement in North America and continuing to shape the contemporary debates concerning reparations for slavery. Despite early problems, the slave trade was enormously financially successful: Britain's colonial status was fueled by wealth from tobacco and sugar plantations in both the West Indies and mainland North America as ports in London, Liverpool, and Bristol prospered, ushering in a modern age dominated by a "plantocracy" of elite slave owners or "absentee" landlords with "interests" (rarely specified) abroad. The later transatlantic slave trade complemented earlier trans-Saharan practices, which had traded primarily in men, by its demographic diversity. European traders preferred male slaves; however, despite popular belief, on the slave ships men were outnumbered by women and children, who were exported in unprecedented numbers and to such an extent that, by the end of the period, the largest numbers of slaves were children. The numbers of human beings involved are staggering: both when considered by themselves and even more so when placed within a context of earlier slave-trading practices. For example, over the course of some twelve centuries, three and a half to four million slaves crossed the Sahara in the trans-Saharan trade of Arabic origins. However, in the transatlantic trade, which lasted less than half that time, a "conservative estimate" (which significantly neglects to consider the recent statistics of Afrocentric

historians) suggests that as many as twelve million (ten and a half million surviving) were transported out of Africa between the mid-fourteenth century and 1867, when a final slave ship arrived in Cuba with its human cargo (it is likely that the last cargoes landed as lately as 1880).

Statistics are almost impossible to verify but research suggests that, by the early nineteenth century, for every European who crossed the Atlantic, two Africans were exported. Approximately one-half of the total number of Africans shipped in the eighteenth century, and one-quarter in the nineteenth, was sent to the Americas. A little-discussed subject concerns the mortality rate among slaves (for which statistics are not known) who died in the African interior. By far the greatest "bulk" of captives for sale had traveled far across the continent, in some cases as many as "a thousand miles," previous to their departure at the Atlantic coast.

European Character and Intervention

The slave trade was primarily European in character, as among those profiting in the trade were Spain, Portugal, Britain, France, and Holland; they were later seconded by Swedish, Danish, and North American participants. Much earlier—in the thirteenth century—Italy had also played an important role in the human trade; bronze sculptures dating from the medieval period and representing shackled Africans can still be found in Venice. While slavery did exist in Africa before 1400 (slaves were traded largely as the result of internal raids and wars for "domestic" purposes), European intervention changed the face of indigenous slavery as it became systematized and organized to a previously unimaginable extent. The slave trade was

Slave Pen. This photograph from the Civil War studio of Mathew Brady shows where Price, Birch & Co., slave dealers in Alexandria, Va., kept their slaves before a sale or auction. NATIONAL ARCHIVES AND RECORDS ADMINISTRATION

operated internationally and combined the economic interests of the Americas, Britain, and continental Europe as it simultaneously exacerbated and contributed to the impoverishment of western Africa. European dominance in the slave trade also encouraged slavery within Africa itself—especially the enslavement of women—and fomented dissensions across and within different African societies while stimulating war and kidnapping between various traders as they represented conflicting national interests.

European intervention into African slavery revolutionized existing systems and internal trading patterns as slave ships participated in the "triangular" trade between Europe, Africa, and the Americas. Slave captains took manufactured goods (rum, textiles, weapons) to Africa, which they exchanged for slaves whom they then sold in the Americas in return for raw materials such as sugar, tobacco, and later cotton, which they then brought back to Europe, completing the triangle. In the early period of the slave trade, Europeans built medieval forts such as Elmina Castle, a Portuguese stronghold that later fell to the British and that survived as a tourist attraction until the twenty-first century. These castles functioned as "barracoons" where slaves were held under horrendous conditions until they were loaded on ships bound for the Americas. Initially Europeans took slaves to the Iberian Peninsula, Madeira, the Canaries, and São Tomé; they were moved from one part of the African coast to the other before they were transported to the Americas. Throughout a four-hundred-year period, slaves were exported from western Africa to Brazil, the Caribbean Islands, Greater Antilles, and North America. Regardless of the fluctuations in trading routes and agreements throughout this period, one factor remained constant: the cost of slaves increased and profits soared.

What was the likely destination for slaves from Africa who made the transatlantic voyage? Brazil and the Caribbean took as much as 90 percent of the slaves—where upon arrival they underwent a process of "seasoning," which even fewer survived—while the American colonies took as little as 8 percent. Within the Caribbean and Central America, Spain dominated the early trade, while Britain, due to its improvements in maritime technology, gained prominence between the mid-seventeenth and mid-eighteenth centuries. Following the abolition of the slave trade by Britain and the United States in 1807 (full emancipation was not to be awarded in the British colonies until 1834, while the Thirteenth Amendment to the U.S. Constitution abolished slavery much later, in 1863), nine-tenths of slaves were taken to Cuba and Brazil. After the above legislation, many illegal voyages took place with paradoxically greater human suffering, as they were forced to operate clandestinely. By far the most important reason for exporting slaves was sugar cultivation; by comparison, tobacco, rice, coffee growing, and mining for precious metals accounted for less than 20 percent of Africans.

Despite popular opinion, the "booming" production of cotton depended not on the transatlantic slave trade

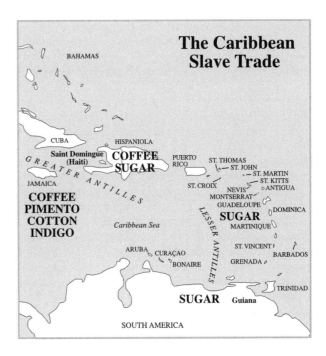

but on the nineteenth-century internal slave trade, which operated from east to west, north to south, and which was made possible only by an expanding black population. This trade brought with it its own horrors, including not only the separation of slave families and suffering under brutal conditions on remote plantations, but also the kidnapping of free blacks into slavery and the wholesale exploitation of the black female slave for "breeding" purposes. In 1790, there were approximately 697,897 slaves in North America as compared to 3,953,760 in 1860, all of whom were indigenous rather than imported.

Slave Resistance and the Abolitionist Movement

Throughout the years of slavery in the Americas, slave resistance played a fundamental role and contributed to the abolition both of the slave trade and slavery as an institution. The earliest recorded slave uprising took place in 1494 as slaves protested Columbus's policy of enslavement in the Caribbean. The methods of slave rebellion were various and ranged from day-to-day resistance (sabotage of machinery, dissembling to avoid work) to escapes involving large numbers of runaways and the establishment of maroon communities. Slaves on the mainland also spearheaded organized revolts such as those led by the black preachers Denmark Vesey (North Carolina, 1822) and Nat Turner (Virginia, 1831). Contrary to earlier scholarship documenting the slave trade, certain areas of the Americas repeatedly drew on particular parts of Africa, so that many more African cultural and social practices have survived than had been previously supposed.

Often compared by historians to the Holocaust, the transatlantic slave trade and the extent to which it legitimized and endorsed the mass enforced migration of enslaved peoples nevertheless remains unparalleled in human history. The full extent of the horrors of the "Middle Passage," by which the transportation of slaves from Africa to the Americas is known, will forever remain insufficiently realized or understood. However, it can be said that this journey was characterized, as a minimum, by annual average losses of between 10 and 20 percent during the six-to-fourteen-week voyage. These deaths were due to dehydration from gastrointestinal disease (known as the "bloody flux") caused by unhygienic conditions in slave ship holds, over-tight "packing" as the slaves were placed close together like "books upon a shelf," and epidemics of smallpox. Life aboard the slave ships was relentlessly oppressive: slaves were chained together, unable to exercise, fed from communal bowls, and provided with minimal sanitation. They suffered from the whites' brutality (including severe whippings and the rape of slave women), starvation in some cases (as supplies ran out), disease, and severe psychological trauma (many of them remained chained throughout the journey to those who had died).

The slave-trader-turned-abolitionist-and-preacher, John Newton, as well as the former slave, Olaudah Equiano, provide moving testimony concerning its perpetual terrors during the eighteenth century and after in their written accounts of the slave trade. John Newton described this "unhappy and disgraceful" trade as contradictory to the "feelings of humanity" and as the "stain of our national character." Captured and placed upon a slave ship, Equiano testified to personal "horror and anguish"; he wrote in 1789: "I saw a multitude of black people of every description chained together, every one of their countenances expressing dejection and sorrow." Each slave ship was designed to hold an average of 330 slaves, although this number was regularly doubled. This is made clear in the notorious case of the Liverpool slaver, the *Brookes*, which is known to have carried as many as 609 slaves on a single voyage. In the eighteenth century, British abolitionist Thomas Clarkson took a plan of this ship (including the illustrations of how the slaves were to be "stowed") to Paris, where a small model was made of it which was used to convert European opinion to antislavery activism. Faced with these conditions and nothing to lose, slave resistance aboard ships was frequent: they refused to eat so that implements had to be devised for force-feeding; they committed suicide in the mythical hope of their soul being freed upon death so that they could "return to Africa" (captains cut off their heads and returned their headless bodies to Africa as proof to others that even in death they were enslaved); and they led slave revolts against the white crews—some of which were successful, including those aboard the *Amistad* (1839) and the *Creole* (1841). Resistance was hardly an issue, however, in one of the most notorious examples of cruelty toward slaves ever recorded, which happened aboard the Liverpool-owned slave ship the *Zong* (1783). The slave captain decided that, in view of their unhealthy status, it would be more profitable to throw his 131 slaves overboard and submit an insurance claim for their loss than to treat them.

The slaves' prospects hardly improved upon their arrival in the Americas; as many as one-third of Africans died within four years of landing, and few survived the "seasoning" process, as they were unable to adjust to the vast changes in climate, culture, and living conditions. In addition to the slaves placed in the holds, large numbers occupied the slightly more fortunate position of working aboard ships as sailors, interpreters, bookkeepers, and cooks (the latter, with their proximity to knives, are historically related to slave revolts).

Paradoxically, however, it was the suffering of white crews—condemned by contemporaries as the "rapid loss of seamen"—which marked the beginning of the campaign for the abolition of the slave trade. While this is a subject for ongoing debate, it seems clear that the slave trade did not die out solely due to economic losses but as a direct result of a number of forces, not least of which included the escalating acts of successful slave resistance—most notably the Haitian Revolution (1794), as well as the American, British, and French abolitionist movements. In its enduring effects for British, French, and Dutch economies, among others, the European-engineered slave trade—described by one historian as a "corrosive commercial and human virus"—encouraged the expansion of merchant shipping, provided a market for goods produced by new industries, and supplied the capital to fund the British Industrial Revolution. Thus, steel products from Sheffield, England, for example, such as hoes and knives, equipped slaves with tools for their labor on plantations in the Americas. By comparison, following the abolition of the slave trade, almost all African regions that had participated in the trade experienced severe financial losses, which continued to have a profound and nefarious impact upon the economic stability of the continent well into the twentieth and twenty-first centuries.

Despite all the efforts of European and North American slave traders to suppress slave culture, enslaved Africans in the Americas nonetheless had the final word, as they developed vast networks across communities. These resulted in rich "creole" cultures and languages as well as an inspirational legacy of art, music, literature, and history the full extent of which remains to be explored.

BIBLIOGRAPHY

Curtin, Philip D. *The Atlantic Slave Trade: A Census.* Madison: University of Wisconsin Press, 1969.

Engerman, Stanley, Seymour Drescher, and Robert Paquette, eds. *Oxford Readers: Slavery.* Oxford: Oxford University Press, 2001.

Equiano, Olaudah. *The Interesting Narrative of the Life of Olaudah Equiano Written by Himself. 1789.* Boston: Bedford/St. Martin's, 1995.

Mannix, Daniel P., and Malcolm Cowley. *Black Cargoes: A History of the Atlantic Slave Trade 1518–1865.* New York: Viking, 1962.

Newton, John. *Thoughts upon the African Slave Trade.* London: J. Buckland and J. Johnson, 1788.

Rawley, James A. *The Transatlantic Slave Trade: A History.* New York: Norton, 1981.

Walvin, James. *Black Ivory: A History of British Slavery.* London: Fontana, 1992.

Wood, Marcus. *Blind Memory: Visual Representations of Slavery in England and America, 1780–1865.* Manchester, U.K.: Manchester University Press, 2000.

Celeste-Marie Bernier

See also **Middle Passage;** and vol. 9: **Voyages of the Slaver St. John; Spanish Colonial Official's Account of Triangular Trade with England.**

SLAVERY. What does it mean to dehumanize a human being? To ponder this question is to approach some definition of slavery, one of the most extreme forms of dehumanization. We know enough about life in the antebellum South to know that slaves resisted dehumanization, that they created a folk culture, a family structure, and a spiritual life that blunted the dehumanizing force of slavery. What was it, then, that made slavery *slavery*?

The problem of slavery, and not just in the American South, was that it defined slaves as outsiders within the very societies of which they were a part. In America this meant that although the slaves got married and formed families, their families were not legally sanctioned and were therefore liable to be torn apart at the will of the master. Put differently, the slave family had no social standing. From youth to old age, from sunup to sundown, slaves spent the bulk of their waking lives at work, for slavery in America was nothing if not a system of labor exploitation. Yet the slaves had no right whatsoever to claim the fruits of their labor. This was "social death," and to the extent that humans are social beings, slavery was a profoundly dehumanizing experience.

What it means to be socially dead, an outsider, varies depending on how a society defines social life. Over the course of slavery's two and a half centuries of life in what became the United States, Americans developed a very specific understanding of social life. In so doing, they were specifying the definition of slavery in America. They saw membership in society in terms of rights, thereby defining the slaves as rightless.

To be sure, social death did not extinguish the slaves' cultural life. The slaves sometimes accumulated small amounts of property, for example, but they had no right to their property independent of the master's will. They bought and sold merchandise, they hired out their labor, but their contracts had no legal standing. In their sacred songs, their profane folktales, and in their explicit complaints, the slaves articulated their dissatisfaction with slavery. But they had no right to publish, to speak, or to assemble. They had no standing in the public sphere, just as their private lives had no legal protection. Thus the distinction between public and private—a central attribute of American society beginning in the eighteenth century—did not apply to the slaves. In all of these ways American slavery dehumanized its victims by depriving them of social standing, without which we cannot be fully human.

Origins of American Slavery

Slavery was largely incompatible with the organic societies of medieval Europe. After the collapse of ancient slavery human bondage persisted on the margins of medieval Europe, first on the islands of the eastern Mediterranean and later in the coastal areas of southern Europe. But western slavery did not revive until the feudal economies declined, opening up opportunities for European merchants and adventurers who were freed from the constraints that prevailed elsewhere. Over the course of the fifteenth, sixteenth, and seventeenth centuries Europe's consciousness of itself expanded to the point where no "Europeans" were considered "outsiders," and as such available for enslavement. This was a far cry from conditions in Africa, where a much more local conception of social membership made Africans subject to enslavement by other Africans. Thus, during those same centuries, entrepreneurs—first from Spain and Portugal and later from Holland and England—took to the seas and plugged themselves into Africa's highly developed system of slavery, transforming it into a vast Atlantic slave trade.

Finally, the collapse of an organically unified conception of European society, reflected in the Protestant Reformation's destruction of the "one true church," paved the way for the critical liberal distinction between the public and private spheres of life. Modern slavery flourished in this setting, for the slaveholders ironically required the freedom of civil society to establish the slave societies of the Atlantic world. Thus did the slave societies of the Americas grow up alongside, and as part of, the development of liberal capitalism. This is what distinguished "modern" slavery from its predecessors in antiquity.

The Atlantic Slave Trade

The Atlantic SLAVE TRADE was in some ways an extension of a much older Mediterranean slave trade. Over the course of the late Middle Ages slave-based sugar plantations spread from Turkey to the islands of the eastern Mediterranean, and westward to coastal regions of southern France and Spain before breaking out into the Atlantic and spreading southward to the Azores, Madeira, and São Tomé. To some extent this line of expansion followed the source of slaves, for by the time sugar was being planted on the islands of the Mediterranean, Arab traders were transporting sub-Saharan Africans across the desert to sell them as slave laborers in southern and eastern Europe. Thus as Europe expanded it grew increasingly de-

Selling a Freedman to Pay His Fine. This engraving from a sketch by James E. Taylor, published in *Frank Leslie's Illustrated Weekly* on 19 January 1867, depicts the return to slavery of an African American in Monticello, Fla. LIBRARY OF CONGRESS

pendent on the continued willingness of Africans to enslave one another.

When the Spanish and the Portuguese first encountered West Africans the Europeans were too weak to establish plantations on the African mainland. But by establishing slavery on the island off the African coast—Madiera, the Azores, and São Tomé—the Europeans created the network of connections with Africans that later allowed them to expand their operations into a vast transatlantic slave trade. Thwarted on the African mainland the Europeans turned westward, leaping across the Atlantic to establish sugar plantations in Brazil and the Caribbean. Over the course of several hundred years, European and colonial slavers purchased approximately thirteen million slaves from their African captors. Perhaps eleven million of those Africans survived the Atlantic crossing to be put to work on the farms and plantations of the New World.

Slavery and the slave trade grew as the economy of western Europe expanded and developed. It peaked in the eighteenth century, when a "consumer revolution" centered in England and North America created unprecedented demand for the commodities produced by slaves, especially sugar. Indeed, the history of slavery in the Amer-

icas can be written in terms of the rise and fall of a series of sugar economies, first in Brazil, and then on a succession of Caribbean islands beginning with Jamaica and ending, in the nineteenth century, with Cuba. By the time the British got around the establishing permanent settlements on the North American mainland, the Atlantic slave trade that fed the booming sugar plantations of Brazil and the Caribbean was fully operational. If the English colonists in Virginia, Maryland, and elsewhere chose to develop slave economies of their own, the means to do so were readily at hand.

From "Societies with Slaves" to "Slave Societies"

In 1776 slavery was legal in every one of the thirteen colonies that declared its independence from Great Britain. Most of the leading ministers in Puritan Massachusetts had been slave owners. By the second quarter of the eighteenth century a significant percentage of the population of New York City was enslaved, and in 1712 several dozen of that city's slaves openly rebelled. By then there were substantial numbers of slaves in Newport, Rhode Island, which was rapidly becoming a center for the North American slave trade. To the south, African slaves first arrived in the Chesapeake region of Virginia and Maryland in

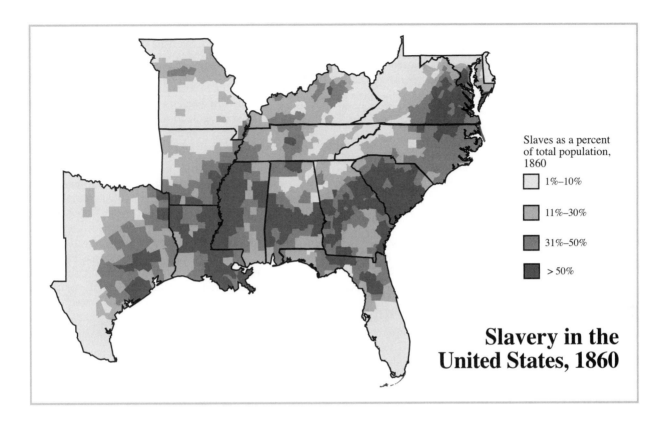

Slavery in the United States, 1860

Slaves as a percent of total population, 1860

- ☐ 1%–10%
- ☐ 11%–30%
- ☐ 31%–50%
- ☐ > 50%

1619. Slaves appeared in the Carolinas a generation or two later. The ubiquity of slavery in eighteenth century America was not unusual, however: slaves had been present in human societies throughout history, and colonial America was no exception.

What made the colonies—and ultimately the American South—exceptional was the fact that the Chesapeake and lowcountry South Carolina and Georgia became full-scale slave societies rather than merely societies with slaves. Slave societies are rare things in human history, and so its emergence in North America is one of the most important historical developments of the eighteenth century. Slave society, not slavery, is what distinguished the northern colonies from the southern colonies and explains why slavery was abolished in the northern states but persisted in the South. Thus the emergence of slave society, rather than the emergence of slavery itself, is the first major turning point in the history of American slavery.

In the Chesapeake slave society developed fairly slowly. For most of the seventeenth century African slaves in Maryland and Virginia numbered in the hundreds. When English settlers first discovered the profitable potential of large-scale tobacco production, their first source of labor was indentured servants, most of them from Great Britain. Thus, tobacco planting was an established business when, in the late seventeenth century, the English economy improved and the supply of indentured servants dried up. It was only then that Chesapeake planters turned to African slaves in large numbers. Between 1680 and 1720 the Chesapeake was transformed from a society with

slaves to a slave society. In those same years, a slave society based on rice planting was constructed in the Carolina lowcountry.

By 1750 the economy and society of both the Chesapeake and the lowcountry were based on slavery. But the two regions differed in significant ways. Tobacco plantations were relatively small; they could be run efficiently with twenty or thirty slaves. Rice plantations were most efficient with fifty slaves or more, whereas the sugar plantations of the Caribbean—and later Louisiana—required so much initial capital that they were most efficient when they had a hundred slaves or more. Because tobacco required some care to cultivate, slaves were organized in gangs that were directly supervised either by the master, an overseer, or a slave driver. Rice planting, by contrast, demanded certain skills but it did not require direct supervision. So in the Carolina lowcountry, slave labor was organized under a "task" system, with individual slaves assigned a certain task every day and left largely on their own to complete it.

Because of these distinctions, slave life in the eighteenth-century lowcountry differed in important ways from slave life in the Chesapeake. Large rice plantations made it easier for slaves to form families of their own. On the other hand, high death rates in the lowcountry destabilized the families that did form. Smaller farms meant that tobacco slaves were much more likely to marry "away" from their home plantations, with all the disruptions and difficulties that such marriages inevitably entailed. On the other hand, Chesapeake slave families were less disrupted by disease and death than were the slave families of the Carolina lowcountry.

Because sugar cane was such a labor-intensive crop, sugar plantations in Brazil and the Caribbean were death traps for slaves; they required constant infusions of new laborers imported from Africa. But sugar could not grow in Virginia or Carolina; and the relative health of slaves working the crops grown there made a family life among slaves possible. As a result, the slave population of the North American colonies developed the ability to reproduce itself naturally over the course of the eighteenth century. In the tobacco regions the slaves achieved a fairly robust rate of population growth, whereas the rice slaves did little more than reproduce their numbers. As a result, the expansion of the rice economy required substantial imports of African slaves throughout the eighteenth century, whereas in the Chesapeake the slave population was largely native-born after 1750. The high density of blacks, combined with sustained African immigration, created a distinctive culture in the coastal lowcountry, a culture marked by its own "gullah" dialect and the persistence of significant African traditions. In Virginia and Maryland, by contrast, a largely native-born population and smaller plantations led to an English-speaking slave community that was more assimilated to the culture of the English settlers.

Although the rice plantations grew more technologically sophisticated, and therefore more productive, over the course of the eighteenth century, the rice culture itself was largely restricted to the lowcountry of South Carolina and Georgia. The tobacco culture of the Chesapeake proved more adaptable. In the upper South, planters shifted readily to wheat production when the tobacco economy faltered. But more important, the tobacco pattern spread at the end of the century into the inland regions of the lower South, where it facilitated the expansion of short-staple COTTON. Thus the form slave society took in the colonial Chesapeake—relatively small plantations, a gang labor system, relatively high birth rates, and a native-born slave population—became the model upon which the cotton economy of the nineteenth century depended. Before that happened, however, the American Revolution had dramatically altered the history of slavery in the United States.

Slavery and the American Revolution

The American Revolution had a profound but ambiguous effect on the history of slavery in the United States. It established the terms of a ferocious debate, without precedent in history, over the morality of slavery itself. It resulted in the creation of the first sizable communities of free blacks in the United States. It made slavery into a sectional institution by abolishing or restricting it in the North while protecting it in the South. And by defining a "citizen" of the new nation as the bearer of certain basic rights, it definitively established the status of American slaves as rightless.

As soon as the conflict between the colonies and Great Britain erupted, the English began to encourage southern slaves to rebel against their masters. Thousands of slaves took advantage of the British offer, thereby transforming the war for independence into a civil war in the southern colonies. As a result, southern slaveholders came to associate their struggle for freedom from Great Britain with the struggle to preserve slavery. The slaves, meanwhile, began to define freedom as the acquisition of rights.

Some of the revolutionary changes had important social consequences. For example, the revolutionary commitment to fundamental human equality inspired the abolition of slavery in every northern state between 1776 and 1804. In the upper South the same ideology, combined with the relative weakness of the slave economy, prompted a wave of MANUMISSIONS (formal emancipations) in Virginia and Maryland. Northern abolition and southern manumissions together produced the first major communities of free blacks in the United States.

There were important legal changes as well. Slave codes across the South were revised to reflect the liberal humanist injunction against cruelty: some of the most barbaric punishments of slaves were eliminated and the wanton murder of a slave was made illegal for the first time. The new Constitution gave Congress the power to ban, by a simple majority vote, the entire nation from participating in the Atlantic slave trade after 1808. In addition the first U.S. Congress reenacted a Northwest Ordinance, first passed by the Continental Congress, substantially restricting the western expansion of slavery in the northern states. All of these developments reflected the sudden and dramatic emergence of an antislavery sentiment that was new to the world.

But the Revolution did not abolish slavery everywhere, and in important ways it reinforced the slave societies of the South even as it eliminated the last societies with slaves in the North. Humanizing the slave codes made slavery less barbaric, for example, but also more tolerable. More important, the new Constitution recognized and protected slavery without ever actually using the word "slave." It included a fugitive slave clause and two "three-fifths" clauses that gave the southern states a discount on their tax liabilities and enhanced representation in the House of Representatives. Finally, the same liberal ideology that provided so many Americans with a novel argument against slavery became the basis for an equally novel proslavery argument. The rights of property in slaves, the claim that slaves were happy, that they were not treated with cruelty, that they were less productive than free laborers: all of these sentiments drew on the same principles of politics and political economy that inspired the Revolution. They became the mainstays of a developing proslavery ideology.

The Westward Expansion of the Slave Economy

Beginning in the 1790s, a previously moribund slavery came roaring back to life. In 1793 Eli Whitney invented

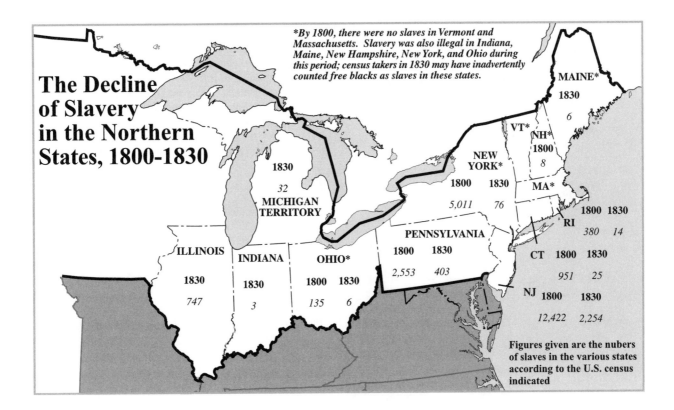

The Decline
of Slavery
in the Northern
States, 1800-1830

By 1800, there were no slaves in Vermont and Massachusetts. Slavery was also illegal in Indiana, Maine, New Hampshire, New York, and Ohio during this period; census takers in 1830 may have inadvertently counted free blacks as slaves in these states.

MAINE* 1830 / 6

MICHIGAN TERRITORY 1830 / 32

VT* / NH* 1800 / 8

NEW YORK* 1800 5,011 / 1830 76

MA* 1800 / 1830

RI 1800 380 / 1830 14

PENNSYLVANIA 1800 2,553 / 1830 403

CT 1800 951 / 1830 25

NJ 1800 12,422 / 1830 2,254

ILLINOIS 1830 / 747

INDIANA 1830 / 3

OHIO* 1800 135 / 1830 6

Figures given are the nubers of slaves in the various states according to the U.S. census indicated

a machine that made the cultivation of short-staple cotton profitable. Almost immediately the cotton economy began a relentless expansion that continued for more than half a century and eventually provided the catalyst for the Civil War.

The COTTON boom commenced with the migration of slaveholders from the upper South down the Piedmont plateau into South Carolina and Georgia. By 1800 slaveholders were spilling across the Appalachians planting tobacco in Kentucky and Tennessee and cotton in Georgia and Alabama. The population of Alabama and Mississippi, 40,000 in 1810, leaped to 200,000 in 1820 and kept growing until it reached over 1.6 million by 1860. By then cotton and slavery had crossed the Mississippi River into Louisiana, parts of Missouri, and Texas. In those same years slave plantations in Kentucky and Tennessee expanded their production of tobacco and to a lesser extent, hemp. And in southern Louisiana the rise of the cotton kingdom was paralleled by the rise in huge, heavily capitalized sugar plantations.

But rice, tobacco, and sugar could not match the dynamism and scope of short-staple cotton. Indeed, cotton quickly established itself as the nation's leading export, in both tons and dollars. Although its growth was erratic—slowing in the 1820s and again in the early 1840s—it never stopped. And far from stagnating, the cotton economy was never more vibrant than it was in the 1850s. Thus on the eve of the Civil War many white Southerners were persuaded that "Cotton is King" and could never be dethroned.

The consequences of slavery's expansion were not confined to economic history, however. For both free and enslaved Southerners, the cotton boom had powerful effects on social and cultural life. Among the slaveholders, the cotton boom bred an aggressively expansionist ethos that influenced everything from family life to national politics. Wives and mothers complained about the men who were prepared to pull up stakes and move westward in search of new opportunities. Sons were urged to leave their towns and families to start up new plantations further west. And slaveholding presidents, including Andrew Jackson and James K. Polk, carried these expansionist convictions with them to Washington, D.C., provoking wars and international confrontations all for the sake of facilitating slavery's expansion. But it was the slaves whose lives, families, and communities were most profoundly disrupted by the rise of the cotton kingdom.

The Deterioration of Slave Life
In the second half of the eighteenth century the lives of most slaves improved. Infant mortality rates among slaves declined; the average height of adult slaves rose, indicating an adequate level of nutrition. With that the slaves reached a healthy rate of natural population growth, the ratio of men to women evened out, and it was possible for most slaves to form families of their own. In addition, the American Revolution had inspired many masters in the upper South to free their slaves, and for the vast majority who remained in bondage the laws of slavery be-

Receiving Corporal Punishment. This drawing shows a slave in Florida bending over uncomfortably, his head and hands in wooden stocks. LIBRARY OF CONGRESS

came somewhat less severe. After 1800, however, this progress came to a halt, and in some ways reversed itself.

In the nineteenth century the conditions of slave life deteriorated. Beginning in the 1790s the state legislatures made it harder and harder for masters to manumit (free) their slaves, further choking the already narrow chances the slaves had of gaining their freedom. After 1830 most southern states passed laws making it a crime to teach a slave to read, adding legally enforced illiteracy to the attributes of enslavement. The health of the slaves declined as well. The number of low-birth-weight infants increased, and the average height of the slaves fell—both of them indications of deteriorating levels of nutrition. With the rise of the sugar plantations of Louisiana, a new and particularly ferocious form of slavery established a foothold in the Old South. Sugar plantations had a well-deserved reputation for almost literally working the slaves to death. They averaged a stunning population decline of about 14 percent each decade. But sugar planting was so profitable that it could survive and prosper anyway, thanks to an internal slave trade that provided Louisiana planters with a steady supply of replacement laborers.

The growth of the internal slave trade in the antebellum South made the systematic destruction of African American families a defining element of the slave system. In colonial times, when new slaves were imported through the Atlantic slave trade, the internal trade was small. But with the expansion of the cotton economy after 1790 and the closing of the Atlantic trade in 1808, a robust market in slaves developed. At first Virginia and Maryland but later South Carolina, Georgia, Kentucky, and Tennessee exported their slaves to the newer slave states further west and south. Eventually even Alabama and Mississippi became net exporters of slaves. Between 1790 and 1860 nearly a million slaves were exported from one part of the South to another, making it one of the largest forced migrations in human history. Between one third and one half of these slaves did not migrate with their masters but were sold through the interstate slave trade.

Slaveholders protested that they sold family members apart from one another only when absolutely necessary. But "necessity" was a flexible concept in the Old South. When the cotton economy was booming and slave prices were high, for example, it became more "necessary" to sell slaves. Furthermore, the ages of the slaves put up for sale suggest that husbands were regularly sold away from wives and children were regularly sold away from parents. The paradox was appalling: cotton cultivation was healthy enough to sustain a natural growth of the slave population through the creation of slave families, but the expansion of the cotton economy broke up those families by the tens of thousands. The forced sale of a close relative became a nearly universal experience for the slaves of the Old South.

The Plantation Regime

Since the late eighteenth century, Americans both North and South accepted that slave labor was less efficient than free labor. Even the slave owners agreed that a slave lacked the incentives to diligent labor that motivated the free worker. Slaves could not be promoted for hard work or fired for poor work. They did not get raises. Harder work did not bring more food, better clothing, a finer home. The slaves could not accumulate savings hoping to buy farms of their own; they could not work with the aim of winning their ultimate freedom; nor could they work to insure that their children's lives would be easier than theirs. Lacking the normal incentives of free labor, the slaves were universally dismissed as lackluster and inefficient workers.

And yet the slave economy grew at impressive, even spectacular rates in the nineteenth century. The returns on investment in slave plantations were comparable to the returns on businesses in the North. Despite the ups and downs of the market for slave-produced commodities, slavery was by and large a profitable system in the Old South. This was no accident. The slaveholders organized their farms and plantations to be as productive as possible. They constructed a managerial hierarchy to oversee the daily labor of the slaves. They employed the latest techniques in crop rotation and manuring. They planted corn and raised livestock that complemented the cash crops, thus keeping the slaves both busy and adequately nourished.

Any free farmer could have done as much, but the slaveholders had advantages that counteracted the weaknesses of their labor system. They put otherwise "unproductive" slaves to work. Slave children went to work at an earlier age than free children, for example. And elderly slaves too old for fieldwork were put in charge of minding very small children and preparing the meals for all the slaves. These and other economies of scale turned a labor system that was in theory unproductive and inefficient into what was, in practice, one of the great economic successes of the nineteenth century.

On a well managed plantation the slaves were kept busy year round, fixing tools and repairing buildings during the winter season, tending to the corn when the cotton was taken care of, slaughtering the hogs after the last of the cotton was ginned. Since most slaves lived on units with twenty or more slaves, most were introduced to some form of systematic management. Slave "drivers" acted as foremen to oversee the gangs in the fields. On larger plantations overseers were hired to manage day to day operations. The larger the plantation the more common it was for particular slaves to specialize in various forms of skilled labor. The "well managed plantation," the slaveholders

agreed, took into consideration not simply the amount of cotton produced, but the overall productivity of the farm's operations.

Yet the fact remained that the slaves lacked the incentive to care very much or work very hard to maximize the master's profits. As a result, much of the management of slaves was aimed at forcing them to do what they did not really care about. This was the underlying tension of the master-slave relationship. It was the reason almost all masters resorted to physical punishment. In the final analysis, the efficiency of southern slavery, and the resentment of the slaves, was driven by the whip.

Slave Culture

Slaves responded to the hardships and disruptions of their lives through the medium of a distinctive culture whose roots were in part African and in part American but whose basic outlines were shaped by the experience of slavery itself.

Slave culture developed in several distinct stages. Over the course of the eighteenth century, as the slave population stabilized and the majority of slaves became native-born, a variety of African dialects gave way to English as the language through which most American slaves communicated with one another. A native-born slave population in turn depended on the existence of slave families.

Planting Sweet Potatoes. Freed slaves—some wearing Union uniforms—work at a plantation on Edisto Island, near Charleston, S.C., during the Union occupation of the island, 1862. GETTY IMAGES

Beginning in the late eighteenth century, a growing number of slaves converted to evangelical Christianity and by 1860 Protestantism was the dominant religion of enslaved African Americans.

Despite the fact that most slaves eventually spoke English and practiced Christianity, elements of West African culture persisted. In some parts of the South, such as lowcountry South Carolina and southern Louisiana, the African influence could be strong. The mystical practices of voodoo common among Louisiana slaves, for example, were only one example of African cultural practices that survived in the Old South. More generally, slaves continued to put their faith in the conjurers and potions that were a part of the mystical life of West Africans. Other African cultural traces could be found in the slaves' funeral practices, their marriage ceremonies, and in the way they treated the sick and the dying. Slave music evinced a rhythmic complexity more common to West Africa than to western Europe. And slave dancing, which masters commonly dismissed as mere wild gyrations, were more often a legacy of African traditions such as the "ring shout."

Even the fact that the slaves spoke English, formed families, and practiced Christianity did not mean that they had simply absorbed the culture of their masters. In important ways the slaves used their language to construct a folk culture of rituals, music, and storytelling that reflected the continuing influence of African traditions and that remained very much the culture of slaves rather than masters. The slaves reckoned kinship more broadly and more flexibly than did their masters, providing some measure of emotional protection from the disruptions of family life. Nor was slave Christianity a mere carbon copy of the religion of the masters. Slaves did not distinguish the sacred from the profane as sharply as their owners did; they empathized more with the Moses of the Old Testament, who led his people out of bondage, than with the New Testament Epistles of St. Paul, which exhorted slaves to obey their masters.

For the masters, however, slave culture was as important for what it lacked as for what it contained. Try as they might, the slaveholders could not overcome the structural constraints of a labor system that gave the slaves no reason to respond to the bourgeois injunctions to diligence, thrift, and sobriety. Slave culture was distinguished less by the persistence of African traditions than by its distance from the culture of the masters.

The Culture of the Masters

Years ago, a pioneering historian of the Old South wrote that slavery was "less a business than a life; it made fewer fortunes than it made men." Maybe so. But slavery made more than its share of fortunes: in 1860 almost all of the richest counties in America were located in the South. And the men who made those fortunes did not do so by lolling about on their verandas, sipping mint juleps and reading the Old South's version of the daily racing form.

Plowing the Rice Fields. This photograph by O. Pierre Havens shows two African Americans (most likely slaves just a few years earlier) working in the vicinity of Savannah, Ga., in the 1870s. Schomburg Center for Research in Black Culture

The slaveholders were a hard-nosed and aggressive lot. Those who inherited their plantations added to their wealth by buying second and third plantations. Sometimes they pulled up stakes, moved west, and built more plantations. Slaveholders who started with a handful of slaves often used their professional careers to subsidize their accumulation of more land and more slaves. It was the rare planter whose wealth did not entail careful management of his farm, constant supervision of his slaves, and a keen eye for a chance to expand his operations or move on.

Because successful slave ownership was hard work, the planters liked to think that they had arrived at their exalted social standing not by the advantages of privileged upbringings but through their steady adherence to the bourgeois virtues of thrift, diligence, and sobriety. No doubt a few generations of wealth smoothed out the rough edges on many a planter family, and the temptation to fancy themselves aristocrats of a sort could become irresistible. But the demands of the slave economy and the plantation regime could not be ignored: to lose sight of the bottom line was to risk financial and social ruin.

Faced with rising antislavery criticism from the North, the slaveholders looked to their experience and filtered it through the prevailing political culture to produce a provocative series of proslavery arguments. If cruelty was immoral, the slaveholders insisted that the slaves were well treated and that brutality was frowned upon. If happiness rested upon a decent standard of living, the slaves were so well treated that they were among the happiest people on earth. Only as slaves did Africans, who would otherwise languish in heathenism, have access to the word of God. Although slave labor was in principle less efficient than free labor, southern slavery put an otherwise unproductive race of people to work in an otherwise unproductive climate, thereby creating wealth and civilization where it could not otherwise have existed. In a culture that sentimentalized the family, the slaveholders increasingly insisted that the families of slaves were protected against all unnecessary disruption. Thus by the standards of liberal society—the immorality of cruelty, the universal right to happiness, freedom to worship, the sanctity of the family, the productivity of labor, and the progress of civilization—southern slave society measured up.

Or so the slaveholders claimed. Northerners—enough of them, anyway—thought differently. As the relentless expansion of the slave states pushed against the equally relentless expansion of the free states, the two regions sharpened their arguments as well as their weapons. When the war came North, with more guns and more machines and more free men to put in uniform, suppressed the slaveholders' rebellion and put down slavery to boot. Thus did American slave society, wealthier and more powerful than ever, come to its violent and irreversible end.

BIBLIOGRAPHY

Berlin, Ira. *Many Thousands Gone: The First Two Centuries of Slavery in North America.* Cambridge, Mass.: Harvard University Press, 1998.

Blassingame, John. W. *The Slave Community: Plantation Life in the Antebellum South.* Rev. and enl. ed. New York: Oxford University Press, 1979.

Chaplin, Joyce E. *An Anxious Pursuit: Agricultural Innovation and Modernity in the Lower South, 1730–1815.* Chapel Hill: University of North Carolina Press, 1993.

Davis, David Brion. *The Problem of Slavery in Western Culture.* Ithaca, N.Y.: Cornell University Press, 1966.

Dusinberre, William. *Them Dark Days: Slavery in the American Rice Swamps.* New York: Oxford University Press, 1996.

Eltis, David. *The Rise of African Slavery in the Americas.* Cambridge, U.K.: Cambridge University Press, 2000.

Fogel, Robert William. *Without Consent or Contract: The Rise and Fall of American Slavery.* New York: Norton, 1989.

Genovese, Eugene D. *Roll, Jordan, Roll: The World the Slaves Made.* New York: Vintage, 1974.

Johnson, Walter. *Soul by Soul: Life inside the Antebellum Slave Market.* Cambridge, Mass.: Harvard University Press, 1999.

Levine, Lawrence W. *Black Culture and Black Consciousness: Afro-American Folk Thought from Slavery to Freedom.* New York: Oxford University Press, 1977.

Morgan, Philip D. *Slave Counterpoint: Black Culture in the Eighteenth-Century Chesapeake and Low Country.* Chapel Hill: University of North Carolina Press, 1998.

Morris, Thomas D. *Southern Slavery and the Law, 1619–1860.* Chapel Hill: University of North Carolina Press, 1996.

Oakes, James. *The Ruling Race: A History of American Slaveholders.* New York: Knopf, 1982.

———. *Slavery and Freedom: An Interpretation of the Old South.* New York: Knopf, 1990.

Phillips, Ulrich Bonnell. *American Negro Slavery: A Survey of the Supply, Employment, and Control of Negro Labor As Determined by the Plantation Regime.* New York: Appleton, 1918. Reprint, Baton Rouge: Louisiana State University Press, 1966.

Smith, Mark. *Mastered by the Clock: Time, Slavery, and Freedom in the American South.* Chapel Hill: University of North Carolina Press, 1997.

Stampp, Kenneth M. *The Peculiar Institution: Slavery in the Antebellum South.* New York: Knopf, 1956.

Tadman, Michael. *Speculators and Slaves: Masters, Traders, and Slaves in the Old South.* Madison: University of Wisconsin Press, 1996.

James Oakes

See also **Middle Passage; Plantation System of the South; Triangular Trade;** *and vol. 9:* **Emancipation Proclamation; Running a Thousand Miles for Freedom; Sociology for the South; The Impending Crisis of the South: How to Meet It; A House Divided; Text of the Pro-Slavery Argument.**

SLEEPY HOLLOW lies about three-quarters of a mile north of Tarrytown, New York, and is famous for both its old Dutch church (1699) and for its association with the writings of Washington Irving. The area was named for a narrow ravine through which flows the Pocantico River. Sleepy Hollow is the site of Irving's tale of Ichabod Crane and the "headless horseman." Irving first visited the Sleepy Hollow region in his youth, and after his death, he was buried in the cemetery behind the Dutch church. Romantic memories of Sleepy Hollow recur in Irving's essays (for example, *Wolfert's Roost*) and attain their most complete and delightful expression in "The Legend of Sleepy Hollow," originally published in *The Sketch Book* in 1819.

BIBLIOGRAPHY

Antelyes, Peter. *Tales of Adventurous Enterprise: Washington Irving and the Poetics of Western Expansion.* New York: Columbia University Press, 1990.

Myers, Andrew B., ed. *The Knickerbocker Tradition: Washington Irving's New York.* Tarrytown, N.Y.: Sleepy Hollow Restorations, 1974.

Stanley T. Williams / H. S.

See also **Literature; New York State.**

SLIDELL'S MISSION TO MEXICO. John Slidell, a Democratic congressman from Louisiana, was sent to

Mexico by President James K. Polk in November 1845 to secure a boundary adjustment between the United States and Mexico. Polk authorized Slidell to offer Mexico up to $50 million for its vast northern territories. Unwilling to part with its territory, the Mexican government formally rejected Slidell's proposal in December 1845. Determined to take the territories one way or another, the Polk administration turned to a military option. After a two-year war, the United States won by force all the territory it had originally sought to purchase through Slidell's mission.

BIBLIOGRAPHY

Bauer, K. Jack. *The Mexican War, 1846–48.* Lincoln: University of Nebraska Press, 1992.

Pletcher, David M. *The Diplomacy of Annexation: Texas, Oregon and the Mexican War.* Columbia: University of Missouri Press, 1973.

Louis Martin Sears / A. G.

See also **Mexican-American War; Mexico City, Capture of; Mexico, Relations with; Westward Migration.**

SLUMS. *See* **Tenements.**

SMALL BUSINESS ADMINISTRATION.

The Small Business Administration (SBA) was founded in 1953 to assist small companies, particularly those serving military interests. It traces its roots to 1932, when President Herbert Hoover established the RECONSTRUCTION FINANCE CORPORATION to provide loans for small businesses during the GREAT DEPRESSION. Ten years later President Franklin D. Roosevelt created the Smaller War Plants Corporation to bolster the ability of small companies to secure military contracts during World War II. The corporation was disbanded in 1946 but reinstated as the Small Defense Plants Administration during the Korean War. President Dwight D. Eisenhower and Congress then consolidated the Small Defense Plants Administration and the Reconstruction Finance Corporation into the SBA, which also took on responsibilities of the Office of Small Business in the Department of Commerce.

The SBA's initial role called for keeping an inventory of businesses that could serve a military purpose in peacetime, providing disaster relief and offering loans and technical assistance. The SBA oversaw a lending program for veterans who wanted to start or expand small businesses. The Equal Opportunity Act of 1964 expanded the SBA's role. The 1964 Equal Opportunity Loan Program allowed applicants living below the poverty line who had sound business proposals to meet credit and collateral requirements. The SBA also began including programs to assist minority-owned businesses. Members of minority races, particularly immigrants, women of all races, individuals with disabilities, and veterans have usually had more difficulty securing loans and credit to further busi-

ness growth. In response to these problems and to growing pressure from advocates of civil rights, President Richard M. Nixon added a minority set-aside program known as the Philadelphia Plan, which allocated a share of federal procurement contracts for minority-owned small businesses.

Enterprises owned by women, the disabled, and Vietnam veterans benefited from SET-ASIDES that were designed to overcome past discrimination. But in 1989, in *City of Richmond v. J. A. Croson Company*, the SUPREME COURT struck down such a program and ruled that public officials would have to offer evidence of past discrimination to justify such policies. In 1995 the Court limited set-asides further when it concluded that the federal government must be subject to the same "strict scrutiny" as state and local governments when attempting to remedy discrimination. In *Adarand Constructors, Inc. v. Pena*, the Supreme Court rejected a federal set-aside program established in the Small Business Act to aid "socially disadvantaged individuals."

In the 1990s, the SBA assisted businesses specializing in high technology, environmental resources, and exports. Its constituency is made up of 21.5 million companies with fewer than five hundred employees, or 99 percent of all businesses in the United States, but directly serves only 1 percent of such businesses. Small businesses accounted for all of the job growth in the nation from 1987 to 1992 and are considered the engine for the national economy. Employing 54 percent of the workforce, they account for half the gross national product.

BIBLIOGRAPHY

Bates, Timothy Mason. *Financing Black Enterprise.* Madison: Institute for Research on Poverty, University of Wisconsin, 1972.

Bean, Jonathan J. *Beyond the Broker State: Federal Policies toward Small Business, 1936–1961.* Chapel Hill: University of North Carolina Press, 1996.

Butler, Stuart. *Enterprise Zones: Greenlining the Inner Cities.* New York: Universe Books, 1981.

Parris, Addison. *The Small Business Administration.* New York: F. A. Prager, 1968.

Erik Bruun / F. B.

See also **Affirmative Action; Business, Minority;** *Richmond v. J.A. Croson Company.*

SMALLPOX.

For most of recorded history, smallpox killed half of all children who died before age five. On 9 December 1979, the World Health Organization (WHO) certified that smallpox had been eradicated globally after a thirteen-year effort. Supposedly, only two remaining stocks of smallpox virus remained, for research purposes, at the Centers for Disease Control and Prevention in Atlanta and at the Ivanovsky Institute of Virology in Moscow. However, subsequent revelations about the Soviet biological warfare program, secretly advanced during the 1980s under Mikhail Gorbachev as a hedge against nuclear weapons reductions, raised the specter of smallpox's return as a means of terrorism and mass destruction.

Early History

Smallpox may have begun as a monkey or a camel pox virus that mutated to infect humans and then evolved into two species: Variola major, the great killer, and Variola minor, with a mortality of less than one percent. In the worst cases, the disease often began with a sneeze or cough beginning twelve to fourteen days after exposure. After an incubation period of twelve days, a high fever, a headache, and muscle pain appeared. From two to five days later a rash appeared, which turned into pustules. By the eighth or ninth day after onset, the pustules dried and crusted before falling off. For about 30 percent of those infected, death occurred, usually in seven to ten days after symptoms first appeared. Dust from the scabs, lingering in and around the sick bed, infected others who encountered it and were susceptible.

The oldest evidence of the disease dates from the mummified body of the Egyptian pharaoh Ramses V (d. 1156 B.C.), although smallpox surely existed for centuries before, from the time when enough people lived in close enough proximity to sustain its spread. The disease only passed from person to person. Human migrations, commerce, and wars spread epidemics, but it was the European colonization of the Americas, southern Africa, and Australia that destroyed the nonresistant native populations between the sixteenth and nineteenth centuries.

Perhaps more than any other single factor, smallpox accounted for the collapse of the Amerindian populations facing European expansion. As Governor John Winthrop of Massachusetts Bay wrote in 1634, "For the natives, they are neere all dead of the small Poxe, so the Lord hathe cleared our title to what we possess." Most of the Amerindian epidemics over the next 250 years probably arose from casual causes, but in 1763 Sir Jeffery Amherst, commanding British military forces in North America, proposed an intentional infection to quell Pontiac's Rebellion. Over time, from the Atlantic to the Pacific, and the Great Lakes to the Gulf, smallpox decimated the tribes, until those finally confined to reservations either acquired immunity and survived or perished like their ancestors.

Ancient observers in China and India knew that afflicted people who survived very rarely became infected again. With that, practices of variolation arose: the Chinese developed insufflation, where a person breathed scab particles; inoculation, or the insertion of a minute amount of virus-carrying pus under the skin, originated in India. Although variolations involved the Variola major virus, and probably caused epidemics from time to time, mortality was slight enough (usually less than 2 percent) to win proponents widely, in both East and West. Zabdiel Boylston's inoculation of 244 people in Boston, during a smallpox

War on Smallpox. A poster created for the Chicago Department of Health and dated 1941 urges parents to have their children vaccinated. LIBRARY OF CONGRESS

outbreak in 1721, was an early and well-documented success in British America.

Modern Eradication Efforts and Dangers

Three-quarters of a century after Boylston, Edward Jenner—an English variolator—realized the merit of a folk belief that farmers and milkmaids who had encountered a mild pox virus of cattle seldom contracted smallpox. He conducted experiments proving the point, and published his findings in 1798 as *An Inquiry into the Cause and Effects of the Variolae Vaccinae.* "Vaccination" and "vaccine" came from the Latin word for cow.

Whether or not Jenner had actually used cowpox virus or, as later authorities claimed, had accidentally applied an attenuated Variola, researchers discovered in 1939 that an altogether distinct virus, *vaccinia*, had mysteriously become the artificial immunizing agent against smallpox. By then, however, the combined effects of vaccination and widespread epidemics of Variola minor had knocked down smallpox incidence and mortality to very low levels. No smallpox deaths occurred in the United States from 1930 to 1943. Nearly fourteen hundred cases, with forty-five deaths, occurred between 1944 and 1949, but the United States remained smallpox-free after 1950.

In 1966, the World Health Organization began a global smallpox eradication project under the leadership of Donald A. Henderson of the U.S. Public Health Service. At the time, between ten million and fifteen million people outside Europe and North America contracted the disease annually. The campaign's strategy was not to vaccinate entire national populations, but to find every case of actual disease and vaccinate everyone in that immediate vicinity. Some 150,000 WHO workers gradually isolated "islands" of the disease and eliminated them. The last case from South America occurred in 1972, the last in Asia appeared in 1975, and the last in Africa happened in 1977. Ali Maow Maalin, a Somali, found on 26 October 1977, was the final person to have naturally occurring smallpox. A laboratory accident in 1978 killed two more people in England, but no further cases were reported. WHO's announcement in 1979 that global eradication had been achieved came as medicine's single greatest achievement—total victory over a human disease.

A dozen years passed between the proclaimed "end" of smallpox and serious reservations about that claim. In 1992, the former deputy chief of the Soviet Union's biological weapons program defected to the West and made startling assertions. Kanatjan Alibekov (later anglicized to Ken Alibek) told American defense officials that during the 1980s a massive stockpile of plague agents, including an annual reserve of twenty tons of liquid smallpox, had been produced and maintained, mainly at a Soviet laboratory in Koltsovo, Siberia. Moreover, by 1990 production facilities existed to manufacture up to one hundred tons of smallpox a year. Investigations after the Soviet Union's collapse were unable fully to confirm or deny Alibekov's details, or the possibility that former Soviet biological warfare scientists found subsequent secret work in several Middle Eastern countries. Yet because of the risk of smallpox's return via terrorism or biological warfare, the U.S. Centers for Disease Control and Prevention in 2001 awarded a contract to Wythe Laboratories, Inc., in Marietta, Pennsylvania to create forty million doses of *vaccinia* as an annual national vaccine reserve. Meanwhile, at the beginning of the twenty-first century the U.S. population remains about as immunologically vulnerable to smallpox as the Amerindians were in the seventeenth century.

BIBLIOGRAPHY

Alibek, Ken. *Biohazard: The Chilling True Story of the Largest Covert Biological Weapons Program in the World.* New York: Random House, 1999.

Crosby, Alfred. "Smallpox." In the *Cambridge World History of Human Disease.* Edited by Kenneth F. Kiple. Cambridge, U.K.: Cambridge University Press, 1994.

Fender, Frank, et al. *Smallpox and Its Eradication.* Geneva, Switzerland: World Health Organization, 1988.

Tucker, Jonathan B. *Scourge: The Once and Future Threat of Smallpox.* New York: Atlantic Monthly Press, 2001.

G. Terry Sharrer

See also **Centers for Disease Control; Public Health.**

SMELTERS. Smelting is a method of separating gold, silver, and other metals from their ores with fire and heat intense enough to melt the ores. A Spanish law of 22 August 1584 required a government smelter to be established in every mining district in the New World and required all miners to bring their gold and lead-silver to a government furnace. Ruins of crude smelters have been found in southern California. A dependence on Spanish and European knowledge of mining techniques continued in the United States throughout the nineteenth century.

In 1750 coal was first used as a fuel for smelting. Beginning in 1830, anthracite coal was used, and by 1860, smelters had nearly attained their present form. However, the era of improved metallurgical and chemical processes had scarcely begun. Colorado's gold sulfide ores defied recovery until a professor of chemistry, Nathaniel P. Hill, after conducting experiments at Swansea, Wales, and Freiberg, Germany, built the Boston and Colorado smelter at Blackhawk, Colorado, in 1867. Its successor was built at Argo (near Denver) in 1878 and managed by Richard Pearce. Pearce had collaborated with Hill on improving smelter design. The Argo facility began the smelting of copper ores in reverberatory furnaces, which radiate heat from the roof onto the treated material. A European-trained mining engineer was also responsible for the mining boom that created Leadville, Colorado. In 1877, August R. Meyer correctly determined that ores believed to be silver were in fact silver-lead carbonates. The new town was born and became a major source of silver and lead as well as a smelting center. Until 1900 the Argo smelter was the only one to smelt gold and silver ores into a crude mixture known as matte exclusively in reverberatories.

A major change in smelter design in the late 1800s was the introduction of much larger furnaces. The Blackhawk smelter had only one small calcining and one small reverberatory furnace. In 1888 Meyer Guggenheim, who had bought two mines at Leadville the year before, decided that he would make more profit if he smelted his own ores. Accordingly, he built the Philadelphia smelter at Pueblo, Colorado, with six great furnaces, each with a daily capacity of sixty tons of ore. In 1893 the largest smelters in the United States were at Denver, Pueblo, and Salt Lake City. The Washoe smelter of the Anaconda Copper Mining Company at Anaconda, Montana, had a smokestack 300 feet high with a thirty-foot inside diameter. Leading up the hillside to the base of this stack were 1,234 feet of flue 60 feet wide.

Toward the close of the nineteenth century, cutthroat competition between the smelters led to combination. On 4 April 1899 the American Smelting and Refining Company brought together eighteen of the country's largest smelting companies. In 1901 the firm of Meyer Guggenheim and his sons, the largest of the independents, joined the trust under terms that ensured them control of American Smelting.

BIBLIOGRAPHY

Fell, James E., Jr. *Ores to Metal: The Rocky Mountain Smelting Industry.* Lincoln: University of Nebraska Press, 1979.

Morrissey, Katherine. "Western Smelters and the Problem of Smelter Smoke." In *Northwest Lands, Northwest Peoples: Readings in Environmental History.* Seattle: University of Washington Press, 1999.

Spence, Clark C. *Mining Engineers and the American West.* New Haven, Conn.: Yale University Press, 1970.

Percy S. Fritz / F. B.

See also **Copper Industry; Gold Mines and Mining; Lead Industry; Mining Towns.**

SMITH V. OREGON EMPLOYMENT (*Employment Division, Department of Human Resources of Oregon et al. v. Smith et al.,* 494 U.S. 872, 1990).

Alfred Smith and Galen Black were fired from their jobs because they ingested the illegal hallucinogen peyote for sacramental purposes during a Native American religious ceremony. When the men applied for unemployment benefits, the Employment Division denied the benefits because they had been discharged for "misconduct." The Oregon Supreme Court held the denial violated the men's rights under the FIRST AMENDMENT, which protects the "free exercise" of religion.

In an opinion written by Justice Antonin Scalia, the U.S. Supreme Court reversed, holding that the free exercise clause permits states to prohibit sacramental peyote use and to deny unemployment benefits to persons discharged for such use. The Court reasoned that the clause does not excuse an individual from compliance with a neutral law not particularly aimed at religious conduct. The Court cited the 1879 case of *Reynolds v. United States,* which upheld the criminalization of polygamy, even as applied to individuals whose religion required it.

Four Justices (Harry Blackmun, W. J. Brennan, Jr., Thurgood Marshall, and Sandra Day O'Connor) disagreed, arguing that the opinion ignored precedent that required the government, unless it could show a compelling interest otherwise, to accommodate religiously motivated activities. *Smith* thus marked a shift in free exercise jurisprudence away from requiring government accommodation of religious activity toward an emphasis on formal governmental neutrality. As the Court admitted, this shift placed minority religions "at a relative disadvantage," because accommodation has to be won in the political process rather than through the courts.

Smith has been the focus of much criticism. The decision's most outspoken opponent on the Court is Justice David Souter, who joined the Court the year after *Smith.* Souter wrote a separate concurrence in the 1993 case of *Church of the Lukumi Babalu Aye v. City of Hialeah* to argue that *Smith* should be overturned.

BIBLIOGRAPHY

McConnell, Michael W. "Free Exercise Revisionism and the *Smith* Decision." *University of Chicago Law Review* 57 (1990): 1109–1153. McConnell is a leading critic of *Smith.*

Rotunda, Ronald D., and John E. Nowak. *Treatise on Constitutional Law: Substance and Procedure.* 3d ed. Volume 5. St. Paul, Minn.: West, 1999. Good overview of freedom of religion jurisprudence.

Kent Greenfield

See also **Indian Religious Life.**

SMITH ACT.

The Smith Act (1940) provided for the registration and fingerprinting of aliens living in the United States and declared it unlawful to advocate, teach, or belong to any group advocating the forceful overthrow of any government in the United States. The act was rarely used during World War II. In the years thereafter it emerged as the primary prosecutorial weapon in the campaign against domestic communists. In *Dennis v. United States* (1951), concerning the conviction of eleven communists under the act, the SUPREME COURT upheld the act's constitutionality. In 1957, however, in *Yates v. United States,* the Court held that the teaching or advocacy of the overthrow of the U.S. government that was not accompanied by any subversive action was constitutionally protected free speech not punishable under the Smith Act.

BIBLIOGRAPHY

Kelknap, Michal R. *Cold War Political Justice: The Smith Act, the Communist Party, and American Civil Liberties.* Westport, Conn.: Greenwood Press, 1977.

Schrecker, Ellen W. *No Ivory Tower: McCarthyism and the Universities.* New York: Oxford University Press, 1986.

Charles S. Campbell / A. R.

See also **Anticommunism; Enemy Aliens in the World Wars; First Amendment; Loyalty Oaths; Sedition Acts.**

SMITH-HUGHES ACT.

The Smith-Hughes Act (1917), a landmark in the advance of federal centralization as well as in vocational EDUCATION, created the Federal Board for Vocational Education for the promotion of training in AGRICULTURE, trades and industries, commerce, and home economics in the secondary schools. Funded by federal GRANTS-IN-AID to be matched by state or local contributions, the act required that state boards submit their plans for vocational education to the board for approval, thus providing for greater federal control than previous education grants. Supplementary acts have extended the original activities to vocational counseling and rehabilitation.

BIBLIOGRAPHY

Kantor, Harvey, and David B. Tyack, eds. *Work, Youth, and Schooling: Historical Perspectives on Vocationalism in American Education.* Stanford, Calif.: Stanford University Press, 1982.

Kett, Joseph F. *The Pursuit of Knowledge Under Difficulties: From Self-improvement to Adult Education in America, 1750–1990.* Stanford, Calif.: Stanford University Press, 1994.

Harvey Wish / A. R.

See also **Curriculum; Education, United States Office of.**

SMITH-LEVER ACT. The Smith-Lever Act (1914) provided for an elaborate system of agricultural extension work conducted through a field force of specialists with the assistance of federal GRANTS-IN-AID based on equal state contributions. Students not attending college received instructions and demonstration work in AGRICULTURE and home economics from county agents, thus enjoying indirectly the benefits of the agricultural colleges and experimental stations. Like other forms of grants-in-aid, the Smith-Lever Act provided for an element of federal control of local activities. This was the first time that federal standards were a factor in aid to EDUCATION.

BIBLIOGRAPHY

Kett, Joseph F. *The Pursuit of Knowledge Under Difficulties: From Self-improvement to Adult Education in America, 1750–1990.* Stanford, Calif.: Stanford University Press, 1994.

Scott, Roy Vernon. *The Reluctant Farmer: The Rise of Agricultural Extension to 1914.* Urbana: University of Illinois Press, 1971.

Harvey Wish / A. R.

See also **Farmers Institutes.**

SMITHSONIAN INSTITUTION, an establishment dedicated to research, education, and national service to science, the arts, and humanities. Headquartered in WASHINGTON, D.C., it was chartered by Congress in 1846 pursuant to the will of the Englishman James Smithson (1765–1829). In 1826, Smithson, who was the illegitimate son of Sir Hugh Smithson, Duke of Northumberland, and Elizabeth Keate Macie, descended from Henry VII, bequeathed his fortune, amounting to about $550,000 (a considerable sum for those days), to "the United States of America, to found at Washington, under the name of the Smithsonian Institution, an Establishment for the increase and diffusion of knowledge among men." Smithson's motivations for this unusual bequest are conjectural, but several influences may have been involved: disillusionment due to the circumstances of his birth, which, in Britain, barred him from certain privileges and inheri-

tances; his keen interest in science (he was an Oxford graduate, a competent chemist, and a member of the Royal Society); his faith in America, generated perhaps from his friendship with Americans traveling in Europe, although he himself never visited the United States; and perhaps the general revolutionary temper of the times, which impelled him to do something original for the benefit of humankind and make his name remembered long after, as he said, "the names of the Northumberlands and Percys are extinct and forgotten."

When, after much debate, Congress accepted the gift, there began a long argument as to what form the institution should take in order to conform most clearly with Smithson's broad prescription. The format that finally evolved and was enacted on 10 August 1846 was due in large part to John Quincy Adams, who was then back in Congress following his presidency and whose articulate championing of science and education was most effective.

The Smithsonian derives its support both from appropriations from Congress and from private endowments, of which Smithson's gift was the nucleus. It is considered an independent establishment in the role of a ward of the U.S. government, the trustee. It is governed by a board of regents made up of the vice-president and chief justice of the United States (ex officio) and three U.S. senators, three representatives, and six citizens named by Congress. The regents elect one of their number as chancellor and choose a secretary, who is the executive officer, or director, of the institution. Since its founding the Smithsonian has had eleven secretaries: Joseph Henry, professor and physicist at the College of New Jersey (now Princeton), noted for his research in electromagnetism, who served from 1846 until his death in 1878; Spencer Fullerton Baird, biologist, secretary from 1878 until his death in 1887; Samuel Pierpont Langley, astronomer and aviation pioneer, from 1887 to 1906; Charles Doolittle Walcott, from 1907 to 1927; Charles Greeley Abbot, astrophysicist, from 1928 to 1944; Alexander Wetmore, biologist, from 1945 to 1952; Leonard Carmichael, psychologist, from 1953 to 1964; S. Dillon Ripley, zoologist, from 1964 to 1984; Robert McCormick Adams from 1984 to 1994; Michael Heyman from 1994 to 1999; and Lawrence Small beginning in 2000.

Henry's original program for the Smithsonian and its plan of organization were based on his interpretation of how best to "increase" and "diffuse" knowledge in order "to carry out the design of the testator." To increase knowledge he proposed to "stimulate men of talent to make original researches, by offering rewards for memoirs containing new truths" and "to appropriate a portion of income for particular researches, under the direction of suitable persons." To diffuse knowledge it was proposed to "publish a series of periodical reports on the progress of different branches of knowledge" and "to publish occasionally separate treatises on subjects of general interest." These objectives have continued to guide the activities of the institution. But this simplicity of design did not last long, and the institution proliferated as Congress began assigning the institution jobs to do and "bureaus" to administer. In 1879, a large rambling structure adjoining the Smithsonian was begun to house exhibits for the National Museum, an outgrowth of the Centennial Exposition of 1876 at Philadelphia. Eventually, the National Museum came under the administration of the Smithsonian. Over the years, the Smithsonian has assembled under its wings yet more MUSEUMS, art galleries, and other branches, making it perhaps the largest museum and cultural complex in the world. The Smithsonian occupies several buildings flanking the Mall between Fifth and Fourteenth streets and other buildings in several other parts of the city and in a number of places outside Washington, including New York City; Cambridge, Massachusetts; and Panama.

The Smithsonian includes sixteen museums. Nine of these are located on the National Mall. They are: the Smithsonian Institution Building, known as the Castle; the Arthur M. Sackler Gallery and the Freer Gallery of Art, both dedicated to Asian art; the Arts and Industries Building; the Hirshhorn Museum and Sculpture Garden; the National Air and Space Museum; the National Museum of African Art; the National Museum of American History; and the National Museum of Natural History, the oldest of the Smithsonian's branches. The National Portrait Gallery and the Smithsonian American Art Museum have, since 1968, occupied the Old Patent Office Building. The Anacostia Museum and Center for African American History and Culture, the National Zoological Park, the National Postal Museum, and the Renwick Gallery of the Smithsonian American Art Museum are located elsewhere in Washington, D.C. The Cooper Hewitt National Design Museum and the National Museum of the American Indian are located in New York City. A National Museum of the American Indian in Washington, D.C., is due to open on the Mall in the early twenty-first century. The Smithsonian also oversees eight research centers: the Archives of American Art, the Center for Folklife and Cultural Heritage, the Conservation and Research Center, the Smithsonian Astrophysical Observatory, the Center for Materials Research and Education, the Smithsonian Environmental Research Center, the Smithsonian Marine Station at Fort Pierce, and the Smithsonian Tropical Research Institute. The International Exchange Service was initiated in 1850 by Baird and Henry to facilitate the international exchange of scientific and other scholarly publications. There are also three agencies technically under the aegis of the Smithsonian but administered by separate boards of trustees: the National Gallery of Art (established 1941), the John F. Kennedy Center for the Performing Arts (opened 1971), and the Woodrow Wilson International Center for Scholars (1968).

The Smithsonian museums, embracing all fields of science, technology, and the arts, are famous for their many unique objects on display. In addition to such show-

pieces as Charles Lindbergh's *Spirit of St. Louis*, the First Ladies' inaugural ball gowns, the Hope Diamond, Benjamin Franklin's printing press, the original "star-spangled banner," and the giant model of the blue whale, the dozens of exhibit halls throughout the museums display much of humanity's knowledge of the earth and human civilization and culture. There are also vast study collections, numbering in the millions of objects and specimens, that form the basis of the research conducted not only by the large staff of Smithsonian scientists but also by students and researchers in history, technology, and the physical and natural sciences. The institution is equally famous for its worldwide exploration programs, which were initiated by Henry and Baird.

The first Smithsonian publication, *Ancient Monuments of the Mississippi Valley*, was issued in 1848, and since that time there have appeared under the Smithsonian imprint (now called the Smithsonian Press) thousands of books, pamphlets, catalogs, bulletins, and periodicals in all branches of science, art, and technology. Most of them are scholarly publications, but a few are popular in nature. Smithsonian publications—some financed by government funds and some by the institution's private funds—are widely distributed to libraries, research institutions, and students. Since 1970, in conjunction with a subsidiary organization, the Smithsonian Associates, the institution has published a popular magazine, *Smithsonian*.

Since the early 1960s, the Smithsonian has expanded its activities, particularly in the field of public education, in an effort to identify the institution more closely with the academic world and with modern educational and research trends. Each of the museums and research centers now includes an Education Department, and, through a program dubbed Smithsonian Affiliates, the Smithsonian has arranged cooperative agreements with museums across the country. Smithsonian Productions creates and manages electronic media for the institution, and ongoing programs of lectures, films, workshops, tours, demonstrations, and performances allow daily access to the "nation's attic."

BIBLIOGRAPHY

Bello, Mark. *The Smithsonian Institution, a World of Discovery: An Exploration of Behind-the-Scenes Research in the Arts, Sciences, and Humanities.* Washington, D.C.: Smithsonian Institution Press, 1993.

Goode, G. Brown, ed. *The Smithsonian Institution, 1846–1896. The History of Its First Half Century.* Washington, D.C., 1897; New York: Arno Press, 1980.

Oehser, Paul Henry. *Sons of Science: The Story of the Smithsonian Institution and Its Leaders.* New York: H. Schuman, 1949.

———. *The Smithsonian Institution.* Boulder, Colo.: Westview Press, 1983.

Paul H. Oehser / F. B.

See also **American Association for the Advancement of Science; Archives; Federal Agencies; Foundations, Endowed; Observatories, Astronomical; Science Museums.**

SMOG. *See* **Air Pollution.**

SMOKE-FILLED ROOM. During the 1920 Republican National Convention a small group of party leaders gathered in a private hotel room to select the Republican presidential nominee. After hours of bargaining and cigar smoking, the group agreed upon Warren Harding as a compromise candidate. A reporter described the selection as being done in a smoke-filled room. Popular distaste with a nomination process that featured too much influence from party leaders and professional politicos sparked reforms leading to the electoral primary system. Nevertheless, the phrase lingers in America's political jargon and metaphorically describes a decision-making process whereby power brokers make deals while hidden from public scrutiny.

BIBLIOGRAPHY

Downes, Randolph C. *The Rise of Warren Gamaliel Harding, 1865–1920.* Columbus: Ohio State University Press, 1970.

Pomper, Gerald. *Nominating the President: The Politics of Convention Choice.* Evanston, Ill.: Northwestern University Press, 1963.

Michael B. Henderson

See also **Elections, Presidential: 1920; Primary, Direct; Republican Party.**

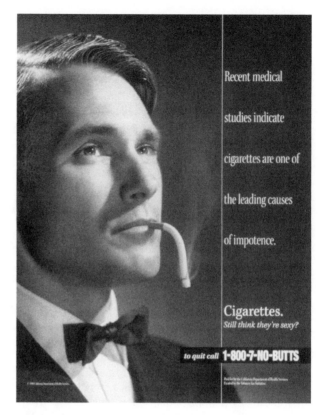

Anti-Smoking Ad. Smoking is creatively cited here as one of the leading causes of impotence, among many other medical problems. CALIFORNIA DEPARTMENT OF HEALTH SERVICES

SMOKING. Tobacco, as it is most often smoked today, is largely derived from the *Nicotiana tabacum* plant, a broad-leafed herb native to the Americas and a member of the nightshade family, to which potatoes and sweet peppers also belong. The indigenous peoples of the Americas used the plant in many different kinds of religious and medical rituals, though no one knows what kinds of health hazards may have been recognized. A Mayan pottery vessel from about the ninth century A.D. shows a man smoking a roll of tobacco leaves tied with a string; Columbus found natives puffing away on tobacco pipes when he arrived in the West Indies in the fifteenth century. Tobacco later became an important staple in the American export economy, with many Southern slave states earning much of their income from tobacco sales and exports.

Pipes, snuff, and chewing tobacco were the most common forms of ingestion prior to the twentieth century. Cigarette smoking did not become popular until the end of the nineteenth century, following the invention of the Bonsack rolling machine in 1884 and flue curing, which gave a milder taste to tobacco smoke, making it easier to inhale. Cigarette smoking was also promoted by the development of mass tobacco advertising and the encouragement of national governments, which recognized tobacco as an easy source of tax revenues. Cigarettes were included with the rations of soldiers fighting in World War I; hundreds of thousands of men returned from com-

bat hooked on the new and fashionable drug. The net effect was a spectacular rise in smoking in the first six decades of the twentieth century. So whereas Americans in 1900 smoked only about fifty cigarettes per adult per year; this would grow by a factor of about eighty over the next sixty years. U.S. smoking rates peaked in 1964, when men and women were smoking an average of 4,300 cigarettes per person per year. Some people smoked more than 20,000 cigarettes per year.

Between 1893 and 1927, fifteen American states banned the sale of cigarettes. Anti-tobacco sentiments were often linked to campaigns to prohibit the sale of alcohol, and although both movements stressed the "moral dangers" accompanying such indulgences, health concerns were also beginning to come into play. Tobacco had been shown to be a health threat in the eighteenth century, when cancers of the nasal passages and lips were linked to smoking. In the nineteenth century, French scientists found that the overwhelming majority of people suffering from cancer of the mouth were pipe smokers. German scholars in the 1920s and 1930s established the lung cancer link, and by the 1950s in both Europe and America, a broad medical consensus had been established that cigarettes were responsible for many serious ailments, including cancer and heart attacks. Many national governments were slow to admit the hazard, however, having become dependent on tobacco taxation as a source of national income. Germany in the 1930s, for example, earned nearly one-twelfth of its total revenue from tobacco taxes, and England in the 1950s earned about 14 percent of its tax revenue from tobacco.

In 1964, the United States Surgeon General's *Report on Smoking* declared cigarettes a major source of health hazards, prompting a decline in U.S. cigarette consumption. By 1994 only about one in four Americans over the age of sixteen was a smoker, and per capita consumption had declined as well—to about 2,500 cigarettes per adult per year. Warning labels had been put on tobacco packaging in the 1960s, though tobacco companies had managed to soften the blow somewhat by camouflaging the labels. New forms of advertising were also sought to compensate for the 1970 ban on television advertising. Tobacco companies became major sponsors of many sporting events (such as race-car driving and tennis) and began to pay actors to smoke in Hollywood movies. Brown and Williamson, for example, in 1983 agreed to pay Sylvester Stallone $500,000 to use that company's tobacco products in each of his next five films.

Tobacco companies won all of the lawsuits filed against them in the 1960s, '70s, and '80s, arguing either that smoking had not been proven hazardous or that smokers themselves were to blame for their illnesses. Tobacco companies spent hundreds of millions of dollars challenging the medical link between smoking and disease. Front organizations such as the Council for Tobacco Research and the Tobacco Institute were established in the 1950s to "balance" the anti-smoking message with "no evidence of harm" propaganda. The industry abruptly changed its legal strategy in the 1990s, however, by conceding that the dangers of smoking had been well known for many decades. Companies began to hire historians to argue that smokers made an informed choice when they decided to take up smoking, and that blame for whatever risks this may have entailed must reside with the smoker.

Tobacco ads were banned on American television in 1970. The U.S. Congress banned smoking on airline flights of less than two hours in 1988, and in 1990 this was extended to all domestic flights. Anti-smoking policies were strengthened in the 1990s. Lawsuits were filed against manufacturers by states seeking to recover medical costs from smoking, and in 1998 the attorneys general of forty-six states agreed to accept a settlement of $206 billion from the five major tobacco companies to offset the public-health costs of smoking. Critics have charged that the increased costs can simply be passed on to consumers and that the settlement, to be paid out over twenty-five years, amounts to only about thirty or forty cents per pack in any event. The U.S. tobacco industry has also responded by shifting the focus of its sales overseas. Today the U.S. market is a shrinking component of U.S. tobacco sales, and more than one-third of the cigarettes manufactured in this country are now being smoked abroad. Philip Morris now sells three cigarettes abroad for every one sold in the United States.

Smoking today is generally regarded as the cause of a global cancer epidemic. While smoking still kills about half a million Americans every year—mainly from heart attacks and cancer—the figure is much higher in places like China, which has become the world's leading consumer of tobacco products. Lung cancer was an extremely rare disease at the beginning of the twentieth century, with only 142 cases recorded in the medical literature worldwide. By the end of the century it was the world's most common cause of cancer death. The World Health Organization has estimated that China is soon going to have a million lung cancer fatalities every year, the majority of these being caused by smoking. The number of Americans dying from lung cancer began to decline in the 1990s as a result of many people quitting, though teen smoking rates actually rose for most of that decade.

Smoking is growing rapidly worldwide, which is why we can expect the global lung cancer epidemic to continue. Global cigarette production in the year 2000 was more than 5.5 trillion cigarettes per annum, and growing. Since one lung cancer death is generated for every 2 to 4 million cigarettes smoked in any given society, we can expect more than 2 million lung cancer deaths per year, worldwide, in the not-too-distant future. Total deaths from other kinds of cigarette-related illnesses (and fires) will of course be greater than this, approaching 10 million per year by the 2020s according to World Health Organization estimates. Cigarettes must already have caused more than 100 million deaths since their invention, and the twenty-first-century toll could be as high as one billion. Anthropologists estimate that approximately 80 billion people have lived since the evolution of *Homo sapiens*, which means that by the end of the twenty-first century cigarettes may have killed more than 1 percent of everyone who has ever lived.

BIBLIOGRAPHY

Kluger, Richard. *Ashes to Ashes: America's Hundred-Year Cigarette War, the Public Health, and the Unabashed Triumph of Philip Morris.* New York: Knopf, 1996.

Parker-Pope, Tara. *Cigarettes: Anatomy of an Industry from Seed to Smoke.* New York: New Press, 2001.

Proctor, Robert N. *Cancer Wars: How Politics Shapes What We Know and Don't Know about Cancer.* New York: Basic Books, 1995.

Robert N. Proctor

See also **Cancer; Tobacco Industry.**

SMUGGLING, COLONIAL. A vital segment of colonial trade, smuggling developed in response to the strict mercantilist policies of England in the seventeenth century. In an attempt to enhance colonial profitability and exert greater control, England passed a series of Nav-

IGATION ACTS that fostered illicit trade and heightened tensions with the colonies.

The earliest Navigation Acts were passed in 1651, and expanded in 1660 and again in 1662, 1663, and 1673. Designed to control Dutch maritime trade, these acts were only loosely enforced, leaving room for colonial merchants to circumvent the laws. With little to hinder their activities, colonial merchants traded illegally in goods enumerated in the Navigation Acts and in the Corn and Manufacturing laws passed in the 1660s. Though the bulk of colonial trade was legal, colonists imported and exported tobacco, sugar, cotton, and wool at will. Had the laws governing trade in enumerated goods been strictly enforced, the economic impact on the colonies might have been disastrous; they engaged in a flourishing trade in many of the goods with other European countries, trade forbidden under the terms of the laws.

Illicit trade between the colonists and European nations did not escape the attention of London merchants, who informed the Lords of Trade in 1676 that their businesses were failing as a result. They warned that the Crown would suffer dramatic losses in customs revenues, losses they estimated at £60,000 per year. When pressed for information by the Lords, colonial merchants admitted they were able to import goods from Europe at a cost twenty percent less than those goods imported from England. Smuggling was profitable indeed, they confirmed.

By 1677, colonial customs agent Edward Randolph estimated that smuggling was costing the Crown over £100,000 per year in lost revenue. By 1684, the Lords of Trade convinced the court to revoke the Massachusetts charter and form the royally governed Dominion of New England, an action justified in part by the intentional violations of the navigation acts.

The MOLASSES ACT of 1733, arguably the harshest of England's laws governing colonial trade, provoked a marked increase in smuggling. The act placed prohibitive duties on molasses and sugar shipped to the colonies from the Dutch, Spanish, and French West Indies. Often bribing customs officials to avoid paying duties, colonial merchants smuggled in large quantities of molasses, used primarily in rum production—an integral product in the so-called triangle trade. The Board of Trade received proof of the breach of the Molasses Act and other trade laws from a variety of sources, but it remained extremely difficult for that body to curb violations. There is evidence to suggest that Rhode Island merchants imported five-sixths of their molasses illegally from the Dutch, French, and Spanish West Indies.

Over the course of the eighteenth century, the Crown passed more trade regulations intended to increase revenue from the colonies and restrict their financial autonomy. These acts, including the Revenue (Sugar) Act of 1764, the TOWNSHEND ACTS of 1767, and the Tea Act of 1773, provoked greater smuggling. In response, England turned increasingly to military strategy to combat the il-

legal trade. Tensions escalated and within three years, the opening shots of the Revolutionary War were fired.

BIBLIOGRAPHY

Bailyn, Bernard. *The New England Merchants in the Seventeenth Century.* Cambridge, Mass.: Harvard University Press, second printing, 1979.

Dickerson, Oliver Morton. *American Colonial Government, 1696–1765.* New York: Russell & Russell, 1962.

Kammen, Michael. *Empire and Interest: The American Colonies and the Politics of Mercantilism.* Philadelphia, New York, and Toronto: J. B. Lippincott, 1970.

Leslie J. Lindenauer

See also **Lords of Trade and Plantation; Sugar Acts; Triangular Trade.**

SMUGGLING OF SLAVES.

The importation of slaves into the United States was not made illegal until 1808, because of a constitutional provision that forbade congressional interference with the SLAVE TRADE until that year. By then, however, most of the states had already passed laws prohibiting the trade. Subsequent federal laws included the act of 20 April 1818, which provided for fines, imprisonment, and forfeiture of the vessel used for slave trading, and the act of 15 May 1820, which defined slave trading as piracy and provided for the death penalty for anyone convicted of engaging in it. Although the federal government authorized cruisers and revenue cutters to capture slave traders, their efforts were largely unsuccessful because U.S. naval forces of the time were insufficient to patrol American and African coastal waters adequately. Federal courts were directed to try offenders, but juries, especially in the South, were often reluctant to convict smugglers. These national measures generally emphasized the punishment of smugglers rather than the prevention of smuggling.

In the absence of effective enforcement, the traffic became a very profitable business, supported by northern capital and dovetailing with the domestic slave trade in the South. Illicit cargoes of enslaved African men and women were either infiltrated into the South through secluded rivers and inlets or boldly unloaded at ports of entry where public apathy or the connivance of local authorities permitted the business. Between 1808 and 1860, more than 250,000 slaves were thus imported. The human cargoes of captured SLAVE SHIPS were occasionally returned to be colonized in Sierra Leone or Liberia. More frequently, however, they were sold at auction in the southern slave market to cover the costs of capture and prosecution, thus paradoxically defeating the original purpose of the laws. Sometimes the seized slaves were turned over to the state governor's agents, who committed them under bond to a planter, often the one from whom they had been captured, who thereupon simply forfeited the normal bond and retained the slaves.

International cooperation to suppress the slave traffic was generally ignored or rejected by the United States until 1842, although the Treaty of Ghent (1815) contained a statement condemning the trade. In the WEBSTER-ASHBURTON TREATY of 1842, the United States agreed to send a squadron with eighty guns to the African coast, but subsequently failed to provide its full quota. More effective was the belated Anglo-American treaty of 7 June 1862, which granted a limited mutual right to search merchant vessels for smuggled slaves and which established three international courts (at Sierra Leone, Cape of Good Hope, and New York) to try the smugglers. The boundaries of the territory in which the mutual right of search existed were greatly extended by another treaty between the United States and Great Britain, signed on 17 February 1863. By 1864, slave trading had come to almost a complete halt as a result of the Union blockade during the Civil War. Finally, in 1865, the Thirteenth Amendment, which abolished domestic SLAVERY, gave the final blow to the slave trade.

BIBLIOGRAPHY

Du Bois, W. E. B. *The Suppression of the African Slave Trade to the United States of America, 1638–1870.* New York: Longmans, Green, 1896.

Noonan, John T. *The Antelope: The Ordeal of the Recaptured Africans in the Administrations of James Monroe and John Quincy Adams.* Berkeley: University of California Press, 1977.

Martin P. Claussen / A. R.

See also *Antelope* Case; Antislavery; Middle Passage; South, the: The Antebellum South.

SNAKE RIVER, formerly the Lewis, a 1,038-mile stream that rises in Shoshone Lake in Yellowstone National Park in Wyoming, forms part of the Idaho-Oregon and the Idaho-Washington boundaries, and cuts across southeast Washington to empty into the Columbia River. Meriwether Lewis and William Clark followed the Snake from the Clearwater River in Idaho to the Columbia in 1805. The Rocky Mountain Fur Company and the HUDSON'S BAY COMPANY battled each other in the fur-trapping business up and down the stream through the early nineteenth century. The OREGON TRAIL paralleled the river closely for some four hundred miles. In the twentieth century, numerous irrigation canals and hydroelectric power projects were established along the Snake.

BIBLIOGRAPHY

Palmer, Tim. *The Snake River: Window to the West.* Washington, D.C.: Island Press, 1991.

Alvin F. Harlow / F. B.

See also Lewis and Clark Expedition.

SNAKES. See Herpetology.

SNELLING, FORT, now Minneapolis, Minnesota, established at the junction of the Mississippi and Minnesota Rivers in 1819 by Col. Henry Leavenworth as part of a general plan of frontier defense. First called Fort Saint Anthony, in 1825 its name was changed in honor of its commandant Col. Josiah Snelling. The fort's commanders mediated between the Dakotas and Ojibwes (St. Peter's agency that was near the fort did this) and protected the headquarters of the AMERICAN FUR COMPANY. Never tested in battle, Fort Snelling lost much of its importance when other northwestern forts were established. It was made a National Historic Landmark in 1960. A museum and state park now surrounds the fort's Round Tower, the oldest structure still standing in the state.

BIBLIOGRAPHY

Hansen, Marcus L. *Old Fort Snelling.* Iowa City: State Historical Society of Iowa, 1918.

T. C. Blegen / A. R.

See also **Dakota Expeditions of Sibley and Sully; Minneapolis–St. Paul; Mississippi River; Sioux Uprising in Minnesota.**

SOAP AND DETERGENT INDUSTRY. Traditionally, soap has been manufactured from alkali (lye) and animal fats (tallow), although vegetable products such as palm oil and coconut oil can be substituted for tallow. American colonists had both major ingredients of soap in abundance, and so soap making began in America during the earliest colonial days. Tallow came as a by-product of slaughtering animals for meat, or from whaling. Farmers produced alkali as a by-product of clearing their land; until the nineteenth century wood ashes served as the major source of lye. The soap manufacturing process was simple, and most farmers could thus make their own soap at home.

The major uses for soap were in the household, for washing clothes and for toilet soap, and in textile manufacturing, particularly for fulling, cleansing, and scouring woolen stuffs. Because colonial America was rural, soap making remained widely dispersed, and no large producers emerged. By the eve of the American Revolution, however, the colonies had developed a minor export market; in 1770 they sent more than 86,000 pounds of soap worth £2,165 to the West Indies. The Revolution interrupted this trade, and it never recovered.

The growth of cities and the textile industry in the early nineteenth century increased soap usage and stimulated the rise of soap-making firms. By 1840, Cincinnati, then the largest meatpacking center in the United States, had become the leading soap-making city as well. The city boasted at least seventeen soap factories, including PROCTER AND GAMBLE (established 1837), which was destined to become the nation's dominant firm. A major change in soap making occurred in the 1840s when manufacturers began to replace lye made from wood ashes with soda ash, a lye made through a chemical process. Almost all soap makers also produced tallow candles, which for many was their major business. The firms made soap in enormous slabs, and these were sold to grocers, who sliced the product like cheese for individual consumers. There were no brands, no advertising was directed at consumers, and most soap factories remained small before the Civil War.

The period between the end of the Civil War and 1900 brought major changes to the soap industry. The market for candles diminished sharply, and soap makers discontinued that business. At the same time, competition rose. Many soap makers began to brand their products and to introduce new varieties of toilet soap made with such exotic ingredients as palm oil and coconut oil. Advertising, at first modest but constantly increasing, became the major innovation. In 1893 Procter and Gamble spent $125,000 to promote Ivory soap, and by 1905 the sales budget for that product alone exceeded $400,000. Advertising proved amazingly effective. In 1900 soap makers concentrated their advertising in newspapers but also advertised in streetcars and trains. Quick to recognize the communications revolution, the soap industry pioneered in radio advertising, particularly by developing daytime serial dramas. Procter and Gamble originated *Ma Perkins*, one of the earliest, most successful, and most long-lived of the genre that came to be known as SOAP OPERAS, to advertise its Oxydol soap in 1933. By 1962 major soap firms spent approximately $250 million per year for advertising, of which 90 percent was television advertising. In 1966, three out of the top five television advertisers were soap makers, and Procter and Gamble was television's biggest sponsor, spending $161 million.

Advertising put large soap makers at a competitive advantage, and by the late 1920s three firms had come to dominate the industry: (1) Colgate-Palmolive-Peet, incorporated as such in 1928 in New York State, although originally founded by William Colgate in 1807; (2) Lever Brothers, an English company that developed a full line of heavily advertised soaps in the nineteenth century and in 1897 and 1899 purchased factories in Boston and Philadelphia; and (3) Procter and Gamble.

Synthetic detergent, which was not a soap, but was made through a chemical synthesis that substituted fatty alcohols for animal fats, had been developed in Germany during World War I to alleviate a tallow shortage. Detergents are superior to soap in certain industrial processes, such as the making of textile finishes. They work better in hard water, and they eliminate the soap curd responsible for "bathtub rings." In 1933 Procter and Gamble introduced a pioneer detergent, Dreft, which targeted the dishwashing market because it was too light for laundering clothes. It succeeded, especially in hard-water regions, until WORLD WAR II interrupted detergent marketing.

In 1940 the "big three" —Colgate, Lever, and Procter and Gamble—controlled about 75 percent of the soap and detergent market. They produced a wide variety of products, such as shampoos, dishwashing detergents, liquid cleaners, and toilet soap, but the most important part of their business was heavy-duty laundry soap, which accounted for about two-thirds of sales. Procter and Gamble had about 34 percent of the market. Lever was a close second with 30 percent, and Colgate trailed with 11 percent. In 1946 Procter and Gamble radically shifted the balance in its favor when it introduced Tide, the first heavy-duty laundry detergent. By 1949, Tide had captured 25 percent of the laundry-detergent market. By 1956, even though Lever and Colgate had developed detergents of their own, Procter and Gamble held 57 percent of the market, as compared with 17 percent for Lever and 11 percent for Colgate. Despite Procter and Gamble's triumph, the big three still competed fiercely.

By 1972, detergents had almost eliminated soap from the laundry market, although toilet soap remained unchallenged by detergents. In the 1970s, bans on detergents by some local governments, which feared contamination of their water supplies, had little impact on the composition or sales of laundry products. In the early 2000s, the smaller firms within the industry still produced a multitude of specialized cleansers for home and industry, although in the highly important fields of toilet soaps, laundry soaps, and detergents, the big three remained dominant, controlling about 80 percent of the total market.

BIBLIOGRAPHY

Claw, Spencer. "The Soap Wars: A Strategic Analysis." *Fortune* 67 (1963).

Lief, Alfred. *"It Floats": The Story of Procter and Gamble*. New York: Rinehart, 1958.

Swasy, Alecia. *Soap Opera: The Inside Story of Procter and Gamble*. New York: Times Books, 1993.

Wilson, Charles. *The History of Unilever: A Study in Economic Growth and Social Change*. 3 vols. New York: Praeger, 1968. The original edition was published in 2 vols., London: Cassell, 1954.

Stephen Salsbury/c. w.

See also **Advertising; Chemical Industry; Hide and Tallow Trade; Manufacturing, Household; Textiles; Whaling.**

SOAP OPERAS are serialized dramas that were presented, usually daily, first on radio and then on television. The name was derived from the fact that manufacturers of soaps and other household products, most notably Procter and Gamble, were frequent sponsors of these programs. The soap opera is broadcasting's unique contribution to Western storytelling art. Although serialized stories had existed prior to the soap opera in printed fiction, comic strips, and movies, none of these forms exhibited the durability of the soap opera. *The Guiding Light*, for example, started on radio in 1937 and moved to television in 1952. Still airing original episodes in 2002 after nearly seventy years, *The Guiding Light* is the longest story ever told in human history.

Soap Operas in Primetime. Primarily a daytime genre, weekly soaps became a hit in primetime with the premier of *Dallas* in 1978 and *Dynasty* in 1981. Shown here are four members of the cast of *Dynasty* in 1985 *(clockwise from left):* John Forsythe, Rock Hudson, Ali McGraw, and Linda Evans.
© AP/WIDE WORLD PHOTOS

Credit for the first soap opera usually goes to Irna Phillips, who created *Painted Dreams* for WGN radio in Chicago in 1930. The first national soap was *Betty and Bob*, created by Frank and Anne Hummert for NBC radio in 1932. Both Phillips and the Hummerts provided a wide variety of soaps for network radio over the next several years; only Phillips, however, would make the transition to television. After many decades, the Phillips-created serials *As the World Turns, The Guiding Light,* and *Days of Our Lives* were still on the air.

Although broadcasting was an industry dominated by men for most of its early history, the soap opera was designed for women and women were frequently employed to create, produce, and write them. Besides Irna Phillips and Anne Hummert, other prolific soap opera artists included Elaine Carrington (*Pepper Young's Family, Red Adams*); Agnes Nixon (*All My Children, One Life to Live*); and Lee Phillip Bell (with her husband, William Bell, *The Young and the Restless* and *The Bold and the Beautiful*). As gender roles changed significantly in the latter half of the twentieth century, the principal audience for soap operas—women who were at home during the day—began to diminish. In the 1970s, many soap operas were rede-

signed to attract younger viewers and college students. By the 1980s, soap operas like *General Hospital* were achieving high ratings among these younger viewers as well as among men. While early soap stories focused almost exclusively on romance and domestic home life, from the mid-1970s soaps often borrowed from other genres, integrating glamorous on-location settings and even elements of science fiction. The soap operas of Agnes Nixon became known in the 1970s and 1980s for their frank depiction of social issues in stories about rape, abortion, infertility, depression, child abuse, AIDS, and a variety of other controversial topics.

The problematic future of the genre became clear in the 1980s with the introduction of the daytime talk and audience participation shows. A soap opera is expensive and labor intensive to produce, requiring a very large cast and a production schedule that runs five days a week, fifty-two weeks a year. The daytime talk show is, by contrast, simple, inexpensive, and amenable to reruns. While the daytime talk show virtually knocked the game show out of the morning and afternoon network schedules, about a dozen soap operas remained on the air. Several long-running soaps have ceased production since 1980, however, and competition from cable has brought overall ratings of the genre down considerably.

The first soap opera on network television, *Faraway Hill*, ran on the Dumont network in 1946 as an evening series. As had been the case in radio, however, the TV soap quickly settled into the daytime schedule. It was not until ABC introduced *Peyton Place* in 1964 that a serious attempt to return the soap to prime time was launched. Like a daytime soap, *Peyton Place* ran multiple episodes per week (up to three); had a huge cast of over one hundred; and did not broadcast reruns, even during the summer. Despite the commercial success of the series, however, the idea was not imitated again for years. In 1978, *Dallas* (CBS, 1978–1991) ushered in the era of the prime-time soap opera. *Dallas* employed multiple ongoing story lines and end-of-episode cliffhangers and, within a few years, became the most-watched series on TV. More prime-time soap operas were introduced over the next few years, including *Knots Landing* (CBS, 1979–1993), *Dynasty* (ABC, 1981–1989), and *Falcon Crest* (CBS, 1981–1990). Although the prime-time soap had begun to wane by the 1990s, its influence was felt in nearly all genres of fictional television series. Before the advent of the prime-time soap, most series episodes were totally self-contained, with little or no reference to events that had happened in previous episodes. Since then, most series have employed some continuing elements from episode to episode.

The soap opera has also become a significant presence on cable. In 2000, Disney/ABC introduced SoapNet, a channel devoted to reruns of daytime and prime-time serials, and another soap channel was expected from Columbia TriStar Television. The Spanish-language networks Univision and Telemundo offer imported soap operas, telenovelas, which play to very large audiences. Even

MTV, the youth-oriented cable channel, introduced its own soap opera, *Undressed*, in 1999.

BIBLIOGRAPHY

Allen, Robert C. *Speaking of Soap Operas.* Chapel Hill: University of North Carolina Press, 1985.

Stedman, Raymond William. *The Serials: Suspense and Drama by Installment.* 2d ed. Norman: University of Oklahoma Press, 1977.

Worlds without End: The Art and History of the Soap Opera. New York: Abrams, 1997.

Robert Thompson

See also **Radio; Television: Programming and Influence.**

SOCCER. Despite its organized origins at East Coast universities in the 1860s, soccer—"football" in its birthplace, Britain—has never truly flourished in the United States. Crowded out of the national sports culture by the "American" sports of football, baseball, and basketball, soccer has also suffered from a succession of failed domestic leagues. Between 1930 and 1950, and again in the 1990s, the U.S. national team had some success in soccer's premier tournament, the World Cup. However, since the 1970s, women's soccer has been more important than the men's game in the United States.

Although Americans often think of soccer as a "foreign" sport, its American roots extend back to 1869, when the first organized soccer match in the United States was played between Rutgers and Princeton universities. In 1884 the American Amateur Football Association was formed, the first such organization outside Britain. Ten years later the United States became the second country in the world to introduce professional soccer. However, these impressive statistics disguise serious early difficulties that determined soccer's marginal role in American sports history. In the 1870s Harvard University opted for a rugby-style "handling game" over the "kicking game." As other universities followed Harvard's example, the handling game developed into the native form of football, at the direct expense of the game Americans (in a telling example of sporting exceptionalism) would call "soccer."

In the late nineteenth century soccer also had to compete with baseball. Although baseball derived from Britain's cricket and rounders, boosters utilized the Abner Doubleday myth to promote baseball as a native-born sport, nothing less than the "national pastime." As the ideology of American nativism accelerated during the 1890s, immigrants realized that playing and watching baseball was an ideal opportunity to demonstrate their allegiance to the United States. By contrast, soccer was viewed as un-American: ominously, the first professional soccer league of 1894 disbanded within months amid controversy over the importation of British players.

In 1921 the American Soccer League (ASL) was formed. The ASL benefited from the economic affluence

Soccer. Stars such as Mia Hamm have inspired girls all over the country to take up soccer. ALLSPORT PHOTOGRAPHY (USA) INC.

and increased leisure time that precipitated a general boom in organized sport during the Roaring Twenties. Crowds at ASL matches regularly outstripped those at games in the nascent National Football League. However, organizational ineptitude, a lack of native talent, and the Wall Street crash of 1929 all contributed to the ASL's demise in 1931. Andrei S. Markovits and Steven L. Hellerman have argued that, as in other industrial capitalist nations, American "sport space" was established and cemented between 1870 and 1930, and that the failure of the ASL sealed American soccer's long-term fate. The game would never attract the blue-collar base of players and fans that powered the "Big Three," baseball, football, and basketball.

Despite these domestic tribulations, in 1930 the national team reached the semifinals of the inaugural soccer World Cup. Twenty years later the United States recorded the greatest upset in World Cup history, beating England 1–0 with a goal by Haitian-born Joseph Gaetjens. Yet it was testimony to the parlous state of American soccer that, while the result was decried as a national disaster in England, it was barely reported in the American media. Having participated in three of the first four World

Cup finals, the United States would not qualify again until 1990.

On a domestic level, organized soccer remained distinctly minor league until 1975, when the struggling North American Soccer League (NASL), founded seven years earlier, was transformed by the New York Cosmos' signing of Brazil's Pele. The greatest soccer player in history brought thousands of spectators through the turnstiles, and his presence (along with massive salaries) helped to attract other soccer superstars to the NASL. However, after Pele's retirement in 1977 it became clear that the NASL's sudden success was a mirage. Audiences tired of a sport in which fading foreigners (Italy's Gianni Rivera memorably termed the NASL an "elephants' graveyard") outnumbered and outshone the few, mediocre American players. The NASL collapsed in 1985.

The league did leave one distinctive legacy. By marketing attendance at matches as a family affair, the NASL helped to establish soccer as an amateur sport among the white middle class, even though this interest has so far failed to evolve into a fan culture for the professional game. By 1997 more than 18 million Americans were playing soccer in some form, particularly organized youth soccer, which flourished because suburban parents perceived the game as nonviolent, coeducational, and multicultural. However, soccer's "yuppification" has compounded its marginalization from America's mainstream sports culture. The soccer boom has largely excluded the working-class and African American constituencies that dominate the professional teams and fan cultures of the Big Three.

In 1994, the United States hosted the World Cup. Beforehand, international commentators expressed outrage that a nation with no significant soccer history or culture would be hosting the apex of "the world's game." However, the tournament proved a great success on and off the field. The United States registered its first World Cup finals victory since 1950 by beating Colombia 2–1, and gave a creditable second-round performance in the 1–0 defeat by Brazil, the eventual champions. Yet the tournament's success failed to translate to the domestic game. The United States Soccer Federation (USSF) secured the World Cup upon the condition that a new national league would be established, but by the time Major League Soccer (MLS) began in 1995, the cultural effect of the World Cup had already waned. Attendance and viewing figures for televised matches remained disappointing. Indeed, until the USSF can convince the networks that soccer—with its few, infrequent scores and single "halftime" break for commercials—is television-friendly, the Big Three will continue to dominate American sport.

After a disastrous display in the 1998 World Cup, the United States exceeded all expectations in the 2002 tournament by beating Portugal and Mexico during a run to the quarter-finals, where the team was unfortunate to lose 1–0 to Germany. However, despite this impressive achievement, the most positive development in U.S. soccer history has been the astounding boom in the women's game. Since the 1970s, soccer has been promoted as a sport for girls—an idea that remains anathema in the male-oriented soccer nations of Europe and South America. In 1997, 39 percent of soccer participants in the United States were female. This base helped the United States win the first women's World Cup in 1991 and the first women's Olympics tournament in 1996. In the 1999 World Cup, the victory of the United States as host nation secured the highest-ever domestic television audience for a soccer match and made national heroes of players like Mia Hamm and Brandi Chastain.

BIBLIOGRAPHY

Kuper, Simon. "Short, Dark, Americans." In *Football Against the Enemy*. London: Orion, 1994. Entertaining assessment of the state of American soccer among women, immigrants, and white suburbanites prior to the 1994 World Cup.

Markovits, Andrei S., and Steven L. Hellerman. *Offside: Soccer and American Exceptionalism*. Princeton, N.J.: Princeton University Press, 2001. Definitive sociological approach to soccer's troubled history in the United States.

Murray, Bill. *The World's Game: A History of Soccer*. Urbana and Chicago: University of Illinois Press, 1996.

Sugden, John. "USA and the World Cup: American Nativism and the Rejection of the People's Game." In *Hosts and Champions: Soccer Cultures, National Identities, and the USA World Cup*. Edited by John Sugden and Alan Tomlinson. Aldershot, England: Arena, 1994. Thorough account of how soccer has been perceived as "un-American."

Martyn Bone

SOCIAL DARWINISM is the application of Charles Darwin's theory of evolution to human society. It is usually being applied when phrases like "survival of the fittest" or "natural selection" are used to explain why some in society prosper while others languish.

Darwin himself remained ambivalent about the social applications of his theory, but three events made it seductive to late-nineteenth-century intellectuals. First, the emergence of huge industrial enterprises deeply divided labor and capital, forcing some to justify increasing social divisions. Second, biblical criticism dislodged Christianity as the central scheme by which people understood their world. And third, the social sciences emerged as an academic discipline proposing to use the lessons of natural science to explain developments in society. Social Darwinism could respond to the needs created by each of these developments, despite perpetual reminders by opponents that Darwin's theory concerned primarily biology, not society.

At the peak of its influence, from roughly 1870 to 1917, two types of Social Darwinism emerged. First, until the 1890s, defenders of laissez-faire capitalism argued that in business as in biology, only the strongest survive. Poverty was the fault of the "unfit"; success was deserved; and, above all, the state should not intervene in natural processes. Charles Francis Adams Jr., president of Union Pacific Railroad, rejected congressional tariffs by saying, "The result of your [tariff] is that you are running in the face of the law of the survival of the fittest."

Among professional social scientists, William Graham Sumner became a famous defender of this sort of individualism. Historians have debated Darwin's influence on Sumner, noting that Sumner also followed philosopher Herbert Spencer, who applied natural selection to organisms and ideas, resulting in an expansive theory of "cosmic evolution." Darwin's natural selection, it seems, appealed to Sumner's individualism while offending his ethics, and one can see a strange reconciliation in Sumner's *What Social Classes Owe To Each Other* (1883), which can be seen as either dark individualism (as his answer to the title is nothing) or a prescription for broad social improvement.

Sociologist Lester Frank Ward represents a second application of Darwin's theory. Ward argued that Darwin's theory supports the view that humans achieved success by cooperation. A generation of sociologists followed Ward, and by the 1890s, Edward A. Ross had articulated the image of society as a "Darwinian jungle" in need of state-sponsored social control of individuals. He was not alone, and his generation began a vilification of Sumner, labeling him an unfeeling "Social Darwinist."

Yet the belief that Darwin's theory justified social control was not always a benign one. At the height of Jim Crow, it was used to justify racism, as when South Carolina Senator Benjamin Tillman argued that "the old struggle of survival of the fittest is beginning . . . and it is not saying too much to predict that the negro must do better or 'move on.'" A bleak fulfillment of this perspective was reached with eugenics, a movement popularized by Darwin's cousin, Francis Galton, who argued that some people should be sterilized to improve civilization's genetic stock. Between 1907 and 1915, twelve states passed sterilization laws.

Debate about Social Darwinism has continued since World War I, although between historians more than policymakers. Since the era of New Deal collectivism, the individualistic use of Social Darwinism has been deployed only as an epithet. Others, however, say the epithet has been wildly overused. Yet despite debate, it remains unknown what Darwin's theory really tells us about societies.

BIBLIOGRAPHY

Bannister, Robert C. *Social Darwinism: Science and Myth in Anglo-American Social Thought.* 1979. Paperback ed., Philadelphia: Temple University Press, 1988. This edition includes a valuable new preface.

Bellomy, Donald C. "'Social Darwinism' Revisited." *Perspectives in American History* new series, 1 (1984): 1–129.

Hofstadter, Richard. *Social Darwinism in American Thought.* Philadelphia: University of Pennsylvania Press, 1944. The first full story of Social Darwinism.

Sumner, William Graham. *What Social Classes Owe to Each Other.* New York: Harper and Brothers, 1883.

Kevin Schultz

See also **Evolutionism; Individualism; Sociology.**

SOCIAL DEMOCRATIC PARTY.

The Social Democracy of America, a radical labor organization, was formed at Chicago, 15–18 June 1897, of sections of the AMERICAN RAILWAY UNION, the SOCIALIST LABOR PARTY clubs, and various religious and trade union groups. The collapse of the Knights of Labor in the 1880s and the violent repression of labor strikes at Homestead, Pennsylvania, and Pullman, Illinois, in the 1890s had convinced radical leaders that they needed to build popular political support for their cause. Eugene V. Debs advocated implementation of a "colonization" plan, whereby the Socialists would concentrate their forces on a western state, such as Colorado, in which unemployment was to be abolished, cooperative industry fostered, and a Socialist government voted into office. This scheme of colonization was repudiated in June 1898, during the Social Democracy's first national convention, by a group of Socialists led by Debs, Victor L. Berger, and Jesse Cox. This group, made up of thirty-three delegates who preferred direct political activism to state colonization, quickly formed the Social Democratic Party of America. Later that year the Social Democrats were able to send two members to the Massachusetts legislature and to elect the mayor of Haverhill, Massachusetts; during the presidential election of 1900, their candidate, Debs, polled 87,814 votes. The subsequent fusion in 1901 of anti–De Leonites in the Socialist Labor Party and the Social Democratic Party led to a new party designation, the Socialist Party of America. During the next two decades Socialist candidates captured seventy-nine mayoralties throughout the country.

BIBLIOGRAPHY

Shannon, David A. *The Socialist Party of America: A History.* New York: Macmillan, 1955.

Young, Marguerite. *Harp Song for a Radical: The Life and Times of Eugene Victor Debs.* New York: Alfred Knopf, 1999.

Harvey Wish / A. G.

See also **Radicals and Radicalism; Socialist Movement; Socialist Party of America.**

SOCIAL GOSPEL

was a movement led by a group of liberal Protestant progressives in response to the social problems raised by the rapid industrialization, urbanization, and increasing immigration of the Gilded Age. The social gospel differentiated itself from earlier Christian reform movements by prioritizing social salvation over individual salvation. Although the ministers and activists of the social gospel based their appeals on liberal theology, which emphasized the immanence of God and the doctrine of Incarnation and valued good works over creeds, they usually showed more interest in social science than in theology. Believing that laissez-faire capitalism's understanding of labor as a commodity and its sole reliance on mechanisms of supply and demand to determine wages and allocate resources was un-Christian, social gospel advocates supported the labor movement and called for an interventionist welfare state. They differed from secular activists in that their ultimate vision was not just a more equitable balance of power within society, but a Christianized society in which cooperation, mutual respect, and compassion replaced greed, competition, and conflict among social and economic classes. Despite all of their efforts to reach the working class and to cooperate with the labor movement, though, the social gospel failed to reach far beyond its middle-class liberal Protestant milieu. Ultimately, the greatest achievement of the social gospel was to prepare the ground of middle-class America for progressivism.

Social Gospel in the Nineteenth Century

Washington Gladden was the first person to formulate the ideas of the social gospel. After failing to have the definite conversion experience required by his family's orthodox Calvinist faith, Gladden discovered liberal theology. His editorial work with the liberal journal the *Independent* and his ministry in several urban churches wracked by labor conflict solidified his liberalism and his concern for the plight of labor. By the mid-1880s, Gladden's name drew audiences across the country to hear his calls for bargaining rights for labor, a shorter work week, factory inspections, inheritance taxation, and regulation of natural monopolies. His charismatic presence, along with his comforting theological exposition of the fatherhood of God and the brotherhood of man, made these ideas, radical at the time, more palatable to his middle-class audiences. Gladden never endorsed socialism, but hoped for a gradual evolution toward a cooperative social order. Although he did write several theological treatises, including *Applied Christianity* (1887) and *Social Salvation* (1901), Gladden's thought relied more on social ethics and reform than on Christian theology.

If Gladden reveals the social gospel's tendencies to reduce Christianity to a system of social ethics, Richard Ely calls attention to the movement's international influences. Ely was a member of a cohort of social scientists who received their academic training in Germany and who regarded the social welfare legislation of the German Empire with great interest. Ely began his career by studying with German historical economists such as Karl Knies, who rejected neoclassical economics and called for economists to attend to differing cultural and historical contexts. As the principal founder of the American Economic Association and a professor at the social science centers of Johns Hopkins and the University of Wisconsin, Ely advocated the application of Christian social ethics to the discipline of economics. In his economic writings, Ely supported such major revisions to the economic order as public ownership of natural monopolies, factory inspections, and consumer protection.

By the mid-1890s, the social gospel had the support of multiple denominations and a strong foothold in interdenominational organizations. The Episcopal church, which had strong ties to English Christian socialism, the Congregational church, which boasted Gladden and social gospel leader Josiah Strong as members, and a small minority within the Baptist Church were the denominational leaders of the social gospel. The social gospel was particularly prominent within interdenominational organizations. The Interdenominational Congress and the Evangelical Alliance evolved into organs of the social gospel, and social Christianity frequently occupied the podium at the Parliament of Religions at the 1893 Chicago World's Fair. Beginning in the 1890s, some social gospel ministers, including Gladden, traveled south with the American Missionary Association to address the plight of southern blacks. Gladden and Walter Rauschenbusch both denounced racial inequality and lynching and explicitly extended the brotherhood of man to include African Americans. However, the primary geographic and intellectual focus of the movement remained the cities of industrial America.

Social Gospel in the Twentieth Century

In the early twentieth century, the social gospel found its intellectual leader in Rauschenbusch. A theologian, Rauschenbusch's social gospel career began while he was the minister of a German Baptist congregation in the Hell's Kitchen neighborhood of New York City. His witness of urban poverty sparked his passion for social Christianity, and after his eleven years of ministry, he became the theologian of the social gospel. In *Christianity and the Social Crisis* (1907), *Christianizing the Social Order* (1912), and *A Theology for the Social Gospel* (1917), Rauschenbusch united German pietistic evangelicalism, theological liberalism, and social Christianity by connecting the Kingdom of God to social salvation. For Rauschenbusch, the Kingdom of God lay in the unknown future, but was latent in the present and active in moments of crisis and change. The Church's and the Christian's role was to enunciate the Kingdom, to find it in the present, and to look to the future with a vision of the Kingdom as one's fulfillment and end. Rauschenbusch accepted a gradualist, Fabian version of socialism. He denounced what he saw as the evils of capitalism and gave his support to workers, but never joined the Socialist Party.

The social gospel reached its zenith in the decade before World War I. In 1908, the Federal Council of Churches, a federation representing thirty-three Protestant denominations, came into being and immediately adopted the social creed of the churches, which affirmed labor's rights to unionize and to bargain collectively. The Men and Religion Forward Movement, an interdenominational campaign that challenged men and boys to de-

413

Walter Rauschenbusch. The German Baptist minister and early-twentieth-century intellectual leader of the social gospel.

vote themselves to Christian social reform, was founded in 1911. An expanding YMCA, the development of institutional churches, and the social direction of the Religious Education Association, which oversaw Sunday-school education, expanded the reach of social Christianity. The social gospel's indirect connection to progressive activist Jane Addams further benefited the movement by drawing attention to the cause of urban social reform. Addams was not, strictly speaking, a member of the social gospel; she did not use the language of social Christianity, and she maintained a skeptical attitude toward the churches, which offered her little financial support. However, her work as a settlement house founder and social activist made her a symbol of the social gospel in action. Hull House workers joined social gospel activists in lobbying for urban housing improvements, shorter working hours, better working conditions for women, unemployment insurance, and against prostitution and other forms of urban vice.

Most members of the social gospel supported World War I, which they saw as a chance to Christianize society and international politics. The Senate's rejection of U.S. participation in the League of Nations and the revelation of the horrors of the war destroyed the cultural optimism that had been the social gospel's emotional foundation. The social gospel persisted through the 1920s, mostly through pacifist and ecumenical organizations. Yet the majority of American Protestants, who remained socially and theologically conservative, had begun to withdraw

their support. Fundamentalism, which began its struggle for denominational power in the 1920s, articulated the growing distrust of the liberal theology behind the social gospel. Fundamentalists did not object to Christian social concern, but to the social gospel's prioritization of social salvation over Christ's regeneration of individual souls. The social gospel, fundamentalists claimed, valued Christian faith only for its inspiration of social action. Furthermore, liberal theology's overemphasis on God's immanence in human society had made God an almost irrelevant component in a largely human project of social reform. As the fundamentalist fight against liberalism and modernism became more strident, fundamentalists identified all social Christianity with the liberal social gospel and associated Christianity with social conservatism.

Criticisms of Social Gospel

In the 1930s, neo-orthodox theology, which originated with the work of Swiss theologian Karl Barth, formed a second major critique of the social gospel. Barth emphasized the transcendental nature of God and the apostolic message of scripture, and criticized liberal theology's willingness to alter Christianity to fit the needs of the middle class, modern scholarship, and social reform. Along with his fellow theologians Paul Tillich and H. Richard Niebuhr, Reinhold Niebuhr expanded Barth's critique of the social gospel. Reinhold Niebuhr took the social gospel to task for its optimism, inattention to human sinfulness, and avoidance of political conflict. In the early 1930s, Niebuhr called for a social Christianity that possessed a more realistic understanding of power structures and human sinfulness and based its appeal on a deep, biblical faith instead of utopian visions. A new, more politically realistic social gospel did develop in the 1930s, as the changing political mood gave a more radical branch of social Christianity the opportunity to express itself. However, World War I, the growth of Protestant political conservatism, and the critiques of neo-orthodoxy divided the social Christianity of the 1930s from its progressive-era precursor.

BIBLIOGRAPHY

Curtis, Susan. *A Consuming Faith: The Social Gospel and Modern American Culture.* Baltimore: Johns Hopkins University Press, 1991.

Hopkins, Charles Howard. *The Rise of the Social Gospel in American Protestantism, 1865–1915.* New Haven, Conn.: Yale University Press, 1940.

May, Henry F. *Protestant Churches and Industrial America.* New York: Harpers & Brothers, 1949.

White, Ronald C., Jr., and C. Howard Hopkins. *The Social Gospel: Religion and Reform in Changing America.* Philadelphia: Temple University Press, 1976.

Molly Oshatz

See also **Modernists, Protestant; Protestantism; Religion and Religious Affiliation.**

SOCIAL LEGISLATION. Laws that seek to promote the common good, generally by protecting and assisting the weaker members of society, are considered to be social legislation. Such legislation includes laws assisting the unemployed, the infirm, the disabled, and the elderly. The social welfare system consists of hundreds of state and federal programs of two general types. Some programs, including SOCIAL SECURITY, Medicare, unemployment insurance, and WORKERS' COMPENSATION, are called social insurance programs because they are designed to protect citizens against hardship due to old age, unemployment, or injury. Because people receiving benefits from these programs generally have contributed toward their benefits by paying payroll taxes during the years that they worked, these social insurance programs are usually thought of as earned rewards for work. Programs of a second type, often cumulatively called the WELFARE SYSTEM, provide government assistance to those already poor. These social programs have maximum income requirements and include Aid to Families with Dependent Children, the FOOD STAMP PROGRAM, Medicaid, and Supplemental Security Insurance.

Although the United States has had social welfare legislation since colonial times, its nature and extent has changed over the years. For much of U.S. history, Americans preferred to rely on the marketplace to distribute goods and services equitably among the population. In cases where the market clearly failed to provide for categories of people such as widows, orphans, or the elderly, families were expected to take responsibility for the care of their members. When family members lacked the ability to do so, private, religious, or charitable organizations often played that role. Help from the town, county, or local government was rarely provided, and even then only in those cases where the need arose due to conditions beyond the individual's control, such as sickness, old age, mental incapacity, or widowhood.

The Nineteenth Century

For most of the nineteenth century, social problems too large for family members or private charities to handle fell under the jurisdiction of local government, consisting of the town, city, or county rather than the more distant national government. Local government's power to pass social legislation was premised upon the power of the state to restrict individual liberty and property for the common welfare. Later, while local governments remained involved, states began to assume a share of the obligation of caring for some of their citizens. Beginning in the late 1820s, a number of states founded asylums for the insane. A series of investigations by the reformer Dorothea Dix played an important role in bringing the plight of the mentally ill to the attention of state legislatures. Later in the nineteenth century, state and local governments created other specialized institutions for dependent persons, such as homes for the blind or mentally retarded.

While states and local communities had an interest in alleviating suffering in their jurisdictions, the U.S. legal system at this time limited the types of aid that could be offered. Natural-law concepts such as social Darwinism and laissez-faire economics stressed that redistributing wealth from certain citizens in the form of taxes to other citizens in the form of government payments was inherently unfair. For this reason, the Supreme Court held it constitutionally valid for a state or local government to create a poorhouse but held it unconstitutional for a state to provide stipends to its blind or other needy citizens to allow them to live independently outside an institution. Such judicial reasoning discouraged state legislatures from considering many social welfare laws.

One important exception to the nineteenth-century legal system's aversion to income redistribution took the form of government pensions granted to Union Civil War veterans. Between 1880 and 1910, the federal government devoted more than one-fourth of its expenditures to pensions for veterans and their dependents. The most important piece of benefits legislation was the Dependent Pension Act of 1890, which made pensions available to all who had served honorably in the war for ninety days or more.

The Progressive Era

As the United States became more urbanized and industrialized during the nineteenth and early twentieth centuries, it experienced new problems caused by rapid social, economic, and cultural changes. The rise of large cities and large-scale corporate capitalism strained the ability of local communities to deal with ever-increasing numbers of impoverished citizens or those with special needs. Despite changing social circumstances, many Americans continued to espouse the traditional idea that providing public assistance would make recipient groups dependent on the government. As the size of both the immigrant population and the industrial workforce exploded in urban areas, however, a group of reformers known as Progressives began to advocate that government, rather than private charitable organizations, offered the best hope for solving society's problems. (See PROGRESSIVE MOVEMENT.) Progressives lobbied for statutes to make industrial capitalism more humane. For example, the SHEPPARD-TOWNER MATERNITY AND INFANCY PROTECTION ACT of 1921 was revolutionary because it provided federal funds to match state funds for establishing maternal and child health services in each state. Under the act, full and part-time doctors and public health nurses were hired by state and local public-health agencies to train mothers and midwives in prenatal and infant care and postnatal care for new mothers. Congress failed to renew the statute, however, and it expired in 1929.

The New Deal

The period of greatest activity in the realm of social legislation occurred during President Franklin D. Roosevelt's NEW DEAL. The Great Depression, which began when the stock market collapsed in 1929 and continued until the late 1930s, caused widespread poverty and economic hardship. Millions of Americans lost their jobs and businesses failed. There were no effective state or federal programs to assist the many Americans who needed help. An elderly California physician named Dr. Francis E. Townsend gained great fame by proposing a system of old-age pensions to be administered by the federal government. The Roosevelt administration responded to the popular pressure for such a program, and in 1935, Congress passed the Social Security Act, the centerpiece of the U.S. scheme of social welfare.

Before the act's passage and its validation by the Supreme Court, such legislation ensuring the welfare of U.S. citizens would have been considered unconstitutional as an invasion of powers reserved to the states under the Tenth Amendment. However, in *Helvering v. Davis* (1937) and *Steward Machine Co. v. Davis* (1937) the Supreme Court held that Congress had the authority to pass the act under its power to tax and spend for the general welfare of the United States. The Court countered the argument that the federal government was intruding into an area of state authority by stating that the Social Security Act was a necessary response to a nationwide problem that could not be solved without national measures.

The Social Security Act's various provisions ultimately included old-age insurance as well as disability and survivors' benefits and Medicare coverage. Under the old-age insurance provisions of the law, pensions were to be paid to workers who reached the age of sixty-five. The necessary funding for these pensions was to be raised through taxes on employers and employees rather than by general public revenues. The size of individual pensions was to reflect the amount of worker contributions so that those with higher wages received higher pensions. While assisting a great many people, the program did not provide coverage to certain groups of workers with the greatest need. These groups included agricultural and domestic workers, many of whom were black.

Title IV of the act created the program known as Aid to Dependent Children (ADC), which provided matching federal money to help states fund mothers' aid programs. In administering the program, states were given wide discretion in determining who was eligible for ADC and how much they received. The result was that one state's benefits might be five or six times the amount of another state's. In 1939, Congress passed legislation making widows with children eligible for social security benefits if their husbands had contributed to the system while working. Thus widows increasingly tended to rely on social security while ADC gradually came to support more divorced, deserted, and never-married mothers. As a result, a certain amount of stigma has attached to ADC, which unlike social security, is limited to those with low incomes.

Post–New Deal Social Legislation

A second period of great legislative activity on the social welfare front occurred between World War II and the end of the 1970s. For example, in 1944, Congress passed the GI BILL OF RIGHTS, which offered a comprehensive set of disability, employment, and educational benefits for returning veterans. Under this legislation, half of all U.S. veterans received benefits for further training or higher education. Federal disability insurance was added to the Social Security Act in 1956.

Early in his presidency, Lyndon B. Johnson put forward an ambitious agenda of social legislation termed the GREAT SOCIETY, which proved to be the most important expansion of the federal government in the United States since the Great Depression. Unlike the New Deal, which was a response to economic hard times, Great Society programs were passed during a time of prosperity. During the Johnson years Congress passed three major civil rights acts. The 1964 act forbade job discrimination and the segregation of public accommodations, the 1965 law guaranteed black voting rights, and a third act in 1968 banned housing discrimination.

The best-known part of the Great Society, however, was a large group of initiatives instituted between 1964 and 1967 known as the WAR ON POVERTY. The Economic Opportunity Act of 1964 generated a number of new programs, including Volunteers in Service to America (VISTA), which was intended to operate as a domestic version of the Peace Corps and sent middle-class young people on "missions" into poor neighborhoods, and Upward Bound, which assisted poor high-school students entering college. Other programs included free legal services for the poor, Neighborhood Youth Corps, the JOB CORPS, and HEAD START. These programs were designed to fight poverty by providing training and educational opportunities to those who otherwise might not have them. A key element of these programs was the idea of community action, or encouraging the poor to participate in designing and running the programs intended to assist them.

In 1965, Congress also added the Medicare program to the existing provisions of the Social Security Act. This provision provides funds for medical care for the nation's elderly and its benefits are available to anyone over age sixty-five, regardless of need. (In 1964, the Food Stamp Act had begun to provide food vouchers for those with minimal income.) In 1966 the government extended medical benefits to welfare recipients of all ages through the Medicaid program. (See MEDICARE AND MEDICAID.) Also during the 1960s, Congress passed legislation to provide significant federal aid to public education. The Elementary and Secondary Education Act of 1965 offered financial assistance to underfunded public school districts throughout the country, while the Higher Education Act of the same year provided aid to needy college and university students.

When compared to most other countries, the extent of social welfare legislation in place in the United States is quite minimal. Nevertheless, such programs have engendered considerable controversy. In the aftermath of the Great Society, few new or significant programs have been implemented. With the election of Ronald Reagan as president in 1980, the federal government began to attempt to cut back on welfare benefits, relying on the theory that the problem of poverty is best addressed by encouraging the growth of private industry and private-sector jobs. In 1996 President Clinton, working together with a Republican Congress, signed into law the Personal Responsibility and Work Opportunity Reconciliation Act, or welfare reform law, which transformed the welfare system by raising recipients' work requirements and limiting the time period during which benefits are available.

BIBLIOGRAPHY

Foner, Eric, and John A. Garraty, eds. *The Reader's Companion to American History.* Boston: Houghton Mifflin, 1991.

LeVert, Marianne. *The Welfare System: Help or Hindrance to the Poor?* Brookfield, Conn.: Milbrook Press, 1995.

Muncy, Robyn. *Creating a Female Dominion in American Reform, 1890–1935.* New York: Oxford University Press, 1991.

Polenberg, Richard. *The Era of Franklin Roosevelt, 1933–1945.* Boston: Bedford/St. Martin's Press, 2000.

Katherine M. Jones

SOCIAL REGISTER.

A semiannual publication listing elite Americans, the Social Register first appeared in Newport, Rhode Island, in 1886. The New York edition followed in 1887, and compiler Louis Keller became the de facto arbiter of aristocratic status in the land of equality during the fluid period of the Gilded Age. Keller incorporated his project as the Social Register Association, which as of the early 2000s still publishes the book from New York City.

Over the four decades following the first edition, Keller produced separate volumes for 24 cities; in 1977 the association consolidated the various lists into a November pre-holiday edition and a supplemental Summer Social Register. The basic format has changed little: each book lists entries alphabetically by family head, along with addresses of first and additional homes, phone numbers, schools and colleges attended, and clubs.

Members of the Social Register are disproportionately eastern and urban. Inclusion is based on birth, marriage, or, occasionally, application. As American "society"—in both the broad and narrow senses—has changed, so has the composition of the Register. Once restricted to Protestant Anglo-Saxons, the Register now includes African Americans, Jews, and those of diverse ethnic groups.

BIBLIOGRAPHY

Cullen, Carole. "Social Register." In *Encyclopedia of American Studies.* Edited by George T. Kurian, Miles Orvell, Johnella E. Butler, and Jay Mechling. Volume 4, pp. 147–148. Danbury, N.Y.: Grolier Educational, 2001.

Higley, Stephen Richard. *Privilege, Power, and Place: The Geography of the American Upper Class.* Lanham, Md.: Rowman & Littlefield, 1995.

Perry Frank

SOCIAL SECURITY.

The social security system in the United States was established on 14 August 1935, when President Franklin D. Roosevelt signed the Social Security Act. The act created a range of government programs, including unemployment insurance and federal welfare grants, but the term "social security" generally designates Old Age, Survivors, and Disability Insurance (OASDI) and related federal programs run by the Social Security Administration. In the second half of the twentieth century, social security grew to become the most expensive federal government program, directly touching the life of almost every American. It enjoyed widespread popularity for several decades, but by the end of the century worries about its future and concerns about its effects on the economy greatly diminished its popularity and led policy makers to consider major changes in its operation.

Before Social Security

Social security is primarily designed to provide income for the elderly by taxing the workforce. Before the establishment of social security, workers pursued a range of strategies to prepare themselves and their spouses for old age—relying primarily on the market and the family. The historians Carole Haber and Brian Gratton have shown that in the late nineteenth and early twentieth centuries, average annual household incomes of those sixty and over were only modestly lower than those in their forties and fifties and were rising over time along with overall economic growth. Most men continued to work into old age, but many were able to retire. The labor force participation rate of men aged sixty-five and over was about 76 percent to 78 percent between 1850 and 1880; thus the retirement rate was 22 percent to 24 percent. The retirement rate rose to 35 percent in 1900 and 42 percent in 1930. Social critics worried that elderly workers were adversely affected by industrialization and that many were becoming unemployable and were being thrown onto the "industrial scrap heap." Research by economic historians has shown that this was probably not the case, as increasing retirement rates were driven by rising incomes. The earnings of their children were an important component of the elderly's income during this period. Surveys from 1889–1890 and 1917–1919 show that children's wages provided about one-third of total income in households headed by those sixty and over. In addition, saving for old age was an important strategy, and nearly 30 percent of elderly households took in boarders. Nearly one million

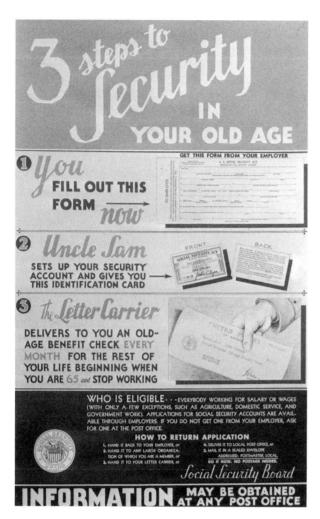

Social Security. This poster gives the public information about this New Deal program, created in 1935. © Bettmann/Corbis

people received Civil War pensions in the 1890s and first decade of the 1900s, declining to about 600,000 by 1920. They covered over half of elderly native-born Northern males and made up 42 percent of the federal budget at their peak. However, by 1930 only about 10 percent of workers were covered by pensions, especially government workers and long-term employees of large corporations such as railroads.

Many of the elderly lived in poverty, especially widows and those who had low earnings before reaching old age. A traditional response was for a poor widow to move in with the family of an adult child. As a last resort, the indigent elderly could move into an almshouse or poorhouse run by a charity or local government. Conditions in these institutions were often harsh and moving there was generally considered to be a deep humiliation. Fear of being consigned to the poorhouse haunted many, but no more than 2 percent of the elderly lived there in the nineteenth and early twentieth centuries.

In 1889 Germany, under Chancellor Otto Bismarck, adopted the first modern social insurance plan, in which workers were taxed to provide money for an old-age fund. Many European countries followed suit, including France (1910), the Netherlands (1913), Italy (1919), and Britain (1925), as did many Latin American nations. The first federal old-age pension bill was introduced into the U.S. Congress in 1909, and Theodore Roosevelt's Progressive Party made old-age insurance part of its platform in 1912, but very little progress was made toward this goal until the Great Depression struck the American economy. The depression caused massive unemployment, forced many employers to cancel pension promises, wiped out the savings of some older people, and squeezed many families who supported their elderly parents. Calls for assistance for the elderly and for a system that would encourage retirement, opening up jobs for younger workers, abounded. As the depression continued, more and more state governments provided relief payments to the elderly poor, but most observers considered these to be grossly inadequate.

Establishment of the Program

On 29 June 1934 Franklin Roosevelt created the Committee on Economic Security (CES), chaired by Secretary of Labor Frances Perkins and led by Executive Staff Director Edwin Witte, a University of Wisconsin economics professor, to study social insurance and recommend legislation. Roosevelt and Congress were faced with a growing call to provide large pensions to the elderly. Most prominent were the "Share Our Wealth" plan of the Louisiana senator Huey P. Long and especially the retired physician Francis Townsend's plan, which called for a pension of $200 per month for those sixty and over—an amount that was more than one-third of per capita annual income—on the condition that recipients not be employed and that they spend their pensions within thirty days. Instead the CES recommended and Congress adopted (by 372 to 33 in the House and 77 to 6 in the Senate) a plan that gave much more modest immediate aid to the elderly through the Old Age Assistance program and created a more permanent system, Old Age Insurance. Old Age Assistance was a joint federal-state venture with the federal government matching state expenditures on a one-to-one basis up to a specified maximum per recipient (originally $15 per month). It allowed states to establish their own eligibility criteria and benefits levels. Meanwhile, the Old Age Insurance system began to tax workers and promised benefits when they reached age sixty-five that were tied to the amount of taxes they had paid, much like a private-sector annuity. This lag between payments and promised benefits made it difficult for future legislation to repeal the social security system. Franklin Roosevelt recognized this, explaining "We put those payroll contributions there so as to give the contributors a legal, moral, and political right to collect their pensions. . . . With those taxes in there, no damn politician can ever scrap my social security program." Alf Landon, the Republicans' unsuccessful 1936 presidential candidate, criticized the Social Security Act as unjust, unworkable, stupidly drafted, and wastefully financed, but Gallup polls showed that voters overwhelmingly approved of it, with 73 percent approving the social security tax on their wages. In late 1936, the federal government began assigning social security account numbers, taking applications at post offices. On 1 January 1937 workers began paying social security taxes and acquiring credits toward old-age benefits. The Supreme Court upheld social security's constitutionality in *Helvering v. Davis* on 24 May 1937. However, the 7 to 2 ruling made it clear that social security taxes are simply taxes like any other, and individuals have no legal right to any benefit based on paying them.

Initially over 9 million workers, including agricultural workers, domestic servants, and government employees, were excluded from the social security system, as were railroad workers, who had their own retirement fund established by federal law in 1934. It was originally planned to begin paying monthly pensions to retirees in 1942, but the Social Security Amendments of 1939 brought this forward to 1940, and on 31 January 1940 Ida May Fuller, a retired legal secretary from Vermont, became the first recipient of a monthly benefit check. The 1939 amendments also added a program to provide dependents' and survivors' benefits—akin to private-sector life insurance—and the program was renamed Old Age and Survivors Insurance (OASI). The acceleration and expansion of social security benefits was driven by the political popularity of spending social security's amassed pool of savings rather than letting it accumulate, especially in light of the "Roosevelt Recession" that struck the economy in 1937. As OASI switched from a fully funded system to a pay-as-you-go system, it became even more difficult to undo the system. Simultaneously, it abandoned the principle of tying benefits exclusively to payments and added a number of redistributive elements, such as providing additional benefits to elderly recipients who were married. With its mix of insurance principles and redistribution, social security carefully straddled the political boundary between stressing self-reliance and welfare.

Expanding Coverage and Benefits

Over the course of the next few decades, as the economy grew rapidly, social security continued to expand, covering more and more workers and adding new benefits. As Andrew Achenbaum observes, "as long as the number of new and current contributors far exceeded the number of beneficiaries, legislators could liberalize existing provisions, expand coverage, and increase benefits—and still point to huge surpluses in the trust funds" (*Social Security*, p. 3). In 1940, 43.5 percent of the labor force was covered by social security's insurance program. This rose to 55 percent in 1949. In 1950 farm and domestic laborers were added to the system. A few years later most of the self-employed were added, as well as military personnel, and coverage reached 78 percent in 1955. Subsequent expansion of occupational coverage pushed this figure to 85

percent by 1968. September 1950 also saw the first across-the-board increase in social security benefits, by a dramatic 77 percent, and Old Age and Survivors Insurance benefit payments became larger than Old Age Assistance payments for the first time. Subsequent benefits increases were often passed just before elections, as they were in September of 1952, 1954, and 1972. Social security's replacement rate—measured as the OASI benefit in the first twelve months of retirement as percentage of employment income in the preceding twelve months—was 39 percent for the average one-earner couple in 1940. Due to inflation, this fell to 23.5 percent before the 1950 benefits increase and then rose to 52 percent in 1955, 58 percent in 1975, and 62 percent in 1995. In 1956 the Social Security Act was amended to provide monthly benefits to permanently and totally disabled workers aged fifty to sixty-four and for disabled children of retired or deceased workers. Old Age, Survivors and Disability Insurance (OASDI) became the system's new name. In 1961 men were allowed to take early retirement at age sixty-two (with lower benefits) for the first time. In 1965 health insurance was added to the social insurance umbrella, with the establishment of Medicare, although the Social Security Administration did not run this program. In 1972 amendments were adopted that expanded benefits considerably, eased earnings restrictions on nonretired workers and began to automatically adjust future benefits for the impact of inflation. In addition, the state-based supplemental payments to the needy, blind, and disabled elderly were federalized as the Supplemental Security Income (SSI) program, administered by the Social Security Administration. By 1972 every major idea of the 1935 Committee on Economic Security had been enacted, coverage had become nearly universal, and older Americans had a deep sense of "entitlement" to their social security benefits. The growth of social security can be seen in tables 1 and 2. (The SSI columns' figures before 1980 are for its predecessor programs: Old Age Assistance, Aid to the Blind, and Aid to Permanently and Totally Disabled.

TABLE 1

Social Security Beneficiaries (thousands)

Year	Retired Workers	Disabled Workers	Wives and Husbands	Children	Others	SSI
1940	112		30	55	26	2,143
1950	1,171		508	700	498	2,952
1960	8,061	455	2,346	2,000	1,981	2,781
1970	13,349	1,493	2,952	4,122	3,778	3,098
1980	19,562	2,859	3,477	4,607	4,988	4,192
1990	24,838	3,011	3,367	3,187	5,421	4,817
2000	28,499	5,042	2,963	3,803	5,107	6,602

SOURCE: Social Security Administration (2001), Table 5.A4; Myers (1985), Table 11.7; and Social Security Administration (2002), Table IV.B9.

TABLE 2

Annual Social Security Payments

Year	Insurance Payments (billions)	Insurance Payments as % of Federal Spending	Insurance Payments as % of GDP	SSI Payments (billions)
1940	$ 0.04	0.4%	0.035%	$ 0.49
1950	$ 0.96	2.3	0.33	$ 1.5
1960	$ 11.2	12.2	2.13	$ 1.9
1970	$ 31.9	16.3	3.07	$ 2.9
1980	$120.5	20.6	4.31	$ 8.1
1990	$247.8	19.9	4.27	$14.8
2000	$407.6	22.0	4.13	$34.1

SOURCE: Social Security Administration (2001), Table 4.A4; Myers (1985), Table 11.8; and Social Security Administration (2002), Tables IV.C2 and IV.C4.

These programs are not part of social security's insurance system.)

Operating Procedures

Before examining social security's evolution in the twentieth century's last quarter, it will be valuable to explain its operating procedures. The insurance portions of social security (retirement, survivors, and disability benefits) have always been paid for by a payroll tax. Initially, the tax was 2 percent of the first $3,000 earned by employees (the "earnings base"). The tax is automatically deducted from payroll and is officially evenly split between the employer and the employee. However, most economists believe that the tax is effectively paid completely by the employee, whose pay would rise by the entire amount of the tax if it did not exist. The tax rate rose to 3 percent in 1950, 6 percent in 1960, 8.4 percent in 1970, 10.16 percent in 1980, and 12.4 percent in 1990 and 2000. The earnings base was also gradually increased, generally much faster than the inflation rate, reaching $4,800 in 1960, $25,900 in 1980, and $76,200 in 2000.

Social security retirement benefits are calculated in several steps. First the worker's Average Indexed Monthly Earnings (AIME) are calculated. Under the procedures adopted in the 1970s, all earnings on which a worker paid social security taxes up until the year he or she turned sixty are "wage indexed" to compensate for past inflation and real wage growth. To accomplish this, each year's wage is multiplied by an "indexing factor" that equals the ratio of the average national wage in the year the worker turns sixty to the average national wage in the year to be indexed. From this set of earnings, the worker's thirty-five best years are selected, added together and divided by 420 (the number of months in thirty-five years). This amount is the AIME. The second step determines the worker's Primary Insurance Amount (PIA) by applying a progressive formula to the AIME to calculate the monthly benefit that the person would receive if he or she retired at the "normal" retirement age. (The normal retirement age was sixty-five from the beginning of the social security system until 2003, when it begins gradually increasing to age sixty-seven by 2025.) The progressive formula has been selected so that low-earning workers receive payments that are disproportionately higher—compared to the taxes that have been paid in—than for high-earning workers. For example, in 2001 the Primary Insurance Amount was 90 percent of the first $561 of the retiree's AIME, 32 percent of the AIME over $561 and up to $3381, and 15 percent of Average Indexed Monthly Earnings above $3381. Adjustments are made to the retiree's Primary Insurance Amount, which is reduced for those taking early retirement and can be increased by as much as 50 percent if the retiree has a spouse who had little or no earnings. Finally, the monthly benefit check is adjusted annually for changes in the cost of living. The adjustment is determined by the rate of inflation in the Consumer Price Index (CPI). Most economists believe that the CPI overstates inflation, so this means that the retiree's monthly benefit buys more over time.

One of social security's initial purposes was to reduce unemployment by inducing older workers to retire. Throughout its history, social security has had a retirement earnings test. The 1935 Social Security Act prohibited any payment when income was earned in "regular employment." In 1939 "regular employment" was defined as earning more than $15 per month—about 25 percent of the minimum wage. The economist Donald Parsons estimates that this earnings test increased the retirement rate for men sixty-five and over by about six percentage points in 1940. In 1950, the income threshold was raised to $50, and the retirement test was eliminated for those age seventy-five and older. In 1960, for the first time, earnings over the exempt amount did not produce total loss of benefits; instead, for income in a certain range, benefits were reduced $1 for every $2 in earnings. In 1990, this rate was cut to $1 for every $3 in earnings for workers above the normal age of retirement. In 2000, as unemployment reached its lowest rate in over thirty years, both houses of Congress unanimously voted to eliminate the retirement earnings test for workers above social security's normal retirement age.

Comparing taxes paid to benefits received, it is possible to calculate the rate of return on a worker's social security "investment," just as one would for a private investment. Such calculations show that social security's rate of return was very high for the first population cohorts covered by the system. Rates of return for those reaching sixty-five in 1950 averaged about 20 percent. By 1965 returns fell to about 10 percent and they continued this downward trend because tax rates had increased and retirees had now been taxed for all or most of their working lives. Inflation-adjusted average rates of return from OASI are given in table 3, which shows that lower-income workers have higher rates of return. Single males' average

TABLE 3

Inflation-Adjusted Lifetime Rates of Return from OASI

Group (earnings level)	Year Cohort Turns Sixty-five				
	1950	1965	1980	1995	2025 (projected)
Single Male					
Low	24.0	10.0	5.3	2.8	1.8
Average	19.2	8.1	4.2	1.8	1.0
High	14.4	6.4	3.8	1.1	0.3
Single Female					
Low	25.4	11.3	6.4	3.7	2.6
Average	21.3	9.8	5.5	2.9	1.9
High	15.9	7.8	4.9	2.1	0.6
One-earner Couple					
Low	28.3	14.3	9.2	5.9	4.2
Average	23.5	12.1	7.7	4.8	3.4
High	18.5	10.0	6.9	4.3	2.2
Two-earner Couple					
Low/Low	24.8	11.2	7.0	3.9	2.6
Average/Low	21.8	10.2	6.2	3.5	2.3
High/Average	16.9	8.1	5.1	2.5	1.1

SOURCE: Steuerle and Bakija, *Retooling Social Security,* p. 290.

rates of return are lower than for single females because women live longer than men and therefore collect more benefits. Studies also show that blacks have lower rates of return due to their lower life expectancies. The table shows that rates of return are projected to continue declining—assuming that taxes and benefit formulas are unchanged.

Problems and Changes

By the mid-1970s, it was becoming clear that the mature social security system could not continue to finance all the benefits it had promised. In 1975, for the first time since 1959, social security ran a deficit, spending more on benefits than it collected in taxes. Deficits occurred again in 1976 and 1977 and were projected to continue, exhausting the Social Security Trust Fund—U.S. government debt owned by the social security system—by the early 1980s. In response, Congress substantially increased social security taxes, and benefits were scaled back by reducing spousal benefits and amending the indexing procedure. President Carter, signing the bill into law, predicted that these moves would make the system sound for decades to come. He was wrong. By 1981 worries about funding shortfalls reappeared and the Reagan administration proposed additional cuts in benefits, including scaling back the cost-of-living inflation adjustment and reducing early retirement benefits. The powerful senior citizens' lobby greeted these proposals with a withering wave of protests and the Senate immediately rejected them, but polls showed that two-thirds of the public were "not too confident" or "not at all confident" in the system. To defuse the issue, the president and Congress appointed the bipartisan National Commission on Social Security Reform, chaired by Alan Greenspan, to make recommendations to solve social security's financing crisis. In 1983, after intense political bickering, Congress accepted the Greenspan commission's proposals to further increase taxes, begin taxing the benefits of higher-income retirees, and gradually increase the normal retirement age from sixty-five to sixty-seven. Taxes were expected to greatly exceed expenditures so that the system's trust fund could be built up in anticipation of the retirement of "baby boomers" born between the end of World War II and the early 1960s. The bill was signed amid predictions that the funding problem was solved for generations to come, and the Social Security Trust Fund, which had never exceeded $40 billion before 1983, began to grow. It reached $214 billion in 1990 and $931 billion in 2000.

Unfortunately, this nest egg did not appear to be large enough given demographic trends and somewhat pessimistic projections of economic growth. By 1993, social security's board of trustees projected that OASDI would begin running deficits around 2015. Social security's spending would then exceed income by an ever-increasing margin, and the board expected the trust fund to be exhausted by about 2035. The number of OASDI beneficiaries per one hundred covered workers, which had been 6.1 in 1950 and 26.6 in 1990, was expected to climb to 42.7 by 2030—there would be only a little more than two workers paying for every beneficiary as the population aged and life expectancies increased. In light of these pessimistic predictions, the 1994–1996 Social Security Advisory Council released its report in early 1997. Unable to achieve consensus, the council offered three options. The "Maintain Benefits" option (supported by six of the thirteen council members) proposed to essentially maintain the historical structure of social security by increasing taxes and slightly reducing benefits. However, the other two options broke with tradition. The "Personal Security Accounts" option (supported by five members) advocated a partial privatization of social security, proposing to divert nearly half of the social security tax into mandatory personal retirement accounts, allowing individuals to put their own social security funds into the stock market. The "Individual Accounts" option (supported by two members) was in between the other two, proposing that social security payroll taxes be increased, but that this money be put into government-run individual retirement accounts.

Leading economists, including the former Council of Economic Advisors chairman Martin Feldstein, began to advocate a transition to a completely privatized social security system. They argued that social security had slowed economic growth by reducing the national savings rate, reasoning that if social security did not exist workers would have saved more for their retirements and this savings would have boosted the investment rate, increasing the nation's capital stock. Because social security is mostly a pay-as-you-go system, however, the money was never saved and any money in the trust fund was lent to the government rather than invested. Feldstein estimated that this effect probably had reduced national income by about 6 percent and that social security taxes further reduced national income by curbing work incentives. Privatization advocates pointed out that inflation-adjusted long-run stock market returns have been about 7 or 8 percent per year—much higher than the returns earned and promised by social security. Privatization would essentially be a forced savings plan, but its critics warned that many individuals were not competent to make their own investment decisions, that the stock market was very volatile, that privatization allowed no room for redistribution, and that privatized plans would have much higher administrative costs than the social security system. Privatization's fans pointed to the success of Chile, which in 1981 replaced its failing pay-as-you-go retirement system with a privately managed mandatory savings program. Chileans earned impressive returns in their new system, which was soon imitated around the world. Amid these developments and a booming stock market, politicians began to advocate similar plans. President Bill Clinton floated the idea of investing surplus social security funds in the stock market, and in his campaign for the presidency in 2000 George W. Bush advocated reforming social security so that it would offer private savings accounts.

Many have seen social security as the most successful government program in American history. It has been credited with bringing true security to American workers, reducing the fear of poverty in old age, allowing more of the elderly to retire and giving them the resources to live independently. Others see it as a flawed system, an intergenerational transfer mechanism that has benefited the earliest cohorts of retirees, but which promises too little to the current and future generations, explaining most of the elderly's rising retirement, income, and independence as extensions of historical trends caused by continued economic growth. By the early twenty-first century, social security had become the subject of an intense political argument.

BIBLIOGRAPHY

Achenbaum, W. Andrew. *Social Security: Visions and Revisions.* New York: Cambridge University Press, 1986.

Berkowitz, Edward D., ed. *Social Security after Fifty: Successes and Failures.* New York: Greenwood Press, 1987.

Berkowitz, Edward D., and Kim McQuaid. *Creating the Welfare State: The Political Economy of Twentieth-Century Reform.* Lawrence: University Press of Kansas, 1992.

Costa, Dora L. *The Evolution of Retirement: An American Economic History, 1880–1990.* Chicago: University of Chicago Press, 1998.

Feldstein, Martin. "The Missing Piece in Policy Analysis: Social Security Reform." *American Economic Review* 86, no. 2 (1996): 1–14.

Ferrara, Peter J., and Michael Tanner. *A New Deal for Social Security.* Washington, D.C.: Cato Institute, 1998.

Haber, Carole, and Brian Gratton. *Old Age and the Search for Security: An American Social History.* Bloomington: Indiana University Press, 1994.

Lubove, Roy. *The Struggle for Social Security, 1900–1935.* Cambridge, Mass.: Harvard University Press, 1968.

Myers, Robert J. *Social Security.* 3d ed. Homewood, Ill.: Irwin, 1985.

Nash, Gerald D., Noel H. Pugach, and Richard Tomasson, eds. *Social Security: The First Half-Century.* Albuquerque: University of New Mexico Press, 1988.

Parsons, Donald O. "Male Retirement Behavior in the United States, 1930–1950." *Journal of Economic History* 51 (1991): 657–674.

Quadagno, Jill. *The Transformation of Old Age Security: Class and Politics in the American Welfare State.* Chicago: University of Chicago Press, 1988.

Rejda, George E. *Social Insurance and Economic Security.* 6th ed. Upper Saddle River, N.J.: Prentice Hall, 1999.

Rubinow, Isaac M. *The Quest for Security.* New York: Henry Holt, 1934.

Social Security Administration, Social Security Online: History Page. http://www.ssa.gov/history/

Steuerle, C. Eugene, and Jon M. Bakija. *Retooling Social Security for the Twenty-first Century: Right and Wrong Approaches to Reform.* Washington, D.C.: Urban Institute Press, 1994.

Weaver, Carolyn. "On the Lack of a Political Market for Compulsory Old-Age Insurance Prior to the Great Depression." *Explorations in Economic History* 20, no. 3 (1983): 294–328.

———. *The Crisis in Social Security: Economic and Political Origins.* Durham, N.C.: Duke University Press, 1982.

Robert Whaples

See also **Medicare and Medicaid; New Deal; Retirement; Retirement Plans; Welfare System;** *and vol.* 9: **The New American Poverty.**

SOCIAL SETTLEMENTS. *See* **Settlement House Movement.**

SOCIAL WORK. The profession of social work emerged in the early twentieth century as charitable organizations began employing trained workers rather than relying on volunteers. Pioneers developed two competing approaches for addressing social problems. Mary Richmond, author of *Social Diagnosis* (1917), is celebrated as a leader of the charity organization movement, while the social settlement movement was epitomized by the work of Jane Addams at Hull-House in Chicago. The profession considers its founding date to be 1898, the year the first social work course was established at the New York School of Philanthropy (now the Columbia University School of Social Work). In 1915, at the National Conference of Charities and Corrections, Abraham Flexner, an educator and expert on professional standards, pronounced that social workers were not professionals, rather they served as mediators between clients and other professionals such as doctors and lawyers. Early social workers took that as a challenge and mobilized workers to produce professional literature, organizations, and a code of ethics.

As June Hopps and Pauline Collins (1995) have noted, the profession of social work responds to wider historical changes, shifting its focus from environmental reform to individual change, as the nation's social climate fluctuates. For example, social workers aimed to radically change institutions and rejected the traditional establishment during the Progressive Era of the 1900s, the depression of the 1930s, and the social unrest of the 1960s. However, in more conservative times, such as the 1920s, 1950s and 1980s, the profession attended to direct service and individual change.

While white Protestant women composed the majority of early social workers, Catholic, Jewish, and African American men and women often formed their own agencies. Segregation laws barred African Americans from white schools of social work, leading African Americans to create Atlanta University School of Social Work. Pioneers like Lawrence Oxley drew from nineteenth-century philosophies of mutual aid and race pride, and the journal *Southern Workman* provided a forum of discussion for African American social reformers of the early twentieth century.

In the 1920s, social workers debated whether the profession would include caseworkers across a broad range of fields or limit membership to a professional elite with high educational standards. The latter position won, and social workers were required to complete masters-level training. Depression-era social workers demanded a federal response to widespread unemployment and poverty. A new political activism was ignited within the profession and the social workers Harry Hopkins and Jane Hoey served in the Franklin D. Roosevelt administration, influencing new emergency relief and social security programs.

In 1952, the Council on Social Work Education (CSWE) emerged to accredit graduate schools, and by the 1970s, baccalaureate programs were accredited to prepare entry-level professionals. The National Association of Social Workers (NASW) was established in 1955, adopting a code of ethics, and merging seven previously scattered organizations for psychiatric, medical, and group workers. In the last quarter of the twentieth century, organizations such as the National Association of Black Social Workers (1968), Latino Social Workers Organization (1992), and North American Association of Christians in Social Work (1954) evolved to address concerns of various groups.

Entry-level social workers are trained as generalists and are expected to provide service to a broad range of clients, maintain a wide scope of knowledge, and practice a great diversity of skills. Advanced practitioners with graduate-level training may specialize in areas such as clinical, medical, or school social work, as well as planning and development, aging, mental health, or corrections. In the late 1960s and 1970s, states began establishing licensing requirements to legally regulate practice. While all states require some form of licensure, current trends are moving toward "declassification": downgrading requirements for social work in order to employ persons with neither a license nor a degree to do case management and other functions traditionally reserved for social workers.

BIBLIOGRAPHY

Carlton-LaNey, Iris. "African American Social Work Pioneers' Response to Need." *Social Work* 44, no. 4 (July 1999): 311–321.

Hopps, June, and Pauline Collins. "Social Work Profession Overview." In *Encyclopedia of Social Work.* 19th ed. Edited by Richard Edwards and June Hopps. Washington, D.C.: NASW Press, 1995.

Popple, Phillip, and Leslie Leighninger. *Social Work, Social Welfare, and American Society.* 5th ed. Boston: Allyn and Bacon, 2002.

T. Laine Scales

See also **Charity Organization Movement; Poverty; Settlement House Movement; Welfare System.**

SOCIALIST LABOR PARTY. Founded in 1877, the Socialist Labor Party (SLP) is the longest-lived socialist organization in the United States. Never rising above a membership of several thousand, the SLP has from time to time exerted influence far beyond its numbers.

Its origins can be found in the communities of German-language immigrant workers who formed labor union bodies, organized social clubs, and published newspapers with broadly socialistic views from the immediate post–Civil War era to the early 1900s. From their ranks mainly arose the earliest U.S. sections of the First International (1864), dominated by the followers of Karl Marx. After the expulsion of American-born followers of the feminist and spiritualist Victoria Woodhull in 1871, this preliminary movement collapsed, although local labor activities continued unabated. A Sozialistische Arbeiter Partei (Socialist Labor Party) formed in 1877, in time to take advantage of working-class outrage following the national railroad strike of that year and to elect members to local and state office in Chicago and elsewhere. (See RAILROAD STRIKE OF 1877.)

The party swiftly declined thereafter and suffered grievously from the defection of "revolutionary socialists" (known widely as anarchists) based in Chicago—the heart of the most influential radicalism of the 1880s. Reaction to the HAYMARKET RIOT (in which anarchists were falsely accused of a bombing, arrested, tried, and executed), the upswing of the labor movement, and the publication of Edward Bellamy's utopian novel *Looking Backward* (1889), followed by the economic depression of the 1890s, all encouraged another wave of political socialism. Once again the little Socialist Labor Party elected a handful of members to local office and bid fair to take over sections of the American labor movement.

Disappointment again followed, as the KNIGHTS OF LABOR collapsed, the American Federation of Labor took a conservative turn, and socialist efforts to organize an all-inclusive union alternative soon failed. In 1897–1899, more than half of the SLP membership defected, soon to join with native-born socialists to form the SOCIALIST PARTY OF AMERICA in 1901.

Now a propaganda group, the SLP had one important mission remaining. Daniel De Leon, a former Columbia University lecturer, had become the voice of the SLP and of antiracist sentiment within the socialist Second International. In 1905 he helped found the INDUSTRIAL WORKERS OF THE WORLD (IWW), and its bitter opposition by employers, the press, and the American Federation of Labor made De Leon and his organization the prime propagandists of radical labor.

De Leon's articulation of a classless society, governed from the workplace rather than the political state (which would be abolished) remains a signal contribution of American socialist thought. But internal disputes led to the expulsion of De Leon from the IWW in 1907.

De Leon's ideas nevertheless continued to exert wide influence upon the strategists of industrial unionism. From the 1910s until the 1960s, SLP loyalists meanwhile distributed many millions of leaflets and ran in countless educational election campaigns, attacking capitalism's unfairness and irrationality and continuing its utopian appeal for a noncoercive society. An aging membership and confusion about the radical movements of the 1960s practically dissolved the remnant, although it has narrowly maintained its existence.

BIBLIOGRAPHY

Buhle, Paul. "The World of Daniel De Leon." In his *From the Knights of Labor to the New World Order.* New York: Garland, 1997.

Laslett, John. *Labor and the Left.* New York: Basic, 1970).

Paul Buhle

See also **American Federation of Labor–Congress of Industrial Organizations; Labor Parties; Socialist Party of America.**

SOCIALIST MOVEMENT. Socialism is a closely intertwined set of liberating ideas and social movements that emerged in the aftermath of the French Revolution. No single definition encompasses the many socialist variants that took root in Europe and America, but socialism enfolds certain key ideas. As products of the Enlightenment, socialists believe in the power of rational thought, in the malleability of economic institutions and social mores, and in a humanistic solidarity that transcends the nation-state. In such a socialist world, the major instruments of production, distribution, and exchange are owned and administered for the welfare of all. Socialism entails the common ownership of the means of production, either through the state or some other mechanism of collective rule, and it seeks a broad and equitable distribution of the wealth generated by capital, especially insofar as early-nineteenth-century industrialism demonstrated a capacity to generate both great wealth and extreme social inequality.

Socialism's Golden Era

American socialism developed from a variety of movements and traditions. Protestant perfectionism, sometimes in tandem with the romantic currents of the early nineteenth century, animated many of the utopian communities and cultural experiments that sought to put into practice an egalitarian, anti-capitalist idealism. Inspired by Charles Fourier, Robert Owen, and Henry George, reform intellectuals established a series of communitarian experiments, among them the transcendentalist Brook Farm, which led an unsteady life in the 1840s; upstate New York's Oneida Community, which marriage reformer John Humphrey Noyes founded in 1848; and the Fair Hope Community of Alabama, inspired by George's single-tax principles.

Such utopias, imagined and experimental, represented an important counterweight to the ideological and legal hegemony of laissez-faire capitalism. By far the most influential utopia was in Edward Bellamy's novel, *Looking Backward* (1888), which captured for millions of readers the disquiet and disgust generated by Gilded Age capitalism. Like so many Christian utopians, Bellamy initially envisioned a socialist future characterized by order, hierarchy, a genteel culture, and an absence of social conflict. The novel appealed strongly to the established Protestant middle class, disenchanted with the chaos of rapid industrialization, but it won an even larger working-class audience that was inspired by Bellamy's combination of rationality and moralism. Indeed, Bellamy came to adopt a much more democratic, feminist, working-class outlook in the 1890s.

Socialism at Its Peak

The socialist movement reached its height during the first two decades of the twentieth century, when the values inherent in Protestant utopianism were linked to the more "scientific" brand of socialism that had arrived on American shores in the wake of the failed European revolutions of 1848. German "48ers" made Americans aware of the early work of Karl Marx, whose ideas forever transformed the way in which both conservatives and radicals would think about capitalism, social class, and the nature of historical causation. Marx saw capitalism as the progressive, dialectical product of the social and economic forces that had ruptured the feudal world and destroyed the power of the landed aristocracy. But capitalism, he contended, was not a stable system: free-market competition tended toward a declining rate of profitability, especially as technological innovations periodically destroyed existing production regimes. Meanwhile, industrial capitalism, with

Brook Farm. Josiah Wolcott's 1844 painting depicts the short-lived (1841–1847) utopian community in West Roxbury (now part of Boston); its members briefly included the writer Nathaniel Hawthorne. Massachusetts Historical Society

its factories, mines, railroads, and urban landscape, generated a strategically powerful proletariat whose own liberation required the socialization of industry and the political and economic liquidation of the bourgeoisie.

The massive coal, rail, and steel strikes of the late nineteenth century and the state violence that suppressed them provided fertile soil for socialist agitation and organization. The most rigorous Marxists were found in the heavily German SOCIALIST LABOR PARTY (SLP), founded in 1877. Led in the 1890s by Daniel De Leon, the SLP became increasingly sectarian and hostile to the multifaceted political reformism of the era and to the more cautious unions of the American Federation of Labor (AFL), presided over by the ex-socialist Samuel Gompers.

The SOCIALIST PARTY OF AMERICA (SP) was a much more pluralistic and successful institution. Its leading personality was Eugene V. Debs, who embodied much that made the pre–World War I SP attractive. A Protestant railroad unionist from Terre Haute, Indiana, Debs moved into the socialist orbit after the courts and the army crushed the 1894 Pullman strike and sent him to jail. After a brief flirtation with a socialist colonization scheme in the West, Debs helped merge existing socialist organizations into the Socialist Party, founded in 1901. By this time he had already conducted the first of his five rousing

campaigns for president of the United States, during which hundreds of thousands heard a message of socialist transcendence delivered in an idiom that resonated well with those Americans, both native-born and immigrant, who were seeking a twentieth-century version of the republican-producer values that had anchored American democracy and citizenship in earlier decades.

Socialism's golden era lasted from 1900 until the 1917–1919 period, when controversies over World War I and the Russian Revolution fractured both the Socialist Party and the very meaning of socialism itself. At its apogee in 1912, when Debs won more than 900,000 votes for president, or 6 percent of the entire presidential vote, the party enrolled about 118,000 members. Socialist ideas and organizations were rooted in three distinct communities. The first was that of the native-born lower-middle class, many of whom were Protestant veterans of Populist, Prohibition, and other rural insurgencies. The second community was intensely urban, immigrant, and activist. German, Croatian, Hungarian, and Jewish Russian immigrants became an increasingly important mass base for the Socialist Party, even as these populations used the party as a way station to their own Americanization. And finally, the SP attracted numerous adherents from the lively world of pre–World War I reform, members of the

Edward Bellamy. The author of *Looking Backward*, the enormously popular, and temporarily influential, utopian novel published in 1888. LIBRARY OF CONGRESS

social gospel, Progressive, and feminist movements. These intellectuals and social movement leaders put the ideas and values of Debsian socialism in fruitful dialogue with other liberal currents and reform institutions. Socialists of both the left and the right played an organic role in the agitation for women's suffrage, the abolition of child labor, and unemployment insurance. Jane Addams, Walter Lippmann, Florence Kelley, Helen Keller, Upton Sinclair, Jack London, Carl Sandburg, and Vida Scudder worked effectively within this milieu.

Aside from Debs, hundreds of socialists campaigned for state and local offices during these years and scores were elected to municipal posts, notably in Milwaukee, Reading, Pennsylvania, Berkeley, California, Butte, Montana, and Flint, Michigan; in various small towns in the upper Midwest; and in states of intense post-Populist conflict such as Oklahoma, Arkansas, and Kansas. With more than three hundred periodicals, mostly weeklies, the party press was even more varied and influential. The Yiddish-language *Jewish Daily Forward* had a circulation of 200,000, while the Kansas-based weekly, the *Appeal to Reason*, peaked at three-quarters of a million subscribers. Scores of immigrant newspapers, like the Slovakian *Rovnost Ludu*, the Slovenian *Proletarec*, and the three Finnish papers—

Tyomies, Raivaaja, and *Toveri*—sustained the socialist idea within that large portion of the American working class whose native tongue was not English.

Internal Divisions and External Repression

This sprawling, multi-ethnic movement was ideologically fractious. No machine ran the party, although in Milwaukee, Victor Berger and other German trade unionists established an organization of considerable durability. In New York City, the Jewish-socialist garment unions were a powerful bloc. Debs was the most famous socialist of his day, but he avoided participation in many of the party's internal disputes. In contrast to socialist practice in Russia and Germany, the party's own publication, the *International Socialist Review*, was a popular and eclectic journal of opinion, not an authoritative ideological organ. This pluralism put the party very much within the American political vein, but as with all third parties in American history, the frustrations endemic to perpetual opposition generated a set of ideological divisions that fractured the party in the second decade of the twentieth century.

Two fissures were particularly important because they layered ideological dispute on top of social and ethnic division. In all socialist parties, tensions arose over trade union strategy and its relationship to political action. This became particularly acute in the United States with the growth of a working-class syndicalism that challenged the increasingly conservative AFL leadership in the years after 1905, when the radical INDUSTRIAL WORKERS OF THE WORLD was founded. Hostile to both electoral action and business unionism, it attracted the allegiance of many socialists, among them William Haywood, who led insurrectionary mass strikes among western metal miners and eastern textile workers. His influence within the SP was opposed by a more reformist wing, led by Berger and the New York City intellectual Morris Hillquit. They thought that Haywood's militant rhetoric on behalf of "sabotage," which they interpreted as meaning violence, and his disdain for an electoral strategy were counterproductive. This wing of the party wanted to function within existing unions and cooperate with the AFL on key issues, including support for immigration restriction and the routinization of a stable, collective bargaining regime. At the party's bitterly divided 1912 convention, the forces identified with Hillquit and Berger pushed through a clause mandating the expulsion of any member advocating sabotage, after which Haywood was recalled from the party leadership in a referendum vote.

This divide in the party ranks turned into a rupture after the Bolshevik Revolution and U.S. entry into World War I. American socialists were far more antiwar than those in the mass European parties who supported their respective fatherlands. Once U.S. belligerency became official in April 1917, the socialists convened in St. Louis and by an overwhelming majority denounced American entry as an imperialistic "crime against the people." Party members were to engage in "continuous, active, and public opposition" to conscription and they were to defend the right to strike. Such principled antiwar radicalism had a dichotomous consequence. On the one hand the party enhanced its strength among all those hostile to the war. These included radical Progressives such as Randolph Bourne and John Reed; pacifists like the young Presbyterian minister, Norman Thomas; an emerging group of Harlem blacks grouped around A. Philip Randolph's *Messenger*; and most important, an increasingly large mass of immigrant socialists, inspired by the Russian Revolution, who were organized into several foreign-language sections of the party. Despite government repression and patriotic fervor, a burst of socialist electoral enthusiasm gave party campaigners up to one-third of the vote in many industrial districts. In the Midwest and Northeast, several socialists were elected to state legislatures and to municipal office.

Despite socialism's appeal during an era when the capitalist nation-state revealed a barbarian visage, American socialism virtually collapsed. First, government repression and patriotic vigilantism proved debilitating. The militantly antiwar Industrial Workers of the World was practically destroyed when, in September 1917, Justice Department agents raided its offices across the nation and arrested virtually the entire leadership. The SP did not suffer such an onslaught, but numerous leaders, including Eugene Debs, spent years in court or in jail because of their vocal opposition to the war.

Divisions within the party, however, were far more debilitating than government repression. Although most socialists were antiwar, many intellectuals, especially those who sought to link the socialist idea to Progressive-Era state building, abandoned the party and supported the Wilsonian war effort. These included both the radical novelist Upton Sinclair and the "revisionist" theoretician William English Walling. A more numerous and consequential defection came on the left after the Bolshevik Revolution split the world socialist movement into those who defended and those who denounced the power of the Soviets. In the United States the socialist Right, oriented toward trade unionism and municipal reform, denounced Bolshevik autocracy and fought to maintain control of the party against a revolutionary Left, whose mass base lay with those eastern European socialists who looked to Moscow for inspiration and guidance. Although the right-leaning functionaries retained control of the party apparatus in 1919 and 1920, their victory was a Pyrrhic one, for a rival set of communist splinter parties emerged out of the factionalism of the SP Left even as tens of thousands of militants drifted from Socialist Party life. In the 1920s and early 1930s the SP remained larger than even a unified Communist Party, but its membership was older, less active, and concentrated in but a few regions, notably southeast Wisconsin and New York City.

The Great Depression and Afterward

Organized socialism in the United States never recovered from this debacle. In the early 1930s the Great Depression made anti-capitalist ideologies attractive to millions, and in Norman Thomas, the SP acquired a most inspiring spokesman who gained 885,000 votes (2.2 percent) in the 1932 presidential vote. But the party could never translate its ethical appeal and economic critique into organizational strength during the depression decade. There were two reasons for this. First, as Thomas would later put it, "Roosevelt stole our program." The main thrust of the New Deal was to stabilize U.S. capitalism and ameliorate class conflict, so Norman Thomas remained a sharp critic of Rooseveltian compromise and failure, especially when it came to the plight of southern sharecroppers, inadequate New Deal relief, and U.S. unwillingness to support the Spanish republic. But few socialists were revolutionaries in the 1930s; since the Progressive Era, they had advanced a social democratic program designed to ameliorate and restructure capitalism. New Deal reforms that regulated business, encouraged trade unionism, and framed a welfare state fulfilled enough of that agenda to rob socialism of its working-class base and union leadership cadre. In 1936 most union socialists, led by a powerful old guard from the garment trades, supported FDR as a Democrat, or in New York state as the candidate of the American Labor Party, which was designed to channel left-wing votes to New Deal candidates.

Equally important, the Socialist Party of the depression decade and afterward never developed an electoral strategy or an ideological posture that avoided a debilitating sectarianism. For a time the American communists did much better. Their ideological and electoral opportunism during the era of the Popular Front did not split the Communist Party because all domestic issues were tangential to the overriding commitment of defending the Soviet Union and adhering to its "line." (The CP collapsed in the years after 1956 not because McCarthyite repression had finally taken its toll, but because long-simmering internal disputes over the character of the international communist movement finally came to a head when Soviet Party leader Nikita Khrushchev demoralized communists by admitting to many of Stalin's criminal blunders.) But the socialists had no foreign lodestar, so the lure of participation in mainstream politics generated division after division within party ranks. When new industrial unions arose in the nation's basic industries, socialists like Walter Reuther and Philip Van Gelder easily ascended to important posts. Unlike the Communists, however, they never formed a coherent bloc and most left the SP before the end of the 1930s. Meanwhile, the most active and intellectually resourceful SP youth were periodically recruited away, often by the Trotskyists, whose rigorous critique of both capitalism and Stalinism proved highly attractive. By 1941 a "silent split" in the party, precipitated by Norman Thomas's pacifist opposition to World War II, had reduced the SP to little more than a sect.

The American Socialist Party abandoned most electoral politics after 1948, and instead sought a realignment of the two-party system so as to more effectively influence labor and the Democrats. Unfortunately, the socialists' flight to mainstream political relevance put them at odds with the new radicalism of the 1960s. Although many leaders of the Students for a Democratic Society had been nurtured within a world of socialist institutions and ideas, socialists in the 1960s distanced themselves from the politics and culture of the New Left. American socialism's most prominent spokesman, Michael Harrington, whose politics had been shaped under the tutelage of Max Schactman's Trotskyist brand of anti-Stalinism, was attuned to the coalition-building strategy of the AFL-CIO leadership and disdainful of the New Left's anti-anti-Communism. Likewise, SP loyalists were at best equivocal about the U.S. war in Vietnam, which many saw as a necessary fight against third-world Stalinism. By the end of 1972 this had engendered yet another party fission, with Harrington leading a left-liberal breakaway faction, the Democratic Socialist Organizing Committee (which in 1982 became the Democratic Socialists of America). The rest of the party also split, with a tiny pacifist fraction retaining rights to the old Socialist Party name, while a well-connected strata of neoconservatives, calling themselves Social Democrats USA, were providing intellectual firepower for the Reaganite assault on Cold War détente, post–New Deal liberalism, and affirmative action policies to aid racial minorities.

Assessments of American Socialism

The ostensible failure of U.S. socialism has long fascinated historians and social scientists. In 1906 the German sociologist Werner Sombart entitled a study of American society, *Why Is There No Socialism in the United States?* He answered, "On the reefs of roast beef and apple pie socialist Utopias of every sort are sent to their doom." In other words, American capitalism was so successful and so "exceptional" that the socialist appeal could make little headway, certainly in comparison to Europe. This argument for an American exceptionalism has been a hardy perennial, with Louis Hartz and Seymour Martin Lipset among the most important late-twentieth-century proponents of this thesis. Hartz argued that the absence of a feudal past meant that America was, in effect, born bourgeois. Like Hartz, Lipset also offered something close to a metahistorical causality, emphasizing the nation's hegemonic Protestant-individualistic culture that he thought mediated against collectivist values and institutions. Other "exceptionalist" features of the U.S. political scene have included ethnic and racial divisions within the working population and the federalist character of the U.S. electoral system.

Another influential answer to the "why no socialism" question was advanced by Daniel Bell, who asserted in *Marxian Socialism in the United States* (1952) that the socialist impulse was an essentially religious, chiliastic one. Whatever their rhetoric or program, socialists were "trapped by the unhappy problem of living in but not of the world, so they could only act, and then inadequately, as a moral, but not a political force in an immoral society." Bell's critique may have had some plausibility at midcentury, when memories of the socialist debacle during the Great Depression decade were still fresh. But he ignored the experience of the western European social democratic parties, which were often members of governing coalitions that built the modern welfare state. Furthermore, his argument for an inherent socialist sectarianism also failed to recognize the incremental, reformist character of socialist (and communist) strategy during the entire second half of the twentieth century.

Indeed, socialism's legacy during the twentieth century has been twofold. First, its values, aspirations, and analysis have always been far more influential than its party organizations. Ex-socialists did not flee a God that failed, but instead sought a more efficacious venue to put their ideals into practice. This has often generated a creatively ambiguous line between socialists and reformers, especially during the Progressive Era and the New Deal and in unions, among many feminists, and in movements for peace and civil rights. In practice, if not theory, liberalism and socialism have been joined at the hip. The second key legacy of American socialism was a highly influential critique of Stalinism and other forms of authoritarian collectivism. From the mid-1920s, most socialists have argued that the Soviet model should be fought, at home and abroad, because of the communist failure to embody core socialist values: industrial democracy, social equality, and anti-imperialism. Remarkably, this was the critique adopted by the more sophisticated proponents of the U.S. posture throughout much of the Cold War, that the communist states of Asia and Eastern Europe were mendacious, not because they abolished capitalism or suppressed religion, but because they generated a new bureaucratic ruling class that presided over regimes that were unfree, inequitable, and imperialistic.

BIBLIOGRAPHY

Bell, Daniel. *Marxian Socialism in the United States.* 1952. Ithaca, N.Y.: Cornell University Press, 1996.

Buhle, Mari Jo. *Women and American Socialism, 1870–1920.* Urbana: University of Illinois Press, 1981.

———, Paul Buhle, and Dan Georgakas. *Encyclopedia of the American Left.* Urbana: University of Illinois Press, 1990.

Buhle, Paul. *Marxism in the United Sates: Remapping the History of the American Left.* London: Verso, 1987.

Harrington, Michael. *Socialism.* New York: Bantam Books, 1972.

Howe, Irving. *Socialism and America.* San Diego, Calif.: Harcourt Brace, 1985.

Isserman, Maurice. *The Other American: The Life of Michael Harrington.* New York: Public Affairs, 2000.

Kipnis, Ira. *The American Socialist Movement: 1897–1912.* New York: Columbia University Press, 1952.

Kloppenberg, James T. *Uncertain Victory: Social Democracy and Progressivism in European and American Thought, 1870–1920.* New York: Oxford University Press, 1986.

Lipow, Arthur. *Authoritarian Socialism in America: Edward Bellamy and the Nationalist Movement.* Berkeley: University of California Press, 1982.

Lipset, Seymour Martin, and Gary Marks. *It Didn't Happen Here: Why Socialism Failed in the United States.* New York: Norton, 2000.

Salvatore, Nick. *Eugene V. Debs: Citizen and Socialist.* Urbana: University of Illinois Press, 1982.

Swanberg, W. A. *Norman Thomas: The Last Idealist.* New York: Scribner, 1976.

Wald, Alan M. *The New York Intellectuals: The Rise and Decline of the Anti-Stalinist Left from the 1930s to the 1980s.* Chapel Hill: University of North Carolina Press, 1987.

Warren, Frank A. *An Alternative Vision: The Socialist Party in the 1930s.* Bloomington: University of Indiana Press, 1974.

Weinstein, James. *The Decline of Socialism in America, 1912–1925.* New York: Monthly Review Press, 1967

Nelson Lichtenstein

See also **Communist Party, United States of America; Newspapers.**

SOCIALIST PARTY OF AMERICA

SOCIALIST PARTY OF AMERICA was formed in July 1901 by a union of the Social Democratic Party of Eugene V. Debs and Victor L. Berger, and Morris Hillquit's wing of the Socialist Labor Party. The Socialist Party gave to American radicalism, normally fragmented and divided, a unique era of organizational unity. The party was well entrenched in the labor movement: the Socialist candidate captured almost one-third of the vote for the presidency of the American Federation of Labor in 1912. In that year, too, the Socialists reached the high point of their electoral success: Eugene V. Debs, running for the U.S. presidency, gained 6 percent of the vote; and some twelve hundred Socialists were elected to public office, including seventy-nine mayors.

The party's growth stopped after 1912, but the following years can be characterized as a time of consolidation rather than as a time of decline. For once departing from its policy of inclusiveness, the party, in 1913, cast out the syndicalist wing led by William D. Haywood. By eliminating the one group not committed to political action, the party became more cohesive without altering the balance between the right and left wings. World War I severely tested, but did not undermine, the Socialist movement. During wartime persecution, Debs and many others went to prison; vigilante action and the barring of Socialist literature from the mails weakened outlying bodies, especially in the western states. These setbacks were more than counterbalanced by the rapid growth of the party's foreign-language federations and by the tapping of antiwar sentiment, as was evident in the party's strong showing in wartime elections.

The Bolshevik revolution in Russia (1917) was the turning point for the party. The problem was not the event itself—this was universally hailed by American Socialists—but whether it provided a model for the United States. The left wing, and especially the foreign-language federations, believed that it did, and they were sustained by instructions coming from the Third Communist International in 1919. The party leaders thought otherwise: they did not think that the United States was ripe for revolution, nor were they willing to reconstitute the party along Leninist lines. With the left wing about to take over, the established leadership in May 1919 suddenly expelled seven foreign-language federations and the entire Michigan party, and invalidated the recent elections to the national executive committee.

A decisive break with the past had occurred. Not only was American radicalism permanently split between Communists and Socialists, the latter had lost their authenticity as a movement of radical action. By 1928, Socialist membership was not even one-tenth of the 1919 level, and, although it experienced some revival during the 1930s under Norman Thomas, the party never regained either its popular base or the electoral appeal of earlier years. After 1956 the Socialist party ceased to nominate presidential candidates and increasingly viewed itself as an educational rather than a political force.

BIBLIOGRAPHY

Shannon, David A. *The Socialist Party of America: A History.* New York: Macmillan, 1955.

Weinstein, James. *The Decline of Socialism in America, 1912–1925.* New York: Monthly Review Press, 1967.

David Brody/A. G.

See also **Communist Party, United States of America; Radicals and Radicalism; Social Democratic Party; Socialist Labor Party; Socialist Movement.**

SOCIETY FOR ETHICAL CULTURE.

SOCIETY FOR ETHICAL CULTURE. See **Ethical Culture, Society for.**

SOCIETY FOR THE PREVENTION OF CRUELTY TO ANIMALS.

SOCIETY FOR THE PREVENTION OF CRUELTY TO ANIMALS. Within a decade of the founding of the American Society for the Prevention of Cruelty to Animals (1866) in New York, citizens in dozens of communities in the United States and Canada established independent organizations to pursue similar work. The proliferation of societies for the prevention of cruelty to animals (SPCAs) in the immediate post–Civil War era reflected a dynamic convergence between rising social interest in animal protection and the numerous practical challenges associated with the incorporation of animals into a burgeoning urban industrial society. The SPCAs pursued a broad agenda, addressing the mistreatment of animals in transportation and conveyance, food production, entertainment, recreation, experimental physiology, and other contexts.

Many SPCAs secured both state charters granting limited law enforcement power and the passage of rudimentary anticruelty statutes, but prosecution of cruelty was only one approach to reform. Advocates also devoted their energy to educating children in the humane treatment of animals and the general dissemination of information concerning animal care. In addition, the SPCAs provided a range of services and programs to better the conditions in which animals worked and lived, particularly in the cities. The movement against cruelty to animals enjoyed strong support from women, and had significant ties to the temperance and child protection movements.

BIBLIOGRAPHY

Finsen, Lawrence, and Susan Finsen. *The Animal Rights Movement in America: From Compassion to Respect.* New York: Twayne, 1994.

Bernard Unti

See also **Animal Protective Societies; Animal Rights Movement.**

SOCIETY FOR THE PREVENTION OF CRUELTY TO CHILDREN.

In April 1874 the American Society for the Prevention of Cruelty to Animals obtained the protection of the state for Mary Ellen Wilson, a mistreated child. In April 1875, because of this case, the first child protective agency, the New York Society for the Prevention of Cruelty to Children, was incorporated. During the ensuing quarter century, more than 150 similar societies emerged. Such agencies aim to protect abused and neglected children. The child protective agency investigates accusations of child neglect or abuse and offers services to correct home conditions and, in appropriate situations, secures protection of the child by legal proceedings. Child protective services exist in every state.

BIBLIOGRAPHY

Cooter, Roger, ed. *In the Name of the Child: Health and Welfare, 1880–1940.* London; New York: Routledge, 1992.

Lawrence, Jon, and Pat Starkey, eds. *Child Welfare and Social Action in the Nineteenth and Twentieth Centuries: International Perspectives.* Liverpool, U.K.: Liverpool University Press, 2001.

Thomas Becker/A. E.

See also **Child Abuse; Domestic Violence; Family; Foster Care.**

SOCIETY FOR THE PROPAGATION OF THE GOSPEL IN FOREIGN PARTS.

Founded in 1701, the Society for the Propagation of the Gospel in Foreign Parts, sometimes called the Venerable Society, conducted the foreign mission work of the Anglican Church in the American colonies and other English possessions overseas. Between 1702 and 1785, when it withdrew from the mission field in the United States, it sent out 309 ordained missionaries and distributed thousands of Bibles, tracts, and prayer books. It also sent out schoolteachers, medical missionaries, and libraries. In 1775 it was helping to support seventy-seven missionaries in the continental colonies, but as the Revolution progressed most of them were forced to retire.

BIBLIOGRAPHY

Butler, Jon. *Awash in a Sea of Faith: Christianizing the American People.* Cambridge, Mass.: Harvard University Press, 1990.

Pascoe, F. C. *Two Hundred Years of the S. P. G., 1701–1900: An Historical Account of the Society for the Propagation of Bible in Foreign Parts.* London, 1901.

Hugh T. Lefler/A. R.

See also **American Bible Society; Church of England in the Colonies.**

SOCIETY FOR WOMEN'S HEALTH RESEARCH,

formerly the Society for the Advancement of Women's Health Research, was established in 1990 out of its founders' belief that biases in biomedical research put women's health at risk. Led by Florence P. Haseltine and Phyllis Greenberger, the society gained political influence through its involvement in federal funding of research. A 1989 report by the General Accounting Office (GAO) found that almost no progress had been made by the NATIONAL INSTITUTES OF HEALTH (NIH) in implementing its 1986 policy to include women as subjects in clinical research. On 18 June 1990, congressional hearings were held to address the issue, and the society led the charge to inform the public of the GAO's findings. As a result, the Women's Health Equity Act of 1990 was introduced by the Congressional Caucus on Women's Issues in July 1990. The society was also involved with the NIH Revitalization Act of 1993, which explicitly required the inclusion of women in federally funded clinical research. The society has also established a Clinical Trials Alliance and created an educational campaign called "Some Things Only a Woman Can Do" to inform women of the importance of participating in clinical trials.

BIBLIOGRAPHY

Alexander, Linda Lewis. *New Dimensions in Women's Health.* Boston: Jones and Bartlett, 1994; 2d ed., 2001.

Mastroianni, Anna C., et al. *Women and Health Research: Ethical and Legal Issues of Including Women in Clinical Studies.* Washington D.C.: National Academy Press, 1994.

Shira M. Diner

See also **Medical Research; Women's Health.**

SOCIETY OF AMERICAN INDIANS

(SAI), the first modern lobby of American Indians, was founded on Columbus Day in 1911 by prominent professional American Indians under the direction of the sociologist Fayette Avery McKenzie, who frequently invited Indian guests to his classes at Ohio State University. The society offered individual, not tribal, membership to American Indians and associate memberships to non-Indians. American Indian members of the SAI were their generation's best and brightest, reflecting assimilation in both their personal and professional lives. Among the SAI's leaders were the Reverend Sherman Coolidge (Arapaho), an Episcopal priest; Arthur C. Parker (Seneca), an anthropologist; Charles Eastman (Santee Sioux) and Carlos Montezuma (Yavapai Apache), both physicians; Laura Kellogg (Oneida), an educator; Thomas Sloan (Omaha), an attorney; and Gertrude Bonnin (Yankton Sioux), an author.

One of the goals of the SAI was to educate the American public about the abilities and aspirations of American Indians. To achieve that goal it began publishing the *Quarterly Journal of the American Indian* (1913–1915), which was renamed *American Indian Magazine* (1916–1920). Conflicting ideologies caused a schism among the society's Indian leaders by 1920. Issues contributing to the dissent were peyote usage on Indian reservations and federal administrative policies. With the exception of 1917, the SAI held a well-publicized convention every Indian summer from 1911 to 1923.

BIBLIOGRAPHY

Hertzberg, Hazel W. *The Search for an American Indian Identity: Modern Pan-Indian Movements.* Syracuse, N.Y.: Syracuse University Press, 1971. The most comprehensive study of the SAI.

Nabokov, Peter. "A Twentieth-Century Indian Voice." In *Native American Testimony: A Chronicle of Indian-White Relations from Prophecy to the Present, 1492–2000.* Edited by Peter Nabokov. New York: Penguin, 1999. Contains testimonials from the opening conference of the SAI in 1911.

Society of American Indians. *The American Indian Magazine.* Washington, D.C.: Society of American Indians (January 1916–August 1920).

———. *The Papers of the Society of American Indians.* Edited by John W. Larner Jr. Wilmington, Del.: Scholarly Resources, 1987. Ten reels of microfilm accompanied by a printed guide.

Susan Dominguez

See also **Indian Policy, U.S., 1900–2000.**

SOCIOLOGY. While the discipline of sociology had its roots in nineteenth-century Europe, it enjoyed its greatest success in the United States during the academic golden age of the mid-twentieth century. Making a science of society was a distinctly modern exercise. Not only did it depend on a modern concept of empirical, experimental science, but it also presupposed "society" as a new object of study. How was one to name, classify, and analyze the forms of human experience in the aggregate—that is, if one sought to discern an aggregate form beyond

relations of kin and distinguished from the apparatus of formal government? A kind of age-old ethnography had long enabled observers to comment on the traits of different peoples, usually by remarking on the exotic look and habits of aliens. Also, the idea of large cultural units or civilizations, usually wedded to imperial domains or great religions, such as Christendom, had a long history. Far less developed was the concept of an order to human relations apart from family, state, ethnicity, or belief that might become the basis for a comparative anatomy of differing communities. Modern notions of "economy" and "society" emerged to name such an order, as European colonial expansion, political revolution, and industrialization stirred consciousness of great change and variation in the form human relations could take. From the Scottish Enlightenment of the late eighteenth century to the universities of Wilhelmine Germany at the beginning of the twentieth century, the terms of economy and society were conjoined and contrasted in various ways. In large part, sociology matured as the second term became clearly differentiated from the first. Surprisingly, it was in the United States, where individualism and the pursuit of wealth seemed to reign supreme, that sociology as a study of the collective, noneconomic forms of human life found its most secure home.

The First Sociologists

Although historians cite the beginning of modern social sciences in the work of Thomas Hobbes (1588–1679), the focus in his masterwork *Leviathan* (1651) on the formation and authority of the state denies him the title of the "first sociologist," which has been bestowed instead on the Scottish writer Adam Ferguson (1723–1816). Ferguson's *Essay on the History of Civil Society* (1767) countered Hobbes in asserting that social sentiments—that is, desires to associate with others due to a dislike of solitude, sympathy with one's fellows and a desire for their esteem, or simple habit—were indeed as "natural" to individuals as their self-regarding appetites. Yet it was the French polymath Auguste Comte (1798–1857) who first used the term "sociology," in 1839 as part of his *Course of Positive Philosophy* and elaborated on its meaning in his *System of Positive Polity* (1851–1854).

Americans generally thought of "society" as the eighteenth-century Scottish writers had, recognizing social sentiments but still putting liberal ideas of individualism, progress, and market relations in the forefront. Comte's sociology was first adopted in the United States in 1854 by two writers venturing a principled defense of southern slavery, George Fitzhugh (1806–1881) in *Sociology for the South* and Henry Hughes (1829–1862) in *Treatise on Sociology.* Both of these authors contrasted slave society with "free society," for them virtually an oxymoron. Principles of individualism and equality, they wrote, eroded social organization as such. From Comte they borrowed the notion that "society" constituted a realm in itself, unified by sentiments concerned with the well-being of the whole and founded, like a family, on hierarchical norms in which superiors governed and cared for dependents incapable of self-rule. Just as Comte fell into obscurity for several decades after his death in 1857, the work of Fitzhugh and Hughes turned out to be a dead-end once the Civil War and the end of slavery made liberal principles all but universal in American society and culture.

American sociology was reborn in the 1880s under different circumstances and with different premises. When William Graham Sumner (1840–1910) began teaching the subject of sociology at Yale University, he relied on its individualistic British exponent Herbert Spencer (1820–1903). In this view human evolution naturally led toward a modern world in which individuals were habituated to peaceful practices of exchange while the power of the state and coercive rule steadily declined. Hence, free will was rendered compatible with social order. This utopia of social order modeled on the ideal of a free market carried a decided moral meaning for Sumner, who insisted that self-sufficiency was the greatest obligation the individual bore toward society and that the plight of the pauper was the rightful consequence of dissipation. Sumner was challenged by a career civil servant, Lester Frank Ward (1841–1913), who brought Comtean principles back to the American scene by advocating an active state that nurtured the common welfare. According to Ward's 1883 book *Dynamic Sociology*, social evolution was to be guided by human intelligence rather than understood in naturalistic terms as a phenomenon impervious to will.

Beginnings of Academic Sociology

These early skirmishes over laissez-faire principles and social reform marked the prologue of institutionalized sociology in the United States. By the beginning of the twentieth century a new generation of intellectuals, coming of age amidst economic instability, industrial strife, and dramatic inequalities of wealth, was ready to combine a reforming spirit with the new repute of science in the emerging research universities. The American Social Science Association (ASSA), founded in 1865, represented an early effort to bring organized intelligence to bear on charitable activities concerned with social problems such as pauperism and crime. In 1885 a group of young American scholars, trained abroad in German universities and eager to see the state bring "social" values to bear on economic affairs, split off from the ASSA to establish the American Economic Association (AEA), the prototype for other specialized professional societies such as the American Political Science Association, founded in 1903. Sociology lagged behind. In 1893 the University of Chicago established the first American chair in sociology, awarded to the social gospel minister Albion Woodbury Small (1854–1926), and under Small's editorship the first issue of the *American Journal of Sociology* appeared in 1895. Ten years later, at the economists' professional meeting, Small and others founded their own organization, the American Sociological Society, later renamed the American Sociological Association (ASA).

Although these academic circles were composed almost entirely of men, women activists in settlement houses helped pioneer the disciplined study of urban and industrial affairs. The social surveys of immigrant neighborhoods conducted by Jane Addams (1860–1935) and her colleagues at Hull-House provided an early model of community research for the University of Chicago sociologists nearby. A few women devoted to studying social problems managed to forge a place in university life, such as Grace Abbott (1878–1939) and Sophonisba Breckinridge (1866–1948), also at the University of Chicago, though they were soon segregated from the male sociologists in a separate school of social work. Elsewhere, W. E. B. Du Bois (1868–1963) made a distinctive contribution to the new styles of social research when his book *The Philadelphia Negro* (1899) demonstrated that "social" conditions, such as poverty and discrimination rather than inbred "racial" traits, accounted for regrettable features of crime and broken families among black slum dwellers.

The reformist mood of early academic social science was, however, quite modest and restrained. The middle-class reformers who entered the new academic social sciences typically recoiled from class struggle and wished instead to foster social peace by ameliorating conditions of deprivation, conflict, and misunderstanding. In any case conservative university administrators and trustees imposed strict limits on advocacy of social change. The prolabor activism of Ward's follower Edward A. Ross (1866–1951) led to Ross's forced resignation from Stanford University in 1900. Other early leaders in the field looked askance at social reform. Franklin Giddings (1855–1931), who assumed a chair in sociology at Columbia University two years after Small's appointment at Chicago, sought instead to frame truly "scientific" means of observation, data collection, and statistical measures for social facts. Nonetheless, Small regarded his Christian ideal of a harmonious society as thoroughly compatible with his aspirations for social science, and he persisted in seeing the discipline as an intimate partner to reformers in the field of social welfare. For years, many colleges in the United States used the term "sociology" for courses dealing with charities and corrections, thus carrying on the tradition of the ASSA.

Sociology Professionalized

A clearer differentiation of sociology from social welfare began in the 1910s and continued into the 1920s. The landmark study by W. I. Thomas (1863–1947) and Florian Znaniecki (1882–1958), *The Polish Peasant in Europe and America* (1918–1920), helped establish the characteristic disposition of Chicago's increasingly professionalized department: the study of change in the life of social groups, understood as a process of "social disorganization" (the loss of traditional norms) and "reorganization" (adaptation to modern life) experienced by recent immigrants from rural villages to the industrial city; a focus, informed by the philosophy of George Herbert Mead (1863–1931) and the "social psychology" of Charles Horton Cooley (1864–1929), on the individual's subjective interpretation of social situations as it emerged in his or her interactions with others; and consequently a style of urban research founded on participant observation, designed both to achieve empathy with the viewpoints of social actors and to map the terrain on which they encountered others, that is, social structure understood as an ecology of social groups. This approach was codified by the new leaders of Chicago sociology in the 1920s, Robert E. Park (1864–1944) and Ernest Burgess (1886–1966), commencing a vibrant body of research on city neighborhoods, ethnicity and racial groups, and youth gangs and other phenomena, such as the lives of con men and prostitutes, on the margins of polite society.

As the "Chicago school" matured, another touchstone of American sociology was in the works. The community study *Middletown* (1929) by Robert S. Lynd (1892–1970) and Helen Merrell Lynd (1896–1982) examined work, family, religion, leisure, and civic life in Muncie, Indiana, under the stress of industrial development, class divisions, and modern transportation and communications. Robert Lynd went on to head the new Social Science Research Council (SSRC), begun with Rockefeller backing in 1923 to fund empirical research and promote scientific development through professional seminars on methodology. Before long, an early sign of government interest in sociology appeared in the publication of *Recent Social Trends* (1932), the work of a committee impaneled by President Herbert Hoover in the fall of 1929 but funded largely by the Rockefeller Foundation and the SSRC. Tellingly, the President's Research Committee on Social Trends was cochaired by an economist, Wesley C. Mitchell (1874–1948), and a political scientist, Charles E. Merriam (1874–1953), representing the more established social science disciplines. But its research was conducted under the leadership of bona fide sociologists, William F. Ogburn (1886–1959), who earned a Ph.D. at Columbia University and then went to Chicago, and Howard W. Odum (1884–1954), another Columbia graduate, who brought academic sociology to the University of North Carolina. Despite its testimony to public interest in sociological research, however, the committee's report was criticized sharply by other sociologists, who considered its dry record of numerical trends in divorce, urbanization, and rates of technological invention unilluminating and uninspired.

By 1928, ninety-nine American colleges and universities had departments of sociology, five times as many as in 1910, and forty-eight others had departments defined as "economics and sociology." In the next decade, sociology achieved a stronger professional footing despite limited prospects for growth during the Great Depression. The membership of the ASA fell drastically, but those who remained were more strictly academic in orientation. As these scholars chafed under the domination of Chicago's inbred sociology department, they demanded that the organization better represent the profession as a whole. Yet the field lacked the kind of unity and coherence customarily claimed by self-conscious professions, and widespread disagreements flourished on what it meant to build a science of society, as the dispute over *Recent Social Trends* suggested. A vigorous cohort of Columbia-bred sociologists spread throughout the country and pursued the ideal of an "objective" science of society in terms bequeathed to them by Giddings. Their ideal was based not on Chicago's intimate observation of groups, their interactions and their sentiments, but rather on statistical generalizations about the attributes and preferences of individuals, a project that flourished in time with the help of new techniques drawn from opinion polling and market research. Other competitors for disciplinary leadership included the pugnacious Luther L. Bernard (1881–1951), the advocate of an updated Comtean social realism.

The real problem of sociology, compared to fields like economics and political science, lay in uncertainty over the definition of its essential subject matter. Since the 1890s, sociology had been defined alternatively as a kind of master discipline offering a comprehensive vision of society and incorporating all other specialties or as a "residual" field covering issues and problems not addressed elsewhere, such as crime and family. In hopes of escaping this quandary, some figures in the 1930s renewed the attempt to build sociological theory out of traditions of social philosophy. Giddings's successor at the helm of Columbia's department, Robert MacIver (1882–1979), moved in this direction. So did the young Talcott Parsons (1902–1979) at Harvard University. The fact that neither of these figures had any prior training in established sociology departments showed how much the discipline was still, during the 1930s, a work in progress.

Harvard had taught sociology in association with economic history and philanthropic "social ethics," moving to found its own department only in 1931 under the leadership of Pitirim Sorokin (1889–1968), a Russian émigré and author of the compendium *Contemporary Sociological Theories* (1928). In contrast to Sorokin's urge to classify the many variants of theory that composed the field, Parsons believed that a scientific discipline rightly had only one theory, a founding charter established by the synthesis of tendencies formerly at odds with each other. Parsons had been introduced to the social sciences by disciples of the dissenting economist Thorstein Veblen (1857–1929) and knew little of Chicago's or Columbia's sociological traditions. In his early masterwork, *The Structure of Social Action* (1937), Parsons portrayed a dawning convergence among exponents of English, French, German, and Italian social thought that overcame the customary divide between "positivist" or empiricist approaches to discovering objective social laws and "idealist" traditions that stressed the unpredictable force of human consciousness and will. But Parsons's synthesis also attempted to get beyond the social "realism" of a Comtean like Bernard and the "nominalist" position of the Giddings school, for whom society was merely a convenient term for an aggregate of individuals. Parsons sought to define "society" as something quite real, even if not a concrete entity in its own right. It was to be understood as an aspect of human experience that, strictly speaking, could be isolated only for the convenience of analysis, namely that element of human action that assured social order primarily by virtue of an integrated set of values held in common by a body of actors.

The Heyday of American Sociology

Parsons was important to the development of American sociology for a number of reasons. Having built his theoretical convergence largely on the work of Emile Durkheim (1858–1918), Max Weber (1864–1920), and Sigmund Freud (1856–1939), Parsons played a crucial role in drawing grand traditions of European social thought into the American milieu. Parsons's synthetic disposition also led him to promote the realignment of sociology with cultural anthropology and social psychology, a tripartite arrangement realized in a new, interdisciplinary department of social relations begun at Harvard in 1946. The result was a clearer definition of sociology's subject matter, the social realm, than the discipline had ever had before. In Parsons's hands, sociology moved away from close associations with the older, dominant fields of economics and political science. Its special concern was those institutions, such as families, schools, churches, neighborhoods, small groups, organizations, and occupations. In these milieus of association and interaction, scholars could see the formation of personalities, roles, values, orientations, perceptions of reality, sentiments of solidarity, and the like. In this way was everyday behavior shaped and social unity fostered. And in these terms sociology defined the essential "structure" of a society, the patterns of behavior that gave it a unique order and disposition distinct from that of other societies, thus permitting a comparative anatomy of societies.

The immediate post–World War II decades marked the heyday of American sociology. Young scholars entering the academy in the 1940s and 1950s, often of immigrant, wartime émigré, and left-wing backgrounds, helped fuel the field's growth. At the same time, funding increased dramatically from private philanthropies. While Rockefeller funds had dominated in the 1920s and 1930s, now the Ford and Carnegie foundations made large contributions. By the 1960s, government sources offered support from the National Science Foundation, the National Institute of Mental Health, the Defense Department, and the Department of Health, Education, and Welfare. The field's infrastructure developed as large-scale survey-research centers at Columbia, Chicago, and Michigan, supported by grants and contracts, provided both jobs and masses of data.

Meanwhile, works such as Gunnar Myrdal's *An American Dilemma* (1944), David Riesman's *The Lonely Crowd* (1950), and William Whyte's *The Organization Man* (1956) garnered popular attention for sociology. Ideas cultivated by sociology along with cultural anthropology and social psychology regarding the "culture of poverty," "deviance" and opportunity structures, as well as schooling and race became part and parcel of public debate, policy formation, and presidential speeches in the era of desegregation and the war on poverty. Sociology became an ever more popular field for students at both the undergraduate and graduate levels, attracting many of the young dissenters who populated campuses in the 1960s and 1970s. As American universities boomed in size, the ASA continued to grow. By 1972 its peak of 15,000 members represented a tenfold gain over its interwar membership. With this kind of growth, American sociology overshadowed developments in the European countries that were sources of the classics in modern social theory, and European thinkers concluded they had to come to terms with American standards in sociological theory as well as empirical methods.

Despite the common impression that Parsons's "structural-functional" theory of the 1950s represented the prevailing paradigm of postwar sociology, the discipline in fact was never so unified that it rested on a single coherent theoretical foundation. The landmark works in empirical sociology during the postwar period, many of them by the Austrian émigré Paul Lazarsfeld (1901–1976) of Columbia's Bureau of Applied Social Research and the students he trained there, rested on refinements of survey and statistical techniques, assisted by computerized data processing, with no special relation to the kind of abstract theory cultivated by Parsons. Also competing with Parsons's theory was the more modest, "middle-range" view of functional analysis promoted by his student Robert K. Merton (b. 1910), a method intended to discover how different parts of society, its institutions and organizations, worked together and influenced each other without presuming that they all meshed neatly in a harmonious whole. Furthermore, reputable theorists such as Lewis Coser (b. 1913) and Reinhard Bendix (1916–1991) challenged the priority Parsons gave to the problem of social order and his insistence that order required normative consensus.

Outside of functionalism per se, Herbert Blumer (1900–1987) codified the social psychology of the old Chicago school in the theoretical current called "symbolic interactionism," and practitioners of Chicago-style investigations of urban communities continued to produce some lively literature, such as *Tally's Corner* (1967) by Elliot Liebow (1925–1994). Other derivatives of interactionism flourished, such as the "dramaturgical" view of roles and rituals in everyday life developed by Erving Goffman (1922–1982) and the iconoclastic "labeling" theory of deviance by Howard S. Becker (b. 1928). More ambitious forays to mount full-bore challenges to Parsonian and Mertonian functionalism, emerging from 1959 to 1966, included the critical sociology of C. Wright Mills (1916–1962), the historical sociology of Barrington

Moore (b. 1913), and the individualistic "social exchange" theory of George Homans (1910–1989). Mills in particular criticized the division of sociology between what he regarded as vacuous "grand theory" (like Parsons's) and "abstracted empiricism" (like Lazarsfeld's work), insisting instead that sociologists must draw on a large canvas the social trends that mark "the salient characteristics of their time—and the problem of how history is being made within it" (Mills, p. 165). Similarly, though without Mills's radical intent, Daniel Bell (b. 1919) defined his own work as "sociography," an attempt to delineate the general form and dynamics of contemporary social life. His influential portrait of the present and the near future is *The Coming of Post-Industrial Society* (1973).

The Mainstream Assailed

Despite the robust appearance of American sociology, it soon encountered a social, political, and intellectual crisis spawned by protest movements in the 1960s and the accompanying revival of radicalism in academic life. Like all the social science and humanist disciplines, established sociology was criticized, mainly by young graduate students, for having provided an essentially conservative ideological rationale for the status quo. In particular, they charged, the functionalist focus on mechanisms of social order obscured the significance of conflict in social life; applauded conformity with social expectations instead of dissent, deviance, and disruption; suggested that the plight of the poor stemmed from their failure to adequately adapt to normative roles rather than from the exploitative and coercive structure of inequitable social relations; and masked the privilege and bias of sociologists themselves under a false ideal of "value-free" science. The most telling criticism aimed at postwar sociology was that the very disposition that gave sociology its own distinctive "social" province, apart from economics and political science, had denied it the ability to recognize the extent to which American society was governed by punitive inequalities in the distribution and uses of wealth and power.

The charge of entrenched conservatism, vigorously advanced by Alvin Gouldner (1920–1981) in *The Coming Crisis of Western Sociology* (1970), misfired in some respects. Parsons, for one, was a liberal Democrat, and his work had emerged just when the rise of welfare states in western Europe (and more modestly in the United States in the New Deal and the Fair Deal) justified a theory that defined distinctly social needs apart from the imperatives of market economics. Indeed, American functionalism, in one form or another, found welcome abroad in Social-Democratic Sweden. Yet it was precisely the modern liberal (welfare-state) assumptions in postwar sociology combined with the anticommunist biases that governed all academic life during the Cold War era that gave social science its deep confidence in the progressive virtues of contemporary American life, including the view, characteristic of "modernization theory," that American society represented the future for all other, less-developed societies. Hence, it refrained from confronting the forms of inequality and injustice that had long shaped the development of the United States.

Consequently, the 1970s witnessed a flurry of studies dealing with the fault lines of American life. In work by William Julius Wilson (b. 1935) and other new black sociologists, racial cleavages were studied more in terms of political economy than in terms of cultural attitudes. In a revival of Marxism, the meaning of class was studied empirically by writers like Michael Burawoy (b. 1947) and theoretically by Erik Olin Wright (b. 1947), among others. Such concerns with race and class were wedded to issues of gender raised by the revival of feminism, yielding sensitive and highly partisan ethnographies, like the study of black women on welfare by Carol B. Stack (b. 1940), *All Our Kin* (1974), which rejected all "blame the victim" scenarios of poverty and family dysfunction.

The number of works on women's status from a feminist standpoint grew through the 1970s and 1980s and included studies of how gender distinctions between men and women are socially maintained, such as the widely read psychoanalytic account by Nancy Chodorow (b. 1944), *The Reproduction of Mothering* (1978). Although several women had earlier achieved distinction, such as Jessie Bernard (1903–1996), Mirra Komarovsky (1906–1999), Rose Laub Coser (1916–1994), Alice Rossi (b. 1922), and Renée Fox (b. 1928), men dominated sociology in its heyday. Beginning in the 1970s, the number of women practitioners increased dramatically, though sociology proved more reluctant than other social science disciplines, particularly anthropology, to revise its general theoretical concepts in the face of feminist criticism, some observers claimed. Paradoxically, the fact that sociology had long recognized a place for studies of women, namely in family dynamics, "ghettoized" such concerns and thus inhibited the understanding that gender inequities were bound up with all aspects of social life. The initiation of the journal *Gender and Society* in 1987 marked an attempt to enforce that broader view of the problem.

Sociology in Distress

At the same time, the fall of functionalism from its pedestal made it seem that sociology, lacking paradigmatic unity, was cast adrift in search of new moorings. Various signs pointed to disciplinary distress. Having enjoyed spectacular growth in the late 1960s, sociology suffered a substantial decline, starting shortly after 1970, in ASA membership and the number of degrees granted. Continued specialization also led many practitioners in the 1980s to lament the fragmentation of their field. The ASA recognized thirty-nine "sections" or research specialties, which included topical concerns as well as distinctive methodologies, ranging from traditional subfields, such as criminology and family, to newer matters, such as comparative and historical sociology, mathematical sociology, Asia and Asian America, aging and the life course, and more.

Highlighting the absence of theoretical consensus, several dynamic intellectual currents during the 1980s and 1990s moved in sharply divergent directions and implied a flight from the discipline's traditional concerns and assumptions. Sociobiology attacked the longstanding assumption that social environment shaped personality, behavior, and social relations more decisively than innate, hereditary traits did. The Harvard biologist E. O. Wilson made sociobiology's first coherent statement in 1975, and the study blossomed by the 1990s along with new studies aiming to isolate genetic sources of behavioral dispositions, such as aggression, sexual promiscuity, and the like. The rise of "rational choice" perspectives in sociology, adopting from economics the principles of methodological individualism, utility optimization, and game theory, reached a new height with the founding of the journal *Rationality and Society* in 1989 and the 1990 publication of *Foundations of Social Theory* by James S. Coleman (1926–1995). Urging an understanding of most social processes as the consequences of actions by individuals seeking to maximize some interests of their own, rational choice renewed the old "nominalist" hostility to notions of society as a reality sui generis.

Meanwhile, another group of sociologists more critical of their society, their discipline, and the discipline's claims to scientific status embraced the disposition known as postmodernism. They emphasized the "social construction" (the historicized, subjective, and social character) of all categories used to grasp reality; regarded modern life as the staging ground for varied techniques of controlling and regimenting unruly people and behaviors; denied that the shape of social life could be understood as "centered" on any essential principles or fully integrated in an overarching whole; and insisted that social action and social change be understood as highly localized, incompletely organized or bounded, strained by contradictory impulses, and largely unpredictable. Such a skeptical view, though antagonistic to rational choice and sociobiology, seemed to share with them a common suspicion of "society" as an entity or structure in its own right. Indeed, "general social theory," which aims to understand societies as wholes and to integrate different dimensions of social life, such as economics, social institutions, politics, and culture, in one view, steadily lost appeal within the discipline.

Other signs also suggested that sociology had entered an era of danger if not disintegration. With the turn to the right in American politics around 1980 and the consequent decline in funding for sociological research geared to public policy and social services, sociologists felt under siege. Sociology departments were eliminated at a few universities. Even the department at Yale University, the home of Sumner and his disciples, was almost closed. Public reception of sociology by this point, strikingly different from the 1950s and 1960s, often appeared hostile. Newspapers were more likely to mock arcane jargon or to assail left-wing biases in ASA proceedings than to seek expert sociological comment on social problems.

Prospects at the End of the Twentieth Century

Nevertheless, graduate student enrollment in the field rebounded in the 1990s, and by the end of the decade, the number of graduate students studying sociology nearly equaled those studying economics. At the same time, while the perennial problems of sociological theory remained unresolved—how to understand the relation between individual and community, how to assess the significance in social action of objective "interests" and subjective "meanings," or whether the field ought to define itself as a scientific or moral discourse—American sociologists continued to generate and develop new techniques, methods, and theories, including sophisticated approaches to understanding social networks, processes of interaction, and dynamic change. Many of these were highly mathematized, others were more historical and ethnographic. However specialized and sophisticated the field had become, a number of sociologists still addressed a broadly educated audience in books concerning "social problems," such as work, immigration, racism, gender inequality, poverty, and homelessness.

By the end of the century, some elder statesmen, such as Neil J. Smelser (b. 1930), director of the Center for Advanced Study in the Behavioral Sciences, greeted late developments of the field with equanimity. Laments over the fragmentation of sociology as a discipline, Smelser suggested, tended to exaggerate the field's unity and coherence at earlier points in its history. In any case, internal specialization, marking off distinct subfields of expertise, inevitably accompanies the growth of a discipline. Smelser pointed out how changes in human organization have challenged the traditional identification of "society" as a unit with the nation-state. New sensitivity was required to both "supranational" and "subnational" phenomena, such as "globalization," racial and ethnic identities, migrations, and community formation and dissolution. He recognized that these factors injected a new complexity to social experience and denied the existence of neatly bounded social units, but he also argued that they made the integrative capacity of general social theory more rather than less urgent if sociological understanding were to advance.

Generally, at the end of the twentieth century, sociologists tended to move away from overarching, architectonic notions of social structure, the metaphor of society as a kind of building, with many levels and rooms configured in a fixed pattern, among which people move and dwell. Instead, they favored more flexible models highlighting purposive action by individuals and groups, processes of interaction, the historical formation and ongoing transformation of social relations in a ceaseless flux, which can never be reduced to a simple story of progressive development. Yet, while these new emphases highlight the active, flexible, complex, and unfinished character of human social behavior, structures of inequality in wealth and power indeed seemed to be deeply entrenched features of the contemporary world. The question had become whether or not the new disposition can contribute to understanding these inequalities and can support efforts to change those forms in hopes of creating a better society, another longstanding aspiration of many modern social theorists.

BIBLIOGRAPHY

Abbott, Andrew. *Department and Discipline: Chicago Sociology at One Hundred.* Chicago: University of Chicago Press, 1999.

Alexander, Jeffrey C. *Theoretical Logic in Sociology.* Volume 4: *The Modern Reconstruction of Classical Thought: Talcott Parsons.* Berkeley: University of California Press, 1983.

Bannister, Robert C. *Sociology and Scientism: The American Quest for Objectivity, 1880–1940.* Chapel Hill: University of North Carolina Press, 1987.

Blackwell, James E., and Morris Janowitz, eds. *Black Sociologists: Historical and Contemporary Perspectives.* Chicago: University of Chicago Press, 1974.

Camic, Charles. "Introduction: Talcott Parsons Before *The Structure of Social Action.*" In Talcott Parsons, *The Early Essays.* Edited by Charles Camic. Chicago: University of Chicago Press, 1991.

Coleman, James S. *Foundations of Social Theory.* Cambridge, Mass.: Harvard University Press, 1990.

Deegan, Mary Jo. *Jane Addams and the Men of the Chicago School, 1892–1918.* New Brunswick, N.J.: Transaction Books, 1988.

Degler, Carl N. *In Search of Human Nature: The Decline and Revival of Darwinism in American Social Thought.* New York: Oxford University Press, 1991.

Fitzpatrick, Ellen. *Endless Crusade: Women Social Scientists and Progressive Reform.* New York: Oxford University Press, 1990.

Furner, Mary O. *Advocacy and Objectivity: A Crisis in the Professionalization of American Social Science, 1865–1905.* Lexington: University Press of Kentucky, 1975.

Haskell, Thomas L. *The Emergence of Professional Social Science: The American Social Science Association and the Nineteenth-Century Crisis of Authority.* Chicago: University of Illinois Press, 1977.

Levine, Donald N. *Visions of the Sociological Tradition.* Chicago: University of Chicago Press, 1995.

Lewis, David Levering. *W. E. B. Du Bois: Biography of a Race.* New York: Henry Holt, 1993.

Matthews, Fred H. *Quest for an American Sociology: Robert E. Park and the Chicago School.* Montreal: McGill-Queen's University Press, 1977.

Mills, C. Wright. *The Sociological Imagination.* Oxford: Oxford University Press, 1959.

Ritzer, George, and Barry Smart, eds. *Handbook of Social Theory.* London: Sage, 2001.

Ross, Dorothy. *The Origins of American Social Science.* New York: Cambridge University Press, 1991.

Seidman, Steven. *Contested Knowledge: Social Theory in the Postmodern Era.* 2d ed. Cambridge, Mass.: Blackwell, 1994.

Smelser, Neil. "Sociology: Spanning Two Centuries." Paper presented at the Frontiers of the Mind in the Twenty-first Century, Library of Congress Symposium, Washington, D.C., 17 June 1999.

Turner, Stephen Park, and Jonathan H. Turner. *The Impossible Science: An Institutional Analysis of American Sociology.* Newbury Park, Calif.: Sage, 1990.

Wagner, Peter, Björn Wittrock, and Richard Whitley, eds. *Discourses on Society: The Shaping of the Social Science Disciplines.* Dordrecht, Netherlands: Kluwer Academic Publishers, 1991.

Howard Brick

See also **American Dilemma, An**; **Learned Societies**; **Settlement House Movement**; **Social Work**.

SODA FOUNTAINS, apparatus for generating and dispensing soda waters. They were developed following a demand created when a Philadelphia perfumer began to serve soda water with fruit juices soon after 1800. In 1834 in New York City, John Mathews started to manufacture machinery to make carbonated beverages. Improvements soon appeared, and about 1858 the marble fountain was invented and patented in Massachusetts. An American soda fountain was exhibited in Paris in 1867, and a popular concession at the Centennial Exposition at Philadelphia in 1876 marked it as a national institution. In 1970 more than half of the approximately fifty thousand drugstores in the United States had soda fountains. By the end of the century, carbonated drinks and their advertisements were so ubiquitous that the idea of making a special trip to the drugstore soda fountain had faded into nostalgia. The fountains themselves fetched high prices as collector's items.

BIBLIOGRAPHY

Palmer, Carl J. *History of the Soda Fountain Industry.* Chicago: Soda Fountain Manufacturers Association, 1947.

Victor S. Clark/A. R.

See also **Coca-Cola**; **Soft Drink Industry**; *and picture (overleaf).*

SOFT DRINK INDUSTRY, the production, marketing, and distribution of nonalcoholic, and generally carbonated, flavored, and sweetened, water-based beverages. The history of soft drinks in the United States illustrates important business innovations, such as product development, franchising, and mass marketing, as well as the evolution of consumer tastes and cultural trends.

Many Europeans long believed natural mineral waters held medicinal qualities and favored them as alternatives to often-polluted common drinking water. By 1772, British chemist Joseph Priestley invented a means to synthetically carbonate water, and the commercial manufacturing of artificial mineral waters began with Ja-

Soda Fountain. A fixture of American drugstores—and life—for more than a century; this one, photographed on 1 January 1940, is in the Sol Drug Store in Camden, N.J. © BETTMANN/CORBIS

cob Schweppe's businesses in Geneva in the 1780s and London in the 1790s. The first known U.S. manufacturer of soda water, as it was then known, was Yale University chemist Benjamin Silliman in 1807, though Joseph Hawkins of Baltimore secured the first U.S. patent for the equipment to produce the drink two years later. By the 1820s, pharmacies nationwide provided the beverage as a remedy for various ailments, especially digestive.

Though the drinks would continue to be sold in part for their therapeutic value, customers increasingly consumed them for refreshment, especially after the 1830s, when sugar and flavorings were first added. Soda fountains emerged as regular features of drugstores by the 1860s and served beverages flavored with ginger, vanilla, fruits, roots, and herbs. In 1874 a Philadelphia store combined two popular products to make the first known ice-cream soda. The first cola drink appeared in 1881.

In the late 1800s, several brands emerged that were still popular a century later. Pharmacists experimenting at local soda fountains invented Hires Root Beer in Philadelphia in 1876, Dr. Pepper in Waco, Texas, in 1885, Coca-Cola in Atlanta, Georgia, in 1886, and Pepsi-Cola in New Bern, North Carolina, in 1893, among others. Reflecting two of the middle-class mores of the period—temperance and feeling overwhelmed by the pace and burdens of modern life—early marketing touted these

drinks as alternatives to alcohol and/or as stimulants. Coca-Cola inventor John S. Pemberton's first print advertisement for his creation read "Delicious! Refreshing! Exhilarating! Invigorating!," while Asa Candler, the eventual founder of the Coca-Cola Company, promoted his product in the years leading up to Prohibition as "The Great National Temperance Beverage."

The history of Coca-Cola reveals how national markets in soft-drink brands developed. To limit the cost of transportation, manufacturers of syrup concentrates licensed bottlers to mix the product, package, and distribute it within a specific territory. Candler underestimated the importance of the bottling side of the business and in 1899 sold the national rights to bottle Coke for a fairly small sum to Benjamin F. Thomas and Joseph B. Whitehead, who then started a national network of bottlers, creating the basic franchising format by which the industry is still run.

Candler and his successor after 1923, Robert Woodruff, were aggressive and innovative in marketing Coke as a leading consumer product and cultural icon. Coupons for free samples and giveaways of items bearing the drink's name and logo publicized the beverage, and pioneering efforts in market research helped define how best to take advantage of advertising and promotions. During World War II, Woodruff opened bottling operations overseas to supply U.S. military personnel, and after the war, Coke was poised to enter these international markets, not only as a consumer product, but also as a symbol of "the American Century."

After World War II, the soft-drink industry became a leader in television advertising, the use of celebrity endorsements, catchy slogans, tie-ins with Hollywood movies, and other forms of mass marketing, particularly focusing on young consumers and emphasizing youth-oriented themes. As health and fitness consciousness and environmental awareness became popular, the industry responded with sugar-free and low-calorie diet sodas, beginning in the 1960s, and later, caffeine-free colas and recyclable containers.

The most famous rivalry within the industry has been between Coke and Pepsi, which waged two rounds of "cola wars" in the twentieth century. In the 1930s and 1940s, Pepsi challenged the industry leader by offering a twelve-ounce bottle for the same five-cent price as Coke's standard six ounces. In the 1970s and 1980s, "Pepsi challenge" taste-tests led Coke to change its formula in 1985, a campaign that failed because it underestimated the attachment Coke drinkers had to the tradition and symbolism of the brand.

In 2001, the soft-drink industry included approximately five hundred U.S. bottlers with more than 183,000 employees, and it achieved retail sales of more than $61 billion. Americans that year consumed an average of 55 gallons of soft drinks per person, up from 48 in 1990 and 34 in 1980. The nine leading companies accounted for 96.5 percent of industry sales, led by Coca-Cola with more than 43 percent of the soft drink market and Pepsi with 31 percent. Seven individual brands accounted for almost two-thirds of all sales: Coca-Cola Classic (itself with nearly 20 percent of the market), Pepsi-Cola, Diet Coke, Mountain Dew (a Pepsi product), Sprite (a Coca-Cola product), Dr. Pepper, and Diet Pepsi. Domestic sales growth slowed in the late 1990s because of increased competition from coffee drinks, iced teas, juices, sports drinks, and bottled waters. The industry continues, however, to tap lucrative international markets; Coke and Pepsi each have bottling operations in more than 120 countries.

BIBLIOGRAPHY

Jorgensen, Janice, ed. *Encyclopedia of Consumer Brands*. Volume 1: *Consumable Products*. Detroit, Mich.: St. James Press, 1994. Features short but detailed histories of many individual brands.

Pendergrast, Mark. *For God, Country, and Coca-Cola: The Unauthorized History of the Great American Soft Drink and the Company That Makes It*. New York: Scribners, 1993.

Tchudi, Stephen N. *Soda Poppery: The History of Soft Drinks in America*. New York: Scribners, 1986.

Tedlow, Richard S. *New and Improved: The Story of Mass Marketing in America*. New York: Basic Books, 1990.

Jeffrey T. Coster

SOFT MONEY has two unrelated meanings. In the nineteenth century "soft money" denoted a monetary policy opposite that of "hard money," which is based on specie. The term originated about 1876 when the Greenback Party was formed by debtor farmers and others from the Republican and Democratic ranks who sought to raise agricultural prices by means of an inflated currency. Greenbackers opposed the resumption of specie payments on the paper notes circulating since the Civil War and called for the free coinage of silver on a par with gold. Later, the Populists held similar views.

In the late twentieth century, "soft money" referred to a popular strategy of financing political campaigns. To elude the campaign finance laws limiting the amount of direct cash contributions, wealthy individuals, corporations, and unions instead wrote their checks to political parties or advocacy groups. Hundreds of millions of dollars, all unregulated, were put to blatantly partisan purposes, most notably, advertisements attacking the opposing candidate. By the closing years of the millennium the practice was coming under greater scrutiny, and calls for reform were growing louder. The McCain-Feingold Act of 2002 attempted to address this problem.

BIBLIOGRAPHY

Magleby, David B., ed. *Outside Money: Soft Money and Issue Advocacy in the 1998 Congressional Elections*. Lanham, Md.: Rowman and Littlefield, 2000.

Timberlake, Richard H. *Monetary Policy in the United States*. Chicago: University of Chicago Press, 1993.

James D. Magee / A. R.

See also **Campaign Financing and Resources; Greenback Movement; Hard Money.**

SOFTWARE INDUSTRY, consists of that part of computer programming activity that is traded between software-producing organizations and corporate or individual software consumers. Traded software represents only a fraction of domestic software activity, whose extent cannot be reliably estimated, since much computer programming takes place within firms and its value is not captured by the industrial census or software industry analysts. According to the industry analyst INPUT, in 2000 the U.S. market for traded software was $138 billion (Table 1). The U.S. software industry is a major exporter, and the total revenues of the top 500 U.S. software firms in the year 2000 were $259 billion, according to the trade publication *Software Magazine*.

The traded software industry consists of three main sectors: programming services, enterprise software products, and shrink-wrapped software products. These three sectors became established in the mid-1950s, the mid-1960s, and the late 1970s, respectively, in response to the technological opportunities and the business environment of the time. The most successful firms developed spe-

TABLE 1

U.S. Software Market (User Expenditures in $ millions), 1970–2000							
Year	1970	1975	1980	1985	1990	1995	2000
Programming Services	744	1,352	2,985	6,233	10,402	15,319	33,400
Software Products	250	810	2,726	13,286	34,066	58,311	104,689
TOTAL	994	2,162	5,711	19,519	44,468	73,630	138,089

SOURCE: Courtesy of INPUT.

cialized capabilities that enabled them to prosper within their sector; however, this specialization made it difficult to move into other sectors, and very few firms have been successful in more than one software sector. It should be noted that the software industry is not confined to independent software vendors, but also includes computer manufacturers such as IBM, Unisys, and NCR who supply programming services and software products alongside their hardware offerings and are among the largest software suppliers. These are sometimes referred to as "captive" markets because computer users have relatively little choice in the supplier of basic operating software for corporate systems.

The United States has been the world leader in the software industry throughout its history, and today accounts for half of global revenues overall, and an estimated three-quarters of the software products market. A notable feature of the industry is its low concentration: there are many thousands of software firms in the United States and throughout the world, but relatively few—mostly American—global players.

Programming Services
The first commercial electronic computers—usually known as "mainframes"—were sold in the early 1950s. They were very expensive, typically renting for $100,000 a year. Most computer-owning corporations undertook their own program development and operations, for which they maintained a staff of up to thirty or forty individuals. This was not a disproportionate expense in relation to the overall costs of running a computer.

By the mid-1950s, however, mainframe prices had fallen significantly, and computer use diffused rapidly—the national computer stock rising from 240 mainframes in 1955 to over four thousand by 1960. Owners of these more moderately priced computers were often unwilling to recruit a permanent programming staff, preferring instead to commission programs from software contractors. Many of the early programming services firms were established by programming entrepreneurs to satisfy this demand. The first such firm, the Computer Usage Corporation (CUC), was incorporated in New York in 1955

by two former IBM programming employees, and the firm initially specialized in developing technical applications for the oil and engineering industries. The capital barriers to software contracting were (and remain) very low, and it was often said that all one needed was "a coding pad and a pencil." The most important capability was the technical knowledge of the principals, usually acquired through working with a computer user or manufacturer. Several dozen firms entered the programming services industry in the second half of the 1950s. In a majority of cases, the firms specialized in particular technical applications, or within a vertical market such as financial services, retail, or manufacturing.

A very different type of entrant came into programming services in the mid-1950s, specializing in the construction of very large programs that were beyond the technical capability of even the largest and most sophisticated users. The first firm of this kind was the Systems Development Corporation (SDC), a subsidiary of the RAND Corporation, Santa Monica. SDC was incorporated in 1956 to develop the programs for the giant SAGE air-defense system. The programs SDC developed for SAGE were unprecedented in size, consisting of more than a million computer instructions. SDC employed several hundred programmers, estimated at the time to be perhaps half of the nation's programming manpower. SDC also trained hundreds of individuals to become programmers. There was, however, a rapid turnover of staff, as experienced programmers left for more remunerative employment in the private sector. At the time, SDC was hailed as the "university for programmers" and it was said that in the 1960s, SDC alumni were to be found in almost every major software firm in the country.

SAGE was a "real-time" system, in which the computer lay at the heart of an information system that responded instantaneously to external events. As the U.S. government deployed more and more real-time defense systems in the late 1950s and 1960s, systems integrators such as TRW, MITRE, General Electric, Westinghouse, Hughes Dynamics, and Lockheed began to develop expertise in software construction. Real-time technologies were hugely expensive to innovate but once established by the military, they quickly diffused into the civilian sector in applications such as airline reservations and on-line banking. When Europe and the rest of the world began to catch up in the 1960s, American independent software firms and the programming services operations of computer manufacturers had a strong first-mover advantage.

By the late 1960s, the most successful of the start-up software contractors had become significant firms. For example, by 1967 CUC had 700 employees, offices in twelve U.S. cities, and annual sales of $13 million. CUC, and firms like it, now offered a broad range of computer services that went well beyond program writing. Another firm, the Computer Sciences Corporation of El Segundo, California, established in 1959 by five programmers to write software for computer manufacturers, grew to become one of the largest computer services firms in the world (which it remains, with revenues in 2000 of $9.4 billion, and sixty-eight thousand employees worldwide).

Nonetheless, giant firms are the exception and the programming services industry is remarkably lacking in concentration. By the late 1960s there were several hundred U.S. programming services firms, but less than fifty of them had as many as a hundred employees. Today, there are several thousand software contracting establishments, but their average size is less than a dozen staff. Of these only the smallest percentage will become global players.

Enterprise Software Products

The 1960s saw an explosion in computer usage in the United States and worldwide. Computer technology evolved dramatically—transistors replaced vacuum tubes, and then microelectronics superceded discrete transistors—with consequent improvements in speed, capacity, reliability, and price. In the United States the computer population grew from 4,400 in 1960 to 46,000 by the end of the decade (63,000 worldwide). The concept of packaged software arose as a technological solution—almost an historical necessity—to the problem of supplying software for the expanding computer population, which by the mid-1960s had begun to outstrip the programming manpower needed to write custom software for each individual installation. A software package was a pre-written program designed for a particular industry, or for a common application such as payroll processing or inventory management. At first software packages were supplied at no cost by computer manufacturers, as part of the bundle of services needed to operate a computer, and which included customer training, field engineering, and so on.

In the mid- to late 1960s a number of established programming services firms began to sell software packages. The packages were usually derived from software assets developed in programming-services contracts, and were called "products" to distinguish them from computer manufacturers' software packages, in order to connote a degree of customer support and service that the manufacturers generally failed to provide with their free packages. Two early examples of software products were Autoflow and Mark IV. Autoflow, a program that assisted computer users with software documentation, was introduced in 1965 by Applied Data Research (ADR), which was founded in Princeton, New Jersey, in 1959. Mark IV was an early form of database launched in 1967 by Informatics (founded in Woodland Hills, California, in 1962). Although Autoflow and Mark IV were perhaps the two best-known software products of the 1960s, they had each achieved only a few hundred sales by the end of the decade.

The manufacturers' distribution of "free" software packages was a major restraint on the growth of the software products industry, because it was extremely difficult to compete against free packages by providing added value that justified a purchase price typically of five thousand

to fifty thousand dollars. As a result of antitrust pressure, and a private lawsuit from ADR, in 1970 IBM "unbundled" its software and services, converting many of its software packages into paid-for software products. Unbundling gave a major fillip to the industry; ADR and Informatics, for example, tripled their sales in as many years. During the 1970s, several hundred of the existing programming services firms and many new ventures entered the software products industry. New entrants included firms such as Computer Associates and Oracle, later to become leading players in the enterprise software industry. However, the 1970s was a somber decade for the software industry, with capital shortages following the stock market crash of the late 1960s, followed by the computer recession of 1970–1971. Hence growth in the 1970s was modest, and total industry sales did not exceed $1 billion until 1978 (a year in which IBM's revenues were $17 billion, for comparison).

During the 1980s, the software products market finally matured and grew at a sustained annual compound rate of 30 percent—from aggregate sales of $2.7 billion in 1980 to over $30 billion by the end of the decade. As with programming services, the software products industry was low in concentration. For example, a survey in 1982 showed that the top fifty or sixty firms accounted for only 50 percent of sales, leaving the remainder to approximately two thousand medium and small firms. (By contrast, in the mainframe computer industry, less than twenty firms accounted for virtually the entire industry, and one firm, IBM, for more than 50 percent.) The software industry was (and is) sometimes characterized as being like "boulders, pebbles, and sand"; that is, a few tens of global players, a few hundred second-tier firms, and thousands of very small firms with a dozen or fewer employees.

The leading firms have generally grown through consolidation or by dominating a particular software genre through organic growth. Consolidation has been particularly important in gaining market share in the software industry for two reasons: it has proved extremely difficult to imitate a successful software product that may have taken years to evolve, and software products have proved insensitive to price, buyers valuing reliability and security of supply above cost. Among the consolidators, Computer Associates, founded in Islandia, New York, in 1976, has been the most prominent and successful. Following its initial public offering in 1981, Computer Associates set out on a course of acquisitions that made it the largest software vendor by 1990 and it has retained its place as one of the top three vendors ever since (usually jockeying for position with Microsoft and Oracle). Computer Associates' acquisitions have included other consolidators, so that if one were to construct a "family tree" of the firm it would contain several hundred names (including ADR and Informatics, mentioned above).

By the 1990s, two major software genres accounted for perhaps a half of all corporate software sales: relational database software and enterprise resource planning (ERP) software. Relational database technology emerged in the early 1970s in the research environment of IBM's San Jose Research Laboratory and the University of California, Berkeley. Relational technology was a major, though technically challenging, advance over earlier database systems. The technology was first exploited by northern Californian software entrepreneurs, including Oracle, founded in Belmont, California, in 1977. The region still remains the world center of relational technology. Oracle has consolidated its early start advantage, out-maneuvering and out-growing all competitors, frequently vying with Computer Associates as the number-two software company. ERP software emerged in the 1980s as a single-product solution to replace the aggregation of numerous application products that computer users typically had to use in the 1970s and 1980s. The leading vendor is SAP, a German firm, which invented the ERP concept in the early 1980s; although there are now several U.S. competitors, none has yet overcome SAP's first-mover advantage. SAP is the only non-U.S. software-product firm in the top ten (and one of only a handful in the top 100).

Shrink-Wrapped Software

The invention in 1971 of the inexpensive microprocessor—a computer on a single microchip—transformed the computer, creating a consumer product from what had previously been a costly capital good. Microprocessors were used in both videogame consoles and personal computers, and a "shrink-wrapped" or "boxed" software industry developed in the 1970s to satisfy the demand for programs for the new computer products. Shrink-wrapped software products were distinguished from enterprise software goods by low prices, high sales volume, and different distribution channels. Consumer software typically sold in tens or hundreds of thousands of units, at a price of a few hundred dollars, at most. Shrink-wrapped software was sold through retail outlets and mail order, with little or no after-sales service, compared with the direct sales forces and account managers employed by enterprise software vendors.

One of the first firms to catch the wave of personal computing was Microsoft, founded in Albuquerque, New Mexico, in 1975 by Bill Gates and Paul Allen. Microsoft specialized in the basic operating software for what were then still known as micro-computers, and which mainly sold to hobbyists. Mass-market personal computers, such as the Apple II and the Tandy TRS-80, arrived in 1977–1978. Within a couple of years two software applications, the word processor and the spreadsheet, made the personal computer generally useful. The word processor concept had existed in the corporate computer world, and many entrepreneurs simultaneously hit on the idea of creating a product for the personal computer market. However, one product, WordStar (produced by a San Rafael-based start-up, MicroPro International), secured a commanding share of the market. By contrast, the first personal computer spreadsheet, VisiCalc, produced by

Software Arts of Cambridge, Massachusetts, had no clear precedent in mainframe computing, and it took the world by storm, initially having the market entirely to itself, although within a couple of years it was imitated by dozens of "clones."

WordStar and VisiCalc were the two top-selling programs, each with sales of more than half a million copies by 1983. WordStar, VisiCalc, and their competitors were known as "productivity applications" because they became the principal tools of corporate information workers. Although productivity applications accounted for around half of software sales, there were many other software genres, each with their leading products—desktop publishing (for example, Adobe Systems' PageMaker), computer-aided design (for example, Autodesk's Auto-CAD), personal finance (for example, Intuit's Quicken), and many more.

The tendency for a single product to dominate a software genre, despite many worthy imitators, is a notable feature of the personal computer software industry and is mainly attributed to "network effects." Because a community or network of users values the ability to share and exchange files and documents, new users tend to adopt the software with the biggest community of users—this favors the most popular product to the detriment of its competitors. The pecking order of top software products tends to change only when there is a major discontinuity in the personal computing environment, which temporarily overcomes these network effects. This first happened following the introduction of the IBM-compatible PC in August 1981. The IBM PC was more powerful than previous desktop computers, and IBM's imprimatur legitimated its use in corporations, and it soon accounted for 80 percent of new sales. Two new productivity applications eclipsed VisiCalc and WordStar, and dominated the platform for a decade: the 1-2-3 spreadsheet by the Lotus Development Corporation (Cambridge, Massachusetts) and the WordPerfect word processor by the WordPerfect Corporation (Orem, Utah). Microsoft, by now relocated to Gates and Allen's home town of Seattle, Washington, developed the operating software for the IBM computer, earning enormous revenues that fuelled its growth.

A seismic shift occurred in the personal computer landscape with the introduction of the Microsoft Windows 3.0 operating system in 1990. Because the productivity application incumbents, Lotus and WordPerfect, did not have Windows-compatible products at this time, Microsoft was able to push its own packages, Excel and Word, with very little competition. At the same time, the company began to bundle its productivity applications into a single product called Microsoft Office. Within a couple of years, Microsoft dominated the markets for both personal computer operating software and productivity applications. This precipitated a restructuring of the industry as competitors repositioned and merged in order to offer comparable "office suites." By the mid-1990s, office suites and individual productivity applications sold some fifty million units annually, with perhaps three-quarters being Microsoft products.

Microsoft's ubiquity and monopolistic practices brought it to the attention of the antitrust division of the Department of Justice in 1995. This exclusive focus on Microsoft has been surprising, since there are comparable monopolies in the enterprise software sector. Moreover, while Microsoft certainly dominates most of the software genres in which it competes, the firm accounts for no more than 10 percent of total software industry sales.

The Internet Era

The diffusion of the PC in the 1980s dramatically changed the working lives of office employees: senior managers began to type their own memoranda, while junior executives spent a disproportionate amount of their days tinkering with spreadsheets. The typewriter was consigned to the dustbin of history, while typists were promoted to being general administrators.

Since the mid-1990s, the Internet has had an equally dramatic effect on the lives of office workers and increasingly the domestic computer user. Although the Internet had been in widespread use in technical communities since the early 1980s, it was the introduction of the World Wide Web in the early 1990s that made the Internet accessible to ordinary users. The enabling software technology of the World Wide Web was the Web browser used in a desktop computer, of which most users are conscious, and the invisible software in "servers" that made Web pages available to remote users on demand. The first and most important supplier of software for the Web was the Netscape Communications Corporation of Mountain View, California, founded in 1994. Run by a 24-year-old wunderkind, Netscape grew from nothing to a billion-dollar corporation in two years. In 1996, however, Microsoft introduced a competing product, Internet Explorer, which quickly achieved a dominant market share. Microsoft's hardball tactics in this achievement added weight to its antitrust prosecution.

At first, the Web was a largely passive experience, but in the late 1990s it became increasingly interactive and participative, with the provision of financial services, travel information, entertainment including pornography, auctions and retail services, and information products of every kind. In a couple of years new brands became household names—Motley Fool, Ameritrade, Yahoo, Travelocity, Amazon, and many more. Some of these are new enterprises, while others are new initiatives from old established firms. Just as the Web is changing the old order of information services and retailing, it is even more profoundly changing the world of software. For example, the metaphor of "shrink-wrapped" software is breaking down as software products are increasingly supplied by electronic download. Some industry observers predict that the concept of a software product or artifact will become obsolete, and programs will be supplied online, on de-

mand, and metered according to use. Whether or not this comes to pass, the phrase software industry will continue to be the collective term for firms engaged in supplying programming goods and services, in whatever way the technology of the day demands.

BIBLIOGRAPHY

Baum, Claude. *The System Builders: The Story of SDC.* Santa Monica, Calif.: Systems Development Corporation, 1981.

Campbell-Kelly, Martin. *A History of the Software Industry: From Airline Reservations to Sonic the Hedgehog.* Cambridge, Mass.: MIT Press, 2003.

Cusumano, Michael A., and Richard W. Selby. *Microsoft Secrets: How the World's Most Powerful Software Company Creates Technology, Shapes Markets, and Manages People.* New York: Free Press, 1995.

Freiberger, Paul, and Michael Swaine. *Fire in the Valley: The Making of the Personal Computer.* 2d ed. New York: McGraw-Hill, 2000.

Herman, Leonard. *Phoenix: The Fall and Rise of Home Videogames.* Union, N.J.: Rolenta Press, 1994.

Hoch, Detlev J., Cyriac R. Roeding, Gert Purkert, and Sandro K. Lindner. *Secrets of Software Success: Management Insights from 100 Software Firms Around the World.* Boston: Harvard Business School Press, 2000.

Liebowitz, Stan J. and Stephen E. Margolis. *Winners, Losers and Microsoft: Competition and Antitrust in High Technology.* Oakland, Calif.: The Independent Institute, 1999.

Manes, Stephen, and Paul Andrews. *Gates: How Microsoft's Mogul Reinvented an Industry and Made Himself the Richest Man in America.* New York: Simon and Schuster, 1994.

Meissner, Gerd. *SAP: Inside the Secret Software Power.* New York: McGraw-Hill, 2000.

Mowery, David C., ed. *The International Computer Software Industry: A Comparative Study of Evolution and Structure.* New York: Oxford University Press, 1996.

Organization for Economic Cooperation and Development. *Software: An Emerging Industry.* Paris: OECD, 1985.

Petersen, W. E. Pete. *Almost Perfect: How a Bunch of Regular Guys Built WordPerfect Corporation.* Rocklin, Calif:. Prima, 1994.

U.S. Department of Commerce. *A Competitive Assessment of the United States Software Industry.* Washington, D.C.: U.S. Department of Commerce, 1984.

Wilson, Mike. *The Difference Between God and Larry Ellison: Inside Oracle Corporation.* New York: Morrow, 1997.

Martin Campbell-Kelly

See also **Computers and Computer Industry; Microsoft; Silicon Valley.**

SOIL is a mixture of weathered rocks and minerals, organic matter, water, and air in varying proportions. Soils differ significantly from place to place because the original parent material differed in chemical composition, depth, and texture (from coarse sand to fine clay), and because each soil shows the effects of environmental factors including climate, vegetation, macro- and microorganisms, the relief of the land, and time since the soil began forming. The result of these factors is a dynamic, living soil with complex structure and multiple layers (horizons). Soils have regional patterns, and also differ substantially over short distances. These differences have shaped local and regional land use patterns throughout history. Because of this, historians have studied soil for clues about how people lived and for explanations of historical events and patterns.

Soil Classification and Mapping

The basis of the modern understanding of soil formation is attributed largely to work in the 1870s by the Russian V. V. Dokuchaev and colleagues. The Russians classified soil based on the presumed genesis of the soils and described the broadest soil categories. Simultaneously but separately, soil scientists in the United States were mapping and classifying soils based on measurable characteristics and focused on the lowest and most specific level of the taxonomy—the soil series. The Russian concepts did not reach the United States until K. D. Glinka translated them into German in 1914, and the American C. F. Marbut incorporated Glinka's ideas into his work. The U.S. system of soil classification that eventually developed considers the genetic origins of soils but defines categories by measurable soil features. Soils are divided into 12 soil orders based on soil characteristics that indicate major soil-forming processes. For example, Andisols is an order defined by the presence of specific minerals that indicate the soils' volcanic origin. At the other end of the taxonomic hierarchy, over 19,000 soil series are recognized in the United States. Research data and land management information are typically associated with the soil series.

Some U.S. soils were mapped as early as 1886, but the official program to map and publish soil surveys started in 1899 by the U.S. Department of Agriculture (USDA) Division of Soils, led by Milton Whitney. The effort was accelerated in 1953 when the Secretary of Agriculture created the National Cooperative Soil Survey, a collaborative effort of states, local governments, and universities led by the USDA Natural Resources Conservation Service. As of 2000, mapping was complete for 76 percent of the contiguous United States, including 94 percent of private lands.

Soil Fertility

Ancient writings demonstrate awareness of the positive effect of manure and certain crops on soil productivity. Modern agricultural chemistry began in eighteenth-century England, France, and Germany, and was dominated by scientists from these countries through the nineteenth century. In the 1840s, the German scientist Justus von Liebig identified essential plant nutrients and the importance of supplying all of them in soil, but this led to a concept of soil as a more or less static storage bin of nutrients and failed to reflect the dynamic nature of soil in relation to plants.

In 1862, state agricultural colleges were established by the MORRILL ACT, and the USDA was created. The Hatch Act of 1888 created experiment stations associated with the colleges. These developments led to the expansion of research plots that established the value of fertilizer in crop production and defined the variations in soil management requirements across the country.

Soil fertility can change because agriculture and other human activities affect erosion rates, soil organic matter levels, pH, nutrient levels, and other soil characteristics. An example of this is the change in distribution of soil nutrients across the country. In the early twentieth century, animal feed was typically grown locally and manure was spread on fields, returning many of the nutrients originally taken from the soil with the crop. Since farms became larger and more specialized toward the end of the twentieth century, feed is commonly grown far from the animals and manure cannot be returned to the land where the feed was grown. Thus, nutrients are concentrated near animal lots and can be a pollution problem, while soil fertility may be adversely affected where feed crops are grown.

Technology and Soil Management

Soil characteristics influence human activity, and conversely, human land use changes soil characteristics. Many technologies have changed how people use soil and have changed the quality of U.S. soils. The plow is one of these technologies. In 1794, Thomas Jefferson calculated the shape of the plow that offered the least resistance. Charles Newbold patented the cast iron plow in 1796. John Deere's steel plow, invented in 1837, made it possible for settlers to penetrate the dense mesh of roots in the rich prairies, and led to extensive plowing. Aeration of soil by plowing leads to organic matter decomposition, and within decades as much as 50 percent of the original soil organic matter was lost from agricultural lands. Until about 1950, plowing and other land use activities accounted for more annual carbon dioxide emissions than that emitted by the burning of fossil fuels. Fossil fuel emissions have grown exponentially since then, while net emissions from land use held steady and have declined recently.

Soil drainage systems expanded rapidly across the country in the early twentieth century in response to technological advances and government support. Drainage made it possible to farm rich lands in the Midwest that were previously too wet to support crops, and it allowed the use of irrigation in arid lands where irrigated soils quickly became saline when salts were not flushed away. The extensive drainage systems radically changed the flow of water through soil and altered the ability of land to control floodwater and to filter contaminants out of water.

A third critical soil technology was the development of manufactured fertilizers. During World War I (1914–1918), the German chemist Fritz Haber developed a process to form ammonia fertilizer. Nitrogen is commonly the most limiting nutrient for intensive crop production.

Phosphorus, another important limiting nutrient in some soils, became readily available as fertilizer in the 1930s. The use of these and other manufactured fertilizers made it possible to grow profitable crops on previously undesirable lands, and made farmers less dependent on crop rotations and nitrogen-fixing plants to maintain soil productivity.

A fourth technology was the development of herbicides beginning after World War II (1939–1945), combined with the refinement of "no-till" farm machinery in the 1970s. No-till is a method of crop farming that eliminates plowing and leaves plant residue from the previous crop on the soil surface. This residue protects the soil and can dramatically reduce erosion rates. The system also requires less fuel and labor than conventional tillage and thus allows a single farmer to manage more acres. The result has been a substantial reduction in erosion rates around the country and an increase in the amount of organic matter stored in the soil. The organic matter and associated biological activity improve productivity and reflect the sequestration of carbon dioxide from the atmosphere into the soil.

Erosion and Conservation

Soil degradation can take many forms, including loss of organic matter, poor biological activity, contamination with pollutants, compaction, and salinization. The most prominent form of land degradation is erosion by wind or water. Erosion is a natural process that is accelerated by overgrazing and cultivation. In *Conquest of the Land Through 7,000 Years* (1999), W. C. Lowdermilk attributed the loss of numerous civilizations to unsustainable agricultural practices that caused erosion, resulting in silting of irrigation systems and loss of land productivity.

The first English colonists in America faced heavily forested lands but gradually cleared the land of trees and planted tobacco, cotton, and grain year after year in the same fields. In the eighteenth century there were references to worn-out land, and by 1800 much farm acreage along the coast had been abandoned. In 1748 Jared Eliot, a Connecticut minister and physician, published a book of essays documenting his observation of the connection between muddy water running from bare, sloping fields and the loss of fertility. John Taylor, a gentleman farmer of Virginia, wrote and was widely read after the Revolution (1775–1783) on the need to care for the soil. Perhaps the best known of this group of pre–Civil War (1861–1865) reformers was Edmund Ruffin of Virginia. Clean-cultivated row crops, corn and cotton, according to Ruffin, were the greatest direct cause of erosion. He urged liming the soil and planting clover or cowpeas as a cover crop. His writings and demonstrations were credited with restoring fertility and stopping erosion on large areas of Southern land.

After the Civil War farmers moved west, subjecting vast areas to erosion, although interest in the problem seemed to decline. In 1927, Hugh Hammond Bennett of

the U.S. Department of Agriculture urged, in *Soil Erosion: A National Menace*, that the situation should be of concern to the entire nation. In 1929, congress appropriated funds for soil erosion research.

The depression of the early 1930s led to programs to encourage conservation. The Soil Erosion Service and the Civilian Conservation Corps began soil conservation programs in 1933 with work relief funds. The DUST BOWL dust storms of 1934 and 1935 influenced Congress in 1935 to establish the Soil Conservation Service (SCS). Within a few years the service was giving technical assistance to farmers who were organized into soil conservation districts. These districts, governed by local committees, worked with the SCS to determine the practices to be adopted, including contour cultivation, strip farming, terracing, drainage, and, later, installing small water facilities. By 1973, more than 90 percent of the nation's farmland was included in soil conservation districts. The SCS was renamed the Natural Resources Conservation Service in 1994.

According to USDA Natural Resources Inventory data, erosion rates declined significantly during the 1980s, largely due to widespread adoption of reduced tillage practices. In the mid-1990s, erosion rates leveled off to about 1.9 billion tons of soil per year.

BIBLIOGRAPHY

Brady, Nyle C. *The Nature and Properties of Soils.* Upper Saddle River, N.J.: Prentice Hall, 2001.

Helms, Douglas. "Soil and Southern History." *Agricultural History* 74, no. 4 (2000): 723–758.

History of the Natural Resources Conservation Service. Available at http://www.nrcs.usda.gov/about/history/

Lowdermilk, W. C. *Conquest of the Land Through 7,000 Years.* Agriculture Information Bulletin No. 99. USDA Natural Resources Conservation Service, 1999.

Simms, D. Harper. *The Soil Conservation Service.* New York: Praeger, 1970.

U.S. Department of Agriculture, Yearbook (1938, 1957, 1958).

Ann Lewandowski

SOLDIERS' HOME. The United States Naval Home in Philadelphia, Pennsylvania, was the first home for disabled veterans. Authorized in 1811 but not completed and occupied until 1831, the home sheltered "disabled and decrepit Navy officers, seamen and Marines." Modern-day applicants must have served during wartime in the navy, marine corps, or coast guard, and be disabled. Each member of the navy and marine corps contributes a small amount per month for the support of the home, which is also subsidized by fines imposed on navy personnel.

A bill introduced by Jefferson Davis, then a senator from Mississippi, and eventually approved by Congress on 3 March 1851, authorized the U.S. Soldiers' and Airmen's Home in Washington, D.C. In addition to serving as a place of residence for both men and women veterans, the home provides medical treatment, nursing, and hospital care as required. Enlisted members and warrant officers of the regular army and air force who have had twenty years of service are eligible. War veterans with fewer than twenty years of service also qualify. Enlisted members and warrant officers of the regular army and air force contribute a small fraction of their monthly earnings to support the home, which also benefits from court-martial fines, unclaimed estates of deceased members, and a portion of the post funds of the army and air force. From 1862 to 1864 President Abraham Lincoln used this home as his summer residence.

On 3 March 1865 Congress created the National Home for Disabled Volunteer Soldiers, an agency to provide a place of residence, complete medical treatment, and hospital care. On 21 March 1866, Congress amended the original act. The first home under its auspices opened in Augusta, Maine, and soon thereafter, others were established in Dayton, Ohio; Milwaukee, Wisconsin; and Hampton, Virginia. By 1930 seven more branches existed, bringing total capacity to approximately twenty-five thousand. In 1923, accommodations for women veterans became available. In 1930 the National Home, the Veterans Bureau, and the Pension Bureau of the Department of the Interior consolidated to form the Veterans Administration (VA). By 1975 the VA had provided additional domiciliary care at eighteen field stations, four of which admitted women veterans.

By the mid-1970s most states and the District of Columbia operated soldiers' homes. All provided residential and nursing care, and some offered hospital care. States receive a subsidy from the VA for the care of eligible veterans and for the construction of nursing homes and the improvement of existing buildings. Some homes admit spouses, widows, and mothers of veterans. At many homes, residents must pay to the institution any personal income in excess of a certain amount.

Thirteen southern states maintained homes for Confederate veterans. These homes, which received no federal support, closed in the 1920s and 1930s. Missouri and Oklahoma maintained separate homes for Union and Confederate veterans.

BIBLIOGRAPHY

Hyman, Harold M. *American Singularity: The 1787 Northwest Ordinance, the 1862 Homestead and Morrill Acts, and the 1944 G.I. Bill.* Athens: University of Georgia Press, 1986.

Kelly, Patrick J. *Creating a National Home: Building the Veterans' Welfare State, 1860–1900.* Cambridge, Mass.: Harvard University Press, 1997.

Resch, John Phillips. *Suffering Soldiers: Revolutionary War Veterans, Moral Sentiment, and Political Culture in the Early Republic.* Amherst: University of Massachusetts Press, 1999.

Rosenburg, R. B. *Living Monuments: Confederate Soldiers' Homes in the New South.* Chapel Hill: University of North Carolina Press, 1993.

Angela Ellis
Carl S. McCarthy

See also **Federal Agencies; GI Bill of Rights; Medicine, Military; Pensions, Military and Naval; Veterans Affairs, Department of.**

SOLID SOUTH. The southern states of the United States became "solid" behind the Democratic Party following the CIVIL WAR. This occurred as a reaction against the Republicans, who had prosecuted the war for the North and inflicted upon the South the depredations of RECONSTRUCTION. As Reconstruction ended in 1877, the South quickly moved to reverse the black empowerment enforced by Northern troops and to restore a culture of white supremacy. Many white southerners realized that a united political front would be necessary to preserve this culture, and the "solid South" was the result. Southerners supported Democratic candidates for office at all levels, from president to municipal dogcatchers.

The first cracks in this unanimity appeared in 1948, when President Harry Truman, a Democrat, supported civil rights reform. Democrats from southern states (known as Dixiecrats) refused to support Truman for re-election, held their own nominating convention, and offered Senator Strom Thurmond of South Carolina as a third-party candidate.

The Solid South splintered in the 1960s, as the Kennedy and Johnson administrations, and their supporters in Congress, backed wide-reaching civil rights legislation and used federal troops to enforce court-ordered racial integration. Southerners began to return to the Republican Party, especially when voting in national elections, and the South is today regarded as a Republican stronghold.

BIBLIOGRAPHY

Black, Earl, and Merle Black. *The Rise of Southern Republicans.* Cambridge, Mass: Harvard University Press, 2002.

Glaser, James M. *Race, Campaign Politics, and the Realignment in the South.* New Haven, Conn.: Yale University Press, 1996.

J. Justin Gustainis

See also **Civil Rights Movement; Democratic Party.**

SOMALIA, RELATIONS WITH. Somalia, in northeastern Africa, attracted American attention for the first time in the 1970s when the military dictatorship of Mohammed Siad Barre solicited military aid from the Soviet Union. In 1980 he switched sides and allied with the United States, which also poured in military aid. As the Cold War ended, Somalia lost its attraction as an ally. Barre's ouster in 1991 allowed clan rivalries, which his dictatorial rule had held in check, to erupt into civil war. The war and severe drought destroyed Somalia's econ-

Somalia. American soldiers patrol the streets of Mogadishu, officially the capital of this war-torn country. AP/WIDE WORLD PHOTOS

omy. In response to televised scenes of starving children, the United Nations in December 1992 introduced troops from several nations, under the command of the United States, to see that international relief aid reached the Somalian people. This food mission initially succeeded, but when its commanders also tried to settle the civil war, troops were caught in a chaotic situation. Thirty U.S. soldiers lost their lives in the course of the conflict, the worst incident being an October 1993 army ranger raid in which eighteen U.S. soldiers were killed and their bodies paraded through the streets of Mogadishu, the capital city. After more than two years and $2 billion, the UN operation left Somalia with no government or administration and controlled by heavily armed rival clans.

BIBLIOGRAPHY

Clarke, Walter, and Jeffrey Herbst, eds. *Learning from Somalia: The Lessons of Armed Humanitarian Intervention.* Boulder, Colo.: Westview Press, 1997.

R. L. Watson / A. G.

See also **Africa, Relations with.**

SOMME OFFENSIVE (8 August–11 November 1918). The first Americans to serve on the western front in

WORLD WAR I were some 2,500 medics and engineers with the British in the Battle of Cambrai, which started in the Somme River area in northern France on 20 November 1917. These detachments were still present for the second Battle of the Somme commencing on 21 March 1918, the first of five luckless efforts by the Germans to win the war before Gen. John J. Pershing's AMERICAN EXPEDITIONARY FORCES could reach full strength. Some Americans were at hand during the German-precipitated crises of the summer of 1918 in the British sector. The 131st Infantry of the Thirty-third National Guard Division from Illinois fought in the Fourth Army under Gen. Sir Henry Rawlinson, helping capture Hamel on 4 July. During the reduction of the Amiens salient, the 131st on 9 August lost nearly 1,000 at Chipilly Ridge and Gressaire Wood, pressing on to help take Etinchem Spur on 13 August.

As the British planned their share of French Gen. Ferdinand Foch's grand offensive, which produced the armistice, Pershing lent Rawlinson the Second Corps of George W. Read. In Rawlinson's attack of 29 September, Read's corps broke through the Hindenburg Line at the Bellicourt Canal Tunnel, an incredible fortification inspiring the later Maginot Line. In October Read's divisions captured Brancourt-le-Grand, Premont, and Vaux-Andigny; crossed the Selle River; took Ri-

447

Somme Offensive, 1918. A two-man crew fires a 37mm gun during an advance against German positions. National Archives and Records Administration

beauville, Mazinghien, and Rejet-de-Beaulieu; and nearly reached the Sambre River—a hard-fought advance of eleven and one-half miles, costing 3,414 killed and 14,526 wounded.

BIBLIOGRAPHY

Cooke, James J. *Pershing and His Generals.* Westport, Conn.: Praeger, 1997.

Cowley, Robert. *1918: Gamble for Victory: The Greatest Attack of World War I.* New York: Macmillan, 1964.

R. W. Daly
Joseph Mills Hanson / A. R.

See also **Aisne-Marne Operation; Champagne-Marne Operation.**

SON OF THE FOREST, A (1829; revised 1831) was the first of five books written by the Pequot preacher and orator William Apess. This narrative of Apess's life and conversion to Methodism excoriates Christian hypocrisy toward, and misrepresentation of, native people, a pronounced theme in all his work. By 1832, Apess had relocated from New York to Boston, where he became associated with both the anti-removal and antislavery movements. His second book, *Experiences of Five Christian Indians of the Pequot Tribe* (1833), shows his exposure to both in its account of the absurdity of color as a signifier of racial inferiority. Enlisted by Cape Cod's Mashpee Indians to aid in their petition for self-government, Apess

recounts their partially successful struggle in his third book, *Indian Nullification of the Unconstitutional Laws of Massachusetts; or, the Pretended Riot Explained* (1835), which was well received by Boston's literary and political elite. Apess's greatest achievement was his final work, *Eulogy on King Philip* (1836), in which he produces an alternative account of King Philip's War that defines both history and politics for native peoples in New England. Well-known throughout his career as a powerful orator, by the time Apess gave the eulogy he had lost the support of sympathetic whites as well as the Mashpee leadership. He returned to New York in 1839, where he died of apoplexy on 10 April.

BIBLIOGRAPHY

Apess, William. *On Our Own Ground: The Complete Writings of William Apess, a Pequot.* Edited by Barry O'Connell. Amherst: University of Massachusetts Press, 1992.

Maureen Konkle

See also **Pequots.**

SON-OF-SAM LAW. Adopted in New York State in 1977 as a response to the public outrage over profits made by convicted serial killer David Berkowitz (also known as "Son of Sam") for selling his story to a publishing house, this law required publishers to deposit money owed to persons either convicted of a crime or who confessed to having committed a crime in a fund used to compensate their victims. In *Simon and Schuster, Inc. v. Members of the New York State Victims Board* (1991), the Supreme Court struck down the New York law because it violated the First Amendment.

BIBLIOGRAPHY

Weed, Frank. *Certainty of Justice: Reform in the Crime Victim Movement.* New York: Aldine de Gruyter, 1995.

Katy J. Harriger / A. R.

See also **Crime; Serial Killings.**

SONS OF LIBERTY (AMERICAN REVOLUTION).

"Sons of Liberty" has three separate meanings. The first is the organized groups of militant colonials who emerged during the Stamp Act crisis and disbanded when the act was repealed. More loosely the term means popular street leaders during the resistance to Britain. The New Yorker Alexander McDougall signed his 1769 broadside "To the Betrayed Inhabitants of the City and Colony of New York" with the pseudonym "A Son of Liberty" although he had taken no part in the Stamp Act resistance. Even more loosely the term recalls its generic use for colonials resisting the STAMP ACT during debates in the House of Commons by the procolonial Isaac Barre.

The issue the organized Sons of Liberty raised and resolved was a combination of general outrage against the Stamp Act and debate about rendering the act null rather than simply protesting. The earliest group was the Loyal Nine in Boston, who coalesced around Samuel Adams. Unlike Adams, who was a Harvard graduate and a gentleman, the Loyal Nine were for the most part prosperous artisans and small traders. They were literate and politically sophisticated but not members of the town elite.

On 14 August 1765 these men staged a public drama beneath the Liberty Tree on Boston Neck, the strip of land that connected town to mainland. Their goal was to show people crossing the Neck how the act would impact their own day-to-day lives. The drama closed when a crowd assembled under the leadership of Ebenezer Macintosh, a shoemaker who was not one of the Loyal Nine. Reenacting and transforming the rituals of a traditional Pope's Day riot, the crowd attacked property belonging to the stamp distributor Andrew Oliver. Oliver resigned his post. Facing similar pressure, distributors from New Hampshire to South Carolina also resigned. Except in Georgia, the act never took force.

New York City's Sons of Liberty operated differently. The Boston group disavowed the destruction of the house of Lieutenant Governor Thomas Hutchinson on 26 August 1765. The New Yorkers, however, disavowed nothing during the rioting in the city through October 1765 to May 1766, including the sacking of a newly opened theater. They also negotiated a mutual-assistance pact with Sons of Liberty in Connecticut. The group in Albany, New York, wrote a formal constitution. Philadelphia had

no organized group. Artisans played large parts in Baltimore and Charles Town, but Samuel Adams was not the only outright gentleman who became involved.

The great achievement of the organized Sons of Liberty was threefold. First, they turned debate about the Stamp Act into outright resistance. Second, they brought many outsiders into street politics, giving them both direction and discipline. Third, by their own militant insistence on a political voice and by the openness of some of them to domestic questions, they helped broaden the agenda of the emerging Revolution from breaking the link with Britain to questioning what kind of place America ought to be.

BIBLIOGRAPHY

Hoerder, Dirk. *Crowd Action in Revolutionary Massachusetts, 1765–1780.* New York: Academic Press, 1977.

Maier, Pauline. *From Resistance to Revolution: Colonial Radicals and the Development of American Opposition to Britain, 1765–1776.* New York: Knopf, 1972.

———. *The Old Revolutionaries: Political Lives in the Age of Samuel Adams.* New York: Knopf, 1980.

Nash, Gary B. *The Urban Crucible: Social Change, Political Consciousness, and the Origins of the American Revolution.* Cambridge, Mass.: Harvard University Press, 1979.

Edward Countryman

See also **Revolution, American: Political History; Stamp Act Congress.**

SONS OF LIBERTY (CIVIL WAR),

a secret organization of Peace Democrats formed by a low-level Indiana Democrat (H. H. Dodd) and implicated in the Indianapolis treason trials (1864). Union investigators depicted the Sons of Liberty as a military outfit with hundreds of thousands of members and accused it of conspiring with Confederate agents to engineer the secession of several northwestern states. Though some of its members worked with Confederates, as a whole the Sons of Liberty was tiny, fractious, and ineffectual. The group appeared more dangerous than it was primarily because Congressman Clement Vallandigham, an Ohio Copperhead imprisoned for disloyalty, served as supreme commander.

BIBLIOGRAPHY

Klement, Frank L. *Dark Lanterns: Secret Political Societies, Conspiracies, and Treason Trials in the Civil War.* Baton Rouge: Louisiana State University Press, 1984.

Jeremy Derfner

See also **Civil War; Copperheads.**

SONS OF THE SOUTH,

sometimes called Blue Lodges, Social Bands, and Friends Society, was a secret society formed in 1854 and devoted to making KANSAS a slave state. Its members, most of whom came from Missouri and organized in paramilitary bands, encouraged southern emigration to Kansas. They also protected pro-slavery settlers in Kansas and in numerous other ways tried to counteract the efforts of northern emigrant aid societies to make Kansas a free state. The violent and illegal tactics employed by the Sons of the South outraged northerners and intensified antislavery sentiment in the North.

BIBLIOGRAPHY

Rawley, James A. *Race and Politics: "Bleeding Kansas" and the Coming of the Civil War.* Philadelphia: Lippincott, 1969.

Henry T. Shanks / A. G.

See also **Alabama Platform; House Divided; Montgomery Convention; Peculiar Institution; Topeka Constitution.**

SOONERS were persons who illegally entered certain lands in the Indian Territory prior to the date set by the U.S. government for the opening of the lands to settlement. The term was first used in connection with the settlement of the so-called Oklahoma Lands in 1889. A proclamation issued by President Benjamin Harrison authorized settlement of these lands as of noon, 22 April, and forbade any person to enter them earlier. Those who did so came to be called "Sooners." The term was also used at later openings of Indian Territory lands to settlement.

BIBLIOGRAPHY

Joyce, Davis D., ed. *"An Oklahoma I Had Never Seen Before": Alternative Views of Oklahoma History.* Norman: University of Oklahoma Press, 1994.

Edward Everett Dale / A. R.

See also **Boomer Movement; Indian Policy, U.S., 1830–1900; Indian Territory.**

SORGHUM. In the 1840s the United States imported sorghum seeds from Liberia and grew the plants with a view to manufacturing sugar commercially from their juice. All such attempts proved futile, however, since glucose is the only saccharine matter in the plant. Colonel Isaac Hedges of Missouri was the greatest promoter of the product. During the Civil War, when Southern molasses was unavailable in the North, sorghum became a popular product in the Upper Mississippi Valley. Farmers used large wooden knives to strip sorghum stalks of their leaves as the plants stood in the field. They then cut the stalks and hauled them to a local mill where they were run between rollers to extract the juice, which was boiled to the proper consistency in large vats. Great quantities of this "long sweetening" were made and used as a substitute for sugar on the prairie frontier.

BIBLIOGRAPHY

Ledbetter, William M. "Isaac Hedges' Vision of a Sorghum-Sugar Industry in Missouri," *Missouri Historical Review* 21, no. 3 (1926): 361–369.

Everett Dick / C. W.

See also **Maple Sugar; Molasses Trade; Sugar Industry.**

SOTO, HERNANDO DE, EXPLORATIONS OF. While Francisco Vásquez de Coronado was seeking the mythical Seven Cities of Cíbola in the southwestern United States, another Spanish conquistador, Hernando de Soto, was similarly in quest of treasure in the Southeast. De Soto, who had been involved in Francisco Pizarro's conquest of the Peruvian Incas, secured a royal grant for the conquest of FLORIDA. Sailing from Havana with a company of about 600 men, de Soto landed on what is now Tampa Bay in the spring of 1539. This was the beginning of a four-year journey of conquest that took him halfway across the continent seeking riches he never found. As he traveled, de Soto ruthlessly pillaged and massacred thousands of Native Americans, while many of his followers were killed or died of disease and exposure.

De Soto passed the first winter at an Apalachee Indian village near the site of Tallahassee. Hearing rumors

Explorations of De Soto and Moscoso

De Soto, 1539–1542

Moscoso, 1542–1543

De Soto dies at Indian village of Guachoya and is buried in the Mississippi River, 1542; Moscoso takes command.

After Moscoso tries unsuccessfully to reach Mexico overland, he returns to the Mississippi, builds seven pinnaces and sails to Mexico.

of wealth to the north, he wandered through Georgia to Creek villages and proceeded through Piedmont country and the western part of the Carolinas—an area that later became CHEROKEE territory but was perhaps occupied by the SIOUX at the time. De Soto advanced through Tennessee and moved south through Creek territory, arriving in October 1540 at Mauvila (or Mabila), a great CHOCTAW town, where a fierce battle ensued. De Soto was wounded, and the Spaniards estimated that three thousand Indians were killed. After they recuperated, the Spaniards headed northwest in November, wintering among the Chickasaws and battling Indians at Cabusto, Chicaca, and Alabamo. In May 1541 de Soto discovered and crossed the Mississippi River. The Spaniards spent the winter of 1541–1542 in northeastern Arkansas and in the spring of 1542 moved down the Arkansas River to the Mississippi once more. De Soto fell ill and died near Natchez on 21 May 1542. The soldiers sank his body in the great river, fearing the Indians would attack if they discovered that de Soto was not immortal—as they had been told Christians were—and reported that he had gone to the sun. After fighting off Indian attacks in east Texas, the Spaniards built barges to float down the Mississippi. Eventually, on 10 September 1543, 320 survivors—of the original company of 600—landed at the mouth of the Pánuco River in the Gulf of Mexico.

BIBLIOGRAPHY

Galloway, Patricia, ed. *The Hernando de Soto Expedition: History, Historiography, and "Discovery" in the Southeast.* Lincoln: University of Nebraska Press, 1997.

Whayne, Jeannie, ed. *Cultural Encounters in the Early South: Indians and Europeans in Arkansas.* Fayetteville: University of Arkansas Press, 1995.

Kenneth M. Stewart/A. R.

See also **Cibola; Coronado Expeditions; Explorations and Expeditions: U.S.**

SOULS OF BLACK FOLK, THE.

Published originally in 1903, *The Souls of Black Folk* is W. E. B. Du Bois's classic collection of thirteen essays and one short story. Assembled from pieces the young Du Bois wrote between 1897 and 1903 (age twenty-nine to thirty-five), the book as a whole is rich and multifaceted. It is a moving evocation of black American folk culture, a poetic rendering of African American history since emancipation, a critical response to the racism and economic subjugation afflicting black Americans at the turn of the twentieth century, and an analysis of political leadership (it contains Du Bois's famous critique of Booker T. Washington's doctrine of accommodation).

Souls can be conveniently divided into three parts: chapters 1–3 have a distinctively historical character; chapters 4–9 display a sociological perspective; and chapters 10–14 demonstrate Du Bois's attempt to capture the spiritual meanings of African American culture. Insisting that "the problem of the twentieth century is the problem of the color-line," Du Bois wrote *Souls* to explore the "strange meaning of being black" in a society that viewed blacks with contempt. To that end, he detailed a sweeping tableau of African American life, emphasizing the struggle for civil rights, the economic and social legacies of slavery, and the contributions of blacks to America's identity as a nation. By expounding on key concepts, such as the notion of "double consciousness" (being black and American), Du Bois described African American efforts to cope with forms of neo-slavery. Most significantly, *Souls* is an original and tragic vision of American history, a gripping revelation of the triumphs, betrayals, and legacies that, in the wake of emancipation, shaped the "souls of black folk" two generations after freedom. The book remains in print in many editions and is widely taught in American colleges.

BIBLIOGRAPHY

Du Bois, W. E. B. *The Souls of Black Folk.* Reprint, edited by David W. Blight and Robert Gooding-Williams. Boston: Bedford and St. Martin's Press, 1997.

David W. Blight

See also **Literature: African American Literature.**

SOUTH AFRICA, RELATIONS WITH.

In 1652 the Dutch East India Company established the first European settlement in South Africa. By the early 1700s they had crushed the indigenous Khoikhoi and usurped their land. The population of Dutch settlers, known as Afrikaners, gradually increased. In the 1790s traders and whalers from New England visited South Africa regularly and trade increased in the mid-1800s. Ships sailed from Boston with barrel staves for the vineyards on South Africa's Western Cape and returned to New England loaded with cowhides for the shoe industry. International interest in South Africa exploded in the late nineteenth century with the discovery of abundant diamonds and gold in the area known as the Transvaal. The most important Americans in this development were mining engineers such as Gardner Williams, who eventually headed the De Beers diamond mines, and John Hays Hammond, who convinced the legendary capitalist Cecil Rhodes that the real wealth was in underground gold mining.

American contributions to the South African economy in the 1800s mainly benefited the white minority. American cultural contributions helped some blacks, particularly through education. John Dube, son of a Zulu leader, studied as a youth at an American missionary school in Natal. In 1889 he entered Oberlin College in Ohio and, after receiving his bachelor's degree, taught in Natal for a few years. In 1901 he opened a vocational school in Natal, based on Booker T. Washington's Tuskegee Institute. In 1912 he was named the first president of the South African Native National Congress, which later became the African National Congress.

Dube's activism was a response to the establishment of the Union of South Africa in 1910, which featured a constitution that denied virtually all political rights to black South Africans. The racist constitution did not deter American officials from carrying on positive, if somewhat limited, relations with the South African government for approximately the next forty years. South Africa fought with the Allies in both world wars and, under the leadership of Jan Smuts, participated in the peace negotiations at Versailles in 1919 and the planning sessions for the United Nations in 1945.

Apartheid and the Cold War

Two developments complicated American relations with South Africa in the years after World War II: the onset of the Cold War and the establishment of apartheid. In 1948 in Pretoria, the Nationalist Party gained control of Parliament. Led by extremist Afrikaners, the Nationalists constructed their system of institutionalized racism known as apartheid. They passed the legal foundations of apartheid in 1950: the Population Registration Act, the Group Areas Act, and the Suppression of Communism Act. These allowed the government to classify all South Africans by race, segregate them in residential areas, and crush any criticism of governmental policies. The emergence of apartheid presented the U.S. government with a dilemma. Maintaining friendly relations with South Africa would open the United States to criticism from black Africans, especially at the United Nations. On the other hand, the international anticommunism of the Pretoria regime was helpful during crises such as the Korean War.

Despite reservations about associating with a racist state, the Truman administration fostered closer ties with Pretoria. The State Department upgraded its presence in South Africa to an embassy, and abstained on antiapartheid measures at the United Nations. The Pentagon negotiated a Mutual Defense Assistance Pact and in 1952 agreed to sell more than $100 million in weapons to South Africa. Following an agreement in 1950, in exchange for scientific, technical, and financial support to South Africa, the United States received a supply of uranium. Over the next fifteen years South Africa shipped more than $1 billion worth of uranium to the U.S. nuclear industry.

In the 1960s and early 1970s, public condemnation of apartheid gradually increased in the United States. The American government occasionally registered protests against Pretoria's excesses; for example, after a 1960 massacre of sixty-nine demonstrators at Sharpeville, the United States recalled its ambassador and supported a U.N. resolution deploring the incident. Nonetheless, Cold War concerns precluded any ruptures in official relations through the mid-1970s.

The situation changed somewhat in 1976, with the election of Jimmy Carter as U.S. president. Carter pledged to break away from traditional Cold War patterns in foreign policy. The central figure in his relations with Africa was Andrew Young, an African American minister and former civil rights activist whom Carter appointed as U.N. ambassador. After police in South Africa murdered Stephen Biko, the extremely dynamic and popular antiapartheid activist, in September 1977, Young called for broad sanctions against Pretoria. Carter was not prepared to go that far, but he did support an arms embargo imposed by the United Nations. Young stated in no uncertain terms that the situation in South Africa needed to change, and official relations were chilly through the end of Carter's term.

Relations warmed up once again after the inauguration of Ronald Reagan. The Reagan administration staunchly opposed sanctions and implemented a policy known as constructive engagement. Engineered by Assistant Secretary of State Chester Crocker, constructive engagement attempted to encourage reform by working with the South African white leadership. Randall Robinson, head of the African American lobby group TransAfrica, emerged as Crocker's leading critic. Robinson and his followers transformed the debate over South Africa into a question of civil rights. Like the American civil rights struggle of the 1960s, the push for sanctions in the mid-1980s became a national grassroots movement. At the same time, Representative Ronald Dellums (D-CA) led a push in Congress for sanctions.

In September 1986, U.S. legislators passed the Comprehensive Anti-Apartheid Act (CAAA). Reagan vetoed the bill, but Congress promptly overrode him. The CAAA banned private loans, new investments, and computer sales by Americans in South Africa. It blocked imports of South African steel, uranium, and agricultural products into the United States and withdrew landing rights for South African airlines. Henceforth the Pretoria regime would pay a concrete price for maintaining apartheid.

Postapartheid Relations

The U.S. sanctions definitely took a toll and were a factor in the decision to end apartheid. More importantly,

Bill Clinton and Nelson Mandela. The two presidents in Cape Town, South Africa, in 1998. GETTY IMAGES

protests within South Africa continued. President F. W. De Klerk began the process of dismantling apartheid in February 1990, when he released Nelson Mandela from jail. Mandela, the African National Congress (ANC) leader who had been sentenced to life in prison in the early 1960s, had spent more than thirty years in jail. During the next few years De Klerk repealed the major legal foundations of apartheid, and he and Mandela reached a final agreement for a new political system in 1993. In April 1994 in the first true national elections in South African history, the ANC won in a landslide and Mandela became the first leader of postapartheid South Africa.

President Bill Clinton announced a three-year $600 million package of aid, trade, and investment for South Africa, which meant that it would receive more U.S. assistance than the rest of Africa combined. In late March 1998, Clinton spent three days visiting South Africa. Mandela and Clinton's tour of Robben Island, where Mandela had been imprisoned, provided the most dramatic footage of Clinton's two weeks in Africa. He emphasized the fact that South Africa was a multiracial democracy like the United States. Mandela responded by praising Clinton for bringing positive attention to Africa. Mandela served a five-year term as president and was succeeded in 1999 by Thabo Mbeki.

Relations with the United States remained strong at the dawn of the new millennium. In May 2000 Mbeki visited the United States. He met with Clinton in Washington and also stopped in Atlanta, where he was hosted by Andrew Young. In 2000, America exported more than $3 billion worth of goods to South Africa—more than half the total U.S. exports to the continent. The United States imported more than $4 billion from South Africa, which ranked second only to Nigeria among African nations. Bilateral relations were more extensive and more positive than ever before, and South Africa had become America's number one ally in Africa.

BIBLIOGRAPHY

Borstelmann, Thomas. *The Cold War and the Color Line: American Race Relations in the Global Arena.* Cambridge, Mass.: Harvard University Press, 2001.

DeRoche, Andrew. *Black, White and Chrome: The United States and Zimbabwe, 1953–1998.* Trenton, N.J.: Africa World Press, 2001.

Lauren, Paul Gordon. *Power and Prejudice: The Politics and Diplomacy of Racial Discrimination.* Boulder, Colo.: Westview Press, 1996.

Massie, Robert. *Loosing the Bonds: The United States and South Africa in the Apartheid Years.* New York: Nan A. Talese/Doubleday, 1997.

Noer, Thomas J. *Cold War and Black Liberation: The United States and White Rule in Africa, 1948–1968.* Columbia: University of Missouri Press, 1985.

Andy DeRoche

SOUTH AMERICA, RELATIONS WITH. *See* **Latin America, Relations with.**

SOUTH CAROLINA. The first inhabitants of South Carolina, an area of some 31,000 square miles along the South Atlantic coast, probably arrived in the region around 13,000 B.C. There were dozens of Indian nations in the area just prior to European contact, with a total population numbering between 15,000 and 30,000. However, after European contact, native peoples were devastated by disease, and their populations quickly declined.

European Exploration and Early Settlement

The Spanish were the first Europeans to attempt permanent settlement in South Carolina. In 1526 an expedition led by Lucas Vásquez de Ayllón founded San Miguel de Gualdape on the coast, possibly Winyah Bay, but the settlement was abandoned within a few months. The French were next when Jean Ribaut led an expedition of Huguenots to Parris Island in 1562, where they founded Charlesfort. Their settlement collapsed within a year. The Spanish returned in 1566 under Pedro Menéndez de Avilés, who founded the garrison town of Santa Elena on Parris Island. The Spanish deserted the site in 1587.

The English attempted to settle the region in the years after the restoration of King Charles II, who in 1663 granted eight prominent noblemen (known as the Lords Proprietors) rights to all the land between Virginia and Spanish Florida, a land they called "Carolina" in honor of their king. The Lords Proprietors sponsored a 1670 expedition, of which only the frigate *Carolina* survived traveling up the Ashley River to Albemarle Point, where settlers established Charles Town. Ten years later, they abandoned Albemarle Point and moved down the river to Oyster Point, near the confluence of the Ashley and Cooper Rivers, where the city that came to be known as Charleston developed. The Lords Proprietors offered generous land grants and religious freedom for settlers, and the colony grew at a healthy pace. By 1700 there were about 4,000 white colonists living in South Carolina, almost all in the coastal plain.

The Peoples of the Colony

A majority of the colony's earliest white settlers were "Barbadians," a term used to describe seasoned settlers from Barbados and other English colonies in the West Indies. The Barbadians were immensely influential, and the acquisitive plantation culture they brought with them set the economic, cultural, and social tone of the colony. After 1700, however, English settlers, whether Barbadians or directly from England, made up less than half of the colony's white population. French, Scottish, Irish, German, Welsh, Jewish, Dutch, and Swiss settlers came to South Carolina in substantial numbers, attracted by incentives such as large land grants and subsidized transportation and provisions. Later, during the 1750s, Scots-Irish settlers from the mid-Atlantic colonies began to

South Carolina

enter South Carolina's largely uninhabited backcountry via a road that ran from Pennsylvania into the Piedmont region. These Scots-Irish farmers filled the region above the fall line, and on the eve of the American Revolution South Carolina's white population stood at 80,000, about half of them in the upcountry.

The Barbadian culture and economy that became established in South Carolina in the late seventeenth century was based on plantation agriculture and African slavery, and black slaves arrived in South Carolina along with the colony's other original founders. In the early years of colonization, a majority of slaves came from the West Indies. After 1700 most were brought directly from Africa to Charleston, the port through which passed 40 percent of Africans brought in to North America before 1775. South Carolina planters were closely attuned to ethnic differences among Africans, and certain peoples were preferred for their technical expertise and ability to adapt to life in South Carolina. Among the Africans brought to the colony were those from the Congo-Angola region (who made up a plurality), Senegambians (preferred), and those from the Windward and Gold Coasts. As a result of the heavy demand for African slave labor, after 1708 blacks made up the majority of nonnatives in South Carolina. Between 1720 and the American Revolution, there were about two blacks for every one white in the colony. The existence of a black majority had a number of important effects, including the development of a distinctive creole culture that combined African and European elements.

Economic and Political Life in Colonial South Carolina

The Indian trade for deerskins was the first economic success in South Carolina's earliest decades, and by the early eighteenth century other lucrative exports included naval stores, salted meats, and lumber products. Commercial agriculture developed slowly, but by the 1720s rice be-

came the colony's first great staple crop and created fabulous wealth for a few Carolina families. It was grown on plantations in the marshy swamps north and south of Charleston, and rice planters relied on the expertise and labor of large numbers of slaves from the rice-growing regions of coastal West Africa. The success of rice fueled the rapid expansion of plantation slavery. Indigo, which produced a blue dye prized in England, was first successfully cultivated in the 1740s and soon became another source of wealth for the colony's planters and farmers. On the eve of the American Revolution, South Carolina was by far the most prosperous British colony in North America. Of the ten wealthiest North Americans, nine were South Carolinians (all from the lowcountry), including Peter Manigault, the richest American. In the upcountry above the fall line, hardscrabble subsistence farms cultivated by white settlers were the norm.

The colony's political character, like so much else, was shaped first by the Barbadians. They were a thorn in the side of the Lords Proprietors, and the Barbadian political faction (the "Goose Creek Men") consistently challenged proprietary rule, seeking stronger defense for the colony and the freedom to pursue wealth as they saw fit. Bitter political factionalism characterized early colonial politics and came to a head after a disastrous war with the Yemassee Indians (1715–1716), fought south of Charleston. The savage Yemassee War severely weakened South Carolina and in 1719 the colonists overthrew the proprietary regime and declared themselves to be under the immediate authority of the king. As a royal colony, South Carolina prospered. Imperial authorities left the wealthy elite to establish a political system that met its needs. The British colonial system operated to the benefit of that elite, providing a ready market for the colony's rice and subsidies for its indigo. Among the most significant challenges to royal government was the Stono Rebellion of September 1739, the largest slave uprising in the American colonies prior to the American Revolution. Originating at plantations along the Stono River just south of Charleston, the revolt left twenty whites and nearly twice that number of blacks dead.

The American Revolution and Internal Sectional Tensions

Seeking to protect their riches and solidify respect for their position in society, the South Carolina planters and merchants who had so profited from the British colonial system became the leaders of revolutionary activity in South Carolina. Sentiment against imperial authority was aroused by arrogant customs officials, the Stamp Act of 1765, the Townshend Acts of 1767, and British political claims. Wealthy low-country Carolinians such as Christopher Gadsden, Henry Laurens, Thomas Lynch, and Arthur Middleton led the colony's independence movement, and in March 1776, a provincial congress set up an independent government with Charlestonian John Rutledge as chief executive. A British attempt to take Charleston by force failed on 28 June 1776 at the Battle of Sullivan's Island, but in the spring of 1780 a British siege led to the city's surrender. In spite of the loss of the colonial capital, in the decisive campaign of the American Revolution upcountry militias rallied behind the leadership of Francis Marion, Andrew Pickens, and Thomas Sumter in late 1780 and 1781. In a brutal civil war punctuated by notable victories at King's Mountain (7 October 1780) and Cowpens (17 January 1781), they held the British army and their Tory allies at bay. Meanwhile the Continental Army under the leadership of Nathaniel Greene drove the British into an enclave around Charleston, which they evacuated finally in December 1782.

In the wake of the Revolution, South Carolina was in disarray. Old rivalries between upcountry and lowcountry resurfaced, resulting in a number of governmental reforms that included the removal of the state capital to Columbia in 1786 near the geographic center of the state. Pierce Butler, Henry Laurens, Charles Pinckney, Charles Cotesworth Pinckney, and John Rutledge, all members of the lowcountry elite, represented South Carolina at the 1787 Constitutional Convention. They then led the movement to ratify the document in 1788, in spite of significant opposition from the upcountry. A political compromise in 1808 helped to end the state's internal sectional rivalry when it amended the state constitution to provide roughly equal political representation in the General Assembly for upcountry and lowcountry.

The Antebellum Era and Secession, 1808–1860

The Compromise of 1808 was possible because the interests of upcountry and lowcountry were converging. After the invention of the cotton gin in 1793, short-staple cotton cultivation spread rapidly into the upcountry, and slave-based plantation agriculture spread with it. Improved transportation in the form of canals and railroads helped to integrate South Carolina's economy, and the South Carolina College, founded in Columbia in 1801, educated the planter elite from both sections and helped create a unified political culture. However, it was the development of a landed elite in the upcountry whose wealth was based on slave labor that did the most to unite the interests of upcountry and lowcountry. White South Carolinians were united in their support of slavery.

After 1820 it became nearly impossible to free a slave in South Carolina and the state had one of the most stringent slave codes in the country. The threat of slave insurrection, vividly demonstrated by the thwarted rising plotted by Denmark Vesey in Charleston during 1822, put whites on the defensive, as did declining cotton prices, worn-out cotton lands, and rising prices for slaves through much of the antebellum era. Besieged by developments beyond their control, South Carolina politicians first focused on the federal Tariff of 1828, which, they believed, put their slave-based economy at a disadvantage. Opponents of the tariff united behind South Carolinian and Vice President John C. Calhoun, who anonymously authored the *South Carolina Exposition and Protest*, a pamphlet

outlining the doctrine of nullification, which held that a state could nullify any federal law it felt was unconstitutional. Despite bitter disagreement between Unionists and Nullifiers within South Carolina, an 1832 convention declared the Tariff null and void, threatening secession if the federal government tried to enforce the law. After Congress passed a compromise tariff, the convention repealed the Ordinance of Nullification, temporarily quelling disunionist sentiment in South Carolina.

As the question of the expansion of slavery in the territories seized the attention of the nation in the 1840s, secessionists in South Carolina (the so-called fire-eaters) argued that if the new territories became antislavery states, they would join with the North and force an end to slavery in South Carolina. The fire-eaters tried to push the state to secede in 1850. Unsuccessful in that year, the election of the antislavery Republican Abraham Lincoln in 1860 gave the fire-eaters the political momentum they sought, and a special state convention ratified the Ordinance of Secession on 20 December 1860. South Carolina was the first state to secede, setting the stage for the Civil War.

Civil War and Reconstruction, 1861–1877

The war began on 12 April 1861, when Confederate artillery bombarded the federal installation at Fort Sumter in Charleston harbor. The war that followed devastated South Carolina. A federal blockade virtually shut down the port of Charleston, and federal troops under General William T. Sherman brought modern warfare to the state in early 1865, plundering and destroying homes, farms, and railroads in a wide swath in their march from Savannah northward. On 17 February 1865, Sherman entered Columbia, and that night a fire destroyed one-third of the city. Between 31 and 35 percent of South Carolina's young white male population died during the war.

With defeat came emancipation for nearly 60 percent of South Carolinians, and white and black Carolinians were forced to work out a new relationship. In late 1865, white Carolinians took advantage of lenient federal policies to create a new state government filled with former Confederates, who imposed restrictive black codes that circumscribed black civil rights and later rejected the Fourteenth Amendment. In response, Congress ordered military rule and a new state government. In 1868, a constitutional convention that welcomed freedmen created a new government recognizing black voting rights, removing property qualifications for office holding, and creating a free public school system. Until 1876, the Republican Party controlled state government, and African Americans held office at every level but governor, achieving a greater degree of political power in South Carolina than in any other state. But South Carolina's whites reacted violently to this turn of events. A reign of terror by the Ku Klux Klan during 1870 and 1871 resulted in so many lynchings and beatings of Republicans that the writ of habeas corpus was suspended in nine upstate counties.

455

However, in the aftermath the federal government failed to make more than a token show of force and terror organizations continued to function in South Carolina. In the disputed election of 1876, the Red Shirts, a white paramilitary organization, managed to engineer an apparent Democratic victory through violence and fraud. The Compromise of 1877 ended federal support for Republican Party government in South Carolina, and the white minority, represented by the Democratic Party and led by former Confederate General Wade Hampton III, regained control of state government.

The Rise of Jim Crow and the Persistence of Poverty, 1877–1941

As Hampton and the old elite (the so-called "Bourbons") returned to power, they tried to recreate the world of antebellum South Carolina. However, their inattention to the state's agricultural problems and mildly tolerant racial policies soon led to political revolt. Benjamin R. Tillman rode the disaffection of the state's white farmers to the governor's office, where he and his allies attacked the symbols of Bourbon power, if not the substance. Tillman focused his "reform" impulse on removing the state's black majority from public life. His triumph was the state's Constitution of 1895, which disfranchised the black majority and laid the groundwork for white supremacy and one-party Democratic rule in the twentieth century. In the last years of the nineteenth century and early years of the twentieth, South Carolina's white government also enacted a host of laws designed to segregate public life, and black Carolinians became virtually powerless. Relations between the races not governed by law were controlled by rigid customs that ensured blacks inferior status. As a result, black Carolinians left the state in droves, most bound for northern cities. After about 1922, South Carolina no longer had a black majority.

Persistent poverty plagued the state in the decades after the Civil War and was another factor in the outmigration. The economy remained overwhelmingly agricultural and the system of sharecropping and farm tenancy led to heavy dependence on cotton, whose prices were in decline because of overproduction. As a result, farmers in the state's northeastern Pee Dee region turned increasingly to tobacco cultivation, which soon witnessed its own cycle of overproduction and declining prices. In the last years of the nineteenth and the early decades of the twentieth century, South Carolinians began to diversify their economy, primarily into extractive industries such as cotton textiles. Textile mills were organized across the Piedmont region, taking advantage of waterpower and a surplus of white labor, but creating new class tensions in the process. These mills were most often built in upcountry towns that boomed with the widespread expansion of railroads after the Civil War. Towns such as Spartanburg, Greenville, Anderson, Rock Hill, and Greenwood became important marketing centers and drew economic activity away from Charleston, which entered a period of decline. In spite of the efforts of an indigenous

Progressive movement, which sought to alleviate the effects of poverty, the economic stagnation that plagued South Carolina through the first decades of the twentieth century proved nearly impervious to change.

As bad as the years before 1930 had seemed, the Great Depression brought economic life in South Carolina nearly to a standstill. With Carolinians literally starving, both white and black Carolinians overwhelmingly supported Franklin D. Roosevelt's attempts to break the Great Depression, and U.S. Senator James F. Byrnes of South Carolina was a key to the passage of New Deal legislation. But the New Deal did little to change things in the Palmetto State. In spite of federal aid, debt-ridden farmers abandoned the land in large numbers, seeking work in cities. The textile industry was a shambles because of overproduction, and the General Textile Strike of 1934 left six dead in the Piedmont mill town of Honea Path.

Modern South Carolina from 1941

With the coming of World War II, a revival began in South Carolina. Military installations boosted the economy in communities all over the state, and defense-related industries helped spur a wartime boom. After the war, agriculture began a long-term decline and by 1980 the state's traditional dependence on farming had given way to a diverse economy. Mechanization eliminated tens of thousands of farm jobs, while crop diversification reduced the importance of cotton, which was replaced by tobacco and soy beans as the state's leading cash crops. For three decades after the war, textiles remained the state's most important industry, and during the 1950s manufacturing employment exceeded agricultural employment for the first time. State government made concerted efforts to attract northern and foreign-owned industry by promoting special tax incentives, tax-free government bonds, technical education, and a revived Port of Charleston. By the 1990s, firms such as Michelin, DuPont, BASF, Fuji, BMW, and Hoffman-LaRoche were a major presence in South Carolina, primarily in the Piedmont, but few had located their headquarters in the state. By the end of the twentieth century, textile employment had declined in importance and, in the long term, appeared doomed in the region. Tourism capitalized on the state's climate and environment and emerged as the state's most lucrative industry, concentrated at coastal destinations such as Myrtle Beach, Charleston, and Hilton Head Island. While the state's standard of living rose considerably after World War II, at century's end South Carolina's 4,012,012 inhabitants still ranked near the bottom nationally in per capita income.

South Carolina's postwar revival included a revolution in race relations. At the end of World War II, the state was a part of the solid Democratic South, its politics was controlled by a rural elite, and Jim Crow ruled race relations. But after the war, the civil rights movement achieved a victory with the U.S. Supreme Court ruling in *Briggs v. Elliott* (a case arising in Clarendon County) as part of its 1954 decision in the landmark *Brown v. Board of Education* case. Though the state's white leaders at first resisted the demands of black Carolinians for civil rights, by the early 1960s they had begun to heed them. A series of strong, moderately progressive governors, including Ernest F. Hollings (1959–1963), Robert E. McNair (1965–1971), and John C. West (1971–1975), urged white South Carolinians to peacefully accept federal civil rights laws and rulings. With the notable exception of the deaths of three students at Orangeburg's South Carolina State College in 1968, South Carolina avoided the violence and unrest that plagued other Deep South states during the civil rights era. By 1970, black Carolinians had begun to take their rightful place in the state's public life. At century's end, racial issues continued to play a prominent role in politics, as black Carolinians supplied the core of Democratic Party voters, while the Republican Party attracted few blacks. But for the first time in its history, the state had a genuine, competitive two-party system. South Carolina was a far different place than it had been even fifty years before.

BIBLIOGRAPHY

Carlton, David L. *Mill and Town in South Carolina, 1880–1920.* Baton Rouge: Louisiana State University Press, 1982.

Edgar, Walter B. *South Carolina: A History.* Columbia: University of South Carolina Press, 1998.

Ford, Lacy K. *Origins of Southern Radicalism: The South Carolina Upcountry 1800–1860.* New York: Oxford University Press, 1988.

Hayes, J. I. *South Carolina and the New Deal.* Columbia: University of South Carolina Press, 2001.

Jones, Lewis P. *South Carolina: A Synoptic History for Laymen.* Rev. ed. Lexington, S.C: Sandlapper, 1978.

Joyner, Charles. *Down By the Riverside: A South Carolina Slave Community.* Urbana: University of Illinois Press, 1984.

Klein, Rachael N. *Unification of a Slave State: The Rise of the Planter Class in the South Carolina Backcountry, 1760–1808.* Chapel Hill: University of North Carolina Press, 1990.

Kovacik, Charles F., and John J. Winberry. *South Carolina: A Geography.* Boulder, Colo.: Westview Press, 1987. Reprinted as Kovacik, Charles F., and John J. Winberry. *South Carolina: The Making of a Landscape.* Columbia: University of South Carolina Press, 1989.

Littlefield, Daniel C. *Rice and Slaves: Ethnicity and the Slave Trade in Colonial South Carolina.* Baton Rouge: Louisiana State University Press, 1981.

Newby, I. A. *Black Carolinians: A History of Blacks in South Carolina from 1895 to 1968.* Columbia: University of South Carolina Press, 1973.

Simkins, Francis Butler. *Pitchfork Ben Tillman, South Carolinian.* Baton Rouge: Louisiana State University Press, 1944.

Tindall, George Brown. *South Carolina Negroes, 1877–1900.* Columbia: University of South Carolina Press, 1952.

Weir, Robert M. *Colonial South Carolina: A History.* Millwood, N.Y.: KTO Press, 1983.

Williamson, Joel. *After Slavery: The Negro in South Carolina during Reconstruction, 1861–1877.* Chapel Hill: University of North Carolina Press, 1965.

Wood, Peter H. *Black Majority: Negroes in Colonial South Carolina from 1670 through the Stono Rebellion.* New York: Knopf, 1974.

Zuczek, Richard. *State of Rebellion: Reconstruction in South Carolina.* Columbia: University of South Carolina Press, 1996.

Henry Lesesne

See also **Albemarle Settlements; Black Codes; Carolina, Fundamental Constitutions of; Charleston; Charleston Harbor, Defense of; Charleston Indian Trade; Fire-Eaters; Menéndez de Avilés, Pedro, Colonization Efforts of; Nullification; Port Royal; Proprietary Colonies; Reconstruction; Red Shirts; Secession; Segregation; Slave Trade; Slavery; Vesey Rebellion;** *and vol. 9:* **Letter Describing Plantation Life in South Carolina; South Carolina Declaration of Causes of Secession.**

SOUTH CAROLINA EXPOSITION AND PROTEST. In the fall of 1828, many South Carolinians were on the point of rebellion against the Tariff of Abominations and the perceived abuse of power by congressional majorities. Seeking redress, state legislators asked John C. Calhoun, then U.S. vice president, to write a justification for a state veto of the offending legislation. In his "draft," Calhoun expanded on the iniquities and dangers of the tariff, and argued that state constitutional conventions had the sovereign authority to declare a federal act unconstitutional. Such a declaration would halt the operation of the law within the state until the federal government secured passage—if it could—of a constitutional amendment confirming the disputed power. The South Carolina legislature did not formally adopt Calhoun's *Exposition*, but printed it with amendments, together with its own protest, in December 1828. Four years later, the state adopted Calhoun's nullification scheme, bringing on a national crisis that showed the impracticality and danger of the procedure, and it was never used again.

BIBLIOGRAPHY

Freehling, William W. *Prelude to Civil War: The Nullification Controversy in South Carolina, 1816–1836.* New York: Harper and Row, 1966.

Wilson, Clyde N., and W. Edwin Hemphill, eds. *The Papers of John C. Calhoun, Vol. 10: 1825–1829.* Columbia: University of South Carolina Press, 1977.

Wiltse, Charles M. *John C. Calhoun.* 3 vols. Indianapolis, Ind.: Bobbs-Merrill, 1944–1951.

Donald J. Ratcliffe

See also **Nullification.**

SOUTH DAKOTA entered the union during 2 November 1889 as the fortieth state, and ranks sixteenth in size among the fifty states. Approximately 77,047 square

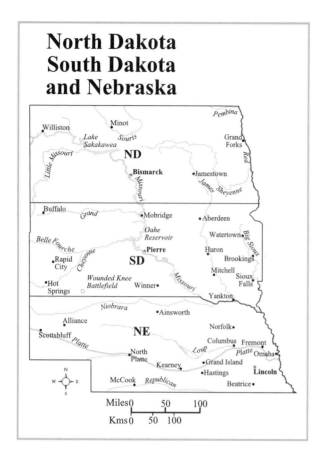

North Dakota South Dakota and Nebraska

miles of land form a rectangle that tilts from northwest to southeast and contains elevations above sea level between 1,100 feet in the southeast corner and 7,242 in the BLACK HILLS at Harney Peak, the highest elevation in the United States east of the Rocky Mountains. A varied terrain contains the geographical center of North America—located near the middle of the state, close to Pierre—and the only true continental divide. From the northeast corner, water flows through the Red River to Hudson's Bay, and down the Minnesota and Mississippi rivers to the Gulf of Mexico.

The most distinctive natural feature is the MISSOURI RIVER, which forms the southeastern boundary and dissects the state. South Dakotans created the term "West River" (meaning west of the river) to identify an area—comprising about three-fifths of the land—from which five principal streams drain into the Missouri River from the west. The term "East River" is used to identify the other two-fifths, from which two principal streams drain into the Missouri near the state's southeastern corner. In West River, rough and porous land with annual rainfall as low as fourteen inches has supported mainly livestock, mineral, and tourist industries. In East River, glacial chernozem soils with annual rainfall as great as twenty-six inches have supported subsistence farming, cash crop production, and livestock feeding industries.

The fertile Missouri River valley sustained a succession of five Native American cultures over nearly 14,000

years before it attracted the first non-Indian settlers as a "Steamboat Society" during the fur trade era. Beginning in the 1860s, white homesteaders and gold seekers used the river for transportation, and settled as rapidly as modern SIOUX tribes ceded acreage to the U.S. Government.

The population that gathered over the next sixty years was as varied as the terrain. Thirteen of fourteen ancestral tribes of Sioux formed nine modern reservation societies that gained recognition by the U.S. Government as "domestic dependent nations." Due to the Sioux's gradual relinquishment of land over more than half a century, South Dakota's first generation of immigrants included representations from most European nations. Immigration records reveal that they included—in order of diminishing numbers—Norwegians, Germans (including Polish), Russians (including Germans from Russia and Finns), Swedes, Danes, Anglo Canadians, Dutch, English and Welsh, Irish, Austrians and Czechs (including Bohemians, Moravians, and Slovakians), Scots, Swiss, and French Canadians. Briefly, Chinese worked in the Black Hills, while both African and Jewish Americans founded agricultural colonies, bringing the total number of enclaves to thirty-six.

Ethnic variety spawned diversity in religious persuasion: the state was home to Lutheran, Catholic, Episcopal, Presbyterian, Congregational, Mennonite, Hutterite, Dutch Reformed, Baptist, Methodist, and Jewish denominations, as well as practitioners of traditional Native American religions. Despite the efforts of Christian missionaries, the tribes preserved the traditional belief system of the Sacred Pipe, and added to it the practices of the Native American (Peyote) Church. Within ten years of statehood, immigrant South Dakotans supported sixteen higher educational institutions and a greater number of academies—an array of choices that encouraged the preservation of cultural variety. When the immigrant population peaked in 1930, there existed no "typical South Dakotans."

Rugged terrain, inhospitable climatic conditions, and economic colonialism have restricted population growth. At the founding of DAKOTA TERRITORY in 1861, more than 20,000 Sioux and approximately 1,000 non-Indians lived in what is now South Dakota. The white citizen population grew to about 348,600 by the time of statehood and by 1930 it had, through gradual increase, become the major part of a total population of 692,849 (a total that, because of the National Indian Citizenship Act of 1924, included Indians). Severe conditions during the Great Depression and the demands of World War II lowered the population to approximately 590,000 by 1945. Following this, a gradual increase brought the census total to 754,844 by the year 2000, at which time at least 10 percent of the population was Native American. A majority of the population was rural until 1960, after which South Dakotans became urban residents by ever-increasing numbers.

In the imaginations of European imperialists, four flags were successively aloft over South Dakota before its purchase by the United States as the center of Upper

Louisiana Territory: the flags of Hapsburg Spain, which controlled the territory from 1494 to 1702; Bourbon France, the dominant power from 1702 to 1762; Bourbon Spain, which reasserted Spanish dominion from 1762 to 1800; and Napoleonic France, briefly ascendant from 1800 to 1803. After Congress acquired the Louisiana Territory in 1803, present-day South Dakota divided politically as well as geographically at the Missouri River into its West River and East River components, each independent of the other and marginally attached to surrounding territorial governments. In the absence of effective territorial administration, federal officials created the Upper Missouri Indian Agency jurisdiction, which remained in place from 1819 to 1868. The Fur Trade Act of 1824 delegated powers to the official in charge that were equivalent to those of a territorial governor. This desultory administration seemed adequate because the only outside economic interest affecting the region was the fur trade, which from 1827 to the end of the 1850s was mainly dominated by St. Louis magnate Pierre Chouteau Jr.

During the years 1858 to 1868, the Upper Missouri Indian Agency collapsed into several smaller Indian agency jurisdictions. The 1861 founding of its replacement, Dakota Territory, created to serve no more than 1,000 citizens, occurred due to an extraordinary combination of circumstances. Extralegal "squatter governments" devised by speculators from Dubuque and St. Paul had started a political movement at present-day Sioux Falls, and began agitating for the creation of a new territory. At the same time, the prospect of secession by southern states after the 1860 presidential election removed an obstacle to political change. Lame duck Democrats in Congress and defeated president James Buchanan claimed a final legacy by extending legal authority to create territorial governments.

Even after the founding of Dakota Territory, political machinations continued. The new town of Yankton on the Missouri River became the territorial capital not only because of its access to steamboat transportation, but also because it was the preference of John B. S. Todd, the cousin of Abraham Lincoln's wife and the first U.S. Delegate to Congress. President Lincoln personally approved the appointments of "Indian Ring" leaders, who collaborated to steal Yankton Sioux tribal assets: these included William Jayne, Lincoln's personal physician, who became governor; and Walter Burleigh and his father-in-law Andrew Faulk, who had stumped western Pennsylvania for Republican votes before Lincoln's election and were now named U.S. Indian Agent and Licensed Trader on the new Yankton Sioux Reservation. Jayne left the territory in 1863 following his defeat by Todd in the second congressional election of 1862. After investigators representing the U.S. Senate exposed fraud and dissolved the Indian Ring, Burleigh twice won election as U.S. Delegate to Congress and Faulk gained appointment as territorial governor. Their escape from retribution set the tone for territorial governance. In 1883, after the seventh territorial governor, Nehemiah Ordway, met his match in

Delegate to Congress Richard Pettigrew, the territorial capital was moved to Bismarck (in present North Dakota) to buttress Ordway's fading political career and enhance his personal economic opportunities.

Largely because Governor Ordway's choice of Bismarck had been based on narrow self-interest, in 1889—after statehood was finally achieved—South Dakotans selected a new capital: Pierre (named after Pierre Chouteau Jr., and his principal trading post, but pronounced "peer"). Its selection not only circumvented competition from population centers at Yankton, Sioux Falls, and Rapid City, but also placed the new political headquarters near the center of the state, within 200 miles of most citizens. Moreover, Pierre was located on a central commercial avenue opened during territorial years by the Dakota Central Railroad across East River, and by the Fort Pierre-to-Deadwood Wagon Road in West River.

Statehood had been so long in coming mainly because of resistance by the Sioux, who refused to relinquish land and bested non-Indian forces during several confrontations outside the borders of Dakota Territory. In two months during the Minnesota Sioux War of 1862, eastern Sioux killed nearly 600 and drove 2,500 whites into flight. At the Grattan Affair in Nebraska (1854), the Fetterman Massacre in Wyoming (1866), and the Battle of the Little Big Horn in Montana (1876), western and middle Sioux claimed decisive victories. Then, whether it was an accident or an ambush by U.S. Army troops, the tragedy at Wounded Knee in South Dakota (1890) broke the will of the Sioux to resist. Their previous victories were fruitful, however: the tribes retained more than 10 percent of their ancestral land, compared to an average 3.5 percent for thirty-seven Great Plains tribes overall. In South Dakota, the Pine Ridge, Rosebud, Cheyenne River, Standing Rock (partly in North Dakota), Lower Brule, and Crow Creek reservations alone contained 12,681,911 acres in 1889 when Congress defined their boundaries (within which tribal groups later sold land, though by 1950 they still retained ownership of 6,114,502 acres). On these reservations, plus those occupied by Yanktons, Sissetons and Wahpetons, and Flandreau Santees in East River, there remained ample space for the survival of tribalism and traditional cultures.

Statehood for South Dakota—achieved through an omnibus act of 1889 that also created North Dakota, Montana, and Washington—was a product of sterling performances by able politicians who made up for the likes of Jayne, Burleigh, Faulk, and Ordway. General William Henry Harrison Beadle accommodated immigrants by organizing an effective survey of rough terrain, then inspired resistance to real estate prospectors (who hoped to purchase federally donated school lands at bargain basement prices) in order to ensure land-sale proceeds sufficient to establish a suitable elementary educational system. Congregational minister Joseph Ward organized a political caucus in Yankton that unified territorial politicians during a succession of constitutional conventions.

The leader of this group of politicians, Arthur Mellette, became the primary architect of the constitution and, for his efforts, gained recognition as both the last territorial governor and the first governor of the state of South Dakota. The constitution gave expression to Mellette's suspicions about politicians, with salutary consequences. It preserved a school-land fund under Beadle's plan to accept no less than $10 per acre, and placed a limit of $100,000 on state indebtedness. At times the latter feature stifled the growth of infrastructure, but it also kept South Dakota free from debt, except on one occasion. Fiscal conservatism fostered a tradition among legislators of carrying surplus funds in the state treasury, and relying on U.S. senators for maximum congressional assistance. The most telling evidence of this tradition came in 2000, when the state received federally funded programs worth $1.7 billion more than South Dakotans had paid in federal taxes that year.

Because of the constitutional restriction on indebtedness, inhospitable natural conditions, and economic colonialism, South Dakotans learned to elect tight-fisted officials to state and local government, but to send liberal spenders to the U.S. Senate. For service within the state, South Dakotans have elected only four Democrats to the office of governor, and have on only two occasions allowed Democrats to control the state legislature. To improve efficiency as well as performance, voters in the 1970s supported referendums that facilitated the consolidation of 160 overlapping state agencies into 16 executive departments and streamlined the judicial system. As far as service in Washington, D.C., was concerned, the long line of fundraisers elected to the U.S. Senate included Richard Pettigrew, Peter Norbeck, William McMaster, Francis Case, Karl Mundt, George McGovern, James Abouresk, and Senate Majority Leader Tom Daschle—all of them charged with the responsibility to bring maximum benefit to a state with limited economic prospects.

South Dakota's economic mainstays have been farming and ranching, which during the banner year of 1991 together contributed $13.2 billion to the economy, enhanced by $436 million in federal subsidies. The livestock industry had taken root before statehood because of insatiable markets that existed in Indian agency jurisdictions, where tribal funds were used to pay market prices for enough livestock to provide about eight pounds of fresh meat per month for more than 20,000 tribal members. Both Indian agencies and U.S. Army installations consumed hay, grain, fruits, and vegetables; contracted for transportation services; and provided part-time jobs for settlers. Because of reliable markets and steady employment through territorial times, farming and ranching fast became the main feature in South Dakota's economic life.

Next in importance has been tourism, which originated when passengers boarded Pierre Chouteau's steamboat *Yellowstone* in 1831 for a ride up the Missouri River. Their primary interests included catching glimpses of Native Americans, exposure to unsullied frontier terrain,

and escape from the monotony of workaday life—touristic interests that have never changed. Railroads replaced steamboats by the outset of the twentieth century, and automobiles and buses replaced rail cars for tourist travel during the 1920s. South Dakotans secured federal funds to install five bridges across the Missouri River during the years 1924–1927 at a cost of $3.1 million, and matched federal funds to build networks of roads during the years 1919–1941 at a cost of $60.4 million. After World War II this transportation system was refined by the completion of 680 miles of freeways running south to north and east to west, at the advantageous funding ratio of 9 to 1. The completion of four earthen dams across the Missouri by the U.S. Army Corps of Engineers during the years 1954–1966 not only stabilized connections between East River and West River, but also added tourist facilities with hunting and fishing opportunities at four large reservoirs behind the dams.

Although Native Americans and untarnished landscapes remained favorite features for tourists, with federal assistance South Dakotans added many other attractions. U.S. Park Service personnel manage the magnificent BADLANDS and the majestic MOUNT RUSHMORE, each of which attracts several million visitors every year. State employees accommodate tourists at serene lodging places named Sylvan Lake and the Game Lodge. Every year Rapid City houses as many as 15,000 in hotels and motels. Local entrepreneurs lure visitors: in East River, Mitchell—with its nineteenth century agricultural exhibition hall, the Corn Palace—is the main destination, while in West River attractions include a snake pit, the Homestake Gold Mine (closed in the year 2000), and exhilarating climbs on Harney Peak and Bear Butte. Since 1935 residents of Sturgis have attracted motorcycle riders to an annual rally that lasts for a week at a cost that sustains the economy of the city the year round. Scenic roads embellished by "pig-tail bridges" slow Black Hills traffic prior to entry into Custer State Park, which contains a herd of buffalo along with countless other species.

A shift in population from farms and ranches to urban centers since the 1960s has required the addition of new industries, though these have not been allowed to encroach on agribusiness or blemish landscapes that sustain tourism. One has been banking, which took off following a 1980 application by representatives from the credit card division of Citibank, which established bank office facilities in Sioux Falls. For banks, the state's special attractions already included the absence of corporate or personal income taxation—and after 1980 a new law promised a guarantee of freedom from legal constraint on usury rates. South Dakotans, as victims of bankers who charged interest rates as high as 24 percent in territorial times, had gradually reduced the usury limit to 8 percent during the Great Depression and had sustained it at that level until the year 1970. Subsequently, however, due to an inflationary economy, state legislators raised the rate to 12 percent and, in 1980, with House Bill 1046 they proposed to eliminate the usury rate altogether to enhance credit opportunities.

While House Bill 1046 awaited the governor's signature, Citicorp, the second largest bank in the world (and Citibank's parent company), faced a dilemma due to the inflationary economy and a legal restriction in New York that held interest rates on credit balances above $500 at 12 percent. Its managers selected South Dakota as the new location for Citibank's back offices in preference to four other states that allowed interest rate charges at 22 percent or greater. After South Dakota's governor signed House Bill 1046, Citibank brought 2,500 jobs to the Sioux Falls business community. Soon other lending institutions relocated to gain the same benefits at urban locations across the state.

More advantageous even than banking to urban economies has been spectacular growth in the health care industry—rendered secure by Medicare/Medicaid support, state employee medical benefits, and private insurance. Its evolution was typical for states in the West. Pioneering country doctors founded makeshift hospitals while officials opened a two-year Medical School at the University of South Dakota (1907) and appointed a State Board of Nursing (1917). Scientific advancements during World War II brought improvements in patient care. The Medical School expanded to offer a four-year degree program (1975). Following national trends, three health management organizations (HMOs) with sprawling networks of hospitals, clinics, and nursing homes came into place. In East River, Sioux Falls became the center of both the Avera managed care and the Sioux Valley Hospital systems. In West River, Rapid City became the center of the Rapid City Regional Hospital network. Although alternative treatment remained available at independent medical and chiropractic clinics, most South Dakotans became customers of the three HMO networks, which could offer easy referral to the Mayo Clinic in Rochester, Minnesota.

Another flourishing urban industry has been education. After state-mandated consolidation during the 1960s, rural elementary schools nearly disappeared. The academic year 1999–2000 opened with the operation of 176 public school district K-12 systems, 26 Alternative Education units, 46 private or parochial academies, 12 public and private colleges and universities, and a suitable array of public and private vocational training institutions. Tradition, ethnic variety, and the realities of urban economics all sustain resistance to change in this complex, costly system.

An additional factor in creating economic stability has been improving living conditions and broadening business opportunities for nine federally recognized Indian tribes on as many reservations. The key to this economic success has been the U.S. government's carrying out of trust responsibilities established by treaties and statutes during the nineteenth century in return for Indian land. One such responsibility was health care, which for Sioux people began with the federal employment of two physicians during the 1840s. The Snyder Act of 1921 and the Indian Health Care Development Act of 1976 stabilized and enlarged this benefit. In 1997, at an annual operational cost of nearly $2 million, U.S. Indian Health Service personnel operated five hospitals and numerous clinics in South Dakota to provide free health care for tribal members. Another responsibility was the provision of housing, which began in the nineteenth century and was formalized by the federal Housing Act of 1937. On the basis of several additional acts, Congress spent at least $30 million a year on South Dakota reservations throughout the final years of the twentieth century.

The freedom from taxation on Indian land under federal trust, or on business profits generated on that land, has led to success in many tribal enterprises, including high-stakes casinos—established on all but one reservation in the state under terms in the National Indian Gaming Regulatory Act of 1988. The Indian Self Determination and Education Assistance Act of 1975 invited tribes to contract for congressional funds to carry out trust responsibilities previously realized by the Bureau of Indian Affairs and other federal agencies. In 1998, the Yankton Sioux tribe (the tribe is about average size—some 7,500 enrolled, half in residence) managed more than $2 million in its business budget (these funds derive from both federal contributions and profits from tribal enterprises), and members have enjoyed congressionally mandated "Indian preference" (affirmative action) regarding all jobs funded by Congress or the tribe for the benefit of Indians. Newly flourishing tribal economies sustain not only enrolled members, but also surrounding non-Indian towns, communities, and infrastructures.

The American Indian Renaissance of the 1970s, which brought cultural traditions from the underground into open use, has affected the economy by making Native American culture a star feature of tourism. This economic mainstay flourishes due to demands for facilities to accommodate visiting scholars and journalists, professional conventions, and Indian arts and crafts displays, as well as recreational travel. For economic as well as cultural reasons, both tribal and non-Indian ethnic heritages are preserved in archives and explained at the Augustana College Center for Western Studies in Sioux Falls, and at the South Dakota Cultural Heritage Center in Pierre.

BIBLIOGRAPHY

Cash, Joseph H., and Herbert T. Hoover, eds. *To Be an Indian: An Oral History.* 2d ed. St. Paul: Minnesota Historical Society, 1995. The original edition appeared in 1971. Contains excerpts from reminiscences by tribal elders.

Hoover, Herbert T. *The Yankton Sioux.* New York: Chelsea House, 1988. The only volume that traces the entire history of a tribe in South Dakota. (Video production available.)

Hoover, Herbert T., and Carol Goss Hoover. *Sioux Country: A History of Indian-White Relations.* Sioux Falls, S.D.: Augustana College Center for Western Studies, 2000. Contains profiles for the histories of seventeen modern tribes on the northern Great Plains.

Hoover, Herbert T., and Karen P. Zimmerman. *South Dakota History: An Annotated Bibliography* and *The Sioux and Other Native American Cultures of the Dakotas.* Westport, Conn.: Greenwood Press, 1993. Two substantial volumes contain a common index.

Hoover, Herbert T., and Larry J. Zimmerman. *South Dakota Leaders: From Pierre Chouteau, Jr., to Oscar Howe.* Lanham, Md.: University Publishing Associates; Vermillion: University of South Dakota Press, 1989. Contains biographies of more than fifty individuals who have affected the history of the state.

Schell, Herbert S. *History of South Dakota.* 3d ed. Lincoln: University of Nebraska Press, 1975. The best single volume on the subject emphasizes political and economic histories.

Herbert T. Hoover

See also **Sioux Wars; Wounded Knee Massacre.**

SOUTH PASS, located in Wyoming at the southern end of the Wind River Mountains, gained noteriety because the emigrant trail to Oregon and California ran through it. There are claims that John Colter discovered the South Pass in 1807 or 1808, and that Robert Stuart and the returning Astorians crossed it in 1812, but both claims are disputed. It is certain that the effective discovery was made in 1824 by Thomas Fitzpatrick, a fur trader. Capt. Benjamin L. E. Bonneville first took wagons over the pass in 1832, and a few years later it became the mountain gateway on the OREGON TRAIL.

Marcus Whitman at the South Pass. This illustration depicts the missionary praying and holding the flag on 4 July 1836, after his party—including his wife, Narcissa, and missionary Henry Spalding and his wife, Eliza—crossed the pass en route to the Oregon region to start a mission near Fort Walla Walla. Cayuse Indians killed the Whitmans in 1847. © CORBIS-BETTMANN

BIBLIOGRAPHY

Sprague, Marshall. *The Great Gates: The Story of the Rocky Mountain Passes.* Boston: Little, Brown, 1964.

Dan E. Clark / F. B.

See also **Fur Trade and Trapping; Rocky Mountains.**

SOUTH, THE

This entry includes 2 subentries:
The Antebellum South
The New South

THE ANTEBELLUM SOUTH

If the United States possesses an official history, it is a heroic tale in which Americans struggle over numerous obstacles to advance the principles of freedom, equality, and democracy. In this story, when so told, one part of the United States, the South, has repeatedly thrown up the barriers whose removal has been necessary for the nation to achieve its destiny. In the mid-nineteenth century, such resistance caused the gravest crisis in American history, as the nation erupted into civil war. Only enormous self-sacrifice and massive carnage allowed the Union to survive and to extend its principles of freedom by abolishing slavery. With its rejection of majority rule, the antebellum South helped bring about this crisis. If for no other reason, this society—the great antagonist to the semi-official United States dream—deserves careful scrutiny. Yet, like other Americans, antebellum southerners saw themselves as defending liberty.

Time and Place

Historically, both for the region and for the nation, there are good reasons to focus on the antebellum period, generally understood as the years from 1830 to 1860. Southern distinctiveness blossomed after 1830, as the region increasingly set itself apart from the rest of the nation in politics, economics, religion, and philosophy. Several related developments occurred around 1830 that paved the way for regional separatism. Among these events were the growth of a northern abolitionist movement, the most famous slave revolt in U.S. history, a definitive decision by Virginia to maintain slavery, and a bitter struggle over tariffs. By the early 1830s, in light of these occurrences, the South saw itself as besieged by hostile forces and organized to defend its institutions. Its philosophers increasingly pictured slavery as a positive good; its churches severed their northern connections; its politicians grew more belligerent in defense of southern rights; its people became intensely suspicious of reformist ideas. Then, to safeguard its perceived interests, to protect its distinctive way of life, and to constitute its own version of republican liberty, the South attempted to create a new nation.

Definitions of the South's geographical borders are often fluid and depend on the criteria used. Using economic measures, for example, one might define the antebellum South as the fifteen slave states. Employing a political yardstick, another definition would focus on the eleven states that seceded from the Union to form the Confederacy, and would thus exclude the slave states of Delaware, Maryland, Kentucky, and Missouri. Applying cultural benchmarks such as dialect and social habits, one might even include parts of some free states in a definition of the South. In essence, there was a central core of Deep South states that included most areas that joined the Confederacy and where southern distinctiveness was strongest, and there were transitional zones of southern influence to the north and west.

Inside the South there existed considerable geographic diversity. The climate was generally warm, normally well watered, but nowhere entirely frost free. In the Appalachian and Ozark Mountains, the climate was cooler and the soil generally poor. Swamps and sandy tracts dotted the coastal plains and were often unsuitable for productive agriculture. Because of early frosts, cotton did not generally thrive in the Upper South, roughly the area north of central Tennessee, and the cash crop was often tobacco or wheat. On the other hand, much of the Lower South, especially the humid climate and rich black soil of the Mississippi Delta, was perfectly suited to production of enormous crops of cotton. Coastal South Carolina and Louisiana were warm enough and wet enough to support the cultivation of rice and sugar cane as well.

Plantations and the Antebellum Economy

The antebellum South was a slave society, but most white southerners owned no slaves. In 1860, slave-owning families composed roughly twenty-five percent of the region's white population. Planter families, usually defined as possessing at least twenty slaves, were much scarcer, comprising only some three percent of southern whites. Yet plantation slavery thrived in antebellum years and continued to expand westward. The key crop was cotton. The South was the world's leading producer of this commodity, which was a vital component of the global economy. Demand for cotton continued strong through the 1850s, and southern cotton fed the world's textile mills. During the 1850s, the South exported more than $100 million worth of cotton per year, comprising more than fifty percent in value of U.S. exports.

Slavery facilitated large-scale, profitable agricultural operations, providing economic opportunities not available in the free states. In most areas, farming would not support high enough wages to attract a reliable work force. Plantation owners, on the other hand, purchased their laborers, provided them with housing and sustenance, and made tidy profits. American slaves were defined as chattel, that is, as moveable property, and few legal restrictions hindered their exploitation. Not tied to the land like Russian serfs, American slaves could be relocated at the will of the owner. Owners were free to pur-

sue economic gain even to the point of breaking up black families. In some areas, particularly in the east, slave sales were crucial to plantation profitability. Plantations enjoyed the advantage of economies of scale. They purchased supplies in bulk at low prices and produced a large enough crop to make money, even if profit per unit was relatively low. Though concentrating on cash crops like cotton, plantations often produced much of their own food and thus reduced overhead expenses. On several levels, then, a plantation was a rational and profitable business investment.

Although there were many variations, plantation management was often quite efficient. Planters used positive incentives to motivate their workers, such as prizes for the most cotton picked or for the most corn shucked. Also present was the negative incentive of the whip. Most cotton plantations used the gang system of labor management in which groups of slaves, often twenty or so, worked systematically at a task throughout the day under supervision of an overseer. Rice-growing areas typically used the task system in which slaves were assigned a specific amount of work per day and toiled with minimal supervision. When the task was finished, the workday ended. In both systems, men and women worked the fields, but men generally did heavy jobs like plowing and women such domestic chores as sewing.

Plantation slavery was a distinctive way of life, not simply a business proposition. Other investment opportunities were available in the South that yielded greater returns than did plantations. For example, southern industrialists, such as William Gregg of South Carolina, often earned higher profits operating factories than planters did farming. But because the southern social ideal was to become a planter, most investment capital nonetheless flowed into agriculture. Even those who made their money as merchants or manufacturers often invested their profits in land and slaves. Most importantly, the relationship between master and slave was qualitatively different than between employer and wage earner. The slave owner invested not just in labor time but in the actual laborer. At least in theory, he had a vested interest in maintaining the health and welfare of the worker, to an extent that employers of hired workers did not. Plantation owners directed the work of slaves but also claimed to safeguard them in sickness and old age. They sometimes equated their role as master with that of a father caring for dependent family members. Many avoided the image of the hard-charging capitalist and embraced the role of manorial lord.

Slavery was a relatively adaptable labor system whose use was not confined to large plantations. On small farms, it was common for slaves to work in the fields beside their owners. Other slaves were rented out, providing cash income for slave owners. Some slaves hired out their own time, receiving wages and remitting a portion to their masters. Industrial concerns used both slave labor and free labor, and slaves worked in iron foundries, textile mills, mines, saw mills, and steamboats. Southern industry developed more slowly than industry in the northern states, but compared with most countries, including many in Europe, the antebellum South experienced substantial industrial growth, including construction of an extensive railway system.

By 1860, the region was one of the wealthier areas of the world, and its per capita income had increased rapidly for the previous twenty years. Relative abundance was widespread and even trickled down to slaves. Slaves ate plain food, mostly corn and pork, but these staples were often supplemented with garden vegetables, fish, and wild game, a diet that provided plentiful energy and sufficient nutrition. Clothing and housing were not luxurious but generally were not much worse than those of poor whites. In material terms, slaves in the antebellum South had a higher standard of living than did many ordinary folk in other countries, much higher, for example, than the standard of living of eastern European peasants.

Meanwhile, the majority of southern whites were neither rich nor poor. Most lived in families headed by yeoman farmers who possessed land but no slaves. Such farmers often practiced an agriculture designed to produce sufficiency and to minimize economic risk rather than to maximize profits. Most of their cultivated land went into food crops, such as corn and sweet potatoes, but they also raised pigs and cattle. Yeomen grew cotton and tobacco to supplement these foodstuffs and thus generated cash to purchase commodities they could not themselves produce. Achieving partial self-sufficiency through this balanced style of farming, yeomen families possessed a degree of independence from market fluctuations.

The People

Some nine million people lived in the eleven states that joined the Confederacy in 1861, and slaves made up about 40 percent of the population. Compared to the rest of the nation, the antebellum South was overwhelmingly rural, as the vast majority of blacks and whites engaged in agriculture. Of the ten largest cities in the United States in 1860, only New Orleans and Baltimore were located within the region. Immigrants tended to avoid the South because wage-paying jobs were scarce. Nonetheless, there were some immigrants, especially Irish refugees, who settled in cotton ports such as Savannah. The region's population continued to grow, quite rapidly in western areas such as Texas, and more slowly in the East, but its population did not increase as rapidly as in the free states. As the South grew more distinctive, its status as a minority within the Union became clearer.

Southern white society had numerous class divisions. Its big planters were among the wealthiest of all Americans, while some ten percent of white families possessed no land and little other property. In economic terms, most whites stood somewhere between these extremes as members of the yeoman order. Clashes and resentments existed, but several factors mitigated class conflict. In a growing economy, upward social mobility was possible and poorer whites often sought to emulate rather than to denigrate planters. Planters shared interpersonal connections with other whites, including kinship, commodity exchanges, and church membership. Common identity as citizens and free men also tied whites together. In contradistinction to slaves, white men defined themselves as independent agents, and even if poor, tended to be little patriarchs who professed to rule their wives and children.

Such men zealously guarded their social reputations, and a violent code of masculine honor thrived in the region. Free men were expected to avoid public humiliation and to resent insults. For many elites, protecting one's honor meant fighting duels. Although dueling was generally illegal and many southerners denounced it, a number of the South's antebellum social and political leaders did fight on the field of honor. Poorer men resorted to knives or fists. The roots of this honor code are partly traceable to Celtic practices brought to America by ancestors of antebellum southerners. But the physical force necessary to maintain slavery, which inured many whites to violence, and the determination of white men to avoid the appearance of servility, contributed mightily to survival of the honor ethic in the South.

Amidst this intensely patriarchal society, southern women carved out fruitful and fulfilling lives. Most white women labored rigorously at household tasks including child rearing, cooking, cleaning, and gardening. Plantation mistresses possessed some leisure, but they also worked hard at supervising servants and nursing sick children. Even more than in the rest of the United States, the lives of southern women were closely linked to the household. Wage-earning opportunities were fewer than in northern states. There was little separation between office and home, as the locus of agricultural production remained in the household. Although free white women sometimes complained about loneliness and hard work, few were neo-abolitionists, itching to escape white male domination. Sharing the racial suppositions of their society and enjoying the advantages of property and freedom, most tended to identify with husbands and fathers, not with slaves.

Even in trying conditions of servitude and racial oppression, African Americans were able to resist many of the dehumanizing aspects of their condition. Only rarely did their resistance result in outright rebellion. Southern slave revolts were short-lived and small in scale compared to those in other slave societies. Individual acts of defiance, including flight, arson, even murder, were somewhat more common, but such actions almost always had grievous consequences for those who participated in them. Most slaves knew firsthand the harshness of plantation discipline and tried to avoid it, and few were prepared to challenge their masters directly or to fight to overthrow the system. They did, however, engage in subtler forms of resistance such as feigning sickness, breaking tools, and pilfering plantation livestock.

Furthermore, African Americans were able to maintain their human dignity by building communities and families. On plantations, the slave quarters were small villages. Living close together, residents provided one another with mutual support and participated in communal rituals, including dances, funerals, weddings, and holiday celebrations. Though unrecognized by law, marriage was normal for slave adults, and after marriage, monogamy was expected. Nuclear families, with a father, mother, and children residing together under one roof, were common but not universal. Fathers sometimes served different masters and were unable to reside with their families. Slave families could not establish truly independent households, for their domestic arrangements were always subject to a master's whim. No laws protected families from being broken up or prevented sexual abuse by the slave owner. Polite society frowned on these practices, but such mistreatment occurred rather frequently.

In 1860, 250,000 free blacks lived in the slave states; the great majority of them lived in the Upper South. Such individuals lived in difficult circumstances, typically eking out small incomes as farm workers. They also suffered social persecution, as they did not possess full civil rights, generally being unable to testify in trials or to vote. Free blacks in the Deep South were fewer in number but usually more prosperous. Often the mulatto offspring of slaveholding fathers, these free people of color frequently worked as skilled artisans for wealthy whites. A small number even became substantial slave owners.

Politics

By 1860, southern states typically allowed all adult white males to vote. With Andrew Jackson elected president in 1828, democracy had become increasingly real for the region but was specifically limited to white men. Riches and refinement faded in importance as criteria for political success. Some social deference toward wealth and education remained, but planters and prominent politicians usually felt obliged to court the goodwill of unlettered yeomen farmers and poor whites. Those excluded from this democracy, however, often suffered—as in the forced westward removal of American Indians. Southern politicians also repeatedly argued that white freedom demanded black slavery, that the reduction of African Americans to the permanent status of manual laborers averted the growth of invidious class distinctions among whites.

Perhaps more than in any other period of southern history, partisan politics thrived in the antebellum era. Voter interest was intense. After 1840, 65 to 75 percent of eligible voters regularly turned out for statewide elections. Democrats and Whigs in the South differed on many issues, especially regarding banks and tariffs, but on slavery there was little difference between the parties. In fact, both parties played games of one-upmanship to see which could pose as the most dedicated defender of slavery. To appear less than ardent in support of the South's peculiar institution meant political death in most of the

region. Even association with antislavery forces outside the region was problematic, as each party portrayed the other's northern wing as tainted with abolitionism. Such party rhetoric helped heat sectional animosity to fever pitch.

Yet this virtually unanimous defense of slavery by southern politicians did not automatically translate into rabid secessionism or into consistent advocacy of states' rights. Even John C. Calhoun, the great theorist of states' rights, viewed secession as a last resort and proposed political solutions that would allow the South to protect its interests as a minority within the Union. Henry Clay of Kentucky, the nation's leading advocate of high tariffs and internal improvements, was a slaveholding southerner who, as an avid unionist, had many followers in the region. Zachary Taylor, a Louisiana cotton planter and the last antebellum southern president, was an even stronger nationalist than Clay. Perhaps more popular with southern voters was the position championed by Andrew Jackson, which argued for reducing the scope of the federal government, but disapproved of letting states veto federal action. As late as the final secession crisis of 1860–1861, advocates of disunion had to overcome strong opposition even in the Deep South.

Religious and Intellectual Life

For blacks and whites, religious belief provided psychological sustenance and helped to make sense of the world. Most southern believers were evangelical Protestants. Methodists and Baptists far surpassed other denominations in membership, but Presbyterians and Episcopalians possessed significant social prestige. By the 1820s, on the eve of the antebellum era, southern churches began to attract increasing numbers of people from all social classes, including planters and slaves. Church membership, as a percentage of total population, grew throughout the antebellum era but never comprised a majority of the southern population, either black or white. Many churches had strict behavioral requirements and expelled members for all sorts of moral lapses.

In the 1840s, southern believers created the Methodist Episcopal Church, South, and the Southern Baptist Convention. Both groups broke with their northern counterparts in disputes related to slavery. Both worked energetically to win black converts, through funding missions to the slaves. These missions began in South Carolina in the late 1820s and soon spread across the region. Initially greeted suspiciously by planters, mission advocates eventually convinced slave owners that their message was consistent with maintaining slavery.

Such missionaries had to please both masters and slaves. To maintain access to the slave population, missionaries often preached a message of obedience. On the other hand, church membership remained voluntary so the missionaries had to tailor their message to African American tastes. They therefore addressed a variety of Christian themes, including those that offered solace and

465

psychological liberation to their audiences. Meanwhile, southern churches provided flexible solutions to some problems associated with slavery, allowing, for example, de facto divorces to slave spouses separated by sale.

This evangelizing sank deep roots into the black community, and religion became a vital part of the identity of many black southerners. African Americans often worshiped in biracial churches, in which members attended services together but sat in segregated sections. Even after emancipation, African American believers generally remained loyal to the Baptist and Methodist church traditions, though not to the southern denominations themselves. Religion became one of the most powerful means by which African Americans resisted the dehumanizing effects of slavery. At least privately, southern blacks claimed a moral superiority over masters who disobeyed the tenets of their own religion. They also took solace in God's promises, for individual glory in heaven and for eventual deliverance as a people from bondage on earth.

Simultaneously, southern whites used religion for their own purposes. In frequent debates with northern churches, they championed a nonpolitical church focused on winning converts and getting believers to heaven. For a church to adopt an abolitionist political agenda, they argued, distorted the Christian message and imposed conditions on believers scripture did not justify. Yet such believers saw the Christian message as egalitarian in that God's offer of salvation extended to all—rich or poor, white or black, male or female. Southern churches practiced organized philanthropy, by building colleges, sponsoring missions, publishing tracts, and supporting temperance legislation, but they rarely challenged the South's dominant social order. In fact, religious arguments provided some of the most popular defenses of slavery. These ideas sometimes dealt with Old Testament themes, depicting biblical patriarchs as slave owners who were the chosen instruments of God. More frequently, southern clergymen focused on New Testament notions. They argued that Jesus had not condemned slavery and that human bondage was therefore allowable in Christian society.

Other southern thinkers broke free of scripture. The antebellum South generated one of the most original episodes in American intellectual history, sometimes labeled as the Reactionary Enlightenment. Perhaps more forcefully than any other group in American history, some southern thinkers severed connections with principles of natural rights and the social contract. Sociological theorists, such as George Fitzhugh of Virginia and Henry Hughes of Mississippi, upheld the virtues of inequality, tradition, and social duty. Well-read in contemporary scholarship, these men argued that slavery was a beneficial system that protected workers from the vicious competition of free society, providing them with protection from well-meaning owners. Also part of the pro-slavery argument were racial theories, propounded by such scientists

as Josiah Nott of Alabama, which argued that blacks and whites belonged to different species.

Conclusion

The antebellum South was the most prosperous and self-confident slave society of modern times. White southerners were ferociously protective of their own liberty, and most, whether slaveholders or not, believed their independence and economic self-interest best served by the preservation of human bondage. Their politicians, ministers, philosophers, and scientists—often able and articulate men—assured them of the righteousness of their way of life. Critical outside voices were ignored. Slaves knew the cruel side of the South, experiencing the special sting of servitude in a land that prided itself on freedom, but they were not allowed to speak. Only the bitter dregs of defeat would humble this proud society and set its captives free.

BIBLIOGRAPHY

Ambrose, Douglas. *Henry Hughes and Proslavery Thought in the Old South.* Baton Rouge: Louisiana State University Press, 1996.

Bauer, K. Jack. *Zachary Taylor: Soldier, Planter, Statesman of the Old Southwest.* Baton Rouge: Louisiana State University Press, 1993.

Berlin, Ira. *Slaves without Masters: The Free Negro in the Antebellum South.* New York: Pantheon Books, 1974.

Faust, Drew Gilpin. *James Henry Hammond and the Old South: A Design for Mastery.* Baton Rouge: Louisiana State University Press, 1982.

Fogel, Robert William, and Stanley L. Engerman. *Time on the Cross: The Economics of American Negro Slavery.* New York: Norton, 1989. Controversial classic which showed that plantations were successful business operations.

Fox-Genovese, Elizabeth. *Within the Plantation Household: Black and White Women of the Old South.* Chapel Hill: University of North Carolina Press, 1988. Nuanced and thoroughly researched, it is much the best book on southern women's history.

Genovese, Eugene. *Roll, Jordan, Roll: The World the Slaves Made.* New York: Vintage Books, 1974. Masterpiece that portrays African Americans as actors in southern history, not mere victims.

Horsman, Reginald. *Josiah Nott of Mobile: Southerner, Physician, and Racial Theorist.* Baton Rouge: Louisiana State University Press, 1987.

Kolchin, Peter. *Unfree Labor: American Slavery and Russian Serfdom.* Cambridge, Mass.: Belknap Press, 1988.

McCurry, Stephanie. *Masters of Small Worlds: Yeoman Households, Gender Relations, and the Political Culture of the Antebellum South Carolina Low Country.* New York: Oxford University Press, 1995.

McWhiney, Grady. *Cracker Culture: Celtic Ways in the Old South.* Tuscaloosa: University of Alabama Press, 1988.

Oakes, James. *The Ruling Race: A History of American Slaveholders.* New York: Vintage Books, 1983.

Quist, John W. *Restless Visionaries: The Social Roots of Antebellum Reform in Alabama and Michigan.* Baton Rouge: Louisiana State University Press, 1998.

Wyatt-Brown, Bertram. *The Shaping of Southern Culture: Honor, Grace, and War, 1760s–1880s.* Chapel Hill: University of North Carolina Press, 2001.

Christopher Owen

See also **Civil War; Confederate States of America; Cotton; Plantation System of the South; Slavery; States' Rights in the Confederacy; Underground Railroad;** *and vol. 9:* **Sociology for the South; The Impending Crisis of the South: How to Meet It; South Carolina Declaration of Causes of Secession.**

THE NEW SOUTH

The expression "New South" has been used and reused in a variety of contexts; in contemporary usage it connotes an emphasis on economic modernization as a cure for regional ills. In historical literature, however, the term has a more precise meaning; it refers to the campaign by journalists and others after Reconstruction for a new orientation for the southern economy. The New South promoters called for a program of economic diversification and industrial development, based on overt solicitation of outside investment.

The New South concept wasn't that new; even in the antebellum South there had been calls for economic diversification and industrialization. A series of commercial conventions, along with manifestoes by southern nationalist sources such as *De Bow's Review*, urged industrialization. During the Civil War the Confederate government's prodigies of wartime production demonstrated the possibility of sweeping industrialization. Defeat, moreover, encouraged a regional reappraisal and demands for economic change. But the political bitterness of Reconstruction distracted public attention; it stilled southern white enthusiasm for an economic program that involved cooperation with northern investors. Only after Redemption, the restoration of white supremacy in 1877, did southern opinion leaders turn their full attention to regaining commercial prosperity. As the national economy boomed in the early 1880s, the improved prospects stirred calls for action. Slavery and the vast financial investment it represented were gone, and, while the plantation system had stabilized after the ruin of Civil War and emancipation, agriculture showed little prospect of growth. But northern industry was expanding dramatically, and Southern journalists and spokespeople rhetorically embraced the national trend.

Even with the losses that the elimination of slavery represented for plantation owners, those envisioning a New South could discern some benefits from ruin. Before the war, the slave states had been notoriously resistant to industrial and urban growth, especially the Deep South region. The profitability of staple crop production under slavery had long discouraged alternative investments. The most striking example of this tendency was in textile production, for while the raw material was near at hand, cotton mills nonetheless remained few. Before the war, the northern states demonstrated marked economic development and consequent transportation and educational advances. For southerners, the sectional controversy with the North had limited the appeal of outside immigration and the entrepreneurial values that would facilitate industrial growth. Both the mores of the slaveholding elite and the structure of the economy had kept industrial development at a rudimentary level, and much of what had existed perished in the war. But the elimination of slavery and the overthrow of the plantation elite eliminated these obstructions to economic diversification. Furthermore, Reconstruction, whatever the cost, had encouraged the spread of a railroad network that could facilitate economic diversification. The region's low wages, weak unions, and the practice of leasing prison inmates to private individuals as laborers had obvious appeal for outside investors as well.

Economic diversification became a priority once Reconstruction ended, at least from the point of view of the region's dominant classes. Investment capital was scarce in the still-impoverished South, however, and the bankrupt and downsized southern governments were incapable of spearheading economic development after Redemption. Outside investment was imperative if industrialization was to happen, and this could take place only with the aid of northern investors and the benign encouragement of the Republican-dominated Federal government. There was also a growing understanding that Republican high-tariff policies—wrong as they were by states' rights principles—might nonetheless facilitate southern industrial development.

Given the partisanship remaining from the struggles of the Civil War and Reconstruction, selling collaboration with the Yankee foe was a sensitive matter. The calls for a New South provided an intellectually respectable rationale. The priority was to persuade skeptical northern investors and the southern dominant classes that they could profit by cooperation, and with positive, or at least defensible, results. The general theme was that the nation must move beyond the bitterness of the war to embrace a new era of industrial prosperity and progress. For civic leaders and promoters of growing urban railroad and industrial centers like Atlanta and Birmingham, this rhetoric had obvious appeal. In the Georgia piedmont, the public campaign for investment textile mills took on evangelical overtones, touting industrialization as the salvation of the white laboring class.

Henry Grady (1850–1889), the youthful editor of the *Atlanta Constitution*, popularized the term "New South" and was its premier spokesman. Grady was troubled by the national public's negative response to Confederate rhetoric, but with the election of Democrat Grover Cleveland as president, a more conciliatory and optimistic approach seemed opportune. In 1886, Grady attracted public attention for his program of national reconciliation before a northern business audience. Before the war, he observed, slavery and agriculture could not sustain healthy economic development. In contrast, "the new South provides a perfect democracy," with "a hundred farms for every plantation, fifty homes for every palace—and a diversified industry that meets the complex need of this complex age" (Bryan, *Henry Grady or Tom Watson? The Rhetorical Struggle for the New South, 1880–1890*, p. 105). Grady also hoped to demonstrate that practical southerners had moved beyond the bitterness of the war. In Grady's words, "we have sowed towns and cities in place of theories, and put business above politics." New leaders in rising cities would provide the flexibility needed for a region reborn.

Grady, and similar spokesmen, like Henry Watterson of the Louisville, Kentucky, *Courier-Journal*, performed a difficult balancing act. For northern audiences, Grady conceded that it was just as well that the Confederacy lost. The aristocratic ethos of the slave regime had yielded an economically stagnant, caste-ridden society. Grady argued that only economic prosperity could move the region beyond its heritage of sectional bitterness. He urged northerners and southerners to cooperate to move into the future together. This conciliatory rhetoric assured Yankee businessmen that they could make a positive contribution through their investments, and that they would not be subjected to northern criticism for funding sectional extremism. For white southerners, Grady praised the nobility of the departed culture of the old plantation South, and he praised the heroism of the lost cause and its adherents. However, his major emphasis was on the economic limitations of the slave system, and the degree to which it inhibited needed diversification. Grady sentimentalized the values of the Old South, but only to laud an urban, industrial New South in which these values had little place.

To forestall regional criticism, Grady assured southerners that economic modernization would not damage plantation agriculture or challenge the racial order too drastically. The distinctive New South enterprise, cotton textile production, was concentrated in the piedmont areas of the Carolinas and Georgia, well outside the Cotton Belt. Textile production was promoted as suitable work for white laborers, and planters were assured that African American labor would not be sought. This New South promise, at least, was borne out; textile laborers remained overwhelmingly white until after the civil rights era. On the other hand, industries like the coal and steel production around Birmingham featured a significantly biracial workforce.

Perhaps the most sensitive obstacle to the New South program of sectional reconciliation, given the Civil War legacy, was the future status of the African American population. It was in this area that the underlying contradictions of the New South approach were most obvious. Before southern audiences, Grady openly proclaimed himself a white supremacist and depicted social segregation as the cornerstone of southern society. He also engaged in a heated press debate with the South's most well-known racial liberal, George Washington Cable. In Grady's tautological formulation, "the supremacy of the white race of the South must be maintained forever, and the domination of the negro race resisted at all points and at all hazards—because the white race is the superior race" (Ibid., p. 49). He repeatedly denounced the proponents of Radical Reconstruction in their efforts to interfere with southern racial practices, maintaining that the concept of social equality was "monstrous" and "impossible."

Despite these racist statements, and within the context of segregation and white supremacy, New South rhetoric tended to emphasize its relative moderation. As Grady pointed out, "we have planted the schoolhouse on the hilltop and made it free to white and black." Grady and his fellow publicists did not target their rhetoric toward the African American population, but it was important to them that their northern audience see proponents of the New South as reasonable—at least in terms of the lowered national expectations after Redemption. The New South model thus encouraged a certain businesslike decorum on racial matters, with proponents predicting that prosperity would improve race relations. Grady and his colleagues emphasized that economic diversification would provide opportunities for black people as well as white, and they tended to oppose lynching, disfranchisement, and other forms of overt racial persecution. Race riots and disorder, after all, would deter outside investment. Ironically, it was only the emergence of African American Booker T. Washington, an educator whose conservative views on civil rights for blacks attracted the support of wealthy white businessmen and politicians, that papered over the inconsistencies of the New South rhetoric on race and gave the whole approach a persuasive spokesman.

The 1880s saw the heyday of the New South movement, aided by northern public willingness to view the new regional emphasis as a positive development. This acceptance presented a plausible rationale for the post-Redemption southern social order, and many former critics of the South endorsed it. For example, the ex–Radical Republican William D. "Pig Iron" Kelley of Pennsylvania, himself the near-victim of a Reconstruction riot, now hailed the New South as finishing the work of national reunion. Northerners, moreover, were mollified by the open admission of the failings of the Old South, which paralleled many of the criticisms of the antebellum free labor critique of slave society. Aided by a widespread sense that the Reconstruction intervention had failed, the national press was generally supportive of the New South vision, seeing it as part of the wider process of reconciliation. Inevitably, however, southern criticism of the priorities of the movement gathered from a variety of directions.

From the beginning, there was dissent against the New South priorities from those most invested in the memory of the Old South and the rebellion. Former leaders like Jefferson Davis and Alexander Stevens, for example, opposed dilution of traditional southern political values, especially states' rights. Various ex-Confederate generals weighed in against forgetting the great struggles of the war in the rush toward interregional commercial cooperation. The battle to lead southern opinion took on a generational quality, as the leaders of the Old South confronted younger, urban New South publicists. The Old South dissenters, often elitists identified with the plantation regime, were articulate and had strong emotional appeal but they were clearly doomed to diminishing relevance. In social terms, the greater challenge was the gathering agrarian revolt that directly opposed the priorities of the New South publicists.

After the late 1870s, dissident activity had grown among the hard-pressed farmers of the hill districts, who were faring badly in the postwar decades. Local protest movements often took the form of "greenbacker" candidacies opposing the dominant Democratic leadership, most spectacularly the "Readjuster" party, which gained power in Virginia. These dissidents tended toward anticorporate, antimonopoly sentiments, and they demanded inflation of the currency to aid debtors. Agrarian discontent spread across the southern (and western) states in the late 1880s; it took the form first of the Farmer's Alliance and, eventually, the Populists of the 1890s, a full-scale third-party challenge to Democratic rule. The agrarian movement demanded aggressive government action to provide for the needs of farmers through inflationary economic policy, direct federal loans to farmers, and regulation, or even nationalization, of railroads and other corporations. Though the Populist revolt was beaten back by the late 1890s—aided by electoral fraud and an improving economy—the agrarian movement permanently redirected discourse away from the New South priorities.

After the defeat of the Populists, emerging southern "demagogues" voiced a class-based rhetoric of hostility toward outside business interests, along with a flamboyant racist discourse in defiance of national norms. Populist rhetoric imbued turn-of-the-century Democratic politics, which substituted agrarian symbolism and white supremacy in place of the drastic reform the real Populists had demanded. Still, the rhetorical climate had changed by the Progressive era. Plebeian tribunes like Senator Jeff Davis of Arkansas, for example, emphasized hostility toward northern insurance companies in his electoral campaigns. South Carolina's Ben Tillman favored higher taxes and rate regulation for railroads, as well as some limitations on child labor. Similarly, demagogues such as James Vardaman and Theodore Bilbo of Mississippi favored raising taxes on corporations to pay for Progressive regulation and government expenditures to benefit the white rural poor. Other leaders, like Cole Blease of South Carolina, spoke more directly to the class resentments of white textile workers. These leaders were often less hostile toward northern corporations in private than their public statements might suggest. Still, by the early twentieth century, southern political discourse became less enthusiastic about promoting northern corporate expansion than had characterized the New South heyday.

Nevertheless, the general New South concept and terminology of outside investment and economic growth as a regional remedy, and specifically as a means of overcoming the legacy of slavery and racism, has remained in the political discourse to the present day.

BIBLIOGRAPHY

Ayers, Edward L. *The Promise of the New South: Life after Reconstruction.* New York: Oxford University Press, 1992.

Bryan, Ferald Joseph. *Henry Grady or Tom Watson? The Rhetorical Struggle for the New South, 1880–1890.* Macon, Ga.: Mercer University Press, 1994.

Foster, Gaines M. *Ghosts of the Confederacy: Defeat, the Lost Cause and the Emergence of the New South, 1865–1913.* New York: Oxford University Press, 1987.

Gaston, Paul M. *The New South Creed: A Study in Southern Myth-Making.* New York: Vintage Books, 1973.

Woodward, C. Vann. *Origins of the New South, 1877–1913.* Baton Rouge: Louisiana State University Press, 1971.

———. *Tom Watson: Agrarian Rebel.* Savannah, Ga.: Beehive Press, 1973.

Michael Fitzgerald

See also **Civil War; Reconstruction; Slavery; South, the: The Antebellum South;** *and vol. 9:* **Black Code of Mississippi, November, 1865; Police Regulations of Saint Landry Parish, Louisiana.**

SOUTHEAST ASIA TREATY ORGANIZATION.

The signing of the Southeast Asia Collective Defense Treaty in Manila on 8 September 1954 by the United States, Australia, New Zealand, Britain, France, Pakistan, Thailand, and the Philippines led to the establishment of the Southeast Asia Treaty Organization (SEATO) in February 1955. The Republic of Vietnam as well as Cambodia and Laos were accorded observer status. But the governments of Burma, Ceylon, India, and Indonesia all rebuffed invitations to be signatories to the Manila Pact, as the Southeast Asia Collective Defense Treaty was known. SEATO was established primarily at Washington's instigation in the aftermath of the French military defeat at Dien Bien Phu in northern Vietnam in April 1954. It was part of an emerging global U.S.-led containment strategy directed at the Soviet Union and "international communism" generally and, in the case of Southeast Asia, at the People's Republic of China and the Democratic Republic of Vietnam (North Vietnam) specifically. It was hoped that SEATO would strengthen the diplomatic and territorial arrangements in Vietnam that had resulted from the Geneva Conference in 1954.

The main significance of SEATO may have been that it formalized the U.S. commitment to Southeast Asia, at a time when the administration of Dwight Eisenhower

(1953–1960) had embarked on an increasingly costly attempt to help turn the Republic of Vietnam (South Vietnam) into a stable noncommunist nation-state under Ngo Dinh Diem (1954–1963). U.S. foreign policy was increasingly constrained by the limits on its military effort to win the war in Vietnam, and SEATO reflected these limits, particularly Washington's inability to gain more widespread multilateral support. Although the United States and three other member governments of SEATO (Australia, New Zealand, and Thailand) sent troops to Vietnam (as did the nonmember government of South Korea), the organization itself played no real role in the conflict.

SEATO was seriously disabled from the outset by internal differences and the lack of an underlying strategic interest around which its member governments could coalesce. The governments of member countries such as Thailand, the Philippines, and Pakistan were as concerned about military threats from other powers in the region as they were about the Soviet Union and China. For example, Pakistan's commitment to SEATO faded in the 1960s because of the organization's unwillingness to support the government in Karachi in its conflict with the Indian government that led to war between the two countries in 1965. Pakistan announced that it was withdrawing from SEATO in November 1972, a year after the second war between Pakistan and India in December 1971 had led to military defeat for Pakistan and the transformation of East Pakistan into Bangladesh.

The French government, meanwhile, boycotted a key 1965 SEATO meeting at which the U.S. wanted member governments to commit to increases in aid and support for the government of South Vietnam. From the beginning of the 1960s the British government was also reluctant to make a military commitment to the looming conflagration in Indochina. Following what was seen as tepid British military support for a U.S.-led effort to counter an apparent threat to northern Thailand by Laotian communist forces in 1962, the Foreign Affairs Committee of the U.S. House of Representatives expressed the view that, unless the British (and the French) governments were more forthcoming, the Manila Pact needed to be rewritten if not terminated. By 1967 Britain was attempting to disengage completely from military affairs east of Suez. SEATO was further undermined in early 1972 when the administration of Richard M. Nixon (1969–1974) embarked on its historic rapprochement with China. In February 1974 SEATO's military structures were abolished, and in June 1977 the organization was disbanded. The treaty on which SEATO was based was not discarded, however, because it represented the only formal security agreement between the government of Thailand and the United States of America.

BIBLIOGRAPHY

Buszynski, Leszek. *SEATO: The Failure of an Alliance Strategy.* Singapore: Singapore University Press, 1983.

McMahon, Robert J. *The Limits of Empire: The United States and Southeast Asia Since World War II.* New York: Columbia University Press, 1999.

Mark T. Berger

See also **Vietnam War.**

SOUTHEAST ASIAN AMERICANS. Geographically, Southeast Asia encompasses a vast region that includes the nations of Cambodia, Myanmar (formerly Burma), Laos, Thailand, Vietnam, as well as the island nations of Brunei, Indonesia, Malaysia, Singapore, and the Philippines. The term Southeast Asian Americans refers to former citizens of these nations and their children who now live in the United States. More specifically, however, "Southeast Asian Americans" frequently designates refugees and immigrants from the nations of mainland Southeast Asia, particularly Vietnam, Laos, and Cambodia. Southeast Asian Americans are an ethnically diverse group comprised of Vietnamese, Chinese, Thai, Khmer (Cambodian), Laotians, Hmong, Mien, and other ethnic minority tribes. Each group has different social backgrounds, cultural practices, languages, and some even have histories of conflict with each other. Nevertheless, the majority of Southeast Asian Americans shares a common immigration history, which is the legacy of U.S. involvement in the Indochina Conflict (1954–1975), also known as the Vietnam War. This catastrophic conflict devastated Vietnam, and destroyed neighboring Laos and Cambodia in the process. The U.S. government's military and political attempts to contain the spread of communism in the region not only divided America, but also produced a massive refugee population for which it had to assume social and historical responsibility. Unlike other Asian immigrants who preceded them, the majority of Southeast Asian Americans entered the United States as refugees. Between 1975 and 1994, the United States received over 1,250,000 refugees from Southeast Asia, of which 66 percent were from Vietnam, 21 percent from Laos, and 13 percent from Cambodia.

Prior to the first wave of refugees in the mid-1970s, the first documented Southeast Asian immigrants arrived in the 1950s and early 1960s. This population of mainly Vietnamese immigrants was small in number—only a little over 18,000—and mostly consisted of university students, diplomats, and wives of American servicemen who entered the country as the war escalated. Dramatic changes in U.S. immigration policy occurred after U.S. forces withdrew from Southeast Asia and communist forces took over Saigon in April 1975. Between 1975 and 1992, the United States admitted over 650,000 persons arriving from Southeast Asia. Though not all Americans welcomed the refugees, Congress strongly supported their plight, granting them "parole" status to enter the United States, and allocations to aid in their resettlement. About 95 percent of these first wave refugees came from Vietnam, with the remaining 5 percent from Cambodia. The majority were

Southeast Asians. Children learn English at Fort Indiantown Gap, Pa., a resettlement center that opened in 1975 to receive thousands of refugees after the Vietnam War. AP/WIDE WORLD PHOTOS

academics, high-ranking military officials, middle class professionals, politicians, and people who worked for the U.S. government or American corporations.

The second wave of refugees (1978–1982) involved two groups: the "land people" from Cambodia and Laos, and the "boat people" from Vietnam. Coming from more diverse backgrounds and social circumstances, refugees in the second wave risked their lives to escape the harsh conditions they confronted under newly installed communist governments. Persecuted and considered traitors by the Laotian communist government for aiding Americans during the war, the Hmong were forced to leave their homeland, and an estimated 300,000 people escaped by crossing the Mekong River to refugee camps in Thailand. Between 1975 and 1979, the genocidal Khmer Rouge regime led by Pol Pot, who ordered the mass execution of "unwanted" bourgeois elements in Cambodian society, instigated a mass exodus. By the end of 1979, conditions were so atrocious that approximately 600,000 Cambodians were living in Thailand's refugee camps. In Vietnam, severe conditions under the communist regime also compelled people to imperil their lives by escaping in small, overcrowded boats to nearby Malaysia, Indonesia, Hong Kong, and the Philippines. These "boat people" risked death by drowning or the danger of piracy rather than endure discrimination under communist rule.

By the early 1980s, global pressure for better humanitarian treatment of refugees forced the Vietnamese government to find solutions for the refugee crisis. The United Nations High Commissioner for Refugees established the Orderly Departure Program to resettle some 200,000 people who awaited their fate in refugee camps, and to reunite family members who had been separated. In addition, Congress passed the Amerasian Homecoming Act in 1987 to allow the persecuted children of American servicemen and Vietnamese women to immigrate to the United States.

The resettlement policy adopted by the U.S. government required the refugees to disperse across the country to ensure their financial self-sufficiency and to prevent overwhelming concentration in any one community. The refugees' desire to build concentrated ethnic communities, however, counteracted this policy. In reconstituting their respective communities, more than 40 percent of the Southeast Asian population resettled in California for its warm climate, employment opportunities, and generous public assistance programs. Southern California's Orange County has become the home of more than 200,000 Vietnamese Americans, the largest number of Vietnamese outside the nation of Vietnam. Sizable populations of Vietnamese Americans have also resettled in Texas, Washington, Louisiana, and Illinois. Hmong Americans reestablished their largest community in Fresno, California, while a surprising number have also concentrated in the "frost belt" states of Minnesota and Wisconsin, where they are the largest Asian American group. And while an overwhelming number of Cambodian Americans live in Long Beach, California, they have also resettled bi-coastally in Massachusetts, Washington, Rhode Island, and Illinois. Of Southeast Asian Americans, Laotians are the most dispersed group, with their largest community in San Diego, California. The 2000 Census enumerates 1,122,528 Vietnamese; 169,428 Hmong; 168,707 Lao; 171,937 Cambodian; and 112,989 Thai Americans living in the United States.

Well-educated and proficient in English, first wave refugees had less difficulty adjusting to life in the United States than their compatriots who arrived later. Linguistic and professional skills enabled many to integrate into American society with ease, and some found self-employment by opening small businesses catering to other co-ethnics. With fewer transferable skills and limited English, second and third wave refugees found work in blue-collar electronic and mechanical industries. By the late 1980s and 1990s, however, global restructuring led many Vietnamese Americans to participate in dot-com industries, particularly in Silicon Valley. Meanwhile, niche service industries such as nail salons enabled many Vietnamese immigrants with low English proficiency and few skills to become lucrative entrepreneurs. Likewise, Cambodians found the proprietorship of doughnut shops, another semi-skilled and labor-intensive enterprise, to be financially rewarding.

Having faced the terrors of war and the daunting task of rebuilding new lives in a foreign land, Southeast Asian

471

SOUTHERN CAMPAIGNS

Americans continue to confront new challenges. Despite government assistance, many people from these communities still live below the poverty line. And although Southeast Asian American youth have often been hailed as the new "model minorities" for their strong academic achievements, gang violence often plagues these communities. The generation gap between immigrant parents and their U.S. born children also divides the community, especially regarding their divergent attitudes toward the homeland and communism. Nevertheless, after nearly three decades of living in the United States, Southeast Asian immigrants and refugees have become productive citizens in American society, contributing as laborers, professionals, and business owners to the nation's economy. And in their efforts to preserve cultural traditions and institutions, Southeast Asian Americans have revitalized many urban areas by creating strong ethnic communities that cater to their compatriots and contribute to the multiethnic landscape of America.

BIBLIOGRAPHY

Chan, Sucheng. *Asian Americans: An Interpretive History.* Boston: Twayne, 1991.

Frank, Anne. "Documenting the Southeast Asian Refugee Experience." Southeast Asian Archive at the University of California, Irvine. Available from http://www.lib.uci.edu/new/seaexhibit.

Haines, David W. *Refugees as Immigrants: Cambodians, Laotians, and Vietnamese in America.* Totowa, N.J.: Rowman and Littlefield, 1989.

———, ed. *Refugees in America in the 1990s: A Reference Handbook.* Westport, Conn.: Greenwood Press, 1996.

Kelly, Gail Paradise. *From Vietnam to America: A Chronicle of the Vietnamese Immigration to the United States.* Boulder, Colo.: Westview Press, 1977.

Kibria, Nazli. *Family Tightrope: The Changing Lives of Vietnamese Americans.* Princeton, N.J.: University of Princeton Press, 1993.

Rambaut, Rubén G. "Vietnamese, Laotian, and Cambodian Americans." In *Asian Americans: Contemporary Trends and Issues.* Edited by Pyong Gap Min. Thousand Oaks, Calif.: Sage Publications, 1995.

Nhi T. Lieu

See also **Asian Americans; Vietnam War.**

SOUTHERN CAMPAIGNS of the American Revolution (1780–1781) were a vigorous effort by the British, after setbacks in the North, to quash rebellion in the Carolinas and Georgia. On 26 December 1779, Sir Henry Clinton and General Charles Cornwallis sailed from New York with eight thousand men. Landing at Savannah, they forced the surrender of the American forces in Charleston. With the British victory at Waxhaw Creek on 29 May, no organized American force was left in the three southernmost states. General George Washington sent two thousand men to the aid of South Carolina, but Horatio Gates promptly lost most of this army at the Battle of Camden (16 August). Meanwhile, Cornwallis detached Major Patrick Ferguson with twelve hundred men, but this force was annihilated at Kings Mountain on 7 October, and another detachment under Colonel Banastre Tarleton was destroyed at the Battle of Cowpens (17 January 1781). Nathanael Greene had succeeded Gates in December 1780. With General Daniel Morgan's aid, he lured Cornwallis into North Carolina and dealt him a crippling blow at Guilford Courthouse on 15 March 1781. The British commander then retired to Wilmington, North Carolina, and prepared for a renewed strike into Virginia. Sir Henry Clinton had sent Benedict Arnold into Virginia with sixteen hundred British troops, but Arnold had delayed. Greene, ignoring Cornwallis's invasion of Virginia, returned to South Carolina, and although he theoretically lost engagements at Hobkirk's Hill (25 April), Ninety-Six (22 May–19 June), and Eutaw Springs (8 September), he so weakened the British forces that by 10 December 1781 he had driven the only remaining British army in the Deep South into a state of siege at Charleston. Meanwhile, Cornwallis had been cornered by a joint American-French force, and he surrendered at Yorktown, Virginia, on 19 October 1781.

BIBLIOGRAPHY

Alden, John R. *The South in the Revolution, 1763-1789.* Baton Rouge: Louisiana State Universtiy Press, 1957.

Higgins, W. Robert., ed. *The Revolutionary War in the South.* Durham, N.C.: Duke University Press,1979.

Lumpkin, Henry. *From Savannah to Yorktown.* Columbia: University of South Carolina Press, 1981.

Morrill, Dan L. *Southern Campaigns of the American Revolution.* Baltimore: Nautical and Aviation Publishing, 1993.

Alvin F. Harlow / A. R.

See also **Camden, Battle of; Cowpens, Battle of; Eutaw Springs, Battle of; Guilford Courthouse, Battle of.**

SOUTHERN CHRISTIAN LEADERSHIP CONFERENCE. Led by the Reverend Martin Luther King Jr., the Southern Christian Leadership Conference (SCLC) was the first major civil rights organization to originate in the South and was one of the guiding forces behind the black freedom struggle in the 1950s and 1960s. The SCLC brought the black church into the forefront of the civil rights movement and helped popularize the tactic of massive nonviolent protest.

The SCLC was founded in early 1957. King and two associates, the Reverend Charles K. Steele and the Reverend Fred L. Shuttlesworth, recognized the need to capitalize on the momentum generated by the Montgomery bus boycott of the previous year and called a meeting of black preachers to found the organization. Although the SCLC made little headway in its first few years, in 1960 the spreading sit-in movement among college students energized the organization. The SCLC sponsored the meeting of student protestors that led to the formation of the Student Non-Violent Coordinating Committee. In 1961, King and the SCLC played a role in the Freedom Rides, which challenged segregation on interstate buses. In 1963 and 1964, the SCLC joined other civil rights organizations in a major project designed to register rural black Mississippians to vote.

The organization was best known, however, for a series of demonstrations it staged in southern cities in an attempt to combat segregation and disfranchisement by focusing national and international attention on the region's Jim Crow practices. The SCLC's 1963 campaign in Birmingham, Alabama, provoked a violent police reaction that aroused the conscience of many white Americans and put international pressure on President John F. Kennedy to act decisively on civil rights. The bill President Kennedy delivered to Congress that June formed the basis of the Civil Rights Act of 1964. In 1965, King and the SCLC launched a campaign of marches and demonstrations in Selma, Alabama, that eventually contributed to the passage of the Voting Rights Act of 1965.

After the passage of the Voting Rights Act, King and the SCLC increasingly turned their attention to creating an interracial alliance of the poor and oppressed. They worked to win housing desegregation and jobs for blacks in Chicago, and to organize a Poor People's March in Washington, D.C., in April 1968. The SCLC, however, faced growing opposition from young blacks, who were increasingly frustrated with the organization's willingness to compromise with whites and with its nonviolent tactics. At the same time, King's outspoken opposition to the war in Vietnam infuriated President Johnson and lost the SCLC the support of some wealthy and influential white liberals. After King's assassination in 1968, the organization was wracked by internal division and lost its preeminent place in the black freedom struggle. The SCLC continues to fight for civil rights.

BIBLIOGRAPHY

Marable, Manning. *Race, Reform and Rebellion: The Second Reconstruction in Black America, 1945–1990.* Jackson: University Press of Mississippi, 1991.

Sitkoff, Harvard. *The Struggle for Black Equality, 1954–1992.* New York: Hill and Wang, 1993.

Williams, Juan. *Eyes on the Prize: America's Civil Rights Years, 1954–1965.* New York: Viking, 1987.

Wendy Wall

See also **Civil Rights Movement; Jim Crow Laws; Voting Rights Act of 1965.**

SOUTHERN COMMERCIAL CONVENTIONS

were convocations in the mid-nineteenth century intended to promote the economic development of the South. The most notable gatherings were the sessions of the so-called Southern Commercial Convention, which met between December 1852 and May 1859. The South was not keeping pace with the North in either population or economic development, which gave the free states an advantage in the struggle over slavery. Although the earlier convention sessions were representative of all of the South and all shades of opinion, as the convention failed to produce results, moderate men ceased to attend. Secessionists of the Lower South came to dominate the sessions and promoted Southern sectionalism.

BIBLIOGRAPHY

Johnson, Vicki Vaugh. *The Men and the Vision of the Southern Commercial Conventions, 1845–1871.* Columbia: University of Missouri Press, 1992.

Angela Ellis

See also **Sectionalism; South, the: The Antebellum South; Southern Rights Movement.**

SOUTHERN RIGHTS MOVEMENT.

For the greater part of American history, a disposition to resist federal authority has flourished in the South. Regional leaders have frequently expressed concern that national majorities would overwhelm southern institutions through control of the federal government. Consequently, southern politicians and intellectuals developed theories designed to prevent such interference. Frequently linked to the defense of slavery, these notions evolved over the first half of the nineteenth century, culminating in the secession of eleven southern states in 1860 and 1861. Yet defense of southern rights continued well into the twentieth century, often aiding white political supremacy and the Jim Crow system of state-mandated racial segregation.

The Virginia and Kentucky Resolutions of 1798 were foundational to the southern rights movement. Written respectively by James Madison and Thomas Jefferson, they argued that the federal government must not trample on powers reserved to the states by the Tenth Amendment, that states could judge the constitutionality of federal laws, and that states should interpose their authority to abrogate unconstitutional federal action. For some two centuries, though often refined and reworked, these ideas provided the core southern case in contesting broad federal authority.

In antebellum days John C. Calhoun built upon the terminology of the resolutions to produce sophisticated defenses of southern rights. In his "Disquisition on Government," published posthumously in 1851, Calhoun maintained that a numerical majority, controlling the levers of government, would inevitably promote its own interests and oppress those of the minority. To prevent this result, he argued that key interest groups must themselves be able to block measures detrimental to their welfare. For true legitimacy, Calhoun argued that government must obtain approval from major interest groups. This step would secure what he called the concurrent majority, thereby minimizing civil discord and violence.

By seceding, southern states endorsed a more drastic means to protect themselves from majority rule. This effort met bloody collapse, but the southern struggle to limit federal authority continued. During Reconstruction, even as the Constitution was amended to provide federal protection of African American rights, southern resistance grew, eventually causing a retreat from federal intervention in the southern states. Decades later, when a re-energized civil rights movement appeared, southern politicians again vigorously opposed extension of federal authority. Echoes of Jefferson and Calhoun appeared in the 1948 platform of the States' Rights Party. The Southern Manifesto of 1956, signed by one hundred southern members of Congress, used similar rhetoric to denounce federally mandated school desegregation.

Defeated in efforts to maintain Jim Crow, many white southerners abandoned their historic ties to the Democratic Party. As Republicans, their criticism of federal authority, expressed in subtler, less racial terms, entered the political mainstream during the 1980s. Within the region only small pockets of support remained for stronger assertions of southern rights. Southern rights arguments were grounded in the region's particular historical circumstances but also involved political and philosophical insights that were more generally applicable. Though presently dormant in its region of origin, the movement had produced a powerful literary legacy. At other times and in other places, forces suspicious of central authority may well draw upon its ideas.

BIBLIOGRAPHY

Frederickson, Kari. *The Dixiecrat Revolt and the End of the Solid South, 1932–1968.* Chapel Hill: University of North Carolina Press, 2001.

John C. Calhoun, A Disquisition on Government and Selections from the Discourse, ed. C. Gordon Post. New York: Liberal Arts Press, 1953.

McDonald, Forrest. *States' Rights and the Union: Imperium in Imperio, 1776–1876.* Lawrence: University Press of Kansas, 2000.

Christopher Owen

See also **South, the: The Antebellum South; States' Rights in the Confederacy.**

SOUTHERN TENANT FARMERS' UNION.

President Franklin D. Roosevelt's NEW DEAL, which was intended to alleviate the economic fallout from the Great Depression, did not benefit all segments of society equally. To boost agricultural prices and, thus, farm incomes, the Agricultural Adjustment Administration (AAA) paid landowners to take land out of production. Because landowners received the government's payments and because they controlled the local administration of the AAA, tenant farmers and SHARECROPPERS received relatively little of this money and, worse, found themselves either out of work or transformed into wage laborers.

In 1934 Arkansas socialists Harry Leland Mitchell and Clay East tapped into the ensuing frustration and formed the Southern Tenant Farmers' Union (STFU). The union sought to use peaceful means, such as lawsuits, speeches, and books and pamphlets to highlight income inequality in southern agriculture. STFU members protested their treatment by landowners and also the local institutions that they believed were responsible for their degraded economic condition, including local school boards, police departments, relief agencies, health agencies, the courts, and poll taxes. After some two years of recruitment and expansion into neighboring states, the STFU still represented highly localized interests. In 1937 it sought broader exposure through an association with the United Cannery, Agricultural, Packinghouse and Allied Workers of America, a CIO affiliate. Conflicts between the STFU and the union and factional fights within the STFU depleted its ranks and ultimately its ability to revive the local activities responsible for its initial organizational success.

The STFU was a reactionary response to economic hardships that southern farmers, particularly non-landowning farmers, faced during the Great Depression. Yet it left a lasting legacy. With its strong religious undertone, its integration of African Americans and women into its membership, and its nonviolent means, the STFU set the stage for the civil rights movement almost three decades later.

BIBLIOGRAPHY

Auerbach, Jerold S. "Southern Tenant Farmers: Socialist Critics of the New Deal." *Labor History* 7 (1966): 3–18.

Dyson, Lowell K. "The Southern Tenant Farmers Union and Depression Politics." *Political Science Quarterly* 88 (1973): 230–252.

Grubbs, Donald H. *Cry from the Cotton: The Southern Tenant Farmers' Union and the New Deal.* Chapel Hill: University of North Carolina Press, 1971.

Mitchell, H. L. "The Founding and Early History of the Southern Tenant Farmers Union." *Arkansas Historical Quarterly* 32 (1973): 342–369.

Naison, Mark D. "The Southern Tenants' Farmers' Union and the CIO." In *"We Are All Leaders": The Alternative Unionism of the Early 1930s.* Edited by Staughton Lynd. Urbana: University of Illinois Press, 1996.

Shawn Kantor

See also **Agriculture.**

SOUTHERN UNIONISTS

during the Civil War were most numerous in the border and upper South states, although across the whole Confederacy many people remained loyal to the federal Union. However, only in Virginia did Unionists precipitate a successful political movement when the counties west of the Appalachians seceded to form the new state of West Virginia. In the main body of the Confederacy, Unionists achieved greatest concentration in the highland counties of east Tennessee. This predominantly yeoman farm region had always opposed the political and economic supremacy of west and middle Tennessee slaveholders and voted overwhelmingly against secession. When war came, the state's eastern counties vigorously resisted Confederate authority. In general, Unionism found most support in the southern uplands, in frontier areas, and, less openly, in the cities. Unionists were also active in ethnically and culturally distinctive areas such as the German-settled counties of north and central Texas and the so-called "Quaker belt" of piedmont North Carolina, where antislavery beliefs were in evidence. In general, hostility to slavery, as distinct from resentment of slaveholders, though present in many communities, was not a defining feature of southern Unionism, which derived from varying degrees of patriotic, ideological, and materialistic factors and embraced a wide spectrum of commitment and, inevitably, opportunism. Unionist support intensified with the growth of popular opposition to Confederate war policies, notably conscription and impressment. At least 100,000 white residents of the eleven seceded states fought in the federal armed forces, with an estimated two-thirds of the total coming from Tennessee and West Virginia.

BIBLIOGRAPHY

Current, Richard Nelson. *Lincoln's Loyalists: Union Soldiers from the Confederacy.* Boston: Northwestern University Press, 1992.

Degler, Carl N. *The Other South: Southern Dissenters in the Nineteenth Century.* New York: Harper and Row, 1974.

Inscoe, John C., and Robert C. Kenzer. *Enemies of the Country: New Perspectives on Unionists in the Civil War South.* Athens: University of Georgia Press, 2001.

Martin Crawford

See also **Civil War; Confederate States of America; Union Sentiment in Border States; Union Sentiment in the South.**

SOUTHWEST may be roughly defined as the southwestern quarter of the United States, although any distinct delimitation of the area is necessarily arbitrary. So considered, it includes OKLAHOMA, TEXAS, NEW MEXICO, ARIZONA, the southern half of CALIFORNIA, and the southern portions of Kansas and Colorado. With the exception of most of Kansas and Oklahoma, which formed part of the LOUISIANA PURCHASE, all of the Southwest was a part of the possessions of Spain, and later of Mexico, well into the nineteenth century and so has, historically, a background that is distinctly Spanish. Kansas is a "marginal state," since its history is partially bound up with that of the Southwest and in part with that of the central prairie states. Oklahoma and Texas each has a history essentially its own. Oklahoma was for more than half a century a great Indian territory, forbidden to settlement by whites. The Five Civilized Tribes, occupying much of it, formed small commonwealths or republics, each with its own government and laws. Texas, settled largely by Anglo-Americans, won its independence from Mexico in 1836. After nearly ten years' existence as a republic, it was annexed by the United States in 1845. The remainder of this southwestern region, except for the small strip of land acquired from Mexico in 1853 in the Gadsden Purchase, became a part of the United States in 1848 with the signing of the Treaty of Guadalupe Hidalgo with Mexico.

The influence of the Southwest on the political history of the United States began early in the nineteenth century. The Louisiana Purchase boundary line, which had been the subject of much controversy, was drawn in 1819, leaving Texas to Spain. Later, the question of the annexation of Texas became an important political issue. After annexation, the dispute over the Texas-Mexico boundary helped to precipitate the MEXICAN-AMERICAN WAR (1846–1848). Disputes over the organization of the new territory acquired from Mexico by this war ended in the much-debated COMPROMISE OF 1850, under which California entered the Union as a free state but slavery was not restricted in the newly created New Mexico and Utah territories. Four years later came the KANSAS-NEBRASKA ACT, allowing the residents of these territories to decide for themselves whether to become free or slave states, and the violent controversies following it attracted the attention of the entire nation.

Significant as the Southwest has been in the political history of the United States, its importance in U.S. economic history is even more apparent. The discovery of gold in California and Colorado in the nineteenth century brought about one of the most picturesque movements in all American history. The settlement of the Pacific coastal region and the increased production of gold stimulated industry, caused the building of the Pacific railways, and created demands for a canal between the Pacific and Atlantic.

Texas, which had early developed as a great cattle-raising area, sent a stream of cattle northward from 1866 to 1890 to stock ranges on the central and northern Plains; thus, it was the chief factor in the formation of the "cow country" that spanned much of the American West. The production of petroleum and natural gas in California and in the great mid-continent field lying largely in Oklahoma and Texas has been of great significance in the economic life of the nation. The fruit-growing industry of southern California, Arizona, and the lower Rio Grande valley of Texas has also been of great importance to the country as a whole. The production of wheat and cotton in this area adds materially to the nation's crops of these two staples. Manufacture and distribution of motion pictures have long centered in southern California, and the industry's influence on the people of the United States as well as much of the world can hardly be estimated. Since World War II, the Southwest has also become a major center for the aerospace and electronics industries. Los Alamos, New Mexico, a major site of atomic research during the war, continues to host a number of university and government laboratories engaged in sensitive research.

Since World War II, the population of the "Sun Belt cities" of the Southwest has swelled with retirees and Mexican immigrants. This demographic trend has transformed LOS ANGELES, PHOENIX, and ALBUQUERQUE into crucibles of conservative thought and important battlegrounds during congressional and presidential elections. It is not coincidence that between 1980 and 2002, three presidents—all Republicans—have hailed from the region. California produced Ronald Reagan, while Texas produced George H. W. Bush and George W. Bush—not to mention the surprisingly strong third-party candidacy of billionaire Ross Perot in 1992 and 1996. Culturally, the Southwest in the twentieth century has produced a flowering of indigenous and blended cultural forms: Mexican *rancheros* inspired the macho style of the Anglo cowboy, a staple of American fiction and movies since the 1890s; in the 1920s, painter Georgia O'Keeffe helped to make the pueblo villages of Taos and SANTA FE, New Mexico, home for the alienated avant-garde; and by century's end, "Tex-Mex" cuisine, a commercialized adaptation of Mexican cuisine, emerged as a mass-market phenomenon. Finally, the status of the Southwest as a borderland between Native American pueblo territory, Anglo-America, and Hispanic Central America has made it a symbol of the increasingly diverse demography of the modern United States.

BIBLIOGRAPHY

Abbott, Carl. *The New Urban America: Growth and Politics in Sunbelt Cities.* Chapel Hill: University of North Carolina Press, 1987.

del Castillo, Richard Griswold. *La Familia: Chicano Families in the Urban Southwest, 1848 to the Present.* Notre Dame, Ind.: University of Notre Dame Press, 1984.

Dutton, Bertha P. *American Indians of the Southwest.* Albuquerque: University of New Mexico Press, 1983.

Kowalewski, Michael, ed. *Reading the West: New Essays on the Literature of the American West.* Cambridge, U.K.: Cambridge University Press, 1996.

Lamar, Howard Roberts. *The Far Southwest, 1846–1912: A Territorial History.* New Haven, Conn.: Yale University Press, 1966.

Nash, Gerald D. *The American West in the Twentieth Century: A Short History of an Urban Oasis.* Englewood Cliffs, N.J.: Prentice-Hall, 1973.

Nichols, Roger L. "The Southwest." In *Encyclopedia of American Social History.* Edited by Mary Kupiec Cayton, Elliot J. Gorn, and Peter W. Williams. Vol. 2. New York: Scribners, 1993.

Weber, David J., ed. *Foreigners in their Native Land: Historical Roots of the Mexican Americans.* Albuquerque: University of New Mexico Press, 1973.

Edward Everett Dale / A. R.

See also **Conservatism; Guadalupe Hidalgo, Treaty of; Mexican Americans; Santa Fe Trail; Sun Belt.**

SOUTHWEST TERRITORY, the title applied to the region established in 1790 and officially named the "Territory of the United States, South of the River Ohio." Although in theory it embraced the future state of Tennessee, the twelve-mile strip that South Carolina had ceded, and, possibly, the Georgia western lands, actual federal governance was applied only to Tennessee. The government of this territory was similar to that of the Northwest Territory, except that it was bound by certain conditions set by North Carolina in its cession of 1789. William Blount was appointed governor and superintendent of Indian affairs, and he served in this capacity for the entire life of the territory, until 1796.

BIBLIOGRAPHY

Durham, Walter T. *Before Tennessee: The Southwest Territory, 1790–1796.* Piney Flats, Tenn.: Rocky Mount Historical Association, 1990.

E. Merton Coulter / F. B.

See also **Northwest Territory; Tennessee.**

SOVEREIGNS OF INDUSTRY was a cooperative movement active in the 1870s that concerned itself with the distribution of the necessities of life. It grew out of the Patrons of Husbandry and at one time numbered forty thousand members. It maintained a number of cooperative stores, some of which followed the principles established by the Rochdale Society of Equitable Pioneers in England. The ultimate goal of the Sovereigns of Industry, however, was to create producer cooperatives, a plan that some critics identified as communist. Though it absorbed some trade unions, the organization began to decline around 1875 and had disappeared before 1880.

BIBLIOGRAPHY

Birchall, Johnston. *Co-op: The People's Business.* Manchester, U.K.: Manchester University Press, 1994.

Pittenger, Mark. *American Socialists and Evolutionary Thought, 1870–1920.* Madison: University of Wisconsin Press, 1993.

Carl L. Cannon / A. E.

See also **Cooperatives, Consumers'; Labor; Socialist Movement.**

SOVEREIGNTY, DOCTRINE OF, has given rise to much spirited debate among lawyers and political theorists. It plays a central role in American law and government and has increasingly become a fundamental issue in international law and relations as well. The doctrine of sovereignty has been the focus of a number of major political theorists, including Jean-Jacques Rousseau and John Austin. It was a key issue in early debates on the structure of American government as well as nineteenth-century debates on the legitimacy of nullification and secession by individual states.

The essential nature of the concept of sovereignty is that of status and power, both de jure and de facto, which gives its possessor both internal and external autonomy. A sovereign is not subject to the control of any other individual or entity and has the right to control all those who fall within its power and jurisdiction. In the United States it is generally held that the ultimate sovereign is the people and that no individual or government entity is sovereign in its own right. Sovereign powers are delegated to both the states and the federal government by grants from the American people.

The notion of sovereignty and the sometimes-competing claims of individual states and the federal government for sovereign powers has been a continuing source of debate and uncertainty in the United States. These issues were a primary focus during the formative period of American government and were specifically treated in the Tenth Amendment to the U.S. Constitution, often referred to as the reserved powers clause. The Tenth Amendment provides that "powers not delegated to the United States by the Constitution . . . are reserved to the States respectively, or to the people." In adopting this amendment to the Constitution, the founders attempted to clarify the system of bifurcated sovereignty between the states and the federal government and to create a system of divided practical sovereignties, recognizing that the states, which had originally joined to form the federal union, retained certain aspects of sovereignty. At the same time, the Constitution recognized that in the act of forming the United States, each individual state had given up certain sovereign aspects to the federal government. Thus, after the ratification of the Tenth Amendment, the United States consisted of both a "sovereign" federal government as well as "sovereign states," each possessing certain sovereign powers. Both state and federal governments retained the right to tax their citizens, for instance, but only the federal government had the sovereign right to deal with foreign countries to sign treaties. During the antebellum period, the extent to which states possessed full sovereignty and rights against the federal government became the subject of national debate and eventually became one of the ideological underpinnings of the conflict between the North and the South. Sovereignty is of immense importance in both domestic and international law. One of the central doctrines of American constitutional law, for example, is that of sovereign immunity. This doctrine holds that because a sovereign individual or entity is autonomous and not subject to the legal, practical, or political authority of any other individual or entity, a sov-

ereign cannot be sued in a court of law, nor can it be compelled to answer any suit filed in any court. The only way a sovereign can be subject to the legal process is if the sovereign agrees to submit itself to such process. The doctrine fit well both with then-current notions of government and with the conservative jurisprudence of the times favoring governmental over individual rights. As political and legal opinion began to favor individual rights, the doctrine of sovereign immunity came into some disfavor. During the latter part of the twentieth century, with the rise of a new theory of federalism among conservative jurists, the doctrine began to experience a revival in regard to states. The importance of the doctrine of sovereignty was also highlighted during the last decades of the twentieth century by the role it played in the resurgent movement for increased political and legal rights claimed by Native American tribes. A number of tribes began to assert their sovereign status, demanding that the federal government recognize them as sovereign nations and accord to them many of the rights and privileges enjoyed by sovereign nations. These claims impacted the legal and political status of the tribes at every level. For instance, as sovereigns, the tribes demanded that tribal courts adjudicate all legal disputes on tribal territory. Several tribes claimed the right to regulate automobile licensing and to issue drivers' licenses, automobile license plates, and registration documents.

In the international arena, the doctrine of sovereignty is closely tied to recognition of political entities by other sovereign nations. Throughout the twentieth century, a number of nations experienced political transitions caused by war and revolution that resulted in successor states that were not always recognized as sovereign by other nations. The denial of sovereign status and the concomitant denial of official recognition by other states and international organizations carried with it serious implications for these states and, among other things, often meant that they were unable to join international organizations, be signatories to international agreements, or receive international aid.

BIBLIOGRAPHY

Hannum, Hurst. *Autonomy, Sovereignty, and Self-determination: The Accommodation of Conflicting Rights.* Philadelphia: University of Pennsylvania Press, 1996.

Norris, Harold. *Education for Popular Sovereignty through Implementing the Constitution and the Bill of Rights: A Collection of Writings on the Occasion of the Bicentennial of the United States Constitution and Bill of Rights.* Detroit, Mich.: Detroit College of Law, 1991.

Karenbeth Farmer
M. H. Hoeflich
William Starr Myers

See also **Democracy; Political Theory; Popular Sovereignty; State Sovereignty.**

SOVIET UNION. *See* **Russia, Relations with.**

SOW CASE, a lawsuit adjudicated in 1643–44 that became famous because it resulted in the division of the Massachusetts General Court into a bicameral legislature. The case arose out of a controversy in which a poor woman, Goody Sherman, accused a well-to-do merchant, Robert Keayne, of stealing her sow. Lower courts decided in favor of Keayne, but Sherman, encouraged by popular sympathy, appealed to the General Court, where the assistants (or magistrates) supported Keayne and the deputies supported Sherman. The two parties clashed over the magistrates' claims to a negative voice (veto power) over the deputies, who held the majority of seats. This disagreement resulted in the division of the two groups into separate legislative houses.

BIBLIOGRAPHY

Bailyn, Bernard. "The *Apologia* of Robert Keayne." *William and Mary Quarterly* 7 (1950): 568–587.

McManus, Edgar J. *Law and Liberty in Early New England: Criminal Justice and Due Process, 1620–1692.* Amherst: University of Massachusetts Press, 1993.

Wall, Robert E. *The Membership of the Massachusetts Bay General Court, 1636–1686.* New York: Garland, 1990.

Viola F. Barnes / s. b.

See also **Colonial Assemblies; General Court, Colonial.**

SOYBEANS. Native to China, the soybean (*Glycine max*) is a legume, like the peanut, and it yields high-quality protein and edible oils. The soybean is the basis of an astonishing range of food items and industrial products. It is the number-one United States crop export and ranks second only to corn as a cash crop. Since the 1950s the United States has been the world's leading soybean producer.

The first documented appearance of the soybean in America was in 1765, when Samuel Bowen, an employee of the East India Company, sent beans acquired in China to the colony of Georgia. Bowen had soybeans planted for several years at his plantation in Thunderbolt. In 1770 Benjamin Franklin sent soybeans from London to botanist John Bartram. James Mease wrote that the soybean grew well in Pennsylvania's climate in 1804. As the nineteenth century progressed, ships plying the China trade dumped the soybeans used as cheap ballast in many United States ports. By the 1850s, the soybean had spread to horticulturalists from Canada to Texas.

Most American farmers discovered the soybean after Japan was opened to western trade in 1854. Japanese soybeans came to the attention of the U.S. government, which distributed them throughout the country to be evaluated as a forage crop. From the 1880s through the end of the century, virtually every agricultural station was testing the soybean. In 1904, the Tuskegee Institute scientist George Washington Carver demonstrated that soybeans provided valuable protein and oil (as he did also with the peanut). By developing new uses for the soybean and promoting its benefit in crop rotation, Carver helped revolutionize agricultural practices in southern states dangerously dependent on cotton.

At this time, only eight soybean cultivars were being grown. Between 1918 and 1931 the Department of Agriculture mounted expeditions to Asia to seek additional varieties. As new cultivars became available and soy processing plants were being built (the first in Decatur, Illinois, in 1922), soybean farming shifted its concentration from the southeastern states to the Midwest. As of the early 2000s, this region was generating more than 70 percent of all United States soybeans, with Illinois and Iowa the leading producers.

Early in the twentieth century most soybeans were grown for forage; however, some notable pioneers were experimenting with the bean's versatility. John Harvey Kellogg, of breakfast cereal fame, made the first soy milk and soy-based meat substitutes in the 1920s. In the 1930s automaker Henry Ford had his chemists create an auto body enamel from soybean oil and made soy meal into a plastic he used to manufacture more than twenty automobile parts.

World War II gave a significant boost to soybean production. Prior to this period, the United States imported 40 percent of its edible fats and oils. When war cut off the supply, the soybean helped make up the deficit. The real boom came in the 1950s with an unprecedented demand for low-cost, high-protein soy meal as an ingredient for livestock feed. This market constitutes more than 90 percent of all soybean use.

The total United States soybean-producing farmland was 1.8 million acres in 1924. By 1975 it had grown to 54.6 million, and the year 2000 set a record with 74.5 million acres planted. Farmers enjoyed a rise in soybean prices from the mid-1970s to a high of $7.75 per bushel in 1983. Prices then declined, with a sharp drop in 1998. In 2000 farmers were paid only $4.40, the lowest price since 1972. United States exports represented 54 percent of all soybeans on the world market in 2000, a value of $6.66 billion.

Major customers for United States soybeans and soy products are Asia, the European Union, and Mexico. Positive industry trends include the demand for soyfood products, which has increased steadily since 1980. By the early 2000s, a thornier and still unresolved issue in trade was the use of genetically modified soybeans. Resistance to that biotechnology continued to be particularly strong among European consumers, a key market.

BIBLIOGRAPHY

Aoyagi, Akiko, and William Shurtleff. *Green Vegetable Soybeans, Edamame, & Vegetable-Type Soybeans: Detailed Information on 1,032 Published Documents.* Lafayette, Calif.: Soyfoods Center, 2001.

———. *Henry Ford and his Researchers' Work With Soybeans, Soyfoods and Chemurgy: Bibliography and Sourcebook 1921 to 1993.* Lafayette, Calif.: Soyfoods Center, 1994.

Liu, Keshun. *Soybeans: Chemistry, Technology, and Utilization.* New York: Chapman and Hall, 1997.

Rinzler, Carol Ann. *The Healing Power of Soy: The Enlightened Person's Guide to Nature's Wonder Food.* Rocklin, Calif.: Prima, 1998.

Christine M. Roane

SPACE PROGRAM.

In the late nineteenth century, fiction writers like Jules Verne and H. G. Wells published novels focusing on space travel in various forms. Although fictitious, these stories would spark the imaginations of several of the early rocket scientists, whose endeavors would ultimately make real the ability for machines to travel through space.

Early Space Pioneers

Several space pioneers soon began distinguishing themselves and giving direction to the new field. Among them, Russian teacher Konstantin Tsiolkowsky (1857–1935) sketched a rocket system in 1903 that was based on an 1883 paper "Modifying the Force of Gravity." He perfected his rocket system throughout the rest of his life, noting in particular the potential of using liquid propellants, a mix of fuel and oxidizer, to effectively move through a vacuum. Tsiolkowsky was one of several European visionaries, including Frenchman Robert Esnault-Pelterie (1881–1957) and Romanian-born Austrian Hermann Oberth (1894–1989), who contributed theoretical knowledge to the notion of human space travel.

Meanwhile, in the United States, Robert Goddard (1882–1945) made great progress in determining the parameters by which a rocket propulsion system might have become more effective. In 1915, this physics professor began using signal ROCKETS, developed in the nineteenth century for the navy by B. F. Cotton. Cotton had tested different rocket shapes and weights of propellant, but Goddard, through multiple experiments, made such rockets over 60 percent more efficient and exhaust velocity went from 1,000 feet per second to 8,000 feet per second. Goddard had long theorized that liquid propellant might be more efficient than solid propellant, but he could not prove it. He soon got a chance to do so.

In the 1920s, Goddard began using liquid oxygen as the oxidizer and gasoline as the fuel (oxidizer gives the oxygen molecules required for the explosion that lets the fuel burn). Thanks to a grant from the Smithsonian, Goddard kept experimenting and on 16 March 1926, he finally succeeded in launching the first liquid-propelled rocket. Goddard was so reclusive, though, that few people learned of his achievement; he did not publish the results until some ten years later.

In fact, even when the American Rocket Society was founded in 1930 (known initially as the American Inter-planetary Society), it drew on space enthusiasts for its membership, but Goddard was not among them. Instead, owing to Charles Lindbergh's intercession with Harry Guggenheim, Goddard was granted additional funds to pursue his research in Roswell, New Mexico, where he spent 1932 to 1940 testing new rockets.

However, until the end of World War II, most of the impetus for space rocketry came from Germany and the Soviet Union. Several German pioneers, including a young Wernher von Braun, eventually went to work for the military after the Nazis came to power, devising liquid-fueled engines, testing optimum ballistic missile shapes, and constructing a series of test machines that, by 1943, led to the flight of the A-4 rocket, later called the V-2. An inefficient and costly machine, the V-2 was an effective weapon and the Nazis fired thousands of them at various cities on the European continent as well as England. The V-2 also became the basis for American postwar experiments with missiles.

After World War II, under Project Paperclip, select German scientists were brought into the United States (in violation of immigration rules regarding former Nazis) and set to work with American experts on various scientific projects. Among the Germans, Wernher von Braun found himself working in Huntsville, Alabama, for the Army Ballistic Missile Agency, and eventually devised a Redstone rocket. At the time, the American space program was nonexistent. Polls taken in the early 1950s showed that most Americans thought atomic-powered ground vehicles were more likely to appear in ensuing decades than any kind of space travel.

The Soviet Shock

Attitudes towards space shifted in the mid-1950s, and were reflected in President Dwight D. Eisenhower's call for the United States to orbit a satellite during the International Geophysical Year (1957–1958). However, the Soviet Union was the first to succeed in this endeavor by sending *Sputnik 1* atop an R-7 ballistic missile on 4 October 1957. President Eisenhower was tempted to minimize the Soviet success, for an American project was under way; yet many in the United States felt this was a reflection of an America slowing down. The failure of the Vanguard TV-3 rocket (a model derived from the U.S. Navy's Viking project) eventually prompted the president to agree to have the army's Redstone rocket, modified into a *Juno 1*, and orbit a scientific satellite, *Explorer 1*, which reached orbit on 31 January 1958. Developed by University of Iowa physicist Dr. James Van Allen, the instrument allowed the detection of the radiation belt that bears his name.

In the meantime, however, additional Soviet success, including the orbiting of a dog aboard *Sputnik 2*, prompted charges of a missile gap and calls for a full-fledged space program. Consequently, on the advice of his science advisor, James Killian, and his team, Eisenhower agreed to create an agency devoted to space matters. Concerned that a military agency would not give a fair share to the need for scientific investigation, on 29 July 1958 Eisenhower signed the act transforming the National Advisory Committee on Aeronautics (NACA, created in 1915) into NATIONAL AERONAUTICS AND SPACE ADMINISTRATION (NASA).

As for early satellites, despite the success of *Explorer 1*, some 50 percent of its 18 launches in 1958 and 1959 had failed; the record improved slightly in 1960. By then, the American space program operated on three main tracks. A military one focussed on robotics that included Corona spy satellites and related tracking devices; a NASA unmanned program of probes designed for orbital and planetary work; and a NASA manned space program.

Mercury

While NASA's focus on scientific experimentation remained an essential part of its function, in the context of the Cold War science often took second place to manned space flight and the need to compete with Soviet successes in space. In the meantime, Project Mercury came into existence in late 1958, with seven astronauts, all chosen from a pool of more than 100 military candidates, presented in April of the following year. A selection of female astronauts for Project Mercury, though made shortly after, failed to go forward due to congressional testimony, claiming this would delay the space program, would offer little of worth in return for the added cost, and would require bending newly established rules that called for all astronauts to be graduates of military test pilot schools (no women were allowed into such schools at the time).

On the technical level, the Mercury capsule was a relatively simple design, cone-shaped for effective ascent into orbit, but with a blunt end to allow for a slowed reentry into the atmosphere. Designed under the direction of former NACA engineer Maxime Faget, the capsule could be launched atop either a Redstone or an Air Force Atlas missile. Early tests of the capsule involved monkeys, but by the time of the first human flight, several design changes had been made in response to astronauts' requests, and included a window as well as redesigned switches and levers.

Because NASA maintained a policy of openness with the media, it became essential that no problems plague a manned flight. This concern for safety prompted added delays to the Mercury manned program. This allowed cosmonaut Yuri Gagarin to become the first human to orbit earth on 12 April 1961, for a little over 100 minutes. American Alan Shepard followed on May 5 aboard a Mercury capsule christened *Freedom 7*, but on a suborbital flight that lasted only fifteen minutes. The propaganda coup of the Gagarin flight was enormous, prompting many around the world to view the Soviet Union as the premier technological and military nation, ahead of the United States. It is in this context of Cold War feats that President John F. Kennedy, on the advice of his science advisors and of Vice President Lyndon B. Johnson, ad-

dressed a joint session of Congress on May 25 and called for the United States to land a man on the Moon by the end of the decade. In so doing, Kennedy framed the manned space program into a special mix of technological achievement and showmanship. Although personally uninterested in space, Kennedy understood that the human dimension of space exploration would encourage the public to go along and support what promised to be an extremely expensive endeavor.

Gemini

A total of six Mercury flights happened between 1961 and 1963 and were soon replaced with the Gemini program, which focussed on the study of navigation and on living conditions in space. Indeed, the Moon program, known as Apollo, required completely new knowledge that could only be gathered in Earth orbit. The first two Geminis were unmanned, but the third included a Mercury veteran, Guss Grissom and a rookie from the new astronaut class, John Young (who would go on to become the longest serving astronaut in the space program). Orbital rendezvous between capsules or other satellites was carried out, as were endurance tests to understand how the human body might react to prolonged living in space. The first space walks also took place aboard Gemini missions. Although Cosmonaut Alexei Leonov was the first to carry out this feat, astronaut Ed White did the first American extra-vehicular activity (EVA) in June 1965. Gemini XII concluded the program in November 1966, and confirmed essential information without which a MOON LANDING would not have been possible.

Apollo

The Apollo program did not begin under auspicious conditions. A total of three unpiloted launches and twelve piloted launches occurred between 1967 and 1972. However, before these happened, on 27 January 1967, a fire broke out during a ground test, killing all three *Apollo 1* astronauts. The tragedy prompted several redesigns, delaying the next manned flight until October 1968, when *Apollo 7* lifted off into Earth orbit. At Christmas 1968, *Apollo 8* had reached lunar orbit, but *Apollo 9* and *10* were still needed to test the hardware, including the lunar module, before the successful walk of Neil Armstrong and Edwin Aldrin on 20 July 1969. Aside from *Apollo 13*, marred by an oxygen tank explosion (which the crew survived), all other missions were successful, with number *17* ending the series on 19 December 1972. By then, the Nixon administration, faced with mounting debts from the Vietnam War as well as broader economic stagflation, ordered the last two missions cancelled and asked NASA to cut costs in all its programs.

As a result, NASA faced a lack of direction in the manned space program. A collaborative effort with the Soviet Union resulted in the Apollo-Soyuz test project in 1975, while in 1973, a modified Saturn V orbited the Skylab laboratory, which became the first American space station, housing three crews of three during 1973.

Apollo 13. The lunar mission, which was aborted and nearly ended in tragedy after a defective oxygen tank exploded onboard on 13 April 1970, began two days earlier with this launch of the Saturn V rocket and attached space capsule. AP/ WIDE WORLD PHOTOS

The Space Shuttle

By 1970, work had begun on a reusable space vehicle, capable of transporting astronauts, satellites, and various cargo into orbit. Although initially designed to be entirely reusable, the shuttle transportation system (STS) eventually became only semi-reusable (the solid rocket boosters can be cleaned and recycled, but the large fuel tank burns up during reentry). Furthermore, added costs meant that NASA contracted for only four shuttles. The fifth, prototype *Enterprise* (named following a write-in campaign by *Star Trek* fans), was never reconditioned for space flight and used only to test the gliding capabilities of the shuttle. Pushed back numerous times for technical reasons, the first flight of the shuttle, carried out by orbiter *Columbia*, took place on 12 April 1981 and was followed by twenty-three other successful missions in five years. These included a series of firsts, such as the first American woman in space, Sally Ride, and the first Afri-

can American in space, Guion Bluford, both in 1983. Foreign astronauts flew on board, from representatives of the European Space Agency, to a Saudi prince and two members of Congress. Impressive though this record is, it masks constant problems NASA faced living up to its promises of a reusable vehicle. From a one-week projected turnaround, the shuttle in fact came to require several months of preparation. Yet after only four test flights, NASA certified the shuttle as operational, even though insiders felt that this would not be the case until the shuttle operated twenty-four flights a year. Pressure to maintain a tight schedule eventually led to catastrophe. On 28 January 1986, the twenty-fifth mission, flown by *Challenger*, exploded shortly after lift-off, killing all on board including civilian teacher Christa McAuliffe. The investigation concluded that a defective rubber O-ring around one of the boosters had caused a leak of hot gas that eventually exploded. For almost thirty-one months, the shuttle program remained grounded while changes were implemented, these included canceling NASA's commitment to orbiting commercial satellites. In late 1988, however, shuttle flights resumed and a replacement shuttle, *Endeavor*, was constructed. Since then, the shuttle fleet has passed the one-hundred mission mark, and no replacement vehicle has been designed to replace the twenty-year old system.

The International Space Station

The latest use of the shuttle has been to visit space stations in orbit. From 1995 to 1998, several shuttles flew to the Russian station *Mir* to drop off astronauts on long-term missions intended to gain experience for missions to the International Space Station (ISS). The ISS represents both an evolution and a scaling down of plans for a permanent presence in space. Initially a Cold War project named "Freedom" intended as a response by the U.S. and select allies to the Soviet-built *Mir*; the ISS underwent scaling down in light of budgetary restrictions and the end of the Cold War. The shift in goals also opened the door to international cooperation between the United States, Russia, Europe and Japan, allowing costs to be cut, while conducting scientific experiments in orbit. In 1993, an agreement was reached that included the funding of several important modules to be built by Russia. Begun in 1998 with the orbiting of the Russian *Zarya* module, and projected to cost over $60 billion, the seven-laboratory installation was expected to be completed in 2004. Yet it has hit tremendous cost overruns that have called into question the advantages of a permanent presence in space. Advocates argue that the ISS will act as a symbolic United Nations in space, where the long-term returns will be as much social and cultural as scientific.

Unmanned Space Program

Ever since its creation, NASA has also proceeded apace in the unmanned investigation of the solar system and beyond, and in the lofting of satellites for other purposes. Although some of its most important scientific planetary projects have been subordinated to the more popular (and more expensive) manned space program, the U.S. space program has continued to assist with many new discoveries. In the 1960s, NASA launched Mariner planetary probes to Mars, Venus, and Mercury, with *Mariner 9* becoming the first U.S. spacecraft to orbit another planet, Mars, in 1971. A series of satellites designed to observe the Sun, the "Orbiting Solar Observatories," proved extremely useful, and *OSO 7*, launched in 1971, became the first satellite to film a solar flare. As for *Pioneer 10* and *11*, launched in 1972 and 1973, these probes conducted successful investigations of the outer planets, and *Pioneer 10*, after passing Pluto, became the first man-made object to leave the solar system in 1983. NASA also sent a multitude of probes to Mars, including the successful *Viking 1* and *2* landers that touched down on the red planet in 1976, and the *Pathfinder* in 1997.

In the early 1970s, NASA also put some of its satellite technology to use for the purposes of examining the climate, predicting crop yield, and charting water pollution as well as the state of the ice cap. This Earth Resource Technology Satellite (ERTS) program demonstrated clearly the advantages of an automated presence in space, and drew considerable attention for the immediate information it could provide, in contrast to long-term scientific exploration. Furthermore, the U.S. space program owns half of the COMSAT corporation, which participates in the International Telecommunication Satellite Consortium (Intelsat), a group that operates a worldwide network of communication satellites.

As an alternative to deep space probes, NASA also began studying the possibility of an orbiting "Large Space Telescope" (LST) that would be able to focus on objects ten times more distant than any earth telescope. The result was the Hubble Space Telescope, launched by the space shuttle in 1990.

BIBLIOGRAPHY

Bilstein, Roger. *Order of Magnitude: A History of the NACA and NASA, 1915–1990*. Washington, D.C.: NASA, 1989.

Bulkeley, Rip. *The Sputniks Crisis and Early United States Space Policy: A Critique of the Historiography of Space*. Bloomington: Indiana University, 1991.

Burrows, William E. *Exploring Space: Voyages in the Solar System and Beyond*. New York: Random House, 1990.

Heppenheimer, T. A. *Countdown. A History of Spaceflight*. New York: Wiley, 1997.

Hudson, Heather E. *Communication Satellites: Their Development and Impact*. New York: Free Press, 1990.

Launius, Roger, and Howard McCurdy. *Spaceflight and the Myth of Presidential Leadership*. Urbana: University of Illinois, 1997.

McCurdy, Howard. *Space and the American Imagination*. Washington, D.C.: Smithsonian, 1997.

McDougall, Walter. . . . *The Heavens and the Earth: A Political History of the Space Age*. Baltimore: Johns Hopkins University Press, 1997.

Vaughan, Diane. *The Challenger Launch Decision: Risky Technology, Culture, and Deviance at NASA*. Chicago: University of Chicago, 1996.

Winter, Frank H. *Prelude to the Space Age: The Rocket Societies 1924–1940*. Washington, D.C.: Smithsonian, 1983.

Guillaume de Syon

See also **Missiles, Military;** *and vol. 9:* **Voice from Moon: The Eagle Has Landed.**

SPACE SHUTTLE. The space shuttle is a reusable orbital vehicle that transports aerospace travelers. Officially titled the Space Transportation System (STS), the space shuttle expands space exploration possibilities and contributes to better comprehension of Earth. The orbiting shuttle enables astronauts to conduct experiments in a weightless environment, deploy or repair satellites, and photographically survey the planet. The shuttle aids building, equipping, and transporting of personnel to and from the International Space Station (ISS). Only selected passengers, based on scientific, engineering, professional, or piloting qualifications, can ride in the shuttle. Americans benefit from the shuttle because of zero-gravity pharmaceutical developments and satellite maintenance.

Throughout the twentieth century, engineers envisioned creating a reusable spacecraft. Military and industrial representatives suggested spacecraft resembling gliders such as the late-1950s Dyna-Soar design. By the 1970s, the National Aeronautics and Space Administration (NASA) focused on developing the STS. Engineers and scientists at NASA centers, universities, industries, and research institutions cooperated to build this unique spacecraft, contributing expertise in specific fields to design components and propulsion, guidance, control, and communication systems. Shuttle orbiters were constructed and tested in California with additional testing at the Marshall Space Flight Center in Huntsville, Alabama.

The winged space shuttle structurally resembles airplanes. Interior areas are designed for crews to live and work safely and comfortably while in space. Externally, the space shuttle is coated with ceramic tiles to protect it from burning up during reentry in Earth's atmosphere. Special bays and robotic arms are created for extravehicular activity (EVA) and satellite interaction.

In 1977, a trial space shuttle orbiter named *Enterprise* was carried on a 747 jet to high altitudes and then released to determine that the shuttle could maneuver through the atmosphere before landing. On 12 April 1981, the shuttle *Columbia*, with Robert L. Crippen and John W. Young aboard, was launched from Kennedy Space Center, Florida. After completing thirty-six orbits in two days, the *Columbia* landed at Edwards Air Force Base, California. NASA built four additional shuttles: *Challenger, Discovery, Atlantis,* and *Endeavour.*

The shuttle enabled the accomplishment of significant aerospace milestones. On the June 1983 STS-7 flight,

Space Shuttle. The launching of the *Atlantis* at the Kennedy Space Center in Florida. U.S. NATIONAL AERONAUTICS AND SPACE ADMINISTRATION

Sally K. Ride became the first American woman astronaut. The next year, Bruce McCandless II and Robert Stewart utilized Manned Maneuvering Units to become the first astronauts to walk in space without being tethered to a spacecraft.

The 28 January 1986 *Challenger* explosion paralyzed the space shuttle program. When O-ring seals on a solid rocket booster failed, the shuttle disintegrated, and the entire crew was killed. A presidential commission determined that NASA was accountable due to ineffective engineering control and communication. After redesigning the O-ring seals, NASA launched the shuttle *Discovery* on 29 September 1988. Shuttle flights became routine again.

Post-*Challenger* achievements included deployment of the Hubble Space Telescope in 1990. Beginning in 1995, the space shuttle occasionally docked with the Russian space station Mir. In late 1998, the shuttle *Endeavour* transported Unity, the ISS core, into orbit. The February 2000 Shuttle Radar Topography Mission (SRTM) aboard the space shuttle *Endeavour* collected information about 80 percent of Earth's surface.

The original space shuttles are scheduled for retirement in 2012. In May 2002, NASA announced that future shuttles would physically resemble their predecessors but would be smaller, safer, more affordable, and not require pilots.

BIBLIOGRAPHY

Harland, David M. *The Space Shuttle: Roles, Missions, and Accomplishments.* New York: Wiley, 1998.

Jenkins, Dennis R. *Space Shuttle: The History of the National Space Transportation System: The First 100 Missions.* 3d ed. Cape Canaveral, Fla.: D.R. Jenkins, 2001. The most thorough compendium of the space shuttle.

NASA. Home page at http://www.nasa.gov

Rumerman, Judy A., and Stephen J. Garber, comps. *Chronology of Space Shuttle Flights, 1981–2000.* Washington, D.C.: NASA History Division, Office of Policy and Plans, NASA Headquarters, 2000.

Elizabeth D. Schafer

SPAIN, RELATIONS WITH. Due to the imperial rivalry between Great Britain and Spain in the New World, American relations with Spain date back to before the Revolution. Upon gaining its independence, the new nation inherited an antagonistic relationship with Spain that persisted throughout the nineteenth century, culminating in the Spanish-American War in 1898. With the territorial rivalry between the United States and the Spanish empire settled in the former's favor by that conflict, the twentieth century saw the relationship increasingly dominated by American interests in Europe rather than Spanish interests in the Western Hemisphere.

Prior to the Declaration of Independence, the American view of Spain was essentially that of the British empire: Spain was not only a territorial rival in the New World, but a religious and ideological one as well. As Protestant Britain developed into a constitutional monarchy, Americans saw Catholic Spain as despotic and interpreted the decline of Spanish power and wealth in the seventeenth and eighteenth centuries as the result of the wicked and deceitful nature of Spain (the so-called "Black Legend").

Americans saw evidence of Spain's duplicity in its reaction to the American war of independence, when in fact Spain's policy was the result of conflicting interests. Torn between its desire to exact revenge upon Britain for loss of colonial territory earlier in the 1700s and its fear that overt support for a colonial independence movement might undermine its own position in Latin America, Spain equivocated. Unlike France, Spain resisted American pleas for recognition and alliance but did covertly supply money to the revolutionaries and declared war on Britain in 1779 in hopes of regaining Gibraltar. As spoils of war, Spain recovered Florida (lost to Britain in 1763), and the United States expanded its territory westward to the Mississippi River, thus setting the stage for future tensions.

Territorial Tensions

For nearly forty years after independence, Spanish-American relations were dominated by these territorial gains, because the new republic shared borders with the old empire in both the south and west. With British strength in Canada rendering northern expansion impractical, American territorial growth would come at the expense of the Spanish. From the American perspective, loosely governed Spanish Florida was a refuge for hostile Native Americans and disreputable characters of all kinds, while Spanish control over navigation of the Mississippi River (New Orleans, its point of access to the Gulf of Mexico, was entirely in Spanish hands) threatened to choke off the economic development of the west.

In the aftermath of Jay's Treaty in November 1794 and the subsequent improvement in British-American relations, Spain's fear of a British-American alliance against it led to the first formal Spanish-American agreement, PINCKNEY'S TREATY (1795). The pact was a clear diplomatic victory for the United States. The Spanish accepted the American claim regarding the Florida border, gave up their claims to territory east of the Mississippi, and conceded American rights on the Mississippi.

Pinckney's Treaty reflected the declining power of Spain in North America, a fact that later led Spain to turn over control of the Louisiana territory to France in 1800 in the secret Treaty of San Ildefonso. Ironically the transfer led just three years later to the purchase of Louisiana by the United States, precisely the result Spain sought to avoid by turning over the territory to its stronger ally.

The LOUISIANA PURCHASE, far from ending the Spanish-American rivalry, merely pushed it farther west. The two powers began to argue again over the proper border between them. The United States adopted the most expansive definition of Louisiana (encompassing not only Texas but West Florida) and sought to acquire the rest of the Florida territories from Spain. President James Monroe (aided by the aggressive military actions of Gen. Andrew Jackson) finally wrested the territory from Spain in return for a definitive settlement of the western border of the Spanish and American territories.

In the midst of protracted negotiations between Secretary of State John Quincy Adams and Luis de Onís, the Spanish minister, Monroe ordered Jackson to suppress the Seminoles in Florida, whom the United States blamed for attacks on Americans. Jackson seized the opportunity to take on not only the Seminoles but the Spanish. Whether Jackson acted with or without permission remains somewhat controversial, but his actions had the undeniable effect of improving the American negotiating position. The resulting agreement, the Adams-Onís or Transcontinental Treaty (signed in 1819, ratified 1821), ceded the Floridas to the United States. It also defined the western border between the United States and Spanish Mexico, affirming the Spanish claim to Texas as well as the U.S. claim to the Pacific Northwest.

The subsequent revolts against Spanish rule by Mexico and other Latin American colonies served not only to give rise to one of the most famous of American foreign policies, the MONROE DOCTRINE, but also to diminish the territorial clashes between Spain and the United States for more than seven decades. President Monroe's statement in 1823 calling for European noninterference was ostensibly a reaction to potential Spanish efforts to regain control of its colonies, but it became a permanent policy toward the hemisphere. The ultimate success of the independence movements in Latin America removed the main cause of Spanish-American enmity.

There was, however, one exception: Cuba. The island remained under Spanish control and had long been desired by the United States. Enthusiasm for the annexation of Cuba reached its height with the OSTEND MANIFESTO in 1854, when three American diplomats in Europe recommended that the United States seize Cuba if Spain refused to sell it, but the idea got mired in the domestic debate over slavery and never gained widespread support.

After the Civil War, a Cuban rebellion (1868–1878) against Spanish rule gave the United States the opportunity to intervene and obtain the island, but the national mood was not conducive to military adventure. When Cubans again rebelled in 1895, however, the American public took a keen interest in events there, an interest both reflected and stoked by the popular press. Advocates of an assertive foreign policy, like Alfred Thayer Mahan and Theodore Roosevelt, argued that growing American economic power needed to be protected by a more assertive diplomacy backed by a more powerful military. Cuba represented an opportunity for the United States to show its growing power. Idealists believed that self-determination required American intervention to end one of the last—and, they argued, one of the most brutal—vestiges of colonialism in the New World. In short, a number of factors converged to revive Spanish-American enmity.

When the battleship *Maine* suffered an explosion and sank on 15 February 1898, most Americans were more than eager to pin the blame on Spain, in defiance of all logic. (Spain ardently hoped to keep the United States out of the conflict, not to give it a pretext for intervention.) On 25 April Congress declared that a state of war had existed between the United States and Spain since 21 April, despite the fact that the Spanish had already agreed to most of the American demands.

In a matter of months, the fighting was over, and Spain had suffered a tremendous defeat, losing the last major remnants of its once worldwide empire. The Treaty of Paris (December 1898) gave Cuba its ostensible independence (in fact, it would become an American protectorate) and gave to the United States the Philippines, Puerto Rico, and Guam. Spain ceased to be an imperial world power, and the United States became one.

Reversal of Fortune

This reversal of the two nations' positions initially led to a diminishment of the importance of Spanish-American relations. Early in the new century, Americans were focused on events in Asia and the Western Hemisphere, precisely the areas from which Spain had been expelled. When World War I broke out in 1914, both nations declared their neutrality. While Spain's caution led it to maintain that stance throughout the war, in 1917 the expanding interests of the United States drew it into the conflict and tentatively into European power politics, thus setting the scene for the next stage in Spanish-American relations.

Just as the American Revolution posed a dilemma for the Spanish, so too did the outbreak of the Spanish Civil War in 1936 for the Americans. The rebellion of Francisco Franco and his generals against the Spanish republican government was a microcosm of the ideological ferment of interwar Europe. Franco received assistance from Nazi Germany and fascist Italy, and the Republicans received assistance from the Soviet Union. Most democracies, including the United States, observed a formal neutrality that had the effect of dooming the Spanish government to defeat.

Franco remained technically neutral throughout World War II, but he favored the Axis when it seemed in command early on and tipped back toward the Allies as the war drew to a close. American policy during the war was to buy Spain's neutrality by overpaying the Spanish for goods with military significance (such as tungsten) in order to keep the Spanish nonbelligerent and the supplies out of German hands.

U.S. policy toward Spain grew harsher with the success of D-Day in 1944 and the growing likelihood of a German defeat. Citing the role played by the Axis powers in Franco's rise to power, in early 1945 Franklin Roosevelt declared that the United States could not have normal relations with his government. The United States joined its allies in barring Spain from the United Nations and recalled its chiefs of mission from Madrid.

Franco blunted American pressure to yield power to a more democratic regime by appealing to growing concern about the Soviet Union. While his quasi-fascist regime remained an international pariah, American leaders gradually reached the conclusion that Franco was preferable to a potential communist government in Spain. The United States did not include Spain in either its economic or military plans for western Europe (the Marshall Plan and the North Atlantic Treaty Organization), but after the outbreak of the Korean War in June 1950, Spain's potential military value in a European war against the Soviets overrode the Truman administration's ideological aversion to Franco.

The rehabilitation of Franco culminated in the Pact of Madrid, signed in September 1953. While Spain remained outside NATO, the agreement (which gave the United States air and naval bases in Spain) effectively allied the two nations during the remainder of the Cold War. The death of Franco in November 1975 and the subsequent return to democratic government in Spain removed whatever residual cloud remained over Spanish-American relations. Spain's acceptance into NATO in 1982 and the European Community in 1986 further solidified the normalization of relations. At the close of the twentieth century, Spanish-American relations resembled those of the United States with other European nations and had lost the distinctive quality of years past.

BIBLIOGRAPHY

Beaulac, Willard L. *Franco: Silent Ally in World War II.* Carbondale: Southern Illinois University Press, 1986.

Cortada, James. *Two Nations Over Time: Spain and the United States, 1775–1977.* Westport, Conn.: Greenwood Press, 1978.

Edwards, Jill. *Anglo-American Relations and the Franco Question 1945–1955.* New York: Oxford University Press, 1999.

Hayes, Carleton J. H. *The United States and Spain: An Interpretation.* New York: Sheed and Ward, 1951.

Little, Douglas. *Malevolent Neutrality: The United States, Great Britain, and the Origins of the Spanish Civil War.* Ithaca, N.Y.: Cornell University Press, 1985.

Rubottom, Richard R., and J. Carter Murphy. *Spain and the United States: Since World War II.* New York: Praeger, 1984.

Whitaker, Arthur P. *Spain and Defense of the West: Ally and Liability.* New York: Harper, 1961. Reprint, Westport, Conn.: Greenwood Press, 1980.

———. *The Spanish-American Frontier, 1783–1795.* Boston and New York: Houghton Mifflin, 1927. Reprint, Lincoln: University of Nebraska Press, 1969.

Mark S. Byrnes

See also **Spanish-American War.**

SPANISH-AMERICAN WAR. The sinking of the battleship *Maine* in Havana harbor on 15 February 1898 provided a dramatic *casus belli* for the Spanish-American War, but underlying causes included U.S. economic interests ($50 million invested in Cuba; $100 million in annual trade, mostly sugar) as well as genuine humanitarian concern over long-continued Spanish misrule. Rebellion in Cuba had erupted violently in 1895, and although by 1897 a more liberal Spanish government had adopted a conciliatory attitude, U.S. public opinion, inflamed by strident "yellow journalism," would not be placated by anything short of full independence for Cuba.

The *Maine* had been sent to Havana ostensibly on a courtesy visit but actually as protection for American citizens. A U.S. Navy court of inquiry concluded on 21 March that the ship had been sunk by an external explosion. Madrid agreed to arbitrate the matter but would not promise independence for Cuba. On 11 April, President William McKinley asked Congress for authority to inter-

Spanish-American War. U.S. troops line up crisply; contrary to this image, thousands of regular soldiers and volunteers found shortages of weapons and supplies, as well as poor food and sanitation, at the camps where they assembled. GETTY IMAGES

vene, and, on 25 April, Congress declared that a state of war existed between Spain and the United States.

The North Atlantic Squadron, concentrated at Key West, Florida, was ordered on 22 April to blockade Cuba. The Spanish home fleet under Adm. Pascual Cervera had sortied from Cadiz on 8 April, and although he had only four cruisers and two destroyers, the approach of this "armada" provoked near panic along the U.S. East Coast.

Spanish troop strength in Cuba totaled 150,000 regulars and forty thousand irregulars and volunteers. The Cuban insurgents numbered perhaps fifty thousand. At the war's beginning, the strength of the U.S. Regular Army under Maj. Gen. Nelson A. Miles was only twenty-six thousand. The legality of using the National Guard, numbering something more than 100,000, for expeditionary service was questionable. Therefore, authorities resorted to the volunteer system used in the Mexican-American War and Civil War. The mobilization act of 22 April provided for a wartime army of 125,000 volunteers (later raised to 200,000) and an increase in the regular army to sixty-five thousand. Thousands of volunteers and recruits converged on ill-prepared southern camps where they found a shortage of weapons, equipment, and supplies, and scandalous sanitary conditions and food.

In the Western Pacific, Commo. George Dewey had been alerted by Acting Secretary of the Navy Theodore Roosevelt to prepare his Asiatic Squadron for operations in the Philippines. On 27 April, Dewey sailed from Hong Kong with four light cruisers, two gunboats, and a reve-

nue cutter—and, as a passenger, Emilio Aguinaldo, an exiled Filipino insurrectionist. Dewey entered Manila Bay in the early morning hours on 1 May and destroyed the Spanish squadron, but he had insufficient strength to land and capture Manila itself. Until U.S. Army forces could arrive, the Spanish garrison had to be kept occupied by Aguinaldo's guerrilla operations.

In the Atlantic, Cervera slipped into Santiago on Cuba's southeast coast. Commo. Winfield Schley took station off Santiago on 28 May and was joined four days later by Rear Adm. William T. Sampson. To support these operations, a marine battalion on 10 June seized nearby Guantánamo to serve as an advance base. Sampson, reluctant to enter the harbor because of mines and land batteries, asked for U.S. Army help. Maj. Gen. William R. Shafter, at Tampa, Florida, received orders on 31 May to embark his V Corps. Despite poor facilities, he had seventeen thousand men, mostly regulars, ready to sail by 14 June and by 20 June was standing outside Santiago. On 22 June, after a heavy shelling of the beach area, the V Corps began going ashore. It was a confused and vulnerable landing, but the Spanish did nothing to interfere.

Between Daiquiri and Santiago were the San Juan heights. Shafter's plan was to send Brig. Gen. Henry W. Lawton's division north to seize the village of El Caney and then to attack frontally with Brig. Gen. Jacob F. Kent's division on the left and Maj. Gen. Joseph Wheeler's dismounted cavalry on the right. The attack began at dawn on 1 July. Wheeler, one-time Confederate cavalryman, sent his dismounted troopers, including the black Ninth and Tenth cavalries and the volunteer ROUGH RIDERS, under command of Lt. Col. Theodore Roosevelt, against Kettle Hill. The Spanish withdrew to an inner defense line, and, as the day ended, the Americans had their ridge line but at a cost of seventeen hundred casualties.

Shafter, not anxious to go against the Spanish second line, asked Sampson to come into Santiago Bay and attack the city, but for Sampson there was still the matter of the harbor defenses. He took his flagship eastward on 3 July to meet with Shafter, and while they argued, Cervera inadvertently resolved the impasse by coming out of the port on orders of the Spanish captain general. His greatly inferior squadron was annihilated by Schley, and on 16 July the Spaniards signed terms of unconditional surrender for the 23,500 troops in and around the city.

At the end of July the VIII Corps, some fifteen thousand men (mostly volunteers) under Maj. Gen. Wesley Merritt, had reached the Philippines. En route, the escort cruiser *Charleston* had stopped at Guam and accepted the surrender of the island from the Spanish governor, who had not heard of the war. Because of an unrepaired cable, Dewey and Merritt themselves did not hear immediately of the peace protocol, and on 13 August an assault against Manila was made. The Spanish surrendered after token resistance.

The peace treaty, signed in Paris on 10 December 1898, established Cuba as an independent state, ceded

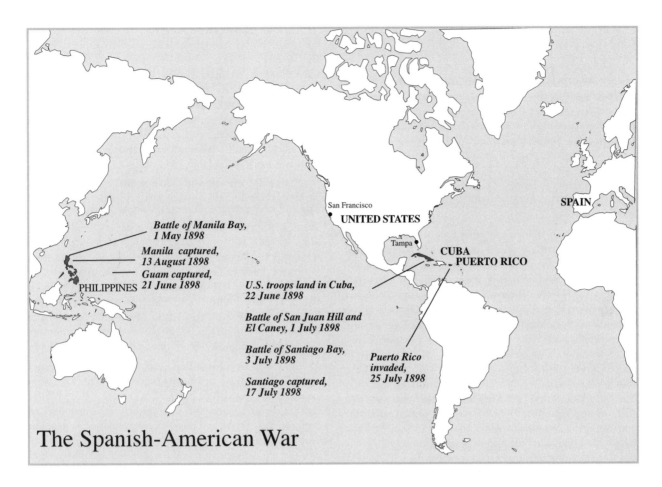

Battle of Manila Bay,
1 May 1898

Manila captured,
13 August 1898

Guam captured,
21 June 1898

PHILIPPINES

U.S. troops land in Cuba,
22 June 1898

Battle of San Juan Hill and
El Caney, 1 July 1898

Battle of Santiago Bay,
3 July 1898

Santiago captured,
17 July 1898

San Francisco
UNITED STATES

Tampa

CUBA
PUERTO RICO

Puerto Rico
invaded,
25 July 1898

SPAIN

The Spanish-American War

Puerto Rico and Guam to the United States, and provided for the payment of $20 million to Spain for the Philippines. Almost overnight the United States had acquired an overseas empire and, in the eyes of Europe, had become a world power. The immediate cost of the war was $250 million and about three thousand American lives, of which only about three hundred were battle deaths. A disgruntled Aguinaldo, expecting independence for the Philippines, declared a provisional republic, which led to the PHILIPPINE INSURRECTION that lasted until 1902.

BIBLIOGRAPHY

Cosmas, Graham A. *An Army for Empire: The United States Army in the Spanish-American War.* Shippensburg, Pa.: White Mane Publishing, 1994.

Hoganson, Kristin L. *Fighting for American Manhood: How Gender Politics Provoked the Spanish-American and Philippine-American Wars.* New Haven, Conn.: Yale University Press, 1998.

Linderman, Gerald F. *The Mirror of War: American Society and the Spanish-American War.* Ann Arbor: University of Michigan Press, 1974.

Musicant, Ivan. *Empire by Default: The Spanish-American War and the Dawn of the American Century.* New York: Holt, 1998.

Traxel, David. *1898: The Birth of the American Century.* New York: Knopf, 1998.

*Edwin H. Simmons/*A. G.

See also **Jingoism;** *Maine,* **Sinking of the; Paris, Treaty of (1898); Teller Amendment; Territories of the United States; Yellow Journalism;** *and vol. 9:* **Anti-Imperialist League Platform; A Soldier's Account of the Spanish-American War.**

SPANISH-AMERICAN WAR, NAVY IN. Shortly before the SPANISH-AMERICAN WAR, growing American interest in a modern, powerful navy had resulted in increased appropriations and a vigorous program of ship construction, especially of battleships and cruisers. The Spanish-American War (1898) lasted only about ninety days, yet it marked the generally successful combat trial of the then new American navy. Following by eight years the appearance of Alfred Thayer Mahan's *The Influence of Sea Power upon History,* the conflict illustrated principles and techniques of war that were sometimes adhered to, sometimes violated.

The main combat areas of the war were Spanish possessions in the Philippines and the Caribbean. In both theaters, American naval ascendancy was first established, although by different means, to assure sea control before undertaking amphibious and military operations. On 1 May 1898, in the Battle of Manila Bay, which involved secondary cruiser forces in a secondary area, Commodore George Dewey easily defeated an antiquated Spanish squadron acting as a fixed fortress fleet. In the Atlantic-Caribbean areas, war strategy and command decisions proved more complex and difficult.

In late April the Navy Department unwisely yielded to the clamor of influential, but ill-informed, East Coast citizens for coastal protection and subsequently divided naval objectives and forces. Rear Adm. William T. Sampson, with new battleships, established a blockade off Havana, the assumed Cuban strategic center. At Norfolk, Virginia, an intended mobile fortress fleet under Commodore Winfield Scott Schley was readied to defend against almost impossible coastal raids by the main Spanish fleet.

In early May, on learning that Spanish Adm. Pascual Cervera had left the Cape Verde Islands, Sampson lifted most of his blockade and steamed eastward on the erroneous assumption that his opponent would first make port at San Juan, Puerto Rico, and then continue to his assumed ultimate destination, Havana. But Cervera, given freedom of command decision, chose a different route and ultimate port than he would have in peacetime. Thus, there was no confrontation of naval forces off Puerto Rico. Cervera slipped into the nearest Cuban port, Santiago, which was then not under American surveillance. Ten days later, after confusion and delay, Schley located Cervera and established a blockade, later joined by Sampson. Soon the Americans landed marines and soldiers and began their military campaign against Santiago. As the city's fall became imminent, Cervera was directed to sortie, if possible, to Havana. However, in the naval battle of 3 July, his fleet was overwhelmed and beached, a significant prelude to further successful American operations against Cuba and, later, Puerto Rico.

There were many important naval lessons learned in the war, from which the Americans profited. Their gunnery required swift technological improvement, which Lt. Comdr. William S. Sims soon provided. Engineering research and development were stimulated by the establishment of the Naval Engineering Experiment Station. Because it took sixty-six days for the *Oregon* to sail from San Francisco around Cape Horn to Key West, Florida, and join the fleet, pressure was exerted for a canal route through Central America. The necessity for overseas bases for logistic support became evident. The Spanish-American War also added strong impetus to the growing demand for an American navy second to none.

BIBLIOGRAPHY

Marolda, Edward J., ed. *Theodore Roosevelt, the U.S. Navy, and the Spanish-American War.* New York: Palgrave, 2001.

Wilson, Herbert W. *The Downfall of Spain: Naval History of the Spanish-American War.* New York: B. Franklin, 1971.

Ellery H. Clark Jr. / A. G.

See also **Manila Bay, Battle of; Navy, Department of the; Paris, Treaty of (1898).**

SPANISH BORDERLANDS refer to the Spanish colonial frontier in what later became the United States. By the late eighteenth century, Spanish claims extended west along the southern rim of North America from Florida to California, and north along the coast to Alaska. The Spanish borderlands vanished as a regional entity in 1821, when Mexico became independent, but its cultural and material legacies endure almost two hundred years later in the borderlands between Mexico and the United States.

Spanish Exploration and Settlement

In the sixteenth century, this vast region was home to a variety of native peoples, ranging from mobile bands in Texas, California, and Arizona to larger farming towns in New Mexico and even larger confederacies east of the Mississippi. This mosaic of local worlds was in constant motion. Ecological, religious, and political forces brought groups together, but also placed them in conflict. Trade connected the humid east, high plains, and arid west. Large-scale migrations—such as that which Apache and Navajo forebears made to the Southwest shortly before the Spanish conquest—were not unheard of.

The Spanish expanded into North America from beachheads in the Caribbean and Mexico. In 1528, after a hurricane landed him on the Texas coast, Alvar Núñez Cabeza de Vaca wandered west into the Chihuahuan and Sonoran deserts. When he finally met Spaniards near the Gulf of California in 1536, he passed along rumors of wealthy cities to the north. This inspired new journeys in the 1540s. Hernando de Soto, formerly with Francisco Pizarro in Peru, searched for another Inca empire between Florida and Texas. The provincial governor Francisco Vázquez de Coronado led a similar expedition into New Mexico and the western plains. Both returned empty-handed, leaving behind a legacy of arrogance, violence, and disease.

Explorations were followed by more sustained settlements. Pedro Menéndez de Avilés founded San Augustine, Florida, in 1565 to displace a colony of French Huguenots and protect Spanish silver fleets sailing through the Bahama Channel. Sir Francis Drake razed the colony in 1586, but it rebounded to become a center for secular and missionary expansion. The 1546 discovery of silver in Zacatecas, Mexico, followed by other mining rushes to the north, opened a new corridor of migration along the Sierra Madres. Juan de Oñate, son of a wealthy Zacatecas family, gained royal permission to settle New Mexico in 1598. New Mexico lacked mines, but offered a harvest of souls for Franciscans. Like Florida, the New Mexico colony was also maintained as a defensive buffer, to protect the mining towns to the south from European rivals to the east. Settlers also migrated along the western Sierra Madres into Sonora, and by the 1680s, Jesuits were setting up missions among the Pima communities of southern Arizona.

The borderlands became contested terrain in the late seventeenth century. In 1680 the Pueblo Indians revolted, driving colonists from New Mexico. When Diego de Vargas retook the province in 1694, he had to acknowledge the limits of colonial power and ease native exploitation. Farther east in 1682, René Robert Cavelier, sieur de La Salle, sailed down the Mississippi, claiming Louisiana for the French. The Spanish sent colonists into Texas to counter the French, and by 1716 established a permanent frontier outpost at Los Adaes, on the Louisiana border. Meanwhile, in 1670, the British founded Charleston as a mainland resource base for Barbados, and within decades British settlers in the Carolinas posed a threat to Spanish Florida. The eighteenth century would be marked by a series of wars between the French, British, Spanish, and their Indian allies to control what would later become the southeastern United States.

These rivalries took a new turn in 1763, when France yielded its North American possessions following the Seven Years' War. Toward the end of the war, France ceded western Louisiana to Spain—perhaps to compensate Spain for its help in the war. In the Treaty of Paris of 1763, England confirmed Spain's title to western Louisiana in return for Florida. Until 1800, when Spain ceded Louisiana back to France, the Mississippi became the new border between English and Spanish North America. When the thirteen colonies revolted in 1776, the Spanish provided financial and military assistance, driving the British from the Mississippi and gulf region. As a reward, the United States returned Florida to Spain in the Treaty of Paris of 1783.

Meanwhile, Carlos III (1759–1788) worked to build Spain's control over western North America. For over a century, Spain had been on the decline as a world power, and its mercantilist policies—which limited the supply and raised the cost of imported goods in New Spain—were hard on frontier outposts. Frontier defense was badly financed and administered. Well-mounted and well-armed Comanches and Apaches took advantage of raiding and trading networks between imperial frontiers to gain an edge over the Spanish. Carlos III therefore set out to reorganize frontier defenses. His administrators attempted to establish a rational line of presidios with mounted patrols, made alliances with Indians to fight other Indians, and set up "peace establishments" to placate former enemies with federally subsidized food, tobacco, and alcohol. As defenses improved, so did economic conditions. From the official perspective, conditions in the Spanish borderlands began to improve by the late 1780s.

Renewed Spanish energy was also reflected by expansion into California and the Pacific Northwest. By the 1760s, Russian fur hunters, with the help of Aleut labor, had made significant inroads into Alaskan sea otter populations. Concerned that the Russian empire would move into California, Carlos III encouraged its settlement in the late 1760s and early 1770s. By 1781, a string of missions, presidios, and towns lined the coast from San Diego to San Francisco. Isolated from the rest of Mexico by strong ocean currents and formidable deserts, California's

ties to colonial markets were weak. Yet Franciscans, in particular, struck it rich. Not only was California rich with potential converts, but here colonists did not have to vie with other empires for native bodies, souls, and trade. In 1790, the Spanish expanded as far north as Vancouver, which they jointly occupied with the United States and England until 1819. But they lacked the resources to settle this far northern frontier. Practically speaking, San Francisco marked the upper limit of Spanish control along the Pacific.

American Expansion

By century's end, then, Spain controlled the southern rim of North America from Florida to California. But newcomers were starting to edge their way west. For instance, the U.S. population of Kentucky rose from 12,000 in 1781 to 221,000 in 1800. Kentucky pioneers began to float flour and bacon down the Ohio and Mississippi Rivers to Spanish markets in Louisiana and Florida. Because this trade was technically illegal, goods often entered the borderlands along well-worn smuggling routes. Worried about their rapidly growing neighbor, and hard-pressed to populate its frontiers from within, Spanish leaders came up with a radical plan to encourage American immigration to Spanish Louisiana. If Americans could not be stopped, why not assimilate them to provide a buffer to westward expansion? In the early American Republic, many frontiersmen were indifferent—and at times even disloyal—to the United States. By 1792, some 45,000 had accepted the new offer by migrating west and taking an oath of allegiance to Spain.

One can only guess how this risky plan might have ended, because in 1800, Spain returned Louisiana to France, and three years later, France sold the province to the United States. Spain and the United States disagreed on the extent of the purchase; the Spanish insisted, for instance, that the vast Missouri River system fell outside Louisiana. In 1804, when Lewis and Clark traveled up the Missouri, Spanish officials tried, unsuccessfully, to intercept them. The U.S. explorer Zebulon Pike was arrested in Colorado in 1806, when his effort to map the southern edge of Louisiana landed him in Spanish territory. Suspecting that he had come to spy, Spanish officials stripped him of his journal and maps and sent him home. In an 1810 account, Pike described New Mexico and Texas as places hungry for manufactures but held back by mercantilist Spain. The lesson was obvious: northern New Spain would be a rich market for U.S. goods, were the rules to change.

And barely a decade later, they would. In 1810, Mexicans initiated a movement for independence, which finally bore fruit in 1821. Two years earlier, in the Adams-Onís Treaty of 1819, Spain ceded Florida to the United States and agreed to a formal boundary with Louisiana. The wars of independence in Mexico had a drastic economic impact. As military subsidies dried up, Indians returned to raiding, making life even more desperate for

Spanish-speaking residents. On the other hand, Mexico opened the frontier to trade in 1821. As northern provinces cautiously embraced U.S. capital, goods, and immigrants, new linkages and tensions emerged, eventually leading to the U.S.-Mexican War and the annexation of Texas, New Mexico, and California. After three centuries of Spanish rule, this contested region lay at the brink of a new borderlands era.

BIBLIOGRAPHY

Cutter, Donald, and Iris Engstrand. *Quest For Empire: Spanish Settlement in the Southwest.* Golden, Colo.: Fulcrum, 1996.

John, Elizabeth A. H. *Storms Brewed in Other Men's Worlds: The Confrontation of Indians, Spanish, and French in the Southwest, 1540–1795.* 2d ed. Norman: University of Oklahoma Press, 1996.

Jones, Oakah L., Jr. *Los Paisanos: Spanish Settlers on the Northern Frontier of New Spain.* 2d ed. Norman: University of Oklahoma Press, 1996.

Spicer, Edward H. *Cycles of Conquest: The Impact of Spain, Mexico, and the United States on the Indians of the Southwest, 1533–1960.* Tucson: University of Arizona Press, 1962.

Weber, David J. *The Spanish Frontier in North America.* New Haven, Conn.: Yale University Press, 1992.

Samuel Truett

See also **Colonial Administration, Spanish; Louisiana Purchase; Mexican-American War; Spain, Relations with.**

SPANISH CONSPIRACY, a series of more or less closely related intrigues beginning in 1786 between Spain and certain Americans living in what was then the western United States. Spain wished to defend Louisiana and Florida by promoting the secession of the West from the United States. To achieve that purpose, Spain manipulated commerce on the Mississippi River and attempted to exploit sectional antagonism between the American East and West. After the United States obtained the right of free navigation of the Mississippi by Pinckney's Treaty in 1795, the conspirators continued to seek commercial privileges, support for colonization schemes, and other advantages from Spain.

In 1786 Congress aroused great indignation in the West by not pressing the U.S. claim to the free navigation of the Mississippi. In 1787 James Wilkinson, a prominent figure in Kentucky politics, went to New Orleans to try his hand at direct negotiation with the Spanish officials of Louisiana. He won some commercial privileges for the West, took an oath of allegiance to Spain, and became an agent in secessionist intrigue. Later, Wilkinson joined forces with a disaffected Aaron Burr, who had treasonous plans for a vast empire in the West and South based on the conquest of Mexico and the separation of the trans-Appalachia states from the Union. By 1806 the conspirators procured boats, men, and supplies and moved on Natchez, Mississippi. When the plans were discovered in 1807, Wilkinson turned against Burr, who was arrested but fled to Spanish Florida. He was intercepted, indicted for treason, yet acquitted due to lack of witnesses. Wilkinson, the government's chief witness, was also acquitted, although deeply implicated in the proceedings.

BIBLIOGRAPHY

Green, Thomas Marshall. *The Spanish Conspiracy: A Review of Early Spanish Movements in the South-west. Containing Proofs of the Intrigues of James Wilkinson and John Brown; of the Complicity Therewith of Judges Sebastian, Wallace, and Innes; the Early Struggles of Kentucky for Autonomy; the Intrigues of Sebastian in 1795–7, and the Legislative Investigation of his Corruption.* Cincinnati, Ohio: Clarke, 1891.

Hay, Thomas Robson. *The Admirable Trumpeter: A Biography of General James Wilkinson.* Garden City, N.Y.: Doubleday, 1941.

McCaleb, Walter Flavius. *The Aaron Burr Conspiracy; and, A New Light on Aaron Burr.* New York: Argosy-Antiquarian, 1966.

Montgomery, M. R. *Jefferson and the Gun-men: How the West was Almost Lost.* New York: Crown, 2000.

Weems, John Edward. *Men Without Counries: Three Adventures of the Early Southwest.* Boston: Houghton Mifflin, 1969.

Arthur P. Whitaker / H. S.

See also **Burr-Hamiton Duel; Spain, Relations with.**

SPANISH DOLLAR. *See* **Pieces of Eight.**

SPANISH LANGUAGE first came to the territory now occupied by the United States as the language of the explorers and settlers who set out from Spain's Caribbean outposts and from New Spain (Mexico) in the early sixteenth century. From that time until Mexico's independence in 1821, the Spanish crown established and maintained settlements from Florida to California. This region, covering approximately the southern third of the North American continent exclusive of modern-day Mexico, received the apposite designation of the "Spanish borderlands" from twentieth-century historians. The easternmost portion of the Spanish borderlands was known as "La Florida" and included the entire southeast quadrant of the present United States, from South Carolina to Mississippi. "New Mexico" extended from Texas to Arizona, while the West Coast was christened "California," after a fabulous island that appears in an early sixteenth-century romance of chivalry. In the last years of the seventeenth century, French explorers claimed the full extent of the Mississippi watershed for Louis XIV, naming it accordingly Louisiana.

In the seventeenth century, English colonists drove the Spanish out of all of La Florida except for the peninsula that now bears the name of that once vast region. It remained in Spanish hands until its purchase by the United States in 1820, if one discounts the British occupation from 1763 to 1783. When the French lost Canada

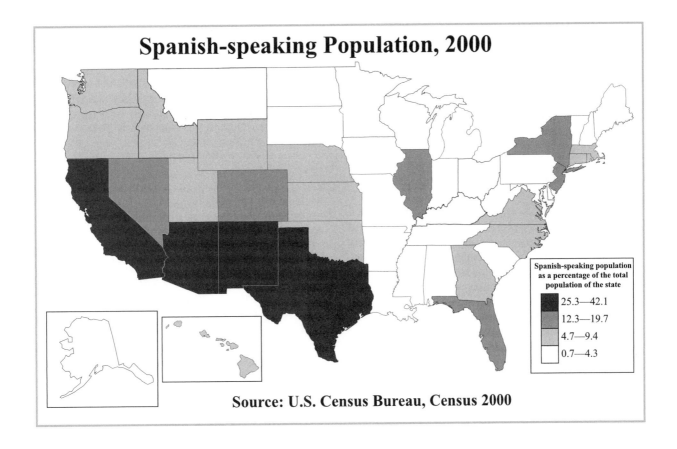

Spanish-speaking Population, 2000

Spanish-speaking population as a percentage of the total population of the state

- 25.3—42.1
- 12.3—19.7
- 4.7—9.4
- 0.7—4.3

Source: U.S. Census Bureau, Census 2000

in 1762, Louisiana was ceded to Spain; Napoleon claimed it back in 1800, only to sell it to the United States in 1803. New Mexico (that is, the present states of New Mexico and Arizona), Texas, and California became part of the Mexican republic that achieved independence in 1821. Texas gained its independence from Mexico in 1836, and in the MEXICAN-AMERICAN WAR (1846–1848), the rest of New Mexico and California was occupied by the United States.

The Spanish borderlands left an immense linguistic legacy. The most immediate and obvious remnants are the thousands of place-names of Spanish origin that pepper maps from Florida to California. American English absorbed large numbers of loanwords from Spanish as the United States extended its sway over Spanish-speaking territories. The Amerindian languages, especially of the Southwest (from Texas to California), incorporated hundreds of Spanish vocabulary items into their languages. An incalculable number of documents in archives from Florida to California (to say nothing of Mexican and Spanish archives containing material relevant to the Spanish borderlands) attest to the use of Spanish not only in its official bureaucratic form but often in ways that reflect many traits of colloquial speech. Finally, and most important, is the survival of Spanish-speaking communities in New Mexico and Louisiana, whose uninterrupted existence from colonial times to the present provides a fas-

cinating example of persistence in the face of overwhelming demographic pressure from speakers of English.

The Spanish spoken in northern New Mexico and southern Colorado constitutes a direct survival of the colonial and Mexican periods of the Southwest. It is also by far the most thoroughly studied variety of U.S. Spanish; in fact, the publication of Aurelio M. Espinosa's *Estudios sobre el español de Nuevo Méjico* (1930–1946) placed New Mexican Spanish in the forefront of the study of American Spanish in general. The Spanish of the *isleños* (islanders) of Louisiana, so named for their having originally emigrated from the Canary Islands, involves a much smaller and less studied linguistic community. Both communities are characterized by a rich folkloric tradition, involving both prose and verse, and in the case of New Mexico, theater as well. This is an oral literature that reflects local patterns of speech and is consequently of great value for linguistic analysis.

However impressive the linguistic legacy of the Spanish borderlands might be, it is rather in the twentieth century that the Spanish language became such an integral part of the national scene. Major currents of immigration followed close upon historical events. The SPANISH-AMERICAN WAR in 1898 brought Puerto Rico into its special relationship with the United States and opened the doors for the establishment of Puerto Rican communities, principally in New York City, but eventually in many other parts of the country. The Mexican revolution that began in 1910 had the effect of driving many refugees north of the border, but the principal magnet for immigration was the economic opportunities offered by U.S. agriculture and industry. Mexican communities all over the Southwest were strengthened by immigration from Mexico, but many immigrants settled in other parts of the country; for instance, Chicago became home to an especially numerous and active community. World War II destroyed many Sephardic Jewish communities in the Balkans; the survivors immigrated en masse to the New World, including the United States. The Cuban revolution of 1959 provoked yet another diaspora, the principal center of which is Miami. The civil wars of Central America in the 1970s and 1980s brought many Guatemalans, Nicaraguans, and Salvadoreans to the United States. Over and above such catastrophic displacements there has been a steady immigration from all Spanish-speaking countries. Spanish is by far the largest non-English language spoken in the United States; indeed, with perhaps 30 million Spanish speakers, the United States counts as one of the largest Spanish-speaking countries after Mexico and Spain.

In studying the numerous varieties of U.S. Spanish, the predominant theme of linguistic research has been to measure the impact of English on immigrant Spanish. English affects the sound system (phonology) and word forms (morphology) in very limited ways, while the influence on vocabulary (lexicon) and phrase and sentence construction (syntax) tends to be notable. Bilingual speakers among themselves often use both languages in the same discourse, a phenomenon labeled "code-switching" in the linguistic literature. The manner in which the rapid transitions from one language to the other are achieved possesses considerable importance for general linguistics. Another favorite subject is the argot or jargon traditionally known as *pachuco* (*caló* is now the preferred designation), an in-group parlance cultivated primarily by young Hispanic males in the Southwest, which is incomprehensible to outsiders. *Caló* involves a massive and systematic substitution of specialized words, often of exotic provenance, for their common equivalents in the standard language.

The Hispanic tradition has enriched American English literature in two ways: first, throughout the nineteenth and twentieth centuries, numerous American writers have shown a special fascination with the Hispanic world in general, and the Spanish borderlands in particular. Their works have helped to propagate large numbers of Spanish loanwords into American English. In the second half of the twentieth century, significant contributions to American English literature have been made by authors of Cuban, Puerto Rican, and Mexican descent. Their works often contain considerable numbers of Spanish words and phrases that their readers are presumed to

know and no doubt penetrate into the language of monolingual English speakers.

The Hispanic presence in the United States shows every sign of continuing the steady growth characteristic of the twentieth century. The already great importance of the Spanish language in the national life of the United States will accordingly be enhanced with each passing decade.

BIBLIOGRAPHY

De Marco, Barbara, and Jerry R. Craddock, eds. *Documenting the Colonial Experience, with Special Regard to Spanish in the American Southwest.* Special Issue, Parts 1–2 of *Romance Philology* 53 (1999–2000).

Kanellos, Nicolás, and Claudio Esteva-Fabregat, eds. *Handbook of Hispanic Cultures in the United States.* 4 vols. Houston, Tex.: Arte Público Press, 1993–1994.

Roca, Ana, ed. *Research on Spanish in the United States: Linguistic Issues and Challenges.* Somerville, Mass.: Cascadilla, 2000.

Rodríguez González, Félix, ed. *Spanish Loanwords in the English Language: A Tendency Towards Hegemony Reversal.* Berlin: Mouton de Gruyter, 1996.

Rudin, Ernst. *Tender Accents of Sound: Spanish in the Chicano Novel in English.* Tempe, Ariz.: Bilingual Press, 1996.

Teschner, Richard V., Garland D. Bills, and Jerry R. Craddock, eds. *Spanish and English of United States Hispanos: A Critical, Annotated, Linguistic Bibliography.* Arlington, Va.: Center for Applied Linguistics, 1975.

Wiegle, Marta, and Peter White. *The Lore of New Mexico.* Publications of the American Folklore Society, New Series. Albuquerque: University of New Mexico Press, 1988.

Jerry R. Craddock

See also **Bilingual Education; Cuban Americans; Hispanic Americans; Mexican Americans; Puerto Ricans in the United States.**

SPEAKEASY, also known as a "blind pig" or a "blind tiger," is an illicit or unlicensed establishment dispensing alcoholic beverages. The speakeasy had been part of the American scene since at least the 1890s, but it reached its heyday after the Eighteenth Amendment took effect in January 1920, ushering in the PROHIBITION era. Though alcohol was officially illegal during Prohibition, bootleggers and distributors of illicit alcohol enjoyed a thriving business serving a public still eager to drink. At the height of their popularity (1924–1933), speakeasies were generally either bars or restaurants to which people gained admission by personal introduction or by presenting a card, usually informally. In social class they ranged from smart restaurants to underworld dens, but whereas before Prohibition, most "respectable" women would not be welcome in a public bar, women as well as men began flocking to speakeasies.

of the House, but in 1789 the House chose a member, Frederick A. C. Muhlenberg, as its first Speaker, and this tradition has continued. The Speaker is usually a senior member of the majority party.

As the leader of the House, the Speaker represents it to outside constituencies, including the president, the Senate, and often the media and the public. The Speaker also serves as the partisan leader of the majority party within the chamber and has come to be regarded as only second in power and importance to the president. Standing behind the vice president in succession to the presidency, several Speakers have been just one step away from the highest office in the land—for example, Sam Rayburn, when Harry S. Truman was without a vice president (1945–1949), and Carl Albert, after the resignation of Vice President Spiro T. Agnew (1973) and again after the resignation of President Richard M. Nixon (1974).

Every two years, at the beginning of each new Congress, the House must select its speaker before it can conduct its business; although the Speaker is elected by the majority of all House members, in practice the House merely ratifies the choice of the majority party. The Speaker's first duty is to preside over the House. The Speaker interprets the rules of the House, and his rulings can be overturned by simple majority vote, though historically this has rarely happened. The Speaker also preserves order, enforces the rules, refers bills and resolutions to the appropriate committees, and prevents dilatory tactics from paralyzing House action.

As the leader of the majority party, the Speaker may use the powers of the office to advance the legislative agenda of the party. The Speaker is influential in determining which bills the House will consider and determines the schedule. The Speaker also places his party's members on committees. The powerful Committee on Rules, which has been called "the arm of the Speaker," sets the rules for debate, including which, if any, amendments may be in order. The Speaker negotiates many internal matters with the minority leader, such as the membership ratio between parties on committees, and the Speaker selects members of conference committees to negotiate differences with the Senate. Henry Clay, Thomas Reed, Joe Cannon, Sam Rayburn, and Newt Gingrich have been among the most influential holders of this office.

Speakeasy. Four men, two sitting on crates, violate Prohibition, like countless others at similar illegal bars all over the country for more than a decade. © CORBIS-BETTMANN

BIBLIOGRAPHY

Allsop, Kenneth. *The Bootleggers: The Story of Chicago's Prohibition Era.* London: Hutchinson, 1968.

Behr, Edward. *Prohibition: Thirteen Years That Changed America.* New York: Arcade, 1996.

Cashman, Sean Dennis. *Prohibition, the Lie of the Land.* New York: Free Press, 1981.

Dumenil, Lynn. *The Modern Temper: American Culture and Society in the 1920s.* New York: Hill and Wang, 1995.

Stanley R. Pillsbury/ D. B.

See also **Crime, Organized; Jazz Age; Women in Public Life, Business, and Professions.**

SPEAKER OF THE HOUSE OF REPRESENTATIVES.

The concept of the Speaker of the U.S. House of Representatives was borrowed from the British House of Commons and some colonial assemblies. The Speaker is the first of only four officers named in the U.S. Constitution: "The House of Representatives shall chuse their Speaker and other Officers . . ." (Article I, Section 2). There is no requirement that the Speaker be a member

BIBLIOGRAPHY

Congressional Quarterly, *Guide to the Congress of the United States.* Washington, D.C.: Congressional Quarterly, 1999.

Davidson, Roger, Susan Webb Hammond, and Raymond Smock. *Masters of the House: Congressional Leadership over Two Centuries.* Boulder, Colo.: Westview Press, 1998.

Peters, Ron M., Jr. ed. *The Speaker: Leadership in the U.S. House of Representatives.* Washington, D.C.: Congressional Quarterly, 1994.

Brian D. Posler

See also **Congress, United States.**

SPECIAL FORCES. As elite, specialized military units, Special Operations Forces (SOF) of each military service have participated in most U.S. conflicts since World War II. Exploiting their unique operational capabilities, SOF units can execute a variety of missions, many entailing the clandestine insertion of SOF by land, air, or sea. SOF most frequently conduct activities such as direct action (raids, ambushes, hostage rescues, and "surgical" strikes); strategic reconnaissance, usually in hostile territory; unconventional warfare, including advising and supporting indigenous insurgent and resistance groups; foreign internal defense (assisting a host nation to defeat insurgency); civil affairs and psychological operations; counterterrorism; humanitarian assistance; and search and rescue operations. The strength of SOF in the active and reserve components of the Army, Navy, and Air Force as of October 2001 was about 43,000, or nearly 2 percent of total U.S. military strength. In recognition of the growing importance of special operations, Congress established a new unified command, the U.S. Special Operations Command (USSOCOM), in 1986 to oversee the doctrine, training, and equipping of all U.S. SOF. Each armed service also has established its own special operations command, which serve as component commands of USSOCOM.

With a strength of about 26,000 in 2001, U.S. Army SOF consist of Special Forces, Rangers, special operations aviation units, civil affairs and psychological operations units, and special operations support units allocated among the Active Army, the Army Reserve, and the Army National Guard. The U.S. Special Forces (USSF) was organized 20 June 1952 at Fort Bragg, North Carolina, as the first permanent unconventional warfare unit in the Army since World War II. Signifying its elite status, USSF was authorized in September 1961 to wear a distinctive green beret, the term "Green Beret" henceforth being synonymous with the USSF.

Under President John F. Kennedy, the USSF's role in counterinsurgency operations, particularly in Southeast Asia, expanded—initially under the auspices of the Central Intelligence Agency and later under U.S. military control. The USSF mobilized Montagnard tribesmen in support of South Vietnam's struggle against the Viet Cong as part of the Civilian Irregular Defense Group program, organizing village defenses and mobile strike forces. Other USSF teams conducted covert cross-border operations as part of the highly secret U.S. Studies and Observation Group. At their peak strength in 1968, more than 3,500 Green Berets were in Vietnam. Green Berets also served in Latin America during the 1960s and, for example, helped Bolivian forces to track down and execute Che Guevara, the Cuban revolutionary, in 1967.

Since the Vietnam War, USSF teams have carried out foreign internal defense training, counterdrug, and humanitarian missions mainly in Latin America and Africa. Together with Rangers and other Army SOF, Special Forces have participated in U.S. operations in Grenada, Panama, Kuwait and Iraq, Somalia, Haiti, and the Balkans. From October 2001 through 2002, Army SOF, joined by Navy and Air Force SOF, have played a significant role in counterterrorist operations in Afghanistan, conducting clandestine reconnaissance missions, advising and assisting anti-Taliban forces, and executing raids and "snatch-and-grab" operations. The First Special Forces Operational Detachment–Delta, or Delta Force, has traditionally conducted highly secret and dangerous counterterrorist, hostage rescue, and other classified operations, often assisted by Rangers and other SOF. The Delta Force took part in the aborted U.S. hostage rescue attempt in Iran in 1980 and in the failed attempt to capture a Somali warlord in Mogadishu in 1993. Civil affairs and psychological operations units are among the most often deployed Army SOF components.

Numbering about 10,000 active and reserve Air Force personnel in 2001, Air Force SOF consist of fixed and rotary wing aircraft units and supporting units whose missions include insertion and extraction, resupply, aerial fire support, air interdiction, force protection, aerial refueling, combat search and rescue, psychological operations, operation and defense of expeditionary airfields, and other specialized missions. Air Force SOF missions often are carried out at night and in adverse weather conditions. During the Cold War, Air Force special operations were conducted in Korea, Tibet, Libya, Cuba, Laos, Vietnam, Cambodia, Iran, Grenada and elsewhere. During the Korean War, Air Force SOF dropped agents behind enemy lines, performed search and rescue missions for downed pilots, conducted psychological warfare and intelligence collection operations, supported partisan warfare, and flew resupply overflights to agents in China and Siberia. Later Air Force SOF were prominent in support of operations in Panama, Saudi Arabia, and Kuwait, in U.S. efforts following the Persian Gulf War to contain Iraq, and in support of U.S. interventions in Somalia, the Balkans, and Afghanistan.

Naval SOF include about 5,000 active and 1,200 reserve personnel organized into SEAL (Sea, Air, Land) Teams, Special Boat Units, and SEAL Delivery Vehicle teams. The SEALs evolved from the Navy's World War II Combat Swimmer Reconnaissance Units, which reconnoitered and cleared beach obstacles to assist amphibious landings, and Navy Underwater Demolition Teams (UDT), or "frogmen," which were organized in 1947 as underwater strike units. In response to President Kennedy's mandate to strengthen American counterinsurgency forces, the Navy formed its first SEAL teams in January 1962, using members of the UDTs. Two SEAL teams, each with a strength of about 200 were activated, one team each assigned to the Atlantic and Pacific Fleets. Approximately 20 SEAL units participated in the Vietnam War, serving as advisers, conducting counterguerrilla operations in the Mekong Delta, and executing covert maritime incursions in North Vietnam to gather intelligence and rescue American prisoners of war. SEALs have taken part in nearly all major Cold War and post–Cold War U.S. military operations through 2002, including the invasion of Grenada, the intervention in Panama (in which four SEALS were killed in action), and the Persian Gulf War, in which SEALs conducted pilot rescue operations, located and disabled mines, carried out sea patrols and deception operations, and executed small raids. Their versatility was again demonstrated in Afghanistan where SEALS, inserted by ship-launched helicopters, were among the first American units to enter that landlocked country in the initial stages of counterterrorist operations.

The Marine Corps has no dedicated SOF units, although a Marine Expeditionary Unit of an infantry battalion and a small air detachment can be trained for special operations as required by circumstances.

BIBLIOGRAPHY

Haas, Michael E. *Apollo's Warriors: United States Air Force Special Operations during the Cold War.* Washington, D.C.: Government Printing Office, 1997.

Hoyt, Edwin P. *Seals at War.* New York: Dell, 1993.

Marquis, Susan L. *Unconventional Warfare: Rebuilding U.S. Special Operations Forces.* Washington, D.C.: Brookings Institute, 1997.

Paddock, Alfred H., Jr. *U.S. Army Special Warfare: Its Origins, Psychological and Unconventional Warfare 1941–1952.* Washington, D.C.: National Defense University Press, 1982.

Stanton, Shelby L. *Green Berets at War: U.S. Army Special Forces in Southeast Asia, 1956–1975.* Novato, Calif.: Presidio Press, 1985.

Vincent H. Demma

See also **Air Force, United States; Army, United States; Marine Corps, United States; Navy, United States.**

SPECIAL INTEREST GROUPS. *See* **Interest Groups.**

SPECIAL PROSECUTORS,

also known as independent counsels, are typically appointed to investigate and prosecute high-profile cases where the ordinary criminal justice machinery cannot be trusted to produce fair results. State and local governments occasionally use special prosecutors. However, throughout American history the most noteworthy special prosecutors have been those appointed to stand in the shoes of the U.S. attorney general, investigating the president or some other high-level executive branch official. In most cases, such an appointment is triggered by a perceived conflict of interest within the Justice Department.

President Ulysses S. Grant appointed a special prosecutor in the 1870s to investigate the Whiskey Ring, a network of whiskey distillers who allegedly conspired to bribe revenue officers and funnel money to government officials, some of whom were close to President Grant.

President Calvin Coolidge appointed two special prosecutors in the 1920s to investigate the Teapot Dome scandal, involving the alleged corrupt leasing of government-owned naval oil reserves by Albert B. Fall, secretary of the interior during the preceding William G. Harding administration.

Subsequently, special prosecutors became a fixture in American government largely due to the Watergate scandal. After President Richard M. Nixon's successful 1972 reelection campaign, burglars linked to the Central Intelligence Agency (CIA) and the White House were charged with breaking into the Democratic National Committee headquarters in the Watergate Hotel. President Nixon was suspected of covering up the break-in. After his attorney general resigned under the cloud of the Watergate scandal, Nixon in the spring of 1973 appointed Elliot Richardson to head the Justice Department, seeking to restore credibility to his shaken administration. Richardson in turn appointed Archibald Cox, a Harvard law professor known for his impeccable integrity, to serve as Watergate special prosecutor. When congressional hearings revealed that President Nixon had installed a taping system in the White House, Cox subpoenaed nine critical tape recordings that would prove or disprove Nixon's complicity in the Watergate cover-up. When the subpoenas were contested, two federal courts ruled in Cox's favor. On the eve of the final deadline for a Supreme Court appeal, Nixon announced he would provide summaries of the tapes but nothing else. The president ordered Attorney General Richardson to fire Cox. Richardson refused and resigned, as did Deputy Attorney General William Ruckelshaus. Finally, Solicitor General Robert Bork carried out the president's order, terminating Cox. In the wake of Cox's firing, in what came to be known as the "Saturday night massacre," a firestorm of public protest erupted. This led to the appointment of a new special prosecutor, Leon Jaworski, followed by the release of dozens of damning tapes and the slow unraveling of the Nixon presidency.

In direct response to Cox's firing, Congress initiated hearings to consider legislation that would create a statutory special prosecutor divorced from the executive branch. Five years of hearings culminated in the Ethics in Government Act of 1978. Under this statute a special three-judge panel of the U.S. Court of Appeals was empowered to appoint neutral prosecutors to investigate alleged criminal wrongdoing in the executive branch in cases where the attorney general might have an actual or potential conflict of interest. Congress later changed the name of this official from special prosecutor to independent counsel, seeking to make clear that this appointee was meant to investigate impartially and to prosecute only where appropriate rather than to act as an aggressive prosecutor bent on convicting his or her target.

Over the controversial twenty-year life span of the independent counsel law, more than twenty separate independent counsel investigations were conducted, some branching out into multiple areas of criminal inquiry. No presidency was immune from its reach. Independent counsel investigations surfaced during the Jimmy Carter, Ronald Reagan, George H. W. Bush, and Bill Clinton administrations.

The Iran-Contra investigation stirred up particular controversy, spanning seven years during the Reagan and Bush administrations. Headed by former judge Lawrence Walsh, this criminal probe involved a scandal in which the government secretly sold arms to Iran and diverted the profits to aid Nicaraguan rebels after Congress prohibited such activity. Walsh obtained a number of indictments and convictions. However, key convictions of Admiral John Poindexter and Lieutenant Colonel Oliver North were overturned on appeal. President Bush, who was implicated in the scandal but never charged with wrongdoing, pardoned the remaining principals.

Opponents of the independent counsel law, many of them Republicans critical of the lengthy and expensive (over $48 million) Iran-Contra probe, argued that the law was fundamentally flawed and had created a monstrous prosecutor unaccountable to any branch of government. In *Morrison v. Olson* (1989) the Supreme Court rejected a variety of constitutional attacks, upholding the indepen-

Kenneth W. Starr. The controversial special prosecutor whose multimillion-dollar investigations culminated in the impeachment and acquittal of President Bill Clinton. ARCHIVE PHOTOS, INC.

dent counsel statute. Yet the drumbeat for the law's demise continued. In 1992, at the end of the Bush administration, Congress refused to reauthorize the independent counsel statute, allowing it to lapse.

In early 1994, Attorney General Janet Reno appointed her own ad hoc special prosecutor, the respected New York attorney Robert Fiske, to head the Whitewater investigation. This scandal involved a failed Arkansas land deal of the 1980s in which President Bill Clinton and his wife, Hillary Rodham Clinton, had invested. Ironically, President Clinton and Reno supported a renewal of the independent counsel law, prompting Congress to reenact it. The special three-judge panel overseeing the Whitewater investigation, believing that reappointment of the attorney general's ad hoc prosecutor would taint the process, unexpectedly replaced Fiske with the more controversial Kenneth W. Starr. Starr, a conservative Republican who had served with distinction on the U.S. Court of Appeals and later as solicitor general during the Bush administration, was viewed by some, particularly Democrats, as politically driven. During Starr's tenure, the Whitewater land-deal investigation expanded into a series of unrelated matters, growing in cost (over $40 million) and escalating in controversy. In 1998, Starr's office received authorization from Attorney General Reno to investigate whether or not President Clinton had committed perjury in denying a sexual affair with the White House intern Monica Lewinsky during his civil deposition in *Clinton v. Jones*, a sexual harassment suit filed by the one-time Arkansas employee Paula Jones.

The Monica Lewinsky affair bloomed into a raging scandal that bitterly divided the nation. After Clinton again denied the affair in front of a federal grand jury, Republicans rallied around Starr, who issued to Congress the lengthy Starr Report, setting forth eleven potential impeachable offenses committed by the president. Enraged Democrats accused Starr of conducting a puritanical witch-hunt fueled by partisan political motives. Relying almost exclusively on the Starr Report, the Republican-dominated House of Representatives voted to impeach President Clinton. After a draining Senate trial, during which the American public grew increasingly weary, the senators voted along party lines to acquit President Clinton in February 1999.

A month later, Congress commenced hearings to debate reauthorizing the independent counsel statute, which was scheduled to "sunset" in June 1999. In an unusual twist, both Reno and Starr publicly opposed reenactment of the special prosecutor law, concluding in hindsight that it had been an unmitigated disaster. Swamped by criticism from both sides of the political aisle, the independent counsel law expired on 30 June 1999.

Following the death of the independent counsel statute, Congress continued to debate possible replacement legislation to deal with scandals in the executive branch without reaching a consensus. Instead, the attorney general and the Justice Department continued to promulgate regulations by which they hire and fire their own special prosecutors as needed, following the ad hoc Watergate model. These special prosecutors, however, remained attached to the executive branch. Thus, they lacked the aura of neutrality envisioned by the ill-fated special prosecutor law of the 1970s that was designed to restore public trust in government after the devastating experience of Watergate.

BIBLIOGRAPHY

Doyle, James. *Not Above the Law: The Battles of Watergate Prosecutors Cox and Jaworski.* New York: Morrow, 1977.

Eastland, Terry. *Ethics, Politics, and the Independent Counsel: Executive Power, Executive Vice, 1789–1989.* Washington, D.C.: National Legal Center for the Public Interest, 1989.

Gormley, Ken. *Archibald Cox: Conscience of a Nation.* Reading, Mass.: Addison-Wesley, 1997.

Harriger, Katy J. *Independent Justice: The Federal Special Prosecutor in American Politics.* Lawrence: University Press of Kansas, 1992.

Kutler, Stanley I. *The Wars of Watergate: The Last Crisis of Richard M. Nixon.* New York: Knopf, 1990.

Schmidt, Susan, and Michael Weisskopf. *Truth at Any Cost: Ken Starr and the Unmaking of Bill Clinton.* New York: HarperCollins, 2000.

Stewart, James B. *Blood Sport: The President and His Adversaries.* New York: Simon and Schuster, 1996.

Walsh, Lawrence E. *Firewall: The Iran-Contra Conspiracy and Cover-Up.* New York: Norton, 1997.

Ken Gormley

See also **Clinton Scandals; Iran-Contra Affair; Teapot Dome Oil Scandal; Watergate; Whiskey Ring.**

SPECIE CIRCULAR. Consistent with President Andrew Jackson's effort to make specie ("in coin") the chief form of money in circulation, the Treasury Department issued several circulars. The first, issued November 1834, ordered collectors of customs and receivers of public money to refuse any form of money not described by an 1816 congressional resolution, particularly drafts of branches of the BANK OF THE UNITED STATES. In April 1835, a second circular directed collectors to accept only gold and silver for all payments of less than ten dollars. The third, of July 1836, directed that nothing but gold or silver should be accepted as payment for public land. By curbing land speculation, the specie circular of 1836 probably hastened the panic of 1837.

BIBLIOGRAPHY

Rousseau, Peter L. *Jacksonian Monetary Policy, Specie Flows, and the Panic of 1837.* Cambridge, Mass.: National Bureau of Economic Research, 2000.

Erik McKinley Eriksson / A. R.

See also **Currency and Coinage; Financial Panics; Hard Money; Legal Tender; Money; Specie Payments, Suspension and Resumption of.**

SPECIE PAYMENTS, SUSPENSION AND RESUMPTION OF. Under a system of specie payments, it is required by law or custom that fiduciary money, usually in the form of bank notes or government paper money issues, be redeemed at par and upon request of the issuing bank or the Treasury in metallic coin. The founding fathers remembered with distaste the paper-money inflation of the Revolution and the excesses of some of the states during the Confederation. The decision for a specie standard of value was therefore implicit in the constitutional grant of power to Congress "to coin Money" and "regulate the Value thereof," and that the states refrain from emitting bills of credit or making anything but gold or silver a legal tender.

The maintenance of specie payments in the United States was difficult from the outset. In 1792, Congress adopted a bimetallic standard of value under which the dollar was defined in terms of both silver and gold. By adopting the then prevailing market ratio of 15 to 1 as the mint ratio, Alexander Hamilton hoped to keep both metals in monetary circulation. Unfortunately, soon after coinage began, the international market price of silver began to fall and gold was hoarded or exported to Europe. It even proved difficult to keep the newly coined silver dollars in circulation because they were accepted at a higher value in the Spanish possessions. In 1834, an attempt was made to bring gold back into monetary circulation by reducing the gold content of the dollar from 24.7 to 23.2 grains while maintaining the silver dollar at 371.25 grains. This meant a new mint ratio of silver to gold of 16 to 1. This ratio undervalued silver, since the international market ratio of the time was about 15.75 to 1. Consequently, silver tended to disappear from circulation while an increasing number of gold coins were minted. Essentially, after 1834 and until 1934, the gold coin reigned as the dominant standard of value in the United States.

America's usually unfavorable balance of trade made it difficult to maintain specie payments during the nineteenth century. In addition, wars and economic crises accelerated the exportation of specie in payment for goods. Also, until 1864, when the National Banking System was established, it was difficult to control the paper bank-note issues of the state-chartered banks. Encouraged by a Supreme Court decision exempting them from the constitutional prohibition against the state issue of bills of credit, the state-chartered banks proceeded to issue bank notes far in excess of their ability to maintain specie payments. In wartime, moreover, the federal government met its needs for revenue through the issue of irredeemable paper money.

In 1814–1815, in response to the unregulated credit expansion of the banks and wartime issue of Treasury notes, most of the banks and branches of the U.S. Treasury suspended specie payments altogether. Coin payments were resumed in February 1817. Soon, another great credit expansion fostered by the policies of the second Bank of the United States culminated in the panic of 1819, and a severe depression during which most banks in the South and West refused to pay specie.

The years 1830–1837 saw solid economic development as well as feverish speculation in land. This eventually led to the panic of 1837 and a nationwide suspension of specie payments. Factors involved in the suspension included a doubling of bank circulation between 1830 and 1837; Andrew Jackson's Specie Circular of 11 July 1836, which halted the land boom; and the distribution of a government surplus, which removed much hard money from the less-developed regions of the country. More importantly, large exports of specie followed the cessation of European investment. Partial resumption was achieved prematurely in 1838. After a premature resumption in 1838, continuing outflows of metallic coin brought another suspension in 1839. Specie payments did not resume until 1842.

The cycle repeated itself in the 1850s. Heavy domestic and foreign investment fueled the rapid expansion of railroads and industry. State bank-note issues increased, and speculation was prevalent. In 1857, capital imports from Europe slackened and the flow of California gold decreased. Money became tight. On 24 August, the failure of the Ohio Life Insurance and Trust Company precipitated a panic in NEW YORK CITY that spread to the rest of the country. Specie payments were suspended. They were resumed six months later.

The most serious deviation from the specie standard occurred in the years 1862–1879. As the Union's military situation deteriorated, precious metals seemed the only secure medium of value. The hoarding and exportation of specie forced the banks and the government to suspend gold payments on 30 December 1861. Also contributing to the crisis was the failure of the Secretary of the Treasury, Salmon P. Chase, to recommend drastic increases in taxes and his use of demand Treasury notes, a form of paper money.

In February 1862, the government began issuing U.S. notes, better known as "greenbacks." These notes were legal tender, and, by 1865, had been issued to the amount of $431 million. While the greenbacks caused no interruption in specie payments, the failure of Secretary of the Treasury Hugh McCulloch's contraction program after the CIVIL WAR made resumption very difficult. Powerful economic groups—namely, creditors—opposed the greenback because of its inflationary effect. The obvious solution would have been a devaluation of the gold content of the dollar. Instead, Congress opted to let the country's economy grow up to the currency supply. On 14 January 1875, Congress passed the RESUMPTION ACT, which provided for coin payments to be resumed on 1 January 1879.

Despite the FREE SILVER agitation of the late nineteenth century, the United States adhered to the GOLD STANDARD. Conservative, hard money presidents rebuffed attempts by western and southern agrarians to restore silver to its ancient monetary function. Such measures as the BLAND-ALLISON ACT of 1878 and the SHERMAN SILVER PURCHASE ACT of 1890 simply provided a subsidy to the silver mine owners of the West. The defeat of William Jennings Bryan in 1896 effectively squelched the silver movement, and the Gold Standard Act of 1900 legally placed the nation's money on the monometallic basis, *de facto* since 1879.

Domestic hoarding and exportation continued to wreak havoc on specie policies through the turn of the century. The Treasury encountered difficulties in maintaining gold payments in 1893 and 1907. Unsound bank investments also contributed to the panic of 1907. The government deviated from the gold standard shortly after the United States entered WORLD WAR I. Large gold exports seemed to threaten the base of the monetary and credit structure. On 7 September and 12 October 1917, President Woodrow Wilson placed an embargo on exports of coin and bullion. These restrictions were removed in June 1919.

The economic cataclysm of the 1930s marked the end of a legitimately defined specie standard of value in the United States. The 1929 stock market crash precipitated more than 5,000 bank failures in three years. When England abandoned the gold standard in September 1931, pressure to follow suit mounted in the United States. In the two weeks preceding the inauguration of President Franklin D. Roosevelt on 4 March 1933, the Federal Reserve banks lost more than $400 million in gold, bringing the reserve down to almost the legal minimum. Several states had already declared banking "holidays" when Roosevelt, on 6 March, issued an executive order closing all banks for four days and prohibiting them from exporting, paying out, or allowing the withdrawal of specie. By the end of March, most banks had been allowed to reopen, but specie payments were not resumed. By further executive orders issued in April 1933, the break with the gold standard was made more complete. No person or institution was permitted to hold gold or gold certificates. Roosevelt also placed an embargo on all international transactions in gold, except under license issued by the secretary of the Treasury. By a joint resolution on 5 June, Congress declared void the "gold clause" in government bonds and private obligations. For the first time, the United States had deliberately abandoned the gold standard *de jure*.

After fluctuating in value in international money markets for nearly two years, the value of the dollar was finally stabilized by the GOLD RESERVE ACT and another presidential order in January 1934. The new dollar was defined as 13.71 grains of fine gold, a devaluation to 59.06 percent of its former value. On this basis, Secretary Henry Morgenthau announced the Treasury's willingness to buy and

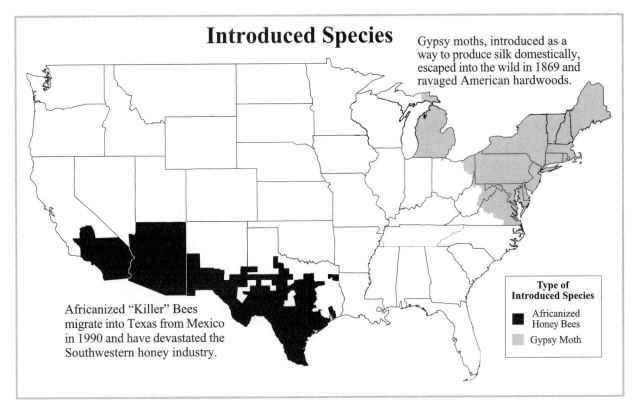

Introduced Species

Gypsy moths, introduced as a way to produce silk domestically, escaped into the wild in 1869 and ravaged American hardwoods.

Africanized "Killer" Bees migrate into Texas from Mexico in 1990 and have devastated the Southwestern honey industry.

Type of Introduced Species
- ■ Africanized Honey Bees
- ▨ Gypsy Moth

sell gold at the new rate of $35 per ounce. It now became possible to obtain gold bullion for making international payments, but domestically the country continued on an irredeemable paper standard, which made gold holdings by citizens illegal.

This partial (some called it "bastardized") gold standard endured for thirty-seven years. Operating under a favorable balance of payments, the United States amassed a gold reserve amounting to more than $24 billion in 1949. After that time, deficits in the international balance reduced the gold stock until it amounted to only about $10 billion by 1971. The continuing deterioration of the balance of payments and the threat to the gold stock impelled President Richard Nixon, on 15 August 1971, to order that the Treasury cease all purchases and sales of gold. As of the year 2000, the dollar was not maintained either at home or abroad at any fixed value in terms of gold; it is uncertain whether gold will regain a place in the monetary system of the nation.

BIBLIOGRAPHY

Friedman, Milton, and Anna Jacobson Schwartz. *The Great Contraction, 1929–1933*. Princeton, N.J.: Princeton University Press, 1965.

Glasner, David, ed. *Business Cycles and Depressions: An Encyclopedia*. New York: Garland, 1997.

Huston, James L. *The Panic of 1857 and the Coming of the Civil War*. Baton Rouge: Louisiana State University Press, 1987.

Kindleberger, Charles P. *Manias, Panics, and Crashes: A History of Financial Crises*. New York: Basic Books, 1978, 1989; Wiley, 1996, 2000.

McSeveney, Samuel T. *The Politics of Depression: Political Behavior in the Northeast, 1893–1896*. New York: Oxford University Press, 1972.

Schweikart, Larry. *Banking in the American South from the Age of Jackson to Reconstruction*. Baton Rouge: Louisiana State University Press, 1987.

Unger, Irwin. *The Greenback Era: A Social and Political History of American Finance, 1865–1879*. Princeton, N.J.: Princeton University Press, 1964.

Wicker, Elmus. *The Banking Panics of the Great Depression*. Cambridge, U.K.; New York: Cambridge University Press, 1996.

*Robert P. Sharkey/*A. R.

See also **Bimetallism; Currency and Coinage; Federal Reserve System; Financial Panics; Greenbacks; Money; Specie Circular.**

SPECIES, INTRODUCED. Introduced species have become a significant ecological problem in the United States and elsewhere. As humans settled in North America over the past fifteen thousand years, they brought with them a variety of species novel to the environment. They intentionally brought many introduced, or exotic, species, such as wheat, potatoes, cattle, pigs, and horses. Many species, however, came uninvited, traveling in the holds of ships or planes, hitching rides on imported produce, or escaping from captivity. Both intentional and unintentional introductions can leave unforeseen and destructive economic and ecological effects. Although most introduced species are poorly adapted to a novel ecosystem and die out, some thrive. Arriving in an ecosystem that evolved without them, introduced species frequently have no predators. Native species may not have the defenses necessary to ward off a novel predator, and introduced species can outcompete native species and drive them to extinction or change an ecosystem by altering relationships within it. At the end of the twentieth century, the United States had thousands of introduced species, some of which the Department of Agriculture estimated were the primary factor in the population decline of approximately 225 of the nation's 660 endangered or threatened species.

The results of species introductions are often dramatic. Introduced species have devastated the ecosystems of Hawaii, which evolved in isolation. Since the arrival of Polynesians one thousand years ago and Europeans two hundred years ago, many of the islands' native plant, bird, and insect species have become extinct because of competition and predation by rats, cats, sheep, goats, and other introduced organisms. In the 1990s the number of introduced species of plants on the islands was triple the number of native plants.

Many introduced species, intentional and not, have been insects that wrought large-scale havoc. In the nineteenth century, merchants imported the gypsy moth caterpillar to the United States in an effort to produce domestic silk. Moths escaped in 1869, spread throughout the country, and continue to cause widespread damage to hardwood forests throughout North America. In 1956 an African species of honeybee that had been imported into Brazil escaped from captivity, established colonies, and hybridized with the European species of honeybee (itself introduced). In 1990 Africanized honeybees began migrating north and crossed into Texas, prompting the Department of Agriculture to predict substantial negative effects on U.S. agriculture. One of the most celebrated cases of an introduced species causing economic damage was the unintentional introduction of the Mediterranean fruit fly, or Medfly, in the 1970s in California. Imported on foreign produce, these small flies caused widespread fruit and vegetable damage.

Other types of species can also be quite disruptive. In the 1990s the zebra mussel began causing widespread economic and ecological disruption. Believed to have been released from the ballast of a European tanker in the Great Lakes in 1988, the mussel population exploded, displacing native mollusks, blocking water pipes and dam outlets, disrupting fisheries, and destroying native aquatic ecosystems. The cost to control them has run well into the billions of dollars, and the urgency of the situation provoked Congress to pass the Nonindigenous Aquatic Nuisance Prevention and Control Act of 1990.

BIBLIOGRAPHY

Drewett, John. "Aliens Not Wanted Here." *New Scientist* 151, 2047 (14 September 1996): 48.

Jones, Clive G., and John H. Lawton, eds. *Linking Species and Ecosystems.* New York: Chapman and Hall, 1995.

Simberloff, Daniel, and Strong, Donald R. "Exotic Species Seriously Threaten Our Environment." *Chronicle of Higher Education* 47 (8 September 2000): B20.

David W. Cash / D. B.

See also **Agriculture, Department of; Endangered Species; Environmental Movement; Environmental Protection Agency.**

SPEECH CODES.   *See* **Group Libel Laws.**

SPEED LIMITS.   In 1973 Congress responded to an oil shortage facing the United States and other countries by instituting a national maximum speed limit of 55 miles per hour (mph). A serious conflict with the Organization of Petroleum Exporting Countries (OPEC) had resulted in a 130 percent increase in the price of oil and eventually

Speed Limit. A sign—and a gentle reminder—on Interstate 5, part of a gasoline-conservation program by both Oregon and Washington. NATIONAL ARCHIVES AND RECORDS ADMINISTRATION

an oil embargo. Prior to 1973, speed limits were set by the individual states, and regulating such safety matters was not considered part of federal jurisdiction. The federal government's only means of enforcing the national speed limit was to direct the Department of Transportation to withhold highway funding from states that did not adopt the 55 mph maximum.

While the speed limit was signed into law by President Richard Nixon to save fuel, many in the public and the government soon recognized that it also saved lives. Studies documented that the higher the speed at which a car traveled, the greater the risk of serious injury or death in the event of a crash. Nevertheless, many Americans were critical of the new law. Some considered the speed limit an unreasonable government restriction on their individual liberty. Others argued that the 55 mph limit was an arbitrary and artificial designation that turned most Americans into law breakers. Opponents of the speed limit also argued that many of the nation's highways, especially in the West, were built for cars to drive at a faster speed than 55 mph. Underlying the debate was the question of whether the federal government rather than the states should set speed limits. As a result of these controversies, in 1987 Congress amended the law to allow states to increase speed limits on rural interstates to 65 mph.

In November 1995, President Bill Clinton signed legislation that returned the jurisdiction for setting speed limits back to the states. This act, which eliminated the national speed limit of 55 mph, passed the Senate by a vote of 63 to 35. States were permitted to raise the speed limits as of 8 December 1995. By 2002, some states had still not changed the speed limit on urban interstates, but most had raised the maximum speed limit to 65 or 70 mph in rural areas.

BIBLIOGRAPHY

Leaf, W. A., and D. F. Preusser. *Literature Review on Vehicle Travel Speeds and Pedestrian Injuries*, publication of the National Highway Traffic Safety Administration, U.S. Department of Transportation. Springfield, Va.: National Technical Information Services, 1999.

Rask, Mark. *American Autobahn: The Road to an Interstate Freeway with No Speed Limit*. Minneapolis, Minn.: Vanguard Non-Fiction Books, 1999.

Shira M. Diner

See also **Automobile Safety; Oil Crises.**

SPELLING BEE. The spelling bee began as a teaching device traditionally employed in American schools. Initially, educators erroneously assumed that spelling proficiency indicated general intellectual capacity. During the nineteenth century, students frequently spelled out loud, competing for the honor of being the best speller in the class; candidates attempted to spell words submitted by an examiner. By the 1840s, communities in the Midwest held spelling matches as part of evening entertainment, and the widespread popularity of the game grew in the West. The term "spelling bee" was first used in Edward Eggleston's *The Hoosier Schoolmaster* (1871). Like the quilting bee, spinning bee, or husking bee, the term "spelling bee" reflects the social nature of the event. Although the popularity of the game declined with the advent of the progressive education movement and the subsequent de-emphasis of spelling and rote learning in general, local communities still supported the enterprise. In 1925 the *Louisville Courier-Journal* sponsored the first national spelling bee. Since then, local communities sponsor individual students to send on to the national event, although no event was held during the war years of 1943, 1944, and 1945.

BIBLIOGRAPHY

Monaghan, E. Jennifer. *A Common Heritage: Noah Webster's Blue-Back Speller*. Hamden, Conn.: Archon Books, 1983.

Nietz, John A. *Old Textbooks: Spelling, Grammar, Reading, Arithmetic, Geography, American History, Civil Government, Physiology, Penmanship, Art, Music, As Taught in the Common Schools from Colonial Days to 1900*. Pittsburgh, Pa.: University of Pittsburgh Press, 1961.

*Harry R. Warfel/*H. S.

See also **Education; Intelligence Tests.**

SPIES are individuals who covertly collect information otherwise not readily available. HUMINT (overt and covert human intelligence) has drawn much public and scholarly attention, although TECHINT (technical intelligence, such as communications, signals, electronics, and image intelligence) is the mainstay of information gathered by intelligence communities today. Particularly in the twentieth century, intelligence collection by individuals constituted only a fraction of the information collected by intelligence gathering agencies, and spies were in most cases considered a last resort to obtain pivotal information.

Revolutionary Period

U.S. history is rich with spies but not with effective intelligence organizations, even though the first espionage network was created before the United States declared independence. The Committees of Safety and the Committees of Correspondence established in the colonies served as intelligence and counterintelligence agencies. They prevented the infiltration of patriot circles by loyalists, broke the code of enciphered British messages, and provided information about impending British activities against the Patriots before the first shot was fired in this conflict. During the Revolutionary War, intelligence facilitated the American victory in more than one way.

George Washington, then commander of the Continental Army, employed spies, relied on intelligence his female and male agents provided, and engaged in deception and disinformation. One of Washington's agents,

Nathan Hale, became the most famous patriot spy of the Revolutionary War. Posing as an art teacher, Hale infiltrated British-controlled Long Island. Without contacts among the local population, no means of communication, and scanty logistics, however, his ill-prepared mission ended in his capture and execution. Many other less renowned agents who helped the revolutionary cause provided a wealth of valuable information to Washington. Posing as loyalists, these were merchants, innkeepers, servants, and farmers who lived and worked where British troops were stationed. They had legitimate reason to be in places where information about troop movements, supplies, and morale could be collected and then forwarded to the Continental Army. Information provided by spies, and particularly by small intelligence cells working behind enemy lines, proved pivotal in a large number of military engagements during the war.

The most notorious spy working for the British during the Revolutionary War was Benedict Arnold. A "walk-in," he defected to the British because of dissatisfaction with being passed over for promotion and because of greed. In 1780 he offered to betray West Point for £20,000 sterling. When his British contact, Major John André, was caught with incriminating documents, Arnold fled on a British ship. Made a brigadier general, he then served on the British side to defeat a cause he had once ardently supported.

Despite Washington's reliance on spies, no organizational structure for intelligence collection was set up after 1783. This did not preclude the United States from using intelligence to pursue its expansion across the continent. A broad definition of the term spy would include Meriwether Lewis and William Clark, for example, a more narrow one the Native American scouts employed by the U.S. Army and the Hispanic agents during the war with Mexico (1846–1848). Although the Civil War would have provided optimal terrain for espionage—with a large number of potential agents in place knowing the habits, speaking the language, and with reasons to be on location—spies were used less than during the Revolution. The most illustrious spy of that period is Belle Boyd, who provided occasional intelligence for Confederate generals Thomas J. "Stonewall" Jackson and Turner Ashby and who made a living telling her story after the conflict.

Intelligence Organizations

When the United States turned to maritime commercial expansion after the Civil War, it became obvious that information about other nations and their naval forces was skimpy at best. The Office of Naval Intelligence was created in 1882 to address this lack of information, and the army followed in 1885 by establishing the Military Information Division (MID—later G-2 of the War Department General Staff). In 1888 service attachés joined American missions abroad and collected information on foreign armies and navies. Intelligence collected by these offices and by individual sources played a part in American territorial acquisitions and military engagements, particularly in the case of Hawaii, the Panama Canal, and the Spanish-American War of 1898.

During World War I a spy-scare ran high in the United States, particularly after German-paid activities committed by saboteurs and strikers had surfaced, and even President Woodrow Wilson feared that the United States was infested with German spies. The Federal Bureau of Investigation (FBI) was charged with counterintelligence operations in the United States, but at the front in Europe, American combat intelligence had to rely mostly on British and French sources. The increased use of communications technology, beginning with the telegraph, shifted the emphasis of intelligence collection to technical intelligence, to cryptography and code breaking. Although the Americans were latecomers to this field, they created a valuable Code and Cipher Section within the MID. After the war had ended in 1918, this section was the nucleus of the so-called "American Black Chamber," headed by Herbert O. Yardley from 1919 until it was closed down in 1929 by President Herbert Hoover's secretary of state, Henry L. Stimson, who strongly disapproved of spying.

Thus, when Japanese forces bombed Pearl Harbor on 7 December 1941 the United States had been virtually without warning from its intelligence services. Some Japanese codes had been broken, but understaffed and ill-coordinated intelligence services within different departments, reliance on communications intelligence, and the lack of HUMINT from Japan had prevented the United States from learning about the imminent attack. Communications intelligence and the U.S. Navy's success in breaking Japanese codes, code-named MAGIC, did play an important part during World War II, as did the information the British Allies supplied after breaking the encryption, code-named ULTRA, used by the Germans on their Enigma cipher machines. But the United States also took steps to create a centralized agency to provide, coordinate, and analyze intelligence. To this end, President Franklin D. Roosevelt formed the Office of the Coordinator of Information on 11 July 1941. However, that attempt failed, and in June 1942, the Office of Strategic Services (OSS) was created, with William J. Donovan as director. With stations around the globe, it collected overt information, ran thousands of agents, and conducted covert operations behind enemy lines and in occupied territory. One of the most efficient station chiefs was Allen W. Dulles in Bern, who had contacts with the German resistance.

The OSS was disbanded at the end of World War II but was soon succeeded by the Central Intelligence Group, created by President Harry S. Truman in January 1946. While the OSS had been under the direction and supervision of the Joint Chiefs of Staff, the director of central intelligence was head of a civilian agency reporting to a National Intelligence Authority composed of the secretaries of navy, war, and state. With the passage of the

National Security Act of 1947, the Central Intelligence Agency was established. Under the supervision of the president, it was to provide the National Security Council with national and strategic intelligence. The deputy director for plans (later deputy director for operations) of the CIA was to be responsible for the clandestine collection of intelligence, a task that proved to be of major importance during the Cold War. Running spy nets in close-knit societies such as the Soviet Union, North Korea, and Cuba, however, turned out to be quite difficult. Because internal security and counterintelligence in these countries was usually operating very well, the United States dramatically increased its TECHINT capabilities to make up for the lack of HUMINT. The photographing of missile launch sites by U-2 planes during the Cuban Missile Crisis clearly demonstrated the advantages of technical intelligence. However, the Bay of Pigs fiasco proved the need for intelligence collected by spies, who might have made clear that the large-scale Cuban resistance movement the CIA counted on for the success of its invasion did not exist. The main targets of American intelligence since the Soviet Union broke apart in the late 1980s are so-called "rogue states" and international terrorism, both of which are quite difficult to penetrate. Here, the United States increasingly has to rely on sharing of clandestine information, particularly within the North Atlantic community.

Spies who operate successfully, with a few exceptions, are unlikely to reveal themselves. But those that have been detected provide a good indication why an individual may choose to take up a dangerous occupation that might end in execution or at least a long prison sentence. Some have ideological reasons, such as Ethel and Julius Rosenberg, arrested in 1950, who provided the Soviet Union with information about nuclear weapons, or Jonathan Pollard, a U.S. Navy intelligence officer with high-level security clearance, who gave secret information to Israel. Others were blackmailed or lured into spying, or they did it because they fell in love with a spy. In many instances, as in the case of Benedict Arnold, greed provided a driving force: Charged with providing secret information to the Soviet Union, John A. Walker Jr. ran a lucrative family spy ring for nearly twenty years. Aldrich Ames, a CIA career official arrested in 1994, revealed to the Soviet Union a large number of covert operations and agents, many of whom were later executed, for more than $2 million. And the first case of espionage in the twenty-first century in the United States has a similar background: Robert P. Hanssen, an FBI agent working in counterintelligence, was arrested in February 2001. From 1985 on, for more than $1 million in cash and diamonds, he had given away the identities of U.S. spies in the Soviet Union, information on highly classified eavesdropping technology, and nuclear war plans.

BIBLIOGRAPHY

Ameringer, Charles D. *U.S. Foreign Intelligence: The Secret Side of American History.* Lexington, Mass.: Lexington Books, 1990.

Bakeless, John. *Turncoats, Traitors, and Heroes: Espionage in the American Revolution.* 1959. New York: Da Capo, 1998.

Dulles, Allen W. *The Craft of Intelligence.* New York: Harper and Row, 1963.

Melton, H. Keith. *The Ultimate SPY Book.* New York: DK, 1996.

O'Toole, George J. A. *The Encyclopedia of American Intelligence and Espionage: From the Revolutionary War to the Present.* New York: Facts on File, 1988.

Polmar, Norman, and Thomas B. Allen. *Spy Book: The Encyclopedia of Espionage.* New York: Random House, 1998.

Michael Wala

See also **Central Intelligence Agency; Intelligence, Military and Strategic; Office of Strategic Services.**

SPIRIT LAKE MASSACRE. On 8 March 1857, a small band of Wahpekute Dakota warriors led by Inkpaduta (Scarlet Point) began attacking white settlements on the Okoboji lakes in northwestern Iowa. The winter of 1856–1857 was unusually severe and both white settlers and Dakota people alike suffered from hunger. While this might have contributed to increased tensions between the two groups, Inkpaduta's attacks were motivated by a desire for retaliation for the previous crimes of murder and rape perpetrated by whites against his own family members in addition to a desire to resist the invasion of his homeland by white foreigners. In all, thirty-two men, women, and children were killed and four women were taken captive. Two of the captives were killed and the other two were eventually released weeks later through mediation and ransoming. Though only one death occurred at Spirit Lake, this event became known as the Spirit Lake Massacre.

In an attempt to capture Inkpaduta, on 9 May 1857, Commissioner of Indian Affairs James Denver issued instructions for Dakota annuities to be withheld until Inkpaduta and his men were delivered to white authorities for punishment. This order violated U.S. treaty obligations to the Dakotas, leading to increased hostilities against whites and nearly causing an immediate war. The tactic proved unsuccessful and, though Inkpaduta was never betrayed by his fellow Dakotas and delivered to white authorities, annuities were finally paid in September 1857. Inkpaduta continued his fierce resistance to white invasion and later participated in the Battle of Little Bighorn. Today he remains a symbol of resistance and freedom to Dakota people.

BIBLIOGRAPHY

Folwell, William Watts. *A History of Minnesota*, Volume II. St. Paul: Minnesota Historical Society Press, 1961.

Seaboy, David. Oral historical account provided during discussion at "The Dakota–U.S. War of 1862: The Seventh Generation" Conference, Southwest State University, Marshall, Minnesota, 4 April 2002.

Teakle, Thomas. *The Spirit Lake Massacre.* Iowa City: State Historical Society of Iowa, 1918.

Angela Cavender Wilson

See also **Sioux.**

SPIRITS INDUSTRY.   The fermenting and distilling of fruits and grains into alcoholic beverages was a practice that the first American settlers brought with them to the new colonies. In the colonial period, Americans made several kinds of beverages, including whiskey, cider, brandy, and most popular of all, rum. Rum was manufactured from imported molasses. Although colonial authorities at times attempted to control consumption, distilled spirits were widely accepted and enjoyed. Distillation was decentralized in rural settings, so mass production was not characteristic of the spirits industry.

The Nineteenth Century: Domination and the Onset of Decline

In the late 1700s and early 1800s whiskey replaced rum as the spirited beverage of choice among Americans. Whiskey, which was distilled from grain, was not only cheaper—especially when turbulent foreign relations made it more expensive and difficult to import molasses—but was also a homegrown product and therefore a symbol of America's newly won independence. Considering the high per capita consumption during much of the nineteenth century—nearly five gallons per person in the early decades—whiskey can be considered America's national beverage during the 1800s.

Although whiskey was made in small distilleries across the new nation, it was a specialty of Scotch-Irish immigrants who settled in western Pennsylvania and then the Kentucky region. Kentucky soon became the center of whiskey production. Distillers there prided themselves on the manufacture of bourbon, which differed from other whiskey because it was made from corn, or corn mixed with other grains, instead of from rye or barley. Furthermore, the distinctive taste of bourbon, which was produced mainly in Bourbon County, Kentucky, derived from the charred wooden barrels in which it matured.

Despite its popularity, whiskey was at the same time often condemned. The TEMPERANCE MOVEMENT, which emerged in the 1820s, targeted spirits, not beer or wine. Historically, Americans have viewed beer and wine as benign in comparison with whiskey and other spirits, which they have regarded as intoxicating and potentially harmful. This explains why taxes on spirits have always been higher than on other alcoholic beverages. Whiskey distillers have often objected to the high tax on their product. In the WHISKEY REBELLION of 1794, farmer-distillers in Pennsylvania objected to the high tax on whiskey and staged a violent revolt. Although the rebellion was quelled, protest was effective enough so that in 1802 the federal government acknowledged that the tax was uncollectable and repealed it. Except for a brief period, the federal tax on whiskey was not reinstituted until the Civil War.

In the second half of the nineteenth century, the whiskey industry experienced overproduction and intense competition, which led to price wars and concentration. A small number of huge distilleries in Peoria, Illinois, had come to rival Kentucky's whiskey industry. The Peoria-based Whiskey Trust tried to control production and raise prices but without much success. By the end of the 1800s, many Americans were switching to beer, which had become cheaper to brew and was less burdened by taxes. It has been estimated that as much as one-third of all whiskey was produced by moonshiners trying to avoid taxes. Another reason whiskey was more expensive than beer was that in the 1860s Congress had created a bonded period that let distillers store their product tax-free until they found buyers. That gave the distillers an incentive to store their whiskey longer, which improved its quality and justified a higher price.

The Twentieth Century: Projecting an Image

Some firms were interested in maintaining high quality standards for their product and fostering public trust in the industry. They turned to federal government officials for assistance. The government responded with the Bottled-in-Bond Act of 1897, the Pure Food and Drug Act of 1906, and the Taft decision of 1909, all of which outlined definitions and standards for whiskey. Afterward, the industry experienced considerable consolidation, with the 613 distilleries of 1909 reduced to only 34 in 1919. The spirits industry was a particular target of the temperance movement into the twentieth century, but now the industry came under increasing attack for its association with big business and trusts. The industry was further damaged by the increasing connection of the consumption of whiskey with Irish immigrants. During PROHIBITION, about thirty distilleries operated legally under medicinal permits.

In the decades after Prohibition, the industry trod carefully, trying to win the goodwill of the American people and establish itself as a good corporate citizen. The industry's trade association, namely the Distilled Spirits Institute (later the Distilled Spirits Council of the United States), pressured firms into complying with government regulation and urged them to be careful in their ADVERTISING. In their Code of Good Practices, established in 1934 and revised several times since, distillers agreed to refrain from radio and television advertising and to ensure responsible and tasteful advertising that did not target youth. In the post-Prohibition period, the industry became further concentrated and was led by the large firms Seagram, Hiram Walker, Schenley, National Distillers, and Brown-Forman. Some small distillers, such as Jack Daniels and the Beam Distilling Company, reorganized. The industry, however, was an oligopoly and new entrants faced high barriers. Major distilling firms maintained plants across the nation.

With the advent of the baby boom generation in the second half of the 1900s, even more Americans chose beer over spirits. Preference in spirits shifted from the brown liquors to clear and sweet spirits such as vodka, gin, and cordials. Although spirits consumption increased in the post–World War II period, its rate of increase was much less than for beer. Beginning in the late 1970s, spirits consumption actually began to fall. The industry largely blamed its misfortunes on government regulation and on an ongoing movement to curtail alcohol advertising. The industry complained often of tax discrimination and claimed that spirits were the most heavily taxed consumer product in the United States. The industry's most important strategy in its battle against increased regulation and taxation has been public relations campaigns that tout moderation and anti–drunk driving messages. In 1991, some members of the industry established the Century Council, an organization to fight drunk driving and underage drinking. At the same time, some firms, led by Seagrams, have favored more aggressive tactics. They have pushed the concept of equivalency, which aimed to show that beer and wine are just as intoxicating as a mixed drink, and broken the taboo against broadcast spirits advertising. At the end of the twentieth century, the spirits industry contributed about $95 billion in U.S. economic activity per year and employed 1.3 million people in the manufacture, distribution, and sale of nearly four thousand brands of spirits.

BIBLIOGRAPHY

Barr, Andrew Barr. *Drink: A Social History of America*. New York: Carroll and Graf, 1999.

Downard, William L. *Dictionary of the History of the American Brewing and Distilling Industries*. Westport, Conn.: Greenwood Press, 1980.

McGowan, Richard. *Government Regulation of the Alcohol Industry: The Search for Revenue and the Common Good*. Westport, Conn.: Quorum Books, 1997.

Pamela E. Pennock

See also **Brewing; Wine Industry.**

SPIRITUALISM is a religious movement whose adherents seek contact with spirits through mediums in gatherings called séances. It emerged in the Northeast amid the transformations of capitalism, industrialization, urbanization, religious revivalism and experimentation, social reform, democratization, and the rising authority of science.

Spiritualism originated in 1848 in western New York, a region swept by religious revivalism and ferment after the opening of the Erie Canal. Radical ex-Quakers and abolitionists there decided that mysterious knockings in the Hydesville home of sisters Kate and Margaret Fox were communications by spirits. Press coverage generated interest in these "spirit manifestations" after the Fox sisters began a series of demonstrations in Rochester, and

Madame Helena Blavatsky. The highly controversial Russian-born spiritualist, who founded the Theosophical Society in New York City in 1875. © Hulton-Deutsch Collection/corbis

they were referred to as the "Rochester Rappings." Advocates claimed scientific proof of immortality. Many Americans thought they could serve as mediums.

Meanwhile, "Poughkeepsie Seer" Andrew Jackson Davis's involvement with mesmerism had by 1847 produced "harmonialism," a system of religious philosophy and social reform he claimed he had received in a trance from the eighteenth-century scientist-mystic Emanuel Swedenborg and other spirits (see Swedenborgian Churches). Rejecting Calvinist doctrines of innate depravity and eternal punishment and advocating perpetual spiritual growth, harmonialism attracted Universalists, Unitarians, Quakers, Swedenborgians, deists, members of evangelical denominations, and radical social reformers, especially abolitionists and women's rights advocates. Spiritualism emerged when Davis and his followers linked harmonialism to mediumship.

Spiritualism spread across the North during the 1850s and subsequently to the West Coast. Associated with abolitionism and other radical reforms, it was less popular in the South. Mediums were usually women, whom Victorian Americans believed had a heightened piety and sensitivity to spirit communication; many were empowered to public social activism by their mediumship. Spirit messages often urged Americans to counteract expanding commercialization, industrialization, and urbanization by retaining communal and republican values thought to be threatened by the emerging order. Spiritualism appealed across race and class lines but was promoted primarily by an anxious new middle class.

Spiritualism had its critics. Ministers, feeling their authority threatened, labeled it necromancy, witchcraft, and a stimulus to free love. Most scientists rejected it, especially after unfavorable investigations in the mid to late nineteenth century, although a few became defenders, and some examined it within the framework of psychic phenomena from the late nineteenth through the mid-twentieth centuries. Debunkers from the 1850s forward have charged mediums with fraud. Some early sympathizers bolted to found Christian Science and Theosophy.

Such challenges limited Spiritualism's growth and appeal, but the new religion persisted and, despite its strong anti-organizational thrust, became institutionalized. Spiritualists formed perhaps thousands of circles nationwide. They founded over 200 newspapers by 1900 and publishing houses in New York City, Boston, Chicago, and San Francisco. The federal census listed 17 Spiritualist churches in 1860, 95 in 1870, 334 in 1890, and 455 in 1906, with tens of thousands of members in 1890 and 1906. Beginning in the 1870s, Spiritualists established camps in New York, Massachusetts, Indiana, Florida, and several other states. National organization efforts began in the 1860s, and the National Spiritualist Association of Churches was founded in Chicago in 1893. Although overall numbers subsequently declined, large-scale organizations proliferated (the NASC remained the largest), giving Spiritualism a permanent institutional presence and an increasingly ecclesiastical character.

Spiritualism revitalized during the 1960s amid increased interest in alternative spiritualities, psychic phenomena, and the subsequent NEW AGE MOVEMENT, whose eclectic practices include spirit "channeling." Yet it remained distinct from New Age religions and continues to express Americans' desire for spiritual grounding amid ongoing change.

BIBLIOGRAPHY

Braude, Ann. *Radical Spirits: Spiritualism and Women's Rights in Nineteenth-Century America.* Boston: Beacon Press, 1989.

Carroll, Bret E. *Spiritualism in Antebellum America.* Bloomington: Indiana University Press, 1997.

Moore, R. Laurence. *In Search of White Crows: Spiritualism, Parapsychology, and American Culture.* New York: Oxford University Press, 1977.

Bret E. Carroll

See also **Parapsychology; Religion and Religious Affiliation; Women's Rights Movement: The Nineteenth Century.**

SPIRO is the name given for an ancient town site in extreme eastern Oklahoma. The site achieved fame in 1935 when an exceptional collection of artifacts was discovered by relic miners in a large communal grave. During the Mississippian Period (1000–1540), these special objects displayed wealth and status. Using these Spiro objects and comparable ones from the Etowah site in Georgia, and the Moundville site in Alabama, archaeologists were able to identify a Southeastern Ceremonial Complex, a belief system and associated symbolic language that appeared to link diverse regional cultures throughout the Southeast.

The Spiro objects included large chipped stone, engraved shell cups and gorgets, copper headdress plates, pearl beads, and well-preserved wooden sculpture and colorful textiles. From a large ossuary of human skeletons, one hundred years of grave goods and bones were collected for communal deposition in a reconstructed tomb. The approximately forty-five square-foot structure, called the Great Mortuary, was created at the base of the main cone of the Craig burial mound in the early years of the 1400s. Preservation of textiles and other perishables was made possible by a hollow cavity formed by the protective cover of clay layers in the mound itself.

The objects found in the Great Mortuary provide a rich foundation upon which to view ancient beliefs and ritual practices, not only of Caddoan-speaking peoples inhabiting the region, but those of others in the Southeast during the Mississippian Period. Extensive external connections are demonstrated through a substantial number of objects from the Cahokia area, near modern St. Louis. Marine whelk shells from the Gulf Coast of Florida were found along with a few objects of distant western sources derived from the Southwest and the Gulf of California.

The site exhibited changes in land use over its 500 years of history. Starting around 900 A.D., it was a thirty-acre village with a ring of burial mounds located on a slight rise to the west. By 1250, the town site took on the character of a large ceremonial center with ordinary habitation off-site nearby in scattered locations.

BIBLIOGRAPHY

Brown, James A. *The Spiro Ceremonial Center: The Archaeology of Arkansas Valley Caddoan Culture in Eastern Oklahoma.* Memoirs of the Museum of Anthropology no. 29. Ann Arbor: University of Michigan, 1996.

Phillips, Philip, and James A. Brown. *Pre-Columbian Shell Engravings from Craig Mound at Spiro, Oklahoma.* 6 vols. Cambridge, Mass.: Peabody Museum Press, Harvard University, 1978–1984.

James A. Brown

See also **Indian Art; Indian Mounds; Native American Graves Protection and Repatriation Act.**

SPOILS SYSTEM. The "spoils system" of distributing government jobs as a reward for political services takes its name from an 1832 speech by the Democratic senator William L. Marcy of New York. Defending President Andrew Jackson's partisan dismissals from office, Marcy avowed that he and his fellows saw "nothing wrong in the rule, that to the victor belong the spoils of the enemy."

Although Jackson is usually credited with inaugurating the system, he never justified it on Marcy's blunt grounds. Under the long reign of Virginia Democratic-Republican presidents, permanent tenure had become the de facto rule in many federal offices. Honoring tradition, Jackson's predecessor John Quincy Adams refused to remove even overt political opponents. Despite this, Jackson accused the federal establishment of opposing his election in 1828. He proclaimed a policy of "rotation in office" to curb official arrogance and corruption and democratize opportunities for public service. Disclaiming anyone's inherent right to continue in office, Jackson dismissed political foes along with some career bureaucrats, replacing them with partisan newspaper editors and other active supporters.

Opponents condemned Jackson for introducing political "proscription," but soon learned to follow his example. By the 1840s both Jackson's Democrats and the opposing Whigs routinely wielded patronage to inspire and discipline party workers. Partisan removals grew ever more extensive, reaching down from Washington bureau chiefs and clerks to land and customs and territorial officials to village postmasters. Thousands of eager supplicants besieged each new administration, making the redistribution of offices every four years a major undertaking.

By the 1850s the spoils system was thoroughly entrenched as an instrument of political warfare both between the parties and among factions within them. Calls for reform surfaced before the Civil War and gathered impetus during Reconstruction from Andrew Johnson's attempted purge of Republican officeholders and the scandals of the Grant administration. Chastising the system for promoting official incompetence and corruption and for adulterating the purity of elections, critics demanded that federal employment be removed from party politics and grounded on merit as determined by competitive examination.

Eradicating the spoils system became a major crusade in the 1870s, championed by good-government reformers, cautiously advanced by presidents, and vehemently opposed by congressional party chieftains. President James Garfield's assassination by a "disappointed office-seeker" undermined resistance and led to the passage of the Pendleton Civil Service Act in 1883. The act inaugurated a merit system of employment for certain classes of federal employees under the supervision of a bipartisan Civil Service Commission and banned the common practice of dunning officeholders for contributions to party coffers.

In the remainder of the century, presidents put more offices under civil service protection, largely replacing the spoils system with a career bureaucracy. Political patronage survives in some federal as well as state and municipal appointments, but its range has been drastically curtailed. Scholars disagree whether politicizing government service improved or damaged its efficiency, integrity, and responsiveness. For good or ill, the spoils system certainly opened office to a broader range of citizens. It also buttressed the operations of mass political parties, and rose and declined in tandem with them.

BIBLIOGRAPHY

Hoogenboom, Ari. *Outlawing the Spoils: A History of the Civil Service Reform Movement, 1865–1883.* Urbana: University of Illinois Press, 1961.

White, Leonard D. *The Jacksonians: A Study in Administrative History, 1829–1861.* New York: Macmillan, 1954.

———. *The Republican Era: 1869–1901, A Study in Administrative History.* New York: Macmillan, 1958.

Daniel Feller

See also **Civil Service.**

SPORTS. Sport in America began as premodern participatory contests of strength, skill, and speed that were unorganized local competitions with simple rules. However, as the nation modernized, sport became highly organized with formalized rules and national competition. Sport became commercialized with expert athletes entertaining paying spectators.

The first sportsmen were Native Americans, who competed for religious, medicinal, and gambling purposes. They had running races, but were best known for team ball sports like lacrosse, which had over forty variations. The colonists defined sports broadly to include all diversions. Colonial amusement reflected their European backgrounds, including social class and religion, and their new surroundings in America. Puritans brought their opposition to pagan and Catholic holidays, Sabbath breaking, and time-wasting amusements. They barred brutal sports, gambling games, and amusements that promoted disorder, but advocated useful activities like wolf hunting, fishing, and training-day (military practice) contests like wrestling and marksmanship. The more heterogeneous colonies had more options. New York, with its Dutch heritage, had bowling, *kolven* (golf), and boat races, and also horseracing after the English took over the colony in 1664. In Philadelphia, control of the community passed from the Quakers to a secular elite who in 1732 tried to separate themselves from lesser sorts by organizing the Schuylkill Fishing Colony, the first sports club in the British Empire.

The South had the most expansive sporting culture. The Anglican Church was more tolerant than the Puritans were, and personal ethics did not prohibit gambling or blood sports. An elite planter class emerged in the late seventeenth century, which tried to emulate the English

Bowling Tournament. Continuing an American tradition since the seventeenth century, bowlers let loose in a 1905 competition in Milwaukee, Wis., sponsored by the American Bowling Congress. LIBRARY OF CONGRESS

country gentry. The great planters originally raced their own horses in impromptu quarter-mile matches and wagered enormous amounts with their peers. By the mid-eighteenth century, they were starting to import expensive Thoroughbreds that competed in long distance races at urban tracks established by elite jockey clubs. This public entertainment helped demonstrate the supposed superiority of the great planters over the masses.

Publicans throughout the colonies were the first sporting entrepreneurs, sponsoring animal baiting, gander pulling, cock fights, skittles (an early form of bowling), shuffleboard, and target shooting to attract thirsty patrons. Moral reformers, particularly evangelical ministers of the Great Awakening, opposed these sports. During the Revolution, many patriots frowned on gambling as unvirtuous and elite sports as aristocratic. The Continental Congress in 1778 recommended that the states suppress racing and "other diversions as are productive of idleness and dissipation."

Antebellum Sport

Sport in the first half of the nineteenth century remained premodern, abhorred by proper Victorians who frowned upon it as immoral and wasteful. The sporting fraternity encompassed a male bachelor subculture, including segments of the elite, skilled butchers, street thugs, volunteer firefighters, and Irish immigrants. They enjoyed blood sports, combat sports like boxing (which was universally banned), and gambling sports. Southern plantation owners employed slaves as cock trainers, jockeys, boxers, and oarsmen.

The leading antebellum sportsman was the industrialist John C. Stevens. He restored Thoroughbred racing to New York in 1823; established the Elysian Fields, the preeminent site of antebellum ball sports, in Hoboken, New Jersey, in 1831; promoted the first major pedestrian race in 1835; and organized the New York Yacht Club in 1844. Seven years later, Stevens sponsored *America*, conqueror of the finest British yachts, promoting pride in American naval architecture, craftsmanship, and seamanship.

American sport began a dramatic transformation at midcentury that led to a boom after the Civil War. This was influenced by the processes of urbanization, industrialization, and immigration; by the development of an ideology that created a positive image for sports; and by the rise of new modern games. The ideology of sports was developed by secular Jacksonian reformers—who thought sports could help cope with such negative features of rapid urbanization as soaring crime rates, epidemics, and class conflict—and by religious reformers inspired by the Second Great Awakening, who saw them as a way to fight sin. Both groups believed that participation in exercise and clean sports would improve public health, build character, develop sound morals, and provide an alternative to vile urban amusements. This positive attitude toward sport was supported by the examples of Scottish Caledonian games (traditional track and field contests) and German *turnverein* (gymnastic societies). Clergymen like Thomas W. Higginson advocated muscular Christianity, the cornerstone of the Young Men's Christian Association movement that harmonized mind, body, and spirit. Health advocates in the 1840s organized the municipal park movement that resulted in the creation of New York's Central Park in 1858. It became a model for large urban parks after the Civil War.

Team sports aptly fit the sports creed. Cricket, a manly and skillful English game, enjoyed a brief fad in the 1840s, but was quickly surpassed by baseball, which had evolved from the English game of rounders. Baseball was simpler, more dramatic, faster paced, and took less time to play. In 1845, Alexander Cartwright drew up the modern rules for his middle-class Knickerbockers club. Early teams were voluntary associations of middle-income men, principally in metropolitan New York, although the game spread quickly along the Atlantic seaboard. Teams were organized by occupation, neighborhood, or political party. The top New York teams organized the National Association of Base Ball Players in 1858 to define rules, resolve disputes, and control the sport's future.

The Late-Nineteenth-Century Sports Boom

The sports explosion was directly abetted by the technological revolution. Communication innovations like telegraphy and telephony helped newspapers report events at distant locations. The *New York World* in the mid-1890s introduced the first sports section. Daily coverage was supplemented by weeklies beginning with the *American Turf Register and Sporting Magazine* (1829) and William T. Porter's urbane *Spirit of the Times* (1831), which promoted angling and horseracing. Other important periodicals included the *National Police Gazette* (1845), the *New York Clipper* (1853), and the *Sporting News* (1886).

The coming of the railroad enabled athletes to journey to distant sites for competition. This potential was demonstrated in 1852, when, to promote rail travel, the Boston, Concord, and Montreal Railroad sponsored the first American intercollegiate athletic contest, the Harvard-Yale crew race at Lake Winnipesaukee, New Hampshire. Railroads enabled baseball leagues to operate and illegal prizefights to take place at out-of-the-way locations. Cheap urban mass transit, especially electrified streetcars, increased access to sporting venues.

Technological innovations also helped sport in many other ways. Thomas Edison's incandescent light bulb improved illumination for indoor events. New equipment was created, such as vulcanized rubber for balls and tires, and new machines made possible cheap, mass-produced sporting goods. The English safety bicycle invented in the late 1880s created a cycling fad among men and women. Riders joined clubs, raced, toured, and attended six-day professional races at Madison Square Garden in New York City.

Social class heavily determined sporting opportunities in this era. The elite, who emulated the English gentry, had the wealth, time, and self-confidence to indulge themselves. They used expensive sports to gain recognition and improved their status by joining restricted athletic, jockey, country, and yacht clubs. Elite colleges became centers of intercollegiate competition, beginning with rowing (1852), baseball (1859), football (1869), and track and field (1873). Participation spread by the 1890s to state and private colleges throughout the nation. Competition promoted manliness, school pride, and the reputation of institutions. Student-run associations ran the teams and recruited gifted athletes through financial aid and easy course loads.

The hardworking new middle class finally became involved in sport because of the sports ideology, the creation of clean new sports, and the accessibility of suburban parks where by the mid-1880s they played on baseball diamonds and tennis courts. Their participation in sport demonstrated "manliness" and offered a sense of self-worth and accomplishment lost in their increasingly bureaucratized work. Manual workers' options were hindered by urbanization, which destroyed many traditional outdoor sports facilities; by the arrival of eastern European immigrants with no athletic heritage; and by the factory system, with its strict time-work discipline, low wages, and long working hours. Lower class urbanites were most active in sports that were accessible and fit in with their environment, like boxing, billiards, and basketball. Progressive reformers promoted sports at settlement houses to help inner-city youth acculturate.

Nineteenth-century sport was virtually an exclusive male sphere. Yet, women, mainly elite daughters whose status protected them from criticism, began to participate after the Civil War. Physicians and female physical educators advocated improved fitness for women to make them more attractive and healthier mothers. Young women partook of sociable coed sports like croquet and ice skating, and individual sports like archery, golf, and tennis, the latter introduced to the United States by Mary Outerbridge in 1875. The cycling fad encouraged the development of sports clothes, including bloomers, shorter skirts, and no corsets. Women's colleges taught physical fitness, but female students preferred team sports and intercollegiate competition. Athletic leaders at the turn of the century modified men's sports, especially the new game of basketball, to make them more "appropriate" for women—that is, less exertive and less competitive. Nonetheless, female physical educators opposed intercollegiate sports as creating undesirable manly values like competitiveness and individualism, and in the 1900s, noncompetitive play days supplanted intercollegiate women's sport.

The Rise of Professional Sport

While most nineteenth-century sport was participatory, the era's most significant development was the rise of professional spectator sports, a product of the commercialization of leisure, the emergence of sports entrepreneurs, the professionalization of athletes, the large potential audiences created by urbanization, and the modernization of baseball, boxing, and horseracing. Baseball started to become a business in the 1860s with the hiring of the first paid players, the opening of Brooklyn's Union Grounds, and the 1869 national tour of the all-salaried Cincinnati Red Stockings. The National Association of Professional Baseball Players, the first professional league, was formed in 1871, supplanted by the more business-minded National League (NL) in 1876. The NL's success led to the rise of rivals, most notably the working-class-oriented American Association—which was created in 1882 but merged with the NL the next season. In the 1880s, major league baseball largely developed its modern character, including tactics, rules, and equipment.

Baseball, dubbed the "national pastime," completely dominated the sporting scene in the early 1900s. Not merely fun, its ideology fit prevailing values and beliefs. It was considered a sport of pastoral American origins that improved health, character, and morality; taught traditional rural values; and promoted social democracy and social integration. Baseball's popularity was reflected by the rise of the American League, the growth of the minor leagues from thirteen in 1900 to forty-six in 1912, and the construction of large fireproof ballparks.

Prizefighting was universally banned until the 1890s, when the bare-knuckle era came to an end—marked by Jim Corbett's 1892 victory over heavyweight champion John L. Sullivan, the preeminent sports hero of the century. Boxing continued to be permitted in just a few locations until the 1920s, when it was legalized in New York. It then became very popular, with heroes like Jack Dempsey fighting in arenas like Madison Square Garden.

509

Athletic Ensemble. Women in Miami in the 1920s demonstrate fashionable dress for different sports. © BETTMANN/CORBIS

Fighters came from the most impoverished backgrounds, hoping to use boxing to escape poverty. There were a few black champions in the less prestigious lighter weight divisions. However, heavyweight champion Jack Johnson (1908–1915) was considered a threat to white supremacy, and there was a crusade to get rid of him. Thereafter, no African American got a heavyweight title shot until Joe Louis, who won the title in 1937. He became a national hero one year later by defeating Max Schmeling, symbol of Nazi Germany. After World War II, boxing was a staple of prime time television, but overexposure and widening public recognition of underworld influences curtailed its success.

Horseracing was rejuvenated after the Civil War under the aegis of politically connected elites. After a successful experiment at Saratoga, New York, in 1863, the American Jockey Club opened New York's Jerome Park (1866), a model for elite courses in Brooklyn; Long Branch, New Jersey; and Chicago. Their success encouraged the rise of proprietary tracks—like those in Brighton Beach, New York, and Guttenberg, New Jersey—run by men closely connected to political machines and syndicate crime. By the early 1900s, every state but Maryland and Kentucky had closed their racetracks, if only temporarily, because of the gambling. In the 1920s, Thoroughbred racing revived because of increasing prosperity, looser morals, ethnic political influence, and underworld influences. Racetrack admissions surpassed admissions for all other sports by the early 1950s, and continued to do so until the early 1980s.

Public interest during the 1920s—the so-called "Golden Age of Sports"—was whetted by increased lei-sure time and discretionary income, by national radio broadcasts of events like baseball's World Series and heavyweight boxing championships, and by the development of a pantheon of heroes. Every major sport had its great hero, role models who symbolized prowess and traditional and modern values. Idols included Babe Ruth in baseball, Red Grange in football, Jack Dempsey in boxing, Bobby Jones in golf, and Charles Lindbergh in aeronautics. While women were largely limited to "feminine" sports like tennis, figure skating, and swimming, some female athletes—notably tennis player Helen Wills—also became widely celebrated.

The Great Depression hurt sport, though people still looked to recreation for escape. Commercialized sports declined, but less than most businesses, as companies curtailed industrial sports programs, and colleges cut back on intercollegiate sports, particularly football. On the other hand, the Public Works Administration and Works Progress Administration constructed thousands of sports fields, swimming pools, and other athletic facilities.

The United States and the Olympics
American athletes at the first Olympics in 1896 came from elite eastern colleges, yet squads in the early 1900s had many working-class ethnic athletes, including Native American Jim Thorpe, gold medalist in the pentathlon and the decathlon at the 1912 games. The first Olympic Games in the United States were held in St. Louis in 1904, but drew only thirteen nations. The 1932 winter games were at Lake Placid, New York, and the summer games in Los Angeles at the Coliseum. The summer games featured the first athletic village. Babe Didrikson starred, winning two

gold medals and a silver in track. An all-around talent, she was the greatest female American athlete of the century. Before the 1936 games at Berlin, there was widespread support for a boycott to protest nazism, but the movement failed. The African American Jesse Owens starred, capturing four gold medals in track, yet returned stateside to a racist society.

Post–World War II Sport

Spectator sports grew rapidly in the prosperous 1950s and 1960s. There were more major sports, the number of franchises rose, and television enabled millions to watch live events. Air travel facilitated major league baseball's opening up of new markets in 1953, when the Boston Braves moved to Milwaukee, and again five years later, when the New York Giants and Dodgers moved to the West Coast. The thirty teams in Major League Baseball, the thirty-one teams in the National Football League (NFL), and the twenty-nine in the National Basketball Association (NBA, founded in 1949) were located throughout the country. This expansion was accompanied by the construction of arenas and stadiums by local governments to keep or attract sports franchises. Television broadcasts promoted growing interest in college football, and created a huge boom in professional football during the 1960s. By the early 1980s, twice as many households watched pro football as baseball. Television also increased interest in golf and tennis, making celebrities of golfers Arnold Palmer and Jack Nicklaus and tennis player Jimmy Connors. Public tastes were broadened, especially through the American Broadcasting Company's *Wide World of Sports,* which went on the air in 1961, and became the longest running series on television.

Professional athletes became empowered through their unions. Marvin Miller, president of the Major League Baseball Players Association, which began in the late 1960s to secure higher salary minimums, grievance procedures, increased pensions, and representation by agents. The union secured salary arbitration in 1973 and achieved free agency in 1976. Average salaries in baseball rose from $19,000 in 1967 to $1.4 million in 2001. Nonetheless, the value of sports franchises appreciated, as with the Chicago Cubs, worth $500 million in 2002.

Major college sports prospered after the war. National College Athletic Association (NCAA) football gained lucrative television contracts, and attendance reached forty million by 1970. Basketball, a much lower cost sport, had to recover from the point shaving scandal of 1951. By the early 1970s, however, the NCAA basketball championships became a prime annual television event, along with the World Series; the NFL's Super Bowl, first played in 1966; and car racing's premier event, the Indianapolis 500.

Race was the central issue in postwar sport. From the late nineteenth century, African Americans had been barred from competing against whites in most professional sports. This custom was shattered by the pivotal integration of Major League Baseball following the hiring

Billie Jean King. The women's tennis champion of the 1960s and 1970s, whose efforts both on and off the court significantly helped not just women's tennis but women's sports in general. GETTY IMAGES

of black player Jackie Robinson in 1947, a huge step in the civil rights movement. Pro football had integrated one year earlier, and the NBA followed in 1950. Desegregation resulted from such factors as the Second Great Migration; African American participation in World War II; political pressure from civil rights workers and politicians like New York's Mayor Fiorello LaGuardia; prointegration columns by African American, communist, and mainstream sportswriters; and the outstanding achievements of Jesse Owens and Joe Louis. Integration moved slowly, and college football teams in the Deep South did not desegregate until the late 1960s. However, in 2002 most players in the NFL, and nearly 80 percent of the NBA, were African Americans, including superstar Michael Jordan, the highest-paid team player of all time.

Women's sports began to boom in the 1970s, as a result of the growing interest of young women in sport, feminism, and improved health, and in reaction to demands for greater American success in international sport. Tennis star Billie Jean King played a major role by demanding equity in prize money, by helping to organize the Virginia Slims circuit in 1971, when she was the first woman athlete to earn over $100,000 in one year, and by defeating misogynist Bobby Riggs in a 1973 nationally televised match. In addition, in 1971, the Association of Intercollegiate Athletics for Women (AIAW) was estab-

511

lished to organize national championships. Then, in 1972, Title IX of the Educational Amendments Act barred sexual discrimination by schools and colleges that received federal assistance. Women were thereafter entitled to parity in athletic scholarships, training facilities, and coaching. By 1996, nearly half of all intercollegiate athletes were women.

The postwar Olympics became an adjunct of the Cold War, supposedly reflecting the relative merits of capitalist and communist social and economic systems. The Soviet Union consistently surpassed the United States, and East Germany nearly matched the United States in 1976, and surpassed it in 1988. One reason for the relatively poor U.S. showing was that it originally had weak women's teams, reflecting national support of only "feminine" sports. National track teams relied heavily on women from historically black colleges, among the few institutions that supported women's track. One black woman runner, Wilma Rudolph of Tennessee State, won three gold medals in track in 1960.

The 1968 Olympics was a target of protest on the part of black athletes encouraged by the civil rights and black power movements, and by the example of charismatic boxer Muhammad Ali. In 1980, President Jimmy Carter forced a boycott of the Olympic Games in Moscow to protest Soviet incursions into Afghanistan. The 1984 Los Angeles games, boycotted by the Soviet Union, and completely organized by the private sector, was a financial success, earning $250 million. American women became much more successful, led by Florence Griffiths-Joyner and Jackie Joyner-Kersee.

At the beginning of the twenty-first century, interest in sport was continuing to grow. Not only were major spectator sports, particularly baseball, football, and auto racing, drawing larger crowds than ever before, but television coverage, especially on cable networks like the Entertainment Sports Programming Network (ESPN), continued to expand. Furthermore, men and women's interest in health and personal appearance sustained the fitness movement that began in the 1970s, promoting mass participatory recreational sport among people of all ages.

BIBLIOGRAPHY

Adelman, Melvin L. *A Sporting Time: New York City and the Rise of Modern Athletics, 1820–70.* Urbana: University of Illinois Press, 1986.

Cahn, Susan. *Coming On Strong: Gender and Sexuality in Twentieth-Century Women's Sport.* New York: Free Press, 1994.

Gorn, Elliott. *The Manly Art: Bare-Knuckle Prize Fighting in Nineteenth-Century America.* Ithaca, N.Y.: Cornell University Press, 1986.

Grundy, Pamela. *Learning to Win: Sports, Education, and Social Change in Twentieth-Century North Carolina.* Chapel Hill: University of North Carolina Press, 2001.

Lester, Robin. *Stagg's University: The Rise, Decline, and Fall of Big-Time Football at the University of Chicago.* Urbana: University of Illinois Press, 1995.

Rader, Benjamin G. *American Sport: From the Age of Folk Games to the Age of Televised Sports.* 4th ed. Englewood Cliffs, N.J.: Prentice Hall, 2000.

Riess, Steven A. *City Games: The Evolution of American Urban Society and the Rise of Sports.* Urbana: University of Illinois Press, 1989.

———. *Touching Base: Professional Baseball and American Culture in the Progressive Era.* Rev. ed. Urbana: University of Illinois Press, 1999.

Seymour, Harold. *Baseball.* 3 vols. New York: Oxford University Press, 1960–1990.

Smith, Ronald A. *Sports and Freedom: The Rise of Big-Time College Athletics.* New York: Oxford University Press, 1988.

Tygiel, Jules. *Baseball's Great Experiment: Jackie Robinson and His Legacy.* Rev. ed. New York: Oxford University Press, 1997.

Wiggins, David K. *Glory Bound: Black Athletes in a White America.* Syracuse, N.Y.: Syracuse University Press, 1997.

Steven A. Riess

See also **College Athletics; Football; Hockey; National Collegiate Athletic Association; Olympic Games; Sports Unions;** *and individual entries, e.g.,* **Baseball; Football; Track and Field.**

SPOTSYLVANIA COURTHOUSE, BATTLE OF

(8–21 May 1864). An advance corps of Gen. Ulysses S. Grant's southward march from the Wilderness in Virginia was stopped northwest of Spotsylvania Courthouse by Confederate troops under Gen. Richard Anderson. After a failed Union assault on 9 May, Confederate generals Richard Ewell and Ambrose Hill entrenched along a front four miles long. Here on 10 May they repulsed waves of attacks by Union forces under Gen. Winfield Scott Hancock and Gen. Ambrose Burnside. Another Union offensive on 12 May captured Ewell's salient but was driven back in hand-to-hand combat. About midnight Ewell retired to an inner line. Thereafter, for some days Grant gradually withdrew south. Grant's losses at Spotsylvania were seventeen thousand; Lee's, eight thousand.

BIBLIOGRAPHY

Gallagher, Gary W., ed. *The Spotsylvania Campaign.* Chapel Hill: University of North Carolina Press, 1998.

Matter, William D. *If It Takes All Summer: The Battle of Spotsylvania.* Chapel Hill: University of North Carolina Press, 1988.

Rhea, Gordon C. *The Battles for Spotsylvania Court House and the Road to Yellow Tavern, May 7–12, 1864.* Baton Rouge: Louisiana State University Press 1997.

Joseph Mills Hanson / A. R.

See also **Civil War; Cold Harbor, Battle of; Petersburg, Siege of; Richmond Campaigns; Army of Northern Virginia; Wilderness, Battles of the.**

SPRINGER V. UNITED STATES, 102 U.S. 586

(1881), a U.S. Supreme Court case that upheld the constitutionality of the federal income tax that had existed from1864 to 1872. By a 7 to 0 vote, the Court rejected the claim that an income tax was a "direct tax" prohibited by the Constitution unless apportioned among the states. The Court concluded that only taxes on real estate and capitation taxes were direct taxes. Although it rendered a seemingly contrary decision in *Pollock v. Farmers' Loan and Trust* (1895), the constitutionality of an income tax was confirmed with the adoption of the Sixteenth Amendment in 1913.

Richard L. Aynes

See also **Income Tax Cases; Taxation.**

SQUARE DEAL, the phrase coined by Theodore Roosevelt during his first term as president to highlight his position on the "labor problem." Its first public utterance appears to have been in the peroration of a Labor Day address given at the New York State Fair in Syracuse on 7 September 1903. In this speech Roosevelt spoke forcefully of the community of interests binding capital to labor and of the danger to this community in allowing either side to pursue overly selfish ends. In order to ensure continued national prosperity, both property owners and the laboring classes must share in the wealth produced. To maintain this balance, labor and capital must remain on an equal footing and subject to the same laws. In the context of the times, his stress on reciprocity was an obvious attack on the prerogatives of the TRUSTS. Furthermore, Roosevelt insisted that "a man" should not be judged on the basis of his social standing but rather on his "merits," including his capacity for work, honesty, commonsense, and devotion to the common good. These virtues were the individual marks of good citizenship, and their preservation was necessary for the future of the republic and the progress of civilization.

Informing Roosevelt's views were his recent experiences during the anthracite coal strike of 1902 and the Miller affair in July 1903, when he enforced an open shop for all government positions. Roosevelt insisted his responsibility as president was to ensure "fair play among all men, capitalists or wage workers, whether they conduct their private business as individuals or as members of organizations" (Gould, *Presidency of Theodore Roosevelt*, p. 115). He advocated an active role for central government to achieve this end and protect the common good. Over the course of the next several years, in correspondence and speeches, he broadened the scope of the Square Deal to incorporate other elements of his reform philosophy. These ideas were gathered together in a volume entitled *A Square Deal*, published in 1906 during his second term.

The Square Deal served as the rallying cry for progressive Republicans, even following Roosevelt's departure from office in 1909. It was refashioned as the NEW NATIONALISM (the phrase coined by Herbert Croly) dur-

Theodore Roosevelt. The president whose Square Deal policies in the early 1900s offered—for the first time—some active federal support in promoting fair treatment of ordinary workers, as well as other progressive domestic reforms. LIBRARY OF CONGRESS

ing Roosevelt's unsuccessful run for the presidency in 1912. In hindsight, the Square Deal was significant to American politics for two reasons. It represented the first attempt by a modern president to promote a unified vision for domestic reform. However, it was less a programmatic blueprint for governmental action than a political philosophy joining his belief in fair play, the virtue of hard work, free labor ideology, and the role of central government in promoting these ends. While innovative in asserting that subordinate groups in society were entitled to fair treatment, it was essentially conservative in its solution, emphasizing "Hamiltonian means" to achieve "Jeffersonian ends." Second, it was the first of three "deals" enunciated by reform-minded presidents in the twentieth century, the other two being Franklin D. Roosevelt's NEW DEAL and Harry S. Truman's FAIR DEAL.

> There must be ever present in our minds the fundamental truth that in a Republic such as ours the only safety is to stand neither for nor against any man because he is rich or he is poor, because he is engaged in one occupation or another, because he works with his brains or because he works with his hands. We must treat each man on his worth and his merits as a man. We must see that each is given a square deal because he is entitled to no more and should receive no less. Finally we must keep ever in mind that a Republic such as ours can exist only in virtue of the orderly liberty which comes through the equal domination of the law over all men alike; and through its administration in such resolute and fearless fashion as shall teach all that no man is above it and no man below it.
>
> **SOURCE:** Theodore Roosevelt, quoted in the *New York Times*, 8 September 1903.

BIBLIOGRAPHY

Blum, John Morton. *The Republican Roosevelt*. Cambridge, Mass.: Harvard University Press, 1954.

Gable, John A.. *The Bull Moose Years: Theodore Roosevelt and the Progressive Party*. Port Washington, N.Y.: Kennikat Press, 1978.

Gould, Lewis L. *The Presidency of Theodore Roosevelt*. Lawrence: University Press of Kansas, 1991.

C. Wyatt Evans

See also **Anthracite Strike; Labor; Progressive Movement.**

STAFFORD V. WALLACE, 258 U.S. 495 (1922). In *Stafford v. Wallace*, the U.S. Supreme Court used the Constitution's interstate commerce power to uphold the Packers and Stockyards Act of 1921, which regulated stockyards, meatpackers, and commission men who facilitated transactions between stock owners, stockyards, packers, and dealers. Writing for a 7 to 1 majority, Chief Justice William Howard Taft rejected the argument that the law regulated intrastate commerce. Rather, he held that stockyards were "in the middle of . . . [the] current of commerce" and that they are "a throat through which the current flows." This holding anticipated a more expansive view of interstate commerce power developed by the Court after 1937.

BIBLIOGRAPHY

Epstein, Lee, and Thomas G. Walker. *Constitutional Law for a Changing America: Institutional Powers and Constraints.* 4th ed. Washington, D.C.: CQ Press, 2001.

Richard L. Aynes

See also **Interstate Commerce Laws; Packers and Stockyards Act.**

STAGECOACH TRAVEL. Stagecoaches were familiar vehicles along the main roads of the East and the South before the coming of railroads in the 1830s and 1840s. Even as the nation's network of iron and steel rails grew larger and more comprehensive, stagecoach connections to small and isolated communities continued to supplement passenger trains well into the second decade of the twentieth century. However, stagecoach travel was most difficult and dangerous across the vast expanse of the American West, where it attracted the most attention. In large measure that was because of the inordinately great distances involved and the Herculean effort required to maintain regular service across the region's dry and sparsely populated landscape.

Stagecoach lines in the East tended to connect pre-existing centers of population, and passengers took regular meals at the established inns and taverns along the way. Nothing of the kind existed in the West in 1858, when John Butterfield undertook an overland stage line connecting St. Louis and San Francisco by way of El Paso, Texas. The route also ran through Tucson and Los Angeles, but neither was more than a village of a few hundred residents at that time. A federal contract paid the stage company $600,000 a year to carry U.S. mail across the continent, and that money helped subsidize way stations at regular intervals, where, in the absence of existing settlements along most of the proposed route, the coaches could change draft animals and the passengers could find food. The Butterfield organization spent nearly a year getting everything into place to support semiweekly stagecoach service.

When Butterfield's Overland Mail Line opened for business on 16 September 1858, the 2,795-mile journey between San Francisco and St. Louis required approximately three weeks of hard traveling, and that was during the best weather. The coaches kept moving all through the day and night except for brief intervals at way stations. Stagecoach fare did not include the cost of meals, which at an average price of a dollar each three times a day for three weeks might effectively add 50 percent to the cost of a through ticket. Sleep had to be obtained aboard the rocking coach.

Antedating Butterfield's line, a stage line connected San Diego and San Antonio in 1857 with semimonthly coaches. Even earlier, in 1849, a stage line of sorts connected Independence, Missouri, and Santa Fe, New Mexico. But these earlier carriers were not as ambitious as the Butterfield line, nor were they run with the attention to detail that a large support structure demanded.

In the spring of 1861, with the threat of Civil War and Texas's secession from the Union, the transcontinental stage line moved north. Following the central Overland Trail, it stretched through the future states of Wy-

Stagecoach. Passengers ride on top as well as inside this coach at Deadwood, S.D., in 1889—well past the heyday of long-distance stage lines. © CORBIS

oming, Utah, and Nevada. Again the Overland Stage Line had to spend a small fortune to build the support structure required for regular operations across the sparsely populated corridor. The long transcontinental journey remained as rigorous as before.

The transcontinental stage line attained its greatest geographical reach under the leadership of Ben Holladay. In the mid-1860s, lines of the Holladay Overland Mail and Express Company extended west from the Missouri River steamboat landings in Kansas and Nebraska to a hub in Salt Lake City. From there additional lines served outposts as distant as Butte, Montana, and The Dalles, Oregon, where steamboat connections to Portland were available. Incurring heavy losses in 1864 and 1965 during the Native American unrest that sometimes prevented overland stagecoaches from running, Holladay in November 1866 sold his interests to Wells, Fargo and Company. Wells, Fargo operated stagecoaches along the transcontinental route between Salt Lake City and Sacramento, California, where steamboats connected to San Francisco. Holladay subsequently acquired and built railroad lines in Oregon.

Railroads generated a great deal of excitement all across the West. As the tracks of the first transcontinental railroad extended east from Sacramento and west from Omaha in the late 1860s, stagecoaches served a shrinking gap. That gap closed when railroad officials drove a last spike at Promontory, Utah, in May 1869 and trains linked California with the rest of the United States for the first time. The era of stagecoaches along the central Overland Trail was over, but thereafter various smaller stage lines linked transcontinental trains to distant outposts. Until buses became popular around the time of World War I, many a road-weary stagecoach continued to meet passenger trains and provide transportation to remote villages in the West. The term "stage" was commonly used to describe any coach, wagon, or sleigh used as a public conveyance. In the 1860s, the heyday of stagecoach lines, the Concord coach, handcrafted in Concord, New Hampshire, by Abbot, Downing and Company, became the quintessential icon of transportation across the frontier West. The first Concord in California, transported aboard a clipper ship that sailed from New England around Cape Horn, inaugurated service out of San Francisco on 25 June 1850.

The familiar egg-shaped body of the Concord coach was renowned for its great strength and its ability to keep passengers dry while floating them across flood-swollen streams. Because the inevitable twisting of the coach body on the rough terrain could easily shatter glass windows, it had only adjustable leather curtains to keep out the dust, wind, and rain. The heavy body, often weighing a ton or more, rode on thick, six- or eight-ply leather belts called thoroughbraces to insulate it from the constant pounding of the wheels over makeshift roads. Nevertheless the swaying made some passengers seasick. Mark Twain aptly characterized the Concord coach as a "cradle on wheels."

Not all stagecoaches were of the familiar type. Vehicles called "celerity" or "mud" wagons were much lighter and cheaper than Concord coaches and, because they had no springs, offered a much rougher ride. They

515

were primarily used on lines where passenger and express traffic was too light to justify the expense of Concord coaches.

A Concord coach could accommodate as many as nine passengers inside and another six or more on the roof, though no one in a crowded coach rode in comfort. In an age renowned for its propriety and formality, perfect strangers, both men and women, might have to interlock knees in the cramped space of the interior or rest a weary head on another's shoulder. Some passengers passed the long hours of an overland journey by drinking themselves into alcoholic stupors, while others organized or participated in impromptu songfests. One common form of entertainment was to shoot at the wild animals, such as antelope and prairie dogs, visible from coach windows. Some passengers probably whiled away the long hours worrying about Indian attacks, even though attacks and stagecoach holdups were both infrequent. The violence associated with stagecoach travel in the West was for the most part an exaggeration fostered by dime novels, Buffalo Bill Cody's Wild West Show, and Hollywood westerns.

Each stagecoach passenger was allowed a maximum of twenty-five pounds of baggage, which rode in a large rear pouch called a boot. The U.S. mail typically rode in the front or rear boot, although, as Mark Twain recalled from personal experience in *Roughing It* (1872), a large load of mail might be shoved among the feet of passengers. Any express shipments, often gold and silver, rode close to the feet of the driver, a skilled horseman who handled the team of four or six draft animals from a seat atop the coach. Sometimes a special messenger accompanied express shipments to guard them from bandits. On occasion a stagecoach might carry a shipment of produce, such as fresh apples from the orchards of Utah to remote towns in Idaho and Montana.

Twain's personal account of overland stage travel in the early 1860s is evocative and true to fact. However, the 1939 Hollywood epic *Stagecoach*, directed by John Ford and featuring a young John Wayne, probably did more than anything else to foster modern perceptions of stagecoach travel as both romantic and dangerous. Louis McLane, onetime head of Wells, Fargo and Company, the most famous name in overland stagecoach travel, wrote to his wife in 1865 about artistic depictions of travel by coach, "I thought staging looked very well to the lithographer, but was the devil in reality." Many hearty travelers who crossed the West by stagecoach in the late 1850s and the 1860s surely would have agreed.

BIBLIOGRAPHY

Frederick, J. V. *Ben Holladay, the Stagecoach King: A Chapter in the Development of Transcontinental Transportation.* Lincoln: University of Nebraska Press, 1989. Originally published in 1940.

Madsen, Betty M., and Brigham D. Madsen. *North to Montana: Jehus, Bullwhackers, and Mule Skinners on the Montana Trail.* Salt Lake City: University of Utah Press, 1980.

Moody, Ralph. *Stagecoach West.* New York: Crowell, 1967.

Schwantes, Carlos Arnaldo. *Long Day's Journey: The Steamboat and Stagecoach Era in the Northern West.* Seattle: University of Washington Press, 1999.

Winther, Oscar Osburn. *The Transportation Frontier: Trans-Mississippi West, 1865–1890.* New York: Holt, Rinehart and Winston, 1964.

Carlos A. Schwantes

See also **Overland Companies; Transportation and Travel; Wells, Fargo and Company; Westward Migration.**

STAGFLATION is a term referring to transitional periods when the economy is simultaneously experiencing the twin evils of INFLATION and high UNEMPLOYMENT, a condition many economists as late as the 1950s considered atypical of the U.S. economy. Stagflation occurs when the economy is moving from an inflationary period (increasing prices, but low unemployment) to a recessionary one (decreasing or stagnant prices and increasing unemployment). It is caused by an overheated economy. In periods of moderate inflation, the usual reaction of business is to increase production to capture the benefits of the higher prices. But if the economy becomes overheated so that price increases are unusually large and are the result of increases in wages and/or the costs of machinery, credit, or natural resources, the reaction of business firms is to produce less and charge higher prices.

The term first came into use in the mid-1970s, when inflation soared to 12 percent and the unemployment rate nearly doubled to 9 percent. This inflation was the result of the quadrupling of oil prices by the Organization of Petroleum Exporting Countries (OPEC), increases in the price of raw materials, and the lifting of Vietnam-era government-imposed PRICE AND WAGE CONTROLS. At the same time, the economy went into recession. In 1979 the high inflation rate was sent spiraling upward when OPEC doubled petroleum prices after the Iranian revolution. President Jimmy Carter established the Council on Wage and Price Stability, which sought voluntary cooperation from workers and manufacturers to hold down wage and price increases. The council could not control OPEC, however, and repeated oil-price hikes thwarted the council's efforts. Years of continued inflation and high unemployment was one of the factors that undermined the Carter presidency and Democratic Party proposals for welfare reform, national health insurance, and reform of labor law.

In 1980, after years of double-digit inflation the Federal Reserve Board (Fed), under Paul Volcker, prodded banks to raise interest rates to record levels of more than 20 percent to induce a recession and break the inflation cycle. Subsequently the Fed pursued a monetary policy designed to head off significant increases in inflation, but in 1994–1995, seven Fed increases in short-term interest rates failed to moderate economic growth. This led to speculation that in a global economy, domestic monetary policy may not be as effective in controlling stagflation as previously thought.

BIBLIOGRAPHY

Ferguson, Thomas, and Joel Rogers, eds. *The Hidden Election: Politics and Economics in the 1980 Presidential Campaign.* New York: Pantheon Books, 1981.

Greider, William. *Secrets of the Temple: How the Federal Reserve Runs the Country.* New York: Simon and Schuster, 1987.

Lal, Deepak, and Martin Wolf, eds. *Stagflation, Savings, and the State: Perspectives on the Global Economy.* New York: Oxford University Press, 1986.

Weintraub, Sidney, and Marwin Goodstein, eds. *Reaganomics in the Stagflation Economy.* Philadelphia: University of Pennsylvania Press, 1983.

Erik Bruun/c. p.

See also **Banking: Overview; Federal Reserve System; Oil Crises.**

STAGGERS RAIL ACT of 1980 (49 U.S.C., Public Law 94-473) was intended to remedy the serious financial troubles experienced by major American RAILROADS during the 1960s and 1970s. The completion of the U.S. interstate highway system in the 1950s increased the use of truck transportation, air transport siphoned off passenger and mail businesses, and pipelines diverted the transportation of petroleum products. The Staggers Rail Act deregulated the railroad industry in the belief that competition should determine freight rates. By restricting the powers and involvement of the Interstate Commerce Commission in determining rates, Congress intended that deregulation would enable the railways to earn adequate revenues.

BIBLIOGRAPHY

Dooley, Frank J., and William E. Thoms. *Railroad Law a Decade after Deregulation.* Westport, Conn.: Quorum Books, 1994.

Himmelberg, Robert F., ed. *Regulatory Issues since 1964: The Rise of the Deregulation Movement.* New York: Garland, 1994.

R. Blake Brown

See also **Deregulation.**

STALWARTS, a term applied to a conservative faction of the REPUBLICAN PARTY during the GILDED AGE. Led by Senator Roscoe Conkling of New York, they supported black male suffrage in the South and opposed the civil-service reform program of Rutherford B. Hayes's administration. Although the Stalwarts were unsuccessful in securing Ulysses S. Grant's nomination for a third presidential term in 1880, the assassination of James Garfield in 1881 elevated to the presidency Chester A. Arthur, the last Stalwart to hold the office. After Conkling's retire-

ment from politics in the 1880s, the designation soon passed out of use.

BIBLIOGRAPHY

Foner, Eric. *Reconstruction: America's Unfinished Revolution, 1863–1877.* New York: Harper and Row, 1988.

Jordan, David M. *Roscoe Conkling of New York: Voice in the Senate.* Ithaca, N.Y.: Cornell University Press, 1971.

Asa E. Martin/t. g.

See also **Civil Service; Liberal Republican Party; Reconstruction.**

STAMP ACT. The formal title of the Stamp Act is seventy words long. Prime Minister George Grenville indicated his intention to impose it in 1763, but it was not enacted until 22 March 1765, to take effect on 1 November. The act's mode of raising taxes was familiar to Britons of the time and was still in limited use at the beginning of the twenty-first century. Colonials understood stamp duties too. For a given document to be legal, a stamp of appropriate value had to be purchased from an official distributor and affixed to the document.

The mode may have been familiar, but the act's avowed purpose of raising revenue directly from colonials by act of Parliament was not. The only precedent also was part of Grenville's program of colonial reform. The Sugar

Stamp Act. Jonas Green's *Maryland Gazette* in Annapolis and other colonial newspapers joined in the unprecedented protests in America, in this case publishing a skull and crossbones in the place on the page where the stamp was supposed to be affixed. LIBRARY OF CONGRESS

Act (or Revenue Act) of 1764 provoked sporadic protest but did take effect. Grenville was not prepared for colonial protest. Neither were eminent colonials such as Benjamin Franklin, who was in London at the time and who nominated his friend John Hughes as stamp distributor for Pennsylvania. Virginia's future militant Richard Henry Lee sought the same post for his province.

Nonetheless the Stamp Act seemed as if it had been designed to provoke protest. The burdens it imposed may have been lighter than their British equivalents, but to colonials they weighed heavily. The act taxed all legal documents, from bills of lading for outbound ships, to indentures of apprenticeship, to marriage licenses. It taxed books, newspapers, advertisements in newspapers, dice, and decks of cards. No free white person in the colonies could live a normal life without paying one or another stamp duty. The duties had to be paid in gold or silver, both of which were in short supply in the colonial economy of barter, paper currency, and private bills of exchange. Violators of the act were subject to trial in a vice admiralty court. The judge would be a royal appointee holding his post "at the King's pleasure," meaning that too many acquittals could bring his dismissal. No jury would address the traditions and procedures that made up "English" liberty.

One goal of the Stamp Act was to reach deep into the economies of the American provinces, possibly for the sake of putting a brake on their development into potential rivals of Britain. But the act was not intended to strip the colonies of their precious metals. On the contrary, money raised would recirculate after paying the costs of royal governorships, Crown courts, and British troops stationed in America.

Even that change, however, was major, especially to elite colonials, who had grown used to the idea that the Virginia House of Burgesses or the Massachusetts Assembly were local equivalents of the House of Commons, fully able to run the affairs of their own provinces. The Stamp Act presented a fundamental challenge not only to the power and the self-image of the colonial elites but also to the material well-being of every free participant in colonial society.

BIBLIOGRAPHY

Bullion, John L. *A Great and Necessary Measure: George Grenville and the Genesis of the Stamp Act, 1763–1775.* Columbia: University of Missouri Press, 1982.

Thomas, Peter David Garner. *British Politics and the Stamp Act Crisis: The First Phase of the American Revolution, 1763–1767.* Oxford: Clarendon Press, 1975.

Edward Countryman

See also **Sons of Liberty (American Revolution);** *and vol. 9:* **Stamp Act.**

STAMP ACT CONGRESS was the first official intercolonial gathering of the revolutionary era. The Stamp Act Congress met in New York City between 7 October and 24 October 1765. Much more than the Albany Congress of 1754, it pointed toward union among white colonial people in the face of external threat, portending the First Continental Congress (1774), the Second Continental Congress (1775–1781), the Articles of Confederation (1781–1789), and debates about the U.S. Constitution (1787–1788).

New Hampshire and Georgia sent no delegates to the Stamp Act Congress. Connecticut, the host province of New York, and South Carolina gave their delegates no power to act. Virginia already was on record against the STAMP ACT in the resolutions of its House of Burgesses. At first glance then the records of the Congress might seem to be a minority report. But in fact the Congress's members laid out a tenable position regarding the Stamp Act and by extension the emerging crisis in colonial relations. They pointed toward coalescence among the separate elites they represented into a coherent leadership. And with their silence on some issues, they addressed the problem of relations among different sorts of colonials who were becoming Americans.

The Congress produced four documents: a general declaration intended for both colonial and British readers, a petition to the king, a memorial to the House of Lords, and a petition to the House of Commons. Each term, declaration, petition, and memorial bespoke a different understanding of the Congress's relationship to the intended readers, but all four documents made the same essential points. (White) colonial Americans were Britons. They had abandoned none of their traditional "Rights and Liberties" by living outside the "Realm" that comprised England, Scotland, and Wales. Self-taxation through representatives was among such rights, because it meant a free gift of the subject's property to the Crown. That right could not be exercised through supposed representatives in the House of Commons, and other British rights, particularly the right to trial by jury, could not be negated. The effect of the Stamp Act would be to stifle the colonial economy, weaken colonial trade with Britain, indirectly harm the British economy itself, and poison relations between the colonies and the metropolis. Colonials were loyal, but they had a duty to seek the Stamp Act's repeal.

The Congress followed Virginia's lead taken in June with resolutions against the Stamp Act by the Virginia House of Burgesses. By the time the Congress met, several colonies had experienced both verbal and violent resistance to the Stamp Act, and it was increasingly clear that the act never would take force. In New York City preparations were under way for the uprising of 31 October 1765 that rendered the act unenforceable there.

The Congress did not address such problems. But both in what it said and what it chose not to say, it did address the complex coalition politics of the revolutionary era. Like the Virginia House of Burgesses, the Congress told discontented colonials that resistance was entirely correct.

BIBLIOGRAPHY

Morgan, Edmund S., and Helen M. Morgan. *The Stamp Act Crisis: Prologue to Revolution.* Chapel Hill: University of North Carolina Press, 1953.

Morgan, Edmund Sears, ed. *Prologue to Revolution: Sources and Documents on the Stamp Act Crisis, 1764–1766.* Chapel Hill: University of North Carolina Press, 1959.

Edward Countryman

See also **Revolution, American: Political History.**

STAMP ACT RIOT in New York City on 31 October 1765 was one among many instances of violent resistance to British policy during the autumn of 1765. The riot was preceded by uprisings in Boston and in Newport, Rhode Island, and it led to continuing unrest in New York City and in other provinces. The total effect was to render the STAMP ACT unenforceable, as stamp distributors resigned their posts one-by-one.

Like the others, the New York uprising was planned. It expressed discontent against the Stamp Act, against the British military and naval presence in New York, and against the pattern of Anglo-American politics.

Stamp Act Riot. This engraving depicts protesters on a New York City street watching a man and a boy burn British stamps. ARCHIVE PHOTOS, INC.

BIBLIOGRAPHY

Countryman, Edward. *A People in Revolution: The American Revolution and Political Society in New York, 1760–1790.* Baltimore: Johns Hopkins University Press, 1981.

Tiedemann, Joseph S. *Reluctant Revolutionaries: New York City and the Road to Independence, 1763–1776.* Ithaca, N.Y.: Cornell University Press, 1997.

Edward Countryman

See also **Riots.**

STAMPEDES were the most dramatic, hazardous, and disastrous events of roundups and cattle drives. Oxen, horses, and buffalo all might stampede, but the frantic flight that the rancheros called *estampida* was especially characteristic of longhorns. A great herd peacefully bedded down might, with the instantaneity of forked lightning, be on its feet, and then with hoofs, hocks, and horns knocking together, the ground shaking from the impact, thunder away in headlong flight. The only way to check them was to circle the leaders and thus swing the mass into a "mill." Causes of stampedes were many: the whir of a rattlesnake near the head of some snoring steer, the flirt of a polecat's tail, the jump of a rabbit, the smell of a lobo, the flash of a match by some careless cowboy lighting a cigarette, or any unexpected sound such as the shaking of an empty saddle by a horse. Cowboy songs were not so much to soothe cattle as to afford a barrier against surprises. Nonetheless, the best preventives were bellies full of grass and water.

Western artists like Frederic Remington, Charles M. Russell, and Frank Reaugh have pictured the stampede. Popular ballads like "Lasca" and "When Work's All Done This Fall" have dramatized it. One of the most powerful stories ever written on any western subject, *Longrope's Last Guard* by Russell, translates it fully. Yet, human fatalities from stampedes were rare. The worst results of the stampedes were to the cattle themselves: animals trampled to death, horns and legs broken, and more "tallow run off" in a night than could be restored by a month of grazing.

BIBLIOGRAPHY

Clayton, Lawrence. *Vaqueros, Cowboys, and Buckaroos.* Austin: University of Texas Press. 2001.

Dary, David. *Cowboy Culture: A Saga of Five Centuries.* New York: Knopf. 1981.

Rifkin, Jeremy. *Beyond Beef: The Rise and Fall of the Cattle Culture.* New York: Dutton. 1992.

Worcester, Donald Emmet. *The Chisholm Trail: High Road of the Cattle Kingdom.* Lincoln: University of Nebraska Press, 1980.

J. Frank Dobie

See also **Cattle; Cattle Drives; Cowboy Songs; Cowboys; Sheep; Trail Drivers.**

STANDARD & POOR'S (S&P) was created by the 1941 merger and incorporation of Poor's, a financial publishing company founded by Henry Varnum Poor in 1867, and Standard Statistics Bureau, a publisher of daily indexes for ninety stocks that its founder, Luther Lee Blake, had begun tracking in 1906. Several government agencies began using the stock index in the late 1950s, particularly after computers enabled the firm to calculate 500 companies' stock on a real-time basis. The company introduced the S&P 500, a capitalization-weighted index of 500 of the largest publicly traded companies in the United States, on 4 March 1957. S&P publishes a number of investment advisories, compendia of statistical information, and financial directories.

BIBLIOGRAPHY

Blake, Rich. "The Rise of the S&P 500." *Institutional Investor,* May 2002.

Downes, John, Elliot Goodman, and Jordan Elliot Goodman. *Dictionary of Finance and Investment Terms.* 4th ed. New York: Barron's, 2001.

Mary Lawrence Wathen

STANDARD OIL COMPANY, an Ohio corporation, was incorporated on 10 January 1870 with a capital of $1 million, the original stockholders being John D. Rockefeller, with 2,667 shares; William Rockefeller, with 1,333 shares; Henry M. Flagler, with 1,333 shares; Samuel Andrews, with 1,333 shares; Stephen V. Harkness, with 1,334 shares; O. B. Jennings, with 1,000 shares; and the firm of Rockefeller, Andrews and Flagler, with 1,000 shares. The company took the place of the previous firm of Rockefeller, Andrews and Flagler (formed 1867), whose refineries were the largest in Cleveland and probably the largest in the world at that time. The company immediately made important extensions. These refineries, superior efficiency, and the threat of the South Improvement Company led Standard Oil to swallow practically all rival refineries in the Cleveland area in 1872.

Coincidentally with the conquest of Cleveland, Standard Oil began reaching out to other cities. In 1872 it bought the oil transporting and refining firm of J. A. Bostwick and Company in New York; the Long Island Oil Company; and a controlling share of the Devoe Manufacturing Company on Long Island. In 1873 it bought pipelines, the largest refinery in the oil regions, and a half interest in a Louisville refinery. The acquisition of the principal refineries of Pittsburgh and Philadelphia was carried out in 1874–1876, while in 1877 Standard Oil defeated the Pennsylvania Railroad and the Empire Transportation Company in a major struggle, taking possession of the pipelines and refineries of the latter. An-

John D. Rockefeller. The oil tycoon and monopolist in his later, more philanthropic years. LIBRARY OF CONGRESS

other war with the Tidewater Pipeline resulted in a working agreement that drastically limited the latter's operations. By 1879, special agreements with the railroads along with strategic use of pools allowed Standard Oil, with its subsidiary and associated companies, to control 90 to 95 percent of the refining capacity of the United States, immense pipeline and storage-tank systems, and powerful marketing organizations at home and abroad.

While Standard Oil of Ohio remained legally a small company with no manufacturing operations outside its state, it was the nucleus of an almost nationwide industrial organization, one of the richest and most powerful in the country. Its articles of incorporation had not authorized it to hold stock in other companies nor to be a partner in any firm. After trying a variety of other methods to skirt the company's articles of incorporation, Standard Oil finally overcame this restriction by acquiring stocks not in the name of Standard Oil of Ohio but in that of a prominent stockholder named as trustee. Flagler, William Rockefeller, Bostwick, and various others served from 1873 to 1879 as trustees. Then, in 1879, the situation was given more systematic treatment. All of the stocks acquired by Standard Oil and held by various trustees, and all of the properties outside Ohio in which Standard Oil had an interest, were transferred to three minor employees as trustees. They held the stocks and properties for the exclusive use and benefit of Standard Oil's stockholders and distributed dividends in specified proportions. But while this arrangement was satisfactory from a legal point of view, it did not provide sufficient administrative centralization. On 2 January 1882, therefore, a new arrangement, the Standard Oil Trust Agreement, set up the first monopoly trust in American history. All stock and properties, including that of the Standard Oil proper as well as of interests outside Ohio, were transferred to a board of nine trustees, consisting of the principal owners and managers, with John D. Rockefeller as head. For each share of stock of Standard Oil of Ohio, twenty trust certificates of a par value of $100 each were to be issued. The total of the trust certificates was therefore $70 million, considerably less than the actual value of the properties. Standard Oil's huge network of refineries, pipes, tanks, and marketing systems was thus given a secret, but for the time being satisfactory, legal organization, while administration was centralized in nine men, with John D. Rockefeller at their head. The new arrangement allowed Standard Oil Trust to integrate the industry horizontally by combining competing companies into one and vertically by controlling petroleum from its production to its sale.

Standard Oil's growth in wealth and power drew the awe of other corporations and the criticism of social critics, most notably muckraker Ida Tarbell, who wrote the scathing "History of the Standard Oil Company" in *McClure's* magazine in 1902. By the time of Tarbell's publication, social criticism was just one of many forces checking Standard Oil's power. The gusher at Spindletop in Texas in 1901 had prompted a flood of new oil companies along the Gulf coast, and they, along with new companies in California and the Plains states, reduced Standard Oil's dominance. Legal challenges beset Standard Oil as well. In 1892, as a result of a decree by the Ohio courts, the Standard Oil Trust dissolved, and the separate establishments and plants were reorganized into twenty constituent companies. But by informal arrangement, unity of action was maintained among these twenty corporations until 1899 when they were gathered into a holding company called Standard Oil of New Jersey. In 1906 the federal Bureau of Corporations filed a report on Standard Oil's operations in Kansas that led directly to a federal antitrust suit against Standard Oil in the U.S. Circuit Court for the Eastern District of Missouri. Three years later, the court ruled against Standard Oil, and in 1911 a decree of the U.S. Supreme Court upheld the ruling. The historic 1911 decision broke up Rockefeller's company into six main entities: Standard Oil of New Jersey (Esso, now Exxon), Standard Oil of New York (Socony, now Mobil), Standard Oil of Ohio, Standard Oil of Indiana (now Amoco, part of BP), and Standard Oil of California (now Chevron). Rockefeller remained nominal head of Standard Oil until 1911, but by 1895 he had surrendered more and more of the actual authority to his associates.

BIBLIOGRAPHY

Hidy, Ralph W. *History of Standard Oil Company (New Jersey)*. New York: Arno Press, 1976.

Wall, Bennett H., et. al. *Growth in a Changing Environment: A History of the Standard Oil Company (New Jersey), 1950–1972 and Exxon Corporation, 1972–1975*. New York: Harper and Row, 1988.

Williamson, Harold F. *The American Petroleum Industry*. Evanston, Ill.: Northwestern University Press, 1959.

Yergin, Daniel. *The Prize: The Epic Quest for Oil, Money, and Power*. New York: Simon and Schuster, 1991.

Allan Nevins / F. B.

See also **Antitrust Laws; Free Trade; Petroleum Industry; Standard Oil Company of New Jersey v. United States; Trusts.**

STANDARD OIL COMPANY OF NEW JERSEY V. UNITED STATES,

221 U.S. 1 (1911), originated in 1906 when the federal government filed a suit against more than seventy corporations and individuals alleging a conspiracy to fix the production and price of oil in violation of the SHERMAN ANTITRUST ACT of 1890. Upholding a 1909 federal circuit court opinion finding the STANDARD OIL COMPANY to be "an attempt to monopolize and a monopolization under Sec. 2 of the Antitrust Act," in 1911 the Supreme Court compelled the cartel to relinquish control over thirty-seven subsidiary companies, essentially creating thirty-eight ostensibly independent companies.

BIBLIOGRAPHY

Bringhurst, Bruce. *Antitrust and the Oil Monopoly: The Standard Oil Cases, 1890–1911*. Westport, Conn.: Greenwood Press, 1979.

Freyer, Tony A. *Regulating Big Business: Antitrust in Great Britain and America, 1880–1990*. New York: Cambridge University Press, 1992.

Andrew C. Rieser

See also **Antitrust Laws; Elkins Act; Government Regulation of Business; Monopoly; Restraint of Trade; Trust-Busting; Trusts.**

STANDARDS OF LIVING

include not only the ownership of consumer goods, but also aspects of living that cannot be purchased or are not under an individual's direct control—for instance, environmental quality and services provided by the government. Social scientists debate how exactly to measure standards of living. In a comparison among nations, often the yardstick is per capita national income, although some scholars prefer the related measure, per capita consumption of goods and services. However, using per capita income, or consumption of those goods and services that are measured by economists, to calculate standards of living can obscure both significant social problems and significant noneconomic values. For instance, despite the high per capita standard of living in the United States, infant mortality in some U.S. cities—including the nation's capitol—equals or surpasses that in some countries with extremely low per capita standards of living. Per capita figures in general do not reveal the extent of gaps between rich and poor. Furthermore, not only do income figures not measure such factors as access to safe drinking water or political freedoms, they also do not measure wealth that does not appear as "income." Thus, for instance, value-producing activities such as unpaid household labor may be rendered invisible, though access to the fruits of such labor improves one's living standard.

On the basis of per capita income, the American standard of living has been among the highest in the world since the early eighteenth century, though such an assessment is more complicated than it appears. Early standards of living of America's free citizens, for instance, were boosted by their access to enslaved labor (slaves' standard of living, though it varied somewhat both materially and nonmaterially, was always low). Numerous immigrants, too, have encountered much lower standards of living than they expected upon coming to the United States, though they often raised them significantly for themselves and their children. Nonetheless, Americans have on the whole enjoyed a relatively high standard of living. Long-term changes in the standard of living were probably modest before the 1840s, but have been pronounced since then. Between 1840 and 1970, per capita income, after allowance for price changes, increased sevenfold. The rate of change has varied from year to year, being affected by business cycles and Kuznets cycles (fluctuations of about twenty years' duration, postulated by Simon Kuznets), and has been slightly higher on the average in the twentieth century than in the nineteenth century. Japan and many Western European countries have experienced roughly comparable rates of improvement in per capita income in the twentieth century, although few of these countries have approached the U.S. level.

Standards of living have varied from region to region in the United States. Incomes of families in the Midwest and, especially, the South have tended to be lower than those of families in the Northeast and Far West. This reflects the concentration of farming, traditionally a low-income industry, in the former regions. (The measured differences may exaggerate standard of living differences, because some components of income on farms are inadequately reflected in national income.) Regional differences, after widening between the middle and end of the nineteenth century (because of the effects of the Civil War), narrowed drastically in the twentieth century. This development was the result of the industrialization of the Midwest and the South and the relative improvement in agricultural incomes.

The distribution of income by size has been roughly the same in the United States as in most Western European nations for which data are available. Just before the Civil War, the richest 5 percent of U.S. families probably had about eight times as much income per family as the remaining 95 percent. There does not seem to have been any major change until after the 1920s, when the degree of inequality diminished somewhat, the rich losing and the poor gaining, in relative terms. By the 1950s, the richest 5 percent had about five times the income per family of the remaining 95 percent. From then to the mid-1970s, the distribution was rather stable, those in the middle-income groups gaining slightly at the expense of both rich and poor. After the 1970s, the distribution began to widen, with working families facing an increasingly declining standard of living. Beginning with the administration of President Ronald Reagan (1980–1988), and due in substantial part to his policies, the income disparity between the richest and poorest Americans has widened significantly. Weakened labor laws and the exploitation of unprotected immigrants have fueled this disparity and pushed a greater share of the nation's wealth upward to the top five percent, while the bottom third or more have experienced a decline in its standard of living.

BIBLIOGRAPHY

Brown, Clair. *American Standards of Living, 1918–1988*. Oxford, U.K.: Blackwell, 1994.

Davis, Lance E., et al. *American Economic Growth: An Economist's History of the United States*. New York: Harper and Row, 1972.

Gallman, Robert E., and John J. Wallis, eds. *American Economic Growth and Standards of Living before the Civil War*. Chicago: University of Chicago Press, 1992.

Robert E. Gallman / D. B.

See also **Consumerism; Work.**

STANFORD UNIVERSITY.

In 1885 a grant of endowment established Leland Stanford Junior College, later Stanford University, in memorial to Jane and Leland Stanford's deceased son, Leland Jr. The $5 million initial grant also included 8,180 acres of Palo Alto farmland owned by Leland Stanford, a former California governor and railroad entrepreneur. Conceived by the renowned landscape architect Fredrick Law Olmsted, the university's campus was constructed over a period of six years and centered around the Inner Quadrangle and Memorial Church. The red tiled roofs and open arches that still distinguish Stanford's campus suggest the architecture of old California missions and marked Stanford as a part of the Western landscape.

Stanford University emerged during a period of transformation and growth in American higher education. During this time many prestigious colleges became universities, and several new schools were founded, including the University of Chicago and Johns Hopkins University. These new universities tended toward a more democratic vision of schooling and embraced the German educational model of including undergraduate and graduate training and emphasizing research as well as teaching among faculty. Stanford's mission and practices in many ways reflected these new shifts in American higher education.

The university was founded as a nondenominational, non-tuition-based, and coeducational institution (although restrictions were placed on women's enrollment in 1899). Leland Stanford hoped that the university would provide a balance between technical education and the cultivation of young imaginations, to "qualify students for personal success and direct usefulness in life; and to promote the public welfare by exercising an influence on behalf of humanity and civilization." In selecting the university's first president, Leland Stanford sought out an educator who would share his educational vision as well as grow with the university. Six months before the opening of the university the Stanfords hired David Starr Jordan, a leading scientific scholar and president of Indiana University, to fill the position.

Stanford University opened it doors in 1891. Located only sixty-three miles from the University of California, Berkeley, the newly founded university faced immediate competition. In its first year Stanford rose to the occasion by enrolling 559 students, from a range of educational backgrounds, into its pioneer class. With a faculty of fifteen, which would triple in the second year, the university established departments based on major subject areas within the humanities and sciences. It also supported an active student life, including a variety of athletic clubs. Under the leadership of Dr. Jordan, who would serve as university president until 1913, Stanford began to build a solid—if not always stable—academic foundation. Yet, in the early years, the most profound challenges to the survival of Stanford University were financial in nature. In 1893, just two years after its founding, Leland Stanford died, sending his estate into legal turmoil. For six years Stanford's funds were held in probate, leading Jane Stanford to consider closing the university temporarily. Stanford University faced a lesser financial setback during the California earthquake of 1906, which destroyed many of the buildings on campus.

In the 1910s, with the retirement of Dr. Jordan as president and the addition of the future president of the United States Herbert Hoover, a pioneer-class graduate, to the board of trustees, Stanford University entered a new period of development. Largely under the leadership of Hoover and his close friend, the president-elect Ray Lyman Wilbur, Stanford began to rise as a research institution. Following World War I President Wilbur reorganized Stanford's departments into schools, including engineering, medicine, the humanities, earth sciences, education, and law, with appointed deans as the head administrators. Wilbur also ended the university's no-tuition policy during this period. Hoover led efforts to build specialized institutions within Stanford University by soliciting donations from private foundations and businessmen to fund the Hoover War Collection (later the Hoover

Institution on War, Revolution, and Peace), established in 1919; the Food Research Institute, founded in 1921; and the Stanford Business School, organized in 1925.

The post–World War II era marked another period of transformation and growth for Stanford, as the university benefited greatly from the U.S. government's increased spending on technological and military research. Stanford University became a key site for government-sponsored research programs. These research programs became a major source of funds and prestige for the university. The Stanford Research Institute, which focused on electrical engineering, was largely funded through governmental support. In 1961 the Atomic Energy Commission provided over 100 million dollars in financial support to build the path-breaking Stanford Linear Accelerator Center (SLAC). Such funding sources not only allowed Stanford to build "steeples of excellence" in specific fields but also made possible other development plans, including the construction of several dormitories and the Stanford Medical Center.

In 2002 Stanford University stood as one of the premier centers of higher learning and research in the country. Enrolling over 6,000 undergraduates and 7,000 graduate students a year, the university continued to attract some of the leading scholars in their fields and has produced a long list of renowned alumni.

BIBLIOGRAPHY

Elliot, Orrin Leslie. *Stanford University: The First Twenty-Five Years*. New York: Arno Press, 1977.

Geiger, Roger. *Research and Relevant Knowledge: American Research Universities Since World War II*. New York: Oxford University Press, 1993.

Lowen, Rebecca S. *Creating the Cold War University: The Transformation of Stanford*. Berkeley: University of California Press, 1997.

Dayo F. Gore

See also **Education, Higher: Colleges and Universities.**

STAR OF THE WEST, an unarmed merchant vessel that President James Buchanan, influenced by Unionist cabinet members, secretly dispatched on 5 January 1861, with troops and supplies to reinforce Maj. Robert Anderson at Fort Sumter, South Carolina. Reaching CHARLESTON harbor on 9 January, the vessel was fired on by the batteries on Morris Island and Fort Moultrie. Neither Anderson nor the vessel's commander returned the fire, and the *Star of the West* withdrew. It was captured by Confederate forces on 20 April 1861.

BIBLIOGRAPHY

Johnson, Ludwell H. "Fort Sumter and Confederate Diplomacy." *Journal of Southern History* 26 (1960): 441–477.

Fletcher M. Green/A. R.

See also **Secession; Sumter, Fort.**

STAR ROUTE FRAUDS bilked the Post Office Department of about $4 million in fraudulent contracts to carry mail, principally in the West, in the 1870s and 1880s. Post Office officials, contractors, subcontractors, and a former senator conspired to obtain congressional appropriations for starting new and useless routes. One $90,000 contract was let on the affidavit of one contractor. Another route with $761 income annually received $50,000 to expedite its service, although for thirty-nine days no papers or letters were carried over that road. Congressional investigations, special agents, Pinkerton detectives, and attorneys brought about more than twenty-five indictments. Trials in 1882 and 1883 proved frauds on ninety-three routes, but no convictions resulted.

BIBLIOGRAPHY

Cullinan, Gerald. *The Post Office Department.* New York: Praeger, 1968.

Louis Pelzer / c. w.

See also **Post Roads; Postal Service, U.S.; Scandals.**

STAR WARS was written and directed by George Lucas and was released by Twentieth Century Fox in 1977. A science fiction tale, *Star Wars* centers on the journey Luke Skywalker (Mark Hamill) makes from innocent young man to noble Jedi Knight. Skywalker eventually teams up with Hans Solo (Harrison Ford) in an effort to save Princess Leia (Carrie Fisher) from the treacherous Darth Vader (David Prowse and James Earl Jones). A classic tale of good versus evil with dazzling special effects, *Star Wars* ushered in the era of the blockbuster. The film grossed over $450 million in United States theaters alone. It inspired Lucas to create his own studio, Lucas Films Ltd., and produce several sequels and prequels, *The Empire Strikes Back* (1980), *Return of the Jedi* (1983), *The Phantom Menace* (1999), and *Attack of the Clones* (2002). *Star Wars* also inspired a spin-off industry of merchandise, from models of x-wing fighters to Pez candy dispensers, that generated over $4 billion in sales. The film earned seven Academy Awards.

Some critics charged that *Star Wars* reproduces racial stereotypes in its representations of both human and alien diversity. No recognizable actors of color are employed in the film, and only a few are in the sequels. James Earl Jones, a black actor, provides the voice but not the performance of Darth Vader. Nevertheless, some count *Star Wars* as a landmark film for both its innovative use of special effects and its problematic racial politics.

BIBLIOGRAPHY

Campbell, Richard, with Christopher R. Martin and Bettina Fabos. *Media and Culture: An Introduction to Mass Communication.* 2d ed. Boston: Bedford/St. Martin's Press, 2000.

Sobchack, Vivian. *Screening Space: The American Science Fiction Film.* 2d ed. New Brunswick, N.J.: Rutgers University Press, 1997.

Daniel Bernardi

See also **Film Industry; Hollywood.**

"STAR-SPANGLED BANNER." In 1931 Congress passed legislation making "The Star-Spangled Banner" the national anthem of the United States. The song began as a poem written by the amateur poet Francis Scott Key on 14 September 1814. On that morning Key was looking at the smoke rising from Fort McKinley in BALTIMORE, which had just endured twenty-five hours of British attack. Through the smoke Key caught sight of the large garrison flag still flying, and this image inspired him to jot a few lines down on the back of a letter.

Key lengthened and revised the poem, and the next day it was published as a broadside with Key's recommendation that the words be sung to a tune he liked, the popular British song "To Anacreon in Heaven." Soon the poem appeared in several newspapers along the East Coast. Shortly thereafter Thomas Carr's music store in Baltimore published the words and music together under the present title. The song had become popular by the start of the Civil War and was frequently played on patriotic occasions. Members of the Maryland State Society, members of the U.S. Daughters of 1812, and Congressman J. Charles Linthicum of Baltimore are credited with bringing about the legislation that made the song the national anthem. The original flag that inspired Key is preserved at the Smithsonian Institution.

BIBLIOGRAPHY

Meyer, Sam. *Paradoxes of Fame: The Francis Scott Key Story.* Annapolis, Md.: Eastwind Publications, 1995.

Connie Ann Kirk

See also **War of 1812.**

Star Wars. The stars of the movie megahit: Mark Hamill *(left)*, Carrie Fisher, and Harrison Ford. THE KOBAL COLLECTION

STARE DECISIS is the principle of deciding judicial controversies on the basis of precedent. It is a principle of the common-law legal systems that distinguishes them from civil-law systems. Adherence to precedent, following the decision rules and reasoning set out in earlier similar cases, is frequently cited as an attribute that gives consistency and predictability to the law and that ensures political stability. However, assumptions concerning the significance and impact of adherence to *stare decisis* have been subjected to serious logical and empirical challenges. The continuing controversy over the scope and significance of *stare decisis* has served to focus greater analytical and empirical attention on the total constellation of factors that may influence judicial decision making.

BIBLIOGRAPHY

Kairys, David. "Legal Reasoning." In *The Politics of Law: A Progressive Critique.* Edited by David Kairys. New York: Pantheon Books, 1982.

Llewellyn, Karl N. *The Common Law Tradition: Deciding Appeals.* Boston: Little, Brown, 1960.

Rantoul, Robert, Jr. "Oration at Scituate: Delivered on the Fourth of July, 1836." In Perry Miller, ed., *The Legal Mind in America: From Independence to the Civil War.* Garden City, N.Y.: Doubleday, 1962.

Tocqueville, Alexis de. *Democracy in America.* Edited by J. P. Mayer. Translated by George Lawrence. New York: Harper Perennial, 1988.

John R. Schmidhauser/c. p.

See also **Judicial Review.**

STARR REPORT. *See* **Clinton Scandals; Impeachment Trial of Bill Clinton.**

STARVING TIME is the term applied to the winter of 1609–1610 at the Jamestown settlement. By spring 1610, only 60 of the 215 settlers remained alive. Research by the Jamestown Recovery Project, which began in 1994, indicates a severe drought in 1609 caused crop failures and poor harvests. Indian depredations and disease also contributed to the deaths. The arrival of a supply fleet in May 1610 saved the colony. The term has also been applied to the Plymouth Colony in spring 1622.

BIBLIOGRAPHY

Barisic, Sonja. "Unearthing Jamestown Hardships: Hastily Buried Bodies Indicate Desperate Times." Associated Press (9 April 2001).

Bradford, William. *History of Plymouth Plantation, 1620–1647.* New York: Russell and Russell, 1968.

Jerry L. Parker

See also **Colonial Settlements;** *and vol. 9:* **Starving in Virginia.**

STATE CONSTITUTIONS. Every state in the United States possesses its own constitution. Historically, state constitutions have been longer than the 7,500-word U.S. Constitution and more detailed regarding the day-to-day relationships between government and the people. For instance, the New York state constitution is 51,700 words long while Alabama's sixth and most recent constitution, ratified in 1901, is 310,296 words long. Differences in length and detail can be attributed to the different purposes of the documents as well as to the different approaches to constitutional uses between the federal and state governments. Both the federal and state constitutions are organic texts: they are the fundamental blueprints for the legal and political organizations of their respective sovereign entities. But both state and federal constitutions go beyond this. While the U.S. Constitution prescribes the limits of federal power, state constitutions describe the details of structure and process of those governmental powers not delegated to the federal government. Many state constitutions also address very specific issues deemed by the states to be of sufficient importance to be included in the constitution rather than in an ordinary statute.

In addition to the bills of rights, which in contrast to the federal Bill of Rights were adopted as part of the original state constitutions and are at their beginning, state constitutions generally contain a large number of statute-like provisions. South Dakota's constitution, for instance, contains provisions, often of very restricted scope, for state hail insurance. Also included is a provision that establishes a twine and cordage plant at the state prison. The Alabama constitution provides specific protection for the loss of peanut crops resulting from disease or bad weather. There are two reasons for including such provisions in the constitution. First, doing so accords them a constitutional status that gives them an enhanced prestige. Second, when a particular rule is included in the state constitution it becomes significantly more difficult to change than if it were simply passed as a statute by a state legislature. It is for these reasons, for example, that the rules protecting the Adirondack Park in upstate New York were incorporated into a late-nineteenth-century revision of the New York constitution rather than simply incorporated into existing statute law.

Most Americans look to the U.S. Constitution as the basis for civil rights. Until passage of the Fourteenth Amendment in 1868, however, it was the bill of rights embedded in each state constitution that enumerated the protections afforded individual citizens of the state. In 1833 Chief Justice John Marshall, writing for the United States Supreme Court, underscored the authority of the state over its citizens by specifically holding in *Barron v. Baltimore* that the federal Bill of Rights provided no protection for individual citizens against any state's action. After ratification of the Fourteenth Amendment, it was the U.S. Constitution that provided the basic protections to an individual's civil rights, while state constitutions provided various additional protections, such as an explicit right to privacy and rights for crime victims. Many legal scholars believe that such provisions in state constitutions provide an important second level of protections of individual rights in areas such as disability laws and privacy rights, areas in which federal courts have tended to narrow such rights under the U.S. Constitution and Bill of Rights.

Revolutionary Era Constitutions

At the time of the American Revolution, two political notions predominated. First was the belief that the new government must be republican in format, taking its inspiration from the political ideas of ancient Greece and Rome, thereby setting America forever apart from the long history of monarchical government in England. The new state constitutions manifested this distrust of monarchy by establishing strong legislative bodies with generally weak executive and judicial branches. Many early state "presidents" or governors were elected every year with term limits in place. To protect government from the sway of the mob and because greater power was placed in these early legislatures, rather than the executive or judiciary branches of state government, in many states it was the legislature that voted on the governor and not the general electorate. Second, it was believed that the new states had to have written constitutions as opposed to the "unwritten" British constitution. The strong belief in the importance of a written constitution infused American life from the beginning at every level. From these intertwined roots, however, the state constitutions evidenced the disparate beliefs and tensions that threatened to overwhelm the new country. There was, and to some extent remains, a constant tension between those who have believed in popular democracy and those who have feared it. In the beginning, and for decades to come, the vast majority of state constitutions did not contemplate a voting population that was other than adult, male, white, and generally possessed of property. It was not until after the Civil War, for instance, that most states granted a right to vote to African Americans, and it was not until the twentieth century that women of any color were allowed to vote in all elections.

The state constitutions adopted between 1776 and 1780 were each the product of a struggle between reactionary forces, loyalists, patriots, great landowners and merchants, and the general populace. The resulting documents directly reflected the success of one group or another in achieving and promoting their visions of the proper political and social order for the new country. In Pennsylvania, the state constitution of 1776 established a House of Representatives to be elected annually, with an Executive Council and an annually elected president who would possess no lawmaking powers. Every adult male taxpayer who lived in the state for one year was eligible to vote. The major qualification to serve in the House of Representatives was a two-year residency in the state. In a further bow to the democratic impulse, each bill considered by the house was to be printed for consideration and comment by the general public in order to afford the public the opportunity to express its views. In short, the Pennsylvania constitution established a form of government strongly inclined to broad public participation and supportive of liberal democratic principles.

The New York state constitution of 1777, on the other hand, was a more conservative document and established a legal and governmental order designed to favor the interests of the wealthy and landed classes. This constitution established a bicameral legislature. The lower house, the assembly, was to be elected annually from counties while the upper house, the senate, was elected in a staggered four-year rotation from only four districts. The governor was to be elected every three years. The assembly had the exclusive right to initiate money bills, but in all other matters the two houses enjoyed equal powers. To vote for an assemblyman, male citizens were required to own land worth at least £20 or possess a renthold of at least forty shillings value. To vote for senator or governor, the elector had to possess a freehold worth £100. A proposal was also put forward to require New York City residency and £10,000 in order to run for senator. This, however, was too biased toward the wealthy elite and was discarded by the drafters. Nonetheless, that proposal illustrates the fears of unbridled democracy among the elite members of the drafting committee.

In Maryland, a state dominated by a small group of large planter-landlords, the constitutional structure of government was even more conservative and anti-democratic. According to its 1776 constitution, general elections were to be held only once every three years and then only for county sheriff and the representatives to the lower house in the state legislature. State senators were to be chosen for five-year terms by a college of electors. The two houses of the state legislature would jointly choose the governor every year. To be elected to the lower house, a man had to prove assets of at least £500; to be elected senator or to serve on the governor's council, a man was required to have assets worth at least £1,000. To be governor, a candidate had to prove a personal fortune of at least £5,000. Only a small percentage of the adult white male population qualified to run for statewide office under these requirements.

These early state constitutions were influenced by such political philosophers as Montesquieu, Rousseau, and John Locke and by English jurists such as Edward Coke and William Blackstone. Most, as a result, reflected the dominant political and legal philosophies of the late eighteenth century. However, they were not intended to be, nor did they remain, static documents. Each constitution contained provisions for revision and supplementation, which almost immediately came into play as states realized their powers and limitations within the framework of dual sovereignty that they shared with the federal government and as the perceived needs of each state changed over time. At each stage in U.S. history, state constitutions have either been amended, often resulting in the bloating of these documents, or simply replaced. For instance, during the populist Jacksonian era, many states sought to curb the abuses of corrupt legislatures, which were under the influence of large and powerful lobbyists and special interest groups. The states did this by giving increased powers to the executive branch and increasing the power of judicial review while limiting the power of the legislative branch. In many cases, the financial power of legislatures was reined in. In Maryland, for instance, the governor's term was increased from one year to four years and the legislature was prohibited from enacting laws using state credit for the benefit either of individuals or private corporations. The state also was prohibited from contracting debts for more than $100,000.

From the Civil War

The Civil War and Reconstruction brought renewed debates on the role and structure of state government. Between 1864 and 1879, thirty-seven new state constitutions were written and ratified as new western states were added and as the political situation changed dramatically. In the South, the so-called carpetbagger constitutions, designed to aid and protect newly enfranchised African Americans, were enacted. They were soon replaced with constitutions designed to ensure white supremacy. The Tennessee Constitution of 1870 prohibited miscegenation and white and black children to attend public school together. To prevent emancipated blacks from exercising political power, state constitutions across the South were amended or rewritten to deprive them of the franchise. Mississippi's constitution of 1890 established a poll tax of two dollars and required that in order to vote a man had to be able to read, understand, and interpret any section of the state constitution. In Louisiana, which added a similar provision to its constitution in 1893, a grandfather clause excused all but African Americans from this exclusionary qualification. The 1895 South Carolina constitution required that a citizen be able to read and understand the state constitution or own $300 in real property in order to vote. By the end of the nineteenth century, voting requirements in state constitutions prevented as many as 90 percent of African American voters in the South from voting. These state constitutional changes were supported by many state statutes and court decisions and by the U.S. Supreme Court in cases such as *Plessy v. Ferguson* (1896), which gave the Court's stamp of approval to the concept of "separate but equal" and prolonged legal segregation in America for another sixty years. This concept was implemented until landmark federal court cases and legislation of the 1950s and 1960s ruled the principle of "separate but equal" to be prohibited under the U.S. Constitution. All state constitutions continue to exist within the complex legal and political context created by dual sovereignty. The U.S. Supreme Court ruling in *Bush v. Gore* (2000) that followed the 2000 presidential elections reflects this complexity. The Court referred not only to the U.S. Constitution but also to the Florida consti-

tution in considering the scope and power of the Florida legislature to set voting standards and processes within the state and the decision that was reached in this case will, inevitably, have an impact on the future shape of state constitutions.

BIBLIOGRAPHY

Countryman, Edward. *The American Revolution.* New York: Hill and Wang, 1985.

Friedman, Lawrence M. *History of American Law.* New York: Simon and Schuster, 1985.

Hammons, Christopher W. "State Constitutional Reform: Is it Necessary?" *Albany Law Review* 64 (2001): 1327–1347.

Robert B. Dishman
Karenbeth Farmer
M. H. Hoeflich

See also **Barron v. Baltimore; Bill of Rights in State Constitutions;** *Bush v. Gore;* **Constitution of the United States; Debts, State; State Sovereignty; Suffrage; Suffrage, African American.**

STATE, DEPARTMENT OF.

President George Washington signed legislation creating a United States Department of Foreign Affairs on 27 July 1789. The department was one of three federal agencies established by Congress during the first session held under the Constitution.

Just a few months later, the Department of Foreign Affairs was renamed the Department of State. The name change better reflected the range of foreign and domestic responsibilities to be carried out by the new agency. Besides executing the foreign policy of the United States, the early State Department was responsible for managing the mint and the patent offices, as well as conducting the census. It was not until one hundred years later, when the United States embarked on a more assertive foreign policy, that these "home affairs" were completely taken over by other branches of the government.

The State Department was initially a tiny agency consisting of the Secretary of State, several clerks, and a part-time translator. The department oversaw a handful of foreign missions in European capitals. In addition, a network of consular posts was established to promote overseas business and protect ships and their crews.

The first leaders of the State Department were the fledgling republic's ablest politicians: Thomas Jefferson, James Madison, James Monroe, and John Quincy Adams. After leaving the post of U.S. Secretary of State, each man was elected President. As secretaries of state, they had two central goals: to secure the United States' newly won independence and to acquire additional territory for settlement and trade. Meanwhile, they wanted to steer clear of alliances with troublesome Old World powers.

Jefferson and his successors succeeded in achieving America's foreign policy aims. The United States managed to stay neutral in the Napoleonic wars. After 1794, favorable treaties were signed with Britain and Spain, resolving borders with Canada and Florida. The U.S. also gained permission to engage in shipping on the Mississippi River, and foreign troops were cleared from American soil. In 1804, President Thomas Jefferson and Secretary of State James Madison struck a brilliant deal with Napoleon. For $15 million, they were able to double the size of American territory with the Louisiana Purchase

Under Secretary of State John Quincy Adams, the United States began asserting its interests in Latin America. Adams was instrumental in formulating the Monroe Doctrine, warning Europe against seeking Caribbean colonies that had become independent of Spain. The United States also pledged to stay out of European conflicts.

When Adams left the State Department to assume the presidency in 1825, it was still very small and had only about twenty employees. It was considered a difficult place to work. All official documents had to be copied by hand, so the State Department's shoestring staff found themselves burdened with clerical duties.

During the years preceding the Civil War, the United States sought to remain aloof from the affairs of the Great Powers. American contacts with Europe were kept to a minimum, and consequently few new diplomatic posts were added abroad. Only seven new missions were added to the fifteen existing overseas posts from 1830 to 1860.

On the other hand, the expansion of American business across the oceans boosted the need for many more new consular stations. To protect and promote this vigorous trade, hundreds of consular posts sprung up around the world during the mid-nineteenth century. In 1860, the State Department was overseeing 480 consulates, commercial agencies, and consular agencies abroad.

Around midcentury, Congress began removing domestic responsibilities from the department and assigning them to new agencies such as the Interior Department and the Census Bureau. Slowly, new management positions were introduced in the department. In 1853, the position of Assistant Secretary of State was added to the State Department's developing bureaucratic structure.

William Henry Seward, Secretary of State during the Civil War, was a key adviser to President Lincoln. He conducted the diplomacy that kept the European powers, especially Great Britain, from actively aiding the Confederacy or declaring war on the Union. He enhanced the prestige and size of the Department of State significantly. During his tenure, there were two assistant secretaries of state to manage the agency's growing workload.

The continued development of international trade continued to be the key factor behind the expansion of the State Department into the twentieth century. As America neared the rank of a Great Power, the department's role in diplomacy became more important, and Congress decided to raise the status of its diplomats. In 1893, the U.S. appointed its first ambassador and established its first

official embassy in London. Soon ambassadors were named to other powerful nations in Europe, the Far East, and Latin America.

The State Department and U.S. Global Involvement

The 1898 Spanish-American war was a turning point for U.S. foreign policy and the State Department. The United States had broken with its tradition of isolationism and non-intervention by going to war against Spain. America's victory over the Spanish led to U.S. possession of its first overseas territories—Cuba, Hawaii, and the Philippines.

During the war against Spain, the State Department established itself as an important source of information for the press and the public. Secretary of State John Hay conducted regular news conferences to help sway public opinion to support this new imperialism.

In response to America's mounting interests around the globe, in the early part of the twentieth century, the State Department was forced to modernize operations and hire many new civil servants and diplomats abroad. In 1900, the department had ninety-one employees in Washington. Two decades later, the department employed 708 employees and had a budget of $1.4 million.

The bureaucratic structure of the department was divided according to political and geographic categories. New offices for disseminating information and managing trade relations were added. Although political patronage was still the surest route to entering the State Department, there were small moves toward the creation of a professional diplomatic corps.

Some who led American foreign policy, however, criticized the department for not changing its ways fast enough. They felt that the Foreign Service was filled with too many amateur diplomats and that the organization operated inefficiently. According to historian Robert Beisner, when Elihu Root became Secretary of State in 1905, he said he felt "like a man trying to conduct the business of a large metropolitan law firm in the office of a village squire." The consular service, Root remarked, was a place "to shelve broken down politicians and to take care of failures in American life . . . at government expense."

Root's concerns about the poor quality of the State Department workforce were addressed somewhat by presidents Theodore Roosevelt and William Howard Taft. Roosevelt signed an executive order in 1906 requiring entry-level consular officers to be appointed only after passing an examination. In 1909, Taft extended the merit system to higher-level Foreign Service Officers below the rank of minister and ambassador. Yet, the pay was so low in the Foreign Service that only men of wealth usually considered a diplomatic career.

The outbreak of World War I in 1914 raised pressing questions of diplomacy, the likes of which the United States had not seen since the era following independence from England. President Wilson looked to the department's leadership and its overseas envoys for assistance in determining what course of action the U.S. should take in response to the European conflict. Once the United States decided to enter the war on the side of Great Britain and Wilson laid out a global role for America in crafting the peace that would follow, the department was called upon to formulate a comprehensive foreign policy.

World War I modernized communications in the State Department. The use of telegraphic codes and ciphers became commonplace during the five-year conflict. The department instituted security measures to protect information and began labeling official documents "Secret" or "Confidential" to designate who would be granted access to them. After the war, the department began a program to interpret other nations' secret codes.

In the decades after World War I, important moves were taken to upgrade the qualifications of those who joined the Foreign Service. The definitive step toward the creation of a professional Foreign Service was Congress's passage of the Rogers Act on 24 May 1924. The Rogers Act made merit rather than political patronage the primary means of selecting diplomats abroad. It created a unified Foreign Service, composed of consular and diplomatic officers. It established a system of challenging written and oral qualifying exams for those seeking to become diplomats.

Under the Rogers Act, a career path was mapped out for Foreign Service Officers, with established requirements for being promoted. A career would encompass regular rotations to a variety of posts and leadership positions. Better salaries were introduced.

Before the Rogers Act was implemented, all the diplomats serving at the rank of chief of mission were political appointees. In 1924, thirty percent of mission chiefs were career appointees. By World War II, half of all chiefs of mission were career Foreign Service Officers. The Foreign Service did not fully shake off the profound influence of patronage until after World War II. By the end of the twentieth century, approximately seventy percent of all ambassadors were career envoys rather than men and women appointed by the president.

American participation in World War II and the onset of the Cold War turned the United States into a global superpower. The United States could no longer isolate itself from overseas developments. After the war, the U.S. would lead the reconstruction of war-torn Europe while working to contain the expansion of Soviet communism. For the first time, the United States became part of permanent military alliances (the North Atlantic Treaty Organization and the Southeast Asia Treaty Organization). Consequently, the State Department was burdened with immense new responsibilities in areas of the world where the nation previously had few interests.

The Cold War and Beyond
During the Cold War, the job of secretary of state became even more important to the crafting of America's inter-national relations. The men that headed the State Department under presidents Truman and Eisenhower—James F. Byrnes, George C. Marshall, Dean Acheson, and John Foster Dulles—were key policymakers who charted America's containment strategy. These department chiefs traveled extensively around the globe to participate in conferences and negotiations. Dulles, for example, logged 480,000 miles of travel during his tenure.

The State Department became more accessible to the public and the press after World War II. In the 1930s, Roosevelt's Secretary of State Cordell Hull began holding news conferences, and his successors also met with the press from time to time. However, starting in the 1950s and continuing to the early 2000s, it became more common to have State Department spokesmen meet regularly with the news media. The department started publishing copies of important speeches by the Secretary of State, and conferences on current international problems were organized for foreign policy experts, the public, and the press.

To meet the burdens of policymaking during the Cold War, the entire State Department bureaucracy was restructured. New bureaus were created, such as Administration, Economic Affairs, Public Affairs, International Organization Affairs, and Congressional Relations. Other geographic policy areas were added—Inter-American Affairs, Far Eastern Affairs, European Affairs, and Near Eastern and African Affairs.

In 1947, Secretary of State Marshall set up the Policy Planning Staff to streamline executive-level decision making. George F. Kennan and Paul Nitze, the original directors of the Policy Planning Staff, were central figures in shaping the United States' aggressive response to Soviet expansionism.

The department grew exponentially after World War II. In 1945, there were 3,700 State employees in Washington and in 1950, nine thousand men and women worked at State headquarters. In 1945, the U.S. managed diplomatic missions in fifty-six foreign capitals. Another 125 posts were added during the next fifty years.

In the 1990s, there were over eight thousand domestic and six thousand overseas employees of the State Department. The State Department also found it necessary to staff its embassies and consulates with thousands of foreign nationals.

In the late 1950s, the department began an extensive program to build embassies and consulates in Europe, Africa, and Asia. Marine guards were deployed to guard embassies in countries considered dangerous because of civil conflict.

To accommodate the growth in personnel, in 1961 the department moved from the State, War, and Navy Building on 17th Street in Washington, D.C., to a four-block site in Foggy Bottom, between Virginia Avenue and C Street and 21st and 23rd streets.

After World War II, the Department of State was no longer the only government entity devoted to foreign policy. The complexities of American foreign policy resulting from the Cold War led to the creation of other agencies to assist in the maintenance of national security. In 1947, the Central Intelligence Agency (CIA) was created to undertake covert intelligence gathering and secret political missions overseas. In 1953, a U.S. Information Agency was established to promote American cultural interests abroad. In 1961, the Agency for International Development was created to manage foreign aid and development initiatives abroad.

To coordinate decision making among the multitude of foreign affairs agencies and offices, in 1947 President Truman established the National Security Council (NSC). Its members were the top ranking foreign policy officials from the White House, State Department, CIA, and the Defense Department.

The department underwent a tumultuous period in the 1950s amidst congressional hearings about communist infiltration of the U.S. government. Fears about communist subversion led President Eisenhower to order the department to conduct background checks on State employees and diplomats to determine whether they were considered security risks. These measures led hundreds of civil servants and diplomats to be charged with treasonous activity. Although some people were rightfully fired on these grounds, many others were innocent victims of the anti-communist "witch-hunt."

Out of concern about communist infiltration, the State Department ousted many of its top Far Eastern experts under suspicion of being sympathetic to world communism. In a case of "guilt by association," the Far Eastern experts were blamed for having contributed to the 1949 "fall of China" by not having been enthusiastic supporters of Nationalist Chinese leader Chiang Kai-Shek. The Asia experts believed Chiang would inevitably fail to repress Mao Tse Tung's revolutionary communist forces and had advised the United States to pull back its financial backing to Chiang. Some diplomatic historians argue that the dearth of Asia experts at the State Department led to flawed U.S. policymaking toward Vietnam.

In the late twentieth century, U.S. leaders grappled with management of the diverse corps of American government employees that were working abroad.

By the early 1960s, there were approximately thirty thousand U.S. government workers abroad, and only one third of them were employed by the State Department. The rest were overseas employees of the Treasury, Agriculture, and Commerce departments. President John F. Kennedy tried to bring leadership to overseas posts by requiring all U.S. government workers in a particular country to report to the chief of a diplomatic mission abroad, usually the ambassador. President Richard M. Nixon reaffirmed that order in 1969.

Coordination between the foreign affairs agencies has also been a source of difficulty for presidents attempting to craft a unified foreign policy. President Truman believed the NSC would streamline foreign policy formulation. But, successive presidents have not been satisfied and experimented with alternate paths for executive decision making. President Kennedy relied heavily on his own advisers in the White House to handle foreign policy crises during his presidency. Presidents Nixon and Ford kept authority over national security matters within the White House and the National Security Council more so than in the State Department. In the late twentieth century, the State Department's ability to lead foreign affairs largely depended on the relationship a particular secretary of state had with the president. For example, Henry Kissinger was an unusually powerful Secretary of State because he was so closely trusted by President Nixon.

U.S. global leadership and the diversity of its interests around the world led to the creation of additional bureaus at State in the 1970s and 1980s. Offices were created to deal with terrorism, science, the environment, human rights, arms control, refugee affairs, and human rights. By 1990, State had 30 different bureaus. These specialized policy offices were designed to address a multiplicity of new crises and problems the U.S. faced overseas. But successive administrations felt that the additional bureaucracy limited the department's ability to offer clear-cut recommendations. Thus, presidents Ronald Reagan and George H.W. Bush often found it expedient to rely on their own set of White House foreign affairs advisers to the exclusion of the State Department's policymakers.

During much of the twentieth century, the State Department and the diplomatic corps were viewed as the government's most elitist institutions. It has taken many years for the department to include more women and men from ordinary backgrounds and people from non-white ethnic groups.

In the early twentieth century, the department engaged in the notorious practice of segregating its workforce. This meant that black and white State Department employees ate in separate cafeterias. It was not until 1925 that the department admitted an African American to the Foreign Service. Segregation quietly ended during World War II, but African Americans have struggled to gain jobs and promotions to leadership positions in the department. President Carter and Secretary of State Cyrus Vance began affirmative action programs to ensure that more African Americans and women were hired and promoted fairly. Because Congress felt the department moved too slowly on this front, it passed the Foreign Service Reform Act in 1980, calling for stricter standards for hiring and promoting diplomats to minimize the chances for discrimination.

Women made their initial inroads at the State Department in administrative jobs and were first admitted into the Foreign Service in the 1920s. President Franklin D. Roosevelt appointed the first two female chiefs of mission. In 1933, he named the daughter of former Secretary of State Williams Jennings Bryan, Ruth Bryan Owen, to serve as the U.S. Minister to Denmark. Florence Jaffrey Harriman served as Minister to Norway from 1937 to 1940. But the presence of women in the diplomatic corps has grown slowly, especially since married women were excluded from overseas assignments until 1971. In 1975, women made up only nine percent of the State Department workforce, and they were concentrated in the lowest levels of the Foreign Service. A class-action discrimination lawsuit filed in 1971 accused the department of discriminating against women, and its settlement nearly two decades later required the department to cancel the Foreign Service entrance examination while corrective actions were taken to prevent further discrimination. In 1995, twenty-eight percent of the department's employees were women and women comprised ten percent of the senior Foreign Service. Promotion rates for women and minorities from 1987 to 1993 were slightly higher than for other Foreign Service Officers.

Even though the United States emerged from the end of the Cold War as the most powerful nation in the world, the State Department was actually one of the smallest government agencies. At the end of the twentieth century, department leaders complained that a shortage of funding was hindering the department's ability to cope with new and dangerous foreign affairs challenges, such as terrorism, nuclear proliferation, and the outbreak of numerous civil wars around the globe.

BIBLIOGRAPHY

Beisner, Robert L. *From the Old Diplomacy to the New, 1865–1900.* Arlington Heights, Ill.: Harlan Davidson, 1986.

Plischke, Elmer. *The U.S. Department of State: A Reference History.* Westport, Conn.: Greenwood Press, 1999.

Slany, William Z. "A History of the United States Department of State, 1789–1996." U.S. Department of State, Office of the Historian, July 1996. Available from http://www.state.gov/www/about_state/history/dephis.html.

Steigman, Andrew L. *The Foreign Service of the United States: First Line of Defense.* Boulder, Colo.: Westview Press, 1985.

Ellen G. Rafshoon

STATE EMBLEMS, NICKNAMES, MOTTOS, AND SONGS must be adopted officially by action of the legislative bodies of the respective states to which they belong before one properly may designate them as such. The table on pages 532–533 lists the state birds, flowers, trees, nicknames, mottos, and songs, although some states have also adopted state gems, state animals, state fish, and so on. Translations of state mottos in languages other than English (Latin, French, Italian, Greak, Spanish, and, in the instance of Washington, Chinook) are also given.

STATE FAIRS. *See* **County and State Fairs.**

STATE LAWS, UNIFORM. In the eighteenth and nineteenth centuries the exercise of state sovereignty resulted in the development of a checkerboard of separate and often conflicting state legal systems. A valid divorce in one state, for example, was occasionally a nullity in another. Toward the end of the nineteenth century, such factors as improved transportation and the increase in commerce persuaded lawmakers that it would be desirable to make some laws uniform throughout the states.

Three methods of adopting laws can establish such uniformity: (1) Congress may pass a law that applies to the states uniformly; (2) state legislatures may adopt identical laws; and (3) representatives of state governments may negotiate an agreement that in turn is adopted by the respective legislatures.

Although only the latter two methods provide for uniform state laws, Congress can develop uniformity merely by exercising its constitutional powers to legislate in substantive areas where its failure to do so permits idiosyncratic state regulation. Long-standing judicial doctrine holds that where Congress has the power to act, its laws preempt or supersede conflicting state laws on the subject.

In 1892, when state representatives met at the first National Conference of Commissioners on Uniform State Laws, they faced two monumental tasks. First, they had to draft acceptable legislation. Second, they had to convince at least some state legislatures that the particular uniform act was wise state policy. Unlike federal laws, uniform acts are not thrust into existence by a superior governmental entity. Each state is free to adopt or reject such acts. (No uniform act has ever met with unanimous success.) States consistently counter powerful arguments of economic or social "necessity," theoretical "rightness," and the convenience of uniformity of culture and attitude with arguments stressing the uniqueness of certain local situations or that a particular area is already covered adequately. Despite the disparity of geographical representation and the sheer numbers of sovereign states (and the District of Columbia, Puerto Rico, and the Virgin Islands), however, the conference has had a surprising degree of success.

The Negotiable Instruments Act and its successor, the Uniform Commercial Code (UCC), have been the most significant of the uniform acts. As of 1975, the UCC was law in all states except Louisiana, and its provisions were the legal framework of most business dealings in the United States. There were over 150 uniform acts, many of which met moderate to great success with state legislatures. Some were not adopted by any states. For example, conflicting laws governing marriage and divorce still allowed for "unknowing bigamists."

The conference successfully constitutes an ever-present machinery to set the wheels of uniformity in motion. Since 1892 the conference has convened every

TABLE 1

State Emblems, Nicknames, Mottos, and Songs

State	Bird	Flower	Tree	Nickname(s)	Motto	Song
Alabama	Yellowhammer	Camellia	Southern pine	Cotton State; Heart of Dixie; Yellow-hammer State	*Audemus jura nostra defendere* ("We dare defend our rights")	*Alabama*
Alaska	Willow ptarmigan	Forget-me-not	Sitka spruce	Land of the Midnight Sun; The Last Frontier	North to the Future (unofficial)	*Alaska's Flag*
Arizona	Cactus wren	Saguaro cactus	Paloverde	Grand Canyon State	*Ditat Deus* ("God enriches")	*Arizona*
Arkansas	Mockingbird	Apple blossom	Short-leaf pine	Land of Opportunity; The Natural State	*Regnat populus* ("The people rule")	*Arkansas*
California	Valley quail	Golden poppy	Redwood	Golden State	*Eureka* ("I have found it")	*I Love You, California*
Colorado	Lark bunting	Columbine	Blue spruce	Centennial State	*Nil sine numine* ("Nothing without Providence")	*Where the Columbines Grow*
Connecticut	American robin	Mountain laurel	White oak	Constitution State; Nutmeg State	*Qui transtulit sustinet* ("He who transplanted still sustains")	(none)
Delaware	Blue hen chicken	Peach blossom	American holly	Diamond State; First State	Liberty and Independence	*Our Delaware*
Florida	Mockingbird	Orange blossom	Sabal palm	Sunshine State; Peninsula State	In God We Trust	*The Swanee River (Old Folks at Home)*
Georgia	Brown thrasher	Cherokee rose	Live oak	Empire State of the South; Peach State	Wisdom, Justice, Moderation	*Georgia on My Mind*
Hawaii	Hawaiian goose (nene)	Hibiscus (Pua Aloalo)	Candlenut (Kukui)	Aloha State; Paradise of the Pacific	*Ua mau ke ea o ka aina i ka pono* ("The life of the land is perpetuated in righteousness")	*Hawaii Ponoi*
Idaho	Mountain bluebird	Syringa	White pine	Gem State	*Esto perpetua* ("May she endure forever")	*Here We Have Idaho*
Illinois	Cardinal	Butterfly violet	White oak	Prairie State	State Sovereignty, National Union	*Illinois*
Indiana	Cardinal	Peony	Tulip tree	Hoosier State	Crossroads of America	*On the Banks of the Wabash Far Away*
Iowa	Eastern goldfinch	Carolina wild rose	Oak	Hawkeye State	Our Liberties We Prize and Our Rights We Will Maintain	*The Song of Iowa*
Kansas	Western meadowlark	Sunflower	Cottonwood	Jayhawker State; Sunflower State	*Ad astra per aspera* ("To the stars through difficulties")	*Home on the Range*
Kentucky	Cardinal	Goldenrod	Tulip poplar	Bluegrass State	United We Stand, Divided We Fall	*My Old Kentucky Home*
Louisiana	Pelican	Magnolia	Bald cypress	Creole State; Pelican State	Union, Justice, and Confidence	*Give Me Louisiana; You Are My Sunshine*
Maine	Chickadee	Pine cone and tassel	White pine	Lumber State; Pine Tree State	*Dirigo* ("I lead")	*State of Maine Song*
Maryland	Baltimore oriole	Black-eyed Susan	White oak	Old Line State	*Fatti maschii, parole femine* ("Manly deeds, womanly words")	*Maryland, My Maryland*
Massachusetts	Chickadee	Mayflower	American elm	Bay State; Old Bay State; Old Colony State	*Ense petit placidam sub libertate quietem* ("By the sword she seeks peace under liberty")	*Massachusetts*
Michigan	Robin	Apple blossom	White pine	Wolverine State	*Si quaeris peninsulam amoenam circumspice* ("If you seek a pleasant peninsula, look about you")	*Michigan, My Michigan (unofficial)*
Minnesota	Loon	Pink and white lady's slipper	Red or Norway pine	Gopher State; North Star State	*L'Etoile du Nord* ("The North Star")	*Hail! Minnesota*
Mississippi	Mockingbird	Magnolia	Magnolia	Magnolia State	*Virtute et armis* ("By Valor and Arms")	*Go, Mississippi*
Missouri	Bluebird	Hawthorn	Dogwood	Show Me State	*Sclus populi suprema lex esto* ("Let the welfare of the people be the supreme law")	*Missouri Waltz*
Montana	Western meadowlark	Bitterroot	Ponderosa pine	Treasure State	*Oro y plata* ("Gold and silver")	*Montana*

[continued]

TABLE 1 [CONTINUED]

State Emblems, Nicknames, Mottos, and Songs

State	Bird	Flower	Tree	Nickname(s)	Motto	Song
Nebraska	Western meadowlark	Goldenrod	Cottonwood	Cornhusker State	Equality Before the Law	Beautiful Nebraska
Nevada	Mountain bluebird	Sagebrush	Single-leaf pinon; Bristlecone pine	Sagebrush State; Silver State	All For Our Country	Home Means Nevada
New Hampshire	Purple finch	Purple lilac	White birch	Granite State	Live Free or Die	Old New Hampshire
New Jersey	Eastern goldfinch	Purple violet	Red oak	Garden State	Liberty and Prosperity	(none)
New Mexico	Roadrunner	Yucca	Pinon (nut pine)	Land of Enchantment; Sunshine State	Crescit eundo ("It grows as it goes")	O Fair New Mexico
New York	Eastern bluebird	Rose	Sugar maple	Empire State	Excelsior ("Ever upward")	(none)
North Carolina	Cardinal	Dogwood	Pine	Old North State; Tar Heel State	Esse quam videri ("To be, rather than to seem")	The Old North State
North Dakota	Western meadowlark	Prairie rose	American elm	Flickertail State; Sioux State	Liberty and Union, Now and Forever, One and Inseparable	North Dakota Hymn
Ohio	Cardinal	Scarlet carnation	Buckeye	Buckeye State	With God All Things Are Possible	Beautiful Ohio
Oklahoma	Scissor-tailed flycatcher	Mistletoe	Redbud	Sooner State	Labor omnia vincit ("Labor conquers all things")	Oklahoma!
Oregon	Western meadowlark	Oregon grape	Douglas fir	Beaver State	She Flies With Her Own Wings	Oregon, My Oregon
Pennsylvania	Ruffed grouse	Mountain laurel	Eastern hemlock	Keystone State	Virtue, Liberty, and Independence	(none)
Rhode Island	Rhode Island red	Violet	Red maple	Little Rhody	Hope	Rhode Island's It for Me
South Carolina	Carolina wren	Carolina jessamine	Palmetto	Palmetto State	Animis opibusque parati ("Prepared in mind and resources") and Dum spiro spero ("While I breathe, I hope")	Carolina
South Dakota	Ring-necked pheasant	Pasqueflower	Black Hills spruce	Coyote State; Sunshine State	Under God the People Rule	Hail, South Dakota
Tennessee	Mockingbird	Iris	Tulip poplar	Volunteer State	Agriculture and Commerce	Tennessee Waltz
Texas	Mockingbird	Bluebonnet	Pecan	Lone Star State	Friendship	Texas, Our Texas
Utah	Sea gull	Sego lily	Blue spruce	Beehive State	Industry	Utah, We Love Thee
Vermont	Hermit thrush	Red clover	Sugar maple	Green Mountain State	Freedom and Unity	Hail, Vermont
Virginia	Cardinal	American dogwood	American dogwood	Old Dominion	Sic semper tyrannis ("Thus always to tyrants")	Carry Me Back to Old Virginia
Washington	Willow goldfinch	Rhododendron	Western hemlock	Evergreen State; Chinook State	Al-ki ("By and by")	Washington, My Home
West Virginia	Cardinal	Rosebay rhododendron	Sugar maple	Mountain State	Montani semper liberi ("Mountaineers are always free men")	The West Virginia Hills and West Virginia, My Home, Sweet Home
Wisconsin	Robin	Butterfly violet	Sugar maple	Badger State	Forward	On, Wisconsin!
Wyoming	Western meadowlark	Indian paintbrush	Cottonwood	Equality State	Equal Rights	Wyoming

year except 1945. Its president reports yearly to the American Bar Association, which in turn passes on the efficacy of new proposals. The assembly thus can respond in timely fashion to needs for uniformity and publicize its utility.

The commissioners, generally three from each state, are appointed by the respective governors, who over the years have made a practice of selecting leading lawyers, judges, and law professors.

BIBLIOGRAPHY

American Bar Association, *Reports* (annual).

Dunham, Allison. "A History of the National Conference of Commissioners on Uniform State Laws." *Law and Contemporary Problems* 30 (1965).

National Conference of Commissioners on Uniform State Laws. "Uniformity in the Law." *Montana Law Journal* 19 (1958).

Eric L. Chase
Harold W. Chase / c. w.

See also **American Bar Association; Congress, United States; Divorce and Marital Separation; Legislatures, State; Sovereignty, Doctrine of.**

STATE SOVEREIGNTY. The doctrine of divided state sovereignty was fashioned by the American revolutionaries. From the signing of the Declaration of Independence in 1776 to the Constitutional Convention in 1787, Republicans (primarily in New England and the upper South) and Nationalists (in middle states and the lower South) struggled to define state sovereignty against the backdrop of a weak national government.

The sovereignty question was unresolved when the federal government commenced in 1789. The belief that sovereignty was divided between the several states and the federal government received validation by the U.S. Supreme Court decision in *CHISHOLM V. GEORGIA* (1793), which held that states could be sued by private citizens. This decision led quickly to the ratification of the Eleventh Amendment, guaranteeing sovereign immunity for states against actions of citizens of another state or a foreign state. Divided sovereignty became the accepted political theory until the 1830s and 1840s.

The South Carolina politician John C. Calhoun became the most prominent advocate for state sovereignty. A former Nationalist, Calhoun returned in the 1830s to the idea that sovereignty was indivisible—the Constitution had been created by the people of the several states, acting as sovereign entities, and not by the Union of the people in those states. During the NULLIFICATION crisis of 1828–1832, Calhoun led South Carolina to the brink of secession by advocating an ideology of state supremacy to nullify a federal tariff.

During the 1840s and 1850s, Calhoun's doctrine became increasingly tied to the defense of slavery. Abolitionists, however, also used state sovereignty as a weapon. The Southern-supported Fugitive Slave Act of 1850 subverted STATES' RIGHTS by ordering free states to return slaves, and ANTISLAVERY advocates (usually staunch Nationalists) used state sovereignty to fight the law in *Ableman v. Booth* (1859). Calhoun's theories ultimately found expression in SECESSION, and in the Constitution of the Confederate States of America (1861).

Although the Union victory in the Civil War (1861–1865) seemed to secure the triumph of nationalism, the Reconstruction-era ratification of the Fourteenth (1868) and Fifteenth Amendments (1870) transformed the sovereignty debate. The Fourteenth Amendment prohibits states from depriving anyone of the rights of citizenship, denying equal protection of the law, or violating fundamental rights without due process of law. The Fifteenth Amendment mandates that federal and state governments shall not deny or abridge the right to vote on account of race. Although the amendments clearly enhanced federal power to protect individual rights, in the decades that followed, the Supreme Court interpreted them narrowly in order to preserve distinctions between federal and state sovereignty. In the *SLAUGHTERHOUSE CASES* (1873), the Court held that Americans had certain rights as U.S. citizens and others as state citizens—the Fourteenth Amendment only guaranteed the former. Both in *U.S. v. Cruikshank* and *U.S. v. Reese* (1876) and in the *Civil Rights Cases* (1883), the Court held that Congress could enforce the amendments only against state actions; federal law could not punish private citizens who violated civil rights of African Americans.

From the end of Reconstruction until the Great Depression, courts interpreted governance of property, family, morality, public health and safety, crime, education, and religion as police powers reserved to states. One result of President Franklin D. Roosevelt's New Deal was a federalism revolution in the 1930s, described by historian Forrest McDonald as an "expansion of federal activity on a scale unprecedented in peacetime." Starting with *NEBBIA V. NEW YORK* (1934), the U.S. Supreme Court transformed federal-state relations by upholding many of the programs of the New Deal.

In 1954, the Supreme Court's decision in *Brown v. Board of Education* delivered what many believed was the fatal blow to state sovereignty. Holding that Southern state laws mandating "separate but equal" schools for black and white students were unconstitutional, the Court ordered local school districts to comply "with all deliberate speed" with federal district judges monitoring their desegregation plans. Southern state and local officials resisted compliance, and states' rights theorists denounced the Court in terms reminiscent of those used in the 1850s. The South once again conflated states' rights with racial issues and gave the Supreme Court great moral authority with the rest of the nation as the protector of individual rights from discriminatory state actions. This trend continued throughout the 1960s and early 1970s, as the Court validated federal civil rights laws and President Lyndon B. Johnson's expansive Great Society programs.

Although conservatives and states' rights advocates had denounced the Court since *Brown* as "judicial activists" and "government by judiciary," the 1980s and 1990s witnessed the resurgence of state sovereignty theories. As Congress enacted laws giving block grants to states for poverty relief and education, the Court shifted toward interpretations of federalism last seen in the 1870s. Legal analysts were stunned by the Court's decision in *U.S. v. Lopez* (1995), invalidating a federal law prohibiting firearms within one thousand feet of a school, public or private. This decision heralded a new era of judicial activism, this time with an emphasis toward states.

In 2002, the Court reinterpreted state sovereignty immunity with an activist reading of the Eleventh Amendment. In *Federal Maritime Commission v. South Carolina State Ports Authority* (2002), a 5-4 majority held that state sovereign immunity prohibits federal agencies from adjudicating an individual's complaint against a state. In the early twenty-first century, state sovereignty is very much alive as a legal and political doctrine.

BIBLIOGRAPHY

Benedict, Michael Les. "Preserving Federalism: Reconstruction and the Waite Court." *Supreme Court Review* (1978): 39–79.

Cushman, Barry. *Rethinking the New Deal Court: The Structure of a Constitutional Revolution.* New York: Oxford University Press, 1998.

McDonald, Forrest. *States' Rights and the Union: Imperium in Imperio, 1776–1876.* Lawrence: University Press of Kansas, 2000.

Rakove, Jack N. *Original Meanings: Politics and Ideas in the Making of the Constitution.* New York: Knopf, 1996.

Patricia Hagler Minter

See also **Brown v. Board of Education of Topeka**; **Fugitive Slave Acts**; *United States v. Cruikshank*; *United States v. Reese*; *and vol. 9:* **Congress Debates the Fourteenth Amendment.**

STATE UNIVERSITY OF NEW YORK.

Public higher education in New York State has an ironic history. The University of the State of New York (SUNY) arguably constitutes the oldest public educational government in the world. But its regents, who oversee all educational institutions in New York, traditionally championed New York's numerous private colleges and discouraged public rivals. Thus, New York, a leader in state control of education, was the last state to create a public higher education system.

When Democratic legislators proposed a $50-million state university in 1946, Governor Thomas E. Dewey, a social progressive and fiscal conservative, blanched at the price tag, but he appointed a commission to design such an institution. Its proposal merely incorporated the existing state-supported institutions into an umbrella organization under the regents' control. However, some members, including several Dewey advisers, wanted a state university free from regents' control. Their portrayal of private institutions' discrimination against Jews and African Americans, particularly by medical and dental schools, convinced Dewey to support an independent state university that, beyond the regents' control, could administer schools of medicine, dentistry, nursing, and public health.

This plan eventually prevailed. On 4 April 1948, Dewey created the State University of New York, incorporating more than thirty existing state-supported institutions of higher education outside New York City and envisioning future medical schools and community colleges. The initial state university consisted of eleven state teachers colleges, six agricultural and technical institutes, five institutes of applied arts and sciences, three temporary veterans colleges, the New York State Maritime Academy, and six "contract colleges" administered by private institutions. Opponents delayed implementation for a year. Finally, on 4 April 1949, the leaders of the various units and the first president, Alvin Eurich (1949–1951), gathered in Albany to formally inaugurate SUNY. Few could have imagined that the fledgling university, with fewer than 30,000 students and just over 2,000 faculty, would grow to become one of the world's largest.

The political imbroglio left scars. Eager to include the legislation among his 1948 presidential election credentials, Dewey compromised. SUNY would create neither research universities or liberal arts colleges. The teachers colleges (except Albany) were barred from training secondary school teachers for a decade, retarding their possible evolution into liberal arts colleges. Private fundraising was banned for two decades. And the regents oversaw SUNY's budget.

Not surprisingly, SUNY's first decade was unexceptional. It acquired medical schools in Brooklyn and Syracuse and a small liberal arts college in Binghamton, and opened a small campus on Long Island. But enrollment remained under 40,000, and SUNY's second president, Frank Carlson (1951–1957), was dismissed for campaigning to purchase Syracuse University as the flagship campus for the system.

In the late 1950s, however, several important developments took place that would spur SUNY's growth in the decade to come. The ban on training secondary school teachers expired. The launch of the Soviet satellite *Sputnik* spurred an increase in spending on education. The first "baby boomers" entered adolescence. And Nelson Rockefeller was elected governor of New York State.

Rockefeller's Heald Commission laid the basis for expansion. Bonds issued by the State University Construction Fund and the first tuition charges would finance capital costs. Budgetary control was extricated from the regents. Potential opposition from private colleges was avoided by offering them public funds for construction and student aid. A parallel structure, City University of New York (CUNY), was created in 1961 as a downstate equivalent of SUNY.

Expansion followed swiftly. The teachers colleges expanded enrollments and evolved into liberal arts colleges. Research universities emerged at Albany, Binghamton, Buffalo, and Stony Brook. Community colleges mushroomed, eventually totaling thirty. A sixty-four-campus system enrolled 280,000 students in 1970. By the late 1960s, SUNY was being compared to the California system and SUNY Chancellor Samuel B. Gould (1964–1970) appeared on the cover of *Time* magazine.

SUNY's upward trajectory soon flattened. Gould retired in 1970; the New York economy slowed; student protests tried taxpayers' patience; and even Rockefeller believed SUNY was overextended. Gould's successor, Ernest Boyer (1970–1977), faced immediate fiscal restraints and then retrenchment, as well as renewed warfare with the regents. Although enrollment (361,000 by 1980) continued to rise, SUNY's prestige declined, while the frustrations over missed opportunities grew. The 1980s and early 1990s witnessed rising tuition, flat enrollments, and shrinking state budgets. The state's share of SUNY college and university budgets plummeted from 90 percent in the late 1980s to well under 50 percent a decade later, necessitating a vocabulary shift from "state-supported" to "state-assisted."

Mid-1990s prosperity underwrote some regeneration. The University Centers at Buffalo and Stony Brook were admitted into the American Association of Universities, while Binghamton was hailed as a "public Ivy." Former teachers colleges evolved into mature, comprehensive colleges. Improved state budgets held tuition constant and funded overdue renovation and construction. SUNY entered the new millennium with 373,000 students, 15,000 faculty, 64 campuses, 1.9 billion alumni, and a physical plant valued at $11 billion.

In a half-century, New York built a system that serves over one-third of its high school graduates and whose acronym is widely respected in academia. But this extraordinary investment and SUNY's many educational achievements have failed to bring public esteem, due in part to the absence of a flagship campus or big-time athletics. SUNY's fiftieth anniversary passed nearly unnoticed and campuses increasingly distanced themselves from the acronym. SUNY's history illustrates the difficult process of creating institutions of mass higher education, especially in northeastern states with prestigious private institutions. SUNY thrived under Governor Rockefeller's aegis but did not sustain the broad public support necessary to replicate the California model.

BIBLIOGRAPHY

Abbott, Frank C. *Government Policy and Higher Education: A Study of the Regents of the University of the State of New York, 1784–1949.* Ithaca, N.Y.: Cornell University Press, 1958.

Bleeker, Samuel E. *The Politics of Architecture: A Perspective on Nelson A. Rockefeller.* New York: Rutledge Press, 1981.

Carmichael, Oliver Cromwell. *New York Establishes a State University: A Case Study in the Process of Policy Formation.* Nashville, Tenn.: Vanderbilt University Press, 1955.

Glazer, Judith S. "Nelson Rockefeller and the Politics of Higher Education in New York State." *History of Higher Education Annual* 9 (1989): 87–114.

Smith, Richard Norton. *Thomas E. Dewey and His Times.* New York: Simon and Schuster, 1982.

W. Bruce Leslie
Kenneth P. O'Brien

See also **California Higher Educational System; Universities, State.**

STATES' RIGHTS advocates believe that considerable governmental authority should be located in the separate and collective states of the United States. The concept of states' rights arose as an extension of colonial rights, which Americans had claimed when they were still under the British Crown. This idea was essential to the American Revolution and under the Articles of Confederation. When the Federal Constitutional Convention met in 1787, states' rights proponents pressed to include their ideas in the Constitution; others advocated a strong national government, with minimal power residing with the states. The federal system adopted at that convention was a reasonably satisfactory compromise that reconciled state and national power. It included an upper house, the Senate, which provided each state with equal input into the legislative process. In 1791, the Tenth Amendment to the Constitution made the states' rights doctrine more explicit: "The powers not delegated to the United States by the Constitution, nor prohibited by it to the States, are reserved to the States respectively, or to the people." From that time until 1865 the tension between national and state governments as they attempted to define their relationships to each other and to protect their respective powers constituted a major theme in American history. In 1798, the promulgation of the Kentucky and Virginia resolutions, which protested acts passed by the national Congress, were manifestations of states' rights. The Hartford Convention of 1814, called by New Englanders who disagreed with President James Madison's wartime policies, was another example of states' rightism.

Although various individual states and groups of states from time to time appealed to the principle of states' rights for their political and economic protection, the South is most often associated with the doctrine. In the first half of the nineteenth century, when disputes arose over the tariff, the national bank, public land policies, internal improvement, and the like, southern leaders used arguments based on states' rights in their attempts to protect their economic interests. They usually lost these battles to maintain their economic power, and their appeals to constitutional principle went unheeded. Overriding all the other disputes was the question of the extension of slavery into the American territories. Southern states fell back on the states' rights principle once again when northerners argued that slavery should not extend into new states. Various events of the 1850s, including the Compromise of 1850, the Kansas-Nebraska controversy, the formation of the Republican Party, civil strife in Kansas, the Dred Scott decision and John Brown's raid, and the election of Abraham Lincoln as president in 1860, were closely related to the slavery and states' rights controversies and led directly to the Civil War. That war established the supremacy of the national government and relegated the states to lesser political and economic positions. Disputes arose from time to time about the relationship of the national and state governments, and invariably the national government emerged the victor. In the first half of the twentieth century, southern politicians continued to speak about states' rights, but this was often nothing more than oratory designed to please southern voters.

After midcentury, when the power, size, and authority of the national government became greater and more complex, many Americans began to have misgivings about the shortcomings of a massive government essentially run by bureaucrats. Those politicians who talked about states' rights often found they had more receptive audiences than previously. Controversies over the administration of welfare programs and other social services gave states' rights advocates issues that they could exploit. More important, the cry for states' rights was often a thinly disguised but firm stand against racial integration in regard to education, public accommodations, politics and voting, housing, and jobs—areas that states' righters insisted were within the sphere of the states. When Senator Strom Thurmond, at that time a Democrat opposed to President Harry S. Truman's civil rights legislation, ran as a candidate for president in 1948, his States' Rights Party carried four states and received thirty-nine electoral votes, the third-largest electoral vote for an independent party in U.S. history. But the revival of states' rights arguments in the third quarter of the twentieth century had little basic impact on the general locus of political power. The national government continued to be more powerful, and the states remained in secondary roles. The attempts of the founders of the United States to divide sovereignty between national and state governments laid the basis for many controversies throughout the nation's history, but on the whole the structures of government that they established functioned well. Except for the Civil War, disputes were settled peacefully. Even as the national government gained more power within the limits of the Constitution after the mid-twentieth century, there appeared to be no prospect of a serious revolt over the diminishing rights of the states.

BIBLIOGRAPHY

Dew, Charles B. *Apostles of Disunion: Southern Secession Commissioners and the Causes of the Civil War.* Charlottesville and London: University Press of Virginia, 2001.

Frederickson, Kari A. *The Dixiecrat Revolt and the End of the Solid South, 1932–1968.* Chapel Hill: University of North Carolina Press, 2001.

Freehling, William W. *Prelude to Civil War: The Nullification Controversy in South Carolina, 1816–1836.* Reprint, New York: Oxford University Press, 1992.

Mason, Alpheus Thomas, ed. *The States Rights Debate: Antifederalism and the Constitution.* 2d ed. New York, Oxford University Press, 1972.

Monroe Billington
Michael Wala

See also **Civil War; Sectionalism; "South Carolina Exposition and Protest"; State Sovereignty; States' Rights in the Confederacy.**

STATES' RIGHTS IN THE CONFEDERACY. The doctrine of states' rights, especially as advanced by John C. Calhoun in his books *A Disquisition on Government* and *A Discourse on the Constitution and Government of the United States,* led to secession of the Southern states, but a faction of some of its strongest adherents impaired the ability of the Confederacy to win the Civil War (1861–1865). Led by Governor Joseph E. Brown of Georgia, Governor Zebulon B. Vance of North Carolina, and Vice President Alexander H. Stephens, the Confederacy attacked conscription as unconstitutional and impeded its operation even after favorable decisions by Confederate courts. The army was crippled by their insistence on the right of states to appoint officers, and by the policy of some states to withhold men and arms from the Confederate government and maintain their own troops. This states' rights faction opposed suspension of the writ of habeas corpus, so that the government was unable to employ that tool for periods aggregating more than a year and a half. They opposed impressment of supplies for the army by entities other than the states. Laws were repealed that had given the Confederate government a monopoly in foreign trade, by means of which it had exported cotton and brought in war supplies through the blockade. This faction hampered the effective prosecution of the war by the Confederate government, and in the end contributed to its downfall.

BIBLIOGRAPHY

Hill, Louise B. *State Socialism in the Confederate States of America.* Charlottesville, Va.: Historical Publishing, 1936.

Owsley, Frank L. *State Rights in the Confederacy.* Chicago: University of Chicago Press, 1931.

Jon Roland

STATISTICS, the scientific discipline that deals with the collection, classification, analysis, and interpretation of numerical facts or data, was invented primarily in the nineteenth and twentieth centuries in Western Europe and North America. In the eighteenth century, when the term came into use, "statistics" referred to a descriptive analysis of the situation of a political state—its people, resources, and social life. In the early nineteenth century, the term came to carry the specific connotation of a quantitative description and analysis of the various aspects of a state or other social or natural phenomenon. Many statistical associations were founded in the 1830s, including the Statistical Society of London (later the Royal Statistical Society) in 1833 and the American Statistical Association in 1839.

Early Use of Statistics

Although scientific claims were made for the statistical enterprise almost from the beginning, it had few characteristics of an academic discipline before the twentieth century, except as a "state science" or *Staatswissenschaft* in parts of central Europe. The role of statistics as a tool of politics, administration, and reform defined its character in the United States throughout the nineteenth century. Advocates of statistics, within government and among private intellectuals, argued that their new field would supply important political knowledge. Statistics could provide governing elites with concise, systematic, and authoritative information on the demographic, moral, medical, and economic characteristics of populations. In this view, statistical knowledge was useful, persuasive, and hence powerful, because it could capture the aggregate and the typical, the relationship between the part and the whole, and when data were available, their trajectory over time. It was particularly appropriate to describe the new arrays of social groups in rapidly growing, industrializing societies, the character and trajectory of social processes in far-flung empires, and the behavior and characteristics of newly mobilized political actors in the age of democratic revolutions.

One strand in this development was the creation of data sets and the development of rules and techniques of data collection and classification. In America, the earliest statistical works were descriptions of the American population and economy dating from the colonial period. British officials watched closely the demographic development of the colonies. By the time of the American Revolution (1775–1783), colonial leaders were aware of American demographic realities, and of the value of statistics. To apportion the tax burden and raise troops for the revolution, Congress turned to population and wealth measures to assess the differential capacities among the colonies. In 1787, the framers institutionalized the national population census to apportion seats among the states in the new Congress, and required that statistics on revenues and expenditures of the national state be collected and published by the new government. Almanacs, statistical gazetteers, and the routine publication of numerical data in the press signaled the growth of the field. Government activities produced election numbers, shipping data from tariff payments, value of land sales, and population distributions. In the early nineteenth century, reform organizations and the new statistical societies published data on the moral status of the society in the form of data on church pews filled, prostitutes arrested, patterns of disease, and drunkards reformed. The collection and publication of statistics thus expanded in both government and private organizations.

Professionalization of Statistics

The professionalization of the discipline began in the late nineteenth century. An International Statistical Congress, made up of government representatives from many states, met for the first time in 1853 and set about the impossible task of standardizing statistical categories across nations. In 1885, a new, more academic organization was created, the International Statistical Institute. Statistical work grew in the new federal agencies such as the Departments of Agriculture and Education in the 1860s and 1870s. The

annual *Statistical Abstract of the United States* first appeared in 1878. The states began to create bureaus of labor statistics to collect data on wages, prices, strikes, and working conditions in industry, the first in Massachusetts in 1869; the federal Bureau of Labor, now the Bureau of Labor Statistics, was created in 1884. Statistical analysis became a university subject in the United States with Richmond Mayo Smith's text and course at Columbia University in the 1880s. Governments created formal posts for "statisticians" in government service, and research organizations devoted to the development of the field emerged. The initial claims of the field were descriptive, but soon, leaders also claimed the capacity to draw inferences from data.

Throughout the nineteenth century, a strong statistical ethic favored complete enumerations whenever possible, to avoid what seemed the speculative excess of early modern "political arithmetic." In the first decades of the twentieth century, there were increasingly influential efforts to define formal procedures of sampling. Agricultural economists in the U.S. Department of Agriculture were pioneers of such methods. By the 1930s, sampling was becoming common in U.S. government statistics. Increasingly, this was grounded in the mathematical methods of probability theory, which favored random rather than "purposive" samples. A 1934 paper by the Polish-born Jerzy Neyman, who was then in England but would soon emigrate to America, helped to define the methods of random sampling. At almost the same time, a notorious failure of indiscriminate large-scale polling in the 1936 election—predicting a landslide victory by Alf Landon over Franklin D. Roosevelt—gave credence to the more mathematical procedures.

Tools and Strategies

The new statistics of the twentieth century was defined not by an object of study—society—nor by counting and classifying, but by its mathematical tools, and by strategies of designing and analyzing observational and experimental data. The mathematics was grounded in an eighteenth-century tradition of probability theory, and was first institutionalized as a mathematical statistics in the 1890s by the English biometrician and eugenicist Karl Pearson. The other crucial founding figure was Sir R. A. Fisher, also an English student of quantitative biology and eugenics, whose statistical strategies of experimental design and analysis date from the 1920s. Pearson and Fisher were particularly influential in the United States, where quantification was associated with Progressive reforms of political and economic life. A biometric movement grew up in the United States under the leadership of scientists such as Raymond Pearl, who had been a postdoctoral student in Pearson's laboratory in London. Economics, also, was highly responsive to the new statistical methods, and deployed them to find trends, correlate variables, and detect and analyze business cycles. The Cowles Commission, set up in 1932 and housed at the University of Chicago in 1939, deployed and created statistical methods to investigate the causes of the worldwide depression of that decade. An international Econometric Society was established at about the same time, in 1930, adapting its name from Pearson's pioneering journal *Biometrika*.

Also prominent among the leading statistical fields in America were agriculture and psychology. Both had statistical traditions reaching back into the nineteenth century, and both were particularly receptive to new statistical tools. Fisher had worked out his methods of experimental design and tests of statistical significance with particular reference to agriculture. In later years he often visited America, where he was associated most closely with a statistical group at Iowa State University led by George Snedecor. The agriculturists divided their fields into many plots and assigned them randomly to experimental and control groups in order to determine, for example, whether a fertilizer treatment significantly increased crop yields. This strategy of collective experiments and randomized treatment also became the model for much of psychology, and especially educational psychology, where the role of the manure (the treatment) was now filled by novel teaching methods or curricular innovations to test for differences in educational achievement. The new experimental psychology was closely tied to strategies for sorting students using tests of intelligence and aptitude in the massively expanded public school systems of the late nineteenth and early twentieth centuries.

The methods of twentieth-century statistics also had a decisive role in medicine. The randomized clinical trial was also in many ways a British innovation, exemplified by a famous test of streptomycin in the treatment of tuberculosis just after World War II (1939–1945). It quickly became important also in America, where medical schools soon began to form departments of biostatistics. Statistics provided a means to coordinate treatments by many physicians in large-scale medical trials, which provided, in effect, a basis for regulating the practice of medicine. By the 1960s, statistical results had acquired something like statutory authority in the evaluation of pharmaceuticals. Not least among the sources of their appeal was the presumed objectivity of their results. The "gold standard" was a thoroughly impersonal process—a well-designed experiment generating quantitative results that could be analyzed by accepted statistical methods to give an unambiguous result.

Historical analysis was fairly closely tied to the field of statistics in the nineteenth century, when statistical work focused primarily on developing data and information systems to analyze "state and society" questions. Carroll Wright, first Commissioner of Labor, often quoted August L. von Schloezer's aphorism that "history is statistics ever advancing, statistics is history standing still." The twentieth century turn in statistics to experimental design and the analysis of biological processes broke that link, which was tenuously restored with the development of cliometrics, or quantitative history, in the 1960s and 1970s. But unlike the social sciences of economics, political science, psychology, and sociology, the field of history did not fully restore its relationship with statistics, for example, by making such training a graduate degree requirement. Thus the use of statistical analysis and "statistics" in the form of data in historical writing has remained a subfield of the American historical writing as history has eschewed a claim to being a "scientific" discipline.

Statistics as a field embraces the scientific ideal. That ideal, which replaces personal judgment with impersonal law, resonates with an American political tradition reaching back to the eighteenth century. The place of science, and especially statistics, as a source of such authority grew enormously in the twentieth century, as a greatly expanded state was increasingly compelled to make decisions in public, and to defend them against challenges.

BIBLIOGRAPHY

Anderson, Margo. *The American Census: A Social History*. New Haven, Conn.: Yale University Press, 1988.

———. *American Medicine and Statistical Thinking, 1800–1860*. Cambridge, Mass.: Harvard University Press, 1984.

Cohen, Patricia Cline. *A Calculating People: The Spread of Numeracy in Early America*. Chicago: University of Chicago Press, 1982.

Cullen, M. J. *The Statistical Movement in Early Victorian Britain: The Foundations of Empirical Social Research*. New York: Barnes and Noble, 1975.

Curtis, Bruce. *The Politics of Population: State Formation, Statistics, and the Census of Canada, 1840–1875*. Toronto: University of Toronto Press, 2001.

Desrosières, Alan. *The Politics of Large Numbers: A History of Statistical Reasoning* (English translation of Alain Desrosieres 1993 study, *La politique des grands nombres: Histoire de la raison statistique*). Cambridge, Mass.: Harvard University Press, 1998.

Gigerenzer, G., et al. *The Empire of Chance: How Probability Changed Science and Everyday Life*. Cambridge, Mass.: Cambridge University Press, 1989.

Glass, D. V. *Numbering the People: The Eighteenth-Century Population Controversy and the Development of Census and Vital Statistics in Britain*. New York: D.C. Heath, 1973.

Marks, Harry M. *The Progress of Experiment: Science and Therapeutic Reform in the United States, 1900–1990*. New York: Cambridge University Press, 1997.

Morgan, Mary S. *The History of Econometric Ideas*. New York: Cambridge University Press, 1990.

Patriarca, Silvana. *Numbers and Nationhood: Writing Statistics in Nineteenth-Century Italy*. New York: Cambridge University Press, 1996.

Porter, Theodore M. *The Rise of Statistical Thinking, 1820–1900*. Princeton, N.J.: Princeton University Press, 1986.

———. *Trust in Numbers: The Pursuit of Objectivity in Science and Public Life*. Princeton, N.J.: Princeton University Press, 1995.

Stigler, Stephen M. *The History of Statistics: The Measurement of Uncertainty Before 1900*. Cambridge, Mass.: Belknap Press of Harvard University Press, 1986.

———. *Statistics on the Table: The History of Statistical Concepts and Methods.* Cambridge, Mass.: Harvard University Press, 1999.

Margo Anderson
Theodore M. Porter

See also **Census, Bureau of the; Demography and Demographic Trends.**

STATUE OF LIBERTY,

STATUE OF LIBERTY, originally named "Liberty Enlightening the World," was a gift from France, unveiled on 28 October 1886 at Bedloe's Island (later Liberty Island) in New York Harbor. There, President Grover Cleveland accepted it as a long-delayed commemoration of a century of American independence. Rising 151 feet above an 89-foot pedestal, it was then the tallest structure in New York City.

The French sculptor Frédéric Auguste Bartholdi had designed the statue with assistance from the great engineer Gustave Eiffel. It was then shipped from Paris in sections. The project's sponsors were a group of French liberals who tirelessly promoted the United States as a model of popular government rooted in stability and order and wanted France to follow the American example. Accordingly, Bartholdi's gigantic classical goddess carries a tablet representing the American Declaration of Independence. Yet she faces outward, stolid, strong, and unmovable as beams from her upraised lamp radiate across the sea.

The history of the Statue of Liberty is largely a story of its growing centrality and importance among the cherished symbols of the American nation. At first it differed chiefly in size and location from numerous other classical goddesses who crowded the nineteenth century's repertory of symbols. But size and location were crucially important. She was an overwhelming presence at the entry to America's greatest city. As more vaporous goddesses faded in the harsh light of modernity, the great statue became the centerpiece of a magical American place, recognizable everywhere through postcards and magazine covers, with the New York City skyline rising behind her.

To many Americans she also conveyed a profoundly personal message. The millions of immigrants who were landing at New York City in the early twentieth century saw in this majestic figure their first intimation of a new life. In her uplifted arm they read a message of welcome that said, "This vast republic wants me!" By 1910 public schools in some large cities were reenacting in pageants (with a teacher as the statue) the gathering of immigrants into an inclusive nation.

The use of the statue to identify America with an active promotion of freedom received further emphasis in the Liberty Bond drives and parades of World War I and from the ideological mobilization of the United States against totalitarian regimes during and after World War II.

Unveiling of the Statue of Liberty. Edward Moran's dramatic 1886 painting depicts the historic event in New York Harbor. © MUSEUM OF THE CITY OF NEW YORK/CORBIS

In domestic affairs, embattled images of the statue also energized campaigns for civil liberties and women's rights.

In the mid-1980s, a fabulously successful fund-raising campaign led by Chrysler executive Lee Iacocca produced a deep restoration of the statue, capped in October 1986 by a four-day extravaganza celebrating its centennial.

BIBLIOGRAPHY

Dillon, Wilton S., and Neil G. Kotler, eds. *The Statue of Liberty Revisited: Making a Universal Symbol.* Washington, D.C.: Smithsonian Institution Press, 1994.

Liberty: The French-American Statue in Art and History. New York: Harper and Row, 1986.

Trachtenberg, Marvin. *The Statue of Liberty.* New York: Penguin Books, 1977.

John Higham

See also **France, Relations with; New York City.**

STATUTES AT LARGE, UNITED STATES.

STATUTES AT LARGE, UNITED STATES. The *United States Statutes at Large* is a chronological publication of the laws enacted in each session of Congress, beginning in 1789. The series is cited as "Stat.," with the volume number preceding and the page number following. The *Statutes at Large* is legal evidence of the laws passed by Congress, which are first officially published as "slip laws." The *United States Code* provides updates, by subject, of the laws in force. The *Statutes* also contained presidential executive orders until the *Federal Register* began publication on 14 March 1936, and included TREATIES WITH FOREIGN NATIONS until the publication *Treaties and Other International Agreements* began on 27 January 1950.

BIBLIOGRAPHY

Barber, Steve, and Mark A. McCormick. *Legal Research*. Albany, N.Y.: Delmar, 1996.

Clement E. Vose / A. E.

See also **Archives; Code, U.S.; Government Publications.**

STATUTES OF LIMITATIONS are laws passed by legislatures that set an amount of time following certain events, after which legal proceedings involving those events may not begin. Statutes of limitations relate to both civil causes of action and criminal prosecutions. A civil statute of limitations may stipulate that the time period begins with the occurrence of an injury or with its discovery. For example, the law may permit an injured party in a car accident only a certain amount of time in which to begin court proceedings against the other party. Statutes of limitation exist for a variety of reasons, but primarily because, as time passes, papers may be destroyed, witnesses may die, or the conditions of a transaction may be forgotten. With the passage of time, it often becomes impractical to attempt to recover damages or to prosecute a crime. Due to statutes of limitations, certain violations of the law, because they are said to have become "stale," are never addressed in court. For some crimes, including homicide, there are no statutes of limitation. A number of states have also begun to abolish time limits for bringing criminal charges in cases involving the alleged sexual abuse of children.

BIBLIOGRAPHY

Engel, Monroe. *Statutes of Limitations*. New York: Knopf, 1988.

Akiba J. Covitz
Esa Lianne Sferra
Meredith L. Stewart

STATUTORY LAW, as distinguished from constitutional law and the common law, is that body of law laid down by a legislature. Both the U.S. Congress and state legislatures enact statutes either by bill or by joint resolution. Federal statutes take precedence over state statutes, and state statutes are superior to the common law. Statutory law is inferior to constitutional law, and courts exercise the power of judicial review when they declare statutes unconstitutional. Statutory law is codified under titles describing the areas of action to which they appertain, and these titles are grouped together in codes. The administrative branch of government enforces statutory law often through the promulgation of administrative rules and regulations that have the effect of law as long as they lie within the limits set by the statutes.

BIBLIOGRAPHY

Burton, Steven J. *An Introduction to Law and Legal Reasoning*. 2d ed. Boston: Little, Brown, 1995.

Hart, H. A. L. *The Concept of Law*. Oxford: Clarendon Press, 1963.

Rantoul, Robert, Jr. "Oration at Scituate. Delivered on the Fourth of July, 1836." In Perry Miller, ed., *The Legal Mind in America: From Independence to the Civil War*. Garden City, N.Y.: Doubleday, 1962.

Walker, Harvey. *Law Making in the United States*. New York: Ronald Press, 1934.

Paul Dolan / C. P.

See also **Code, U.S.; Executive Orders; Initiative.**

STEAM POWER AND ENGINES. The first useful steam engine was developed in England by Thomas Newcomen and was put into operation by 1712. By 1730 the engine was not uncommon in western Europe, and in 1755 the first steam engine began operation in the American colonies, at a copper mine in Belleville, New Jersey. This engine, built by the British firm of Joseph Hornblower, was followed by another in PHILADELPHIA, built in 1773 by Christopher Colles. Three years later a third engine was at work, raising water for New York City waterworks. The Newcomen engines were large, expensive, and cumbersome. Except for draining valuable mines or providing water for large cities, they were not economically attractive in America, where waterpower suitable for manufactures was reasonably plentiful along the eastern seaboard.

Providing power for transportation was a greater problem. The Newcomen engine was too bulky for such purposes, but after the improvements made by James Watt beginning in 1764, it occurred to many that the steam engine might be applied to propelling boats. Beginning in 1785 more than a dozen American inventors tried to build STEAMBOATS, including Jehosaphat Starr, Apollos Kinsley, Isaac Briggs, William Longstreet, Elijah Ormsbee, John Stevens, Daniel French, Samuel Morey, James Rumsey, and Nathan Read. They were all slowed by the necessity of building their own engines (the export of which was forbidden by England) with inadequate machine-shop facilities and limited knowledge of steam technology. The most successful inventor was John Fitch, who established regular steamboat service between Philadelphia and New Jersey in 1790.

The complexity of applying steam power to navigation led some of these inventors to turn to the simpler problems of supplying stationary power. The Soho works in New Jersey, which had helped Stevens on his steamboat, began in 1799 to build two large engines for a new water-works in Philadelphia. The head of the shops, Nicholas J. Roosevelt, later partnered with Robert Fulton in operating the first commercially successful steamboat (1807). Robert Livingston, a partner of Fulton and brother-in-law of Stevens, knew Benjamin Henry Latrobe, a British physician-architect with a knowledge of steam engines, and a number of workmen who had built and operated engines in England. Prominent emigrant British engineers such as James Smallman, John Nancarrow, and Charles Stoudinger provided an important source of new technological information for American inventors and engine builders.

In 1802 Oliver Evans of Philadelphia became the first American to make steam engines for the general market. Smallman followed in 1804, and with the addition of Daniel Large and others, that city soon became the center of engine building. New York City, where Robert McQueen and James Allaire had been patronized by Fulton, became another center of engine manufacture. During the War of 1812 the building and use of engines spread to the western states. The first engine built in Pittsburgh (for a steamboat) was completed in 1811. The following year Evans opened a Pittsburgh branch of his Philadelphia Mars Iron Works. With the addition of such pioneer builders as Thomas Copeland, James Arthurs, Mahlon Rogers, and Mark Stackhouse, Pittsburgh too became a center of steam engineering. Thomas Bakewell and David Prentice opened Kentucky's first engine shop in Louisville in 1816. Work in Cincinnati, Ohio, began soon afterward, and by 1826 that city had five steam-engine factories. The widespread use of steamboats on western riverways spurred this western activity; the demand for engines on southern sugar plantations, the easy accessibility of iron and coal around Pittsburgh, and, initially, the dislocations of eastern trade caused by the War of 1812 also contributed to the vitality of western steamboat production.

By 1838 steam power was widely accepted all over the United States. The federal census of that year counted 3,010 steam engines. Of these, 350 were used on locomotives, 800 on steamboats, and 1,860 were stationary. This last category included those that ran mills of all descriptions, were at work on farms and plantations, and raised water for cities. Pennsylvania accounted for the largest number (383) of stationary engines, Louisiana was second with 274, and Massachusetts had 165. Except for Louisiana, where the engines were typically used on large sugar plantations to grind cane, most of these were located in cities. Of the 383 engines in Pennsylvania, 133 were at work in Pittsburgh and 174 in Philadelphia; of the 165 engines in Massachusetts, 114 were in or around Boston. The steam engine had a profound effect on the economy, culture, and aesthetics of cities. Formerly centers only of trade, culture, and government, they now became centers of manufacturing and, consequently, the home of a large class of factory operatives. As long as factories and mills had depended on waterpower, such a

development in cities had been impossible. Unskilled and semiskilled jobs proliferated in factories powered by steam engines, thus sparking a demand for cheap labor and fueling a demographic shift towards ever larger cities that would continue throughout the nineteenth century. Indeed, the technology of the steam engine contributed mightily to the urbanization and industrialization of the American landscape.

By the middle of the nineteenth century, virtually every American city contained shops producing steam engines and had a large number of the machines at work. Imported engines were not important in the trade, although American engines were regularly exported. Northern-made engines in the South were used not only on plantations, but also in other extractive processes carried out in rice mills, cottonseed oil mills, cotton gins and presses, and the saline wells of western Virginia. Most important, these engines found increasing use in cotton textile mills scattered throughout the region. Southern cities, notably Charleston, South Carolina, and Richmond, Virginia, became manufacturing centers in their own right, basing their activity to a considerable extent on steam.

As the first machine necessarily made of iron, the steam engine had a critical influence on the development of the iron industry. Previously, most iron had been used in a wrought form. Most engine parts were cast, however, and the improvements in casting technique forced by engine development were available for use in making other machines as well. In addition, rolling mills began to multiply only when boiler plate came into demand from engine builders. These boiler-plate makers in turn became the first to construct iron boats. The harnessing of steam engines to railroad locomotion, of course, increased the demand for rails as well as engines. In a circle of improvement, steam engines were used to drive rolling mills, provide blast for furnaces, and run drilling machines, lathes, and other iron-working machines, all of which made it easier to produce and work iron and led to improved steam engines. The demand for coal, both for iron furnaces and steam boilers, was also greatly stimulated.

There were essentially three types of steam engines used in the country before the introduction of the turbine late in the nineteenthth century. The first engines were of the Newcomen type. After the introduction of Watt's improvements in this engine, no more of the old style were built. Watt's atmospheric engine was widely popular for both stationary use and for the eastern steamboats, such as Fulton's *Clermont*. It was largely superseded by Evans's high-pressure engine. The piston of the Newcomen-type engine was actuated by introducing steam under it, condensing the steam with cold water, then allowing the weight of the atmosphere (about fifteen pounds per square inch) to push the piston down. Watt's key improvement was to provide a separate condenser, which would conserve heat and make the piston "double-acting" by introducing steam alternately on both sides of the piston. Evans's further improvement consisted of using the force of the steam itself (at 100–200 pounds per square inch) to drive the piston directly, allowing it to escape into the atmosphere uncondensed. The power of the Watt engine could usually be increased only by enlarging the cylinder. With Evans's Columbian engine, only the steam pressure need be increased. Because it provided more power in a smaller space, his engine quickly became standard on western steamboats and eventually on locomotives.

Subsequent efforts at improvement went in two directions: first, toward further refinements of the reciprocating engine, especially by such improved valve actions as that of George Corliss of Rhode Island, and second, toward a rotary engine. Hundreds of patents were taken out for such devices before the successes of such late nineteenth-century inventors as Charles Gordon Curtis in developing the steam turbine. In the twentieth century, steam power has remained of primary importance only in the generation of electricity in power plants, although its potential use in automobiles periodically receives attention.

BIBLIOGRAPHY

Hamlin, Talbot. *Benjamin Henry Latrobe*. New York: Oxford University Press, 1955.

Hills, Richard L. *Power from Steam: A History of the Stationary Steam Engine*. Cambridge, U.K.: Cambridge University Press, 1989.

Philip, Cynthia Owen. *Robert Fulton, A Biography*. New York: F. Watts, 1985.

Pursell, Carroll W. *Early Stationary Steam Engines in America*. Washington, D.C.: Smithsonian Institution Press, 1969.

Rolt, Lionel. *The Steam Engine of Thomas Newcomen*. New York: Science History Publications, 1977.

Carroll Pursell / A. R.

See also **Agricultural Machinery; Fulton's Folly; Industrial Revolution; Locomotives; Manufacturing; Railroads; Transportation and Travel; Water Supply and Conservation.**

STEAMBOATS. The origin of steam-powered boats in America is typically traced to Robert Fulton's experiences on the Hudson River with the *Clermont* in the first decade of the nineteenth century. The idea dates at least to sixteenth-century Spain, when Blasco de Garay, a native of Barcelona, experimented with a steamer. Work on the concept continued in England and France through the eighteenth century, but in almost every case, the boats were too heavy, unwieldy, and underfinanced. By 1784, innovation met demand when the Scotsman James Watt and others improved the efficiency of the steam engine at about the time America needed better transportation systems for its struggle westward.

James Rumsey, on the Potomac River, and John Fitch, on the Delaware, worked with steamboat ideas in the 1780s that were used by future entrepreneurs. With the successful commercial application of steam by Fulton and

his financier, Robert R. Livingston, boats were soon plying the Hudson, Delaware, Connecticut, and Providence Rivers, as well as Lake Champlain. The first steamboat on western waters, the 116-foot sternwheeler *New Orleans*, was built by Nicolas J. Roosevelt, a partner of Fulton's and ancestor of the future presidents, in Pittsburgh.

The most dramatic improvements in steamboat design came at the hands of Henry Shreve, whose name lives on in the river city in Louisiana. Shreve's second steamboat, the 148-foot-long sidewheeler *Washington*, featured the machinery and a high-pressure engine on the upper deck (rather than below deck), allowing the flat, shallow hull to draw less water and more safely navigate the treacherous shoals, rapids, and chutes of the Mississippi River system. His round trip from Louisville to New Orleans in 1816 took forty-one days, a journey that would have taken a keelboat several months to complete. Shreve also deserves credit for the design of the snagboat, first seen in the Heliopolis; a snagboat was a steamer with a Samson's chain, A-frame, and block-and-tackle system at its bow that could remove trees and other obstructions from inland waters.

More specialized steamboats, with higher tonnage, were constructed for the Great Lakes beginning in 1818. The following year, the first ship with steam power, the *Savannah*, crossed the Atlantic to Europe, although it ran mostly under sail and it was thirty years until regular steamship service began on the ocean. By 1825, the steamboat, fueled by wood or coal, was becoming the vehicle of choice for long-distance inland travel, replacing the keelboat, flatboat, barge, and canoe. Ten years later, 700 boats were registered in U.S. waters. The cost of shipping raw materials and manufactured goods dropped considerably, beginning at the deep-water ports of the lower Mississippi and Gulf of Mexico, and after the work done by the U.S. Army Corps of Engineers, shallower ports in other inland river systems. Steamboats soon plied the Red, Colorado, Rio Grande, Arkansas, Savannah, Sacramento, and Columbia Rivers. Ocean steamships, powered by coal and drawing four times as much water as steamboats, began to use a screw propeller instead of paddlewheels as early as 1851.

The first steamboats were crude, dangerous contraptions with short life spans. Fires, boiler explosions, collisions, snags, ice, and rot took their toll throughout the steamboat era. Various estimates put the average life of an inland steamboat at between three and five years. Shreve's *Washington*, for example, exploded on the Ohio River on 9 January 1819, killing eight but sparing the captain. Perhaps the worst inland shipping disaster in U.S. history came on 27 April 1865, when the steamer *Sultana*, carrying more than 2,300 people (mostly Union soldiers returning from Confederate prison camps) exploded seven miles up the Mississippi from Memphis, killing more than 1,700.

In the early years, captains tended to be boat owners, but corporations soon replaced them. By the 1850s, the

General Slocum. Remains of the excursion steamer that burned and sank in New York's East River, just off the Bronx, on 15 June 1904; most of the 1,021 dead were German Americans from the Lower East Side of Manhattan. © BETTMANN/CORBIS

fancy packets and floating palaces made famous by Mark Twain were churning American rivers. Steam lines like those owned by Diamond Joe Reynolds on the Mississippi and the Fall River line on the East Coast fought smaller firms in court and at the wharves. Boats increased in tonnage and opulence: bars, staterooms, dance halls, and lounges decorated the upper decks, while orchestras, stewards, chefs, and barbers served the needs of travelers. One of the most opulent steamboats was the third boat named *J. M. White*, finished in 1878 at Louisville for $200,000. It was 325 feet long, powered by 10 boilers—each 34 feet long—and had cylinders 43 inches in diameter. Its cabin stretched 260 feet, featuring chandeliers and a single piece of Belgian carpet 19 feet wide, and its hold carried 8,500 bales of cotton. It could easily carry 300 cabin passengers, 500 deck passengers, and 90 roustabouts. The boat burned only eight months into service.

Steamboat racing was a popular activity. Many captains needed only a slight excuse to start a match with a rival, even with a load of dry goods and decks full of passengers. Perhaps the most famous race took place in 1870 from New Orleans to St. Louis between the *Robert E. Lee* and the *Natchez*. The *Robert E. Lee* won the race in a time of three days, eighteen hours, and fourteen minutes. Racing added to the romance of the steamboat era, which also took in gambling, drinking, music, and other pursuits as part of life on the waters.

During the Civil War, steamboats were used to transport troops and in battle, but the coming of the railroad (it had reached the Mississippi in 1854) was a warning sign. The peak period of the steamboat lasted from about 1850 to 1875. With the exception of the great lumber boom of the 1880s in the northern forests of Minnesota, Michigan, and Wisconsin and the shipping of cotton from the Mississippi Delta, steamboats were reduced to short runs, day trips, and ferrying by the early twentieth century. After World War I, diesel-powered towboats and barges increasingly provided the muscle to move goods on the inland rivers; by the end of the twentieth century, only a handful of working steamboats, including the *Delta Queen*, were in operation as tourist attractions.

BIBLIOGRAPHY

Corbin, Annalies. *The Material Culture of Steamboat Passengers: Archaeological Evidence from the Missouri River.* New York: Kluwer Academic, 2000.

Dayton, Frederick Erving. *Steamboat Days.* New York: Tudor, 1939. Written by a former riverman.

Hunter, Louis C. *Steamboats on the Western Rivers: An Economic and Technological History.* Cambridge, Mass.: Harvard University Press, 1949. The definitive economic history.

Morrison, John H. *History of American Steam Navigation.* New York: Stephen Daye Press, 1958. The original edition was published in 1903.

Petersen, William J., *Steamboating on the Upper Mississippi.* Iowa City: State Historical Society of Iowa, 1968. An anecdotal account.

Mark Neuzil

See also **Great Lakes Steamships; Mississippi River;** *New Orleans;* **River Navigation;** *Savannah;* **Steam Power and Engines.**

STEEL STRIKES. The mass production of steel began in the United States during the 1870s. Since that time, the American steel industry has gone back and forth between being heavily unionized and hardly unionized at all. It was highly unionized until the Homestead Lockout of 1892, almost entirely nonunion from 1892 until U.S. Steel recognized the Steelworkers Organizing Committee in 1937, and highly unionized again from 1937 until steel production capacity began to disappear in the late 1970s. At present, the industry is largely nonunion. Major steel strikes have marked periods of both union growth and decline.

The First Union Era

The Amalgamated Association of Iron, Steel and Tin Workers, the first national union to include steelworkers, formed in 1876 after winning a series of local labor struggles across the steelmaking areas of Pennsylvania and Ohio. That union's strength, however, was in the iron industry. As iron manufacturers began to switch to steel production during the 1880s and early 1890s, skilled ironworkers fought to maintain power over production. Many manufacturers managed to switch from iron to steel without incident simply by closing their iron plants and opening up new steel mills with less-skilled, nonunion workers.

The Amalgamated Association lost its most important foothold in steelmaking during the Homestead Lockout of 1892. Carnegie Steel, the largest firm in the world at that time, instigated the dispute because it wanted to better compete with an increasing number of rival companies who operated on a nonunion basis. The 6 July 1892 gun battle between strikers and Pinkerton guards hired to protect their replacements has made this one of the most famous incidents in American labor history. Since the company's primary owner, Andrew Carnegie, had once expressed support for trade unionism, many Americans saw the lockout as an act of hypocrisy.

The Nonunion Era

After Homestead, the Amalgamated Association gradually disappeared from the scene. In 1901, the union struck the newly formed United States Steel Corporation, which controlled approximately 65 percent of the industry. This action gave U.S. Steel an excuse to drive the union from most of the small number of plants it controlled that still bargained with them. After a small lockout in 1909, U.S. Steel, along with the vast majority of firms in the steel industry, was union free.

In 1919, steelworkers made a strong but ultimately unsuccessful attempt to regain their previous power in the industry. During World War I, John Fitzpatrick, president of the Chicago American Federation of Labor, and the future Communist candidate for U.S. president William Z. Foster formed the National Committee for Organizing Iron and Steel Workers. On 22 September 1919, the committee called a national strike over a wide range of issues, most notably union recognition and the eight-hour day. Fiercely protective of their managerial prerogatives, industry leaders chose to fight the strike at any cost.

Confrontation over Steel. Chicago police use guns, clubs, and tear gas against strikers outside the Republic Steel plant on 30 May 1937—the most violent moment of the so-called Little Steel Strike. AP/Wide World Photos

Steel companies played on ethnic and racial difference among their workers in order win the dispute. Immigrant workers responded to the call to strike in greater numbers than their native-born counterparts. To make matters worse, the Amalgamated Association, which benefited handsomely from dues paid by new members the committee brought in, did little to support the strike. Under the influence of company propaganda, Amalgamated Association members, mostly better-skilled, native-born workers, voted to end their involvement in the walkout on 14 December 1919. These developments made it possible for many steel plants to continue operating during the strike, or at least wait out the trouble until a few strikers returned to work. Steelmakers and their friends in the media also made a big deal over Foster's connections to the Industrial Workers of the World in order to drain support for the strike. On 8 January 1920, the committee called off the strike. It disbanded shortly thereafter.

At the beginning of the Depression, the Amalgamated Association had very few members and no interest in organizing. John L. Lewis formed what would become the Congress of Industrial Organizations (CIO) in large part to get the American Federation of Labor to organize steel and other largely nonunion major manufacturing industries. In 1936, Lewis appointed the United Mine Workers vice president Philip Murray the head of the Steelworkers Organizing Committee (SWOC), the group within the CIO charged with organizing steel.

At first, the SWOC concentrated its efforts on the industry giant U.S. Steel. This campaign bore fruit in March 1937, when U.S. Steel recognized the SWOC without a fight. But other large firms, collectively dubbed "Little Steel" only because they were smaller than U.S. Steel Corporation, fought hard against the SWOC. The Little Steel Strike of 1937 was really separate strikes against Bethlehem Steel, Republic Steel, Inland Steel, and

Youngstown Sheet and Tube. It began when the Republic Steel president, Tom Girdler, locked employees out of the firm's Massillon, Ohio, mill on 20 May. The most famous incident of the strike occurred on 30 May 1937, outside a Republic Steel plant in Chicago. Chicago policemen shot into a crowd of strikers who had wanted to march on the plant. Ten marchers, seven of whom were shot in the back, died of their wounds. The gunfire injured thirty others, nine of whom were permanently disabled.

None of the "Little Steel" firms recognized the SWOC as a result of the strike. However, the strike did provide fodder for many complaints that the union brought before the newly formed National Labor Relations Board. Pressure from the board as these complaints wound their way through the legal process and pressure from the Roosevelt administration to keep production going during World War II led each of these firms to recognize the SWOC in the years following the strike. In a few cases, this required additional strikes, such as at Bethlehem Steel's South Bethlehem, Pennsylvania, plant in 1941. The SWOC's successor organization, the United Steelworkers of America (USWA), represented nearly every steelworker in America by the end of the war.

The USWA Era

Between 1946 and 1959, the USWA struck five times in an effort to win higher wages for its members. Each of these strikes shut down the industry. Because of the importance of the steel industry to the national economy, the government became deeply involved in these disputes. The 1952 strike led to President Truman's historic decision to seize the entire steel industry. In *Youngstown Sheet and Tube Company v. Sawyer* (1952), the Supreme Court ruled this action unconstitutional. The 1959 strike lasted 116 days, until the Supreme Court upheld a presidential injunction that ended the dispute on the grounds that it created a national economic emergency.

Union wage gains made during these strikes contributed to the collapse of the steel industry. In each of these disputes, employers tended to make wage concessions to the union rather than cede control over the production process. This and the failure of American producers to innovate made American steel expensive in relation to its foreign competition. Because these strikes continually disrupted supply, steel consumers increasingly looked to foreign sources for cheap, reliable product. The collapse of the industry began in the mid-1960s. By the early 1980s, the American steel industry had shrunk to a shadow of its former self.

As a result of this crisis, the United Steelworkers of America voluntarily gave up the right to strike. The Experimental Negotiating Agreement (ENA), a contract with employers under which the union agreed to settle all collective bargaining disputes through arbitration, prevented strikes that would further destabilize the industry and drive consumers to foreign suppliers. It lasted from 1973 to 1983. The parties never invoked the arbitration clause,

settling all the disputes themselves. Unfortunately, because steelworker wages continued to increase over the life of the agreement, the ENA did not stop the steel industry's disastrous decline.

Industrywide bargaining between employers and the USWA broke down in 1985. This led to many isolated strikes, often motivated by the union's desire to limit the damage that deindustrialization inflicted upon its members. The strike against USX (the successor company to U.S. Steel) in 1986 and early 1987 is perhaps the most important of these because the company and the union managed to find common ground. Other disputes, such as the strike and lockout that started in 1997 at Rocky Mountain Steel Mills in Pueblo, Colorado, have become battles to the death resulting in either the destruction of the union or the bankruptcy of the firm. Most new steel mills built in the United States over the last twenty years have been nonunion from their inception. Therefore, few of these facilities have faced strikes.

BIBLIOGRAPHY

Brody, David. *Steelworkers in America: The Nonunion Era.* Cambridge, Mass.: Harvard University Press, 1960.

———. *Labor in Crisis; the Steel Strike of 1919.* Urbana: University of Illinois Press, 1987.

Fitch, John A. *The Steel Workers.* Pittsburgh, Pa.: University of Pittsburgh Press, 1989.

Hoerr, John P. *And the Wolf Finally Came.* Pittsburgh, Pa.: University of Pittsburgh Press, 1988.

Tiffany, Paul. *The Decline of American Steel.* New York: Oxford University Press, 1988.

Jonathan Rees

See also **American Federation of Labor–Congress of Industrial Organizations; Arbitration; Collective Bargaining; Homestead Strike of 1892; Strikes; United Steelworkers of America.**

STEERING COMMITTEES are committees frequently found in legislatures and generally concerned with such matters as the scheduling of legislation. In the U.S. Congress they are party committees, and as such perform a number of functions. In some cases they may be involved in the formulation of party tactics and positions for particular bills. In the Senate, both the Republican and Democratic Parties established such committees in the late nineteenth century, and each prepared a legislative schedule when its party was the majority party. In the late 1940s both parties assigned such scheduling duties to their newly created policy committees. The Republican steering committee was displaced, but the Democrats reconstituted their steering committee as a committee on committees, responsible for assigning party members to standing committees. In the House, both parties established such committees in the twentieth century to assist the leaders in formulating strategy. For a short time in the 1920s the Republican Steering Committee dominated the House. In 1949 it was renamed the Policy Committee to act as an advisory body for the Republican leaders. The House Democrats established such a committee in the 1930s, but it has met only infrequently and has had no great impact on party decisions.

Steering committees took on far greater importance in the 1970s. In the aftermath of the Watergate scandal, congressional rules underwent substantial reform. Traditionally, committee chairs enjoyed almost dictatorial power over the committees they headed. In the 1970s, however, new rules put forth a partial democratization of the committee system, in that the respective committee chairs were forced to share at least a degree of power with ranking members of each committee. As part of these reforms, the Democratic majority in the House and Senate gave to steering committees the committee assignment function formerly exercised by the members of the Ways and Means Committee. Consequently, steering committees began to play a more active role in party decision making. Within both the Republican and Democratic Parties, steering committees have become the scene of intraparty jockeying for committee assignments. Under the House and Senate rules, the majority party decides committee assignments for its members, and the minority party decides committee assignments for its members. Thus, with a large number of members competing for a relatively small number of key committee assignments, the parties' respective steering committees take on tremendous importance within the Republican and Democratic caucuses. Even for new members, who lack the seniority to head the most powerful committees, steering committees are very important. Assignment to a powerful committee, even at a junior rank, affords the representative or senator prestige and political capital. Not surprisingly, therefore, steering committees have emerged as an important aspect of the legislative process.

BIBLIOGRAPHY

Redman, Eric. *The Dance of Legislation.* New York: Simon and Schuster, 1973.

Reid, Thomas R. *Congressional Odyssey: The Saga of a Senate Bill.* San Francisco: Freeman, 1980.

Smith, Stephen S. *Call to Order: Floor Politics in the House and Senate.* Washington, D.C.: Brookings Institution, 1989.

Dale Vinyard/A. G.

See also **Delegation of Powers; Rules of the House.**

STEM CELL RESEARCH. *See* **Bioethics; Genetic Engineering.**

STEVENS, ISAAC, MISSION (1853–1855). Isaac Stevens was thirty-five years old in 1853 when he was appointed the Washington Territory's first governor and also Superintendent of Indian Affairs. As a West Point graduate, he was commissioned in the Corps of Engineers and gained experience as a surveyor and engineer. After military service in the War with Mexico (1846–1848), he joined the U.S. Coast and Geodetic Survey.

Stevens's trip to his new post in the Washington Territory was combined with the additional job of commanding a survey team in mapping out a northern route for a proposed transcontinental railroad. Of the four surveys commissioned for the railroad, Stevens's was the most comprehensive, including records of flora, fauna, and Indian tribes.

Stevens assumed the governorship in November 1853 and set up a territorial government. With white people moving to the territory and settling on prime land claimed by Indian tribes, conflicts were inevitable. Stevens's solution was to divide the territory into districts and send agents out to select Indian representatives of each tribe to sign treaties.

Stevens traveled to Washington, D.C., to lobby for funds to build roads and to buy Indian lands and establish Indian reserves. He returned in December 1854 with $45,000 for negotiating treaties with Indians in Washington Territory and another $80,000 for tribes along the eastern boundary of the territory.

Stevens appointed a commission to draw up a treaty patterned after those already signed with several Oregon tribes. Once it was ready, he set up a treaty council at Medicine Creek with tribes of Puget Sound Indians. On Christmas Day 1854, Stevens presented the treaty through an interpreter who used the Chinook Jargon, a language of some 500 words that crossed Indian language barriers.

The tribes were regarded as separate nations, but not foreign nations. They could make no treaties with any other country and were totally under the dominion of the United States. Representatives of the tribes signed the treaty on 26 December 1854, exchanging most of their land and gaining graduated annuity payments and an agricultural and industrial school. Their fishing rights were guaranteed on their usual grounds not included in the reservation land. Congress ratified the treaty on 3 March 1855.

Similar treaties were signed with other Puget Sound tribes at Point Elliott, Point No Port, and Neah Bay in January 1855. The ratification of these treaties was delayed in Congress until March 1859 because an Indian War, consisting of mostly small skirmishes, was waged with these tribes before they were settled on reservations.

Stevens's method of signing treaties continued with great councils held in Walla Walla (May–June 1855), and in present-day Montana at Hell Gate on the Clark Ford (July 1855) and at the mouth of the Judith River (October 1855).

Indian fishing rights outlined in the Treaty of Medicine Creek were challenged in court cases that lasted from 1968 to 1979, resulting in a Supreme Court decision, *U.S. v. Washington*, on the side of the Indians, ensuring their rights to fifty percent of the harvestable number of fish allowed within conservation regulations of the state of Washington.

BIBLIOGRAPHY

Marks, Paula Mitchell. *In a Barren Land: American Indian Dispossession and Survival*. New York: William Morrow, 1998.

Prucha, Francis Paul. *American Indian Treaties: The History of a Political Anomaly*. Berkeley: University of California Press, 1994.

Richards, Kent D. *Isaac I. Stevens: Young Man in a Hurry*. Provo, Utah: Brigham Young University Press, 1979.

Veda Boyd Jones

STOCK MARKET.

Originating in the Netherlands and Great Britain during the seventeenth century, stock exchanges initially enabled investors to buy and sell shares of companies to raise money for overseas expansion. Called "bourses," these exchanges eventually began dealing in the public securities of banks, insurance companies, and manufacturing firms. Until World War I, the London Stock Exchange was the largest and busiest in the world. Although inaugurated in 1792, when twenty-four New York merchants signed the Buttonwood Agreement, and formally organized in 1817, the New York Stock Exchange (NYSE), which is located on Wall Street in New York City, was small by comparison to the European bourses, with an average of only 100 shares traded per session. The NYSE attained preeminence only after World War I, which had disrupted the financial markets of Europe and transformed the United States into an economic power of the first order.

The Stock Market Crash

Flourishing throughout the 1920s, the stock market crashed on 29 October 1929, bringing to an end the era of economic prosperity and ushering in a new, impoverished age that few understood. Yet the stock market crash did not cause the GREAT DEPRESSION of the 1930s. Rather, the crash was one of the more dramatic symptoms of structural weaknesses in the national and international economies. Between February 1928 and September 1929 prices on the New York Stock Exchange steadily rose. For eighteen months, investors enjoyed a "Bull" market in which almost everyone made money. The cumulative value of stocks in 1929 reached an estimated $67.5 billion, with 1 billion shares traded. The price of stock, however, had long ceased to bear any relation to the earning power of the corporations issuing it. The ratio of corporate earnings to the market price of stocks climbed to 16 to 1; a 10 to 1 ratio was the standard. In the autumn of 1929, the stock market began to fall apart.

On 19 October 1929, stock prices dropped sharply, unnerving Wall Street financiers, brokers, and investors. Big bankers tried to avert a crash by conspicuously buying stock in an attempt to restore public confidence. Ten days later, on "Black Tuesday," all efforts to save the market failed. By 13 November, the crash had wiped out $30 billion in stock value. Most knowledgeable Americans, including Herbert Hoover who had been elected president in November 1929, viewed the crash as a necessary and healthy adjustment provoked by inflated stock and undisciplined speculation. Only paper empires had toppled, Americans reassured themselves. The crash, though, brought down the economies of a number of European countries. The American economy followed. The Great Depression had begun.

What Went Wrong

By 1928 the value of such stocks as the Radio Corporation of America, Radio-Keith-Orpheum (RKO), Westinghouse, United Aircraft, and Southern Securities were grossly inflated, exceeding any reasonable expectation of future earnings. Brokers, however, encouraged speculation in these and other stocks by permitting investors to buy shares on "margin," that is, on credit. Investors paid as little as 25 percent of the purchase price out of their own capital reserves, borrowing the remainder from brokerages or banks and using the stock they were about to buy as collateral. The abrupt decline in stock prices triggered panic selling and forced brokers to issue a "margin call," which required all who had borrowed from them to repay their debts in full. Many had to liquidate their remaining stock to meet their financial obligations, thereby precipitating the crash.

Remedying Abuses

Investigations conducted during the 1930s by the Senate Banking and Currency Committee, under the direction of chief counsel Ferdinand Pecora, uncovered ample evidence of fraud, corruption, misrepresentation, and other unsavory practices in an essentially unregulated stock exchange. To remedy these abuses, Congress passed the Securities Act of 1933 and the Securities and Exchange Act of 1934, initiating federal regulation of the stock market. The Securities Act required all companies issuing stock to inform the Federal Trade Commission of their financial condition. Complaints that the new law was too intrusive prompted Congress to revise it. The resulting Securities and Exchange Act established the Securities and Exchange Commission (SEC) and granted it extensive authority to monitor stock exchanges, brokerage houses, and independent dealers. The SEC gained additional regulatory powers through the Public Utilities Holding Company Act of 1935, the Investment Companies Act of 1940, and the Investments Advisers Act of 1940, symbolizing the intention of government to intervene more fully than ever before into the economic life of the nation.

The American Stock Exchange

Located only blocks from the New York Stock Exchange, the American Stock Exchange (AMEX), which was founded during the 1790s, is the stock market for small

548

companies and small investors. The stock issues of organizations that do not meet the listing and size requirements of the NYSE are commonly traded on the AMEX. Once known as the "New York Curb Exchange" because dealers traded on the street outside brokerage houses in the New York financial district, the AMEX moved indoors in 1921.

Trading on the AMEX reached new heights as the 1990s drew to a close. Average daily trading volume was a record 29 million shares in 1998, up from the previous high of 24.4 million set only a few years earlier. More than 7.3 billion shares changed hands on the AMEX in 1998, up from 6.1 billion a year earlier. By 2000, the number of shares traded on the AMEX had reached 13.318 billion. On the NYSE, by contrast, 307.5 billion shares valued at $10.5 trillion changed hands in 2001, an increase of 17 percent over the 262.5 billion shares traded in 2000.

The National Association of Securities Dealers
In addition to organized exchanges, where brokers and dealers quoted prices on shares of stock, an Over-The-Counter (OTC) market had existed since the 1870s. Congress exerted control over the OTC market with passage of the Maloney Act of 1937, which created the National Association of Securities Dealers (NASD). Since its inception, the NASD has traded the shares of companies not large enough to be included on the New York Stock Exchange, the American Stock Exchange, or one of the other regional exchanges. In 1971 the NASD developed the National Association of Securities Dealers Automated Quotations (NASDAQ), becoming the first exchange to use computers to conduct business.

The volume of shares traded made the NASDAQ the largest stock exchange in the world at the end of the 1990s, with a record 202 billion shares changing hands in 1998 alone. Yet, the market value of the NASDAQ, a mere $2.6 trillion in 1998, paled by comparison to the market value of the NYSE, which totaled a staggering $10.9 trillion.

The Dow Jones Industrial Average
The principal index for assessing the performance of the stock market, the Dow Jones Industrial Average, dates from 1893 and at present includes thirty NYSE blue-chip stocks chosen by the editors of the *Wall Street Journal*. The blue-chips are comparatively safe investments with a low yield and a high price per share, but are issued by companies with a long history of good management and steady profits. Included among the blue-chips are the Aluminum Company of America (Alcoa), American Express, AT&T, Coca-Cola, Eastman Kodak, General Electric, General Motors, IBM, McDonald's, Philip Morris, Proctor and Gamble, Wal-Mart, and Walt Disney.

Bulls and Bears
Until the early 1980s, market analysts heralded the arrival of a "Bull" market when the Dow Jones Industrial Average reached 1,000 points. In a "Bull" market, the price per share rises and investors buy now intending to resale later at a handsome profit. A "Bear" market, by contrast, produces lower share prices; investors sell stocks or bonds intending to repurchase them later at a lower price. The Dow surpassed the 1,000 mark for the first time in 1972. A decade later it reached the unprecedented 2,000 mark before crashing on "Black Monday," 19 October 1987, when it plummeted more than 500 points in a single day and lost 22 percent of its value.

Riding the Bull: The Stock Market in the 1990s
During the 1990s the performance of the stock market was erratic. On 17 April 1991, the Dow Jones Industrial Average closed above 3,000 points for the first time in history. By 1995 the Dow had gained 33.5 percent in value and passed the 4,000 mark. In 1997 the Dow reached a high of 8,000, but began to fluctuate more wildly and unpredictably. In late October 1997, for instance, the stock market came as close to crashing as it had in a decade, when the Dow fell a record 554 points in a single day, equaling 7.2 percent of its total value, only to rebound with a record 337-point rise the following day. At the end of the week, the market had ebbed and flowed its way to a mark of 7,442.08, the loss of a mere 4 percent in value.

Even when the Dow fell, the value of stocks remained far greater than it had been at the beginning of the decade. By 1998 the Dow had reached 9,000; it closed the century near 11,000 with no apparent limits on its ascent. But analysts could not predict how the market would perform over the short or the long term. Although the market continued to rise steadily, and at times dramatically after 1997, by the end of the decade many experts feared that its volatility suggested the bottom could drop out at any moment.

The Growth of the Stock Market
The unparalleled rise in stock values attracted hundreds of thousands of new investors. By 1997 more than 42 percent of all American families owned stock either directly or through pension plans and mutual funds. Easier access to stock trading through Internet brokerages, which enabled investors to trade stocks without a broker for commissions as low as $5 per trade, added significantly to the numbers of those who ventured into the market. By 1999 more than 6.3 million households in the United States had on-line trading accounts, with assets totaling $400 billion. The popularity of on-line trading encouraged people to conduct more transactions, and to buy and sell more quickly in order to take advantage of short-term changes in the market.

During the 1990s the percentage of wealth invested in the stock market grew at an alarming rate. As recently as 1990, Americans had entrusted only 16 percent of their wealth to the stock market. Even during the "Bull" market of the 1980s, the portion of income devoted to securities never exceeded 19 percent. At the end of the twentieth century, by contrast, stock investments composed a record 34 percent of Americans' aggregate wealth, amounting to more than the value of their homes. A prolonged decline in stocks would thus prove cataclysmic for the millions who relied on the market to ensure their financial welfare now and in the future.

Permanent Prosperity?

Market analysts, nevertheless, remained optimistic. Many looked forward to an endlessly prosperous future, believing that the American economy had undergone a fundamental structural change. The advent of information technology, the global market, and world peace promised to generate unprecedented corporate earnings and continually rising stock prices. Those who shared this perspective postulated a "long boom" that would carry the American economy past all the difficulties and limitations that had hampered it in the past.

By the end of 2000, however, a series of government reports disclosed surprising weaknesses in the economy, giving rise to speculation that the eight-year period of uninterrupted growth was about to come to an end. In response to rumors of a general economic slowdown, the stock market fell. By 21 December 2000, the NASDAQ Index, dominated by high-tech stocks, had lost nearly half of its value, declining to 2,332.78. The Dow Jones Industrial Average held steadier, closing above 10,600 points, but by the end of the year optimism on Wall Street had evaporated amid apprehension over corporate earnings that were lower than expected. Stock prices tumbled, losing approximately $1 trillion in just a few months. Throughout 2001 and 2002, especially after the terrorist attacks of 11 September 2001, economists were concerned that the continued decline in stock values would trigger a reduction in capital investment and consumer spending, the two forces that had sustained the economic boom of the 1990s.

In the wake of corporate scandals and the resultant loss of public confidence, the stock market plummeted during the second quarter of 2002. After reaching its peak in January 2000, the Dow lost 34 percent of its value over the next two-and-one-half years. During the same period, the NASDAQ composite plunged 75 percent, the worst decline for a major index since the Great Depression. The market subsequently rallied, but few analysts were willing to predict what would happen next during one of the most volatile periods in the history of the market.

BIBLIOGRAPHY

Friedman, Milton, and Anna J. Schwartz. *The Great Contraction, 1929–1933*. Princeton, N.J.: Princeton University Press, 1965.

Galbraith, John Kenneth. *The Great Crash*. Reprint ed. Boston: Mariner Books, 1997.

Geisst, Charles R. *Wall Street: A History*. New York: Oxford University Press, 1999.

Longman, Philip J. "Is Prosperity Permanent?" *U.S. News & World Report* 123 (November 10, 1997): 36–39.

Parrish, Michael E. *Securities Regulation and the New Deal*. New Haven, Conn.: Yale University Press, 1970.

Seligman, Joel. *The Transformation of Wall Street: A History of the Securities and Exchange Commission and Modern Corporate Finance*. Rev. ed. Boston: Northeastern University Press, 1995.

Sobel, Robert. *AMEX: A History of the American Stock Exchange*. Frederick, Md.: The Beard Group, 2000.

———. *The Big Board: A History of the New York Stock Exchange*. Frederick, Md.: The Beard Group, 2000.

White, Eugene N. "The Stock Market Boom and Crash Revisited." *Journal of Economic Perspectives* (Spring 1990): 67–83.

Mark G. Malvasi

See also **Wall Street.**

STOCKBRIDGE INDIAN SETTLEMENT. At the beginning of the twenty-first century, the Stockbridge-Munsee band of the Mahican Nation occupied a 46,000-acre reservation in northeastern Wisconsin. Seven hundred of the tribe's fourteen hundred members lived on the reservation, which boasted a health clinic, services for the elderly, a historical museum and library, a golf course, and a casino. The Stockbridge people, formed from an amalgamation of Mahicans, Wappingers, and Housatonics, began their journey to Wisconsin in western Massachusetts during the 1730s, when a small band of Mahicans joined a mission at the town of Stockbridge. Even though the Stockbridges fought for the Americans in the revolutionary war, successive waves of immigrants and land speculators took their territory from them. They moved further and further west, settling in New York, then Indiana, then several locations in Wisconsin, where some Munsee Delawares joined them. The Stockbridge-Munsee band, as this new combination was called, experienced a revival in the 1930s and 1940s, both because of Bureau of Indian Affairs reforms made under John Collier's leadership, and because of an intense sense of community history and identity.

BIBLIOGRAPHY

Davids, Dorothy W. "Stockbridge-Munsee (Mohican)." In *Encyclopedia of North American Indians: Native American History, Culture, and Life, from Paleo-Indians to the Present*. Edited by Frederick E. Hoxie. New York: Houghton Mifflin, 1996.

Frazier, Patrick. *The Mohicans of Stockbridge*. Lincoln: University of Nebraska Press, 1992. Treats the eighteenth-century experiences of the Stockbridge people.

Savagian, John C. "The Tribal Reorganization of the Stockbridge-Munsee: Essential Conditions in the Re-Creation of a Native American Community, 1930–1942." *Wisconsin Magazine of History* 77, no. 1 (August 1993): 39–62.

Matthew Holt Jennings

See also **Mahican.**

STOCKS, a device for punishing petty offenders, consisting of a frame in which the culprit's hands, or hands and feet, were confined while he remained seated. Required by law in some of the American colonies, stocks existed in every English town in which a court or magistrate sat. This PUNISHMENT was designed to publicly humiliate offenders and make vagrants known to honest citizens. Onlookers often added to the punishment by throwing things at the culprit, by pulling the stool from beneath him, or by tipping him backward so that he hung head down. As late as the early nineteenth century, American gentlemen sometimes amused themselves by baiting the victims.

BIBLIOGRAPHY

Pestritto, Ronald J. *Founding the Criminal Law: Punishment and Political Thought in the Origins of America.* DeKalb: Northern Illinois University Press, 2000.

Clifford K. Shipton/s. b.

See also **Crime; Ducking Stool; Manners and Etiquette; Pillory; Prisons and Prison Reform.**

STOCKTON-KEARNY QUARREL. On 23 July 1846, Commo. Robert F. Stockton relieved Commo. John D. Sloat as commander of the U.S. naval force fighting the Mexicans on the Pacific coast. Stockton aggressively extended Sloat's conquest to the south, which precipitated revolt among the Californians. When Gen. Stephen W. Kearny, under orders to take possession of CALIFORNIA and to set up a temporary civil government, arrived at San Diego in December, he found Stockton unwilling to relinquish his command. Strained relations existed until the middle of January 1847, when Stockton passed the governorship over to John C. Frémont, whom Kearny in turn succeeded early in March.

BIBLIOGRAPHY

Gutiérrez, Ramón, and Richard J. Orsi, eds. *Contested Eden: California before the Gold Rush.* Berkeley: University of California Press, 1998.

Harlow, Neal. *California Conquered: War and Peace on the Pacific, 1846–1850.* Berkeley: University of California Press, 1982.

Robert J. Parker/a. e.

See also **Bear Flag Revolt; Kearny's March to California; Mexican-American War.**

STOCKYARDS. Travelers along the Cumberland Road and other highways leading into the American West of the 1820s and 1830s were accustomed to the familiar sight of droves of cattle fattened on the frontier farms of the Midwest on their way to the markets of eastern seaboard cities. The extension of the railroads into the West in the two succeeding decades changed this, so that by the outbreak of the Civil War, livestock had become one of the chief freight items of the western roads. This change in the marketing of livestock resulted in new business methods. At the various western termini, accommodations for holding livestock, commission firms to handle consignments for the shipper, and packing plants to process a portion of the shipments appeared as component parts of a great business community.

The early stockyards in these terminal cities were either private yards or yards owned and operated by the railroads. As the traffic increased, need for a consolidated yard became clear to all. On 25 December 1865, the Union Stock Yards, founded by John B. Sherman, opened in Chicago. Under a charter granted by the Illinois legislature, a company known as the Union Stockyard and Transit Company was formed with a capital of $1 million. The railroads running into Chicago took most of the stock, and officials of most of the railroads served on the board of directors. As the trade in western cattle grew, yards were opened in other cities. Kansas City opened in 1871, St. Louis in 1872, Cincinnati in 1874, Omaha in 1884, and St. Paul and Denver in 1886.

The rise of Chicago to a position of supremacy was due to its favorable location—nine important railroad lines converged there—and to the advantage given it by the concentration of supplies for the Union armies during the Civil War. Equally important was the enterprise of its citizens in furnishing factors indispensable for the efficient marketing of livestock, including commission houses, stockyards, and packing plants. With cattle pouring in from the western ranges, the large packing companies, including Nelson Morris in 1859, Armour in 1867, and Swift in 1875, began concentrating in Chicago, making it the greatest livestock center in the world. By the early 1970s, Omaha, Nebraska, had become the largest livestock market in the world, and Chicago's Union Stock Yards were closed in 1971.

Distinctive communities grew up in and around the yards in the various cities. The great packing companies built their plants nearby, and around them sprawled the "packing towns" made famous in Upton Sinclair's 1906 novel, *The Jungle,* about exploitation of immigrant workers. Commission men, cattle and horse buyers, railroad men, reporters of stock news, cattlemen and their cowboys from the western ranges, and stock detectives representing western livestock associations could all be found in the yards. They formed a vigorous, distinctive, and colorful group in the business community of the West.

BIBLIOGRAPHY

Cronon, William. *Nature's Metropolis: Chicago and the Great West.* New York: Norton, 1991.

Jablonsky, Thomas J. *Pride in the Jungle: Community and Everyday Life in Back of the Yards Chicago.* Baltimore: Johns Hopkins University Press, 1993.

Wade, Louise Carroll. *Chicago's Pride: The Stockyards, Packingtown, and Environs in the Nineteenth Century.* Urbana: University of Illinois Press, 1987.

Ernest S. Osgood / H. S.

See also **Cumberland Road**; **Jungle, The**; **Livestock Industry**; **Meatpacking**.

STONEWALL RIOT. *See* **Gay and Lesbian Movement**.

STONEY CREEK, BATTLE OF (6 June 1813). Generals John Chandler and William H. Winder, with about fourteen hundred Americans, encamped on 5 June at Stoney Creek at the western end of Lake Ontario, near the British camp at Burlington Heights. The following morning, shortly before daybreak, British general John Vincent, with about seven hundred British regulars, attacked the Americans, and heavy casualties were suffered on both sides. The two American commanders, eighteen other officers, and eighty men, as well as ordnance, were captured. Fearing a renewal of the attack, the American army withdrew.

BIBLIOGRAPHY

Babcock, Louis L. *The War of 1812 on the Niagara Frontier.* Buffalo, 1927.

Pierre, Berton. *The Invasion of Canada.* Boston: Little, Brown. 1980.

Robert W. Bingham / A. R.

See also **Niagara Campaigns**; **War of 1812**.

STORES, GENERAL, have been characterized by their great variety of goods and services. From colonial times through much of the nineteenth century, they constituted the typical retail unit; but in 1967 they made up less than 50,000 of the 1,763,324 retail units in the United States, and by the end of the century their numbers had been reduced still further. In their heyday general stores that were owned and operated by individuals or partners quickly followed peddlers into newly occupied regions. To survive in such limited markets, storekeepers sold great varieties of merchandise to customers, marketed crops taken in trade, operated local post offices, and provided credit and elementary banking services. Many did ultimately turn to banking, manufacturing, processing farm crops, or other specialized business services. General stores thus met an economic need at a vital stage of community development, and they also served as training schools for people who would ultimately concentrate on more specialized commercial enterprises.

General Store. Though greatly reduced in number and scope, convenience stores like this one, photographed in 1975 in tiny Helen, Ga., and operated by Warren Brown and his wife *(shown here)* for more than twenty years, continue to serve towns all over America. NATIONAL ARCHIVES AND RECORDS ADMINISTRATION

BIBLIOGRAPHY

Atherton, Lewis E. *The Frontier Merchant in Mid-America.* Columbia: University of Missouri Press, 1971.

Jones, Fred M. *Middlemen in the Domestic Trade of the United States, 1800–1860.* Urbana: University of Illinois Press, 1937.

Lewis E. Atherton / A. R.

See also **Consumerism**; **Country Store**; **Pharmacy**.

STRATEGIC ARMS LIMITATION TALKS. In 1968 President Lyndon B. Johnson and Leonid I. Brezhnev, Soviet Communist party chairman, agreed to open the first of an eventual two Strategic Arms Limitation Talks (SALT). By this time, the three basic issues that had stalled previous major Soviet-American disarmament agreements no longer posed problems. First, the détente that followed the Cuban missile crisis of 1962 improved the political climate greatly over the days of Joseph Stalin and Joseph R. McCarthy. Second, the development of the spy satellite made irrelevant the thorny issue of on-site inspections. Third, America's nuclear superiority over the Soviet Union was eroding because of a massive nuclear building program undertaken by the Soviets after the Cuban crisis, which eliminated the problem created because the United States was unwilling to give up its nuclear lead while the Soviets refused to negotiate except on terms of equality. So, in 1968, Johnson offered to open SALT with the clear implication that the United States would accept Soviet nuclear parity.

Unfortunately, the 1968 talks never came off. First, the Soviet Union and other Warsaw-Pact nations invaded Czechoslovakia. Then Richard M. Nixon, Johnson's probable successor, attacked the president for considering abandonment of America's nuclear superiority. With Johnson already discredited by his Vietnam policy, Nixon's attack forced postponement of the talks.

With the defeat of the Democrats in the 1968 presidential election, SALT had to await a new administration and its review of defense and foreign policies. After Nixon's election, presidential assistant Henry A. Kissinger undertook a study that showed the Soviet Union would indeed soon achieve nuclear parity. Nixon now talked of nuclear "sufficiency" rather than superiority. Still, the president took a hard line. He insisted that the Soviet Union prove its good faith in Vietnam and the Middle East before convening SALT. He applied even more pressure by pushing a new, albeit limited, antiballistic missile (ABM) program through Congress and by quietly accelerating deployment of sophisticated independently targeted multiple warheads.

SALT I opened in November 1969. The official delegates met first in Helsinki and later in Vienna. Nevertheless, the real negotiations took place in secret meetings between Kissinger and Soviet ambassador Anatoly Dobrynin, which culminated in the SALT I agreement hammered out at the Moscow summit of 1972. SALT I consisted of two accords: the Antiballistic Missile (ABM) Treaty, which severely limited ABM defenses, and the Interim Agreement on the Limitation of Strategic Offensive Arms, which froze the total number of strategic missile launchers pending further negotiation of a more comprehensive treaty limiting strategic missiles and bombers. The United States and the Soviet Union had concluded a separate agreement in September 1971 on measures to avert accidental use of nuclear weapons. The ABM Treaty, of indefinite duration, restricted each party to two ABM sites, with one hundred ABM launchers at each. In the only later amendment, a 1974 protocol, the two parties agreed to forgo one of those sites. Further constraints included a ban on the testing and deployment of land-mobile, sea-based, air-based, and space-based systems. The United States and Soviet Union could deploy only fixed, land-based ABM systems at the one allowed site. The Soviet Union kept its existing ABM systems around Moscow. The United States completed its deployment at a site for defense of intercontinental ballistic missile (ICBM) launchers near Grand Forks, North Dakota, but in 1975 mothballed the complex as too expensive. The ABM treaty was a solid achievement in arms limitation, although both nations found it easier to agree to it because they doubted the cost-effectiveness of available ABM systems.

While the treaty temporarily headed off a costly and useless ABM deployment race, it did not have the desired effect of also dampening down deployment of strategic offensive missiles. Furthermore, in June 2002, President George W. Bush unilaterally withdrew from the 1972 ABM Treaty because it limited the ability of the United States to develop new antimissile defenses. Bush had come into office stating his intent to remove the United States from this agreement, and the terrorist attacks of 11 September 2001 only hardened his resolve to revive President Ronald Reagan's attempts to develop a missile shield. Opponents of the withdrawal pointed out that the United States has more to fear from biological war and that the defense industry is yet to create a workable national missile defense system.

The second accord, the Interim Agreement, froze the level of land- and sea-based strategic missiles. The Soviet Union had a quantitative advantage with 2,348 missile launchers to 1,710 for the United States. Two important facts, however, offset this imbalance. First, the accord did not apply to strategic bombers or forward-based nuclear delivery systems, and the United States had a significant advantage in both categories. Second, although the Soviet Union had more missile launchers and deployed missiles, the United States had a larger number of strategic missile warheads, and by 1972 had already begun deploying multiple, independently targeted reentry vehicle warheads (MIRV). Overall, the Interim Agreement placed only modest limits on strategic missiles. In contrast to the ABM Treaty, it was not significant as an arms control measure.

The American public widely cheered SALT I, but it had two significant gaps: it lacked controls on manned bombers and on multiple warheads. At the Vladivostok summit of 1974, President Gerald R. Ford announced that he and Brezhnev had already reached a tentative SALT II agreement limiting all strategic weapons. They promised to restrict their arsenals to 2,400 strategic missiles each, 1,320 of which could have multiple warheads. Although Soviet missiles carried larger payloads, two provisions compensated for this advantage. The United States could have 525 bombers to the Soviets' 160, and American planes and missiles already stationed with the NORTH ATLANTIC TREATY ORGANIZATION (NATO) in Europe would not count against its quota of 2,400.

SALT II refers to the subsequent negotiation of a treaty to replace the SALT I Interim Agreement. These talks lasted from November 1972 to June 1979. The SALT II Treaty provided equal levels of strategic arms and included strategic bombers as well as strategic missiles. Intended to be in effect for ten years, during which the United States and Soviet Union would negotiate a third SALT agreement for further reductions, the SALT II treaty fell afoul of the collapse of the Soviet-American détente of the 1970s after the Soviet occupation of Afghanistan in 1979. Neither the American Senate nor the Soviet Duma ever ratified it. Nonetheless, both sides formally observed its constraints until 1986, and, for all practical purposes, even after the dissolution of the Soviet Union.

In 1982, under the administration of President Ronald Reagan, a new series of negotiations, the Strategic Arms Reduction Talks (START), succeeded SALT. In July 1991, President George H. W. Bush and Soviet President Mikhail Gorbachev signed the START I treaty in Moscow. In January 1993, Bush and Russian President Boris Yeltsin met in Moscow to discuss the START II treaty. These treaties involved increasingly substantial reductions, but even so, START I brought the level of strategic warheads down only to about the SALT II level, and START II down to the SALT I level. Moreover, the START II treaty proved largely irrelevant because although the U.S. Senate ratified the agreement in 1996, the Russian Duma refused to do so until 2000 in protest of the North Atlantic Treaty Organization's accepting new members from the former Soviet Bloc, American policies toward Iraq, and NATO intervention in Kosovo. In May 2002, President George W. Bush and Russian President Vladimir Putin signed a nuclear arms reduction treaty to shrink strategic nuclear forces by about two-thirds over the next decade. The Senate and the Duma have yet to ratify this treaty, and even if they were to approve it, the agreement only requires each nation to store rather than destroy the missiles that it cuts. Critics of the treaty identify this stipulation as seriously undermining the effectiveness of the agreement since both countries can easily reactivate missiles in a conflict.

The SALT process was a success in demonstrating that adversaries could reach arms limitation agreements, but owing to the very cautious and conservative approaches of both sides, the limitations on strategic offensive arms were unable to keep up with the military technological advances given precedence by the two countries. The ABM treaty, buffeted mainly by revived American interest in President Reagan's Strategic Defense Initiative (SDI) of 1983, survived the decade before the SDI lost favor. It remained an effective arms control agreement until 2002. Pursuant to the SALT I agreements, a Standing Consultative Commission (SCC) came into existence to resolve questions regarding the meaning of and compliance with the SALT agreements. It was also stipulated that there would be no interference with the use of national technical means of verification, such as observation satellites. SALT thus helped at least to stabilize, if not greatly reduce, the military balance. The SALT process and the agreements reached, while causing some friction and disagreements, contributed to the overall political détente of the 1970s. While not sufficient to sustain that détente, the SALT process helped ensure that even under renewed tension, the risk of nuclear war remained low.

BIBLIOGRAPHY

Caldwell, Dan. *The Dynamics of Domestic Politics and Arms Control: The SALT II Treaty Ratification Debate.* Columbia: University of South Carolina Press, 1991.

Carter, April. *Success and Failure in Arms Control Negotiations.* Oxford: Oxford University Press, 1989.

Goldfischer, David. *The Best Defense: Policy Alternatives for U.S. Nuclear Security from the 1950s to the 1990s.* Ithaca, NY: Cornell University Press, 1993.

Shimko, Keith L. *Images and Arms Control: Perceptions of the Soviet Union in the Reagan Administration.* Ann Arbor: University of Michigan Press, 1991.

Weber, Steve. *Cooperation and Discord in U.S.-Soviet Arms Control.* Princeton, N.J.: Princeton University Press, 1991.

Jerald A. Combs
Raymond L. Garthoff/A. E.

See also **Air Defense; Arms Race and Disarmament; Cold War; Defense, Department of; Foreign Policy; Missiles, Military; Russia, Relations with; Summit Conferences, U.S. and Russian.**

STRATEGIC DEFENSE INITIATIVE (SDI), also known as Star Wars, was a research project to create a missile defense system that would protect the United States from nuclear attack. Begun by the administration of Ronald Reagan, few military programs have been the subject of more intense, even emotional, debate than have SDI and its successors.

By the late 1960s, the primary means that the United States and the Soviet Union had of directly attacking the other was with nuclear weapons delivered by intercontinental ballistic missiles (ICBMs). Despite experimentation by both sides with nuclear-tipped defensive missiles, the difficulties of "hitting a bullet with a bullet" proved immense and military planners concluded that any prospective missile defense could be easily overwhelmed. In 1972 the two countries agreed in the Anti-Ballistic Missile (ABM) Treaty to build no more than two defensive missile sites each, a number reduced to one in 1974. When Congress shut down the sole U.S. missile defense base in 1976 only months after it had become operational, strategic defense appeared to have been abandoned by the United States for good.

Research quietly continued within the U.S. Army, however, now with an eye toward creating interceptor missiles that would not require nuclear warheads of their own. Partially as a result of the deployment of a new generation of Soviet ICBMs, by the early 1980s U.S. military leaders were growing increasingly concerned about the possibility of suffering a crippling first strike in a future war. In February 1983 the Joint Chiefs of Staff recommended to President Reagan a renewed national program for missile defense, a cause that had already been championed for years by the nuclear physicist Edward Teller and others. Reagan found this emphasis on defense, rather than offense, appealing on both moral and domestic political grounds and in a nationally televised address on 23 March 1983 he delivered a dramatic plea for this new Strategic Defense Initiative. By asking "Wouldn't it be better to save lives than to avenge them?" however, he raised the stated goal from the arcane but plausible one of protecting the nation's second strike capability to the unrealistic but emotionally appealing goal of creating an infallible space shield that could withstand even a massive nuclear attack.

SDI immediately became the subject of intense political controversy. Critics argued that it would extend the arms race into space and cause the Soviet Union to expand its own offensive nuclear forces. Furthermore, many of the proposed weapons—including neutron particle beams, rail guns, and lasers—represented exotic and unproven new technologies. Defenders of SDI responded that the Soviet Union was already expanding its strategic forces at a rapid rate and that missile defense research continued in the Soviet Union as well. Reagan's immense personal popularity triumphed over a reluctant Congress, and by 1987 annual spending on SDI-related programs was more than $3 billion. Although the effect SDI had on the last years of the Cold War remains the subject of heated disagreement, it is apparent that Soviet leaders did take very seriously the threat it represented of a new and very expensive arms race that they could not hope to win.

In 1991 the program's goal was changed to intercepting only a small number of intermediate and long-range missiles, perhaps launched from a rogue state such as Iraq or North Korea. Though public interest had waned, funding quietly continued in the range of $3 billion to $4 billion annually throughout the administration of George H. W. Bush. In 1993 the Clinton administration surprised many by retaining the program, although it was renamed Ballistic Missile Defense and moderately scaled back. By the late 1990s, however, funding was again comparable to that of the years from 1987 to 1993, and following the commencement of a high-profile series of tests in 1999, the subject became once more a matter of great public debate. In 2002 President George W. Bush changed the program's name to Missile Defense Agency and withdrew from the 1972 ABM Treaty in order ultimately to deploy a national system of missile defense.

BIBLIOGRAPHY

Baucom, Donald R. *The Origins of SDI, 1944–1983*. Lawrence: University Press of Kansas, 1992. A revised version of the official history.

Fitzgerald, Frances. *Way Out There in the Blue: Reagan, Star Wars, and the End of the Cold War*. New York: Simon and Schuster, 2000. A critical account focusing on the personal role of Ronald Reagan.

McMahon, K. Scott. *Pursuit of the Shield: The U.S. Quest for Limited Ballistic Missile Defense*. Lanham, Md.: University Press of America, 1997.

Missile Defense Agency. Homepage at http://www.acq.osd.mil/bmdo. Includes histories, congressional testimony, biographical sketches, and other information.

David Rezelman

See also **Arms Race and Disarmament; Missiles, Military.**

STRAUDER V. WEST VIRGINIA, 100 U.S. 303 (1880), a case in which the SUPREME COURT declared that a WEST VIRGINIA statute restricting jury service to whites violated the Fourteenth Amendment because it denied AFRICAN AMERICANS equal protection of the law. The Court also upheld the Civil Rights Act (1866) provision for re-

moval of cases to the federal courts when equal rights were denied in state courts.

BIBLIOGRAPHY

Engle, Stephen D. "Mountaineer Reconstruction: Blacks in the Political Reconstruction of West Virginia." *Journal of Negro History* 78 (Summer 1993): 137–165.

Ransom E. Noble Jr. / A. R.

See also **Civil Rights Act of 1866; Civil Rights and Liberties; Constitution of the United States; Equal Protection of the Law; Jury Trial;** *United States v. Harris.*

STREET RAILWAYS. *See* **Railways, Urban, and Rapid Transit.**

STRIKES. A strike is an organized collective work stoppage undertaken by employees to pressure their employer or employers into meeting their demands. A strike differs from a lockout, which is a cessation of work that occurs when an employer precludes employees from taking up their work posts. During the twentieth century, most strikes were organized through labor unions. Although the possibility of striking enhances the bargaining power of unions, strikes are a tool of last resort for workers. Strikes are called only when the demands or claims of labor remain unresolved in the collective bargaining process and in grievance procedures.

Workers rarely strike over a single issue. Nonetheless, strikes can be categorized according to the primary goal that striking workers seek to achieve. In an "organizing strike," union workers seek an employer's recognition of the union as the representative of the workers. In an "economic strike," workers seek to obtain higher wages, reduced working hours, or more extensive benefits. "Grievance strikes" erupt when employers have failed to meet contract terms, or when employers and unions do not agree on the interpretation of a contract. Other types of strikes include "general strikes," which are organized across industries and plants; "wildcat strikes," which are not authorized by the strikers' union, or which take place despite a no-strike clause on a particular issue; and "sympathy strikes," in which workers strike in support of other striking workers rather than to advance their own claims.

Historically, many of the earliest (1850–1900) and most violent strikes in the United States were "organizing strikes," waged primarily to obtain union recognition. Without such recognition, these strikes were considered illegal and often were enjoined by courts.

Between 1900 and 1925, the government softened its antilabor stance to a more neutral position. The need for "organizing strikes" was largely obviated between 1925 and 1959 when legislation and court rulings provided mechanisms for unions to be established and to obtain

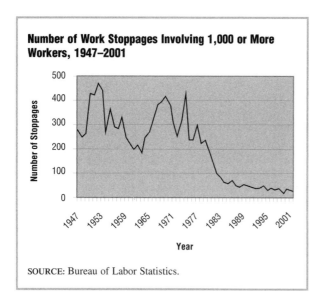

Number of Work Stoppages Involving 1,000 or More Workers, 1947–2001

SOURCE: Bureau of Labor Statistics.

recognition from employers, bringing bargaining power parity between labor and management. From 1960 to 1980, strikes by government employees gave rise to legislation and executive orders that continue to govern public sector strikes. In the 1980s, several strikes were defeated when employers hired permanent replacement workers. These defeats, along with the mixed success of other strikes, raised questions about the continuing efficacy of strikes, some of which remain unanswered.

Strike Activity and Court Rulings Before 1850

Philadelphia was not only the birthplace of American liberty, but also the cradle of American labor activism. In 1786, Philadelphia's employing printers collectively attempted to reduce the wages of skilled print craftsmen to $5.83 per week. In response, on 31 May 1786, twenty-six Philadelphia craftsmen jointly resolved to "not engage to work for any printing establishment in this city or county under the sum of $6.00 per week," and to "support such of our brethren as shall be thrown out of employment on account of their refusing to work for less than $6.00 per week." Standing by their resolution, these craftsmen waged what was probably the new nation's first labor strike, successfully procuring a $6-per-week minimum wage for skilled printers citywide.

Philadelphia was also the site of an early, influential court case that constricted the permissible scope of collective action by laborers. In *Commonwealth v. Pullis* (1806), shoemakers associated with Philadelphia's Society of Journeymen Cordwainers were convicted of criminal conspiracy after striking for higher wages. These convictions apparently did not chill further labor strikes in Philadelphia. In 1835, several unions simultaneously staged a walkout in one of the nation's first "general strikes."

Following the Philadelphia court's lead, New York courts in 1809 and 1835 characterized both labor strikes and labor unions as unlawful conspiracies designed to injure employers or their businesses. Most other states followed suit. One notable exception was Massachusetts, whose Supreme Court ruled in *Commonwealth v. Hunt* (1842) that strikes in and of themselves were not criminal conspiracies.

1850–1900: Violence and Suppression

In the late nineteenth and early twentieth centuries, most labor strikes were undertaken in violation of contemporary laws. Consequently, strikers often clashed violently with law enforcement officials.

In 1886, steel magnate Andrew Carnegie published a popular essay defending workers' right to organize into unions. In 1892, however, Carnegie's pro-worker image was forever tarnished when he authorized the use of violence against striking and locked-out workers at his steel plant in Homestead, Pennsylvania. The "Homestead Strike" (which began as a lockout) left many dead and wounded, and set back the labor movement considerably.

The Homestead Strike arose following a downturn in steel price (from $35 to $22 per ton). Carnegie's Homestead plant manager Henry C. Frick, with Carnegie's blessing, locked out 1,100 steelworkers in an effort to cut wages and rid the plant of union labor. After implementing the lockout, Frick announced he would no longer negotiate with the workers' union, the Amalgamated Association of Iron and Steel Workers. In response, although only 750 of the 3,800 workers at Homestead belonged to the union, 3,000 of them met and voted overwhelmingly to strike.

To penetrate the threatening picket lines that had formed around the closed-up plant, Frick retained a large, armed cadre of Pinkerton Detective agents. When the Pinkerton agents approached the plant, however, an armed confrontation ensued. After a twelve-hour clash that left three Pinkertons and nine workers dead, the Pinkertons surrendered. Many of the Pinkertons were then beaten by the victorious workers, and twenty were severely injured. The state militia was called in, and replacement workers took up the striking men's positions. Four months after the Homestead Strike was declared, it was broken. Strike leaders and about 160 other strikers were arrested and charged with treason. Although juries refused to convict any of the strikers, all were fired and blacklisted. Many of the remaining strikers did return to work, but the effect of these events was to evict unions from Homestead and to limit unions among steelworkers throughout the Pittsburgh area.

One year later, another failed strike dealt another setback to organized labor. Employees of the Pullman Company, which made railroad sleeping cars, were required to live in company-owned housing in the company town of Pullman, Illinois, near Chicago. In 1893, Pullman laid off workers and reduced wages, without reducing housing rents for remaining workers. In response, the Pullman workers struck, demanding lower rents and higher wages. Urged by the American Railway Union (ARU) and its president, Eugene V. Debs, railway workers nationwide boycotted trains carrying Pullman cars, including trains carrying U.S. mail. Declaring the strike a federal crime, President Grover Cleveland sent 12,000 troops to Pullman to break the strike.

On 3 August 1894, the Pullman Strike was broken. Debs was imprisoned, the ARU was disbanded, and Pullman employees signed a pledge never to unionize again. In 1895, the U.S. Supreme Court *in re Debs*, 158 U.S. 564, affirmed Debs's conviction for conspiring to obstruct interstate commerce. The Court's opinion also sustained the power of lower courts to order striking workers to return to work.

1900–1925: Government Neutrality

In 1902, President Theodore Roosevelt became the first U.S. president to intervene personally to resolve a labor dispute. In May, 150,000 anthracite coal miners in Pennsylvania struck, seeking higher wages, shorter workdays, improved coal weighing processes, and recognition of the United Mine Workers of America (UMWA) as the representative of the workers. At that time anthracite coal was one of the nation's most important industrial and home heating energy sources. Thus, a winter fuel shortage threatened if the strike could not be resolved.

On 3 October, President Roosevelt personally urged miners and mine operators to settle their dispute. John Mitchell, president of UMWA, agreed to meet with mine operators, but the operators refused to meet with the union. After threatening to send in military forces to operate the mines, President Roosevelt instead established the Anthracite Coal Strike Commission to arbitrate a settlement. These events marked the first time the U.S. government worked to settle, rather than break, a strike.

On 23 October, the striking miners returned to work. In November, the new government commission commenced public hearings in Scranton and Philadelphia. In March 1903, the commission awarded the miners a ten-percent wage increase, a nine-hour workday, and a neutral board for resolving operator-worker disputes. Although the UMWA was never recognized by the mine operators, miners continued to organize through the UMWA.

A decade later, Congress codified Theodore Roosevelt's policy of neutrality in the 1914 Clayton Antitrust Act. That act declared that labor was not an article of commerce or a commodity, and that combinations of workers were not conspiracies in restraint of trade. These provisions were designed to ensure that the federal government would remain neutral when faced with private sector labor-management disputes.

Government neutrality toward private sector labor-management disputes did not extend to public sector disputes. One such dispute arose in 1919, when Boston Police Commissioner Edwin U. Curtis refused to negotiate with the Boston Social Club, a police fraternal organization, over the hours, wages, and working conditions of

Strikers. Pickets walk along a street in New York in 1937, during a period of extensive union activism and successes, in large part the result of unprecedented federal support for organized labor. COURTESY OF THE FRANKLIN D. ROOSEVELT LIBRARY

Boston police officers. In August 1919, the Social Club applied to the American Federation of Labor to become a full-fledged union. Social Club members soon learned, however, that Commissioner Curtis had amended the Department's rules to prohibit police officers from forming virtually any outside organization. Curtis had also recruited a volunteer police force in anticipation of a strike.

This rule change precipitated a police strike, with three-quarters of the regular force walking out. Disorder ensued. The Massachusetts State Guard was deployed, and several fatalities resulted from subsequent violence. In response, Massachusetts Governor Calvin Coolidge famously proclaimed that "there is no right to strike against the public safety by anybody, anywhere, anytime." Facing public disapproval and rigid opposition from Governor Coolidge and Commissioner Curtis, the Boston police strike was broken. None of the striking policemen were rehired.

1925–1946: Congressional Attempts to Equalize Labor-Management Bargaining Power

During the second quarter of the twentieth century, for the first time in American history, the U.S. Congress championed organized labor. Rather than reflexively supporting management (as in the nineteenth century), or remaining neutral (as in the early twentieth century), Congress sought to use the power and prestige of the federal government to elevate the bargaining power of organized labor to parity with that of management. To do so, it enacted laws that regulated management activities such as lockouts and injunctions, while also regulating labor activities such as strikes and picketing.

The Railway Labor Act of 1926 (RLA) was the first federal statute to require employers to recognize and bargain with labor unions. Specifically, the RLA required railroad companies engaged in interstate commerce to bargain collectively with employee-designated representatives. Subsequently, the RLA was expanded to cover other transportation industries, including airlines and bus lines. In 1932, the Norris-LaGuardia Act provided additional protections for organized labor activity by limiting the power of federal courts to issue injunctions prohibiting certain strikes, pickets, or boycotts.

During Franklin D. Roosevelt's presidency, Congress greatly expanded the scope of legal protection afforded labor organization and strike activity. The most important New Deal labor statute, the National Labor Relations Act of 1935 (Wagner Act), guaranteed to most nonagricultural private sector employees not covered by the 1926 RLA the rights to organize, to bargain collectively, and to strike. The Wagner Act prohibited both employers and unions from engaging in certain specified unfair labor practices, and obliged both sides to engage in good faith collective bargaining. In addition, the Wagner Act established the National Labor Relations Board (NLRB), a permanent, independent federal agency charged with enforcing the Wagner Act and mediating labor-management disputes. The NLRB was also charged with resolving disputes between competing labor organizations over the right to represent particular groups of employees. The following year, Congress further protected labor activity by enacting the Byrnes (or Strikebreakers) Act of 1936, which protected workers engaged in picketing, labor organizing, or collective bargaining against threats or actual uses of force or violence.

1946–1959: Congress Seeks to Check Labor's Power

In 1939, two years before the United States entered World War II, every major American labor organization except for the UMWA took—and honored—a pledge not to strike for the duration of the war. This pledge expired with the end of the war in 1945. A tidal wave of strikes followed, making 1946 the most strike-torn year America had faced. In that year, strikes were called by the United Auto Workers and by unions representing steel, rubber, meatpacking, oil refining, and electrical appliance workers. In addition, the cities of Pittsburgh, Oakland, and Rochester (New York) faced general strikes.

The disruptions caused by these strikes led Congress to enact, over President Truman's veto, the Labor-Management Relations (Taft-Hartley) Act of 1947. Taft-Hartley placed new and substantial limits and qualifications on organized labor's legal right to strike or engage in other coercive activity. Under the act, unions were required to provide a 60-day no-strike notice period before canceling a collective bargaining agreement. During this period, the government could order further delay, or even an outright aversion, of the proposed strike, by declaring a "national emergency." Taft-Hartley flatly prohibited government employees from striking, and nullified certain parts of the 1932 Norris-LaGuardia Act by allowing courts to enjoin certain specified unfair labor practices. Finally, Taft-Hartley prohibited "jurisdictional strikes"— that is, disputes between unions to determine which union should represent particular workers.

A decade later, Congress reacted to allegations of linkages between organized labor and organized crime by enacting the Labor-Management Reporting and Disclosure Act of 1959 (Landrum-Griffin Act), which sought to "clean up" and democratize labor unions. The Landrum-Griffin Act required unions to allow their members to vote on decisions to call or terminate strikes, to raise dues, and to select officers. In cases where more than one union sought to represent a particular group of workers, Landrum-Griffin mandated that the union receiving the most votes would serve as the exclusive employee representative.

The labor laws developed during the 1920s and 1930s, as modified in the 1940s and 1950s, created mechanisms to establish unions and obtain recognition from private employers. By establishing such mechanisms, these laws played a key role in reducing the incidence of economic disruption and violence previously associated with labor-management clashes.

1960–1980: Public Sector Unionism

Before 1960, government employees shared few of the benefits of labor organization enjoyed by their private sector counterparts. Many public sector positions were considered to provide essential services that could not be disrupted without endangering the public. Based on this reasoning, the 1947 Taft-Hartley Act prohibited public sector strikes and imposed harsh penalties on striking federal employees: immediate dismissal and a three-year bar to reemployment. In 1947, eight states, including New York, enacted similar legislative strike prohibitions for their state and local public employees.

In 1962, however, President John F. Kennedy issued an Executive Order that encouraged union representation and collective bargaining on behalf of federal employees, and authorized the use of limited advisory arbitration of employee grievances. Consequently, federal employees joined unions in large numbers during the 1960s. State and local government employees, including many schoolteachers, followed suit.

Although federal employees and most state and local employees are prohibited by law from striking, such laws have not always prevented public sector strikes from occurring. Nor have these laws always been enforced. In January 1966, New York City's transit workers struck for two weeks, shutting down the world's largest subway system and creating monumental traffic jams across the city's five boroughs. Rather than invoking the state law that prohibited public sector strikes, however, the New York State legislature passed special legislation exempting transit workers from the statutory penalties. In 1967, New York created a new process for resolving stalemates in the public sector collective bargaining process aimed at heading off public sector strikes before they occurred.

Perhaps influenced by New York's approach, the federal government adopted measures to improve its own collective bargaining process to prevent its employees from striking. In 1969, President Nixon ordered that disputes concerning the terms and conditions of federal employment that remained unresolved in the collective bargaining process would be referred to a neutral arbitrator, whose decision would bind all parties. The Civil Service Reform Act of 1978 substantially codified the approach taken in President Nixon's 1969 executive order, creating a new independent Federal Labor Relation Authority (FLRA) to serve as arbitrator.

The 1978 act was intended to avoid creating the conditions that might lead federal employees to strike, by providing fair and orderly procedures for resolving impasses in the collective bargaining process. Nonetheless, in 1981, just three years after the 1978 act, almost 13,000 federally employed professional air traffic controllers (PATCOs) struck, seeking higher pay and reduced working hours. Within 48 hours, President Reagan fired every one of the 11,350 PATCOs who did not heed his order to return to work, and declared a lifetime ban against their rehiring. The government's success in recruiting and retaining replacement PATCOs without substantially disrupting the nation's commercial air traffic inspired some private sector employers to make similar use of replacement workers when confronted with strikes. Consequently, strikes and the threat of strike by unions lost substantial ability to impact negotiations with both private and public sector employers.

1980s–Early 2000s: Whither Strikes?

Soon after President Reagan defeated the PATCO strike, the Supreme Court dealt organized labor an additional blow when it ruled in 1983 that a replacement worker hired during a strike had a right to retain the striking worker's job after the strike was settled. Two years later, the Court in *Pattern Makers' League of North America, AFL-CIO v. National Labor Relations Board*, 473 U.S. 95, ruled that union members could resign from their unions at any time, without notice. This ruling left a striking union without recourse if a member resigned and crossed a picket line to return to work.

Despite these setbacks to organized labor, however, several major strikes occurred in the 1990s. In 1990, following eight years of annual pay cuts, 6,300 Greyhound bus drivers began a bitter three-year strike marred by shootings, beatings, and threats of violence from both sides. The Greyhound strike ended in 1993, when the drivers accepted Greyhound's offer of a 20-percent wage increase over six years, plus $22 million in back pay.

In summer 1996, the United Auto Workers struck General Motors Corporation over the issues of excessive overtime and outsourcing of jobs. After being forced to briefly shut down most of its manufacturing plants nationwide, General Motors ended the strike by meeting the lion's share of the union's demands.

Although strikes most often are waged by unions representing middle-income workers, some of the nation's highest-paid employees—professional athletes—struck during the 1980s and 1990s. In both 1982 and 1987, the National Football League Players Association (NFLPA) struck, seeking free agency and a higher salary scale for professional football players. Both times, the players quickly returned to work without achieving their strike objectives. In 1993, however, without waging another strike, NFLPA secured both free agency and substantially higher salaries for its members through a collective bargaining agreement negotiated with the National Football League.

In professional ice hockey, team owners locked out players for half the 1994–1995 season in a dispute over salary cap and free agency rules. The National Basketball Association also lost a third of its 1998–1999 season when the league locked out its players in a bid to renegotiate league salary cap rules. Both lockouts were ultimately resolved by compromise negotiations.

In 1994, professional baseball players struck for the entire season when team owners sought to impose a league-wide salary cap. Because of the strike, the World Series was canceled in 1994 for the first time since 1904. Although the players returned to work the following season, the salary cap issue remained unresolved.

Despite the scope and the success of some strikes during the 1990s, strikes are waning as a tool of organized labor. In 2001, the Bureau of Labor Statistics reported that the number of idle days, and the percent of working time lost because of strikes and lockouts, had both reached historic lows.

BIBLIOGRAPHY

Dunlop, John T., and Neil W. Chamberlain, eds. *Frontiers of Collective Bargaining*. New York: Harper and Row, 1967.

Freeman, Joshua B. *In Transit: The Transport Workers Union in New York City, 1933–1966*. 2d ed. Philadelphia: Temple University Press, 2001.

Ross, Arthur M., and Paul T. Hartman. *Changing Patterns of Industrial Conflict*. New York: Wiley, 1960.

Steinfeld, Robert J. "The Philadelphia Cordwainers' Case of 1806: The Struggle over Alternative Legal Constructions of a Free Market in Labor." In *Labor Law in America: Historical and Critical Essays.* Edited by Christopher L. Tomlins and Andrew J. King. Baltimore: Johns Hopkins University Press, 1992.

U.S. Department of Labor, Bureau of Labor Statistics. Home page at http://www.bls.gov/

Zieger, Robert H. *American Workers, American Unions.* Baltimore: John Hopkins University Press, 1994.

Linda Dynan

See also **Taft-Hartley Act;** *and vol. 9:* **The Pullman Strike and Boycott.**

STRONTIUM 90.

STRONTIUM 90. When anyone discusses the harmful effects of atomic fallout, that discussion primarily relates to strontium 90 (^{90}Sr), an isotope created during both nuclear detonations and nuclear-power reactions.

The parent chemical, strontium (Sr), is a silver-yellow alkaline-earth metal with physical and chemical properties similar to calcium. Strontium itself serves as a popular ingredient in fireworks and signal flares. The element also exists in the form of four stable and twelve unstable isotopes, including ^{90}Sr.

A nuclear explosion creates ^{90}Sr, one of the most lethal of the 300 radioactive products formed during detonation. Such a detonation can send a mushroom cloud thousands of feet into the atmosphere and carry radioactive isotopes thousands of miles, depending on wind trajectories. Precipitation can then deposit the isotopes on soils, waterways, vegetation, and cities in areas covered by the cloud. Because of ^{90}Sr's chemical similarity to calcium, plant and animal tissues readily assimilate the isotope. At this stage, ^{90}Sr may enter the human food supply, mainly in milk. The hazard occurs because the body treats ^{90}Sr as though it actually were calcium, and the isotope subsequently concentrates in bone where it damages stem cells of the bone marrow as well as the body's immune functions. Strontium 90 has a half-life of 28.1 years, which means that it emits radioactive energy for that period of time. It is particularly dangerous for growing children and is believed to contribute to bone cancer and leukemia.

Scientists observed the effects of ^{90}Sr at the end of World War II (1939–1945), when the United States dropped atomic bombs on the Japanese cities of Hiroshima (6 August 1945) and Nagasaki (9 August 1945); the two bombs killed in excess of 200,000 people. Prominent atomic physicists such as Enrico Fermi and Niels Bohr, both involved in the Manhattan Project that assembled the first two atomic bombs, began to advocate for peacetime applications of the new technology in the form of nuclear power.

Atmospheric nuclear weapons testing in Nevada began in January 1951, and by 1953, studies detected radioactivity levels in humans and animals, especially the presence of ^{90}Sr. The following year, the U.S. Atomic Energy Commission began to measure ^{90}Sr in healthy adult New York City residents who died in accidents. A 1958 study of ^{90}Sr in 60,000 baby teeth in the St. Louis area revealed that levels of the radioactive element rose steadily during atmospheric nuclear weapons testing, except during a testing moratorium between 1959 and 1961. By 1962, the U.S. Public Health Service established an expanded program of ^{90}Sr analysis in thirty-four U.S. cities. Levels peaked in 1964, shortly after the Limited Test Ban Treaty passed, and levels dropped rapidly after that.

Various U.S. governmental agencies began terminating ^{90}Sr studies between 1970 and 1982, despite the fact that ^{90}Sr concentrations in the urban areas of the northeastern United States remained at the 1957 levels. These concentrations suggest that another source of radioactivity—possibly nuclear power reactors—has added to ^{90}Sr levels in the American environment. Researchers have linked radioactive emissions from reactors to increased childhood leukemia rates in the United States and abroad.

BIBLIOGRAPHY

Makhijani, Arjun, Howard Hu, and Katherine Yih, eds. *Nuclear Wastelands: A Global Guide to Nuclear Weapons Production and Its Health and Environmental Effects.* Cambridge, Mass.: MIT Press, 1995.

Miller, G. Tyler, Jr. *Living in the Environment: Principles, Connections, and Solutions.* 9th ed. Belmont, Calif.: Wadsworth Publishing, 1996.

Miller, Richard. *Under the Cloud: The Decades of Nuclear Testing.* New York: Free Press, 1986.

Mark Todd

See also **Nuclear Power; Nuclear Weapons; Physics: Nuclear Physics.**

STUART'S RIDE.

STUART'S RIDE. As General Robert E. Lee prepared to resist Union general George B. McClellan's march on Richmond in 1862, Confederate general J. E. B. Stuart's cavalry staged a daring reconnaissance mission. On 14 June Stuart rode behind McClellan, surprising him completely; on 15 June the cavalry rode into Richmond with 165 prisoners, having traveled more than one hundred miles and having lost only one man. Stuart's ride demonstrated McClellan's vulnerability and forced him to switch his supply base to the James River; Lee obtained with the information he required. Although of questionable military value, the ride girded Confederate morale.

BIBLIOGRAPHY

Sears, Stephen W. *To the Gates of Richmond.* New York: Ticknor and Fields, 1992.

Thomas, Emory. *Bold Dragoon: The Life of J. E. B. Stuart.* New York: Harper and Row. 1986.

Thomason, John W. *Jeb Stuart.* New York: Scribner, 1958.

Thomas Robson Hay / A. R.

See also **Cavalry, Horse; Richmond Campaigns.**

Stokely Carmichael. A leading proponent of Black Power while head of SNCC from 1966 (before moving to Guinea in West Africa in 1969). LIBRARY OF CONGRESS

STUDENT NONVIOLENT COORDINATING COMMITTEE

(SNCC) was founded in April 1960 to coordinate southern black college students in nonviolent protests against lunch counter segregation. As many chain and department store dining facilities in Texas and the Upper South dropped the color bar, this phase of the southern black protest movement subsided toward the end of the year. SNCC changed from a committee coordinating campus-based groups to a staffed organization that initiated its own projects in local communities. It played a central role in the desegregation and voter registration campaigns that followed in the Deep South. Operating in the most oppressive areas, its dedicated workers became celebrated for their courage in the face of white intimidation. Beginning in 1961, SNCC met with publicized hostility after sending integrated buses through the most segregated areas of the South on "Freedom Rides." In 1963 SNCC organized the Freedom Ballot in Mississippi to prove that blacks would vote if given the opportunity. Despite violent opposition from whites, almost eighty thousand blacks voted, nearly four times the number registered in the state. This event paved the way for SNCC to organize the Mississippi Freedom Democratic Party and register voters. Three men associated with this party disappeared and were later found dead with gunshot wounds. Sometime after 1964 the idea of

Black Power emerged in SNCC, and it later came to prominence when Stokely Carmichael became head of the organization. With this transition SNCC declined as an organization, but it continued to act as a catalyst for civil rights activity and social change.

BIBLIOGRAPHY

Carson, Clayborne. *In Struggle: SNCC and the Black Awakening of the 1960s.* Cambridge, Mass.: Harvard University Press, 1981.

Greenberg, Cheryl Lynn. *A Circle of Trust: Remembering SNCC.* New Brunswick, N.J.: Rutgers University Press, 1998.

Moody, Anne. *Coming of Age in Mississippi.* New York: Dell, 1968.

Stoper, Emily. *The Student Nonviolent Coordinating Committee.* Brooklyn, N.Y.: Carlson, 1989.

August Meier/H. S.

See also **Black Power; Congress of Racial Equality; Freedom Riders;** *and vol. 9:* **Black Power Speech; Student Nonviolent Coordinating Committee Founding Statement.**

STUDENTS FOR A DEMOCRATIC SOCIETY.

SDS was the main organizational expression of the campus-based radical movement known as the New Left in the 1960s. An almost moribund organization of about three hundred students at the start of the decade, it grew to the point where probably well over fifty thousand people took part in the activities of local SDS chapters in 1968–1969.

SDS originated as the student department of the League for Industrial Democracy, a mildly social-democratic educational service. In the 1950s, under the name Student League for Industrial Democracy, the campus affiliate consisted of a dwindling number of campus discussion groups. When sit-ins at segregated lunch counters revived student political activism in the South in 1960, SDS began to orient toward the new movement. Gradually, a core of articulate student leaders emerged who were interested in such issues as civil rights and nuclear disarmament and in the relations between them. Under the leadership of Tom Hayden and Al Haber of the University of Michigan, SDS in 1962 issued the "Port Huron Statement," a sixty-four page document that proclaimed independence from traditional radical and liberal formulas. The statement became a manifesto for student activists of the New Left.

SDS's own membership grew slowly until the escalation of American military intervention in Vietnam in 1965. SDS sponsored a march on Washington in April 1965, the first national demonstration against the war, which drew upward of twenty thousand mostly young people. From then on, SDS grew rapidly, although it ceased playing a leading role in the antiwar movement. The organization became progressively more radical in the late 1960s, cutting its ties to the League for Industrial Democracy in 1965. At the same time, SDS members began turning their attention to large problems within American society. Several women who held the first national SDS "women's meeting" in 1965 later became key figures in the feminist movement of the 1970s. Civil rights leaders began turning toward "black power," which influenced SDS members.

By the end of the decade, SDS at the national level was an avowedly revolutionary organization. Its influence within the student movement came largely through its insistence that the alienation felt by many young people had its roots in the same social system that carried on the Vietnam War and oppressed racial minorities in the United States. At many schools, notably at Columbia University in 1968 and Harvard University in 1969, SDS chapters led disruptive protests against university ties with the military and other issues.

The momentum of protests in the late 1960s caused many in SDS to believe that a social revolution was not far away, and this feeling, in turn, exacerbated factional divisions. SDS split into two groups at its annual convention in June 1969. One group, led by members of the Progressive Labor Party, advocated a worker-student alliance, while the other group, led in part by people who later formed the "Weather Underground," placed their main emphasis on support for Third World and black revolutionaries. The former group still existed under the name SDS in 1974, but its following was only a tiny fraction of that commanded by SDS in the late 1960s.

BIBLIOGRAPHY

Heath, G. Louis. *Vandals in the Bomb Factory: The History and Literature of the Students for a Democratic Society.* Metuchen, N.J.: Scarecrow Press, 1976.

Miller, Jim. *Democracy Is in the Streets: From Port Huron to the Siege of Chicago.* New York: Simon and Schuster, 1987.

Sale, Kirkpatrick. *SDS.* New York: Vintage Books, 1973.

Unger, Irwin. *The Movement: A History of the American New Left, 1959–1972.* New York: Dodd, Mead, 1974.

James P. O'Brien/H. S.

See also **Antiwar Movements; Civil Rights Movement; Vietnam War.**

STURGES V. CROWNINSHIELD, 4 Wheaton 122 (1819), examined at length the respective powers of state and federal governments over bankruptcy and what constitutes that "impairment of the obligation of contract" that the Constitution forbids. Ruling on the constitutionality of a New York State bankruptcy law, the Supreme Court maintained that state bankruptcy laws were permitted since congressional legislation was lacking. The Court concluded that the power of Congress to enact "uniform laws on the subject of bankruptcies" was supreme. But the New York law was declared invalid because it applied retroactively to contracts made prior to its enactment.

BIBLIOGRAPHY

Coleman, Peter J. *Debtors and Creditors in America.* Madison: Wisconsin Historical Society, 1974.

Harvey Pinney/A. R.

See also **Bankruptcy Laws; Contract Clause; Debt, Imprisonment for; Enumerated Powers;** *Fletcher v. Peck*; *Ogden v. Saunders*; **State Laws, Uniform.**

SUBMARINES. The first operating submarine was tested by the Dutch inventor Cornelis Drebbel from 1620 to 1624, but a submarine was not used in combat until 1776, when David Bushnell's one-man wooden craft, the *Turtle*, failed in its submerged attack on the British ship *Eagle* in New York harbor. Later, Robert Fulton, a famous American artist and inventor, built the *Nautilus* (1801) out of wood covered by iron plates. Although successful in submerged tests against wooden ships, the *Nautilus* failed to interest the government of France, England, or the United States. Bushnell produced another submarine for the War of 1812 against England, but his craft was unsuccessful.

During the Civil War the Confederacy undertook the construction of various submarines. Horace L. Hunley financed the building of the *Pioneer* (1862) by James McClintock and Baxter Watson, but it never entered combat. A second vessel was lost en route to the fighting. The first submarine to sink a ship was the hand-powered *Hunley.* This cigar-shaped boat was made of boiler plate and manned by a crew of nine. It took the lives of thirty-five volunteers in five trial runs and became known as the Peripatetic Coffin. On the night of 17 February 1864, it drove its spar torpedo into the Union *Housatonic* anchored at the entrance to Charleston harbor, South Carolina, and both vessels sank. The Union's one attempt to construct a submarine proved abortive; the main effort went into semisubmersibles and monitors.

England, France, Sweden, Russia, and Spain pursued submarine development in the ninettenth century. Modern undersea craft in America evolved from the pioneering work of John P. Holland, an Irish immigrant, and Simon Lake. Holland built six submarines (1875–1897), one of which, the *Plunger,* won the U.S. government's competition for a practical submarine design in 1893. It was never completed. His most famous craft, the fifty-three-foot *Holland,* was built at his own expense and became the U.S. Navy's first submarine in 1900. Lake, Holland's chief competitor, envisioned submarines mainly as salvage and exploration vehicles. Lake's company built seven submarines for Russia (1901–1906) and twenty-seven for the United States, with the first completed in 1911.

England and Germany had a delayed interest in submarines. England's first order came in 1901; the first German vessel, the 139-foot U-1, was not completed until 1905. At the outset of World War I, there were subma-

John P. Holland. The prolific inventor of early submarines, sitting in the turret of one of these in 1898. © CORBIS-BETTMANN

drop" hull with a nuclear propulsion plant to produce the Skipjack (1956–1957), and later the Thresher, Sturgeon, and Los Angeles, classes of very fast submarines, capable of underwater speeds exceeding thirty knots.

The majority of U.S. nuclear submarines are primarily intended to destroy enemy submarines; the remainder are the fleet ballistic-missile submarines armed with strategic Polaris, Poseidon, or Trident missiles for use against land targets. The Navy commissioned forty-one Polaris-Poseidon submarines between 1959 and 1967. Displacing between 5,900 and 7,320 tons each, these vessels were a vital part of the U.S. nuclear deterrent force.

The submarine played a vital role in America's COLD WAR military strategy. Beginning with the Poseidon missile (1970), all U.S. submarines carried submarine-launched ballistic missiles (SLBMs), all of which carried multiple warheads, dubbed multiple independently targeted reentry vehicles (MIRVs). The *Trident* carries twenty-four Trident C-4 or D-5 missiles, each loaded with eight warheads. In 1988, the United States had sixty-six hundred warheads on thirty-two submarines and the Soviet Union thirty-four hundred warheads on sixty-three submarines. Both forces were reduced under the terms of the first Strategic Arms Reduction Talks Treaty (START I). The START II agreement in 1993 downgraded the U.S. force to about seventeen hundred warheads on eighteen submarines. The accuracy of SLBMs was greatly improved with the introduction of the global positioning system (GPS). Signals emitted from satellites in orbit enable the missile's computers to calculate its position with very high precision.

rines in the fleets of all the major navies. The standard submarine was about two hundred feet long and displaced several hundred tons. German U-boats sank more than five thousand merchant and fishing ships during the conflict. After the war, the U.S. Navy built a series of classes leading to the successful Gato and Balao classes of submarine of World War II.

Germany again used submarines to good advantage during World War II, although its attacks failed in the end because of a devastating Allied antisubmarine campaign. In the Pacific, U.S. submarines sank 1,314 naval and merchant ships (1941–1945). Two wartime developments—radar and the snorkel (breathing tubes to draw in air from just under the surface)—made a major impact on submarine combat.

After World War II, the United States was quick to adapt advanced German submarine technology. War-built submarines were converted to the improved GUPPY-configuration (1946–1962), and the world's first nuclear-powered submarine, the *U.S.S. Nautilus*, was launched in 1954. With a three-thousand-ton displacement and 320 feet long, the *Nautilus* traversed the Arctic Ocean under the ice cap, crossing the North Pole on 3 August 1958. The U.S. Navy married the advanced Albacore "tear

BIBLIOGRAPHY

Alden, John D. *The Fleet Submarine in the U.S. Navy: A Design and Construction History*. Annapolis, Md.: Naval Institute Press, 1979.

Burgess, Robert F. *Ships Beneath the Sea: A History of Subs and Submersibles*. New York: McGraw-Hill, 1975.

Cochran, Thomas B., William M. Arkin, and Milton M. Hoenig. *Nuclear Weapons Databook*. Vol. 1. Cambridge, Mass.: Ballinger, 1984.

———, et al. *Nuclear Weapons Databook*. Vol. 4. New York: Harper and Row, Ballinger Division, 1989.

Hoyt, Edwin P. *From the Turtle to the Nautilus: The Story of Submarines*. Boston: Little, Brown, 1963.

Polmar, Norman. *The American Submarine*. Annapolis, Md.: Nautical and Aviation Publishing Company of America, 1981

———, and Jurrien Noot. *Submarines of the Russian and Soviet Navies, 1718–1990*. Annapolis, Md.: Naval Institute Press, 1991.

Roscoe, Theodore. *United States Submarine Operations in World War II*. Annapolis, Md.: United States Naval Institute, 1949.

Leo Sartori
Ken W. Sayers/A. R.

563

See also **Atlantic, Battle of the;** *Lusitania,* **Sinking of the; Merchantmen, Armed; Missiles, Military;** *"Nautilus";* **Navy, Confederate; North Sea Mine Barrage; Philippine Sea, Battle of the; World War II, Navy in.**

SUBPOENA. *See* **Presidents and Subpoenas.**

SUBSIDIES. The United States has been exceedingly liberal in granting subsidies to various commercial enterprises, despite frequent doubts concerning the constitutionality of such action. The debate over government subsidies had its roots in the conflict between Hamiltonian and Jeffersonian visions of American development. As George Washington's Treasury Secretary, Alexander Hamilton enthusiastically advocated federal aid to manufacturers, believing such aid was crucial to placing the nation on a firm economic foundation. Hamilton's support for subsidies also reflected his belief that anything not explicitly prohibited by the Constitution was a legal and proper power of the federal government.

Thomas Jefferson held the opposite view. According to Jefferson, the federal government should not exercise any power not explicitly granted to it by the Constitution. Federal subsidies flew in the face of a strict constructionist interpretation of the Constitution, and thus received Jefferson's ire. Jefferson also had regional and partisan motivations for opposing federal subsidies. As a southern planter, he deeply distrusted Hamilton's effort to establish a large manufacturing base in the United States. Jefferson believed that such policies would undermine agriculture and transform the nation from an agrarian democracy into an urban, industrial empire.

Jefferson's protégé and presidential successor, James Madison, represented a middle position between the Jeffersonian and Hamiltonian extremes. Although a southern planter like Jefferson, Madison shared Hamilton's belief that federal transportation subsidies were necessary for American economic development. However, Madison also shared Jefferson's narrow interpretation of federal power under the Constitution. Consequently, as president, Madison vetoed a bill that would have allocated federal funds to the construction of highways and canals. At the same time, however, Madison encouraged the bill's supporters to propose an amendment to the Constitution that would explicitly provide for federal subsidies to internal improvements. Madison's ambiguous position on the subsidy issue personified a debate that would continue in the United States for more than half a century.

Despite the fractious debate over the constitutionality of subsidies, throughout U.S. national history state and privately owned transportation improvements have been freely subsidized. Between 1825 and 1829, Congress voted to subscribe $235,000 to the Louisville and Portland Canal, $1 million to the Chesapeake and Ohio Canal, $225,000 to the Chesapeake and Delaware Canal, and

$80,000 to the Dismal Swamp Canal. At about the same time, land grants were made to aid in the construction of three canals to connect the Great Lakes with the Ohio and Mississippi rivers; one of these waterways, the Illinois and Michigan Canal, was still receiving assistance from the state of Illinois in the mid-1970s. The Sault Sainte Marie Canal also received a large land donation from Congress. Railroad promoters also sought federal subsidies, and between 1850 and 1871, more than 131 million acres of public lands were given to them. The first transcontinental railroads, the Union Pacific and the Central Pacific, received twenty million acres of public lands and a loan of $53 million.

Debate over subsidies constituted one of the major partisan divides of the nineteenth century. The Whig party advocated federal transportation subsidies, which they usually referred to as "internal improvements," as a vital step in the creation of a national transportation infrastructure. In keeping with the spirit of the Hamiltonian tradition, Whigs such as Sen. Henry Clay of Kentucky contended that without government aid, the nation's transportation system would develop in an inefficient, haphazard manner. This inefficiency, they feared, would slow western expansion and undermine economic development west of the Appalachian Mountains. According to the Whigs, all Americans would suffer as a result.

The Democratic Party took a more ambiguous position on the issue of subsidies. On the whole, Democrats generally supported transportation subsidies at the state level, and some also supported federal subsidies for the construction of a transcontinental railroad. Most southern Democrats, however, adamantly opposed transportation subsidies at the federal level. According to southern Democrats such as Sen. John Calhoun of South Carolina, federal transportation subsidies represented an unconstitutional expansion of government power, just as Jefferson and Madison had argued a generation earlier. The southern Democrats' concern had a deeply pragmatic motivation. They feared that federal expansion into the realm of private economic development would eventually and perhaps inevitably pave the way toward federal intervention in state affairs, particularly in regards to the explosive issue of slavery. With the North's population rapidly surpassing that of the South, southern Democrats feared that a powerful federal government would one day be capable of removing slavery where it already existed in the southern states. In addition, southern Democrats believed that subsidies unfairly benefited northern industry while providing nothing in return for southern farmers.

The Civil War largely resolved the debate over federal subsidies. The defeat of the Confederacy and the rise of the Republican Party as a national force in American politics ensured that federal subsidies would remain a permanent feature of the political landscape. In the decades following the Civil War, Republicans aggressively promoted federal subsidies for producers and manufacturers in virtually every sector of American industry. The proliferation in federal subsidies reflected the close relationship between the Republican Party and corporate America. By the late nineteenth century, Great Britain stood as the only economic rival comparable in size to the American economy. Republicans justified subsidies in part on the grounds that they gave American industry a boost in its competition with British manufacturers.

Mail subsidies to the merchant marine were generously granted during the years 1845–1858, 1864–1877, 1891, and after World War I, but in each case they failed to establish a shipping industry comparable to that of Great Britain. The subsidies given to aviation have been more successful. Between 1926 and 1933, $87 million in mail subsidies were given to various air transport companies, and although excessive in amount and accompanied by corruption, they were largely responsible for the present far-flung air service. Airplane manufacturers not only profited from this boon to commercial flying, they also received many lucrative contracts for the sale of their planes to the War and Navy departments.

Newspapers have also enjoyed government subsidies. In the nineteenth century, many newspapers were largely financed by government advertising, and a change in administration meant a goodly number of the old party organs would be forced to suspend because of the loss of patronage. Cheap postage rates on fourth-class matter have also served as a subsidy to newspapers and periodicals.

Under the Newlands Reclamation Act of 1902, the U.S. government has spent billions of dollars on reclamation projects. Farmers benefiting from government-supplied water were expected to pay reasonable charges, but poor planning raised costs so high that farmers could not meet the charges and substantial parts of both interest and principal have been written off. Irrigation projects necessitate the construction of dams and reservoirs, many of which provide electric power. This power has been sold at low rates to distributing companies, which have thus been saved from undertaking expensive construction work. Electric power companies further benefited by the government land policy, which, until Theodore Roosevelt's administration, permitted them to preempt power sites at little cost.

The establishment in 1932 of the Reconstruction Finance Corporation and in 1933 of the Public Works Administration with their "pump priming" programs marked a new era in government subsidies to business and local governments. Not only were loans made to banks, railroads, and industrial corporations at low rates, but outright grants were offered to state and local governments for permanent improvements such as sewage-disposal plants, waterworks, parks, public schools, municipal buildings, and settlement houses. Federal subsidies and grants-in-aid have assisted agricultural colleges, vocational training schools, state road construction, state forests, and parks.

Tariffs, although not strictly speaking subsidies, have the effect of subsidies, because they artificially increase the income of producers of protected goods. The very first tariff gave some protection to American manufactures, and that protection was progressively increased until 1833, when the free-trade elements succeeded in forcing a compromise that brought rates down to a lower level. But at no time has the policy of indirectly subsidizing business by tariff protection been abandoned. The farmers who have been more hurt than helped by tariffs obtained their subsidy in 1933 in the Agricultural Adjustment Act, which provided for benefit payments to farmers who cooperated with the government in the adjustment program. Payments to "farmers" to reduce their output of basic crops kept on increasing until in 1970 nine individuals or corporations each received more than a million dollars; the largest payment was $4.4 million. Between $3 billion and $4 billion annually was being paid to larger farmers, to a considerable degree to corporate—conglomerate agribusiness—farmers. These government subsidies tended to eliminate the small farmer and sharecropper and to concentrate the production of basic crops in the hands of the more efficient larger owners.

Most industries, businesses, and major population groups have received generous subsidies, directly or indirectly, since 1933. Mining industries, especially the oil companies, benefited enormously from the generous depletion allowance that reduced their taxes on income. The cattle and sheep industries in the eleven far western states benefit through the privilege of grazing their livestock within Bureau of Land Management districts and national forests at less than commercial rates. Cane and beet sugar producers have profited from a series of protectionist rates alternating with outright subsidies. Middle- and low-income families and the construction industry and the building trades have been subsidized by public housing programs. Federal regulations have at times required government agencies to use only certain American-made or -raised goods.

The extraordinary growth in the number of federal subsidies was no accident. Politicians both at the federal and state levels aggressively used subsidies as a means to appease constituents and to solicit campaign contributions from private industry. Subsidies made it possible for members of Congress to direct federal money to their own congressional districts, which thus allowed the members to present the subsidies as evidence of their commitment to constituent service. Members of Congress, therefore, naturally came to see federal subsidies as a critical feature of their reelection campaigns.

These subsidies, commonly derided as "pork barrel" projects, became an unavoidable feature of the annual federal budget in the twentieth century, and they included every conceivable industry. Indeed, by the end of the twentieth century, federal subsidies included a staggering range of pork barrel projects, ranging from the timber industry to the beekeeping industry, and from Navy base expansions to state highway projects.

By the last quarter of the twentieth century, advocates of government reform focused their attention on "pork barrel" federal subsidies. Common Cause and other good government non-profit organizations began to publish lists of pork barrel projects, which soon received growing coverage in the print and television media. In the view of many observers, Congress's willingness to spend public money on unnecessary subsidies seemed to provide striking evidence that it placed provincial concerns over national interest.

The passage of the NORTH AMERICAN FREE TRADE AGREEMENT (NAFTA) in 1993 marked, at least on paper, a watershed in the history of federal subsidies. On an unprecedented scale, the United States government agreed to abandon key subsidies in agriculture and industry in return for concomitant reductions in Canadian and Mexican subsidies. Since NAFTA's passage, however, disputes have arisen because each of the signatory nations has taken advantage of loopholes in the treaty to continue subsidies.

As the federal budget deficit soared to record heights in the 1980s, advocates of a balanced budget joined in the attack on federal subsidies. The Concord Coalition, the Reform Party, and other political organizations identified pork barrel projects as a major obstacle to a federal balanced budget, and called for their elimination. However, the entrenched nature of congressional support for pork barrel subsidies made reform extremely difficult, if not impossible, to achieve.

The most important congressional opposition to wasteful subsidies emerged in 1991 with the inception of the congressional Porkbusters Coalition, a bipartisan organization of House members. The Porkbusters Coalition identifies particularly unnecessary congressional spending and organizes legislative opposition to pork barrel spending. Predictably unpopular with the rest of Congress, the membership of the Porkbusters Coalition membership remains quite small, including only a small fraction of members of Congress.

BIBLIOGRAPHY

Drews, Roberta. *Federal Subsidies for Public Housing: Issues and Options.* Washington, D.C.: Congress of the United States, Congressional Budget Office, 1983.

Ferris, Sally A. *Federal Subsidies to Rail Passenger Service: An Assessment of Amtrak.* Washington, D.C.: Congress of the United States, Congressional Budget Office, 1982.

Fitzgerald, Randall, and Gerald Lipson. *Porkbarrel: The Unexpurgated Grace Commission Story of Congressional Profligacy.* Washington, D.C.: Cato Institute, 1984.

Hufbauer, Gary C., and Joanna Shelton Erb. *Subsidies in International Trade.* Washington, D.C.: Institute for International Economics, 1984.

Roodman, David Malin. *Paying the Piper: Subsidies, Politics, and the Environment.* Washington, D.C.: Worldwatch Institute, 1996.

Tuckman, Howard P., and Edward Whalen, eds. *Subsidies to Higher Education: The Issues.* New York: Praeger, 1980.

Paul W. Gates / A. G.

See also **Citrus Industry; Dairy Industry; Electric Power and Light Industry; Government Regulation of Business; Land Grants: Land Grants for Railways; Sugar Industry; Trade, Foreign; Wool Growing and Manufacture.**

SUBSISTENCE HOMESTEADS. Programs to relocate indigent families to places where they can subsist on the land are ancient. Many political leaders have responded to pressures of overpopulation by planting colonies, either within their country or in remote lands. These efforts were sometimes successful when good land was available, perhaps as the result of victory in war; depopulation by a plague; or discovery of new lands occupied by primitive nomadic peoples, as in the Americas and Australia. Conquerors often rewarded their troops with free land. Sometimes settlements were less successful, or a complete failure, usually because the land or climate was poor, or the location subject to attack by predatory neighbors.

In 1862 the United States, although engaged in a civil war, adopted the Homestead Act, which granted 160 acres in frontier areas to any family that would stake a claim and work the land for a period of time. However, by around 1890 all the public land that anyone might be able to farm using only labor and simple hand tools had been claimed, and people began to seek ways to settle less favorable land, such as that in the Great Plains, that would require some capital investment to be economically viable. Explorer John Wesley Powell was one of these. He proposed the creation of communal settlements built around irrigation projects funded by the government.

Small farms had played an important role in the earlier stages of the nation's industrialization, since workers frequently supplemented their wages by cultivating small plots of land to supply the food required by their families. This kept a great many people from starving during the 1930s depression. The practice declined with increasing agricultural mechanization, although it was encouraged by some employers—such as George M. Pullman and Henry Ford—who located industrial plants in communities where subsistence farming was or could be undertaken.

In section 208 of the National Industrial Recovery Act (1933), Congress stipulated that

> To provide for aiding the redistribution of the overbalance of population in industrial centers $25,000,000 is hereby made available to the President, to be used by him through such agencies and under such regulation as he may make, for making loans for and otherwise aiding in the purchase of subsistence homesteads. The money collected as repayment of said loans shall constitute a revolving fund to be administered as directed by the President for the purposes of this section.

The Federal Subsistence Homestead Corporation proceeded to build communities of new homes located on tracts of from one to five tillable acres, offering them at low payments to the eligible unemployed. Production facilities appropriate to the skills of the populations were also provided in most cases.

Subsistence homesteading, as distinct from subsistence farming, settles a family on a plot of land where it can grow most of its food and make many of its goods, but near part-time or full-time jobs for cash income. This has often meant near existing settlements, when land is available from foreclosures and tax sales.

The first project to receive a federal loan was the Dayton Homestead Unit. In the fall of 1931, groups of unemployed and partially employed families in ten sections of the city were organized into production units. Each unit was to manufacture for the group's needs and to barter a portion of their products for raw materials that they could not produce themselves. They differed from most self-help barter organizations in their emphasis on production for use.

The first Homestead Unit was organized in the spring of 1932. A farm of 160 acres, purchased for eight thousand dollars, was divided into thirty-five three-acre plots, with fifty-five acres reserved for community pasture and woodlot, commons, and public roads. Thirty-five families took possession.

Although helpful in supplementing meager incomes, the project could not take its membership completely off relief. Distribution and overhead costs, the inability to grow or manufacture their own material in the city, and the necessity of paying rent for headquarters and individual residences made it impossible for the members to secure enough for their labors to make them self-supporting. If the units had been charged fully with all that was donated to them—rent, land for gardens, tools, implements, materials, and supplies—the project could never have broken even.

One of the most successful communities was Arthurdale, West Virginia, where employment in native crafts was emphasized. An effort to provide employment for garment workers from New York City in a cooperatively managed plant across the Hudson River at Jersey Homesteads was less successful. Only about one hundred such projects were undertaken, and the program was of little significance as relief or recovery policy. Interest declined with improved economic conditions, and the program was terminated in 1942.

BIBLIOGRAPHY

Lord, Russell, and Paul H. Johnstone, eds. *A Place on Earth: A Critical Appraisal of Subsistence Homesteads.* Washington, D.C.: Bureau of Agricultural Economics, 1942.

Jon Roland

See also **Agriculture; Homestead Movement.**

SUBSTANCE ABUSE is characterized by repeated use of a substance or substances in situations where use leads to—or contributes to—markedly negative outcomes. Defining substance abuse can be difficult. "Substance" refers to the spectrum of drugs that can be potentially abused, such as illicit drugs (marijuana, heroin), licit drugs (alcohol, tobacco), and prescription drugs (Vicodin, Xanax). "Abuse" refers to the use of a substance when it is not medically indicated or when its use exceeds socially accepted levels. Technically, substance abuse is one in a spectrum of substance use disorders outlined in the American Psychiatric Association's *Diagnostic and Statistical Manual of Mental Disorders.* In order to meet diagnostic criteria, an individual, over the course of one year, must experience one or more of the following: significant impairment in the fulfillment of role obligations due to use of a substance, continued use of a substance in dangerous situations, recurrent substance-related legal problems, or continued use of a particular substance despite having continued social or interpersonal problems caused or compounded by the use of the substance.

The continuum of substance-related disorders begins with substance use, intoxication, and withdrawal, followed by substance abuse, and then dependence. This progression marks an escalation in the use of substances that leads to numerous medical, social, and psychological difficulties. Numerous medical problems have been linked to use of substances. Cigarette smoking, for example, causes heart disease, stroke, chronic lung disease, and cancers of the lung, mouth, pharynx, esophagus, and bladder. Smokeless tobacco can lead to gum recession, an increased risk for heart disease and stroke, and cancers of the mouth, pharynx, and esophagus. Prolonged use of the drug can impair or reduce short-term memory and lead to respiratory problems, cancer, reproductive problems, and immune system problems.

Socially, substance abuse has been implicated in relational, occupational, academic, and living difficulties, such as loss of a job, housing, or a spouse; spousal and child abuse; social rejection; economic collapse; and social isolation. Psychological difficulties can occur, as the repeated misuse of substances can lead to numerous other psychiatric disorders, such as mood and anxiety disorders, sleep disorders, sexual dysfunction, delirium, dementia, amnestic disorder, and psychosis.

Substances of Abuse

In the early 2000s, the three most popular drugs of abuse were alcohol, tobacco, and MARIJUANA. Each has an extensive history dating back thousands of years. Beer was consumed as far back as 8000 B.C. There is evidence of the production of wine as far back as 3000 B.C., and possibly even farther back to 5400 B.C. In the United States, beer tends to have an alcohol content of 3 to 5 percent; wines, 8 to 17 percent; and distilled spirits, 20 to 95 percent. These concentrations often exceed the limit imposed by nature, as alcohol concentrations in excess of 15 percent are toxic to the yeast that help produce alcohol during the fermentation process. Higher concentrations are obtained through the process of distillation. In the United States, alcohol is among the most widely used of the substances of abuse. In 2001 roughly 80 percent of U.S. high school seniors had tried alcohol. Sixty-four percent reported having been drunk at least once in their lives. Approximately 14 million Americans meet the diagnostic criteria for alcohol abuse or ALCOHOLISM. It has been estimated that on an annual basis alcohol use leads to the loss of 100,000 lives. Research has demonstrated that alcohol abuse can lead to liver disease, heart disease, cancer, and pancreatitis. Additionally, alcohol use by pregnant women can lead to fetal alcohol syndrome.

Tobacco products are the second most commonly used drug, and are the delivery system for the addictive substance called nicotine. Tobacco products are available in smokable forms such as cigarettes, cigars, and pipes, and smokeless forms such as chewing tobacco and snuff. The tobacco plant is native to the Americas; it is believed that the native peoples used tobacco, in particular during religious ceremonies, long before the arrival of the Europeans to the continent. The consumption of tobacco spread to Europe and beyond as the explorers returned to their countries of origin. Native tobacco is thought to have been much more potent than the current plant and to have contained more psychoactive substances. The Europeans, however, grew different varieties of the plant and arrived at milder versions more like those available in the early 2000s. Production of smoking tobacco was limited until the early 1800s when an American, James Bonsack, patented a machine that could produce 200 cigarettes per minute. This invention allowed for a more affordable product. The popularity of cigarette smoking spread throughout the world, as well as into lower socioeconomic classes within the United States. Tobacco is implicated in 430,000 deaths in the United States each year. In 2001, 61 percent of high school seniors had tried cigarettes and almost 20 percent had tried smokeless tobacco.

The third most commonly misused substance in the United States is marijuana. Marijuana is a plant that contains chemicals that, when smoked or ingested, lead to altered mood states. Marijuana use has been documented as far back as 2737 B.C. in China. In the United States, marijuana was used in the nineteenth century to treat migraine headaches, convulsions, pain, and to induce sleep. Recreational use has been documented to have begun in the 1920s, coinciding with the Prohibition era. At the end of Prohibition, marijuana use dwindled. The Marijuana Stamp Act (1937) required that a tax be imposed on those carrying marijuana. Late in the twentieth century, groups began advocating the legalization of marijuana for medicinal purposes. The first such legislation passed in California in 1996. Arizona, Alaska, Colorado, Hawaii, Maine, Nevada, Oregon, and Washington have since enacted similar laws. Opponents of these laws have launched fierce legal battles. In the meantime, almost half of high

school seniors reported in a 2001 survey that they had used marijuana.

Other Substances of Abuse

Barbiturates and similar drugs. Introduced in 1870 as a treatment for sleep disorders, chloral hydrate was a hypnotic drug with a high potential for addiction. Other drugs—paraldehyde and bromide salts—were also used to induce sleep, but they were highly addictive and had other negative side effects. Once barbiturates were introduced in 1903 these drugs were discontinued as a treatment. Barbiturates were used as the primary line of defense against anxiety and insomnia until the introduction of benzodiazepines. Barbiturates are highly addictive, and they serve as a sedative at low doses and as a hypnotic at high doses. In the years 1950 to 1970 barbiturates were the most common drug of abuse, second to alcohol. In 2001 almost 9 percent of U.S. high school seniors reported that they had tried barbiturates.

Benzodiazepines. Drugs such as Librium, Valium, and Xanax fall into this category. When first introduced in the 1960s as an alternative treatment for sleeplessness and anxiety, benzodiazepines were well received by doctors and patients. While benzodiazepines have been popular prescription drugs to treat anxiety disorders, they are also popular drugs of abuse. Overuse of these drugs can lead to respiratory difficulties, sleeplessness, coma, and death.

Amphetamines. This class of medications is used and abused to ward off fatigue and to increase energy. First discovered in 1887, amphetamines were found to have medicinal value in 1927 for breathing disorders such as asthma. It quickly became apparent, however, that a concentrated version of the treatment drug could be used to attain an altered mental state. During World War II, amphetamines were used by soldiers—with the support of the military—to stay awake and work longer periods of time. In the mid-1960s legislation was introduced, such as amendments to the federal food and drug laws, to curb the black market in amphetamines. Many pharmaceutical amphetamine products were removed from the market altogether. More than 16 percent of high school seniors in 2001 reported having tried amphetamines.

Central nervous system stimulants. Central nervous system (CNS) stimulants, which include cocaine and drugs such as ephedrine and methylphenidate (Ritalin), have energizing effects very similar to those of amphetamines. The latter two are of particular importance given their frequent prescription in populations of children. Ephedrine has been used in Eastern medicine for thousands of years but was introduced into the United States and other Western markets much later. The first Western medical journal report of its effectiveness in treating asthma appeared in 1930. Ritalin is used in treating attention-deficit/hyperactivity disorder (ADHD) as well as narcolepsy and depression. ADHD is the most commonly diagnosed childhood disorder. Unfortunately, young children are now buying and selling Ritalin among their peers, leading to problems of abuse by young children as well as medication noncompliance among those youth who have been prescribed the drug.

Cocaine. Cocaine, a by-product of the coca plant, was isolated in the late 1850s and scientists began investigating the potential use of pure cocaine for European and U.S. populations. The leaf was used in a variety of brews, the most popular of which was the initial recipe for Coca-Cola. Reportedly, the Coca-Cola Company did not remove cocaine completely from its recipe until 1929. Sigmund Freud, the renowned psychodynamic clinician, hailed cocaine as a potential cure for depression and some addictions. Cocaine was a valuable anesthetic, providing local, fast-acting, and long-lasting effects during some surgical procedures. Outbreak of cocaine abuse in the United States in the late 1800s and similar ones abroad were thought to be related, however, to the use of cocaine in numerous medical preparations. In 1914 cocaine was officially classified as a narcotic, and its widespread use in the medical community stopped. In the early 2000s, more than 8 percent of high school seniors in the United States had tried cocaine.

Heroin. Heroin is in the opiate family, a broad and complex category that includes drugs such as morphine and codeine. Heroin abuse accounts for 90 percent of the opiate abuse in the United States. Like other substances of abuse, heroin has changed over time from an estimated 6 percent purity in the United States in the 1980s to 65 to 80 percent purity in the early 2000s. During the same period, there has been a reported decrease in price. Perhaps the greatest problem that heroin users face is the exposure to diseases, especially the HIV virus, when using dirty needles to inject the substance. In the early 2000s, almost 2 percent of high school seniors reported having tried heroin in their lifetime.

Hallucinogens. Hallucinogens are drugs that cause hallucinations. Hallucinations may be visual, auditory, or sensory and may produce rapid, intense emotional swings. Lysergic acid diethylamide (LSD) is the most commonly known hallucinogen and is the most widely used. Other hallucinogens include mescaline, psilocybin mushrooms, and ibogaine. Usually thought of as hallucinogens, PCP (phencyclidine) and ketamine were initially developed as general anesthetics for surgery. They distort visual and auditory perceptions and also produce feelings of detachment from the environment and self. They are, more accurately, dissociative anesthetics. In 2001, almost 13 percent of high school seniors had tried some form of hallucinogen.

Inhalants. An unusual class of substances, inhalants can be found among traditional household items and include gasoline, glue, felt-tip pens, pesticides, and household cleaners. The origins of inhalant use are not known for certain, although historical evidence suggests that nitrous oxide had been used recreationally as far back as the 1800s, with gasoline and glue emerging as substances for recreational use in the 1950s. The practice of glue sniffing has been traced to California adolescents who accidentally discovered the intoxicating effects of their airplane model glue. Inhalants have been referred to as "kiddie" drugs because younger rather than older adolescents use them. Of a group of U.S. eighth graders surveyed in 2001, 17 percent reported having tried inhalants.

Treatments for Substance Abuse and Related Disorders

The treatment for substance abuse varies by substance, severity of abuse, and the theoretical approach of the clinician. The main therapy approaches include biological treatments, behavioral therapy, and social treatments. Research findings suggest that a combination of therapy approaches is more effective than one approach by itself.

Biological treatments include detoxification, antagonist drugs, and drug maintenance therapy. Detoxification is the process by which a health professional monitors the patient's withdrawal from a drug. Detoxification involves either giving a patient smaller and smaller doses of the drug until the person is no longer taking the drug, or replacing the original drug of abuse with medications that help minimize withdrawal symptoms. Antagonist drugs interfere with the effects of other drugs. Antagonist drugs vary by drug of abuse. Disulfiram (Antabuse), for example, is used for patients trying to end alcohol abuse. Drinking any alcohol while on disulfiram produces a violent physical reaction that includes vomiting, increased heart rate, and other effects. Less common is the use of narcotic antagonists or partial antagonists in the treatment of patients who abuse or are dependent on opioids. Narcotic antagonists block opioids from attaching to endorphin receptor sites, eliminating the "high" and making the abuse pointless. These narcotic antagonists, however, are thought to be too dangerous for regular treatment and are reserved for extreme cases. Finally, drug maintenance therapy has been used primarily for treatment of heroin dependence. A drug such as methadone replaces the heroin, creating an addiction that is medically supervised. For people who are addicted to heroin, the oral medication methadone is cleaner and safer, and its availability through a clinic can eliminate dangerous drug-seeking behaviors.

In the behavioral therapy realm, aversion therapy has been used mostly to treat alcohol abuse and dependence. There are various ways to apply the therapy, which is informed by the principles of classical conditioning. That is, the stimulus, such as alcohol, is paired up with an aversive response that can be a thought or a physiological response such as that of Antabuse. Behavioral self-control training (BSCT) is a cognitive-behavioral treatment also used to treat alcohol abuse and dependence. It involves having the patient track their drinking behaviors as well as emotional, cognitive, and other important changes associated with drinking. In addition to increased awareness, the patient learns coping strategies to better manage their drinking and related cues. A similar approach, also cognitive-behavioral, is relapse-prevention training. In addition to the other BSCT tasks, patients in relapse-prevention training plan ahead, focusing on what is an appropriate amount to drink, what are acceptable drinks, and when it is all right to drink. Relapse-prevention has been used somewhat successfully to treat marijuana and cocaine abuse. Another behaviorally informed approach, contingency management treatment, has been used to treat cocaine abuse. The treatment involves developing a set of incentives that are given once a patient proves, such as through a urine sample, that they are drug-free.

Social treatments have been popular, especially Alcoholics Anonymous, a self-help group in existence since the mid-1930s. Self-help groups are often led by community members and exist outside of professional settings. ALCOHOLICS ANONYMOUS, for example, provides support from peers and guidelines for living with a strong spiritual component. Meetings take place often and regularly. In addition, group members are available to each other around the clock. Similar programs, such as Narcotics Anonymous, are available for other substances. Some self-help groups have expanded into more encompassing settings, offering residential treatment facilities to ease the transition into a drug-free lifestyle.

An important debate in treatment of substance abuse has centered on whether the main goal of therapy is abstinence or reduction. While the traditional approaches—supported by existing laws—advocate for complete abstinence, some people in the field advocate for reducing the harm potential of the use of a substance. Harm reduction programs arrived in the United States in the 1990s, having been successful elsewhere. Advocates of this approach view it as "humane" and "practical" in that it focuses on the effects of the drug (rather than the drug use) and seeks to minimize negative effects for people who use substances and for those around them. This debate is quite charged given that some proponents of harm reduction also support the use of marijuana for medicinal purposes. The intersection of academic perspectives on substance use and social policy makes this area of study controversial.

Prevention Efforts

While the debate on treatments for substance abuse and related disorders will likely continue for some time, both camps would agree that the best treatment for substance abuse is to prevent it altogether. Given the personal and social cost of substance abuse it is not surprising that prevention of drug abuse has, itself, become an important activity. Substance abuse prevention has generally taken the form of suppression or interdiction efforts, although more recent activities have targeted demand reduction.

Suppression efforts include the use of punitive measures to thwart substance use and abuse. Historically, suppression efforts occurred in China in the eighteenth century, when opium-den owners were executed, and in the

United States during the period of Prohibition (1920–1933) when the Eighteenth Amendment to the U.S. Constitution outlawed the production, distribution, or sale of alcoholic beverages. Suppression efforts in the early 2000s centered on enforcing existing laws and establishing new laws designed to stop drug trafficking, distribution, and use. Research has shown that public policy strategies such as raising the minimum drinking age to twenty-one and increasing alcohol prices has resulted in fewer deaths, such as from motor vehicle accidents. In 2002 the Office of National Drug Control Policy requested a budget of $19.2 billion for drug control strategies.

Demand reduction includes all efforts whose primary goal is to decrease the underlying desire for substances to abuse. Demand reduction theorists argue that if there is no market demand for substances, then their use has been effectively prevented. Demand reduction strategies for prevention of substance abuse include a broad range of activities that are designed to stop substance use before it begins, provide people with the tools to prevent relapse, or build resilience among those who are at high risk for substance use. Demand reduction prevention activities can be broadly categorized into three levels: primary, secondary, and tertiary.

Primary prevention activities are intended to reach a broad audience in an effort to avert the onset of use. An example of a primary prevention program is that of Drug Abuse Resistance Education (known as Project DARE), which was developed in the early 1980s as a prevention program targeting substance use by adolescents. In the early 2000s it was implemented in 80 percent of school districts in the United States. In the program, specially trained police officers conduct classroom lectures and discussions on how to resist peer pressure and lead drug-free lives. While Project DARE remains undeniably popular, its effectiveness in reducing substance abuse has been consistently questioned. No scientific study of the program's outcomes has revealed an impact on substance use by youth.

Generally, secondary prevention includes efforts to reduce the underlying causes of substance abuse among populations that are at risk for use. Studies have shown that substance abuse is predicted by both individual and environmental factors. Theories of problem behavior prevention identify the factors that are predictive of a particular problem behavior and target them for intervention. Such predictors are classified as risk or protective factors. Within such a model, a risk factor is any variable that increases the likelihood that a negative outcome will occur, while a protective factor is a variable that decreases the likelihood that a negative outcome will occur. By successfully targeting the appropriate risk or protective factors with a prevention/intervention program, a reduction in negative outcome behaviors may occur.

Tertiary prevention includes activities that are designed to minimize the impact of substance use. The harm reduction approach can be considered a tertiary prevention strategy, inasmuch as it attempts to minimize the harmful consequences of drug use and the high-risk behaviors associated with drug use.

BIBLIOGRAPHY

"Alcohol." National Institute on Alcohol Abuse and Alcoholism. Available at http://www.niaaa.nih.gov/publications/harm-al.htm

Doweiko, Harold E. *Concepts of Chemical Dependency.* 5th ed. Pacific Grove, Calif.: Brooks/Cole-Thomson Learning, 2002.

"High School and Youth Trends." National Institute on Drug Abuse. Available at http://www.nida.nih.gov/Infofax/HSYouthtrends.html

"Marijuana: Just the Facts." Texas Commission of Alcohol and Drug Abuse. Available at http://www.tcada.state.tx.us/research/facts/marijuana.html

Marlatt, G. Alan, and Gary R. VandenBos, eds. *Addictive Behaviors: Readings on Etiology, Prevention, and Treatment.* Washington, D.C.: American Psychological Association, 1997.

Scott C. Bates
Melanie M. Domenech-Rodríguez

See also **Alcohol, Regulation of; Drug Trafficking, Illegal; Tobacco Industry.**

SUBSTITUTES, CIVIL WAR.   No conscription in the North during the CIVIL WAR was absolute. The drafted man could always hire a substitute if he could afford it. Starting in 1862, the U.S. government allowed this escape from military service on the theory that, so long as each name drawn from the wheel produced a man, it made no difference whether the drafted person or one hired to take his place appeared for muster. The Conscription Act of 3 March 1863 legalized this method of draft evasion. Until the act of 24 February 1864, the conscript could choose between hiring a substitute or paying the government $300 as commutation of service. Thereafter, the government only permitted substitution, except for conscientious objectors. Furthermore, exemption by furnishing a substitute extended only until the next succeeding draft, at which point the principal again became liable. Immediately, the prices of substitutes rose far above the $300 to which the commutation clause had held them. For this reason, legal draft evasion became the prerogative of only the unusually well-to-do.

From the early days of the war, the Confederacy also allowed a limited substitution system. The first Confederate Conscription Act permitted substitutes from men not legally liable to service to the extent of one man a month in each company. The second conscription act made men previously furnishing substitutes again liable to serve, thus causing much dissension and legal action. By the end of 1863, the Confederacy had abolished the whole system. Scholars have never accurately compiled the number of substitutes.

BIBLIOGRAPHY

Geary, James W. *We Need Men: The Union Draft in the Civil War.* Dekalb: Northern Illinois University Press, 1991.

Madden, David, ed. *Beyond the Battlefield: The Ordinary Life and Extraordinary Times of the Civil War Soldier.* New York: Simon and Schuster, 2000.

Wert, Jeffry D. *A Brotherhood of Valor: The Common Soldiers of the Stonewall Brigade, C.S.A., and the Iron Brigade, U.S.A.* New York: Simon and Schuster, 1999.

Fred A. Shannon / A. E.

See also **Army, Confederate; Army, Union; Bounty Jumper; Conscription and Recruitment.**

SUBTREASURIES   are the regional banks and repositories charged with the stewardship of the federal government's funds. After President Andrew Jackson removed government deposits from the second BANK OF THE UNITED STATES they were placed in so-called "pet banks." This system did not prove to be satisfactory, and an act, approved 4 July 1840, set up an independent treasury. Until 30 June 1843, part of the payments to the government might be other than specie ("in coin"). The law was repealed 13 August 1841, but was re-enacted in August 1846, with the intent that receipts and expenditures were to be in specie or Treasury notes. Subtreasuries were established at New York, Philadelphia, Charleston, New Orleans, Saint Louis, and Boston; and later at Chicago, San Francisco, and Cincinnati.

The gravest trouble came when government surpluses caused a shortage in the money markets. The situation was helped after the establishment in 1863–1864 of the national banks, which were made government depositories. Secretary of the Treasury Leslie M. Shaw, from 1902 to 1907, used many devices to smooth the effect of Treasury operations on the money market. The Federal Reserve Act of 1913 provided that the Federal Reserve banks might act as fiscal agents for the government. This made the subtreasuries unnecessary. But political pressure caused them to be temporarily retained. By an act of Congress dated 29 May 1920, the nine subtreasuries were terminated; the last one closed its doors on 10 February 1921.

BIBLIOGRAPHY

Moser, Harold D. *Subtreasury Politics and the Virginia Conservative Democrats, 1835–1844.* Madison, Wis., 1977.

James D. Magee / A. R.

See also **Banking: State Banks; Federal Reserve System; Money; Pet Banks.**

SUBURBANIZATION   describes the general trend of city dwellers to move from the city into residential areas in ever-growing concentric circles away from the city's core. The trend began briefly in the nineteenth century and then exploded after World War II (1939–1945). Sub-

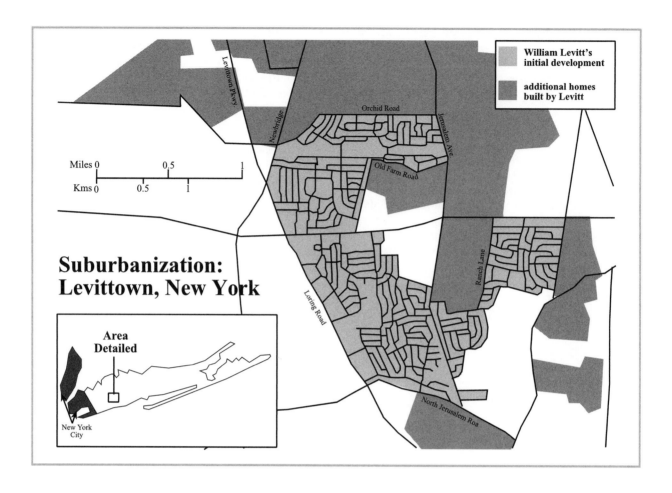

**Suburbanization:
Levittown, New York**

Area
Detailed

New York
City

urbs developed their own shopping and service districts and bred their own distinct lifestyles.

Historians and sociologists have long had difficulty defining the start of suburbanization. Researchers have noted that even before the American Revolution (1775–1783), land speculators were offering land outside of cities like Boston and New York for development as residential areas. The term "suburban" was in use by 1800.

Crowded Urban Centers

Large American cities at that time were heterogeneous. They contained no distinct boundaries for commerce centers, artisan shops, stores, or residences. All existed side by side, often with one building performing several different functions. Indeed, contiguousness was one of the hallmarks of presuburban American cities. Kenneth T. Jackson, author of the classic *Crabgrass Frontier: The Suburbanization of the United States* (1985), has termed these areas "walking cities." Jackson notes that walking cities were very congested. Lots were small, usually no more than twenty feet wide; streets were narrow; buildings were crowded together and tended to grow up rather than out. Any visitor to modern Wall Street—one of lower Manhattan's earliest developed streets—will quickly note the narrow, choked character of the street. People added to the congestion. While early American city population

densities would be something less, average European densities ranged from 35,000 to 75,000 people per square mile. Because of the congestion, but also because foot- and horse-travel were the only transportation options for city denizens, inhabitants lived close to their work. Indeed, many lived in apartments above or behind their shops.

City elites tended to congregate near the centers of power, which included governmental buildings and dockside entry points. In the preindustrial days, those were the true seats of commerce. The first areas termed "suburb," in fact, were not pleasant escape destinations for city leaders, but rather odious peripheral sites where city law relegated such malodorous businesses as tanneries, slaughterhouses, and soap-making shops. On the periphery, houses of prostitution, vagrant camps, and, later, homes for urban slaves also grew. When the elite did begin moving away from the bustle of commerce centers, it was usually because commercial real estate developers offered them lucrative sums for their homes, or perhaps they wanted to enjoy a country life more fitting a moneyed, genteel society. However, it was important that their homes remained within easy walking or carriage distance of commerce.

Transportation Advances

Transportation advances were the key to modern suburbanization. One of the first was the adoption from Europe of omnibus lines. An omnibus was a large, horse-pulled carriage capable of carrying many passengers. Omnibus lines typically ran to and from city centers, dropping off and taking on paying passengers at different established depots along their line.

After the advent of steam power in the early nineteenth century, it was but a short time before steamer ferries offered easy and practical escape from city congestion. In 1810, using technology perfected by Scottish inventor James Watt, Robert Fulton demonstrated the effectiveness of steam power for river travel. By 1814, steamer ferries connected Manhattan with Brooklyn across the East River. Brooklyn, then isolated and rural, offered a pastoral setting away from the bustling docks and Wall Street for New York's new wealthier class.

Steam-powered railroads, another English invention but one that Americans would exploit to magnificent effect, also helped drive early suburbs. New York City had railroad commuter service by 1832; Boston had it by 1834. Railroads helped transform suburbs into higher-class areas because only the wealthier citizens of a city could afford the rail fare.

Industrial Growth and Immigration

The Industrial Revolution, which began in the United States in the 1830s and continued into the 1880s, had a major impact on the creation of suburbs. Industries, located at first near ocean or river ports, situated themselves near established cities. They drew workers from rural areas, adding to the urban congestion. As more people crowded in, a percentage of people left for the suburbs.

Foreign immigration also fed the urban flight. Revolutions across Europe in 1848, the Irish potato famine of the 1840s, and nationalist unification movements in Italy and Germany in the 1860s all created a class of European émigrés seeking relief in the United States. Immigrants arrived in the United States full of hope, but frequently found those hopes dashed when they discovered it difficult to escape urban areas. Ward heelers working for city municipal "boss systems" or "machines" often met immigrants at their point of entry, gave them a grubstake of money, and offered them jobs and residences—both in the crowded urban core—in return for perpetual political support. To scared new arrivals, the offers sounded good, but they trapped many in cities, compounding the congestion and grime.

Suburban Growth

As urban cores grew, suburbs grew by a parallel rate. For example, New York City continued to grow throughout the nineteenth century. By the 1890 census, it held more than 2.5 million people. Suburban Brooklyn's population always remained less than half that of New York City's. By the 1890 census, Brooklyn had slightly more than 800,000 people. Philadelphia and Boston experienced similar urban/suburban growth rates.

As Jackson points out, the movement of middle and upper classes to suburbs was "not inevitable." Indeed, such had not necessarily occurred in the great cities of Europe. But Americans carried with them certain emotional, romantic baggage leftover from the early days of the Republic. Thomas Jefferson and other Enlightenment thinkers had vigorously connected republican virtue with agrarian (or at least rural) lifestyles. Reformers during and after the Second Great Awakening (c. 1825–1840) equated rural lifestyles with health. Periodic smallpox, yellow fever, and dysentery outbreaks in crowded cities tended to prove them correct. But the cities could not be erased: by 1870, cities and agricultural areas existed in a state of mutual support, and too many urbanites made their living off the commercial centers.

People with enough money to achieve mobility, however, could enjoy the benefits, both healthful and aesthetic, of the country by moving to the suburbs. In suburban homes they would not have to rely on subsistence gardens for food, as rail transportation ensured adequate produce from the countryside. Rather, they could turn their grounds into romantic garden areas, replete with manicured lawns, shrubs, and relaxing fountains.

The Automobile Age

The twentieth century saw the rise of the machine that would cause the explosion of modern suburbia—the automobile. Like so much other technology, autos came to the United States from Europe. But it took American entrepreneur Henry Ford to make them accessible to average Americans. Using the assembly line system to speed and cheapen the production of cars, then enabling Americans to buy them on credit, Ford revolutionized not only the auto industry, but American roadways and city growth as well.

After World War I (1914–1918), when the United States experienced an economic boom that lasted until 1929, modern suburbia began to take shape. The Ford Model T, long the staple of American auto consumers, was quite durable and could, in fact, negotiate dirt roads and ditches, but paved roads became the preference of the driving public. Macadamized roads led into the suburbs, creating a freeway system that fed both metropolitan area sprawl and urban deterioration. As historian Lewis Munford criticized in his book *City in History: Its Origins, Its Transformations, and Its Prospects* (1961), city planners began to subjugate every other consideration to the car. Still, suburban growth was slow. Only 17 percent of the nation's population lived in suburbia in 1920. As with everything else, the Great Depression retarded growth. By 1940 only 20 percent of the population was classified as suburban.

The great suburban explosion, however, came after World War II (1939–1945). In 1945 and 1946, millions of servicemen returned home, all entitled to education benefits under the G.I. Bill and housing benefits under the Veterans Administration (VA) and Federal Housing

Administration (FHA). The subsequent issuance of thousands of new bachelors' degrees created a new professional class in the United States, and those veterans who chose vocational education beefed up the service sector. Both classes began having the children that would become the baby boomers, and they needed low-cost housing. Despite the federal backing of home loans, a postwar housing shortage proved an obstacle. The suburbs provided a resolution.

Suburbs, in fact, were an ideal solution to the problem, for transportation was no longer an obstacle. New car sales slowed during the war for obvious reasons: first, men—the primary buyers of cars then—were out of the country by the millions; second, gasoline rationing impeded travel during the war; third, American auto manufacturers produced no new models after the 1942 model year, their plants turned over to military production until the end of the war.

But after Japan surrendered in September 1945, Americans began buying cars once again. They bought a staggering 70,000 cars in the last few months of 1945; that number jumped to more than 2 million in 1946, and more than 5 million in 1949. Many American families, with men drawing army pay and women working in war industry plants, emerged from the war with tidy nest eggs. That gave them plenty for a down payment on a house, and it enabled many to buy their first car or perhaps buy a second car. The advent of two-car families eased any commute for the breadwinner from suburbia: he could take one car while his wife had a second vehicle at home for shuttling children to school and running errands.

Levittowns

Nevertheless, with Americans eager to buy, the housing shortage remained. It took enterprising real estate speculators to break the logjam. None became more famous than builders William and Alfred Levitt. William, a salesman, and Alfred, an architect, wanted to apply mass production techniques to housing. They bought land in Hempstead, Long Island, New York, some thirty miles from New York City, then put together teams of nonunion builders who erected simple two-bedroom, one-bathroom homes on sixty-foot by one hundred-foot lots. There the Levitts built 17,000 homes that would ultimately house more than 80,000 people. They integrated parks and swimming pools, and buildings for schools and churches, into their neighborhoods. The first "Levittown" was born, offering mass-produced homes and prepackaged neighborhoods.

When the first LEVITTOWN houses went on sale, New Yorkers stood in line to get them. The average price for a two-story, Cape Cod–style home was $7,900. Down payments were about $90; monthly payments averaged $58; that at a time when the average family income was about $3,000 a year. The Levitts followed up their Long Island success with Levittowns in Pennsylvania and New Jersey.

Other speculators and developers followed suit, so that more "Levittowns" sprang up outside other American urban areas. Between 1947 and 1960, the population in suburbs grew by 50 to 100 percent. By 1960, one-third of the nation's population lived in suburban areas. In fact, by 1960, a new phenomenon had occurred—that of "strip cities": one, two, or perhaps more urban areas connected by almost continuous suburbs and suburban shopping areas. The U.S. census counted thirteen of those areas by 1960, obviously including Boston to New York to Washington, D.C., but also Albany to Erie, New York; Cleveland to Pittsburgh; Detroit to Muskegon, Michigan; Toledo to Cincinnati; Atlanta to Raleigh; Miami to Jacksonville, Chicago to Milwaukee, St. Louis to Peoria; Kansas City to Sioux Falls; Dallas–Fort Worth to San Antonio–Houston; San Francisco to San Diego; and Seattle to Eugene.

The Levitts became famous. In 1950, William's likeness appeared on the cover of *Time* magazine. But they also became the subject of criticism from architects, sociologists, and city planners. Some said Levittowns were undermining vital urban sectors. In truth, the automobile had been doing that for three decades. Other critics, like Lewis Mumford, decried the homogeneity—the sameness—of the Cape Cod homes in Levittowns.

But of course, one man's cookie-cutter, prefab house is another man's castle. The people moving into Levittowns were not architectural designers or enlightened romanticists. Rather, they were working people desiring, like their suburban forebears, a chance to get out of the congestion, grime, and, with thousands of cars on the streets, pollution of the cities.

Levittowners tended to love their new homes. They had spacious closets and ample cooking room in the kitchens; the Levitts even supplied television sets with each new home! On weekends, homeowners could putter in their new lawns, planting shrubs and trees. Children could safely bicycle up and down the wide streets of their neighborhoods. Adults, accustomed to the dark, cloistered, often lonely existence of the city, suddenly found themselves sharing backyards with neighbors and actually taking time to visit with them. Neighborhood coffee or bridge clubs sprang up, giving mothers a weekly break from housewifely duties. (Routinely in the 1940s and 1950s, it was the man who made the daily commute from suburbia to the city.) The backyard barbecue became a symbol of suburban freedom, and many a couple struck enduring friendships over the grill. Many suburbanites recall the thrill and pride of moving from a crowded city apartment into their own homes; of having the chance to create a new neighborhood as they had never done before. In that, suburbia reflected the great American optimism of the immediate postwar years.

The Downside of Suburbia

But Levittowns and other suburbs were not all "beds of roses." The togetherness and friendships that suburbs of-

Suburbia. An early 1950s aerial view of Levittown, Pa., one of the many planned communities that sprang up in the years after World War II. © UPI/corbis-Bettmann

fered could often become double-edged swords. Proximity and the fact that neighborhoods, especially front yards, were open—hence many a suburbanite's activities were open to neighborly review and criticism—gave rise to an intense competition often called "keeping up with the Joneses." The second car (especially a Cadillac, Lincoln, or perhaps a sports model), a boat parked out front, the grass in the front yard, even the barbecue grill could all become competitive status symbols. The comings and goings of teenagers was hard to hide, and sometimes harder to explain. The Tuesday afternoon coffee club was both a time for women to get together and an invitation to engage in intense, often cutting, criticism. If a woman's floor was not clean enough or her cups and saucers not spotless, the news was soon all over the neighborhood. The flight to the suburbs also frequently cut families off from traditional support groups such as parents, grandparents, uncles, and aunts. With those connections harder to maintain, many a young woman found herself home alone with nothing but diapers to wash and floors to clean, and, in fact, doubting her abilities to do that properly. Suburban living played no little part in the women's liberation movement of the 1960s and 1970s.

An element of racism also crept into the suburbs. The rise of suburbia did indicate a "white flight" from the urban core, and critics charged the Levitts and other suburban developers with racism. Levittowns and other neighborhoods had restrictive covenants barring African Americans from buying homes there. The covenants also

extended to renting. William Levitt, a Jew who had seen what horrors racial prejudice had wrought in Nazi Germany, chafed under the accusations, and he countered that he was only selling the type of neighborhoods that buying suburbanites wanted. In that Levitt had hit the root of the sociological phenomenon of suburbs: most homebuyers were white, and they wanted to settle in homogenous neighborhoods.

Civil rights advocates also charged in the early 1970s that largely white suburban schools were in violation of the desegregation mandate the Supreme Court handed down in the 1954 *Brown v. Topeka Board of Education* case. In *Milliken v. Bradley*, a 1974 case that attempted to desegregate urban and suburban Detroit schools, the Court maintained that no constitutional violation existed, as the suburban schools were not created with overt intent to segregate. The Detroit area school system remained the same.

Urban businessmen also griped about the loss of business to the suburbs. All suburban areas, given their distance from cities, generated their own support services and businesses—grocery stores, five-and-dime stores, gas stations, restaurants, laundries, doctors' offices, movie houses. Businesses left in downtown areas not only suffered from an undermining of their customer pool, but the customers who were left tended to be of a lower class with less disposable income.

Simultaneously, by 1960, New York, Chicago, and other large cities had ceased to grow; soon their population would start to decline as more people fled to the suburbs. Consequently, the urban tax base also dwindled, cutting into revenues for capital improvements. Inner cities started a period of decline and decay. Tenements remained overcrowded; gangs began offering inner-city youth some type of affiliation and made robbery the order of the day; murders increased as police became overworked and were unable to maintain an authoritarian presence; graffiti defaced public transportation and buildings. By the late 1960s and 1970s, inner cities had become synonymous with—if not stereotypical of—crime, violence, and filth. Public-housing projects (often notoriously known simply as "the projects") sprang up in cities as alternatives to run-down tenements, but they often quickly deteriorated into new centers of crime.

Not until the 1990s did cities effectively get control over, and in fact revitalize, run-down urban areas. Cities as vastly different in size and culture as Boston and Oklahoma City funded projects to clean up downtown areas, attract businesses back to the city, and pull customers back into the city by cleaning up streets, lighting them, ridding them of crime, and building public attractions like parks, river-walks, and sports facilities. By 2000, Mayor Rudolph Giuliani of New York was being praised for drastically lowering the crime and homicide rates there.

While the flight to suburbia has by no means abated, an interesting phenomenon occurred in the early 1990s. Researchers recognized that some professionals were in fact moving out of the suburbs and back into cities. They could spend less time commuting; commutes in some areas, including mileage and traffic tie-ups, might eat up three hours a day, seriously eroding sleep and family time.

Nevertheless, suburban areas continue to grow. The new millennium, however, has seen downtown urban areas strive to create a more beneficially symbiotic relationship with suburbs.

BIBLIOGRAPHY

Dobriner, William M. *Class in Suburbia*. Englewood Cliffs, N.J.: Prentice-Hall, 1963.

Jackson, Kenneth T. *Crabgrass Frontier: The Suburbanization of the United States*. New York: Oxford University Press, 1985.

Norquist, John O. *The Wealth of Cities: Revitalizing the Centers of American Life*. Reading, Mass.: Addison-Wesley, 1998.

Patterson, James T. *Grand Expectations: The United States, 1945–1974*. New York: Oxford University Press, 1996.

R. Steven Jones

See also **City Planning; Urbanization.**

ISBN 0-684-80529-4

9 780684 805290

90000